THE LABOUR GOVERNMENT
1964-1970

A PERSONAL RECORD

Also by Harold Wilson

NEW DEAL FOR COAL

IN PLACE OF DOLLARS

THE WAR ON WORLD POVERTY

THE RELEVANCE OF BRITISH SOCIALISM

PURPOSE IN POLITICS

THE NEW BRITAIN

PURPOSE IN POWER

Harold Wilson

THE LABOUR GOVERNMENT
1964-1970

A PERSONAL RECORD

Weidenfeld and Nicolson
and
Michael Joseph

First published in Great Britain by
WEIDENFELD AND NICOLSON
5 Winsley Street
London W1
and
MICHAEL JOSEPH LTD
52 Bedford Square
London WC1
1971

7181 0947 3

Set and printed in Great Britain by
Tonbridge Printers Ltd, Peach Hall Works, Tonbridge, Kent
in Times ten on twelve point on paper supplied by
P. F. Bingham Ltd, and bound by James Burn
at Esher, Surrey

To the hundreds of thousands of members of the Labour party whose efforts and idealism created the Government of 1964–1970 and who, in dark days and brighter ones, sustained it with their unwavering loyalty

Acknowledgements

This book was begun on 2nd September, 1970, and the first full draft was completed on 1st February, 1971.

I am indebted to all those friends who so willingly gave me their help in its compilation; too many, I regret, for me to acknowledge them all here. But I am especially grateful to my colleagues in the Labour Administration of 1964–1970 who readily helped me when I asked them to refresh my memory on individual events in which they were particularly and personally involved.

Above all, I would wish to thank Mrs Marcia Williams, my secretary, and Mr Joe Haines for their unstinted assistance at all stages in the writing, reading and checking of the script, and Miss Peggy Field who typed, in all, well over 400,000 words of the earlier and final hand-written drafts.

Mr Martin Gilbert generously gave up time from his major historical work to read the entire script, making many valuable comments and corrections as well as providing the maps. He was helped throughout by Mrs Jane Cousins who also worked hard in assisting Mr Haines in the preparation of the final draft for the printers.

Contents

Illustrations

20 Talks at No. 10 on the Government's industrial relations proposals, June 1969

Between pages 636 and 637

21 Mr Wilson and his Soviet hosts in Moscow, January 1968

22 With President Johnson in Washington, February 1968

23 The 1969 Commonwealth conference

24 Visit to Nigeria, March 1969

25 Meeting with President Nixon at Mildenhall, Suffolk, August 1969

26 With Mrs Golda Meir and Herr Willy Brandt at the eleventh socialist international conference, June 1969

The author and publishers are grateful to the following for permission to reproduce pictures in their collection: Associated Press for numbers 5, 6, 7, 10, 21, 22, 24 and 26; Kelvin Brodie of the *Sunday Times* for number 8; Camera Press for numbers 3, 17, 23 and 25; Fox Photos for number 12; the Labour Party Photographic Library for the frontispiece and numbers 2, 8 and 9; Sidney Martin of Thomson Newspapers for number 1; Popperfoto for number 3; Press Association for numbers 11, 14 and 19; *The Times* for number 20; Thomson Newspapers for number 15.

CARTOONS

MAPS

Foreword

This book is the record of a Government all but a year of whose life was dominated by an inherited balance of payments problem which was nearing a crisis at the moment we took office; we lived and governed during a period when that problem made frenetic speculative attack on Britain both easy and profitable. In our last year of power that balance of payments problem had been overcome, and had been seen to be overcome. But the harsh measures which we had to take, and from which we did not shrink, bit deep. By June, 1970, confidence in the Government had returned, but it was, perhaps, still fragile. The effect of a bad set of trade figures published three days before polling day – and, ironically, since proved to be substantially wrong – must have caused some hesitation and doubt – momentarily, perhaps, but decisively. Yet looking back from today, the detached observer might agree that Britain and Britain's Government, working together, had transformed a crippling deficit into one of the strongest balance of payments surpluses in the world. The sneers abroad about Britain's sickness had given place to admiration. Nor could this transformation have been brought about by reliance on the drift or the weak surrender to blind market forces which had characterised the years of our predecessors. It had meant the application of specifically Socialist measures, some of them newly-designed for the problems we were facing, to secure national policies in industry and a more purposive use of our national resources for overcoming a national malady. It had meant, equally, through our social policies – including taxation and greater public expenditure – the creation of a fairer order of society, without which we could not appeal, with any hope of success, for the sacrifices, restraint and efforts which were necessary from a united people, and which alone made possible the achievement of a situation of national strength.

It was a Government which had faced disappointment after disappointment, and none greater than the economic restraints on our ability to carry through the social revolution to which we were committed at the speed we would have wished. Yet, despite those restraints and the need to transfer resources from domestic expenditure, private and public, to the needs of our export markets, we carried through an expansion in the social services, health, welfare and housing, education and social security, unparalleled in our history.

But the Socialism of those six years was not confined to the measures necessary to modernise industry or to expand and humanise our social services; in a far wider sense it was seen in the transformation of many of Britain's political and social institutions, including the modernisation of the law and the mobilisation of our people in our policies at home and abroad against racialism and discrimination.

If in all these things we had not gone as far as we would have wished, we achieved far more than most would have expected. As we went forward for a mandate to continue what we had begun, we were determined to use our newly-developed economic strength as a basis for faster economic expansion, based on full employment, and for a more rapid rate of improvement in the welfare service.

In the event, we were denied that mandate; once again, a Labour Government was prevented from building on the foundations which it had laid.

1st February, 1971

There is one important problem facing representative Parliamentary Government in the whole of the world where it exists. It is being asked to solve a problem which so far it has failed to solve: that is, how to reconcile Parliamentary popularity with sound economic planning. So far, nobody on either side of this House has succeeded, and it is a problem which has to be solved if we are to meet the challenge that comes to us from other parts of the world and if we are to grout and to buttress the institutions of Parliamentary Government in the affections of the population. . . .

I would describe the central problem falling upon representative government in the Western world as how to persuade the people to forego immediate satisfactions in order to build up the economic resources of the country. . . . How can we persuade the ordinary man and woman that it is worthwhile making sacrifices in their immediate standards or foregoing substantial rising standards to extend fixed capital equipment throughout the country?

—Aneurin Bevan, in his last speech
in the House of Commons,
3rd November, 1959.

Chapter 1

'LORD Attlee once said that it was not possible in our parliamentary system to maintain a government with a majority of less than ten. What do you think of that?'

These words were put to me in a television interview in my constituency in the early hours of Friday, 16th October 1964. At that time the television computers were crediting Labour with a probable over-all majority of thirty, and early editions had gone to press headlining a Labour landslide.

In all the interviews that night, and on the train from Liverpool the next morning, I strongly discounted the predictions. There was no certainty we should win at all. The majority, if any, might be very narrow; there could be a stalemate with no party holding an over-all majority. I hoped I was wrong.

At 2.47 p.m. on that Friday afternoon, Labour reached a bare over-all majority with the announcement that we had gained, net, 56 seats, bringing our total to 316. The final figures were:

Labour	317
Conservative	303
Liberal	9
The retiring Speaker	1

As soon as the figure of 316 seats was reached, Sir Alec Douglas-Home, who until then had rightly refused to concede defeat, asked for an Audience of the Queen and tendered the resignation of his Government. I was told to stand by. A Palace car would be sent for me.

No. 10, imperturbable as ever, had made all the necessary arrangements for a change of Government. Herbert Bowden, our Chief Whip in Opposition, had been told the previous evening, before polling ended, what I must do. I would be asked to make Chequers available to the outgoing Prime Minister. I found an invitation to him already awaiting my signature and this went off to him immediately. I would need to have morning coat and striped pants ready at Transport House to put on for the Audience. In fact I had asked Tony Field, a friend who had driven me throughout the election, to call at my North London home on his return from Liverpool and bring me a *short* black coat. It turned out that no constitutional issue was raised.

1

While I was changing, two detectives were ushered into the room, an inspector and a sergeant of Special Branch. Even while I was dressing they were briefing me on what 'protection' for a Prime Minister was to mean. They – or their successors – were never to leave me unescorted, except at home or in the House of Commons, for nearly six years.

On arrival at the Palace I was conducted to the Queen's private apartment. She simply asked me if I could form an Administration. Exactly a year earlier, Sir Alec Douglas-Home – in the different circumstances of a Cabinet divided over his nomination – had answered the same question, saying that he would have consultations to see if he could form a Government and, if successful, return to the Palace.

Despite the narrowness of my majority, I was in no doubt that a Government could be formed and I was made Prime Minister on the spot. Strangely to me and contrary to all I had understood about the procedures, there was no formal kissing of hands such as occurs with the appointment of all other senior ministers. It was taken as read.

I then left for No. 10 in the official car, driven, as I had asked, by my old Board of Trade driver of the forties and early fifties, Bill Housden, who in most of the intervening years had been Harold Macmillan's driver in all his ministerial posts and later when he was Prime Minister.

After saying a few words to press and television reporters on the steps of No. 10, I went along that long corridor from the front door to the Cabinet Room, a little bewildered, more than a little lonely, but above all else conscious of our small majority and the utter unpredictability of even the immediate future.

I was greeted as 'Prime Minister' by Sir Alec Douglas-Home's private secretary, as I still regarded him. Sir Alec, meanwhile, had disappeared through the back door, quietly.

Within minutes the private secretaries had converged upon me to work out the arrangements for forming the Government, to discuss with me urgent Foreign Office telegrams awaiting my attention, and to inform me about the economic situation.

It was a stormy welcome. The Chinese had, the previous day, exploded their first nuclear weapon. There was a Foreign Office draft of an immediate Government statement it was recommended I should issue. I told them to hold it until we had a Foreign Secretary and an Administration.

There was a telegram appraising the situation in the Soviet Union following the overthrow, less than twenty-four hours earlier, of Mr Khrushchev and the appointment of Mr Kosygin. It was an open question whether, if the news from Moscow had come an hour or two before the polls closed, there would have been an electoral rush to play safe and to vote the existing Government back into power.

There was a telephone call from President Johnson.

There was ominous news of the 'confrontation', the war between

Indonesia and Malaysia, an area of fighting to which the previous Government – with Labour support – had committed the largest force of troops sent to any area of fighting since the Second World War.

And, grimmest of all, there was the economic news. The monthly trade returns for September showing a serious continuing deficit had been published that morning. There had been talk in the last hours of the Conservative Government of raising bank rate by a point to stem any selling of sterling as a result of the trade figures. But it was decided to take no action. Worse, there was the Treasury's assessment of the forward balance-of-payments position. Prepared, as is the practice before every election, for a possible new Government, it showed a position still more serious – to judge from the ex-Chancellor's subsequent statements in the House of Commons, where he was talking of much smaller figures – than the last assessment prepared a month earlier for the Conservatives.

In the face of all this, there could be no question of 'low-profile government' or of having a period of three months or more in which no decisions needed to be taken.

The pattern our first hundred days would have to take was set in the first hundred minutes.

But the immediate task was to form the Government. In my own mind I had decided who the first appointments were to be and had decided to recommend their names to the Queen that night, so that they could begin to take charge. Six senior ministers were, in fact, seen by me and their appointment announced that evening. Neither the foreign nor the economic situation allowed any delay.

The appointments would be conditioned by a machinery of government decision I had taken, eighteen months before, on becoming Leader of the Opposition, about the handling of economic affairs under a Labour Government. The decision was that while the Chancellor of the Exchequer should be responsible for all actions necessary in the monetary field, foreign exchange, internal monetary management, Government expenditure and taxation, Britain could hope to win economic security only by a fundamental reconstruction and modernisation of industry under the direction of a department at least as powerful as the Treasury. This new department would be concerned with real resources, with economic planning, with strengthening our ability to export and to save imports, with increasing productivity, and our competitiveness in domestic and export markets. This idea I had, in fact, favoured before I even became Leader of the Opposition, and as soon as I was elected in February 1963 I made this clear to the shadow Chancellor and others. My detailed plans had been announced in October 1963. The legend that the Department of Economic Affairs, as it was to be called, was all worked out in a taxi with George Brown on the way back from a meeting with the TUC at the St Ermin's Hotel to a division at the House of Commons – a distance of less than a mile – was just not true. It was in that taxi, however, that I first suggested to him that the right job for him would be Secretary of State for Economic Affairs.

Whitehall is always well prepared for a change of Government. In July 1964, the civil service mandarins were clearly expecting a Labour victory and wanted to be prepared for it. At the suggestion of Lord Plowden, an eminent public figure with close Whitehall contacts – he had been responsible for the Macmillan reforms in the senior levels of the civil service – I was invited to dine with Sir Laurence Helsby, the joint permanent secretary of the Treasury, whose duties included the responsibility for the home civil service and for the machinery of government. When I was invited to meet Sir Laurence, I asked whether this proposal had the assent of the then Prime Minister. I was told that he was prepared to agree to this meeting provided, quite fairly, that I did not announce it as an indication that he was conceding in advance the result of the General Election and that the meeting would not take place until the last week of July, which, since we were near the end of the statutory life of the 1959 Parliament, effectively meant at the end of the sittings of that Parliament. He was concerned lest questions might be raised in Parliament if news of our secret dinner party were to leak. I accepted these conditions.

At that dinner with Sir Laurence I indicated some of my ideas for changes in departmental responsibilities. In fact, I had underrated the civil service. Earlier in the year I had recorded an interview with Dr Norman Hunt for the BBC Third Programme. The recording had lasted for over an hour. The programme was in the event cut for transmission to twenty-five minutes. The text of the broadcast itself was reprinted in the *Listener*. Sir Laurence showed the most intimate knowledge of my broadcast and I suspected that he had had the sixty-minute and not the twenty-five-minute version. He gave me his advice on a number of ideas I had, and also his own proposals for adding overseas shipping and civil aviation to the trade and tourist responsibilities of the Board of Trade. He raised no argument against my proposals either for a Department of Economic Affairs or my proposed Ministry of Technology.

So that first night, 16th October, George Brown became Secretary of State in charge of the new Department of Economic Affairs (DEA); James Callaghan, Chancellor of the Exchequer; Patrick Gordon Walker, who had lost his seat at Smethwick and would be looking for an alternative seat, Foreign Secretary; Lord Gardiner, Lord Chancellor; Denis Healey, Secretary of State for Defence; and Herbert Bowden, Lord President and Leader of the House of Commons.

But although Jim Callaghan, as Chancellor of the Exchequer, and George Brown, as First Secretary and Secretary of State for Economic Affairs, had accepted the broad division of function between the two departments, there was an immediate need, in the light of the advice each was getting from his departmental advisers, to settle a concordat as to the division of duties between them, and it had to be settled that Friday night. The draft I was given, which had been prepared by civil servants, set the division as between short-term responsibilities (Treasury) and long-term planning (DEA).

This was not what I had in mind. The concordat which emerged from my meeting later that evening with George Brown and Jim Callaghan made clear the fundamental distinction between monetary responsibilities on the one hand, which must come under the Treasury, and, on the other, the co-ordinating responsibilities for industry and everything to do with the mobilisation of real resources for productivity and exports.

George Brown went away to recruit his department and worked wonders, both in terms of a strong civil service team and of high-powered industrial advisers headed by Mr Fred Catherwood, at that time managing director of the British Aluminium Company. George Brown quickly and rightly added to his departmental duties responsibilities for prices and incomes, though there were moments in succeeding years when I felt that the DEA had become so overborne by prices and incomes questions that it was not driving ahead sufficiently fast with industrial planning and productivity questions. He also added – I now think I was wrong to agree – responsibility for the main issues of overseas economic policy. This caused endless problems with the Board of Trade and to some extent abutted onto Treasury responsibilities in the field of overseas finance.

Once the concordat was set up – it did not take more than a few minutes to dictate its terms – the three of us, the Chancellor, the First Secretary and myself, were faced with a much more fundamental problem. During the election campaign, the Treasury had produced a forecast of the economic situation for presentation to the incoming Government, be it Labour or Conservative. This was on our desks that night.

This formidable memorandum made it clear that Britain was facing a deficit of £800 millions on our overseas payments for the year 1964, and a scarcely less daunting prospect for 1965.

This presented us with a far more serious economic position than anything we had expected. I had gone so far in an election speech on 1st October – one which was dismissed by the Conservatives as 'scare-mongering' – as to suggest that we were running into deficit at a rate of a million pounds a day, less than £400 millions a year. The reality was more than twice as serious.

It was this inheritance which was to dominate almost every action of the Government for five years of the five years, eight months we were in office.

It was arranged that the new Secretary of State for Economic Affairs and the new Chancellor should meet me at No. 10 on the Saturday morning to review the economic position. The memorandum we had studied overnight insisted that decisions were not only urgent, but overdue. In addition to action on the domestic front, a decision was needed immediately to take effect on the foreign balance. There were three courses before us, all worked out in detail by the Treasury in consultation with the other departments concerned: devaluation of sterling; quantitative restrictions on imports (quotas); and a surcharge, in effect a temporary additional tariff, on a very wide range of imports.

There was comment, and this has been subsequently echoed, that we made an initial, even a fatal, blunder in our decision not to devalue within twenty-four hours of taking office, when we could have put all the responsibility on our Conservative predecessors. Politically, it might have been tempting and we were not unaware of the temptation. But I was convinced, and my colleagues agreed, that to devalue could have the most dangerous consequences.

The financial world at home and abroad was aware that the postwar decision to devalue in 1949 had been taken by a Labour Government. There would have been many who would conclude that a Labour Government facing difficulties always took the easy way out by devaluing the pound. Speculation would be aroused every time that Britain ran into even minor economic difficulties – or even without them. For we were to learn over the years that it was all too easy for those so minded to talk the pound down on the most frivolous of pretexts.

When, three years later, devaluation was forced upon us, the whole world recognised that there was no alternative – central banks and governments accepted the decision as necessary, recognising the courage and determination we had shown in our fight to hold the parity. And for these reasons they backed us wholeheartedly, and only a few countries followed our example by devaluing their own currency. In 1964 there would have been no such acceptance; in 1964 the true facts of Britain's deficit were not known and politics, rather than economic necessity, would have been blamed.

But there were other considerations. We might well have started off an orgy of competitive beggar-my-neighbour currency devaluations – similar to those of the 1930s – which would have plunged the world into monetary anarchy, and left us no better off – even, perhaps, stimulating economic nationalism and blind protectionism abroad.

There were also strong reasons in terms of the domestic, economic and political scene. I had always argued – and continued to argue for the next three years – that devaluation was not an easy way out; that, by its very nature in cheapening exports and making imports dearer, it would require a severe and rapid transfer of resources from home consumption, public and private, to meet the needs of overseas markets. This would mean brutal restraints in both public and private expenditure over and above what was required by the domestic situation we had inherited.

So devaluation was ruled out by a deliberate decision.

Quotas, after careful consideration, we rejected. I had had enough experience of administering them in the forties to know the damage they could inflict on industrial production, no matter how selective the system, and, in particular, their effect in ossifying the industrial structure, penalising new or growing or efficient firms and feather-bedding the uncompetitive.

We were thus faced with the third proposition in the Treasury brief. But the imposition of a temporary surcharge on imports was not easy, either. It would be argued abroad that a sudden rise in the tariff over a wide range of commodities was contrary to our international obligations, particularly those of the General Agreement on Tariffs and Trade (GATT), and of the European Free Trade Agreement (EFTA). Other nations with close economic relations with us – for example, Commonwealth countries, the Irish Republic, the United States – might have strong grounds for protest. There would be the fear that, once imposed, the surcharge would not be easily removed. There was the fear – against which I warned when we made our announcement – that some of our own manufacturers enjoying a temporary protection against foreign competition would slide into easy ways, instead of responding to the challenge by making themselves still more competitive.

Despite these anxieties, since action had to be taken, we decided to recommend the import surcharge to the Cabinet. We decided in principle that it should be imposed at a rate of fifteen per cent on all imports, except food, tobacco and basic raw materials. The departments – and here it was essential to bring the Board of Trade into the picture as soon as the President was appointed – were left to work out the details for submission to the Cabinet.

But first the full Cabinet had to be appointed, together with all the junior ministers and whips.

The ministers appointed who were not already Privy Councillors – as George and Patrick Gordon Walker were – had to be sworn of the Privy Council on the Saturday afternoon. All six kissed hands on their appointments and, where appropriate, received their seals of office. I had to attend to be appointed First Lord of the Treasury, where I was *not* required to kiss hands, on the ground that I had kissed hands as Prime Minister – which I had not.

This Privy Council marked a new step towards informality. I had been informed by the Palace that in place of the previous insistence on morning dress, lounge suits would be acceptable both for Council and for Audiences.

In forming the rest of the Administration I was determined on a number of innovations in the machinery of government, with new ministries relevant to Britain's priority problems, and with the appointment within existing departments of specialist junior ministers with special responsibilities. Many of these changes had been foreshadowed in speeches and broadcasts I had made in our last year and more of Opposition. A good deal of work had already been done, not only by us, but also by the ever-perceptive civil servants who had studied our proposals.

In addition to the DEA, the other major new department was the Ministry of Technology. I had long felt that we needed a ministry to discharge two functions which existing departments were inadequate to perform. It was to be a 'Ministry of Industry', starting with a relatively small number of industries, but taking on a wider and wider sponsorship, with a very direct responsibility for increasing productivity and efficiency, particularly within those industries in urgent need of restructuring or modernisation: industries such as machine tools and other branches of engineering, and shipbuilding, which, in the early sixties, had been the subject of report after report showing a worsening balance of trade between exports and imports, industries which, with shining exceptions, still relied too much on the structure and techniques of a bygone age.

The second task of the Ministry of Technology would be to speed the application of new scientific methods to industrial production. This had been the main theme of my speech at Labour's Scarborough conference in October 1963, which had attracted considerable attention. Britain had always been good in the scientific laboratory, but all too often the results of fundamental research done here had been clothed with the necessary know-how only by foreign industrialists. This had been a not unfamiliar process before the war. During the war some of our major inventions – such as jet propulsion, radar and other electronic developments, and antibiotics – had been handed over to the United States under the lend-lease arrangements from 1941 to 1945, and developed there – to the point where, in some cases, we were paying royalties on what were essentially British inventions or discoveries. The process had continued apace after the war and I decided something must be done about it.

I once described the Ministry of Technology in our pre-Government days as 'NRDC writ large'. The National Research Development Corporation, an idea of Sir Stafford Cripps, had been set up by me in 1948 after I had succeeded him at the Board of Trade, to develop, to the production stage, inventions by British scientists and research workers. The main purpose was to develop discoveries from our Government research establishments, such as the Royal Aircraft Establishment at Farnborough, as well as discoveries in university research laboratories. Over its sixteen years of life it had achieved considerable success on a modest scale. I felt not only should NRDC be transferred to the new ministry, but that over a far wider field this kind of activity should become a central theme of the ministry's work.

As I envisaged it, the Ministry of Technology would take over the technological, as opposed to the pure scientific work previously presided over by the Lord President of the Council, together with such little work on industrial technology as was done by a very small department of the Board of Trade. I intended that it should in due course incorporate the aircraft production section of the Ministry of Aviation, including the department's responsibilities for electronics, avionics, etc. This obviously would take time, as would the transfer to the department of the engineering, shipbuilding and related industries.

But there was one industry, computers, where time was not on our side. My frequent meetings with leading scientists, technologists and industrialists in the last two or three years of Opposition had convinced me that, if action was not taken quickly, the British computer industry would rapidly cease to exist, facing, as was the case in other European countries, the most formidable competition from the American giants. When, on the evening we took office, I asked Frank Cousins to become the first Minister of Technology, I told him that he had, in my view, about a month to save the British computer industry and that this must be his first priority. He succeeded.

Another newly-launched ministry, though one which was not destined to last long, was the Ministry of Land and Planning. I felt that the Housing and Local Government Department could not mobilise land resources, or ensure that planning decisions were taken with the speed necessary to enable the housing drive to proceed at the rate we wanted. In the event the ministry, which I set up under Fred Willey, failed to achieve its purpose, through no fault of his. The very powerful civil service structure in the Ministry of Housing and Local Government was not going to let the responsibility for local authority planning decisions pass out of its control. Within days of its conception the MHLG had won a battle – on which, perhaps, I should have acted more firmly – to ensure that this part of the planning work was left under its control.

Looking back on it – and conscious six years afterwards of how far our housing drive suffered later, not to mention the relative failure of the Land Commission to get moving, due to excessively slow planning decisions and zoning of land for housing purposes – I believe my first thoughts were right and that the new ministry should have had this power. Even so, it had plenty of work to do during the years of its existence. I gave it responsibility for the problems of land development, with particular reference to the problem of land cornering and speculation, and it was also entrusted with what has been a major revolution in many of our older cities, the enactment of leasehold enfranchisement.

Of great importance to over two and a half million people was the creation of the Welsh Department under the Secretary of State for Wales, with a seat in the Cabinet. Based to a considerable extent on the Scottish Office, which had existed since 1885, it was given full responsibility for local government, housing and planning, economic planning, roads, forestry and derelict land clearance and later for tourism and health, together with shared responsibility for agriculture with the ministry.

Within the field of ministries already in existence, I appointed a number of junior ministers with special responsibilities for subjects essential to Britain's economic and social development which had not been given an adequate priority in the past. In the Ministry of Labour, I appointed an additional Parliamentary Secretary, Richard Marsh, who began a distinguished ministerial career with a successful attack on the long-neglected problems of industrial training. In the Ministry of Housing and Local Government, Bob Mellish was appointed as Parliamentary Secretary with a special responsibility for London housing. In Education, Denis Howell, who had an unrivalled knowledge of sporting problems, was appointed as a junior minister with a special responsibility for sport. Indeed he rapidly acquired the title throughout the press and the sporting world of 'Minister of Sport'.

I decided that priority must also be given to the field of arts and amenities and appointed Miss Jennie Lee to this position. There was a problem in deciding to which department she should be formally allocated. In the past the responsibility for the arts had been, improbably, with the Treasury. While some dedicated people were involved in the work, it was always difficult for the Treasury to provide adequate finance, for even though its total spending was very small compared with that of the major spending departments, there was always the danger that when the Treasury was on an economy drive it would have to cut its own minuscule spending department to set an example. I felt that a spending department ought not to be in the Treasury anyway. Temporarily, I put it in the Ministry of Public Building and Works, where Jennie Lee also had the responsibility, under the minister, for a number of decisions affecting architectural development, particularly of public buildings, and some responsibility for design within the building industry. But this was not entirely satisfactory and at the turn of the year, after some doubt whether she should be in Housing and Local Government or in Education and Science, I transferred her to the latter.

Overseas there were three important new decisions. First a new ministry, that of Overseas Development, was set up under Barbara Castle, with a seat in the Cabinet. Its duty was to administer Britain's aid programme abroad, previously the responsibility of a minor department – the Technical Co-operation Department – and to do it with a new instruction that aid was to be granted not so much as a charity but as a real means to development, particularly within the Commonwealth. I intended also that it should have wide responsibilities. In my very early ministerial career I had seen a good deal of the work of the Food and Agriculture Organisation (FAO) of the United Nations, and other specialised agencies. I was very anxious that all Britain's responsibilities in relation to these organisations should be centred in the Ministry of Overseas Development. With one exception (the World Health Organisation) responsibility was so transferred and a new zest was put into the job of overseas development, despite the fact that Barbara was never able, against the background of financial stringency, to get the funds that she really wanted to have at her disposal.

The second appointment in the field of foreign and Commonwealth policy was a Minister of Disarmament, with the rank of Minister of State at the Foreign Office. I felt it right that the minister should be under the general control of the Foreign Secretary – but with strong and expert connections with the Defence Department – not a separate agency as in the United States. Alun Gwynne-Jones, raised to the Lords as Lord Chalfont, became the new minister and brought his considerable expertise and ability to the task of helping forward the United Nations' disarmament programme.

The third decision in the overseas field was no less a break with the past. I decided that Britain's representative at the United Nations should be a member of the Government. Sir Hugh Foot, distinguished colonial administrator and expert on the developing countries, who had resigned from the diplomatic service and from his post at New York in protest against the Conservative Government's African policies, was raised to the Lords as Lord Caradon and made Minister of State in the Foreign Office and permanent representative at the United Nations. His success there was mainly due to his own personality and reputation and particularly to the respect he enjoyed among the representatives of the growing number of third-world delegates. But it owed not a little also to the fact that he was a minister of the Crown, and that he had direct access to the Prime Minister. This was not a fiction. I told him when I appointed him that there would be occasions when the Foreign Office, or even the Cabinet, might be tempted to make decisions which, against a wider world context, would appear wrong, and that from his vantage point in New York he could return to us and act, as it were, as a conscience, as a goad, to persuade us to reconsider our policies. This happened on a number of occasions.

No ministers were appointed to No. 10, though the non-departmental ministers were to operate in the Cabinet Office. George Wigg, as Paymaster-General, was given a special responsibility in the field of security. The last few years of the Conservative Administration suggested that there was still too much laxity in the operation of security procedures, with all too obvious confusion of where responsibility lay. For example, many in high places had been surprised to find, in Lord Denning's Report, that in addition to the Prime Minister's over-all and direct charge, there was a specific instruction to the security service that, where questions arose outside the normal run of their duties, advice should be sought from the permanent under-secretary at the Home Office. But ministerial responsibility was blurred and I had to issue a new directive. (The then principal private secretary at No. 10 who has very special duties in this field, told me at the time of the Denning Report that he had not known of the Home Office provision, though a brief reference had been made in the House years earlier.) Another matter which had caused concern at the time of Denning had been the clear fact that, for whatever reason, the then Prime Minister had not been made aware of facts which were common gossip – not all of it accurate – among MPs and in Fleet Street.

George Wigg's remit, which I put in writing and circulated to all the departments concerned, was not to cut across existing departmental re-sponsibilities, but nevertheless it charged him with the duty of keeping me fully informed, and at the earliest moment, of any developments of which I ought to know. In addition he was to satisfy himself, and me, that departmental procedures were adequate for the task laid on them. Both the security services, and the departments, especially Defence, welcomed his intervention, and a lot of necessary changes were made and procedures brought up to date. I believe that his three years on this – and other – work, did more for our security services, and their place in the system of government, than has ever been guessed at. For obvious reasons it can neither be described nor fully evaluated.

With one or two exceptions, the entire Government was formed by the early part of the week following the election. The members of it I set out below, excluding the whips and Royal Household appointments in both Houses:

CABINET

Prime Minister and First Lord of The Treasury	Harold Wilson
First Secretary of State and Secretary of State for Economic Affairs	George Brown
Secretary of State for Foreign Affairs	Patrick Gordon Walker
Lord President of the Council	Herbert Bowden
Lord Chancellor	Lord Gardiner
Chancellor of the Exchequer	James Callaghan
Secretary of State for Defence	Denis Healey
Secretary of State for the Home Department	Sir Frank Soskice
Secretary of State for Commonwealth Relations	Arthur Bottomley
Secretary of State for Scotland	William Ross
Secretary of State for Wales	James Griffiths
Secretary of State for the Colonies	Anthony Greenwood
President of the Board of Trade	Douglas Jay
Lord Privy Seal	Lord Longford

Secretary of State for Education and Science	Michael Stewart
Minister of Housing and Local Government	Richard Crossman
Chancellor of the Duchy of Lancaster	Douglas Houghton
Minister of Labour	Ray Gunter
Minister of Technology	Frank Cousins
Minister of Power	Fred Lee
Minister of Transport	Tom Fraser
Minister of Overseas Development	Barbara Castle

MINISTERS NOT IN THE CABINET

Minister of Health	Kenneth Robinson
Minister of Pensions and National Insurance	Margaret Herbison
Minister of Public Building and Works	Charles Pannell
Minister of Aviation	Roy Jenkins
Postmaster-General	Anthony Wedgwood Benn
Minister of Land and Natural Resources	Frederick Willey
Deputy Secretary of State for Defence and Minister of Defence for the Army	Frederick Mulley
Minister without Portfolio	Sir Eric Fletcher
Minister without Portfolio	Lord Champion
Paymaster-General	George Wigg
Chief Secretary to the Treasury	John Diamond
Minister of State, Department of Economic Affairs	Anthony Crosland
Minister of Defence for the Royal Navy	Christopher Mayhew
Minister of Defence for the Royal Air Force	Lord Shackleton
Minister of State, Department of Education and Science	Lord Bowden
Ministers of State for Foreign Affairs	George Thomson, Lord Caradon, Walter Padley, Lord Chalfont
Minister of State, Home Office	Alice Bacon
Minister of State, Commonwealth Relations Office	Cledwyn Hughes
Ministers of State, Board of Trade	George Darling, Edward Redhead, Roy Mason
Minister of State, Scottish Office	George Willis
Minister of State, Welsh Office	Goronwy Roberts

Minister of State, Department of
  Education and Science   Reginald Prentice
Attorney-General   Sir Elwyn Jones
Lord Advocate   Gordon Stott
Solicitor-General   Sir Dingle Foot
Solicitor-General for Scotland   James G. Leechman

OTHER MINISTERS

Parliamentary Secretaries, Ministry of
  Agriculture, Fisheries and Food   James Hoy, John Mackie
Parliamentary Secretary, Ministry of
  Aviation   John Stonehouse
Under-Secretaries for the Colonies   Lord Taylor,
                                    Mrs Eirene White

Under-Secretary of State for Common-
  wealth Relations   Lord Taylor
Under-Secretary of State for Defence,
  for the Royal Navy   J. P. W. Mallalieu
Under-Secretary of State for Defence,
  for the Army   G. W. Reynolds
Under-Secretary of State for Defence, for
  the Royal Air Force   Bruce Millan
Joint Under-Secretaries of State for
  Economic Affairs   Maurice Foley,
                                    William Rodgers

Joint Under-Secretaries of State,
  Department of Education and Science   James Boyden,
                                    Denis Howell

Under-Secretary of State for Foreign
  Affairs   Lord Walston
Parliamentary Secretary, Ministry of
  Health   Sir Barnett Stross
Joint Under-Secretaries of State to the
  Home Office   Lord Stonham,
                                    George Thomas

Joint Parliamentary Secretaries,
  Ministry of Housing and Local
  Government   James MacColl,
                                  Robert Mellish

Joint Parliamentary Secretaries,
  Ministry of Labour   Richard Marsh,
                                  Ernest Thornton

Joint Parliamentary Secretaries, Ministry
of Land and Natural Resources

Lord Mitchison,
Arthur Skeffington

Parliamentary Secretary for Overseas
Development

Albert Oram

Joint Parliamentary Secretaries, Ministry
of Pensions and National Insurance

Harold Davies,
Norman Pentland

Assistant Postmaster-General

Joseph Slater

Parliamentary Secretary, Ministry of
Power

John Morris

Parliamentary Secretary, Ministry of
Public Building and Works

Jennie Lee

Under-Secretaries of State for Scotland

Dr J. Dickson Mabon,
Judith Hart,
Lord Hughes

Parliamentary Secretary, Ministry of
Technology

Lord Snow

Parliamentary Secretary, Board of Trade

Lord Rhodes

Joint Parliamentary Secretaries, Ministry
of Transport

Lord Lindgren,
Stephen Swingler

Parliamentary Secretary to the Treasury
(Chief Whip)

Edward Short

Financial Secretary to the Treasury

Niall MacDermot

Under-Secretary of State for Wales

Harold Finch

Chapter 2

Cabinet procedure – legislation and the small majority – statement on the economic situation – Southern Africa, Rhodesia, and the threat of UDI – the first ten days of office

ON Monday, 19th October, we held our first Cabinet. Apart from myself, only two of the twenty-three members had sat in a Cabinet before. Patrick Gordon Walker had been Commonwealth Secretary in Clem Attlee's Government, from February 1950 to October 1951 and for that same period Jim Griffiths – now appointed, at the age of seventy-four, as a kind of 'Charter' Secretary of State for Wales – had been Secretary of State for the Colonies. George Brown had been a senior departmental minister at the Ministry of Works, but not a member of the Cabinet.

I had to lay down the rules, and as far as possible, and to the best of my memory, I based them on those insisted on by Clem Attlee. Strict timekeeping: the Cabinet could not be kept waiting for one or two laggards. Circulation of documents in adequate time for colleagues to read: only in an emergency would I give authority for a paper to be circulated on the day before Cabinet met. Departmental disagreements should be thrashed out before Cabinet met: where possible an agreed statement should be submitted where more than one department was involved. Where disagreement remained, this should be clearly stated and the arguments set out either in joint or separate papers. Any proposals involving expenditure should be fully discussed with the Treasury first, and Treasury agreement – or disagreement – recorded. The cost to the public purse should be set out in the paper. The figure, agreed by the Treasury, should be shown, even if the Treasury opposed the expenditure. In subsequent years I insisted more and more that the cost, too, in terms of civil service manpower should also be set out; before the end of the Government I accepted a Conservative backbench suggestion that such estimates, in addition to statements of financial cost, should be attached to the explanatory memorandum which accompanies public Bills when they are presented to Parliament.

There was one other – minor – procedural decision to be taken. Was smoking to be allowed in Cabinet? In Winston Churchill's Governments it was of course the rule, as it was in the first two years and more of Clem Attlee's. But in November 1947, following restraints on tobacco imports due to dollar stringency, the then Cabinet accepted a suggestion of Hugh Dalton's that, to set an example, Cabinet should not smoke – an indulgence being permitted from one o'clock if Cabinet business was not completed. (Ernest Bevin's watch was always five minutes fast.) I rehearsed the arguments before Cabinet was asked to decide. A non-smoking Cabinet would have shorter meetings: smokers would tend to speed their decisions and curb their loquacity. On the other hand, meetings might be less good-tempered and co-operative. And even the incentive to shorter meetings might lead to decisions being deferred, referred back for further consideration or inter-departmental discussion – a procedure which I always sought to avoid and usually succeeded in doing so.

The Cabinet decided. The right way.

But it was not only Cabinet rules which had to be settled. We had to give deep consideration to the Cabinet's posture, in the face of its unprecedentedly small parliamentary majority.

We had Clem Attlee's warning ever-present in our minds. We knew what it would mean for the Leader of the House, for the Chief Whip and his team. In addition to their heavy departmental duties and problems, ministers would have to be in almost constant attendance at the House. We all knew what would be involved.

I began by referring to the problem we faced. We did not know how long the Parliament would last, or whether the timing of the next election would be decided at a moment chosen by the Prime Minister, or forced upon him by parliamentary defeat.

I recommended the Cabinet to plan on the basis of a Queen's Speech covering a full and hard-working session, with one or more further sessions to come. Further, in the development of our policies we should proceed exactly as if we had a majority not of four but of a hundred, and press on with all the policies in which we believed, the policies we had been elected to carry out. If the main strategy of policy was trimmed because of our narrow majority, we should quickly become a Cabinet of political opportunism, operating on short-term considerations, pushed around by every form of pressure. Worse, if we started picking our way among possible political traps and minefields, we should lose our sense of the direction we had to travel. The same applied if we were to shirk introducing unpopular measures which we considered to be necessary, but which might be electorally damaging if we had to go to the country early, and at short notice.

The country had suffered from eighteen months of electioneering, of a Government, albeit with a hundred majority, fearful to take necessary measures because of electoral consequences. The previous Prime Minister on his election as leader of the Conservative party had said, in October 1963: 'So from this moment on, the fact that there is a General Election ahead of us must never be out of our minds. Every act that we take, every attitude that we strike, every speech that we make in Parliament or elsewhere, must have that in mind. . . .'

Neither the country nor the Government could survive, still less make progress, on that basis. We had to live dangerously, and that meant we had to act responsibly. The Cabinet fully agreed. It was never in doubt.

One of the first decisions to be taken by the new Cabinet was the endorsement of the economic proposals put before it by the three of us who had met on that first Saturday morning. There was no disposition to argue. Action had to be announced and taken quickly. As the new Parliament had not yet met, it was not possible to publish a White Paper. On 26th October, ten days after taking office, we issued our 'statement' on the economic situation. It covered the results of the Government's 'first review of the financial and economic state of the nation. . . . The Government take the view that the country is entitled to know the full facts of the situation. . . .'

On the international financial position, it concluded that while, with the facilities available, the strength of sterling could and would be maintained, the underlying economic situation remained profoundly unsatisfactory. The balance of payments deficit for 1964 was most unlikely to be below £700 millions and might well reach £800 millions. While a considerable improvement was expected, in 1965 'the deficit would still be at an unacceptable level'.

The position on imports and exports was surveyed together with the domestic economic situation, the problem of 'continually rising prices' – and the position on public expenditure. We saw 'lack of balance and absence of proper sound and economic priorities. . . .' And there was a sharp rejoinder to the Conservative spending-spree in the election year: 'The large public expenditure programmes which the Government found on taking office would, if left unchanged, fully absorb for the years ahead the future growth of revenue at present rates of taxation, even on the assumption of a regular four per cent per year rate of growth of gross national product; and without a growing increase in the rate of personal saving, higher rates of taxation would be needed. . . .'

The statement then went on to announce the action we had decided to take, which I summarise:

The introduction of surcharges, at fifteen per cent, on all imports, except food, tobacco and basic raw materials;

The enactment of an export rebate scheme, under which exporters could recover part at least of indirect taxes paid by them in the process of production;

The establishment of a Commonwealth Exports Council, for which I had long pressed in Opposition, and which the Conservatives had steadfastly resisted;

Consultations with industry on a plan to deal with productivity, prices and incomes, and the establishment of a Price Review Body;

Severance payments, improved transfer grants and other measures to help labour mobility between industries, and, where necessary, areas;

New measures to help areas of under-employment;

A strict review of Government expenditure, with particular emphasis on scrapping 'prestige projects'. The statement announced that the French Government had already been told of our wish to re-examine urgently the Concorde project;

Consultation with the International Monetary Fund on the use by Britain of her drawing rights.

The reaction to the Government statement was predictably mixed. The Conservative press was hostile on Tuesday, 27th October, and again on the Sunday, 1st November. Some of it bitterly so. Mr Maudling, on the other hand, said that we had inherited his analysis – and his solutions.

The reaction from certain countries overseas was furious. For obvious reasons we had not been able to consult them and we were much criticised by the Opposition in Parliament for failing to do so. We had informed our Commonwealth partners, who were, for the most part, very understanding, and I had exchanged personal messages with President Johnson. He was within ten days of his presidential election but he was surprisingly forthcoming, recognising our difficulties and our desire to avoid severe deflationary measures, or higher interest rates, which could have hurt the US economy more directly.

The Irish Republic, our closest and most integrated trading partner, was much more anxious, and the Prime Minister, Mr Sean Lemass, was over to see me on 5th November. But the sharpest reaction was from member countries of EFTA, some of whom felt that their exports and economies would be severely hit, and who, in any case, felt that our action was a breach of the spirit, and – it was argued – the letter of the EFTA Treaty. We were to hear more of this and in critical circumstances.

The other priority task of the new Cabinet was the preparation of the Queen's Speech, the legislative programme for the new parliamentary session.

Once again, the civil servants responsible, under the leadership of the Secretary to the Cabinet, Sir Burke Trend, had anticipated our needs. Neutral and non-political though the civil service is, it is as sharp as any other body of men in recognising political realities. They had read the election manifesto, and studied every statement. The first draft of the Queen's Speech was ready within days, perhaps hours, of the opening of the ballot-boxes; or was it, I wondered, ready even before? Had two drafts been prepared, on alternative election assumptions? Whatever the answer, it was a first-class draft: all our major policy commitments were there, and we felt it right to endorse them. An increase in pensions; the abolition of the widows' earnings rule; the repeal of the Rent Act; steel nationalisation; the abolition of health charges; leasehold enfranchisement; the Land Commission: all were there.

At our first Cabinet, the usual sub-committee on the Queen's Speech was set up under the chairmanship of the Lord President to prepare a definitive draft for the Cabinet's approval and submission to the Queen.

But before the Queen's Speech committee could meet, Southern Africa had moved into the centre of the stage. Northern Rhodesia was to attain independence as Zambia at midnight on 22nd–23rd October. There was a thorny problem which had to be settled before the Union Flag was lowered for the last time, namely the conditions on which the British South Africa Company (Chartered) could continue to operate in the newly-independent Zambia. This problem took quite a lot of ministers' time, including my own. British interests were very much involved; world interests, too, in the supply of vital raw materials. The new sovereign nation had its rights. Instructions were given on my authority and Arthur Bottomley, the new Commonwealth Relations Secretary, who represented the Government at the celebrations, was highly successful in the settlement he negotiated at the fifty-ninth minute of the last hour with Zambia's leader, Dr Kenneth Kaunda, an agreement covering the future operations of the Chartered company.

But, even before this problem was settled, with the new Labour Government fewer than four days old, there had been a major eruption from Southern Africa: Rhodesia.

It was a problem we had foreseen. It had nearly reached breaking-point under the Conservative Government but the final crisis had been successfully postponed until the British election was over.

The problem had a history.

The abortive Central African Federation of Northern and Southern Rhodesia and Nyasaland had finally broken up, unmourned, on 31st December 1963, and each country became legally a British colony, with varying degrees of internal self-government. Northern Rhodesia and Nyasaland had the classical pre-independence model of a Chief Minister and a virtually autonomous Government, under a British-appointed Governor, but with no responsibility for defence and foreign policy. Southern Rhodesia reverted to the status it had enjoyed since 1924, with full internal self-government, and, uniquely among non-independent Commonwealth countries, its own highly efficient armed forces. It had no responsibility for foreign affairs, but had its own High Commission in London, and in important capitals, such as Washington, had its own minister, who for diplomatic purposes was attached to the British Embassy.

When the Federation had broken up the Federal Air Force reverted to Southern Rhodesia, a matter of some controversy in the British Parliament. The Labour shadow cabinet had considered opposing the transfer, but after an exchange with the Northern Rhodesian Chief Minister, Kenneth Kaunda, we decided to withdraw our opposition on the ground that he had, albeit reluctantly, agreed to the transfer at the Victoria Falls Conference, which had dealt with the residual assets of the Federation.

Nyasaland, first, and then Northern Rhodesia were on the road to independence within the Commonwealth, under legislation passed at Westminster. Nyasaland had become independent as Malawi in July 1964, and Northern Rhodesia, as Zambia, celebrated the final hand-over of power exactly a week after we took office.

Southern Rhodesia presented an entirely different problem. Never – since South African independence in 1909 – had a British colony been granted full autonomy, except on the basis of universal adult suffrage, 'one man, one vote'. Southern Rhodesia had a constitution in which only five per cent of the population had the vote. Almost all of the electorate were Europeans, either descendants of the original, mainly British, settlers, or recent – mainly postwar – immigrants from Britain, though a growing number of postwar immigrants, approaching parity with the British, were white South Africans.

The 1961 constitution had been passed by the British Parliament in a highly controversial atmosphere. The Labour party had voted solidly against it. (So did Mr Ian Smith and his supporters in the Rhodesian Parliament, but for different reasons.)

It was a sharply regressive constitution, with two main rolls of voters. The A-roll was confined to Europeans, the B-roll to a small proportion of African, Asian and coloured voters. Registration – after a severe literacy test – depended on educational, property or income qualifications. On Rhodesian Government figures 60,000 were entitled to register; only 10,700 had done so by 1964. Of these, only 1,443 voted in the 1965 General Election. The small registration was attributed by the Government to African nationalist propaganda, backed by physical intimidation; by the nationalists to lack of effort by the registration authorities, combined with the restrictions imposed by the literacy test.

There was also a complicated provision for cross-voting, under which B-roll voters were able to vote in A-roll constituencies, but on a severely devalued basis in that four B-roll voters counted only as equal to one A-roll voter. Cross-voting in the early sixties, as for very many years to come, gave no hope of any decisive African influence in even a single A-roll seat, African representation being limited to the fifteen reserved B-roll seats.

In April 1963, the Welenskyite right-wing European Administration, headed by Sir Edgar Whitehead, had been heavily defeated at the polls, and replaced by the Rhodesian Front, then headed by Mr Winston Field. Few of the Salisbury Establishment expected them to last – they were contemptuously written off as ignorant 'cowboys'. But the Establishment underrated their tenacity, their racialist grass-roots backing, and their determination to go independent on the 1961 constitution: legally, if a

British Government could be persuaded to carry the necessary legislation through Parliament, or, in default of legality, by a 'Unilateral Declaration of Independence' (UDI).

Labour was vehemently committed against any grant of independence on the basis of the 1961 or any similar constitution. At the eve-of-conference rally at the Labour conference at Scarborough in October 1963, the first I had addressed as leader, I had devoted the central part of my speech to this theme of the disenfranchised Southern Rhodesia Africans who outnumbered the Europeans by fifteen to one.

The Conservative Government under Sir Alec Douglas-Home for a time appeared equivocal and ready to give in to pressure – including the pressure of their own powerful Central African parliamentary lobby, which had already won a victory over Sir Alec on Katanga. Week after week we pressed the Conservative Government in the House, and ultimately the Government grew tougher. Whether this was due to pressure by African and Asian Commonwealth countries – and Canada – or whether it was the brutal replacement of Mr Winston Field by Mr Ian Smith in April 1964, or to our own pressure, can only be surmised. When Mr Smith replaced Mr Field, Sir Alec Douglas-Home asked me to see him, and I could see that his earlier hopes of taming Mr Smith had now evaporated. Very soon afterwards, Sir Alec gave what seemed to me a clear commitment when, across the floor of the House, he agreed with my proposition that 'majorities, as well as minorities, had their rights'.

From that time, Sir Alec, together with his Commonwealth Secretary, Mr Duncan Sandys, took a very firm line with the Smith Government, consistently asserting that 1961 had never been put forward as an independence constitution.

Every statement by Sir Alec Douglas-Home and Mr Sandys made it clear that independence could be granted only by the British Parliament, on the basis of proposals put before it by the British Government. There was no commitment to any automatic independence. The 1961 constitution was not a basis for an independence constitution. The strongest warnings were given about the bilateral and international consequences of a purported UDI.

No less tough and forthright were the Conservative Government's strictures in the government-to-government talks in September 1964, a week before Sir Alec announced the election date. He had made clear that independence had to depend on the proved 'genuine desire' of the great majority of the Rhodesian population; that a referendum from the predominantly European electorate, insufficiently representing the Africans, would not suffice; that Mr Smith's prescription of an 'indaba' of chiefs (all of whom were paid creatures of the Government) was not acceptable. Finally, he insisted that 'independence could only be conceded on the basis of majority rule'.

The communiqué included these words: 'The British Prime Minister said that the British Government must be satisfied that any basis on which it was proposed that independence should be granted was acceptable to the people of the country as a whole.'

This was the first statement of what came to be known as the fifth principle. The Conservative Government remained firm to the end. On 15th October – polling day itself – Mr Sandys went into his office, and drafted a telegram for immediate transmission to Mr Smith, rejecting the latter's proposal for an 'indaba' of chiefs and headmen as a means of testing the views of the African population, and rejecting an invitation to send observers. (All the Conservative Government's exchanges with the Southern Rhodesian Government are set out in the Blue Book (Cmnd. 2807) which I presented to Parliament after UDI in November 1965, as are the subsequent telegrams, messages and oral exchanges which we had with them up to the UDI declaration.)

On 19th October, the Monday after we took office, Arthur Bottomley, the new Commonwealth Secretary, wrote a stiff letter backing the Sandys message and proposing that he should visit Salisbury the following week after attending the Zambian independence celebrations.

But the 'indaba' took place on 22nd October, and Mr Smith made preparations for an independence referendum of the Rhodesian electorate on 5th November. Mr Smith refused to accept Arthur Bottomley's proposals for a visit if it meant, as it must mean, seeing representative Africans, including the two Nationalist leaders, Mr Joshua Nkomo and the Reverend Ndabaningi Sithole. He would be allowed to go to Rhodesia only for discussions with Mr Smith, as the letter put it, 'in my capacity as Prime Minister of Rhodesia'.

On 23rd October, I countered the rejection by inviting Mr Smith to London. He refused to come. I then warned him in the strongest terms about any action he might take after the referendum, particularly a UDI, and I demanded a categorical assurance that no such action would be taken. Otherwise, I said, I would have to make our views public on the lines of a draft statement I sent him.

Our anxieties had been increased by Mr Smith's summary dismissal of the Chief of Staff of Rhodesia's military forces, Major-General Anderson, because of his opposition to UDI. Mr Smith's unconvincing excuse was that the fifty-one-year-old General was due for retirement. He was not. The General commented, 'I have taken an oath to the Queen and to me that means one is an upholder of constitutional government.' After his dismissal he emphasised that the Services supported his opposition to UDI and said that if he had been in command when one was declared, he would have had to disobey orders.

Mr Smith refused to give me the categorical assurance about UDI. Reports reached us from Rhodesia that he would announce UDI at the debate in the Salisbury Parliament, on Tuesday 27th October. We decided to publish the warning which he had seen in draft, and it was issued from 10 Downing Street at 6 a.m. on the morning of the 27th, 8 a.m. in Rhodesia, where it would be heard on every car radio.

After reaffirming that Her Majesty's Government looked forward to Southern Rhodesia taking her place as an independent sovereign state within the Commonwealth, we re-asserted that the decision to grant independence rested entirely with the British Government and Parliament. They would have a solemn duty to be satisfied that the terms of independence were acceptable to the people of Southern Rhodesia as a whole.

Turning to reports of UDI, we said we:

find it necessary to declare what serious consequences would flow from such an act. . . .
– A mere declaration of independence would have no constitutional effect. . . . A declaration of independence would be an open act of defiance and rebellion and it would be treasonable to take steps to give effect to it. . . .
– No Commonwealth Government would be able to recognise a unilateral declaration.
– Commonwealth membership would be out of the question, with all the related economic consequences.
– The British Government would be bound to sever relations with those responsible for such a declaration.

There would be no relations with the Crown. Southern Rhodesians would cease to be British subjects.

– The economic effects would be disastrous to the prosperity and prospects of the people of Southern Rhodesia. All financial and trade relations between Britain and Southern Rhodesia would be jeopardised. Any further aid or any further access to the London market would be out of the question. . . .
In short, an illegal declaration of independence in Southern Rhodesia would bring to an end relationships between her and Britain, would cut Rhodesia off from the rest of the Commonwealth, from most foreign Governments and international organisations, would inflict disastrous economic damage upon her, and would leave her isolated and virtually friendless in a largely hostile continent.

When Parliament debated the Queen's Speech a week later, on 3rd November, Sir Alec Douglas-Home described the language as 'rough, but right'.

In its first ten days of office, the new Labour Government had been through a baptism of fire. The economic situation; an explosive foreign situation; Rhodesia at danger-point: on each of these, far-reaching decisions had to be taken before the Government was a week old.

Looking back on those first few days, from six years on, I derived a little ironic amusement from articles in Conservative newspapers advocating the virtues of leisurely, even inactive, decision-free government.

Chapter 3

The Queen's Speech of 3rd November – Labour's programme – the Conservative reaction – speculation against sterling – Government expenditure – the drain on reserves – economic dictation and social policy – the Governor of the Bank of England

PARLIAMENT was summoned for Tuesday, 27th October. The previous day the Parliamentary Labour Party was called to Church House, Westminster for the election of the leader and deputy leader for the duration of the Parliament. At this meeting Ted Short, the Government Chief Whip, told the party what would be involved in trying to run the Government with so small a majority. He said that pairing would have to be unprecedentedly strict and under his own personal control. He did not want anyone to be sick during this Parliament; still less could he afford any abstentions or careless absences. He said that the task he had given himself was to ensure that the next election would be called at a moment of the Prime Minister's choosing and that it would not be forced upon him. It was a mark of the success with which he fulfilled his task, and the loyalty of the PLP to everything he asked of them, that when the Parliament did end in March 1966, it was, in fact, at a moment of my own choosing.

The first days of Parliament as usual were occupied with the election of Mr Speaker and the swearing-in of members. There had been doubt whether the former Conservative Solicitor-General, Sir Harry Hylton-Foster, who had been Speaker in the previous Parliament, would go forward for re-election. After the Government was formed he told Herbert Bowden, our Chief Whip in Opposition, that, while he was willing to serve in the new Parliament, he would refuse if he felt our support for him was dictated by the narrowness of our majority. Herbert Bowden reminded Sir Harry that I had told him in the summer, when a substantial Labour majority was widely expected, that a Labour Government would wish him to continue in office. He accepted nomination.

Because of the narrow majority the Opposition agreed to share with us the appointments of the non-voting chairman and deputy chairman of Ways and Means. From our side of the House, Dr Horace King became chairman and deputy Speaker; from the Conservative side, Sir Samuel Storey became deputy-chairman. Our effective majority, consequently, became five over-all, fourteen over the official Opposition.

On Tuesday, 3rd November the Queen's Speech was delivered from the throne to both Houses of Parliament.

27

In addition to the usual references to overseas affairs, where the Speech laid particular emphasis on interdependence on nuclear questions and on the United Nations and its agencies, the main stress was on economic strength and social progress at home. There was great emphasis on regional planning and the development areas, and the first Bill mentioned was legislation to create a Highlands and Islands Development Board.

Then followed public ownership and control of the iron and steel industry; a Bill in the industrial relations field to clear up a highly controversial court decision – Rookes *v.* Barnard; action would be taken to require companies to disclose political contributions in their accounts; a major review of the whole field of social security; immediate legislation to increase existing rates of national insurance and associated benefits; prescription charges for medicines were to go. New Bills were to be introduced – largely inherited from the work of Sir Edward Boyle – for determining teachers' pay.

In the field of housing, we promised a Bill to restore rent control and, in effect, repeal all the odious provisions of the highly controversial Conservative Rent Act of 1957. A Crown Lands Commission with powers to acquire land for the community was to be introduced, and there was to be a measure to provide for leasehold enfranchisement. A Bill to provide for the appointment of Law Commissioners to recommend reforms in the law was announced, and also new measures for the impartial investigation of individual grievances – the Ombudsman proposal to which I had committed the incoming Government in a speech at Stowmarket the previous July. In addition to Government Bills, it was announced that facilities would be provided for a free decision by Parliament on the issue of capital punishment.

It would have been an ambitious programme, even with a three-figure majority. It embodied a great part of the election programme of industrial modernisation and social advance. *The Times*, in a leading article the next day, commented: '... The speech contains a useful programme which, with one provocative exception [Steel], establishes a sensible order of priorities. ...'

In the debate that followed, the Leader of the Opposition, Sir Alec Douglas-Home, opened the major discussion after the mover and seconder of the Address had spoken. His speech was a delightful blend of the sardonic and the serious. He ribbed me, as he was entitled to, about the size of the Government – which, because of the special appointments and new ministries, exceeded the statutory limit, thus requiring new legislation. He described some of the senior appointments as having been based on the demobilisation formula, 'age and length of service'. He had something of a point here, because though I had a considerable number of young ministers, especially in the junior positions, any incoming Labour Government is to some extent influenced by the fact that the

Prime Minister has been presiding over an elected shadow cabinet which tends to represent sectional or regional differences and is not necessarily chosen, in every case, with a view to the election of those best suited to become senior members of an Administration. In addition, my predecessor, Hugh Gaitskell, had nominated some forty or fifty front bench spokesmen, not all of whom would have been my choice. Most of those had to be slotted into position. In the few instances where I did not appoint them to ministerial office, I had nothing but trouble for years ahead. In the case of one or two of those who were appointed to, or offered, posts junior to those which they felt their abilities qualified them, there was more trouble to follow. Sir Alec was perfectly entitled to stir it up.

My own speech was mainly related to the contents of the Queen's Speech, though I took particular pleasure in announcing that our first Bill would be one to legalise the action of local authorities providing free or cheap bus fares for old-age pensioners and others. Ted Short, Bessie Braddock and I had tried over a period of years to promote such a Bill and had been frustrated by the Conservative Government, Sir Alec Douglas-Home as Prime Minister himself giving our proposals the *coup de grâce* in 1964.

There was one incident towards the end of my speech which caused great controversy. I referred to the absence from the House of the Foreign Secretary, Patrick Gordon Walker, who had lost his seat at Smethwick following 'the utterly squalid' campaign of the Smethwick Conservatives.

My words inevitably produced some barracking from the opposite side and I then let fly with what I had said when I had first heard the Smethwick result during my own count in Huyton. Pointing out that Sir Alec Douglas-Home had specifically repudiated any campaign which exploited anti-immigrant feelings, I asked him, then and there, to get up and say whether he endorsed the successful Conservative candidate, Peter Griffiths, or whether he repudiated the means by which he had entered the House. If the former, I said, then Sir Alec would have fallen a long way from the position he had taken up. If the latter, then the honourable member for Smethwick would, for the lifetime of Parliament, be treated as a parliamentary leper.

This created an immediate outcry and some Conservatives walked out in protest. The first 'early-day motion' on the Order Paper for the new Parliament was a backbench censure signed by the majority of Conservative members against the language I had used. Bitterness followed for a considerable period of time. There was much press comment as to see why I had let fly in this way. Perhaps James Margach of the *Sunday Times* produced the best rational argument when he said it was not possible to believe I was still fighting the last election, but that I had already begun to fight the next. My decision to use this phrase – not very fully thought out – was not, in fact, calculated for such a purpose; it was an expression of my anger about what had occurred.

The greater part of the debate on the Queen's Speech, which lasted a week, centred inevitably on the economic situation. This was the main theme, of course, of the speeches of George Brown and of Jim Callaghan, both of whom foreshadowed legislation to give effect to the announcements in the economic statement of 26th October, concerning import deposits and export rebates. A Ways and Means statement was promised for 11th November.

On the last day of the debate there was a Conservative amendment deploring the decision to go forward with steel nationalisation. This showed us what we were up against in the matter of maintaining a parliamentary majority. The sickness tally the weekend before the debate showed one or two of our people in hospital, but sufficiently fit to be brought by ambulance to New Palace Yard, from where their vote could be credited. Then one of our whips, Brian O'Malley, inconveniently went down with appendicitis, and there was doubt whether we should make our total. On the day of the vote, a Scottish member was taken ill with bronchitis, bringing our majority down to three. Then a fog in Scotland prevented thirteen of our Labour members from flying down from Glasgow. Four came on the Royal Scot; the other nine rushed over to Prestwick by coach. The debate was reasonably lively, though good-tempered, but the principal attention centred on the fog-bound Scots. But by 8.30 they had all arrived; we had secured our numbers and we won through with a majority of five.

In fact, the Government would not have fallen on an accidental defeat caused by Scottish fog. We should have had to put down a motion of confidence to give our underlying majority, small though it was, an opportunity to overcome the vagaries of the climate. But this experience showed the very narrow margin on which we were operating and would have to continue to operate.

Once the Queen's Speech had been approved, parliamentary interest was directed on the statement Jim Callaghan was to make in the Committee of Ways and Means on 11th November. It was, in fact, an autumn Budget. He took the opportunity of announcing the increases in social benefits. An increase of 12s 6d to £4 a week in the old-age pension for single people, and of 21s to £6 10s for a married couple. There would be corresponding increases in war pensions, and industrial injuries benefit. The 10s widows' pension was increased to 30s and the 'earnings rule' for widows was abolished, ending a long-standing and bitter grievance. All this was estimated to cost £85 millions a year. But it could not come into effect until the following March, because of the time taken to alter the papers, records, pension books and the rest.

Jim Callaghan announced a corresponding increase in the National

Assistance Board rates, which, he said, he hoped could be got through by the end of the year, to give much-needed help over the winter. He raised the dependants' allowance for income tax purposes and the age-exemption provision, to take account of the new pension increases. He then came to his proposals for taxation: 6d a gallon on petrol and hydro-carbon oils to take effect immediately and a rise of 6d in the standard rate of income tax to take effect from the beginning of the next financial year on 6th April, though with no increase for the reduced rates of tax on lower incomes. He announced two major tax reforms. One was the introduction of our new capital gains tax. The other involved a funda-mental change in company taxation, by creating a corporation tax to replace the former profits tax and the income tax on companies.

There were also Ways and Means resolutions to give effect to the export rebate tax and to the import deposits scheme. The only votes were on the petrol tax, which we won by the comfortable margin of ten, and the resolution for the increase in income tax, which, with Liberal help, we won by twenty-six.

We were soon to learn that decisions on pensions and taxation were no longer to be regarded, as in the past, as decisions for Parliament alone. The combination of tax increases with increased social security benefits provoked the first of a series of attacks on sterling, by speculators and others, which beset almost every action of the Government for the next five years. I should therefore say something about how these raids on sterling are brought about.

British citizens are virtually precluded by the exchange control laws from speculating in sterling, that is from speculation based on selling sterling to obtain foreign currencies. Where speculation has occurred, it has been either through specifically illegal transactions or, occasionally, by highly devious routes, just within the law but difficult to identify, and still more difficult to prevent. But in London there is a number of large international companies who, in normal times, hold considerable amounts of working capital in sterling, but who, when there is doubt about the future of sterling – particularly about the exchange rate itself – tend to move their money out, even at a relatively high cost in terms of interest, to some currency they regard as more secure.

At a time of heavy balance of payments deficit there is, of course, a large quantity of sterling splashing about in the markets of the world and, when confidence in sterling is low, dealers in many markets sell sterling for US dollars, German marks, Swiss francs, or anything deemed safer. The only way in which British citizens can in effect take a position in sterling, because they expect either a marginal fall in the parity or an outright devaluation, is by postponing receipt of the payments due to them in some foreign currency, since after the fall in the sterling rate such foreign currencies would be worth more in sterling terms. Similarly, importers who have to make payments in foreign currency would tend to advance their payments, paying the bill on the nail or even before, lest they might have to raise more sterling to pay for a given amount of a foreign currency. In really difficult times there was clear evidence that importers were increasing the physical quantities of their imports, buying their raw materials for three or six – or, in one or two cases of which I got direct evidence, even twelve – months ahead, and, of course, paying as quickly as possible for the imports thus ordered. These 'leads and lags', as they are called, could have an effect running into many hundreds of millions of pounds at a time on the sterling position and thus on the reserves.

On top of all this, there was, on critical occasions, the direct speculation which grew to fantastic proportions, usually near a weekend when a devaluation was expected or prophesied. Such dealings were confined to foreign exchange dealers or speculators. They usually took the form, either of the dealers getting rid of any sterling they held or, if they held none, of selling sterling they did not possess with the idea of buying it back some days later, usually after the weekend. This sometimes meant that if they had to pay bills in sterling they had to borrow at extortionate rates of interest. But this was of little concern to them if a major change in the external value of sterling was expected. Although British citizens could not take part in such transactions the voice of, at any rate, a few of them was seldom found wanting, even at times of comparative calm, when for one reason or another they thought that sterling should be sold.

Experienced journalists, even in Conservative newspapers, repeatedly expressed their wonderment at some flurry or even major crisis in sterling, starting abroad, but which experts in foreign capitals, and journalists in a position to know, said had originated in rumours or selling advice from people in the City. It was hard to feel, in our position, that there was not a great deal of political malice, or, at the least, political misunderstanding and misrepresentation, behind some of this advice. There were sometimes suggestions that it was being organised for specifically political motives. This could never be proved and perhaps the fair comment would be that in times of greatest difficulty the Conservative party, shall we say, did nothing to help. Strikes against the national interest are always to be condemned; strikes of capital are no less, and in certain circumstances are infinitely more, damaging.

It is difficult to describe what it meant to live against a background of this persistent speculation, speculation in the main made possible only by the balance of payments deficit. Indeed it virtually disappeared as a threat once we moved into strong surplus some five years later. But until we were in surplus it meant that every action we took had to be considered against a background of the confidence factor, particularly against our assessment of what the speculators might do. It meant, and this is not only inhibiting but humiliating for any Government, that things we had decided to do, right in themselves – for example, an increase in old-age pensions, even as late as 1969, when we were moving into a strong surplus – had to be timed in such a way as to minimise possible speculative consequences, and wherever possible to coincide with an occasion when some further confidence-winning factor in the monetary field was taking place.

It meant watching the physical movements of the Chancellor, the Governor of the Bank of England, or the Prime Minister. Once, we virtually had to order the Governor, Lord Cromer, to proceed with his plans for a holiday in the South of France, lest cancellation might be construed as portending immediate devaluation. There was one period, in 1966, when I was proposing to return from holiday the Friday before the autumn bank holiday Monday, and senior officials virtually had to plead with me to postpone my journey until the Saturday when the markets would be closed – or, if I must return on the Friday, to leave it as late as possible in the day, when the markets had closed, and to make no prior announcement of my movements. This has not been a problem facing a Prime Minister who inherited, from us, a balance of payments surplus of £600 millions.

On television four years later, asked to name some of the mistakes we had made as a Government, I said that we had always underestimated the power of the speculators against a Government of whose politics, policies and even personalities they did not approve. It was interesting that Mr Maudling, who did not stay long enough at the Treasury to get the full force of the speculation which his Government's £800 millions deficit might have provoked, said, in a radio programme in December 1968, that we had all underestimated the power of the speculators. That was why, learning fast as we went on, we were determined more and more to strengthen the basic position of sterling, which meant to strengthen our balance of payments – and this in turn could only be done by strengthening the competitiveness of British industry. Though, increasingly, recent comments have recorded the view that it was in fact these measures which in the end led to our defeat in the General Election of 1970.

The run on sterling which began, following the Chancellor's Ways and Means statement on 11th November, was, I think, easy to explain. There was, as I have said, a considerable surplus of highly volatile sterling in world markets because of the balance of payments deficit. These foreign owners of sterling, concerned as they were with its safe lodgement – apart from those who were speculating more directly – needed little briefing for them to conclude that in Britain we now had a Government of 'softies'. A Government concerned, even at a difficult time, with payment to the old-age pensioners and others in need, concerned to provide charitable largesse which our foreign critics felt Britain could not afford. A Government which was at the same time attacking the sacred principles of personal and co-operative incentive by our apparent willingness to pay for this social generosity – as they saw it – out of taxes on the managerial and professional classes, and on public companies.

For the weeks which followed the Chancellor's statement, he was rarely out of the Cabinet Room where I did most of my work, and the Governor of the Bank of England became a frequent visitor. The Chancellor and the Prime Minister receive a daily tally of the movements on foreign exchange markets, recording not only the exchange rate, but the amount of money which the Bank of England has had to throw, hour by hour, into the market to stabilise the sterling rate, together with payments on Government account, or otherwise, across the exchanges. Just as, in happier days, these reports record the amount of money taken in by the Bank of England, by selling sterling for other currencies at a time when confidence in sterling is riding high. Never did a Chancellor and I enjoy those daily tallies more than in the months from September 1969 right through to the midsummer of 1970, recording as they did the remarkable intake, mainly of short-term money, which had fled the country and now wanted to come back.

As I have said, the greatest danger was always Friday. The Friday after the Chancellor's statement was the first really bad one of which we had experience. By the early part of the next week the Chancellor, senior Treasury and Cabinet officials, the Governor and the deputy-Governor and I were in pretty constant session.

The Governor, Lord Cromer, was in a peculiarly difficult position. He had to maintain the confidence of sterling; he was regarded as the voice of the City, not only to the Government but to other central banks and to the world financial community. Whatever his personal views or his political views – and in later years after his retirement he made little secret of what these political views were – it was his duty, at any rate, to represent to the Chancellor and the Prime Minister the things that were being said abroad or in the City; to indicate to the Government the issues on which, in the City's view, it was necessary to win confidence if a disastrous haemorrhage were to be averted.

That was why we had to listen night after night to demands that there should be immediate cuts in Government expenditure, and particularly in those parts of Government expenditure which related to the social services. It was not long before we were being asked, almost at pistol-point, to cut back on expenditure, even to the point of stopping the road-building programme, or schools which were only half constructed – for every Government learns pretty quickly that it is easier to talk about restraining public expenditure, easier to cut Government expenditure in the long term, than to make cuts which can have any immediate impact. For so many spending programmes are committed for years ahead. Indeed, in January, 1965, at a private lunch at No. 10, I challenged him specifically on this point, I told him that Government expenditure was committed far ahead; schools which were being built, roads which were part-way to completion, had been programmed by our Conservative predecessors in 1962–63. Was it in his view, I asked him, that we should cut them off half-finished – roads left as an eyesore on the countryside, schools left without a roof, in order to satisfy foreign financial fetishism? This question was difficult for him, but he answered, 'Yes'. That was, in fact, what he felt he had to ask. And this discussion took place not against the background of a critical run on sterling, but in the period of calm, following his successful swap operations.

My first encounter with the Governor made a deep impression on me. After he had spoken in grave terms about the forward situation, I calmly asked him whether the Bank had been engaging in operations in the market in forward selling. He asked the deputy-Governor whether they had or not. He was told the answer was 'no'. Rightly or wrongly, and it is clearly a highly arguable question whether they should have so operated in the forward market, I was glad to hear by the end of the week that they were doing so.

Day by day we faced a heavy drain on the reserves. We could lose £50 millions in a day, sometimes more, and our total gold and convertible currency reserves barely totalled £1,000 millions. Short-term central bank assistance was near exhaustion and there was no immediate prospect of the International Monetary Fund borrowing on which we had decided. The pound was at its support level. Rumours were reaching feverish proportions.

There had been a crisis meeting of EFTA in Geneva, attended by Douglas Jay and Patrick Gordon Walker; Tony Crosland had been sent out from DEA earlier to deal with the general economic situation. On the night of Thursday, 19th November I had an emergency, almost panic, call from Patrick Gordon Walker in Geneva. He needed my clearance for a firm assurance that the fifteen per cent import surcharge would be reduced in a matter of months. Otherwise the discussions would break down, and country after country would be likely to retaliate against our trade. I gave him the assurance and at 4.00 a.m. the conference reached an uneasy agreement.

For the weekend of 21st – 22nd November we had arranged a meeting of ministers, advisers and Service chiefs at Chequers.

Ministers gathered there for dinner on the Friday evening, with the exception of Jim Callaghan, who was closeted with the Governor. When he arrived, he, George Brown and I adjourned to the Long Gallery to consider his report. Action, it was clear from his report, had to be taken at once. This meant bank rate, which would have to be raised by two per cent. George Brown, who, on expansionist grounds, had opposed a suggested one per cent increase a week earlier, now dropped his objection. We decided that since it had to go up there was no point in leaving it till the following Thursday, with sterling's defences down for three days of intense speculation. It should be announced the following Monday morning at opening of business.

It was important that we should inform Washington urgently.

Sir Eric Roll, who had been appointed permanent secretary to DEA, was in Washington, winding up his affairs as the Economic Minister in the Embassy. The problem was to catch him before he left for London. We got a message through in the small hours and found that he was on his way to New York, where he would have to change planes. We asked the Embassy and the Consulate staff to track him down and order him, as soon as he was found, to cancel his booking to London and return to Washington, at the same time asking him to put through an emergency telephone call to London. He was found and I spoke to him personally, though as it was an open line I had to speak to some extent in riddles. However, he understood that the bank rate was going up by two points and that he must immediately inform the relevant American authorities. I told him that a full telegram would be waiting for him when he got back to the Embassy in Washington, and also that I was sending my principal private secretary, Derek Mitchell (who had been a Treasury civil servant until coming to No. 10), to Washington to brief him more fully. Mitchell left in the early hours of Saturday. As soon as Roll got back to Washington he saw the American Secretary of the Treasury, Douglas Dillon, and Dillon's deputy, Robert Roosa. They fully understood our action and decided to put up their own rate at the same time as we raised ours.

Lord Cromer was authorised to act. He announced the increase in bank rate at the opening of business on Monday, the 23rd. For an hour or two sterling rallied; it looked as though the action we had taken had done the trick. But during the afternoon heavy selling developed and at the end of the day sterling was up only by less than half a cent. Reports suggested that British companies and international companies were selling sterling short, since our action was regarded as showing not so much determination as panic. There was a feeling that perhaps the situation was worse than we had said.

At 3.30 p.m. on the same day, Jim Callaghan announced to the House the action that had been taken and gave the reason. The Tories were cock-a-hoop, and Mr Maudling's comment was anything but helpful: 'The speculative movements,' he said, 'both by their nature and timing clearly derive from the recent action of the Government, including, in particular, the Budget, the taxation proposals and the inept handling of the surcharge.'

We had a defence debate that day, on the adjournment, and I took the opportunity to say something about the economic crisis. The Conservatives soon made clear their anger that I was using a defence debate to deal with the sterling crisis, and I was not allowed to get very far with it. I did point out, however, that during the sterling crisis which had followed Suez – a policy which we had totally opposed – the Labour Opposition, once sterling was in danger, had backed the Conservatives one hundred per cent, and had done everything in its power to restore confidence in sterling.

The market reaction was no better on the Tuesday, 24th November. That night we had our most desperate meeting with the Governor of the Bank. Claiming that our failure to act in accordance with his advice had precipitated the crisis, he was now demanding all-round cuts in expenditure, regardless of social or even economic priorities, and fundamental changes in some of the Chancellor's economic announcements.

Not for the first time, I said that we had now reached the situation where a newly-elected Government with a mandate from the people was being told, not so much by the Governor of the Bank of England but by international speculators, that the policies on which we had fought the election could not be implemented; that the Government was to be forced into the adoption of Tory policies to which it was fundamentally opposed. The Governor confirmed that that was, in fact, the case.

I asked him if this meant that it was impossible for any Government, whatever its party label, whatever its manifesto or the policies on which it fought an election, to continue, unless it immediately reverted to full-scale Tory policies. He had to admit that that was what his argument meant, because of the sheer compulsion of the economic dictation of those who exercised decisive economic power.

I said that if that was the case, I was not prepared to accept it. What he was telling me was that not only were social progress and indeed the whole of our mandate for reform in danger; so was democracy itself. To accept his argument would mean that the Queen's First Minister was being asked to ring down the curtain on parliamentary democracy, by accepting the doctrine that an election in Britain was a farce, that the British people could not make a choice between policies, and that the policies were directed from outside the country, mainly by people who did not understand Britain and relied for their information upon the advice of people whose motives varied from ignorance to malice. In these circumstances, I concluded, there was nothing left for me to do except to appeal to the democracy I was being asked to repudiate, to go back to the electorate for a mandate giving me full powers to handle the crisis.

The Governor recognised my constitutional right to do this. Not unfairly, he warned me that if I did so – and the process would occupy some four weeks – the run on sterling would continue and indeed intensify; that our reserves, which had already fallen considerably, would have run out long before polling day, long before I had any mandate for any other action. I told him that I recognised the force of his arguments. In these circumstances, I said, there was nothing left for us to do but float the pound, and let it find its own level. While it might go down substantially at first, there was a limit beyond which it could not go, and then it might start to pick up, and confidence of a sort would be restored.

I warned him that if I went to the country on this issue of dictation by overseas financiers, I would have a landslide. He said ruefully that he believed I would, but clearly felt that the means of achieving such a landslide would be bad for Britain and bad for sterling. He said further that it would have a very bad effect on other currencies; we might be plunged into a world financial crisis.

That was what I was waiting for. 'Precisely,' I replied, and went on to point out that the international financial community, his central banking colleagues, would be the last to want Britain either to float or to be forced by speculation into devaluing. They had a vested interest in exchange stability and the strength of sterling. He agreed.

I asked him, therefore, why he didn't get on to them and ask them what they were prepared to do to avert a crisis which was based largely on speculative factors and had little to do with the basic position of sterling, weak though our balance of payments was. He said he would try, but was doubtful whether this could be done unless he was able to convey to them news of major changes of policy. I wished him well, but I re-asserted my determination, rather than sacrifice the constitutional rights of a newly-elected Government responsible to a free Parliament, to float and go to the country.

The following day, 25th November, the haemorrhage continued, but in the late afternoon when I was addressing a meeting for the Freedom from Hunger Campaign at Church House, I received a message that the Governor had successfully raised $3,000 millions from the central bankers. He had done a magnificent job. Heaven knows what he said about my possible intentions on the international telephone as he explained the alternatives. I did not inquire.

Sterling was safe – for a time. Long enough, we hoped, for the measures we were taking to strengthen exports to the point where day-to-day speculation would no longer be reinforced by a chronic balance of payments deficit.

Chapter 4

Defence policy – the Chequers conference – the defence debate – visit to Washington – discussions with President Johnson – visit to Ottawa

AFTER Friday night's economic decisions at Chequers we were able to proceed, at the time we had set, on the Saturday morning with our weekend defence conference of 21st-22nd November.

Our aim was to discuss the whole of our defence problems so that decisions could be taken on the main strategy, on weapon procurement, particularly aircraft, and at the same time be ready to discuss all these issues in depth at the White House talks in Washington three weeks later. Denis Healey would also be enabled to begin planning his first Defence White Paper, for presentation the following February.

Denis Healey had already taken a firm grip on the department, which was in the early stages of inter-Service integration, announced as a policy by the previous Government in 1963, but barely begun. Defence policy had suffered from the velocity of circulation of Conservative defence ministers – nine in thirteen years – only one or two of whom stayed long enough to get a real sense of the issues involved, let alone to plan any long-term strategy. Denis Healey, who remained as Minister of Defence for the whole of our period in office, had been appointed shadow Minister of Defence when I was elected leader of the party in February 1963, and was certainly thoroughly versed in the problems, and particularly the international implications, of defence issues.

Inevitably, decisions on the economic problems in our first week in office had called in question 'expenditure on items of low economic priority, such as "prestige projects" ' – a reference to the expensive new military aircraft we had inherited.

We had decided, and felt it right, to maintain a full British contribution to the defence of Malaysia. In particular, we had tightened up arrangements for defensive responses to Indonesian probings and infiltration, and embarked on a programme of sharply increasing jungle mobility by a substantially greater use of helicopters. But Britain's deployment of about thirty thousand men on confrontation, out of a total of fifty-four thousand on duty in south-east Asia, represented a heavy strain on services which for a very long time had been over-stretched by the former Government's acceptance of virtually unlimited commitments unrelated to our resources.

But in the previous decade the most far-reaching decision so far taken had related to nuclear problems.

In the late fifties and early sixties there had been violent lurches of policy as minister succeeded minister and nuclear fashion succeeded fashion. Duncan Sandys had turned down the American Polaris missile-carrying submarine in favour of Britain's ill-fated Blue Streak missile, with a flourish of press headlines. The London *Evening News* had said: 'POLARIS OUT, BLUE STREAK IN: Now Macmillan will talk from Strength.'

By April 1960, Blue Streak, obsolete before it was built, was itself 'out' after a formidable waste of public money, and the American airborne Skybolt missile was presented as Mr Watkinson's nuclear response. (Mr Watkinson, who later had a spectacular success selling Schweppervescence, was the eighth Tory Minister of Defence in eight years.) By the end of 1962 the Americans themselves had become disenchanted with the cost of Skybolt and its prospective performance, and decided to cancel it. At the Nassau conference in December 1962, Mr Macmillan, fearful of a major revolt from his right wing, managed to wring from a reluctant President Kennedy an undertaking to provide the know-how for the building of Polaris submarines, together with the missiles to stock them. Skybolt was now 'out' and Polaris 'in' again.

In the debate which followed, and in my twenty months as Leader of the Opposition, we had opposed the decision, and opposed still more the pretence that Britain had an 'independent' nuclear weapon.

In the first days of the new Government in October 1964, I had discussed with Patrick Gordon Walker and Denis Healey the future of the Polaris project in the light of the information now available to us. It was clear that production of the submarines was well past the point of no return; there could be no question of cancelling them, except at inordinate cost. We decided to go ahead with four of the projected five submarines, and to ensure their deployment as a fully committed part of the NATO defence forces. There was to be no nuclear pretence or suggestion of a go-it-alone British nuclear war against the Soviet Union. This decision was endorsed by the Cabinet Defence Committee, and later by Cabinet, and was, therefore, not under review at Chequers.

The conference there was really faced with four main issues:

1. Against the background of the necessity to reduce defence expenditure, what was to be the current defence posture of Her Majesty's Forces, having regard to the strain placed on them by excessive inherited commitments and by the Indonesian confrontation?

2. With the need to cut spending conditioning our decision, we had to consider the question of the three new aircraft: TSR 2, the Canberra replacement which would carry the airborne nuclear weapon; HS 681, a relatively short-take-off transport aircraft to replace the Argosy; and the P 1154, a replacement for the Hunter and the Sea Vixen.

3. We had to decide, for approval by the Cabinet, the line to be

taken on the whole range of defence questions in the discussions which, together with the Foreign and Defence Secretaries, I was due to have in Washington three weeks later.

4. As part of this, but of much wider importance – not least in our own parliamentary setting – was the contentious question of the American proposal for the so-called mixed-manned Fleet, the multilateral force (MLF) which for some two years had divided the previous Government, though not the Labour Opposition, since we totally opposed it. This was a proposal, in effect, forced upon President Kennedy by his policy-planning people in the State Department. He had told me in April 1963 that he had never been very keen on it,

'Ahoy Old Chap, Need Any Help?'

and was not pushing it, but he thought Europe wanted it. A few weeks later, I found from Herr Brandt and others that the Germans for whom he spoke certainly did not want it, but thought President Kennedy was insisting upon it. The State Department's Mr Walt Whitman Rostow was a persuasive salesman – to both sides. As for the German Government, the naval aide to its Defence Minister was quoted as saying that, speaking for himself, he would never join a multilateral force; thank you, he would rather swim.

The division in the British Conservative Government had been deep, and had indeed, in a manner uncharacteristic of Whitehall, reached a point familiar in Washington, where one department was actively briefing the press against the other. The Ministry of Defence had been totally opposed to the MLF, doubtful both of its practicability and whether it could serve any military purpose. The Foreign Office, on the other hand, anxious to please the United States, had been in favour of it. But no definitive position was ever reached. This problem, in common with many others, they successfully swept under the carpet before the election. But the election was now over: the new Government had to decide a firm line before the Washington conference.

The defence weekend at Chequers, attended by all leading ministers and their permanent secretaries, the Chiefs of Staff and their advisers, including the defence planning staff, was one of the most thorough ever undertaken by a British Government.

We began on the Saturday morning in the Hawtrey Room, which was laid out for a screen 'presentation' of Britain's defence commitments, posture and deployment. Each area of the world where British troops were stationed was set out in slide after slide, with full statistics – each type of equipment, military, naval, air. These, together with the presentation – Malaysia, Hong Kong, the Caribbean, the South Atlantic and South Pacific, Cyprus, Aden, the Gulf, the NATO forces by land, sea and air – confirmed our long-held view, so forcibly expressed by George Wigg in our years of Opposition, that Britain's defence forces were over-stretched almost to breaking-point. There was an excessive strain on the troops themselves, especially unaccompanied service. Something had to give: it had to be commitments.

The pressure on manpower was such that the following year the Trooping the Colour ceremony would have had to be cancelled if there had been one further call for troops to deal with an emergency situation. I remember one State visit at the height of the Malaysian confrontation, when driving to Victoria Station for the welcoming ceremony I saw the streets lined – at long intervals – almost exclusively by boys from the training ships.

We moved from the Hawtrey Room to the Great Parlour, where I began the serious talks by insisting that in this review there would be no sacred cows. Everything had to be questioned, justified where it could be justified, and costed. At the end of the day some projects and commitments would be justified, and be included in the programme, though even they would have to be re-questioned from time to time. And the first defence Bill must represent a sharp cut in the figure of £2,400 millions (at 1964 prices) for 1969–70 which we had inherited from our predecessors.

A session was spent on the problem of the three aircraft, for each of which Service chiefs put up a strong case. While we were not seeking to take immediate decisions, it became clear that Denis Healey was moving to a recommendation that further development on P 1154, the Sea Vixen and Hunter replacement, likely to be very costly, should be scrapped in favour of a further purchase of American Phantoms, which the previous Government had decided to buy for the Navy earlier in the year.

It was also clear that however attractive the HS 681 transport aircraft might be, a great deal of further development expenditure would be necessary. It was the almost universal experience with all new aircraft projects up to that time – and since – that the first, and many subsequent, estimates of costs, turned out to be only a small proportion of the final figure.

TSR 2, despite the brilliance of its conception and design, was clearly marked for stringent review. Its costs were escalating out of all relation to earlier estimates, and it was a favourite Treasury target for cancellation under both the Conservative and the Labour Governments. Although it had flown successfully as an empty shell, it had not yet incorporated the expensive and untried avionic equipment on which one of its principal combat roles depended, its contour-flying capacity, flying just above ground level, too low for detection by hostile radar screens. The impossibility of forecasting the cost of getting this equipment right made further cost escalation a virtual certainty.

While no decisions were taken for several weeks, we were moving towards a policy, later categorically endorsed by the Plowden Report on the aircraft industry, that the development of an expensive and untried major aircraft was beyond the capacity of Britain's economy. For without the certainty of large export sales, hundreds of millions of development expenditure had to be concentrated on the relatively small number of aircraft needed to meet RAF and RN requirements. In immediate terms, it would mean turning to the US, where we could meet some of our needs off the shelf, and since the development costs would have been met by the US Defence Department, this would mean that we should get them more cheaply.

If we were to cancel TSR 2 we would have to turn to an alternative US aircraft, the TFX (F 111 A) – not yet proved, still less in quantity production – where again our purchase would be only a small fraction of the US order, with correspondingly limited development costs per aircraft.

The other major question was the line we were to take in Washington. We knew that President Johnson was pressing the MLF with even more fervour than President Kennedy, though his enthusiasm was the result of fanatical pressures from his top officials, particularly Mr George Ball, Under-Secretary of State, and Mr Walt Whitman Rostow. Our line on this had been taken and announced in Opposition, and everything we had heard, with expert military – and above all naval – advice available to us, confirmed that we had been right.

It took little time at Chequers, therefore, for us to conclude that we would maintain our opposition to the MLF, and make it clear to the President why we were doing so. But we felt that it was desirable to work out an alternative plan which would cover our own proposal to internationalise the British deterrent through NATO, while avoiding the insoluble problems of mixed-manning, and the political objections of appearing to give the Germans a finger on the nuclear trigger.

This was the genesis of the Atlantic Nuclear Force (ANF) under which we would commit our Polaris submarines, and the Americans an equivalent number of theirs, to NATO, under the unequivocal control of the Supreme Allied Commander, Europe (SACEUR). These vessels would be irrevocably committed to NATO as long as NATO lasted as an effective organisation. Only in the event of a break-up of NATO would they revert to British control.

This was our answer to the controversial Nassau Agreement, which we had said we should 'renegotiate'.

In returning from this, our first major defence conference at Chequers, to Downing Street on the Sunday evening there was a long night's work ahead. There was a further late-evening meeting on the economic crisis measures due to be announced the next day. There was a defence speech to prepare for Monday's debate, which the Opposition had called for so that our general strategy would be fully probed before Washington.

It was not an easy speech, since, although we had reached fairly definite conclusions, a final decision still had to be taken by the Cabinet on a programme to be submitted to them. I had laid down that the purpose of the meeting was fully to identify, examine and dissect the problems. It would then be for the minister responsible to submit fully-prepared position papers to the appropriate Cabinet committee and Cabinet itself, papers which would reflect the discussion, deal with unanswered problems and take full account of the views expressed by colleagues, including, in this case, the Chancellor, the Foreign Secretary and the Minister of Aviation.

This procedure was to apply at every subsequent Chequers conference, even when the full Cabinet was there.

In accordance with the practice which I followed in every parliamentary speech or Commons statement I made in our five and a half years, I dictated the whole speech in draft to a series of Garden Room girls (so called because their office overlooks the Downing Street garden). After it had been examined with my private office, it was then despatched to the departments for checking, for amendments – sometimes necessitated by diplomatic considerations, sometimes by the need to avoid provoking speculative movements in the foreign exchange markets – filling in statistical gaps and occasional quoting of authorities. It was, and is, my strong view, that, in modern Britain, the Prime Minister's grip on every major subject, particularly finance and economic affairs, industrial policies and industrial relations, foreign and Commonwealth affairs, including such major issues as Rhodesia and the Nigerian crisis, should be such that he can dictate, without a departmental brief, the main text of any speech he has to make, in Parliament or in the country. More than that, speeches of ministers – of all Governments – which clearly emanate from a departmental brief are frequently insensitive in political terms. It is particularly important that a Prime Minister's speech on any subject is part of and consistent with a general and political philosophy which inspires every sector of government. Every Prime Minister's style of government must be different, but I find it hard to resist the view that a modern head of government must be the managing director as well as chairman of his team, and this means that he must be completely *au fait* not only with developments in the work of all main departments, including the particular responsibility of No. 10, but also with every short-run occurrence of political importance. And all he does, and says, must be part of a coherent political strategy.

In the event, the debate on 23rd November passed off reasonably well (with no vote) and apart from the economic crisis we were able to concentrate on preparations for Washington.

The Americans seemed to be preparing themselves for the talks as seriously as we were. They were keenly interested in the line the new Government would be taking, and No. 10 was besieged with their emissaries, official and unofficial. They were particularly determined that the talks should not be ruined by any misunderstanding. From their point of view, the Nassau conference of December 1962 had been a calamity. They had not appreciated what the Skybolt cancellation would mean for a beleaguered Prime Minister, under severe pressure as his economic policies went awry and his Common Market initiative was nearing disaster. (Indeed, Nassau was the decisive factor in destroying that initiative.) The President was unprepared for his request for Polaris, and lack of preparation and continual misunderstanding led to an unsatisfactory outcome.

So much so that President Kennedy had set up a high-level inquiry to see what had gone wrong. He had entrusted a Harvard professor, Richard Neustadt, to carry out the inquiry, involving months of work in Washington departments and discussions with British ministers and officials, as well as Opposition leaders. Professor Neustadt told me afterwards that the document which he finally prepared, the length of a full-sized novel, was presented to the President the Sunday before his death. The President had intended to study it in great depth after his return

C

from Texas and to use its lessons as a model for preparing future conferences.

On 25th November Dick Neustadt was again sent to London, this time to see me to ensure that the White House talks were fully prepared on both sides, and on a basis that would prevent misunderstanding. He made it clear to me, as did the US Ambassador, David Bruce, in a series of meetings, that the success of the talks would depend on the acceptance of MLF. This was also the message coming from our Ambassador in Washington, Lord Harlech, the former Conservative minister appointed by Mr Macmillan when Mr Kennedy was President and whom I had asked to continue in his post. A British newspaper editor, who visited Washington at the same time, and met President Johnson, saw me before and after his visit. He confirmed the MLF pressures. But there was a more ominous note.

President Johnson had told the editor bluntly that he would never trust a British Prime Minister again, because all his experience showed their Washington visits to be concerned mainly with domestic electioneering. The President had, in fact, spoken in similar terms to me when, as Leader of the Opposition, I had met him in the spring of 1964. He was then incensed at the recent visit of Sir Alec Douglas-Home, who, intending to raise with him the question of the American objections to the export of British buses to Cuba, had omitted to do so, and being reminded of this only as he left the White House made a perfunctory reference to it. At a subsequent press conference, reporters took his public utterances as an assertion that he had banged the table and expressed himself in no uncertain terms on the issue. He was so reported in Britain.

We had another visitor during the run-up to Washington – Mr George Ball, Under-Secretary of State, a committed pro-European, indeed a fanatic for European unity, who was one of the most passionate advocates of the MLF. Always friendly, his manner, as I knew from past meetings, was very direct. He made it clear that there could be no question of going back on the MLF, that the American Government would expect us to support it and that unless I was going to be in a position to say so, it would be better if I cancelled my visit. I said I would begin the negotiations when I reached Washington, not before. I was not certain then, and became still less certain when I reached Washington, whether the line he had taken had been authorised by the White House.

The party set out for Washington on the morning of Sunday, 6th December. It included Patrick Gordon Walker and Denis Healey, the Secretary of the Cabinet, senior Foreign Office and Defence officials and the Chief of the Defence Staff, Earl Mountbatten.

We flew by a chartered BOAC aircraft. My predecessors had always used chartered Boeing 707s for these visits but I had decided from the outset that I would fly only in British-built aircraft. The only one available from BOAC at that time was the much slower Comet and, with the head winds, we had to come down at Prestwick and Gander.

We reached Washington at 8.15 p.m. local time (1.15 a.m. GMT) and were met by Lord Harlech. We had a short meeting with him and his advisers to discuss what we could expect when the talks began the following day.

The next morning, 7th December, we were greeted by the President at a short ceremony on the White House lawn, with troops, bands, a nineteen-gun salute and the rest, and brief general speeches by the President and myself. We then went into the receiving line for some of the principal American and British guests after which, at 11.30 a.m., the President and I went up to the Oval Room. Meanwhile Dean Rusk, the US Secretary of State, Robert McNamara, the Secretary for Defence, and other leading members of the Administration went into the Cabinet Room with Patrick Gordon Walker, Denis Healey and the rest of our delegation. While the President and I got down to the top-level talks, the others spent most of the morning opening up the various subjects they would want to discuss during the week.

The President and I began on a personal note. He repeated that after his previous experience he had come to the conclusion that he would never trust a British Prime Minister again. I said I was aware of this and remembered that he had said it to me. I then repeated what I had said on that occasion. I understood what he meant. For my part, I wanted to make it clear that I intended to say nothing outside the White House that I had not said to him inside. I would probably have to say a lot of things to him inside. I believe that what we then agreed was never broken either in my exchanges with him or in my subsequent exchanges with his successor, President Nixon, to whom I renewed the undertaking.

As in all my later meetings with him, we got down first to a political discussion. President Johnson, supreme politician of his time in America, was always interested in explaining his own political problems, difficulties and triumphs and, equally, showed a professional's interest in the political problems of his guest. He was fascinated with the hazards created by our smallest-ever parliamentary majority, but was genuinely impressed by the reports he had received from his London Embassy about our determination to act in domestic and international affairs as we should if our parliamentary situation were secure.

On occasion I had difficulty in explaining what a small majority meant in Britain's system of democracy. His political reputation had been built up by his success as Senate majority leader with, at times a small, and always unreliable, majority, so he felt that he understood the problems facing our parliamentary leadership. It was harder for him to see that while failure to carry a vote in the Senate did not mean the end of a presidency, which was secure for a four-year period, a serious parliamentary defeat might mean the end of the Government, or at least an immediate general election.

We discussed the economic problems for a time.

Economic issues were not his primary interest, but he showed a great deal of understanding and sympathy, stemming, as I came to learn, from his deep Texan suspicion of all bankers, particularly Eastern ones. He was ready to extend that suspicion to the international banking fraternity, with their esoteric preoccupation with spot and forward exchanges, gold and convertible currencies, which, essentially a populist of the 1890s, he distrusted.

I was with the President until lunch-time.

Meanwhile, our two Secretaries of State had opened up with their American colleagues most of the subjects on the agreed agenda. We returned to the Embassy, where, with the exception of the President himself, we entertained the American delegation to lunch. In the afternoon, while our two Secretaries of State held a further meeting with their opposite numbers, I returned to the White House, for a brief meeting *à deux* with the President, after which we joined our colleagues in the Cabinet room, each of us flanked by our senior colleagues, advisers and note-takers.

The discussion was world-wide. A brief and agreed discussion on NATO apart from the question of MLF, which we brought up at the end of the meeting. We went over the situation in the Congo; we had moved RAF transport aircraft to Ascension, ready to fly out missionaries and beleaguered Belgian officials and businessmen.

We emphasised the special role we could play in Africa, through our close relations with Commonwealth countries, though I stressed that those relations would depend on our firmness in handling the Rhodesian situation and, to a lesser extent only, on our policies in relation to developments in Portuguese Africa. Our position in Africa, and our intentions to maintain and use it, were welcome to the Americans, for they had little leverage there, and at the same time had to face considerable domestic pressures on African problems. They were very concerned about both Chinese and Russian penetration in Africa. This at least helped them to understand why we were not planning to do more in Asia.

The President raised the question, without excessive enthusiasm, of our co-operating with him in South Vietnam, even if only on a limited – even a token – basis. I made it clear that we could not enter into any such commitments. We were co-chairman of the Geneva conference, under the Agreements of 1954 and 1962, and would have a role to play in seeking a way to peace. But I stressed the fact also, which seemed new to him, that we had as many as fifty-four thousand troops in Malaysia.

There was a short discussion on our joint approach to multilateral nuclear disarmament, with priority for a fully comprehensive test ban and a world-wide non-proliferation agreement. It was agreed that Alun Chalfont should visit Washington for discussions with the US Disarmament Agency.

We put on the record what had been said in the President's study about the financial situation. I then raised the outstanding question of the multilateral, mixed-manned fleet. I explained in detail our objections to the proposal; the technical objections, none of them resolved by the test operation of the experimental mixed-manned surface vessel. The problems of international politics – opposition in Europe, not least in Britain, to any suggestion, however indirect, of a German finger even influencing the nuclear trigger. I pointed out that on two successive visits to Moscow I had vigorously repudiated Mr Khrushchev's insistence that MLF would, in fact, mean German nuclear participation, but without convincing him. Mr Gromyko, with his Premier's approval, had produced a gesture of the hands, in which a finger of one hand – German – was pressing on another finger, the trigger finger. What mattered was not so much whether we in the West were satisfied that the Germans had no power to influence a decision to use nuclear weapons, but whether the Soviet Union would believe it. If our hope were for a progressive easement of tension, however gradual, MLF could be a fatal provocation. Even if the Soviet reaction were simulated for propaganda purposes, we should be giving them a valuable card – and for what purpose in terms of the strength and cohesion of the Western Alliance?

But, I went on, we recognised there were problems to be solved, not least anxieties on the continent of Europe. On the one hand, there were those – including many in Britain – who after Cuba helplessly felt that the world might one day be plunged into nuclear war by a unilateral decision in the White House; nuclear fall-out and perhaps nuclear weapons themselves would not observe political frontiers. A proper machinery of consultation was essential. On the other hand, there were those who feared that, at the moment of mortal crisis for Europe, a future American President might lose his nerve and leave Europe to its fate. Collective planning and a collectivised deterrent answerable to NATO were needed: but the deterrent should be one which made military (and naval) as well as political sense.

I asked President Johnson to study our proposal for an Atlantic Nuclear Force, which Denis Healey had handed over to his opposite number. He agreed that this should be closely studied overnight, and discussed on the morrow.

That night we had the big dinner at the White House – receiving line, bands and a dinner which, on the whole, was informal and enjoyable. There were formal speeches, in President Johnson's case carefully prepared and elegantly worded, in my case impromptu. But I took the opportunity of stressing Britain's determination to co-operate with the US in world peace, and to refashion NATO on more modern principles. I made a great point of the role of race and colour in world affairs:

> We hear arguments, I've heard this often enough, about whether there is a special relationship between the United States and Great Britain. Some of those who talk about the special relationship, I think, are looking backwards and not looking forward. They talk about the nostalgia of our imperial age. We regard our relationship with you not as a *special* relationship but as a *close* relationship, governed by the only things that matter, unity of purpose, and unity in our objectives. We don't come to you at any time on the basis of our past grandeur or of any faded thoughts of what that grandeur was... we have, and we always shall have, a close relationship. . . .

In subsequent discussions over the next four years, most of them constructive, and usually helpful, there was never any talk of grandeur, indeed there was little of past grandeur to show.

The following morning, 8th December, we had a delegation meeting at the Embassy. Patrick Gordon Walker and Denis Healey, with their advisers, were to meet Dean Rusk, Bob McNamara and their team at 9.00 a.m. I had a number of formal engagements, including laying a wreath at the National War Memorial and another on President Kennedy's grave. I was due to meet President Johnson at 11.30 a.m. and after a further talk with him, the two delegations would meet in plenary session.

But when I reached the White House I found that there had been no meeting of the Secretaries of State. The President had called Rusk, McNamara and their advisers in to a separate meeting while our team had waited in the Cabinet Room for well over two hours. It was clear that he was trying to settle, once and for all, the question of the mixed-manned fleet. When I arrived I was taken into the Cabinet Room, and told that the President would see me as soon as he was free. In the event their domestic meeting did not end until 12.15 p.m. It was plain that the President, who had never been personally very far committed to the mixed-manned fleet, was moving towards our position. As time went on, Denis Healey described what was going on in the Oval Room as 'Ball's last stand'. So it proved.

When the President met us he said that he was very prepared to consider our idea of the Atlantic Nuclear Force, and at a further meeting with him and his advisers at 3.45 p.m. we went through a list of US queries and comments on the draft. The official record showed that I raised in tabular form eighteen points on their memo. The President then made clear that he was not accepting it there and then, nor committing the US Administration to it, but he was instructing his delegation at NATO to enter into full discussions with us and other colleagues and to prepare a full study of what was involved. Clearly we had won the day.

We left Washington with a very satisfactory communiqué and a good press. Most of the comment was inevitably concentrated on the end of MLF. The private briefing by the President to both American and British journalists and the on-the-record briefing by the State Department showed that they shared our view of the success of the discussions.

One 1964 election myth had been disposed of: Sir Alec Douglas-Home's frequent gibe that Britain under a Labour Government with our distinctive nuclear policy would never be invited to sit at the 'top table'. This was because of his obsession with what he regarded as the 'independent nuclear deterrent'. In fact our approach, less obsessional and more realistic, had led to a much warmer welcome at the top table. Both sides could feel we had laid down the basis of a satisfactory working relationship for the years ahead.

Henry Brandon in the *Sunday Times*, who never on such an occasion writes without the most authoritative indication of the President's views, concluded:

> The key question that is being asked in the White House in the wake of Mr Wilson's visit is whether he will be able to see his opportunities over the mountain of difficulties he is facing.... If Mr Wilson now is regarded as having great opportunity for leadership, it can be taken as eloquent testimony of the qualities he displayed in Washington. But this is also due to the reluctance of the President to take the lead.
> ... The Prime Minister seems to have struck the right note with the President, with whom he discussed principles and politics. In the open meetings he tended to give the advisers on both sides something of an inferiority complex by his command of the substance discussed.

The *Daily Telegraph* reprinted a cartoon from the *Christian Science Monitor* showing a ship – 'Multi-lateral force' – having been torpedoed by a submarine with myself in the conning tower. It was never to surface again.

On Wednesday, 9th December we flew north for Ottawa. The talks there, which included a meeting with the full Canadian Cabinet, were just as satisfactory but inevitably much more relaxed. I had known the Canadian Prime Minister, Lester Pearson, for many years, indeed first when he was Canadian Foreign Secretary and I was in the postwar Attlee Government. He was anxious to know what had gone on in Washington and was very pleased with the results. There was no substantial difference to iron out between the position of our two Governments, apart from our formally raising for the first, but not the last, time the effect on Britain's exports of some of the built-in quirks in Canadian customs legislation and procedures.

Chapter 5

The Labour party conference at Brighton – defence policy and foreign affairs – the control of public expenditure – incomes policy and the DEA – Sir Winston Churchill's illness – Leyton – a majority of three – death of Sir Winston Churchill – end of the 100 days

I RETURNED to London in the early hours of Friday, 11th December, after a tiresome diversion to Manchester because of fog at Heathrow.

Apart from the work which had accumulated during my absence, there was a succession of overseas visitors to see and entertain, including Dr Hastings Banda, Prime Minister (later President) of Malawi, and Dr Schroeder, the German Minister of Defence, eager for news about the MLF.

That same night I had to go to Brighton for the annual Labour party conference, postponed because of the election and compressed into a single weekend. As with every other conference, as party leader I had to deliver a key-note speech and I was working on this until I left London and, again, for part of the Saturday morning. Unfortunately, dictating late at night, I was carried away into including a reference to Dunkirk, despite my earlier and repeated insistence that Britain was facing not a once-for-all miracle operation, but a long and sustained haul. A more accurate historical parallel, if one were needed, would have been the long period after Dunkirk and through to victory.

At Brighton I had to answer some murmurings and anxieties from the party. The most serious related to the increases in old-age pensions and other benefits, which we had announced in the Queen's Speech. Details had been given by the Chancellor in his November Budget statement – with the results in foreign exchange markets which I have described. But through sheer administrative difficulties it was impossible to bring them into effect until early spring. Peggy Herbison, the Minister of Pensions and National Insurance, tried all she knew to get them speeded up. But it was simply not possible. Not satisfied with the ministry's replies, I asked the Chancellor of the Duchy of Lancaster, Douglas Houghton, a pensions expert and chairman of all the Cabinet committees concerned with the social services, to conduct an independent investigation. He confirmed the ministry view and we had to explain that no increase would be possible before Christmas. By this time the problem of pressure on sterling had asserted itself and even if we could have speeded up the increases, there would have been strong Treasury objections to doing so. This was not the reason for the delay, although speculative reactions were mentioned by George

53

Brown in his conference speech and some play was made of the apparently contradictory explanations. There was in fact no contradiction: we could not have done it more quickly.

Nevertheless, I was still anxious that something should be done for those in greatest need at Christmas time. I asked for examinations to be made of the possible supply of free coal, together with corresponding payment of gas or electricity bills for those who did not use coal. In the event what we decided to do was to make a special Christmas bonus of £4 to all on National Assistance, and at the same time to announce the largest increase in National Assistance scales ever made. There was some criticism by certain of our members on behalf of the pensioners who did not qualify, but certainly in my own constituency – and this was the experience of other ministers – it was an extremely popular move.

It was a pity that this could not be announced at conference. Nevertheless, the party, with its own Government in office for the first time for over thirteen years, was excited, pleased with some of the social reforms we had instituted – especially the abolition of the widows' earnings rule and the repeal of the Conservatives' Rent Act. At the same time it was impatient and angry about the financial obstruction we were facing, and little inclined to accept what it regarded as bureaucratic delays on pensions and other parts of our programme.

The conference over, there was only a week of Parliament left before the Christmas recess. But the Opposition had demanded, and we had promised, a two-day debate on foreign affairs and defence following my visit to Washington.

The Conservatives, led by Sir Alec Douglas-Home, were extremely critical of the proposed Atlantic Nuclear Force, though they were still divided among themselves about their support for the mixed-manned force.

Sir Alec Douglas-Home and Mr Peter (later Lord) Thorneycroft, the former Minister of Defence and by that time shadow defence spokesman, were as divided in Opposition on the question as they had been in Government. But they were united on one thing. They were determined to prove that Labour's nuclear policy involved the surrender of Britain's so-called 'independent deterrent', which had been the virility symbol of Conservative policy and propaganda in their last year or two of office, indeed ever since the Nassau Agreement. They were on the watch for any re-negotiation of Nassau. We had said that it would be our policy to remove the clause in that agreement which was based on a fictitious assertion of independent nuclear action by Britain. This clause had never been taken seriously in the United States or in Britain. It had, of course, been a sop to the right wing of the Conservative party, traditionally opposed to what they conceived to be the subordination of Britain's defences to the United States. But the Conservatives were in fact backing the nuclear horse both ways. If they failed to prove that we had destroyed

Britain's so-called nuclear independence, then they would still be happy. For they would be able to taunt our own left with acquiescence in the fact that a Labour Government had continued the Tory policy in full.

But the truth was that, apart from our elderly V-bombers, Britain would have no genuinely independent deterrent, in so far as we should be dependent on the US both for the know-how necessary for the building of the Polaris-armed submarines and for the supply of weapons.

The Conservative argument was that once these had been delivered, by 1968, Britain would then enjoy independence.

In the concluding stages of the debate, amid uproar, I set out to destroy this argument once and for all. I pointed out that the British war-head, which was to be incorporated in the Polaris missile, had not been tested, and – apart from the testing of certain components which could safely be done underground – could almost certainly not be tested within the terms of the nuclear test ban. But, more important, I made it clear that we should still be dependent, after the completion of the Polaris programme in 1968, on the Americans for certain specialised materials essential to the maintenance of our missile force. To make sense of their argument the Conservatives must postulate some future row with the Americans, neatly postponed, of course, until after the Polaris fleet was in being; a row in which, incredibly, Britain would want to use the bomb and America would not.

In these hypothetical circumstances, I asked whether the US might not say that, having fulfilled the agreement in terms of supplying know-how, and missiles, they would 'feel free to withhold some essential component or material not covered in the contracts'.

Sir Alec Douglas-Home refused to answer the question whether he was satisfied that Britain could, without long delays capable of wrecking the whole programme, supply every essential component for the Polaris programme, without dependence on the Americans. He challenged me to justify my charge. I said that I could 'give chapter and verse to both right honourable Gentlemen about fundamental components, which it had been intended that we should manufacture but which were not covered in the contracts and for which it was necessary to turn to the Americans for help'.

I invited Mr Thorneycroft to inspect the evidence on which I was basing my reply – with the usual provisions for secrecy, as between Privy Counsellors. I added this:

> The question is whether, after 1968, we shall be in a position to supply all the fissile materials required to maintain the effectiveness of our warheads, having regard to the half-life of these materials and so on. The Leader of the Opposition knows what I am talking about, I will not specify these materials. I am prepared to give them to the right honourable gentleman. I will give him their numbers in the Atomic Table. I will tell him anything that he wants to know.

Sir Alec interrupted, and I gave way to him. But all he could say was:

> Is not the Prime Minister going to buy these "rotten" submarines and put them into his force as a credible deterrent?

I replied that what I was proving was that this programme was not as he had always claimed, independent, it was inter-dependent . . .

> The fact is that there is no independent deterrent because we are dependent on the Americans.

There was such uproar by this time that I could barely get in a few more sentences, though there was much I wanted still to say.

But I put the issue, in the concluding moments of the debate, on the question of the credibility of any British Prime Minister embarking on a nuclear war on the 'go it alone' basis:

> Finally, we want to know what sort of war they were going to have the deterrent for. Obviously not some nuclear Suez. We acquit them of that. Obviously not as a contribution to a trigger mechanism to bring the American bomb into action when the American Government did not want to do it. The argument which we have had is that one day we may get some lunatic American President who, when the crunch came, was prepared to retire to Fortress America and to leave Europe to its fate. We have now answered that point, because we have made it clear that this is committed to NATO as long as the alliance lasts. So I put to the Leader of the Opposition – what are they voting about tonight? It is not a nuclear Suez. It is not the trigger for the American strategic deterrent. We are left with one possibility – that the Leader of the Opposition is talking about embarking on a go-it-alone war with the Soviet Union when the rest of the alliance does not wish to do so. Is that it? Our credibility depends on this – it depends on the credibility of the Government. I want the Leader of the Opposition to tell us, as a former Prime Minister, as the head of the alternative Government, knowing that a go-it-alone war would mean a certain amount of posthumous revenge against the Soviet Union and total annihilation of all human life in Britain, whether he would be prepared to press that button in that kind of war. If he is not prepared to answer that . . . question [Interruption] – hon. members cannot take it – this has proved that their argument is a charade.

There was no doubt who had won the debate. This was the clear view of our side of the House. The Tories were still angry and shouting, but our people felt that the debate had marked the end of a long chapter of sterile argument about the so-called independent deterrent before and since the election. The press next morning were clear in their judgment of the debate. Clearest of all was William Barkley, in one of the last pieces he wrote for the *Daily Express* after forty distinguished years in the Parliamentary Gallery, when he said,

> The nuclear debate in the Commons finished last night in a crescendo of fury unparalleled since Suez. Mr Harold Wilson, the Prime Minister,

was at once fighting mad and perfectly controlled in a towering attack on the Tories for their demand to maintain Britain's independent deterrent. By the time he had finished – and he was only counted out by the clock – it seemed that he had left Sir Alec Douglas-Home and Mr Peter Thorneycroft, the late Minister of Defence, stricken on the field.

There was one other important item of parliamentary business before the recess. On 21st December, with time provided by the Government, the House debated the second reading of Sidney Silverman's private member's Bill: the Murder (Abolition of Death Penalty) Bill for which the Government had provided time. Every member of the Cabinet had voted for abolition every time the matter was before the House.

Over the years, even with a large Conservative majority in the House, the number of MPs voting on a free vote for abolition had risen steadily, and in 1957, even with a Conservative majority, the House had shown a majority in favour of abolition. But there had been deep divisions at that time within the Conservative party, and the then Home Secretary had introduced the Homicide Bill. This had set out degrees or types of murder, only some of which would carry the death penalty, while others would involve life imprisonment only. There were many anomalies – shooting in passion carried the death penalty; slow, systematic, calculated murder by poison did not. But it was more than just argument or logic: Parliament and the public had been affronted by cases where it was virtually certain that innocent men had been executed.

The Labour party, in common with the other parties, did not regard this subject as one for a party programme or manifesto. We felt that, as with many other issues involving decisions based on conscience, there should be a free vote of the House. We had made it clear throughout, however, that we would provide Government time for getting such a bill through if it were the free will of the House.

When, in December 1963, I had been invited by Sir Alec Douglas-Home to nominate six life peers in order to bring up our severely eroded numbers in the Lords to working strength, I had invited Gerald Gardiner, a passionate abolitionist, to be one of the six – my intention being that he should learn something of the workings of the Lords, ready for his appointment as Lord Chancellor if Labour won the election. He mentioned to me that he had never sought preferments, still less a peerage. He had refused a judicial appointment, even though it would have been in the Chancery Division, because he could not accept collective responsibility with his prospective brother judges for the enforcement of the death penalty. He asked what a Labour Government would do about it. I told him simply that it would be left to a free vote. But it would be impossible to conceive of a House of Commons, so constituted as to provide a majority for a Labour Government, which would not show persistently higher majorities in favour of total abolition, should an Abolition Bill be introduced.

On 21st December, after one of the best non-party debates the House had heard for many years, the second reading was carried, on a free vote, by 355 to 170.

At this point the Conservatives put the whips on – perhaps owing to some promise to their back-benchers – and voted as a party that the Bill, instead of being sent to a standing committee upstairs, should have its committee stage on the floor of the House. With the help of the Liberals, we defeated this manoeuvre by eighteen votes.

This was not the end of it, however. For on a Friday early the following year, when the House was debating private motions selected by ballot, a Conservative motion, carefully prepared and carefully whipped for, decided that the Bill should be re-committed to a committee of the whole House. This would mean either that essential Government business would be lost while the Bill occupied a great deal of parliamentary time – and delaying tactics were inevitable – or that the Bill would have to be dropped. In the event, we got it through by carrying a resolution that the House would meet every Wednesday morning for the committee stage of the Bill. It finally passed the Commons at 3.00 a.m. on 14th July 1965. Even then its troubles were not over, for the Lords carried a Conservative amendment to limit its operation to a trial period of five years, in such terms that the death penalty would automatically be resumed on the basis of the 1957 Act, unless both Houses carried motions providing for permanent abolition. These motions were in fact carried through both Houses in December 1969. Sidney Silverman, who had fought for abolition for more than a quarter of a century, did not live to see the final decision.

Those last few days before the Christmas recess of 1964 were as hectic as any of the others had been. There was the visit of the Prime Minister of Malta, Dr Borg Olivier, to discuss the dockyard position in Malta; a meeting with Sir Alec Douglas-Home and Mr Duncan Sandys about Rhodesia, where the situation was becoming increasingly difficult; and a visit to Manchester to open a new technological college. And on the last evening before I went away for Christmas a meeting of economic ministers and Treasury, DEA and Board of Trade officials at Downing Street to discuss forward economic programmes, with particular reference to new means of encouraging exports.

Before we went away there was one very special party at No. 10 – for Britain's paraplegic Olympic team. Early in November, I had given a reception for our notably successful Olympic team from Tokyo, after which I went to the Festival of Remembrance at the Royal Albert Hall. When I arrived there, I told the wife of one of the Defence chiefs what we had been doing. She asked me pointedly if I was going to give a party also for the British participants in the paraplegic Olympic Games in Tokyo.

I went into this and set up the party on Friday, 18th December. It was

the beginning of a very close and, for Mary and me, deeply moving, relationship with Stoke Mandeville, and with British paraplegic sufferers
from that and other hospitals. They came in their wheel-chairs; gold-
medallists in archery, table tennis, swimming and other games. It was one
of the most truly memorable occasions their hosts, including myself, had
ever experienced.

On Wednesday, 23rd December we caught the midnight train from
Paddington to Penzance, and flew by helicopter to the Isles of Scilly for
Christmas, New Year and our silver wedding anniversary, and the first
break of more than a few hours I had had since coming into office, indeed
since the election campaign had started.

New Year's Day saw the first Honours List of the new Administration.
These lists are usually in fairly final form by mid-October, and we had
inherited from our predecessors the usual departmental recommendations
for State servants and for industry, the arts, journalism, and the social
and other services. I asked each of our incoming ministers urgently to
reconsider his department's recommendations and then proceeded to add a
number whose recognition I felt had been too long delayed – perhaps not
even considered.

This list when published was welcomed by the press as less stuffy, more
original and more representative of the kind of people who made Britain
tick. There were no hereditary peerages, no baronetcies. Life Peerages
then, and subsequently, were based not only on the test of distinction
but on that of having something of importance to say, in the national
forum which the House of Lords provides: not a reward for past services
but an opportunity to do a job of work. New Year and Birthday lists were
not to be a means of appointing political nominees to be lords – there
would be separate lists for that as our number of active peers fell below
the working level through death or incapacity.

Sports, entertainment and the arts had more representatives – including
such long overdue recommendations as Stanley Matthews for a knighthood – and many leading industrialists, surprisingly the forgotten men of
Conservative lists, were included. It was at this time I instituted a new
citation in my recommendations to the Queen for 'services to export'; in
each list from then on some forty to sixty industrialists, traders, exporters
and technicians at all levels received recognition from the British Empire
Medal to life peerages.

I returned to London on Saturday, 2nd January 1965, and found the
conduct of the Administration momentarily somewhat quieter. There were
of course the Foreign Office telegrams and the daily submissions and
reports from ministers. Some of the urgent preoccupations of the first few
weeks were no longer pressing. Sterling was having a quiet period. The
major strategic decisions in foreign and defence policy had been taken
and were being worked out by the ministers and departments concerned.

The final decisions on defence expenditure would have to be taken in time for February's White Paper.

There were other problems overseas – the troublesome negotiations for independence in British Guiana, rumblings in Aden, above all the continuing fighting in Malaysia. Contingency plans had to be made against further escalation in the fighting there, and the Commander-in-Chief, Far East, Sir Varyl Begg, came home from Singapore to report, and gave the Defence and Overseas Policy Committee a full briefing.

Meanwhile, there was intense activity on the Estimates front, where the key role was played by Jack Diamond, the Chief Secretary to the Treasury – with Cabinet rank, though not then in the Cabinet – whose function I envisaged as equivalent to the US Director of the Bureau of the Budget. I had spent some time in Opposition discussing US methods with the Director, Mr Kermit Gordon, a former pupil of mine at Oxford. Jack Diamond, while reporting to the Chancellor and working under his general direction, was given a reasonably free hand to exact economies.

An important part of this was of course the annual price review for the farmers under the Agriculture Acts of 1947 (which provided guaranteed markets and guaranteed prices for most items of farm produce) and the 1957 Act, where the Tories introduced deficiency payments in place of the public buying which had underwritten the 1947 Agreement.

This is always, each year, a difficult negotiation. Ministry officials sit down with the farmers' unions and discuss the estimates, prepared independently by agricultural colleges and universities, of the farmers' income area by area, before agreeing on the total figure. This is usually a little higher than the year before to take account of rising costs, though, at the same time, discounting cost to a considerable extent to allow for increased farm productivity. It is always a difficult battle and there can be no guarantee that it will be an 'agreed' settlement. The Treasury, under any Government, presses for the lowest possible total payment, and, after a good harvest, even for a recoupment by a 'negative price review'. The agricultural departments, naturally, are more responsive to the position of the farmers. The Government's negotiating position is usually worked out, and recommended to Cabinet, by an Agricultural Policy committee or Farm Price Review committee of senior ministers. I always insisted on this being presided over by a non-departmental minister, in 1965 by Douglas Houghton, Chancellor of the Duchy of Lancaster, in later years by Michael Stewart, after he left the DEA, then by George Thomson when Minister without Portfolio, and finally Peter Shore. But it is always a headache for a Cabinet and comes at a critical time of the year, when Budget questions and the preparation of the Defence White Paper are pressing hard on ministers.

It was becoming increasingly clear that all three of the controversial aircraft, HS 681, P 1154 and TSR 2 would go, and be replaced in the main by American purchases, the first two by Hercules and Phantoms, supplemented by an increased order for British Buccaneers.

Aviation questions almost invariably leaked. I had always suspected Conservative ministers, but when I found how prone our own decisions and discussions were to get into the press, I revised my view. (I received warm thanks from Julian Amery – by this time out of the House – for saying in Parliament that I now knew I had misjudged him.) But our probable intentions – though no final decision had been taken – became the matter of press discussion, and immediately the aircraft manufacturers were knocking on our door.

As they saw it, it would mean the end of British airframe production and the disbandment of British airframe design teams. It would also have grave repercussions for the development of new jet engines, which, ordered and paid for on the military programme, could have a valuable overspill or 'spin-off' in the civil market. The aircraft industry chiefs had told the press that they would ask to see me at No. 10 to make representations on the military aircraft – and on Concorde. Workers in the aircraft industry had already marched down Whitehall, their lost day's pay and rail fares, the press reported, being paid by their employers. Their fears were groundless.

I felt that it was better to invite the aircraft industry leaders to Chequers where we could have a full evening's discussion over and after dinner, and without all the attendant publicity which surrounded the door of No. 10. It was arranged that they would come on the night of Friday, 15th January to Chequers, where I had to go for the weekend, for a Saturday and Sunday working conference on economic policy.

Roy Jenkins, Minister of Aviation, was with me. The industrialists were utterly frank about the position and we were warned that in addition to the problems they foresaw, there was a danger that the major company in the industry, the British Aircraft Corporation, might break up, since some of its joint owners were anxious to pull out and apply their investments elsewhere.

In December, we had appointed the Plowden Committee to make a full-dress inquiry into the aircraft industry. But while we were able to encourage our guests on Anglo-French joint projects, and to press them to go wholeheartedly for the proposed European airbus, we were not able to give them any reassurance on the question of HS 681, P 1154 or TSR 2.

Another worry for them was Concorde.

In the economic statement of 26th October we had indicated that we were reviewing the 'prestige aircraft', including Concorde. Roy Jenkins, after discussions with the French in October 1964, had soon found that they were totally unwilling to cancel or even to review the project. What is more, the Concorde arrangement was not a commercial agreement which could have allowed the two parties to break off the programme when costs escalated or commercial prospects grew dim. It was the subject of an international treaty, registered at the United Nations and subject to all the procedures of the International Court at the Hague. Had we unilaterally denounced the treaty, we were told, we could have been taken to the International Court, where there would have been little doubt that it would have found against us. This would have meant that the French could then have gone ahead with the project no matter what the cost, giving us no benefit either from the research or the ultimate product. But the Court would almost certainly have ruled that we should be mulcted for half the cost. At that time half the cost was estimated – greatly underestimated as it turned out – at £190 millions. This we should have had to pay, with nothing to show for it, the result of what we considered a highly improvident treaty on the part of Julian Amery, Roy Jenkins's predecessor at the Ministry of Aviation. Faced with this situation, we had little alternative but to go on. The total cost of research and the production of the two prototypes to which we were bound by the treaty had escalated from an original figure of £150 millions, as stated by Julian Amery, to £380 millions in 1964. By 1970 it had reached a total estimated cost of £800 millions.

The following morning we began our weekend conference on economic affairs. All the senior economic ministers, together with the officials of the principal economic departments, and the Government's economic advisers, were there to consider our industrial and trading policies, with particular reference to the strengthening of assistance to exports and the tightening of safeguards on foreign exchange leakages, particularly on capital account.

By this time DEA was well advanced on its work of preparing plans for expansion, and identifying and stirring up the laggards in industry – including those whose export performance was inadequate and deteriorating, while at the same time failing to meet the challenge of rising imports of manufactured goods – particularly technical goods – coming into the country. The Ministry of Technology was increasingly pressing research and development projects on industry. I was working on plans ultimately to transfer the responsibility for aircraft production from the Ministry of Aviation to Technology and, in advance of that, engineering and shipbuilding. I was always told that this was unnecessary since the Board of Trade were responsible, though I found the engineering divisions of the Board of Trade – machine tools, etc. – pathetically small and very *laissez-faire* in concept. In a Board of Trade document arguing against transfer, I was actually told that production in one of the key sectors had risen by ten per cent in ten years!

No one seemed to have taken much action on the Stewart Mitchell Report of two years earlier which had shown that in the whole machine-tool industry there were only twenty-three graduate scientists or engineers.

Incidentally, I was heartened to hear that as aircraft production was temporarily cut back, a considerable number of skilled aeronautical engineers went into machine-tools and other sections of the engineering industry and greatly improved their design and research performance.

The Ministry of Technology had made a tremendous start on saving the indigenous British computer industry, which, as I had warned Frank Cousins on the day we took office, was on the verge of extinction. He personally took charge of talks between the various parts of the industry which led ultimately to the creation of International Computers Limited (ICL), which in our time became the biggest computer enterprise in the world outside American ownership and which, within a year or two of its establishment, had over £100 millions' worth of orders in Europe alone. But this salvage operation meant money. Frank Cousins introduced a Bill to increase the financial provision for the National Research Development Corporation and took other measures to assist the industry, including pre-production orders, to encourage the development of new types of products.

The Chequers meeting gave us time, which the critical days of the first two months had denied us, to review progress in industry, industrial relations and regional policy.

George Brown had interpreted the DEA mandate liberally. Besides his responsibility for 'real resources', he had rightly concluded that economic expansion depended on restraint on prices and incomes. The Conservative Government had preached, threatened, and failed. In no time, George was discussing the general outline of a prices and incomes policy with unions and employers, formally, informally, at all times of the day and night. At the same time, he was intervening in individual prices and wages decisions.

Manufacturers collectively, and trade by trade, would receive from him a peremptory demand to justify the current wave of price increases. One moment he was banging the table at the bakers who were intent on raising bread prices; the next he was holding the baking unions in check on their wage demand. But George Brown recognised that whatever had to be dealt with in this way, he had to set up more independent machinery to review incomes and prices, and that planned expansion of incomes meant that money wages and salaries had to be related to a real and measurable increase in productivity.

It was a tribute to his unique methods of persuasion – private sessions with George Woodcock, General Secretary of the TUC, and his employers' and FBI counterparts, and formal cocked-hat sessions with the two sides sitting together – that he had succeeded where all his predecessors had failed in getting the managerial side (incorporating manufacturers in their price capacity, and employers), trade unions and Government to sign a mutual Declaration of Intent on Productivity, Prices and Incomes on 16th December 1964. The setting, in the gilded salon of Lancaster House, was appropriate to an international disarmament treaty, but it was an historic occasion. The test was to be its implementation.

The other significant achievement of DEA, whose full implication we were able to review at the Chequers weekend, was the development of regional policy. I had insisted, in the first few days of the Government, on the maximum regional devolution of Government departments, and sent a minute calling for a new system of regional machinery. The embryo arrangements under which regional representatives of Whitehall departments were to be grouped together as Regional Boards were to be greatly strengthened. As far as possible they should be sited together in regional mini-Whitehalls. The very limited Boards for Industry should be upgraded to Regional Economic Planning Councils, and in membership and terms of reference should be enabled to extend far beyond industrial consultation, to cover regional economic planning – including transport and industrial diversification – as well as social planning, housing, education, and amenities in the widest sense.

The bare instructions of my minute were set alight by George's enthusiasm and drive. Touring the country, in vigorous formal meetings and turbulent evening sessions, he strengthened the Regional Boards – now Regional Planning Boards under DEA chairmanship, covering all the departments – to service Regional Economic Planning Councils consisting of nominated members, capable of speaking for both sides of industry, for local government, social and other interests, and for regional universities. Universities were given research contracts on different aspects of regional development, transport, land planning, industrial and economic development, social development, derelict land clearance and comprehensive schemes such as a regional barrage proposal, a combined operation involving economic, transport, hydrostatic and other experts.

The appointment of the Regional Economic Planning Boards and the Regional Economic Planning Councils for the eight regions, together with their national equivalents in Scotland and Wales, became effective on 25th February, a month after the Chequers meetings.

A great deal of our time at Chequers was concerned with further stimulation to exports. We had got the joint-stock banks to extend the scheme under which they would lend for export at specially favourable rates. We were also concerned to see what could be done to stop the capital drain, particularly in portfolio investment to the United States. I had dictated for the meeting a list of some twenty or thirty suggestions which might help with the particular industries, even going so far as a proposal for a language diploma to be organised by colleges of further education, university crash-courses and so on, each holder to be rewarded by his employers with a specific supplement to his salary.

When the meeting broke up on the Sunday morning, we had an outline of the statement ready for Parliament.

But we decided to hold it over. For in the previous few days Sir Winston Churchill had been taken gravely ill, and it was clear from medical bulletins that it could only be a matter of time.

This week marked our first two by-elections, with polling on Thursday, 21st January. Seats had to be found for Patrick Gordon Walker and Frank Cousins. Two senior MPs, Frank Bowles and Reg Sorensen, with some reluctance on their part, were persuaded by the whips to go to the Lords. Frank Cousins was adopted for Nuneaton, and Patrick Gordon Walker for Leyton. I had tried to persuade him to go for a much safer seat which he could have had in the north, but he preferred a London constituency.

These were difficult constituencies, despite the apparently safe majorities. The weather was cold, and after a year and a half of intense electioneering culminating in the October General Election, the voters needed more incentive than they had to go to the polls. Moreover the Conservative campaign, particularly in Leyton, was well-designed to exploit issues which might lead, if not to a turnover of votes, at any rate to substantial abstention.

Conservative canvassers confined themselves in the main to exploiting the grievance that MPs had increased their salaries within days of Labour's return to office, while old-age pensioners still had months to wait for their promised increase.

True, the Conservatives had not opposed the increase in MPs' pay, which implemented a report by the Lawrence committee set up by Sir Alec Douglas-Home when still Prime Minister, with a general all-party understanding that it would be carried through by whatever party formed the Government. The Lawrence recommendations for ministerial salaries, however, were implemented only as to half of the proposed increase. It was equally true that the old-age pensioners, whose long wait was exploited by Conservative canvassers, had been refused any increase at all by the Conservative Government just before leaving office. But for them it was good door-step stuff, as was the exploitation of the immigration questions, mainly by the fascist fringe, once again directing their vicious campaign against Gordon Walker, who had long been one of their favourite targets.

As the results came through on television, it was clear that there had been a very poor vote. In Nuneaton the poll had fallen to 60.8 per cent, against 81.1 per cent in the General Election; in Leyton to 57.7 per cent, from 70.2 per cent.

Frank Cousins held the Nuneaton seat, but with a majority reduced from 11,702 to 5,241, a bad result. But there was a far bigger shock at Leyton, where Gordon Walker was defending a majority of 7,926. A recount was announced, and, just after midnight, it was confirmed that the Conservatives had won the seat by 205.

Patrick telephoned me at once to offer his inevitable resignation. Knowing what he was going through, I said, having expressed my commiseration, 'Let's not talk about that: come and have a chat in the morning, when you've had some sleep.' There could be no question of his going on, though I undertook to bring him back into the Administration at some future time when he was back in the House.

Meanwhile, I had to fill the gap. I decided to appoint Michael Stewart, whom I had long regarded as a wise and authoritative figure capable of filling any position in the Government. In one sense only, it was a pity that I had to take him from the Department of Education. He was a dedicated educationalist, and in three months, as Secretary of State for Education, he had recharted the education policy of the country and smoothly redirected it on comprehensive lines. In a debate on the day of the polls the Conservatives had launched an all-out attack on our policy to end selectivity in secondary education, and Michael had enjoyed a triumph such as few enjoy in a lifetime in Parliament.

Now his post had to be filled. By far the outstanding success among ministers outside the Cabinet was Roy Jenkins. I decided he must be invited, though I knew that his inclinations were far more in the direction of the Home Office than Education. Whoever went to Education I hoped would stay for two or three years at least, and his heart must be in the job. Roy confirmed that he would prefer to wait until the Home Office – for which he was so obviously fitted – became available. A brave decision: few politicians would refuse their first chance of joining the Cabinet.

The obvious alternative was Tony Crosland, then Minister of State in DEA, who in addition to his economic brilliance had always taken a close interest in education. He accepted and his stay of nearly three years in the department was a great success.

Meanwhile we had to take stock of the new situation. Our majority was now down from five to three, because of Leyton, and the task of keeping afloat correspondingly increased. It meant, for one thing, that if a Labour MP were to die – as three did in the remainder of that Parliament – our majority would be down to two for the period required to select a candidate and mount an election, even if we were confident of holding the seat. If two were to die at about the same time...

Anthony Shrimsley, writing shortly afterwards in his book, *The First 100 Days of Harold Wilson*, doubted whether there was a single member of the Parliamentary Labour Party who thought Labour would be able to carry on – except, he said, the Prime Minister. I was still hopeful, against heavy odds, that we would keep going until we had some real achievements to put before the people.

Certainly the press were in no doubt that the end was in sight. One Conservative newspaper, referring to a photograph of me taken on the steps of 10 Downing Street by my father in 1924, confidently forecast that

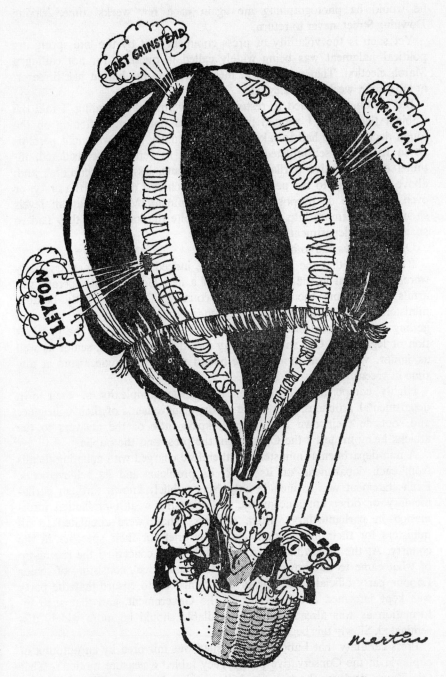

"Brothers! We're running out of gas!"

he would be photographing me again in a few weeks' time, leaving Downing Street, never to return.

Yet such is the volatility of press comment that by the late spring my political judgment was being widely called in question for not calling a March election. That would have meant pressing the button just three or, at most four, weeks after Leyton.

But action was needed to restore the Government's standing. I told the Cabinet that, while I wanted no changes of policy, no softening on the tough decisions we had to take to get the country right, we might perhaps go in for fewer self-inflicted wounds, such as certain ill-considered, ill-timed or provocative parliamentary statements, less 'ministerialitis', and, above all, an end to the persistent leaks which cast doubt on the unity, or even the sense of purpose, of the Government. Ministers at all levels should get out more into the country, despite the long hours they had to spend in their departments and in the House.

Other changes had to be made, too.

It was clear that the Government and, indeed, the parliamentary party were, as is usual in the early months of a new Government, operating at arm's length from the party in the country. This was partly because ministers at all levels were heavily engaged in learning their jobs and getting on with the decisions that had to be made, including the preparation of legislation. Our small majority meant that ministers, senior as well as junior, were much more House-bound than their predecessors at any time in recent memory.

Highly competent ministers, mastering the complexity of their own departmental problems, knew little of the achievements of their colleagues and, outside their own departments, knew little of the answers to the attacks being made by the Opposition, the press and the public.

A non-departmental minister was therefore charged with collating details from each department, on its work, its problems and its achievements. Each statement was to include only facts publicly known through parliamentary or other announcements, including the wealth of factual information in parliamentary written answers. These were circulated to all ministers for their information, and as a brief for their speeches in the country. At the same time I arranged with those concerned the setting-up of what came to be known as the 'Little Committee', consisting of senior Labour party officials, and one or two ministers, to ensure that the party was kept informed about actions of the Government, and that such information as was already publicly available should be more widely disseminated. Slowly this began to happen.

Press certainty that Labour was finished was mirrored by an outburst of euphoria in the Conservative party. They tabled a censure motion: 'That this House deplores the hasty and ill-considered actions of Her Majesty's Government during their first hundred days of office and has no confidence in their ability to conduct the nation's affairs.' They were all geared up for an early election. Mr Edward Heath, who had been appointed by Sir Alec Douglas-Home as co-ordinator of election preparations, had already made a dramatic and highly-publicised flight on New Year's Day to Sir Alec's home in Scotland, to lay before his leader a draft election programme, which came to be known as the 'Instant Manifesto'. So far as I know, this was the first time that the word 'instant' was used as a description of political style: it was not then a term of abuse.

Early on the morning of Sunday, 24th January, I was telephoned at Downing Street with the news that Sir Winston Churchill had died. I was soon in hurried consultation with the Leader of the House and the Chief Whip, since we had decided that in the event of his death, the House should adjourn, not just for the one day which is customary on the death of a former Prime Minister, but for the period until the funeral.

My first task was the tribute to Sir Winston. It had been decided that it should be the opening of the BBC's comprehensive programme of national and world tributes, together with an impressive film of Sir Winston's life and achievements. I had to speak my tribute live from 10 Downing Street. I was more nervous than ever before on television. I spoke at eight o'clock, trying in eight minutes to underline the qualities which had shone through more than half a century of public life. I spoke of his humanity: 'The man who could move armies and navies and embrace the world in one strategic sweep, could himself be moved to uncontrollable and unashamed tears at the sight of the old soul's cheerfulness in a shelter or of a street of devastated houses – at the thought of the human realities which lay behind the war communiqués.'

I went on to speak of his power over the written and spoken word, which, I said, had illuminated his own historical writings and which:

> ... was itself thrown into clearer relief by his sense of making history and writing history, not as distinct occupations but as part of a wider whole. And it is because of this that the words and deeds of Winston Churchill will form part of the rich heritage of our nation and of our time as long as history comes to be written and to be read.
>
> Now his pen and his sword are equally at rest. The tempestuous, restless vitality of a man who would have scorned the ease of a peaceful retreat has ended today in quiet, in peace, in stillness. But what every one of us can know is that Winston Churchill's life, his monumental achievements, have enriched forever – not only our nation which he led, not only the world which he bestrode – but the hearts of each of us whose lives he touched with his greatness.

Meanwhile, the necessary preparations were made for Parliament, the lying-in-state, and all else that had to be done. Contingency preparations had been made long before, in which Sir Winston had himself played some part. When one of his defence ministers had, with some trepidation, approached him about his department's proposals to abolish certain military units, he had satisfied himself that other named units would not be affected, since he envisaged their deployment at his funeral.

But first there would be the parliamentary tributes. I was engaged on that grey Sunday afternoon on the brief speech I was to deliver in the Commons, when the clock in Horse Guards struck four o'clock. Unnoticed by me, it marked the precise end of our first hundred days, begun in bewildered excitement, ended on this sombre day.

It was my duty the following afternoon to appear at the bar of the House bearing a message from the Queen, informing Parliament of her royal wish that the body of Sir Winston should lie in state in Westminster Hall. I had given instructions that the seat he occupied for so many years after his retirement from office, below the gangway immediately next to the Government front bench, should be left empty throughout the afternoon. One unthinking back-bencher sought to claim it and was sharply hustled on to another bench.

I ended my tribute with these words:

We are conscious only that the tempestuous years are over; the years of appraisal are yet to come. It is a moment for the heartfelt tribute that this House, of all places, desires to pay in an atmosphere of quiet.
For now the noise of hooves thundering across the veldt; the clamour of the hustings in a score of contests; the shots in Sidney Street, the angry guns of Gallipoli, Flanders, Coronel and the Falkland Islands; the sullen feet of marching men in Tonypandy; the urgent warnings of the Nazi threat; the whine of the sirens and the dawn bombardment of the Normandy beaches – all these now are silent. There is a stillness. And in that stillness, echoes and memories. To each whose life has been touched by Winston Churchill, to each his memory. And as those memories are told and retold, as the world pours in its tributes, as world leaders announce their intention, in this jet age, of coming to join in this vast assembly to pay honour and respect to his memory, we in this House treasure one thought, and it was a thought some of us felt it right to express in the parliamentary tributes on his retirement. Each one of us recalls some little incident – many of us, as in my own case, a kind action, graced with the courtesy of a past generation and going far beyond the normal calls of parliamentary comradeship. Each of us has his own memory, for in the tumultuous diapason of a world's tributes, all of us here at least know the epitaph he would have chosen for himself:
'He was a good House of Commons man.'

Early on the Saturday morning, the last of the three hundred thousand who had filed past the bier in Westminster Hall came through. I had arranged, as a parliamentary tribute to Sir Winston, that in place of the rota of soldiers who mounted guard in Westminster Hall, three party leaders – Prime Minister, leader of the Opposition and leader of the Liberal Party – together with Mr Speaker, should mount guard for a short period. This we did late on the Friday evening. The four of us, in full morning dress, took up our positions at the corners of the catafalque.

It was only for a few minutes. It was for an age.

The next day there was the great procession from Westminster Hall to St Paul's – the service of tribute, attended by presidents, prime ministers and war leaders from all over the world. Then the solemn progress following the coffin down to the river, where it was taken by launch to Waterloo and then to the train – and so to Sir Winston's last resting-place at Bladon.

Chapter 6

THE Queen had invited the world's leaders who had gathered for the funeral to a reception at Buckingham Palace. Nearly every Commonwealth country was represented, most of them at presidential or prime ministerial level. It was the greatest assembly of the world's leaders, and recent leaders, ever gathered together.

General de Gaulle was there. I had called on him the previous evening at the French Embassy. After our fifty-minute talk he let the press know that we had made an extremely good start in our relationship. Ministerial and even official relations with France had been at a discount ever since the Common Market veto of January 1963. At one point during the reception I was caught, without an interpreter, with General de Gaulle and Marshal Koniev, principal representative of the USSR. With my barely tolerable French and my much less conversational Russian I had to keep the two in some degree of rapport until help came.

At my Audience with the Queen earlier in the week I had formally recommended that, in addition to the heads and other official representatives of sovereign governments to be invited to the Palace reception, she should also be graciously pleased to invite Mr Ian Smith, who we had heard was attending the funeral. I felt this to be appropriate even though Rhodesia, while self-governing, was not juridically independent.

After the reception had continued for over an hour – by this time it was nearly two o'clock – the Queen commented on the absence of Mr Smith. I could not answer for his whereabouts and she ordered an equerry to seek him out. He was duly found eating a steak in the restaurant of the St Ermin's Hotel.* He informed the equerry that he had never received the invitation. I was told later by his High Commission that it was, in fact, in his pocket all the time.

He stammered out his excuses to the Queen, I thought unconvincingly. He and I then had a private word. It had been arranged that we should meet at 4.00 p.m. It was our first meeting since I went to No. 10. I suggested that as the reception was clearly going to break up early, and as some ten or twelve overseas visitors were planning to meet me, we might meet at 3.00 p.m. He agreed, but made a great point about coming into

---

* Since the serialisation of this book it has been suggested that Mr Smith was at the Hyde Park Hotel, not St Ermin's Hotel as I was informed at the time.

10 Downing Street secretly, by the back entrance, as it might be difficult for him if he were seen coming through the front door.

He arrived at three o'clock and we talked in the Cabinet Room for ninety minutes. He was extremely difficult, extremely sour, and not a little offensive about his obsessional aversions – the Labour Government, the previous Conservative Government, the United Nations and the Commonwealth – and particularly, in a phrase I came to know more and more in succeeding months, 'the countries to the north of us' – the newly-independent African states.

It was difficult to penetrate his thinking about UDI. He had won his independence referendum overwhelmingly. Though he claimed this subsequently as a mandate for UDI, he had made clear just before the poll that a vote for independence was *not* a vote for UDI. At Downing Street, however, he seemed to regard UDI as anything but urgent. Even if Britain refused him constitutional independence, he said, he was advised by his South African lawyers that, living under the 1961 constitution and putting his own interpretation on its provisions, there need be no question of majority rule for 150 years. This seemed adequately to cover his oft-repeated statement: 'Not in my lifetime.'

We made no progress. But at the end of the meeting I proposed to him that I should send the Lord Chancellor, Gerald Gardiner, and the Commonwealth Secretary, Arthur Bottomley, to Salisbury for meetings with him and his colleagues. They should also, I added, meet representatives of all other sections of the community – including the African leaders in prison whom Arthur Bottomley had been specifically precluded from meeting when we had previously discussed a ministerial visit. He now showed a reluctant acceptance of the idea of a mission, and after an exchange of telegrams this was duly set up. He left, again insisting on going out through the garden. I made no objection but said that if I were asked by the press if I had seen him, I should certainly have to make it clear that we had met. He agreed.

But his behaviour at the Palace earlier was not the end of his curious conduct for that day.

Ninety minutes after Mr Smith had left, Lester Pearson, the Canadian Prime Minister, came to see me. He began by telling me that he had had a talk with 'that strange fellow, Smith', and went on to say what a pity it was that Mr Smith and I could not meet. In answer to Lester Pearson's suggestion that Mr Smith and I should meet, Mr Smith had said that we had not met, that we would not be meeting, and, that, indeed, it would be politically impossible for him to meet me. I told Lester Pearson exactly whom I had seen, and asked the Cabinet Secretary, Sir Burke Trend, to come in and say where he had been, and with whom, from 3.00 p.m. till 4.30 p.m. When he answered, Lester Pearson was astounded. Not only, I think, that Mr Smith should have misled him, but also that the Rhodesian

Premier should think he could get away with it. It was obvious that Lester Pearson would discuss the question with me.

The following Monday morning Sir Robert Menzies also told me that in a talk 'with that queer laddie, Smith', the latter had said no meeting had taken place. The explanation this time was that I refused to see him. The whole episode did cause some little doubt in my mind about the involved character of the man with whom I was to be dealing.

After Lester Pearson left No. 10, during the same afternoon I saw the President of Zambia, Dr Kaunda, and the German Chancellor, Dr Erhard, whom I already had arranged to visit in the spring. Throughout the Saturday and Sunday following the State funeral, the visits continued. One of the most significant, on the Sunday morning, was that of the Irish Foreign Minister, Mr Frank Aitken. It was then that we completed arrangements for something I had proposed to his Government soon after we took office: namely, the return to Ireland of the remains of Sir Roger Casement, who had been hanged for treason in 1916. The refusal to return his body had soured Anglo-Irish relations for almost half a century and I felt the time had come for us to put it right. What we had been concerned about – and on this we had as yet no assurance from the Irish Government – was the danger that the Irish Government might seek to have him reinterred, not in Southern Ireland, but in Belfast where he came from. He was able to give me the assurance, and we were able to arrange for the remains to be flown over on 23rd February.

It was to be a grisly operation. Long before dawn, Sir Roger Casement's remains were exhumed at Pentonville, under the supervision of Home Office officials, including one of my private secretaries, Philip Woodfield, who was on secondment from the Home Office. The coffin was taken during the morning to Northolt Airport where an Aer Lingus aircraft, chartered by the Irish Government, was diverted a few minutes before its expected landing at Heathrow. Within minutes, the coffin was aboard and the aircraft took off for Dublin. Its arrival was timed so that a simultaneous announcement could be made by me in the House of Commons and by Mr Sean Lemass, the Irish Prime Minister, in the Dail. There was no doubt that this action, followed by the much closer trade relations – including the Anglo-Irish Free Trade Area Agreement – developed later in the year, did a great deal to improve friendship between the two countries. Indeed almost throughout our period of office they remained at the best level known since the Government of Ireland Act nearly half a century earlier.

During the time of Sir Winston's illness and the succeeding period of mourning, a number of Government announcements had been deferred. One of these was put out from No. 10 on the Sunday night. It announced the appointment of Mr R. A. Butler as Master of Trinity College, Cambridge.

Mr Butler had been treated disgracefully by the new Conservative Opposition after October 1964. Looking for a scapegoat, they settled on him, using a report of an apparently injudicious conversation between him and a *Daily Express* journalist, during the preceding election. If they had had the wit – or if they had not been expecting an early general election – the best thing they could have done would have been to have elected him leader *pro tem* while the young lions fought for the succession. But he was given no standing at all, and I wondered whether he might in the circumstances welcome the opportunity of a break from politics, and whether he would accept the Mastership of Trinity.

Some months before the post became vacant I had sent a message to the Fellows asking them whether, instead of having a Royal appointment on the Prime Minister's recommendation, they would not prefer to come into line with most Oxford and Cambridge colleges and elect their own Master. This, however, they refused.

Shortly afterwards the position became vacant. At a No. 10 reception I approached Rab Butler, who, somewhat to my surprise, was extremely attracted by it. Just before Christmas he came to see me and told me quite firmly that he would like to accept. I told him that informal soundings taken by my appointments office had suggested some considerable hostility, mainly on the ground that he was not a Trinity man, but also because there was some resentment at a 'political' appointment, of all things. I said, however, I felt that he should have the recommendation if he wanted it.

Despite further rumblings of a probable mutinous reception, the appointment, when announced, was warmly welcomed. There was considerable interest taken by the press in my motives for appointing him. I learnt that in a discussion of my reasons in one of the very high reaches of the Establishment, a great constitutional pundit finally concluded that it was 'an act of unprecedented magnanimity'.

The other announcement that had been held over until after Sir Winston Churchill's funeral was the statement on the economic situation, which we had prepared at Chequers.

Now that Parliament was sitting again, Douglas Jay announced the export measures. The Commonwealth Exports Council had been formed, with – in addition to the existing Committee on Exports to Canada – Committees for Australia, New Zealand and Commonwealth countries in Africa, Asia and the Caribbean respectively. The 'piggy-back' scheme, under which large exporters took on the exports of small firms with no export experience; the encouragement of export clubs and groups fostered by local Chambers of Commerce; a study of a proposed marketing organisation to sell on behalf of small firms; a publicity campaign on Government aids to exporters; a scheme prepared by the British National Export Council to encourage more inward and outward missions concerned with British exports, with Government financial help up to half the cost; a scheme for collective market research with, again, Government help of up to fifty per cent of the cost of individual projects; the strengthening of the commercial services in embassies and high commissions abroad: all these were announced. On finance the statement included approval for the Export Credits Guarantee Department (ECGD) to make long-term guarantees over a wider range of exports, while the joint-stock banks' related schemes for finance at a five and a half per cent interest rate was extended in scope. Finance for overseas buyers was made available at the five and a half per cent rate.

Meanwhile we were heavily involved in the preparation of the Government's first Defence White Paper. The bulk of the work was done by Denis Healey who had, by this time, got a grip on his department unapproached by any of his predecessors. But the successive drafts had to be examined line by line and finally cleared in the Defence committee, and in the Cabinet: the policy had to be geared to financial realities, and far-reaching expenditure decisions had to be taken in time for the Estimates which were published with the White Paper (Command 2592) on 22nd February.

Under the heading 'The Legacy', paragraph 1 began:

> The present Government has inherited defence forces which are seriously over-stretched and in some respects dangerously under-equipped. The expenditure of over £20,000 millions since 1952 has failed to provide the necessary incentive for voluntary recruitment in some fields or to produce all the weapons needed for current tasks. There has been no real attempt to match political commitments to military resources, still less to relate the resources made available for defence to the economic circumstances of the nation.
> The 1963–64 Estimates provided for an expenditure of £1,838 millions, while those for 1964–65 provided for £1,998 millions, an increase of 8.7 per cent, or more than 5.5 per cent in real terms. The plans for 1965–66 which we inherited would have made necessary Estimates of £2,176 millions, a further increase of 8.9 per cent, or 5.1 per cent, in real terms. . . . To continue on these lines would mean imposing an increasing burden on the British people which none of their competitors in world trade are carrying. It would mean that Britain was steadily raising the percentage of her national income devoted to defence at a time when Russia and the United States were reducing theirs. Moreover, there is no guarantee in the plans of the previous Government that this expenditure would give value for money or provide our forces at the right time with the arms they need.

The Estimates cut our predecessors' projects by £56 millions to £2,120 millions. Defence, in common with so many other areas of public expenditure, has so many long-lead items involving commitments many years ahead that it is hard to secure economies except over a long period, and then only by major changes in policy and commitments.

The White Paper for the most part set out – in its sections dealing with the Atlantic Nuclear Force, the land and air defence of Western Europe, peace-keeping outside Europe, cost control and operational requirements – the policy decisions already announced in Parliament. Denis Healey, however, outlined the new systems of cost-benefit analysis, based to a considerable extent on techniques, well-publicised in Washington, which were being rapidly developed. On organisation he was able to give a valuable progress report on integration and the desperately difficult problem of getting away from the inward-looking preoccupation of individual Service departments and inter-Service rivalries and disputes.

The major spending decisions were on aircraft. The purchase of US Phantoms and British Buccaneers as the Hunter/Sea Vixen replacement, and of C 130s to replace the projected HS 681 was ratified. To save foreign exchange and provide some help to the domestic industry, the Phantom was to be powered by British engines, and fitted with a proportion of British components. In the event, this well-meant decision proved extremely costly to the taxpayer.

The defence debate on 3rd and 4th March ran on well-worn lines. We had had too many debates on defence, and aviation, in our twenty-one weeks of office for the arguments to make any impression. Sir Alec Douglas-Home and I had a routine clash on the second day. The lines of attack were *vieux jeu*, but I concluded on a novel note. Conscious that defence debates had been bedevilled for years by electioneering and obscured by security considerations, I offered joint talks with the Opposition on Privy Counsellor terms. We would withhold nothing from them, however secret, and we should not seek to limit their freedom to oppose. But that freedom would be exercised on the basis of the real facts, and they would learn enough, in the conduct of a political argument, to avoid embarrassing Britain, however much they might fairly wish to embarrass the Government.

The Opposition viewed this offer with some suspicion. The argument put forward that this would inevitably help the Government and hobble the Opposition did not, in fact, hold water, since I had put forward the same proposal from the Opposition in January 1964. It was rejected by the then Government because they sought – and indeed gained – mileage through making nuclear policies an election issue. This time they were more wary, and after some weeks were ready, more for appearances' sake it seemed, to enter into 'talks about talks'. Meetings were difficult to arrange and the soundings were to drag out through the spring and summer. In the event, a tentative trial discussion with the Opposition leaders, on an agreed agenda, was fixed for 11th November; on that morning the Rhodesian UDI occurred, and the meeting was cancelled.

I cannot help feeling that if a Conservative Government (or Opposition) had made such a proposal, the entire press would have praised their statesmanship, and condemned a reluctant Labour party for putting politics before the nation's defence. Since we were the authors of the proposal, there was no such reaction. All I remember is newspaper comment insisting that this was an obvious political ploy by an incumbent Government, just as they had argued – when we had put it forward before – that it was an obvious ploy for an Opposition.

Meanwhile, the situation in Vietnam was deteriorating sharply. We had, in Opposition and in Government, always opposed the idea of any extension of the war from the South to the North. I knew the pressures on President Johnson to escalate the war by bombing. Indeed, as Leader of the Opposition I had been visited by the chief hawk in the Administration, Mr Rostow, who had tried to persuade me not only of the virtues of MLF but of the desirability of instituting a selective programme of bombing public utilities and other essential parts of North Vietnam's economic infrastructure. He got no encouragement from me. Neither had the proposal been raised with me by the President during my Washington visit just before Christmas.

As North Vietnamese army penetration into the South increased, US involvement in the hostilities grew – naval patrols, including the concentration of warships in the Tonkin Gulf, and the training of the South Vietnamese armed forces, including pilots – up to the point where American airmen accompanied South Vietnamese pilots in a 'non-combatant' capacity.

On 7th February, 1965 there was a heavy attack by the Vietcong-North Vietnamese forces on the American airfield and 'billet-base' at Pleiku. In retaliation, the US for the first time launched a heavy bombing attack on North Vietnam from the heavy concentration of aircraft-carriers in the Gulf.

There was a sharp world reaction. Mr Kosygin was on a short visit to Hanoi and strongly condemned the bombing. There was an appeal by North Vietnam to the three-power International Control Commission to investigate the attack. Pressure grew in Parliament, with emergency questions and a motion signed by fifty back-benchers, many of them, as press comment rightly pointed out, not among those who usually supported left-wing *démarches*.

At the Security Council, Adlai Stevenson, the US Ambassador to UN, described the action as defensive and pleaded as justification the infiltration of thirty-four thousand DRV troops into the South, as well as the daily breaches of the integrity of Laos, contrary to the Geneva Agreements, by the movement of troops and supplies along the 'Ho Chi-Minh trail'.

On the late evening of 10th February we received a report of an extremely vicious attack by the Vietcong in the Saigon area, involving the destruction of a club used largely by American servicemen. Knowing the pressures on the President to escalate the war, if need be by the use of nuclear weapons, I feared that his patience might falter and that he would give way to the hawks in the Administration and Congress, and above all, in the Services. Knowing equally the reaction that would follow in the House of Commons, I felt that this was a time for a personal discussion with him to remind him of the attitude his friends, and indeed the rest of the world, might take up if he were provoked too far.

I therefore arranged to telephone him on the 'hot-line' and got through about 3.30 a.m. our time, 10.30 p.m. Washington time. I expressed concern to him about the Vietcong attack, and suggested I might come over to talk with him. To my surprise, he let fly in an outburst of Texan temper:

> I think a trip, Mr Prime Minister, on this situation would be very misunderstood and I don't think any good would flow from it. If one of us jumps across the Atlantic every time there is a critical situation next week I shall be flying over when Soekarno jumps on you and I will be giving you advice.
> ... As far as my problem in Vietnam we have asked everyone to share it with us. They were willing to share advice but not responsibility. Let me send you the exact situation as I view it on classified cable.
> ... I have met escalation in many places and I take it in my stride and I do not think our personal visits would do anything but dramatise and heat it up.

Taking up an earlier reference to Clem Attlee's visit to President Truman over the danger of Korean escalation in December 1950, he shortly pointed out that we had troops in Korea, not in Vietnam:

> ... I won't tell you how to run Malaysia and you don't tell us how to run Vietnam. ... If you want to help us some in Vietnam send us some men and send us some folks to deal with these guerillas. And announce to the press that you are going to help us. Now if you don't feel like doing that, go on with your Malaysian problem. ...

His view was I should not cross the Atlantic with my 'shirt-tails flying'. Cooling down a little, he widened the canvas. After he had claimed that he was supporting us in all international matters – he referred to his adoption of the Atlantic Nuclear Force – I said we were getting anything but help from him with Spain: 'We are facing a hell of a problem in Gibraltar where a lot of bloody fascists are treating our people abominably.'

By the end we were on better terms, and early the next morning a most contrite and friendly telegram arrived, suggesting a visit a few weeks later.

We had received discouraging replies from our messages to our Soviet co-chairman, under the Geneva Agreements, proposing a reconvening of the Geneva powers. On 20th February we made a less ambitious suggestion. In a message to the Soviet Government we proposed that the two co-chairmen should at least agree to approach the Geneva Govern-

ments to seek their individual views 'on the circumstances in which a peaceful settlement' might be reached. There was no reply until 15th March, when we received a routine denunciation of the United States and a renewed call for the withdrawal of all American forces and equipment. Mr Gromyko was due to arrive in London the following day, 16th March. Before he came, I carried out my scheduled visit to West Germany and West Berlin.

At 8.15 a.m. on 6th March I left No. 10 for the weekend visit to Berlin, where I was met by the governing Mayor, Willy Brandt, and the chiefs of the Allied Military Government missions. After a short welcoming ceremony, I went on to the *Rathaus* to sign the Golden Book and make a speech, followed by lunch, toasts and a long talk with Herr Brandt, and then by a tour of West Berlin – including the Wall. I had visited this three years earlier, leading a Labour party delegation of forty-two MPs, when our extremely robust attitude – even by pacifist and left-wing members – had created a deep impression and lasting friendship.

Later in the afternoon I had discussions with the British Military Representative at his headquarters, followed by a dinner with leading German and Allied guests at the Ambassador's residence.

Next morning I read the lesson at the Garrison Church morning service, and then had drinks in the sergeants' and other messes. After lunching with the Allied commanders I left for Bonn, where we had a delegation meeting and worked on briefs; in the early evening I went –

to quote my No. 10 diary, 'to take a glass of wine' with Chancellor Erhard, and to have a preliminary talk which went on till midnight. He was a great deal preoccupied with the crisis in relations with the Middle East. The German establishment of diplomatic relations with Israel was followed by Arab recognition of East Germany, with all that meant for Bonn under the inhibiting Hallstein doctrine.

But Dr Erhard was relaxed and communicative about Anglo-German relations and European affairs. I was interested, though not surprised, to hear the words in which this great preacher of free-market discipline condemned the EEC arrangements for agricultural price support, market-rigging and the inequitable machinery for financing the Common Agricultural Policy, which so far as cereal prices were concerned had been laid down the previous December. But it was obvious that the Germans were powerless to do anything about it.

In the morning we had our first round of talks with the Federal German Chancellor and his staff. We met again in the afternoon, after the *Bundeskanzler*'s lunch, when there were formal speeches at the Palais Schaumberg. We did not have much difficulty with the political side of the agenda – our Berlin visit had gone down well in Bonn. But we attached no less importance to economic issues, particularly the cost which Britain had to meet in maintaining close on fifty thousand troops in Germany. This cost was running at nearly £100 millions a year, and was a heavy burden both in budgetary terms and in the loss of foreign exchange.

Jack Diamond, Chief Secretary to the Treasury, was with me. We gave notice that we should not continue with the current agreement, due to expire in April, and made clear that we should insist on considerably more favourable terms in the two-year agreement which, we said, must replace it. It was agreed that Jack Diamond should return to Bonn shortly thereafter, making it clear that we could not accept the current drain, either on the taxpayer or on the reserves.

After the meeting with Fritz Erler, leader of the Social Democratic party in the *Bundestag*, I attended a dinner given by our Ambassador. But both before dinner and at intervals after it I was being plagued with lengthy telegrams from London.

Following a series of meetings in a Cabinet committee chaired by Herbert Bowden, the Lord President, the Government was due to make a statement on immigration. Agreement had not been easy to reach, and Bowden and some other colleagues were afraid that the Home Secretary, Sir Frank Soskice, who was a hard-liner, would be negative, and possibly provocative to our own people, in supplementary answers. They wanted me to make the statement instead. The draft I had from the Home Secretary certainly seemed too negative to me, and I dictated a whole series of amendments, virtually requiring its rewriting. Late in the evening further telegrams made it clear that the amendments were unwelcome in the Home Office, but I refused to argue the matter further by telegram, saying that the Home Secretary and his people should go on working on my draft. I would consider major amendments – though not many – on my return, but warned London that my programme gave all too little time for discussion. I wanted to spend as much time as possible on preparing a parliamentary tribute to Herbert Morrison, who had died while I was in Germany.

I had prepared, also, my answers for questions the following day, and had struck out a Foreign Office suggestion both for the main answer and 'drafts for supplementaries' to a question on Vietnam, where the parliamentary situation – on our side – was becoming critical. The Foreign Office came back on these and again I made it clear I was not in a mood for changes – they could have a few minutes, not more, on my return.

After a final round of talks with the Germans there was the formal farewell ceremony, with military bands and national anthems, followed by a press conference. The conference was easy, relaxed and stimulating. But there were a number of questions about sterling, where as usual I advised speculators not to burn their fingers by selling the pound short, and there was great interest in the views of the famous Professor Rueff, President de Gaulle's economic adviser. My dismissal of his views as 'out-of-date thirty years ago when I first failed to understand him' was to lead to a sequel on my visit to Paris a month later.

I reached London Airport at 1.15 p.m. and I was plunged into urgent work on the mass of documents which my private office had brought to the airport lounge; indeed I had to work on them all the way to Downing Street. From the airport the Home Office were told by telephone that I would accept only one not very major amendment to the immigration statement, and that was that.

It took me an hour to dictate the tribute to Herbert Morrison and I had just five minutes before going into the chamber for my question time, during which George Thomson, the Minister of State at the Foreign Office, with strong Foreign Office pressure behind him, tried to get me to take a much more committed pro-American line on bombing in Vietnam. I refused.

The questions to me that day related, in the main, to a private enterprise effort by General de Gaulle to get a Franco-Soviet sponsored conference going in Vietnam. We were asked to support the initiative, with its scarcely-veiled French condemnation of the Americans. I was quite sure the Americans would not have responded, and was extremely doubtful – rightly, as it turned out – about the Russians. I stuck to our settled line. We were co-chairman of the Geneva Conference, we were pressing our co-chairman in Moscow for action leading to a conference. Mr

Gromyko's visit to London was about to take place and shortly afterwards the Foreign Secretary was going to Washington.

There was another issue. The International Control Commission, consisting of India, Poland and Canada, had just reported, with India joining Poland in condemning the American attacks on North Vietnam as a violation of the 1954 agreement, and with the Canadian representative dissociating himself from the condemnation.

I refused to join with the majority report, but from our left (and from many centre and right-wingers who disagreed with American policy), as well as from the Conservatives, whose policy was all the way with L.B.J., I had a rough time. I stuck to my line, stressing our policy of pressing the Americans and the other parties to the fighting to get round the conference table. But for weeks more I was finding the Americans as obdurate as the Soviets in refusing even to consider the idea of negotiations.

After questions, I made my statement on immigration, beginning with an assertion of the clear doctrine that 'once immigrants are here, they should be treated for all purposes as citizens of the United Kingdom, without discrimination'. I then set out our policy for co-ordinating action to encourage assimilation and better community relations area by area, especially in the big cities. I announced that Maurice Foley, at that time Under-Secretary at DEA, would be put in ministerial charge. (He was later transferred to the Home Office, with the same duties, when Roy Jenkins replaced Sir Frank Soskice.)

I announced that we were introducing a Bill to forbid racial discrimination in public places and to provide penalties against the evil of incitement to racial hatred.

There was justifiable concern in all parties, and especially in immigrant areas, about the number of immigrants coming into Britain through the widespread evasion of existing statutory controls, by fake passports, impersonation and false or unfulfilled statements about the purpose of entry into the country. I announced that we were undertaking a fresh examination of the machinery of control and, as a preliminary to this, that the Government was sending a high-level mission to discuss with the relevant Commonwealth governments the problems that had arisen. In particular, the mission was to see what could be done to stamp out evasion at source by establishing adequate controls, as well as health checks, in the countries from which the immigrants came.

Our first choice to head the mission was Lord Butler, but preoccupation with his forthcoming academic duties and a slight temporary concern with his health caused him to refuse. We then invited Lord Mountbatten, who was due to retire later in the year as first Chief of the Defence Staff. We were able to announce his appointment on 23rd March, and he carried through the assignment as only he could do.

From early March until Easter we were preoccupied by further critical developments in the Vietnam situation, and with the preparation for the Budget.

Mr Gromyko's visit to London, from 16th to 20th March – though he was friendly and reasonably constructive on bilateral questions – produced no results on Vietnam. In a series of meetings with the Foreign Secretary, and a tough two-hour session at Downing Street, he stonewalled on every proposal to re-call any form of Geneva conference. He was no less opposed to our suggestion of a more limited conference consisting of the two co-chairmen, Canada, India and Poland (the ICC countries) and the parties to the fighting. This would have had the merit, from the Soviet point of view, of excluding China and reducing Chinese pressures on Hanoi. But to this, as to all else that we urged, every response was a flat repetition of their denunciation of America and a demand for unconditional withdrawal of US troops, equipment and advisers.

In a meeting with MPs Mr Gromyko went a little farther. He was reported as saying the Soviet Union would be willing to resume her role as co-chairman, but not until air attacks stopped. In the official talks, he continued to insist on prior withdrawal as an essential condition of any diplomatic moves.

Two days after Mr Gromyko's return to Moscow events in Vietnam took a grave turn. On 22nd March, General Maxwell Taylor, US Ambassador in Saigon, made a statement to the effect that 'no limit existed to the potential escalation' of the war. On the same day the US Defence Department announced that they were using a variety of gas in Vietnam. Michael Stewart arrived in Washington that evening and found awaiting him a telegram from me warning him to make no public statement until the following morning. I was fearful that Foreign Office pressure would be exerted on him to express support; this was, in fact, unfair to Michael Stewart, who reacted as strongly as I did.

Throughout the morning, while Washington still slept, I was dictating and repeatedly strengthening the terms of two telegrams to Michael Stewart, one on the issue itself and its handling, one on the domestic political aspects. Predictably and rightly there was a storm in the PLP. Six senior members, including Philip Noel-Baker and Arthur Blenkinsop, the vice-chairman of the PLP, sent the Foreign Secretary a telegram demanding that he express the 'horror and indignation' felt in Britain at this action.

Neither this telegram nor mine was needed. Michael breakfasted with Dean Rusk and saw the President later in the morning. He spoke to both in the strongest terms. Words he addressed to the President privately he said he must use in his address to the National Press Club at lunchtime: 'In the choice of measures everyone responsible should consider not only what is militarily appropriate for the job in hand but the effect on people around the world. What I am, in fact, asking the United States to display is what your Declaration of Independence called "a decent respect for the opinions of mankind".'

Answering questions about General Taylor's outburst, he said he had discussed this with the President and was satisfied that the President's previous statement – 'We seek no wider war' – still stood, and that 'any utterance that seems to go beyond that or can be construed as going beyond it is wrong'.

The terms in which the Foreign Secretary spoke were hailed in the British press as the bluntest straight-talking Britain had indulged in in Anglo-US relations since the war. But he was widely supported, and his uncompromising approach won the approval of Labour MPs.

This was not all he had achieved. With his firm, persuasive and often underrated authority, he had a marked effect in helping domestic US pressures to steer American thinking away from negative attitudes to negotiations. He reinforced a message I had sent to the President, in which I had drawn attention to the symbolism of Harry Truman's re-drawing of the presidential crest, arrows in the one claw, olive branch in the other, heart-side, with the head turned to the olive branch. 'If we give you support in using the arrows in the circumstances of the fighting in Vietnam,' we said, 'we should like to see more of the olive branch.'

Two days after Michael Stewart's meeting with the President, the White House issued a statement which, after reiterating American concern to ensure the security and independence of countries in south-east Asia, and their policy of furnishing assistance to South Vietnam, went on:

> The United States will never be second in seeking a settlement in Vietnam that is based on an end of Communist aggression. . . . I am ready to go anywhere at any time, and meet with anyone, wherever there is a promise of progress towards an honourable peace. We have said many times, to all who are interested in our principles for honourable negotiations, that we seek no more than a return to the essentials of the agreements of 1954. . . .

Recalling now the press vilification and the violence of the demonstrations that marked so much of Michael Stewart's two periods at the Foreign Office, I have every reason for saying that his critics were as wrong in their misrepresentation of what he was seeking to achieve as in their persistent undervaluation of his untiring efforts, his influence – and his achievements.

Chapter 7

Budget strategy and procedures – the decision about TSR 2 – visit to General de Gaulle – economic discussions in Paris – Aden – the New York bankers – more talks with President Johnson – Chequers conference of world socialist leaders – audience with the Pope – the Rann of Kutch – Captain O'Neill's visit – problems of a parliamentary majority of three – the Finance Bill – steel nationalisation – gloomy political progress

W HILE the Vietnamese crisis was at its height, work was going rapidly ahead on the Budget.

The main lines had been laid down in the Chancellor's Ways and Means statement of 11th November, and from that time he had been fully engaged with his two lieutenants, Jack Diamond and Niall MacDermot, in translating the announcement into budgetary and legislative terms.

The normal procedure in government, at any rate in our period, has been that the Chancellor, from the end of December or very early January, begins to work out the Budget strategy, first, in what have come to be known as macro-economic terms. By that time the expenditure Estimates are – or should be – agreed and firm, and the Treasury, with the assistance of the revenue departments, makes its forecast of the revenue at existing rates of taxation. The resultant balance between expenditure and tax revenue has to be corrected by an amount necessary to bring the economy into balance, the net disinflationary off-take – or, much more rarely these days, reflationary boost. This must be related to Treasury strategy on monetary policy, domestic and international.

Pledges (for instance, in previous Finance Bill debates) and priorities – every budget should have its theme, be it, for example, exports, savings or investment incentives – together dictate the pattern of tax changes. Usually the Chancellor, by the turn of the year, is discarding certain options; on some, indeed, because of the administration time required, the decision to close an option has to be taken some months ahead of the Budget.

At each stage the Chancellor discusses his developing strategy with the Prime Minister: first, the broad size of the Budget surplus; second, the selective tax changes. Here, every tax change has to be assessed in real terms, in resource terms as well as in terms of the tax yield, in the current year and in a full year. Tax changes, like changes in the Government expenditure pattern involving, say, £100 millions, in cash terms may have only minimal effects in their call on real resources, if, for example, they are merely a 'transfer payment' from one group of taxpayers to another. The cost-of-living effect has to be assessed. In our period, the Treasury worked out for each of the indirect taxes a ready reckoner showing that a £100 millions increase or decrease of tax on Commodity A would have a direct effect on the retail price index of x points, against y points for a similar yield in the case of Commodity B. In preparing the unprecedentedly severe Budget of 1968, Roy Jenkins had a whole series of alternatives, each of them costed in terms of the effects on industry and the cost of living.

In modern conditions the Prime Minister is, roughly, in weekly contact with the range of options so that his advice is available not only on economic but on social and political strategy. This is useful to the Chancellor when it is a question of going back and fighting his decision through a Treasury machine almost too fully immersed in the Budget to be able to gauge outside reaction.

Where changes in direct taxation are concerned the options are almost infinite in number, with the possible permutations of standard rates, reduced rates, surtax, earned income relief at different levels, and personal and child allowances. Schemes A, B, C to Z and, in theory, right through the Greek and Chinese alphabets as well, are available, reflecting different calculations of financial and real resource effects and different scales of fiscal progressiveness. In the preparation of the 1970 Budget, for example, Roy Jenkins had these narrowed down to a dozen or so, then three, and in time the Prime Minister became familiar with the refinements of the Inland Revenue alphabet.

Week by week, the Budget takes shape; week by week, options are closed. The arrangement I had with our two successive Chancellors was that no option was excluded before the general strategy and the specific options were discussed with me. Since, by long practice, the Cabinet is not involved in the Budget decision until the very eve of its presentation, the involvement of the Prime Minister at each stage helps the Cabinet to accept that the Prime Minister's ability to 'advise, encourage and to warn' throughout the process means that political realities have not been ignored. In fact any Chancellor is likely to be as well-endowed as his chief with all these necessary attributes; the system works because it enables a heavily-immersed Chancellor, often under weighty bureaucratic pressure, to take a second opinion.

In our early years I tried to involve the Cabinet more in the successive stages of preparing the Budget, by borrowing a procedure Sir Stafford Cripps had tried. He had found his colleagues suspicious and difficult at the Budget Cabinet, since both his overall strategy and his specific proposals were called sharply in question by that most democratic of bodies, the Attlee Cabinet. On an earlier occasion, in 1947, a key element in Hugh Dalton's Budget had been thrown out on Budget eve. Stafford therefore introduced the idea of a two-stage Budget consultation. At the first, the strategy, the main aims of the Budget, had to be decided; the Cabinet had to accept, amend or reject the Chancellor's view about the Budget balance, in particular the size of the disinflationary surplus. Beyond that he would listen, without saying how his mind was working, to any suggestions about individual taxes.

This meant that when the final decision was taken no one could fairly argue that this or that unpopular element was not needed, because the strategy was too tough; the strategy carried prior Cabinet endorsement. If this or that disagreeable proposal was not acceptable, its critics must propose a fiscally equivalent alternative. Stafford tried, but this system did not succeed. Nor was it wholly successful when I reintroduced it. Cabinets tend to say, 'We'll accept that strategy when we see what it means in specific tax charges.' But both the Chancellor and I found a pre-Budget airing useful. Without tying the Cabinet down to a specific strategy, and in particular a specific Budget balance, we were able to get some idea of the Cabinet's thematic thinking on the strategy as a whole, and on priorities. The rest was unexpectedly easy.

Little of this was necessary, however, in 1965. The principal decisions had been announced in November, and the general balance then agreed had not changed. The Budget task was not so much political as administrative, with the whole effort of the Treasury, the revenue departments and the three Treasury ministers deployed for every possible hour of every possible day on the complexities of the corporation and capital gains taxes. My advice was limited to a few thoughts on the economic aspects – especially on overseas financing – and on what we might hope to get through in an unusually long Finance Bill, with a majority of three.

But a major spending decision had still to be taken. The Estimates had been agreed and published and, so far as defence was concerned, the main strategy both of expenditure and policy had been debated and approved early in March. But a decision still had to be taken about TSR 2.

Parliamentary pressures were formidable – and those of industry no less so – and there was a sharp difference in the Cabinet. We had to reach a final decision at our meeting on Thursday, 31st March, before the Chancellor opened his Budget the following Tuesday, and I had to leave for Paris early on the Friday morning. We had a long agenda and the issue was not settled by 1.00 p.m., nor could it have been adequately considered if we had gone on even an hour beyond our normal time. That Thursday, most unusually, we failed to reach agreement within normal Cabinet time. It was most unusual because I can claim that the total number of times in nearly six years that a decision had to be deferred to an adjourned Cabinet was less than in any period of three or four months in which I sat in the postwar Cabinet. But we had to have a decision, and Cabinet was called again for 10.00 p.m. By midnight I had to resolve a difficult – indeed, I think, in all our time, a unique – situation. The Cabinet was split three ways: some favoured continuing with TSR 2; some favoured its outright cancellation, with no replacement; and the third group supported the Defence Secretary's view that TSR 2 should go but that its military role should be taken over by an order for American Phantoms, together with one for a number of F 111As. There was not, in fact, a clear Cabinet majority for any one of the three propositions. I summed up, and this was accepted, that a clear majority was for cancelling TSR 2. The question of the replacement, if any, should be further examined in the Defence committee, subject to final Cabinet approval.

It was further decided, on my suggestion, that the decision on TSR 2 should be announced in the Budget speech. And, in view of our plans for a joint Anglo-French military aircraft programme, and recalling President de Gaulle's sharp reaction after Rambouillet to the Polaris contract, it was decided that I should tell him, in strict confidence, of the possibility of a further purchase of US aircraft. I left for Paris early the next morning, Friday, 1st April, with the press screaming stories about the Cabinet split on TSR 2. I was received by General de Gaulle at the Elysée. He invited me into his study and we sat down on his settee, each of us flanked by an interpreter, his being the multilingual Prince Andronikov, and on my side Oliver Wright, Foreign Office private secretary at No. 10. In the event the Prince translated both ways, leaving Oliver free to take a very full note.

I told him about the TSR 2 decision and the likely American purchase, stressing the confidentiality of the decisions, which he respected. He was at pains to show that we were, and had been for years, satellites of the Americans and economically over-dependent on them. I rebutted this and instanced our Government's decision to establish a firmly-based computer industry, British-owned and controlled, in contrast to French experience, where the only sizeable French concern, Machine Bull, had been taken over by the Americans. In the world of the 1970s and 1980s, I said, where a country's strength would depend more and more on industrial technology, independence in computers and advanced electronics would matter more than a national independence in nuclear weapons.

We covered the whole range of world affairs, with particular reference to East–West relations, the growing crisis in Vietnam, the Middle East and Africa. I felt then – and I was to see how devastatingly events in 1967 brought it home to him – that his *soi-disant* middle position between the two power blocs earned him far less political dividend than he hoped for. But it was clear that at that time, before his major policy switch in 1967, there was nothing dividing us on the Middle East, and we found a pretty high common denominator of agreement on African questions. He agreed to my suggestion that ministers and officials should get together for discussions on these two questions and this followed in the spring.

We had an agreeable lunch, with short but informal speeches, and in the afternoon, somewhat to my surprise, he showed an interest in pursuing financial questions. He paraded a full ministerial team, including Prime Minister Pompidou, Foreign Minister Couve de Murville and Finance Minister Giscard d'Estaing.

M. Pompidou had to leave us after a little time for a censure debate in the Assembly, but Giscard and Couve kept their respective ends up. Couve was at least as articulate as Giscard; as a former *Inspecteur des Finances*, he always felt that he could hold his own with any Finance Minister, not least Giscard. Besides, he had a close continuing relationship with his old tutor, Professor Rueff, who had the General's ear on all financial matters.

The General presided benignly from the settee, saying nothing. I remembered the story of the banker who had urged the President to take a closer interest in certain economic developments as being vital to the future of France, and the General replying by dismissing the whole of economics as 'quartermaster stuff'. So it was for him, but economic questions had importance in his relations with America. In a world where France could no more challenge the US for world leadership than pit her atomic weapons against the Americans, Rueff's persuasions convinced the General that he had one weapon – gold – which could be decisive against an America labouring under a severe balance of payments deficit. That this was more than accounted for, at that time, by America's aid programme meant nothing. While other countries, including Britain, were helping the US by converting gold holdings into dollars, the General sat tight on his gold, always ready to frustrate efforts to ease the world liquidity position. For these efforts, he felt, would ease the position of the Americans and postpone the increase in the gold price which it was French policy to increase and from which he was waiting to profit. Battles have been won by aggressive and far-sighted quartermasters.

At 5.30 p.m. I left him to go to the Hôtel Matignon for an hour with M. Pompidou. Once again the subject which the French wanted to discuss was gold, and the purpose of the French approach to my visit became clear. But I was on my home ground.

The Prime Minister spoke for some length right down the Gaullist line. In his view, all the world's financial troubles were caused by the American payments deficit. I countered by saying that the argument was the other way round. The continuing American deficit was pouring billions of dollars into the rest of the western world. At a time when world liquidity was lamentably failing to keep pace with the growth of world trade, the exiguous trickle of newly-mined gold was being supplemented by the influx of deficit dollars on to world currency markets. The time to worry about the Americans would be when they turned the deficit into a surplus and we were all plunged into an acute liquidity squeeze. This thesis received some support in the Euro-dollar squeeze a year later, and France herself felt the draught of the withdrawal of dollars from Europe in the summer of 1969, when the hopes of French and other gold lobbyists were dashed by international action to defuse speculation in gold.

M. Pompidou flatly rejected this thesis, and I tried again. I saw the world monetary system as fed by gold from three large gold mines, South Africa, the Soviet Union and Fort Knox. All were pouring out gold, and yet there was still not enough. There was a limit to what South Africa and the Soviet Union could produce, a limit far below the needs of world liquidity; the gap was made good by the mining and sale of US gold reserves from Fort Knox. If Fort Knox ceased 'production' or, worse still, if the flow were reversed and gold started to go back into the mine, then the world liquidity situation would become critical. M. Pompidou refused to accept this argument but said we might talk further about it at the Quai d'Orsay dinner that evening. Clearly he was finding me a slow, not to say perverse, pupil. More education was needed. This explained what happened later.

At the reception before dinner I was hailed by Professor Rueff, who made a joking reference to what I had said about him at the Bonn press conference. We briefly discussed his prewar works, which I remembered I had been set to attempt to savage at a G. D. H. Cole seminar at Oxford in 1936. He hoped we could discuss the situation further after dinner. My own view was that I should perhaps meet others of the two hundred or so Frenchmen there.

After dinner we assembled in one of the ante-rooms for coffee, but I suddenly found myself being piloted by one of Couve's secretaries through long corridors, across an enormous salon, and then away to the right, far from any visible human being. The inevitability of my abduction reminded me of one of the more frightening inter-war French films. Not a Briton in sight.

Finally I was steered to a corner table where I found M. Pompidou, Couve, Giscard and, of course, Professor Rueff awaiting me: it was a seminar at the summit. I felt decidedly lonely, not so much because I feared my inability to hold my own in this company – in any case, I felt Giscard might be helpful – but because there would be no witness to what was said. At that point I saw Sir Burke Trend in the far distance, passing the end of the room, and hollered 'Burke' at the top of my voice. He looked startled, saw me and came over.

Rueff was put in to open the seminar. He made some good theoretical points. When I said that gold production was totally inadequate to meet world requirements, he said the same could be true of world wheat supplies if we all insisted on keeping its price at the 1924 level; all that was wrong in economic terms was the artificially low price of gold. Gold prices should be raised.

In the cut-and-thrust that followed they were at great pains to throw the blame on the Americans. I soon noticed, however, a very sharp division between Giscard on the one hand and Couve on the other, who echoed all that Rueff was saying, M. Pompidou remaining silent. Rueff and Couve were opposing all moves to ease the liquidity shortage, whether by the scheme for Special Drawing Rights which Jim Callaghan was pressing, or any other means of creating 'paper gold'. This opposition clearly extended to Giscard's proposals for a Currency Reserve Unit (CRU), in which we saw considerable merit. Rueff and Couve were pretty cutting about it, despite those of its provisions which rewarded countries earning gold. Some of Rueff's comments led me to venture the thought that he was misrepresenting Giscard's precise proposals and Couve rushed to Rueff's defence. Without recounting all the technical details, I asked whether Rueff was not confused in thinking that the CRU bonus would depend on total holdings of gold and convertible currencies, rather than, as I understood, the annual increment in gold and currency holdings. Couve was certain that I was wrong, so was Rueff. Giscard came down crisply in favour of my interpretation and, for good measure, went on to make it clear that he had always suspected that neither Rueff nor Couve had ever understood his proposals.

But it was clear that I had failed to pass the examiners. I had not, at least not yet, shown the degree of economic perception qualifying me for entry to the anti-American, anti-liquidity gold club.

The next morning I had another series of talks with the General, again very cordial, and on a number of quite important issues we were clearly in close agreement. He had been fully briefed about the discussions of the previous evening and talked of it with some amusement, though he was obviously not concerned, as he said, to go into the technicalities we had discussed.

For the last forty-five minutes we were joined by our principal advisers. I then went for a final press conference. Here I found, and the French press in the following days confirmed it, that the briefing about the talks, both from the Elysée and the Quai d'Orsay, had been unusually friendly.

From Paris I flew to Southport, where I had to address the annual dinner of the Guild of British Newspaper Editors. On Monday we had the Budget Cabinet, where the Chancellor's proposals went through with very little question.

By this time I had gone down with influenza, the only time I took to my bed in No. 10, apart from a half-day in May 1969. I went through my question time in the Commons, feeling more dead than alive, unfortunately missing Jim's first Budget speech; though I had the fun of seeing the presentation of the succeeding disclosures, together with comment thereon, on television.

From then on my scarcely attenuated flow of visitors had to be received in my bedroom, and I had only a little time to prepare a speech for a Labour party meeting at Reading the following Sunday.

I was due to go to the United States on Wednesday, 14th April. President Johnson, in the course of now most affable exchanges, appeared by this time most ready to discuss the Vietnam situation with me. I spent three days clearing the decks for my visit, with meeting after meeting on every considerable subject – defence, foreign affairs, the details of legislation we were preparing on rents, land-planning and leasehold – where no agreement had been possible at Cabinet committee meetings, the only relaxation being a Free Church dinner at the House.

But on the Wednesday evening, a few hours before I was due to leave, a storm arose out of a decision of the Defence Committee to call out a small number of 'ever-readies', part of the stand-by civilian reserve, for service in Aden. Very few were needed, but our over-stretch throughout the world and a sudden crisis in the South Arabian Federation required us to call up some specialist tradesmen for service there.

George Brown, who, after some hard demur, had agreed to it, approached me during the evening saying that he could not now agree, and that I must rescind the decision; indeed, that he was going to resign if I refused. This was the first of many threatened resignations. He was obviously very concerned; he thought it would hit every headline, and that there would be serious trouble in the party because for the first time since conscription ended civilians were being called up for service. In the event, it rated two or three inches on the odd inside page, and there was no reaction at all from the PLP.

He would have liked me to cancel my visit to the United States. I made it clear that the recall of the specialists had been a collective decision; nothing had happened since the Defence committee meeting ended at 7.30 p.m. to justify a change of policy or even, at that hour, recalling the committee. He continued to approach me, on the telephone and by a number of personal visits. I was worried that George, who, although not officially deputy Prime Minister, was – as always – in charge of the Government in my absence, might himself take action to reverse the decision. I therefore left with Bert Bowden, Lord President, a handwritten instruction that there was to be no reversal of the decision, unless, because of some new development, the Cabinet as a whole so decided. I went downstairs for a few minutes for a party which left-wing MPs were giving to Frank Bowles on his entry into the Government as a whip in the Lords, and then, ignoring further requests to telephone George Brown, left for Washington, physically and emotionally exhausted. On arrival at New York

I found a telegram from him in peremptory terms, demanding that I telephone him on arrival. Realising that it was 3.00 a.m. in London, I decided not to reply and left the matter to await the morrow. Nothing further happened.

Most of Wednesday, 14th April I spent in New York; I discussed exports for ninety minutes with the British Commonwealth Chamber of Commerce, then went to the United Nations, where I had a long private talk with U Thant and a lunch attended by the ambassadors of most of the leading powers. There was a press conference in the afternoon followed by talks with Adlai Stevenson and Averell Harriman. In the evening I had to make a major speech to the Economic Club at the Waldorf Astoria. This is one of the prime American dinner audiences and some two thousand leading bankers, industrialists, economists, Government leaders and officials were there.

It was a robust speech, dealing with some of the speculative talk which had flared up from time to time in New York, which I contemptuously dismissed. I made it clear that we could have devalued on taking office and blamed it on our predecessors; the fact that we did not do so showed our determination not to do so then, as in the future. There was an aggressive passage in which, after recounting the changes we were forcing in British industry, I said, 'Given the response of which our people are capable, be under no illusions we shall be ready to knock hell out of you.' The speech had a tumultuous reception and favourable reporting on a major scale on both sides of the Atlantic. The next day the Bank of England reported an intake of £37 millions of foreign currency, largely through buying in New York. It was welcome.

Early the following morning, 15th April, I flew to Washington and was met by Dean Rusk, who stressed the importance of the talks which had been arranged with the new Secretary of the Treasury, Mr Fowler. 'You'll like Joe,' he said, 'you'll feel you've known him all your life. He fits you like an old shoe.' He was right. I called on him that morning and had a most constructive discussion with him. He was on our side.

I then had lunch with the President. He was in an expansive mood. This time our discussion on Vietnam was much more constructive. His White House statement of 25th March had been reinforced by his speech at John Hopkins University, Baltimore on 7th April, where he offered 'unconditional discussions'. When I used the word 'negotiations', a word which he himself had, in fact, used on 25th March, he still demurred; he stressed the 'three Ds': determination, development – here he referred to his billion-dollar scheme for development in the Mekong valley – and 'discussion'. After the President had explained exactly what he had in mind I was much more reassured and I pledged our full support in pressing our Soviet co-chairman to build on this new American willingness to secure a settlement round the conference table.

Apart from an occasional moment in future years when President Johnson revived the notion of a British military presence in Vietnam, these April talks set out a division of function which he more than once stressed publicly. The American Government would not be deflected from its military task; but, equally, he would give full backing to any British initiative which had any chance of getting peace-talks on the move.

One was already in train. I had asked Patrick Gordon Walker, following his retirement from Government, to make a tour of south-east Asian capitals as my personal emissary to discuss the Vietnam situation. In the event – while he produced a useful report on his talks in Saigon, Vientiane, Rangoon, Bangkok, Kuala Lumpur, Pnom Penh, Tokyo and Delhi – Hanoi and Peking barred the door to him.

After a short talk with Willy Brandt, who was also in Washington, I held a reception at the Embassy for American finance ministers, administrative financial advisers and bankers, including the top officials of the IMF and the World Bank, and then left the Embassy for the airport, reaching Heathrow early on the morning of Good Friday, 16th April.

At 10.00 a.m. I caught the train for Penzance and worked for the whole journey, partly catching up with telegrams and Cabinet committee minutes and papers, as well as dictating to the Garden Room girl a full record of my private talks with the President. Also on the train was Sir John Stevens, British Economic Minister in Washington, on his way to a Devon holiday. He had been with me on the Washington financial talks, and I took the opportunity of full discussions on the next steps in both bilateral and multilateral monetary questions.

After a short Easter break I was back at Downing Street the following Wednesday, 21st April. I found the usual accumulation of red boxes, and took the opportunity of seeing a number of ambassadors, high commissioners and foreign visitors, and also of interviewing those I was proposing to recommend for life peerages to strengthen our ever-dwindling numbers in the Upper House.

The following weekend, 24th-25th April, we were due to have a conference at Chequers of democratic socialist party leaders from all over Europe. The delegates included a number of socialist leaders in government, some at head of government level, others as foreign ministers or deputy prime ministers in coalition governments. Willy Brandt was there.

It was an opportunity to hammer out the difficult problem of relations between the Six and EFTA. This was a subject on which I had represented the Labour party in conference after conference in Europe over our last six or seven Opposition years and I had come to know most of my Chequers guests on intimate personal terms.

I proposed to them that the time had come for a new initiative. Europe could not continue at 'Sixes and Sevens'. The proposal I put forward, therefore, was that we should call a meeting of EFTA prime ministers in the following month to consider, at top level, not only our internal EFTA problems but also the question of an approach to EEC, on which we had heard encouraging noises from certain countries within the Six.

Such an approach would raise a number of possible approaches. One would be the integration of the two European economic blocs; another the terms on which negotiations could be reopened for the entry into EEC of any countries who wished to join the Market, and for appropriate means of association for the rest. Alternatively, if the Market could not do business on these lines, we might consider a simple bridge-building operation between EEC and EFTA, aimed at a low-tariff or, preferably, a free-trade area within Europe. The Six attached importance to the totality of their economic integration; EEC was not simply a free-trade area, it was an economic union, a community. Some EFTA countries could not proceed so far. One idea we might explore – and it was currently much canvassed within EEC countries – was a free-trade area consisting of eight or nine economic units, seven EFTA countries (eight if Finland were included) and one, single integrated EEC customs union. EFTA – or FIN EFTA – countries would preserve their several independent constitutions within a relatively loose free-trade area, the other members of which would be a fully integrated western European economic community.

The proposal for a prime ministers' conference was warmly supported by the EFTA prime ministers and other leaders at Chequers. It was agreed that each of us would consult our fellow heads of government and, at the same time, our friends within EEC. The first opportunity open to the British Government to inform EEC heads of government of our ideas was my visit to Rome, due to take place on 27th April.

My first meeting with Signor Moro, the Italian Prime Minister, whom I had met as Leader of the Opposition on his 1964 visit to London, began in a somewhat eerie way. My full delegation paraded at his office, and he expressed a desire to see me alone. It immediately became clear that one of the things he hoped for from my visit was my intervention in one of the perennial Italian internal political crises, then threatening the existence of the Government. Sr Moro knew of the part I had been asked to play in 1963 as leader of the Labour party – through my talks with Guiseppe Saragat and Pietro Nenni – in creating the conditions in which the warring Italian socialist parties could unite. Pietro Nenni, as deputy Prime Minister, held a key role in the *apertura a sinistra*. But he was subject to continuous trouble with the uneasy marriage partners of the 'United' Socialist Party. There was every danger that he would throw in his hand – even during my visit. Sr Moro asked me to use my influence with Nenni to ensure that he did all in his power to keep the Government together. I had private talks with Nenni and, indeed, he had to withdraw from the inter-Government talks for half a day, while he sorted out his party problems. In the end all was well – for the time being.

My talks with Sr Moro, and Sr Fanfani, the Foreign Minister, were themselves relaxed and useful. There was no real difference on any issue; they were particularly keen on closer technological co-operation, especially on nuclear questions. Both were eager to see Britain play a greater part in Europe, and they welcomed our EFTA initiative as a first step, since, with General de Gaulle's attitude dominating the EEC, they saw little prospect of any of us gaining entry to the Community.

One of the most memorable events during my visit was my Audience with His holiness Pope Pius XIII on 28th April. He spoke in English and greeted me most warmly. He was aware of the fact that my East Liverpool constituency probably included more Roman Catholics than any other constituency in Britain; he had been well briefed on all I had tried to do over twenty years in helping the local churches to solve their educational problems in a rapidly expanding area. But he was warmest on the question of foreign affairs. While not interfering in any way in British domestic politics, he felt that our entry into Government held out a new and real hope for peace, partly because of our links with the non-aligned world and our influence in the Commonwealth, particularly Africa.

Above all he was concerned about Vietnam. He interrogated me about my views, and my judgment about the US President's real willingness to take the steps necessary for peace. He told me with deep sincerity that he prayed about Vietnam every night; he was always ready to take any steps anyone could suggest to him which might help a solution.

There was a personal note. Just as I left, I mentioned our young Irish housekeeper, whose rosary I had brought for his blessing. He not only blessed it, he presented me with one of his own, and one for Mary, who was with me throughout the Audience.

I promised him that I would keep in close touch with him on Vietnam, and from that time forward we had a continuing, almost regular exchange of views and analyses, through HM Minister to the Vatican. On every issue – Vietnam principally, but also Rhodesia and the Nigerian tragedy – I felt free to approach him for help and, where appropriate, personal intervention.

On my return to London on 29th April there was a particularly difficult dispute between two Commonwealth countries. Fighting had broken out between India and Pakistan in the Rann of Kutch over the disputed ownership of a small stretch of unproductive territory, which was, in fact, under water for the whole of the rainy season and not much use the rest of the year. But prestige was involved, and all the passions released from the unsolved problem of Kashmir found vent in the Rann of Kutch.

I sent personal messages to President Ayub Khan and Prime Minister Shastri, and with their goodwill put our two High Commissioners in Delhi and Rawalpindi on the job. At a later point the High Commissioners, John Freeman and Sir Morrice James, each of them well-briefed on the attitude of his host Government, met in Ceylon to discuss the basis on which a settlement could be reached. The work they did, as both Governments later recognised, was decisive in the final outcome, reached in June during the Commonwealth conference.

On 9th May Captain O'Neill, the Ulster Prime Minister, flew over to see me. He had paid a courtesy visit soon after we came into office. But now we had to get down to realities.

Northern Ireland had not at that time erupted into the troubles we had to face later, but I was anxious that the Ulster Unionist Government under Captain O'Neill should be encouraged to press on with their programme of ending discrimination in housing allocations and jobs and generally improving the lot of the minority in Northern Ireland. Since coming into office he had, by Northern Ireland standards, carried through a remarkable programme of easement. The problem was that a high proportion of his Stormont parliamentary party would have used the word 'appeasement' to describe his policies. He had been successful in arranging, on 14th January of that year, the first meeting in over forty years between the Northern and Southern Ireland Premiers. He told me that his Special Branch advisers had warned him that while they would be happy to see him walk through the Catholic area of Falls Road without a bodyguard, even with a full bodyguard they could give him no guarantee of security in the extremist Protestant areas.

An acute political situation had arisen in our own Parliament following the Budget. Our majority of three was temporarily reduced to two when the member for Abertillery died in February: but we held the seat without difficulty. Every vote in Parliament was an agony for the whips. During those all-night sittings when I was allowed to go to bed – and the Chief Whip was very understanding – I frequently put out the light wondering whether we should still be a Government when day dawned. On every key division we were still dependent on ambulances and the vagaries of air and rail travel. Labour members were almost chained to the House.

For the walking sick we had what could be only described as a hospital ward attached to the whips' office, with Harriet Slater, the first-ever woman whip, detailed by the Chief Whip to act as matron to ensure their comfort, and, above all, their survival, while he 'nodded them through' and registered their vote in the division lobby. Legends proliferated. If a member sneezed in the tea-room, macabre colleagues surrounded him to ask him what his majority was. Since the House of Commons was part of the Palace of Westminster, where no one ever officially dies, but waits to expire on the way to hospital, there was morbid speculation on the question whether, if a member were to die at say 9.00 p.m., the Chief Whip would be justified in 'nodding him through' a ten o'clock division, while the ambulance was still on its way.

Of course sterling suffered, since Westminster rumours are always exaggerated by the time they reach the City. Feverish City gossip regularly spread the certain, but untrue, news of the death of a sick Labour member, particularly on a Friday. One Friday the gold reserves were mulcted of some £50 millions on the definite news of the death of a well-loved, though delicate, backbench colleague; he in fact survived another year, but very much less than the £50 millions returned to the reserves when the rumour was proved false. Such was British democracy in Anno Domini, 1965.

Set-piece divisions could be prepared for. But the spring and summer of 1965 saw almost continuous divisions on the committee stage of Jim Callaghan's Finance Bill. It comprised ninety clauses and twenty-one schedules of infinite complication, inviting divisions on the most esoteric, not to say factious amendments; in its progress through committee it faced eighty-three divisions, all of them won by the Government, until, the committee stage concluded, I unwisely claimed credit for our success.

The Tory conduct of the Finance Bill, to judge from the Tory press, was a classic of organisation. Yet it was in no way different and in its impact less efficient than the organisation of Opposition to every Finance Bill which Hugh Gaitskell and I led as successive shadow Chancellors from 1951 to 1962. But their publicity was better, and this contributed to the emergence of the Conservative shadow chancellor, Edward Heath, as a potential leader later in the year.

All was well, as long as the Parliamentary Party was united. As Prime Minister, following my practice as Leader of the Opposition, I was available to every member who wanted to see me. This practice was not dependent on our majority; it continued up to 1970.

But new strains came in the May of 1965. The Queen's Speech had made clear the Government's intention to proceed with the Bill to nationalise the steel industry, and this had been approved by the House against an abortive Opposition amendment six months earlier, though we had paid a price in foreign exchange speculation for our determination to carry through a measure for which we had a clear electoral mandate. A White Paper setting out our detailed proposals had been prepared by Fred Lee, the Minister of Power, and this was laid before Parliament. It came up for approval on 5th May.

Our problem was that one or two members, notably Woodrow Wyatt and Desmond Donnelly, had declared their hostility to nationalisation. Donnelly was opposed on principle, and he discovered many other things to oppose on principle in succeeding years. Woodrow was more pragmatic, and had done a great deal of homework in consultation with leading figures within the industry. He felt that an alternative, involving a more limited degree of public ownership, would be more effective. He took

'I've got a tiger in my tank'

(With apologies to Esso Petroleum)

advantage of my open-door policy to see me a number of times, and was extremely persuasive, though I could not accept that the Steel Federation, as he hoped, would agree to his proposals for qualified nationalisation.

A crowded party meeting on 5th May endorsed the White Paper, though with just enough opposing speeches to cause concern. Two were enough. George Brown, who wound up, had sweated blood with Donnelly and Woodrow Wyatt and, dedicated though he was to the measure, tactically indicated his willingness for further talks. Winding up the debate the same evening he appeared to incline more to their views than anyone expected, though his determination on the issue was not in doubt. In the last few minutes, anxious for a full vote, he addressed himself to Woodrow Wyatt, who had said that the degree of control over the research, production, development and manpower policies of the industry could be adequately exercised by taking a fifty-one per cent holding in thirteen of the fourteen major companies we were proposing to take over.

George disagreed, but Hansard reported the closing exchanges of his speech in these words:

Mr Brown: I am prepared to say that, if the industry and its friends, the Tory Party, will come to us and say that they are prepared for the Government to assume the control which we and my hon. Friend agree is essential, we shall, of course, listen to what they have to say.
Mr Wyatt: Do I understand my right hon. Friend to say that, if the industry will come forward and concede the complete control which we both agree is necessary on something less than 100 per cent, he is prepared to listen? If so, I shall vote for his White Paper.
Mr Brown: 'Listen' is the word. Listen, certainly.

Question put: –
The House divided: –
Ayes: 310
Noes: 306

Our majority was, therefore, four.

The Liberals supported the Conservative Opposition. Wyatt and Donnelly, at the last minute, decided to vote with us.

Within minutes, my room at the House was thronged with Labour members protesting against George's words. I was in no doubt about what he meant, and I made clear that the legislation we should introduce would be based on the unadulterated policy of this White Paper. Quite understandably, this was not the view of the press or television interviewers who asked me for a statement as I boarded the aircraft for an official visit to the new, primarily technical, university in Newcastle, and an industrial tour of West Cumberland. 'Labour party split', and our early political demise, provided the theme. They were right to perceive that a revolt confined to no more than *two* Labour MPs could, on an issue involving confidence in the Government, bring us down.

This was, of course, one of the major difficulties of a majority as small as ours, and on occasions, fortunately rare, we did not lack those who were at least tempted to take advantage of the Government's vulnerability. More than once a group of four or five asked to see me to press a particular point and make clear that, between them, they represented more than the whole of our majority. The first time this happened, I reacted sharply and said that once any group of people in the party decided to abuse that position, and once the Government showed itself willing to submit to blackmail, then government as such would become impossible. I pointed out that within a party such as ours, there were many minorities – for example, a small number of adherents to some rarefied monetary or tax theory, or members concerned with some small, but to them important, issue of foreign affairs. For all I knew there might be enough members of the Flat Earth Society capable of bringing the Government down. But if they were to exert that power, and I was stupid enough to give in to it, then the Parliamentary Labour Party would quickly become a rabble, and the Government would have to commit itself to a whole series of contradictory postures, from flat-earthism downwards. After one or two such meetings I let it be known in the party that I would not meet any group who came breathing threats to use its power to erode or destroy our majority.

So we continued to live dangerously. The public, we were told, likened our week-by-week parliamentary encounters to the *Perils of Pauline* and rather enjoyed it. But there was a sense of adventure and comradeship, and no words are adequate to pay tribute to the general parliamentary gallantry and loyalty of our members, rarely able to pair, confined to the House night after night, often until daybreak. When our numbers were strengthened by the 1966 election, the newcomers had to listen to unending and nostalgic memories of the great days of 1965.

Chapter 8

Britain and the UN – trade and speculation – plans for a Common-wealth peace mission to Vietnam – the Commonwealth conference – discussions at Chequers and Dorneywood – Rhodesia – the instructions to the Vietnam mission – the conference communiqué – speech at Glasgow – Mr Heath and the Conservative party – mission to North Vietnam

THE EFTA heads of government conference was held in Vienna on 24th May. After an official welcome by the Chancellor of Austria, Dr Josef Klaus, I was asked, as initiator of the meeting, to open the discussion. In a lengthy statement I dealt with three main subjects. The principal one related to the serious, and worsening, division in Europe between the two trading blocs. EEC was consolidating its economic union and raising stiffer and stiffer barriers against the rest of Europe and the world, whatever hopes we might have of world-wide negotiated tariff reductions in the 'Kennedy round' GATT talks. For our part, we were engaged in improving and strengthening trade relations within EFTA. While supporting these measures in EFTA, I suggested that we should make clear our willingness to enter into talks with the Community about possible 'bridge-building' between the two organisations. There might be direct and mutually agreed reductions of tariffs and other barriers between us; we might move to some kind of association, such as that envisaged in Article 238 of the Treaty of Rome. We might alternatively try to create some loose free-trade association covering EFTA, EEC and any other countries willing to join. A number of possible schemes had been put forward. There was the plan of Herr Munchmeyer, a leading German industrialist, under which EEC as a single economic unit might itself join EFTA or some wide grouping, maintaining and, as it sought fit, strengthening its own integrated union as between EEC members. This was similar to an idea I had put from the Opposition front bench in 1962, when I referred to a free trade area of eight members, seven EFTA countries and the Six joining as a single unit.

Secondly, I dealt with our own proposals within EFTA to strengthen our association and stressed that if talks were to be held with EEC we should in no way weaken our own links; we should indeed press on with improving them, unless and until we could see a more advantageous future opening up as a result of the bridge-building operations.

Thirdly, I referred to the concern which, I said, I realised was felt throughout EFTA as a result of our import surcharge. I made clear that it would be scrapped at the earliest possible opportunity. It had, in fact, been reduced from the original fifteen per cent to ten per cent on 27th April 1965 and was finally abolished on 30th November 1966.

In the discussion which followed there was a general welcome for the initiative I had proposed, and several alternative approaches were examined. At the same time there was to be no slackening of our effort to strengthen EFTA and we agreed on a 'mandate' of instructions to the EFTA council of permanent representatives, to work out proposals for the next quarterly conference of EFTA ministers.

In the communiqué we issued that evening, 24th May, we referred to this mandate, and set out our conclusions on bridge-building in these words:

> Ministers examined the situation as it exists today in Europe, after five years of successful development of EFTA. They discussed the likely consequences for Europe of the deepening division resulting from the continued separate evolution of EFTA and the EEC. A heavy responsibility rested on Governments to seek to ensure closer co-operation between EFTA and the EEC and to pursue such policies as would promote to the greatest extent possible the growth of trade, the expansion of their economies and the welfare of all the peoples of Western Europe.
>
> Ministers considered that a hardening of the division could only be arrested by new initiatives. They firmly believed that steps could and should be taken to bring about closer and more continuous contact between the two groups, in order to facilitate the removal of trade barriers and the promotion of. closer economic co-operation in Europe, which are the fundamental objectives of EFTA. They agreed that it would be desirable to seek to arrange meetings at ministerial level between the two groups at the earliest opportunity which offered prospects of a fruitful result.
>
> Ministers therefore decided that the Council should be charged with the task of recommending what procedural arrangements might best facilitate contacts between EFTA and the EEC and what substantive issues of policy might be the subjects of discussion between them; and that this report should be submitted to the Ministerial Council of EFTA at its meeting in Copenhagen in October with a view to a meeting between EFTA and the EEC as soon as possible thereafter.

When I returned to London, on 25th May, it was to discussions about monetary policy. I had been pressing the Treasury for some time to get bank rate down. It had remained at the crisis level of seven per cent for over seven months. The speculative drain had been halted, temporarily at least, and our rates were certainly above comparable rates abroad. We had quite strict controls over the quantity of bank lending; it seemed less important to ration lending by price. I was concerned about possible trouble in the autumn, a seasonally unfavourable period for sterling.

The Bank of England was not averse to coming down half a point, but Jim Callaghan pressed them successfully to go down by a whole point, contrary to the old Bank doctrine of 'up by ones, down by halves'. But we felt it right to tighten up somewhat on the use of real resources by strengthening the controls on hire purchase. On the Wednesday evening, 26th May, George Brown, Jim Callaghan and I met in my room at the House to discuss the package. George, who both personally and departmentally represented the case for expansion, was pleased with the proposed bank rate cut, but feared that its good effects would be more than offset by the hire purchase proposals. In the event, at 3.00 a.m., we agreed to report our discussion to Cabinet the following morning, with the Bank standing by for our decision. The Cabinet endorsed the whole package and George with a good grace accepted it.

On 4th June, the House adjourned for the Whitsun recess, most of which I spent at Chequers discussing primarily departmental problems and assessments with a succession of individual Ministers. Lord Caradon flew over from New York and we had a general discussion on Vietnam and Commonwealth anxieties about Rhodesia. But the main purpose of his visit was to ask Britain to take a lead on the financial crisis facing the UN. Some countries were seriously behind with their subscriptions, notably the Soviet Union and her friends, who, while paying their annual quota, refused to contribute to the costly peace-keeping operations undertaken in the early sixties in the Congo. The US refused to increase her quota unless the USSR at least accepted the obligation in principle and made a token contribution. Hugh Caradon asked that we should authorise him to take a dramatic lead in heading an international rescue operation by pledging $10 millions, without condition or qualification. This was supported by the Foreign Secretary, and I undertook to press the Chancellor, who, despite the tightness of the monetary situation, agreed. Our lead was widely followed, and UN finances were soon on a healthier basis.

On 11th June Mary and I went to Bradford for the formal opening of the buildings of Bradford University of which I was Chancellor-designate. It was while I was there that a message came through informing me of bad trade figures for May. These figures vary considerably from month to month, and every successive President of the Board of Trade has to warn against optimistic or pessimistic deductions from a single month's figures. But our situation was too sensitive – the fear was that speculation, 'leads and lags' and reduction of idle balances would once again reach feverish proportions.

As soon as I returned to London I had an urgent meeting with the economics ministers on the evening of Saturday, 12th June. Against an average deficit on visible trade of £17 millions in the first four months of the year, the May figure had slumped to £57 millions. Our fears about the selling of sterling which would follow publication were justified.

Meanwhile, we had to prepare for the Commonwealth conference, due to begin on 17th June, the first I had chaired as Prime Minister. I had attended a previous meeting under Clem Attlee's chairmanship seventeen years earlier. On that occasion nine countries, including Southern Rhodesia, were represented round the Cabinet table at Downing Street. Now, in June 1965 there were to be twenty-one, and, by the conference held in January 1969, twenty-eight.

The Sunday before the conference, I had another all-day session at Chequers on defence, and stayed over until the Monday morning.

I was extremely concerned about the worsening Vietnam situation, and the negative response to proposals for talks about peace. This would obviously be a central subject at the Commonwealth conference, where it was virtually certain that a majority – including almost all the Asian, African and Caribbean delegates – would take a strong anti-American line. No less the PLP, and not only the left, were deeply anxious about the trend of events, and in this they represented the views of many millions, probably a majority of our people.

Pacing the terrace at Chequers early on that sunny Monday morning, I had an idea which, after sorting out in my mind, I discussed with my principal private secretary, Derek Mitchell, and Oliver Wright, my Foreign Office private secretary. This was the concept of a Commonwealth peace mission. The Commonwealth conference would represent more than a sixth of the total UN membership of 117 countries, and almost exactly a quarter of the world's population. Almost every political philosophy was represented there, including a majority of non-aligned nations. On the Vietnam issue there were pro-Americans, anti-Americans and the totally uncommitted: a microcosm of the UN and of the world itself. A peace mission sponsored by so widely representative a conference should therefore be accepted – as an individual nation's initiative from any quarter could not be.

We hammered out the pros and cons, the obstacles to overcome, the key people to consult. As soon as I returned to London I sent for the Foreign Secretary to discuss the project with him. What I had in mind, I told Michael Stewart and his advisers, was that I should put to the conference at its opening session a proposal to set up, with the authority of the whole Commonwealth, a mission of four prime ministers – or five, if this became necessary to secure balance – representing every point of view on the Vietnam issue. No party to the dispute could feel that the mission was in any way rigged in favour of some preconceived solution.

The immediate reaction of Michael Stewart and his advisers was to say that they saw great merit in this proposal if we could get it through the conference. They felt, however, that it would be necessary to consult the White House as a matter of urgency. For if the President were to refuse to receive the mission, or to pour cold water on the idea – which was unlikely – or if any State Department or Pentagon hawks were to engage on hostile briefing – which was much less unlikely – the success of the mission would be prejudiced from the start. He considered that it was right to put my proposal forward at the first meeting of the conference, and if agreement were reached to announce it that evening – even if this meant a certain degree of 'bouncing' of individual delegates. To proceed slowly would enable non-Commonwealth Governments hostile to the idea to get to work on the delegates. There were, within individual delegations, officials of varying degrees of influence, who could be relied upon to represent the Chinese and Soviet points of view, without any pressures from outside governments. To delay announcements would mean leaks, possibly tendentious, within minutes of the end of the session.

There was agreement on my proposal that the mission should visit Moscow, Washington and Peking, as well as Hanoi and Saigon, and that in the course of its travels there should be meetings with the three members of the International Control Commission.

The officials went off to work out the idea in greater detail. I said to Michael Stewart that it was vital to get Sir Robert Menzies's reactions at the outset: fortunately I was due to dine with him at the Australian High Commission that evening, 14th June. In the event he warmly endorsed it, even before its acceptance by President Johnson, though he agreed that the President's support was essential.

As the Commonwealth presidents and prime ministers gathered for the meeting one after another came to see me at Downing Street, or, where a head of state was concerned, I called on him at the hotel where he was the British Government's guest. I had to be very careful about floating the idea of the mission because of the likelihood of leaks, but it was welcomed by Lester Pearson of Canada and President Ayub Khan of Pakistan. President Kaunda of Zambia gave it his support, and on my eve-of-conference call upon President Nyerere of Tanzania he appeared to be prepared to accept it, without question, though equally without enthusiasm. He was more concerned to talk about Rhodesia, and in particular to get me to commit Her Majesty's Government to be ready to use troops to quell the rebellious members of the Rhodesian Front.

On the Wednesday, Mr David Bruce, the US Ambassador, called to express the warm support of President Johnson.

The conference met at Marlborough House for its ceremonial opening on Thursday, 17th June, and adjourned – after a brief ceremony, with a speech of welcome from myself as chairman, and supporting speeches from the senior and junior heads of government – for photographs and an outdoor reception for the Commonwealth press.

When we met that afternoon, at 3.30 p.m., I got them to agree that we should meet in restricted session in the chairman's room: one

E

delegation leader plus one, instead of the large numbers which, despite our agreed rules, nearly every delegation insisted on parading in the main conference room. At this restricted meeting I put the proposition to them. It was warmly endorsed by most of my colleagues, by some in enthusiastic terms. But Julius Nyerere unexpectedly raised difficulties; the longer the argument continued and the greater the number of Commonwealth countries who supported me, the sharper became his objections.

There was no doubt about where he stood on the Vietnam issue, though the terms of my opening speech had made clear that it was a strength, not a weakness, that every point of view was represented round the table. On the contrary, he felt that for us to put forward even the neutral posture of an independent mission would appear to condone 'American aggression'.

He was also deeply concerned about the reaction our proposal might have in China. As the evening wore on he made very clear, what I had feared all along, that while he was quite willing to attend a Commonwealth conference and play an active part in it, he was concerned also to take no action which would prejudice the success of the conference which was immediately to follow ours, the second Afro-Asian 'Third World' conference, in Algiers. More than half the Marlborough House delegates had booked their return tickets *via* Algiers. President Nyerere urged on his Afro-Asian brethren, particularly those who were backing me, that the Bandoeng Conference, Mark 2, might have something far crisper to say about Vietnam than anything that could be agreed in London; the appointment of a Commonwealth mission might affect their freedom of action in Algiers.

I insisted that we must take a decision, and refused to agree to any adjournment to the morrow. Now that the matter had been so fully discussed, press reports would concentrate on our disagreement, not on the high level of agreement which had been expressed. We had evening engagements: dinner for all the Commonwealth heads of delegation at No. 10, television interviews and the possibility of a parliamentary statement. The pro-mission supporters were getting impatient.

By 8.30 p.m., by which time I had pronounced a dispensation on changing for dinner, the conference had agreed on an interim communiqué. Tanzania alone objected but did not press this to the point of overturning the long-established convention of unanimity at Commonwealth conferences.

Four heads of government were appointed, those of Britain, Nigeria, Ghana and Trinidad. There was no Asian country. It would be difficult to appoint India or Pakistan without offending the other or, for that matter, Malaysia, and we therefore asked the Prime Minister of Ceylon; but, mainly on grounds of health, he felt unable to accept. What was surprising was the great enthusiasm of President Nkrumah of Ghana, who, throughout the meeting, countered every argument Julius Nyerere put forward.

Bob Menzies and I had to leave No. 10 after dinner in order to record our television interviews on prospects for the conference, and on the mission. Bob praised the initiative: 'Full marks,' he said. If it failed, well, 'we will have tried – and it is better to have loved and lost than never to have loved at all ...'. His strong support of the Vietnam initiative proved to be something of an embarrassment for the Conservatives, who, after the first announcement, were determined to crab the whole idea as an ill-thought-out gimmick. Yet no world leader more strongly supported the American Vietnam policy than Sir Robert.

A little before midnight, held up by the archaic parliamentary rules in these matters which then prevented intervention except at a break in business, I announced the proposal to the House.

Sir Alec Douglas-Home welcomed the initiative:

> ... when the Commonwealth Prime Ministers are in conference everyone would hope and expect that they would take any action open to them to further the processes of peacemaking.
> The situation in Vietnam is most difficult and baffling. It is one of great danger because it could lead to an escalation to a war which would be of concern to the whole world.
> We on this side of the House, therefore, hope that the contacts which the Prime Minister will make, led by the right hon. Gentleman, will assist towards a peaceful settlement. I welcome the statement made by the Prime Minister.

Mr Grimond and, more ecstatically, our hard-line left-wingers, echoed the same sentiments.

So did the press, in unaccustomed harmony the following morning. Many of them drew attention to the risks I had taken, but equally they drew attention to Britain's success in getting a Commonwealth of such varying views to come to an agreement on so divisive an issue, though Tanzania's reservations were noted. Even the *Daily Mail* felt moved to say:

> There has never been a diplomatic initiative quite so original as the Commonwealth Mission. ...
> It is an exciting idea for which it seems Mr Wilson must be given the full credit. It is a bold and imaginative stroke. ...
> To have appointed such a delegation before the Governments it proposes to visit agree may appear to invite the risk of refusal. But any capital which declined to receive it would lay itself open to a charge of turning down a possible chance of peace in Vietnam.

On the Friday we began, as is usual in Commonwealth conferences (1966 proved an exception), on a review of the world situation. Some delegations insisted on harking back to the Vietnam decision. Mr Murumbi, of Kenya – President Kenyatta unfortunately not being present

– tried to reopen the issue. He objected to the proposal that I should lead the mission. His friendship with Marshal Chen Yi, the Chinese Foreign Minister, whom he had recently visited, meant this was taken by the press, rightly or wrongly, as reflecting the first Chinese reaction to our decision. Julius Nyerere – I quote from inspired press reports – 'feared that our decision would put China in the dock'. Certainly China's first reaction was discouraging. Chou-en-Lai the following day referred to it as 'a manoeuvre in support of the United States "peace talks" hoax'. Two days later the Peking *People's Daily* modestly contented itself with calling me a 'nitwit'.

On Friday night the first group of prime ministers came to Chequers for dinner; most of them stayed the night. Another group were entertained simultaneously by the Commonwealth Secretary at Dorneywood, the Foreign Secretary's official country residence some fourteen miles from Chequers. These nights away from the conference atmosphere have proved their value over the years for thrashing out conference difficulties and getting on closer personal terms.

We were able to make progress with the Rann of Kutch dispute, which had become more dangerous with the outbreak of fighting on the Kashmir border. Mr Shastri was at Chequers, President Ayub at Dorneywood. After dinner, when my guests went up to the Long Gallery for coffee and drinks and informal discussion, I took the chance of sounding out the Indian Prime Minister about the dispute, and we were soon looking at maps. 'Was this track essential? Could Pakistan move along that one? Suppose it were only police and not troops involved in this area, and guns moved back in that one?' Gradually the sticking-points became clearer. Meanwhile, a similar process was going on at Dorneywood. Each tentative advance or embryo concession was passed through private secretaries from one house to the other and we began to make progress.

On the next evening the roles were reversed. I took Ayub aside after dinner, Arthur Bottomley engaged Shastri. First I asked Ayub, who was on good terms with President Soekarno of Indonesia, what he could do to help promote a settlement of the Malaysian confrontation. This he was most ready to do, though doubtful of the outcome. Before he left London a week later he had all the necessary information.

We then passed on to the Rann of Kutch problem, again exchanging messages point by point with Dorneywood. By midnight, putting together the moves in both houses, we were moving towards a possible settlement. Both our guests accepted my proposal that, with the Queen's permission, we might retire for a few minutes from the Royal dinner for the Commonwealth prime ministers to see if an agreement could be worked out. Detailed briefing was prepared in the Commonwealth Office, and on the night of Tuesday, 22nd June, when we were all at Buckingham Palace, by prior arrangement with Her Majesty we went to a prepared room and quickly reached the basis of a settlement. The two British High Commissioners followed this up with their host Governments and, a cease-fire was signed on 30th June and announced by me in Parliament.

A great part of that weekend, 18th–20th June, was devoted to the Vietnam mission, mainly by a series of telephone calls. Whatever difficulties we encountered my three colleagues were devoted to the idea, and determined to press on. Messages were sent to all the capitals we were proposing to visit. President Johnson and South Vietnam welcomed the mission, President Johnson explaining to me that he was doing this in the most restrained way to help counter the line being put out in Communist capitals that my initiative was a put-up job on behalf of Washington. On the 23rd, our four ambassadors in Moscow handed a joint message to Mr Kosygin asking for his support.

But there was another development which went far to ease relations in the conference. Listening to the radio on the terrace at Chequers on the Saturday morning I heard news of the army coup in Algiers which had ousted Ben Bella. I asked Oliver Wright to check with the Foreign Office. For once they were caught napping. They had not heard; indeed it was an hour or two before we got the North African desk manned. But there was no doubt about the facts.

Ben Bella was to have been host at the non-aligned nations' conference. But more than that, he was looked up to by many leaders, and by none more than Julius Nyerere, as the patron saint of the Bandoeng ideology. His imprisonment and replacement by Colonel Boumédienne were bound to have an effect on some of my African colleagues.

This materialised on the Sunday evening, when the guests at Chequers included Presidents Nyerere and Kaunda. I had heard the last words of the repeat headlines at the end of the six o'clock news, and was pretty sure that I had heard that Chou-en-Lai, in Cairo, en route for the Algiers conference, had recognised Colonel Boumédienne and cabled his congratulations. We could get no immediate confirmation from the Foreign Office, and I asked my office to try to get the full text from the BBC. I was sitting between Julius Nyerere and Kenneth Kaunda, and mentioned what I thought I had heard on the BBC. They were incredulous. Shortly afterwards the full BBC text was brought in.

The reaction was sharp. 'Indecent:' Julius Nyerere almost hissed the word. More sadly, Kenneth Kaunda, looking very strained, said: 'It almost makes you want to be physically sick.'

There was animated discussion across the table and, after dinner, urgent consultations and frantic telephoning. The outcome was that I was approached as conference chairman by some of our guests, speaking for the dozen or so Bandoeng countries, who asked for the postponement of the meeting the next morning for half an hour, while they met in the chairman's room. I agreed. The meeting, in fact, lasted well over an hour. They decided unanimously that they would not go to Algiers, and that telegrams should be sent to other participants asking them to join in demanding that the conference be cancelled. The god had failed and, whatever our difficulties, Britain seemed just that little bit more acceptable.

The rest of the day, Monday, 21st June, was a good test of the new atmosphere – it was spent on the most controversial subject of all, Rhodesia. Arthur Bottomley, from the chair always reserved for the British minister introducing or replying to any discussion, opened up with a fully prepared statement on all the developments since July 1964, when the Rhodesian question had almost led to the break-up of the previous conference. He set out the progress of negotiations with the Rhodesian Government and our warnings on UDI.

He was followed by Nkrumah, clearly speaking on behalf of all his African colleagues (except President Banda of Malawi), for there had been a series of all-African meetings in hotels and High Commission residences almost from the first arrivals. He put forward a six-point plan. Britain must convene a constitutional conference of all parties and groups in Rhodesia. Britain must tell Smith to release all political prisoners. Smith should be given a specific time in which to carry out this instruction. Failing that, Britain should suspend the Rhodesian constitution. An interim and representative government should be appointed, charged with the repeal of all repressive legislation. A general election should be held on a franchise based on 'one man, one vote'. Rhodesia was to be given independence as soon as a genuinely representative government was formed after the election.

His plan and his arguments were supported by all the African leaders, except Hastings Banda, though Sir Akubakar, the Prime Minister of Nigeria, while generally supporting Nkrumah's line, made a strong appeal that the final outcome must be one which would enable both the European and African peoples of Rhodesia to learn to live together. He supported Milton Obote and Albert Margai on the release of Africans who were imprisoned or detained: 'Although the primary responsibility rests with Britain, the political prisoners must be released, and this release would pave the way for a constitutional conference.' Most of the Asians and the Caribbean representatives supported the African line.

But not Hastings Banda. Tired, almost bored, with the arguments, he contemptuously attacked those who were demanding British military intervention. He said flatly that British public opinion would not tolerate it, and hinted that there would be trouble in the armed forces. He was the only African I have ever heard use the phrase 'kith and kin' except as a term of abuse.

Also resisting African pressures were New Zealand and Australia,

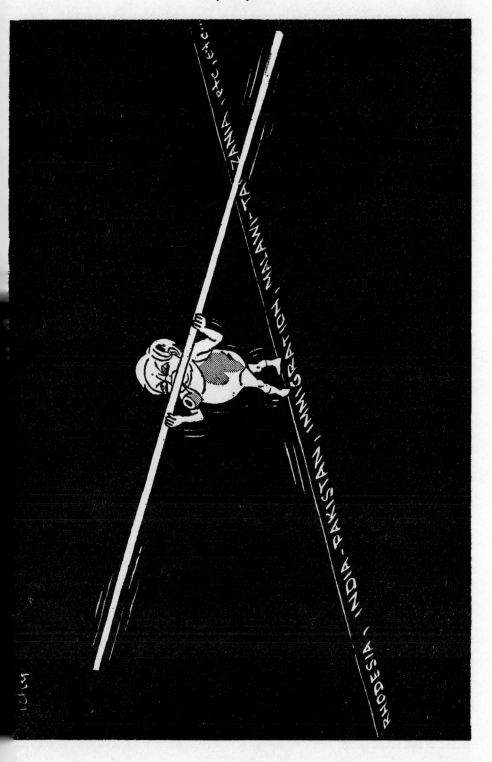

with Bob Menzies, as always, relishing the opportunity to reprove the Africans on their use of the word 'democracy', outlining the number of one-party states in independent Africa. Lester Pearson certainly did not go all the way with the Africans, particularly on military intervention, but he felt that we should be doing more. He had formed a low opinion of Mr Smith when he had met him in London in January.

But the main contribution to the debate was made by Julius Nyerere. With his brilliant forensic powers, supported by the grave pleadings of Kenneth Kaunda, he put us in the dock on charge after charge. He condemned our failure to use force, contrasting our inaction with earlier British intervention in Cyprus, Kenya, Aden and British Guiana. When we pointed out the historical and geographical realities he dismissed them. There was nothing, he argued, in the fact that the colonies he had named had had no forces of their own, while Rhodesia had had powerful military forces for forty years: juridically she was a colony, as, indeed, in law she was. Equally, he dismissed the difficulties of a military operation in a land-locked country five hundred miles from the nearest sea and sheltered therefrom by almost uniformly friendly territory. As we pointed out, in our colonial period we had troops stationed in all trouble-spots, regular naval visits, and easy access from the sea. But for him history and geography could not overcome an issue of principle.

Nor, he urged, was it any argument to say how we would react to a UDI. Action was needed now. UDI, if we let it happen, would merely confirm the case for swift military retribution. Negotiations were useless, indeed dangerous. We were negotiating with the wrong people. Smith would never accept 'one man, one vote'. It was not enough to talk of guarantees of unimpeded progress to majority rule. Independence should come only after the introduction of universal franchise.

I made a long statement in reply, standing by our arguments, and urging that what they were advocating could plunge Africa into armed conflict going far beyond the borders of Rhodesia.

It was clear that the big battle, yet to come, would be on the communiqué.

The remaining days were devoted to constructive discussion, economic affairs, world development and the working of intra-Commonwealth institutions, consultation on the world situation, following the opening review on the previous Friday, East-West relations, disarmament, problems of the Caribbean, the Indian sub-continent, south-east Asia, Cyprus and Malaysia. It was a bitter blow for Tunku Abdul Rahman of Malaysia when the cool reception given to his plea for a combined Commonwealth appeal for an end to Indonesian aggression was followed by a flat refusal to include any reference in the communiqué other than an agreement to 'take note'.

We had a useful day on Commonwealth institutions, and agreed on the appointment of a new and independent full-time Secretary-General of the conference, Mr Arnold Smith of Canada.

On economic co-operation within the Commonwealth, Britain took the initiative. I proposed a three-point plan:

First, a conference of Commonwealth trade ministers, preferably to follow the usual meeting of Commonwealth finance ministers on the eve of the annual IMF meeting;

Second, a meeting – leading, I hoped, to permanent machinery – between the development and planning officials of individual countries to co-ordinate development programmes, so that each could see how we could help the underdeveloped countries; for example, by laying out new, and where necessary, specialised capacity to help with forward development programmes;

Third, closer Commonwealth consultation on aircraft requirements, including the reactivation of the former Commonwealth committee for exchanging information on aircraft development and plans, which had not met for some years.

All these were agreed in principle, but I was acutely disappointed at the outcome. Despite the initiatives proposed by Douglas Jay, who led our delegation at the Commonwealth trade ministers' conference ultimately held in London the following year, there was virtually no willingness to improve intra-Commonwealth trading arrangements. The developing countries were more concerned with aid programmes. The developed – particularly Australia but, to a smaller extent, Canada, too – were resistant to closer trading relations. For while they welcomed the continuation, and encouragement, of their long-established agricultural exports to Britain, they were not disposed to adopt arrangements which put their own domestic manufacturers at risk. There was the fact, too, that long years of neglect of Commonwealth trade had led to the development of strong non-Commonwealth ties, such as those of Australia with Japan, and the continuing permeation of Canada's economic life by the United States. There is in fact nothing under the sun more *laissez-faire* than Commonwealth trade.

On Friday, 25th June we went straight into the discussion on the draft final communiqué, which had been prepared by officials on the daunting basis of 'one delegation, one draughtsman'. I knew it would be a long day – in fact it took eleven hours with only a short break for lunch.

We began with Vietnam. We recorded the decision to set up the mission, and the statement made by its four members on 24th June, making clear that, whatever the views of its member-governments, the mission as a whole, was appointed as representative of the whole Commonwealth, and had no preconceived notion about the road to peace. The conference agreed also on the 'Memorandum of Guidance' to the mission. Although we never got airborne, this was a remarkable summary of

Commonwealth policy on Vietnam, despite sharply differing view-points.
It was quoted for years afterwards as an authority, in Parliament after
parliament throughout the Commonwealth. After agreeing on 'certain
basic considerations', we stated the 'instructions to the mission', by which
it should be guided:

    (i) a suspension of all United States air attacks on North Vietnam;
   (ii) a North Vietnamese undertaking to prevent the movement of any
       military forces or assistance or material to South Vietnam;
  (iii) a total cease-fire on all sides to enable a conference to be convened
       to seek a peaceful settlement;
  (iv) the objectives of such a conference might be to:
      (a) end the war in Vietnam;
      (b) secure the withdrawal of all foreign military presence from
         Vietnam and the neutralisation of the area;
      (c) establish, for a period, an international peace force, under the
         auspices of the Geneva Agreement, to safeguard peace in
         Vietnam;
      (d) establish principles for the eventual unification of the country
         through free and internationally supervised elections.

No fully representative international conference, even five years and more
later, ever produced so specific a list of objectives and means to peace.
It was no mean achievement to get it through a top-level conference of
twenty-one states.

The remainder of the communiqué, issued close on midnight and later
presented to Parliament as a White Paper (Cmmd 2712), set out our
conclusions on the world situation; Cyprus; Africa – with a particularly
trenchant condemnation of Portuguese colonialism; the Caribbean, including an expression of concern over American intervention in the
Dominican Republic; nuclear disarmament – including the problem of
associating China with future developments; dependent territories –
accounting by this time for only ten millions out of a Commonwealth
population of 750 millions – with a likely five newly-independent
countries due to emerge in the following three years; economic affairs,
including development problems; the distinctively institutional affairs of
the Commonwealth, including the establishment of a Commonwealth
Foundation, and the development of the Commonwealth Secretariat.

The key issue, however, which took most of our eleven-hour drafting
session was Rhodesia.

This was an essentially compromise draft. We secured a reiteration of
the admission that the final responsibility was Britain's, which was all
that my predecessor had been able to salvage from the disastrous 1964
conference. The views of the Africans were clearly set out; so was the
position of the British Government. We insisted on our right to continue
discussions and undertook to take full account of all the views that had
been expressed. We conceded that 'in this process of seeking to reach

agreement on Rhodesia's advance to independence a constitutional conference would, at the appropriate time, be a natural step'. If negotiations did not produce speedy results, having regard to our insistence on 'unimpeded progress towards majority rule', we would be ready to take the initiative in that we would 'consider promoting such a conference'.

But it was stiff going. Julius Nyerere fought hard. He moved again and again, hour after hour, the inclusion of a passage insisting that any independence settlement should be 'on the basis of majority rule'. He rejected the argument that unimpeded progress thereto should be a sufficient guarantee. In the event, though the majority of delegates undoubtedly agreed with him, he was isolated; our draft, amended and amended and amended, was agreed. It was to his credit that he did not carry his disagreement to the point of seeking a veto, which would have produced a vacuum in the middle of the communiqué, but reserved only his right, which all conceded, to make public his dissociation from the words on which we were agreed.

But the Commonwealth had survived a crisis. I had driven my colleagues hard, first on Vietnam, but above all on Rhodesia. My insistence on standing by our position on Rhodesia had subjected the conference to great strain.

With the communiqué so precariously agreed at 9.15 that evening, I had, as chairman, to face almost endless press conferences, and eight or nine television interviews, including the two British channels, Commonwealth companies, a Central Office of Information broadcast to Africa and most of the American networks. Someone calculated that I had addressed 140 million people on television that night – not a figure easy to check. All I know is that I got into bed well after midnight, and had to rise early to fly to Glasgow the following morning for my first major political speech for some months.

I went through my notes on the BEA Glasgow flight. After a brief topical reference to the Commonwealth conference, it consisted in the main of a progress report on action we had taken to fulfil the election programme I had outlined in Glasgow nine months earlier. But there was also a comment on the economic situation, designed to dampen down the speculation which was beginning to build-up following the publication of the May trade figures. Jim Callaghan had told me, at a late-night meeting during the conference, that his City advisers attributed a good deal of the growing pressure on sterling to expectation of an early general election, with all the uncertainties, not excluding a change of parity, which might follow the expected Conservative victory.

I told Jim Callaghan that I was aware of this and might, in the Glasgow speech, announce that I did not intend to recommend a dissolution of Parliament in 1965. In the few minutes I had on the aircraft I thought about the implications. One was very clear to me – the possibility of an immediate change in the Conservative party leadership. The young lions, and more particularly their friends in the press, were urging a change. *The Economist* ran an 'Alec must go' article.

What no doubt held them back was the fear of a repetition of the Byzantine excesses which had been so highly publicised after the retirement of Mr Macmillan. Were this to happen, they feared that I might go to the country with the Opposition in disarray. True there was no magic circle now: the Conservatives, of whom it had been said in October 1963, by one of their most loyal supporters, that they had ceased to be gentlemen without becoming democrats, had adopted an elective system in April 1965. Even a leadership election could rack the party. But they might recognise, as I had sometimes pointed out to my colleagues, that anything which occurs on the eve of the summer holidays, or Christmas, is very quickly forgotten; holidays have an amnesic quality. There was a real likelihood that the *putsch* might succeed, since the whole business could be concluded in July. If it were late enough in July, most of the country would be on holiday.

I knew what the consequences might be, but – all in three or four minutes – decided not to pursue that line of argument further. More important was the need for some quietus, however slight, however temporary, on sterling speculation. So my speech included these words:

> Let me make this clear now, to those who are given to intellectual and other forms of speculation about the political scene, it is not my intention to recommend a dissolution of Parliament this year.
> ... Given that condition, our continued ability to put our legislation through Parliament, there will be no election. I thought it better to say this now and to end uncertainty and speculation by a straight statement rather than to play the silly 'Will-it-be-June?' or 'Will-it-be-October?' game that was played with the British people and British industry with so much harm a year ago.

Norman Dodds, one of our most popular members, died just two months later, and press comment just before the by-election was pessimistic about our chances of holding the seat. Meanwhile my predictions on the Conservative reaction proved correct. Sir Alec Douglas-Home resigned on 22nd July and Mr Heath was elected on the 28th. Indeed I had given him a little help.

It was in another passage in this Glasgow speech, dictated more by hubris and a desire to pay tribute to my parliamentary colleagues on the platform, that I claimed that we had taken a highly contentious Finance Bill through its committee stage, in the face of sustained and bitter attack, with a majority of three, without losing a single division. As I said it I realised that this might prove an irresistible challenge.

Retribution followed swiftly. Late on the night of 6th–7th July, indeed well after midnight, some of our members, expecting no further division, and seeing Conservatives leaving, had eluded the whips' net and slipped off home. Many of the departing Conservatives had adjourned only as far as the area bounded by Great Peter Street and Smith Square and, returning, were led by Mr Heath into the Division Lobby. We were beaten twice, on totally unimportant issues, it is true, but it was a famous victory, recalling to veterans a precisely similar operation conducted years earlier by Generals Wigg and Byng.

In the week following the Commonwealth conference I had separate meetings with nearly all the prime ministers, before each returned to his country. One was with Sir Robert Menzies, whom I had sounded, in an interval during Friday's communiqué drafting session, about the wardenship of the Cinque Ports, vacant with the death of Sir Winston Churchill. Who, in fact, *could* follow Sir Winston? Bob Menzies was not only one of his close wartime Commonwealth colleagues, but had something of his pugnacity. But more, as I put it to him, in historic times the Warden had been charged with the defence of the Ports against aggression from across the Channel. Twice within a generation that defence had depended on help spontaneously provided by the forces of the Commonwealth; it was entirely fitting that a Commonwealth statesman should take up the appointment. Besides, I knew he always sought to visit England in the cricket season – he had come on to Chequers from the New Zealand test. He accepted, and my prediction that the Canterbury Cricket Festival would have a new patron duly came to pass.

On Sunday, 27th June I had a meeting with the designated members of the Vietnam peace mission, to review the response from the five capitals. Washington and Saigon had accepted it. In a broadcast on 1st July Hanoi Radio flatly rejected it, in a routine assertion that peace would come only if the US ended their 'aggressive war', combined with some homely animadversions on my own role in the Vietnam question. Mr Kosygin informed our ambassadors that Moscow would not receive the mission. The Soviet Union had no intention of intervening in the matter unless North Vietnam asked them to do so: it was a matter entirely between the parties to the fighting, which would end if America withdrew. China also rejected the mission: their note, handed to our Chargé on 25th June, described the proposal as a 'manoeuvre'. We decided to remain in touch, ready to go if circumstances changed. But as soon as President Nkrumah returned to Ghana he began to bombard me with proposals that he should go on a one-man mission to the five capitals, representing the four of us and pressing for the mission to be received.

I was extremely doubtful. He was the one committed anti-American of the four, and I feared the line he might take in our name. He received discouragement from Washington, which persuaded him to wait. In the event he did not reach Peking until the following February – and never returned to Ghana.

After discussions with Michael Stewart about the responses we had received, I tried another means of getting through to Ho Chi-Minh, to urge the *bona fides* of the Commonwealth mission. Harold Davies MP, then parliamentary secretary to the Ministry of Pensions and National Insurance, later my parliamentary private secretary, had been a regular visitor to Hanoi, and written extensively about Ho Chi-Minh, whom he knew well. Harold and I had been close friends for very many years, sharing political platforms all over the country.

From time to time he was approached on the Vietnam issue by the two North Vietnamese journalists in London, who, in addition to their journalistic activities, constituted an unofficial North Vietnamese presence in London. I authorised Harold Davies to consult them about the possibility of a visit, the idea of which, I found, was very acceptable to Washington. The President was keen to see any direct line into Hanoi, provided he could keep below the horizon.

I was convinced that he was perfectly genuine. He was ready for meaningful talks to see whether more organised negotiations could begin. In any case, he wanted any information he could get about the thinking of Ho Chi-Minh. In later years his growing desperation led his advisers into dependence on some strange and unreliable contacts – one, the subject of scathing comment to me by Mr Kosygin in January 1968, which will be described in a later chapter.

After a visit to Paris the journalists confirmed that Harold Davies would be welcomed in Hanoi, and his visa would be waiting in Pnom Penh. He was accompanied by Mr Donald Murray, a very able Foreign Office Vietnam expert. But there was no time for further messages to go about Mr Murray's visa.

Unfortunately, whatever hopes the Davies visit might have justified were dashed by a serious, indeed disastrous, leak in London, while he was on the way. This led not only to the inevitable private notice question from the Opposition front bench, but to a refusal of a visa to Mr Murray, who was grounded in Pnom Penh. On my instructions Davies went on alone, though I felt that the damage had been done. I had little doubt that he would at any rate see Ho Chi-Minh; but on arrival he was greeted with bitter complaints about the leak, and he was punished by being allowed to see only party officials – headed by a top DRV foreign ministry official – for some seven hours. This was not entirely useless, but the mission had clearly failed, to the unconfined joy of Conservative MPs and their press allies. Condemnation of 'gimmicks' filled the air, together with sententious lectures on the advantages of secret diplomacy, which this would have been, but for the leak. We had tried every secret channel open to us.

The Conservative doctrine apparently meant: 'Don't try anything unless you are sure it will succeed.' Our view was set out in a rough exchange between Mr Maudling, leading for the Opposition, and myself on 15th

July, concluding with these words: 'Is this not,' he said 'a humiliating rebuff when a British Minister cannot ever see the minister of another Government? . . .' (with which, be it noted, neither under the Conservative Government nor ourselves had we any diplomatic, as opposed to consular, relations). 'As to rebuffs,' I replied, 'if anyone here is going to try to play the part which I believe we can play in order to get peace, we have to be prepared to accept rebuffs. I would rather have the rebuffs than the attitude of the right honourable Gentlemen who would be prepared to let this war go on another two years without making any effort. . . .'

While the fate of the Davies mission was still undecided, Adlai Stevenson came to spend the Saturday with me at Chequers. He was passionately interested in every move in the Vietnam situation, and unburdened his mind to me on his task at the United Nations. Three days later he died in a London street. It was a melancholy moment when, after a sad and almost silent lunch at the Embassy, we gathered to see his coffin borne into Grosvenor Square to be flown in the President's plane, Air Force One, to his own country.

Chapter 9

IN the first weeks of July the pace of government showed no diminution. I went to Durham for the 1965 Miners' Gala, as every Labour party leader has done every year, whether in Government or in Opposition. We had a number of economic meetings on the financial position over the weekend and throughout the following week.

Overseas visitors came and went, Prince Souvanna Phouma of Laos was my guest at a working lunch and I saw the chairman of the World Bank, the Soviet Ambassador and the Chief Minister of Gibraltar. There were visits to the Crafts Council exhibition and the Royal Tournament at Olympia, and another to Buckingham Palace, to discuss with the Duke of Edinburgh the report he had prepared, on my invitation, about my proposal for a new honour, the Queen's Award for Industry, for export and technological achievement.

Meanwhile, the trade figures were exacting their toll, and press speculation forecasting an early election, to be followed by a Conservative government, was not helping sterling. My Glasgow announcement ruling out a June election had had little effect, mainly because widely-read financial pundits, taken more seriously abroad than at home, were forecasting an economic apocalypse. *The Economist* had written us off a few weeks earlier. Under the heading 'Three Times Round went his Gallant Ship', it said, '. . . The behaviour of the Labour Government in the past week has done nothing except confirm the impression that the ship really is going down. What is more, the gales are blowing and the sea is heaving outside. Three times round has gone Labour's gallant ship. How soon does it sink to the bottom of the sea . . . ?'

There was still too much free sterling 'splashing around the world' (Jim Callaghan's phrase to me) and there was too much encouragement to convert it into 'safer' currencies or into gold.

The consequences of the run on sterling following the May trade figures were recorded in the gold figures at the end of the month and started off a fresh run. It was as though the individuals concerned in the first run were surprised at the results of their first reaction – and this surprise scared them into a second panic. The Chancellor and I agreed that new measures were needed. I foreshadowed them in a speech at a party rally at Newtown, Montgomeryshire on 24th July. I said that against the background of a rapidly improving balance of payments position, with over-all balance in prospect: '...we have to set this flurry of loose and uninformed talk at home and abroad about our economic situation. It is not for me – at any rate here and now, to analyse the motives of those who at home and abroad want to sell Britain short. They have been wrong before. ...' I referred to the steps we had already taken, and said that new economic measures would be announced 'in the next few days'.

On the evening of 26th July the Governor of the Bank of England came with the Chancellor of the Exchequer.

The economic package we were preparing was approved by Cabinet, though there were some extremely tough and unhappy measures in it. The Chancellor announced our proposals to Parliament on Tuesday, 27th July. It left nothing to chance.

He announced that all starting dates for public expenditure, with the exception of industrial building, housing, school-building and hospitals, would be postponed for six months. We would ensure that the nationalised industries did the same with the greater part of their own investment proposals. Local government building would be similarly controlled by a firm exercise of loan sanctions. Local authority mortgages to private house-buyers, which had been rising from a figure of some £83 millions in the early sixties to £179 millions the previous year and were now running at £190 millions, were to be cut back to £130 millions. There were to be new defence economies. We announced the postponement of two major measures which had been in our election programme, the proposed income-related guaranteed pension for those retiring from industry and our proposals for further reductions and removals of National Health charges. We announced that in the field of private building a new licensing procedure would be introduced, providing for starting dates with some delay. We extended the control over office building, which we had already introduced for London, to the Birmingham conurbation. Industrial development certificates in London and the south-east, the midlands and the eastern region, would be required for all new industrial development over ten thousand square feet. We tightened up hire purchase, cutting the three-year repayment period to thirty months. We provided a further extension of exchange control. The Governor sent a letter to the joint-stock banks insisting on a tightening of bank credit. We required prepayment by importers on goods imported into the country, in an attempt to deal with the 'leads and lags' question. At the same time, on the positive side, we announced improved Export Credit Guarantee Department help for medium-term exports and also some reductions in the cost of short-term credit for British exports.

It was a formidable package and was taken as such. Sterling began to pick up, though in the next week or two there were periods when we were doubtful whether confidence had been sufficiently re-established to ensure the security of the pound.

To our opponents, who had just elected Mr Heath as their leader, it was of course a gift from the gods. The implementation of two election pledges postponed! But worse – or, for them, better – a crisis statement affecting building, hire purchase and a wide range of other decisions. Unfortunately, during the summer, when we had had to press on with the highly controversial Finance Bill, Government time had had to pre-empt most of the parliamentary days. So the usual ration of Supply Days – when the Opposition can choose the subject for debate – had not been made available to them. Now, at the very end of term, there were three of these days, when they could indulge themselves in a series of censure motions. The day after Mr Heath's election they tabled a censure motion on the cost of living, and, on the following day, a second censure motion on 'The Government's failure to honour their election pledges'! At the same time they gave notice of a general censure motion for the last day before the adjournment.

As Prime Minister, I had hardly spoken at all in a political debate, as opposed to debates on foreign affairs and defence, and felt it was time that I entered the fray. I chose the election pledge debate. This was moved by Anthony Barber, with his usual Conservative Central Office brief of carefully selected figures, together with what we were later to learn was his main stock-in-trade, a choice line in personal abuse. I pitched into him with what I felt was not a very good speech, though our people cheered it to the echo, saying, as did the press, that I had at last returned to my old Opposition style of lively debate. Indeed, at the end of my speech all our members chanted, 'Divide, divide' on the assumption that the debate was now over – as it very largely was.

My main line, of course, was to point out that having been in office for only nine months, we could hardly be held accountable for the failure to carry through all the legislation necessary to fulfil election pledges, which, when they were given, were clearly stated to be carried out over an entire Parliament. All this, and the inherited £800 millions deficit. I had a lot of fun at the Opposition's expense until, towards the end of my speech, with the Tories by this time pretty silent, I heard an agonised cry from a Scottish Conservative MP, asking about the pricing scheme for white fish. All I could say to this was: '... After all we have heard about the great, rasping attack that we were to get from honourable Gentlemen opposite – three days of attack that we should not have had, if it were not for the new Sir Galahad who is leading them – the whole censure motion has come down to a plaintive cry about white fish.'

Even so I was able to answer the Opposition about our plans in that area of the economy.

The Tories' final motion of censure came the following Monday, 2nd August. It was opened by the new Leader of the Opposition. I had wondered whether to speak immediately after him, but I felt that all the attention, both of Parliament and the press, would be properly concentrated on the new leader: I thought it right for me just to wind up briefly, rather than follow him in what would inevitably become a gladiatorial display. When I heard him I rather regretted this decision, because his speech was less good than I expected, no light and shade and a sustained attack at a consistently shrill level. It would have been easy to deal with on the spot, but in the event I wound up. The House was in a holiday mood and in any case I had noticed during previous debates a marked unwillingness on the part of Opposition MPs at that time of night that I should be heard at all. In a winding-up speech in a previous debate there had been no fewer than nineteen points of order, which had proved almost impossible for the Speaker to control. In this particular debate, the last ten minutes were almost continual uproar, interruption and points of order designed to ensure that whatever kill they thought I was working up to should not be allowed to get across. However, for the third time in a week, we won the censure motion division, this time with a comfortable thirteen majority. The following day the House adjourned for the summer recess.

But though I was due to go on holiday on the Thursday night, 5th August, our troubles were not over. Apart from a rush to catch up with all the end-of-term work – including a fascinating lunch I gave to the feudalist, almost pre-biblical rulers of the South Arabian Federation – the foreign exchange situation was still giving anxiety. The main rush of speculation had eased off, but there was as yet no sharp influx of the money that had left the reserves. There was acute anxiety about what might happen in August, when markets tended to be thin but feverish; when there might be in the minds of the morbid some expectation that we were working up to a devaluation in September, at the time of the annual meeting of the International Monetary Fund.

I was somewhat reassured on my way to my final pre-holiday Audience at Buckingham Palace to be told by Derek Mitchell that he had just got the first flash of the export figures for July, showing not only a record figure, but a fantastic increase over any previous month. 'Assuming,' he said, 'that it's not that a fly has settled on the computer, this should have a very good effect on the foreign exchange market.'

But the Governor was still extremely anxious. He felt that we had not done enough and had made his views known to the Chancellor. Jim Callaghan felt it right to bring the Governor and deputy Governor, Mr Leslie O'Brien, round to see me at ten o'clock on the Thursday evening, just a couple of hours before I was due to go for my train.

The Governor was in his gloomiest mood and clearly felt that the financial end of the world was near. More speculation, more trouble for the pound could only mean the collapse of the world monetary system. The dollar would be engulfed: it might even go first. I said again, as I had said nine months earlier, that in that case, perhaps the rest of the world might take a hand in curbing the speculators. He pressed the point further and I said that if the issue was as bad as he thought, then I would be ready to fly to America for talks with the President and the Federal Reserve authorities there because, obviously, we were all in it together. I went so far as to have a call put through to the President on a contingency basis and to make provisional arrangements to have a plane ready to pick me up. Meanwhile, I said, I was going to catch my train and felt that if the Chancellor, who was due to go to the Isle of Wight, and the Governor, who was due to go to the south of France, and I were all to go away, it might be the most reassuring thing for the markets.

The Governor said that in no circumstances would he go to the south of France in such a situation. The Chancellor and I virtually ordered him to go – in so far as it is possible for orders to be given to the Governor. For him to have announced that he was not going would, of course, have stimulated much more dangerous speculation, since it would have been assumed that devaluation, floating or some other grave move was in immediate prospect. When I made it clear I was still going, and the Chancellor did the same, the Governor, finally, with great reluctance, decided to leave on the Saturday for France. I left No. 10 at 12.15 a.m. on the morning of 6th August with only a few minutes to catch the train. The RAF had a plane standing by to pick me up at St Mawgan ready to fly to Washington, if it should prove necessary.

It was a troubled journey through the night, and before catching the RMV *Scillonian* from Penzance to the Isles of Scilly, I put a call through to my office. Everything was relatively quiet and it seemed there was no reason why I should not go on. I would, of course, get a full report on the condition of the markets as soon as they opened, and if necessary I might have to come back to the mainland and go to St Mawgan.

In fact, sterling had its best day for many weeks. This was, we were told later, due to the fact that the Chancellor and I were going away as usual, as would not have been expected if action was imminent. It was also due to a non-attributable, but very clearly identifiable interview I had given, some hours before the Governor's visit, to the *Guardian*. In this interview I had taken an extremely robust line about sterling. On the Friday, therefore, the crisis was over and indeed the money began to flow back into the reserves. The Governor went on holiday on the Saturday.

This was my first summer holiday on Scilly since going to No. 10. I was in the closest touch with Downing Street. A scrambler telephone had been installed in my bungalow, but since GPO telephone communications with the mainland depended on an open radio link, this was anything but secure. An office had been set up in the Customs House, with an unbreakable teleprinter line with No. 10. If I had to speak in general terms with the White House, facilities were available; a more secret talk would mean a helicopter journey to RNAS Culdrose. (In later years improved facilities were made available on Scilly.) A succession of Garden Room girls was appointed to the Customs House to operate the teleprinter and keep in touch with No. 10.

The first few days of the holiday went quietly, give or take a purported assassination attempt and the unceremonious return of an armed gunman to the mainland.

Inevitably, there were many press demands to photograph my family on holiday. To avoid my being followed around every day, my office arranged, and Fleet Street fully co-operated in, a day for press photographers to come and take any pictures they wanted. We hired a launch for them and went off to an uninhabited island. The photos they took of me in holiday garb provided material for the cartoonists for five years – so far. Although I had not expected this, reporters came with them. To avoid disappointment, I agreed to a highly informal press conference. (This was positively the first occasion a representative of Tass interviewed a Prime Minister on an uninhabited British island.) It happened that this was the day when the very good set of trade figures was published, though, as ever, I insisted that extravagant deductions should not be made from a single month's figures.

I was in hourly touch with Downing Street. The Foreign Secretary also was on holiday on the island. My arrangement with him was that the mass of foreign telegrams addressed to him by the secret teleprinter I would not read, unless either my office or he felt that I should. One evening he stopped me in the little island's main street. The Geneva disarmament conference was deadlocked. The Foreign Office wanted us to support the Americans. Lord Chalfont wanted to take a new initiative. At Michael Stewart's suggestion we supported him. If we had not done so, I believe the non-proliferation treaty now in force might never have been signed. It was the breakthrough.

But a new and potentially dangerous problem was developing in southeast Asia. Some three or four months earlier, we had received a warning that Tunku Abdul Rahman, the Prime Minister of Malaysia, was losing his patience with his parliamentary colleague, Lee Kuan Yew (Harry Lee), the Singaporean leader, to the point where Lee was in danger of being arrested and imprisoned. Singapore, which had been an independent Commonwealth country in its own right, had in September 1963 merged with Malaya, Sarawak and North Borneo to form the new territory of Malaysia. Harry Lee decided to go into Opposition, in the ultimate hope of leading a Federation-wide Opposition large enough eventually to become the Government of the greater area. The Tunku was becoming more and more incensed with his lively Opposition. Some weeks before the

Commonwealth conference we had received news of an impending crisis, involving a possible coup against Harry Lee and his colleagues.

I felt it necessary to go so far as to let the Tunku know that if he were to take action of this kind, it would be unwise for him to show his face at the Commonwealth conference, since a large number of his colleagues – including myself – would feel that such action was totally opposed to all we believed in as a Commonwealth.

In the event nothing happened, but on the weekend of 13th–15th August news came through that the Federation had broken up. There had been angry scenes between the Tunku and Lee. This had led to Singapore being virtually expelled from the Federation and told to set up on its own account. Lee was in a desperate state, bursting into tears in front of the television cameras and regretting the break-up. Nevertheless, he determined to make a go of the newly-independent Singapore. There was great anxiety in Whitehall and I decided to fly across to the mainland to Culdrose on the Sunday for meetings with Cledwyn Hughes, Minister of State, Commonwealth Office (in the absence of the Secretary of State), the Secretary of State for Defence and our advisers. We took the necessary decisions and made the dispositions that had to be made, sending very strong messages to both leaders to avoid any action that could lead to an outbreak of hostilities, or, indeed, of internal subversion. We authorised talks to take place to review the Anglo-Malaysian defence agreement, on a basis fair to all the parties concerned.

Many months afterwards, in April 1966, Lee Kuan Yew came to Britain and spent the day with me at Chequers. On that occasion he said quite simply – and he repeated it publicly, in my hearing, at a party conference rally in 1967 – that the action I had taken both before and after the Commonwealth conference in 1965 had 'saved my life'. With all that we were hearing in the summer of 1965 I believe this was not an exaggeration.

Although the foreign exchange situation was relatively easy during this period of my August holiday, a great deal of my time was spent in telephone calls about the monetary position. These took place, usually at six in the evening, though occasionally in the morning as well, on a hook-up basis with the Chancellor, the chief Treasury advisers and the Secretary of the Cabinet. They were associated with the concern about sterling which Joe Fowler, the American Secretary of the Treasury, was expressing. He was extremely helpful to us, but was anxious both about sterling and for the dollar, if anything were to go wrong. Looking to the future, he was afraid of an inflationary situation developing and in particular doubted whether the voluntary prices and incomes policy which George Brown had negotiated would be able to withstand the pressure for wage increases to which we were subject. While he did not attempt in any way to make terms or give us orders, he was apprehensive that if further central bank aid were required it would be difficult to mount if we had no better safeguard against inflation than the voluntary system. It was in these circumstances that we began first to think in terms of statutory powers.

George Brown, who was minister responsible for prices and incomes policy, was on holiday in the South of France, and after we had taken our discussions a good deal further it was decided to despatch Sir Eric Roll, the permanent secretary of DEA, to visit him. George took the problem on board with remarkable composure, but cut short his holiday to return to London for talks with the Chancellor and myself at the end of the month. It would be necessary for him to make an impact on the Trades Union Congress, which was meeting in Brighton early in September.

I had recognised that what we were turning over in our minds would create acute difficulties within the Cabinet, particularly with Frank Cousins, the Minister of Technology, still nominally General Secretary of the Transport and General Workers' Union. Frank had repeatedly expressed considerable scepticism about – indeed opposition to – what was still only a voluntary policy. His life's work had been based on the doctrine that a trade union leader's job was to get more wages for his men; even a voluntary incomes policy seemed incompatible with that life-long objective. It was for this reason that while I was over at Culdrose for the meeting on Malaysia I had had a talk not only with Herbert Bowden, Lord President, who was holidaying near, but also with Frank Cousins over tea at his farmhouse cottage. He took the first intimation of what we were discussing extremely calmly, and I felt that we might not have too much difficulty about it when it had to be raised in Cabinet.

On Friday, 27th August, appropriately after the foreign exchange markets had closed for the long weekend, I crossed to Penzance and caught the night train for Paddington. I arrived at half past seven and on leaving the sleeper, I was surrounded by reporters who, before I was properly awake, asked my views about the outburst of unofficial strikes in the car industry. My answer was not very coherent but I had already decided to take immediate action about it and when I got to No. 10 I asked my office to call together a meeting of both sides of the industry for the following week.

But the immediate issue facing us was the decision that had to be taken on prices and incomes policy, on which George had been having private talks with Mr George Woodcock in advance of the Brighton Congress. It was clear that the voluntary procedures, resting on the Declaration of Intent, were proving inadequate. Wage settlements were racing ahead of the targets envisaged in the declaration: worse, they showed little sign of helping the lower-paid. The strong were prospering; in industries where trade union bargaining power was weak, wages were hardly rising.

The one encouraging factor was the success of the National Board for Prices and Incomes (NBPI) under Aubrey Jones. Its fearless reports, whether on wage claims or settlements, were commanding wider and wider respect. Its report on bread and flour prices, (Cmnd 2760), published on 1st September following an earlier report on the bakers' pay claim, recommended a standstill on all prices in the industry.

A Cabinet had been arranged for 1st September to thrash out the future of prices and incomes policy. Earlier on that day the Defence committee met to deal with a crisis in our relations with Singapore, arising out of the defence treaty we had had with the united Malaysia.

At the Cabinet, which lasted for three hours, Jim Callaghan explained the necessity for statutory powers. George was given the mandate he sought. The NBPI was to be made a statutory body, with the Secretary of State having power to refer any price or wage issue to it. He would be given power to enforce its decisions by ministerial order, and to defer the implementation of any wage or price settlement while the Board's inquiries were continuing. The legislation would provide also for an 'early-warning' system for price increases and wage salary settlements. It was arranged that he would leave for Brighton where the General Council was in session, preparing for the following week's Congress.

His meetings lasted twelve hours, and as we heard from the regular reports phoned through to No. 10, became very rough in the evening, not least when the General Council met in private to consider George's proposals. Late at night a statement was agreed with the Council. The only issue on which George was forced to compromise was an undertaking that the legislation, even though passed by Parliament, could only be 'activated' by a specific Order in Council requiring the assent of both Houses. This would give time for the voluntary system to prove itself, strengthened by a recommendation, which George Woodcock urged on the Council, that Congress should agree that all wage claims by individual unions should be submitted to the General Council for 'vetting' by new machinery. These recommendations of the General Council were adopted by Congress on the following Monday.

Events were coming thick and fast in what was to prove a grave week.

On 1st September terrorists in Aden shot Sir Arthur Charles, Speaker of the Legislative Council.

Despite the Rann of Kutch settlement, clashes had occurred between India and Pakistan over Kashmir early in August. Arthur Bottomley had called in the High Commissioners for India and Pakistan to the Commonwealth Relations Office. As the probability of open war drew nearer, I sent, on 3rd September, personal messages to President Ayub Khan and Prime Minister Shastri. But on 6th September, after disputed frontier crossings by both sides, fighting began across the Indian border with West Pakistan. Arthur Bottomley had just set out for a brief holiday in Scotland and found, on arrival at his hotel, a message instructing him to return immediately to London. CRO officials briefed me on the situation and inveigled me into issuing, on 6th September, a statement – justified as they said by cast-iron evidence – condemning India for an act of aggression. I was wrong in this; all the facts were too much in dispute. Anglo-Indian relations were in consequence embittered for many months to come. When Arthur Bottomley returned to London the following morning, he said that if he had been in London on the previous day no statement would have been issued from No. 10. I had been taken for a ride by a pro-Pakistani faction in CRO; it did not remain there for long.

On Thursday, 2nd September, I was telephoned by the No. 10 press secretary in the late morning with the sad news that Sir Harry Hylton-Foster, Speaker of the House of Commons, had collapsed in St James's and died almost immediately. He had been well-liked and presided with fairness and distinction over one of the most potentially difficult parliamentary situations of modern times.

But his death presented a clear threat to the future of the Government. It was not to be expected that the Conservatives, hungry for an election after the encouraging public-opinion polls in August, and watching with interest the clash between the Government and the unions, would be willing to make available one of their back-benchers to fill the gap. For nearly a year they had provided two of the three full-time occupants of the Chair. They lost no time in making clear that they were not going to help.

Never was the early demise of the Government so confidently predicted as in the press headlines the following day:

Guardian:	'Speaker's death threat to Government. Tories leave Mr Wilson with vacancies problem.'
Daily Express:	'Election this autumn? Tories in no-co-operation mood.'
Financial Times:	'Labour's majority may be cut to one.'
Daily Mirror:	'Speaker's death a blow to Wilson. Majority is one – but Labour press on.'
The Times:	'The Speaker dies in London street. New Government crisis over majority.'
Daily Telegraph:	'Speaker's death cuts majority. Prospect of one-vote lead for Wilson.'
Daily Sketch:	'Wilson walks the one-vote tightrope.'
Daily Mail:	'Wilson on the edge of the precipice.'
The *Mail* went on:	'The moment for the reckoning in politics has arrived. Death brought Mr Harold Wilson's Government to the precipice last night. Only through reliable support from the ten Liberal MPs or by constant incredible luck, can he hold power for long.'

Never in that short Parliament was the press so united in proclaiming an early election – be it voluntary or forced by parliamentary defeat – followed by a Conservative victory. For a few moments I wondered if they were not right.

The Leader of the House and the Chief Whip came to see me. We thought that Dr Horace King, deputy Speaker and chairman of Ways and Means, was the obvious choice. But we decided to await the inter-party talks we had proposed. The Conservatives immediately called for the election of Dr King, less, we felt, through admiration for his qualities than through voting arithmetic. Their subsequent treatment of him justified this judgment. We hoped – though the Tories were reported as saying that no Conservative would occupy any of the three chairs – that Sir Samuel Storey, deputy chairman of Ways and Means, would succeed Dr King as deputy Speaker. The problem was the No. 3. Herbert Bowden and Ted Short went to work. They hoped to find a Conservative back-bencher, or perhaps a Liberal, for either would leave our *over-all* majority unimpaired.

For the next month practically all press comment was in the nature of a premature wake. The only way out, many of them appeared to think, was a deal with the Liberals and there was much speculation about the terms which they would seek to exact and our likely reaction to them. Yet within a day or two political correspondents were commenting on my relaxed approach. Was this just my incurable optimism, they asked, or had I a plan?

They need not have worried. Sir Samuel accepted the deputy Speakership, and as time went on soundings of the Liberal, Mr Roderic Bowen QC, appeared not unhopeful. What was not known, while the speculation continued throughout the month, was that a Conservative back-bencher of long experience had privately approached me and told me he would be willing to serve.

But *The Economist*, in successive weeks, knew better. 'The reason why he does not [go to the country],' it said on 11th September, 'is because he believes that, given the opportunity, the country would sack him ignominiously. . . . The political danger for Labour is that Mr Wilson may be postponing a defeat in order to reap a landslide.' The over-all majority we reaped six months later, though not a landslide, was ninety-seven.

But these things were read overseas. Again sterling came under pressure.

The day after Sir Harry's death on 2nd September saw the conference at No. 10 on the motor industry, which I had convened on returning from my holiday – 'a dramatic move, unparalleled in peacetime,' one paper called it.

It was a high-level meeting, representing most of the principal corporations and each of the many unions involved in the industry. I have seldom heard such blunt talk at any industrial confrontation, particularly from the employers. The Minister of Labour, Ray Gunter, and I stressed the severe damage the national economy, particularly exports, was suffering from one unofficial dispute after another. Various ideas were discussed: developing and strengthening the existing fact-finding commission; a special inquiry to be set up by the Government; a 'flying-squad' ready to intervene immediately to establish the facts in an individual dispute.

We asked the two sides of the industry to give urgent consideration to the problem, and, in about a month's time, to report to a further meeting, under Ray Gunter's chairmanship. We asked them to consider, in particular, a series of proposals he had outlined. The principal one was the appointment of an industrial relations 'trouble-shooter' for the industry. This was agreed at subsequent meetings and the appointment of Mr Jack Scamp was eventually announced on 12th October. Although he had a number of spectacular successes in the early years, settling or preventing really crippling strikes, the problem grew more serious as the sixties wore on.

A speech I made at Bristol the following day, 4th September, calling for specific productivity measures including the establishment of factory production committees was widely reported as a message that Labour would carry on. Though not all were convinced. In a leader, 'Half a league, half a league...' the *Guardian* editorialised: ' "The Government is determined to carry on", the Prime Minister says, but is it practicable? The Government's majority is down to one. To survive the winter would be almost miraculous....' It then went on to advocate a deal with the Liberals. But the more hopeful economic situation helped sterling. Mr Fowler, the US Treasury Secretary, was touring European capitals proclaiming American views for world currency reform, and quietly building up a sterling support operation. In the latter task, though not the former, he was successful. He had something to report about a toughening of incomes policy. On 10th September a further massive $1,000 millions international programme of short-term lending was announced to fight the speculators. Sterling, already strengthening, rose to unassailable levels, and the bears, political and otherwise, rushed to cover.

Meanwhile, President de Gaulle announced a virtual withdrawal from NATO counsels, and foreshadowed further problems within the Common Market.

In the intervals of a minor war with certain prominent railwaymen about the introduction of liner trains, where I was first rebuffed, and finally successful, and with almost daily rumours about the identity of the next Speaker, from Jo Grimond to Frank Soskice, I was planning a full Cabinet Sunday session at Chequers. The agenda I laid down for it was to look ahead over the next six months, reviewing policies and analysing the forward political situation. This took place on 12th September and was the first opportunity for many months to review the political situation as a whole. I told my colleagues not to worry about the Speakership, that I had a feeling this would sort itself out, and that we should plan on carrying on well into 1966. We discussed the favourite legislative priorities of individual ministers, for inclusion in the Queen's Speech for the 1965–6 session. I said that our developing plans for fulfilling our 1964 election manifesto should be brought forward and put in the shop-window. A great deal of work had been done which should see the light of day. With the exception of the specific issues affected by the July measures – namely our long-term superannuation scheme and subsidised mortgage rates – the other issues should be embodied in Bills, or at least White Papers. These would show that our electoral aspirations were not just aspirations, but facts, capable of implementation by a Government that meant business. Where Bills or White Papers were bogged down in committees with bureaucratic or legalistic difficulties, or inter-departmental dissension, the issues should be brought to me for settlement, either by Cabinet or by *ad hoc* ministerial meetings under my chairmanship.

It was a programme for survival, and for fighting back. Public comment took the point that steel nationalisation would not be in the Queen's Speech. A gesture to the Liberals it was thought: it was in fact a decision that we should go on without them, provided – steel now being postponed – that we could now safely carry the whole Parliamentary Party with us.

At the same time rumours about our solution of the Speakership problem began to circulate; the name of Mr Roderic Bowen, as someone who was prepared to accept the deputy's position, began to be canvassed. But the Conservatives were confident that the problem could not be solved. They came out strongly and publicly for Dr King, not knowing the issue was settled. They discounted stories of Mr Bowen: he would not accept; if he did they would vote him down. How was not clear, unless they put up a Tory. We were, in fact, home and dry, without involving the Conservative offer I kept in my knapsack. But a few days later a statement by an extreme left-winger, William Warbey, that he could no longer accept the Labour whip, because of his feelings on Vietnam, again underlined our vulnerable position. Once again we were written off. Comment revived about a Lib-Lab deal.

This same week saw the publication, on 13th September, of Labour's National Plan, marked by the most remarkable example of instant opposition the political world had seen. It was denounced by Mr Heath, bell, book, candle and statistics, before publication.

The Plan was a remarkable and thorough piece of work. National economic strategy up to 1970, with priority for exports and the balance of payments, was set out with all its implications in terms of financial planning, national income and its components, public expenditure – and its implications in real resources – with an analysis of what it meant in terms of production, labour requirements and exports and imports, industry by industry, including agriculture. The main work had been undertaken by Sir Donald McDougall, formerly deputy-Director-General of NEDC and from October 1964 Director-General of DEA. So much was involved that publication fell further and further back, and I kept sending urgent messages throughout the summer asking George to give it all priority. Before and after the holidays I chaired a number of meetings on the individual chapters, and the Plan was published in a blaze of press and television conferences on 13th September.

It was a brave effort. It was right. It was the events of 1966 and 1967 which proved that we did not have the time for the Plan to work in real terms – production, exports, import-saving – before short-term speculative factors overwhelmed us. What it did set out to do was fulfilled – but two years later.

When Labour was recording great strength in the public-opinion polls in the late October and early November of 1965, I was amused to read a series of condemnations of my lack of political acumen for not going to the country in October, when we would have clearly won. To have done so would have meant announcing the election at the very moment when not a single political commentator gave me even the slightest chance of survival. They did not understand that there was work to do before I was ready to go to the country.

The last four days of September were as stormy as the first. I went on a political speaking tour in Lancashire – Bury and Liverpool. We had an international crisis when China, intervening in the Indo-Pakistan dispute, presented an ultimatum to India, whom we backed with our limited resources. Aden was aflame, and I was presiding over meetings at No. 10 preparing for the inevitable martial take-over, suspension of the constitution and declaration of a State of Emergency. Not all my colleagues were happy that this should happen on the eve of the Labour party conference. But it was necessary and it was announced on 25th September, two days before conference opened.

The main political comment was still about the Speakership. We could not win, they said, though the *People* ran a story 'Wily Wilson will outwit them all'. In fact, a simple, straightforward solution had done so.

As the Liberal conference gathered, the story was still 'Jo holds the key – or is it a knife?'. He was not quite sure himself. He stirred the political scene with an unexpected speech at the opening of his Edinburgh conference; he had not been expected to speak until the last day. It was a remarkable oration accurately summarised in the *Financial Times*'s headline: 'Mr Grimond gives terms for a Lib-Lab alliance. More an ultimatum than an invitation.'

Assuming a minority Government in the very near future, he fairly recognised that it might be Liberal action in the Commons which forced an election. For, as he pointed out, a Conservative censure motion or amendment to the forthcoming Queen's Speech would force Liberal support if it concentrated on an issue to which the Liberals were committed; he instanced industrial co-ownership or Europe. Only if there were a prior general understanding between Labour and the Liberals on broad principles could the Liberals undertake to keep Labour in office: '... Certainly it is not something which can be done at the last minute in an atmosphere of crisis.' He was quite right to set out the Liberals' dilemma, and he drew the only possible conclusions from it, rejecting, as he had to, a deal with the Conservatives which would inevitably mean an electoral as well as a parliamentary alliance.

But his proposal would have meant agreement on a programme and scrapping policies which were central to our election mandate. It would have meant more – scrapping basic beliefs and philosophy as Socialists. I never considered accepting his proposal for one moment, but decided that I would briefly discuss it in my speech at the conference the following Tuesday.

I was reinforced in this by the Liberals' reception of our proposals for dealing with land profiteering. During the Liberal conference the Minister of Land and Natural Resources published a White Paper setting out our detailed proposals. Instant rejection of it by Mr Grimond released a new flow of gloomy predictions, though by the latter part of his conference he seemed to be moving towards supporting us. Not a satisfactory basis for the kind of alliance Mr Grimond appeared to be holding out. Besides, while most political comment concentrated on the size of our majority, I was concerned – as our party would be – with a different kind of arithmetic. Set against seats actually held, the Liberals' proposals would mean a nine-inch tail trying to wag a three-hundred-inch dog.

But as our conference assembled and the press moved into Blackpool from Scarborough, all comment and speculation was concentrated on the Liberal 'offer'. I disposed of it in five minutes:

> .... in this Finance Bill battle there were 107 divisions in which the Liberals – shades of the 1909 People's Budget – voted 13 times with the Government for fiscal modernisation and 94 times with the Opposition, against it. There they were, Conservatives and Liberals alike, with modernisation on their lips, voting with their feet against urgent measures of fiscal reform ...
> ... In this session so far, there have been 268 divisions, 39 of these were free votes, 229 were straight confrontations between Government and Opposition. Three of these were lost when the Tories were playing their midnight game of cowboys and Indians in the houses of Smith Square and Lord North Street. The other 226 we won. Our average majority was 13. In only a handful of divisions did we have a majority below our nominal three – and to put Scarborough in perspective, perhaps it is right that I should record that the Liberal party, what Mr Grimond quaintly calls the 'Radical Left', voted 68 times with us and 157 times with the Conservatives. To be fair, on four occasions they abstained. ...

Referring to our land proposals, I said:

A Socialist theme, yes. I should have thought a Liberal theme too. That great 'modernising' party on this theme at least at Scarborough last week carried through an exercise in recidivism which places its present leadership some years behind the Liberals of sixty years ago. In 1909, in 1910, they filled the land with song, 'God gave the land to the people.' Now, in 1965, we have the first fruits of Liberal revisionism: while they would not intend to throw doubt on the Almighty's intention in this respect, their researches suggest that He did not intend this decision to be taken too literally. . . .

I concluded with a review of our achievements, our programme for the year ahead:

We are clear what our mandate means in terms of our parliamentary programme and in terms of executive Government. I hope that others will feel able to support these measures which we put forward because we believe them to be in the national interest. If they can, we shall welcome their support. If they cannot, we shall have to go on without them. . . .
So, if others find themselves unable honourably to support the measures we put forward – and I intend no reflection on their motives – this must be a matter for them. But if this leads to a seizure in our parliamentary government, or a situation in which effective government cannot be carried on, then let this be understood – this will not be an issue to be settled in the back corridors of the Palace of Westminster, it will be an issue to be settled by the sovereign and independent decision of the British people.

On the election forecasts, to quote an observer, 'he contemptuously brushed aside what he called "press gossip about an early and unnecessary election" '.

That was the end of that.

In passing, I commented on the intensive Conservative preoccupation with 'image', the image of their new leader, of their party and of its policies:

. . . for us men, at least, our shaving mirror tells us what the image is – something never very far removed from the face that we present. Nikolai Gogol had the last word on this Colman, Prentis and Varley technique in the foreword to his play, 'The Government Inspector', a century and more ago, when he quoted the Russian proverb, NA ZERKALO NYETCHA PYENYAT KOLI ROSHA KRIVA – or in the words of the authorised translation, 'Don't blame the mirror if the mug is ugly'.

The conference was an opportunity for ministers to present our achievements and to indicate the thinking on new policies. Perhaps the most important was Dick Crossman's speech on the Monday, on housing. He spelt out our plan to give a much higher priority to local authority house-building, including new financial aid for councils to shield them against high interest rates. For medium-income owner-occupiers he detailed the new mortgage-option scheme, involving subsidies on mortgages, whatever the ruling rate of interest, if there were a disclaimer of tax relief at the standard rate. He dealt with the proposed Land Commission, with measures to ease the rate burden, and with leasehold enfranchisement.

It was a good conference. Even a press which had arrived in Blackpool with many doubts recorded an almost unanimous verdict that the leadership had firmly received from the great majority of delegates: 'their loyalty, enthusiasm, in some cases adulation'. And the leadership knew how sorely they had been tried.

There was a major row over our immigration policies, about which a very wide section of party opinion, understandably, felt very strongly, but the Government's incomes policy, already accepted by the TUC, was endorsed by a comfortable majority.

Though the conference exacted its full toll in terms of evening engagements, regional parties, union dinners, receptions, Scots, Welsh and Lancastrian nights and receptions for overseas visitors, I had to keep a close watch on Government business, with teleprinter messages, red boxes, scrambler telephones. Mr Ian Smith was active, and reports, press and private, reached me about another lurch towards UDI. A warning I gave that this would be treasonable led to severe criticism, though the words I had used were precisely the words used by our predecessors.

As our conference ended it was to an intensification of the Rhodesian crisis that we were returning.

" Don't need the Liberals, George! Better, maybe, to have a tiny majority ALWAYS!"   London Express Service.

F

Chapter 10

Rhodesia – the 'five principles' – rumours of UDI – Mr Smith's second visit to Downing Street and a warning – Mr Smith rejects the Menzies mission – the Conservative position on Rhodesia – my visit to Rhodesia – meeting with President Kenyatta at Nairobi – arrival in Salisbury

THE rumours of a move to UDI were growing, though there was nothing in our exchanges with Rhodesia, throughout that spring and summer, to justify any Rhodesian claim of a breakdown.

After the strange meeting I had had with Mr Smith on the day of Sir Winston Churchill's funeral in January, the Rhodesian Government had agreed to the visit of the Lord Chancellor and the Commonwealth Secretary and placed virtually no bar on their meeting African leaders, as well as other representatives of public opinion.

It was during this visit, at the end of February, that the 'five principles' first came to be formally stated:

1. The principle and intention of unimpeded progress to majority rule, already enshrined in the 1961 constitution, would have to be maintained and guaranteed.
2. There would also have to be guarantees against retrogressive amendment of the constitution.
3. There would have to be immediate improvement in the political status of the African population.
4. There would have to be progress towards ending racial discrimination.
5. The British Government would need to be satisfied that any basis proposed for independence was acceptable to the people of Rhodesia as a whole.

The talks which Lord Gardiner and Arthur Bottomley had with the Rhodesian Cabinet were directed, in the main, to firm constitutional guarantees that if independence were granted, as proposed, long before majority rule became a reality, no action would be taken subsequently to hold up the progress to majority rule as more Africans qualified for the vote. But their urgings fell on stony ground, as did my colleagues' pressure for immediate action, in conformity with the fourth principle, to get rid of the discriminatory system of land tenure enshrined in the Rhodesian Land Apportionment Act.

But on the mission's last night in Salisbury, 3rd March, the two ministers had a private talk with Mr Smith in which he indicated – on a personal basis – a way round the impasse over constitutional guarantees. We were pressing for effective 'entrenched' clauses, to prevent a European

143

majority in the legislature from amending or revoking, in a retrogressive sense, the constitutional guarantees which were necessary to give effect to the first four principles. We therefore proposed that the entrenched clauses could be changed only by a two-thirds majority in a legislature in which elected Africans – or Europeans elected by the African voters – together with any elected representatives of the Asian and coloured population – should have *more* than one-third of the seats.

This had been firmly resisted by the Rhodesian Cabinet. But at the private meeting Mr Smith indicated that he would not be averse to an effective blocking quarter, with sufficient non-European MPs to guarantee it. This raised our hopes somewhat. In a message to Mr Smith on 29th March, I had proposed that 'the suggestion you put forward in your private conversation with them on 3rd March' should be further and urgently examined through contacts with our respective High Commissioners.

But little progress was made. Mr Smith telegraphed me scathingly about the Commonwealth prime ministers' conference: '... I am willing at all times to receive suggestions from you and to listen to what the British Government has to say on Rhodesia, but, frankly, I am not interested in what the other members of the Commonwealth say about our affairs, and what they do say will not turn us from what we consider to be the right thing to do in the interests of our country.' On the reference in the Commonwealth communiqué to a constitutional conference, he said: '... I must make it clear that to Rhodesia such a conference is absolutely unnecessary and out of the question, and that if such a conference were to be called the Rhodesian Government would not attend, nor would anyone from our country.'

During the summer, rumours, some from reliable sources, kept arriving from Salisbury, reporting that UDI was imminent. There had been a scare which reached me at Chequers in July that the Rhodesian Front would act on the following day, 13th July, a national day to commemorate the life and work of Cecil Rhodes. If there were anything in the rumour, the Rhodesian ministers must have changed their minds, for nothing happened. But Mr Smith was putting on the pressure.

On 18th July he invited Arthur Bottomley to visit Rhodesia. The Secretary of State had a number of other Commonwealth tours on hand and suggested that the Minister of State, Mr Cledwyn Hughes, should go. He did, but no progress was made. Arthur Bottomley then suggested he himself should go in October, after the Labour party conference. Mr Smith's reply showed increasing impatience: '... I regret to say the impression is gaining ground that your Government has no intention of granting independence to Rhodesia.' He had asked our agreement to the appointment of a Rhodesian envoy, with independent diplomatic status, to Lisbon. We had refused, to his intense annoyance. He again pressed

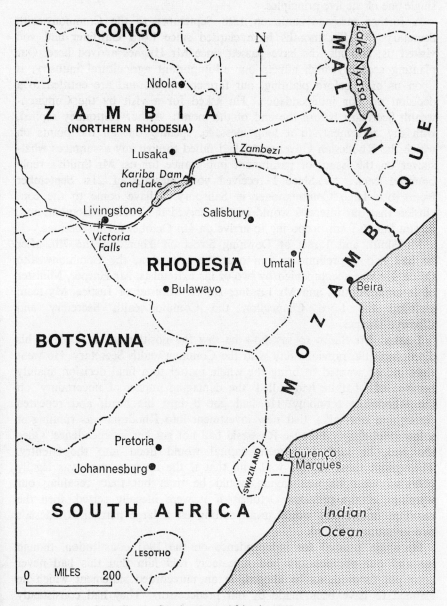

South-eastern Africa in 1965

'for a decision'. On what, was not clear; presumably on his proposal for immediate and unconditional independence on his terms, regardless of a single one of the five principles.

A further message came on 15th September to the Commonwealth Secretary: '... Six months have elapsed since Lord Gardiner and you visited us; two months have passed since Mr Hughes arrived here. Our planting season, which affects our all-important agricultural industry, is upon us and, before planting, our farmers expect and are entitled to a decision on our independence.' He asked for a visit by the Commonwealth Secretary before the end of the month. Arthur Bottomley replied, with my agreement, in a long message, spelling out all the points on which the Rhodesian Government had failed to give any assurances whatsoever on the issues of paramount importance for us. Mr Smith's reply bounced back: '... Since I received your message of 21st September from your High Commissioner in Salisbury, I have come to the conclusion that our interests would best be served if I came to London, and, as you know, I am proposing to arrive on 4th October for discussions.'

Mr Smith and I met at Downing Street on Thursday, the 7th, after he had had a preliminary run over the ground at the Commonwealth Office. He was accompanied by two of his extremists, Mr Harper, Minister of Internal Affairs, and Mr Lardner-Burke, Minister of Justice. My team included the Lord Chancellor, the Commonwealth Secretary and Cledwyn Hughes.

I asked Mr Smith to say how he saw the position, as a result of his discussions the previous day with the Commonwealth Secretary. He went right in: he wanted to bring the whole matter to a final decision, mainly because of what he had called 'the damaging impact of uncertainty' on the Rhodesian economy. He had got it into his head, and repeated throughout our talks, that new investment into Rhodesia was running at a low level simply because Rhodesia had not got her independence. Once she had, he said, investment capital would flood into the country. Throughout these talks I told him that if the independence was legally obtained what he was saying would be true, but that – recalling our warnings of the previous October – if it were illegally seized, then the resultant uncertainty would mean cutting off a large part of Rhodesia's new investment capital.

He again pressed for independence on the 1961 constitution, though we and our predecessors had repeatedly told him that this had never been put forward, as he alleged, in an unrecorded statement which he claimed to have been made by our predecessors. They had consistently denied having made such a statement. He said the British Government were concerned only with the Africans in Rhodesia, not with the Europeans. We were proceeding on racial lines. He put forward proposals in which the entrenched clauses could be safeguarded by a senate, which they were even prepared to fill with Africans. But the control over the blocking vote would, on his proposals, have depended upon twelve chiefs. We had repeatedly pointed out – and he well knew – that these hereditary noblemen were, to a man, paid by the Rhodesian Government.

He said they were prepared to concede what he called 'virtually universal' adult suffrage on the B-roll, to the extent of adding about a million voters. They would not, of course, have any more seats. Three years later on board HMS *Fearless*, when he made this suggestion again it became clear that he and his colleagues were pretty confident that the stringent literacy test would delay the registration of even half that figure for something like a decade, perhaps longer.

For two days the argument went back and forth. We insisted on the five principles. We pointed out that in every country to which independence had been given, democratic suffrage, one man, one vote, had been achieved before sovereignty was conceded. If we were to depart from this principle, not only we, but Parliament, public opinion and the world would need to be satisfied that there would be no retrogressive action on the agreed road to majority rule.

We were also concerned that under the 1961 constitution, even if no steps were taken to hold up African enfranchisement, it would be very many years before majority rule was reached. We asked for his estimate and he said that several estimates had been made, varying from fifteen to fifty years. I asked whether the education programme could not be speeded up, with our financial assistance, to advance the progress of enfranchisement. Mr Smith replied: '... the Rhodesian Government would think it wrong to accelerate the educational advance of the Africans simply in order to improve their political status in the community....' When I said that the rate of advance we envisaged would not yield majority rule within the next few years, the official record stated: 'Mr Smith agreed: indeed, the Rhodesian Government would oppose any deliberate acceleration for this purpose. Nor would they widen the franchise because, when this had been considered some years earlier, Europeans had begun to leave the country in large numbers.'

So the argument continued across the table throughout the day, and in private talks at lunch. We probed them on the other principles. On non-discrimination, we asked about the Land Apportionment Act which Mr Smith rushed to defend, even for its 'value in protecting the Africans from exploitation', though, as the Commonwealth Secretary pointed out, the Act had been criticised by Rhodesia's Constitutional Council.

Summing up the first day's discussion, I said it was clear that the two sides were very far apart on all five principles, and that only the concept of a senate offered some possibility of advance. Even here, there was still a great gulf between the opposing sides. We agreed to meet the following day, though it was clear we were moving towards a break.

I began on the Friday afternoon, 8th October, by repeating our minimum terms and summarising where we had reached on each of the five principles. The gap was still very wide, not only on the first and second principles but also on his proposals for increasing the number of B-roll electors. There was nothing specific and, in any case, no suggestion of providing any more seats for Africans. On the fourth principle, non-discrimination, he appeared to have some improvement in mind, though there was apparently no question of the repeal of the Land Apportionment Act. But on the basic questions, including the senate and the means of testing Rhodesian opinion, there was no move forward at all.

No basis had been found, I said, on which the United Kingdom Government could recommend Parliament to grant independence to Rhodesia. There was no early prospect of majority rule; indeed, he had again said that he would resist proposals to do anything to accelerate the education of the Africans, on which we were prepared to give financial help, so that more could be helped to meet the educational qualifications; and I added, 'The United Kingdom Government could not countenance a transfer of sovereignty on the basis of so slender a guarantee of early majority rule.'

As the afternoon wore on, the signs of a break became clearer. Mr Smith said, '... the two sides were clearly as far apart as ever'. When he and his colleagues returned to Rhodesia, he said, they could do nothing but face up to what they considered the only alternative. The question, therefore, was how this could be implemented in a way which would cause the least trouble to both parties.

I said it would be tragic if an irrevocable decision were taken without full realisation of all the facts. So many tragedies in world history had been caused by a failure fully to appreciate, in advance, the possible consequences of a leap in the dark. But I gave him a severe warning about what the consequences would be, economically, in terms of world opinion, together with the dangers for southern Africa as a whole. Mr Smith could not get away from his obsession, which he repeated in these talks and, indeed, on almost every occasion whenever we met. This was the assertion that the people of Rhodesia – the Europeans – knew that their country and their lives were at stake, and that the situation facing them was exactly that facing Britain in 1939. Britain had not then been deterred from going to war. The Rhodesian people themselves would rather fight it out than go voluntarily from Rhodesia. I pointed out shortly that when Britain had decided to fight in 1939, and to fight on alone in 1940, she had not been without friends, and it could not be said of Britain that the whole of the rest of the world was against her. Rhodesia could make no similar claim.

He again rejected any constitutional conference. It was independence on his terms or nothing. To quote the official record: 'If Rhodesia could not obtain independence, he would not seek to remain; and there were many like him.' He had to say, he went on, that they had no option now but to take their independence: there might be advantage in discussing now how a 'unilateral' declaration might be implemented. I replied flatly that the British Government could not discuss how an illegal act might be carried out. He replied cheerfully that he had expected such a reply, but had felt it right to make the offer.

We briefly discussed the communiqué which, as finally agreed, merely recorded our total disagreement on the constitutional principles for independence. Mr Lardner-Burke, who was clearly in a hurry to get on, said they would wish to publish all the correspondence which had passed between the two Governments since June 1963. I said that our conventions would require me, in such a case, to seek the agreement of our predecessors for the publication of any documents relating to their period of office.

During the weekend Mr Smith had talks with Mr Heath and Sir Alec Douglas-Home. Mr Smith mentioned an idea which aroused their interest – the proposal that while the constitution should remain unamended, any settlement reached could be safeguarded by a solemn treaty between Britain and an independent Rhodesia. This was not a new idea. The Rhodesian High Commissioner had put it forward as a personal suggestion several months earlier. It had made no progress. Both sides recognised that the form of the settlement was unimportant; what mattered was the content, be it enshrined in a constitution or in a treaty. The problem of guaranteeing the treaty would be exactly the same as that of safeguarding the constitution.

But Sir Alec Douglas-Home and Mr Heath, anxious to avoid a breakdown, raised it with me. To make doubly sure, I asked Mr Smith to come to see me on the Monday. Clearly he did not take the proposal at all seriously, and Mr Lardner-Burke was particularly light-hearted when we discussed how the treaty could be enforced. On my visit to Salisbury later in the month I raised the question again; Mr Smith dismissed it. It is interesting, however, to note that when he met me on HMS *Tiger* fourteen months later, with, as he had undertaken, 'full powers to reach an agreement', he complained when I raised the issue of a treaty, registrable with the UN, saying that this was an entirely new proposal of which he had had no notice. Indeed he used it as a reason for going back on his word, insisting that he had to go back to Salisbury for consultation.

Mr Smith returned to Rhodesia on 12th October. There was general expectation that UDI would come within a very few days. That night I made a television broadcast, explaining why we had stood by the principles and policies of successive Governments and warning in the strongest terms against reckless action in Rhodesia. I concluded:

We are not giving up. Too much is at stake. . . . Last night I was in direct touch with 19 other heads of Commonwealth Governments. This evening Her Majesty's High Commission in Salisbury took to Mr Smith a personal message from me, pressing him, if he continues to reject independence on the terms we have offered, to agree to a new Commonwealth initiative, to a mission of senior Commonwealth Prime Ministers representing all the Prime Ministers and Presidents and peoples of the Commonwealth. . . . I know I speak for everyone in these islands, all parties, all our people, when I say to Mr Smith, 'Prime Minister, think again.'

I was told by observers at the Conservative party conference gathering that evening in Brighton that this broadcast was heard in silence, and with very deep feeling.

But Mr Smith was in no mood to think again, as became clear five days later, when he summarily and contemptuously rejected the proposed Commonwealth mission, which Sir Robert Menzies had agreed to lead. He would be welcome, said Mr Smith, if he were to come in a personal capacity. On the same day Mr Lardner-Burke signed a restriction order on the former Liberal Premier, Mr Garfield Todd, confining him to his house for a period of twelve months.

Serious messages were coming in. Reliable sources warned that UDI might be accompanied by the use of force against the Governor – possibly involving his arrest. Doubts – as it turned out unworthy ones – were circulating that Sir Humphrey Gibbs, whose health was giving him cause for concern, might in any case resign. But we had to prepare to meet action against him. Should he be taken into custody, the governorship would fall on Sir Hugh Beadle and, after him, right down the list of high court judges, by seniority.

We had to resume consideration of an idea we had considered earlier – the appointment of an alternative Governor, possibly sent out from Britain.

A number of names had been considered, including distinguished Rhodesians, particularly those who had held high positions in the Rhodesian armed services. But, after a great deal of thought, the view of my colleagues and myself was that we should approach Lord Mountbatten, recently retired from the position of Chief of the Defence Staff. It was not only that his authority and personality would be of vital importance in influencing the opinions of, at any rate, the moderate Rhodesians, and perhaps many others whose loyalty to the Crown might give them pause when presented with illegal independence. There was the further point that Lord Mountbatten's unique record in the history of Indian independence meant that no one could be more fitted for handling a difficult negotiating problem of this kind.

But there was a problem. He was not only a distinguished war leader, and the first to hold the high office of Chief of the Defence Staff. He was also a member of the Royal Family. There could be no question of even approaching him without seeking at least the informal approval of the Queen, and one had to take account of the fact that the circumstances in which he might be asked to assume the Governorship might involve some personal danger.

It was for that reason that after the breakdown of the talks with Mr Smith on 11th October, I sought an Audience at Balmoral and flew from Heathrow to Dyce early on the Wednesday morning. I had hoped to keep the flight secret, at any rate until I reached Aberdeen; but the Heathrow authorities have a charming habit on being notified of VIP flights, of passing on the information to the resident press representatives. So the fact of my flight was on the early-morning news and, of course, I was seen off by a number of journalists and photographers.

Subsequent reports indicated that this news had a somewhat disturbing effect on the opening of the Conservative party conference that morning. As soon as it became known, so one understood, distinguished political writers left the press table to confer on the implications of my visit to Balmoral and distinguished delegates to the conference followed them to find out what might be happening. There was a great deal of speculation, expectation even, that my purpose was to advise the Queen to grant a dissolution of Parliament, to be followed by an immediate general election. Faced with this possibility, not every delegate was able to concentrate as fully as they would have wished on the words of wisdom from the Tory platform. One press report added that some were heard to say, bitterly, as though realising for the first time that the Conservatives were no longer in office, 'We've just sung the Queen: he is seeing her.'

After my Audience I returned quickly to Dyce, where I was interrogated by pressmen. I answered the question that was uppermost in their minds and said it had nothing to do with a general election.

But the purpose of the visit was undeniably necessary and the timing of it unavoidable, even if it did have an unsettling effect at Brighton.

Mr Smith's refusal to receive the proposed Menzies mission reached me on 18th October. I answered at length, on the same day, rejecting his arguments and again urging him to accept not only the necessary safeguards in the constitution, but – what was coming into growing prominence as the dark Salisbury night closed in – safeguards for the freedom of the press and for the freedom of the individual. I ended my reply with an appeal:

> ... before any irrevocable step is taken, I beg you, yet again, even at the eleventh hour, for the sake of your country, for the sake of Africa and for the sake of future generations of all races, to pause before bringing hardship and misery, perhaps even worse, to your own people and to countless others far beyond your borders, who have no power to influence your decision but whose lives may be gravely affected by it. ...

In reply I received, on 20th October, another argumentative historical review on what was and was not said by our predecessors in 1961.

On 21st October I sent him yet another telegram, again challenging his claim that Sir Alec Douglas-Home's Government had put forward the 1961 constitution, unamended, as an independence constitution. But after putting all this formally, once more on the record, I concluded:

> ...need we go on bandying arguments at arm's length, when the future of so many people of all races is in such suspense? For my part I do not want to go on like this. Accordingly I propose to fly with the Commonwealth Secretary to Salisbury in the next day or two in order to discuss the whole matter further with you, including all the suggestions I have put to you. I shall naturally expect to have an opportunity of meeting anyone whose views I feel to be relevant to a solution of this grave problem. But I want you to realise that my sole purpose in this visit will be to try to find some means of breaking the deadlock and to avert the tragic consequences which otherwise I see no way of avoiding. ...

Mr Smith accepted my proposal three days later, and I made it clear to him that I would expect to see representatives of all the parties to the 1961 constitutional conference, be they in detention or not. Mr Smith agreed and I said that I should expect to see them at Government House.

Just before I left, I was diverted by some correspondence with Mr Heath, which I could interpret only as meaning that, under pressure from his right-wing as he was, he was seeking to move into a position of dissociation from Government policy on Rhodesia, indeed from the posture firmly adopted by the Conservative Government up to October 1964.

On 18th October I had written to him to express my concern about a statement made by Mr Iain Macleod on television saying that, with regard to a unilateral declaration of independence, 'the law in this matter is by no means clear'. In my letter to Mr Heath I quoted this, and stressed that Sir Alec Douglas-Home had told Mr Smith, in London in September 1964, that a UDI would be 'a revolt against the Crown'. This warning, I recalled, had been repeated by me in my statement of 26th October 1964, in this case the word 'rebellion' being used – no legal difference being involved – and I quoted Sir Alec Douglas-Home's subsequent support in Parliament for my statement. Unfortunately, in a letter of 22nd October, Mr Heath sought to slide out of his predecessor's statement by invoking the claim that Sir Alec had said only that the words were 'rough', not, as the House had heard and leading newspapers and the BBC had reported, 'rough but right'. *Hansard* nevertheless had no record of the words 'but right'. It was unfortunate that the letter from Mr Heath did not reach me in time for me to compose a reply before I left for Rhodesia, and my reply had to be written out in the aircraft and sent back from Salisbury. Mr Heath's letter showed not only that he now, for the first time, disputed our definition of the consequences in the statement of 26th October 1964, but that he was also quibbling about what Sir Alec Douglas-Home had said in the House about it. There was, too, a claim in a further letter that he and his colleagues had invented the proposal to guarantee any constitutional settlement with Rhodesia through a treaty. As I told him in a further reply, Mr Smith himself had claimed the authorship:

> But does it matter? When I was asked by a pressman about this I said that if this idea proved to be viable, I should be happy for the royalties to acrue to the rightful owner, whoever he might be; if it is not viable there is not much purpose in pursuing it further. It is perhaps to be noted that in an interview with a London Conservative newspaper this weekend Mr Smith said 'he' had put it to you and your colleagues.
> Frankly, I am more concerned with getting a solution. And I should like to be quite sure, in view of recent doubts about this, that you and your colleagues are not in any way resiling from the vital fifth principle, the issue on which Sir Alec and Mr Smith broke off a year ago, namely the insistence that any agreement reached must be acceptable to the people of Rhodesia as a whole.

Neither Mr Heath nor Sir Alec Douglas-Home had in any way publicly dissociated themselves from our policies or warnings; indeed, as a loyal constitutionalist party it was difficult for them to get into a position where they might be construed as giving any aid to a group of men poised on the edge of an act of open disloyalty to the Crown. I had been disturbed to be told by a Cabinet colleague that Mr Heath had said to him that while there was no divergence on basic policies, they were watching for one false step, after which Rhodesia would become an issue between the parties.

We flew in an RAF Transport Command Comet by way of the British sovereign base at Akrotiri, Cyprus, and on to Nairobi, where I was met at the airport by President Kenyatta. He had not been to London for the Commonwealth conference in June and this was my first opportunity of discussing Rhodesia with him since taking office. Speaking quietly, but with all the authority of the acknowledged father of his people, he took a very different line from that taken by the Kenya delegate at the Commonwealth conference. He was particularly robust in his strictures on the African nationalist leaders in Rhodesia. Not only were they sharply divided and quarrelling publicly – he and other African leaders, he said, had tried to get them together – they were no more than agitators, unwilling to come to terms with the realities of power. I should tell them to attempt to work for what they believed in just as other African leaders had done.

We reached Salisbury Airport at 7.00 p.m., local time, on Monday, 25th October. It was only after UDI occurred that we found that this was the date stamped on the petrol ration coupons subsequently issued. This confirmed the suspicion I was later in the week to express to Mr Smith that UDI was a firm decision and that my visit had merely postponed it.

Despite the reinforced numbers of Special Branch officers together with some RAF police, whose duty it was to protect the aircraft, there was some expectation of trouble at the airport. There was a big crowd – friendly and otherwise – to welcome me, and many on the observation roof under which I had to pass. The *Guardian* described my entry into the VIP suite as 'showing the demeanour of a landlord who had come to deal with a tenant who had mismanaged the property entrusted to him'.

Waiting at the airport was one of Mr Smith's ministers, the Governor's private secretary and the deputy leader of the African Parliamentary party, who took the opportunity hurriedly to warn me of anything I might be told by the Government about the real attitude of his parliamentary colleagues. The roads all the way to Government House were lined by thousands of Africans, mostly cheering, many bearing placards, 'One man, One vote' and 'No sell-out'. There were many friendly Europeans, clearly of the liberal persuasion, and a small number who were actively hostile and had their distinctive ways of showing it.

Chapter 11

Talks in Salisbury – statement to the Rhodesian people – Mr Smith's proposals – meeting with President Kaunda at Livingstone – with Sir Abubakar at Lagos – with President Nkrumah at Accra – return to Britain – Gibraltar – cold-line telephone call to Mr Smith – UDI declared

I BORE letters from the Queen to the Governor and to Mr Smith. Sir Humphrey took his when I arrived and read it gravely, much affected, Mr Smith had called a dinner-party, attended by European and African MPs, businessmen and representatives of the Constitutional Commission. I handed Mr Smith's letter to him there: he read it out the next night at a civic banquet in Salisbury, prefacing a very hard-line speech; the expectation had been that the occasion would have been used to celebrate the declaration of UDI. Mr Smith said, 'Things have changed. The arrival of the British Prime Minister has spiked my guns.' He concluded by quoting King Henry V before Agincourt – 'He which hath no stomach to this fight, let him depart.'

After dinner, my colleagues and I had a long talk with the Governor and with Sir Hugh Beadle, who appeared more optimistic than I had expected. I had not at that time learned to discount his optimism about a settlement, nor, despite the scathing terms in which he referred to 'Smith' and his colleagues, how supple, indeed devious, he was prepared to be to get us to concede a settlement, however tangential its connection with the five principles. But he was able to tell me that his predecessor as Chief Justice, Sir Robert Tredgold, who had resigned from his post in protest against the actions of the United Federal Government, had recently visited African nationalist leaders in their detention camps at Gonukadzingwa and Sikombela. He had formed the view that Mr Joshua Nkomo, leader of the Zimbabwe African People's Union (ZAPU) and the Reverend Ndabaningi Sithole, leader of the rival Zimbabwe African National Union (ZANU) would be willing to accept an independence settlement which did not involve prior majority rule, provided there were adequate guarantees for the assured achievement of majority rule over a reasonable period of time. Sir Hugh was also convinced that there would be some give on the part of the Rhodesian Government.

On the following morning we met Mr Smith in his office at Milton Buildings. He welcomed us, and underlined what Sir Hugh Beadle had told me by saying that although there was no overt change in the situation there was now a ray of light about the nationalists' attitude, and he sensed

155

a significant move on the part of the African Parliamentary party. He felt that I should be able to form my own view of this when I saw Nkomo and Sithole; he, of course, had no contact with them.

He came straight to the question of a treaty: this should simply be a means of reaffirming the obligation about the entrenched clauses, but it could not go beyond the 1961 constitution. Mr Lardner-Burke was more direct. He agreed that the question was the content of the guarantees, not the document in which they were recorded. As to registration with the United Nations, 'the Rhodesian Government were not enthusiastic about this idea'. I raised the question of the right of appeal to the Judicial Committee of the Privy Council. Mr Smith said – in direct contradiction to the line he was to take on what came to be one of the main breaking-points in 1968 – that 'the Privy Council was already the ultimate Court of Appeal for Rhodesia and would therefore be acceptable to the Rhodesian Government in the context of the proposed treaty'. He went out of his way to dismiss Conservative claims, published at the time of my Downing Street talks with him, that they were the authors of the treaty proposed; he himself, he said, had invented it a year earlier. He was certainly right that it had come from a Rhodesian source some time before.

The greater part of our discussion on that Tuesday morning followed the well-worn lines of the London discussions, though the Rhodesians seemed more relaxed and, on the whole, slightly more friendly. In addition to Mr Lardner-Burke, I was very glad to see that Mr Dupont was there in place of Mr William Harper. There was always some doubt whether it was Dupont or Lardner-Burke who was the evil genius of the UDI campaign, but it was good to get Mr Dupont in direct range of our arguments. There had been some suggestion that he discounted reports by Mr Smith, Mr Harper and the High Commission about the toughness and determination of the British Government, and I took every opportunity, when he was being contumacious, to let him have it with both barrels.

We got down to a number of detailed questions including the role of the Constitutional Council, which had shown considerable independence in its rejection of certain Rhodesian Front measures. We asked how many Africans could be registered immediately, given a drive to put them on the electoral roll. The Rhodesians gave us higher figures than we had been told before, up to sixty thousand on the B-roll, and some ten thousand or more on the A-roll. We again offered financial help with education, which would speed enfranchisement. Again it was firmly rejected.

We then discussed the fifth principle, and the test of 'acceptability to the people of Rhodesia as a whole'. Mr Smith suggested that if Sir Robert Tredgold was right about nationalist attitudes, then a statement by them as well as the leaders of other groups and parties might be held to be an adequate test. I said this was not excluded, but I reserved my position until I could hear the nationalist views at first hand. On the blocking quarter Mr Smith seemed more reasonable; African representatives, he said, need not be confined to the hereditary chiefs.

In the afternoon I began my round of consultations at Government House. At 2.30 p.m. I saw the African leader of the parliamentary Opposition, Mr Gondo, and his colleagues – no sign there of the changing view Mr Smith had claimed to detect; at 3.45 p.m. Mr Palley, the white liberal, elected by B-roll Africans; at five o'clock a delegation from the Asian community, at 5.30 p.m. one from the coloured community; and at six o'clock the representative of a second and separate coloured community. All of these were flatly opposed to Rhodesian Front proposals, almost all to any independence before majority rule.

At 6.30 that evening I had a private meeting in my room with Sir Roy Welensky. I had been warned that both the conference room at Government House and my private apartments were almost certainly bugged; whether Sir Roy did not believe this, or just did not care, he hit out in his characteristically pugnacious manner. He used the most scathing terms about the Rhodesian Front Government and went on to say that his own biggest mistake as Prime Minister had been the decision that the Government should take over responsibility for the Rhodesian Broadcasting Corporation, both radio and television. The Rhodesian Front had adopted the RBC as a weapon of Government propaganda. All criticism was silenced, and exclusively Government-slanted news and views put over the air. Sir Roy was with me an hour; he was totally pessimistic and discounted the rumours about the African nationalists.

After dinner, a very movable feast that week, I had a deeply moving meeting with the Rhodesian newspaper editors, who, to a man, had presented the truth as they saw it, despite the volume of virulent letters from their readers – some of which I read during the week I was there – and despite, equally, threats of censorship and imprisonment. They gave me their analysis, their pessimistic prognosis; at the end I asked all my colleagues to rise with me and raise our glasses in tribute to a very courageous band of men, standing up, as they so fearlessly had done, for the highest traditions of their profession.

The next morning, Wednesday, 27th October, after a brief social call from Sir Len Hutton, who was in Salisbury on business, I had a long talk with the members of the Rhodesian Constitutional Association. These were, in effect, the liberal successors of Roy Welensky and Edgar Whitehead, though since the election of the previous May without a single MP in the House. I formed the opinion, as did many of my colleagues who met them on subsequent visits, that their hearts were in the right place but that, for reasons not entirely their own fault, they were almost totally ineffective. They had no leader with even a fraction of the charisma of Ian Smith. Lord Malvern, who as Sir Godfrey Huggins had been Prime Minister for twenty-three years, from 1933 to 1956, followed them. By this time he was old and frail, but he expressed himself in terms that made Sir Roy Welensky sound moderate.

At 11.15 a.m. Mr Nkomo was brought in, with his colleagues of the Zimbabwe African People's Union, some from Gonukadzingwa, others – whom they had not seen for months – from other detention centres. They were accompanied by Mr Nkomo's assertive legal adviser, Mr Leo Baron, a European, himself soon to be behind bars for professional activities which would have been considered normal in any civilised country.

Mr Nkomo was in an angry mood. His arm was in a sling, and he complained that at the camp he had received no proper medical attention for it, only a rough dressing from orderlies. My personal doctor, Joe Stone, examined him and found that there was not much wrong – he had fallen and cut his arm on a bottle. But his complaints about maltreatment were confirmed when I found that no arrangements had been made to provide food at lunchtime – and that they had been picked up from the camp early in the morning, without breakfast, flown to Salisbury, and kept in a hot van in a blistering temperature without air-conditioning or any ventilation. Finding that no food was to be provided, I had a blazing row with the Rhodesian authorities, and sent a British army colonel who was with me to act as my representative and satisfy himself that my visitors were properly fed.

Our talks rapidly made it clear that Mr Nkomo and his supporters had no intention whatsoever of accepting any settlement without prior majority rule. There was no question in his mind at all of accepting the 1961 constitution, however amended, as a basis for independence. Throughout, the Africans spoke quickly, reasonably and with great sadness, looking to us to protect them and the other four million Africans. I asked them why they had not tried to work the 1961 constitution; indeed, had campaigned in the villages to persuade Africans to boycott it. They strongly denied the allegations – which Mr Smith and his colleagues repeated in every talk we ever had – about terrorisation of the African population with threats and, worse, hut-burning and murder. But they said the constitution was so rigged against the Africans that it was unworkable; were they to try to work it, they would be supplanted by more militant leaders.

The High Commission gave a lunch for me to meet representatives of industry, finance and the farmers, including the powerful – and then prosperous – tobacco growers. The businessmen in general were, of all the groups I saw in Rhodesia apart from the churches, the most insistent on the need for a settlement, the most ready to make concessions from the European hard line, and the most ready to criticise Rhodesian Front intransigence. At 2.30 p.m. I met Mr Garfield Todd, the former Prime Minister, who strongly supported the Nkomo–Sithole line. At five o'clock the Reverend Sithole came in with his supporters. They immediately dismissed any suggestion of working with ZAPU, but they argued reasonably and intelligently. The delegation, no doubt representing their movement, was more intellectual and contained a high proportion of teachers and office workers. Whatever the personal antipathies, they took exactly the same line as Nkomo and his friends: 'one man, one vote'.

There could be no question of a deal with Mr Smith. What they unitedly wanted was a constitutional conference, and the imposition of a constitution by the British Government.

When we had fully covered the political and constitutional issues I had a spare half-hour, and went round the room asking each their personal history, education, job, whether free or detained and getting a brief account of their political activities – and, where relevant, as it was with the majority, the reasons for their detention and imprisonment. One was an accountant, unable to practise because of racialist laws, and forced to become a doorstep-salesman.

At the end of the meeting, I inquired whether Mr Sithole had eaten. He too, like Nkomo, had been given no breakfast; he, too, had been kept in a hot police van, and had eaten nothing all day. I asked the police who were in attendance what arrangements had been made to provide food for him. None had.

It was at this point that, for the first time in my life, I totally lost my temper to the point where I was out of control. This was the first time I had ever known what 'seeing red' could mean. On going in to harangue the Governor, I was unable to see him because of red flashes before my eyes. I made it clear that I was not having this treatment of the Africans by the Rhodesian Government and their police. I told the Governor that the African leaders had come at my invitation and they were to be treated in a civilised manner. I was already incensed by reports I had had from British and American journalists – some of whom had been reasonably friendly to the Rhodesian Government, but had become progressively disenchanted in their writings since their arrival in Salisbury – about their sense of outrage at seeing police dogs deliberately set loose on Africans peaceably gathered at the Government House gates to cheer Nkomo or Sithole on their arrival.

I told the Governor that if in half an hour from the time I was speaking Sithole and his colleagues were not sitting down to a three-course meal, the menu of which I had personally approved and which would be supervised by my own staff – then I would take a hand. I would personally lead all my staff into the streets of Salisbury, visit every café and snack bar and with our money – I flourished my wallet – we would ourselves buy enough food and would feed my visitors in Government House. What was more, every one of the thousand pressmen and television reporters from Britain, America and the whole free world would be there to see, to photograph and to film what was happening. Half an hour later, they were sitting down to an excellent meal, the menu having been brought to me for approval.

In the evening I saw Sir Robert Tredgold. He was not altogether surprised at the line Nkomo and Sithole had taken, though he had hoped for some movement. He again expressed himself in the strongest terms about the Rhodesian Government, and the disaster he was certain was only a matter of days away.

Thursday, 28th October was certainly the most colourful day of my visit. The Council of Chiefs paraded on the lawn, gorgeously dressed and extremely affable, even condescending. I took them to the conference room and put the problems to them as I saw them. I asked them whether they would support a UDI if the Rhodesian Government claimed to seize one. I told them it was illegal. They said that certainly they could not support anything illegal. I then made clear my concern to test Mr Smith's claim that the chiefs clearly represented the opinion of the four million Africans. In response to question after question, they assured me that they did.

I asked them how they came to know what the Africans were thinking; what were their methods of consultation and discussion? Two or three of them insisted that they simply knew, because they owed their position to the divine law of chiefly blood and this made them the best judges of what the Africans wanted. But were there any consultations? I asked. Yes, they replied, regularly; they described their local tribal customs with the chief sitting surrounded by the villagers discussing affairs of the village or even affairs of state.

I thought I would test how far they themselves were aware of the issues. I therefore described with great care – and I repeated the point a number of times – one of the big issues which was at present standing in the way of a settlement, namely the Rhodesian Government's desire to amend the 1961 constitution in a retrogressive direction by providing that as more Africans qualified for the A-roll vote and began to win A-roll seats, there should be a simultaneous reduction in the number of B-roll seats reserved for Africans. What would be their method of consultation on this? Had they in fact discussed this very fundamental issue with their constituents? Yes, indeed they had, this was one of the issues, apparently, on which there was almost nightly discussion.

When the point had been properly established, I stopped and asked whether there was a single one of the thirty chiefs present who had the remotest idea of what I had been talking about. Would, perhaps, one of them like to explain to me the issue and say what he himself thought about it? There was a prolonged silence until one of the chiefs, more learned than the rest, essayed an attempt at it but did not get even near to a correct rendering of what the problem was about. This test satisfied me that their claims to be a representative consultative group capable of expressing the opinion of the Africans were totally false.

I discussed Mr Smith's proposal for a senate with them, and found them extremely resistant to the idea that men of chiefly blood should actually take their place and sit down in a chamber with elected Africans. This would be an offence against their dignity. In return I explained that Britain, which for centuries had a feudal, even a chiefly, system based on heredity had emerged from that state of affairs. Indeed two leading peers, Sir Alec Douglas-Home himself and Mr Quintin Hogg, had only recently renounced their hereditary peerages and moved along the corridor from the House of Lords to the House of Commons. I illustrated this with gestures, indicating movement in a horizontal direction.

We had two interpreters for all this discussion, Matabele and Mashona. I was amused when the first of these explained the regrettable apostasy on the part of the two ex-peers I had named, and illustrated it not by a horizontal motion, but by moving his hands to indicate that they had stepped down from a high altitude to the low altitude of the elected chamber. I interrupted and pointed out that in our country we felt that it was a truly horizontal movement, both geographically and in terms of parliamentary dignity. It was no use. The other interpreter insisted on signifying by the same hand signals that it was a very marked step down for my two distinguished parliamentary colleagues. The chiefs parted from me in the most friendly way, denying as they went the suggestion which they knew had been put to me, that since every man jack of them was paid by the Rhodesian Government – a significant part of the pay depended upon discretionary allowances or expenses – they were in any way subject to Government influence or pressure. But to meet them had been an education; undoubtedly, a fine body of men!

I then met the Christian Council of Rhodesia, including the courageous Bishop Skelton, the other Anglican bishops, the no less determined Roman Catholic leaders, the nonconformists, the Salvation Army and an extremely articulate and progressive professor of theology at the university. Of all the people I met, these impressed me most for their liberalism, their vigour and the courage with which they expressed themselves. And this vigour and courage, as I had reason to know – and as the world has learned since – was not confined to the privacy of a conference room at Government House.

That day I had a private lunch with Mr Smith and our own High Commissioner at the High Commissioner's residence. I reported to Mr Smith that the hopes he had expressed of some movement towards an amended 1961 constitution on the part of the African leaders were entirely without foundation. But he knew that I would be meeting Nkomo and Sithole again, together. A state of total enmity had existed between them for years and there had been clashes, even fatal ones, between some of their followers. But I was concerned to see whether either or both of them was expressing an exaggeratedly militant line for fear of being over-bid by the other.

I then gave Mr Smith some of my impressions. I said that I had been struck by the personal support for him over a wider range of public opinion than many, perhaps even he himself, would have expected. Even the liberal Europeans and some of the Church leaders had not entirely given up hope of him. I felt that his powers of leadership – what in the western world was increasingly known as 'charisma' – were such that if he would give a bold lead for a liberal constitution, in accordance with the five principles, he might be surprised how many people fell into line with him, including a lot of progressive, but not ultra-nationalist Africans.

I said that it was not for me to interfere in his domestic politics, though we had a common interest in reaching a solution. But as a student of politics I could not understand why he allowed himself to be pushed around by the right-wing, almost fascist, element in his Cabinet. It would be the easiest thing in the world for him to move to the centre and ditch some of his extreme supporters. He would soon find others of much more use to him, much more representative of a united Rhodesia. He smiled and said, 'That's what they all tell me.' But he then said that, with others, he had led the fight against the Welensky Administration, from the time when he had resigned as Welensky's Chief Whip. These men had been loyal to him and he could not let them down now. I was still uncertain whether he was simply expressing a basic loyalty, or whether, as I had reason to feel later, he himself was to some extent a prisoner of some of the extreme right.

That afternoon I talked first for an hour with Mr Nkomo and then with Mr Sithole and told them of my desire that they should get together. They raised no objection and it was agreed that they would meet alone. Neither they nor I doubted that, had any of their followers been there, relations might have been very disturbed, perhaps violent. We went along to a small room. The police guards were around, but not too visible, but I felt it right to have my two Special Branch officers with me, not so much to protect me against either or both of them, but in case the two got into physical conflict. The two leaders met, shook hands, sat down and chatted agreeably to one another, and I left them alone to talk there for a while. When I got back they were obviously exchanging detention camp stories, and roaring with laughter; guessing that some of their jokes were at my expense I regretted my ignorance of African language. With the aid of an interpreter I discussed the situation with them. Together – and separately – they stated their total opposition to any settlement which was not based on the prior achievement of majority rule.

That evening, my party was invited to a reception given by Mrs Smith at the Prime Minister's residence. The whole Rhodesian Cabinet and their wives were there. I got the opportunity of a private talk with one or two known reactionary members of the Cabinet, whom I had not previously met, and warned them very straight about what sanctions could mean.

The ladies then withdrew and we went into dinner. I sat on Mr Smith's right and on my right was the egregious Duke of Montrose, a settler of long standing in Rhodesia, still known there as Lord Graham, despite his succession to the dukedom. I was aware that he was one of the most passionate supporters of UDI, a committed reactionary, and because of his title he was much spoken of as the likely 'Regent' of Rhodesia if independence were declared. I did not find him impressive, and this judgment was strengthened in the course of the evening.

After the loyal toast, Mr Smith said that he would start off the contribution to the evening's gaiety with a cricket story, since his chief guest was a Yorkshireman. He then recounted the oldest of the Roses' match stories. I was prepared to settle for that, because I wanted a serious talk round the dinner-table with the whole Cabinet. Arthur Bottomley, however, felt it polite to respond with an Essex cricket story and one of the Rhodesians capped the stories with a tale of incredible prurience. It became clear that I was not going to get any serious discussion. Then one after another of the Rhodesians called for a story by Lord Graham; it was explained to me that he was the greatest of all story-tellers. I forbear recounting his story. Suffice it to say that it was about an American girl who was not a very good dancer, particularly in relation to the physical gestures with which she displayed her charms while dancing and her inability to master such a technique of the art as related to bumps, grinds and other advances of modern terpsichorean technology. How she was trained in these arts was dramatically recounted by Lord Graham, who found it necessary to the point of his story to act the part in full, with every gesture carried out by his enormous frame. Each time he went into one of the motions of the dance, he brushed his capacious frame against my face. Although I am normally tolerant, I found myself unimpressed by his performance.

At the end of it he sat down, with roars of approval from his colleagues. Rhodesia's finest hour. In a moment of silence I said menacingly, 'I see.' I had the audience and in an icy voice I repeated, 'I see.... now I understand what qualifications you have to have to become the Regent of Rhodesia.' The temperature fell about forty degrees. There was a shocked silence and then one after the other the Rhodesians began to laugh. I have often wondered whether that one remark – and the fear that it would become publicly known – ended Lord Graham's chance of becoming 'Regent' when UDI was finally declared.

When we returned to Government House we were met with alarmist rumours from the press and from friendly Rhodesian sources that UDI was to be declared the following morning. There were even panicky stories that we should not be able to get to the airport, but that we should be arrested and held as hostages. Almost anything seemed possible in that land-locked, introvert community. I discounted the rumours, but attached more credence to those which said that UDI would be declared after our visit.

I spent an hour preparing a final statement to the Rhodesian people, to be broadcast – as I hoped – on Rhodesian television. It contained a sincere warning, but made clear our real understanding of what the whites feared most. While progress to ultimate majority rule must be embodied in the independence constitution, there would be no time-scale set for majority rule. After what I had seen of the African political parties and, above all, their fratricidal divisions, progress to majority rule should depend not on time measured by clock or calendar but by co-operation, progress and achievement in making democracy work. I was dealing with people who assumed that independence on our terms would mean that their daughters would be raped by marauding Africans the following morning. Indeed that was what Front propaganda had convinced them was the prevailing way of life in, to quote Mr Smith's favourite phrase, 'the countries to the north of us'.

We had arranged a meeting in the Prime Minister's office on the Friday morning, 29th October. He was accompanied by Mr Dupont, Mr Lardner-Burke and the Minister of Local Government, Mr A. P. Smith. Mr Ian Smith invited me to summarise my impressions. I described my talks with African nationalist leaders and my refusal to accede to their demand for military intervention. They did not expect majority rule in the immediate future, I said. They understood there would be no set time for majority rule; that it was up to them and the date would depend on their co-operation in working the 1961 constitution.

But I was conscious that we were approaching a crisis. I said that I wanted to put two new propositions to Mr Smith, which I had worked out, alone, in the small hours and discussed with my colleagues and advisers that morning. The first was that the two Governments should now work out a detailed independence constitution, based on 1961, but with essential amendments to provide guarantees for the effective fulfil-ment of the five principles. I proposed that the Commonwealth Secre-tary and the Attorney-General, Sir Elwyn Jones, should stay behind to discuss our essential requirements with Rhodesian ministers. So far I had no confidence that these were acceptable to the Front.

If agreement could be reached, it should then be put to the Rhodesian people 'as a whole'. There were two possible ways of consulting Rhodesian opinion, as the fifth principle required. One would be a referendum – not, certainly on the present electorate, but perhaps on a special electorate consisting of all adult taxpayers, for the Africans registered as taxpayers far exceeded the B-roll electors. If Mr Smith felt, as he so often said, that the majority of the population would accept the kind of independence constitution I was putting forward, he could not object to a referendum, for the 1961 constitution itself provided for a referendum of the four Rhodesian communities, European, African, Asian and coloured. I underrated Mr Smith in that remark: he did object.

For that situation I had a second proposal ready.

I recalled the procedure which had been followed in Malaysia with the Cobbold Commission, followed by the UN mission. Neither would be acceptable to the Rhodesian Government; I proposed instead a Royal Commission, appointed by both Governments. It would be predominantly manned by representative Rhodesians. I had in mind men such as Sir Victor Robinson, chairman of the Constitutional Commission, who, with his colleagues, had greatly impressed me when I had met them. The chairman, I felt, should be the Chief Justice, Sir Hugh Beadle, whose capacity for manoeuvre I had not yet fully grasped. But it would include a respected elder statesman from Britain. I instanced Lord Butler (not the most popular Englishman in Rhodesia), Lord Amory or Sir Jocelyn Simon, plus perhaps a distinguished Australian jurist to be nominated by Sir Robert Menzies. The Commission's terms of reference might be to recommend the constitutional arrangements on which Rhodesia could proceed to independence. It would have power to take formal evidence, but it would also move freely around the country to obtain informally the views of all sections of opinion.

Mr Smith said they would give these proposals careful thought. He was against a referendum, but he would think about the Royal Commission, though he doubted whether it would be able to produce a solution acceptable to both sides. He promised to put it to his Cabinet at once. We then briefly went over the whole ground again. I warned him once again of the consequences of UDI. We came around again to the representative quality of the chiefs, and I said that it was clear that they had little comprehension of the terms of the existing constitution. Mr Smith said that this merely reinforced his argument that the majority of Africans were not capable of applying their minds to constitutional issues! We then came to the question of the Royal Commission and agreed that, subject to further consideration by both Governments, its terms of reference might well be 'to recommend such amendments to the 1961 constitution as will provide the basis on which Rhodesia may proceed to independence as rapidly as possible in a manner which will give effect to the principles enunciated by the British Government in their statement of 9th October 1965, and will be acceptable to the people of Rhodesia as a whole'.

The Rhodesian Cabinet met in the afternoon. In the early evening there was some frenzied coming-and-going by Sir Hugh Beadle, whose irrepressible ingenuity led to an incredible succession of proposals for a settlement.

Finally, around six o'clock, he came with a small, dirty scrap of paper on which, following his talk with Mr Smith, had been scribbled what he regarded as the final proposals of the Rhodesian Government and which he thought I could accept. The exact text was as follows:

1. Independence on the 1961 constitution, Creation of House of Chiefs of 12.
2. Two-thirds majority of House of Chiefs voting with our Parliament have full power to alter any entrenched clauses.
3. Commission: Sir Hugh Beadle: Chairman
   1 UK choice
   1 Rhodesia choice

Mr Wilson to sign that he will grant independence if Commission finds that this is acceptable to the people of Rhodesia as a whole.

I told Sir Hugh Beadle that we could not continue on the basis of scraps of paper being ferried by Chief Justices from the Prime Minister's residence to Government House. I said that I did not think it was, indeed, the function of a Chief Justice, however anxious he was to promote a settlement, to act as a telegraph boy. If Mr Smith had anything to say, he should say it to me. I would therefore propose that all my colleagues should cancel their engagements – the Attorney-General was dining with the Rhodesian judges – and that we should meet Mr Smith and his Cabinet wherever he chose at nine o'clock.

Mr Smith agreed, and we met at his residence.

He asked me what conclusion I had reached on the alternative proposal they had put forward. I said I had no idea what this alternative proposal was. I had had a scrap of paper handed to me by the Chief Justice and it was not my conception of the duty of the Chief Justice to act as a messenger boy. If Mr Smith had anything to propose he would tell me. He then set out the scrap of paper proposals more fully. He said that my suggested Royal Commission should be charged with the task of recommending amendments to the constitution and seeing if these were acceptable. But of course the amended constitution must first be acceptable to the Rhodesian Government. I felt there was some force in this but I asked that as an alternative we should try to work out with them some proposals to satisfy the first four principles and that, if we could agree on them, they would then be put to the Royal Commission purely to test acceptability; in other words, the Royal Commission would not have the task of drawing up the proposed document. Its duty would be to report that the Rhodesian people as a whole accepted our agreed document; or they might say they would be likely to accept it with certain specific amendments; or report that it was unacceptable to the Rhodesian people.

We then discussed the possibility of the Royal Commission's putting in an interim report to us on the method by which it would test acceptability. The two Governments could then give the Commission the go-ahead to carry out the acceptability test.

We argued long into the evening. Mr Smith and one or two others, I felt, were genuinely trying to see if anything could be worked out on this basis. But other members of the Cabinet, particularly in the quarter of the table where Lord Graham was sitting, were muttering imprecations against Mr Smith and shooting menacing looks every time he started to move towards something I had proposed.

At the end of our talks I said I would have to take this proposal back to the British Cabinet for approval and that I could not commit the British Government. There was some further muttering and anxiety that I was delaying a decision once again but Mr Smith supported my proposal, provided that we gave a speedy answer. 'How long,' Mr Smith asked, 'would it take the United Kingdom Cabinet to make up their minds? For the past week or ten days, Rhodesia has been virtually at a standstill and this cannot go on.' I said that there had been a very long delay throughout, and it was not unreasonable that the United Kingdom Government should require time to examine this new proposal, which had only been put forward in summary form a few hours before.

But in view of what Mr Smith had said I felt bound to tell the Rhodesian Cabinet that I could not help suspecting that they had already decided that they were going to assume their independence – illegally – in the very near future; that they were not prepared to delay implementing their decisions any longer even in order to allow the British Cabinet, which bore the ultimate responsibility in this matter, adequate time in which to consider their latest proposal. If this was their attitude it was wholly irresponsible and they had no grounds for asking me to agree, virtually at pistol-point, to fall into line with their wishes. Mr Smith said that this criticism was unfair and that there was no pistol held to my head.

I asked him what action the Rhodesian Government would have taken if I had not come to Salisbury on the previous Monday. Mr Smith replied that my guess on this point was as good as his own. I said that he had answered my question.

We then agreed that, over the weekend, the Commonwealth Secretary and the Attorney-General would meet with Mr Lardner-Burke and the legal officers of the Rhodesian Government to see what progress they could make in drafting terms of reference and procedure for the Royal Commission. They were to seek to reach agreement on the outstanding issues, particularly those relating to the blocking-proportion and the treatment of constitutional amendments, and, in particular, amendments of the specially entrenched clauses.

Just before I left Mr Smith's house, Mr Harper approached me, rather sheepishly, with his son's autograph book, saying he would not be forgiven if he did not ask me to sign it. Seeing the black looks from the Graham quarter of the room, he sought to recover by saying that he hoped we should not see a situation where, as a result of British policies, you would need six autographs of a British Prime Minister to swap for one of Colin Bland (the Rhodesian cricketer). I replied, as I signed, that I hoped we should not see a situation where as a result of the policies of the Rhodesian Government six autographs of a British Prime Minister would be traded in Rhodesia for one of Colin Jordan.

I left Salisbury on the Saturday morning, 30th October, leaving my two colleagues behind. We were resoundingly cheered on the way by a small number of whites and by a larger number of Africans. But the last poster we saw as we left the Salisbury suburbs and headed for the airport was one demanding 'Home Rule for Scotland'.

We were due to spend that night in Lagos, where I was the guest of Sir Abubakar. But with the load we were carrying, the Comet could not carry enough fuel for the whole journey. This gave me the opportunity to touch down in Zambia for a meeting with President Kaunda. The Lusaka runway was not then long enough for the Comet, so we landed at Livingstone where, unfortunately, the fuelling apparatus broke down and, in a temperature of 135 degrees, the Comet had to be fuelled by hand. This gave me time not only for a long talk with Kenneth Kaunda, but also the pleasure of a short flight with him to see the Victoria Falls.

We reached Lagos at ten o'clock that evening and had a meeting with Abubakar until very late. We reported to him on what had happened. He supported the line we had taken, but warned me that other African leaders would oppose any move in that direction – since, unlike himself, a number would continue to insist on no independence before majority rule.

Early the next morning we flew to Accra where we were due to be met by President Nkrumah of Ghana. On arrival, we found the local Rentacrowd organisation out in force with placards and several hundred troops. There was a red carpet and a microphone for our joint speeches. But no Nkrumah. My staff, in informing him of the time of arrival, had failed to allow for the time difference between Lagos and Accra. We were taken to the VIP lounge and entertained by other ministers, notably my unfavourite Quaison Sackey. Finally, Nkrumah arrived. He kept me there a very long time, as he argued again and again that we should not proceed on the lines being proposed. We then took off for Gibraltar, where I had the most enthusiastic reception I have ever known, even though knowledge of our visit had not been in the papers and was only communicated by radio and by word of mouth an hour or two before our arrival. What they welcomed was a gesture of support by Britain. Then home to London.

On the Monday, 1st November, the Cabinet accepted the proposal for a Royal Commission, but already grim messages were coming through from the Commonwealth Secretary and Attorney-General, indicating a complete breakdown on almost every issue relevant to the implementation of the first four principles. Mr Smith sent me a menacing telegram: 'The talks ended here this morning without managing to bring the two sides any closer. After you departed no progress was made, I regret to report.' He then again reminded me of his claim that he had made an agreement with Sir Alec Douglas-Home that Rhodesia could have independence on the 1961 constitution – the claim we had told him repeatedly was totally untrue. But he felt now that the Royal Commission would be itself sufficient to test Rhodesian opinion – not on an agreed constitution, but on his proposals.

I replied to him on 3rd November following a full briefing by my colleagues, now returned, and a Cabinet meeting to consider their report. I once again denied his claim that Sir Alec Douglas-Home had made any such offer about the 1961 constitution and, indeed, contradicted him by reference to the joint communiqué, issued by Sir Alec and himself, in September 1964. I then put forward a number of other proposals about the Royal Commission that might help to reach a solution. For a day or two more we were bogged down in exchanges about what would happen if the Commission, which on their proposal would have two Rhodesian members and one British, could not agree; whether the majority report would carry validity or whether it would be necessary to have the matter examined further. The exchanges – all set out in the British Government's Blue Book following UDI – became more and more serious, more and more urgent.

Right up to 10th November we were resisting the demand that any majority report should be automatically accepted by the British Government and, Mr Smith sought to imply, by the British Parliament.

On the night of 10th November we received clear evidence that the Rhodesians were moving to a UDI early the following morning.

I decided to try to telephone Mr Smith. Such are the frustrations of Anglo-Rhodesian telephonic communication that we were barred from speaking, first by atmospherics and then by the night closure of the relevant section of the South-African telephone system. In the event I spoke to him between 5.00 and 6.00 a.m. after having been up all night. In view of the gravity of the situation, I felt it right to have the conversation tape-recorded so that there could be no subsequent misunderstanding. Even this precaution was criticised subsequently in Parliament and in certain sections of the press by supporters of Mr Smith.

The way Mr Smith talked suggested that he was still ready to discuss one or two points of substance and, following a talk the High Commissioner had held with him the previous night, it seemed to me that one or two of the difficulties could be overcome. I gave him the necessary assurance on one of these – which he accepted – and then we went on to other points, particularly the one about the unanimity of the report. Mr Smith said he had got most of this and seemed to discuss it in quite a friendly way. He said that while this point was causing his Cabinet concern he would take my message to them. I spelled it out again to make sure that he had got it right. He then said that the last written message which his Cabinet had received gave him the impression that we were further apart and not closer together. Again we went over the ground as though we were genuinely negotiating. But then he said this:

> Well, now as I said, we are in the midst of discussing this and I take it that it would not be right of me if I do not tell you that the feeling seems to be that it looks as though this thing has gone too far. I would be wrong to say the feeling was optimistic.
> My Cabinet and I regret that this has happened at this stage because you find yourself in the position that it has gone too far, not because of actions on your part. Is this not irreconcilable?

This was not the first time that he had indicated – indeed he had been explicit in our conversation in Salisbury – that if there were a break it would not be the fault of the present British Government. Like Sir Roy Welensky he felt that it was our predecessors who had sold Rhodesia down the river; that, in fact, all the damage had been done before.

In truth, this was unfair, in that both British Governments had pursued the same attitude throughout. But in view of later charges – not only by Monday Club supporters and by leading Conservative newspapers but even by members of the Conservative leadership – that the break had been the result of our handling of it, it was helpful to know, for what it was worth, that Mr Smith felt that the fault lay not in Britain's Labour Government.

All the time he was talking, the UDI machinery was moving inexorably ahead.

I repeated that the matter was now capable of being reconciled and offered to send a senior minister out that day to settle all outstanding issues, with full authority from the Cabinet and myself. I then said that the suspicion I had voiced on the Friday night in Rhodesia was right: the decision had been taken,

> ...that members of your Cabinet – whether a majority or not, only you can say – have pretty well decided to take the law into their own hands, irrespective of any effort to reach agreement.... If anybody can now say that this position is irreconcilable or justifies illegal action I think they want their heads examining or they must have a death wish on them that is beyond what can be dealt with by ordinary rational argument such as you and I have conducted....

Every word of this exchange was published and every line of every discussion, every telegram exchanged between us was included in the

Blue Book we subsequently laid before Parliament. This was not planned 'open government'; words exchanged in the heat of the moment across the negotiating table, or even in the extremities of that last agonised telephone call, were published without editing or censorship.

'I am grateful to you for taking all this trouble . . . ,' he concluded. At 11.00 a.m. on Thursday, 11th November, UDI was declared. Mr Smith called on Sir Humphrey Gibbs to inform him. The Governor, in accordance with instructions which had been in his hands for weeks, dismissed the ministers.

Chapter 12

First ministerial reshuffle – election rumours – the Government's achievements – the Queen's Speech and our programme for the new session – the Steel Bill – the problem of Zambia – the Winter Emergencies Committee – Dr Beeching – meeting with President Ayub Khan – Anglo-Irish talks – visit to the United Nations, Washington and Ottawa – return to Britain – vote on the oil embargo – Cabinet reshuffle – the Vietnam Christmas truce

MEANWHILE, Rhodesian distractions notwithstanding, the pace of government had been speeding up on the domestic front with the return of Parliament and the Queen's Speech at hand. And while Cabinet committees, under my or my colleagues' chairmanship, were preparing the programme for the following session, other problems were pressing upon us, ranging from a visit from the railway unions worried about closures of railways and railway workshops under the 1962 Act, to a call by the Iraqi Prime Minister who came to complain – and threaten – about our policy in Aden.

On 9th October I had announced my first, very minor, ministerial reshuffle. Lord Bowden, in title Minister of State at the Department of Education and Science, in effect the Minister for Higher Education, resigned at the end of his secondment from the Manchester Institute of Technology and was replaced by Ted Redhead, an experienced educational administrator, until then Minister of State at the Board of Trade. In his place as 'Minister for Exports', Lord Brown, a prominent industrialist, was appointed to the Board of Trade. In subsequent years I enunciated a 'law' about the co-efficient between the publicity attaching to a minister's work and the reality of his achievements. In the past I had known very high co-efficients: Frank Cousins I felt had a co-efficient less than unity. But of all our ministers, over nearly five years, there was none who for quiet, effective effort, in negotiations or trade fairs abroad, still more in required visits to small groups of young exporters or potential exporters, was so successful but received so little publicity as Wilfred Brown.

Lord Taylor resigned from the Colonial Office on becoming Vice-Chancellor of Newfoundland University and was replaced by Lord Beswick. Dick Marsh was moved from his duties at the Ministry of Labour to help Frank Cousins at the rapidly expanding Ministry of Technology.

On 12th October we published the White Paper setting out our proposals for the Parliamentary Commissioner – the 'Ombudsman' –

G   173

promised, after the Conservatives had rejected the proposal, in the speech I had made at Stowmarket in July 1964. One of our big problems was the understandable feelings MPs might have if their constituents were to go straight to the Ombudsman for redress, bypassing traditional parliamentary methods of scrutinising the executive. We provided that all references to the Parliamentary Commissioner should be made through a Member of Parliament.

On the 13th, I attended the third of a series of dinners arranged by the Governor of the Bank of England to enable the Chancellor and me to meet leading City figures in an effort to remove the misunderstandings, and even mistrust, which had marked our first year.

About this time the press began to print a new series of election rumours. The story now was not that I should be forced to the country and inevitable defeat; it was that I should be stealing a mean advantage over my opponents by a snap election. It was no nearer the truth, though I was amused to read in November the criticisms of my inferior judgment in not going to the polls in October. Had I done so I should have had to recommend a dissolution early in September, when the death of the Speaker had been widely acclaimed as the death-knell of the Government.

Dr King was elected as Speaker on the return of Parliament at the end of October. I was unable to move the traditional resolution of congratulation on his election, as I was in Rhodesia. After all the speculation, Sir Samuel Storey became deputy Speaker, and Mr Roderic Bowen deputy chairman of Ways and Means.

As the Rhodesian crisis mounted, plans were aired for proxy voting to make a government less vulnerable to casual illness. The polls moved our way and previously sceptical newspapers suddenly rediscovered me as a silver-haired father-figure, and trusted I would not abuse our new-found popularity by an appeal to the country for an increased majority.

On 6th November, with UDI imminent, I went to Cardiff for my niece's wedding with a police car outside the Church tuned in by short-wave radio to my office to handle urgent messages.

But on the 7th another political catastrophe struck. Henry Solomons, who had won back the Hull North seat in 1964 with a majority of 1,181, suddenly died. It was a highly marginal seat, held by the Conservatives since 1950, but in 1955 and 1959 only by three-figure majorities.

Erith, where our prospects had only recently been written off by commentators, had not yet polled, so our majority was down to one. If we held Erith and lost Hull, it would still be one; if we lost both, Labour would be in a minority. Against this background the Government had to go on governing.

On 8th November our first session of Parliament ended with the Prorogation Speech. Prorogation would normally have taken place on the previous Thursday or Friday, 4th or 5th November, but we feared a crisis in Rhodesia at a time when Parliament would not be in session so the speech was postponed to the Monday.

The brief interval before the Queen's Speech opening the new session the following day provided a moment for those with time to ponder on our achievements over rather more than twelve months.

We had weathered the financial storm resulting from the £800 millions deficit: we were getting close to balancing our accounts, though it was a long time before the figures appeared showing how close we were.

We had entered a new era with our international initiatives, notably the ending of the independent nuclear pretence, the torpedoing of the MLF; NATO – and Europe – were moving into a new phase; industry was on the move, with the new technology accepted by Britain's industrial leaders; industrial drift and financial manoeuvring were giving way to a new sense of purpose based on the drive for export and industrial modernisation.

We had carried through a major fiscal revolution centring on the corporation and capital gains taxes.

And, despite the pre-emption of parliamentary time on the Finance Bill, we had completed a legislative programme which not only exceeded, in size and scope, any two legislative sessions of 1951–63, but which stood comparison with the best of the Attlee years, when the majority was not three but 190.

Sixty-five Government Bills, in addition to the Bill abolishing capital punishment which occupied thirteen sittings in Government time, including nine morning sessions, were on the statute book. The Prorogation Speech listed the main legislative and executive achievements:

aids to exporters; the tax reforms; the establishment of the National Board for Prices and Incomes; the establishment of the Regional Economic Planning Committees and Boards; the strengthening of scientific research, and the greater modernisation of science for technological advance in industry; the establishment of the Science Research Council and the National Environment Research Council; the enlarged and strengthened Monopolies Commission; the appointment of the Royal Commission on Industrial Relations; increased pensions and other benefits under the national insurance, industrial injuries and war pensions schemes, and increased national assistance. The abolition of the earnings rule for widows; the freedom restored to local authorities to provide for cheap travel for the aged and disabled; provision for redundancy payments and industrial retraining; the lead to local educational authorities to spread comprehensive education and end the 11-plus; new measures to increase the supply of teachers (which led to the number of student teachers being more than doubled in our period of office); unprecedented provision for the arts and the establishment of the Sports Council; legislation passed 'to restore security of tenure to tenants of decontrolled houses, to provide machinery for fixing fair rents for privately rented accommodation, and to make the harassment of tenants an offence'; measures to integrate immigrants within the community, to prohibit racial discrimination and to make incitement to racial hatred a criminal act; an act to strengthen the law on firearms; the control of office building development; the establishment of the permanent Law Commissions for England and Wales and for Scotland, the biggest step forward in law reform in centuries.

All this with a majority of three; with the inhibiting effects of the £800 millions deficit, and with the manoeuvrings of speculators who seemed determined that we should never escape from the weakness that deficit created. With, too, the preoccupations of Vietnam and Rhodesia and the Indonesian confrontation.

But there was little time for looking back. Parliament met less than twenty-four hours later for the Queen's Speech, setting out the programme for the new session. It was an exercise in continuity: Bills to give effect to White Papers we had already published and which were being turned into draft legislation, together with Bills we had hoped to introduce and which were now ready, or nearly ready; Bills to extend principles already asserted in the 1964–5 session.

To summarise, the Queen's Speech foreshadowed: the Prices and Incomes Bill; legislation and executive action for dock – and dock labour – modernisation, following the Devlin Report; new agricultural legislation, including farm structure, agricultural co-operation in buying and selling, help for the hill-farmers, and the establishment of the Meat and Livestock Commission; a consumer protection Bill on 'misleading trade descriptions'; legislation to enable nationalised industries to enter more widely into manufacturing; a bill to reorganise the coal industry's financing, including the writing off of much of the unrealistic capital burden resulting from compensation to private coal-owners (who ought, as I had argued twenty years earlier, to have been fined, not compensated); the Bill to establish the Land Commission 'to acquire land for the community and to recover a part of the development value realised in land transactions'; legislation to reform the leasehold system, including provision for leasehold enfranchisement; new Exchequer subsidies for local authority housing to ensure that new housing developments paid only four per cent interest, whatever the ruling market rate; a Bill to give legislative backing to our July decision to restore building licensing; legislation 'to lessen the injustices of the rating system and to lessen the burden of rates'; new developments in higher education, in teacher supply, and comprehensive education, and the establishment of a Public Schools Commission; 'earnings-related' benefits, to provide over and above the fixed-rate benefits and supplementary benefits for sickness, unemployment and widowhood, based on previous earnings; the supplementation of workers' compensation, and minimum rates of sick pay for agricultural workers; increased public service pensions; new Bills to reform the administration of justice and promote law reform; a move forward in company law, requiring directors to be much more forthcoming in reporting to their shareholders the real figures underlying company accounts – including contributions for political purposes; a Bill to establish the Ombudsman; Bills to provide more effective co-ordination of public transport, and improved road safety legislation.

It was a formidable programme. No one could know – certainly I did not – how long the session would last. But I was determined that we should press on with it. Ministers were instructed to introduce every Bill within the programme, even if parliamentary time was not immediately available, and, where policy had at long last been decided, White Papers should be laid if Bills were not ready.

But one measure was not in the programme. This was the nationalisation of steel, based on the White Paper approved in such difficult circumstances the previous May. It was clear that with a majority of three, even if we were able to maintain that majority, we would have the utmost difficulty in carrying a Bill through every stage of the legislative process. I was not prepared to become a hostage to Messrs Donnelly and Wyatt, to say nothing of their possible allies. We preferred to wait until we had an adequate majority.

Mr Heath, however, was more impatient, and he lost little time in coming to it in his speech on the Address: 'Is the Prime Minister not now going to tackle a problem which he described at the time as . . . "basic to our industrial effort, to exports, to our industrial efficiency"?' He even attributed our omission of steel nationalisation to 'a squalid act of political expediency by a Prime Minister who puts political power before his principles and beliefs . . .'.

I replied in the spirit of his comments: '. . . If he will give us reasonable facilities for getting the Bill through quickly, he can have the Steel Bill. . . .' But I made it clear that we proposed to go on with it at the proper time – few MPs were in doubt what I meant – but I warned '. . . in the event of serious dissipation of the assets of the companies to be nationalised or the adoption of other measures to frustrate the manifest objectives of nationalisation, we reserve the right to strengthen those provisions of the White Paper, including, of course, the terms of compensation.'

A small diversion at that point illustrated a matter of considerable constitutional importance, which was highlighted in the Northern Ireland developments five years later. I quote *Hansard*:

> *Sir Knox Cunningham* (Antrim South) *rose* – *Hon. Members:* Sit down.
> *The Prime Minister:* It really has nothing to do with the hon. and learned

Member, because under the White Paper all legislation on steel in Northern Ireland is a matter for the Northern Ireland Parliament.

For, Donnelly and Wyatt notwithstanding, the Conservatives could hold up our legislation only because they could command the votes of their twelve Ulster Unionist allies, voting on steel policy in Great Britain even though the measure could not affect Northern Ireland. As I commented soon afterwards, twelve Ulster Tories had voted to prevent us from legislating to outlaw Rachmanism, even to determine local government ward-boundaries in Northampton, when no English, Welsh or Scots Member could vote on Rachmanism in Belfast or Derry, or on ward-boundaries in any local government area in Ulster.

But this constitutional diversion had little effect on the left of the Parliamentary Labour Party, who were furious about the delay in legislating on steel. Deputations were awaiting me in my room within minutes of the end of my speech. I explained the facts of life. But, I pledged, the Bill would become law in the next Parliament, given an adequate majority. It did.

The Queen's Speech debate was dominated, however, not so much by steel as by Rhodesia. Indeed Mr Heath and I both devoted a considerable part of our opening speeches to the position there.

UDI was declared on the 11th, two days after the opening of Parliament. I broke off a Cabinet meeting to see Mr Heath and Mr Grimond. In a statement before the Queen's Speech debate was resumed I set out the most recent exchanges, culminating with the early-morning telephone call. I announced that an enabling Bill to deal with all the legal and other issues arising from UDI would be debated the following week. Since there would be a general desire for an immediate debate, the Whips were discussing changing the following day's programme, intended to cover foreign affairs, into a specific debate on Rhodesia. I announced that we were taking the initiative in raising Rhodesia at the Security Council immediately and that the Foreign Secretary would fly to New York to take charge. All the exchanges written and oral between the two Governments would, subject to the agreement of our predecessors, be published and laid before the House.

I then summarised our position:

We did not seek this challenge. The House will concede that we did everything in our power to avoid it; but now it has been made, then, with whatever sadness, we shall face this challenge with resolution and determination. Whatever measures the Government, with the support of this House, judge are needed to restore Rhodesia to the rule of law, to allegiance to the Crown, these measures will be taken....

Mr Heath played it coolly. He joined with us in deploring UDI and questioned me mainly about the Governor's action in dismissing Rhodesian ministers. Was it true, he asked, that the Governor had suspended the constitution? As for our decision to raise the matter at UN, would the Foreign Secretary continue to emphasise that Rhodesia remained a British responsibility? An impeccable statement: there was no sign of any hedging, no attempt to create what he later called 'the great divide'. I answered in the same spirit. The constitution had not been suspended, nor could it be without legislation at Westminster. The enabling Bill would deal with that. On the reference to the United Nations, I confirmed that the Foreign Secretary would continue to emphasise that Rhodesia was a British responsibility:

> ... Indeed, in one sense this is another part of the tragedy of the situation. It is more of a British responsibility today than it was yesterday, because now the responsibility is directly on this country and on this House, as no other House and certainly no other Court will have any legal right to exercise power in Rhodesia. But the extent to which what has happened in Rhodesia will create a difficult situation in Africa and the Commonwealth makes it a matter of world concern, and those who deny this are burying their heads in the sand. ...

A British responsibility – a world concern. All our policies had to recognise both these realities.

The dissent from the Tory benches at these last words was, in fact, the beginning of the great divide.

When the House debated Rhodesia the following day Mr Heath was beginning to shift his position. While conceding that we had done all we could in the last exchanges, especially on the question of the Royal Commission and on our willingness in advance to accept a unanimous report, he queried whether UDI could not have been averted if I had stayed on in Salisbury. On sanctions, he had a new phrase – they should not be 'punitive'. Mr Grimond interpreted him as meaning that they should not be effective. Mr Heath pressed more and more about the use of force, which I had rejected. He questioned the need to suspend the constitution and reserved his position on individual orders made under the enabling Bill.

I defined our attitude to the use of force in an intervention, at Mr Heath's invitation, during his speech. He was concerned that my rejection of force had been qualified by a reference in an answer to Mr Grimond the previous day to possible intervention if 'our troops are asked for to preserve law and order and to avert a tragic action, subversion, murder and so on'. 'Asked for by whom? Mr Smith?' My answer was:

> The legal Government of Rhodesia is the Governor. If the Governor were to approach Her Majesty's Government for forces, police or any other assistance to help restore law and order, we would, of course, respond to the request; we would naturally give very full consideration to it. If the Governor is pressed, whether by Mr Smith or any other private person – because Mr Smith is a private person – then the Governor, naturally, will weigh the importance of the pressure of Mr Smith and of others.

But the use of force was of concern to others as well as Mr Heath. The Foreign Secretary was having the roughest possible ride at the United Nations, where almost every 'non-aligned' nation, headed by the Africans, and supported by the Soviet bloc, was pressing for immediate action. They demanded use of troops to quell the rebellion and to arrest the illegal regime, and the imposition of a new constitution based on immediate majority rule. Although a resolution on these lines was carried by the General Assembly it had no binding force; we made it clear that any attempt to pass a mandatory resolution of the Security Council on similar lines would be met with our resistance, by veto if necessary.

Public comment in Britain has been so narrowly confined to what was to become a party political struggle, that far too little recognition has been given to the dilemma, in governmental terms, which we faced. Much too often, difficult decisions of government are dismissed in terms of a Prime Minister's reaction to pressure from the Opposition, or minority – sometimes majority – pressure from Government back-benchers, so that the real task of government is almost always reduced to parliamentary manoeuvring. In nearly every case a Government has to decide on other grounds, and in four cases out of five it has probably had to set its course – irrevocably perhaps – before it becomes a public issue, before Parliament or press has had the opportunity to react. Our policy for a Rhodesian UDI had in fact been made public from the day we issued the early-morning statement, ten days after taking office, and it had been repeated in Parliament, in negotiations with Mr Smith, and in clear public statements in Rhodesia.

So far from domestic political considerations swaying our judgment there were, in fact – I used the phrase frequently – four 'constituencies' we had to consider. In the parliamentary debate four days later I summarised the pressures and considerations:

> I do not believe that a British Government have ever had to face a problem so complicated or so apparently insoluble. I have to use a mixed metaphor to explain how the problem strikes me. What we are trying to do is to go straight down the middle of the road in a four-dimensional situation. There is the dimension of Rhodesian opinion – and that is not uncomplicated; the dimension of public opinion in Britain, and that is not entirely uncomplicated; the views that our Commonwealth colleagues have; and the dimension of world opinion, as expressed particularly in the United Nations, where it can take the form of a mandatory and possibly dangerous resolution.

The complications of Rhodesian opinion and the difficulties of assessing it had dominated months of exchanges before UDI. Now new forces and arguments were taking charge.

There were the Labour and Conservative parties at home, and British public opinion. The line we were taking because we believed it was right was, in fact, the one the party would support, though a minority – never more – consistently urged the use of force to quell the revolt. And there was always the danger of a breakaway on the right. Not more than one or two, but on the day UDI was declared our majority was only one.

From the Conservatives we expected trouble. Mr Heath had to trim his sails, conscious of the pressures, on the one hand, of a small but articulate group of liberal Conservatives, some of them ex-Commonwealth Relations Office ministers, and on the other, of the right-wing reactionaries, later identifying themselves as the Monday Club. All he could do – all he did – was to shift uneasily between them and, after a humiliating three-way split in a parliamentary division, to move to the right. I did not seriously have to consider Conservative manoeuvrings, though in early 1966 during the election – and again in 1967 and 1968 – I kept a wary eye on his pressure for resumed negotiations. It is true, of course, that had we decided to intervene by force of arms he would have led a united party, and almost certainly won majority support in the country. But this was never on.

The third and fourth constituencies were the Commonwealth and the United Nations. True, the prevailing Commonwealth attitude was reflected in the UN, but there was another force at work there, the Soviet bloc, already busy in seeking to win clients among African countries.

Taking the Commonwealth first, there was the clear fact that if we failed to react strongly against UDI, the Commonwealth, as we knew it, would break up or perhaps be reduced to a handful of the older dominions, plus perhaps Malaysia and Malawi. Two African countries, Tanzania and Ghana, did break off diplomatic relations over our refusal to intervene with force. In the first case, Julius Nyerere continued to write to me from time to time through the ordinary post and through other channels, while, in the second, President Nkrumah was not destined to survive as head of his Government for much more than three months after UDI. Their reaction was caused by our refusal to use force; to have failed to respond to the challenge of UDI in all other ways open to us would have meant a far wider breakaway. And the result would have been at least to drive one Commonwealth country after another into greater dependence on the Russians or, worse, to force them to choose between the Soviet Union and China, in what was rapidly becoming a major competitive enterprise in African penetration.

That was why it was not an exaggeration to say that the speed and direction of policy on UDI was part of 'a battle for the soul of Africa'.

But the struggle was not in political terms only. Conservatives could and did sneer at these arguments. For many of them, the Commonwealth would be a better place without the new independent countries. But even a Conservative Government would have had to count the economic cost of appeasement. And the principal key – though not the only one – was Zambia.

Zambia's economy was utterly dependent on Rhodesia. Her electricity supplies came from the Kariba dam and power-station, situated on the south bank of the Zambesi; her coal came from Wankie; much of her food supplies and nearly all of her consumer goods came from Rhodesia; her oil was from the Rhodesian refinery; her exports to, and imports from the trans-oceanic world were largely dependent on Rhodesian rail transport to Beira in Portuguese Mozambique. Kenneth Kaunda was acutely conscious of his weakness. His copper mines would stop production if Wankie coal or Kariba current were cut off. Yet he wanted to establish his independence. His demand was that we send troops via Lusaka, not only to man the northern bank of the Zambesi, but to occupy Kariba.

This we could not do, though we were concerned about a possible Rhodesian pre-emptive strike against Lusaka and the mines. And because his oil was cut off, as a Rhodesian counter-sanction, we had to embark on a major airlift with RAF Britannias and all the charter aircraft we could muster. It was not helped by a refusal by Tanzania, the nearest ferrying-point, to allow RAF personnel to stage there and pick up oil-drums.

I was anxious that Zambia's requirement for consumer goods should be switched from Rhodesia to the western world. I invited Sir Norman Kipping, retiring director-general of the Federation of British Industries, to spend some weeks in Zambia, working alongside the British economic team, identifying Zambian requirements and assisting British firms to meet them. But even three years later, when, because of her continuing dependence on Rhodesia, Zambia was rightly exempted from the UN resolution on total sanctions on Rhodesian trade, she had switched more of her purchases to South Africa than to Britain.

We were concerned – and had reason to be worried – about the dangers of a possible pre-emptive strike from Rhodesia. We offered to send troops to man the northern bank, but President Kaunda refused to have them unless they had orders, within days, to occupy Kariba. This would have been futile as a military operation. Had they succeeded in crossing the river, one civilian in a white coat could have pulled the switches before the power-station could be occupied. Dr Kaunda, however, was willing to accept the RAF, partly to counter possible Rhodesian air-strikes, partly to protect the air-lift of oil supplies. On the information available to us it could be a difficult operation. RAF fighters would be at risk without radar cover. To send the radar equipment and teams without fighter cover could be equally dangerous. In the event, the flight of the Argosies with the radar equipment was covered by Sea Vixens of HMS *Eagle*, conveniently available in the Mozambique channel.

But Kenneth Kaunda's main demand was for an air-strike capability and when this was refused he asked for the RAF to be withdrawn.

Zambia was, in a real sense, part of the third constituency. Britain was utterly dependent on her copper supplies. Had they been cut off, either by the Rhodesians or by a Zambia made sullen by our refusal to use force, we would have had two million unemployed within a matter of months. This was not just speculation; it was more than a gesture when two Zambian ministers were despatched to Moscow to discuss copper sales. True, had the Russians taken over Zambia's output we might have hoped to buy from other suppliers whose production would no longer be used by the Russians. But suppose the USSR bought in order to stockpile? It was an ugly situation and justified our sensitivity to Zambian demands for help.

The fourth constituency was the UN with the anti-colonialist world against us, even aiming at new heights of irresponsibility, whipped up by competitive Soviet and Chinese pressures. It was an unenviable position for a Government, precariously in power and with an Opposition increasingly ready to make party capital out of our difficulties. An Opposition perhaps a little deflated in mid-November, however, when a National Opinion Poll survey gave us a surprise lead of 18.5 per cent.

At home at this time there was an unseasonable cold spell which caused a failure of both gas and electricity supplies. It was no solace that the odds against so low a temperature in November were, on Meteorological Office calculations, a hundred to one: the breakdown was universally attributed to socialism.

I called the gas and power chiefs to No. 10 on 17th November. There was plenty of explanation. Electricity demand had been seriously under-forecast in the early 1960s and the plant was not there to meet it. The plant available had been kept hard at work for three years, and was long overdue for maintenance. It had been taken out of service for the summer and was not back in use when the November temperature fell. No less pathetic was the lament by the gas chiefs. A new plant at Coleshill had broken down – the new Tipton plant was still awaiting spares. I expressed myself in suitably terse language and gave directions for preventive action for the future. The gas grid was to be speeded up so that a breakdown in one plant could be made good from others, or from imported methane.

A Winter Emergencies Committee was to be set up to look ahead and take necessary action well before crisis hit us. In particular, it was to speed work on the grid, and to bulldoze through essential supplies of components and equipment. For it was clear to me that there had been serious deficiencies in supplies from the private enterprise contractors, though I had to tone down my strictures in public – lest they hit our exports! It was equally clear that the public industries concerned had not pressed their requirements adequately. From now on this would be done at ministerial level.

Few announcements gave the Opposition and their press more good clean fun than the Winter Emergencies Committee. A gimmick if ever there was one, they said – it was held uniquely responsible when there were more plant breakdowns in the West Midlands two months later. But its work in progressing plant supplies and maintenance, its action to deal with winter coal distribution and the effect of the weather on rail movements produced real results in the severe cold spells of succeeding winters, when the growing margins of electrical generating capacity over peak winter demands, and the new flexibility of the gas grid, gave us a freedom from power-cuts and lowered gas pressures such as we had not known for years.

There were problems about the pit closure programme and the miners came to see me. The Danish Prime Minister, Jens-Otto Krag, a friend of twenty years' standing, paid an official visit. Dean Rusk and Bob McNamara came to call, en route to NATO with a last attempt to revive the ghost of MLF. I said I would discuss these matters with the President when I visited Washington on 17th December.

There were transport problems. Dr Beeching, whose term of office in British Railways had expired, declared his wish to return to ICI. I wanted him to stay. No one had been more critical in 1963 and 1964 than I of the policies he was carrying through, though I blamed them on his political masters. I was impressed with his vision for the future and his plans to ensure that the new streamlined rail system should get the traffic necessary to make it viable and relieve road congestion at the same time. I pressed Beeching, and used my persuasion on the ICI chairman, Sir Paul Chambers, to agree to his being engaged, free of day-to-day responsibilities, on a survey of our transport needs and policies. Unfortunately I had not reckoned with certain of my colleagues who, road-conscious, regarded Beeching as an enemy of road transport. It was an occasion when I yielded to sectional Cabinet pressure and, looking back on it, I was wrong. Dr Beeching, shortly afterwards Lord Beeching, returned to ICI.

There were telegrams from the Foreign Secretary who was visiting Moscow and arranging a visit for me in the New Year. There was an outburst of controversy over our new building controls. In a speech at Bletchley I justified them, at a time when we had to hold back pressure on resources, by saying we wanted 'houses not casinos'.

President Ayub Khan of Pakistan was in London on his way to Washington. My colleagues and I were worried about his apparent flirtation with the Russians *and* the Chinese. Was this because he disliked and feared them less than he feared and disliked the Indians? Was he moving over, or was it the problem of a country bordering on the one and only a few miles from the other? Breaking away from a state dinner I had a very intimate talk with him and was much reassured – as was President Johnson a few days later.

On the eve of my pre-Christmas visit to Washington, the most important Anglo-Irish talks since the war took place at Marlborough House on 13th and 14th December. For months we had quietly worked, without publicity, for an Anglo-Irish free-trade agreement. By mid-December officials and visiting ministers had taken the discussions as far as they could without top-level talks. Mr Sean Lemass, the Irish Prime Minister, and I thrashed out the main points and then set up appropriate working groups. I had known him seventeen years earlier when Stafford Cripps and I and the then Premier of Eire, Mr de Valera, and he had reached an agreement ending the trade war of the thirties. This time our aim was higher, to sign an agreement which over ten years would progressively eliminate all restrictions, whether by quota or by tariff, on our two-way trade, and create a total free-trade area between our two countries.

The going was tough. Sean Lemass and his colleagues were hard bargainers. I left the negotiations to the Commonwealth Secretary and the economic ministers, making clear that I was available if needed. Hours after an agreement was expected, there was still no news from Marlborough House, but I was advised not to come as it might suggest there was a crisis. Fifteen minutes later I was asked to go round. There *was* a crisis.

I took the chair, as if I were an independent conciliator, and asked the Taoiseach and the Commonwealth Secretary to report their disagreement. We argued for some time and then Sean Lemass and I adjourned: it was a question of the lamb quota, a narrow disagreement on store cattle, some problem about British car exports, and a few details about trade across the border. There was no more we could offer, except a last-minute concession which I authorised on lamb; and there was also the fact that on a night when Marlborough House heating was excessive, the down-stairs bar, because of staff troubles, could not remain open for more than another twenty minutes. Good sense, good will, and lamb quota and thirst produced an agreement in fifteen, and the next day, 14th December, the Anglo-Irish Free Trade Treaty was signed with great ceremony at Downing Street.

The next day, 15th December, I flew to New York, to be greeted by hundreds of wild Irishmen, unimpressed, indeed uninformed, about the historic agreement signed the previous day. I was due to address the General Assembly and it was not going to be easy in the post-UDI situation. Lord Caradon had invited Commonwealth representatives to meet me on the evening of my arrival. Not all of them turned up, though an exchange of telegrams with their capitals confirmed that in many cases their instructions were much more co-operative than their subsequent behaviour. This was – and to some extent, still is – a UN problem: new countries, often short of trained personnel, are represented by ambassadors with little experience and little sense of responsibility to their home Governments, exaggerated desires to create an individual reputation and an even more exaggerated herd instinct. And the herd had decided on boycott.

The next morning, as I spoke, some twenty African delegates walked out. There is no denying that it hurt; I was a passionate believer in the independent Commonwealth. I had gone to great lengths, and risked not only political unpopularity but even parliamentary defeat in our total opposition to the policies of the Rhodesian Front. But all one could do was to be good-tempered about it. At the end of my scripted speech I made an appeal to the African delegates, *in absentia*, 'when they are able to listen': 'Today we see some of our friends, passionate to intervene and unable to do so, directing their understandable anger not against Rhodesia but against Britain. All right, I understand that. But the British Government is not going to be deflected from the course that we are convinced is right, in which I believe the whole British people are behind us.'

The speech was a reasoned defence of our Rhodesian policy and a passionate attack on racialism. But I dealt at length also with decolonisation, with nuclear disarmament, non-proliferation, including our determination that any developments within NATO must be anti-disseminatory; with Vietnam; economic and social development; and with the need to accept China into the community of nations – for, as I said, 'disarmament and history cannot wait'. I referred to our decision to provide a logistic force to help mount UN peace-keeping operations. My main theme was the need to move towards a world authority, overriding national sovereignty. And as a first step new procedures – not so much remedial, for dealing with conflicts when they arise, but preventative, for dealing with conflicts before they become acute – were needed. Michael Stewart and Hugh Caradon had done a great deal of work on this peace-making initiative, and we had a new resolution before the General Assembly for the creation of machinery designed to act in time. It was a sad reflection on the 1965 Assembly that the preoccupation with Rhodesia, with frustration leading to malice, led the delegates involved to block Britain's initiative.

The end of the speech led to an ovation which I felt was earned not so much by what I had said, but as a demonstration against those who refused to listen.

Then, in the afternoon, on to Washington, where, as had become our usual form, the President and I had a private talk. We began with exchanges about domestic politics. The old professional was still enthralled by our parliamentary cliff-hanging. To survive with that majority etc., etc. I looked at my watch, 5.00 p.m. Washington time, 10.00 p.m. at home. 'At this moment,' I said, 'the House is dividing on our proposals about the Territorial Army. I know that one of my Merseyside colleagues has announced that he will abstain. There may be more. Perhaps within ten minutes our Government will have fallen.' It did not prevent us from entering into world problems. What matters in these meetings is whether you have something to say.

In fact the President was able in an impromptu speech the next day to rib me about my 'pessimism'. 'Here he is,' he said, 'telling me last night that his Government might fall, and we have had the figures – he won by a majority of one.' Higher than on some occasions in his Senate experience – he could still not get used to the fact that while American Presidents can be defeated in Congress on a major issue and survive, for British Prime Ministers a Commons defeat can be the end.

Vietnam was high on our agenda. On arrival in Washington I received a telegram from sixty-eight Labour MPs – not from the left only, but right across the party – demanding that the US should stop bombing North Vietnam. The telegram was touched off by a report that a power-station only fourteen miles from Haiphong had been bombed, and by reports that Secretary McNamara had spoken at NATO of 'the near certainty of war with China'.

I pressed the President hard, as I had in a number of Downing Street–White House exchanges, at least to suspend the bombing to test the sincerity of North Vietnamese hints that there might be a response on their side, possibly leading to negotiations. It was clear that his mind was not closed to this, and we discussed the modalities. At the same time I repeated that if US aircraft were to bomb Hanoi or Haiphong we should be forced publicly to dissociate from that action. It was right that there should be no misunderstanding or subsequent recriminations between us.

Other subjects we discussed were Britain's military presence east of Suez and Rhodesia. At that time the Government was still committed to an effective, if limited, presence in south-east Asia, even after the end of the Indonesian confrontation. But I had to make clear that substantial cuts must be made in our Defence Estimates, then under discussion, and that these had to be reduced over a very short period of years by £500 millions in real terms. We were not prepared to carry our European and Asian burdens alone, and at a cost, measured in terms of the proportion of our national product spent on defence, far higher than that of all our industrial competitors, bar the US. When confrontation ended, I said, we should expect to cut back sharply on the military establishment in Asia. I was not even asked on this occasion for British troops in Vietnam.

On Rhodesia L.B.J. was backing us all the way, partly, I think, because though it was our responsibility his conception of Anglo-American relations dictated full support; partly because the State Department, with Africa Desk officials such as Governor Mennen Williams, pressed on him the need to keep on close terms with black Africa. He had immediately followed us in applying the sanctions which our own Parliament had approved, but there was still the outstanding question of oil. The Cabinet had decided in principle to introduce oil sanctions, though it was recognised that these would be meaningless if they were not backed by other countries with big oil interests. I did not refer to oil in my United Nations speech, as had been expected. I wanted to make sure that the US, and the American oil companies, would go the whole way with us. The President made it clear beyond all doubt that they would. As we were getting a similar response to our soundings in other capitals, we were free to announce it. The timing, inevitably, was such that Parliament could not be told first – the announcement was early Friday evening – and this, understandably, added to Mr Heath's anger and kindled his already growing opposition to our policy on sanctions.

After lunch we found that we had virtually exhausted our agenda. We then embarked on a new procedure in international discussions. I cannot remember which of us suggested it – it just grew – but it is one I subsequently found useful in other negotiations. We sat down with our advisers and quite informally discussed what each of us would say to the press – the formal communiqués of earlier visits had been dropped as our talks became more relaxed. For an hour we raised questions, and encouraged our advisers – particularly the two press secretaries – to think of the kind of questions that might be asked. It had the merit of presenting an agreed position – and also of ensuring that everything relevant, or anything which outside commentators might think relevant, was discussed.

In the evening the President, obviously well-pleased with the talks, invited Mary and myself to go with Mrs Johnson and himself to the annual ceremony of switching on Washington's Christmas lights: the first invitation to a British Prime Minister since one to Mr Churchill, twenty-one years earlier. In his speech the President referred to the hundreds of thousands of 'our boys' in Vietnam at that time. Then, touching again on my presence on the platform he referred to Britain's position as Geneva co-chairman, and said that he wanted his people to know he regarded our task as that of trying to get the parties to the conference table. He would support any initiative we proposed to that end. It was a far cry from the hot-line explosion ten months earlier.

It had been a good visit, the President clearly felt the same: very obvious briefing to a trusted British correspondent was summed up in an article headed 'How Wilson gained President Johnson's trust'.

> ... Mr Wilson's performance here was a masterly exercise in the art of the possible. He obtained full American support for the next and riskiest move against Rhodesia – international oil sanctions. . . .
> Wilson was not pressed by Johnson for any new aid to Vietnam. Instead he was left free to apply his fertile mind to exploring new avenues to bring the war to the conference table. Johnson has every confidence that Wilson is practical enough not to propose anything he could not accept.

The following morning, Saturday, 18th December, we flew to Philadelphia to spend a few hours with our elder son, then on a post-graduate course at Pennsylvania, before going on to Ottawa to meet Lester Pearson. I was sorry to read in the British press criticism of my spending part of Saturday in this way – I was, in any case, returning in time for the two-day foreign affairs debate starting the following Monday.

The Ottawa talks were uneventful, mainly covering the ground already discussed in Washington, but with more exchanges about our respective roles in NATO, and our hopes of getting nuclear talks there steered into a more constructive and less internationally provocative context. There was complete agreement on Rhodesia, and Mr Pearson gave the first indication of Canadian help in the Zambian oil air-lift. The Canadian C 130s when they came had a much bigger and speedier lift than our superannuated Argosies and Britannias. We discussed also the proposed two-day Commonwealth conference at Lagos which Sir Abubakar Tafawa Balewa had flown to London to suggest to me. Neither Lester Pearson nor I was particularly keen, but we both felt that we could not turn the proposal down and aggravate feelings in the Commonwealth still further.

I flew back through the night, reaching London Airport at 8.30 a.m., in good time for the foreign affairs debate on which hard things had already been said. It had been understood that the Foreign Secretary would open the debate and that I would speak early on the second day to report on my Washington and New York discussions. But the announcement of the oil embargo had upset the Opposition.

I anticipated the debate with a statement, after questions, on Rhodesia and the embargo. Mr Heath took this calmly enough, saying that we were to have two days' debate. But even he must have been surprised by the explosive reaction of his right-wing fringe. By the evening, therefore, the Opposition sought to change the following day's business by tabling a motion about the use of force in Rhodesia. This was not in question, but it did provide what I described the next day as 'the lowest common denominator of agreement on Rhodesia' within the Conservative party, which showed every sign of splitting wide open over the subsequent vote on the order imposing the oil embargo, for it was mildly critical but combined with a declaration against the use of force. We tabled an amendment, but refused to change the business to a narrow debate on the motion, since the House had been told that all matters of foreign and overseas affairs would be in order on both days; I had undertaken to report on my Washington visit and many of our members wished to debate Vietnam, NATO, Aden and other questions.

In the opening part of his speech Mr Heath was unusually angry at this decision, and made it clear that for his part the debate would be confined to Rhodesia. I replied to his attacks upon us, but covered a much wider canvas, as did many members of all parties who were subsequently called. His 'fears' about the use of force were fully answered: we would not attempt to restore legality by an expeditionary force. But while it was not then our intention to introduce what became known as the Beira patrol, I refused to rule out naval action to stop tankers taking oil to the Rhodesian pipeline at Beira, as part of a multilateral UN decision. Again, the World Bank was holding meetings in Lusaka and Salisbury, seeking to guarantee Kariba. If there were agreement – and this would involve the illegal regime

– to have a Commonwealth force there, we would feel free to contribute – but it would not be an 'invasion'. Nevertheless, it provided enough of a straw to enable the Conservatives to go more or less unitedly into the division lobbies. They were defeated by 299 votes to 272.

But they presented a different spectacle in the vote on the oil embargo order. The earlier sanctions orders, made under the Southern Rhodesia Act passed by both Houses after UDI, had gone through the House without a division, but with growing criticism from the Tory right.

In the oil embargo debate the official Opposition was represented only by a junior front-bencher who made some legalistic points without dealing with the principle before the House. The House divided – Ayes 276, Noes 48. The official Opposition abstained, their leaders sitting there silently and unhappily watching their party split not two ways, but three. There were the abstainers, there were the thirty liberal-minded Tories, including former CRO ministers, who voted with the Government, and there were fifty (including tellers) who voted against the order. One of our members, Reggie Paget, abstained.

From that time onwards Mr Heath moved to the right, and the political divide over Rhodesia became a reality.

But for the greater part of the day, when I was not in the House, my time was devoted to domestic matters. Among them we had to consider the report of the Plowden Committee on the aircraft industry, set up a year earlier. We had many meetings on its findings before it was published on 16th December. Its main conclusion was that Britain should not again attempt, single-handed, to produce a major military aircraft, or missile, or a new long-range civil aircraft. Joint projects with other countries which shared the cost and increased the market could be economic and should be pursued. Where they were not possible high-cost aircraft and missiles should be bought off the US production line. There should be Government participation in the shareholding of the two main airframe companies, but not in the (then) two aero-engine concerns. The other main recommendation was that a conference of European aviation ministers should be held to formulate a long-term plan to develop a 'European aircraft industry, including Britain, capable of competing with the United States'.

The Government accepted the broad recommendations, particularly the warning against costly, go-it-alone projects; but attached less importance than the committee to the share-holding in the two companies. Our view was that a single company was the right answer, with an agreed degree of Government participation. Before long the two engine companies did merge and European co-operation was pressed hard on bilateral, trilateral and multilateral projects, civil and military.

Just before Christmas I announced my first Cabinet-level reshuffle of ministers. I had discussed with Frank Soskice at the party conference in

Blackpool the likelihood that he would be rested from the arduous duties of the Home Office. He would be recommended in due course for a life peerage – but there were to be no avoidable by-elections in this Parliament. Meanwhile he became Lord Privy Seal. To succeed him I wanted Roy Jenkins, who had proved his administrative ability and courage in one of the most difficult of departments (Aviation) – and who, on refusing the Department of Education had been held in reserve for the Home Office. His going there marked a revolutionary change both in the out-dated administration of the department and in Home Office attitudes.

To make possible the appointment of Barbara Castle as Minister of Transport I intended to move Tom Fraser to Aviation. But I found him only too anxious to retire altogether. He had enjoyed the work, and in a quiet way had done well. But he – and I – had entirely miscalculated the glare of publicity which beats down on the ministry – mainly because so many newspaper readers are motorists. He had been treated pretty cruelly and he told me that neither he nor his wife could take any more of it. Fred Mulley, Denis Healey's deputy at Defence, went to Aviation instead.

Barbara's appointment received a predictable reaction from those commentators who felt that her inability to drive a vehicle was of more importance than her manifest ability to drive a ministry. I wanted not only an effective and untiring minister, but above all one who had the intellectual capacity and sense of economic issues to bring some order into Britain's confused and inefficient transport system.

She was replaced at the Overseas Development Ministry by Tony Greenwood, until then Colonial Secretary. When I had appointed him I had told him that his task would be to work himself out of a job by bringing dependent territories more rapidly forward to independence. His report on progress to independence to the Commonwealth conference showed how well he had succeeded. Lord Longford, who had been pressing for an administrative job to combine with his part-time leadership of the Lords, succeeded him at the Colonial Office.

Then to Chequers for Christmas. I was not able to leave Downing Street until very late on Christmas Eve. My colleagues, as usual, had cheerfully cleared their desks before departing, and cleared a good deal of it on to me. It was this which led to No. 10 issuing what came to be known as the 'endearing' circular. It began 'My colleagues have an endearing habit' – that of leaving me with a week's work as they went on holiday. From the following Easter onwards, they were given a date, well in advance of the statutory holiday, to work to. Papers – other than those of great urgency, or those which by the nature of the problem could not have been submitted earlier – which failed to arrive on time would be left unread until after the holiday.

But another problem kept me at my desk. President Johnson and I were in direct touch about the proposed Christmas truce in Vietnam, including a bombing pause, which I – and no doubt others – was pressing him to make open-ended after ground fighting was resumed. We were still exchanging messages until almost midnight on Christmas Eve.

A quiet Christmas with not too many red boxes to go through or telegrams to read, but one made memorable by my first visit to Stoke Mandeville Hospital on Boxing Day where Mary and I spent several hours touring the paraplegic wards. It had been the Downing Street party for the paraplegic Olympic team which had introduced me to that heroic community, and I was to be in close touch with them throughout my premiership.

Then to Scilly. More telegrams from the US. The President told me that he had decided to extend the bombing pause, and was sending Arthur Goldberg, Adlai Stevenson's successor as American Ambassador to the UN, on a world tour to explain his decision and to seek the help of those countries who had pressed him to cease the bombing in exerting pressure, now, on Hanoi to respond by a move towards negotiations. He was due to fly in to London on New Year's Day and I arranged to come back early to meet him.

The only domestic flurry was over infected corned beef. It had been established that substantial quantities which had been stored for cooling in a badly polluted river had been imported from South America and were on sale in Britain. A typhoid epidemic was reported from areas where the beef was on sale and there was public demand for the sales to stop. The Ministry of Agriculture seemed to be moving too slowly and I phoned the Minister, Fred Peart, asking him to take action at once in banning further sales. My intervention became known, and was immediately greeted as a publicity gimmick. Admittedly, I laid myself open to this: but what I was concerned with was the perennial sensitivity of ministries to the trade groups they sponsored – the Minister welcomed my giving a lead. And I had after all spent four months in hospital with typhoid fever when I was fourteen.

Chapter 13

*The Lagos conference – Mr Smith and the Hull North by-election – a
March election – Cabinet and NEC meeting at Chequers – gas and elec-
tricity crisis – the Vietnam bombing pause – the Commonwealth Food
Relief Scheme for southern Africa – national rail strike averted –
Downing Street intervention in strikes – east of Suez policy – the
Defence White Paper – discussions with Mr Kosygin – the abolition of
National Assistance – the election campaign*

ARTHUR Goldberg called at No. 10 on the evening of 1st January.
The bombing pause was now firmly in force. We responded to the
President's appeal by seeking to involve the USSR in pressures on
Hanoi to respond – but in vain.

By Monday, the 3rd, the full rhythm of the Government was re-
established. We had meetings to help forward George Brown's Fairfields'
enterprise. This Clyde shipyard was nearing bankruptcy and facing closure.
Efficiency was low, and wages more than the yard could afford. George
had conceived the idea of a new venture in workers' participation and
joint management. He proposed a new structure – financed jointly by the
unions, the Government and certain private interests – on terms which
gave the shipyard workers every incentive to co-operate in making the
yard competitive. Brilliant management by Mr (later Sir) Iain Stewart, who
had long been urging this kind of approach to the problems of industry,
led to a short-term miracle, but, as events proved, success was achieved on
the basis of tenders which proved unrealistic in the face of rising costs. In
the event, in the re-organisation of the industry which followed the passage
of the Shipbuilding Industry Act, and the establishment of the Government-
financed Shipbuilding Industry Board, operating on a system of mergers,
estuary by estuary, Fairfields was incorporated, with John Brown's and
Yarrow's, into Upper Clyde Shipbuilders.

Later in the week, on Thursday, 6th January, I had yet another
working dinner, this time for industrialists – most of them the young
men of industry who, with or without Government help, were daringly
transforming the pattern of industry by their merger and restructuring
policies.

Before I left for Lagos, for Sir Abubakar's Commonwealth conference
on 10th January, I opened the new research and library section of the
Amalgamated Engineering Union at their Peckham, London, headquarters.
I used the occasion to appeal to the trade union movement to move forward into the age in which we were living by themselves forcing the pace
for higher productivity in industry.

I had been greatly impressed over the years by my contacts with Walter Reuther, leader of the American Automobile Workers. It was his sophisticated approach to the challenge of automation, which we had discussed in Sweden in July 1963, which partly inspired my Scarborough speech of that year. He had been my guest at No. 10, and at my request had given me a brief on modern union organisation. His approach was to force the pace in industrial efficiency – the dividends of which would accrue in full measure to his members – by a ruthless approach to unorganised and backward employers. Were he to find such a firm within, or on the fringe of, the motor industry, he would proceed, by strikes or in any other appropriate manner, to organise it. Perhaps, he would say, its inefficiency was such that it could pay only half the wage his members could expect. In that case he would give them three years to come into line. Fifty per cent now would become sixty-six and two thirds per cent after a year, eighty-three and one third per cent after two years and the full rate after three. No excuses would be accepted: if the firm did not know how to raise productivity at the time rate he would put in the union's efficiency experts. He had 170 industrial consultants at Ph.D. level on his staff.

This was the basis of my appeal to the AEU, and through them to the union movement: insist on high wages, but force the pace on productivity so that every organised firm could meet them. This was, I said, 'make-or-break year', a phrase which was to be thrown back at me six months later. At that time it looked like 'make'. We were getting very close to a balance in our overseas payments, though the full figures were not available in time for us to quote, or the ever-defeatist speculators to assimilate, before we were forced into a new crisis.

I had to leave the lunch which followed the AEU ceremony to catch the plane to Lagos. We arrived about 10.00 p.m. on 10th January, and were submitted to a wildly unorganised press conference in the heat and humidity of Lagos Airport. The local press were extremely enthusiastic, being concerned to put questions that sounded more like propaganda. One importunate journalist who had had more than an innings seemed determined to monopolise the questions; I, on the other hand, was anxious that journalists from the rest of the Commonwealth should have an opportunity. Somewhat exasperated, I appealed to him, 'Look friend, do belt up, there's a good chap, and give the others a chance', a phrase which appeared on British television. It was followed by a magisterial rebuke in a letter to *The Times* regretting that a British Prime Minister should use such idiomatic language.

Sir Abubakar and I drove to the city, along a road that I came to know so well three years later. There was great enthusiasm at the roadside, but behind the cheers sounded the ominous if distant crackle of insurgent gunfire, which from time to time we were able to hear from the heavily guarded conference hotel.

When we reached our quarters, tragic news awaited us. Agreement on the Kashmir issue between President Ayub and Prime Minister Shastri in Tashkent had been followed by the collapse and death of Mr Shastri, a greatly loved Commonwealth colleague. Our conference would be over-shadowed by the news, and by our fears for the future of India, even though Mr Shastri had not been expected in Lagos. I sent an immediate telegram to George Brown asking him to fly to New Delhi for the funeral and nominated the Lord President of the Council, Bert Bowden, to take charge of the Government in our joint absence.

There were other telegrams. One informed me that the ever-ready Sir Hugh Beadle was proposing to fly to Britain for consultations with all aspects of opinion there on the Rhodesian question. I sent a reply to the Governor asking him to ground his effervescent Chief Justice and defer his visit until I was back in London.

The two-day conference opened the next day, 11th January: almost every Commonwealth country was represented at head of government or deputy level, Australia alone being represented by her High Commissioner as an observer.

There was only one subject before us, Rhodesia. And Britain was in the dock, as we had been a month earlier at New York, though this time we were dealing with principals, rather than distant plenipotentiaries, not all of whom represented their principals' views.

I presented Britain's position and then the debate began. It was hard-hitting, though somewhat repetitive, as one African leader after another sought to prove how much more African he was than his neighbour. From Asia, Cyprus, the Caribbean, the message of condemnation was the same. Then Lee Kuan Yew of Singapore spoke – an off-the-cuff unprepared speech of some forty minutes at a level of sophistication rarely achieved in any of the Commonwealth conferences which I attended. I said to my secretary that it should have been recorded and published in a journal such as *Encounter* to get on record what the modern world was really about. Lester Pearson said exactly the same to me after the morning's session.

But most of the speeches were on predictable lines. When some of the countries represented had been colonial territories, subversion – for which a number of those round that Lagos table had suffered imprisonment – had been crushed by imperialist forces. Rhodesia was a colony, why had we not acted? Towards the end of the evening, Albert Margai of Sierra Leone rose to administer the *coup de grâce*; in a devastating speech he set out the case for military intervention. Not unaware of my colleagues' propensity to brief the press, I passed a note to Abubakar asking for the right of reply. I took twenty-five minutes, in straight, almost crude, parliamentary debating style, with not a little reflection on the military fallacies of Sir Albert. But I was right – in the earlier edition of the British press next morning it was his speech, not mine, which was reported. And serious British journalists forecast – wrongly – the breakdown of the conference, if not the Commonwealth, in circumstances humiliating to Britain.

On the Wednesday Dr Banda of Malawi joined the conference. His speech was mystical and historical. After an hour, by which time he had reached 1924, he was sharply brought to order by Abubakar, who gave him five minutes to wind up. I gathered Dr Banda was vaguely supporting Britain. By tea-time we were further from an agreement than ever. I proposed an adjournment, followed by a meeting of heads of delegates only, plus one observer per delegation, for the larger the meeting the greater the temptation to play to the gallery. This was agreed and we retired to our separate delegate meetings. Ours was gloomy and prepared for a break. Malcolm Macdonald, our roving commissioner in Africa, had sounded his clients and saw no hope of an agreement.

An hour later we were back, fully agreed – on our terms – subject to a short drafting session. But this was partly achieved by my phrase 'weeks not months', based on advice we were receiving that the oil sanctions and the closure of the Beira pipeline would bring the Rhodesian economy to a halt. We had good reason to believe that Portugal would not challenge the determination of the UN, nor seek to encourage sanction-breaking. We were misled but what I said to my colleagues appeared at the time to be a safe prophecy.

The conference ended in an atmosphere of unity, even euphoria. On behalf of my colleagues and myself, as the only British Prime Minister who had attended a Commonwealth conference other than as chairman, I made a presentation of a silver plate to our highly successful chairman. Then Abubakar, full of justified pride, insisted on riding with me to the airport. Again we heard the rifle-fire. As we turned into the airport entrance he said to me, 'You have a great future as Prime Minister of our mother country. You are fortunate. One thing only I wish for you, that you never have to become Prime Minister of a federal and divided country.'

That was on Wednesday, 11th January. On the Saturday, 15th January, he was dead, and his body was later found in a ditch, the victim of a communal uprising.

Our aircraft headed south. I had promised Kenneth Kaunda, who had not felt it right to come to Lagos, that I would return to Britain via Zambia, just 3,300 miles further. He greeted us at the airport and we breakfasted with him. I met with his Cabinet and he and I then strolled alone together in the garden of State House. The talk was about Kariba, military forces, the airlift, and RAF protection against possible Rhodesian aggression. I stood firm on the line we had taken and explained our support of the Governor. I was a little shocked to hear Kenneth Kaunda describe Sir Humphrey Gibbs as a racialist.

We then toured Lusaka and visited the RAF contingent there. Lightnings

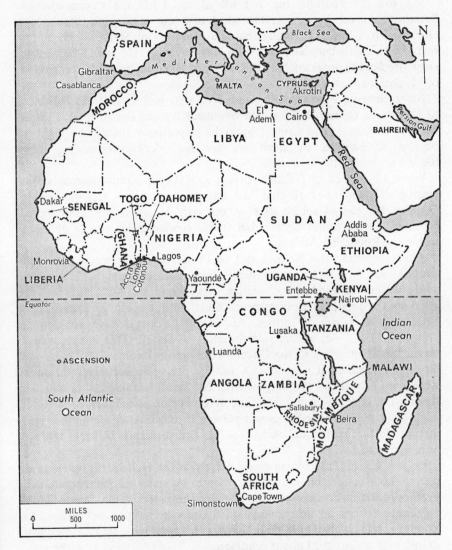

Map of Africa showing principal places mentioned in text.

flew overhead. I do not know what effect they would have had on any potential enemy – though they could have controlled Rhodesian skies – but they impressed me. We saw the air-lift in operation, and the radar establishment.

We left for Nairobi; but not all of us. I left the Commonwealth Secretary, Arthur Bottomley, behind. I had sent a message through the Governor to Mr Smith saying that the Secretary of State would, at my request, visit Salisbury and stay with the Governor. He would be glad to meet Mr Smith, provided that this was not taken as implying recognition of Mr Smith's regime.

Before leaving I saw British journalists who had flown from Salisbury to Lusaka to report on the rough treatment handed out to three Labour MPs by Rhodesian racialists. I took the opportunity during the flight to Nairobi to issue a statement via the flight-deck – condemning these Rhodesian barbarities.

When we arrived at Nairobi Airport at 4.00 p.m., Jomo Kenyatta was waiting. We discussed all that had happened since our last meeting in October. He was as robust as ever, not only in supporting international resistance to the Smith regime, but in his condemnation of the divisions within the Rhodesian Africans.

After inspecting the Nairobi end of the RAF air-lift we rejoined the aircraft, but were held up by flight-deck messages from RAF Lusaka, where Arthur Bottomley was waiting to speak to me. Mr Smith had re-acted to the proposed Bottomley mission: Arthur could go to Salisbury – but only as a private citizen. Above all, he would have no security protection. I was not having HM Secretary of State treated in that way. I sent a further message to the Governor for transmission to Mr Smith and set off for London. It was difficult meeting pressmen and television inter-viewers on arrival, not knowing whether Mr Smith had relented or whether Arthur Bottomley was by that time returning on a commercial flight. I might have guessed. Mr Smith was playing it tough. After all, he had read that an election was in the offing, and his British friends had told him we were bound to lose.

He was already intervening provocatively in the Hull North by-election, due to be held at the end of the month. A series of anonymous and electorally illegal documents, issued under the name of the 'White Rose' organisation from an accommodation address in London but printed in Rhodesia, was circulating in Hull North with urgent pleas that the recipient should vote against the Labour candidate.

I was back at No. 10 at 2.00 a.m. and had to catch a train for Sheffield at 9.45, with a speech to prepare, for a series of housing functions Then to Huddersfield, where I was due to present the prizes at the speech-day of Royds Hall, my old school. The following day I addressed a party meeting before flying back to London.

I returned – to a critical situation. A police pay claim and the railway-men's pay claim were reaching a decisive stage. The underpaid railwaymen had a strong case, on which they had been to see me months earlier. It had been referred to the Prices and Incomes Board, which reported on 14th January (Cmnd. 2873). It was an austere, almost unfeeling report, recommending virtually no improvement on the employers' offer of three and a half per cent on basic rates, with the exception of clerical workers. I put it in my box to read on the train the following weekend. It was while reading it that my mind began to harden on a March election, which until then I had not seriously contemplated. I recognised that we were in for a stormy industrial period. The Board (NBPI) was interpreting its terms of reference tightly and applying the most severe of norms in this case, which covered some of the lowest-paid workers in Britain. On the other hand, to yield incontinently to strike threats would mean the end of any meaningful prices and incomes policy, with serious effects abroad. Nor would the legislation to which we were committed make things any easier. Sooner or later there would be a confrontation, with the likelihood of a prolonged and damaging strike. It was not a welcome prospect with a majority of, at most, three, whether we were going for early legislation or not.

A great deal has been written about the decision to hold the election in March, almost all of it wrong. It has been assumed that I decided to call it following on our remarkable victory in the Hull North by-election on 27th January, when our majority was increased from 1,181 to 5,351, a four and a half per cent swing to Labour from 1964. The truth is almost precisely the opposite. I had decided on an early election quite firmly, before Hull polled. Indeed, had we lost Hull I should have had to go to the country, as the majority would then have been down to one. And there were serious reports coming in about the deterioration in the health of one of our comrades, Harold Hayman, who had been killed off in a costly stock exchange rumour one Friday in the previous summer. (He died in February.)

If anything, Hull was a signal not to go to the country. I interpreted the Hull vote not as a decisive vote of confidence but as a vote to tell us to get on with our job. Hull was not going to be responsible for forcing an election which probably few people wanted – certainly the polls suggested there was a strong majority against holding an election. The electors of Hull probably felt we needed more time before they could really decide whether we had earned their support.

If I was correct in that, it was a reason for second thoughts. Indeed, from the Hull result until well into the election my one doubt was whether the country, which had been not so much electioneering as electioneered against for well over two years, would not greet a further contest with a mighty yawn – expressed in a low poll.

But I had no intention of changing my mind about the decision I had taken to recommend a dissolution.

There was a lot to think about. There had not been a March election since 1880 (when the Government lost). There was a risk of bad weather, as in 1963 – or indeed as there was to be in March 1970 – which not only lowers morale and, therefore, Government support, but which also makes many families worse off – building and other outdoor workers are unable to work, an extra bag of coal to buy or, in other cases, more shillings needed in the meter for heating. On the other hand, there is usually a better feeling as the country emerges from winter into spring. These are difficult things to assess in electoral terms.

The timing of Easter was all right: there were no county council elections in early April. When I said on announcing the 1970 election that I had planned this in 1966, my remark caused some hilarity. But one of my worries in 1966 was that I might limit my freedom of manoeuvre for the succeeding election. I had looked up the 'golden numbers' in Whitaker's Almanac, and found that Easter in 1970 was inconsiderately early, and was followed at the wrong interval by the county and GLC elections, with the borough elections and Whitsun following. I was anxious not to be forced into a premature autumn election in 1969, nor to have to leave a decision until late 1970, when, if the omens were unfriendly, we should have to continue through a final, perhaps hard, winter, postponing the election to the very end of the statutory life of the Parliament. I worked out that it would still be possible to go on 19th March, 1st May or late June, the last depending on the date of the wakes weeks. So all was well.

What was clear was that March would mean the freshest possible electoral register; Labour is always penalised by a stale register. The registers are always issued in February on material compiled the previous October; in that sense they are four months old when published: more people have moved and may be difficult to trace. Every month after the early spring is an additional penalty for Labour.

In broader terms would it not be said – especially after Hull – that we had a mandate to stay in office, and that the country would like to see more of our 1964 manifesto pledges on the statute book before making their judgment on us? This was true, but one thing was plain to me. We might well not have much more on the statute book by the time of an October election – and I certainly was not prepared to go through another winter. It is too often forgotten that the effective parliamentary year is half over by late February or early March, and that the number of days available for new legislation is strictly limited. Though the shape of the Budget was not then known, it was more than likely that there would be a long Finance Bill. Edward Heath had climbed to the leadership on the long-drawn-out Finance Bill of 1965; his new and determined successor as shadow Chancellor, Iain Macleod, was not likely to be less assiduous in his committee-stage duties.

Moreover, some of our major commitments – such as leasehold enfranchisement, municipal housing, cheap home loans, and our proposals for dealing with land speculation – had been worked out only to White Paper stage, and many months of complicated legislative drafting lay ahead. Some could be introduced by March, but not legislated for. On my insistence, we had pushed on with legislation and White Papers, so that at least our policies were, or would shortly be, in the shop-window. There was advantage in being able to show that what we had promised in general terms made workable legislation.

A decision on election-timing is a lonely one. Whatever the consultations, it is one man's decision and if things go wrong he is as likely to be criticised for missing a favourable tide as for plunging in too early. But – before Hull – I decided to consult George Brown as deputy leader, and found he had reached the same conclusion.

I called in the Chancellor, for it was clear that a March election would be greeted with the charge that we were going to the country to anticipate an unpopular Budget. Jim's advice from the Treasury at that time was, in fact, for a neutral Budget, with little, if any, net increase in taxation. But we knew what would be said. Strangely, weeks after the decision had been taken, when I was trying to get interest shown in the possibility of a March election because I feared apathy, the press in general would not take it seriously; they had worked out that I dare not lay myself open to a charge of Budget-dodging. Jim Callaghan agreed that since we could not have a formal Budget ready before dissolution, he would make a Budget-type statement early in March, setting out the Budget forecasts and prospects, together with his broad Budget judgment.

In December I had proposed to the National Executive committee of the Labour party, who were restive about the increasing remoteness, to them, of their own Government, that Cabinet and NEC should meet all day together at Chequers on 6th February to review the course of political affairs for the months ahead. This was, as it turned out, a most useful exercise. Minister after minister opened up discussions on all the main areas of government; NEC members probed, criticised and made suggestions. Right up to that weekend there was little expectation of a general election, but the Chequers meeting revived speculation. Throughout the day there was no mention, at any rate by me, of a March election. But the meeting accepted my proposal that we should jointly work out a document on the way ahead for presentation to the annual party conference in October. I was anxious that the drafting of an election manifesto should be set in hand: I had already set my PPS, Peter Shore, MP for Stepney – who had written most of the 1964 manifesto – to put pen to paper. But a conference document, we agreed, should be worked out – I wondered how many of those present felt it might have another purpose. Certainly the press the following morning had got the message.

But there was a great deal to do regardless of the election. In fact, the first two months of 1966 were as busy as any I had known.

On the industrial front we announced that the system of investment allowances would be replaced by investment grants. The allowance system permitted a business firm to offset against the tax on its profits a percentage of any expenditure on new capital investment. This scheme had the disadvantage that investment incentives went only to the established, profit-making firm. They provided no help to new businesses, many of which we were persuading to set up in development areas. There was a further disadvantage which I had come across in my Public Accounts committee work: the system seemed unable to prevent a situation where large tax allowances were claimed without a penny having been spent on investment – one large public company had received an allowance of £12 millions in this way. We were concerned to secure a more speedy and certain repayment against new investment, similar to the milk-cheque farmers receive from the Milk Marketing Board. The investment grant was set at twenty per cent on approved capital expenditure, forty per cent in development areas.

A week later George Brown announced a new and more revolutionary change, the establishment of the Industrial Reorganisation Corporation. This idea, worked out in the Ministry of Technology, envisaged a statutory body equipped with state funds to help promote rationalisation, mergers and restructuring of industries and firms, where this was needed to help exports or to pool resources for new technological advance. Working alongside existing financial institutions, it could act either after an approach from firms interested or it could itself take the initiative, usually acting with the appropriate sponsoring department in approaching an industry or a number of firms. George Brown assembled for its board what must have been the highest-powered group of industrialists and financiers ever to sit round one table as co-directors.

The Conservatives immediately reacted, seizing on the proposal that we could safeguard the taxpayers' money by taking a share in the equity, as an alternative to providing loan capital, as 'back-door nationalisation'. They fought the proposal up and down the country and made it one of their principal targets in the general election in March.

Meanwhile – poor preparation for an election – in the last week of January there were widespread industrial stoppages through further gas and electricity breakdowns, mainly caused by mechanical failures and late deliveries of plant and components. The situation was worst in the West Midlands where there was an almost total closure of factories dependent on gas and many other stoppages through electricity breakdowns. When the crisis broke, the Conservatives were, of course, cock-a-hoop. It was the fault of the Labour Government, nationalisation and my recently announced Winter Emergencies Committee, in that order. Nightly television spelt out the crisis and our case was going by default. I sent for Fred Lee, Minister of Power, and told him to go to the areas affected, knock the heads of the fuel industries and the plant suppliers together, and get some grip on the situation.

At the worst point in the crisis I was due to address the Birmingham Chamber of Commerce, always an agreeable occasion. From past experience I knew that the predominantly small manufacturers who attend these functions are pretty right-wing in their approach, and, as the evening wears on, good-naturedly vociferous. But they were dedicated exporters, the Chamber itself sponsoring group sales missions all over the world. I was able to announce further help to exporters, including sales teams.

On the gas and electricity crisis I replied to the Opposition's attack:

> I see some of my parliamentary colleagues – across the House – have been asking about the Winter Emergencies Committee that was set up in November after the first crisis in this area.
> That committee was set up to ensure that so far as humanly possible all the actions of Government Departments were co-ordinated to deal with the problems that might arise if we had another severe winter.
> But a Winter Emergencies Committee cannot mend broken pumps, nor can it retrospectively build a gas works.
> There has been here a breakdown in national planning, through a failure to provide a sufficient margin of capacity (and we have been very near the limit through inadequate capacity in electricity as well) and, in particular, so far as gas is concerned, to provide the necessary facilities for dealing with a crisis in one area.

I went on to spell out our plans for speeding the construction of the gas grid and to increase underground storage for imported methane. With the help of two mild winters, and the work of the Winter Emergencies Committee in ensuring that the capacity problems were dealt with on time, we were virtually free of interference with production for the next few years, until further breakdowns, this time of a mechanical or structural character, particularly in nuclear plants, brought fresh strain early in 1970.

Meanwhile other radical reforms were under way. The Law Commissions were appointed. An inquiry was set up under Lord Fulton into all aspects of the civil service, the first major look at the service since the Harcourt–Trevelyan reforms of 1854.

After long, mainly bureaucratic, delays, I was able to make progress in changing the fifty-year rule about the publication of state documents. This had been pressed for years by historians and writers but our predecessors had refused to move. I was advised against shortening the period, mainly because, with the twenty-five years I was proposing, the Cabinet and related documents of a statesman who had become a minister when a young man would be laid bare and criticised during his lifetime. Even under the fifty-year rule, this could have happened to Sir Winston Churchill and others. Speaking for myself, I said I would rather be alive to hit back at all who would in the seventies wish to savage my infant documents of 1947–51. In the event, I settled on thirty years, but had the devil's own trouble in getting the Opposition's agreement, since these matters must carry the assent of all parties before a recommendation can be made to the Queen. In the end, with the election near, I told the Opposition that if they could not agree, our respective cases should be threshed out in public. Mr Heath finally agreed and, in addition to the general thirty-year period, it was provided that on matters of great public, perhaps international, interest – we had in mind such events as Indian independence – the Government might publish volumes of the relevant documents ahead of the thirty-year period and, where appropriate, commission outside historians to write an 'official history'. These operations were to be supervised by an all-party committee of Privy Counsellors.

On 10th February I announced the appointment of two Royal Commissions on local government, for England and for Scotland. Wales was excluded, as proposals for local government reform in the principality were far advanced through the consultations of the Secretary of State with all the interests affected. The pattern of local government had – and still has – remained virtually unchanged since the early 1890s, being governed by the Acts of 1889 and 1894, passed before the advent of the motor-car and the need for a modern road system, before Parliament laid on local authorities the responsibility for secondary education, for teacher training, for the people's housing, and health and welfare – including the welfare of children – and for town and country planning. Local authorities, following a pattern prescribed three-quarters of a century earlier, were inhibited in dealing with so many issues where decisions had to transcend local boundaries.

Sir John Maud, now Lord Redcliffe-Maud, and Lord Wheatley were subsequently appointed as chairmen for the English and Scottish Royal Commissions respectively.

Then, suddenly, the Labour party was deep in a new crisis over Vietnam. Hanoi had made no response to the continued American bombing-pause and on 31st January President Johnson ordered the resumption of the air attacks. The Foreign Office, falling over itself to get into line, issued a press statement supporting the President's action. By an error, this was not submitted to me for approval. I would not have agreed to a statement in those terms. The left was justifiably outraged and an attempt was made to secure a Standing Order No. 9 Adjournment debate; ninety MPs, again going far beyond the conventional left, telegraphed Senator Fulbright supporting his attack on the President.

At the Parliamentary Party meeting the next morning – which would normally have been the occasion for drawing the lessons from Hull North – there was a major storm, and I replied for some thirty minutes on Vietnam. It was disappointing that with an election so near – though my friends on the left could not know that – we were presenting the image of a badly split party. Manny Shinwell, chairman of the Parliamentary Party, who had formed his own views about election-timing, warned them that the country would not re-elect a Labour majority if they became a 'disunited rabble'.

The following Tuesday, 8th February, the Opposition chose to devote their day on the Consolidated Fund Bill to a debate on Asia, including Vietnam. One reason was their fear that the Defence White Paper then in preparation would foreshadow a run-down in our presence in southeast Asia. It was no less clear that after recent comment about divisions in the Conservative party, they wished to exploit Labour's differences over Vietnam. They were not disappointed.

I put the Government's point of view. We had pressed in Washington for the Christmas truce, both in ground fighting and bombing, to be extended. The President had agreed, and we had exchanged telegrams throughout Christmas. On ground fighting, America promised not to re-open hostilities by firing the first shot. It was, in fact, the Vietcong who started the ground fighting. Even then the bombing did not begin again: the pause lasted forty days. In addition to the American 'peace offensive' in non-aligned capitals, we had sent repeated messages to Mr Kosygin and to Hanoi. We had pressed throughout January for the pause to continue through to the Vietnamese New Year, because the North Vietnamese needed time to think their position through. Because the President had agreed to our demand for the extension, because, in forty days, there had been no response, we must understand his position now. As interruptions from our back-benchers grew stronger, I concluded:

> I hoped that it was true that if America would agree to the cessation of bombing, that would create conditions in which Hanoi would come to the conference table. This is why I find it difficult to understand why those who urge this so strongly on me – although I did not need any urging: it was one of the cardinal principles stated in the report of the Commonwealth conference – were not so vocal and demonstrative, once the 40-day bombing truce had begun, to see that the same pressure was put on the other side in Hanoi. . . .
>
> We have had speeches, resolutions, demonstrations and telegrams, but I would have been more impressed if the international cables during the 40-day truce had been sizzling with messages to Hanoi and to Ho Chi Minh saying, when one thinks of all the pressures brought on the United States, 'Now conditions for talks exist. Now play your part. Your friends in this country who want peace expect you now to respond.' I should like to have seen 'Peace in Vietnam' outside the Chinese Embassy. . . .
>
> I should have liked to have seen the peace lobby outside the Chinese

H

Embassy demanding that the Chinese Government should use their influence ... on Hanoi ... to make peace.

Conservative back-benchers – and some on the front bench – had reacted to the debate on the greatest human tragedy of the postwar world with great merriment, and not for the first time or the last. Referring to the sincerity of Labour back-benchers' feelings on Vietnam, I said that I had often wanted to see 'similar passion shown by hon. Members opposite on this – I should sometimes like, when we are going through these questions, to have the smirks taken from the faces of some hon. Members opposite, who look on this question not in terms of the tragedy it is, but in terms of a little innocent fun in regard to the front bench and back benches on this side. ...'

Vietnam was not the only question at this time to engage the Tory sense of humour. They were in full cry on a humanitarian issue in Africa.

A great part of central and southern Africa, particularly Bechuanaland and Basutoland, but also Rhodesia, was suffering from a prolonged drought, involving the danger of severe malnutrition and the slaughter of livestock herds. So far as Rhodesia was concerned, our sanctions were strictly limited to those directed against the economy and industrial development. They were not directed towards starvation. But the Rhodesian press was reporting that whatever the terrors British sanctions might hold, divine sanctions were more immediate and devastating in their effects. It was not only urgent that our sanctions should not endanger the lives of innocent people; we had a duty to help, regardless of constitutional controversy, regardless of illegality. I therefore telephoned Lester Pearson and Bob Menzies, Prime Ministers of the Commonwealth's two major grain-producing countries, proposing an immediate Commonwealth food relief scheme, in the cost of which we would participate, to bring help to the countries concerned, which must include Rhodesia. They responded, and we approached South Africa for help in getting relief through to the High Commission territories. A message was sent to the Governor of Rhodesia offering help and authorising contact with Mr Smith for the purpose.

But the grain we were sending to Africa provided grist to the Conservatives; it was all huge fun; it was a gimmick, like the Winter Emergencies Committee. It passed into Conservative mythology and was still a good cheer-line for the faithful five years later. As the crisis grew, Tory MPs played out a comedy on the Westminster stage. By that time the help we had given was already feeding 105,000 of Bechuanaland's 540,000 population, to say nothing of animal feed, and a new programme was just starting for Basutoland. Zambia had not yet calculated her import requirements. 'In the case of Rhodesia,' I told the Commons on 3rd February, 'the information which has reached us suggests that the situation with regard to food supplies for the human population there is not critical but may become so, in which case we will take action to deal with it as soon as the crop figures are known . . .'.

One pro-Rhodesian MP, Mr Patrick Wall, did in fact take the problem seriously and asked us to step up action to help the Matabele. I told him:

> . . . We took immediate steps to see what were the requirements in Rhodesia, in spite of some scathing remarks of Mr Smith about this exercise and his unwillingness to co-operate in working out what was required. We have got information suggesting that with the recent falls of rain there is no immediate crisis so far as foodstuffs are concerned. We shall hear from the Governor what requirements are and we shall take immediate steps to see that supplies get there.

In the event the belated rains saved the situation in Rhodesia and Zambia. But how the Conservatives would have condemned us if we had not acted – and the rains had not come! The fact that we had – evidence of another 'gimmick' – provided a continuing charge against us long after the details were forgotten.

It was not only Rhodesian food which was becoming a party issue; on Rhodesia itself the Conservatives were busy distancing themselves from the position they had taken up when in Government and, indeed, up to and after UDI. After the humiliating three-way split in the parliamentary vote on oil sanctions, Mr Heath lost no time in moving towards his party's big battalion, the fifty hard-liners who had voted against us while he and his front bench abstained.

This change began in January and, I suspect, was touched off by a visit of Sir Hugh Beadle. My proposal to the Governor from Lagos that Sir Hugh should postpone his projected visit was accepted and he came later in January. He was already shifting his attitude away from the Governor's staunch position to some kind of accommodation with Mr Smith. Looking back I could see that Mr Smith's puzzlement when I met him on my last night in Salisbury might have been due to the fact that Sir Hugh, in his self-chosen role of messenger boy between us, had spoken in two voices to Mr Smith and myself. In London he spoke to me in firm support of the line the Governor was taking, but an article he wrote for the *Sunday Express* was construed as a rejection of our policies and a call for direct negotiations. When I asked him about this he said he had been misunderstood. I am not sure that Mr Heath misunderstood him, and Sir Hugh was embarked on a course which finally led to his summary ejection from Government House by an angry Governor who had put up with his presence for over two years following UDI.

Within days Mr Heath, who not long before had said that there could be no talks with the regime, was nailing his flag to negotiations, and attacking my 'stiff-necked' attitude. This was the same Opposition leader who had reacted sharply when I had referred to the regime as a 'police state', and was criticised by me for so doing, but who – perhaps under pressure from his moderates – had himself a few days later used the same phrase. It was clear to me that in the coming election Rhodesia would become a major party issue, not so much, I think, because Mr Heath thought there were any votes in it – there were not – but because his conception of leadership meant an undue degree of responsiveness to his party's intransigent right wing.

In the middle of these preoccupations we were faced with the threat of a virtually certain national rail strike. The National Union of Railwaymen was angered by the Government's decision to refer its major pay claim to the NBPI, the first action of this kind that we had taken. It was still more angered by the Board's report recommending no improvement on the employers' offer of three and a half per cent on basic rates, giving a possible increase of earnings of six and a half to seven and a half per cent; clerical workers were to have only five per cent, against British Railways' offer of three and a half per cent. The railwaymen made it clear that they would not accept the NBPI recommendations. On 4th February they formally rejected British Railways' final offer – which, while not going beyond the NBPI figures, proposed that it should take effect at an earlier date and suggested also specific measures to improve productivity which would give more time off. The strike was announced for 14th February.

During the week efforts were made – first by the Ministry of Labour, then by DEA – to get the parties together. The Government was faced with a dilemma. A rail strike could be very damaging, despite the emergency measures we had prepared. It would not help politically on the eve of an election and it might last through the greater part of the election period. At a ministerial meeting which I chaired at 3.15 p.m. on 7th February, we agreed that we could not put pressure on British Railways to offer more; not only NBPI but the wider prices and incomes policy could be fatally prejudiced.

On the Friday, 11th February, less than three days before the announced start of the strike, George Brown called both sides in to DEA. The talks went on through the morning and through lunch-time.

George suggested, and the employers accepted, a further short antedating of the proposed settlement. There was some movement among members of the union executive, and George had the bitter disappointment of seeing a motion to accept British Railways' offer defeated by only one vote. In the early afternoon the meeting broke up, with no apparent prospect of avoiding the strike.

All the ministers concerned – George Brown, Ray Gunter and Barbara Castle – felt that I should now intervene. This had to be done quickly, for most members of the NUR executive were working railwaymen, drawn from every part of the country. Some would be leaving London that afternoon. I called them to a meeting at No. 10, with the British Railways Board standing by.

First, I saw Mr Stanley Raymond, chairman of British Railways. I confirmed what I had told him when he had come to see me two days earlier, that we were not pressing the Board to go any further, either in cash terms or in advancing the date of first payment.

So much legend has grown up, particularly since the change of government in June 1970, about beer and sandwich parties at No. 10 with ministers, led by myself, twisting the arm of employers to make inflationary settlements, that it is time to state not only the facts, but what I regard as the principles that should regulate intervention by the Prime Minister in an industrial dispute.

He should intervene only as a last resort and no party to a dispute should be encouraged to believe that he will intervene at all. In no circumstances should he be regarded as a court of appeal ready to reverse or amend what the ministers responsible have urged on the parties. In the main – there can be exceptions – he should be prepared to intervene only when there is a procedural deadlock which cannot be resolved without his intervention. One exception is a strike which could inflict severe damage on the economy and where there is a chance that there could be a last-minute change of heart. Another is where the Prime Minister's authority is needed to make clear beyond all doubt that what his ministerial colleagues have told the unions and employers is the last word. A rare case is where someone's face needs to be saved, with no real issue at stake, with perhaps one side refusing to meet the other.

During my five and a half years as Prime Minister I intervened directly in only five disputes.

The first was that railway dispute in February 1966, where the margin on the executive was only one vote, where there was doubt about the Government's determination and a distinct unwillingness to look ahead to all the rich prospects in terms of increased wages of a genuine long-term productivity agreement.

The second was the seamen's strike in May-June 1966, which was not only likely to be severely damaging to Britain's prospects of recovery, but in which it was essential to make clear that, on grounds of incomes policy, the Government could not press the employers for a higher offer; in which, too, a basic cause of the dispute was deep-seated bitterness about an issue only the Government could resolve, namely the seamen's demand for new legislation to amend the hated Merchant Shipping Act of 1894.

The third was the Liverpool dock strike in October 1967, the damage from which aggravated the foreign exchange movements which forced devaluation. I was in Liverpool on constituency business, and in touch with the progress of discussions. Even so I should certainly have refused to intervene had not a procedure deadlock occurred at 4.00 a.m., when the employers decided to break off talks and to issue a provocative press statement. Faced with this, it was the ever-patient Jack Scamp, who had presided over the talks for some eighteen hours, who recommended my intervention. All I did was to get them back round the table; by breakfast-time they had hammered out an agreement which led to a resumption of work the following week.

The fourth – another rail strike – was in December 1967. This was the famous 'who-sits-where?' dispute when ASLEF, the drivers' union, called a strike on the question of where guards should sit on a diesel loco. Here I was asked by Mr George Woodcock to call the union to No. 10 at 11.30 p.m. for one reason only: to make clear that what the TUC General Council members had already told them was not going to be changed – it was a face-saving operation.

The fifth was the newspaper strike which occurred in the middle of the General Election of June 1970. The issue I had to resolve was purely procedural, though of prime importance. The proprietors refused to sit down with the union which had made the claim (SOGAT) unless the other unions, particularly the National Graphical Association, whose claim would come later in the year, were there too. The reason was their determination to end the leap-frogging system which had worsened industrial relations and made newspaper economics impossible for years. SOGAT rejected a multilateral meeting, nor were NGA willing to attend. Every newspaper faced a shut-down the following day and, at that stage, over a purely procedural issue. I called in all the parties and put to them an idea of my own for breaking the deadlock. This was accepted in each case within minutes and led to a fully representative meeting that evening. The ultimate wage-deal – whether inflationary or not my newspaper critics must decide – was a matter purely between the parties, with no pressure or intervention by myself or any other minister. I withdrew from the discussions once the procedure for further talks had been agreed.

Since the legend to which I have referred was much invoked at the time of the national dock strike in July 1970, I put it on record that the criteria I have outlined would have justified intervention then by No. 10, since a procedural deadlock had occurred in that the employers refused to sit down with the unions in view of the state the negotiations had reached. Had the Prime Minister intervened, a wholly unnecessary strike would have been avoided and the ultimate settlement, reached after two weeks of damaging disruption, could have been secured on exactly the same terms without a stoppage.

In the railways dispute of February 1966 I had to do two things. First, to make clear, lest there was any element of brinkmanship among the executive members, that there could be no question of any agreement going beyond what George Brown had discussed with them earlier in the day. This I did, though it took hours for it to be accepted. Again, contrary to the legend of inflationary settlements, the final agreement varied by not a penny in amount, nor a day in terms of dating, from the one which George Brown had so narrowly failed to persuade them to accept eleven hours earlier. Secondly, I had to try to raise their eyes beyond the immediate grievance about which they and their members felt so strongly. Here Barbara Castle, who as sponsoring minister took an almost parental interest in those who worked within her ministerial sphere, was most helpful. With little encouragement she spoke for twenty minutes, weaving a web of hope: higher productivity and higher wages in the not very distant tomorrow. I seized on this, and all the evening until well past midnight we were offering this as the solvent. I said the Government would ensure that meaningful productivity talks were held and, if they wished, they would open under my chairmanship. A little after midnight the NUR executive asked to have a private meeting, and they retired to the Cabinet offices. After what seemed an age they returned: by thirteen votes to ten they had decided to accept the agreement and call off the strike.

It was most welcome news. The lines were cleared for the election. *The Times* in its leading article on that Saturday morning, 12th February, began: 'All credit to Mr Wilson for getting the railway strike called off without the payment of any further ransom money.' They had taken the point, though it did not prevent the 'surrender' legend developing.

As for beer and sandwiches, the facts were funnier than the fiction. Expecting late-night talks, I had asked that the Government Hospitality Fund (GHF) should be ready to serve drinks and sandwiches at any time during the night. They are good at most things, even at short notice. But the sum total of their provision was an inadequate number of paper-thin smoked salmon and cream cheese sandwiches, not much larger than postage-stamps. In a hungry moment during one of the adjournments I ate six, and felt no better for them. The railwaymen had had hardly any lunch. At this point my political office and household took charge. My wife, secretaries and housekeeper started to cut sandwiches, filling them with everything in our kitchen. Our bread was soon running out – emissaries were sent to the police canteen at Cannon Row. (A Scotland Yard legend subsequently had it that a police van with loaves in the back for us received a 999 call and the loaves were taken on a chase round Lambeth before being delivered, too late, to No. 10.) A friend of mine was seen among the waiting journalists and despatched to tour the main-line stations' all-night refreshment rooms, buying up their entire stocks of cold sausages. When the bread ran out a member of my staff, not content that the Chancellor's family should be sleeping through all this, went through the ever-open door to No. 11 and burgled Jim of his one remaining loaf. All my stocks of whisky and beer were mobilised to help in lubricating the machinery of industrial relations, as were the cigars I kept for visiting statesmen.

So much for the legend. A slightly sheepish civil service machine whose action to invoke GHF had failed so lamentably asked me for an account to cover the running down of household food stocks, to say nothing of the run on liquidity. I refused to charge a penny but insisted that since the Chancellor had been inconvenienced an account be sent to the Treasury to reimburse him. Somewhere in the recesses of the labyrinthine financial machine of the Treasury there must exist to this day an approved expenditure chit for 1s 3d for the reimbursement of the bread account of the Rt. Hon. L. J. Callaghan MP.

Later, on 11th March, the opening day of the election campaign, the *Guardian*, under the heading, 'Mr Wilson redeems his pledge to the railwaymen', reported, as did others, the meeting I chaired at No. 10 of representatives of railway management and the three railway unions to inaugurate the new machinery for creating increased productivity with higher wages, and a new pay structure for the industry. They worked hard – it was a longer job than expected – and before long Barbara Castle was once again using all her considerable charm and persuasion to break the deadlock over rail containers. But when the productivity agreement which we had envisaged at Downing Street was finally carried through, it brought about a totally new structure and a new deal for Britain's railwaymen, paid for out of higher productivity.

Another issue which caused trouble in this pre-election period was defence. We were engaged on the difficult task of securing the required saving on defence while still maintaining some post-confrontation presence east of Suez. Our left wing and a minority of the Cabinet favoured pulling out totally; a majority, including myself, moved more by thoughts of a contribution to international peace-keeping than by considerations of imperial splendour, favoured the retention of a minimum force there.

But in immediate terms the issue was not so much the strategy as the decisions we had to take about air and naval forces. Denis Healey, after long consideration, had come down in favour of phasing out the existing aircraft carriers in the seventies, when they became unviable, and to place no orders for new carriers, relying on shore-based aircraft to support our other arms. We had some talks with Australia about the possible use of a base in north-west Australia but these came to nothing. There was a tremendous battle within the Defence Department, involving Service ministers as well as chiefs of staff, on the carrier controversy. The final defence advice was to phase the carriers out. There was a sharp revolt from the Navy and, in the event, the First Sea Lord, Sir David Luce, resigned with quiet dignity. The Minister of Defence for the Navy,

Christopher Mayhew, also resigned. It was a difficult situation, just nine days before an election was due to be announced.

The Defence White Paper was published on Tuesday, 22nd February, followed by Mayhew's resignation statement, made while I was in Moscow.

We announced that the final withdrawal from Aden would be in 1968. (It was, in fact, achieved in 1967.) There would be reductions in Malta, Cyprus, Guyana and, after confrontation, in south-east Asia. We considered a major transfer from Germany to Britain because of the continuing foreign exchange cost, even after securing an improved off-set agreement. But it was clear that the budgetary costs of building accommodation in home bases would far exceed the budgetary and foreign exchange savings which withdrawal would bring. It was decided to purchase a number of American variable-geometry F 111As as a Canberra replacement, to strengthen our shore-based aircraft. These were to be paid for by off-setting orders for British equipment to be negotiated with the American Defence Department.

When the White Paper was published I was in Moscow, accompanied by the Minister of Technology, Frank Cousins – for a large part of our discussions were to be about trade and technological exchanges – and by the Minister of Disarmament, Alun Chalfont. We were due to arrive on Monday, 21st February at Vnukovo Airport, where Mr Kosygin and his colleagues, military bands and a massive guard of honour were waiting. As we came down in thick fog, we suddenly saw trees on both sides; our Trident pilot swooped the plane up almost off the ground and we made for Sherematievo, thirty miles away. While the reception party dashed along icy roads – one of its cars crashed in a ditch – we circled, and finally landed to be warmly received by Mr Kosygin and the members of the supreme Presidium. We were taken to our *dacha* and talks began almost immediately.

On trade and technology we made considerable headway: I had known Mr Kosygin for many years, long before anyone ever forecast that either of us might reach the premiership, and had discussed these questions with him long into the night. But on Vietnam we got nowhere. In plenary sessions Mr Kosygin and his colleagues took a hard line, and in a long private talk with Mr Brezhnev, the Party Secretary, he took an even harder one, combining with it a long and baleful analysis of the German problem. In private Mr Kosygin was more ready to talk – particularly in the intervals of a Kremlin performance of *Baktchisarai Fontan*, when we had food and drink and a much franker discussion with only his interpreter and Lord Chalfont, who was acting as mine. We went over the history of the bombing-pause and our disappointment at the lack of any response from Hanoi. But what became clear – and this really confirmed the terms of his response the previous June to the projected

Commonwealth peace mission, and his lack of response to our appeals during the bombing-pause – was the inability of the Soviet Government to exert any real pressure on Hanoi in the face of continuing militant Chinese pressure. I tried to explain to him – and at an Embassy function I think I partly succeeded – something of American thinking and the sincerity of the President's desire to get round the table and ultimately to effect a total withdrawal of American troops.

We did manage to get a line through to Hanoi. With Mr Kosygin's agreement Lord Chalfont had a six-hour talk at the North Vietnamese Embassy with a high-powered delegation then in Moscow, but without any concrete result. He had successful talks with the Soviet disarmament ministers, leading to an invitation to him to visit Moscow a month later for more detailed talks on the proposed non-proliferation treaty, talks which, I believe, helped to break the deadlock.

My talks took place in an atmosphere of unusual cordiality, far more friendly than Mr Macmillan's visit in 1959 had been. The British press reports reflected this. The *Daily Express* began their mid-visit report:

> Mr Harold Wilson established one fact of paramount importance at the start of his meetings with Soviet Prime Minister Kosygin, here in Moscow today.
> The Russians want to talk. They may not be ready to make any major moves, but they are anxious to keep open the line to London – and through London to Washington. . . .
> Since his arrival he has been loaded with marks of favour. *Pravda* has most unusually front-paged his biography and picture.
> There was a tremendous turn-out of the Soviet top men at today's luncheon of welcome in the Kremlin.
> Most Ministers and 12 members of the Supreme Presidium were present – a big gesture from the Russians.

The following day I had an open press conference at the Moscow Press Club, where I enjoyed ribbing some of their top journalists whom I had met in many previous visits. This was followed by a nation-wide television broadcast seen, it was reported, by forty million Soviet viewers. It was partly in English, with dubbed translation, partly in my inadequate but quasi-phonetic Russian. In both, as in my Kremlin speech, I stated our position on Vietnam: 'We agreed this morning that there can be no military solution in the interests of the people of Vietnam.' I stressed – as I had done in an earlier broadcast on Russian television when Leader of the Opposition – that we were and would remain loyal to our alliance and friends, as they would to theirs. Any proposals we would make would be from a position foursquare within our alliance; but we and they, each loyal to our friends, could begin to build a bridge which recognised world realities, but could seize world opportunities. I tried to shake their long-established and understandable German obsession, and said: 'No Government of which I am head will ever agree to a German finger on the nuclear trigger. But the problem of non-proliferation is not a problem of Germany alone.' I went on to warn of the danger of a nuclear arms race getting beyond the power of any nation to finance and beyond the power of any nation to control.

The visit was, I think, a success. When we drove from our last Kremlin meeting via the *dacha* to the airport on Thursday, 24th February, every lamp standard bore the British and Soviet flags, and the streets were lined with thousands of flag-waving 'factory workers who had come to cheer', which always spontaneously happens when the Kremlin is pleased with the way a visit has gone. This was the conclusion, too, of most of the British press. The *Daily Express* summarised the visit with a second headline: 'Wilson's visit succeeded brilliantly – but only because the Russians wanted it to.' There was much comment on its effects on the now-expected election, and on my motives for the visit. In fact it had been arranged long before I had seriously considered a March election. I doubt if it affected the voting one way or the other. I would have preferred from the political point of view to have been at home during the defence difficulties.

In my last Audience with the Queen on 27th January, before she left for her Caribbean tour, I had informally mentioned the probability that I should be recommending a dissolution for the early days of March, by which time she would be back in London. She agreed that the formal recommendation to enable the forthcoming dissolution to be announced in advance could be sent by secure telegram. A fortnight before this was sent I wrote a letter setting out my recommendations, to which the Queen replied in her own hand.

I decided that the announcement should be made on 28th February, a full calendar month before polling day on 31st March. On the 26th I had to speak to a political rally in Carlisle; it was fearfully difficult to avoid a slip about the announcement. Members of my political staff, sitting in the front row, had their hearts in their mouths when I began a sentence, 'And next Monday...'. In fact, my disclosure about 'next Monday' was the result of a quick mental calculation I had just made: the Labour Government would have been in office for five hundred days.

Parliament continued to meet for a further eleven days in a mounting election atmosphere. There was a great deal of essential parliamentary work to get through, particularly routine financial business, including the Defence and Civil Estimates, Supply days and the Consolidated Fund Bill.

On 1st March Jim Callaghan opened an economic debate with the pre-Budget speech we had agreed he should make. He was able to present a reassuring picture of the improved trade position and the rapidly improving balance of payments; to report progress on repayment of short-term debt and on a much healthier position in the development areas;

of the twenty-nine thousand fall in unemployment in the year to February 1966, twenty-eight thousand had been in Scotland, the north-east and the north-west. He followed what he called the 'Budget judgment' by giving advance notice of a number of tax changes.

Although in July 1965 we had had to announce, amid gibes and accusations of broken pledges, that we should have to defer our promised help to owner-occupiers, he said that in the Budget proper he would introduce the mortgage-option scheme. This would give anyone taking out or holding a mortgage the option either of paying the full mortgage interest rate and claiming income tax relief, or of forgoing tax relief and paying mortgage interest at two per cent below the ruling rate. With building society rates running at six and a half per cent this would mean a mortgage rate of four and a half per cent for anyone deciding to join the scheme. The calculations were such that any householder paying less than the standard rate of income tax would benefit by taking the option.

The Chancellor also announced a tax on betting and gaming, and set out the details.

A measure of rate relief, over and above our quite generous legislation to help low-income ratepayers, had already been announced, and the Chancellor explained how this would work – £30 millions of Exchequer aid to local authority rates, to bring about a reduction of 5d in the pound on the domestic rate, in the first year; £60 millions (10d in the pound) in the second year; £90 millions (1s 3d in the pound) in the third year, and so on. He pointed out that Mr Heath, who the previous week had made a pledge to cut taxes, had complained that the rate of subsidy was not enough; it should be at least £100 millions in the first year alone.

In the last week before dissolution we had the annual defence debate, which Denis Healey handled with the greatest of ease. The Chris Mayhew 'sensation' was as though it had never been.

Also in the last week – and the rush of statements about Government decisions, which I had asked three months earlier should be speeded up, must have appeared a little blatant – was the announcement by Margaret Herbison, the Minister of Pensions and National Insurance, that National Assistance was to be abolished and replaced by supplementary benefit, as of right. Entitlement and payment would be by a single pension book, ending the humiliation of the two-book system, under which proud old people could not help showing to their neighbours that they were 'on National Assistance'. We attached great importance to this change. The National Assistance Board and the relevant departments of the Ministry of Pensions and National Insurance would be merged into a new Ministry of Social Security. When the election came I found the abolition of the two-book system to be one of the most popular of all our reforms. Hundreds of thousands of old people so hated the indignity of 'going on assistance' that wrongly, but understandably, they failed to claim help to which they were entitled. One result of the reform was that 450,000 of the least well-off members of the community now claimed their rights.

On 10th March, the Prorogation Speech was read and Parliament was dissolved later in the day. Twenty-one Government Bills had received the Royal Assent in the short four-month session, but most of the major measures foreshadowed in the Queen's Speech the previous November were in a long list of unfinished business, brought before Parliament but not yet law. Many of them, together with other announced Bills on which we were working, were among the principal issues in the election.

The election campaign proper began the following day, 11th March. I celebrated my fiftieth birthday by opening Labour's campaign in Glasgow.

This book is not the place to describe the 1966 election, which was lively and exhausting but in the main enjoyable. I would refer only to two issues of major Government policy.

Mr Heath decided to make the opening of negotiations with Mr Smith a major election issue. It made little impact, but to make assurance doubly sure I attacked him strongly for the general change of mind in his policy in a speech which I made at Southampton half-way through the campaign.

But that was not all. Unknown to Mr Heath, I had sent a senior Commonwealth Office official, Mr Duncan Watson, to discuss how a return to legality might be worked out. Mr Watson was not authorised to enter into any discussions with Mr Smith or his colleagues without specific authority from No. 10. Nothing emerged; Mr Smith was too busy making statements to British newspapers calling on the electors to throw us out. Mr Watson's visit did, in fact, leak into the press from Salisbury, but no harm was done.

The other issue was the Common Market. After the campaign began there was a meeting of Western Europe Union in London, presided over by Michael Stewart, where the principal subject of debate was the announcement by President de Gaulle that France would withdraw from any effective role in NATO. In a discussion on economic co-operation, a French under-secretary used delphic words which were interpreted by some as a sign that France was moving towards support for an enlarged Community, to include Britain. This was quite soon discounted in Paris, but Michael Stewart (as chairman, not as the British representative) felt it right to refer to these remarks at his press conference after the meeting. They were immediately seized on by Mr Heath, who had been seeking to make the Common Market a major election issue. After some days of this, I angered Mr Heath in a speech at Bristol by saying, 'One encouraging gesture from the French Government and he rolls on his back like a spaniel' – then, remembering that I should probably receive thousands of letters from dog-lovers, went on to explain that some of my best friends were spaniels. Mr Heath was deeply upset and in his first – though not his last – venture into political abuse, expressed himself with a choice collection of epithets: 'Lies, stooping to abuse, revolting, poisonous lies, deplorable, personal hostility, nauseating, filthy insinuation – absolutely filthy. God, it's a filthy speech.'

At least it enlivened the campaign. But the less excitable commentators noticed that I had said that we should continue and intensify our probings and exchanges, leading, if they showed favourable conditions to exist, to 'negotiations'; I concluded my speech on this subject: '. . . given a fair wind, we will negotiate our way into the Common Market, head held high, not crawl in. And we shall go in if the conditions are right. . . . Negotiations? Yes. Unconditional acceptance of whatever terms we are offered? No. We believe that given the right conditions it would be possible and right to join EEC as an economic community.' But I went on to reject any notion of a supranational body controlling foreign affairs and defence – still more the suggestion, favoured by leading Conservatives, that we should be willing to accept a European nuclear deterrent as part of the price of entry. 'If the conditions are right, and we are able to enter the wider European community from a situation of industrial strength, we shall be facing a challenging adventure.'

From the first results declared it became clear that we had been returned with a large majority. Seats we had never previously held, or not held since the 1945–50 Parliament, fell to us – Exeter, Oxford, Hampstead, York, Plymouth Sutton, Cambridge. What pleased me most was the recapture of Smethwick.

When the final results were declared, the state of the parties was:

Labour	363	Republican Labour	
Conservatives	253	(Northern Ireland)	1
Liberals	12	The Speaker	1

(49 gains, 1 loss to the Liberals)

Our majority over the Conservatives was 110; over-all, 97.

Chapter 14

*Government changes after the election – meeting with Mrs Gandhi –
the Queen's Speech – Rhodesia and sanctions – the new Parliament –
parliamentary reform – the seamen's strike – the Budget – negotiations
with the South Arabian Federation – the strain on sterling after the
seamen's strike – State of Emergency – end of the strike*

FOLLOWING the election victory, I embarked immediately on a
Government reshuffle; the changes were announced on 5th April.
Four senior ministers left the Government. Sir Frank Soskice, who
had not stood at the election, went to the Lords as Lord Stow Hill.
Jim Griffiths, now seventy-five, offered his resignation – it had always
been understood between us that, as one of the best-loved sons of Wales,
he would hold office for only a year or so, to launch the new Secretaryship of State. Charles Pannell, who had brought a pugnacious energy to
the somewhat placid Ministry of Works – and had 'nationalised' the
Commons building – stood down. He had not been in the best of health.
Sir Eric Fletcher, Minister without Portfolio and the House of Commons
minister working with the Lord Chancellor on law reform, became
chairman of Ways and Means and deputy Speaker. With our larger
majority the Government followed the usual practice by taking all the
three Commons chairs.

Beginning with these vacancies, I moved a number of ministers to
different posts. Cledwyn Hughes became Secretary of State for Wales.
Lord Longford, as Leader of the Lords, returned to his original position
of Lord Privy Seal. Fred Lee left Power for the Colonial Office and
took very readily to the job until the position of a separate Secretary of
State was abolished the following year. In his place Dick Marsh, one of
our best Parliamentary Secretaries, was appointed Minister of Power,
with the immediate task of preparing the Bill for steel nationalisation
and piloting it through the Commons. Douglas Houghton, in a change of
titles rather than functions, became Minister without Portfolio. He continued to preside over a large number of Cabinet committees, including
all those concerned with co-ordinating social service policy.

The new Chancellor of the Duchy in place of Douglas was George
Thomson, until then Minister of State at the Foreign Office. He was
given, under the Foreign Secretary's direction, a specific responsibility for
European affairs.

I described his tasks when Parliament met, as to

... seize every opportunity, in the political field, in his contacts with
European organisations – such as WEU [Western European Union],

219

the Committee of Ministers of the Council of Europe at Strasbourg, and so on – as well as any bilateral opportunity that presents itself as a result, for example of his responsibilities within NATO, to probe in a very positive sense, the terms on which we would be able to enter the European Economic Community and its related organisations.

Reg Prentice, Minister of State, Education and Science, followed Charles Pannell at Public Building and Works, and was succeeded by Goronwy Roberts who moved from the Welsh Office – it was a little difficult to have two north Welshmen in the two senior Welsh posts. George Thomas became Minister of State for Wales, and Eirene White, who had carried more than Under-Secretary responsibility at the Colonial Office, became another Minister of State at the Foreign Office, the first woman minister ever to enter that department. Judith Hart was given a similar appointment in the Commonwealth Office.

These moves, and a number of voluntary retirements among the older junior ministers, gave me the opportunity to bring in some of our brighter and young MPs, including, for the first time, some of the 1964 vintage: Shirley Williams (Ministry of Labour), David Ennals (Army Under-Secretary, Defence), and Peter Shore (Technology). Other younger ministers, including by-election victors of the early sixties, were Jeremy Bray (Power), Merlyn Rees (RAF Under-Secretary, Defence), Dick Taverne (Home Office), Edmund Dell (Technology) and Bruce Millan (Scottish Office). John Stonehouse moved laterally from Aviation to the Colonial Office, Ifor Davies from the Whips' Office to Wales, Julian Snow, a former whip of Lord Attlee's time, went to Health, and two new peers joined the Government: Lord Kennet (Housing) and Lord Winterbottom (Navy Under-Secretary, Defence) replacing 'Very Ordinary Seaman' J. P. W. Mallalieu, who had moved up into Mayhew's post as Minister of Defence for the Navy.

Cabinet committees were streamlined and remanned. The principal chairmen had been George Brown, who chaired the leading economic committees; Bert Bowden, the committees on legislation, immigration, rent and leasehold legislation, and broadcasting policy; and Douglas Houghton, the committees covering social services, agricultural price review, and general home policy. Frank Longford had, of course, duties in the Lords, but his keenness in the field of social policy, especially in areas which cut across departmental boundaries – children's work, delinquency, charitable foundations – meant that in addition to membership of all the main Cabinet committees he was frequently given special responsibilities in his chosen field.

From my earliest ministerial experience under Lord Attlee, I had always maintained that the strength of a Government lay in its non-departmental ministers. They are the half-back line of a modern administration: they get few chances to score goals or secure massive publicity, but without

Mr Wilson with Lord Attlee at the Transport House celebrations of the election victory, 16th October 1964

Mr and Mrs Wilson leave Transport House for Buckingham Palace, where the Queen asked Mr Wilson to form a Government

Mr Wilson and Mr Smith leaving Milton Buildings in Salisbury after their talks in October 1965
With them is Mr Arthur Bottomley, Secretary of State for Commonwealth Relations

Mr Wilson with the nationalist leader, Mr Joshua Nkomo

Some of the members of the African Council of Chiefs – 'a splendid body of men'

On his way back from Salisbury the Prime Minister visited President Kaunda of Zambia. Anti-UDI banners can be seen in the background

Another stop on the way home was Lagos where Mr Wilson met the Nigerian Prime Minister, Sir Abubakar Tafawa Balewa

them the team could never prosper. We were then – and, indeed, at all times – well-served by our chairmen, and in those earlier years Bert Bowden was in a very real sense the pivot of the Administration, and certainly the closest to me of all my Cabinet colleagues.

I had to do something about the heavy burden falling on George Brown, especially as I wanted him to chair a new and very senior committee to examine all the economic and social implications of joining EEC.

His work on economic co-ordination and as a departmental minister – DEA had developed more than I had originally intended – his successful regional work, his work on NEDC, new legislation and executive tasks such as the creation of IRC, placed a heavy burden on him. I was not happy that he should spend so much time dealing with individual price applications, or wage-claims, often until far into the night. With his agreement, therefore, I laid down that while he would be responsible for general prices and incomes policy, negotiations on broad policy with the CBI and the TUC, for the framing of the prices and incomes legislation, and – in consultation with the appropriate minister – for NBPI references, departmental ministers would have the task of handling individual price and wage questions. The Minister of Labour would be at the centre of the stage when needed in wage negotiations; the sponsoring departments, mainly Agriculture and the Board of Trade, but also Transport, Works and Power – when price questions were involved.

The new Cabinet met for the first time on Maundy Thursday, 7th April – a week after polling day – and we were soon back into the rhythm. Although the tempo was somewhat slower, problems pressed at home and abroad.

On the Saturday morning following my return to London I had gone to meet the Indian Prime Minister, Mrs Indira Gandhi, at London Airport, where she was changing planes on her way back from New York. We talked for two hours and were able to do something to repair the harm done by the statement of the previous September. I explained what had happened and made clear what I felt about the mistake.

We had to send our reply to General de Gaulle's *démarche* announcing his withdrawal from NATO. This was delivered and published over Easter weekend. I had to speak at the annual dinner of the National Farmers' Union, a somewhat unhappy occasion since the farmers, not for the last time, had that day voted their president, Sir Harold Woolley, out of office. There was no doubt that this was a reprisal for his part in finalising the spring farm price review. The negotiations were very far advanced before the election was announced and then took place in that atmosphere of increasing militancy which always seems to go with the imminence of an election. Like the doctors in 1970, though less blatantly political, the farmers saw a once-for-all opportunity of playing off one party against the other. Our offer, high by historical standards, did not satisfy their demands and, just before a breakdown occurred, Sir Harold Woolley asked to see me. There was no time for the long-drawn-out bilateral talks at the Ministry. With the Minister of Agriculture, Fred Peart, present, we had three meetings: I was anxious that a breakdown in talks should not become an election issue, and the Cabinet had given me a little more room for manoeuvre. Sir Harold Woolley and I settled – a good agreement, though one for which he had to pay. Despite his summary dismissal, I was anxious that his wisdom and great knowledge of agriculture should not be lost to our national counsels and he was recommended for a peerage in the next New Year honours list.

The most urgent task facing the new Cabinet was the preparation of the Queen's Speech – urgent, but not very difficult since there was so much unfinished legislation before Parliament at the time of the dissolution. Other Bills were now ready or nearly ready; where drafting had not been set in hand we had taken the necessary policy decisions in our pre-election White Papers. Steel, omitted from the 1965 legislative programme, could now go ahead. I was a little surprised to be met with an attempt by a number of senior ministers to draw back and to seek a compromise with the industry. With full Cabinet authority I had given the Parliamentary Party a pledge that we should proceed with steel nationalisation as soon as we had an adequate majority. It did not seem to me or, fortunately, to a majority of the Cabinet, that the election had changed anything, except to confirm our mandate and to free us from mavericks in the division lobbies. So the decision was taken and the Lord President's Queen's Speech committee was instructed to keep it in their draft.

The decision to go ahead with legislation to give the National Board for Prices and Incomes statutory backing, to legislate for early warning of increased prices and wages, and to invoke a standstill for a limited period subject to specific parliamentary authority, was confirmed, despite a last-ditch stand by Frank Cousins.

But, once again, the most urgent problem was Rhodesia. We had closed the Beira–Umtali oil pipeline by our air reconnaissance and frigate patrol. Our action had not been challenged, but news had reached us of a determined exercise by the regime, together with some members of the shipping underworld, to run the Beira gauntlet. As I described the situation in the House when we met a fortnight later on 21st April, '. . . Our naval forces had identified a tanker – a tanker of whose past murky history, despite its frequent changes of name, we had abundant information – which was approaching Beira. The Government in whose country it was then registered – it changed its registration with a rather high velocity of circulation – had already issued a decree forbidding its vessels to transport oil destined for Rhodesia. . . .'

In front was *Joanna V*, followed by *Manuela* and five other tankers, already chartered, some loaded with oil, were in the queue behind them.

The Government concerned – that of Greece – had repeatedly warned the owners and master of the serious consequences of ignoring that decree, though it was in some difficulty – as was our frigate commander – partly because the master swore blind that he was going into Beira only for bunkering and provisions (this was shown to be a lie), partly because the owners were in process of changing the flag to another state the very afternoon in question. Since the naval commander had not had a specific request from the flag state to intercept her, and since there was doubt who the flag state was, the frigate allowed her to proceed to Beira. Our job was now to stop her getting out.

There was considerable doubt about the legality of our interception. Moreover, I had given Parliament an assurance, under Opposition pressure, that we would not use force unilaterally to make the oil blockade effective. We would seek international action, and act only under United Nations authority.

The matter was already being pressed at the United Nations. The Committee of 24 on Decolonisation had met and demanded a meeting of the Security Council. We decided to take the initiative and Lord Caradon was instructed to ask for a meeting of the Council. Had we left matters where they were, sanctions would have become totally ineffective and our Rhodesia policy would have been destroyed. Pressure for the use of force would have become stronger and stronger, with incalculable results, particularly if eastern-bloc countries joined in the struggle on the ground.

We tabled a mandatory resolution under Chapter VII of the United Nations Charter, giving us authority to take the necessary action. I sent the Attorney-General overnight to help Lord Caradon. Feeling was running so high that it appeared almost certain that the mandatory resolution which finally emerged – and this would have been a certainty if we had not tabled our own resolution – would contain totally unacceptable clauses involving the use of military force and action against Portugal and South Africa. Throughout Good Friday and the Saturday I was receiving ominous telegrams over the No. 10 secret teleprinter to my holiday home. Then, as a result of brilliant negotiations by Hugh Caradon and Elwyn Jones, and without the necessity which we might have had to face of using the veto against unacceptable amendments, our own resolution went through. The amendments we could not accept, though supported by a majority of the Council, just failed to get the required nine votes to carry the Council.

Joanna V was locked in Beira, her master and owners knowing that if she unloaded her oil she would not be allowed to sail free. She stayed there for months, until finally she sailed, still laden, and was courteously escorted by the Royal Navy away from all the places where her presence was not desired.

There was a tremendous storm from the Conservatives, which reached its crescendo in the debate on the Queen's Speech on 21st April.

Over the Easter weekend changes in the Whip's Office were announced. The deputy Chief Whip, Sydney Irving was to become deputy chairman of Ways and Means. In his place I appointed John Silkin, a relatively new MP, who had joined the Whips' Office in 1964, and who had been pairing-whip when we had a majority of three.

Parliament was called for 18th April. As in 1964, the Parliamentary Party met in the morning. I was elected party leader, and George Brown deputy leader, for the whole Parliament. Addressing the PLP, I said, without anticipating the contents of the Queen's Speech, that I felt most members would be satisfied by it. This was widely and rightly interpreted as meaning that steel was in. We had over seventy new members, forty-nine of them Labour gains. I was quickly meeting them to form an assessment. They came to a reception at No. 10 and I had evening meetings with groups of them subsequently, each Tuesday evening, with parties of twenty or thirty from the different regional groups.

The 1966 intake was very different even from that of 1964. With a few exceptions, they were difficult to classify; the old division of right and left seemed to have less meaning. Some, far-left on world affairs, were relatively staid on domestic questions; others, quite passionate on domestic affairs, were strongly in favour of entering EEC. The majority seemed to feel more strongly on racial questions and on human rights than on issues which had divided the party in the past, even Vietnam.

The other common denominator seemed to be a high degree of irreverence about established parliamentary procedures, particularly those stemming from long-past struggles for supremacy between King and Parliament. In the first two days of formalities, concerned with the re-election of Mr Speaker, many of them grew increasingly impatient with Black Rod and the repeated journeys which they had to undertake to the House of Lords. Soon they were talking of getting rid of this 'flummery', and dressing Mr Speaker, the Serjeant-at-Arms, and the clerks and officers of the House in modern dress. Above all, they wanted to be involved in active party work. There had never up to that time been an intake which looked less like lobby-fodder.

The Queen's Speech contained few surprises. Most of the Bills were inherited from the previous session, plus steel. The speech foreshadowed investment grants, legislation to create the Industrial Re-organisation Corporation, the Prices and Incomes Bill, new agricultural legislation – including the creation of a Meat and Livestock Commission – steel, Bills to forward the Devlin Report on the docks, rate relief, new measures on Exchequer support for local authorities, legislation to provide the new housing subsidies so that, whatever the market rate, local councils would pay no more than four per cent on their borrowing for house-building loans, the Land Commission, legislation to impose licensing on less essential building, the Leasehold Bill, the Bill to create the new Ministry of Social Security and to replace National Assistance by the new supplementary benefits, road safety measures, new legislation on law reform, reform of the judicial system, penal law and fugitive offenders.

The debate on the Speech was quiet, apart from the opening storm on Rhodesian sanctions. A considerable part of my speech was about parliamentary modernisation, designed to bring more and more members into the affairs of the Government. I proposed talks with the other parties about the establishment of new select committees, to supplement the existing Public Accounts, Estimates and Nationalised Industries committees. What we had in mind was, for a start, two new committees each, perhaps, working on the problems of a given department for a single year, or for two years, then moving on to the problems of another department. I stressed the importance of selecting departments in which there was close concern with human problems. In my speech I instanced the Home Office and the Education Department, while leaving the final choices to be settled by the inter-party talks. In the event, we accepted a suggestion from Mr Heath for a Select Committee on Science and Technology, and another, departmentally, on Agriculture. This latter spent most of its time on the Common Market, producing valuable comment, and in time gave place to a committee on the Education Department.

In the opening weeks of the new Parliament the tempo of government had slackened a little, mainly because the Cabinet and its committees were not so preoccupied with new legislation, thrashing out policy problems before a Bill went for drafting, or going through the draft legislation clause by clause. For me it meant far fewer minutes from sponsoring ministers, fewer draft Bills before Cabinet, fewer White Papers which, under rules, had to be approved, paragraph by paragraph, by the full Cabinet, before being laid; fewer of the meetings – which had taken so much time in our first year and more – where because a Cabinet committee had failed to reach agreement on a fundamental issue of principle, a meeting of the disputing ministers was held under my chairmanship so that clear and binding instructions could be given to the committee. The main lines of our legislation were laid down, and most of the Bills drafted for a session which was due to last until the autumn of 1967.

As life grew less hectic, I decided to spend more time in the country, looking at housing progress and other social problems, and more particularly visiting industrial organisations, research stations and trade union conferences. I had, whenever possible, in the previous Parliament addressed trade unions and employers' gatherings on our industrial and wider economic problems – probably more in seventeen months than any of my prime ministerial predecessors in their whole term of office. Now I was starting from a balance of payments position which gave some hope for an ending of the chronic deficit under which we laboured. We had no figures until well after the event, but figures later published showed us to be almost in balance. For 1966, the statistics published in 1967 showed a current deficit of £59 millions, and an overall deficit of £175 millions, each little more than half the 1965 figures, and far below the 1964 adverse balances of £402 millions on current account, and £776 millions over-all. A truer comparison for 1964 would show an over-all deficit of some £830 millions, since in that year, unlike 1966, we exercised the right under the 'bisque' arrangements not to make the annual payment on the North American postwar loan.

Successive revisions of the figures, published in later years, showed even these deficit figures for 1966 to have been set too high.

My first big industrial occasion was the Scottish Trades Union Congress, which I had addressed two years earlier as Leader of the Opposition – and eighteen years earlier as President of the Board of Trade. Part of my speech dealt with the transformation we were bringing to all parts of Scotland by scheduling almost the whole country as a development area, by our vastly extended financial incentives to private industry, our advance factory programme, by the creation of the Highlands and Islands Development Board, by the establishment of science-based industries, as exemplified by a recent decision to set up the advanced fast breeder reactor at Dounreay in the far north. But the rest of the speech was an appeal for restraint in incomes and measures to promote higher productivity. I concluded:

> The last time I was in Scotland, six weeks ago tonight – on a different mission to herald the opening of Labour's election campaign – your Secretary of State spoke in that meeting; many of you were there. I want to repeat to you the challenge with which he ended his great speech that evening. He had been talking of what this Government had done, is doing, will further do. He said and I echo these words 'This is your country, work for it'.

At the end of the month I addressed the annual meeting of the national committee of the Amalgamated Engineering Union, whose headquarters I had visited in January. I took the opportunity to make a major speech on productivity and income restraint. In particular I made an impassioned appeal for modernisation of trade union practices: '... The sooner your rule book is consigned to the industrial museum, the more quickly the union will be geared to the challenge facing industry and the nation. ...'

This was warmly applauded by about half the fifty members of the national committee and coldly received by the communist members and their friends.

I repeated the warning two days later at the Merseyside May Day meeting at Kirkby stadium in my constituency, when I condemned the 'Maginot line' of outmoded defensive practices behind which so many industrial workers vainly sought to shelter. I said:

The defensive work-spreading practices bred in the years of depression, so far from defending full employment and wage standards, are the surest way of endangering them. While we honour on May Day the pioneers of the Labour movement and re-dedicate ourselves to the work they began, we must guard against keeping the attitudes they had to adopt and at the same time losing their vision.

I returned from Liverpool to face the threat of an official strike of Britain's seamen. I was not concerned with the terms of wages and hours. This was a matter for the parties, though from the outset we made clear that we could not, in the jargon of the post-1970 Conservative Government, 'lean on' the employers to produce a settlement which we should have to oppose on grounds of incomes policy.

I had told Ray Gunter that we were in for a 'long, hot summer'. But anyone who seeks to judge the seamen must have some regard for their grievances. If the union was militant – and before the strike ended no one had more to say than I on the mechanism of militancy – this was in large part due to a generation of union complacency. For years the NUS had been little more than a companies' union, and shipowners and union officials had an equal responsibility for the utter frustration of union members, many of whom felt that their interest had been entrusted to a union which was little more than a 'stooge' of the employers. Frustrations outside the field of wages and conditions related to such matters as the failure to press for the modernisation of the 1894 Merchant Shipping Act. In 1960 an unofficial strike, mainly on Merseyside, should have acted as a sharp warning to both sides. I saw a good deal of it, because of the number of my constitutents affected, and spoke out strongly at the time. But the warning went unheeded. 1966 was the pay-off, for though talks were taking place about reform of the Act they had not reached an agreed settlement.

The seamen's struggle was a test of Government determination to preserve the criteria we had laid down for incomes policy. We certainly were not helped by the publication, on the day I addressed the AEU, of the report of the Kindersley inquiry into doctors' and dentists' remuneration, calling for an immediate increase of about thirty per cent for the GPs, and varying amounts for hospital doctors and dentists. There was a strong case for an increase going far beyond national income criteria: the report on doctors' pay covered a longer period and there were basic inadequacies in national scales. But to pay thirty per cent in a single year would be inequitable and, in the context of incomes policy for manual and other workers, highly provocative. We decided to stage the payments over two years, from 1st April 1966, with retrospective effect, and 1st April 1967. The result was the kind of explosion we later came to regard as inevitable whenever doctors' remuneration was involved. They had a strong case and always succeeded in alienating public opinion by the way in which they asserted it.

This was the week of the Budget, anticipated by the Chancellor's statement in March. More than in most Budget statements, the Chancellor dealt in great detail with overseas financing, borrowing and the overseas capital account. He was in a position, too, greatly to refine the detailed operation of both the capital gains tax and the corporation tax imposed a year earlier.

Broadly, his Budget assessment was the same as that put forward in the House on the eve of the election. In so far as he needed to raise more revenue, it was because of new assessments by the Treasury experts. The Treasury forecasters have to operate on huge sums with totally inadequate means of assessing even current trends. They usually become more pessimistic in the spring months, and always qualify their prophecies by looking to an expected surge in the late summer and early autumn. There was hardly a Budget appreciation in my experience which did not admit that internal demand was a little sluggish at the time of forecasting, and then went on to advise that that should not be invoked to justify an expansionary Budget – because of the expected natural increase in demand later in the year, an expected demand which did not always materialise.

The advice was in this case for a more disinflationary Budget than had been considered necessary in the March 'Budget assessment'. With the wisdom of hindsight I would feel that on that occasion the judgment was right. Certainly the argument that the Chancellor took an optimistic line in March for electoral reasons and a gloomier view in May cannot be sustained. His appreciation on both occasions, strictly based on Treasury advice, was an honest, non-political assessment.

He had to raise taxation to the tune of some £250 millions. I have never seen the process of Budget-speech titillation carried through more teasingly. First, he had the House expecting an increase in the Chancellor's traditional friends, beer, spirits and tobacco – and then rejected it. Then it seemed purchase tax would be taking the strain. Or perhaps income tax. But no, 'there will be no increase of income tax, surtax, purchase tax, vehicle licence duty or other Customs and Excise revenue duties'. The House was dumbfounded, and well-prepared for the Chancellor's announcement of the new selective employment tax (SET).

Work had been going on upon this for some time. It was, in effect, a pay-roll tax on services, a means of raising considerable sums of revenue at little administrative cost, and with less effect on the cost of living than most other forms of indirect taxation; while at the same time it would help to get some transfer of workers from service trades to manufacturing. There was also an argument in equity. Consumer expenditure on goods bore tax at high rates; freely spendable income was going more and more on consumer services, which were tax-free. Even so, SET was equivalent to a purchase tax on services of only about three to four per cent.

The Friday after the Budget, 6th May, Ray Gunter met the seamen's executive and urged them to accept the employers' offer, at the same time proposing an inquiry into the conditions of seagoing employment and a review of the Merchant Shipping Act. This was turned down the next morning during a forty-five-minute meeting.

On the Monday, the Minister of Labour met the employers, the Shipping Federation; on the Wednesday he met the NUS again with a strong appeal to consider the damage a strike would inflict on the economy. The following morning, 12th May, the seamen again turned him down and were due to go to their home ports and not to return until the strike had begun. Ray Gunter came round to No. 10 just before midnight and advised me to send them, before they had time to disperse, an invitation to No. 10 the following morning. Meanwhile, Mr George Woodcock was urging the seamen's leaders for over two hours to reconsider their decision – but to no avail.

On 13th May I met the forty-eight seamen's leaders at noon in the State dining-room at No. 10, laid out as a conference room. I urged on them the damage they would do to Britain and to their own industry and emphasised the benefits of Ray Gunter's proposed inquiry. Their reaction was militant and bitter and with many offensive comments on the shipowners' methods, and their excessive profits, and with political attacks on us for backing the bosses against the workers. We argued through and through the subject. But the gap was too wide. The employers, who had granted a thirteen per cent increase in March 1965, had offered five per cent, with four per cent to follow in each of the next two years. The seamen were demanding that all work over forty hours a week should be paid at overtime rates; this would be equivalent to a seventeen per cent increase in earnings averaging £20 a week. The employers pointed out that the thirteen per cent of the previous year had included a payment of £8 per month over and above the basic rate, to compensate for working more than forty hours a week at sea. The executive withdrew to a room in the Cabinet Office, where once again they took just forty-five minutes to reject our appeal.

Nothing could now avert the strike. Henceforth our efforts had to be directed to making it as short as possible and to prevent it from spreading.

From Monday, 16th May, the docks slid into paralysis. Ships loading for export were immobilised. Each new incoming vessel tied up, and stayed. Each night television screens showed dismal pictures of docks at a standstill with congestion growing. Port emergency committees tried to ease the congestion, so that foreign-owned ships could still enter and leave. Naval officers were standing by to take over responsibility if voluntary action failed. All exporters who could do so booked space on freight aircraft.

The NUS was seeking to involve the dockers, so that foreign shipping would be blocked. The Communist party, which was playing a much bigger part in orchestrating the strike than the public at that time knew, was seeking to influence its friends in the docks. But men like Jack Dash knew just how far they could go with those who had so often followed them before; Mr Dash was not, in order to help the seamen, willing to invite a rebuff which might become a precedent for future occasions when he was fighting for the interests, as he saw them, of his own dockers.

Without dockers' intervention the results would be serious enough. Food stocks were adequate for a short strike, but we had to warn against panic buying and hoarding. No less serious were the dangers for employment, as raw material stocks ran down, and for exports, since markets once lost might not be regained. There were problems of maintaining supplies to remote Scottish islands. Before long these were being carried by landing-craft and naval auxiliaries. The Cabinet Emergencies committee was meeting daily under the chairmanship of the Home Secretary, serviced by the officials' committee which met twice daily.

The pound fell on the first day of the strike and had to be supported by sales of dollars from the reserves.

That evening, I broadcast on television. I warned: 'This will settle nothing. . . . This is not the way.' I expressed sympathy for all the seamen had been through and repeated our pledge about the Merchant Shipping Act. But I had to re-emphasise our incomes policy, and – stressing that maintenance of that policy was the only means to full employment – made clear that we could not accept an inflationary settlement:

> To accept the seamen's demand would breach the dykes. This would mean higher and higher living costs and we would be priced out of export markets. . . .
> The Minister of Labour and I made it clear to the union that if our urgent advice were not taken it would be the duty of the Government to resist the action taken, for this would be a strike against the State, against the community. . . . This is a challenge we did not seek, and do not want.

But it was now one that had to be met.

Until we saw how the strike developed, I said, we should not move to declare a State of Emergency, but would be ready to do this when it became necessary.

One or two of my colleagues and some MPs close to the NUS felt that this broadcast was unwise, but I believed that it was essential if we were to make a reality of prices and incomes policy, that the whole country, including members of other unions, should know what was involved. This was the confrontation which in January I had recognised must one day be faced; the tragedy was that it had to be done in an industry where a strike was so damaging to the nation.

On Thursday, 19th May the Leader of the House warned that after Parliament adjourned the following week for the Whitsun recess, members might have to be recalled if a State of Emergency were declared.

The union was as intransigent as ever. Even the mild Mr Hogarth, its general secretary, was making militant speeches and threatened me that if naval vessels were used to move strike-bound vessels to make room for incoming foreign ships, it could mean the downfall of the Labour Government. Speaking at Liverpool, he said, 'If Wilson uses Navy ships we will go to the precipice and we will go right over, and take him with us.'

We remained ready to use the Navy if it became necessary.

On the Monday, 23rd May the Minister of Labour saw both sides. But no progress was made. The NUS was threatening to rough things up and was making new appeals to the dockers and to foreign transport unions. We decided to advise the Queen to declare a State of Emergency, so that regulations made under it could be debated by Parliament before the recess. The danger was that that might exacerbate the dispute and drive workers in other industries to support the seamen.

During this time we were facing a parliamentary crisis in other directions. Deadlock had been reached with the South Arabian Federation in negotiations for our withdrawal. Mr Duncan Sandys, who vehemently opposed either withdrawal or the break-up of the unworkable Federation he had created, received information from some of the feudal sheikhs which he felt would destroy our case. Day after day the press screamed such headlines as 'Challenge to Wilson', 'Wilson faces new Crisis', 'Wilson lashed in Aden row', 'Wilson misled MPs', 'Move to censure Wilson'. The day the seamen's strike began, Michael Stewart in the House accused Mr Sandys of mischief. Just as the Foreign Secretary had announced the convening of a conference, Mr Sandys had picked out one speech by a member of the South Arabian Federation negotiating team, which was not representative of the final considered view of the Federal Government, and had made it public.

Mr Sandys then tabled a backbench motion of censure. Mr Heath, willing to wound but fearing to lead, half associated himself with it. The row dragged on. Mr Heath wrote to me and demanded a statement and immediately sent his letter to the press. I replied the next day:

> It is not the practice of the Government to act on a motion tabled by Opposition backbenchers.
> Your letter does not make clear whether you supported the motion or not. If you do you will presumably sign it.

I suggested talks through the 'usual channels' about how the matter should be handled. The Conservatives were unwilling to proceed to a motion of censure. I agreed to make a statement the following week. To such headlines as 'New Aden Shock for Wilson', the story was stirred up again by the sheikhs' delegation changing their story.

When the statement was made on 24th May, I was helped by Mr Heath, who badly muffed an intervention, and I had little difficulty. 'Mr Wilson routs Aden critics,' wrote the *Guardian*; 'Wilson wins on points over Aden,' more cautiously wrote the *Daily Telegraph*.

I took the opportunity of criticising certain ex-ministers for making our task more difficult by their manoeuvrings with 'certain South Arabian groups and individuals'. I could have gone further. We had one difficulty after another arising out of Mr Sandys' ministerial obsession with federations: Rhodesia was a problem deriving from the failure of the Central African Federation; there had been the Malaysia break-up and now there was South Arabia. Still more difficult was the problem I met in dealing with ministers of more than one country. 'But Mr Sandys,' they said, 'had given us a pledge' that the British Government would do this or that. The trouble was there was no written record, note or minutes, and we were more than once accused of bad faith over an alleged Government pledge whose existence we could neither confirm nor deny.

There were other diversions to take up our time, despite the concentration we were giving to the strike and its industrial consequences. George Brown had used words at a function in Bergen suggesting a clearer commitment to entering EEC than the Cabinet had ever agreed. The party was in uproar.

At the last party meeting before the recess on 25th May, a storm broke out about our east of Suez policy. Woodrow Wyatt went so far as to say we were staying there only for American dollar aid – which I intervened to deny. It was agreed that there should be a full-dress party meeting on the subject immediately after the recess.

On the same day there was a new development in the shipping strike. Over the weekend Ray Gunter had been to see me with a new proposal, that a Court of Inquiry under the 1919 Act should be set up immediately. He had offered an inquiry when we were seeking to avert the strike, and after the strike had begun had offered to set it up immediately work was resumed. What was now proposed was to set it up even though the strike continued. He reminded me that such an action was unprecedented, since it had always been the practice to insist first on a return to work. But this was what he and his experienced and wise conciliation staff advised. I agreed, and the court was set up on 26th May, under the chairmanship of Lord Pearson. It included a member of the Prices and Incomes Board, but Ray Gunter made it clear that its report would not be submitted to the Board for comment.

The NUS said the strike would go on while the Court was sitting, and Mr Hogarth told his Southampton members that it would last at least three weeks, perhaps six. NUS leaders put out feelers to foreign maritime unions asking them to cut off their ships from entering British ports.

The House adjourned on 27th May for Whitsun, having approved the emergency powers without a division.

The Whitsun recess, as usual, provided little respite for me: it somehow always happened that though most MPs and nearly all ministers got a holiday, my desk was more crowded than ever. (It was still worse with the Middle East crisis a year later.) I took a little time off to prepare a fully scripted speech ready for the Parliamentary Party meeting on the east of Suez question, but the greater part of the time was dominated by the strike and the action which had to be taken to keep supplies flowing, production going, and prices down.

The NUS, who had turned down Lord Pearson's appeal at the start of the inquiry for a return to work, declared an embargo on foreign-owned oil tankers and declared them 'black'. A major struggle began between the Government – aided by the TUC – and the NUS to prevent a blockade of oil supplies, which could have brought industry, as well as transport, to a standstill.

But one piece of good news cheered us all – the announcement in Bangkok that following talks there between Malaysia's deputy Prime Minister, Tun Razak, and the Indonesian Foreign Minister, Adam Malik, confrontation would end. This was going to mean a major change in our defence deployment and the chance to bring thousands of men home.

On 2nd June the gold figures were published for May: a loss of £38 millions from the reserves, the largest fall since July 1965. And few in the City thought that this was the full extent of the damage, for it was known that the Bank of England had repeatedly intervened to maintain sterling. We were back in the situation where not only daily but almost hourly figures of the foreign exchange position were being sent by the Treasury to No. 10. The publication of the figures caused further moves against the pound. During the week it fell to the lowest level for fifteen months.

A touch of humour came in a report from Washington: 'Mr Edward Heath said today that if he had been Prime Minister there would not have been a seamen's strike.' Asked at a National Press Club luncheon how he would have handled the strike if he had been in office, he replied briskly: '... The situation would not have arisen.' One could only assume that he would have 'leant' on the employers.

The Court of Inquiry submitted its interim report on Tuesday, 7th June. It recommended a speed-up in the introduction of the forty-eight-hour week, and of the forty-hour week in June 1967, on terms which would mean a marginal improvement in earnings, as against the five, four and four per cent previously offered.

Two days later, on 9th June, the seamen's executive rejected the court's report. In the absence on holiday of Mr Woodcock, Mr Vic Feather intervened and called the seamen's leaders to the TUC. More and more unions were concerned about the effects of the strike on their members' jobs: experienced leaders felt that the NUS had gone too far in rejecting the report of the court. There was a move to block any approach by the NUS to foreign unions for an all-out blockade on Britain's trade. The

Transport and General Workers was resisting attempts to bring the dockers out, but feelers were being put out by NUS militants to leaders of some of the smaller dock unions.

Mr Woodcock flew back from his holiday for the TUC meeting, where the seamen were shortly told that their trade union colleagues would not support them. The TUC would assist in negotiations, but otherwise would dissociate from their action and give them no help. The NUS briefly withdrew and came back to report a refusal to consider any compromise. TUC and transport leaders immediately moved to inform the international trade union movement and the International Transport Workers' Federation, to which the NUS had appealed, that the TUC were not supporting the seamen. In one or two ports, notably Harwich and certain of the cross-Channel ports, where seamen were losing their inflated summer pay-packets, there were moves to persuade the NUS to negotiate, but the executive remained apparently monolithic.

The following day George Woodcock, who was keeping in close touch with us, decided to 'invite himself' to the NUS headquarters, where he addressed the executive for an hour. He pulled no punches. After he had left, the executive issued a statement saying that they felt they had a solution to the present dispute, which would mean bringing together the four parties, seamen, shipowners, TUC and Government. George Woodcock reported to Ray Gunter, who reported on the development to me on 13th June. But it became clear that the proposal simply amounted to a Government subsidy to meet the cost of introducing the forty-hour week. This was a proposal we could not even consider.

The strain on sterling continued, and at the central bankers' monthly meeting in Basle new 'swap' arrangements were worked out, giving Britain the chance to draw on short-term loans while we were bearing the strain. When this was announced, the pound rose on world markets.

The NUS were checking carefully port by port on the state of morale. Signs of willingness to compromise were crushed and in the larger ports the executive line was being held. What made it harder for all of us who sought to end the strike was that many seamen, in addition to receiving strike pay, had taken well-paid jobs ashore. On the other hand, determined NUS attempts to involve the dockers, which for a few hours seemed to have some success, were fought off. One of the militant NUS leaders, Mr Gordon Norris, addressed London dockers, saying: 'Make the red ensign the black ensign.' He recalled that earlier in the dispute he had said he did not want them to take action which would inconvenience the public, or the dockers' wives and families. But, 'now the storm is about to break'. It did not. After half an hour's conferring, the dockers were back at work, as the TGWU officials directed them.

Again the TUC tried to help. The Finance and General Purposes Committee came to see me on 14th June. They suggested that I should meet the nine-man NUS negotiating committee. I arranged this for the following day.

It was a busy couple of days. Parliament was back, and the Conservatives were in full cry over Aden. We were involved in a bitter row with European countries over the European Launcher Development Organisation (ELDO); the party meeting took place on east of Suez policy, with a major speech from me; the Iron and Steel Federation came to see me, asking me to halt our nationalisation plans – and found me as disappointing as the NUS did later in the evening. I made it clear to the NUS that subsidies were out and that we could not agree to a settlement which went beyond the Court of Inquiry report, except in return for specific, immediate, guaranteed and 'copper-bottomed' improvements in productivity.

After meeting the seamen I met the shipowners. The NUS had reacted to its meeting with me by summoning its executive, which met on the 16th. On the 17th I called in both sides for separate meetings at No. 10. The seamen listened politely to my words, returned to their Clapham headquarters, where they were joined by TUC leaders who pleaded with them for resumed negotiations, and then announced a categorical refusal to negotiate. Mr Hogarth said, 'The TUC can do nothing for us. The position is wide open. We are going to ask for some positive support, not just sympathy. This is a fight with the Government, not with the shipowners.'

The strike entered its sixth week. On the Monday, 20th June, I made a full report to Parliament on the discussions of the previous week and announced that the proclamation of a State of Emergency and the regulations which were due to lapse later in the week would have to be renewed by parliamentary resolution. I announced the use of RAF Transport Command planes for help with urgent export shipments, and for postal services – the Northern Ireland ports were the worst affected. More naval vessels would be put into service.

Concluding my statement I dealt with the underlying causes of the strike. I reported that I had told the employers that they had a heavy responsibility for the union's unhappy history, '... by the cynical way in which for so many years they were content to transform the union into a creature of the companies. This led to a naturally democratic revolt, which is now giving way, in the name of militancy, to pressures which are anything but democratic. . . .' Then I went on:

> ... It has been apparent for some time – and I do not say this without having a good reason for saying it – that since the Court of Inquiry's report a few individuals have brought pressure to bear on a select few on the executive council of the National Union of Seamen, who in turn have been able to dominate the majority of that otherwise sturdy union.
> It is difficult for us to appreciate the pressures which are being put on men I know to be realistic and responsible, not only in their executive capacity but in the highly organised strike committees in the ports, by

this tightly knit group of politically motivated men, who, as the last General Election showed, utterly failed to secure acceptance of their views by the British electorate, but who are now determined to exercise back-stage pressures, forcing great hardship on the members of the union, and their families, and endangering the security of the industry and the economic welfare of the nation.

I did not use the word 'Communist', though no one in the House or in the press, which next morning headlined my words as a sensation, had any doubts whom I had in mind. The fact was that the moderate members of

the seamen's executive were virtually terrorised by a small professional group of Communists or near-Communists who planned their tactics with outside help and were able to impose their ideas on the mesmerised and timid secretariat and rank-and-file members of the executive. From various sources we began to receive undeniable evidence of what was going on, even to the point where we could predict the exact line the group would take at the next meeting, as well as the approaches made to Communist sympathisers in unions whose support the seamen were canvassing.

I gave some of the facts to the House, eight days later, when challenged to produce my evidence.

I began by pointing out that there were no Communists on the executive, though this was not true of the negotiating committee. Indeed, in the union as a whole, there were not enough to man more than one or two picket lines. I was impugning not the integrity of executive members, but their lack of guts. I went on:

... The House will be aware that the Communist party, unlike the major political parties, has at its disposal an efficient and disciplined industrial apparatus controlled from Communist party headquarters. No major strike occurs anywhere in this country in any sector of industry in which that apparatus fails to concern itself. ...
It may be because of the political impotence of the Communist party

'... Now is the time of night the graves, all gaping wide, every one lets forth his sprite ...'
(*A Midsummer Night's Dream*)

that it has sought expression in industrial organisation. But hon. Members would delude themselves if they imagined that there was not a most efficient organisation on the industrial side, that it has not got full-time officers ready to operate in any situation where industrial troubles are developing. Equally, we would under-estimate its power if we did not recognise that however misguided we may consider Communists' objectives or methods, in their own way they desire to see an improvement in working-class standards. They would not be effective if this were not so. ...
None of us would wish to curtail the basic legal rights of freedom of speech and action in this democracy – equally, those of us who regard their activities as harmful have our rights, including the right to take such action as we may think appropriate.

I

I have had to think a great deal about this in recent weeks, and my statement of eight days ago was not made without a great deal of anxious consideration. Some of us, owing to the position that we hold, have not only an equal right to take any action within our power to ensure that these activities are known and understood for what they are, but we have a duty to exercise that right. Otherwise, I would not have spoken as I did or as I now intend to speak.

...For some years, the Communist party has had as one of its objectives the building up of a position of strength not only in the Seamen's Union, but in other unions concerned with docks and transport. It engages in the struggle for power in the Seamen's Union because it recognises the facts which I have outlined to the House: not only that democracy is shallow-rooted in this union, not only that grievances and exploitation have festered for so many years, but that the very nature of sea-going employment makes infiltration from outside easier than in most other industries.

The bid that the Communists are making is directed to next year's conference at which the rules can be changed and at which steps can be taken also to change the full-time officers. In this union, for reasons I have given, the full-time officers have an unusual degree of power to influence the conduct of the union's activities, even if this power has not been very much exercised of late. This is a take-over bid, and take-over bidders on all sides of industry are notorious for their single-mindedness and their ruthlessness. The whole formidable power of the Communist party's industrial apparatus has for some time been directed towards this end, and the seamen's strike, with all its background of justification for industrial action, has provided the ground.

...The Communist party's industrial organiser is Mr Bert Ramelson, who in January succeeded Mr Peter Kerrigan. He has three full-time officials on his staff and in the London area, where the docks provide his hunting ground, his principal lieutenant is Mr Dennis Goodwin. Round this full-time nucleus has been gathered a small group of active trade unionists in the NUS and other trade unions.

...I have referred to the numerical weakness of the Communists in the NUS. Yet, despite this, as soon as the strike began, they were successful in ensuring that the chairmanship of the strike committees in the country's two major ports, London and Liverpool, were taken by two Communists, Mr Jack Coward and Mr Roger Woods. Again, in the union's negotiating machinery, a leading member of the negotiating committee, not himself a member of the executive council, who was elected from the floor at the annual general conference, was also a highly articulate and effective Communist, Mr Gordon Norris, who in certain of his activities has operated under the name of George Goodman.

The objectives of the Communist party in this dispute were, first, to influence the day-to-day policy of the executive council; secondly, to extend the area of stoppage; and, thirdly, to use the strike not only to improve the conditions of the seamen – in which I believe them to be genuine – but also to secure what is at present the main political and industrial objective of the Communist party – the destruction of the Government's prices and incomes policy.

First, let me deal with the organisation of the union and the strike. I have referred to the Communists' success in capturing two of the major strike committees. They are also effectively represented in other areas. When Mr Norris, who has not paused for breath during the last six weeks, visited Glasgow, he made it his business to contact certain members of the strike committee, but omitted to contact the secretary, who happened to be a loyal and efficient member of the union. The same thing, according to newspaper reports, happened in Belfast. At various stages since the strike began, these individuals I have mentioned have met to decide their policy and have sought, through whatever means have been open to them, to influence the executive council.

As I have said, they started with the disadvantage of having no Communists among the members of the executive council. They had to operate through any who were responsive to their suggestions, including a circle of members whose conception of the strike made them amenable to the type of proposals the Communist party was advocating....

...If I refer to Mr Joseph Kenny and Mr James Slater, neither of them a member of the Communist party, I must acknowledge their political and argumentative skill. I have had five meetings with the executive council, or with committees appointed by that council, and I can testify to their ability and to their mastery of the details of the seamen's complaints, to their ability to absorb skilled briefing and to their dominance amongst their colleagues.

They live in Liverpool and South Shields respectively and over the past few weeks, when attending the executive council in London, they have stayed at the same flat as Mr Jack Coward. Of course, they are free to stay where they like, but Mr Ramelson has visited the flat when they were there and Mr Norris has been in constant touch with them. They have been in continual contact with Mr Ramelson and Mr Norris.

I need no evidence, other than my eyes and ears, to recognise that these two have dominated the executive council throughout the negotiations. Again, they were predominant in the executive council's brusque and unanimous rejection of the appeal my right hon. Friend the Minister of Labour and I made to the executive council a week last Friday....

All this was said more than a week later, and I quote it to show what we were up against.

My earlier statement led to strong denunciations from the left, and a challenge from the press and Opposition to publish my evidence. Mr Heath asked to see me and the press were informed of his concern at my statement. He pressed me to give more facts and to produce the evidence on which I relied. I decided to make all the facts available to him on Privy Counsellor terms, and for good measure to bring to our meeting their senior people responsible for these matters, and one of the operators 'in the field'.

In doing this I was following an action taken by Mr Macmillan as Prime Minister, when I had just become Leader of the Opposition. At the time there had been great public and parliamentary criticism of the Secret Service, following 'Kim' Philby's flight to Moscow. I asked to see Mr Macmillan. He was accompanied by the head of MI6, whom the Prime Minister asked to tell me the whole facts. While what was public knowledge could not have justified the manifest failure of the Secret

Service to keep Philby under control, one simple fact I was given made sense of the story. I was satisfied, and I felt it my duty to say so in the House without giving any reason, and to ask my 'hon. Friends' to let it go. (I was promptly criticised in the press for gagging my back-benchers.)

Mr Heath was given every facility to satisfy himself on the nature and reliability of our evidence. I found it a matter for regret, therefore, when he did not follow up the meeting by saying so, as I had done with Mr Macmillan. Indeed, knowing the facts and knowing exactly why I could not reveal my sources, he exploited my weakness. In addition to scarcely veiled press briefing, he followed my announcement of a State of Emergency with a question demanding that I give the House 'more information to justify my assertion that he [that is, I] doubted whether the executive of the NUS was its own master'. That was a few minutes after his meeting with me and the officials concerned.

I gave some of the facts later in the day to George Woodcock, without saying anything about my sources. When he met the press he rightly refused to say whether he accepted the allegations, but he commented that if they were true, it was a 'crime against trade unionism. We can stand a hell of a lot, but a crime is a crime.'

The talk with George Woodcock led to a meeting between Ray Gunter, myself and the Finance and General Purposes Committee of the TUC, who were in almost constant session at this time. We agreed that Lord Pearson, whom we had sounded out, should be asked to chair a meeting between the two sides. The TUC persuaded the NUS executive to attend. The outstanding problem was that of leave arrangements which under the Court of Inquiry report would be cut from fifty-one to thirty-nine days a year. Lord Pearson's intervention led to a move forward and further meetings on the basis of an increased number of leave days in return for specific and measurable steps to increase productivity. It looked more hopeful, but those who were working to prevent a settlement threw in everything.

On the Monday, 27th June, hard information reached me that a new ploy was to be tried at the make-or-break meeting of the executive the following Thursday. I sent for Bill Hogarth, who was being pressed by TUC leaders and members of his secretariat to show more firmness against the militants. I told him what the group was proposing. First, a ballot of the entire union membership; and, if this failed, a recall delegate conference.

Hogarth was clearly disbelieving. They couldn't make such proposals, he said. Under union rules the only provision for a ballot, in the case of the election of the General Secretary, required a six-month period so that seamen in distant seas or ports could vote. Nor was a recall conference feasible. But he was uneasy that *if* I were right, all the progress made towards an agreement would be wrecked. I put a proposal to him:

'What I have told you just now, the two moves that will be made on Thursday morning, I will dictate for you and hand to you in a sealed envelope. When the proposals are made I want you to open it, read it out and say how long the envelope has been in your possession.'

In the event the sealed envelope was not needed.

Moderates on the executive got to work. For the first time there were other private meetings than those where the militants used their persuasion. I spoke on the telephone to Ted Hill, who had recently retired as president of the Boilermakers' Union. By a strange rule he was a member of the executive as a union trustee; he decided to throw his considerable weight into the fray. When the meeting began the usual group tried to stem the move to accept the terms for a settlement, and, when they proceeded to make their proposals for a ballot or a recall conference, they were outvoted. Bill Hogarth did not need to show his hand. But, despite an executive protest, there was general agreement that my speech in the Commons the previous day had caused a revulsion of feeling against outside pressure, for rank-and-file members of the executive now were more aware of what manoeuvrings had gone on.

When, the day before, Parliament had debated the regulations made under the renewed emergency powers, there was some hope of an agreement. I had let it be known that I would go as far as I could in giving more information about outside pressures, and did so in the words I have quoted above.

The immediate reaction was that I might have had a counter-productive effect on the executive. Mr Heath was highly critical of my original action in mentioning outside pressure. He was very doubtful whether it would shorten the strike; it may even be that it would lengthen the strike: '... Only time will show.' It did, less than twenty-four hours later, when the strike was called off.

My action had been justified, despite gloomy predictions in the press that morning. But pressure on space meant that there was no room to say so. 'Wilson's Dilemma' headlined the fact that American forces had bombed Hanoi.

Chapter 15

THE problems of the month of June were not confined to those presented by the shipping strike. There had been the row in a packed party meeting over east of Suez policy. With the meeting's agreement I made public my speech, as I was anxious that, since there would be leaks, reports of what I said should be accurate. It was hard-line, mainly centring on our peace-keeping role in the area. I could not understand colleagues who pressed for me to attack Rhodesia with force of arms and denied the means in terms of essential bases. With headlines like 'Wilson crushes revolt', a vote of 225 against 54 was widely reported. But feeling smouldered and my task was made no easier when the Vietnam row blazed up again.

Three years afterwards when I was asked about mistakes I had made in office, I instanced my clinging to our east of Suez role when facts were dictating a recessional. I was, I said, one of the last to be converted, and it needed a lot of hard facts to convert me. Other of my colleagues, left-wing and pro-European alike, were wiser in their perceptions.

There was the crisis in that June over ELDO. Britain had joined ELDO under our predecessors, mainly, I felt, to provide a respectable repository for the costly Blue Streak project. As with almost every other aircraft or missile project, the cost of ELDO escalated, and we were shocked to see that there was no means of cancelling the project if the expense became unacceptable. Indeed I found that when European countries had proposed a cut-off point providing for review and possible cancellation, it had been the British delegate, on the instructions of our ministerial predecessors, who had objected and won the day. We had to bear, and, despite a scaling-down of our contribution, continue to bear, an excessive proportion of an excessive total cost. We gave notice of our intention to withdraw. This promptly leaked, and there was a parliamentary row about that. I was pressed by the Opposition to institute leak inquiries; in so far as they elicited anything, it was a fairly clear indication that the disclosures came from industry.

The Conservatives, while still advocating cuts in public expenditure, attacked our policy and demanded that we maintain our ELDO member-ship.

Our European partners were up in arms too. In the event, our tough attitude paid off. We agreed to remain in the organisation in return for a substantial reduction in our percentage contribution, and for an agreement that the project could be reviewed if the cost increased still further.

Throughout the month there were countless meetings on Rhodesia. A ministerial mission returned from Zambia to press for a much bigger con-tribution to Zambia's policy of becoming more independent, in economic terms, of Rhodesia. There were meetings on aid for Zambia. There was the Chuter Ede Memorial lecture at the National Union of Teachers headquarters to dictate and deliver.

There was also a flurry over words used in a weekend speech by Denis Healey, who was reported as saying of General de Gaulle: 'No one in Europe trusts him to speak for them. He is regarded as a bad ally in NATO and a bad partner in the Common Market.' He made an apology and withdrawal in the House on 27th June. Mr Heath, stung by right-wing Conservative charges that he was not tough enough with us, sought to raise the matter in the House by the almost unprecedented technique for a Leader of the Opposition of a private notice question. It was his second spectacular attempt in a week. It failed; the House accepted my view that once a member has made an apology it is in-variably accepted. But he pressed it, and I pointed out that in 1963, after General de Gaulle's veto in the Common Market negotiations, Sir Alec Douglas-Home had answered a question seeking to know whether the General had deceived Britain, by an unqualified 'Yes'. Mr Heath expostulated; Sir Alec Douglas-Home asked whether he had not been right to say that General de Gaulle had misled the then Conservative Government. I replied that the word was not 'misled' it was 'deceived'. The House accepted that Mr Heath had been, as I claimed, 'clobbered', and the new technique of private notice question was dropped. *The Times,* usually uncritical on the Opposition side, commented:

> Self-immolation is a rarity in British political life, but if ever a man soaked himself with petrol and waited for someone to strike a match it was Mr Heath in the House of Commons yesterday. With one act of staggering ineptitude, Mr Heath delivered his parliamentary reputation into the hands of the Prime Minister. Mr Wilson applied the torch with-out mercy. Mr Heath's mistake was so glaring, its outcome so inevitable, that the newest member on the outermost backbench might well have been ashamed to make it.

There were machinery of government questions to be dealt with. After long discussions with Frank Cousins, and a last-ditch stand by Douglas Jay, briefed by the Board of Trade to maintain its *laissez-faire* attitude to the engineering industries, I announced the transfer of responsibility for the engineering industry to the Ministry of Technology. On 16th June I announced that shipbuilding would also be transferred to that department, and at a later stage, the production functions of the Ministry of Aviation.

These were not the only discussions I had with Frank Cousins. He had, to be fair, throughout all our later Cabinet meetings on incomes policy reserved his position and made fairly clear that he would resign if we introduced the legislation foreshadowed in the Queen's Speeches of November 1965 *and* April 1966. It was not that he was opposed to any form of incomes policy. On the contrary, he was ready to advocate a very simple approach, under which we would impose a strict control of all significant prices. Given this, the employers would be very tough on wage claims. This was an idea which has been tried in a number of countries, as a short-term expedient, and which in recent months in 1970–1 has gained new adherents. The practical problem was how to maintain an effective control of prices. In the consumer trades, fashion and design changes make it impossible to set price criteria: in capital goods so many of the products are custom-built. In the forties I had tried to maintain in being an attenuated form of wartime price controls, when President of the Board of Trade, but this had become increasingly difficult as the economy became more consumer-orientated and new lines for export were being designed daily. The view of my colleagues responsible for these matters confirmed my view of the impracticability of the idea, and we were forced back on the legislation we had announced. Frank could not accept it.

I had given him the chance gracefully to withdraw at the time of the election. When he did not do so I concluded that the fulfilment he was deriving from his increasingly successful work at the Ministry of Technology was gaining the upper hand. I was wrong. June saw meeting after meeting about his intentions. At 11 a.m. on Sunday, 3rd July he came to see me to say that he had decided to resign, and it was clear that I could not talk him out of it. I had been long prepared and, after the necessary submission had been sent to the Palace, I saw the ministers who would be affected.

I offered Tony Benn, who had proved a successfully technological Postmaster-General, the Ministry of Technology. He was more than a little overcome by the magnitude of the job. I suggested to him that he should go easy on publicity until he had mastered the intricacies of this large and expanding ministry. It had to take on responsibility for the engineering and shipbuilding industries from the Board of Trade, and it was preparing in a few months' time to take over Whitehall's monster, the aircraft production side of the Ministry of Aviation. Frank, I felt, had underplayed the achievements of his ministry, and I had said so at a Royal Society dinner. But with a new minister a period of quiet assimilation was needed.

I invited the Chief Whip, Edward Short, to take Tony Benn's place. He had been promised an administrative post as soon as possible. He must go down to history as one of the great Chief Whips, if only for his success in the seventeen months when our majority was practically unworkable.

There is always a doubt when a long-serving whip is moved to a department of his own. These doubts were quickly resolved. At the end of his period as PMG, when discussing my idea to promote him to Education and Science, I said to Michael Stewart, by that time No. 2 in the Cabinet, that Ted Short was in my view, as an administrator, the most successful minister in the administration. 'Oh,' said Michael, 'Barbara is surely the best administrator.' I told him I had meant 'outside the Cabinet'. He agreed.

John Silkin, Ted Short's deputy in the Whip's Office, became Chief. He was under no illusion about the task that faced him in getting the Prices and Incomes Bill through the House. That task was more than doubled before the month was out.

There was a full head-of-government visit from Chancellor Erhard on 23rd–24th May necessitating, as these visits do, many hours round the Cabinet table and exchanges of meals at Downing Street and the German Embassy. Our meetings were affable, friendly on the European question, but tight-fisted on off-set costs, driving us to consider unilateral action. We were making no progress on bridge-building between the Six and the Seven.

There was an agreeable interlude during the month. A chance remark by Lord Attlee at Trooping the Colour led me to make soundings of his family about a possible weekend at Chequers. No Prime Minister had spent more time there, but I was not sure whether, so soon after Lady Attlee's death, he might find it too painful. But he was keen to come and he spent the weekend of 18–19th June with us. Communication was difficult, because of his deafness and the slurring of his speech following a stroke. But there were two memorable Attlee-esque replies to questions I put to him.

Q: Clem, yourself excluded, and politics apart, who of all the Prime Ministers Britain has had since you became old enough to take an interest, do you consider the best, as Prime Minister?

A: Salisbury.

Q: If you were in this chair, again, and apart from all the day-to-day problems that press upon a Prime Minister, where would you throw your weight? What subject would you give higher priority than it is getting?

A: Transport.

He was right, though he could not know the priority that Barbara Castle was giving it, in preparing the biggest and most far-reaching Transport Bill in our history – nor the time I myself had to spend on successive policy-drafts.

But above all, there was Vietnam. Early in the month President Johnson sent the Ambassador to tell me that he was sending a senior military officer as a personal emissary to discuss certain pending operations in Vietnam. When he came it was to explain to me the decision that had been taken in principle to bomb targets within the city of Hanoi and the port of Haiphong.

The President knew from repeated exchanges, and our agreement the previous December about what I should say if I were asked about the bombing of populated areas, that I was committed to public dissociation from any such action. Now he had decided – the principle, though not the timing. Presumably he hoped that I could still be persuaded, at any rate to mute my criticism, if not to support the policy. Certainly his military emissary did his best. A more humane colonel never did exist in Vietnam. He produced map after map, with the target areas marked: the calculations of his macabre computer, with grisly details of the material fed into it, of the likely civilian death toll. There was an x per cent possibility of twelve deaths and a y per cent probability that two would die.

I repeated our total objection to the policy, and followed this up with a series of exchanges with the President. He was left in no doubt that we would dissociate.

On the night of 28th–29th June the bombs fell. I had no subsequent reason to doubt that the colonel's computer had proved accurate. But I decided that I would not wait for the inevitable private notice question. My office gave notice to the Speaker that I would make a statement. But before that I had prepared a statement to issue from No. 10, for the world's press were demanding answers from Downing Street and the Foreign Office to their questions. The Foreign Office were warned that there should be no private enterprise comments – even on non-attributable terms – such as had occurred the previous January over the end of the bombing pause.

The Foreign Office sought to water down my draft. At the very last they were hoping for a less forthright statement. Hopefully, they prepared a counter-draft of the controversial passages. Politely, but firmly, I indicated to them into which part of their filing system they were free to put it.

My statement to the House, after reciting the facts, repeated the terms of the Downing Street announcement:

Her Majesty's Government have noted with regret that United States aircraft have attacked North Vietnamese targets touching on the populated areas of Hanoi and Haiphong.

It is difficult for the British Government, which is not involved in the fighting in Vietnam, to assess the importance of any particular action which the United States Government regards as militarily necessary in this conflict. Nevertheless, we have made it clear on many occasions that we could not support an extension of the bombing to such areas, even though we were confident that the United States forces would take every precaution, as always, to avoid civilian casualties. We believe that the value of each application of force must be judged not merely in terms of the military needs which it is designed to meet, but also in terms of the additional suffering and distress which it inflicts upon innocent people and the effect it can have on the prospects for an early move to a political solution.

For these reasons, when President Johnson informed me that the United States Government judged it necessary to attack targets touching on the populated areas of Hanoi and Haiphong, I told him that while we naturally accepted his assurance that these attacks would be directed specifically against the oil installations and that everything possible would be done to avoid harm to the civilian population, we should, nevertheless, feel bound to re-affirm that we must dissociate ourselves from an action of this kind. . . .

I went on to repeat our general support of American policy, emphasising the now firm American acceptance of unconditional negotiations, originally put forward by Britain in the Commonwealth conference and independently.

Mr Heath moved into the attack. The Conservative party, despite a spasm of anti-Americanism during the recent election campaign, was now all the way with L.B.J. I replied:

It is perfectly possible, reasonable and logical to support a general policy without committing oneself to every action taken in support of that policy. To assume in advance that one will support every action taken in support of a given policy might lead Her Majesty's Government, or even Her Majesty's Opposition, into a very difficult situation.

I repeated that our attitude had been made clear to the President on many occasions. Mr Heath continued to press. If I had entertained any hopes that our own left would be mollified by dissociation they were removed by one intervention after another. To take one intervention of many from our backbenches:

. . . While many of us warmly welcome my right hon. Friend's statement dissociating Her Majesty's Government from the American bombing of Hanoi and Haiphong, may I ask whether he will not go further, dissociate the Government from American policy in Vietnam altogether and take a new initiative this afternoon, with the Soviet Union, designed to call an early peace conference and a cease-fire in that unhappy country?

I reminded the House that the Commonwealth Prime Ministers a year earlier had unanimously called for an end both to the bombing of North Vietnam and to infiltration from the north to the south. I referred to our continued pressure on the USSR to call a conference without conditions, and stressed the added urgency which the day's events had added to our appeal. I could not tell them that I was hoping to visit the Soviet Union within a few days.

The early days of July brought a new crisis. And it hit us with incredible rapidity. On Friday, 1st July George Brown, Jim Callaghan and I met to discuss the economic situation. 1965 had taught us what July could mean, and how suddenly crisis could hit us. The Chancellor, with all his Treasury and Bank of England briefs before him, drew a picture of blue skies in every direction. (The meeting subsequently became known as the 'blue skies meeting'.) There was no sign of any foreign exchange market problem. He was advised that we should not need to take any special action, either on the foreign exchange or on the domestic front. The seamen's strike had caused great speculative raids on the pound, but the agreement between the central banks had stabilised the situation and markets had eased after the ending of the strike.

Then came the publication on 4th July of the June gold figures showing a further drain on sterling. There had been the immediate rush to sell sterling short because of the strike, and then – even though the strike was over – a fresh rush started to sell it short again when the speculators saw how much damage they had done. They had first slashed with their razor, and then fainted at the sight of blood. Within a week the Chancellor's hopes were dashed. I recalled that at the end of July 1957, the then Chancellor, Mr Thorneycroft, had spoken in the most optimistic terms to the House of Commons, and that by mid-August we had lost a fifth of our reserves following speculation against the pound.

But this was not the only factor. The French Prime Minister came on a head-of-government visit on 6th July. The talks as a whole were agreeable, though of little profit so far as our approach to Europe was concerned. But I had reason to feel that M. Pompidou was somewhat annoyed, and understandably so, when we had to postpone part of the talks scheduled for the afternoon of the 7th, and at the same time to apologise for our inability to attend the dinner he was giving for Her Majesty's Government at the French Embassy the same evening. The reason was that we were forced into a debate on Vietnam on the Wednesday, despite all our efforts to postpone it until the Prime Minister had returned to Paris. The Opposition were keen to capitalise on the deep feeling on Vietnam in our Parliamentary Party by drawing attention to our divided counsels. They had a Supply day with the choice of subject. They would have been willing to debate it on Tuesday, but we had a party meeting on the Wednesday morning and the Government were anxious for our case to be properly heard there. We wanted to defer the debate, but the Conservatives refused. I had to wind up the debate, which we won easily with far fewer abstentions than expected. M. Pompidou courteously accepted my explanation, and he no doubt remembered that on my visit to Paris the previous year he had had to withdraw from our talks because of a debate in the *Assemblée*. But press reports showed that the incident rankled.

More serious was French briefing about the Common Market. The French were reported as saying that British entry would not be possible unless the 'UK takes tough action first'. The *Financial Times*, one among many, reflected their views in this way:

> ...A high French source, questioned last night on what would constitute an improvement sufficient to permit British entry into the Market, said that as an example one would no longer expect there to be a sterling crisis every few months. The same source, asked whether France thought Britain would have to devalue the pound before entry, said it was up to Britain to decide. He really did not know, but it might finally prove unavoidable. ...

Inevitably, the word flashed through the foreign exchange markets that M. Pompidou was convinced that devaluation was unavoidable. I referred to this in a private talk with M. Pompidou during a lunch at the Embassy the morning the reports were published. M. Pompidou deprecated the press stories and I fully accepted his sincerity. But someone had talked. And there were those in Paris who made no secret of the fact that in their unceasing war against the dollar-sterling axis the road to success might well lie in attacking the then soft underbelly of sterling.

Raids on sterling intensified, and the Bank of England had to pour out more and more of the reserves in the attempt to stop the haemorrhage. Undoubtedly, foreign doubts were strengthened by messages from London, many of them emanating from sheer political prejudice, that the end, if not of the world then of the pound, was at hand. Politically motivated men were not confined to the seamen's executive.

In fact, figures published early in 1967 showed that in the second half of 1966 our current balance had a surplus of £48 millions, our over-all balance a minimal deficit of £12 millions. Since the export–import component of the current balance had been distorted by the effects of the dock strike in May and June – the trade figures recovering from July onwards – it is probable that, discounting the effects of the strike on export-timing, we had reached a current account balance in the spring.

But the intense speculation – and here, of course, I include 'leads and lags' and the actions of prudent traders covering their positions – took no account of the fact that Britain was nearing balance on her overseas payments. It is interesting to ask why, in a summer when we had a deficit running at the annual rate of £800 millions, there were few selling sterling short, while in a summer when we were running at a deficit only a fraction of that figure, anti-sterling speculation ran riot. Whatever explanation is given must transcend economic considerations. Some would advance the political explanation; others what is called the 'psychological' one. If that is so, then, on the facts then available, it was morbid psychology with which we had to deal. For from early July – be it the publication of the trade figures or the rumours surrounding the French visit – the pressure never let up.

We had a new Governor of the Bank of England. Leslie (later Sir Leslie) O'Brien had replaced Lord Cromer soon after the election.

The Chancellor had decided not to renew Lord Cromer's appointment. I decided to mark his retirement by recommending him for a Privy Counsellorship. His retirement did nothing to mar his subsequent career. After four years' further service with Barings, he was selected by Mr Heath for appointment as Her Majesty's Ambassador in Washington. On his appointment, *The Times* noted – what I had not realised – that he had been a close friend of Mr Heath's for many years. Subsequently it was reported that, during his period as Governor, he had 'interfered in Conservative party politics by making known his preference' for Mr Heath as Leader against Mr Maudling. He was chosen by the BBC to appear on 'Panorama' as its independent witness to open the television election campaign in May 1970.

Of the possible candidates to succeed him, Leslie O'Brien was certainly the one I would have chosen and I was glad, therefore, when the Chancellor recommended him as his choice. We now had a totally professional, cool and competent central banker, who rapidly showed his ability to win respect in the City and abroad. What is more, he was a non-political Governor, provided that phrase is taken as meaning that he was utterly fearless, and rightly so, in speaking his mind privately and publicly to Governments – as has been shown since we left office – regardless of political complexion. Now he was to be blooded in one of the nastiest and most inexplicable crises sterling had faced. Through all the difficult days of July and beyond, his calm and reasoned advice made a deep impression on my colleagues and myself.

M. Pompidou left our shores in an atmosphere of goodwill, even on the Common Market. A report on the record summed him up in these terms: '... he was glad to see that, on the British side, the possibility of joining the Common Market seemed closer than a few years ago. Once the British Government considered it possible and opportune to join, France would be only too pleased, and would strive to seek, with her partners, the necessary transitions.'

Just before M. Pompidou left, Mr Harold Holt, who had succeeded Sir Robert Menzies as Prime Minister of Australia six months earlier, arrived. After Harold Holt's tragic death by drowning, and the accession of Mr John Gorton, a wise counsellor summed up the three premiers as, 'Menzies – British to the bootstraps; Holt, all the way with L.B.J.; Gorton – Australia first.' Mr Holt was, in fact, reorientating Australian policy in an Asian and American direction. His visit to London was incidental to that central aim. Nevertheless, we established a good working relationship, which was helpful in the Commonwealth conference later in the year. He and Mrs Holt spent the weekend with us at Chequers and we both spoke at the Australian Club during the week.

But before we reached mid-week the economic situation took a further turn for the worse. The press – particularly the financial press – was excessively gloomy, and inclined to take more account of the short-term psychological feelings of the market than of the basic improvement in the balance of payments. Even so, I now feel I was almost certainly unfair and unduly sharp in my reaction to a leading article in a Sunday newspaper which I described as 'wet'. That was in my speech at the Australian Club. Because of our meetings on the financial situation, I had to miss the dinner and arrived just in time to deliver a strong speech making clear that we should defend the sterling rate.

But there was plenty to worry about. Visits from the Governor again became a regular part of the Downing Street pattern. He was firm on maintaining the parity of sterling. I would judge from his remarks that he felt we might have to devalue if and when we joined the Common Market, but unilaterally and out of the blue, no. At the same time he felt that, since short-term rates, particularly the Treasury Bill rate, were now up to the limit possible for six per cent bank rate, we could defer an increase in bank rate no longer. We were in any case badly hit by rising interest rates abroad, and especially in European rates as a result of a successful American squeeze on the Euro-dollar market. Our declared intentions on prices and incomes policy needed to become a legislative reality and there had to be cut-backs in Government expenditure. We decided to raise bank rate a full point, and set in hand a reappraisal of our general financial policies forthwith.

On Wednesday, 13th July – the day Mr Holt flew to Washington – I went to Sussex University to receive an honorary degree. On my return I found a difficult situation had arisen. George Brown for some days had been advocating devaluation. I do not criticise him; he was personally, and in his official capacity as head of DEA, an apostle of industrial expansion. The measures we had to take would undoubtedly involve a degree of inflation and set back the growth rate; they would be bound to prejudice the fulfilment of the National Plan, on which he had expended so much labour and, indeed, affection. Where I think, and thought then, he was wrong was in his belief that devaluation would have eased our problems and, in particular, facilitated a more rapid rate of industrial expansion. The measures we should have had to take to make devaluation effective, involving a substantial diversion of real resources from the domestic market to exports, would, at a time when our reserves were pretty fully strained, have involved a sharper deflation. Indeed when we did devalue, with a much less strained economy, this was shown to be the case.

But on my return from Sussex I heard a suggestion that under George's pressure Jim Callaghan was weakening. It was the first time this had been suggested, and I made it plain that there would be no devaluation. We were going to fight. If, in the end, we lost, then the world would know we had done everything to avoid it, and would know that we had not chosen devaluation as an easy way out. Jim was certainly glad to hear this: it confirmed the robust attitude he had taken up from the outset. That settled it, and I had no idea until the events of a week later that George Brown still had anything beyond philosophic reservations, still less that he would push them as he did.

We agreed on the bank rate increase and a call for £100 millions of special deposits to get a tighter grip on bank lending, and on the outline of a statement I would make in Parliament the next day, which I proceeded to dictate when they had left me.

I began with the pressure on sterling as a result of several abnormal pressures, predominant in which had been the seamen's strike. It had been costly in its effects, doubly so when the consequential reserve figures were published. Not that I was apologising for our policies on the seamen's strike: '... This short-run price was something which we deliberately accepted from the outset, not least because of our determination to make the prices and incomes policy effective. . . .'

Had we taken the opposite line and let the incomes policy go, we should have been facing a precisely similar run on sterling for having done so.

I announced the review we had set in hand:

> This review is now proceeding and I intend to make a further statement in the House in the near future about the measures we shall propose, which will have the effect of providing the restraint that is necessary in internal demand, public and private, particularly the redeployment of resources according to national priorities, and also the steps needed to make a substantial reduction in overseas Government expenditure, which is running at a rate excessive in relation to our resources and is a major impediment to the restoration of balance in our overseas payments.

After my statement, on 14th July, George Brown moved the second reading of the Prices and Incomes Bill, drafted on the lines announced the previous autumn.

Polling was proceeding that day in Carmarthen, to fill the vacancy created by the death of Lady Megan Lloyd-George. I doubt if recent electoral history could produce another example of a Government increasing bank rate, and foreshadowing a grim statement on a wide range of economic issues, at the moment of maximum electoral impact. We lost the election to the Welsh Nationalists.

On the Saturday, 16th July, I flew to Moscow. This visit had been arranged several weeks earlier. Indeed there had been press reports earlier in the year of my talk with the Soviet Ambassador when we had agreed that I should visit the British trade fair due to be held there in July. As shadow Chancellor I had visited the previous fair in 1961, on the Soviet Government's invitation, stemming from the part I had played in getting Anglo-Soviet trade started after the war and my keen interest in it in all the years thereafter.

But I had other reasons, as the Soviet Government clearly appreciated. I wanted to assess the latest Soviet feelings on Vietnam. It was not, as some commentators naïvely suggested, that I had any new peace proposals to put forward. The situation had deteriorated so sharply that the best one could hope for was to prevent it escalating to a dangerous degree. Even more silly was Sir Alec Douglas-Home's suggestion that the Russians had suddenly put out the welcome mat on hearing of my dissociation from the bombing of Hanoi and Haiphong. The visit had been arranged long before.

The idea had been warmly supported by President Johnson both before and after the statement of dissociation. He knew what my parliamentary and press critics did not know, and were not prepared to acknowledge afterwards, that the key issue in the Vietnam issue at that time was the very hard report that Hanoi was giving out that they intended to put captured American pilots on trial, with all that would inevitably mean in terms of American reprisals.

With President Johnson's personal approval, echoing the message he had sent to me, the State Department issued a statement saying, 'His efforts have our heartfelt best wishes.'

I reached Vnukovo Airport on Saturday, 16th July. Mr Kosygin met me at the airport, and we had a long talk in the car which took us to the *dacha* he had reserved for us on the Lenin Hills.

On the Sunday, I went round the trade exhibition with Mr Kosygin for several hours. It was almost intolerably hot and humid, and our accompanying press reporters were wilting; only a very few stayed the course.

Serious talks with the Russian leaders began on the Monday, 18th July. Most of the morning was devoted to Vietnam. Clearly, as I expected, they were not going to move towards a conference, or in any way to seek to influence Hanoi on negotiations. I had not seen them so grave and they spoke, as we did, about the dangers of an escalation. This brought me to my main point. Spokesmen in Hanoi had said that the captured US pilots would shortly be put on trial as *franc-tireurs*, since there was no state of war between the US and North Vietnam. I urged them as strongly as I could to bring home to Hanoi what this would mean. Clearly they were impressed; their fears of escalation were very real and I was left in no doubt at the lunch we held at the Embassy that they were going to act. They did.

The British press at home, worked up about the economic crisis, regarded my visit as a purposeless and irrelevant interlude. The *Daily Telegraph* headlined it 'The lost week-end'. It was anything but that. President Johnson later privately said, and Senator Mansfield, Senate majority leader, clearly on the President's briefing, publicly said that it was my intervention which had stopped the trials, and headed off the most dangerous situation in the war. Without doubt, US opinion, sharply divided on Vietnam, would have lurched violently to the side of the hawks if the pilots had been put on trial and I have little doubt, from all the President told me, that he would have had to respond.

Just before lunch at the British Embassy, while we were having drinks on the balcony facing the Kremlin, Mr Kosygin took me aside and addressed me very urgently. 'You said this morning,' he said, 'that the Chinese will fight to the last drop of North Vietnamese blood. This is frequently said in western countries. It is not true at all. The truth is the very opposite. The danger is that the Chinese *will* intervene with volunteers, in numbers you cannot imagine. What will the West say then? When will the war ever end?'

This rang a bell. A few days earlier, a Warsaw Pact meeting at Bucharest had issued a communiqué on Vietnam, expressing the readiness of East European countries to send volunteers to fight alongside the DRV and Vietcong forces. This had puzzled western diplomats and commentators, who had tended to dismiss it as sabre-rattling. I said that presumably this offer was meant as a warning, or at least as an intimation to Hanoi that she should not accept Chinese intervention. He gave no answer.

In the afternoon we met alone, apart from one interpreter on each side, for two hours in the summer-house of the *dacha* where I was staying.

Together with the lunch-time aside, the conversation confirmed one thing I had frequently suspected. This was Mr Kosygin's allergy to a recall of the Geneva conference. The last country the Soviets would want there would be China. If there were ever to be a multilateral conference – and this would take place only if both parties to the fighting wanted us – it would be a more select gathering.

On the Lenin Hills and at and after dinner I tried to emphasise and re-emphasise what I had said about the proposed trials in Hanoi. This got across, but on progress to end the war there was nothing at all, as we had expected.

Meanwhile I was being kept in close touch with the situation in London. As we expected, the interim statement had done nothing to staunch the bleeding. Saturday's financial press recorded: 'Government urged to act quickly as pound takes a hammering' (*Guardian*) and 'Pound wilts as market falls' (*The Times*), though one city report said that my decision to continue with my Moscow visit had provided some reassurance.

Monday was no better. The pound was at support level and large sums were being poured out to stop it going through the floor. A flood of telegrams kept me in touch with the work of the committee of senior officials appointed to fashion the details of the package the Cabinet had authorised in general terms the previous Thursday. On the Monday, one of my private secretaries arrived with the latest draft, and with reports on the political temperature from some of my closest associates, and on some of the manoeuvrings in the Commons tea-room and elsewhere.

"HE WANTED POLITICAL ASYLUM, BUT I'VE TOLD HIM TO GO BACK AND FACE THE MUSIC."

I left Moscow at 7.00 a.m. on Tuesday, 19th July and reached London just before lunch, where I was brought up to date on the latest moves in the crisis.

So much was subsequently written about my suspicions of plots and conspiracies that I should here set out the facts. There was no plot, no conspiracy, no cabal, no organisation. There was a great deal of concern and a lot of loose talk. Some members – a minority – of the Cabinet were in favour of devaluation, though most of those would have wished to 'float' the rate. One or two were concerned about the effect of the economies on their departments.

A number, quite fairly – and this included one or two ministers with considerable economic expertise but in non-economic departments – felt that too much was being settled by too small a number of senior ministers, George Brown, Jim Callaghan and myself. We had kept it too long to ourselves, they felt, and when the news had broken it was too late to do anything except embark on a dreary exercise in cutting back public and private expenditure. It was no use saying that the storm had hit us early in July as suddenly as it hit them, and that Jim had warned the Cabinet of the growing crisis in the first week of July.

Seminars were taking place all over the Palace of Westminster; Dick Crossman in the tea-room was instructing the young, and George Brown, whose voice tended to get a little loud when analysing the intricacies of monetary economics, was also involved, principally with junior ministers. But there was no organised movement.

The Cabinet met at 5.00 p.m. on Tuesday, 19th July and went on until 9.45; I had to adjourn it since four senior ministers were due at the Palace for a function in honour of King Hussein's State visit. Though concern was expressed about the way the crisis had arisen and at our lack of preparedness and alternative options, the Cabinet was remarkably good-tempered. A small number put the case for floating the pound, though almost all agreed that it would be impossible to float at a moment of extreme crisis. Once the crisis was over we should examine the idea in a calmer atmosphere. There was virtually no pressure for devaluation to a fixed, lower parity. Grim, and resigned to taking the measures which had been worked out, ministers concentrated their arguments mainly on details of the expenditure cuts.

George Brown stated his position quite early in the meeting. He was for growth; we had fallen back into the old Treasury position of past years. In his view, we could break free only by devaluation. He must reserve his position until he saw what the Cabinet decided. Having said this he then sat on through the meeting, saying very little as we went through the measures, occasionally proving very co-operative on individual items, particularly the proposed incomes freeze.

By the time we adjourned most of us, I think, felt that George Brown's earlier hints of resignation had receded and that he would stay. He said nothing further that evening, and I sat up till 1.30 a.m. dictating my statement for the morrow. It had been a twenty-one-hour day. At Cabinet the next morning the package was approved, and George played a full, if slightly reserved, part in the proceedings. It was agreed that, before my statement, he would see the TUC and the CBI in separate meetings, while I went on revising the statement to take account of the Cabinet's decisions. He left me at 1.30 p.m. to make the necessary arrangements.

At 1.45, while still revising the statement and snatching coffee and sandwiches, I received a message that George would not see the TUC or CBI. I must see them myself. He was going to resign and would want to see me. He did, in fact, send a letter of resignation, which I returned to him asking him to think more about it and see me later. I hurriedly arranged that I would see the two industrial organisations before the statement. I heard from a colleague, who sat for two hours drinking tea with George, that George was protesting his total loyalty to me. He finally agreed to come to see me at 10.30 p.m. By this time, however, the press gallery was buzzing with reports of his resignation, fed by George's ostentatious absence from the front bench when I made the statement. Even Granada Television's 'Coronation Street' was interrupted with a news-flash that he was going.

When I met the CBI and the TUC the general indications of the position, which was all I could then give them, came to them as a shock. As I had to be in the House, we adjourned the meeting until 6.30 p.m. at No. 10.

At 3.30 p.m. I made my statement to the House. I began with the analysis. Sterling had been under pressure for the past two and a half weeks. '... after improvement in the early weeks of May we were blown off course by the seven-week seamen's strike and when the bill for that strike was presented in terms of the gold and convertible currency figures in June the foreign exchange market reacted adversely.'

I went on to speak of more fundamental, underlying causes. The most important was the squeeze on world liquidity. '... Action taken by the United States' authorities to strengthen the American balance of payments has led to an acute shortage of dollars and Euro-dollars in world trade and this has led to a progressive rise in interest rates in most financial centres and to the selling of sterling to replenish dollar balances.' I went on to set out the two areas in which action had to be taken:

> Action is needed for the purpose of making a direct impact on our payments balance, and particularly on certain parts of our overseas expenditure which, in recent years, has been growing rapidly. Action is needed equally to deal with the problem of internal demand, public and private, and to redeploy resources, both manpower and capacity, according to national priorities, and check inflation.

I reported on progress with exports. In the first five months of 1966 they had been nine per cent higher in value, and six per cent higher in volume, than in the previous year, a faster rate of improvement than that set out in the National Plan. Our exports were competitive in price, quality and performance, but opportunities were being lost by shortage of labour, long order books and protracted delivery dates. Hours of work had been reduced and incomes were rising faster than productivity.

Beginning with home demand, I then set out the ten measures we had decided to take.

> 1 HIRE PURCHASE: 'Too high a proportion of today's production is being paid for by a mortgage on tomorrow's earnings.' The hire purchase controls would be tightened. Repayment periods would be cut to a general limit of twenty-four months. The down payment on cars, motor cycles and caravans would be raised to 40 per cent, on furniture to 20 per cent, on domestic appliances to $33\frac{1}{3}$ per cent, cookers and water-heaters being exempt from the changes. This should cut borrowing by £160 millions.

2 THE REGULATOR: The provision – first introduced by Mr Selwyn Lloyd in 1961 – in successive Finance Acts to enable a Chancellor to raise or lower indirect tax rates by ten per cent was invoked, for the first time since Mr Selwyn Lloyd had himself invoked it, with the full ten per cent increase taking effect on drink, oils and petrol and purchase tax: a total of about £150 millions. Public service vehicles were to receive a subsidy to offset the increased tax on petrol and derv.

3 POST OFFICE CHARGES: Certain increases in postal and telephone charges, adding up to £20 millions.

4 SURTAX: A one-year surcharge of ten per cent on the year's surtax liabilities, yielding £26 millions.

5 BUILDING CONTROLS: Under the bill to license private building, then before Parliament, an order would be made reducing from £100,000 to £50,000 the cost limit above which a licence was required. The development areas were excluded. It was estimated that building would be cut back by £180 millions. Office building controls were extended to the whole of Britain lying south of a line from the Wash to the Hampshire/ Dorset borders.

6 PUBLIC INVESTMENT: Cuts of £150 millions in central and local government (£55 millions) and publicly owned industries (£95 millions). Housing, schools, hospitals, Government-financed factories, including advance factories built in development areas, were to be exempt from the restrictions.

7 OVERSEAS EXPENDITURE: Cuts in overseas expenditure, military and cicil, by 'at least £100 millions'. Expenditure on British forces in Germany would be cut so that total foreign exchange costs were at a level covered by off-set and other payments. If agreement could not be reached we should propose to NATO and WEU substantial cuts in our forces to achieve corresponding savings. The Chancellor flew to Bonn that afternoon for negotiations with the Germans.

8 PRIVATE OVERSEAS EXPENDITURE: A travel allowance of £50 per person outside the sterling area. To encourage tourism in Britain I announced a scheme to provide development loan assistance for building, expanding and modernising hotels where it could be shown that this would result in a significant increase in earnings from overseas visitors.

9 FOREIGN EXCHANGE CONTROLS: A tightening up on evasion through capital transferred abroad by emigrants.

10 INCOMES AND PRICES: To help contain domestic inflation and to prevent increased costs and prices from hitting exports, I announced the staggering six-month standstill on wages, salaries and other types of income, followed by a further six months of severe restraint, and a similar standstill on prices. Where a definite commitment existed to increase pay or reduce hours, at a further date, this should be deferred

for six months. (This included the case of the railwaymen.) No new commitments should be implemented during the rest of 1966, and in the following six months only in exceptional circumstances. Similar rules would apply for dividends, and also for prices, except where an increase was caused by seasonal factors, the cost of imported materials or Government action, such as increased taxes.

I then faced, as was to be expected, the roughest House any Prime Minister had faced for a very long time. But it was nothing to the evening that lay ahead.

I had to prepare a television broadcast. At 6.10 p.m. I began to dictate it and as each page was ready it went for checking and revision. My adjourned meeting with the CBI and the TUC was at 6.30 p.m. and went on longer than I had planned. It ended just after 7.30 p.m. and I returned to my broadcast script with all too little time to complete it. While I was dictating, freshly typed pages were brought in, which I had to revise, before returning to the dictation. As always with such broadcasts the problem was length, which had to be not more than ten minutes. Owing to the way in which I had to prepare it I could not forecast whether the draft would come out as five minutes or twenty. I was fortunate; when the draft was ready some fifteen minutes before the time of the broadcast, a trial run showed it to be a few seconds less than the limit. There was no time to record it: I broadcast it live.

Messages were coming to me from the Leader of the House and the whips saying that the tea-room at the House was seething, and letters, telephone calls, round robins and memorials were going to George beseeching him to stay in the Government.

He came, as agreed, at 10.30 p.m. He began by saying that he had no alternative to resignation, since the position he had taken up was by this time so widely known. I said that I would not attempt to dissuade him, but that I was trusting him – and this was imperative – neither in his resignation speech, nor in any other public statement, to say anything on the devaluation theme which would make the position of sterling still more difficult. He was very thoughtful, and asked whether he could be transferred from his economic post to such a position as Lord Privy Seal. I told him that this would not be possible; his views had become known and he could not partly dissociate from the required degree of collective Cabinet responsibility by changing his job. He asked if he could consult the Lord President and the Paymaster General. They told him that he should stay, accept full Cabinet responsibility and, as he left, tell the assembled television and press reporters that this was his position. This he did, and by the next day he was hard at work on the draft of the prices and incomes policy I had announced and other parts of the economic statement falling within the jurisdiction of DEA.

Sterling rose sharply in the hour following my statement, and stood up well the following morning. Then the market became erratic, with heavy forward selling and a fairly strong spot position. By the afternoon the Bank was again having to provide support.

The Conservatives tabled a short, sharp motion of censure on the Government. The TUC began to express deep reservations about incomes policy. Frank Cousins had, on the day of my announcement, stated that the Transport and General Workers' would not observe the freeze. Now other trade union leaders were joining him. Even right-wing members of the General Council expressed doubts about whether it could possibly work.

The TUC called on the Chancellor on the Friday, and then went on to discuss the wages freeze with George Brown and arranged meetings with him and Ray Gunter for the following week, before the monthly meeting of the General Council on 27th July.

On the Saturday I had an hour or two off, fulfilling a long-standing date with Bessie Braddock to open the rebuilt Cavern Club, the Liverpool cellar where it is claimed the Mersey beat was born and the Beatles began their career. On Sunday I was busy on my speech for the censure debate.

On the Monday, 25th July, there was an anxious party meeting to attend. But first I received an urgent request from George Woodcock that I should meet the TUC economic committee. We arranged it for my room at the House.

It was a rough meeting, with most of the talking, on the TUC side, by implacable opponents of the freeze. I made it clear that we had no option, and dismissed the view that devaluation would provide an easy way out of facing reality. If the six months' pay pause were excluded from the proposals, the package as a whole would have to be slanted in a much more deflationary direction and this would inevitably mean a much bigger increase in unemployment, over and above the limited rise we foresaw.

One right-wing union leader almost plaintively commented, 'You asked us for voluntary restraint to avoid a freeze, and we agreed. Now you're asking us for a freeze to avoid unemployment.'

From the comments of those round the table it seemed that the TUC would refuse to co-operate. But two members who had remained silent said that I should not assume that what had been said by the more vociferous of their colleagues would necessarily represent the views of the whole council. We adjourned to the following day.

The full party meeting, immediately afterwards, was no more happy. After my speech the chairman, Manny Shinwell, invited questions, almost all of which were hostile. *Before* meeting forty-seven left-wing members, including Frank Cousins, had put their signatures to a motion condemning the Government's action and calling for a new policy, including an urgent review of the role of sterling as a national currency; restrictions on inessential imports – gambling machines were specified; stringent licensing of capital exports; direct planning of the economy; huge cuts in defence spending.

But there was never any likelihood that the signatories would make common cause with the Conservatives in the censure vote.

The two-day debate was predictable; predictably bad. There was just one cheerful moment in the opening speech. Just as Mr Heath was declaiming about the need for 'fresh and virile leadership', George Brown came in beaming, and took his seat alongside me for the first time since his resignation crisis. He was loudly cheered by all our members.

That evening I met the TUC leaders again. They produced a document saying they would 'acquiesce' in the incomes policy provided social equity were preserved. I undertook to give consideration to the proposal that the lowest-paid workers and men involved in genuine productivity agreements should escape the full rigours of the freeze. The document was ratified by the General Council at its meeting the following Wednesday, by a majority of twenty to twelve.

I opened the second day of the debate. It was a hard-hitting speech, taking up some of the points Mr Heath had made. But the Opposition adopted a new tactic. There had been one occasion in the previous Parliament when they had denied me a hearing by raising some eighteen bogus points of order, which the Chair seemed unable to control. On this occasion their game was to chatter among themselves, ostentatiously ignoring my speech, in the hope of throwing me off my stride. It did not succeed, but it was mightily discomfiting. It was nothing to the disgraceful treatment they gave George Brown, winding up the debate: howls of laughter throughout his speech, the Tory benches at their traditional post-prandial worst.

By this time the pound was holding its own without Bank of England support, and was helped by the TUC 'acquiescence' in the incomes policy. But what worried me was that the hundreds of millions of pounds of speculative money which had poured out of the country during the seamen's strike, and on a still greater scale in July, showed no signs of returning. It had been covered by short-term borrowing from the central banks. We were counting on the reflux for paying it back.

The day after the debate, Thursday 28th July, I flew to Washington for a visit planned and announced some weeks before. For the first time at No. 10 I was desperately tired. The late nights, the Moscow visit, social commitments and meetings associated with King Hussein's State visit, the debate, a great deal of intense work earlier in the week helping George to finalise his White Paper on prices and incomes policy, the Cabinet to approve it and the new clauses to strengthen the Prices and Incomes Bill, had all taken their toll. As the RAF Comet's doors closed I suddenly felt once again like a schoolboy going on holiday. I had some ten hours free of meetings, telephones and colleagues, though I had all the volumes of briefing to read for the Washington visit. In general, these briefs were not really necessary on the major items, but there was always a score or more of fringe issues – many of them technical – some of which I had to raise, some of which might be raised by the President. I hated to negotiate with a file open in front of me. This meant not only studying the 'speaking notes' but memorising the main points in the 'background briefs'. Then there was a similar, if slightly smaller, set of briefs for the visit to Ottawa.

Because of the acute pressure of the previous weeks I had not had my customary pre-visit meeting with HM Ambassador. Instead, I had suggested he should return to London as usual, co-operate with my office in preparing briefs, and then discuss all the issues with me on the aircraft.

All this took me most of the way to Gander, Newfoundland, but to be able to eat, drink, sleep a little and quietly to work on accumulated red boxes was the nearest I had been for many weeks to a Prime Minister's idea of heaven. It was like a weekend at Chequers, plenty of work, plenty of interest – but without the telephones. We were in touch through the flight-deck, on the Ministry of Defence network, for the occasional message, but on this flight, unlike some others, this facility was sparingly used.

After refuelling at Gander, we had a three and a half hour flight to Washington. This, for me, meant sleep on the bed which VIP aircraft carry. I was wakened just as we approached Andrews Field, rapidly combed my hair, and emerged to reply on US television to Dean Rusk's welcome.

We were the President's guests at Blair House, across the road from the White House. After a quick drink with Dean Rusk I went to bed. For the first time since going to No. 10 I asked for a sleeping pill, in case I came to at English waking-time, 4.00 a.m. in Washington. Wake I did, and then slept on until Washington waking-time. I had enjoyed eleven and a half hours' sleep, and was fully recovered. The President, who was coping with an aviation strike, and who in any case had the unfortunate habit of going down to the White House communication room at three or four in the morning to read telegrams, told me he had had just an hour and a half's sleep. I never did believe this recent nonsense about needing a day or two's rest before negotiations. On an east–west flight the sun's movements give the English the chance to over-indulge. It is true that if, to save working days, one flies west–east overnight, there is a problem. One answer is slower aircraft.

At 11 a.m. on Friday, 29th July I met the President. No overseas visit had a worse build-up. Even before the financial blizzard hit us, I had read authoritative pronouncements that my dissociation from the bombing of Hanoi and Haiphong would earn me the frozen mitt from the President. After the financial crisis, it was said he would have little time for 'a down-at-heel mendicant', particularly one who was scaling down defence commitments.

I had some doubts myself about the reception I should get. Mr Harold Holt, who preceded me by three weeks, had had a hero's welcome as a result of his decision to commit Australian troops to Veitnam. Mr Keith Holyoake of New Zealand had received a similar encomium *in absentia* for following suit. The President had decided to follow up his good fortune by sending a round robin to all his friends asking them to join the bandwagon.

A very urgent and personal message reached me at the worst moment in the July financial crisis, at a time when the US were in the lead in providing short-term financial help, and that help was desperately needed. The President had said that he understood our problems as co-chairman of Geneva; he knew, too, how stretched our forces were, and the heavy commitment we were bearing in NATO. But could we not send even a token force? A platoon of bagpipers would be sufficient; it was the British flag that was wanted. I replied courteously but firmly – there could be no British troops. At no time was any link suggested, or even hinted at, between financial help and our policy on Vietnam, nor following my refusal was there any slackening in America's unstinted monetary co-operation. So much for the oft-repeated smear, insulting equally to America, that financial considerations were dictating Britain's Vietnam policy.

Forecasts, and my own anxieties, proved liars. The President's greeting was as warm as ever and, as usual, we got down to a politicians' chat about our recent miseries. He was fascinated by our parliamentary problems and our relations with the unions. What really amazed him was that we had secured parliamentary approval and union 'acquiescence' for an incomes policy that no democratic country had introduced even in wartime. Unlike outside comment, he was deeply appreciative of the pressure we had exerted against the Hanoi 'war criminal' trials. There was no reference to a British expeditionary force for Vietnam, no criticism of our defence cuts, or of our intentions to reduce the BAOR commitment.

At the informal lunch he gave, attended by members of the Administration, Senators, and leading American and British pressmen, he amazed the company, and myself most of all, by the hyperbole he used in proposing my health:

England is not a nation of amateurs. We know her as a country whose greatest resource is 'the strong heart of her sons'. That is why I am confident she will prevail. . . .
To those who urge you to think small I can only reply 'Impossible!'.
A nation that has given us the tongue of a Shakespeare, the faith of a Milton, and the courage of a Churchill must always be a force for progress, an influence for good in these days.
You, personally, are asking of the British people today the same fortitude – the same resolve – that turned the tide in those days.

Then in a really astonishing tribute – I quote the *Daily Express* report, 'his voice rising to declamatory heights' – Mr Johnson said:

> I must say that England is blessed now, as it was then, with gallant and hardy leadership. In you, sir, she has a man of mettle....
> She is blessed with a leader whose own enterprise and courage will show the way. Your firmness and leadership have inspired us deeply in the tradition of the great men of Britain.

Wildly exaggerated though it was, it was good to hear in a week when most epithets aimed in my direction had been as wide of the mark the other way.

In our talks the President promised full backing to the pound and he authorised his spokesman to use a concept I had urged on him, that 'the dollar and sterling should link arms'. We were both under attack.

Our 5½-hour talks ended at tea-time and I flew to Ottawa, where, because of the tight time-table, Lester Pearson met me in the RCAF building. We briefly covered all the ground we had to cover, and we went on to a short press and television conference. He knew that I was due to arrive in London in time for the World Cup Final at Wembley. He suggested that he should join the aircraft and go to Wembley with me. I said he would be most welcome – it was only on his next visit to London that he told me that he was at least half-serious. Then cutting off the press conference because, he said, I had an important engagement

"Why not? If President Johnson can think I'm a Churchill, you can think I won the World Cup"

the following afternoon, he bet me $5 before the television cameras that England would lose. I took the bet, with an abundance of witnesses.

The RAF had told us before we left London that the aircraft's doors would open on the Saturday afternoon at 1.10 p.m. They were fifteen seconds early. After a quick press and television conference I drove to Wembley – the British reading and viewing public were not interested that weekend in international affairs.

That dramatic final put heart into everyone, not least myself, and it was a great celebration at the Royal Garden Hotel that evening. Across the floor I saw George Brown on his feet leading his table in the singing of the West Ham United anthem, 'I'm for ever blowing bubbles'. I was conscripted later in the evening to propose a number of toasts in Russian to the Soviet team and to inscribe a message of goodwill to them in their programme – later given wide circulation in the Soviet Union.

A few days later our gold and convertible currency reserves gained $5 (Canadian), as Lester Pearson cheerfully paid up.

Chapter 16

The Prices and Incomes Bill – the bankers at No. 10 – meeting with Captain O'Neill – Rhodesian 'talks about talks' – the Blackpool Congress – the Lancaster House National Productivity conference – the Commonwealth conference – Rhodesia and demands for the use of force – the Labour party conference at Brighton – hostile demonstrations – the wage freeze

PARLIAMENT sat longer into August than had been the practice in previous years in order that the Prices and Incomes Bill, now to be strengthened by the addition of Part IV on the lines foreshadowed in my statement of 20th July, could conclude its passage through the Commons.

Even without the addition of Part IV its passage was bound to be difficult, as the new Chief Whip had realised on taking up his appointment. In its original form the Bill had been given a second reading on 14th July by 340 votes to 236 and was already having a rough time in committee, before the Part IV clauses were added. The Conservatives had inevitably opposed it. The temptation to make capital out of the fissures on our own side was irresistible; moreover, they were opposed to the powers we proposed over prices. They succeeded in clothing these motives in a set of vague philosophic utterances about the attack on inflation being best achieved through increased competition, but no one was in any doubt about their tactics. With their solid vote against us, their hope lay in breakaway votes, or at least abstention by a substantial section of our own supporters.

On 29th July George Brown tabled the Part IV clauses. There was a major row on the floor of the Commons on the ground that Part IV was substantially a new Bill, emboding a different principle from the Bill then before committee. The Opposition tabled and Mr Heath moved a motion for which we had undertaken to find time, that the Bill be brought out of standing committee and continue its committee stage on the floor of the House. When the vote was put we had a large number of Labour abstentions and the motion was defeated by only fifty-two votes.

The battle continued in Standing Committee B, meeting morning, afternoon and evening. In all there were seven sessions of the committee stage, taking forty-two hours of debate. On the last day upstairs on Part IV the committee met all morning, and again at 4.00 p.m., sitting, with a three-hour break, until 11.20 the following morning, nearly nineteen hours in all.

While George Brown was fighting the Bill through, reporting to me from time to time, there were other major concerns to be dealt with. On incomes policy, I had to receive the doctors, whose pay settlement, due to date from 1st April following the Kindersley Report, was caught by the six months' deferment. They were understandably infuriated, since the time from April had been spent in working out administrative details. It was a predictably rough meeting and doctors were only partially mollified by our pledge to proceed to implement the Report as soon as the six months were up, with a limited degree of backdating so that they did not lose nine months. The minister, Kenneth Robinson, paid a tribute in the House to the 'responsible' attitude of the Council of the British Medical Association in accepting, with qualification, the deferment of the award.

On 3rd August I was again host to a representative group from the City, continuing the series of meetings which had taken place alternately at the Bank of England and No. 10 over the previous few months.

I suppose it was inevitable in the highly neurotic state of the financial world that even the announcement of this dinner caused an upset in the markets. Press headlines the next morning recorded: 'Bankers at No. 10 start a scare', and 'Bankers' meeting with Wilson unsettles markets'. Clearly something must be afoot, and it could only be devaluation, or floating the pound – which Mr Maudling, far from helpfully, was reported as having advocated. Rumours were flying around the City and we had to deny them – for once the denial was immediately accepted – and the pound picked up as the day moved on. My visitors, of course, were of a different mettle from the rumour-mongers; it was agreed that the Governor had assembled a very high-powered group.

I wanted to take the opportunity of hearing their views on the prospects for sterling after the measures of 20th July and, in particular, to ask them their assessment of the reasons for the very slow reflux of 'funk money', in contrast to our experience in July 1965.

The bankers proved to be constructive and friendly, One after another said how right the Treasury had been to publish the token figure of £25 millions for the July gold loss; everyone knew that the real loss was very many times greater, and to publish a patently derisory figure had had the right effect. (The £25 millions figure, as with all other monthly gold and convertible currency figures, was a true one, but was struck only after the borrowing of substantial short-term aid, mainly central bank 'swaps'; true, but as a guide to the strain taken by sterling, quite unhelpful.)

On the question of the reflux, most of the bankers were relaxed. They said – as our Treasury advisers had said – that we should expect it to start flooding back in September. Their forecast proved correct. Almost without exception they stressed that we were right to stand firm on parity, and to go on asserting it.

Referring to the very remarkable turn-round on the balance of payments – though we had as yet no figures later than those for the first
quarter of the year – and to the undisputably tough measures we had
taken, I asked why in their opinion so sour a view was taken about
sterling abroad?

The reply, from one of the most respected merchant bankers in the
City, took me by surprise, but one after another of his colleagues
supported him. The trouble, he said, was that in an age of speedy communications, nearly all British newspapers were available at the breakfast table over a wide part of Europe. A few years ago there had only
been the *Continental Daily Mail*, printed in Paris. The trouble was that
a high proportion of the press was still fighting the last general election.
Their sustained political attacks on the Government could not but have
a deleterious effect on sterling.

The extension of the parliamentary sittings gave me the chance to clear
a great deal of outstanding Government business. I chaired a series of
meetings of the ministerial housing committee which I had set up to try
to stimulate greater activity, especially in the public sector, and to concentrate the housing drive, particularly, on housing priority areas and on
cutting the over-long period of construction. The same committee had to
deal, too, with the tricky problem of housing mortgage rates under the
prices and incomes standstill.

Another meeting I chaired was the first of the Cabinet's Steering
Committee on Economic Policy (SEP), which I had set up in response
to feelings expressed in the recent crisis that Cabinet members were not
taken fully into collective discussion of economic questions at a sufficiently early stage.

The drive for restructuring industry was being pressed ahead. The
Industrial Reorganisation Corporation was hard at work, under temporary powers, pending the passage of the IRC Bill. We had planned
to take the second reading before the House went up, but it had to be
postponed until the autumn because of the timetable for the Prices and
Incomes Bill. We settled our policy for shipbuilding and Douglas Jay,
President of the Board of Trade, announced our decision to introduce
legislation in the autumn to create the Shipbuilding Industry Board, and
its appointment meanwhile on an interim basis. It would be provided with
adequate finance to help in the restructuring and modernisation of the
industry, on the basis of local mergers, with, in almost every case, one
integrated company for each main shipbuilding area or river basin.
Valuable work was going on between the two sides to cut back the
restrictive practices and costly 'who-does-what?' disputes which had bedevilled the industry for years. Financial assistance and, therefore, the
maintenance of employment would be dependent on adequate progress
being made, nationally and locally. What was achieved in the years

K

immediately ahead was the biggest step forward in the industry in our lifetime, especially in industrial relations and working practices.

Immediately following Douglas Jay's statement, responsibility for shipbuilding and marine engineering passed, as I had earlier announced it would, from the Board of Trade to the Ministry of Technology.

On 5th August I had my most important meeting up to that time with Captain Terence O'Neill, the Prime Minister of Northern Ireland. The Home Secretary and I had a private lunch with him, then went on talking well into the afternoon.

Captain O'Neill had already made more progress in a matter of two or three years in attacking problems of discrimination and human rights than all his Stormont predecessors in more than forty years. But this progress had aroused open hostility on the part of his atavistic grass-roots supporters and many of his back-benchers, to say nothing of a black reactionary group in his Cabinet. It was essential that the progress be maintained for, as the world learnt three years later, time – after so many years had been wasted – was not on our side. The Westminster Parliament, and particularly many of our 1964 and 1966 new entrants, was deeply concerned about human rights. It seemed inconsistent to assert human rights in Africa or the darkest areas of Europe when they were patently denied in Ulster, part of the United Kingdom.

The Government of Ireland Act, 1920, had provided a great measure of devolution to the Northern Irish Government and Parliament, but Section 75 provided: 'Notwithstanding the establishment of the Parliaments of Southern and Northern Ireland or anything contained in this Act, the supreme authority of the Parliament of the United Kingdom remains unaffected and undiminished. . . .' Moreover, even in default of constitutional action, our members were concerned with the very great increase in financial assistance from the Westminster Exchequer to Ulster, and without constitutional reform and more liberal policies it was becoming more difficult to justify to MPs, and to some members of our Cabinet, the large sums we were being asked to vote.

Captain O'Neill readily took these arguments. He stressed how much had already been done and explained his plans for the future. But he gravely underlined the threats to his position and to the reform movement. When the crunch finally came, he said, he would stand firm, whatever the cost. Three years later this was seen to be no empty promise. But he had moved so far and so fast by Northern Ireland standards that he felt there must be a period of consolidation, certainly for the rest of the year, or a dangerous and possibly irresistible tide of reaction would set in.

There was no doubt about his courage and resolve. Roy Jenkins and I agreed not to press him to go further for the next few months and I later defended this attitude in Parliament. I was satisfied then, as I am today, that we had not been taken for a ride. It was the right decision. But more time, the most precious commodity in the explosive Northern Ireland situation, was being inevitably lost.

Rhodesia, too, was in the news again. I had promised to make a statement before the recess on the 'talks about talks' which, as I had previously told Parliament, had been going on in Salisbury for several weeks. Following the visit of Mr Duncan Watson of the Commonwealth Office in March, I had sent my Foreign Office private secretary, Oliver Wright, with a Commonwealth Office team to enter into informal talks with Mr Smith about a return to constitutional rule and a possible basis for a constitutional independence settlement. The talks were held under the aegis of the Governor, and it was made clear that this did not mean any degree of recognition of Mr Smith and his colleagues, other than as leaders of a political party. Talks were going on with other Rhodesian parties and interests at the same time.

The officials had returned to London to report. In my statement I announced that they were returning to Rhodesia to continue their discussions, on the same exploratory and non-committal basis, to see whether a basis could be found for negotiations, and with whom. The key issues were the form of the restoration of legality and the acceptability test under the fifth principle. I undertook to recommend a recall of Parliament if there were any change in the situation requiring one, certainly if any final commitment were in prospect. Another mission had gone to Zambia to discuss how further we could help her in dealing with her economic difficulties.

Mr Heath wrongly took my reference to 'two issues' only as indicating that we had made progress on principles 1 to 4. I made it clear that he would be wrong to draw any such conclusion. He pressed me on the use of force and I said that we stood by our declared position; certainly I should be ready to discuss a recall of Parliament with him if there were any change in our position.

There was progress to report in two areas of modernisation. I announced the appointment of Sir Edmund Compton, who had been Comptroller and Auditor-General in my Public Accounts Committee days and still held the position, to the post of Parliamentary Commissioner (Ombudsman). This announcement was made ahead of the passage of the necessary legislation and this led to a factious parliamentary row. The other announcement was that of the appointment of a Royal Commission, presided over by Lord Beeching, to inquire into the administration of judicial assizes and quarter-sessions.

As the Prices and Incomes Bill reached its final stages, I was concerned with the arrangements for a further reallocation of ministerial duties. Its main element was an exchange of roles between George Brown and Michael Stewart.

From the night of his abortive resignation, George Brown had gone through a very difficult period. Though he applied himself with dedication and drive to the amendments in the Prices and Incomes Bill and to the task of steering it through the House, his morale had been seriously affected. He had said too much – too publicly, and too loudly – about his attitudes to the crisis, and he has since made clear that what he felt, and was known to feel, about certain basic economic issues made it hard for him to carry on. I was aware of the problem. With that ammunition in their belts the Tories would have massacred him; indeed by common consent, including his own, his all-time parliamentary low had been the treatment of his speech winding up the economic censure debate on 27th July.

He was imagining slights where none were intended. One evening, he arrived late for the Parliamentary Party meeting and found that his usual seat, next to mine, was already occupied by one of the PLP vice-chairmen, who failed to vacate it – he probably had not seen George Brown arrive. George sat below the platform. Later that evening he telephoned my office, holding me responsible. He now knew where he stood, he said, but he was not going to resign; he would wait for me to sack him. Little did he know that I was about to offer him the one job within a Prime Minister's gift which, above all others, he wanted.

It was not easy. Many members of the Parliamentary Party, and, I soon learnt, leading members of the Cabinet, felt that he had not the precisely right temperament for the Foreign Office. Doubts on this issue had played a prominent part in the leadership election in 1963. I had doubts, but I hoped that the George Brown we had seen for the past few months – the night of 20th July alone excepted – dispelled them. He had fought a great and soberly conducted election campaign, and for months afterwards we had consistently seen him at his unrivalled best. He had done the job he set out to do in creating DEA; it was running well and the transfer to other ministers of responsibility for individual price and wage cases had eliminated some of the late-night explosions. DEA I felt needed now, not the inspiration of its creating genius, but a period of quiet and orderly administration and Michael Stewart, I was equally sure, had the temperament required. The Foreign Office, at the same time, could do with a shake-up and a little more dynamism. We seemed to be drawing nearer to the point where we would have to take a decision about Europe, and George Brown seemed to me the appropriate leader for the task which might lie ahead.

I had just one worry: whether the excitability he had kept so well under control for these past months could stay under control. In asking him to take the job I made it clear that this would be the test I should have to apply to his stewardship in the months ahead. George was overjoyed, and his morale rose some forty points. He asked that I should defer the announcement until the third reading of the Prices and Incomes Bill was secured. It was announced in fact, at 10.00 p.m. as the division bells were ringing. Michael Stewart, though a little disappointed at leaving the Foreign Office, readily accepted the move and brought his great administrative talents to his new task. He was listed at No. 3 in the Cabinet order of precedence, which aroused great press interest. I could not understand then, as on all subsequent occasions, the great fascination the press – and no less some of my colleagues – took in what was known as the 'pecking list'. If anyone had asked me at any time in Clem Attlee's Administration where I stood in the batting order, I should not have known; it was, in any case, somewhere suitably low down on the list.

The other element in the reshuffle involved the Leadership of the House. Bert Bowden had done this job with quiet efficiency and was generally popular, but I wanted to see a little play given to the inventiveness and iconoclasm of Dick Crossman, who would be likely to call in question everything in the field of parliamentary procedure and practice. This was just what many of our back-benchers were wanting, particularly the somewhat frustrated new intake. I also needed Bert Bowden's cool, wise counsel and firm persuasion at the Commonwealth Office, particularly if we were shortly to be moving into fresh negotiations on Rhodesia. This was one of the reasons why I wanted to make my changes before the holidays; as it was, he would have little enough time to learn the job before the Commonwealth Prime Ministers' conference in September. Arthur Bottomley moved to Overseas Development, in turn enabling me to complete the circle by releasing Tony Greenwood, whom I wanted at Housing. No one, I felt – and rightly – could better handle local authorities and individual deputations with more charm and tact, or, where needed, firmness.

With the Prices and Incomes Bill through the Commons and the new ministers at their desks, I left the next day, Thursday 11th August for a belated holiday in the Isles of Scilly.

The previous month had been the hardest and most disappointing of our period of office. The suddenness and devastating character of the crisis had undeniably thrown us off course, wrecking hard-worked-out policies, deferring hopes of some of the reforms we had planned for the future. Without bitterness even at some of the public comments, I wondered what the position would have been if the seamen's strike could have been averted, or quickly ended. And yet, if that had been regarded as being at the expense of our incomes policy, the result would have been the same, certainly with the speculators in the neurotic mood they had shown.

Would it be, as much comment, then and since, has argued, the turning-point of the Administration? I resolved that we would press on in the new situation, carrying through our domestic social policies, and, above all, redoubling our efforts to get the balance of payments right. Still more concentration on the industrial task was needed. It was hard that this blow had fallen just when our balance of payments position was nearing equilibrium. Looking back on July 1966, from four years later, the overriding thought must be what a difference there would have been, how much more we would have done – and how much earlier we could have done it – if, as our successors were to do, we had inherited not a record deficit, but a *surplus* of £612 millions on the international payments.

The holiday, shorter than usual, was – for the only time in my Administration – undisturbed by a crisis requiring my return to London. I kept in close touch – I now had a walkie-talkie to keep contact with base – and when required I could speak to London from any point on the islands. The flow of teleprinter reports and the twice-weekly arrival of the red box also helped to keep me in touch. Confidence in sterling was slowly returning. There were few major international disturbances calling for action. The main political interest was in my acceptance of the TUC invitation to address its annual congress. This was variously interpreted by the press as an act of unexampled courage, or the onset of lunacy. Well-informed industrial correspondents were daily drawing up their tally, union by union, of how the votes would be cast for acceptance or rejection of the incomes policy. It was clearly going to be a very close-run thing.

On Sunday, 28th August I was back at my desk – having yielded to official pressure not to travel on the Friday, with the markets open. The newspapers described me as bronzed and 'fighting fit'. That was how I felt.

My first task was to prepare my speech for the TUC the following week. But there was the usual accumulation of work – plus new telegrams from Rhodesia and preparations for the Commonwealth conference.

On 3rd September I went to Nottingham University to receive an honorary degree at a special ceremony held to commemorate the meetings there of the British Association. I was able to claim the distinction, of being the only Prime Minister to have once read a paper at an ordinary session of the BA – in 1939, when any attention that might have been paid to it was lost by the news coming in that Hitler had invaded Poland.

Two days later, Monday, 5th September, I flew to Blackpool where the Congress was being held. I had taken great care with the preparation of my speech. The national problem we were facing meant that there were home truths that had to be stated. On such occasions – there was another at the TUC in 1969 – I wonder at some of the comments I read afterwards, commenting on the cool reception. One could always have a warm hearing if one evaded the issues and invoked, for the purposes of attack, the traditional bogey-figure of the gathering one is addressing. My style, designed neither for standing ovations nor a friendly press, is based on the proposition that if you have anything unpopular to say, say it – not behind the backs of those to whom it is directed but to their faces. It is always possible to get cheers by attacking the unions at a conference of Conservatives, or in the City of London. I have reserved my criticisms and warnings to trade unionists, in the main, for trade union conferences: it is in the City that I have made most of my criticism of speculative excesses and unpatriotic attacks on sterling.

So my speech at the Blackpool Congress made some clear and – I hoped – telling points. It was described by one commentator as 'the frankest and toughest report ever made by any Prime Minister in peacetime on the state of Britain'.

During my speech I said:

Productivity is an essential to a planned incomes policy but it cannot be a substitute for it. . . .

The biggest challenge facing the trade union movement in the productivity drive is the elimination of every avoidable restrictive practice, whether at national or workshop level. And the biggest problem here is overmanning, deliberately employing more men than are needed to do a given job. In the conditions we face today, so far from being a protection against unemployment they are the surest road to it.

The restrictive practices that are still too prevalent today amount simply to a means of laying claim to a full day's pay for less than a full day's work. . . .

It might be tempting to some to say, let things rip, and let the balance of payments go to hell. I told your General Council what this would mean. One false, careless, regardless step – could push the world into conditions not unlike those of the early thirties. . . .

And if it were to happen we, as a nation more dependent than almost any other on overseas trade, could well be plunged into a depression such as we have not seen in this generation, where the workless might be numbered not as one and a half to two per cent, but at one and a half to two millions. . . .

There are still scandalous cases of 'who does what?' holding back production, and even frustrating the installation of new and revolutionary techniques in products. The trade union movement will have to tackle this problem. . . .

It is of paramount importance, however harsh this may seem, that where demand and real employment fall, the labour is released to meet the urgent demands of the export and other key industries. At this time, hoarding of labour by employers, and work-sharing by employees, must be scheduled as practices totally inimical to our national recovery. . . .

And on the issue of the day, the expected card vote on the Government's pay policy, where block votes were almost daily shifting one way or the other, as one man, or two, on an individual delegation decided the votes of hundreds of thousands, I said: 'If our costs rise and our trade balance goes wrong, other figures than card votes will take over – figures of under-capacity working and redundancies and short-time and unemployment.'

I then reminded them of past votes on foreign policy: '...I frequently receive letters and resolutions from unions asking, often demanding, that Britain's influence, Britain's weight, be thrown behind some great issue in world affairs. As I said to Congress in Blackpool two years ago on the eve of the 1964 election, in the last resort no one will listen to a nation in pawn.'

My final message was: 'There will be no letting up in the severity of the Government's economic measures until we are paying our way and seen to be paying our way. And this means that *the Government must govern.*'

Our policies were endorsed two days later, in somewhat confusing votes on a series of conflicting resolutions. All the votes showed majorities for the Government's policy, varying from 1,112,000 on one pledging 'full support' for the incomes policy, to 344,000 on the endorsement of the General Council's report expressing 'acquiescence' in that policy.

Whatever the differences in their views of the Government, there was no difference about a clumsy attempt by Mr Heath on the eve of Congress to dictate to them. His message called on them to 'knock some sense into Government by making the freeze voluntary'. It was treated with contempt.

But an increasing worry was the growth in short-time working as the economic measures bit deep. BMC, Britain's biggest car combine, issued short-time working notices to fifty thousand employees. Some of the under-employment was due to our measures, but much more to a decision on the part of employers to end the hoarding of labour. Industry was forced by the squeeze to become much more cost-conscious. We paid a hard price in July as our measures forced a cost-cutting revolution on many thousands of firms who had freewheeled through every crisis of the postwar world. More than we realised, it was leading not only to increased labour productivity but to a clearing of unproductive deadwood from the board-rooms.

Later in the month, on 27th September, I chaired the Lancaster House National Productivity Conference, representative of British industry in the widest sense. I was struck by one of Britain's leading industrial consultants saying that whereas in every previous economic crisis the demand for consultants fell away, as firms felt they had nothing to offer, in that of 1966 the call for consultative advice on cutting costs was almost beyond the capacity of the firms concerned to meet.

Already Commonwealth leaders were gathering in London for the conference, due to start on 6th September, which promised to be even tougher than the TUC. As I paid my courtesy calls on those delegates who were heads of state, ominous reports reached me of caucus meetings of African leaders to plan, and virtually to take over, the conference. The main topic – as it proved, almost the only topic – was to be Rhodesia. They were going to ensure that nothing else was discussed until they had secured satisfaction on that subject.

We decided that there was no point in trying to force the meeting to take another issue first, such as the traditional debate on the world situation. Sir Alec Douglas-Home had tried to hold Rhodesia back in 1964 and practically a whole day had been wasted on a wrangle over the time-table. It was better, with a good grace, to put Rhodesia on as the first item and, one hoped, get through it in reasonable time.

I wondered whether it would be wise for me to exercise the right of taking the chair and sent a message to some of the leaders proposing that Rhodesia be taken in 'committee of the whole House', in which every delegation would be represented, but under another chairman. I suggested Lester Pearson. But the message was fed back politely that they would insist that I took the chair; less politely, that the view had been expressed at caucus meetings that 'Wilson was not going to be let off the hook in that fashion'. Apparently the right seat, for the man in the dock, was the chair.

The conference began the morning after I returned from Blackpool. It turned out, in fact, to be a nightmare conference, by common consent the worst ever held up to that time, just as that of January 1969 was equally widely regarded as the best of the whole series since Commonwealth Prime Ministers' meetings began. Twenty-two out of twenty-three independent members of the Commonwealth took part, Tanzania boycotting the meeting.

As soon as the formalities were over I proposed that after making the introductory statement on Rhodesia, as I had been asked to do, I should vacate the chair so that I could take a full part. Dr Milton Obote (Uganda) who, we soon became aware, was tending to take the leadership of the African delegations, opposed the idea. It would be wrong to start the discussion on the basis that the chairman would abuse his position, he said; they had the fullest confidence in my impartial chairmanship, even where Britain was very directly involved. Mr Kapwepwe, the fire-brand foreign minister of Zambia, in Kenneth Kaunda's absence, went further, stating that it would be wrong to give the impression that Britain was the accused in this case. (This was encouraging, but within a week he was branding me as a 'racialist'.) Others took the same line. So I was firmly in the chair, at their wish, and there could now be no criticism of me if as chairman I tried to steer the discussion in any particular channel. In fact, I had decided to play it quite differently. I would not be goaded into making any comment on any individual contribution. I would listen to each speaker in silence – and then call the next. To aid in this process I had armed myself with an enormous Tanzanian pipe which, despite our severed relations, I had received as a present; its capacity enabled me to smoke it for two hours without a refill and I suggested that any speaker whose eloquence outran a full smoke should be ruled out of order. I further suggested, not very seriously, that the length of each contribution should be in proportion to the financial and material help the speaker's country was giving to Zambia. On the basis of one hour for Britain, I said, that would give Sierra Leone forty-five seconds. In the event, and very predictably, it was Sierra Leone's Sir Albert Margai who alone spoke for longer than the pipe's two hours.

Before proceeding to business, I laid down guidelines for press briefing. The new and independent Commonwealth Secretariat would brief the press each day. While it was too much to ask individual delegations not to speak to their own national press, I asked them to brief only on their own contributions and not seek to paraphrase the speeches of others. It would also be helpful, I said, if delegates could refrain from excessive and above all slanted reports of the conference's proceedings to the press of countries other than their own. This was agreed, but observed almost exclusively in the breach.

During the lunch interval we received news of the assassination of Dr Verwoerd, the Prime Minister of South Africa. I briefly mentioned it at the opening of the new session; there was no reaction. As speculation grew that Dr Vorster was the probable successor, real anxiety grew that this could lead to an intensification of apartheid, and possibly the spread of conflict to other areas of southern Africa.

I opened the discussion with a full statement of our position on Rhodesia, including an analysis of the problems caused by forty years of history. I covered all the events before and after UDI, and the action subsequently taken by Britain and by the United Nations. Then came an estimate of the economic effect of sanctions, so far, on the Rhodesian economy – and I indicated how much they were costing Britain. I explained why my earlier optimism in Lagos, about the time required for sanctions to have a decisive political effect, had proved wrong.

I then came to the 'talks about talks' which had caused so much suspicion among African leaders. There would be no sell-out, I said; any agreement must be with a Government which had returned to a state of constitutional grace; it must be a broad-based Government not confined to a single party or race; and it must be fully within the six principles. For to the five basic principles I had spelt out a sixth – designed in fact to reassure the Rhodesian Europeans about the position after majority rule was reached; it laid down that just as, in the period *before* majority rule, there must be no exploitation of the majority by the minority, in the period *after* majority rule was reached the minority must equally have built-in guarantees against exploitation by the majority. In particular, I stressed that the fifth principle, requiring that the settlement must be acceptable to Rhodesia as a whole, adequately tested, must provide a safeguard for the African population whose interests my colleagues were strongly, and rightly, fighting to defend.

The discussions had started on Mr Smith's initiative but, I told the meeting, his attitude seemed to have hardened in the second phase of the talks. He perhaps thought – there were too many people in Britain sending him this signal – that our economic difficulties would soften our attitude to Rhodesia. He was certainly ready to seize on any rumour from his friends in Britain suggesting that our Government was about to fall, or any silly Westminster or City rumour that we were about to form a coalition.

I was followed by Dr Obote, who spoke firmly but with a restrained choice of language. He expressed some suspicion about the Salisbury talks, and did not see how they could be unofficial if British officials acting on the instructions of HMG were talking with officials of the illegal regime. The Africans had asked for my statement to be circulated and I agreed. Dr Obote felt that all delegates should have time to study it before the debate was resumed. This was generally agreed and we accordingly adjourned early.

The next morning, Wednesday 7th September, the attack was opened by Mr Kapwepwe, who spoke for an hour in language which was anything but restrained. He began by asking for an immediate answer to a challenge about the use of force. I replied that I would deal with all points raised at the end, and not deal with individual speeches. His language was particularly violent when he came to the 'talks about talks'. There were now grave doubts as to Britain's attitude towards the rebellion, he said. Britain was willing to ride roughshod over the Commonwealth partners when it served her own interests. It had been suggested that the purpose of the talks was to pave the way to a legally independent Rhodesia. This would be to pave the way to another South Africa; one might as well pave the way to hell. He ranged over past sins of past Governments. Britain talked about sanctions biting. Africans did not want them to bite, but to kill. He called for a Commonwealth declaration demanding, first, a period of direct rule imposed by HMG and, second, no independence until there was a Government elected by the majority of the people on the basis of one man, one vote.

He went on and on. I was wrong to have said we would not use military force; he likened it to a situation in a family where the father assured his children beforehand that he would never use the whip against them no matter what they did. In the strongest terms he demanded the use of force now.

No doubt a great deal of this was designed for home consumption in the Zambian internal power struggle. Mr Wina, the Finance Minister, then his principal rival, had asked for time to follow him. In fifteen minutes he put Kapwepwe's points far more effectively and far more woundingly. Zambia had occupied the whole morning.

The speeches were so long that there was only time for three in the afternoon. Dr Sangster, acting Prime Minister of Jamaica, followed the African line. Lee Kuan Yew of Singapore spoke next, but in more moderate terms, though even he called for destruction by force of Rhodesia's rail links with the outside world. Keith Holyoake for New Zealand supported Britain.

I had hoped to end the debate on Rhodesia by the Thursday evening but those hopes were receding. Our problem was made the more difficult in that each morning there was a caucus meeting consisting of all the Africans except Malawi and all the Asians (Malaysia were invited but the Tunku soon tired of attending), where the day's tactics were carefully planned: the order of speakers, who was to press for this or that commitment by Britain. As the conference wore on, the caucus meetings took up more of each morning. The excluded minority, mainly of experienced Commonwealthmen, was getting more restive at the caballistic and discourteous methods which were being adopted.

On the Thursday morning the Indian Foreign Minister, Swaran Singh, opened the discussion briefly, right down the caucus line. He was followed by Sir Albert Margai, wilder, more ebullient even than in Lagos and much longer. I predicted two hours for him, which would see the morning through. I was wrong. He shouted and bellowed, plenty of humour but more malice. He was clearly infuriated by my refusal to reply to his more hyperbolic rhetorical questions – except one. He dismissed my historical argument about the almost complete self-government Rhodesia had had since 1923, including her own armed forces and police, by saying: 'It was you, Mr Chairman, who had given it them.' I pointed out that I was only seven years old at the time. 'Then,' he said, 'if it wasn't you, it was your father.' As I was able to assure him of an infrangible paternal alibi, he settled on my grandfather as the culprit.

Towards the end of the morning, and the two hours, Sir Albert reached what seemed to be the end of his seventh or eighth peroration, and actually stopped, for breath as it turned out. I briefly thanked him, and said that Kenya, Ceylon and Australia had sent in their names to speak in the morning, Guyana, Trinidad and Tobago and Canada for the afternoon. But it was now too late to call another speaker. We were running very late and it was clear that we should not complete the Rhodesia discussion that day. We had not touched on any other item on the agenda and the conference might have to lengthen the sittings. Officials were instructed to meet and prepare a fresh time-table. They met, but we had not reckoned with the caucus. Nor had I reckoned with Sir Albert. He had nowhere near finished, he said, so we asked him to resume in the afternoon.

After he had formally ended we had the recommendations on the time-table. We should start each morning at 9.30 and add half an hour in the afternoon. We should aim to complete the Rhodesian discussion by Friday afternoon but if not, we might have to meet on Saturday morning.

Nigeria, Cyprus, Kenya, Malaysia, Ceylon and Australia spoke. Harold Holt was robust in our support, the Tunku in general critical but against the use of force. He could not forgive the Afro-Asian countries for their scant support of Malaysia during confrontation. The others followed the Zambian and caucus line.

Before we adjourned I brought the meeting firmly up against the time-table problem. Thirteen had spoken; nine were waiting to speak; then they would expect me to reply. I proposed that all nine should speak on the Friday, and I would reply to the debate at the outset of Monday's meeting (this would give us time for some hard work at Chequers). They might then adjourn to study what I had said. But we must finish Rhodesia on Monday. Even so, that would allow only Tuesday or Wednesday for all the wider issues we had to discuss, and Thursday for the communiqué. This was agreed, though Dr Obote warned that unless my statement was acceptable to his friends and himself, the debate would go on for very much longer.

On the Friday, the representatives of Ghana, Pakistan, Canada, Guyana, Malawi (at great length), Trinidad, the Gambia, Malta and Uganda spoke. Lester Pearson supported us, while reserving the position of the use of force for a later time, and then only under a mandatory Security Council resolution. He recommended world-wide mandatory sanctions on selective items. Dr Banda of Malawi broadly supported us. Syed Pirzada, the Foreign Minister of Pakistan, and Dr Borg Olivier of Malta were in favour of the declaration, though opposing force. Dr Borg Olivier, however, disagreed with the proposal for a period of direct rule, for he had experienced direct rule, and it had not been a happy experience.

Dr Obote's lengthy speech was clearly the planned reply of the African delegates. It was all the more effective for being restrained in tone and language, more in sorrow than in anger. But he criticised us strongly for the failure of sanctions and for the 'talks about talks'; he was in favour of using force, but the tactics and strategy must be for Britain to determine; we ought not to keep giving assurances that force would not be used. Above all, whatever the 'talks about talks' were designed to achieve, there must be no question of any settlement ahead of majority rule on the basis of one man, one vote.

On one question Dr Obote was helpful. He rejected the advice of those who had proposed that we should take the lead in UN in proposing sanctions against South Africa to force her to cease sustaining Rhodesia. This would weaken Britain's trade – we should certainly have borne the brunt of it. They must not do anything, he said, which would weaken

Britain and then hope that they would get the results which they wanted. The strength of Britain was necessary for solving the Rhodesian issue.

We adjourned for the weekend in a sense of very great strain. Few could be confident that the Commonwealth would not break up.

Yet when the first of the three dinner-parties assembled at Chequers the atmosphere was warm and friendly. African leaders were cracking jokes with me, there were roars of laughter – even singing. But it would have been wrong to count on this. I spoke separately to one or two of the key figures, not making much impression on their thinking but making very clear that whatever I said on the Monday morning would be as far as we could go.

I returned to Downing Street for a Cabinet I had called for the Saturday morning. We found a serious situation. The dissolution of the Commonwealth seemed imminent unless we agreed categorically to the statement the majority of the Commonwealth demanded: no independence before majority rule. That would mean the end for that year, and all time, of any possible negotiated settlement and, in the absence of a settlement, a continuation of the deadlock in Rhodesia, with sanctions only slowly biting, and with no way out until the Rhodesian liberals succeeded in taking over – an unlikely event – or bloody revolution created a new situation.

In the event, the Cabinet gave the Commonwealth Secretary and me a free hand, including the power, virtually an instruction, to agree to 'no independence before majority rule' rather than see the Commonwealth break up. I returned to Chequers for the second Prime Ministers' dinner.

On the Sunday the third group came. At the previous conference most guests stayed the night. On this occasion President Obote, alone, had arranged to stay. After the others had left he and I stayed up until well into the small hours. I knew that he was accepted as temporary leader of the African Commonwealth; I knew that he was prepared to help, given no breach of the principle he had advocated.

We began with the position as it was, sanctions limping because of South Africa's sanctions-breaking. He repeated what he had said in the conference: no one could expect Britain to cripple herself in an economic war with South Africa.

I told him that public opinion in Britain would expect us to make, at any rate, one final effort to reach an accommodation with Smith, provided that it embodied in full the guarantees called for in the six principles. This attempt must be made, and the Commonwealth would be wrong to seek to prevent it. On the Monday I would assert our right and duty to make it. Mr Smith must be warned that if this failed, Commonwealth and world opinion would demand a tougher approach. Milton Obote was thoroughly understanding, but he could not accept this proposal, nor could I ask him to. I left him to consider it, and at 3.00 a.m. I returned by car to London to prepare for my statement.

There was an expectant mood that Monday morning. I made a long speech, replying to the serious points made in four days' debate but avoiding provocation. I dealt at length with the arguments about using force and underlined the understanding attitude a number of delegates had shown about the alternative – economic confrontation with South Africa. I re-emphasised the meaning of the six principles and the issues on which we should insist for any settlement and dealt with the precondition of a return to constitutional rule.

I set out the basis on which the British Government would approach further talks. If they were unproductive, then Her Majesty's Government would be ready to agree during the forthcoming session of the United Nations General Assembly, due to begin on 1st December, to mandatory sanctions, binding on all nations, on exports, including, at a later stage, oil, to Rhodesia. In other words I was asking for rather less than three months to get an agreement based on the six principles.

My colleagues said they wanted time to study what I had said. They wanted the text, which would take time. I suggested that we should meet in the afternoon, in restricted session, on head of government plus one adviser, to thrash out an agreement.

In restricted session we argued the issue through and through. In the end we mandated Lester Pearson, who carried the confidence of almost every delegate, to consult with all delegates and put forward proposals for ratification by the conference. I put to him our final proposals. We would claim rather less than three months for final discussions with Rhodesia. No agreement would be concluded which did not fully implement the six principles, with full guarantees. If by the beginning of December agreement was not reached we would support mandatory sanctions at UN and agree to a statement that there would be no independence in advance of majority rule.

Lester Pearson worked far into the night and by the morning had his recommendations, broadly acceptable to us, available for circulation.

But the Commonwealth atmosphere was hardening. Messages reached us that the caucus was out for the kill. Despite our mutual pledge to secrecy, every point made in the discussions was leaked, in the most slanted way, to the press.

When I saw the papers the next morning even my equable temper was outraged. In addition to highly tendentious and inaccurate briefing about Britain's position, there was a further report in the *Guardian*. Mr Simon Kapwepwe, head of the Zambia delegation, who had flown back to Lusaka on the previous evening, was reported as saying at the airport, 'This conference makes us know that Mr Wilson is coming to be a racialist.'

I decided that enough was enough and I had reached the end of the road. I called my people together and laid down the tactics.

As we entered Marlborough House, we were all looking grim and determined. This was no act. I met Mr Murumbi of the Kenya delegation. I told him that I had had enough and was ready for a showdown where I would respond in kind to all I had put up with in the past week. I instructed Malcolm Macdonald, our roving Ambassador in Africa – and no one was more respected in Commonwealth African countries – to make contact with all his friends and make clear that I had said my last word. I ran into Arnold Smith, bearing the news that the caucus was meeting and that the start of the conference would be delayed. He was left in no doubt that the delay had better not be too long. I then told him – knowing that this information would rapidly permeate to national delegates – that as far as I was concerned the conference was over. If there was no move to accept a reasonable settlement, I would adjourn the conference as soon as it resumed and then feel free to act on the lines I had indicated. I would propose that the conference should meet again in three months' time in an appropriate Commonwealth capital; I would suggest Nairobi, under the chairmanship of President Kenyatta. If I had reached a settlement in that time, I would justify it to the adjourned conference. If there was no settlement I would stand by my proposals both about UN and the commitment on no independence before majority rule (NIBMR). Meanwhile I said that the Cabinet would meet at 3.00 p.m. to announce the breakdown of the conference. It had in fact been called, on a standby basis.

All the non-caucus heads waited in the chairman's room, where restricted meetings were held. As time went on – half an hour, an hour, an hour and a half – my colleagues grew restive. Lester Pearson, veteran of more conferences than any of us, protested that it was intolerable that the conference should be held up while a majority of delegates met upstairs to present us with an agreed position.

I went to my office and made it clear to my advisers that when the restricted meeting finally convened it would not begin by an invitation to a nominated caucus member, as the caucus would suggest, to record their views. They would listen first to a statement by the chairman, and I was going to blow my top, under suitable control, but they would be left in no doubt about what I felt, and what I intended. There was some attempt on the part of my advisers to calm me down, but I rejected all they said. I was, in fact, calmer than they were and sat down to prepare my speaking notes. When these were ready I returned to the conference room. Messages kept on coming – five minutes more; ten minutes more; ready to come down.

Finally the caucus members arrived and I was told that they had appointed Swaran Singh, the Indian Foreign Minister, to speak for them. I said that before I spoke I had a few words to address to the conference, which I proceeded to do in a cold but controlled fury. The manuscript notes, from which I delivered a twenty-five-minute speech, have survived and the following is a summary of them:

Before we begin consideration of the composite draft prepared by the Canadian Prime Minister, it is necessary to review the situation, which in my view is the most serious the Commonwealth has faced.

1. Every word I have said in restricted seminar has been systematically fed out to the press, despite our solemn pledge to maintain secrecy. And in the most slanted way. We have done no press briefing, but all night our press office has been asked what did Mr Wilson mean when he said this or that. Think of the effect of all this in Salisbury, on the Governor.

   There has been the most systematic use of the opposition press in Britain – I ask those responsible what their feelings would be if I were your guest and systematically briefed the opposition press against you, where there is an opposition press.

2. It is not only the fact of the press briefings – it is the nature of them. Some things I have read in this morning's British press, and I do not blame the press, I can only describe as character assassination. One statement – and I do not need to tell you what it is, you have all read it – is plainly actionable.

   It would suggest that we have a group here which has now totally lost interest in the Smith regime – they seem to be bending all their efforts bringing down the Wilson regime. Well, if that's what you want. . . .

   Some of our colleagues are saying things to the press they haven't got the guts to say inside. If anyone thinks I am a racialist let them say so here and we'll see if it is the general view. And if you think I am, why are we waiting? And why did you insist, against my own proposal, that I should take the chair?

3. Now as to the present position. I have gone as far as I can. I have done everything in my power to help this conference reach agreement, and I should now like to see a corresponding willingness shown by others.

4. Unfortunately, the mechanism of this conference is becoming too rigid, in a way we have never seen before, and which is causing much resentment. We have no objection to meetings of the like-minded. But it seems that a majority of the delegates are meeting each morning to decide the conduct of the day's meeting. I take an example. Yesterday in response to some words of Albert [Margai] I made an important concession. No interest was shown because the attitude of a large number of delegates was already decided on the basis of the facts as they already stood the previous night.

   Individual delegates tell me they have a different view – but can't express it because of a collective decision.

   We cannot do business on that basis. No doubt decisions have been taken about the Canadian document and amendments to it agreed upstairs. No provision for give and take such as we have always had in the past.

5. I repeat, I have gone as far as I can and I must be frank with my colleagues. One or two things are unacceptable to me in the Canadian draft.

   One of the difficulties, as I said on Monday evening, we might be a lot more agreed about in two or three months' time. For example, what I then might say, and will not now say on NIBMR.

   If, therefore, there cannot be a more constructive attitude shown, with give and take, and if we are to have all negotiations – and what delegates really think said to the press and not here – my only suggestion is that we should adjourn today for three months, and on this I shall have a concrete proposition to make, three months from now in some suitable Commonwealth capital, for example, Nairobi.

But if that happens I make it clear now that I shall have to withdraw all the proposals I have made, and we shall have to seek to solve the problem in the way we believe to be right. I would do nothing to make the situation worse – but I must from now on reserve the right to speak to the British press with the same freedom others intend to use.

The effect on the heads of delegates meeting was cataclysmic. All were angry at the accusations about racialism, the author having deemed it more convenient not to be present that morning.

Within half an hour, a working party of Canada, India, Jamaica, Uganda, Zambia and Britain was hard at work drafting the Rhodesia section of the communiqué in a fully constructive spirit.

At lunch-time when I retired to my room I phoned George Brown and told him we were home and dry. He could not believe it. 'You conceded NIBMR, I take it,' he said. I replied I had not and told him of the three months' plan. He was staggered and very pleased.

While a number of us were drafting the communiqué, the main conference went on, at my suggestion, under the chairmanship of Mr Holt. Rapidly and perfunctorily it reviewed the world political situation – usually one of the most valuable and searching parts of a conference's work. Equally perfunctory was the discussion on the world economic situation and, the following day, on world development and a number of questions affecting Commonwealth institutions. All we were able to do, virtually without discussion, was to ratify a number of decisions proposed by the meetings of senior officials.

By mid-afternoon we had completed our work, and I was able to resume the chair. Early in the evening I suspended the discussion on the world economic situation and presented the draft communiqué on Rhodesia to the meeting. It went through in less than half an hour, with only the most minor drafting amendments.

The communiqué again set out the basis on which independence would be granted within the six principles. Then came the key passage, paragraph 10, which in its final and agreed form read:

The heads of government also noted that the British Government proposed immediately to communicate its intentions as indicated above through the Governor to all sections of opinion in Rhodesia and to inform the illegal regime there that if they are not prepared to take the initial and indispensable step whereby the rebellion is brought to an end and executive authority is vested in the Governor, the following related consequences will ensue:

(a) The British Government will withdraw all previous proposals for a constitutional settlement which have been made; in particular, they will not thereafter be prepared to submit to the British Parliament any settlement which involves independence before majority rule.

(b) Given the full support of Commonwealth representatives at the United Nations, the British Government will be prepared to join in sponsoring in the Security Council of the United Nations before the end of this year a resolution providing for effective and selective mandatory sanctions against Rhodesia.

The conference ended on Thursday, 15th September, in an atmosphere of mutual friendship, cordiality and self-congratulations on the part of all concerned. But there were many of us who feared for the future of the Commonwealth and doubted whether it could survive a similar traumatic conference. It was two and a quarter years before we met again – in a conference as constructive and united as 1966 had been divisive. Wednesday, 14th September, was the last time we had to endure the caucus.

It was almost with relief that I turned to the problems of the home front.

As the party conference at Brighton drew near, there were fresh and ominous rumblings about a possible defeat on incomes policy. Activists in some of the unions which at the TUC had switched their votes to support of the Government were determined to secure a different casting of the vote at conference.

But their activities were as nothing compared with an exercise successfully carried through by Clive Jenkins, the ingenious secretary of the Association of Supervisory Staffs, Executives and Technicians (ASSET), as it was then named. Our six months' incomes freeze was designed to be voluntary, carried through by the acceptance of both sides of industry. But TUC 'acquiescence' did not bind industrial unions who had agreements with trade associations and individual employers, some of whom were in a position to enforce those agreements. ASSET took a test case to the Edmonton (London) County Court. It was on behalf of one of their members, against the Thorn Electrical Industries, and asked for a declaration that a wage increase, during the pause period, must be paid. ASSET won. This decision placed a number of employers in a difficult situation. On 30th September the Newspaper Proprietors' Association (NPA), now the Newspaper Publishers' Association, had an agreement with employees to pay a cost-of-living bonus based on movements in the retail price index. An increase of 2s a week was due to some of their staff, and after the ASSET case it seemed impossible to refuse it.

Their decision to pay it reached the minister after we had arrived at Brighton for the party conference. On the Saturday morning I called a meeting in my hotel room with Michael Stewart, Ray Gunter, Dick Crossman, as Leader of the House, and the Attorney-General, at which Ray Gunter's permanent secretary, Sir Denis Barnes, who had been asked to discuss the situation with the NPA, reported to us. Clearly the newspaper employers felt unable to challenge the court's ruling. We issued a statement,

> ... on the situation arising from the statement issued by the Newspaper Proprietors' Association on Friday night and other recent developments in the position on prices and incomes.
>
> It was decided that Mr Stewart should enter into immediate consultations with the TUC and the Confederation of British Industries about the question of bringing Part Four of the Prices and Incomes Act into force. . . .

But this was not the only problem we faced on the fringe of conference. The demonstrators were out in force: Vietnam and the car workers; to say nothing of some photogenic ladies who had been hired and dressed by a PR firm with one, and only one idea in mind, to get me photographed with the product they were advertising.

On the Sunday morning, as usual, I was due to read the lesson at the pre-conference service, on this occasion at the Dorset Road Methodist Church. Just before I left the hotel, I was tipped off by a friendly television employee that there would be trouble in church from anti-Vietnam demonstrators. Not for the first time television was involved in situations where demonstrators – in this case gaol sentences were in the event imposed – had sought its aid for publicity purposes. (We had not yet reached the position where telegenic situations were planned in advance between a television authority and the demonstrators, or where television crews were to be seen invoking trouble in the course of some public ceremony. I was to learn more of these practices later.) As I reached the pulpit to read the second lesson, pandemonium broke loose. The minister vainly appealed for quiet. I decided to carry on with the lesson, though, despite the public address system, little could be heard by the congregation, whose attention was, in any case, distracted by the arrest by uniformed police of the men and women demonstrators. It was one of the most unpleasant experiences of my premiership.

Towards the end of the Monday morning session of conference, the promenade outside the conference hall was occupied by thousands of car workers who had descended on Brighton by special trains from Birmingham and Coventry. They were led by the most clearly identifiable communist shop-stewards in the industry, though by no means all of the demonstrators themselves were members of that particular faith.

I had to leave conference early to deal with red boxes which had arrived from London, and just missed their solicitations; many of my colleagues were less fortunate and they were very roughly handled.

During lunch-time, as I worked on my papers, thousands of demonstrators converged on the Grand Hotel, their loudspeaker slogans repeated again and again. Work on my papers delayed my return to conference, though from my room I could hear the gibes at colleagues who had to fight their way past a mob which the police had unaccountably allowed to form a crescent-shaped blockade round the hotel entrance: such cries as 'Ray Gunter wants a halter round his neck, and we can all go marching home'.

Dick Crossman, a Coventry MP, forged his way through to cries of 'traitor'. Others of my colleagues were greeted with no less objectionable comments. But with respect to them, my colleagues were not the principal target.

'You've got to come out sometime, Wilson.'

They were, of course, right. I was not going to plead the exigencies of State papers to keep me confined to the hotel.

The Brighton police were very worried, despite – or because of – their failure to keep the pavement clear. Did I have to go back this afternoon? Yes, I did. They then suggested that I should leave the hotel by a back entrance, through the kitchens. I decided to leave by the main entrance, and meet the demonstrators head on. A senior police officer feared that the result could be dangerous, and that 'heads would be broken'. I thought not – if I could get a chance to speak to the crowd.

As we went through the front door, the booing and the cat-calling reached a crescendo. I stopped – there was no alternative – and through the noise called to a demonstrator to give me the microphone he was holding. He made no move and I repeated the request, less politely – 'Give me that bloody microphone'.

To my intense relief, he handed it over and I began to speak; after a number of false starts, I got a hearing and said, 'I've been listening to you and your slogans for the last half-hour. Now you listen to me for a minute.'

I told them that I understood their anxieties, but that they could not be removed by shouting slogans. I asked them to choose three of their number to come into the hotel for a quiet talk with me. After hurried consultations, they asked if they could nominate six. I agreed – and *twelve* of them entered the hotel with me, led by a veteran Communist shop-steward, Mr Dick Etheridge. 'That's what's wrong with BMC,' I told them, 'always needing twelve men to do what six should be doing.'

For over an hour we talked, smoked and drank tea. Each explained what worried him most, whether it was factory organisation, lay-off procedures, or redundancy payments. A full record was made of their complaints and I promised that each of the responsible ministers would look into the grievances. When I eventually left for the conference hall, the booing had given way to cheers of 'Good old Harold!'.

Conference itself was surprisingly relaxed. My speech on the Tuesday was carefully calculated not to play to the gallery. No Tory-baiting; I ignored the Opposition. My theme was 'change' – the need not merely to accept change but to promote it – what we were doing in industrial and institutional change by inquiry followed by action. Change in society too: I announced the end of political honours. The speech was set against the background of the economic crisis, with the same sombre warnings I had addressed to the TUC. And to the escapists of the far left, one warning: '...we cannot afford to fight the problems of the sixties with the attitudes of the Social Democratic Federation, nor, in looking for a solution to those problems, seek vainly to find the answer in Highgate Cemetery.'

The applause was friendly, 'dutiful' as it was put, to a speech which set out not to raise passions but to force conference to face the responsibilities of Government. It was, predictably, panned by the critics for that very reason.

But the real drama was not on the conference floor. By the early evening of Monday, 3rd October, the full Cabinet was meeting in my room. Michael Stewart's talks with the TUC and the CBI had failed to find a solution. Our incomes policy was in danger of dying the death of a thousand judicial cuts. But a decision to activate Part IV could be taken only by the full Cabinet. Constitutional pundits in London tried to tell me that there was no precedent for a Cabinet meeting outside London. I reminded them that in Inverness Town Hall there was a framed set of Cabinet signatures, which I had seen two years earlier, commemorating a meeting there of Lloyd George's Cabinet: he had been on holiday, and rather than return to London he ordered his colleagues all to take the long journey north to join him.

It did not take long to reach the inevitable decision, which was unanimous, and it was announced that evening. Four ministers flew to Balmoral the following day for the Privy Council necessary to make the order.

It was living dangerously; conference was to debate hostile resolutions on incomes policy the morning the ministers flew north.

In the event, the TGWU resolution opposing wages legislation was defeated by 3,925,000 against 2,471,000. Six other resolutions showed pro-Government majorities.

Frank Cousins' only compensation was a narrow 150,000 majority on a resolution demanding that the fall in the demand for labour, resulting from the squeeze measures, should be met by work-sharing and short-time, not by dismissals and redundancies.

It was a grim autumn, with unemployment rising month by month, and widespread short-time, mainly in the car industry. The numbers of wholly unemployed were rising as employers cut their costs and ceased to hoard labour.

The CBI business survey showed that the firms sampled expected a very serious fall in new capital investment in 1967 – a pessimism not, in fact, realised when the final figures for the year became available, for in that year investment in manufacturing industries, at constant prices, fell by only 2.8 per cent, and was well above the 1964 rate.

When Parliament met later in the month, these anxieties were expressed in a debate initiated by the Opposition on redeployment. A day later, the motion to approve the activation of Part IV of the Prices and Incomes Act was agreed, after a rough debate, by 307 votes to 239. Some thirty Labour back-benchers abstained.

The wages freeze was total, and was honoured without exception. More surprising, there was not a single strike against it. The only major dispute in the whole six months' period was a strike against redundancies in BMC's radiator factory at Oxford.

Chapter 17

A GREAT deal of work had gone on since the General Election on the question of closer relations with Europe. George Brown's committee had painstakingly produced a number of reports, and we were nearing the time for a decision about our next step.

I felt that, instead of taking this further through Cabinet committees and formal Cabinet meetings, it was the kind of decision which would gain from a full-day meeting at Chequers. Many ministers felt strongly on this issue; it was better to have a 'second reading' debate, with no vote. We were due to meet on Saturday, 22nd October.

On Friday, 21st October I visited Wigan to open a new housing project, and went on to Skelmersdale New Town. On the train I re-read the papers which had been prepared for the Chequers meeting the following day, and considered what I should aim for at the end of the discussion. The case for applying to join EEC had been strengthened in my mind. But on what terms? What would the European reaction be? It seemed to me impossible to take a formal decision to apply, as some of my most senior colleagues wanted, without further contacts, and at the highest level. I decided to discuss with George Brown that evening the idea that he and I should visit each Government of the Six.

After the housing ceremony Wigan Corporation entertained me to lunch. Half-way through, a message was brought in from my mobile private office. A pit-heap had collapsed in South Wales, engulfing a school in the village of Aberfan, with a heavy loss of life feared. I asked immediately to be kept in touch, and told my secretary to tell the Secretary of State for Wales, Cledwyn Hughes, to fly at once to the scene of the disaster. In fact he was already on his way by helicopter from the RNAS base in Anglesey.

I went to Skelmersdale, where more news was coming in from Aberfan. I spoke to the Secretary of State in Merthyr. While there was little hope that lives could now be saved, there was still a faint chance that a few children might have been trapped behind some wall or partition and be still alive. I told the Secretary of State to take complete control of all the life-saving and other services. If anything had to be done to avert further disaster – or if anything could be done to save just one life – he was to order it and override all objections. He was specifically authorised to break the law, if necessary, to save life, with my undertaking that retrospective legislation to validate his actions would be introduced as necessary. Equally, I feared that some official might refuse an order on financial grounds – a civil servant conscious that Treasury agreement had not been obtained; or a local government servant, conscious that there was no statutory authority or financial agreement.

Cledwyn understood, and repeated his instruction. I was still unhappy, and felt that I ought to be there: it might be necessary to give orders about the emergency deployment of troops. I told him that I was coming on the strict understanding that no one on any kind of operational duty was to cease performing their duties to meet me.

My principal private secretary, Michael Halls, who was listening from London, had anticipated this decision and broke into the call to say that an Andover was already on its way to Liverpool Airport, ready to fly us to RAF St Athan. For the rest of that tragic evening I reproduce, without amendment, the note I dictated on my return from South Wales:

...I was taken by RAF car with police escort to Merthyr where – I was told at St Athan – a meeting of all those in charge of operations would assemble at 9.30 p.m. We were rather badly delayed outside Merthyr but the police car radioed for assistance and the police broke the jam and let us through. Two miles outside Merthyr we could see across the valley the scene of the disaster, the floodlights and also smoke rising from the wrecked houses. There was a big crowd in Merthyr when I arrived but I went straight in, being met at the car by Cledwyn. First we went to the Chief Constable's room where the Mayor, the Chief Constable, the Minister of Power and the three Welsh Ministers put me quickly in the picture. We then went to the main room. I began by saying, let us not have introductions, but would each present who spoke give his name and his job. I then said that if there was any man there who had a job to do on the site or any man by being on the site could even remotely help to save the life of one child, he should leave at once.

The Chief Constable then took charge and gave his own brief report and called each in turn. The Borough Engineer, who had done a remarkable job, reported he had all the equipment he needed; the Director of Production, NCB (their specialist in pit disasters) who reported on what they were doing to secure the tip from further movement; the head of Civil Defence; the head of the gas, electricity and water undertakings; the Director of Education just back from a meeting with the parents where he had tried to get a list of the missing children; the Brigadier, Western Command; each gave a brief report. I put a few questions and asked them if there was anyone there who felt anything more was needed, whether powers, equipment, or men. All agreed there was nothing they could ask for. Operationally I felt it had been very well done, for example, there were emergency telephones erected direct to the site, walkie-talkies, emergency feeding services and a tremendous assortment of drag lines and other civil engineering equipment. The Chief Constable then went to take his press conference, while I went up to the site.

We were driven one and a half – or two – miles back up the main road, then turned right across the valley and into the road immediately below the road where the houses and school were. We could only get half way along because of vehicles, and walked the rest through thick squelching black mud, varying an inch to three inches in depth. We then turned left to where the houses were – what looked like a smoking heap of match-board, bric-à-brac and mud, no one could have told there had been houses there at all. Men were digging and machines were scooping mud away under the searchlights. We then went down back along the road and turned up the path – which as we all felt was probably the path where the children had gone to school that morning – and then along to the school where we scrambled up the slope through all the workers, diggers, baulks of wood being carried and even banging into us. A number of the workers came up, shook hands and some of the bereaved parents just came and shook hands saying nothing.

The school hall where we went was open to the sky. And then half way along it was a great heap of black mud rising higher than the roof would have been and then merging with the pit heap itself. On the wall where we were standing were children's drawings, safety posters, etc. We watched the digging for some time, talked briefly to some of those who were working and then walked slowly back – one or two pressmen and then a television interviewer asked for my reactions, and I refused to comment at that stage. On getting back we heard the latest operational reports of the decisions given on various offers of help from outside. I had a further conference with the Chief Constable and Ministers. Dick Marsh was there looking very ashen and obviously worried about charges that were already spreading about negligence by the NCB and the warnings that had been given. George Thomas was perhaps the most affected as he had taken on the job of comforting the relatives and had attended the meeting of relatives held by the Director of Education.

I had a brief informal press conference, again refused TV interviews and then being satisfied that all concerned had the necessary powers, left for St. Athan, leaving at 1 a.m. and reaching London Airport soon after 2 a.m. I was driven to Chequers, shoes thick with mud and suit badly spattered, with that murderous mud we had seen. In the press conference I had simply announced that there would be a full and independent inquiry to be held in public. I discussed the form with Cledwyn and said we must have a senior judge. He said Lord Justice Edmund Davies would be the right choice but I said the Lord Chancellor was at Chequers for the Common Market meeting and I raised it with him before the meeting began. He himself suggested Edmund Davies and a line was put out to find him, though we did not get him until 6 p.m. Lord Gardiner had left Chequers by the time the Judge came through, so I spoke to him and found him very keen to do the inquiry – he mentioned to me that he was born only a few miles away and knew Aberfan and the school very well. On the Sunday he was announced and on the Monday the Secretary of State, in his statement to the House, said the inquiry would be established under the 1921 Act. On the Tuesday after questions I moved the necessary resolution in the House.

First thing on Saturday morning I had been in touch with the Palace about a visit by the Queen. Prince Philip was on his way and Lord Snowdon was already there. The Palace was anxious that the Queen's presence should not be allowed to stop any of the work. It was therefore decided that she should settle the date and the timing – possibly Sunday, possibly Tuesday – after hearing from the Duke.

On the Tuesday afternoon George Thomas, who had by this time returned to London and who was still pretty moved and shattered, told me of the reaction of some of the people to the visitors. They were obviously glad that I had gone – but the highest praise was for Lord Snowdon. He had gone spontaneously and, instead of inspecting the site, had made it his job to visit bereaved relatives. George Thomas told me some of the things he did – sitting holding the hands of a distraught father, sitting with the head of a mother on his shoulder for half an hour in silence. In another house he comforted an older couple who had lost 13 grandchildren – in another where they were terribly upset he offered to make a cup of tea, went into the kitchen and returned with a tray with cups for them all. He helped an older man persuade his son, who was clutching something in his tightly clenched fist, to open his hand. It was a prefect's badge, the only thing by which he had been able to identify his child. . . .

I reached Chequers at 2.30 a.m. that morning. When I awoke, beside the sudden waking realisation of those hours I could see my suit hanging and my filthy shoes, both covered with Aberfan slurry. Somehow it was weeks before I could bear to have them cleaned, and much longer before I could wear them.

George Brown arrived early at Chequers. I had not been able to see him on the Friday evening, so we met briefly before the Cabinet. I put to him an idea of a visit to the six EEC capitals. There was a momentary suspicion that he would prefer to go alone in the first instance, but this quickly disappeared. As a convinced pro-European I think he suddenly sensed that it was important that I should go, too, not only because it would emphasise to our hosts our sense of purpose, but also because I should be able to put directly to European heads of government the doubts which were still troubling me and get them answered.

It was an excellent Cabinet discussion, with senior officials there to help ministers in answering queries and doubts. I sought no final decision on the principle, though a majority by this time felt we should be ready to move forward. Just before summing up, I put my suggestion of the six capitals' tour to my colleagues, and it was universally supported. I directed that the matter be put on the formal Cabinet agenda, for decision, and said that I would put before my colleagues the draft of a parliamentary statement for endorsement; for while we should be making no final decision to apply for membership, we had to make clear that the series of visits had a serious purpose.

Most of the Cabinet left Chequers before dinner, but I had asked a number of senior colleagues to stay for a discussion after dinner about defence. Denis Healey had been working hard on a new defence pattern, designed to make still bigger savings in the Estimates over the next four or five years on the basis of reduced commitments. He had told me that he was ready to propose an approximate terminal date for our deployment east of Suez, though this would have to be worked out in all its implications – diplomatic equally with military and economic – and nothing could be announced before the Defence Estimates of the following year. I wanted to hear, in strict privacy, the views of the ministers principally concerned.

In our discussions in the Long Gallery there was general agreement with his proposals. But there was a sudden and serious disturbance to our talks. We had only just begun when the news came through that the spy George Blake, serving a sentence of forty-two years at Wormwood Scrubs, had escaped. This really was a shock, and it was clear there would be a rowdy parliamentary reaction. The Home Secretary went off to the telephone to deal with the situation.

The next few days saw the parliamentary sequels to our decisions and to Blake's escape.

On 24th October, the day of Cledwyn Hughes's statement on Aberfan and the establishment of the tribunal, Roy Jenkins answered a private notice question by Quintin Hogg about Blake's escape and announced an independent inquiry into prison security, to be headed by Lord Mountbatten. The Conservatives seemed determined to make it a party political issue, regardless of certain sensational escapes in their period of office. A week later, replying to an opposition censure motion, 'Conduct of the Home Secretary', Roy produced so scathing a reply that one went away feeling that the Opposition leaders could not have been more devastatingly castigated if he had produced irrefutable evidence that they had, severally and collectively, been responsible for springing Blake. His account in the closing sentences of his speech of the conspicuously unsuccessful manoeuvrings of Mr Heath himself, was a classic. He concluded: '...I believe that this problem will be met by the constructive measures we are taking, and taking quickly; but it will not be met by that combination of procedural incompetence and petty partisanship which is the constant characteristic of the rt. hon. Gentleman's parliamentary style.'

Meanwhile an unseemly argument had blown up around the Aberfan inquiry. The television producers were conducting their own examinations, with all the difficulties that can arise in trial by television. Some of those interviewed were men who would be key witnesses before the tribunal of inquiry. The searching style of television interviewing, which may hold few terrors for politicians and other experienced interviewees, involved dangers for the tribunal's statutory function to seek out the truth. But even the most experienced politician, schooled by years of parliamentary questions and answers, knows that a sudden unexpected television question – 'Answer yes, or no' – before twenty million viewers, can force an ill-considered answer, regretted afterwards. How much more might a Coal Board employee, a local government officer or a Government inspector, asked such a question, rush out an answer – probed with the aid of neither examining nor friendly counsel – which he would then stick to throughout the inquiry's proceedings? It was to guard against this conditioning and leading of vital evidence that the Attorney-General, rightly, issued a warning. It was immediately, and wrongly, interpreted by the press as a gag on free press comment. It was not. Free press comment could only be helpful to the tribunal, who could judge it against the evidence taken; press comment never, and press reporting rarely, is capable of conditioning evidence.

What Sir Elwyn Jones had in mind was not any issue of contempt of court: a tribunal composed of men of such authority and experience would not be influenced by press and television comment, except in so far as they found such comment helpful in indicating lines for inquiry. It was a matter of witnesses committing themselves under the pressure of television questioning. But from the moment of his warning, editorial comment and cartoonists' nightmares were such as to suggest that fascism had been introduced in Britain overnight. The Attorney-General was under such attack that I felt it right to support him with a statement in the House.

It was interesting that when the tribunal held its first meeting, its judicial chairman endorsed Sir Elwyn's statement. This support for the Attorney-General received only a fraction of the publicity which had been accorded to the attacks on him. Looking back on this not un-important incident, I feel, as I thought then, that the press genuinely believed that an issue had been raised affecting freedom of comment and had reacted accordingly.

The week after the Aberfan disaster, I was in Cornwall opening a new county infants' school designed to replace a Victorian building, of which my sister was head. Linked with us by closed-circuit television was seven other Cornish schools, which I opened simultaneously. It should have been – and, in a sense, was proud and happy family occasion. But, less than eight days after Aberfan, I could not get out of my mind, however illogical and unfair though it was – what was almost a sense of resentment at these happy innocent children, with all they had to look forward to, compared with the children of that Welsh valley, who had no future. Irrational and unjust, not least since every child was contributing to fund-raising efforts for Aberfan.

On 10th November I made a statement in the Commons on the

subject of Europe. Following Chequers I had circulated a draft of it to the Cabinet, who had gone through it line by line, and endorsed it.

I repeated the commitment in the election manifesto about entry into the Community, given the necessary safeguards, and referred to the probings which had taken place. The Government had conducted a deep and searching review of all aspects of our relations with the EEC, including our EFTA and Commonwealth membership. We had examined in depth all the implications for Britain of the Treaty of Rome and of decisions taken under the Treaty.

I continued:

> ... In the light of this review the Government have decided that a new high-level approach must now be made to see whether the conditions exist – or do not exist – for fruitful negotiations, and the basis on which such negotiations could take place.
>
> It is vital that we maintain the closest relations with our EFTA colleagues. Her Majesty's Government therefore now propose to invite the Heads of Government of the EFTA countries to attend a conference in London in the next few weeks to discuss the problems involved in moves by EFTA countries to join the EEC.
>
> Following that conference, my right hon. Friend the Foreign Secretary and I intend to engage in a series of discussions with each of the Heads of Government of the Six, for the purpose of establishing whether it appears likely that essential British and Commonwealth interests could be safeguarded if Britain were to accept the Treaty of Rome and join EEC.
>
> In the light of these discussions the Government will then take its decision whether or not to activate the arrangements for negotiating for entry, and what the appropriate time for such negotiations would be. . . .
>
> I want the House, the country, and our friends abroad to know that the Government are approaching the discussions I have foreshadowed with the clear intention and determination to enter EEC, if, as we hope, our essential British and Commonwealth interests can be safeguarded. *We mean business.*

And, to counter the inevitable rumours that entry would mean devaluation, I stressed that we should enter only when we had secured a strong economy, a strong balance of payments, and a strong pound. I ended by suggesting that the usual channels should discuss the timing of a debate, which I was sure the House would want before our European visits took place.

In subsequent questioning, I answered fears of a 'go slow' by saying, 'We intend to start – I was going to say at a hell of a pace, but that would have been out of order. . . .'

The debate took place a week later and though strong reservations, indeed outright opposition, were expressed from a minority on both sides of the Commons, we were able to feel that we had been given a fair wind for our initiative.

The EFTA Prime Ministers' meeting was fixed for 5th December at

Chequers, and arrangements were set in hand for the six visits in the spring. On 14th November I told Parliament that – as foreshadowed in our Moscow communiqué the previous February – Mr Kosygin had accepted an invitation to visit Britain, and would be arriving in London on 6th February for the first visit by a Soviet leader since Mr Khrushchev and Mr Bulganin came in April 1956. Meanwhile, the Foreign Secretary was due to visit Moscow.

That evening was the occasion of my annual speech at Guildhall, in response to the toast, 'Her Majesty's ministers'. Though traditionally these speeches tend to be devoted to foreign affairs, I had in the two previous years devoted as much time to economic questions. In 1965 I had naturally concentrated the overseas part of the speech on Rhodesia. This time I decided to speak mainly on Europe.

Nevertheless, I was speaking from a much stronger economic position, with our payments balance moving into surplus. I stressed the need for cool heads, cool nerves and a determination not to be panicked into easing up before we had achieved balance; for cutting out waste, whether through restrictive working practices or unnecessary overheads, from the board room downwards; for firm criteria, after the six months' statutory freeze ended, by which prices and incomes increases must be justified during the period of severe restraint. In this part of the speech I spoke in exactly the same words I had used a few days earlier not far away, 'to your neighbours and partners in this great national effort, the dockers of Poplar. . . .'.

But the main stress was on our hopes of what entry into the EEC on the right terms could mean for Britain and Europe, in particular in technology, where we had so strong a lead to give. It was in this speech that I first put forward my proposal for

> . . . a drive to create a new technological community to pool within Europe the enormous technological inventiveness of Britain and other European countries, to enable Europe, on a competitive basis, to become more self-reliant and neither dependent on imports nor dominated from outside, but basing itself on the creation of competitive indigenous European industries. I can think of nothing that would make a greater reality of the whole European concept. And in this field of technological co-operation no one has more to contribute than Britain. . . .

Nothing did more in Europe, as we found from our visits there, to convince opinion that we really did 'mean business' and were ready to provide new motivation and a fresh, characteristically British, driving force to the European economic idea.

But while our European initiative was hitting the headlines, the routine press of Government business continued, with the usual parliamentary storms – on real or imagined issues – and with the Cabinet locked in a new and tougher approach to the coming year's Estimates.

There was a great row over Gibraltar. Spain had been getting rough in asserting her claim to sovereignty over the Rock. New travel and trade restrictions had been imposed at the frontier; there had been scarcely spontaneous mob attacks on our consulates.

I was resolved that if Gibraltar wanted to remain with us she should do so. Equally, we all felt, and had the full reassurance of the law officers, that the fresh Spanish claim, reasserted first in 1964, was utterly bogus. The Treaty of Utrecht in 1713 had laid down that Gibraltar was to be British, but that if there were any question of the alienation of sovereignty to any other country, Spain should have first claim. No question of alienation was involved. Under our predecessors, a step towards modified self-government was made, in effect giving to the Chief Minister and his colleagues powers similar to those exercised by a city council in Britain. A limited measure of devolution to the people of Gibraltar could by no stretch of imagination invoke the requirements of the treaty concerning sovereignty. But in 1964, just before we came into office, the Spanish Government had asserted their claim.

There was never then, or subsequently, any possibility that we should admit the Spanish claim or consider any of the much canvassed compromises. The decisive factor was the attitude of the Gibraltarians. I had seen something of this on my brief visit a year earlier, on my way home from Salisbury, when, although the visit was announced on Gibraltar Radio only an hour or two before I arrived, the streets were packed with cheering crowds expressing support for the British connection. A referendum showed the almost total unanimity of the Gibraltarians in their decision to stay British. It would have been morally and politically inconceivable to have ever considered handing them over to a dictatorship, particularly – so far as the Labour party was concerned – Spain.

But press stories that we were likely to go soft on Gibraltar led to vociferous parliamentary pressure, and a rough question-time for the Colonial Secretary, Fred Lee, did not help. He was, in my view wrongly, put up to answer a private notice question. His responsibilities covered the colonial responsibility for Gibraltar, but he was not concerned directly with the negotiations and caused suspicion by stalling when asked about them. I directed that in future all such questions should be dealt with by the Foreign Office. George Brown decided that a number of questions tabled to him for 31st October, but unlikely to be reached, should be answered orally after questions. He began by reaffirming that 'Gibraltar is British by right', and said that no recent actions by the Spaniards could affect this fact. But as a country committed to setting an example in the peaceful settlement of disputes by referring them to a world authority, he announced that we had proposed to Madrid that all the legal issues in dispute should be referred to the Permanent Court of International Justice. He went on to say that we were sure of our case and had nothing to fear.

L

A White Paper would be published setting out the exchanges.

After Sir Alec Douglas-Home had welcomed the statement, Mr Heath rushed in with an attempt to draw a distinction between the isthmus and the Rock which, as George Brown pointed out, could only do a disservice. Four times he was up, concluding excitedly, in total distinction from Sir Alec Douglas-Home, who knew all the facts, that the Government's action was weakening our case.

I was sickened by the hypocrisy of the Conservative party over Gibraltar. In the spring of 1964, the then Conservative Government had agreed to provide Spain with the technical drawings and all the necessary know-how and equipment to build a new frigate force. I had attacked this from the Opposition benches, and was immediately subjected to a concerted press and political attack. Sir Alec Douglas-Home in a contrived but much-publicised speech at a private dining-club had gone so far as to say that, by taking this line, I had demonstrated my unfitness not only to be Prime Minister, but even to be Leader of the Opposition. He gained a great deal of mileage from these attacks and the Conservative press claimed that the recovery in the Tory party's fortunes in the summer of 1964 owed a great deal to them. Yet it was at this time that Spain had formally asserted her claim to Gibraltar. But now, in 1966, the Conservatives were donning their Palmerstonian mantles to express their detestation of Spain and her claim. It was not long after this, when Spanish frigates exercised close in to Gibraltar, that I acidly reminded the Conservative leadership across the floor of the House that if they had had their way the frigates infringing Gibraltar's territorial waters would have been of British origin.

Another parliamentary row was about telephone-tapping. To judge from my correspondence, a surprisingly high proportion of the population is convinced that it is the target of an eavesdropping Secret Service. Members of Parliament are not immune from this syndrome, and every click or hiatus on the line is taken as proof that they are being 'tapped'. Suddenly in November 1966, questions appeared on the order paper of the House of Commons. I decided to answer them myself, since this type of question is peculiarly within the responsibility of the Prime Minister. In the time of the previous government, anxieties arising from the transmission to the Bar Council of information so obtained about a barrister, had led to an inquiry by a committee of Privy Counsellors which had explained the rules, and shown how very few, even among suspected criminals or others possibly concerned with activities inimical to the security of the State, were covered.

But there were new fears, and there was a sensational build-up in the press. One Conservative newspaper went so far as to say, in the context of telephone tapping, 'The Labour party, once again, is involving itself in a sense of conspiracy. And one Minister – Mr George Wigg, the Paymaster-General – is not far from the scene. Truth or lies, fact or fiction, it is becoming believed by too many Labour MPs that Mr Wigg is keeping a close watch on either themselves or members of the Government.'

This was rubbish. How much it was rubbish did not become clear until I spoke in the House of Commons. Without prejudice to the normal practice of not replying to questions on security techniques, my answers made clear, first, that there *had* been tapping of MPs' telephones up to the time Labour came into office; second, that this had covered members of more than one party; third, that I had peremptorily stopped it when I became Prime Minister. From that moment no member had his telephone tapped so long as Labour remained in office.

Unfortunately, the press was unable to give as much coverage to the facts as had been previously given to the lie. Now the attack was concentrated on accusations that I had smeared my predecessors by suggesting that MPs' telephones had been tapped until 1964. I might have replied, had I wished to pursue the matter further, in the laconic words of Clem Attlee; invited after his retirement to appear at a London schools' brainstrust, he was asked, 'Why have you always preached class-war?' and replied, 'Didn't preach it, found it.'

During this period we were moving fast to our new initiative for a Rhodesian settlement. Three days after the Commonwealth conference ended, the Commonwealth Secretary flew out to Rhodesia for talks under the aegis of the Governor. He was there from 19th to 28th September. His task was to warn Mr Smith that he had rather less than three months in which to reach a settlement, otherwise we would institute the processes foreshadowed in the Commonwealth communiqué.

During his ten days' stay in Salisbury Bert Bowden saw every section of opinion, except those represented by Mr Nkomo and Mr Sithole. On every request to see them Mr Smith stalled, and he gave a flat refusal only on the Commonwealth Secretary's last day there. There was no progress with Mr Smith, either on the return to legality or on the implementation of the six principles. All he had to offer was a proposal that each time the Africans, by qualifying for A-roll votes, won a seat, new European seats would be created.

It was calculated that this device would delay the achievement of majority rule by a further ten years as against the period which would have been possible under Section 37 of the 1961 constitution, which dealt with the creation of new seats. At the end of the visit Bert Bowden and Mr Smith managed to agree on one thing: a statement listing the areas of disagreement. It was almost total.

When the Commonwealth Secretary returned to London and reported to the Cabinet we agreed to draw up a definitive statement setting out a number of alternative offers we were prepared to make; Mr Smith clearly regarded the situation as a battle for public opinion in Britain, where he had many friends.

We outlined, first, the proposals put forward by the Commonwealth Secretary, a simple six-principles solution. Second, we said we were prepared to agree to a proposal, much canvassed in Rhodesia, which provided for the safeguarding of the entrenched clauses of the constitution through a mechanism involving, in the first instance, a Rhodesian Constitutional Commission – the existing Constitutional Council writ large with more African representatives – and then the Judicial Committee of the Privy Council.

Third, we proposed as an alternative procedure that constitutional experts from the Commonwealth – we had in mind a commission headed by an eminent jurist from Australia – should visit Rhodesia to work out a new constitutional approach.

Fourth, we proposed that a mission of Commonwealth Prime Ministers should visit Rhodesia and work out a new basis for settlement.

Fifth, we proposed an entirely different situation – an 'Act of Union' between Rhodesia and Britain, under which Rhodesia would become part of Britain, with representatives in the British Parliament. This was based on a proposal put forward in a newspaper article written by Sir Edgar Whitehead, former Rhodesian Prime Minister.

The document embodying these five proposals was sent to the Governor on 15th October for discussion with Mr Smith. For nearly a month there was no reply. We then received a reply trying to throw upon us the onus of a breakdown. We decided to send a further short message to Salisbury for the purpose of elucidating certain deliberately obscure parts of Mr Smith's reply. If he wanted to play a game of musical parcels designed to ensure that we should be holding the parcel when the music stopped we could play it as well as he could; the difference was that we wanted a settlement if it could be honourably reached. Our reply went on 11th November.

He replied on 17th November in the most negative terms. It looked as though a final breach was near. Only the most desultory exchange went on through the Governor, assisted by Sir Hugh Beadle, by this time exercising his ingenious mind from a bed in Government House, to which he was painfully confined by a slipped disc.

The Governor felt that we had reached the end of the road so far as written exchanges were concerned. He was pressing in the most urgent terms that the Commonwealth Secretary should fly to Salisbury again. Once again we reached the point where we might have to face the resignation of the Governor.

On 21st November we had a meeting of the Rhodesian committee of the Cabinet in my room at the House of Commons. There was a general anxiety to respond; one or two ministers even feared the effect on sterling of a break – such is the weakness of a Government when the balance of payments is still in doubt – but this fear was not shared by Bert Bowden, who was determined not to fly out to Salisbury again. He indicated that if pressed it could be a resignation matter: I knew he had personal and family reasons for his unwillingness. I adjourned the meeting for a talk with him. I said he had to go. I think I had half persuaded him when a message came in that Mr David Frost was going to visit Salisbury to interview Mr Smith and wanted a safe-conduct from us. This was not in doubt, but I took the opportunity of pointing out to the Commonwealth Secretary that it would look damn funny if Mr Frost went, and Mr Bowden did not. He agreed to go.

Bert Bowden left on 24th November. For the account of what happened I rely on some diary notes I dictated at the time. Bert left for Rhodesia on the evening of Thursday, 24th November. He arrived Friday evening, talked to the Governor and Beadle and on the Saturday saw Smith. In the late morning I received a telegram from him saying that Smith had opened up certain propositions on which Bert had made no comment but said that he must report them to his colleagues in London. For a moment I considered what had gone wrong with him since he knew our attitude completely and should have been able to say yes or no. When, however, the longer telegram came in the afternoon, I realised his difficulties and for a time I was as bewildered as he was.

What had happened – Bert gave us a fuller picture on his return – was that he and Smith had met. Smith had asked him what propositions Bert had come with. Bert said he had none, but had Smith anything to say? Smith said, 'You came all this way to see me.' Bert said no, he had come to see the Governor. The telegram went on to say that they then sat and glowered at one another for some minutes at the end of which Smith said, 'We must go and see the Governor and tell him where we stand.' (Smith, Bert thought, was obviously trying to get the Governor on his side in establishing the responsibility for the break.)

Bert said, 'You mean, I take it, the Queen's Governor.' This was the first time Smith had used the words 'the Governor'. Smith said, 'Yes'.

The Governor immediately said he must have Beadle there. Beadle, who was downstairs, had to be found, so Smith and Bert sat there in the Governor's presence continuing to glower at one another for a further ten minutes. When they opened up no progress was made until Beadle (who, Bert suspected – and later confirmed – had had a long talk with Smith on the Friday evening) asked Smith whether it was not a fact that he was prepared to entrench the whole of Chapter III of the Constitution, including section 37, provided that the Delimitation Commission (the equivalent of our Boundary Commission) was protected in the fulfilment of its duties.

Smith gave a moderately encouraging answer and when Bert pointed out that after more than two months from his previous visit, there had been no progress on the return to constitutional rule, Beadle asked Smith if he was prepared in any circumstances to return to the 1961 constitution. When Bert asked him whether that would mean he was prepared to consider giving up his 'independence', Smith said, 'Yes'.

Bert then insisted that a note of this discussion be agreed, and he himself dictated it, asking Smith to interrupt him to correct any point. When it was complete it was agreed, and each retained a copy.

Bert reported to London and I had a worrying few hours working out the implications. By the evening of Saturday, I was pretty clear what the next step should be – a direct confrontation, under, of course, the aegis of the Governor.

I felt, however, that Bert would almost certainly resist the idea of any further meeting, especially if it involved me in direct dealings with a rebel, with all that would mean for his department's relations with African countries. I knew equally that he would not wish to remain in Salisbury any longer and that there could in any case be no question of getting Cabinet authority for him to negotiate in Salisbury, at any rate without reporting back personally to his colleagues. And time was getting short. Smith had waited more than two of the three months envisaged in the Commonwealth communiqué.

I therefore called in Sir Morrice James, Bert's permanent secretary, and other CRO advisers to prepare draft instructions to Bert, concentrating on the further questions he should put to Smith, since we had heard a BBC report from Salisbury that the two were to meet on the Sunday morning. I then dictated a telegram couched in such words that he would know it came from me personally. (Having been abroad on negotiations as long ago as 1947, I knew there was always a time, sometimes very quickly developing, when one thinks London has gone mad: I wanted him to know that I was personally dealing with this.)

My telegram 'For Bert from Harold' began by telling him what I thought he most wanted to know, that I agreed he should return at once. At his discretion he could stay another day, but since the new situation would mean a collective decision, we needed him home quickly.

After outlining the questions, I enjoined on him a total ban on news statements and interviews, and suggested that if photographed at airports he should wear his well-known saturnine expression.

In the event he did not see Smith, but three of Smith's officials came to Government House to see if he wanted to see him, and to inquire whether there were any points Bert wanted to elucidate. They were, therefore, given the three questions we had telegraphed to Bert.

We were surprised to hear that the Commonwealth Secretary had left for Malawi without seeing Mr Smith again, but were told that a long telegram giving his appreciation would arrive in the afternoon. It was ready for me early in the evening. But preparations for a meeting were going ahead. On Saturday night I had asked the Defence Department, with

Denis Healey's support, to prepare contingency plans; the alternatives were to be the sovereign base area at Akrotiri; Malta; or Gibraltar – probably off-shore in a naval vessel. It reported that HMS *Hermes* was available, but she was in dry dock and to move her would excite comment. HMS *Tiger* was at Casablanca on a goodwill visit and could reach Gibraltar in time for the following Thursday.

By Sunday night, 27th November, when we had settled on Gibraltar, the Defence Department had prepared flight plans. A Comet would pick up the Governor's party and Smith's party in Salisbury, and fly them *via* Luanda to Ascension, where two Britannias would be waiting.

(The Comet did not have the range for the sea crossing from Ascension to Gibraltar – for, apart from Angola, we could not have safely asked permission for Smith to overfly any other West African country.) Two aircraft were needed in case of breakdown; in any case, I wanted the Governor's plane to reach Gibraltar ahead of Mr Smith's so that he could receive him on board HMS *Tiger*.

From Saturday evening, 26th November, I had been consulting those of my colleagues most directly concerned. My impression of their reactions can be seen from the following further extract from the note I dictated at the time:

When I informed George Brown of developments on the Saturday evening, he was decidedly enthusiastic and thought a settlement now possible. On re-reading the telegrams on the Sunday morning he was even more euphoric. I saw the Lord Chancellor, who was emphatic that Bert and I should now meet Smith in appropriate circumstances, but he was equally clear that Smith was not trying to get a settlement, and that it was a last-minute public relations exercise.

The Chancellor and the First Secretary, whom I saw in the evening, strongly supported the idea that we should have a go. Dick Crossman had phoned me in the morning and I had indicated to him that there was some move that perhaps ought to be followed up, but I did not give him any details. He had telephoned because of uncertainty about the parliamentary timetable in relation to Rhodesia. He was in touch with the Chief Whip, who asked to see me. He began by telling me that Dick had said, 'Do not divert Harold from what I think he wants to do'. Dick had said that if we got a settlement we might have 50 abstentions but that it would still be worth it. The Chief Whip thought the figure would be lower.

On the Monday Bert returned and immediately fell in with the idea of a meeting, provided that we secured some understanding from Smith about the basis for the meeting.

Meanwhile, I had asked Sir Morrice James to be ready to fly to Salisbury by commercial flight on the Monday evening, 28th November. But there was no flight that evening, so we decided that the Comet which was being got ready for the Rhodesian party should take him and he should wait there for instructions.

Bert Bowden and I gave Sir Morrice James draft instructions – confirmed by telegram while he was in the air – for until the Tuesday morning the Cabinet had had no opportunity to approve the proposal we were putting forward. The Cabinet fully backed us both on the broad issue and the instructions given to Sir Morrice James. He was to extend the invitation 'under the Governor's aegis', but the meeting would take place only on one condition – that Mr Smith would have full power to settle on the spot.

Mr Smith reacted most favourably. He agreed he must have power to settle, but said he would like more time, suggesting that the meeting be delayed by twenty-four hours. I was worried at this because I had to be back for the EFTA heads of government meeting on the Sunday night.

But we agreed to his request, pressing him to leave as early as he could. There was a complication about flight times, in that Ascension could be used only in the hours of daylight. In the event, Mr Smith met his colleagues on the Wednesday morning, secured clearance of his plans, and informed Sir Morrice James that he had full and unequivocal powers to settle. Mr Smith wanted to leave after dark to avoid the press – we had agreed a joint release-time of the announcement for 9.30 a.m. Thursday, and both sides had observed strict secrecy. As it happened, he was seen by a South African photographer, who had been tipped off by the then landlord of the hotel where the RAF crew were staying that they were packing their bags and had asked for an early-morning call. The news broke at once and beat the agreed deadline.

In London, two Rhodesia committee meetings finalised our negotiating brief. On the Thursday the Cabinet gave us their blessing, with, quoting my diary record, 'some quite emotional comments from George'. In the afternoon I made a brief statement to the House in answer to questions on the order paper which secured a friendly cheer from both sides.

I said that there had been signs of movement in the past week, but that there was still, so far as I could at the moment judge, a considerable gap to bridge. 'There can be no question,' I said, 'of a settlement which does not honour the principles which all of us in the House stand by.'

The Labour member who had the first question down warned that if any of the six principles were to be abandoned many of his hon. Friends would not be able to continue to support the Government on this issue. I replied: 'My hon. Friend need have no anxiety. If there were any question of abandoning the six principles, which the House has endorsed, I could not support Her Majesty's Government, either.'

I was particularly gratified by the reaction of our own members.

My PPS, Ernie Fernyhough, told me on arrival that members in the tea-room and corridors had warmly greeted the news in the morning's papers. What pleased me were the words of a deputation of our MPs who were active on African questions. Once reassured that there would be no sell-out, no agreement except on the basis of the six principles and the Commonwealth communiqué, they were very friendly. Andrew Faulds, the victor of Smethwick, waited to shake my hand and wish me luck. There was wild cheering at a brief PLP meeting I had called to enable our members to express their views. They were all friendly and not disposed to delay me.

The Commonwealth Secretary, the Attorney-General and I went straight from the party meeting to the airport. We had to take a long route, over the sea, to avoid overflying Spain in a military aircraft. We reached Gibraltar at 9.30 p.m. in a heavy, squally, force-10 gale and driving rain. We were driven to the dockyard and taken in a sea-rescue launch to *Tiger*, a mile or so outside the harbour. We had arranged to have our meetings at sea, to ensure privacy for our talks. It was an almost dangerous leap from the launch to the platform with each vessel moving up and down some five feet in the rough seas. When we reached the deck we noticed four frogmen in full operational attire, waiting to rescue any who had missed their footing. After a brief reception by the admiral and captain, we inspected the conference room and went to our cabins to await the Rhodesians.

At 1.30 a.m. the Governor and Sir Hugh Beadle, the latter in a harness because of his back troubles, were hoisted aboard and Mr Smith and his colleagues, Mr Howman and Mr Clark (Solicitor-General), arrived half an hour later. I had a brief meeting with the Governor and Sir Hugh, and, on Mr Smith's arrival, a short talk with him in my cabin. In the morning I had another private talk with him there, before the full meeting assembled in the ward-room. I said to him that whatever had happened over the past year we were genuinely seeking a settlement, within the six principles. There was no point in looking backwards, or in engaging in recrimination. But we were both adult: I must make absolutely clear what the consequences of a breakdown would be.

At the Commonwealth conference, I said, we had fought for a three-month period in which we should seek to reach a settlement, which, to become effective, had to be acceptable to the people of Rhodesia as a whole. Failing that, mandatory sanctions at UN and our NIBMR declaration must follow.

He should not assume, as some of his British political friends had told him, that our economic position meant that we were desperate for a settlement. The British press for two days past, stimulated by a reference by the Chancellor – who was not in fact speaking in that context – had printed alarmist stories of the possible economic consequences of a confrontation with South Africa.

Mr Smith said that he had never been taken in by all he had read and been told about Britain's economic weakness. He recognised, he said, our latent economic strength.

I then told him that, as I saw it, we were on board *Tiger* to see whether we could reach an honourable constitutional settlement which could be a basis for independence. But there was also the question of a return to constitutional rule. No agreement could be signed except with a constitutional Government. Given agreement on board, we could proceed to agree a constitution, but that would have to be submitted to the fifth-principle test before the proposed constitution was put before Parliament. That test could not take place against the background of illegality. He would have to face, therefore, a period – under the 1961 constitution – without independence while the Royal Commission was at work. He had to face, too, the possibility that the Commission would rule that the proposals were not acceptable to the Rhodesian people. If this happened, I warned him, a second UDI would create a very different situation. He would face mandatory sanctions from the outset, and he could not count on further assurances about the non-use of force; such assurances would be withdrawn. He said he was not impressed by that kind of thing, and we went to the ward-room for our more formal talks.

The minutes of the successive formal sessions on the Friday and Saturday have been published in the Command Paper (Cmnd. 3171) we issued after Salisbury's rejection of what we worked out.

We quickly reached agreement on the entrenchment of the vital Chapter III constitutional safeguards, and sent our respective experts down to Sir Hugh Beadle's cabin to secure his assistance in drafting.

We then came to the question of the number of seats, and the franchise questions, vital to Principles I, II and III. At this point I put forward a new proposal, designed to reassure the Europeans and to clothe in constitutional form the new, sixth, principle I had enunciated earlier in the year, namely: 'It would be necessary to ensure that regardless of race, there was no oppression of majority by minority or of minority by majority.'

I found that Mr Smith welcomed this new principle. He liked, too, my new proposal. I had worked this out on the eve of the talks, and found that our expert advisers, as well as the ministers who accompanied me, found no fault with it. It provided, in addition to a blocking quarter of African seats, a blocking quarter also of European seats to safeguard European rights in the period when African capture of A-roll seats put the Africans in a majority of the legislature. The details were set out in the Command Paper, which further set out our complicated higher mathematics on the African blocking quarter, with the perennial arguments on the proportion between chiefs and elected Africans in the Senate which I proposed. The suffrage question, again, seemed nearer a settlement. On guarantees, we revived the proposal he had once favoured – a bilateral treaty registrable, as all treaties must be, with the United Nations.

But there was still the question of the return to constitutional rule and our requirement of a broad-based Government. On this I suggested an informal, restricted meeting between British ministers, Mr Smith and Mr Howman, since it must raise invidious questions about Mr Smith's colleagues.

Our proposals were:

1. If we could reach agreement on the constitutional terms for a settlement he could indicate his willingness to return to legality under the 1961 constitution. He could, in fact, leave the ship as Prime Minister-designate, with the Governor's approval:

2. The 1961 constitution would operate pending the Royal Commission's determination about the acceptability of our agreed constitutional proposals 'to the Rhodesian people as a whole';

3. If they were found acceptable, we would proceed to put them before Parliament, and proceed to unwind sanctions;

4. He would undertake to form a 'broad-based' Government in agreement with us, which would be the Government of Rhodesia during the interim period.

5. Since there might be a period when law and order was threatened, there would be a Governor's Defence Council, consisting of five Rhodesians and one British officer, to advise the Governor in the interim period. But the Governor could, in fact, act only on the advice of the constitutional Rhodesian Government.

I asked him point-blank whether he felt that if he signed an agreement on these lines, to which he had not demurred, some of his right wing would resign. He was very direct in reply: it would not be a question of resignation, he said, he would get rid of them. I felt that he would be glad to. So far as the broad-based Government was concerned, we were thinking of the inclusion of five additional ministers not of the Rhodesian Front, including, for example, businessmen, and one or two 'constitutional' Africans. The Front would still constitute a majority, but we should have to insist on the removal of 'one or two' of his colleagues. I asked him how big his then 'Cabinet' was – the answer was thirteen. Given, then, five new names, how large a Cabinet would he envisage? To my surprise he said, categorically, that he would want a Cabinet of twelve. Given the five newcomers, this meant that he was ready to drop six of his existing colleagues – more than I was pressing upon him.

We then started to go through the list of possible newcomers which Bert Bowden had prepared. It was interesting to see how many eminent Rhodesians – lawyers and businessmen – Mr Smith seemed, or affected, never to have heard of. At this point we invited the Governor and Sir Hugh Beadle to join us. Very quickly Mr Smith agreed on Sir Evan Campbell, Mr J. Quintin, a former Federal minister, and Mr A. D. Butler, the Welenskyite party leader. He was ready to accept an elected African, and agreed on the name, and also an African businessman, non-political and a member of the Constitutional Council. He was known to us also, though surprisingly not to Mr Smith, as a vice-chairman of the multiracial National Club.

We reached agreement on the five names and on one or two reserves, in case any individual refused to serve. We had, in fact, made surprising progress.

The afternoon session was no less harmonious, once again dealing with the content of a constitutional settlement. The question of detainees was discussed and settled in principle; the Attorney-General and Mr Smith's Solicitor-General were left to work it out in detail. They, and advisers on both sides, were instructed to turn the proposals on the franchise and on seats into a firm constitutional draft.

We then went back to the question of the return to constitutional rule. I repeated, in full session, the warning I had given to him privately about an issue on which some of my colleagues, and many in Parliament, were anxious – the danger of a second UDI, if after a period of legal rule under the 1961 constitution the Royal Commission reported that the proposed independence constitution was not acceptable to the Rhodesian people.

We then discussed the time-table in detail, Mr Smith reserving his position on two points. The first was whether the return to constitutional rule, which we said must come at once, should precede or follow the period in which the Royal Commission was testing opinion; the second, for the record, was the question of the broad-based Government, despite his private agreement with us earlier.

Before we adjourned for dinner, I proposed that the legal and other experts who had been instructed to prepare drafts should meet after they had eaten and report to us at a meeting at 10.30 p.m. Mr Smith pleaded that his people, and he, were tired. Could we not resume early in the morning? he asked. I suggested 8.00 a.m. and he agreed.

Then came a new proposal. Though he had specifically come to the meeting with full power to settle and to sign, he asked that he might telegraph the proposals we had given him since some involved new issues of principle. When I asked him to specify these, he mentioned the treaty registrable with the UN. This surprised me, as he had himself put it to Conservative leaders in London in October 1965. But I agreed to his proposal, advising him to warn his colleagues not to disperse for the week-end, so that he could have comments on the substantive issues as early as possible on the Saturday. He agreed. Sir Hugh Beadle said that surely anything he found acceptable would be endorsed in Salisbury. He agreed, but said there were one or two new issues, and again reserved his position on the two points he had previously mentioned.

At the long meeting on the Saturday morning, 3rd December, we continued to make good progress on the constitutional points, on detainees – where the experts were asked to prepare an agreed draft – and on a second Royal Commission to inquire into racial discrimination. We adjourned early before lunch for the drafters to get to work. Meanwhile we heard a disturbing story from Sir Hugh Beadle: Smith had told him that he could go no further without reporting back to his colleagues in person. When we met in my cabin he confirmed this.

This was Mr Smith's second major shift, and it did not increase our confidence in him. He had come – he had confirmed this before leaving Salisbury – with full powers to settle. On the Friday evening everything had been *ad referendum* to Salisbury, on the basis of a telegraphed report. Now, he said, he had to go back personally.

I was in a difficulty. If I agreed to his return, there was a danger that all the progress we had made, and even the possibility of an agreement, would be at risk once the rats got at him. On the other hand I would be vulnerable to political criticism at home, and possibly among Rhodesian moderates, if I refused him extra time. I said I would like to think things over during lunch and give him my answer later. When we met I told him with reluctance that I agreed that he should go back; but on condition that when the text which was being finalised was before us in the afternoon we should discuss it together, and then he should tell us – at once or, if he wished, after an interval for study – whether he would reject it as a whole, or, before leaving the ship, accept it for himself, and agree to commend it to his colleagues. In a private conversation with the Governor and Sir Hugh during the lunch interval he indicated that he would have no difficulty in accepting the constitutional proposals, but might have a little trouble on the return to legality. I reminded him that he had undertaken to come with full plenipotentiary powers to settle and that if he had acted as he had promised, he could have left the ship that evening or the following day, as Prime Minister-designate, with an Anglo-Rhodesian agreement in his pocket.

In our private talks I raised another matter with him, the question of the Rhodesian 'Parliament' during the period when the Royal Commission was engaged in testing opinion. In the morning I had pointed out that under an Order in Council made under the Southern Rhodesian Act, their Parliament was in abeyance. We could, of course, on the return to legality, make a new order restoring the validity of parliamentary proceedings. But, I asked him, what were his own views?

If a substantial number of Front members opposed the terms of the settlement, he might face difficulties – possibly the parliamentary rejection of legislation or refusal of 'supply'. He discounted this fear, saying that probably little legislation would be required. In any case, as I pointed out, if the situation did become impossible, he could as legal Prime Minister recommend the Governor to dissolve the Salisbury Parliament. The British

Parliament could then, by agreement, be asked to pass any necessary legislation under the Southern Rhodesia Act.

Sir Hugh Beadle put another suggestion in the private discussions: that if agreement were reached, the Governor should dissolve Parliament and under the 1961 constitution, to which Rhodesia would have returned, a general election must be held in not less than four months. This would be long enough for the Royal Commission to inquire and report and, meanwhile, the Government would take all necessary decisions, exactly as a British Government does in the (shorter) period of an election in our country. Mr Smith had told Sir Hugh, and he confirmed this, that he would welcome an early election for the purpose of 'getting rid of thirty of my chaps'.

Some of our advisers were worried about the idea of an immediate election, because if the new Parliament were still Front-dominated it would be difficult to reconcile the continuance of the broad-based Government with the responsibility of the Government to Parliament. There was the further problem that a second election would be required when the new constitution came into force. However, we agreed to leave the choice to Mr Smith; he told us he had no strong views one way or the other.

When we put the draft agreement before Mr Smith in the afternoon, the reference to an election was in square brackets – to be deleted if necessary. But Mr Smith agreed that the brackets should be removed, so that the relevant section carried the same validity as the rest of the draft. If this meant anything, it meant that Mr Smith on the whole favoured the idea of an election, recognising that the decision would be his. Or was it, I wondered later, that he was looking for an emotive debating point to justify rejection of the proposals we had worked out together?

I have dealt with this question in detail, because, after Salisbury had rejected the *Tiger* proposals, Mr Smith utterly misrepresented and perverted our discussions by claiming that we had insisted on sending Parliament packing and instituting a period of direct rule by the Governor.

By tea-time we had reached a substantive draft and Mr Smith had no further points to raise. He asked – and it was agreed – that when the amendments were typed in he be allowed to take the document to his cabin and study it. He would need time for reading and thought. If on reading it, it was unacceptable to him the discussions would end, and we should revert to the pre-*Tiger* situation. If, however, he could commend it to his colleagues, arrangements would be made for him to leave for Salisbury that evening.

We left him adequate time for study. After two hours I sent my principal private secretary, Michael Halls, to inquire how Mr Smith was getting on; he returned with the disturbing report that the document had not been touched and that Mr Smith had been going on a conducted tour of the ship. A few minutes later Mr Smith sent a message, in reply to our inquiry, and said that he had ordered his dinner; he would read the document over dinner and see me 'in ten minutes'. Half an hour later he had not done so, and we were within forty-five minutes of the scheduled time for his leaving the ship. He then sent a message saying he had finished his first course, and would be down 'in five minutes'. But when Michael Halls reminded him that he was due to reject or to sign the document he said he did not mind signing it as a correct record of our meetings.

This he confirmed when we met in the ward-room – his third broken pledge, in little more than twenty-four hours.

I began by saying that it was a question of accepting the document in its entirety, or rejecting it. The deadline could not be extended beyond a day of his return. Even if Mr Smith had gone back on the agreed intention of reaching agreement on *Tiger*, he should at least undertake to commend it to his colleagues. He replied that it was impossible since he himself could not accept the document. But he would try to give an answer, 'Yes' or 'No', within the time I had laid down.

I made clear that though I had come with power to settle, I was now in some difficulty; if he was reserving his position in order to consult his colleagues, the British Cabinet must equally be free to take their own decision on the document we had produced.

I then adjourned the meeting so that I could consider, with appropriate advice, the implications of Mr Smith's third exercise in backsliding. He did not take this very seriously. He was too busy packing. Shortly after 9.00 p.m. he appeared on deck ready to board the launch to the shore. When I heard this, I gave instructions that he was not to leave. Just as he prepared to enter the boat I intercepted him while the executive officer gave the order, 'Boat away'. I took Mr Smith down to my cabin.

I had already summoned the Governor and Sir Hugh to my cabin and put them in the picture. They were devastated, since earlier in the day, following a talk with Mr Smith, they were convinced that a settlement, then and there, was 'a hundred to one on'. I therefore expected that Sir Hugh would agree that Mr Smith had gone back on the agreement we had made at lunchtime – that the document should be accepted *ad referendum* Salisbury or rejected. Sir Hugh then wavered, and asked if there could not be a compromise. I replied that if the issue was now that of whether the return to legality should precede or follow the appointment of the Royal Commission – which Sir Hugh so patently wanted to chair – no Commission could function with credibility against a background of illegality, press censorship and oppression. I wanted a simple answer. I regret that I was moved to say, of Sir Hugh, that I could not understand how any man could have a slipped disc whom Providence had failed to provide with a backbone. We then met with Mr Smith.

It was a rough interview. I took him through all his successive postures: full power to settle, a request to telegraph the proposals to Salisbury, a request to go back for consultation with either a document he rejected, or one he commended, and then a refusal to take any line at all. How could we do business? Looking back on it, I feel that I underrated the fears he had always had that, even while he was in the air, his colleagues would 'do a Winston Field on him'.

After seventy minutes of vigorous, not to say emotional exchanges, the more polite of which were recorded in Command Paper 3171, I proposed a fifteen-minute adjournment to allow each side to take stock. We met again at 11.00 p.m. I then said that we should regard what had been drawn up as a draft agreement, a working document, to be signed as an accurate record by both sides. It should be considered by the British Government and by Salisbury. Since Mr Smith's departure had been delayed, we would extend the time by which we expected them to decide their attitude until noon on Monday, 5th December. Mr Smith agreed. I then addressed him in a final exhortation, with no punches pulled. I quote the official record:

> The Prime Minister said that he had proposed this course because he still believed that Mr Smith wished to reach a settlement, if only because the alternatives were so terrible to contemplate. Since this might be his last meeting with Mr Smith on this basis, he hoped that Mr Smith was under no illusions about the consequences if he and his colleagues rejected the proposals.
>
> Since IDI [Illegal Declaration of Independence] both sides had made mistakes and miscalculations. Mr Smith and his colleagues had said that IDI would be a nine days' wonder; but it was still a matter of intense and anxious discussion. They had predicted that it would result in an inflow of new investment into Rhodesia; but investment had virtually ceased. They had been confident that it would secure early recognition by other countries; but no country had recognised a pseudo-independent Rhodesia. The British Government had also made mistakes – particularly in predicting that sanctions would bring the rebellion to an end in a matter of weeks rather than months. But if the last chance of a settlement was now lost, it would not necessarily be a matter of weeks or even months; it might be a matter of years. The problem was a moral problem, on which the British Government were not going to give in. If there was no settlement now, things would never be the same again. Mandatory sanctions, even though on a limited basis, would be unavoidable, equally the British Government were committed to withdraw all their previous proposals for a settlement, including those which had been under discussion during the present weekend, and to adopt a policy of 'no independence before majority rule'.
>
> The Rhodesian problem was not unlike the United States Civil War. That, too, had started with a constitutional issue and had ended with the abolition of slavery. Similarly, the Rhodesian problem in its fundamentals was not simply a question of constitutional provisions; it was a question of African advancement. The British Government would go on to the

end; and they would not compromise. Moreover, once the problem reached the United Nations, that organisation could not afford to lose; and other powerful countries could not afford to let it lose. Mr Smith should not assume that, if he and his colleagues in the illegal regime now rejected the proposed settlement, it would ever be possible for them to discuss the question with Britain again on the present basis. Nor should the regime assume that, although the British Government had not reversed their earlier undertaking not to use force to bring the rebellion to an end, they would necessarily be able to maintain this position. They should also remember that, if they now rebuffed our own offer to accept the proposed settlement, they would have very few friends left.

Perhaps they had not been very well advised by British visitors to Salisbury. Perhaps they had paid too much attention to gossip and speculation about British economic weakness. It was true that the loss of some £30 millions of exports to Rhodesia in the last year was unfortunate. But over the same period our total exports had increased by nearly ten times as much. Mr Smith and his colleagues should therefore beware of trusting people whose only motive was to write Britain down. We were basically a strong country, and we had never yet been defeated in any task to which we had really set our hands. If it took us years to solve the problem we should not give up, however much we might be hurt in the process. Once mandatory sanctions were introduced, once the principle of 'no independence before majority rule' was formally adopted, there could be no going back and no more concessions of the kind the British Government had been ready to make in order to promote this last meeting and to give Mr Smith and his colleagues a final chance.

If, on the other hand, it proved possible to reach agreement on the settlement at this eleventh hour, there would be other and more constructive subjects which would need urgent consideration – e.g. the lifting of sanctions; the formation of the broad-based Government (on which he and Mr Smith had already exchanged suggestions privately); the release of detainees; the suspension of outstanding death sentences pronounced by the Salisbury regime; the establishment of the Royal Commission; the exchange of new High Commissioners; and so forth. He still hoped that a wise decision in Salisbury might allow him to be in early touch with Mr Smith on these and similar questions.

We then signed the working document and parted at midnight. I spent a few hours in Gibraltar discussing with the Chief Minister the Spanish threat and repeated our unalterable decision to stand firm by the people of Gibraltar.

By 12.30 p.m. on Sunday, 4th December I was in London, and held a Cabinet from 2.30 p.m. to 5.30 p.m. The Cabinet virtually unanimously accepted the working document. I then left for Chequers for the EFTA Prime Ministers' dinner. What a relief it was to meet with serious heads of government who knew what they wanted and meant what they said!

But Rhodesia was a matter of importance to our EFTA colleagues. Because of the force of public opinion in their own countries, the Scandinavians were at least as concerned with the Rhodesian situation as with European trade. At dinner, Jim Callaghan sat next to the Portuguese economics minister, known to be very close to Dr Salazar. Jim Callaghan told him where things stood after *Tiger* and the minister asked to have a private talk with me. Immediately afterwards he left for London to phone his Prime Minister. The following morning when the conference formally convened, he told me that Dr Salazar had particularly wanted me to know that he had intervened strongly with Mr Smith before Gibraltar and, on that very morning, had again pressed him in the strongest terms to settle.

During the conference we heard that the Rhodesian 'Cabinet' had not reached agreement by noon and had told us they wanted more time. We agreed.

At 6.00 p.m., after a flood of conflicting rumours, we received the news that they had rejected the agreement.

I decided to make a statement to the House that evening. In the Comet on the way back from Gibraltar I had dictated the greater part of it in a form which could be used whether the Rhodesians accepted or rejected the proposed settlement. Now I had to 'top and tail' it on the basis of the latest news.

Under Commons rules it is not possible to intervene in the business of the day, except at the end of a given debate. A message was sent that I would make my statement at the end of the debate on the Tribunals and Inquiries Bill then before the House. My over-long statement took some time to type and check, but the Attorney-General filibustered bravely, sitting down as I arrived. Never has the House been so fully and authoritatively informed on tribunals and inquiries.

The House was sympathetic with my disappointment. My answers to questions were passionate and over-long but Mr Speaker, and the House, showed their traditional tolerance to a minister at a moment of crisis. I was, however, disturbed at some of the undertones of official Opposition questioning. The 'great divide' – the phrase used by Mr Heath on Rhodesia at his party conference two months earlier – was becoming a reality. I wanted no divide, but if there were to be one, I wanted it to be on our terms.

On my return to No. 10, exhausted though I was, I drafted a motion for the two-day debate I had promised. It was in three parts:

That this House endorses the decision of Her Majesty's Government to accept the Working Document worked out by the Prime Minister and Mr Ian Smith on 3rd December; deplores its rejection by the illegal regime in Rhodesia; and supports the decision of Her Majesty's Government now to implement the undertakings given in the Commonwealth Prime Ministers' communiqué.

It was understandable that the Opposition, in view of the line they had taken since the Prime Ministers' conference, should dissociate from the third part of the resolution, even though to do so would invite the riposte that to fail to proceed with mandatory sanctions would mean acquiescence in illegality and a major split with the majority of Commonwealth nations.

The question was how the Opposition would vote on the first two legs of the resolution: endorsement of the working document, and condemnnation of its rejection by Salisbury. If the Opposition moved an amendment opposing sanctions and NIBMR, that was one thing, and we should oppose them; if they opposed the whole resolution they were formally aligning themselves with Salisbury. They recognised the dilemma in which I had placed them, and, presumably with their eyes open, they decided to meet the whole resolution in head-on opposition.

I was shocked and angry. In the impassioned speech I made – lasting some eighty minutes, including interruptions – I never ceased to make this clear. It was probably the most aggressive speech of my parliamentary career.

I set out to deal with the issues as calmly and factually as I could. But the Opposition were determined to interrupt and create as much noise as they could. This proved to me a stimulus. I had intended to leave to the concluding part of my speech my strictures on an Opposition which aligned itself with Salisbury on all the issues raised in our motion.

But the interruptions were so sustained that I replied immediately:

Since the document was rejected, we are told, purely because we insist on legality, this means that by their vote they are no longer insisting on legality. It is no good their trying to wriggle out of this.... They are voting against a motion which endorses the Government's acceptance of the working document – they are against endorsing it....
They are voting against the criticism (An Hon. Member – They are voting against you....

This was it, of course. I replied:

Yes, against me, not against Mr Smith. Every one of the hon. Gentlemen opposite is more interested in trying to get rid of the legal Government here than the illegal regime in Southern Rhodesia.

I went on to point out the three successive stages by which Mr Smith on board *Tiger* had gone back on his power to settle. On the question of a possible dissolution – which Mr Smith by this time, despite all he had said to me, was whipping up into a major reason for rejection – I disclosed the facts and exposed his utter dishonesty.

I set out all the alternatives we had proposed to him over the three months since the Commonwealth conference: the Commonwealth Prime Ministers' mission to be led by Mr Lester Pearson, the commission of Commonwealth constitutional experts under Sir Douglas Menzies, the Australian judge and cousin of Sir Robert; our dramatic offer, based on a suggestion of Sir Edgar Whitehead, for an Act of Union between Rhodesia and Britain, with Rhodesian representatives in the British Parliament.

My conclusion was a passionate denunciation of the hypocrisy of the

Opposition – who had themselves neatly swept the Rhodesian question under the carpet until the 1964 Election was safely out of the way – over the whole period from the time we had taken office. I warned that their vote would be a vote to break our obligations to the Commonwealth:

> They may feel that we ought not to have entered into such obligations and if this is their attitude, let them say so, because I know that had we not done it the Commonwealth would have been destroyed....
> A year ago, the Leader of the Opposition was shattered at my suggestion that this was a moral issue. He looked surprised when I said it. He himself went on, a month later, to admit that it was a moral issue....
> I would remind him of this – his recognition that it is a moral issue – before he decides where he will stand, when all of us have to stand up and be counted in the Lobbies tonight.

I had never spoken in the House with so much passion. I drew the contrast with Suez, when Mr Heath as Chief Whip had whipped his unwilling supporters into line; the suppression of the facts by the then Government; now we were publishing every exchange in a further Blue Book. For us there would be no secret treaty of collusion:

> If they vote tonight it will be for party unity and not for principle. There will be sad hearts among many who will vote. If the leaders of the party opposite call upon the same hon. Members to sacrifice principle to the dictates of party, this will be the most despicable parliamentary manoeuvre in the history of the Conservative party. If they do that, then they must accept responsibility for every action of the Salisbury regime from now on. Above all – in our parliamentary system which, on an issue such as this, ultimately rejects the tepid Laodicean spirit of compromise on the greatest moral issue which Britain has had to face in the post-war world – they must range themselves irrevocably on one side or the other.

I concluded with a historical parallel which had never been far from my mind. The words and interruptions are taken straight from Hansard:

> It is more than a century ago that the great issue of constitutional legality and racial slavery imperilled the future of a great nation across the Atlantic. The Tory Establishment of those days supported illegality and condoned slavery and racialism (Interruption). But there were men, poor men, in Lancashire, who suffered deep hardship, privation and near starvation. Yet remained firm on what they were able to recognise as a moral issue (Laughter). I assure hon. Gentlemen opposite that this is not a laughing matter. Some hon. Gentlemen opposite cannot take the truth. They are smiling because they know that it is true.
> The sacrifice suffered by these people was commemorated in the imperishable words of Abraham Lincoln's Memorial to the Working Men of Manchester.
> Hon. and right hon. Gentlemen opposite are tonight not asked to accept privations for their principles. Nor are we. But it will be on principle – on a moral issue – that we shall divide tonight.

When I sat down it was to cheers from our side such as I had never known before. All our back-benchers rose to their feet and waved their order papers, a totally spontaneous and unexpected act. Standing ovations are not unusual in party conferences, and are indeed *de rigueur* at some. But none of us could remember one in the House of Commons at the end of a speech. More predictable was the news we heard later that the Conservative whips had passed the word round that Mr Heath should be given a spontaneous ovation when he made the concluding Opposition speech that evening.

Our motion was carried against the Conservative amendment by 353 to 244.

Rhodesia, and progress towards the Common Market, continued to dominate the political scene and the work of government to the end of the year.

Reports were coming into London, not always easy to evaluate, about the Rhodesian 'Cabinet' meeting on 5th December. What appears to have been true was that by lunch-time there seemed to be a majority in favour of accepting the *Tiger* document. Mr Smith was said to have advocated this course and it is widely accepted that when the tireless Lord Graham set out to lecture him, saying that he would never accept it, Mr Smith pointed to the door and said he was free to leave. If the reports were true, Mr Smith could have clinched the agreement by lunch-time, but he weakly agreed to an adjournment, during which interval the extremist party bosses exerted their pressure and invoked all the grass-roots threats of which they were capable.

By the afternoon the die-hards were gaining ground and Mr Smith went along with them. From then on their main preoccupation appears to have been how they could falsify the record.

For our part we joined in the United Nations in a mandatory resolution, under Chapter VII of the UN constitution, setting up a wide-ranging system of international sanctions on trade with Rhodesia.

The other great issue during these stormy days was Europe. The EFTA Prime Ministers on that same Monday, 5th December, gave their blessing to our plan to visit the capitals of the Six and the meeting concluded with a general undertaking to keep in the closest touch throughout. We agreed that while none of us would seek to negotiate for any other EFTA country, each would, in their own discussions, bear the interests of their partners in mind.

As Christmas drew nearer, our programme for the European visits was settled. Most public comment during that period was based on optimistic or pessimistic forecasts of what we should find in Europe – and above all, in Paris.

Chapter 18

Crisis in the newspaper industry – Cabinet changes – visit to Rome – discussion with Signor Moro – Common Market problems – speech at Strasbourg – visit to Paris – discussions with General de Gaulle – visit to Brussels – the problem of agriculture

WHEN I returned to work on New Year's Day, 1967, it was to find a growing crisis in Fleet Street. More than one newspaper was reported to face imminent closure as circulation and advertising revenue failed to keep pace with sharply rising costs. There were reports that the Government would have to intervene, and various specifics, such as a subsidy on newsprint, were proposed. I was under strong pressure from a number of MPs and from journalists to take action.

But any measures which might have to be taken would have to be most carefully prepared, to avoid not only the charge but the fact, however indirect, of Government interference with the press. Clearly, any non-discriminatory action to help the press generally would be extremely costly. The prosperous would become much more prosperous before the threatened papers could be saved. On the other hand a selective policy could be represented as interference and however careful the Government might be, the charge would lie that it had placed an independent newspaper in its debt. Moreover, some of the more powerful and prosperous proprietors were arguing that Britain could do with fewer newspapers.

The day after my return to London I was guest speaker at a television celebration of ten years of Granada's 'What the Papers Say'. I began by referring to the 'present grave position in Britain's newspaper industry'. Then I set out the doctrine that in a free and democratic country such as ours the British people need, and are entitled to demand: a free press representing every point of view, however poisonous any of us might feel that certain of those views – or the expression of them – may be. I went on: 'If this is to be achieved this country needs and is entitled to have something like the present number of papers, national and local, recognising that circulations and reputations will wax and wane as individual papers are more or less successful in catering for the particular type of demand at which they aim.'

I said I was urging this both from the consumers' point of view and from that of the hardship falling on Fleet Street, on journalists and other staffs when a great paper – or a local paper – closed its doors. There was something fundamentally unhealthy in newspaper economics when the balance between circulation revenue and advertising revenue had become so distorted that almost no price increase could guarantee viability. I asked if we should not be looking more widely at the communications industry as a whole. Referring to television advertising, then much more profitable than today, I said that while it had:

> ...undoubtedly tapped a new source of advertising revenue, none can deny that the net effect of commercial television has been to draw away from the press advertising revenue which it would have had, and which would have been sufficient to guarantee viability on much smaller circulations.
>
> And if this is true, it is equally true that so far as the press is concerned television advertising revenues do not fall with an even hand: that where the lifegiving waters of television advertising do come down to irrigate the arid plain, they are channelled in an arbitrary fashion as between newspapers and their groups, certainly not representing need, nor for that matter directed to the areas of greatest potential fertility.

I set out the problems within the industry; above all, restrictive practices, not only on the labour required in a rapidly changing industrial scene where ancient craft rules had lost any meaning they ever had, but also on recruitment. I said:

> In my area, where my constituency is, and it's a great printing centre, it is still easier for a rich man to get through the eye of a needle than for a young alert school-leaver – 'O' levels and all – to get a training apprenticeship in the printing industry. Restrictive practices in the newspaper industry have reached the dimensions of a national scandal.

That last sentence was the one headlined by most papers the following day. I blamed management for part of the responsibility:

> There is too much fear and timidity on the part of some managements – a fear of interference with production which probably will have to be faced one of these days. Many here are familiar with the late night threat – rarely, if ever, an official demand on the part of a great union – which can paralyse production for a night or longer.

I said that the old solidarity of employers – 'one closed, everyone closed' – had been abrogated but the newspapers might consider a group insurance or indemnity policy to cover for each the cost of such unofficial disruption, '...to enable the industry as a whole to deal with what I can only describe as blackmail'.

In conclusion, I referred to the role of Government. The possible disappearance of one or more great newspapers was a matter of national concern, and for this reason must be a matter for Government concern. I spelled out the 'appalling risks' of Government intervention:

> This is particularly true where the immediate dangers are not generalised but are concentrated on a small number of our great papers, because Government intervention involving discrimination would not only of itself be a very grave step, whatever safeguards there might be. It is not only a question of what would be done but of what some might think

was being done. And even if it were possible to provide any assistance that were needed on a non-discriminatory basis – here providing help where help is not needed by the very definition – there might still be a lingering suspicion of obligation – and even if this were untrue, it might threaten the whole philosophy of the free press.

I do not believe the solution should be sought through further concentrations of closures. And no one should assume further concentrations which are a question for the Monopolies Commission, over which I have no influence, and for the Government over which I have. A tidy book-keeping solution which might get the accounts right over-all, particularly if those accounts are put right by closure, is not a solution that the nation could accept.

Government not as government – government certainly not as a political organisation, but government as trustee for the people as a whole, who want to maintain a free choice of newspaper, will be watching this urgent work with anxiety mixed with hope. Anxiety, for all the reasons I have mentioned. Hope, because I believe this industry is capable of solving its own problems.

But should there be any matter – I have referred to restrictive practices, to the work of the joint board and there is the Cameron inquiry – or should there be any other matter where the industry feels that the Government can assist, on a basis which does not threaten – or even be capable of being represented as threatening – the existence of a free press, then the Government stands ready to give what help it can.

In the event, disaster was very narrowly averted. There was a moderate pick-up in advertising as the economy began to recover. Hard-hit newspapers drove tougher bargains with the unions and, faced with the choice between acceptance or heavier unemployment, in individual cases the unions agreed to somewhat more efficient working practices. Newspaper prices were raised, with Government agreement. Cross-printing arrangements helped to make the use of expensive plant more economical.

In the first week of the new year I made further changes in the ministerial team, including the Cabinet. Patrick Gordon Walker had regained Leyton at the 1966 General Election and it had been understood that he would be brought back into the Government. He replaced Douglas Houghton as Minister without Portfolio. Douglas had been a most successful 'half-back' and a great deal of the Government's success in the social services and other fields owed much to his expertise and almost infinite capacity to take pains in going through the most abstruse and technical detail.

But he was sixty-eight, and though showing no signs of age or tiredness – a characteristic he has gone on to display in the discharge of his no less exacting duties as Parliamentary Party chairman – I was under pressure, rightly, to reduce the average age of the Government at all levels. Two other ministers left the Cabinet but remained in the Administration, with the incorporation of the Colonial Office into the Commonwealth Relations

Office. Fred Lee became Chancellor of the Duchy of Lancaster – the first Lancastrian with a Lancastrian seat to hold the post for a half a century – and was allocated to the Department of Economic Affairs to give Michael Stewart much-needed help on the industrial side. Much of his working life had been at the bench, and during the war he had been chief convener of shop-stewards at the Metrovick complex at Trafford Park, Manchester. As a young minister at the Ministry of Labour, he had impressed Clem Attlee with his fresh ideas on industry and industrial relations. It was unfortunate that he was less successful in the House than in his department (and for some reason the press had it in for my Freds – Fred Peart alone enjoying a measure of exemption). Arthur Bottomley remained at Overseas Development, but outside the Cabinet, which I reduced to twenty-one.

The Ministry of Aviation was due to be formally wound up a few weeks later and its aircraft industry work transferred to the Ministry of Technology. Fred Mulley moved to the Foreign Office to become, with George Thomson, joint-deputy to George Brown, with responsibilities for Europe and economic questions. John Stonehouse became Minister of State in the enlarged Ministry of Technology and for a few weeks, pending Parliament's approval of the relevant 'ministerial transfer of functions order', titular Minister of Aviation, though at the salary of a Minister of State. Lord Shackleton left the position of Minister of Defence for the RAF to become deputy Leader in the Lords.

There was a major change at Defence. Before the election Denis Healey had told me that the process of unifying the department had reached the point where he would be ready to replace the three Ministers of Defence for the separate services by two functional ministers, one for general administration, including personnel questions, and one for equipment, each dealing right across the board. Gerry Reynolds, who had been Minister of Defence for the Army, became Minister of Defence (Administration), and Roy Mason, Minister of Defence (Equipment). The third former Minister of Defence, Bill Mallalieu, replaced Roy Mason as Minister of State, Board of Trade, with special responsibilities for civil aviation, shipping and tourism. Denis made a statement that the ministerial regrouping did not mean the end of the separate Chiefs of Staff for each service, or of the individual services.

A number of ministers of state retired, most of them over sixty, one over seventy – still doing a good job but I had to think of future recruits for the Cabinet. Lord Champion, deputy Leader in the Lords, Austen Albu (DEA), Walter Padley (Foreign Office), Ted Redhead (Education and Science), and George Willis (Scottish Office), left us; as did Lord Rhodes and Harold Davies, Under-Secretaries respectively at the Board of Trade and the Ministry of Social Security. Harold Davies became my PPS. All reshuffles involving the departure of tried and trusted colleagues are painful: this one was particularly so.

These resignations enabled me to promote promising Under-Secretaries – Shirley Williams to Minister of State, Education and Science (higher education); George Thomas to Minister of State, Commonwealth Office and Dick Mabon, Minister of State, Scottish Office. Eirene White moved from the Foreign Office to Minister of State, Welsh Office.

Maurice Foley, who had specialised on immigration, moved to Defence as Under-Secretary for the Navy, and his place was taken by David Ennals. The work on immigration was specialised and dedicated and I did not want any young minister to do more than a relatively short stint; but I was extremely fortunate in all the three who held the post. Peter Shore moved across from Technology to the DEA and was replaced by Jeremy Bray. Jim Boyden became Under-Secretary for the Army, and his place at Works was taken by Lord Winterbottom. Charles Loughlin moved from Health to Social Security, Julian Snow transferred to Health, and Bill Rodgers from the DEA to the Foreign Office, replacing Lord Walston, who went to the Board of Trade.

The newcomers were Harold Lever (DEA); Roy Hattersley and Ernie Fernyhough, till then my PPS (both to Labour); Norman Buchan (Scotland) and Reg Freeson (Power).

On Sunday, 15th January the Foreign Secretary and I left for Rome, on the first of our Six visits. Rome was put first because any other order could have invited criticism – but no one could be affronted by our going first to the capital where the Treaty was signed. Before leaving we had held a final briefing and tactics meeting at Chequers. It was agreed that I would open with a general statement and George Brown would then make a statement on the special problems we were facing on agricultural financing. We found that this worked well on every one of the six visits; as monetary questions came more and more to be raised by our hosts I dealt at length with these.

We were warmly welcomed, above all by President Saragat, who was able, in a long private audience and at the dinner he gave for us at the Quirinale, to indulge with old friends his passion for discussing the cut-and-thrust of the political world, both British and Italian, which his official position normally precluded. It was very clear that Signor Moro, the Prime Minister, strongly supported British entry and would go to great lengths to achieve it, and if it were possible for anyone to feel even more strongly, that man was Signor Nenni. The Foreign Minister, Signor Fanfani, outwardly seemed much more reserved and cautious, very anxious to press points of concern to the French – though I think that this marked not an absence of enthusiasm, but an expert's view that all would depend on Paris.

It might be convenient to describe the main course of the Rome talks, setting as they did the pattern for the rest. On subsequent visits – Paris was, of course, a special case – I shall refer only to divergences from the pattern, including any new points raised. One thing we knew: as we expected, and as was right, the full trend of our talks in each capital was known in the other five within hours. For our part, we kept our EFTA partners and the Commonwealth in the picture as the discussions progressed.

Signor Moro welcomed us, happy that we should have come to Rome first – he took it as a mark of respect to the city where the Treaty was signed, and as a recognition of Italy's favourable attitude to our entry. 'Europe is not Europe without Britain.' Thanking him, I went straight into a statement of our position. We were there not to begin a negotiation, but to establish whether, as we hoped, conditions might be favourable to a negotiation. We were concerned not so much with the wording of the Treaty, but the reality of its practical working.

I explained the statement I had made in the Commons on 10th November. After the Six discussions, Her Majesty's Government would decide whether or not to activate arrangements for entry. (It was not necessarily a question of applying, for the application of 1961 remained on the table.) As we had said, we meant business and a majority of the House of Commons was favourable. I referred to the EFTA Heads of Government conference, which had welcomed our move.

On the Treaty of Rome, I repeated that we were prepared to accept it and not to seek such amendments or revisions as would fundamentally alter its character. We would accept the Treaty, subject to the necessary adjustments consequent on the admission of a new member and provided that we received satisfaction on the points of difficulty we envisaged and would proceed to outline. Despite some hostile comment, we saw our entry not as weakening, but as strengthening the Community.

Dealing with the economy, I said that our decision was based not on weakness, but on economic strength. The £800 millions balance of payments deficit of 1964 had been halved in 1965, and further reduced in 1966. (I did not then know that the final 1966 deficit would prove to be £67 millions and that, as I spoke, we were in fact in surplus.) Our monthly visible trade deficit had fallen from £45 millions in 1964 to £23 millions in 1965 and to £12 millions in 1966.

I then came to the problems that had to be solved if Britain were to contemplate entry. These were, briefly, problems arising from the European Community's Common Agricultural Policy as it had emerged over the past few years; Commonwealth questions; problems related to freedom of capital movements; and problems of regional policy. Regional policies, I said, we were raising not because I thought they constituted a major difficulty, but because we wanted to hear of Italian experience here – they had problems in their south as we had in our north.

Of course, the fact that I had listed these major issues did not mean that there would not be others of great importance; more appropriately they should be part and parcel of the negotiations. They might well include other agricultural problems not directly arising from the CAP; the time-table for our acceptance of the common external tariff; and the abolition of tariffs within an expanded Community. We did not need to explore these in detail at this stage. On our general approach to negotiations, I said that I hoped that we should not have to get involved in all the details which had dominated the arguments of 1961–3. We had embarked on a great effort and would not like to see great issues bogged down in discussions of such questions as kangaroo meat; though we should take into account the provisional agreements reached in the earlier negotiations.

I stressed the importance of our contribution to a European technology, and my proposal for a European technological community. On political unity, I said that we were prepared to play our part and gave them a preview of what I was going to say at Strasbourg.

Signor Moro welcomed my statement, both in general and in detail, and we got down to specific issues. After a good deal of constructive cross-table discussion, Signor Fanfani set out a list of nine questions he wanted to put. I had every reason to think that these had been agreed with other members of the Six, to draw us out at the very outset of the talks. They were concerned with:

1 Britain's economic situation: the relation in time between achieving balance and the beginning of negotiations.
2 The relation in time between such negotiations and the Kennedy round of tariff negotiations.
3 The scope, extent and duration of the adaptations to the Treaty, or regulations made thereunder, which we should be seeking.
4 The extent to which we were prepared to accept results of the 1961–3 negotiations as a starting-point for resumed negotiations.
5 The changes we should want to press on Commonwealth issues.
6 The question of adjustments in the social field, not then urgent as the Community would require two or three years more to complete their arrangements. By mid-1968 there should be total freedom of movement of labour within the Community.
7 Our relations with EFTA. Did we envisage individual or collective negotiations? Would there be two sets of negotiations, involving those who sought full entry and those who sought some form of association?
8 Our proposals on technology. Italy (which always stressed Britain's technological potential, whether in bilateral or wider discussions) Welcomed our initiatives, but should we not be clearer about

institutions when Euratom was integrated with the other communities? Were we proposing technological collaboration in advance of entry?

9 Political unity. What was our attitude to discussions then going on within the Six on matters which might involve amendment of the treaties? Signor Fanfani did not expect us to support supranational proposals, though Italy hoped ultimately for a supranational Europe – achieved gradually and quietly and in a way which would not make our negotiations for entry more difficult.

I dealt briefly with all of the questions except those relating to agriculture. There was no come-back on anything I said.

When we met again in the afternoon, George Brown went straight in on the agricultural issues. First, the cost of living: he gave our then estimates of an increase in food prices from ten to fourteen per cent and stressed the effect this would have on incomes policy, and he underlined the case for a more realistic price-level in the Community. He then dealt with the problem of the period of transition.

Turning to the problem for our farmers, he made it clear that he rejected the simple view that since we should be moving into a higher-priced agricultural system, British agriculture must benefit. The CAP cereals premium would hit us in two ways. Very many of our farmers, especially the smaller ones, depended on cheap cereal for feeding-stuffs; at the same time subsidised imports from the Community would injure our producers. Some cereal producers would benefit, but the effect of the CAP would be to divide British agriculture between the north and west on the one hand, and the south on the other. The first group, with its higher rainfall and in the main poorer land, included the greater part of our small agricultural holdings, rearing livestock and producing pig meat, dairy produce and eggs. While they would suffer, the south and east would prosper. This led us to feel, first, that a really adequate transitional period should be agreed and, second, that since there would be major changes in the pattern of our agriculture, we should want to be free to make calls on production grants under the provisions of the CAP 'Guidance Fund' for 'structural improvement'. Both of us referred to the existing British production grants, hill-farming subsidies and the rest, and the need for such assistance to be available – and indeed intensified – on a Community-wide basis.

Turning to the Commonwealth, the Foreign Secretary, while referring to problems affecting Australia and Canada, described in full detail the effects on New Zealand and on present and former dependent territories in tropical and sub-tropical areas, and pressed the special need for action to continue the benefits many of them enjoyed under the Commonwealth Sugar Agreement.

He took issue with Signor Fanfani on some (inadequate) estimates the

Italian Foreign Minister had been given of the effect of the CAP on Britain's balance of payments; the Community estimates of some £200 millions he regarded as totally unrealistic. He laid all the weight of his argument upon the level of prices fixed by the CAP and on the inequitable system of CAP financing. Unless changes were made, the burden imposed upon Britain as a new member would be so unfair as to be politically unacceptable. He then spelt out in fuller detail our views on Signor Fanfani's questions, in so far as they related to agriculture, the Commonwealth and regulations made under the Treaty.

Our talks then went deeper and deeper into issues such as the free movement of labour and, in detail, into the operations of the Guidance and Guarantee Fund of the CAP. We were particularly concerned about how far grants from the Fund would be available for structural improvement, and for correcting the worsening regional imbalance which CAP decisions would involve. Signor Restivo, the Italian Minister of Agriculture, then treated us to a detailed and helpful account of Italian experience under CAP. He stressed, in particular, how Italy had taken advantage of its provisions to even out regional disparities. His speech was impressive – but, as we commented, Italy was a food exporter, living under a Community regime created for food exporters; for this very reason it would create great difficulties for us, the world's largest food importer, which could not be fully met by transitional arrangements and adjustments in our system of farm production and food supply.

On the second day we continued with agricultural problems and, in particular, problems of CAP financing. George Brown, again, was at his best in summarising the issues. It had been in our Opposition days – when he had wound up a debate on the Chief Enaharo case – that I had said that, if he had taken up the law, George could have been one of the great lawyers of our age.

We then turned to capital movements and regional policies. On capital movements, I said that we had attempted to evaluate the consequences for Britain of the Community's arrangements for dealing with capital movements, distinguishing as they did between direct investment – investment, for example, by industralists in production or assembly plants abroad – and portfolio investment – investment by private individuals or financial institutions in stocks and shares. This was a very real distinction for Britain. Given a transitional period for adjustments, we would welcome a system of free movements of capital for direct investment, under which our businessmen would be able increasingly to invest in our sister nations within the Community, as European firms invested in production facilities in Britain.

Portfolio investment, however, raised different issues. I had every confidence in the ability of the City of London to take advantage of freer movements of capital; indeed as one of the world's two major capital markets we should be able to add a further dimension to the financial ambience of the Six. But there were special problems for us. Our foreign exchange controls involved a fairly strict control on overseas portfolio investment.

We were not afraid, over a reasonable period, of freedom of movement, both ways, between Britain and the existing EEC countries. But the liberalisation requirements of the Community might well expose Britain to the risk of a capital drain, via the Community, to third countries such as the United States. Our own ring fence on British portfolio investment in the outside world might well be removed, given time and adequate safeguards, to allow freedom of capital movements to other members of the enlarged Community we envisaged. But there was no fence round the Community; this was understandable since the capital markets of the Six were mainly orientated in domestic terms. I would see no objection, over a period, to European capital being used to develop European industry and trade. I would see every objection to its being used to invest in the United States. Existing rules might mean that British savings went, through Europe, to Wall Street to build up an American industrial strength which might then reinvest in Europe.

I said that I would rather see British and Community capital and technology mobilised in order to develop, let us say, a strong and independent European computer industry than have our portfolio investment flowing *via* the Community to the United States, to be used there for the purpose of building a still stronger American computer industry which might then dominate the individual, or collective, computer industry of Community countries.

It would be interesting, I said, to know the effect of this financial *démarche* on other members of the Six when it was circulated to them. (That it led to some furious thinking became clear when, a few weeks later, we visited Luxembourg, which was obviously designated by the Six as the centre for a further and more detailed confrontation on the issues I had raised.)

We then turned to regional policies. Both George Brown and I set out the questions. We suspected that the Italians – and the Belgians, too – had got away with murder on securing acceptance of their regional policies by the Community. We were concerned to enjoy the same freedom. The answers we received, both on the freedom we required for our existing regional policies and on our plans to extend them, and on interventions we intended to practise through such instruments as the Industrial Reorganisation Corporation – itself partly based on the Italian IRI – were reassuring. It was important to us that we should be able to report not only to our colleagues but to Parliament, that in the matter of regional policies, Community law, but still more important, Community practice, allowed a great deal of latitude.

At the end of the meeting I summed up our conclusions. We were encouraged by what we had heard. Some problems which outside commentators had felt might divide us seemed unlikely to do so. Given a reasonable attitude on Commonwealth problems, foreign exchange policies and certain other issues, the big outstanding problem was the agricultural policy, particularly so far as its financial operations were concerned. The Community regulations had been drawn up for countries which were, in the main, food exporters. This fact must inevitably create a serious problem for a country such as Britain, which was a major food importer. It was possible that other issues we had raised might, in the event, constitute a stumbling-block, but there could be no escape from the fact that agriculture and agricultural financing would be the central issue. It would need the total resources of European ingenuity and goodwill to overcome it.

The following Sunday, 22nd January, we left for Strasbourg, where I addressed the Assembly of the Council of Europe on the invitation of my parliamentary – and former governmental – colleague, Geoffrey de Freitas, the President of the Assembly. I had dictated the speech at Chequers before our visit to Rome and it was intended as a major declaration. Certainly it was so regarded in Strasbourg.

I began with an excursion into history. Two thousand years ago – only the last one-ten-thousandth of the period man had been recently estimated to have been on earth, less than half a second of man's hour of history – the British people were already indistinguishably created from a score of areas represented at the Council that day. A thousand years ago, the name 'England' itself reflected the origins of European invaders and settlers. Then came the superimposition of Norman French laws and forms of law, brought to England from France and themselves of Scandinavian origin. Similarly, North American civilisation was created by European colonists and settlers – and the United States constitution itself was largely based on theories deriving from a Frenchman's misreading of the manner in which Government was conducted in eighteenth-century England.

Apart from my full explanation of the Government's initiative which preceded the visits to the Six, there were two themes I tried to stress. The first was the evolution of the nineteenth-century nation-state into a greater concept of unity and international co-operation, together with, not the negative concept of the retreat from imperialism, but the forward move from Empire to Commonwealth, in our own case, and that of France and others. And in all this I stressed the need not for uniformity but for drawing strength from the diversity of national, political and cultural characteristics.

The second theme was that of modern technology and the great impetus that a market of three hundred millions could give – in contrast to smaller, divided national markets. Repeating my favourite theme, and one which M. Jean-Jacques Servan-Schreiber was shortly to argue more fully in his book *The American Challenge*, I went on:

> Let no one here doubt Britain's loyalty to NATO and the Atlantic Alliance. But I have also always said that that loyalty must never mean subservience. Still less must it mean an industrial helotry under which we in Europe produce only the conventional apparatus of a modern economy, while becoming increasingly dependent on American business for the sophisticated apparatus which will call the industrial tune in the '70s and '80s.

I had taken the precaution of formally sending the text of my speech, *via* HM Ambassador, Sir Patrick Reilly, to President de Gaulle. There had been some doubt in my mind whether the General would resent my making a major speech on French soil, the contents of which he might not wholly endorse. On arrival at the Elysée I found that these fears were ill-founded. He began by expressing his deepest appreciation of my action in sending him a copy of the speech I had delivered; it was of the greatest interest. He did not say to what extent he agreed with it.

From Strasbourg we had flown to Paris, where we were met by M. Couve de Murville.

There had been one or two difficulties about the procedure to be followed. I had reason to know that the General wanted to meet me alone, before the wider talks. But I discovered that George Brown had sent a telegram – which he had omitted to clear with me – instructing HM Ambassador to insist that all our talks should be together, four or five of us, depending on whether both the French Prime Minister and the Foreign Minister were going to be present. I decided not to press the matter – but at a crucial point in the talks the General did.

We met at the Elysée at 10.00 a.m. on the morning of Tuesday, 24th January. It was a foursome – the General, M. Couve de Murville, George Brown and myself – plus Prince Andronikov, and my new Foreign Office private secretary, Michael Palliser.

Throughout these discussions, unlike those of April 1965, the task of interpreter was shared. This job is highly skilled, requiring qualities beyond those of linguistic fluency. Michael Palliser, now HM Minister in the Paris Embassy, was commended to me by officials and ministers alike as one of the high-flyers of the diplomatic service – and so he proved throughout his three-year period at No. 10. He is totally bilingual and totally European – he is the son-in-law of Paul-Henri Spaak. In international negotiations there is always a secondary prestige confrontation between the interpreters on both sides, and throughout my period at Downing Street I was well served, particularly in negotiations with the Russians and the Italians. The test, apparently, is the number of occasions when one's own interpreter is able to intervene in a translation by his opposite number to say that the other interpreter has not correctly translated what his man was saying; the usual convention was that each interpreter translated the words not of his own principal, but of the foreigner. By this test – and it became a secondary interest of our talks – my calculation recorded a seven to two victory by Michael Palliser over the redoubtable Andronikov.

To be fair, some of the goals were scored by Michael Palliser's superior knowledge of my thinking on esoteric questions of international finance, in which he had perforce been frequently engaged. But it was, in a minor way, good for prestige and the General, both on this occasion and on my next visit in June 1967, courteously went out of his way to pay tribute to Michael Palliser's command of the language and his power as an interpreter.

It was agreed that, as in Rome, I should begin by setting out at length the purposes and intentions of the British initiative. I spoke very much as I had in Rome, stating the purpose of our visit and the facts – and our hopes – about the economic situation. Figures at last available showed that we were by this time paying our way abroad.

I stressed the importance of technology in our approach. Both of us attached the greatest importance to our bilateral collaboration, defence and civil. But Europe must do more collectively in industrial technology. I reminded him that however much we built up our military defences in Europe all this would be barring the front door and leaving the back door open. Industrial independence was the prerequisite of political and, even more, military independence. Both France and Britain had been forced to pay the price of not building up that rugged industrial independence which could make them proof against humiliating industrial take-overs.

After setting out the main problems that would have to be dealt with in any negotiations, I turned to the role of France and Britain in Europe.

What our initiative might produce could not be measured purely in terms of the detailed economic issues that had dominated the discussions four or five years before. The essential issue was whether we could hope to build up Europe, as the General and I understood Europe, with the clear purpose of breaking down tension between East and West. We both had a special role – slightly different perhaps. We should play our respective roles together. Unlike some of our friends in the West, we both had quite close relations with the Soviet Union, in personal terms as well as governmental.

This brought me to the theme of my Strasbourg speech. Europe had an even wider role to play in the world at large, but she could not do so unless she were powerful – and that meant economically powerful. The task of the great European powers – and I instanced France and Britain – was not to be mere messenger-boys between the two power-blocs. We had a bigger role to play – and other nations wanted us to play that role – bigger than merely waiting in the ante-rooms while the United States and the Soviet Union settled everything directly between themselves. That was why France and Britain had to make effective their enormous potential industrial strength by giving that strength a chance to operate on a European and not on a limited national base, or on a series of national bases. Only if France and Britain did this could they exert all that went with industrial strength and independence in terms of Europe's influence in world affairs.

The President thanked me courteously, and then opened up. As ever he was relaxed, speaking quickly, fluently, without any notes; yet the whole speech was as logical in its framework and order as if he had written down every word. This he could not have done, as he replied almost point by point to what I had said.

He was, he said, greatly interested by my statement and by the way in which it was expressed. First, he said, he was particularly struck by the great difference between what I was now saying about Europe in general and the Common Market in particular, compared with the British attitude throughout the years since he had had the honour of directing French affairs. He remembered Britain's refusal to participate when the Common Market was being negotiated. He recalled Mr Macmillan speaking about 'economic warfare' – a reference, recently confirmed by Mr Macmillan, to a comparison between EEC and the Bonapartist continental system – and how Mr Macmillan made clear to him his hope that the Common Market would fail. He remembered Mr Heath involving the European governments in interminable negotiations in Brussels which had inevitably produced no result. He also remembered, he said, my own statements before I came to office, and, indeed, thereafter he had understood that we were not at that time favourable to the possibilities of economic integration with the Common Market. But now he took note of the very substantial change in the British position and he had listened with great attention to my exposition of it. He took note, with great interest, of the great difference between the past and what was apparently the present British attitude.

He went on to say that he had also been greatly struck by what I had said, and had implied, in my remarks about independence. For many years he had observed that Britain appeared to wish, at almost any cost, to maintain a special role with the United States. This had even been true in regard to Britain's relations with continental Europe; Sir Winston Churchill had expounded the doctrine of European unity, but had made it clear that such unity was all right for the Europeans but not for the British. It had been the same in NATO and the NATO nuclear force.

Now, as he understood it, I was saying that things had changed and that Britain sought independence, especially in the economic field, in industrial development and in the field of capital investment. He went on to deal with sterling; he had not, he said, found me too explicit about the future role I envisaged for the pound sterling. France paid tribute to the great effort made by the British Government to restore the nation's economic strength during the past two years. But they were not clear about the British attitude in the financial field; our policy towards sterling still seemed to be very closely linked with United States financial policy. Nevertheless, he wished to re-emphasise the great difference that struck him in my remarks about Britain's attitude towards her own independence, and, he said, he warmly welcomed this.

He then went on to a theme which was to become familiar during the year – the nature of the Community as it was, and was becoming, and how the entry of new countries might affect it. The Treaty was not itself a reality – it was simply a treaty – but its application had created certain realities, difficult as that application had been, both in the industrial and economic field and also – and here the difficulties had been very great indeed – in agriculture. This was the situation as it had developed at present among the Six and without taking account of the possibility of British entry, which would clearly be a matter of major significance both economically and industrially. Its consequence would be profoundly to change, if not the text of the Treaty, certainly its practical application. Moreover, others would wish to join: it would be a Community not of six, but of – and here he went up the ordinal scale – *'huit neuf, dix, onze, douze, treize'*, and its whole nature would be different. Naturally, he said, I realised this, and he was not saying it was an inconceivable proposition; indeed, he did not regard it as such. But it would be very difficult.

These words, he said, disposed of the problems that British membership would involve for the machinery and operation of EEC. But there was a number of practical problems. He instanced agriculture. Coal and steel would be others. But perhaps most important of all would be finance and the problem of currencies; it could not be denied that sterling was in a different international position from the other European currencies in that it was a reserve currency and, because of the vast size of the sterling balances, presented certain very special difficulties which placed it in a different situation from the currencies of the Six.

On technology, he was impressed by my arguments, though he felt that Anglo-French collaboration, such as we had been successfully developing over the past two years in military aircraft, could go on equally well whether Britain entered EEC or not.

He concluded by saying that he would reflect very carefully upon what I had said, upon what he had heard about the talks the Foreign Secretary and I had had in Rome, and the account of them he had received from us. He would look forward to hearing from me in due course how my talks in the other capitals of the Six had gone. The French Government would then wish to reflect very carefully on the outcome and to weigh the various considerations involved.

We then settled down to a short exchange on points he had made, dealing in particular with the Nassau Agreement and our own policy on nuclear weapons, and on Anglo-French aircraft collaboration, as a result of which the RAF's major aircraft for the middle and late seventies would now be Anglo-French in conception, design and production. But the essence of this successful bilateral co-operation, I reminded him, was the increasing of a market where the orders were placed by Governments. Collaboration meant that the cost to each of us was halved, and the market was doubled, because the two Governments could guarantee that what was produced would be bought. This would not apply in civil technology; however close our collaboration the products would be bought in the main by private enterprise firms, and sales would be across an eighteen per cent tariff frontier.

We broke off for lunch, and in the afternoon had a meeting with M. Pompidou and M. Couve de Murville at the Hôtel Matignon, where we examined the issues which had been raised in the morning in much greater depth. M. Pompidou was friendly, urbane and businesslike. Couve's superb intellect, not unmixed with the charm one always met with in private, was deployed on highlighting some of the difficulties he saw. Practically the whole afternoon was spent on the problems created by sterling's reserve currency role, and the sterling balances, and on capital movements. We replied on the same lines as in Rome, but the discussions went much deeper.

The next morning the French Cabinet had its weekly meeting and our talks were resumed at the Hôtel Matignon in the afternoon. They were mainly on agriculture and regional problems and George took over the job of exposition very much on the lines of his statements in Rome; again, very clear and to the point, as were his comments in the cross-table duel with Couve. The French ministers were very concerned to assess the scale of British cereals production then and, on the best assumptions we could make, on British entry into the Six.

At 4.00 p.m. M. Pompidou broke off the meeting, because the President was waiting to greet us at the Elysée for our final meeting. He asked me if I would drive by a somewhat less direct route than he was taking, as the President would want him to report on our meeting and then be on the steps when we arrived.

The General said he would like a private meeting with the two Prime Ministers and interpreters. He was very friendly and hoped we had enjoyed our talks. He commented briefly on our talks at the Hôtel Matignon about financial matters and agriculture and the question of levies. I said that it was a question not only of the levies but the whole complex of the Community's arrangements on agricultural financing. He asked me about the Commonwealth and I briefly summarised our sticking-points. At the same time I felt that world food prices might rise over the next few years as China, perhaps, became established as a continuing food importer and as US surpluses were run down.

He then turned to domestic agriculture. M. Pompidou, he said, had reported something from our talks which had surprised and impressed him, namely the large amount of cereals produced in Britain. Yes, I said, thirteen million tons. He repeated his surprise – France was then producing twenty millions with far more people on the land, and at a correspondingly higher price. We imported, I went on, seven million tons. With Common Market incentives, if prices were not changed, we should soon be producing twenty millions and importing a further three to four millions more. Though, I said, this did not seem to make sense to us, it was at least arguable that, longer term, we should maintain our concentration on livestock, and import more of those of our cereal needs we could not meet ourselves from the outside world. I was concerned that he should not use my twenty millions estimate as an indication that EEC entry might make us independent of imports. But the size of our cereal production continued to surprise him: it was as though he thought we were playing in the local Sunday School League and suddenly discovered that we were in the First Division.

We then went into the conference room where our two delegations were waiting. The General summarised the course of the talks and invited me to comment. I went over those points where I wanted to be sure that we had been fully understood: questions arising from the Treaty, CAP financing, New Zealand and other Commonwealth problems, the Commonwealth Sugar Agreement, sterling and the sterling balances.

I then turned to what seemed to be the main French point, changes in the character of the Community. Obviously it would have to accept change. But what changes would there be if there were no new members? The EEC had changed remarkably in the past ten, or even the past two years. The French Government should consider what changes they would still have to face, even if there were no enlargement. But where would the Community be in the 1970s with no British entry? Change, yes, but not the intensified technological dynamic we foresaw, with all that would mean in terms of Europe's influence in world affairs. Europe would remain divided. I ended by thanking the General for the reception accorded to us. The Foreign Secretary added his final comments, as did M. Pompidou – with a sting in the tail. He had been impressed, he said, with the Foreign Secretary's account of the extent of British interests outside the Community; this suggested that there might be great difficulty in absorbing those interests within a Community which was more restricted in terms of its geographical horizons and more protectionist in terms of its economic policies.

M. Debré, the Finance Minister, who had joined us, raised afresh the monetary issues, to which I briefly replied, and Couve characteristically said how much he agreed with George Brown when he had said that the political issues raised by British entry overshadowed the economic issues.

The General then announced that he wished to express the impressions he had formed from our meetings: impressions not of results, for there could be none at this stage, but of the exchange of views we had had.

Now we had a classical statement of the Gaullist philosophy. First of all, he said, he had the impression of a British Government which, as always in his past experience, was acting with the greatest solidity and dignity. He had the impression of an England (his word) which had evolved much from the position it used to take, which he personally had known so well in the past. He had the impression of an England which now really wished to moor itself alongside the Continent and was prepared, in principle, to pledge itself to rules in the formulation of which it had played no part and which would involve it in definite links with the system which had grown up on the Continent. He had the impression of an England which seemed disposed to detach itself to some extent from the special relationship which it had, or had had, with the United States, thus enabling it to be a European country; for the basic element of his idea of Europe was that it must be an enfranchised – '*affranchi*' – continent, as indeed it must be to play its proper part in the world.

If these impressions of his were correct – and he referred to their importance for our relations with Eastern Europe – then he welcomed this development.

But, he asked, what conclusions should be drawn?

The Common Market existed. It was a reality. He emphasised the difficulties involved in its construction and the similarity of its members in their industrial, commercial and financial make-up, and their currency arrangements, agriculture, technology – not identical, but similar.

Would the presence of Britain enable the Community to remain what it was? If we had to face the fact that Britain could not enter EEC without changing its fundamental character, could some other means of British participation be found; a means, he emphasised, other than membership? An arrangement? An association? An agreement between Britain and the Six? This was the question he asked himself, he said. He came to no conclusion, except to note Britain's evolution, which corresponded to his wishes. He was disposed, for himself, to study fully the question which the British had put to themselves: did the conditions exist – or not exist – for Britain to join the Community?

He invited the British, he said, to study, for their part, two alternatives:

either (his words) 'something entirely new', or an agreement for 'association' – again his word.

I felt I should comment. His reference to 'mooring alongside the Continent' was important, even historic. I had in mind that when the General had abruptly ended the 1961–3 negotiations he explained his action publicly in terms of the refusal of Britain to moor herself alongside continental Europe, and her insistence on a 'mid-Atlantic' position. I then commented on his other words, including his references to Eastern Europe, and reminded him that we had taken a leading part in preserving the option of closer relations with the Soviet Union by rejecting the multilateral force.

But I was at pains to make clear that there was no solution in his alternatives, 'something entirely new' or 'association', presumably under Article 238 of the Rome Treaty. Under such arrangements the British ship would not be moored alongside the Continent, but would come and go. It would be a commuter relationship; at best, an offshore relationship.

General de Gaulle then pronounced his benediction, his pleasure at the talks. His appreciation of Britain had been enhanced by them; he could only hope that our regard for France had been in no way diminished.

Classical, courteous. But what did it mean? Some members of my delegation were encouraged, because of the reference to 'mooring alongside Europe'. On the other hand there were the references to the alternatives. What, if anything, did they mean?

A week later we were in Brussels for discussions with the Belgian Government, and with the EEC and Euratom Commission.

The first meeting with the Belgian Government followed dinner at the Château de Val Duchesse. (George Brown, incidentally, was depressed that evening: his beloved West Ham, having only drawn with Swindon Town in a cup-tie the previous Saturday, faced a replay. When the news came through that Swindon had won, I had a forlorn Foreign Secretary on my hands; when the reason for his gloom was made clear, we witnessed an animated discussion which revealed the divisive effects of Belgian football on a communally and politically divided Cabinet. We agreed to discuss more unifying issues.)

Most of the discussion followed what had been said in Rome. But the Belgians were keen in pursuance of their political objectives, as M. Paul Van der Boynants, the Prime Minister, put it, to stress the 'tripod' thesis of M. Harmel, the Foreign Minister. In essence, they explained, they believed that Europe could develop healthily only if there were a balance between the three 'great European powers' – Britain, France and Germany – on a basis of equality. Given this balance, smaller powers such as Belgium were prepared to accept a larger measure of influence in the Community of the three great powers.

Europe must include France, whatever the difficulties. Europe must include Germany, who had shown her determination to pursue the idea of Europe rather than that of nationalism, but she could resist nationalism only in so far as progress was being made to build Europe. Europe must include Britain. It was inconceivable for Belgium to be associated with Germany in Europe while Britain remained outside, or for Europe to develop a policy towards the East without Britain.

M. Van der Boynants went on to develop his argument with special reference to European technology, the possibility of an economic *détente* with the East, and the formation of a European political front at international conferences.

I replied briefly, on the same lines I had taken in Rome and Paris, and we adjourned until the morrow, when I outlined more fully our position on the main questions affecting negotiations for entry.

This was followed by a series of questions from the Belgian delegation, more on institutional issues than on the issues of substance which I had emphasised as vital. The Foreign Secretary replied to these in some detail.

This led to a detailed discussion on agricultural questions, where George again took the lead, once more explaining our position in terms of the cost of living in Britain, the effects on British agriculture, the Commonwealth, and on Britain's balance of payments.

M. Harmel (the Prime Minister had by this time left to attend the Assembly) pressed George Brown point by point. I could not help feeling that the reiteration and development of the questions were part of an agreed EEC operation planned by, and to be reported to, the Six as a whole.

We met again in the afternoon and traversed well-worn paths as we discussed Community institutions and problems of capital movements and the position of sterling. I had to deal with some misrepresentations or misunderstandings of what had been said in Paris: the French report clearly had implied that I had stressed the prestige implications of the sterling system. The truth was quite the reverse, and I hoped that my reply would receive an equally wide circulation.

We went on to technology. The Belgian Prime Minister was also the minister responsible for science and technology, and he was clearly aroused by my speeches in Guildhall and at Strasbourg on this subject. He stressed our clear multilateral approach, in contrast with the bilateral emphasis favoured by France and Germany, and referred to Belgian initiatives on this question, mainly, apparently, related to outer space and satellite development.

My reply was more earthbound, and emphasised the importance of industrial collaboration on new productive processes and repeated the arguments I had urged on General de Gaulle.

On an institutional point that they had pressed strongly, I said that the European technological community I had proposed in Guildhall was not intended to be a separate organisation, with its own council or high authority and secretariat. There might be a case for superimposing it on Euratom, in the hope of breathing life into that somewhat disappointing organisation. But, as I understood it, since the three Communities were to be fused into one it would not be sensible to set up a technological institution outside the new organisation. Just as in Britain the Ministry of Technology had the duty of integrating technological development and industry, so in a Community that included Britain there would be advantage in the integration of European technological activities with the industrial and economic work of the new three-in-one Community.

In the evening, the Belgian Prime Minister invited us in for a restricted meeting to discuss an initiative his Government, and particularly M. Harmel, wished to take in the field of European political unity. We probed for more details of what at that stage seemed not to have been worked out very far and, in particular, asked what the French and German reactions would be likely to be, and whether non-NATO members or associates of an enlarged EEC would be included. We did not commit ourselves in any way, but left our hosts to make what progress they might with other members of the Six so that we should have something a little more definite to consider.

Earlier in that day we had a working lunch, followed by a meeting, with leading members of the EEC and Euratom Commissions. There was a somewhat arid discussion on the procedure to be followed should Britain decide to seek entry. Should a new application be made, or should we merely reactivate the 1961–3 application, where all that had happened had been a 'suspension' of the negotiations, the file remaining open? We did not get much of a lead and decided that the matter at that stage was somewhat academic.

Most of the time was spent on agricultural financing, with Dr Mansholt, the member of the Commission responsible for agriculture, doing most of the talking. He had done his homework and produced calculations to show that our financial contribution based on paying ninety per cent of the yield of import levies, in a Community expanded to include Denmark, Norway, Ireland and ourselves, would amount to some $685 millions. But decisions had been taken in the Market only to the end of 1969. If a hundred per cent payment of levies were decided, our tally would be $760 millions. The total due from us would depend on the contributions called for, according to the so-called 'key' setting out each country's proportion, to make up any deficit in CAP financing. He estimated that Britain would pay thirty-five per cent of the total budget, Germany and France twenty per cent, Italy twelve per cent, and the rest smaller amounts.

I pointed out that on current CAP decisions we should get little back from the agricultural fund in terms of assistance to Britain's farms and such a schedule of contributions would be intolerable. As the greatest importer we should be paying the lion's share of the levies, probably more than the rest of the enlarged Community put together and, at the same time, more than one-third of the budgetary contributions. Dr Mansholt then hurriedly said that he felt the current arrangements, based on transferring ninety per cent of the levies, plus the fixed 'key' of direct national contributions, were suitable only for the Community of Six.

As the meeting ended, it was clear that the Eurocrats had been left in no doubt that there could be no question of British entry on anything like the figures they had been discussing.

We left Brussels for London on the Thursday morning, arriving in time for my parliamentary questions.

There was urgent work to do, to prepare for a very different international negotiation. Mr Kosygin was due to arrive in London the following Monday morning.

Chapter 19

The search for a settlement in Vietnam – Mr Kosygin's visit to Britain – proposals for a de-escalation of the war – draft terms for agreement – victory for the hawks – Mr Kosygin at Chequers – the attempt to rescue negotiations – President Johnson's proposal – meeting with Mr Kosygin at Claridge's – final search for a formula – the bombing resumes

FOR some weeks before Mr Kosygin's visit I had been in close touch with President Johnson. The President was now clearly and actively working for a Vietnam settlement and had been involved in a number of secret initiatives, not all of them through the most suitable instruments.

The previous November there had been the farce of the Lewandowski affair. M. Lewandowski was the Polish member of the International Control Commission. Through the US Embassy, reinforced by experts from Washington, he had been briefed about the terms under which the Americans might be prepared to stop the bombing of the North. Thus armed, M. Lewandowski set off in the ICC aircraft on one of its regular flights to Hanoi and discussed the propositions with the DRV. He was overjoyed to find them showing very considerable interest. Unfortunately, on returning to base, it transpired that the terms he had put to Hanoi were very different from those on which the Americans had so painstakingly briefed him. There was another case a year later, and the result was to deepen Hanoi's cynicism about American peace initiatives.

It also meant trouble for us. George Brown was in Moscow at the time and the Soviet Government, genuinely I think, were continuing their policy of keeping us as a useful channel to Washington. But when they raised questions about M. Lewandowski's activities, George Brown was unable to comment. The US had failed to inform us. The Russians swiftly dismissed George from that particular case as unable to act as *interlocuteur valable*.

I was determined that this should not happen during Mr Kosygin's visit. There were straws in the wind to suggest that he might be prepared to change his previous policy of refusing to intervene to get the parties to the conference table. Weeks before, when he had proposed the exact dates for his visit, I had immediately noticed that this was the period of Tet, the Vietnamese New Year, when – if the experience of previous years was followed – there would be a cease-fire. It would be easier to extend this, or a bombing pause associated with it, than to seek to create a cease-fire at any other time. But there could be no repetition of the Lewandowski affair.

I made this clear to President Johnson and asked him to send a representative in whom he had confidence to put me fully in the picture before Mr Kosygin arrived. Some ten days before the Russian talks he sent Mr Chet Cooper, the right-hand man of Averell Harriman, who had been charged on behalf of the US Administration with all the duties associated with getting negotiations started for a political settlement. When Mr Cooper arrived, he told me that he had instructions to give me the whole picture, including the full details of the President's proposals for stopping the bombing and getting to the conference table. He emphasised the almost total secrecy of what he was telling me, saying that it had been kept so close in Washington that there were only four persons in the whole US Administration who were in the know. He then set out the proposals. The American Government were hoping to pass them to the DRV at a secret rendezvous, 'under a palm-tree', arranged for some eight or ten days hence, when the Tet truce became effective. But, and the President had confirmed this to me direct, they wanted me to do all I could to get the Russians behind the proposals and, if the omens looked right, to get Mr Kosygin himself to pass them on to the DRV Administration.

I knew that a great deal could change in Washington in a week, so I asked the President to send Chet Cooper back to London for last-minute briefing before the Russians came and to stay here for a day or two for consultation, as soon as we saw what line the Russians were taking. If it was going to be an active one, then I hoped he might stay longer. The President agreed and on the Saturday before the Russians came Mr Cooper brought me fully up to date. The 'palm-tree' meeting appeared to be arranged for the following Wednesday, but the President set great store by my involving the Russians.

On the morning of Monday, 6th February Mr Kosygin was due to arrive at Gatwick Airport, where a full-dress welcome with troops, military band and speaking platform had been arranged. I was in the Pullman coach at Victoria Station, just ready to leave, when we heard that, because of fog, there was considerable doubt whether the Soviet party could land. The train was held in the station for a few minutes. We were then told that Mr Kosygin had been diverted to London Airport. We rushed back to No. 10, awaited a police escort, and then reached the airport in eighteen minutes. The Government Hospitality Fund and the Ministry of Defence were equal to the emergency, and a small detachment of troops, a band, a platform with a public address system, and facilities for reporters, photographers and television were there in time.

After brief speeches we went in my car to Claridge's, where Mr Kosygin was staying as guest of the Government. As always, he was ready to talk very frankly in private, free from the presence of advisers, secretaries and note-takers.

It rapidly emerged that he was most anxious to discuss Vietnam; we had to see what we could do together. But as far as possible this should be discussed in private.

That afternoon we met privately for an hour. Mr Kosygin directed the conversation straight to Vietnam. He asked whether there were any DRV representatives in London. No official representatives, I told him, but two or three press representatives whose duties seemed to me to go much wider than news-gathering. We also had a consul-general in Hanoi.

We agreed on how the talks in plenary session should be handled. When we were all formally gathered together, I welcomed him officially, and he responded warmly. We decided that we should begin on Vietnam.

I set out the position as we saw it, bringing Mr Kosygin up to date on the latest Washington position and the state of opinion in the United States. I referred to an interview given in Hanoi on 28th January to an Australian journalist, Mr Wilfred Burchett, and confirmed as authentic by the DRV party journal. This had suggested that bilateral talks could begin between the US and North Vietnam if the bombing and, it seemed, 'all other acts of war against North Vietnam', ceased.

I reminded him of the Foreign Secretary's proposals in Moscow the previous November – he had been speaking not only for himself and not only for HM Government. He had put forward, with authority, a two-phase programme to meet the requirements of both sides. The DRV required proof of an 'unconditional' cessation of bombing; the US an assurance that some measure of 'de-escalation' would follow if the bombing was stopped. The two-phase agreement, agreed secretly in advance, would be, first, overt action by the US in stopping the bombing; second, further action in de-escalation by the US responded to by the DRV and the National Liberation Front by similar acts of de-escalation. Two phases, three factors, the US acting in phase A, both in phase B. But both phases must be covered by a previous understanding.

I was holding back on US refinements in this basic position and I emphasised the need to use the Tet truce to get a continuing bombing pause, balanced and responded to by an equivalent North Vietnamese response. Our hope was that Mr Kosygin, with his special contacts with Hanoi, could impress on the North Vietnamese leaders the importance of giving the Americans a firm sign, during Tet, of a readiness to make a positive and visible response to a cessation of bombing. I was not pressing him to say at *this* meeting whether he could send such a message. But if he could, I would press the US to respond, promptly and visibly. It was, in every sense, an issue of confidence, both ways. Mr Kosygin had stressed to us the North Vietnamese fear that unless the bombing stopped unconditionally the Americans might resume it. The Americans, for their part, might well fear that de-escalation would stop, or be reversed, or that the situation might worsen in other ways. The Americans would want any cessation of bombing to be permanent, but this meant convincing action by way of a signal from Hanoi.

I added another key point. If Hanoi insisted on the participation of the NLF (Viet Cong) in talks – if this were a prior condition for them – I did not see there need necessarily be any problem here. The best thing, I felt, would be a direct contact between the Americans and the North Vietnamese but this was not indispensable. I then raised the possibility of a Geneva-type conference, recognising the problem for our Soviet co-chairman.

Mr Kosygin's reply was full of meaning. For the first time he was prepared to talk business. True, at one point he checked himself to make clear that what he was saying did not mean that he had reached an agreement with North Vietnam; he was relying on what they had said publicly. I took this statement in the spirit in which it was said and solemnly hastened to say that I accepted this; indeed that that was in my mind when I referred to the subject.

He felt it was premature to talk about a new-style Geneva conference; such ideas were unrealistic in the absence of direct contact between the United States and the North Vietnamese; and, anyway, what about the Chinese? He was addressing himself – and this was for the first time – to the steps that had to be taken now to get the parties talking. Basing himself on public statements, and particularly the Burchett interview I had cited, he could see similar phrases in public utterances by President Johnson and Mr Dean Rusk. Warming to his subject, he said that if we, if he and I, could together take the North Vietnamese statement (the DRV Foreign Minister's statement in the press interview) as a basis and say to the President – together or separately, privately or publicly, in the communiqué or in a special message – that the statement was an acceptable basis for discussion, then that was the best move for us to take, leading to bilateral talks. He specifically agreed that because of Tet the present time was the most appropriate one. He said – and this again was new – that our task was to advise and assist the US and the DRV to meet and discuss their problems at the negotiating table.

The Foreign Secretary raised the question of movements of North Vietnamese troops through the demilitarized zone (DMZ). It would help if, during this period, there could be a shut-down on movement through the zone to the south. Mr Kosygin retaliated that all the time US ships were bringing in new troops. We should get nowhere talking about troop movements – our task was to concentrate on getting the two sides in contact. He had suggested how this should be done.

I felt that we should not go much further forward in a gathering of this size, and was sure that this was his view. We agreed to adjourn, Mr Kosygin asking that no reference should be made in press briefing to the subject of our discussion.

Between that meeting and a private dinner at No. 10, both sides were

Mr Wilson and the Foreign Secretary, Mr Michael Stewart with the Mayor of West Berlin, Herr Willy Brandt looking over the Berlin Wall in March 1965

With Mr Kosygin at the British Industrial Fair in Moscow in July 1966

December 1965. Many
African delegates walked out
of the United Nations
General Assembly during
Mr Wilson's speech in
protest against Britain's
Rhodesian policy
(radioed photograph)

Below:
Mrs Gandhi made a brief
visit to England in April 1966
on her way back to India
from the United States. With
Mrs Gandhi and Mr Wilson
are Mr Arthur Bottomley
and Dr Jirah Mehta, the
Indian High Commissioner
in London

The opening day of the Commonwealth Prime Ministers' conference at Marlborough House in September 1966

With Mr Lee Kuan Yew, Prime Minister of Singapore in October 1967

The procession of miners and their families passing through Durham during the annual Durham Miners' Gala in July 1965

An angry scene during the Labour party conference in October 1966. Mr Wilson addressing nearly a thousand aggrieved carworkers

busy. I called in the US Ambassador, David Bruce, and Chet Cooper. I had no compunction about this. Clearly Mr Kosygin expected me to do it: I learnt later in the week that he would have felt he was wasting his time if he had not been sure that we were in the most intimate contact. The American reaction was one of surprise and satisfaction. For the first time the Soviet leaders were active in trying to get the parties together, without any posture of detachment or of waiting to be approached.

Mr Kosygin was busy, too. When I asked him at dinner if I could take it that he was in direct touch with Hanoi, he gave me an old-fashioned look. How did I think he had been spending his time since our meeting? He wanted me to understand that every signal would be passed on and he was equally concerned that I was in at least as close touch with Washington. I remarked that before the weekend we should both be short of sleep. Because of the time-factor I should be up very late (Washington was five hours behind London time) and he would be up very early (Hanoi was seven hours ahead). It might well be that the two of us would never be in our beds at the same time. We again agreed that the Tet truce created a vitally important opportunity.

The next morning was devoted mainly to discussions on trade. They were valuable and constructive and led to an important agreement that in future trade discussions should not be limited to contacts between our respective trade ministries: both sides should include representatives of the department responsible for long-term planning, *Gosplan* on their side, Technology and DEA on ours. In our Opposition years I had been involved in many talks in which I had witnessed the central importance of *Gosplan* not only in general trade planning, but even in industrial projects involving exports of turn-key factories, or industrial know-how. We wanted to know their thinking in the next five-year plan so that we could gear programmes for increased industrial capacity to meet specific Soviet import requirements. This worked well in the years ahead.

Mr Kosygin then launched – mainly I think for his 'gallery' – into an attack on western trade embargoes, the agreed NATO schedules of goods embargoed on broad military grounds for export to the Soviet Union – the so-called COCOM lists. When speaking recently in Vladivostok, it appeared, he had been much heckled on this subject. It was an issue with which I had been personally involved for over fifteen years; few knew it better, and I had devoted a great amount of energy at No. 10 into getting some sense into the system. Endeavouring to help him, I asked whether he would favour a separation of the lists for China and for the Soviet Union, involving less stringent controls on the latter: in effect a reversion to the distinction between COCOM and 'CHINCOM', which a few years earlier had been merged into a single list. He took note that this was an idea we were considering.

In the afternoon we continued with other bilateral questions – civil aviation agreements, financial claims, and navigation, where an Anglo-Soviet navigation agreement was nearing signature.

We briefly adjourned, and met again a few minutes later in restricted session, to discuss Vietnam. With discretion I thought it right to say that in this important discussion Mr Kosygin had his own channels of communication for consulting certain people; he could assume that I also was in a position to have certain consultations. I began by picking up a reference he had made the previous day to the Lewandowski affair, which I said had been badly mishandled. I was not attributing blame. Nor could I; Mr Rapacki, the Polish Foreign Minister, in a private conversation with me at Downing Street had put a very different interpretation on the event from the one accepted in Washington, but I was not going into that, in present company. What the whole affair had proved was the need for improved confidence on both sides. I seized on the word he had used the previous evening – 'assist' – in other words, to do all in our power to promote confidence.

I felt that he was best placed to give me an impression of the thinking in Hanoi, while I could explain to him the thinking in Washington and describe in more detail the pressures on the American Government. In realistic terms, those American leaders who deeply desired a settlement had to be able to convince those who were urging that the military activities must be maintained, that by stopping the fighting the other side would not be placed in a position of military advantage.

Now, I went on, I would come to the guts of what I had to say. Despite what I had said, I was satisfied that the Americans would now be prepared to move to further actions to strengthen mutual confidence if they were able to secure some assurance that this move would be reciprocated. I believed that they were now seeking to get word to Hanoi on lines I was about to describe. The Foreign Secretary interposed to say the crucial word was 'now'. For I knew – and I suspected that Mr Kosygin knew – that the 'palm-tree' discussions were scheduled for the following day.

The Americans recognised the need for a first and visible step by them, and equally they recognised that this step must be the cessation of the bombing. This I believed they would do, and they realised it must be presented as being done unconditionally. Therefore, we had to use our ingenuity to find a means of divorcing, in presentation, the stopping of the bombing itself from the consequential actions, which Mr Kosygin and I knew were essential if we were to get the bombing stopped.

The consequential actions which I outlined were as follows. The US were willing, over and beyond the two-phase formula previously discussed, to stop the build-up of their forces in the South if they were assured that the movement of North Vietnam forces from the north to the south would stop at the same time. Essentially, therefore, the two stages were kept apart. But, because the United States Government would know that the second stage would follow, they would therefore be able first to stop the bombing, even if there was a short interval between the first stage and the actions to be taken by both sides at the second stage. There would be balanced concessions at the second stage, while the first stage would mean action only by the United States. They would be able to take that action only because they knew that the second stage, involving DRV action as well as US action, would follow in a short period of time. This proposal would meet Mr Kosygin's requirement of the previous day about American reinforcement of Vietnam.

I said that I thought this really did demonstrate US determination to create the conditions in which both sides could meet to talk peace. Despite the pressure of public opinion, they were prepared to take two specific and overt acts of de-escalation, and the one act asked of Hanoi would not take place until the Americans had acted visibly. All the US would have would be a secret assurance about stage two, and I understood why, with the special problems facing Hanoi, it would have to be secret.

Mr Kosygin welcomed the fact that the US were getting into contact with Hanoi and handing over a message to them. The North Vietnamese would study it. But he could not regard a decision to stop the bombing as praiseworthy – it was only stopping something which had been condemned, anyway. It was not an act of de-escalation. I told him I had difficulty in understanding the view that stopping the bombing was not de-escalation since it had always been argued that starting the bombing had been an act of escalation.

Mr Kosygin felt that the US were asking too much if in return for stopping bombing and the balanced actions of non-infiltration, they expected North Vietnam to stop the guerillas and the NLF from further hostilities. I said that was not in the package; he was right, conditions there were such that it could not be ensured in that way. It would be difficult to police. The assurance required from North Vietnam was not that all fighting had to stop throughout the whole of Vietnam, but that the movement from north to south would stop – this would be easy to observe and to carry out. Stopping all the fighting, everywhere, would be a matter, surely, for the negotiations? It was important that there should be no misunderstanding and I suggested that I should send him a text, which he welcomed.

That evening we had a formal dinner for our guest. For the first time we rearranged the large state dining-room at No. 10 in horseshoe fashion, so that we could seat sixty-three instead of the usual thirty or so. Another three hundred came to the reception after dinner.

Mr Kosygin was on my right with my wife on his right: Mme Gvishiani, his daughter, was on my left. For some minutes we each chatted with our lady neighbour, but I guess that Mr Kosygin, though charming and a great hit with ladies, does not enjoy dinner-table talk as much as an exciting discussion about the design of a new power-station. Quite suddenly he slewed his chair round some forty degrees, signalled his interpreter to move, and in no time we were once again immersed in the problems of south-east Asia, followed by deep discussions on Soviet fears of a *'revanchiste'* Germany.

On the Wednesday morning, 8th February, Mr Kosygin visited Elliott Automation's factory at Boreham Wood, where he had a hero's reception from the crowds of housewives and others. One lady rushed up to kiss him and granted him the accolade of 'old fruit', which I later translated for him literally as *'stary frukt'*, though a more idiomatic translation would have been *'starina'*. He was warmly received by the Lord Mayor of London at Guildhall, where he made a very hard-line speech on Vietnam and Germany, more, I felt, for the record back home. In the afternoon he opened the Anglo-Soviet Historical Exhibition at the Victoria and Albert Museum and later attended a thousand-strong reception given by the Government at Lancaster House. In the evening I was his guest at the Soviet Embassy, where once again we followed up the private conversation of the previous evening, concentrating this time on Germany. I raised as strongly as I could – as I had on my earlier visits to Moscow – the case of Mr Gerald Brooke, a British citizen imprisoned in the USSR, and made an appeal for clemency. But I made no more progress than in the past. He carefully repeated that there was no direct relationship between the Krogers' case and the Brooke case; but, he said, the fact remained that if the Krogers, Soviet-bloc spies serving long-term sentences in British prison, were released, action on Brooke would follow.

On the Thursday morning, 9th February, we resumed at Claridge's, beginning with a private meeting between Mr Kosygin and myself. He first raised the question of the communiqué: in particular, he wanted to include a 'pact of friendship, non-aggression and peaceful development'. On economic questions, he hoped that we should stress co-operation on science and technology equally with trade and economic co-operation. Our bilateral economic relations, he said, should be based on both current and long-term agreements which would make it possible for trade to develop unaffected by fluctuations in world markets. There might well be an agreement, he thought, on these lines for three years up to 1970, with a view to concluding a long-term agreement thereafter. Financial claims, the treaty on navigation and co-operation in aviation should also be included. We then went on to a long private discussion on non-proliferation and the nuclear arms race.

After an hour we were joined by the Foreign Secretary and by Mr Kosygin's principal advisers.

In the afternoon Mr Kosygin addressed a crowded meeting of members

of both Houses of Parliament in the Royal Gallery at the House of
Lords. He was very well-received, though again it was the hard line he
took. Meanwhile I was hard at work with the Americans on Vietnam.

In the evening the Queen gave a dinner for him at Buckingham Palace,
a rare honour for a visiting Prime Minister, not head of state. Mr
Kosygin, who clearly enjoyed his reception, spent a good deal of time
pressing the Queen and Prince Philip to pay a State visit to the Soviet
Union. An urgent message reached me about this, while we were having
coffee, and I took action to steer the invitation into the proper channel
through which incoming and outgoing State visits are arranged.

The next morning we met for our final plenary session. We began
with financial claims. The Chancellor attended the meeting for this item
and quite quickly we reached agreement about the settlement of almost
the last of the outstanding, twenty-year-old wartime claims.

We then went on to European questions. I explained the purposes,
economic and political, behind our EEC initiative. From that we
turned to problems of European security, the proposed security conference, and the question of Germany and Berlin. The Foreign Secretary
led the discussion from our side, and it took a very predictable course,
with the frequently stated positions of both sides asserted and repeated.
Mr Kosygin did go so far as to say that the Soviet Union did not regard
the Federal Republic as an 'area of plague' and that they wished it to
take part fully in any discussions of European affairs. But they were
alarmed at recent developments in Germany revealing the growing
power of the neo-Nazis, who at a *Land* election had just polled ten per
cent of the votes.

The next subject on the agenda, disarmament, led to a detailed discussion on non-proliferation and anti-ballistic missiles (ABMs). George
Brown expressed our view that an arms race in ABMs would interfere
with progress towards a reduction of nuclear stockpiles and even with
progress towards genuine non-proliferation. As he said, I had already
raised this with the Russians.

Mr Kosygin said that the USSR had not taken any final decision so
he could not give a considered reply at that time. But it seemed to him
that the United Kingdom had posed the question in a very odd way, as
had President Johnson and Mr McNamara, when they approached the
subject. Their attitude seemed to be one of asking why they should start
making anti-missile systems when it was cheaper to make offensive
weapons. He was surprised that we should support this attitude, which
was one of obscurantism and misanthropy. Every child knew it was
cheaper to buy offensive rather than defensive weapons; but what kind
of philosophy was it that concerned itself with killing people in the
cheapest possible way?

The Foreign Secretary said that the whole point was that we were not trying to encourage new and cheaper offensive systems – quite the opposite. Those who entered this new field would stimulate others who would decide that the only answer was more and more offensive weapons. Our policy was to stop development and production of new nuclear systems; to stop increased production of present weapons; to agree on a cut-off of fissile material and to begin to get on with genuine disarmament.

Mr Kosygin said he fully understood the view that if one side produced defensive systems it stimulated the other to increase and develop new offensive ones. It was, moreover, very costly. But if all countries had perfect defensive anti-missile weapons, nuclear weapons would have been neutralised, and mankind could live in peace. He must express his criticism of the Labour Government for taking the line that it was cheaper and better to go on with offensive systems.

I took him up on this, referring first to China as a proof of the need for non-proliferation. It was not simply that money which might have been spent on ABMs would be spent on offensive weapons. Quite apart from our view that there should be an agreed limitation on offensive weapons, leading to their ultimate elimination, there was the simple historical fact about an arms race between offence and defence.

Armour *versus* anti-tank guns; naval gun-power against battle-ship cladding – all were costly in terms of money and resources and increased the risk of war beginning when one side felt it had a temporary, but effective, advantage in the arms race. But costly though these were, they were as nothing compared with the cost to both sides of an ABM race. At this Mr Kosygin reacted very sharply for practically the only time during the week's talks. He misunderstood me as suggesting that we – as agents, no doubt, for the US – were asking the USSR to take risks on their defence to save money. No decision had been taken, he repeated, but the issue would not be decided in terms of costs. I quickly reassured him on the point: I was talking of both sides. But if one side or the other went ahead it would mean a new twist to the arms race.

In addition to raising, yet again without success, the case of Mr Gerald Brooke, I pressed him, as I had in Moscow in July 1966, on his attitude towards progress for agreed and phased troop withdrawal in Europe, both sides, East and West. In view of the sensitivity he had shown, I made clear that I was raising this not to save money – though that would be one effect – but to preserve the military balance and ease tension.

He said that as there had been no real discussion of this he could not give a conclusive reply. His opinion, however, was that to bring this about there was one prerequisite – a declaration of the inviolability of existing boundaries. If that could be settled we could take up the question of mutual balanced force reductions.

We broke off early because we had agreed that before lunch we should have a further meeting on Vietnam. Time was getting late.

Nothing had been heard about the 'palm-tree' talks. But Mr Kosygin was obviously hopeful that we faced a unique opportunity, though he did not spell this out and I was loath to press him too far. I had the strong impression that Soviet influence in Hanoi was being listened to – perhaps the Chinese influence was at an unusually low point because of the Red Guards' crisis.

But the Americans were getting worried. At our request they had agreed to maintain the truce – provided that the other side did not fire first – and the bombing pause so long as Mr Kosygin and I were meeting. But they felt that any spirit of hope, any possibility of building up confidence, had been dimmed by an increase during the truce in infiltration of DRV forces to the south, free of any interdiction by bombing. They sent me the figures – far higher than the average pre-truce daily rate – and urged me to press them upon Mr Kosygin and warn him that this conduct was damaging to any hope of a settlement. This I had done at dinner, and he took the figures very seriously. I did not learn, however, whether he pressed the point in Hanoi; I would guess that he did.

I said I would be brief. I had been in touch with friends. So had he. There were two propositions to consider.

George Brown had been pressing a simple reconvening of the Geneva conference, which I had little hope the Russians would accept, but I felt it right to urge Mr Kosygin to say whether it was a possibility.

The other was the two-phase solution which involved Hanoi giving a private assurance in return for a cessation of the bombing. I was authorised to say that if this was done, he could be sure that my friends would take the necessary action, provided he could ensure that his friends would also take the action they were asked to take.

Mr Kosygin suddenly looked interested. It seemed that the way I had put it was in some way more attractive than what had been said earlier in the week, though I had said nothing new. As he understood the proposal, the US would stop the bombing and make a statement to this effect, while North Vietnam would give an assurance in confidence, without publicity, that it would take certain steps in response. I repeated it again: North Vietnam would be required to give an assurance that it would not move troops from the north to the south; thereafter the United States would make a further statement about not moving further troops into Vietnam. But before they did so, the US would need the secret assurance that the second stage – the North Vietnamese standstill on troop movements – would follow the first, the cessation of bombing. Again Mr Kosygin said that, as he understood it, the first stage would consist of stopping the bombing *and* not introducing any new troops.

I said, again, that provided the appropriate secret assurance were given by North Vietnam, the United States Government would stop the bombing and make a public declaration to this effect. This would therefore appear to all the world as being an unconditional stop. But the Americans could only do this if given a private assurance from the DRV that it was ready, i.e. that the DRV would stop moving troops into South Vietnam. At the same time the US would stop reinforcing their troops.

Mr Kosygin asked whether he could have this in writing; I agreed. He said this would be a very important document. We were together assuming a considerable responsibility. He would like to have the proposal in writing so that he could send it to Moscow; the sooner he was given it, the sooner this could be done.

I said that the North Vietnamese assurance could be given either direct to the Americans, or alternatively through the Russians to the United Kingdom Goverment. In the latter case, I would then pass it on to the Americans.

I wanted to make absolutely certain that the text was approved by the Americans. The American Ambassador, David Bruce, and Chet Cooper were called in and were told what I had said. They were then invited to draft the letter to hand to the Russians, to make sure that it was confirmed as the Amercan position. This was done, and in the early evening before I went to the Soviet Embassy reception a text was handed to me, authenticated by the US Embassy. I was assured that there had been the fullest consultation with the State Department at top level.

The document I handed to Mr Kosygin on arrival followed almost word for word what I had said in the morning, except that my remark that any secret assurance could reach the United States direct or *via* the Soviet and British Governments was expanded to include a further route, namely *via* the Soviet Government to Washington.

George Brown and I had a further talk with Mr Kosygin before we left the Embassy; Mr Kosygin was taking the day's developments very seriously and clearly with some hope.

We returned to No. 10, where the US Ambassador and Chet Cooper were waiting; we told them of our talks in Kensington Palace Gardens.

David Bruce, one of the most respected and experienced diplomats in the world and one who, as the President had told me, enjoyed his highest confidence, far and above that accorded to a most senior ambassador, then delivered himself of a judgment: 'Prime Minister,' he said, 'I think you've made it. This is going to be the biggest diplomatic coup of this century.'

I demurred, and said that we had not yet seen what Hanoi would do, nor how China would react.

Then at about 10.00 p.m. the telephone rang. It was the White House –

Walt Rostow had tried to phone Michael Palliser, who had gone home with 'flu, and had been told to ring Downing Street. The gist of his message was that on the President's instructions our text had been re-drafted. A new text would come over the White House–Downing Street teleprinter, starting now, and should be the one to be used with the Russians. If the earlier text had not been handed over, we should use the new text; if it had, the new text should be substituted.

We were staggered, all of us, ministers, civil servants, Americans. No one could understand what had happened. Before contacting Mr Kosygin I said we had better see the text. He was due to catch the train at Euston for his Scottish visit in less than an hour.

While we awaited the text we tried to assess what had happened. David Bruce, with all his experience, was not the man either to be misled, or to mislead me about Washington's policy. Both he and Chet Cooper had been certain that the earlier text represented the considered view of the US Government 'as of' the early evening of that day. But – we knew from Rostow – there had been a meeting. Indeed it was still going on.

I was furious, I hope I can say icily so, though as the evening wore on the language in which I expressed myself was less and less parlia-mentary. The Americans who were with me in Downing Street were equally angry.

I said that there could be only three possible explanations. One, which I was reluctant to believe, was that the White House had taken me – and hence Mr Kosygin – for a ride. Two, the most likely, that the Washington hawks had staged a successful take-over. Three – and here I paraphrase – that the authorities in Washington were suffering from a degree of confusion about a possible and unfortunate juxtaposition of certain parts of their anatomy, one of which was their elbow.

David Bruce, who had been placed in a most difficult position, charit-ably suggested that the third was the most likely hypothesis. My view that it was the second later received authoritative confirmation; it was, simply and tragically, a victory for the hawks.

The message from Rostow changed the basis of what I had said, and been authorised to say, to the Russians. Phase A – B and the rest all went. We were right back, further back, than in the proposals put *via* Lewandowski. The new terms now read – the italics are mine:

A. The US would order a cessation of bombing of North Vietnam, *as soon as they were assured that infiltration from North Vietnam to South Vietnam had stopped.* ['Had stopped' – not 'would stop following the cessation of bombing'.]

B. Within a period to be agreed between the two sides before the cessation of bombing, the US would stop further augmenting their forces in South Vietnam. Stopping the bombing would be an action which was immediately apparent and public. This would require, therefore, that the stopping of North Vietnam infiltration should become public very quickly thereafter. If Hanoi were unwilling to announce this, the US would have to do so when it stops augmentation of American forces. And in that case, Hanoi must not deny it.

This was a total reversal of the policy the US had put forward for transmission to the Soviet Prime Minister. All the briefing I had received had been based on the A – B formula: it had come from the President's personal emissary on two visits – the week before Mr Kosygin's visit and from 4th February – and he had been charged specifically to speak on these lines. So had the United States Ambassador to the Court of St James. No degree of mental confusion in Washington – my third hypothesis – could possibly be adduced in defence of such a fundamental change. It was a reversal of policy, and it had been deliberately taken just when there was a real chance – one thinks of Ambassador Bruce's words earlier that evening – of a settlement based on the prolongation of the Tet truce from the end of the week when it was due to end.

This was not all. Such action could only have the worst possible effect on the Russians. For the first time since the Vietnamese fighting had begun, they had shown willingness to use their good offices in Hanoi, even to the point of risking their always precarious influence there. What would that influence amount to on a subsequent occasion? What use could China make of all this? They would be sure to learn of it from the pro-Chinese faction in Hanoi. What might be the reaction in Moscow, where perhaps not all of Mr Kosygin's colleagues would approve of his getting out so far on a limb with these Western Governments? Would he be willing to try again?

In its new orientation, the formula was unrecognisable. Instead of a secret advance assurance about stopping infiltration as a means of securing the bombing pause, infiltration had to stop first, and become public very quickly afterwards.

The new American formula had to be given to Mr Kosygin, already on the way to Euston. My office telephoned the station and asked for facilities for my secretary, Michael Halls, who was charged with the distasteful task, to get through the barriers and the security men. If necessary, and if this were possible without endangering safe railway working, the train should be held back until his arrival. In fact he arrived on time, flashed his No. 10 pass at the inspectors, and handed over the message a minute before the train was due to leave.

Meanwhile I was expressing myself in a short message to the President, on the Downing Street–White House teleprinter, dictated by me after consultation with the bewildered Ambassador and the outraged Chet Cooper. Before sending it I gave myself time to cool down: my considered reaction was despatched at 2.40 a.m. on the Saturday morning. It is too soon after the event to reproduce it in full, but perhaps the opening paragraph will suffice:

You will realise what a hell of a situation I am in for my last day of talks with Kosygin. My immediately following telegram sets out what seems to have happened over the past weeks as I understand it, but I want to concentrate here on the immediate way ahead. I have to re-establish trust because not only will he have doubts about my credibility but he will have lost credibility in Hanoi and possibly among his colleagues. . . .

The 'immediately following telegram' set out the history of the week with brutal frankness, including an account of the successive proposals I had put to the Russians with what I had been clearly told at the highest level carried White House authority. Every line was based on the advice of the US Ambassador and of Chet Cooper, sent by the President personally with the President's *cachet* of his personal confidence. I reminded President Johnson that my oral statement on Tuesday, confirmed in writing, was communicated at once to Washington. So was the Friday statement. Yet both were repudiated by Rostow's telephone call and subsequent telegram. 'I cannot understand why I was not told earlier [that the Washington line had been switched]. Kosygin will find it even more difficult to understand.'

I then felt it right to turn to the future, and particularly my talks at Chequers with Mr Kosygin. I said that I intended to be frank with the Soviet Prime Minister, while telling him that the present situation had arisen, in my view, from deep American concern about the intensive North Vietnamese infiltration into the south during the Tet truce. I would remind him of my earlier warning that these movements might prejudice the situation, a warning reinforced by a statement I had made to him on the Friday lunch-time, that in the first two days of Tet they had been on a shocking and provocative scale. I then outlined possible action, saying that while George Brown and I had discussed this with David Bruce and Chet Cooper for three hours, the responsibility for what I was now saying was entirely that of HMG. I would do my best in a very difficult situation. I could not say that I thought the proposals put forward in my first message to Mr Kosygin of Friday evening were wrong: all I could say was that they were no longer acceptable in Washington.

I reminded the President that, for the first time in the war, Mr Kosygin was no longer saying that these matters had nothing to do with the USSR but were a matter for Hanoi: 'He now says he and I must do all we can to get a settlement.'

The hope was almost certainly gone that we could extend the truce long enough to secure an arrangement, which had appeared so near, capable of bringing the parties immediately to the conference table. The best we could hope for would be words in the communiqué which would make a new initiative possible. But it would be infinitely harder – for America no less than Hanoi – to move in that direction once the bombing had restarted and the ground fighting had resumed, than it would have been to extend the bombing pause and the truce a day at a time while a solution was sought.

I told the President that in my talks with Mr Kosygin I would try to give effect to the US concern about infiltration. I said that perhaps the best we could hope for would be for Mr Kosygin and me, each knowing the views of our friends, to seek a solution, which each could commend to his friend, like two solicitors seeking to settle a matter out of court, *ad referendum* to the two clients.

The President telegraphed his reply immediately in warm terms. He understood the difficulty I was in. How much, he said, he appreciated my dedicated effort during this week; he would express publicly 'our thanks'. But he was at pains to say that he could not give me 'power of attorney' – which I had not suggested. On this point I replied, shortly, that he had misunderstood me in suggesting I was proposing a power of attorney. Clearly that would be out of the question: 'That was not my phrase. The key words were *ad referendum*, repeat *ad referendum*.' I wondered who was drafting his telegrams. I knew who was drafting mine. I was.

All day Saturday, 11th February, George Brown and I met with our advisers. At 11.30 p.m. we called in David Bruce yet again: I did not leave for Chequers until 3.15 a.m. During what was left of the night, I thought the matter through, and awoke fresh and with a clear view. If I could get nothing more reasonable to offer than the existing US attitude, I would put my own views as the British view and attempt to sell it to the US on the one hand and Mr Kosygin on the other. Thereafter that would be the British Government's definite proposal for the ending of the war.

I dictated this message from my bed for President Johnson to see when he awoke a few hours later. To meet his expressed fear that between the cessation of bombing and the stopping of infiltration the DRV would rush three or four divisions through the DMZ I proposed that the 'prior two-way assurance' should contain a time-table, if possible underwritten by, or at any rate communicated through, the Russians, under which the US would agree in advance to stop the bombing in return for the DRV's prior assurance to stop the infiltration, say, six hours later, or an even shorter time-table if necessary. I said this proposal would be on my responsibility; I was not asking him to comment at that stage. I would air it with Mr Kosygin that evening specifically as my own idea without committing Washington. If I got 'any mileage' out of it I would let the President know and ask for him to state his attitude, preferably while Mr Kosygin was still at Chequers.

Mr Kosygin, meanwhile, had spent Saturday in Scotland. He had a great success, and clearly enjoyed all he saw. He was escorted throughout the day by Willie Ross, the Secretary of State, who had been told about the American exercise in switch-selling the night before and had been asked to watch out for any signs of reaction. But Mr Kosygin made no reference to it.

He was due at Chequers for dinner and for the signing of the communiqué at 6.00 p.m. on Sunday. I was waiting for a reply to my overnight message to the President. And this time, though I feared the damage was done, I wanted to make sure that there should be no breakdown in communication. The President gave his approval to Chet Cooper's spending the Sunday at Chequers, incarcerated in the 'Prison Room' on the upper floor, where Queen Elizabeth I had imprisoned Lady Mary Grey, sister of Lady Jane. He was connected by direct line to David Bruce and to the White House. When the line was being tested on the Saturday afternoon, the White House engineer said he hoped that, if used, we shouldn't keep the President up as late as we had done the previous evening. Late! Washington was five hours behind London, so we were much later to bed.

Chet Cooper arrived after lunch and was installed in his room, with a tray of food, a bottle of Scotch and one of Bourbon, and my transistor radio.

At 6.00 p.m. Mr Kosygin arrived. By this time the President had called his National Security Council together. The Chequers–White House hot-line was in operation, tested and tested again.

We met alone for a short period before the Foreign Secretary arrived. I told Mr Kosygin what had happened, and what I thought was the reason for it. I emphasised the extreme concern of the US about infiltration and their fears of further infiltration between the agreement and the bombing pause and the DRV's invocation of the second stage.

Our conversation was not minuted, but we went over the ground again, with a full record, when the Foreign Secretary and Mr Soldatov, former Soviet Ambassador in London, joined us. I summarised it thus: we had hoped that the two sides might get together and desert the battlefield for the conference room, or even that we might see the more limited de-escalation through the bombing pause and the stopping of DRV infiltration into the south. These hopes had not materialised and we were now faced with a difficult, and perhaps dangerous, situation. The Soviet Union and Britain should maintain close consultation so that, if the moment came, we could give all the assistance in our power to resume moves to peace. For the moment, what should we say in the communiqué? Here Mr Kosygin became difficult, and this was understandable. He could not agree to words in the communiqué going beyond previous Soviet statements: in particular, he could not agree to my reference to our specific efforts together. To find the correct path on Vietnam it was necessary to remain in the shadow and not to publicise contacts. Anything done must remain profoundly confidential. He had in mind possible Chinese exploitation for propaganda purposes, if there were anything more public.

I told Mr Kosygin that I had put a new draft to Washington, based on the earlier Friday formulation, but reflecting American anxieties about infiltration. I made no secret of the direct contact we had set up between Chequers and the White House, so that there could be speedy consultation in case there was any hope of progress. The extended Tet truce had only hours to run.

We adjourned to the Great Hall for a pre-dinner drink, while a report was taken to the Prison Room. Chet Cooper had a message for us. How long, Washington was asking, would Mr Kosygin be staying at Chequers? The National Security Council meeting was unlikely to reach a decision before 10.30 or 11.00 p.m., our time.

Before we went in to dinner Mr Kosygin said that he would be ready to sign the communiqué after we had eaten. He had only small drafting points on it. As I was anxious to delay his departure until Washington was clearer in its views, I said we had a number of points, some of them substantial and all of them constructive.

After dinner we had a long talk in the Long Gallery, helped by the presence of the ladies. I raised the subject of our Common Market initiative and explained our purposes.

By this time we were past ten o'clock. Still no news from the Prison Room: the National Security Council was still meeting. I had usefully employed twenty minutes or more in an exercise in the higher technology, to which Mr Kosygin was always ready to respond. In addition to his great knowledge of industry he had a keen interest in geology and had told me of his intentions to speed the work of exploration in the USSR, particularly in the north, describing his hopes of what might be discovered. One of the two Premiers on his delegation, Mr Djavakishvili, the head of the Georgian SSR, was a professional geologist, and I had invited a geologist friend of mine to the dinner. Starting with a polite criticism of the uneven quality of phosphate rock shipped from the Kola peninsula to Britain, I embarked on a flight into the higher realms of chemical engineering. Mr Kosygin recalled that in Moscow many years earlier, before either of us was Prime Minister, we had had an animated discussion on the best methods of making phosphoric acid and its derivatives, in which I had described his attitude as somewhat reactionary. At Chequers I drew a fanciful picture of a new multinational industry, with Russian phosphate rock linked with Norwegian electric power, and a world-wide distribution network of acid-carrying tankers. Further, I understood that in the Kola area there were substantial quantities of anhydrite (calcium sulphate), which we had used to build up a competitive sulphuric acid industry. Britain could supply the know-how. By this time he had in prospect a major chemical complex, extending through sodium tripolyphosphate into detergents. Not wishing to appear unambitious I referred to the presence of common salt: visions began to appear of hydrochloric acid, urea and a vast fertiliser and plastics complex, PVC – the lot. This filibuster took a little time, though Mr Kosygin was genuinely interested.

We went into the Great Parlour to agree and sign the communiqué and the Russians prepared to leave. Message after message went up to the Prison Room asking if Washington was ready to talk. No; but ten minutes at the most, then five more; then the message was to keep the Russians there at all costs. As Mr Kosygin and his party went downstairs to go, the fleet of official cars came round into the courtyard; Chet Cooper told me afterwards that he held the telephone outside the open window so that the noise of the exhausts could be heard in Washington. But despite a presentation of a book about Chequers to each of our guests, with a laborious half-page inscription for each, the message came too late. As Mr Kosygin left I told him that a message was expected from the President within minutes. If it seemed important, I would send a message asking him not to go to bed on reaching Claridge's, and would speed after him. He said it would have to be a good one.

Five minutes later the White House were through to us. The President had a further offer to make, reflecting, it seemed, my proposals of the morning, but with a stricter time-table. This would be set out in specific terms in a telegram on the direct teleprinter. I decided that to save time we would pick it up at Downing Street and I asked that Ambassador Bruce should be there to endorse anything I might want to put in writing. Mr Kosygin's suite at Claridge's was alerted.

The President's telegram – drafted one would think for his local domestic gallery – began by pointing out that the A – B offer had been outstanding for about three months. So it had; but Chet Cooper had brought a radically new formulation. He had had no reply from Hanoi.

Then came the emollient:

> ... Nevertheless, you have worked nobly this week to bring about what all humanity wants: a decisive move towards peace. It is an effort that will be long remembered. I feel a responsibility to give you this further chance to make that effort bear fruit.
> We will go more than half-way. I am prepared to go the last mile in this week's particular effort: although none of us can regard a failure tonight as the end of the road.

After referring to his responsibility to US troops, and to South Vietnam, he said, '... Nevertheless I agree with you that you should go forward and try once again with Kosygin saying to him ...' He then set out the precise proposals.

If I could get a North Vietnamese assurance, either direct to the US, or through us, 'before 10.00 a.m. British time tomorrow' (Monday) that all movements of troops and supplies into South Vietnam would stop at that time, I could promise an assurance from the US that they would not resume bombing from that time. The US build-up would stop within a matter of days. All of us concerned with the week's operation could then build on these acts to promote 'further balanced measures of de-escalation'. There could then be a prompt move 'to a neutral spot' to engage in unconditional negotiations designed to bring peace.

It was a formulation somewhere between the American Friday statement, Mark 2, and my own proposals. Given time, it might have been a basis for a move forward. But in my view it was certain to founder on the utterly unrealistic time-table. Even if Mr Kosygin agreed to forward the message forthwith to Moscow to pass to Hanoi, then, even given instant transmission, which I doubted, the President was giving just nine hours for this to be done; nine hours for the Hanoi Government – known to be divided – to meet, take a decision and send it back to Washington. And all this would be against the background of the breakdown of trust caused by the events of the previous Friday.

The Foreign Secretary and I reached Claridge's at 1.00 a.m. I read the proposal. Mr Kosygin's first reaction was that this provided nothing new compared with the original A – B formula. I contended that it was a major advance. There was no bombing now; there would be none, given the assurance asked for. By that night, Monday, we should have the result we both sought. If not, there would be a resumption of bombing and the peace effort would have to start all over again, with a much greater weight of mistrust to remove. The confirmation letter, endorsed by the US Ambassador, which I had left to be typed, was then brought in and handed over.

Mr Kosygin was grave. The proposal, he said, was in ultimatum form, with a final hour of 10.00 a.m. I said that if sheer lack of time were the problem I would try to get an extension from Washington. But Mr Kosygin said it was dictation. No one could give an answer in such a period, and he was assuredly right.

We went over and over the ground for a few minutes, then Mr Kosygin began to write. He said he would pass the message on at once; he had just written a draft, and he would ask Moscow to pass it on to Hanoi. He was sure that they would do so but he could not count on success. His draft was passed outside to his staff.

He emphasised that he could not be hopeful. The North Vietnamese could not be expected to abandon the south or to stop all movement of supplies to the south, for it would imperil the security of a hundred thousand of their fighting men there. (This was, I think, the first time that he or any Communist leader had given a figure of the number of DRV forces in the south, and clearly repudiated many statements made from Hanoi.)

As the meeting broke up, he asked me to stay for a private word. It was to emphasise the point about supplies. The DRV forces would be denied food – which I said could not have been intended – and ammunition. Such a course would be appropriate only if there were a cease-fire – a fair point. Moreover, there was a problem of rotating troops, what is known in the West as *roulement*.

As I left Claridge's at 2.00 a.m. I was approached by a *Daily Express* journalist near the door. His editor had posted, on a continuous twenty-four-hour rota for the whole week, a series of men to watch comings and goings, at considerable expense and, no doubt, involving much tedium and cold for the men concerned. Not a story had resulted. Now they had their reward – a front-page exclusive. I was not able to satisfy the reporter's curiosity about the reason for my unscheduled visit, and I found him markedly incredulous at a suggestion I made that perhaps I had gone to collect a box of matches I had lent Mr Kosygin at Chequers and which he had inadvertently taken away.

Before going to bed I sent a further message to President Johnson, pressing for more time. In the morning, before meeting Mr Kosygin to conduct him to Gatwick, I received a grudging further six hours – until 4.00 p.m. – after which bombing would restart.

In the train to Gatwick Mr Kosygin confirmed that he had passed the message on overnight. He noted the few hours' extension, but was sure that this was not enough. He confirmed receipt of a message from the Foreign Secretary saying that if any signal were received from Hanoi – e.g. stating that more time was required to consider the message – our Government would immediately go into action with Washington to press for an extension. No such message came. The bombing recommenced a few hours later.

The farewells at Gatwick, including the public speeches, were friendly, confirming the great success of the visit from the bilateral and public point of view. Mr Kosygin had had an enthusiastic reception everywhere he had been and greatly improved the Soviet image in the public mind. We both agreed that Anglo-Soviet relations were now at 'an all-time high'.

Press and public knew nothing of the central preoccupation of our visit or how near we had been to success – nor the deep disappointment we both felt. It was not for many months that even the first stories leaked – in Washington – and then with significant omissions.

A historic opportunity had been missed. The Washington decision on the Friday was decisive and disastrous. Some two years later I had the opportunity of discussing these events with a senior US statesman who had been involved in the Washington policy reversal at the operative time. I expressed the view that, in terms of influence on his master, the more I saw of certain of the White House advisers the more I thought that Rasputin was a much-maligned man. There was no dissent.

On the day that these words are being written, 17th November 1970, a

N

Guardian editorial has said the last word, for the time being. Reviewing Chet Cooper's book on these events, just published in the US, the *Guardian* concludes, in anticipation of my own account:

> ...It [Mr Cooper's book] shows that the Wilson-Kosygin attempt to stop the war was serious. It shows that, as some of us guessed at the time, Washington mishandled it badly. And since it all happened during the Tet truce of 1967 it casts a still more sad and ironic light on the Tet offensive of 1968. That, coming just one year after the abortive peace effort in London, finally proved to President Johnson that the US could not win in Vietnam. ... When Mr Wilson besought Washington to delay a resumption of the bombing at the end of the extended Tet pause, the White House put off a decision. Then it demanded a reply from Hanoi within 12 hours – having itself taken three times as long to consider a simpler request. So the mission failed, and so, in the end, President Johnson lost his job.

For, as the *Guardian* hinted, Tet 1968 was a very different story. Not of hope, but destruction. It was the time of the DRV offensive, penetrating, with great devastation, Saigon itself, and involving the shelling of the US Embassy. Within weeks of that offensive, President Johnson announced a unilateral cessation of the bombing, with no stage A – stage B prior assurance that infiltration would cease, still less any prior condition that it had ceased; still graver, in personal terms, he announced in the same statement his decision to stand down from the presidency at the end of the year. As one who was so close to him in these years, and in these moments of decision, I have never been able to get away from an impression of a classical Greek tragedy. February 1967 was the re-enactment, in our time, of the Sibylline books.

Chapter 20

TWO days after Mr Kosygin left us, George Brown and I resumed our series of visits to the Six with a journey to Bonn, where Dr Kiesinger had just became Chancellor of the 'great coalition', and Willy Brandt deputy-Chancellor and Foreign Minister. Since this was my first meeting with the new team – indeed, Dr Kiesinger welcomed me as the first head of government to visit him since he became Chancellor – there was naturally some discussion of issues other than EEC. The Germans were keen to know all that we could tell them about the Russians' visit. On Herr Brandt's proposal meetings were arranged during our visit, at Foreign Minister and official level, to discuss non-proliferation and the recurring off-set problem.

In a restricted meeting – Dr Kiesinger, Willy Brandt, George Brown and myself – which lasted all morning, we dealt with all these questions, but most of our time was spent on the Common Market. Because of the General's emphasis, not now on Britain's suitability for EEC membership, but on the effect of enlargement on the nature of the Community, I addressed myself particularly to this problem.

I repeated what I had said to the General, that the Community would in fact be strengthened by the entry of new members. Not only would the entry of five or so additional countries increase the market for the products of each country to three hundred million people – larger than either the US or the Soviet domestic market – but the Community would derive additional productive power from what we and others had to contribute from our wide range of technological skills.

I stressed that the outcome of our talks would depend to a great extent on the exercise of German influence in Paris. I did not want to put any strain on Franco-German relations, which were very close. In Paris the General had made an important pronouncement when he said that Britain was ready to moor alongside the European quay. It was his emphasis on the changes he feared in the Community which was disturbing. And, talking to some members of the Community, at least, we discerned evidence of a feeling – as in Paris – that over ten years the Community had developed into a cosy family home which newcomers might upset, especially if they were noisy children. Was it for that reason that President de Gaulle had said we might have to build 'a new house'? George intervened to ask the Chancellor to use his influence to head off proposals for new arrangements, be they a totally new set of machinery or, simply, British association, under Article 238, which at one point the General had clearly indicated.

The Chancellor, who reiterated Germany's full support for British entry, said that his Government, like its predecessors, had had long discussions with the French about the question. He had himself raised the subject with the General, drawing his attention to our declaration of 10th November, and had sent him a letter from German industrial leaders urging the case for British entry. The General had been resistant, but he felt that we had made progress in Paris. As to German influence in Paris, this was difficult to assess so early in his Chancellorship, not least because there were serious differences between Bonn and Paris on such questions as NATO and the stationing of French troops on German territory. The revived Franco-German friendship, so carefully fostered by Dr Adenauer, was still a tender plant.

We got the impression that Dr Kiesinger's approach was very much 'softly, softly, catchee General'. But how softly? Then, and subsequently, we became increasingly convinced that he would never be prepared to press his undoubted conviction that Britain must be admitted to the Six to the point of annoying General de Gaulle.

The Chancellor belonged to that section of his party which was strongly orientated to Paris, for geographical and cultural reasons. The historic Franco-German partnership was an achievement of Dr Adenauer; under Dr Erhardt, the quintessential quartermaster, there was less emotional content and fewer points of contact, but the partnership was still very much of a reality. Dr Kiesinger was likely to be another Adenauer, but with less ability to press an unpopular course on the General.

How, he asked, could the Germans exert an influence in Paris? He did not believe that they could impress General de Gaulle by attempting to bring pressure on him, for they knew his personality and they knew how strongly he felt about certain things. He did not think that it would be good for Germany to exert much pressure so soon after overcoming the unpleasantness which had existed between France and Germany. But his Government could try to convince the General by producing good arguments in support of the British initiative and by seeking to dissect and dispel French anxieties, especially the fear that British entry would destroy the Community.

The Chancellor was concerned about maintaining the momentum, for British public opinion would expect results following the six visits; he feared that if French resistance blocked further moves there would be a hiatus. It would be intolerable not only for as great and important a country as Britain but 'for all of us, and I repeat all of us', if the experience of 1963 were to be repeated.

I warned him that if this were to happen things would not stand still. The fact that EEC and EFTA existed side by side meant that there was already a divisive barrier in Europe, though across that barrier there was no hostility. It might be that a spirit of competitiveness – I would not, I said, use the term 'trade war' – might enter into the relations between the two groups. But there was more. Some of the EFTA countries were already suffering to a growing extent from the Common Agricultural Policy: the CAP could not be said to be in accord with GATT. But because there was a real understanding that a wider, fuller economic union would follow – the type of development blessed by GATT – objection had not so far been raised by any EFTA member. But that situation could change.

In the afternoon, in full plenary session, and on the Thursday morning, we outlined more fully the Government's position on the Market, almost exactly as we had done in our three previous visits. We deployed our arguments on agricultural financing, capital movements, the Commonwealth problems and regional policy, and answered their questions – in particular, on the problem of sterling balances.

At the end of our meetings the Chancellor took up a point I had made in a speech at the dinner the previous evening. I had asked them to do more than just support Britain's initiative and to do all in their power – he stressed these words – to forward British entry.

Again, his note of caution. Germany genuinely wanted to help, and to be firm in doing so, but she must manoeuvre with caution. They would discuss these matters very thoroughly with their French friends; they would convey their impressions of the current talks; they would try to dispel French anxieties. But they must set about this carefully, not weakly, and with wisdom and prudence. The task would not be easy but they would faithfully try, as honest brokers, to overcome the difficulties in Paris. He asked us to understand if they did not make any solemn public declaration.

Little more than a week later we went to the Hague for our fifth visit and, early in March, to Luxembourg. These were two of the most agreeable of our visits. Both countries were unequivocally in favour of the British initiative, though Luxembourg was understandably more concerned with French attitudes.

The Dutch have traditionally been Britain's closest friends on Common Market questions: as in 1961–3 so in 1967. At the very outset they urged us to maintain the momentum of our approach by submitting an application for membership of the Community as soon as possible after the six visits were complete. The application should be as simple as possible; and here was the rub: we should, they thought, be content to seek solutions to our principal problems by means of transitional periods only, though they conceded later that there might have to be a 'footnote' about New Zealand butter.

The Prime Minister, Dr Zijlstra, who was soon to give up the premiership to become head of the Dutch Central Bank, was extremely interested in the position of sterling, our balance of payments and the role of the sterling balances.

He reverted to the problem at our third meeting on the Monday afternoon, submitting us to a rigorous cross-examination on the possible use of Article 108 of the Treaty of Rome. There was every indication that there had been consultation among the Six on this, and that this distinguished economist-banker had been instructed to press us upon it.

Article 108 had been included in the Treaty as a mutual assistance clause, to encourage members of the Community to give help to any member country with balance of payments problems. But, Dr Zijlstra argued, none of the currencies of the signatories was a reserve currency. Would it, he wondered, be possible to distinguish normal assistance to EEC members with balance of payments problems from the problem of sterling as a world currency?

I replied that Article 108 had, in fact, been invoked by Italy when she had had balance of payments problems. It was, I felt, an article which dealt with two specific problems, such as we had experienced. The first was a disequilibrium in a member country's balance of payments, the second a situation where, at a time when there was no serious imbalance in a country's overseas payments, there was nevertheless a shortage of a particular currency, or speculative pressure. While we had, it was true, been subject to heavy speculative pressures even when we were close to equilibrium, the position of sterling in the main should reflect the basic condition of Britain's balance of payments.

Now, on the question of sterling as distinct from Britain's own balance of payments, one had to distinguish between our role as an international currency and the question of the sterling balances. Many countries were willing to hold their reserves, and many trading and financial institutions their working balances, in sterling because it suited them; unlike gold, sterling balances earned interest. Even in 1966, the total of the sterling balances had remained fairly constant. From time to time there had been fluctuations and big changes in the distribution of the balances as between countries; but taking one year with another, the over-all level had been steady. Under the then Basle Agreement, a fall in the level of the balances could be offset by temporary financial assistance from the signatories to the Agreement, who included the members of EEC. To that extent the Six were already involved in the problem.

I well understood that the Six might feel anxious that a recurrence of balance of payments troubles, causing a violent movement in leads and lags, could, if Britain were in EEC, create a situation in which deflationary action in Britain might lead to the export of unemployment to the Six. But they might be reassured not only by our improved balance of payments – and the fact I had mentioned of the long-term stability of the over-all total of the sterling balances – but by two other factors. The first was that recourse not only to Basle but also the IMF was available should sterling come under pressure; the second was the fact that Britain's international financial assets comfortably exceed her liabilities.

Dr Zijlstra asked whether, as a reassurance, the operation of Article 108 should not be limited to normal balance of payments fluctuations and not extended to cover problems arising from the reserve currency complication. Dr Luns, the Foreign Minister, went further: could it in law be invoked for problems arising from sterling being a reserve currency?

I replied that we would leave the legal arguments to the lawyers, but that, as I read it, Article 108 as drafted covered both problems. Should the Six wish to redraft it, or to seek a derogation in the sense suggested, Britain would be happy to give such a proposal sympathetic consideration! More seriously, I went on to say that international help for any currency in difficulties had not in the past – nor would it be in the future – been limited to the Six. In the case of Italy, for example, as well as the members of EEC, Britain, the United States and other members of the world financial community had rallied round. So it had been with sterling in 1964 and with India, Ceylon and Ghana. But the Six need not fear that if Britain became a member of the Community we would place a legalistic interpretation upon the mutual assistance provisions of Article 108 in order to meet pressures arising from sterling's international role, e.g. to underwrite the sterling balances.

Dr Zijlstra and Dr Luns welcomed this assurance, and said that the other members of the Six should be told of it. The redoubtable Jonkheer van Lennep, central banker and later Secretary-General of OECD, supported me. He pointed out that whatever the Article said in law, it had been drafted at a time when currencies were not generally convertible and he felt it right that what I had said in the changed conditions should be set on the record.

Convertibility and other factors had changed the situation EEC currencies might face. For example, a change in the position of the United States, arising perhaps from an ending of the fighting in Vietnam, could lead to a Euro-dollar squeeze affecting all EEC members, present and prospective. Once again it would be international action on a world scale, not limited to EEC, that would have to be taken.

We had a similar, largely technical, discussion about capital movements, where once again I drew the distinction, in our thinking, between direct and portfolio investment. We should be willing to liberalise investment movements within an enlarged EEC to a greater extent than movements to the outside world. But we still feared, in conditions of a free capital market, exchange operations under which funds were transmitted from London to an EEC capital and subsequently, or even simultaneously, passed on to a third country such as the United States. Jonkheer van Lennep agreed that when the Treaty was drafted an undue net outflow of investment from the Community to third countries had not been considered. But he felt that a ready-made solution was provided by Section 2 of Article 70, which provided that where free transfer within the Community led EEC residents to take advantage of it in order to evade rules about the transmission of funds to third countries, the state concerned, after consultation, could take appropriate measures. I agreed, and Dr Zijlstra added that he felt that there was no real difficulty so long as the Community was not called on to face a sustained and heavy net outward flow of capital. He added that we should find France on our side in any question about the restriction of the free flow of portfolio investment to third countries.

When we visited Luxembourg eight days later there was further discussion on these questions, which had clearly been the subject of animated exchanges between the Six. M. Werner, Prime Minister and Minister of Finance, felt that what we had said clarified the position on both Articles 108 and 70, and thought that there would be little difficulty in agreeing on an interpretative document during the negotiations for entry.

While in Luxembourg we had a meeting with leading members of the High Authority of the European Coal and Steel Community, whose headquarters are in the city. No issues of principle were raised by them, but they seemed anxious to raise points about the negotiations then proceeding on the Kennedy round of tariff and trade negotiations under GATT. They had one or two questions about our programme for the nationalisation of steel, and we, in turn, put a number of questions about pricing policy under the Authority.

The one clear impression my colleagues and I took away with us was the complaisant attitude of the Authority when the national interest of any member country was involved. The contrast could not have been greater with the Commission of EEC. No matter what the issue – protection, pricing policies, differential interest rates to help, indeed virtually to subsidise, national industries or regional policies – there seemed little disposition on the part of the Authority to insist on 'harmonisation'. And from the examples mentioned, it seemed that France had no cause for complaint when the interests of her national industries were involved.

The Luxembourg visit completed the round of the Six capitals. I intended that there should be a very full process of consideration by the Cabinet, which should provide every minister with the best possible opportunity of studying the issues involved and making up his mind on them. I accordingly gave instructions that the full minutes of all our meetings, restricted and plenary, with individual countries, with the Commission and with the High Authority should be printed and circulated in a single volume to my colleagues. It extended to 140 pages of fairly closely printed foolscap; nothing was omitted. Points and exchanges capable of being interpreted for or against a decision to enter were fully and neutrally reported; nothing was altered or presented anew.

This was circulated to the Cabinet a week before Easter, together with a covering note by the Foreign Secretary and myself, giving a summary of the main points raised in each capital and our general impressions.

For over two months – with Mr Kosygin's visit and the European tour – more than I would have wished of my time, and that of a number of colleagues, had to be devoted to international affairs. But the general work of government continued apace. Domestic issues requiring collective decision were concentrated in meetings which I would chair between these engagements.

The economic position was improving: sterling was strong; international payments, certainly on the monetary movements basis now used by the present Government, were in balance; the trade figures were showing a remarkable improvement. The foreign exchange which had poured out of the country the previous summer was returning on a flood tide. By the end of February we had paid back all our short-term borrowings ('federal swaps') from the US; by the end of March, all the short-term borrowings incurred in the 1966 crisis were repaid. Bank rate was reduced to six per cent. There were signs of a pick-up in the economy, though unemployment had settled on a seasonally corrected basis at a higher level. The numbers wholly unemployed on this basis, averaging about 569,000, were in March 1967 some 255,000 higher than in the same month of 1966. The numbers 'temporarily stopped' – mainly on organised short time – had fallen to 44,000 against a peak of 104,000 which had followed the July measures, but were still running at 37,000 above the figures for early 1966. The statutory wage-freeze had ended and railwaymen, doctors and others were receiving their delayed increases. We had moved into the period of 'severe restraint', rigorously enforced and widely observed. The City and industry voiced their hopes of a better year ahead.

But there were problems. One of these, the D-Notice affair, I can only describe as self-inflicted, in personal terms one of my costliest mistakes of our near six years in office.

The D-Notice system had operated virtually unchanged under successive Governments for many years. It was a voluntary system under which a number of Notices were issued to editors, the BBC, publishers and other agencies engaged in the communications industry for their general guidance as to the kind of information which should not be published in the interests of national security. These D-Notices were drawn up and agreed by a committee under the chairmanship of the Permanent Under-Secretary of State of the Ministry of Defence (for a time the Permanent Secretary of the Ministry of Aviation), consisting partly of officials and partly of nominated representatives of the press. It was the duty of the secretary of the committee to give guidance to editors and similar people in other parts of the communications industry as to whether particular pieces of information were covered by a D-Notice or not. In the main, the system was designed to relate to developments in aircraft missiles, military nuclear matters and equipment of the armed forces. But it extended also to troop movements in an emergency where security was vital, and also to secret information about the working of the security and intelligence services, including, for example, the names of the heads, and other officials of MI 5 and MI 6, even though the identity of the chiefs of these services was fairly widely known.

At the beginning of 1967 the number of current D-Notices was sixteen. The most recent of these had been issued in June 1964.

As I have explained, the purpose of the D-Notices was advisory only. Moreover, any opinion given by the secretary of the D-Notice committee as to whether a particular piece of information was covered by a D-Notice or not was also only advisory. The editor was perfectly free in the exercise of his own discretion to publish what he thought fit, though he would be aware that in doing so he might put himself at risk in relation to the Official Secrets Acts.

D-Notices were loyally observed, almost without question, by the press and the other media, and most were scrupulous in asking clearance for any story they proposed to publish which might come near the scope of a Notice in force.

On 22nd February I was due to answer a question from an Opposition member about the number of D-Notices issued in each of the last three years. None had, in fact, been issued. But, outraged by a story which had appeared in the *Daily Express*, I gratuitously added this comment:

As the House knows, the system under which these notices are issued had worked well on a voluntary basis for many years, and that means on the basis of confidence and trust between the authorities concerned and the press. The procedure is described in Chapter 9 of the Radcliffe Report (Cmmd. 1681 of 1962) which stresses that 'Its success depends upon goodwill and, in effect, upon very little else'.
Unfortunately, the confidence and trust which are the basis of the whole system have been called into question by the action of one newspaper in initiating this morning a sensationalised and inaccurate story purporting to describe a situation in which, in fact, the powers and practice have not changed for well over 40 years.

In answer to a subsequent supplementary question, I went further and referred to a clear breach of two D-Notices, despite the fact that the newspaper concerned was repeatedly warned that it would be contravening the Notice.

Before questions I had asked Mr Heath to call, and had told him of my intentions.

The story – which had reached two newspapers from a disgruntled ex-employee of a cable company – described the daily collection from cable offices of hundreds of international cables and their transport to a department of Government. It contained substantial inaccuracies and it described a system unchanged for a generation, but its drift and presentation had the effect of suggesting that under the Labour Government there was a 'big brother' system of snooping into private affairs.

I was categorically assured by the relevant department, and by the legal advisers of the Foreign Office, that this story was a breach of the Notice and that the newspaper concerned had been so informed, first at official level by the secretary of the committee, and then by a telephone call from the Foreign Secretary himself to the proprietor of the paper. This seemed hard enough for the statement I wanted to make, but it was still a mistake to make it. For one thing, I should have allowed the authorities to take it up with the paper concerned. What is more, I had no idea that there was a weak link in our case, which was to emerge the next morning. The reason for my haste was that this one breach of the system – which I was told it was – might lead to others and to the undermining of a vital part of our defences. It may be that, as with other Prime Ministers, I was inevitably preoccupied with security questions. But anyone who has held this responsibility knows just what can be at stake, even if he can never be explicit. I was justified, when the issue became one of major controversy, in saying that this kind of thing could put lives at risk, though I could not explain why.

Looking back on it, I would say that my concern on the question was justified, but my method of handling it was heavy-handed and over-hurried. What I should have foreseen was the almost unanimous press attack which followed. It was inevitable that they should see it as a threat to the freedom of the press. At least it could be said that I had succeeded in uniting the press – though not on my side. But with such heavy responsibilities for security even that disagreeable risk had sometimes to be taken by a Prime Minister.

I must at this point repudiate two legends which gained currency. I was not advised, still less pressured, by the then Paymaster General, George Wigg, to make the charge I did in my parliamentary answer. Nor was I pressed to do so by Sir Burke Trend, the Secretary to the Cabinet, who advises the Prime Minister directly on security questions. On the contrary, though he satisfied himself and me, on the departmental advice he was so clearly given, that the facts were right, he asked me, in the sense of one putting a question to advise against, whether I was really sure that

I felt I should make the statement. I said that I was. The decision and the responsibility were entirely mine, on the facts as I had them.

The next morning, the paper concerned published a statement that the author of the article had been informed by the D-Notice secretary, Colonel Sammy Lohan, that the proposed publication would not be a breach of the relevant Notice, though he urged that there should be no publication.

Later in the day Mr Heath came to see me. I felt, from the way he talked, that he was in possession of some facts unknown to me. I made a statement in the House, carefully prepared by those concerned, and even more carefully scrutinised by the Cabinet Officer, standing by my previous statement. The department, after examining the details of the conversation over lunch between the journalist concerned and Colonel Lohan, was totally satisfied that there was a breach, and that the newspaper was properly so informed. I said that the 'Services, Press and Broadcasting Committee' was being called to look into the incident.

Mr Heath pressed for a committee of Privy Counsellors to be appointed. I replied that another newspaper which had the story had, at the request of the secretary, decided not to publish it and was severely prejudiced by that fact. But I went on to say that if following the meeting of the D-Notice committee there were any dispute about the facts I would discuss the situation with the Leader of the Opposition.

In the event, the press representatives on the committee refused to carry out an examination of the facts. They were not willing to sit in judgment on an individual newspaper. When this became clear I decided to set up a committee of Privy Counsellors, under Lord Radcliffe. The other members of the committee were Mr Selwyn Lloyd and Manny Shinwell.

At the same time we were facing a major revolt in the PLP on defence. Denis Healey's 1967 White Paper, one might have hoped, would have been more acceptable to the left than its predecessors. For the first time it was possible to show economies in defence spending which were actually realised, with substantial further reductions in prospect. Our military commitments in the Far East were being reduced after the end of confrontation and both the White Paper and Denis's speech in the defence debate held out prospects of a continued run-down; indeed the main limit on the speed of withdrawal was not a desire to maintain an inflated establishment there, but accommodation problems at home. There was to be a run-down in the Persian Gulf, and we were to leave Southern Arabia – Aden and the surrounding territories – in 1968. Here, the limitation was not our desire to maintain a military establishment, but the speed with which we could negotiate a viable constitutional settlement in Aden and the wider Federation.

But a substantial section of the PLP, going much wider than the traditional left, wanted more, and wanted it more quickly. Defence spending and the spread of British forces had been a central argument of our party critics in the economic crisis of the previous July: now, they felt, was the time to express their strongly held views. Looking back on those weeks, I now see that more time and care should have been given to anticipating the trouble which broke when the vote was called on the Defence White Paper on 28th February. That it was not, was due, I suppose, to my preoccupation with Mr Kosygin's visit, Vietnam and the European tour. Certainly I was surprised when the White Paper was approved by a majority of only thirty-nine with some sixty-two abstentions.

This vote could not be ignored, and at the party meeting which followed on the Thursday evening I felt it necessary to warn the party. It was not in any sense a harsh speech – though it was later portrayed as such – still less one conceived in panic. My reason for it was that, under the Crossman–Silkin regime, we were moving towards a degree of liberality in party management seldom risked with a Government party; indeed, going far beyond anything the Labour party had conceived possible in our Opposition years throughout the fifties and early sixties. I had given my full support to Dick Crossman, as Leader of the House, and John Silkin, as Chief Whip, and the last thing I wanted to do was to clamp down with rigid party discipline, withdrawals of the whip and the like. I was disappointed, therefore, with what had happened.

In my short speech to the meeting I said simply that we could not go on in this manner. The last thing I wanted to do was to move back to any tightening of discipline. But many of those who embarrassed the Government did so in the safe knowledge that their revolt was sufficiently limited in numbers to avoid a crisis which might force the Government to resign or go to the country; I contrasted their behaviour with that of the days when our majority was three or less. Those who abstained did so only because they knew that our majority would be safe through the support of others, many of whom were subject to exactly the same constituency pressures. The member for 'Coketown West' was a hero in his constituency, and no doubt equally in 'Coketown East', simply because he could count on his neighbour to support the Government in the lobbies. This was not political courage: it was the opposite.

I was concerned also at the reaction of some hard-line members of the right wing, one or two of whom had abstained merely to draw attention to the laxity of party discipline and many of whom were proposing to do so on the next occasion. My strictures at this attitude were much more vehement: they had not even the excuse of 'conscience'. I was at pains to make clear that the parliamentary leadership, while prepared to overlook this particular occurrence, were still more concerned to see that it should not happen again. (I was very much aware that we should soon be putting a strain on a wider section of the party with the proposals we were then preparing for new legislation on prices and incomes.) This led me, very much in a throw-away reference, to say that every dog is allowed one bite, but if biting becomes too much of a habit its owner tends to have doubts about renewing the licence when it comes up.

There was literally no reaction in the meeting to this remark, apart from some mild amusement. Certainly no suggestion that I was enunciating a new parliamentary or constitutional doctrine; still less behaving like a Prime Minister in a petulant panic. But the phrase was a good headline, and the press the next morning hailed it as an enormity of almost Hitlerian proportions. The story ran for days, gaining momentum by repetition. It was, of course, a gift to the cartoonists, picked up again and again in the period of by-election and local government election reverses which followed. (Looking at the cartoons one can see what inspiration was derived also from the arrival, a short while earlier, in my family establishment, of the most unfractious canine, Paddy, my golden Labrador.)

The dispute between the libertarians and the disciplinarians in the party was personalised by the clash – first in private, then in public – between Dick Crossman and Manny Shinwell, chairman of the PLP, seconded, respectively, by John Silkin and George Wigg. I tried to reconcile these conflicting factions at meetings in my room at the House, but a speech by Dick Crossman at Morden, Surrey, glorying in his liberal policies led to an equally vigorous response by Manny, followed a few weeks later by his resignation. This I greatly regretted. He had been a great success as chairman and his good humour, eternal youth and vigorous support of the Government had been of classic quality. Equally valuable had been his advice to me as he would sit in my room, one afternoon after another, puffing his pipe or cigar and drawing on his vast experience and his shrewd judgment in one potential crisis after another. Our survival and unity in the 1964–6 Parliament owed far more to him than was recognised at the time; it is given to few in their eighties to play so decisive a part at the very centre of the political process. But now the lifetime rebel had become an archetypal disciplinarian, and he felt that he could not accept the methods of the parliamentary leadership.

He was succeeded by Douglas Houghton, who with a different though increasingly successful style of chairmanship saw the party through the no less grave problems which followed devaluation later in the year.

During these weeks the Government was giving a great deal of thought to the prices and incomes policy which was to replace the six-month freeze. A policy of severe restraint was then in force, but we had to decide the statutory framework within which incomes policy would work when severe restraint ended in June. Michael Stewart had given a great deal of thought to this and was almost ready to put proposals to the Cabinet for publication and, later, legislation. We knew that this would not be easy, either within the PLP or in the context of our relations with the TUC. A White Paper (Cmnd. 3235) was published on 21st March: it set out tight criteria, with exceptions only for lower-paid workers and productivity bargains, and proposed that Part II of the Prices and Incomes Act should be put into effect. This would provide for a delay in implementing proposals to raise either prices or wages until a decision could be taken whether or not to refer them to the Prices and Incomes Board. Where they were referred, a further freeze would take place, while the Board was examining the claim.

Press reports during March and April, starting from the defence debate and the 'barking dogs' episode, were of an apocalyptic character, suggesting total crisis in the PLP. This was not apparent to me. But certainly morale was shaken by our defeat in the Pollok (Glasgow) by-election on 9th March, where the Conservative was elected mainly through the loss of Labour votes to the Scottish Nationalist. Labour's vote fell from 21,257 in 1966 to 12,069 while the Scottish Nationalists, who had not run in the 1966 General Election, polled 10,884. The Conservative vote fell from 19,282 to 14,270, but this was enough for them to gain the seat by a majority of 2,201. A Gallup poll afterwards suggested that enough of the Nationalist voters would vote Labour in a General Election for us to regain the seat. This poll was vindicated in June 1970. Although on the same day we held Nuneaton, with a sharply reduced majority, 4,054 against 11,403 in 1966, a third by-election in the Rhondda revealed a massive swing to the Welsh Nationalists, reducing our majority from 16,888 in March 1966 to 2,306, in both cases over the Welsh Nationalists. The Conservative poll fell from 1,955 to 1,075, which put their candidate at the bottom of the poll, below the Nationalist and below the Communist. In April we suffered severe losses in the counties, including the Greater London Council, where a 1964 victory by 64 seats to 36 was turned into a Conservative majority of 82 to 18. Most galling of all was the loss of our majority on the inner London seats, corresponding to the old London County Council area, which we had controlled since 1932.

The other big event – or, as the press held it to be, non-event – was the Budget. Jim Callaghan, again keeping me fully informed about his assessment and proposals, accepted the Treasury's advice that no fundamental changes were needed following the action taken the previous July. No further net increases in taxation were required; equally, there was no cause for any easement.

In his Budget statement on 11th April, the Chancellor was able to claim considerable success with the balance of payments. From 1964 to 1966, on a comparable basis, there had been an improvement of £633 millions. Now, on visible trade alone we had a deficit in the fourth quarter of 1966 of only £112 millions, partly helped by anticipation of the ending of the import surcharge. In the first quarter of 1967, we were again nearly in balance. Exports were ten per cent higher than in the same period of the previous year. All the signs were of a surplus on our over-all balance of payments, sufficient over the years immediately ahead to pay off our Monetary Fund borrowings. He announced that there would be no major changes in the taxation system and almost no changes in individual taxes. He concluded: 'We are back on course. The ship is picking up speed. The economy is moving. Every seaman knows the command at such a moment, "Steady as she goes".'

There was another development of some importance in economic affairs in those weeks; perhaps more significant in constitutional terms than in its not insignificant content. Michael Stewart had been giving a great deal of thought to the need for further incentives to industrialists to invest in development areas. His proposal, which was finally included in legislation, came to be known as the Regional Employment Premium. This provided a simple premium payment to manufacturing employers in the development areas, based on the numbers employed. The new departure was that his proposals were published not as a White Paper, but as a 'Green Paper'. This innovation was designed to enable the Government to put forward a new proposal not as a firm decision of Government but as a question for consultation and public discussion. A White Paper is essentially a statement of Government policy, in such terms that a withdrawal or major amendment, following consultations or public debate, tends to be regarded as a humiliating withdrawal. A Green Paper represents the best that the Government can propose on a given issue, but, remaining uncommitted, it is able without loss of face to leave its final decision open until it has been able to consider the public reaction to it.

The Green Paper proved, in fact, to be one of our major contributions to the concept of public participation in public decisions. In this particular case, public opinion was favourable, and the proposals became law later in the year. In the next three years, up to the change of Government, twelve Green Papers were issued and the practice has been followed by our successors.

In overseas affairs, there were important developments to record. One which did not involve us directly, though it had been the occasion of very tough discussions with Mr Kosygin, was concerned with Soviet–American talks on the nuclear arms race. Mr Kosygin had told me in February that the Soviet Government had not at that time taken a decision on anti-ballistic missile systems, though he had been critical of our view that there should be direct talks before either major power embarked on a major programme of development of ABMs. On 2nd March President Johnson announced that Mr Kosygin had agreed to Soviet–American discussions on the limitation of defensive as well as offensive nuclear weapons. That development was much more at the centre of my thinking than the question of dog licences, on which the press concentrated at that time.

The other major question was Aden. All our efforts to secure a settlement there had broken down, thanks equally to the feudal rulers and the divided, indeed fratricidal, terrorist organisations. Incidents of violence multiplied: no fewer than 256 in the first two months of the year, almost as many as in the whole of 1965.

We decided in principle that the time-table for independence, which we had announced for 1968, should be speeded up and George Thomson flew out for urgent consultations with the Federal Government and to put before them the outline of a proposal for independence in November 1967. Meanwhile, the Foreign Secretary made a holding speech in the debate in the House of Commons after a violent argument with Mr Sandys.

A peaceful settlement was not assisted by the arrival in Aden of a three-man mission from the United Nations, which almost immediately decided to leave the country, accompanying their departure with an *obbligato* of hysterical and, in some cases, unprintable comments. On arriving in Rome they were intercepted by our people and by U Thant and persuaded to come to London for discussions with the Foreign Secretary, who, with enormous patience, managed to talk a little sense into them. Then, and right to the end, George Brown handled the Aden problem with great skill.

On 17th March when I was in my constituency, George telephoned. He wanted to appoint one of his juniors as a minister resident in Aden, on the Churchill wartime model. I pointed out that ministers could not be appointed in that manner and suggested that Lord Shackleton, Minister without Portfolio, was the right man to go out – on a temporary basis – with a specific remit to help the High Commissioner. George Brown agreed and the mission was announced that evening.

On Saturday, 18th March, a very different crisis – localised but serious – broke. At 9.11 a.m. an American-owned tanker sailing under the Liberian flag, the *Torrey Canyon*, 118,285 tons, ran, in perfect weather and broad daylight, on to the Sevenstones Reef 18½ miles west of Land's End, eight miles north-east of the Isles of Scilly. The impact of the wreck broke open a number of the 18 oil compartments, and an estimated 30,000 tons of her cargo of 117,000 tons of filthy crude oil gushed out into the Atlantic, slowly heading east towards the beaches of the western and southern mainland. The departments concerned were asked to report urgently on the situation and the C-in-C Plymouth was put in operational charge. Local authorities bombarded the departments and Downing Street with demands for immediate action to protect their beaches.

On the Sunday morning, at Chequers, I received the first assessments. They and the press were unanimous in warning of the grave dangers of pollution – of the sea, the beaches, the fishing-grounds, the nesting areas and the oyster fisheries – and the certain massacre of wildlife.

With the agreement of the Defence Secretary, I asked Maurice Foley, Under-Secretary for the Navy, to go at once to Plymouth, to hold a watching brief, to take any decision the naval authorities might put to him and to keep Denis Healey and me informed. He was to return to report as soon as he had formed an assessment.

Late on the Tuesday night he came to No. 10 to supplement the detailed information he had been sending by telegraph. It was a grim situation. The tanker was firmly caught on the Sevenstones and the view of the Admiralty was that she would never be towed off. (This view was authoritatively supported by an octogenarian friend of mine, Captain Phillips, a former Trinity House pilot, whom I saw when in Scilly at the end of the week: 'Ah,' he said, 'the Sevenstones, she never gives up a ship.') The *Torrey Canyon*'s owners and the Dutch salvage company which had arrived on the scene thought otherwise. But it would be another week before the spring tides, which would provide the only hope of getting her away – if she didn't break her back first. It was not possible to pump her oil out of the compartments which were undamaged, for the force of the impact had damaged the engines and pumps beyond repair. Oil of this kind cannot be sucked out by the pumps of a relief tanker moored alongside, even if, in the gales then blowing, one could have been so moored.

Any attempt to install pumps aboard, or to repair the ship's own engines and pumps, involved the near certain risk of an explosion, for the ship was a trap of highly volatile and explosive gases released from the oil. The Queen's Harbour-Master, Plymouth, who was in operational charge for the Admiralty, told me the following weekend that even to hammer a nail into a piece of wood might well have fatal consequences. The captain of a Dutch salvage tug was, in fact, tragically killed by an explosion of the trapped gas when he boarded her.

There were virtually no precedents to follow. Experts were flown to Plymouth, and one was able to confirm that a small tanker which had run aground in the Persian Gulf had been set on fire and burnt out, oil as well. It might be possible, he said, to set fire to the oil, but first it had to be extracted from the sealed compartments by some safe 'can-opening' operation. She could be bombed or shelled, but there was no guarantee that the oil would ignite – the action might add tens of thousands of tons to the slick already pouring towards the beaches. In any case, such an operation would require the assent of her owners, who still hoped to float her off. The Sevenstones were outside territorial waters; to bomb her without the owners' consent would have been an act of piracy.

Priority was given to action aimed at protecting the beaches. As early as Sunday, 19th March the Navy had been spraying the surface oil with the best detergent then available. The following day, fishing and other vessels locally available were impressed into the operation. Factories went on overtime to build foam-plastic booms to protect river estuaries, fisheries and oyster-beds. The Defence Secretary announced a Government grant of £500,000 for the attack on beach and sea pollution. The Minister of Housing, with his responsibility for relations with local authorities, was put in over-all charge of the landward attack on polluted beaches with a full call, in consultation with the Defence Secretary, on Service detachments. Central co-ordination of operations was entrusted to the Cabinet Emergencies committee, under the chairmanship of the Home Secretary. This met daily, and when necessary twice daily, serviced by the officials' Emergencies committee. Sir Solly Zuckerman, Chief Scientific Adviser to the Government, was put in charge of the scientists of all the departments concerned and he rapidly mobilised the aid of Government and private research establishments.

On 24th March, Good Friday, I crossed to the islands for my Easter holiday, but there was to be little time off. The BEA helicopter in which I flew went over *Torrey Canyon*. Even before we saw her we could smell the oil and see the great oil slick stretching out to the mainland.

I had taken a private secretary, Roger Dawe, with me to keep in touch with London and Plymouth. On the Saturday evening I was coming down the last fairway at the golf club when he met me with a message. The owners, hopeful of towing off the tanker during the spring tides of Monday and Tuesday, had decided that she was then to be anchored in Crow Sound, between St Mary's and St Martin's in the Isles of Scilly, reasonably protected from the prevailing south-west winds; failing that, off a Cornish beach. I said, shortly, that they were not going to do any such thing. They had done enough damage to our beaches. The nearest haven I would be interested in would be Bantry Bay, in Ireland.

I told Roger Dawe to get in touch with London and Plymouth and to call a meeting for the following afternoon at Culdrose Air Station, including the Home Secretary, the Minister of Defence (Administration), the Attorney-General, the Minister of Housing, Maurice Foley and Sir Solly Zuckerman, together with our chief naval advisers, and the owners and their legal representatives. Meanwhile I put through a call to my friend Captain Thomas, the master of RMV *Scillonian*, who knew Crow Sound as well as anyone could. *Torrey Canyon* would take months to be made seaworthy, he said. It only required a strong south-easterly, such as one which devastated unprotected coastal areas of Scilly a few years earlier, to break her up. Moreover, I had doubts whether the sea-bed there would provide a grip for her anchor. Captain Thomas confirmed that there was no more unsuitable place. I asked him to put his local information at the disposal of the Admiralty and to stand by at Culdrose the following afternoon.

I flew there by helicopter, the pilot taking me over a number of Cornwall's most famous beaches, black and revolting with the glutinous crude oil. The Government team was waiting for me while the owners and their lawyers waited in another room. The Queen's Harbour-Master and other officers made a full report on every maritime and technical aspect of the problem. They were willing to stake their reputation that she could not be towed off; but how long she would remain before breaking up, and how much more oil would pour out when she began to do so, they could not guess. The Attorney-General and his advisers then came up with the proposal that, if she were towed off, we should offer to buy her, see her with an attendant naval vessel to a suitable point – the Admiralty advisers nominated one west of mid-Atlantic – and there send her to the bottom. He was authorised to negotiate this with the owners, and told that he could go up to £1 million as the price – that is if she was towed off as a floating concern; we were putting in a much larger claim for damage to our beaches. Agreement was accordingly reached.

Meanwhile, Sir Solly Zuckerman reported on the work of the large group of scientists he was heading, who had been working night and day on the problem. The question we had to face was the problem of the remaining eighty to ninety thousand tons or more of oil still remaining on the tanker, if, within the next two days, she were not floated off. Scientists at the Ministry of Technology's Warren Spring Laboratory, Stevenage, had succeeded, in laboratory conditions, in burning a thousand gallons of Kuwait crude, the only residue being a bucketful or so of ash. The question was whether – if *Torrey Canyon* broke her back, or was destroyed by bombing – her oil could be ignited as it poured out across the sea. Authority was given for an attempt to fire an oil-slick measuring four miles by two near the Wolf Rock, to see if it would ignite. The question was whether the much lower temperature, and several days' loss of volatile gases, would make it impossible to set it ablaze.

The helicopter flew me back to Scilly. Just after I had left the airport, our pilot received a signal that *Torrey Canyon*'s attendant destroyer had reported 'something strange happening'. He was told to fly over her and reported that she had broken her back and shifted her position. Fresh oil – an official report estimated a further thirty thousand tons – was pouring out. Our legal and other preparations for her last resting-place were now unnecessary.

In this new situation Roy Jenkins and his Emergencies committee took the decision in principle, subject to my agreement, that she should be destroyed by bombs and rockets on the Tuesday, by which time we should have a report on the attempt to fire the oil-slick off the Wolf Rock. All the preparations were made. Naval Buccaneers, flown down from Lossiemouth, and RAF Hunters from Chivenor, in Devon, took part.

On the Tuesday morning I went over to another island, Tresco, for lunch. Walking across the island from the quay I had a message that the attempt to fire the Wolf oil-slick had failed.

We were presented with a most difficult choice. If we did nothing, the tanker would break open, and all her remaining oil – far more than the amount which had already escaped – would pour on to the Cornish beaches and right up the English and Bristol Channels over a period of time. Just as the council workers and troops had cleaned up a beach, a fresh load would arrive.

On the other hand, to 'open the can' by bombing would produce an immediate surge of oil, which, after the Wolf Rock operation, we could be anything but sure of firing. Our hope must lie in the bombing itself igniting the oil, but there were no precedents to guide us; no one had bombed a modern tanker, designed to be as fireproof as possible. The Emergencies committee met to decide whether or not to bomb the ship that afternoon. After a quick lunch I rushed back to the quay. Just as I boarded the small boat the walkie-talkie bleeped. The Home Secretary told me that the recommendation was to release the bombs in half an hour's time. Did I agree? I gave approval and reached St Mary's just in time to get to the coastguard tower as the first Buccaneers flew over *Torrey Canyon*. The first stick of bombs missed, as did the second. The third was a direct hit, followed first by smoke and then by those welcome flames. *Torrey Canyon* was ablaze from stem to stern. The Hunters flew over jettisoning kerosene on the vessel and the oil which was pouring out of her. The oil was ignited and spread far beyond the ship. More bombs followed.

The next day I returned to the mainland. I was told that reconnaissance had shown that three or four oil compartments were still intact; they were bombed that afternoon. At a press conference I was asked pointed questions about the use of napalm. There was great interest in where it had come from. I hazarded the suggestion that it might have come from the stocks of the Isles of Scilly Council. Another question put to me earned me a rebuke from the Leader of the Opposition. In replying I felt moved to criticise the standard of navigation, with some terse comments on the standards sometimes in force in ships sailing under flags of convenience. Procedurally, I should have awaited the inquiry due to be held by the Liberian Government. But I had already had full reports, both from the Navy and locally. When dawn broke on the 18th, the *Torrey Canyon* had found herself going to the south of Scilly instead of taking the usual northern route to Milford Haven. The airport staff on St Mary's had seen her pass so close to them that they expected her to founder on Scilly's southern rocks. East of the islands she headed to the north. The Sevenstones lightship signalled to her frantically to alter course, but to no avail. My strictures on this navigational skill were solemnly criticised by Mr Heath the next day; I replied that if he saw political advantage in linking his party's future with the navigational ability of those responsible for the *Torrey Canyon*, he was welcome.

Mr Heath's comments were overbid – not for the last time – by his then shadow cabinet colleague, Mr Enoch Powell, who, denouncing me as 'a street urchin', attacked me for my 'gutter language' on the flags of convenience question.

Mr Heath had a final fling. If bombing was so successful, he asked, why had we not done it before? Knowing maritime law would have precluded such action until the owners conceded total loss, it was a challenge relying on the safety of hindsight on the results of the bombing, which was in doubt until the bombs fell. Had the bombing produced nothing but the release of tens of thousands of unignited oil, he would have been free to attack us for our lack of foresight. Such are the delights of that particular style of Opposition.

It had been a successful operation, and the Cornish beaches were cleared by Whitsun. Comparisons have been made with the ease with which the *Pacific Glory* incident in October 1970 was dealt with. But she was aground on sand, not fatally trapped on solid rock; her engines and pumps were not put out of action; it was quite safe to pump out enough oil to float her off on a favourable tide. A new detergent had been developed (by BP) much more suitable for dealing both with floating oil and polluted beaches. I had seen it tested at Warren Springs in the previous January; above all, there was the advantage of the previous experience. From the time *Torrey Canyon* struck, the Navy first, and then those concerned with dealing with the pollution, had to act and act quickly with no previous experience to guide them. Despite some later criticism by a sub-committee of the Select Committee on Science and Technology, a good deal of it concerned with co-ordination and absence of advance preparation, I believe that the Navy, the scientists and the rest did a great job.

When I returned to London on 30th March I was plunged immediately into a series of Cabinet discussions on the Common Market. Colleagues had by this time had the opportunity to study every word of the discussions in the six capitals. A further series of authoritative papers, some of them very lengthy and on almost every issue raised, was prepared for circulation. They covered the balance of payments, monetary problems, tax policies – including 'fiscal harmonisation', agriculture, the cost of living, regional questions, mobility of labour and immigration policies, social policy – including 'harmonisation', human rights and a very full statement on the constitutional issues involved, prepared under the direction of the Lord Chancellor. With that last exception, all the papers were prepared, without ministerial intervention, by the special unit I had set up in the Cabinet Office under Mr (later Sir) William Neild with experts drawn from the departments. Individual ministers who wanted to circulate their own papers were not precluded from doing so.

I was anxious that no colleague should feel that the decision was in any way rushed, that any relevant issue – even the most tangential – was not examined and discussed, or that he, or the Cabinet as a whole, was being 'bounced' into a decision.

To get through the Cabinet a proposal that Britain should apply for entry into EEC was a formidable task. To succeed and to produce a firm decision without any resignations seemed a near miracle, but perhaps this was assisted by an answer I gave to a question in a television interview on the possibility of resignation – that I felt there might be one, or even two, but that would not stand in the way of a decision whatever that decision might be.

I told my colleagues that the fullest time would be available for so important a matter and that the final decision would not be taken until every minister felt that it had been adequately discussed. We met roughly twice a week from Easter until the beginning of May, taking one or two subjects at each meeting. Where any asked for more information, or a further paper – or for a matter to come back to us for reconsideration – this was agreed. If anyone had asked for a document on the effect of entry into the Market on British pigeon-fancying, he would have got it; but no one did.

As each subject was discussed I tried to get a preliminary view of it before we passed on to others. Sometimes the Cabinet was only too ready to move on. George Brown was a little impatient on occasions to rush decisions, but he had to take my view on one morning or another that the matter had not been adequately discussed by the time we reached 1.00 p.m. and should be further argued.

I was concerned also with the debate in the Parliamentary Party. Recalling 1962, when I had presided over five marathon meetings of the PLP groups concerned, I proposed that there should be three full-scale party meetings exclusively directed to the subject. George Brown opened the first and I was to wind up the third. There was some alarm at one of his – unpremeditated – phrases about General de Gaulle. He was reported as saying that he felt that on this occasion there would be no French veto because the President was no longer strong enough to make one effective. There was some fear that this might stiffen the General against us.

The PLP debates were vigorous and well-informed, but much less passionate than those of 1962. A very clear majority supported British entry and an early application. My final speech at the third meeting was taken as a strong lead in favour of an application, with no commitment about entry until the terms which emerged from the negotiations became known.

By the last week of April I felt that the Cabinet discussions were reaching the point where my colleagues would soon be ready to take a decision. Even those who had pressed for more and more information were silent. At this point, I asked for a full discussion on the well-documented choices before us: entry, or those attractive sisters, NAFTA and GITA. The North Atlantic free-trade area, which had been much urged on us by friends in North America, envisaged a loose free-trade area of the EFTA countries, Canada and the US. In a wider formulation, which belied its North Atlantic title, the free-trade area might extend to Australia and New Zealand. GITA was, simply, 'go it alone', Britain standing on her own feet and making her own terms with all the main trading groups. (The alternative title was '*Sinn fein*' – in English '*ourselves alone*'.)

In our very thorough discussions on these alternatives there was general agreement that NAFTA was unreal. There was no guarantee, no indication even, that it could become a reality in any foreseeable period. Its American supporters were engaged in a desperate fight with resurgent American protectionism. All experience suggested that the powerful Australian manufacturing lobby would resist any permanent association which laid their domestic market open on equal terms to American and British competition.

GITA, it was widely agreed, was not so much a constructive alternative as a fall-back if entry were denied to us. It was vital that we should not negotiate on the basis of economic weakness. In or out of the Community we must be strong. If entry were denied to us or if, after negotiations, the terms were unacceptable, then we must be in a position to stand, and prosper, outside. The one conclusion which emerged from all our discussions was that we must press on relentlessly with the policies necessary to make Britain strong.

On the last Thursday in April, the 27th, I decided to move forward. I said that while I was prepared, if colleagues so desired, to continue the discussions for a week, even weeks, longer, my impression was that most of us were ready to take a decision. But this was a vital issue. It must not be rushed. I suggested, therefore, that we should spend the whole of the next weekend on it in a relaxed and free debate – the Saturday at Downing Street, the Sunday at Chequers. When minister after minister, including those who had pressed for fuller examination, and postponement, said they felt that one day would be enough I knew that we were within sight of a decision. We agreed to meet on the Sunday, 30th April.

The Chequers meeting was agreeable but still very much to the point. There was no doubt that the decision would be to apply for entry. But, following the line I had taken at all Chequers discussions, I made clear that we should not take any decision there. Summing up the meeting quite early in the evening, I said that I felt I could sense the general view of the Cabinet. At our formal meeting on the Tuesday I would put a concrete proposition for acceptance or rejection, together with a draft parliamentary statement. To ensure that there were no leaks, I should have to insist that the statement – after Cabinet approval, paragraph by paragraph – would be made in Parliament that afternoon.

That evening I dictated the draft statement for circulation on the Monday. One procedural question which had to be settled was the form of the application. This was a matter which had been much discussed with the jurists of EEC on our European tour. Technically, we were told, our application was in, merely adjourned. On the other hand I felt there was some doubt in that the motion which Parliament had adopted, in August 1961, said no more than 'this House supports the decision of Her Majesty's Government to make formal application under Article 237 of the Treaty of Rome in order to initiate negotiations to see if satisfactory arrangements can be made to meet the special interests of the United Kingdom, of the Commonwealth and of the European Free Trade Association . . .'.

I decided to recommend a fresh application.

The formal decision and my draft statement went through Cabinet very quickly on Tuesday, 2nd May. That afternoon I made my statement. It began: 'Her Majesty's Government have today decided to make an application under Article 237 of the Treaty of Rome for membership of the European Economic Community and parallel application for membership of the European Coal and Steel Community and Euratom . . .'.

I recalled my statement of 10th November, described the visits to the Six, and went over the main issues. I set out our position on the Treaty in the terms I had used in November and said that, while there were anxieties, the Treaty need not be an obstacle. Negotiations should not be unnecessarily complicated with lesser issues, many of which could be best dealt with after entry. I then dealt with the main problems – agricultural, financing, matters of Commonwealth concern, capital investments and regional policies – before dealing with the broad issues facing every member, the effect on exports and imports, technology and economic dynamism and the political issues.

The House, I said, would have unprecedentedly full opportunities for debate. The statement I was making would be presented as a White Paper and submitted for approval in a three-day debate. In 1961 the House, on the eve of the August adjournment, had been vouchsafed only two days, without any of the prior debates which we had had in 1966–7.

In the debate, on 8th, 9th and 10th of May, I arranged for all the ministers concerned with the principal issues to speak. I opened on the first day, and the Commonwealth Secretary, Bert Bowden, wound up. On the second day, following a speech by Mr Heath, the Chancellor of the Exchequer opened the debate for the Government, and Fred Peart, the Minister of Agriculture, wound up. On the final day, George Brown opened and Michael Stewart wound up. An amendment tabled by Mr Robin Turton, the Conservative 'father of the House', was defeated by a large majority, and on the main question, to approve the White Paper, including the decision to apply for membership, the vote was 488 for, 62 against. It was the biggest majority on a contested vote on a matter of public policy for almost a century. Historians were not wanting to point out that the vote on the Tichborne case in 1875 showed a larger majority; that apart, it was almost certainly the biggest majority on a major issue since the development of the modern system of party political alignments more than a century before.

Chapter 21

THE early days of May were dominated by controversy over the Common Market and by analysis of the Commons voting, which showed thirty-five Labour members in the 'No' lobby. There was much speculation about what General de Gaulle would do.

But on the domestic front there were other worries. The GLC electoral cataclysm of April and the general massacre of Labour councillors in the counties were followed by the worst borough election results we had experienced since the war. After the GLC election I had made clear, in a speech in Fulham on 15th April, that there would be no change in our policies: they were necessary, and they would continue. The night after the borough elections, on the day the House adjourned for the Whitsun recess, 12th May, I was speaking in Croydon. I made no apology for our bad showing. We had pursued our stern economic measures, '... without fear or favour, and we have faced periods of great electoral unpopularity'. Those measures, our economic policy, would continue, '... until we have got the country firmly established on a sound economy'.

Parliament went into recess; I did not. I had taken on some eleven speeches up and down the country, some of them on major occasions or major themes. But the growing pressure of events, indeed crises, meant there would be no time off at all for me or for a small number of senior ministers.

The Kennedy round of tariff reduction negotiations was coming to a head and we had day and night meetings to give final instructions to our negotiators. Agreement was reached at midnight on 18th May and formally signed on 30th May.

The ever-sensitive situation in Hong Kong erupted into strikes, riots and murder, following the imprisonment of a number of Chinese Communist journalists.

There was deadlock in the Aden negotiations, and a new and more dangerous outbreak of violence. The High Commissioner was recalled and Sir Humphrey Trevelyan sworn in as his successor with almost full powers.

Gibraltar faced a new crisis as Spain imposed fresh restrictions on access to the Rock, including restrictions on flights by civil aircraft and the threat of physical interference with their safety.

King Faisal of Saudi Arabia was due in London during the recess, for critically important talks on the situation in the Gulf and South Arabia, particularly about the consideration we were giving to a programme of withdrawal from the Gulf states as well as Aden.

At home, the conference season saw one union after another pressing resolutions condemning Government policy on prices and incomes. Defeat became certain at the TUC Congress and the Labour party conference. A grumbling row over the siting of London's third airport erupted into a full-scale campaign by the 'not at Stansted' lobby; the issue had not been well-handled by the departments.

On a somewhat lighter side, a campaign developed against the Government's decision to clamp down on the maritime pirate radios, adding a new and mainly youthful element to the demonstrators I had to face whenever I went about the country.

Some of these matters provided a formidable agenda for a fortnight's recess.

There was also a serious development on the Common Market front. Following a number of not discouraging remarks by certain of his ministers – and then a dampener by M. Giscard d'Estaing on the difficulties presented by the sterling system – General de Gaulle finally broke silence at a press conference on 16th May. He began:

> Dear friends, I am going to answer your question about Britain and the Common Market. Of course, I am not going to prejudice what the negotiations, if they take place – I repeat, if they take place – would be be about.... Today I will restrict myself to general ideas, to a view of the subject as a whole which I think needs to be clearly stated.
>
> I will start by saying that the movement which seems at present to be leading England to link herself to Europe instead of keeping herself apart is a movement which can only please France.
>
> This is why we note with sympathy what appears to be indicated by the British Government's declared aim and the step it has taken.
>
> For our part, there is no question of there being a veto, nor has there ever been one. It is simply a question of finding out whether this conclusion is possible within the framework of the Common Market without bringing about destructive upheavals; or in what other situation and in what other conditions this conclusion could be possible; or whether it would be desirable to preserve what has been built until such time as it would appear conceivable to welcome an England which, for its own part, would have undergone a profound transformation....

He then went on to develop, at very considerable length, the twin themes of his allocution to me in the Elysée four months earlier – the position of sterling and the effect on the 'developed' Market.

His arguments about sterling were reinforced by the argument that, unlike the Six, we feed ourselves to a very great extent with food bought cheaply all over the world and especially in the Commonwealth. If we accepted the rules of the Six our balance of payments would collapse and dearer food would lead to dearer wages, thus pricing our exports out of world markets. We could not accept the freedom of capital movements insisted upon by the Six.

EEC countries, on the other hand, were in a perfectly solid position:

> ... And so, while one does not despair of the pound holding its own, the fact is that it will be a long time before one is certain about this because, in its relationship to the currencies of the Six, the pound is in the special position of being what is called a reserve currency.

He went on to develop this theme:

> In fact, parity and monetary solidarity are essential rules, essential conditions of the Common Market. They cannot be extended to our neighbours across the Channel, unless some day the pound sterling appears in a completely new position so that its future value appears assured, it is freed from its character as a reserve currency, and the mortgage of Britain's sterling balance within the sterling area disappears. But when will it be so? ...

He drew parallels with our overseas political arrangements, again going far beyond Europe. But his chief concern was with the future of the Six, whose ten-year development he surprisingly held to have been consummated by the role of the EEC Commission in the Kennedy round negotiations. To the extent that that was true, it owed little to the General.

If the Community were changed to admit Britain, he said, or if there were agreement to envisage changing it, one of three outcomes must follow, which he summarised in these words:

1 The destruction of the Community:

> ... building a totally new edifice and in razing what has just been built. In this case, what would result if not the creation of a free trade zone in Western Europe, pending an Atlantic zone, which would take away from our continent its own personality?

2 Association of Britain and the EFTA countries under Article 238:

> to install ... a regime of association which is, in any case, provided for in the Treaty of Rome and which would multiply and help the economic relations of the contracting parties.

3 A waiting game:

> Finally, to wait for the change to be brought about by the internal and external developments of which, it seems, England is showing signs. In other words, that this great people, so magnificently gifted with ability and courage, should on their own behalf and for themselves achieve the profound economic and political transformation which would allow them to join the Six continentals.

He concluded:

...I truly believe that this is the desire of many people who wish to see a Europe appear which would have its natural dimensions and who have for England a deep admiration and a sincere friendship. If Britain one day reached this stage, with what joy would France then greet this historic transformation.

It was what one British newspaper called 'the velvet veto'.

The following day I had a mad rush to make three speeches, opening the new offices of the General and Municipal Workers' Union in Esher; then speaking at the Labour party's annual women's conference at Southend, and finally at the first annual dinner of the Confederation of British Industry in London. It was there, as part of a general speech on relations between Government and industry, that I replied to General de Gaulle, repeating simply what I had said earlier, that we should not take 'No' for an answer. But, I said, we must, all of us, know before many months are up exactly where we stand.

But as public comment for some days was mainly concentrated on General de Gaulle's speech, critical European reactions to it, on analysis of the General's position, and discussion of what Britain's strategy should be, the smouldering crisis in the Middle East began to reach danger-point.

Until the spring of 1966, the settlement made after the Suez crisis was holding reasonably firm. Units of the United Nations Emergency Force served as a stabilising influence in the Gaza/Sinai area, observing and patrolling the 59 kilometre demarcation line in the Gaza Strip and the 209 kilometre frontier between the UAR and Israel, and also observing and guaranteeing the safety of shipping passing through the narrow Straits of Tiran. These straits provided Israel's means of entrance from the Indian Ocean to the Gulf of Aqaba, and her port of Eilat. In 1957, Israel had removed her troops from this critical port only with the utmost reluctance and on the firmest assurances that the UN detachment would provide adequate safeguards.

From the spring of 1966 there had been a succession of incidents on Israel's borders, some from the UAR side, some from the Palestinian refugees in Jordan, and some of the most provocative from Syria. Some of these were referred to the Security Council, whose membership was quantitatively and qualitatively unbalanced to the disadvantage of Israel. George Brown, who before entering the Government had been widely regarded as friendly to the Arabs, himself commented in the House, in a debate on the Middle East at the end of May, that a terrorist raid on Israel led to no action or condemnation while an attack shortly afterwards by Israel on her neighbour was condemned outright by the Security Council. The worst problems were in the north on the Israeli–Syrian border. Attempts by U Thant to calm the situation by invoking the Israel–Syria Mixed Armistice Commission, strongly backed by Britain, led to little improvement and Syria became more and more provocative. After an incident in April in the demilitarised zone south of Lake Tiberias (Galilee), Israel struck back at Syrian positions. From then on the situation worsened, but it is fair to say that during this period the UAR showed considerable restraint and speeches and demonstrations were not then reflected in any military needling of Israel.

In the second week of May Israeli leaders made strong pronouncements about the Syrian provocations and warned that they could not continue to tolerate them.

At this point the UAR moved into the conflict. In the years immediately before, Egypt had been powerfully reinforced by Soviet arms supplies on a prodigious scale, both in the air and on the ground. On 14th and 15th May, with a great fanfare of aggressive speeches and broadcasts, President Nasser moved up troops and supplies towards the Israeli borders. Whether he feared that the Israelis were contemplating a pre-emptive attack on Syria, or even outright invasion; whether he felt that his large-scale military build-up would deter Israel; whether he was engaging in a risky round of inter-Arab politics: all these are matters for history to clarify. What is not in doubt is that the UAR military posture, with its loud orchestrated propaganda support, looked to the Israelis like a formidable threat of imminent invasion.

On 16th May President Nasser, perhaps carried away by his own propaganda offensive, took the grave step of demanding the withdrawal of the UN Emergency Force. The Secretary-General agreed on the ground that UN troops could not remain on the territory of a member without the consent of that member. We considered the action ill-judged, indeed procedurally wrong, in that U Thant had made no attempt to secure the consent of, or even to consult with, the appropriate organisations of UN including the Security Council, under whose aegis the arrangement had been reached which included the stationing of the buffer force. We expressed our deep concern to the Secretary-General but the decision could not be reversed. To Israel, it was a clear signal that President Nasser either was hell-bent on war or at least had been carried by his own pronouncements and actions to a point from which he could not easily withdraw.

There was worse to follow. On Monday, 22nd May President Nasser announced that following the removal of the UN troops he had moved UAR troops into Sharm-el-Sheikh, immediately overlooking the Straits of Tiran, and that he intended to close the Straits to Israeli ships, and to the carriage of strategic goods to Israel. The UAR was reported to be laying mines in the Straits. Tanks and guns commanded the narrow strip of deep water through which ships must pass. From that time events moved fast, and at any moment it seemed that war might break out, with either side seeking to gain the advantage to be derived from a pre-emptive strike.

King Faisal of Saudi Arabia was still in London, expressing his concern about our proposed evacuation of Aden and Southern Arabia. On the Friday, 19th May, we had long talks in which he gravely urged us not only to leave military units in the area but to accept a binding military commitment to use them to defend the new South-Arabian state against attack or infiltration from UAR-inspired Arab nationalism. He spoke passionately about President Nasser's expansionist aims; in most of the affected Middle-East states including the Gulf sheikdoms, he said, there were seditious groups ready to go into action when President Nasser gave the signal. Unless we held firm in Southern Arabia, the Gulf would be subverted within months. He showed us – and his Embassy later released this to the press – his maps and other information on the extent of UAR penetration, and bitterly attacked President Nasser for his aggression in the Yemen and for UAR attacks on Saudi-Arabian forces. He clearly feared an invasion of his country by Nasser. In a speech at Chatham House on 15th May he publicly repeated his warnings and spoke in the strongest terms of the UAR threat to independent Middle-Eastern countries.

When King Faisal and I met again on Monday, 22nd May for further discussions, as I thought, on British policies in the area, the situation had entirely changed. He told me that whatever he might have said about President Nasser before the weekend was of no account now. An Arab brother was in immediate peril from an attack by the common enemy and he would join his brethren in resisting such an attack to the uttermost.

During this developing crisis, I was in the closest touch with the Foreign Secretary, the Defence Secretary, the Chiefs of Staff and all our advisers, meeting either in *ad hoc* meetings at any time of the day or night, or more formally in the Defence committee.

We were urging the USSR to press restraint on their Arab friends, and were, of course, in the closest contact with Washington. George Brown postponed for a day or two his announced Moscow visit.

The Cabinet met on Tuesday, 23rd May, the day after President Nasser's declaration about the Straits of Tiran. We had one of our gravest discussions. Though several ministers were committed friends of Israel and of Israeli leaders, we were all agreed to urge the utmost restraint, at a very difficult time, on her, while doing everything possible by direct diplomatic pressures and at UN to urge that similar pressures be put on the Arab countries by those in a position to influence them. U Thant announced a visit to Cairo.

After the Cabinet meeting we made it publicly clear that we could not compromise on the principle that the Gulf of Aqaba and the Straits were international waterways, and that this must be asserted internationally. Israel, we said, rather than taking unilateral action should seek UN assurances or, failing that, international assurances that the right of maritime passage remained inviolate.

We decided, and announced, that we would consult with leading maritime nations to make a declaration to this effect. The consultations began immediately.

On the Wednesday morning, 24th May, I was due to go to Margate for the annual conference of the Electrical Trades Union. My speech – on productivity and prices and incomes – was ready. Because of the crisis I arranged to fly there by helicopter, go straight into the hall and make my speech, and return forthwith. I began the speech with a prepared statement on the crisis, including a reaffirmation of the statement made by the then British delegate at the UN in 1957.

> It is the view of Her Majesty's Government in the United Kingdom that the Straits of Tiran must be regarded as an international waterway through which the vessels of all nations have a right of passage. Her Majesty's Government will assert this right on behalf of all British shipping and is prepared to join with others to secure general recognition of this right.

In the afternoon, Abba Eban, the Israeli Foreign Minister, came to No. 10 for an urgent meeting with me. In the evening Mr Heath and Sir Alec Douglas-Home came to express their concern and to satisfy themselves that we were doing all in our power not only to avert hostilities, but to stand firm on the maritime rights of all nations in the disputed waters. They went away reassured. Throughout the crisis, including the debate on the day Parliament resumed, there was a completely bipartisan approach to the problem.

President de Gaulle, who was moving from his role as the principal arms supplier to Israel into a more pro-Arab position, called for four-power talks between Britain, France, the US and the USSR. We supported this proposal but it was rejected by the Soviet Union. During this period I kept in close touch with the General by personal messages and through the British Ambassador. It was announced in both capitals that I should shortly be visiting Paris. This had been agreed between the General and myself when we had met at Dr Adenauer's funeral in April, though General de Gaulle had suggested I should wait until after his half-yearly press conference, lest anything he said there might be construed as a comment on our talks!

George Thomson, Minister of State at the Foreign Office, was sent to Washington to discuss the maritime position and his work was later reinforced by the despatch of a senior member of Denis Healey's naval staff for talks with the State Department and the Pentagon.

George Brown left for Moscow, where, in an hour-long public lecture to the Soviet Foreign Affairs Institute, he set out our position and urged the Russians to press restraint on the UAR and other Arab countries. But

o

Moscow's line was set. We had little doubt nevertheless that they were pressing their friends not to go too far. After George Brown's return there was an angry public warning to Britain to stop supporting Israel and ten Soviet warships were ordered to the Mediterranean.

On Wednesday, 31st May Parliament met and debated the situation as a matter of urgency. George Brown, who opened, gave the House a sombre recital of the facts, and of what we were seeking to do. His approach was welcomed on both sides of the House. Mr Heath and Sir Alec Douglas-Home spoke firmly, seeking to make sure that we were not diverted from our declared position, and I was able to leave for North America with full, all-party backing from the House.

The visit I had planned to Canada and the US was cut to under three days. It had been intended that I should visit one or two Canadian provincial capitals, as well as Montreal for Britain's day at Expo 67, and Ottawa, for our contribution to the centenary celebrations of the British North American Act. Because of the crisis and the debate I had to omit all save the Ottawa visit, before going on to Washington.

Lester Pearson was firmly in support of our line, and made this clear publicly, though he shared our doubts whether we could get a sufficiently universal declaration by the maritime powers to impress the Egyptians. Certainly, he thought, if we asserted our position sufficiently strongly it would be unlikely that there would be any interference with a British vessel or that of other signatories; in any case we could provide naval cover. We might hope to persuade Nasser to remove the mines. The one thing that we could not do would be to guarantee freedom of passage for an Israeli ship, short of escorting her with a British or Allied warship. This was not in our plan, nor would such a rash venture be likely to find much international support. Lester Pearson would certainly not have contributed armed support; he was, in any case, still bruised by President Nasser's action in dismissing the UNEF. The Canadians felt they had been bundled home in the most inconsiderate and humiliating manner.

In Washington I found the President in full support of our proposals, but anxious that, for his own domestic reasons, we should take the lead in presenting them and organising support for them. He had sent messages to me, in this sense, over the previous week. His reason, I think, was that he was so heavily committed in Vietnam that he did not want to strain US public opinion any further.

The President did, however, make a concession on Vietnam in order to influence international opinion in the Middle East context. He stopped the bombing of Hanoi and Haiphong, to help win the support of non-aligned countries in urging restraint on the Arabs.

He told me that things were not going well in the Senate. Hubert Humphrey and Dean Rusk had spent the best part of the day seeking bipartisan support for what we had agreed, and had run into unexpected apathy and even resistance. I expressed the view – while it was not fitting for me to comment on his domestic political scene – that that would change within a day or two when senators and congressmen received their weekend mail, particularly from areas where the Jewish vote was strong. Hubert Humphrey told me afterwards that this was exactly what did happen.

It had been widely expected that my Washington visit would be the occasion for presidential strictures about our policies in Aden and the Gulf and our run-down in the Far East. But these were not even raised. It was, I think, an occasion where the US felt they needed us more than we needed them, both on general Middle-Eastern policy and in the assertion of free passage through Tiran.

On the Saturday, 3rd June, after breakfast with the Vice-President, I flew to New York for talks at the United Nations. I had lunch with U Thant – back, empty-handed, from Cairo – then a meeting with the President of the Security Council and flew back through the night, reaching Downing Street on the Sunday. The following morning, Monday, 5th June, I was wakened with the news that war had broken out.

Most of that day I had meetings with colleagues to deal with the new situation. The Foreign Office were in constant touch with Arab embassies, with the Israelis, and with Washington and Moscow and with our representative at UN, who was aiming, with others, to secure a cease-fire. But within hours it became clear that our own interests were likely to suffer directly.

Cairo and other Arab radio stations broadcast a series of allegations: first, that British aircraft had taken part in Israel's attack on the UAR and, second, less ambitiously but with no less mendacity, that we had helped the Israeli attacks by the use of our communications system. This was what came to be known as the 'big lie'. It was not true and could not have been true. We offered to make available to UN observers all the information about movements of ships and aircraft in the area and to give them facilities for inspection at all our RAF stations, including Cyprus and Malta and on board HM ships. Weeks later the lie was withdrawn – but the damage was done. British embassies and consulates were attacked and damaged in many Arab cities. The UAR closed the Suez Canal. Iraq, Kuwait, Algeria, Syria and the Lebanon cut off oil supplies, in some cases to Britain and the US only, in others to western countries generally. There were threats to withdraw sterling balances. In general, the further a country was from the fighting, or the more loath a country was to become involved in the fighting, the more shrill were its attacks and the more militant its gestures. One country in this category – Sudan – was reputed to have withdrawn the whole of its sterling balances, some £30 millions, from Britain where it was getting some seven per cent interest and transferred them to a Swiss bank at around three per cent. The latter, having no immediate use for the money, reinvested it in Britain, the Swiss gaining the four or so per cent which the Arabs surrendered as a means of punishing Britain.

The economic consequences of this June week were extremely serious for Britain. The closure of the Canal alone, it was authoritatively estimated, was costing Britain £20 millions a month on our balance of payments. No less serious was the loss of Middle-East oil. We had to seek to replace this from other areas at a higher price and, in the main, at much higher freights. Supplies from Libya, the one source west of the Canal, were cut for a time. Nor could we make up any substantial part of the loss from Nigeria, our other short-haul source. Within weeks, the civil war there cut off all our Nigerian supplies, too. We had to shop for supplies in the US and Latin America, at high cost, high freights and in competition with other hard-hit countries. We had many anxieties for the following winter. In the event, a decision by a number of Arab countries to rescind the ban, together with the deployment, after the loss of several weeks and at great cost, of giant tankers using the Cape route, improved the supply position, but it was touch and go for naphtha supplies until the end of the winter.

This crisis was a serious blow. By the early autumn with other difficulties arising it seemed almost a fatal one to our economic recovery. Exports, the balance of payments and sterling were all strong before the Six-Day War.

Our current balance of visible and invisible trade, including all Government expenditure abroad, was in deficit only to the extent of £67 millions in the twelve months ended June 1967; the over-all balance, at minus £87 millions, was also within close haul of a surplus. (Revised figures published subsequently showed us actually in surplus during the latter months of 1966 and early months of 1967.) Confidence in sterling was sturdy, and in May bank rate had been reduced to $5\frac{1}{2}$ per cent, the lowest figure for $2\frac{1}{2}$ years. Jim Callaghan was able to claim in the Common Market debate that we approached the EEC negotiations from a strong economic position, a phrase which was quoted with approval by newspapers of differing political views.

The Middle East crisis of June 1967 was the biggest contributing factor to the devaluation which came five months later. Confidence in sterling was eroded by the war and further weakened when the monthly figures reflecting its consequences were published. From a strong and improving balance of payments position, we had returned by the autumn once again to a vulnerable position and domestic events, notably two damaging dock strikes together with some manoeuvring on the Continent, were sufficient to bring sterling down. Without the impact and continuing effects of the Middle East crisis we could have weathered these disturbances without a grave deterioration in confidence in the pound. It was to be two years more and at heavy cost – economic, social and political – before we were able to regain our surplus position.

The first of several Security Council resolutions calling for a cease-fire was approved on the evening of Tuesday, 6th June, was accepted by Israel and rejected by Syria and the UAR. Sporadic fighting continued, particularly on the Israel–Syria front. On 10th June the fighting ended with Israel occupying former UAR territory in Gaza, Sinai, including Sharm-el-Sheikh, former Syrian territory on the Golan Heights, and the west bank of the Jordan. Her military position was for the time much more secure on the frontiers north, east and south. The UN settled down to devising means to secure a settlement. We were anxious that the problem of arms supplies should be dealt with. The precarious balance of the early fifties had been shaken by the Russian supplies to the Arab countries and only partly redressed by supplies to Israel from France and other western countries. When the fighting began, we moved immediately to place a ban on arms shipments to the combatants and George Brown tried to secure international agreement to honour it. It was a brave attempt, but after some days of effort it became clear that others would not follow our lead. We had never intended the embargo to be unilateral, so with regret the ban was rescinded.

Nearly three years after the fighting ended the *Daily Mail* published a sensational story alleging that George Brown and I had sought to intervene, with British forces, in the Six-Day War. It was stated, as though a fact, that as soon as Israeli aircraft bombed the Egyptian airfields, I called the Cabinet to No. 10 to hear a 'startling proposition' which I and George Brown had prepared. On the grounds that our oil supplies and the Suez Canal were threatened, we were supposed to have proposed that an aircraft-carrier, cruisers, destroyers and several smaller ships, plus Royal Marines, should be sent into the Gulf of Aqaba (no such ships were, in fact, within steaming range). Our purpose, apparently, was to enforce security for Israel and freedom of the Gulf for her shipping. Then, a still more incredible flight of fancy, 'Cairo would be told that unless the war stopped, British forces would have no alternative but to start a bombardment'. The story ended with an account of our humiliating rejection by the Cabinet.

Not one sentence, or thought, contained in the article had the remotest connection with fact. Because such legends can be believed and foul up international relationships, a flat denial was issued by No. 10. This was printed by the *Daily Mail*, but the newspaper refused to retract; instead they sought to justify their story by reference to a different point in history – though equally inaccurate. There were questions in Parliament, where Sir Alec Douglas-Home completely accepted our denial.

I called in the Lord Chancellor to conduct an independent investigation, with access to all Cabinet and Cabinet committee minutes. His report to me, setting out the results of his inquiry, ruled that the *Daily Mail* story was 'completely untrue' and confirmed the accuracy of the No. 10 statement. Fortunately, the *Daily Mail*'s version was not believed abroad and no damage was done.

It was clear that my visit to General de Gaulle would be devoted as much to the world situation after the events of early June as to anything else. When the meeting was first broached in Bonn after Dr Adenauer's funeral we had intended it to embrace a wide scope.

As ever, General de Gaulle had greeted me in Bonn with great warmth. I pointed out that when we had met at the Elysée in January our talk had been confined to Britain and the EEC. There were many other questions we should be discussing. I suggested that, perhaps in the forthcoming Whitsun recess, I might come to Paris, Colombey or wherever he liked; as the excuse, I said my wife could do some shopping. *'Paris est à vous,'* he replied and it would be good if she were to shop there. Any time. Then, remembering, he said that it would be better if I came after his mid-May press conference. Yes, he added, there were many questions, much broader than those we had discussed. I said that it would give us an opportunity to look at the problems of Europe, and still wider issues, for the next ten years ahead. 'Ah,' he replied, 'ten years – I shall not be there.' Recalling the rough way in which he had responded to a question by Mr Macmillan about 'France after de Gaulle' I reflected that this must be the first time he had indulged in public in intimations of mortality.

On the Sunday evening, 18th June, I flew to Paris, where I had a briefing meeting at the Embassy, and went on to Versailles the following morning. I was the President's guest at the Petit Trianon, originally built as a hunting-lodge for the Grand Palace, and much used by Louis XIV and his successors. It had recently been renovated by the French Government – at very great expense, said General de Gaulle – and this was the first time it had been used for an international *rencontre*. I was, he said, the first person to sleep there since Louis-Philippe, leading me to murmur *'absit omen'*.

We immediately entered into a discussion of the Middle East situation. The President was more depressed than I had ever seen him. This was partly, I think, because Mr Kosygin had virtually bypassed him; clearly the Soviet Premier's visit a few days before had not been a success.

Not only had the USSR summarily rejected the President's proposal for four-power talks but there was much discussion about a bilateral meeting between Mr Kosygin and President Johnson in the US. General de Gaulle felt he had been spurned and if this was so it was a sad ending to all his hopes about Franco–Soviet relations. But there was more than that. He believed that we were nearing a world crisis, that war, world war, could be very near and that there was no one to listen to him. He considered that Mr Kosygin, while taking a hard line about the need for Israel to retreat from the territory she occupied and for the UN to condemn her 'aggression', had not formed any clear idea of what Soviet policy should be. For his part, he said, he had not given his guest any clear indication of French policy.

I explained our objectives and emphasised how we had supported the French proposal for a four-power approach, which we still supported. We had been very close in our basic approach, and we had both taken the same line in cutting off arms; it was a disappointment that our lead had not been followed.

General de Gaulle then set out his despairing attitude to the world situation. The problem of Israel mattered less now than the grave international context within which we had to consider the Middle East position – a context which included such problems as the war in Vietnam, the recent Chinese detonation of a thermonuclear weapon and many others. We could not look at the Middle East alone, because these other factors would encourage certain powers to stand out against any Middle East settlement; he did not specify what these were. The world was now passing through a very dangerous period. None of us – not Britain, not France, not America, not Russia – was holding the reins any longer, nor likely to do so. No one could say how long this would last, still less how it would end. Nobody was in control of the situation.

That was why he had proposed four-power consideration. He would have insisted that the four should agree that whichever side struck first, Israelis or Arabs, should be condemned as the aggressor. The US and Britain had supported the four-power approach, but the Soviet Union had refused. Perhaps they were now regretting this decision. But the war had broken out and now we were in a different and totally incalculable period.

Let us look at the Middle East first, he said, and then at the wider international scene. Public opinion in France – doubtless in Britain, too – was sympathetic to Israel: understandable after two thousand years of history and the sufferings of the Jewish people, including the massacres of the last war.

In France, too, there was still a feeling of hostility towards the Arabs, because of Algeria. But the Government must approach the problem dispassionately. Britain, the US and the Soviet Union had created the state of Israel. France had accepted this. Israel had taken root and flourished.

He offered no view on the Suez episode in 1956; he had not been in charge at the time. But Britain and France had been forced to abandon the Canal, while Israel, he said, had gained. The French Government of the day had made a firm public declaration about free passage into the Gulf of Aqaba, even when the Algerian war was producing bad relations with the Arabs. But the situation had changed. The Algerian War was over. France's relations with the Arab states had improved. She was on reasonably good terms with many of them. Given this, there was no reason for France – 'or, I would suggest, the United Kingdom' – to ruin its relations with the Arabs, merely because public opinion felt some 'superficial sympathy' (his phrase) for Israel because she was a small country with an unhappy history.

France had hoped that while supplying arms to Israel she could improve her relations with the Arabs. I reflected that this was de Gaulle's genius, not only in the Middle East: he could supply arms to South Africa, yet seem to identify with emerging African countries. Trying to remain dispassionate, he had met the present crisis by saying that whoever attacked first was the guilty party. He named Israel. She had been successful in the contest of arms, she had effected a drastic change in the balance of power in the Middle East, but she had created a situation which was more difficult than ever for the Arabs to accept. It might well be the case that no lasting agreement could be achieved for perhaps another quarter of a century. In effect, the two sides were still at war; and they would stay at war.

He then turned to the wider world situation. The main issue was the continuing effect of the war in Vietnam. It dominated everything. There could be no lasting peace in the world while it continued. It was Vietnam which prevented the four big powers taking up the reins of the Middle East situation. Their impotence would last as long as the Vietnam war lasted; worse, so long as it lasted there would be the danger of its escalating to an international war. Now an already dangerous situation was aggravated by the explosion of the Chinese thermonuclear weapon. All the USSR could do in response was to raise the stakes still higher and to abuse the US still more stridently, as they were, no doubt, doing at this moment in the General Assembly of the United Nations. The United States would have to react and the rift between the two super-powers would become even deeper.

He asked rhetorically where we stood on Vietnam. The French Government had said clearly, time and time again, that the US should leave Vietnam. The US paid no attention, of course. But the longer they stayed there, the nearer would become the prospect of general war. Partly because of this, France had left NATO. She was not going to be drawn into somebody else's war. The French were not so rich that they could afford to ruin themselves for this kind of reason. They were too fond of life. They would not go down this road with the United States.

I replied at some length describing our position, as set out in the Government's public statements in Parliament. General de Gaulle took up a reference I had made to Ho Chi-Minh. The Government of North Vietnam, especially Ho Chi-Minh himself, he said, would not yield. The future of their country was at stake. So long as the war continued at the present tempo they could go on fighting indefinitely. They would negotiate only if the US agreed to stop the bombing and to leave Vietnam within a specified period. Perhaps two years, he said – and without any conditions. Then – only then – would the North Vietnamese be prepared to negotiate. Otherwise, there was no hope. They could not negotiate at present: quite impossible. For the way in which their country was being treated made it inevitable that any negotiations must be regarded as no better than surrender. In any event, China would never agree that North Vietnam should go to the conference table. It was clear that the Americans were not ready to stop the bombing of the north. *Enfin*, the war would go on, even if the US put still more troops into Vietnam. The situation, he had to say, was the greatest absurdity of the twentieth century. He, de Gaulle, could see no answer to the problem.

Returning to the Middle East, he said his Government had noted our intention to withdraw from Aden. They welcomed this as friends of Britain. But we must recognise that the real reason why we were involved in the Middle East at all was because of our basic relationship with the United States. All our difficulties there, whether on oil or on the Suez Canal, would not be eased by withdrawal from Aden. It was for this reason: the Arab countries were hostile to the US because of American support for Israel, which 'rubbed off' on Britain because of our fundamental link with Washington.

It was the same in the Far East. The French Government recognised our commitments in Hong Kong and Singapore. But here again, whenever international tension developed and we had to choose one side or the other, we always chose the same side. It was inexplicable to him, since it brought no benefit to us at all. The only realistic solution for Britain, as for France, was to have no external commitments. We, of course, might not agree: that would not affect France's friendship for us!

Again I replied in some detail explaining our position in Hong Kong, and our policy for contraction in south-east Asia and withdrawal from Aden. The President thanked me for my exposition. His Government, he said, would understand the importance which we attached to contracting our effort and expenditure overseas. But on the critical issue of the growing tension between the US and the Soviet Union, both in the Middle East and the Far East, where – he kept returning to this – the situation had now been aggravated by the detonation of the Chinese H-bomb, his Government did not see clearly where our real sympathies lay. Sooner or later we should have to choose whether to side with the United States – and this would mean siding with them in their quarrels – or leaving them. He guessed that we had not finally decided, for reasons which he fully respected. The French Government, had, however, taken their decision. In both the Middle East and the Far East, they had disengaged. US disputes were not their disputes. If they led the US into war it would not be France's war. This was not because of any hostility to the US but because France realised that now the United States was the greatest power in the world they would behave as France and Britain had behaved when we had occupied this position – that is, they would consider only themselves and their own interests. For a country like France – and perhaps the United Kingdom – this inevitably posed the basic question: whether to go down the same road as the United States or not.

Again I replied at length, and my words were chosen not so much to explain our position as to cheer him up and even accept that the end of the world was, perhaps, after all, not at hand. All to no avail: he said that he thought we might well be involved in a world war by September.

As I walked back on those slippery marble floors to my apartments, M. Burin des Roziers, the President's Chef de Cabinet, said he thought that the President was very depressed. Apocalyptic, I suggested. 'Ah,' he said, 'the General is seventy-six, and has little to look forward to.' (I was sure he was referring to the General's disappointment following Mr Kosygin's visit.) I replied that I was fifty-one and, if I were to take so dejected a view, what purpose was there in remaining in public affairs?

The General had decided that our lunch was to be, as he put it, *en famille*. It was fascinating. He was lively, charming, all the depression of the morning was set aside. We talked on personal matters, family matters. The President deferred throughout to 'Yvonne', his wife.

I said it was June; in a month or so, there would be the holidays. Where would he go? Colombey? The President said, certainly Colombey. I asked him why it was *'deux églises'* when there was only one. He explained that one had been closed.

I asked him how he spent his time. Well, he walked in the woods, and thought deeply. (I said that I liked to walk, but not to think about public affairs – hence my preoccupation with golf.) But in the evening, well, he read – I knew from a former secretary of his that his favourite reading was westerns. But beyond that, he played patience. I compared notes with him: in my days as Leader of the Opposition from 1963–4 I used to enjoy patience. If I had been working late at night I would play a few games of patience before going to bed to allow my brain to slow up, otherwise it would be racing, even while asleep. Yet, I said, having tried it after going to No. 10, I found it unnecessary; I was always asleep within seconds of putting out the light.

But, I asked him, 'do you cheat?' This led to a fascinating discussion. His short answer was that there were situations in which this was justified; this led to a discussion about the ethical rules about patience.

After lunch, we became serious again. For about half an hour we discussed the Middle East situation and, in particular, the proposed four-power summit. I said that I was not disposed to go to the United

States unless he proposed to go. He said that he could see no point in going. It was impossible to predict how the situation would develop. Despite Mr Kosygin's inevitable need to strike attitudes in New York, he had received from him the impression of an almost physical attitude of uncertainty and indecision. He was quite sure that if he saw President Johnson he would receive exactly the same impression. No one was really in charge of the situation any longer; nor would it be possible, until the lessons of the disastrous conflict between Israel and the Arabs had really sunk in – always assuming that general war had not broken out in the interval – to approach the question of a settlement in rational terms. And this would take a very long time.

I suggested that this might be a negative view of the situation. A more positive view would be to work for a solution whereby all Arab states would recognise Israel's right to exist and her rights to enjoy freedom of navigation through the Straits of Tiran – and also through the Canal – while at the same time the Arabs would receive satisfaction of their claims as regards the settlement of the refugees.

The President replied that this might be so; but any such settlement lay a long way ahead.

In the early afternoon members of my delegation and I walked in the magnificent Trianon gardens. I was due to meet the General again at 4.00 p.m. Just as we were returning to the Trianon we received a message that the General thought we might meet outside. The weather was glorious and we agreed. Shortly, officers were bringing out the high-backed Second Empire-style chairs, with their deep purple upholstery, which we had admired in one of the ante-rooms, and we sat under the trees.

I began by recalling that we had decided to have a brief exchange on Africa, where in our former colonial territories we had pursued similar policies and where there was little disagreement between us. But there was the problem of Rhodesia, which I explained to him. My purpose was to ask him to clamp down on sanctions-breaking by French oil interests sending oil to Rhodesia through Mozambique. He promised to study the matter, but went on to say that the Portuguese faced great difficulties in Angola and Mozambique, and now in Macao, and France tried on the whole not to make life too difficult for them.

We then turned to Europe. I suggested that the drift of the morning's discussions might lead to the suggestion that we must leave the two super-powers to become the world's arbiters. This was not our view and I presumed not his. He replied that they did not – and indeed could not – so act. No one could.

I asked whether we should not aim at working more closely together through exercising our combined national experience and wisdom rather than by relying on military or economic power. As he had commented, there had been great changes in British policy. We were less dependent on the US for military supplies. We had just decided not to ask for the Poseidon missile in place of Polaris. To that extent I was presenting him not with a new Nassau but a Nassau in reverse. Trianon was the opposite of Rambouillet. To have influence we should build up European economic strength and, hence, economic independence. We had a long way to go. For example, Britain led the world in the civil application of nuclear energy, with our fast-breeder reactors. Yet when we were in competition with France for a Belgian reactor order the French experts were pressing the Belgians to take an American water-cooled reactor. There was a similar problem on aero-engines.

The President welcomed our assertion of greater independence; in aviation he welcomed Anglo-French co-operation. And certainly we should co-operate more wholeheartedly on nuclear questions. Our aim should be a situation where neither France nor Britain depended on US technology, especially for defence purposes.

None the less, he went on, there would always remain the question of British policy generally and especially of Britain's policy in relation to the United States. Was it possible for Britain at present – and was Britain willing? – to follow any policy that was really distinct from that of the United States, whether in Asia, the Middle East or Europe? This was what France still did not know. The whole situation would be very different if France were genuinely convinced that Britain really was disengaging from the US in all major matters such as defence policy and in areas such as Asia, the Middle East, Africa and Europe.

I told him that in all these matters we took our own decisions and they were based on our view of where our national interest lay.

I then proposed I should comment on some of his statements in his press conference, which I had studied with great care. He would have seen my prompt reply that Britain was not prepared to take 'no' for an answer. Admittedly, the President would say that he had not said 'no', only that more time was needed. But more time was not available. Our application was clear and unconditional; had it not been, the General could have said, as he did say in January, that there was no proposition before him or the rest of the Six. I then set out our position on each of his points.

I reminded him that we had killed the multilateral force. But if the President were afraid of a trend to Atlanticism, he should realise that his policies might in fact strengthen pressure for an Atlantic grouping. There were some in Britain who felt that we should turn away from a European alignment towards an Atlantic one. Our application showed what we had decided. If we were rebuffed we should face a difficult choice. But not only Britain. The pressures on his European partners would be very great.

I instanced monetary policy, proposals for increased world liquidity, the gold problem and the like, where France was standing virtually alone. If this continued, he might find in the context of the Group of Ten, or of

IMF, European countries, and especially Germany, breaking away and making common cause with the US. In the financial field Germany might have much to gain. At the least, the process would be unsatisfactory and divisive, but it might well have increasingly political overtones. Indeed, he – and we – had to face the possibility that a time might come, perhaps quite soon, when the US and Germany would be linked more closely together in political matters. He could surely see the dangers if France and the US were engaged, as had happened before, in a struggle for the soul of Germany?

The General said he had listened, not only with interest, but with real gravity to what I had said. I had depicted an Atlantic grouping which would constitute an even greater and more complete domination by the US in technology, industry, finance and politics than ever before. I had implied that if Britain were unable to join the Communities this grouping would be the consequence. This certainly did not appeal to France. Indeed, they had accepted with resignation a policy of European integration – he corrected himself, 'organised co-operation in Europe' – precisely in order to escape from such domination.

But they could not be completely certain that, if Britain joined the Communities, such an Atlantic Community would not one day emerge. Britain in the Communities, even if she changed substantially, might seek this. But if she stayed unchanged, and even if the British Government and I did not seek this, the fact remained that British entry would introduce to the Communities an element broadly favourable to the 'Atlantic' concept. Moreover, as I well knew, certain members of the Six were also favourable to it, though possibly less so than Britain. He then proceeded to list them, in lofty tones, with the indication that they were only restrained from the mortal sin of Atlanticism by the firmness of the General.

'*Les Hollandais*' – they were strongly in favour of the Atlantic concept. '*Les Belges*' – more or less equally so. '*Les Allemands*' – they would be very tempted. '*Les pauvres Italiens*' – they, being directly dependent on the United States, could not hope to prevent it.

British entry, therefore, would not enable Europe to avoid such an Atlantic prospect; the purpose of French membership on the other hand was to prevent it. He had always observed, in war and in peace, and whether or not Britain really wanted it, that she was linked to the United States. Thus, if Britain joined in her present condition and even if the British Government did not state or think that this was their purpose, Britain would introduce an element that inclined towards an Atlantic type of Community. And within the Six, they would no doubt find Germany and Italy, '*les pauvres Belges*' – the epithet had shifted this time – and the Dutch all favourable to their ideas. This was why he was cautious. In this attitude there was no hostility to Britain and it did not result from any failure to recognise British capabilities. It was simply because he saw Britain as she had been so far.

True, there had been recent changes. Again he spoke approvingly about missiles and aircraft and nuclear energy, where, though we had begun in close association with the United States, we now had our own capability. Similarly in electronics and computers, where the British were now beginning to acquire a national *amour propre*. All this was welcome, but the question remained: where did Britain stand? If we joined EEC in two or three years' time what would be our attitude, in discussion within Europe, to the United States? And in such matters as agriculture, food products, currency questions and capital movements – all fundamental to the EEC – what would Britain's attitude be?

At Rome, France and her partners had all been favourable to British entry, but in practice the other five agreed with her that they should carefully examine the likely effect upon the EEC of British membership in respect of agriculture, monetary matters, capital movements and also political affairs. They would, therefore, examine this, as provided by the Treaty. This would naturally take some time. At present they had taken note, without comment, of the British application and they had to see where it would leave the Six. But this depended essentially on Britain – what our attitude would be towards agricultural problems involving New Zealand or Canada, towards the movement of capital and in regard to sterling.

He then repeated: would British entry lead simply to an Atlantic Community, or possibly some free-trade area arrangements even looser than the Kennedy round? He himself had had no part in the establishment of the EEC; it might well have been preferable to set up something wider. But this was what had been established – what existed was a Community with certain rules and obligations.

He then concluded by widening the discussion. The world was not advancing towards peace, to a *détente*, to a great-power agreement; on the contrary, the movement was towards possibly greater conflicts. The Vietnam problem was threatening to involve China.

The Middle East crisis was resulting in a confrontation between the US and the Soviet Union. In Europe, no one could tell exactly what relationship would develop between the US and the USSR.

Against all this background he knew that I was aware of the French approach. It was possible that this approach would be unsuccessful; it was conceivable that one day the Atlantic concept would submerge them. But in that case there would be no Europe, or at least no European Europe: no specifically European character or personality. The French Government did not wish this to happen. But they recognised that they might be unable to prevent it.

I dealt briefly with some of the points raised, though more for the record than in the hope of converting him. We had a brief discussion on the latest exchanges on the Middle East, described in telegrams which had just come in. We agreed to have a further meeting in the morning to review overnight developments.

In an atmosphere of great amity, we adjourned to dress for dinner, a much more formal occasion, with ministers and senior advisers brought out from Paris.

After the speeches, the General took us round the Trianon State apartments, *Le Président Soleil* loftily pointing out the particular rooms where individual favourites of *Le Roi Soleil* were wont to stay. After dinner, he asked me to go with him in the car for a short drive through the park, to the floodlit Grand Palace. It was a small French car, about the size of a British 1100 saloon. Prince Andronikov sat in the front with the driver, the General and I sat at the back, the General, somehow, wrapping his legs into the small space available. He spoke a little about Versailles and then reverted to some of the themes of the afternoon.

I told him that there was one matter I wished to raise privately. There had been a strong rumour that the French Government had decided, on public expenditure grounds, to cancel the Anglo-French variable-geometry ('swing-wing') aircraft. This we would regret, though, unlike Concorde, it was regulated by an agreement under which either partner could withdraw. He said that the French Government had not yet reached a final decision, though a major review of defence expenditure was in progress. (It was, in fact, cancelled within days.) I went on with the question I wanted to put: there were rumours that the French Government would then place an order with Dassault for a specifically French V–G Model. Was this so?

The General contorted his face in an expression full of meaning, without saying a word. But that prince of interpreters was equal to the occasion. 'The President,' said M. Andronikov, 'says that this is hardly conceivable.'

The President's facial expression was not designed to mislead: no order was placed with Dassault.

I then asked if it was agreeable to him, as we had envisaged in April, that we should discuss the next ten years: there were things I wanted to say which were best said in private. He agreed, again repeating that he would not be there all that time. I asked him how he would forecast a France without de Gaulle. Almost repeating the words he had used to Mr Macmillan, who had recently told me of it, his forecast was again *'les délices de l'anarchie'*. Throughout history, he said, the French people had always responded to a period of strong rule by a relapse into anarchy. This would happen and it would not be possible to prevent it.

I asked him how the standing of France, after a period when his leadership ensured that her every act counted, would be affected when, finally – not too soon, I hoped – he retired to Colombey? He shrugged his shoulders, and said that it was difficult to say. So much would depend on the internal state of France. A France given over to mob rule would count for little abroad. The de Gaulle period would be over; it would be a matter for history.

I said that I should like to make an observation, if he had no objection. His contemporaries, at home and abroad, recognised how much he had done for France. His allies and friends abroad might not agree with all his actions and policies, but France counted as she had not for many years past. At home, while there were no doubt many who disagreed with internal policies, that was a matter for democracy in France; it was not for me, a foreigner, to express an opinion. Nor was it for me to express a view about internal affairs in France after his retirement. But France's friends overseas had the right to ask themselves about the future of Europe, and that meant asking about the strength and influence of France in Europe, and more widely.

He was listening intently, refusing to take up any hint that I was on ground he would like me to leave untrodden. On the contrary, these were matters of great gravity. Clearly, I said, as he would know, his place in history was secure; not only in French history but also in world history. There was no doubt about the judgment of historians upon his period in office, about the sense of purpose he had brought to France herself, about the great international prestige he had earned for France. But historians, perhaps writing years afterwards, would not only describe the de Gaulle years but would look back on those years in the light of later developments. The statue would be viewed across a great deal of intervening territory and the lens used by the historians might be such as to enlarge that territory, to the detriment of their appreciation of the statue. Their judgment would be not only: what did de Gaulle achieve?, but: how durable was that achievement?

In international affairs, surely the one thing he had to fear was an increase in the relative strength of Germany, which he had contained throughout his period of power; indeed, grappled to France by the Franco–German treaty and relationship. Did he not fear that post-de Gaulle France, particularly if his forecast of a period of anarchy and division were realised, would be relegated to a second-class status against the power of a strong Germany?

He warmed to this theme. '*Les Allemands,*' he said, '*seront toujours les Allemands.*' He had no doubt what would happen – but he would not be there to prevent it. The de Gaulle days would be over. I asked whether he did not feel that history would then say, France had been strong, but with his going it relapsed into weakness? This, surely, was a case he must see for greater British involvement in the political affairs of Europe. Knowing his strong sense of history, I said that he would know that traditionally in the sixteenth, seventeenth, eighteenth and nineteenth centuries, Britain – not always consciously, sometimes almost instinctively – had thrown her influence behind the second and smaller European powers, against the most powerful. Would he want to see a Europe with, on his estimate, a weakened France, but without the balancing factor of Britain? He said he was very well aware of these questions. But he would not then have the responsibility. *Après moi* – probably what was in his mind was what he had said in the afternoon was the determinant; Europe would become 'Atlantic', and while he had the power, he was not going to speed the process.

It had been a remarkable discussion, friendly above all, with the General fully involved in his exposition. Since our meeting the next morning, 20th June, was very brief – there had been no significant overnight developments in New York – it was my last memory of him. Against the setting of that June Versailles night, it was one I could never forget.

Chapter 22

THOSE midsummer weeks of 1967 were without respite at home or, more particularly, abroad. The Middle East situation dominated the scene. Now, day by day, we had to assess its consequences, especially the economic effects. These were real enough but containable: what was to be harder to contain was the serious damage caused by speculation.

What worried me was the speed with which the confidence factor in industry and in finance – above all, international finance – had turned adverse specifically because of the Middle East. Our hard-won recovery in exports and the balance of payments was discounted because of our vulnerability to these overseas factors beyond our control.

Abroad, Gibraltar, Rhodesia, Nigeria, Aden, defence policy were continuing to press on us. But immediately there was an extremely difficult political situation arising from the inquiry into the D-Notice affair.

When it reported on 13th June (Cmnd. 3309) we found the committee of Privy Counsellors had ruled against us. They had taken evidence from all concerned in the incident, and in my view, we made a further blunder in not being legally represented before the committee. The newspaper, the journalist and the editor concerned were most ably represented by the Conservative 'shadow' spokesman on legal affairs, now the Attorney-General, Sir Peter Rawlinson. We were in a weak position in that the principal Government witness was Colonel Lohan, secretary of the Services, Press and Broadcasting Committee.

A well-known and popular character – in every way a character – he was in a weak position in that it transpired that his discussion with Mr Chapman Pincher of the *Daily Express* about the applicability of D-Notices to the case in question took place over lunch at a London restaurant.

As the committee observed, it did not think that the selection of a lunch meeting in a public restaurant was a wise choice for an occasion of this nature, which was urgent, important and dealt with matters of some secrecy. The committee added that, on the other hand, the men were friends who had had working contacts for years and no doubt the appointment seemed to them a natural arrangement. The committee went on to observe that it felt bound to conclude that Colonel Lohan did not manage to convey to those he spoke to on the afternoon of Monday, 20th February, including Mr Pincher, that he himself regarded the cable-vetting story as a D-Notice matter. The instructions he had received from the Foreign Office department concerned was that he was 'to try to get the story stopped on D-Notice grounds'. It is probable, too, that the Foreign Secretary's evidence failed to impress the committee. On being told late in the evening that the article was being published, George Brown, who was at a private party, rightly phoned the newspaper proprietor involved, who took the matter very seriously, but was reassured on speaking to his editor by what Colonel Lohan had told the journalist.

My statement in the House had been based on the clear advice of Foreign Office officials and the FO legal department, but in the light of what Colonel Lohan had said over lunch, and subsequently, the committee naturally concluded that I was wrong in saying that those concerned had been told that the article contravened the Notice. On the question whether the Notice was, in fact, contravened, the committee supported the paper: our case was never argued before it by counsel and, on advice, my colleagues and I felt that we could not accept the finding. It was very clear, however, that the practice so sensationally described was not new; still less, as so much public comment at the time inferred, was it a diabolical 1984 invention of the Labour Government. As the committee reported, 'No new practice has been introduced in recent years in the procedure for the interception of telegrams which departs from the principles previously observed.'

It is not easy for a Government to go against the findings of so high-powered a committee, though there was a notable precedent in the derisive rejection by Mr Macmillan's Government of the Devlin Report on the Nyasaland massacre in 1959. But because we felt that, however misled about Colonel Lohan's activities, we were right in accepting the advice we had been tendered, we issued a White Paper (Cmnd. 3312) accepting the committee's findings on the working and future of the D-Notice system, and dissociating the Government from its findings on the issues raised by the publication of the article.

It was the Government's view that the Department was right in informing Colonel Lohan that the press story fell within the scope of the relevant D-Notices; that, as the committee report concluded, Colonel Lohan accepted these instructions; but that, in the event, he appeared to have based his case less on the D-Notices themselves than was envisaged in his instructions, nor indeed did he appear to have accepted his instructions as soundly based.

The rejection of the committee's findings, of course, compounded my original offence in the eyes of the press, and comment upon the Government, particularly on me, became even more bitter.

What was of more concern was the danger that the affair might destroy relations between the press and the defence and security authorities, which, as the Radcliffe Inquiry of 1962 had said, confirmed again by the 1967 Committee, were based essentially on goodwill. I was concerned to repair the damage as far as possible, and arranged a meeting with the editors. Once the subject had been brought to my attention I felt that certain of the D-Notices were outdated, and should, in consultation with the press, be revised and liberalised. I felt also that there should be changes in the personnel responsible for administering the system. I indicated that we would be willing to have as chairman of the Services, Press and Broadcasting Committee an independent person with Fleet Street experience – and suggested a former editor, Mr Donald McLachlan, who had had experience of high-level intelligence and security questions during the war: I was willing to nominate also an ex-military officer, a respected press defence correspondent, as secretary. The editors, however, felt that things should be left as they were, with the PUS at the Defence Department as chairman. Colonel Lohan suddenly resigned and made a number of unauthorised press statements; Admiral Denning was appointed in his place, with the general approval of the press; confidence was fully restored, and he applied himself speedily to revising the relevant Notices in consultation with the press, as I had suggested.

The debate on 22nd June was inevitably extremely rough. It was opened by the Attorney-General, who moved a motion approving our White Paper, 'noting' the report of the Privy Counsellors' committee, welcoming the Government's acceptance of its recommendations on the D-Notice system, and, '... conscious of the need to provide adequate protection for the nation's secrets while safeguarding the freedom and independence of the press, endorses Her Majesty's Government's expressed intention to discuss with the press, measures designed to maintain and strengthen the D-Notice system.'

The Opposition, obviously, moved an amendment to accept the report. Mr Barber's speech, in common with most of the Opposition speeches which followed, was concerned more with Wilson-baiting than security. This was inevitable. Mr Heath's winding-up speech was in the same spirit, and I rose to reply to the debate in a turbulent House. Interruptions and bogus points of order prevented me from getting a hearing for several minutes.

I ended with the specific point about the information given to the journalist concerned by Colonel Lohan. The other paper with the story – the *Daily Mail* – had agreed, after representations from Colonel Lohan, not to publish. I then quoted from the Privy Counsellors' report of the evidence given by Colonel Lohan about his luncheon with the *Daily Express* journalist.

'We parted,' said the Colonel, 'in an extremely good mood. He said he would represent to his editor quite fairly what I had said. He made a joke as we left, saying "you know jolly well if you were the editor, you would publish, wouldn't you?" I made no comment, except to laugh. We took a taxi together....'

I mentioned that relations between the Colonel and the journalist had been the subject of inquiries by the Conservative Government. I was asked by the Colonel's MP, a Conservative Privy Counsellor, if the Colonel had been positively vetted. I said he had not. (When I had discovered this, I was astounded, as he had to know the most secret information for the fulfilment of his duties.)

The Times described my answer about positive vetting as a 'pitiless innuendo', and Mr Heath, who seldom knew the precise moment to stop, insisted on a further inquiry. This took place and, when it was completed, he dropped the subject as suddenly as he had taken it up.

Though my motives had been concerned with protecting the security and intelligence services for which I was responsible, I was wrong to make an issue of it in the first instance. It was a very long time before my relations with the press were repaired, and I was entering upon a period when I needed justice at least, if mercy was too much to expect. I had neither, though on the D-Notice issue the public-opinion polls suggested that the electorate had not the slightest interest in the subject.

There were in fact before the House more real issues of public policy. The day that the Radcliffe Report was published, 13th June, the House debated the second reading of the Prices and Incomes Bill, 1967 vintage.

During the period of 'severe restraint' which followed the ending of the total wages freeze in December 1966, we had been engaged in discussions with the TUC and the CBI about the criteria which should govern prices and incomes decisions from the middle of the year. In a score of meetings with the TUC, at individual union executives and at trade union conferences, I had sought to make two points.

The first related to the 'social wage'. The TUC was always pressing us to improve our provision for the social services in the widest sense – health, housing, education and social security. Every extra pound spent on these services was an addition to the real standard of living of every family in the land. But we could not spend the national income twice over. Every pound devoted to the social wage was a pound that could not accrue in increased private income through the wage packet.

Secondly, we could increase the private wage packet to the extent that wage increases were matched by increased productivity.

This was the reasoning behind the speech I had made in Greenford, Middlesex, in March, in which I had put forward the concept of the 'national dividend'. It was the day after a conference – convened by the

TUC – of all trade union executive members had ratified a TUC proposal for a voluntary incomes policy, administered by the TUC on the basis of vetting individual wage demands and wage settlements. This I described as an 'historic decision', as indeed it was. 'It is right,' I said, 'to welcome the TUC proposal of an annual appraisal between Government and industry of the prospects for production and for incomes in the succeeding year.' I went on:

> As we see it, what it means is this. Each year we will sit down together, Government and industry, with all the figures and forecasts available to us. We then work out together an assessment of what, in relation to production and to calls upon that production, the National Dividend can be for the year ahead. A National Dividend for distribution between all forms of income, for distribution to workers by hand and by brain. It will then be for the trade union movement, through the machinery it is developing, to ensure that what is distributed is related to the workers' share – which will of course be the predominant share in that National Dividend – on a basis of steadily rising incomes, and on a basis which ensures that the amount distributed does not run ahead of the amount we earn by our production.
> This will be a new concept, unique in a democracy in this or any other country, and I pay my tribute in saying that it was the events of yesterday [the TU executives' conference] which make it possible.

But my words fell on stony ground. Speeches delivered 'Friday for Saturday' normally receive only the most perfunctory of reporting and press interest was centred mainly on my 'barking dogs' reference of the previous day. Had I announced that dog licences were to be abolished in the forthcoming Budget, I would have been better reported. George Woodcock, perhaps basing his remarks on a travesty of what I had said, perhaps because he was aware that the Croydon conference had laid on the TUC more than they could deliver, gave a cold reception to my speech.

Following consultations with the CBI and the TUC after the publication of the Prices and Incomes White Paper (Cmnd. 3235) in March, the House was asked to approve the Prices and Incomes Bill based on the activation at some future time of Part II of the 1966 Act. Clause I built on the Part II provisions. The standstill provided for could be extended for a period of six months from the time of referring a proposed wage and price increase to the Board; Clauses II and III provided that if action to raise prices and incomes had been taken in advance of a report to the Board, an adverse report of the Board would permit the Government to ask for the situation to revert to whatever the Board recommended. Later clauses removed anxieties which had arisen in the operation of Part IV of the 1966 Act: employers who had frozen a wage increase could pay it retrospectively, but could not be taken to court for failure to do so.

There was sharp criticism of this measure within the Parliamentary

Party, though it was, in fact, a stage in the unwinding of the statutory freeze powers of the previous year. Our task was made easier by George Woodcock – though he was criticised for it – when he said that he had no doctrinal objection to the Government's decision to take these powers. What mattered was how the powers were operated in practice, and on that he expected to be consulted.

The Second Reading of the Bill on 13th June was carried by 288 votes to 235, the Opposition voting against the legislation. On our side there were some forty abstentions, but our people were not going to go into the lobby with the Conservatives. The Conservatives were, in fact, prepared to oppose any form of incomes policy, even measures to provide for a short standstill while the case for an individual increase was being examined and for a short period thereafter.

Concurrently, we were working on a fresh attack on poverty. All that we had done in successive increases in pensions and National Assistance had been directed towards relieving poverty in the main sectors – retirement pensioners, the sick and disabled and war pensioners. But there was accumulating evidence that, once these groups had been helped, the principal area of poverty was to be found in large families, whether or not the head of the household was at work. Patrick Gordon Walker had been charged with the responsibility for working out means of help. We were examining a 'claw-back' scheme, under which family allowances would be increased while provision was made by an off-setting reduction in income tax child allowances, to ensure that any relief provided should not accrue to better-off families. But this would take some time to work out, and poverty could not wait. Gordon Walker was therefore authorised to announce a scheme under which an increase of seven shillings a week for the second and subsequent children of each family would be paid from the following April. To help in the coming winter, five shillings of this increase would be paid for fourth and subsequent children (about one million in all) in 609,000 families. The seven-shilling scheme would cost some £83 millions a year. The cost of school meals was to be raised by 6d, and welfare milk by 2d a pint, to provide £25 millions of the £83 millions. And to deal with environmental poverty measured in terms of educational provision, an additional sum of £16 millions was to be provided over the succeeding two years for new educational building – over and above existing programmes – in the 'educational priority areas' highlighted by the report of the committee headed by Lady Plowden on primary education.

Simultaneously with these announcements, the Government suffered a shock by the resignation of Margaret Herbison, our Minister of Pensions and National Insurance from 1964 – subsequently the first Minister of Social Security – and pioneer of all our great reforms in social security. It was attributed to disappointment about the Gordon Walker announcement, but that was not the reason. The previous autumn, when we had settled the expenditure Estimates for the financial year 1967–8, provision had been made for an increase in basic pensions, though this was not to be announced until mid-1967. Peggy Herbison had fought for a higher increase than the Chancellor and the Cabinet were able to accept and had promptly informed me that she must resign. I told her that while all of us would regret her resignation at any time, she could not state her reason for resignation in advance of a Government announcement on the issue on which she was leaving. She loyally accepted this ruling, and continued with her work. I hoped that with the passage of time she would be prepared to acquiesce in the decision but, as the pensions announcement drew near, she was adamant about going, although making it clear that in the manner of her going, and by her continuing support of the Government, she would do nothing to embarrass her colleagues. Peggy was as good as her word. I asked Judith Hart, Minister of State at the Commonwealth Office, to succeed her.

In the concluding days before Parliament adjourned for the summer recess we had two major debates, on economic affairs and defence.

The first, a motion of censure moved by Mr Macleod, lasted two days and was noteworthy for Jim Callaghan's estimate of our payments position, and his full report about Government decisions on public expenditure.

The overseas deficit had been progressively reduced, he said, and we were now basically in balance. The figures for the first quarter showed a surplus. We were convinced that we could reconcile a growth rate of three per cent per annum, the equivalent of £1,000 millions a year in real resources, with a healthy balance of payments and an improvement in the standard of life of the people. But we had never attempted to hide the fact that we would still be walking an economic tightrope from which a slip would have serious consequences. The Chancellor said:

> The fact that this should be so and the fact that the margin of safety is so small represents the real crushing indictment of the failure of the party opposite to act in the years between 1951 and 1964. . . .
> It would be frivolous to be deflected from our present course because one quarter's trading figures are not as good as we would like and because the temporary closure of the Suez Canal has worsened our balance of payments. It is a long-term operation that we are engaged in.
> The economy and the pound are much stronger than they were in 1964 to sustain the closure of the Suez Canal – much stronger. When I look back over the last three years I reflect how sterling, for example, has come through the Middle East crisis, and I realise that it could not have done it either in the summer of 1964, or even subsequently, this is a measure of the progress that is being made.

On public expenditure, Jim Callaghan announced the result of our annual Public Expenditure Survey Committee (PESC) review, providing that the increase in real terms would be limited in the financial years

1967–8 to 1970–1 to three per cent per annum. Central to this was our further decision about defence spending.

Three days later, on 27th July, in the last debate before the summer adjournment, the House discussed the White Paper on Defence (Cmnd. 3357), which we had laid following a further exhaustive defence review.

The 'supplementary statement on defence policy' recalled that in the White Paper presented in February a further announcement about the size and deployment of the forces over the coming decade had been promised. Emphasising more strongly than hitherto that the main deployment would be increasingly concentrated on Europe, the July statement foreshadowed that the forces in Singapore and Malaysia, after confrontation, would be reduced to about half by 1970–1, from eighty thousand to around forty thousand. The reduction would continue after 1970–1, though it was not possible to plan it with exactitude. But the key to the White Paper lay in these words: 'We plan to withdraw altogether from our bases in Singapore and Malaysia in the middle 1970s; the precise timing of our eventual withdrawal will depend on progress made in achieving a new basis for stability in south-east Asia and in resolving other problems in the Far East.'

There was considerable speculation about a massive abstention by our back-benchers. But, partly because our people, gratified by the further moves we had made, were simply not going to go with the Conservatives into the division lobby and partly because our Chief Whip, recalling my warnings of the spring, had made clear that even he would not tolerate a repetition of earlier events, the expected revolt did not materialise. Our majority was ninety, very close to our 'theoretical majority', and abstentions were minimal. The House adjourned in good order for the long recess.

In July I had again taken the opportunity to get out of Westminster and to see the real Britain: a visit on the 7th by helicopter to the National Gas Turbine Research Establishment at Pyestock, Hampshire, and, on the 8th, to the International Eisteddfod at Llangollen. On the 21st I went to Clydebank to see the *Q4*, to be named *Queen Elizabeth II*, nearing completion. It was an opportunity to look at the Clyde's problems, on which I had had so much to do, at first hand. The shipyards were short of orders. Once *Q4* was launched, there would be no employment at Clydebank for craftsmen, except in the finishing trades, and a few hundred employed on constructing oil-drilling rigs. I asked to meet trade union representatives. It was a gloomy meeting, though in the event our fears were not justified and – following devaluation four months later – new orders were forthcoming.

I was steered into an office for a pre-arranged meeting with Sir Basil Smallpeice, chairman of Cunard. He was utterly depressed about the prospects for shipping. There was the likelihood, he told me, of a massive lay-up of many Cunard ships, including the bearers of many famous names. Even the launching of the *Q4* was in doubt. Government participation in Cunard was essential. He was ready to offer fifty per cent participation. I asked whether this would include a corresponding share of the equity in Cunard freight subsidiaries, including those due to be containerised. He did not rule this out. To a Socialist Prime Minister this offer of agreed, back-door nationalisation might have been tempting, but I was cautious. I told him that we would examine the proposition. What was really ironic was the great show of ideological indignation then being staged by Mr John Davies, Director-General of the CBI, and his colleagues about Government proposals – later embodied in the Industrial Expansion Act – to provide statutory backing, under appropriate safeguards, for loans to industrial enterprises needing finance.

I returned to London overnight, to be phoned on arrival by an early-rising Minister of Technology. Apparently there was a meeting in Amsterdam to allocate shipbuilding orders on behalf of a new European container consortium. Six ships were involved and the report to the principals recommended the placing of orders on the basis of tenders, subject to two being placed in France; General de Gaulle had insisted. British tenders were way out of line, but Tony Benn felt that if we were to demonstrate the same degree of intervention as the General we might yet secure an order or two. There were British interests among the shipowner members of the consortium. The General's success had been secured by twisting the arms of French shipowners. Tony Benn recommended similar action by me. Cunard were involved.

Loath as I was to interfere with the complicated workings of the shipping market, I agreed that intervention was necessary. I knew something of the basis on which certain continental shipyards did business. There was, of course, no question of Government subsidies in those classical areas of free enterprise. There was one simple, pure law, in operation on the Continent, and more widely: no one should be caught out paying subsidies.

I gave directions that our shipowners should be approached and persuaded to secure an adjournment of the decision to place orders to allow fresh bids to be made. Meanwhile the minister should ensure that certain named British shipbuilders should have representatives present at the Amsterdam Hilton before the start of business. Once bids were re-invited, the tenders could be reconsidered in the light of the help the Shipbuilding Industry Board was ready to extend to our restructured yards. In the event, after the adjournment we received two of the orders. I went to my breakfast confident that Adam Smith would have approved of my actions; and Mr John Davies, too, could he have been contacted. Such are the duties of a modern Prime Minister.

The parliamentary recess gave no immediate respite. The untimely death of Lord Normanbrook, on 15th June, meant that I had to nominate a new chairman of the BBC. My choice fell upon Lord Hill, a former Conservative Cabinet minister, who had distinguished himself by the scrupulous fairness with which, as chairman of the Independent Television Authority, he had administered the Television Act in respect of comment on public affairs. Memoirs later published suggested that certain BBC chiefs, dining with the Conservative party chairman on the night of the announcement, 26th July, greeted the news with singular lack of enthusiasm. But then, all change is painful and they endured to applaud the appointment. Bert Bowden was designated to succeed Lord Hill at the Independent Television Authority. This meant another by-election.

In the week between the adjournment of Parliament, on 28th July, and my departure on holiday, on 5th August, events continued to press.

Overseas, there was another major dispute with Spain over Gibraltar. The UN Committee of 24, more motivated by hostility to Britain than by concern for what 23,000 Gibraltarians wanted, continued to needle us – this was to be the subject of a measured rebuke by George Brown when he visited UN soon afterwards. We had decided that the wishes of the inhabitants of Gibraltar should be tested by a referendum, which we proposed should be conducted under the supervision of observers appointed by the United Nations. The referendum, held on 10th September, was decisive. Out of 12,762 registered voters, 12,138 voted for the maintenance of the British connection, only 44 voted against.

Rhodesia continued to concern us. I had invited Lord Alport, a former Conservative Commonwealth Office minister, and subsequently British High Commissioner to the Central African Federation, to visit Salisbury. He had met representatives of all sections of opinion there, including Mr Smith, and returned with a totally negative report. There was no sign of any movement towards our minimum conditions.

After the adjournment of the House, I stayed on in London for a few days, as I usually did, to clear my desk, to settle outstanding issues with colleagues, and to put work in hand for officials and official committees. But that week saw the publication of the report of the Tribunal on Aberfan. It was a devastating criticism of the National Coal Board, criticism which was, in the main, fully and honourably accepted by the Board's chairman, Lord Robens. Indeed, in the witness-box towards the end of the hearings Lord Robens had accepted full responsibility for the tragedy. The chairman of the Tribunal witheringly commented that if that had been done at the outset, the Tribunal could have been saved months of evidence-taking.

There was much speculation about whether Lord Robens would offer his resignation or, if he did not, whether the Government would ask for it. With my agreement the ministers concerned asked the Board for a report within a month, setting out their proposals, both in terms of internal organisation and tipping practice, to ensure that such risks were avoided in future. Only when that was received and its effectiveness assessed would a decision be taken about individuals. The report was thorough and showed that all the lessons of the disaster had been learned. The question of resignation did not arise. In any event, the minister reported to me that he understood that Lord Robens was considering whether to resign – not over Aberfan – at the end of the Board's financial year, though he had not finally decided. We decided no action was called for.

At the end of the first week in August I went on holiday to the Isles of Scilly. I was not greatly disturbed; an hour in the morning and two hours in the evening was enough to deal with telegrams. But I was getting a little more worried about the economic situation. There had been one or two flurries on the exchange markets in July. The trade figures for June, published in late July, were not encouraging and sterling suffered. Any market operator who had passed his 11-plus in economic realities would have realised that the closure of the Suez Canal had distorted the trade figures, but this did not stop speculation, heightened by a tightening of US interest rates. By mid-August the financial press was reporting the lowest parity for sterling since 1964.

There was also a backbench storm, expressed in telegrams to my holiday home, about the latest wave of bombing in Vietnam. Then on 15th August, new trade figures were published, remarkably good ones, and they brought an instant reaction in favour of sterling, just as irrational, in the circumstances, as the previous bear reaction. The Treasury announced a further balance of payments surplus for the *second* quarter of the year.

I hoped I might get through this holiday without having to return to London. It was not to be. The troubles which had begun in Hong Kong spread to mainland China.

'Spontaneous' reactions to the sentencing of the Chinese journalists in Hong Kong led to mob attacks on the British legation compound in Peking. The main buildings were attacked and burnt down. We did not retaliate in kind against the Chinese in Portland Place, but an Order in Council approved at Balmoral tightened up restrictions on the movement of Chinese diplomats in London and refused permission for them to leave Britain. This was designed to last as long as restrictions on the movement or repatriation of British officials in China. To enforce the order the Chinese Legation was picketed by police: this led to a mad attack on them by Chinese diplomats, axes and other weapons being produced. There was no senior Secretary of State in or near London and the situation was threatening. I decided to spend a day in London. On 23rd August I received reports from the ministers in acting charge of the Home Office and Foreign Office and gave the necessary instructions.

In the afternoon the High Commissioner to Nigeria, Sir David Hunt, came to report on the worsening situation in the Nigerian civil war. Before leaving London I met a number of ministers involved in a Government reshuffle on which I was working. I flew back to Cornwall in the evening after a brief meeting at Heathrow with George Brown, on his return from his holiday in Norway.

I had two days more in Scilly before returning to London. Michael Stewart was there for a holiday and I discussed my ministerial plans with him. He had done a painstaking and thorough job at DEA and had brought order and a sense of system to its work. The view was much put about that, under his direction, the department seemed to be losing authority as against the Treasury. This was not so. But though, on his appointment, I had transferred responsibility for individual price and income cases to the executive departments, he remained bogged down in general incomes policy to a point where, in Whitehall and more widely, this seemed to be DEA's only role. Nevertheless, during these critical months he had succeeded in holding down cost inflation more successfully than at any time for years past and in marked contrast to the record of some of our principal industrial competitors. And he had pioneered new and successful incentives for regional development.

But I now wanted Michael for a full-time co-ordinating role – previously discharged by Douglas Houghton – and it was time to give Patrick Gordon Walker a department. I doubted whether Michael would last very long in that role, however; it could only be a matter of time before one of George's late-night resignations stuck and I would want Michael back at the Foreign Office.

Although a great deal had been done in modernising and restructuring industry, I was not satisfied with the pace. While as Prime Minister I interested myself closely in modernisation plans, it had to be largely at second remove or by chairing ministerial committees over some inter-departmental dispute. I did not want us to go on to the end of our term relying on purely monetary measures and demand management; my whole strategy from the time of my Swansea speech in January 1964 had been aimed at strengthening the competitive base of British industry so that sustained growth without balance of payments repercussions could be possible. I therefore told Michael that I would propose myself to take charge of DEA with a Secretary of State to assist me. In addition I would take over the chairmanship of the National Economic Development Council and strengthen contacts with industry at the highest level.

To avoid too many comings and goings around No. 10, I arranged to see three ministers who were affected in the reshuffle on my journey home on Saturday, 26th August. Peter Shore, who was to become the new Secretary of State for Economic Affairs, and Harold Lever, marked out for Financial Secretary, dined with me in Penzance. I broke my journey at Plymouth, where I had arranged for Douglas Jay, who was on holiday in the west country, to meet me – I did not want to bring him all the way to London to hear that I was asking him to stand down.

We met in the station-master's office and, understandably, he took it badly. He suspected that it was because of his clear anti-Market stance and some calculated indiscretions – which had won him press headlines at critical times – suggesting divided counsels among the economic ministers. This was not my reason. He knew how highly I regarded his great success in development area policy, which had been one of his main interests from his days with Hugh Dalton at the Board of Trade, twenty-five years earlier. But he was now over sixty, above the 'retiring age' which I had informally laid down, except for very special cases. I was anxious also to bring Tony Crosland into the economic team.

On the Sunday, 27th August, I invited George Brown to lunch with me, and explained my proposed changes. He pressed me to promote George Thomson to a Cabinet post and was keen that it should be Education, to be vacated by Tony Crosland. I was equally keen to bring George Thomson into the Cabinet, but was doubtful about Education: George was a Scot and it might be difficult to put him in charge of the English and Welsh departments. I decided to send Gordon Walker to Education and not the Commonwealth Office as I had first intended: a last-minute thought raised doubts in my mind about his degree of acceptance to many of our own people, in whose minds the Seretse Khama episode of 1951 still rankled. I spoke to George Thomson just as he left for the Continent and told him he would be in the Cabinet and that he would receive *via* the British Consul at Basle, where he was leaving the train early in the morning, a telegram setting out my decision. He was then to telephone me. He was delighted to go to Commonwealth Relations and eminently fitted for it.

Arthur Bottomley stood down from Overseas Development and was replaced by Reg Prentice, Minister of Public Buildings and Works, a proved administrator and good in the House, who had been a devoted supporter of world development efforts for many years. He was succeeded by Bob Mellish, then Parliamentary Secretary at the Ministry of Housing; his appointment meant that the two departments would work more closely together, with an increased concentration on house-building. Fred Willey, who had done a painstaking but ill-published job on all the complicated legislation on planning, including the Land Commission and leasehold enfranchisement, also left the Government.

There were switches at, and promotions to, Minister of State level. Goronwy Roberts moved from Education to the Foreign Office; Alice Bacon from the Home Office to Education; Niall MacDermot from Financial Secretary, Treasury, to Minister of State, Housing and Local Government; Lord Stonham and Stephen Swingler were promoted to be Ministers of State in the Home Office and in Transport, respectively.

Among parliamentary secretaries, Edmund Dell, already marked out as a high-flyer, moved from Technology to DEA and two back-benchers, Alan Williams and Neil Carmichael, went to Technology and Transport respectively. There were still two vacancies at this level, which had to wait until I could contact back-benchers on holiday abroad. Later in the week I announced the appointment of Gwyneth Dunwoody to the Board of Trade and Gerry Fowler to Technology. Gwyneth's appointment produced the first case of a mother-and-daughter team in the same Administration – her mother, Lady Phillips, widow of Morgan Phillips, being a member of the front bench in the Lords. (Two years later, with the appointment of Gwyneth's husband, Dr John Dunwoody, we had a unique family combination in Government.)

The two back-benchers were not the only colleagues I had difficulty in tracking down on the Continent. I wanted Dick Marsh, the Minister of Power, back urgently from his Yugoslav holiday. He was finally traced to a wine *fest* in Northern Yugoslavia, intercepted by Marshal Tito's security police and hurriedly despatched to the nearest airport.

The Electricity Council had suddenly, and without warning, announced substantial increases in electricity charges, with domestic consumers differentially bearing a heavier burden than industrial users. In one sense this was not unexpected; in May, as the House had adjourned for Whitsun, the Minister had announced that the Central Electricity Generating Board were to increase their 'wholesale' price to the area councils. This system invariably meant a succession of announcements, with headlines at each stage. But the timing of the Council's September announcement could not have been worse. It was on the eve of the TUC Congress, where at best it would only be with the greatest difficulty that resolutions approving, or acquiescing in, the Government's prices and incomes policy could be got through. The TUC were understandably critical of the fact that tough measures on wages were made unfair by price increases in the public and private sectors. Moreover, with a further burden on industry, it would be harder to enforce the early-warning system and NBPI scrutiny of increases in the private sector. To private industry, it appeared that neither early warnings nor the subjection of their price increases to independent investigation had any reality in the public sector.

I had long been dissatisfied with the quasi-independence of the public sector in the matter of prices, and never felt – with my knowledge of the civil service machine – that sponsoring departments were capable of discharging the function of vetting and, where necessary, vetoing increases. They appeared too often in the role of apologists for their statutory protégés. I held a series of meetings with the ministers responsible for public industries, and it was decided that henceforth these industries, in all major cases, should submit proposed price increases in good time for NBPI investigation and that the NBPI should be authorised not merely to study the financial accounts purporting to justify the increases, but, where necessary, to carry out an efficiency audit of the industry concerned, either with their own staff or by involving the aid of outside consultants. But I was able to get an assurance from both electricity and gas, who also were busy putting up prices, in their case to raise finance for the costly North Sea gas programme – designed to *lower* prices in the seventies – that they did not contemplate a further increase for at least three years. This was honoured.

The Congress went badly for the Government with the passing of hostile resolutions on Vietnam, prices and incomes and unemployment. The majorities were not all that large, mainly because the president of the Engineers, Lord Carron, insisted on using 'Carron's law' – where as president of the union he claimed to decide what general union policy meant on any Congress or Labour Conference vote – to throw a million votes on the Government side. He would not be there another year.

It seemed certain that we should go down on similar resolutions at our party conference, to be held at Scarborough from 2nd to 6th October.

The Labour conference met in a gloomy mood. We had done badly in further by-elections. On 21st September we were defending Cambridge and Walthamstow West, vacant through the deaths of Labour members. Cambridge we expected to lose, though a swing from a Labour gain by 991 votes in 1966 to a Conservative lead of 5,978 votes in the by-election was anything but comforting. Walthamstow West was regarded as a safe Labour seat – held by us since 1929. It was the constituency to which Clem Attlee had repaired when his East London seat disappeared through redistribution. But a majority of 8,725 in March 1966 gave place to a narrow Conservative win by 62.

There was growing anxiety about unemployment and the effect of the previous year's crisis measures. The Government had, in fact, begun on a gentle reflation, supplemented by a £50 millions 'winter work' programme for the development areas. Public works and other schemes – such as road improvements and 'mini' projects in school-building and hospitals – were authorised in these areas, provided that the work could be put in hand immediately and be completed by the end of the winter.

Our special concern about unemployment in the peak winter months was reflected also in a Government decision to defer a number of scheduled colliery closures until the following year. The Coal Board's plan, accepted with great courage and statesmanship by the miners' union, envisaged a run-down of some thirty-five thousand miners a year through closures and concentration of work on the more economic pits. But by 1967 the closure programme had dealt with all the relatively 'easy' cases; easy, in that most of the miners affected could be re-employed in other pits within reasonable travelling distance, though the closure of any colliery round which a whole community has grown up cannot in any circumstances be

P

regarded as easy. But in addition to mines which had to be closed for geological reasons, such as exhaustion of reserves or a fault – many of which were in utterly remote areas – the list of uneconomic pits now to be closed included a number where men made redundant would have no hope of finding alternative employment inside or outside the industry.

In July, in a list of some twenty economic measures which I had dictated at Chequers for circulation to my colleagues, I had given high priority to a review of pit closures, with special reference to the winter. The Chancellor had agreed to accept the financial cost involved, which could not be absorbed by the Board within its financial obligations. Representatives of Regional Economic Planning Councils, and others, during my industrial tours, my meetings with regional groups of MPs during the recess, and deputations from the National Union of Mineworkers, and the TUC, emphasised the urgency of action. Together with the relevant ministers I met Lord Robens at No. 10. While he was troubled about deferment of any part of the closure programme, because it would mean an almost unmanageable closure programme when it ended, he made a useful suggestion governing closure procedure. Recalling my own proposal, endorsed by Cabinet in 1964, that all proposed rail closures be submitted, with adequate notice, to Regional Economic Planning Councils (EPCs) for examination and comment before action was taken, he proposed that due notice of pit closures should similarly be given to the EPCs who would report on the likely effects on employment, having regard to alternative factory jobs in the area.

On 29th September, on the eve of conference, three of my colleagues and I met the executive of the NUM in Scarborough, and told them of our decision to defer sixteen projected colliery closures until the following spring and to seek financial provision to allow us to defer for a further period closures where the Government was satisfied, after Regional Economic Council scrutiny, that the unemployment situation would be seriously worsened. Our announcement was welcomed, though there was strong criticism of the fact that the deferred closures would take effect in the second half of the year, together with the closures of the pits scheduled for the summer and autumn. Their request that the whole programme be set back by six months would have been far too costly.

The interest at conference, in the main, surrounded critical economic motions. The time-table and agenda of a Labour conference is not under the control of any party managers; neither the National Executive Committee, nor the party leader, can decide the subjects or the resolutions chosen for debate; nor can they decide their timing. I was due to speak on the Wednesday, 4th October, somewhat late for a key-note speech. But it was felt that in past years my Tuesday speech had been to some extent overshadowed by speculation and comment on some great policy clash due to take place on the Wednesday or Thursday. We would get the arguments over, for good or ill, on the Tuesday.

It was almost universally expected that the anti-Government resolutions would be carried, as they had been at the TUC. Jim Callaghan, the spokesman appointed by the NEC, wisely decided not to speak until the end of the debate. Conference rarely fails to respond to a good speech; even more

'ERE, IT BOUNCES !

rarely does the best speech influence a set-piece vote, on which many delegates – particularly union delegates – arrive in the conference hall with their minds made up or mandated on. On this occasion, however, it was a truly brilliant speech and it certainly affected the vote. To the surprise of many, including myself, the main resolution – 'This Conference records its continued support for the Government's economic policies...' – was carried by 3,213,000 to 3,091,000 votes. Resolutions opposing the Government's prices and incomes policy, condemning the rise in unemployment, calling for a national minimum wage of £15 per week, and regretting the economic policies of the Government, were all defeated by majorities varying from 1,300,000 to over 1,700,000; one only – supporting Government policies but protesting that we had done too little to restrain prices and dividends – was carried, but by fewer than 200,000.

My speech on the Wednesday, nominally presenting the parliamentary report, was, as on each of the three previous occasions, a progress report on the work of the Government.

First, in addition to a description of the problems we were facing in economic affairs and the anxieties facing conference, I decided to give a detailed account of our achievements in the social services. Hardly a delegate realised how much had been done, even against the background of the critical economic situation we had inherited. Moreover, these achievements had hardly been recognised in the country; press reports about us were inevitably directed much more to crises, inquests and divisions than to social reform and social achievement.

Second – since this was Scarborough – I gave a brief progress report on the Scarborough programme I had outlined four years earlier on technology, the mobilisation of science for industrial modernisation, and education for skill.

Third, and this was a new departure, I decided to spend a few minutes – not more than four or five, in a speech of an hour – attacking our opponents. This was what conference invariably wanted, and in recent years I had not given it to them. For three years I had put up with sustained personal attacks in almost every speech Mr Heath and his colleagues made in the country, and especially at their conference, where approximately fifty-five minutes in every hour's oratory was flatteringly devoted to me. I did not intend to respond in their chosen vein, nor have I ever done. I have never felt that speeches consisting of such crudities as 'liar', 'cheat', 'twister', 'hypocrite', 'swindler', which were their regular stock-in-trade, formed the best currency of political exchange; I thought I could find more expressive ways of summarising Conservative inadequacies as I saw them.

I began by pointing out that this progress report covered three years of Labour Government, less than half-way between our election in 1964 and the statutory date for the end of the Parliament elected in 1966. I told the conference:

Today I am going to give you the facts. In the three years we have been in office we have ended the slide to social inequality and public neglect. We have put in hand a dramatic deployment of resources in favour of those in greatest need, in favour of the under-privileged, on all fronts of social action – social security, health and welfare, the housing of our people, the education of our children and our young people – the most massive ever carried through. We have set out to make good the damage done to our society by Tory Government. Tory Government which upheld a two-standard system that in another country won recognition in the phrase 'private affluence and public squalor'.

We have carried through this programme of social advance against a background of inherited economic difficulties. When they were faced with economic crises the Tories cut the social services again and again. When economic crises overtook them, as it did every four years, they placed new burdens on those least able to bear them. Twice they increased the weight of the prescription charges. They cut school building, they cut the building of houses to rent. To be fair to them they did not cut the hospital building programme. They had hardly any hospital building programme to cut.

I then proceeded to give details:

Provision for the old, the sick, the disabled:

In 1963/64, the Tories' last financial year – this was a peak year for them, because they deliberately pushed up their social service spending as the Election drew nearer – in 1963/64 the total they provided for social security was £1,970 millions. This year we are providing £2,831 millions, an increase of £861 millions. For every £100 they spent, we are spending £144.

Provision for the young:

Education. Their last full year, £1,363 millions: this year, £1,936 millions – an increase of £573 millions. For every £100 they provided on education, we are providing £142. Nor is our provision confined to school hours: on sport and other youth activities we are spending exactly twice as much as the figure they had worked up to in their pre-election programme.

Provision for health and welfare services:

Their last full year £1,118 millions: this year £1,619 millions, an increase of £501 millions. Again, for every £100 they provided in their peak year, we are providing £145.

Housing and slum clearance:

Their last full year £657 millions: this year £1,018 millions, an increase of £361 millions. Again, for every £100 they provided in their peak year, we are providing £155.

Our total provision for social services of all kinds for which they allotted £5,144 millions in their last full year, their peak year: our provision is now £7,457 millions, an increase of over £2,300 millions, 45 per cent. Fine words? Proud facts – achieved by your Labour Government.

The figures I have given you represent our social priorities, against an economic background which would have driven a Tory Government into social retreat and panic demolition. Some will ask, 'What about defence?' Quite right. In 1951, when there was a great debate about the rearmament programme, I expressed my doubts about the priority between defence expenditure and social expenditure. We had then committed ourselves to a defence programme of £1,700 millions. That had to be set against a total expenditure on the social services of £2,069 millions: for every £100 allocated for defence £122 were being spent on the social services. Today, for every £100 we are spending on defence we are spending £340 on the social services, and in 1970/71 our planning provides that for every £100 we shall be spending on defence we shall be spending £390 on the social services. In real terms allowing for increased prices, defence expenditure this year has been already cut by one-third compared with that 1951 defence plan.

I doubt if there is a delegate here who in 1964 – even though the gravity of the economic position was at that time deliberately concealed from us – would have expected that three years later we would be able to report an increase of £2,300 millions, or nearly a half, in our provision for the social services.

And for those who say we could spend more on the social services, if we spent less on defence, let me remind them of this. The *increase* in our total provision for the social services, not the total spending, the *increase* alone, in three years, is considerably more than the *total* amount we are spending on defence – which we have cut. We have switched resources from defence to the social services – the right priority for a Socialist Government.

And now what these socialist priorities mean in human terms. Let us go into the home of an old age pensioner. Of course we haven't abolished poverty yet. But for everyone in receipt of the basic pension, in three years we have raised the benefit paid by 22/6d. a week for a single person. In thirteen years they only managed 37/6d. And on top of this the Social Security supplement as of right to those who need it.

Or suppose we take the case of a newly bereaved widow. Her husband was 55, he'd worked forty years and he was earning the average wage in British industry. In 1964 his widow would have had £4. 15s. 0d. for the first thirteen weeks: now that newly-bereaved widow would receive £10. 8s. 0d. for 26 weeks. And after that she gets the Labour Government's increased rate of benefit – with all that she can then gain from our abolition of the earnings rule for widows.

Or take housing subsidies. On a typical house, the subsidy is now over £85 a year against £24 when we came into office; on a flat costing £5,000 in one of our big cities £112, against £24 three years ago.

Record completions, record starts, an all-time record in nearly half a million new houses now under construction. Houses built to let – in a year of Tory squeeze, 1963, after twelve years in office, they built 124,000. This year, despite economic difficulties we shall complete getting on for 200,000: 16 for every 10 they built.

Schools: they averaged 475 new schools a year. We are building well over 600 and we have just allocated more in the areas of greatest need. Primary schools, our first need: they averaged 295 per year, we are building 500.

Hospitals: new hospital building – in their thirteen years they spent £22.6 millions a year – this year we are spending £97.3 millions. For every £100 they spent each year, we are spending £431.

I summarised the progress in making my Scarborough speech on industry and educational opportunity a reality:

1 *Education:*

We have increased teacher training, the first guarantee of smaller classes. We have stepped up primary school building. Our determination to end the vicious system under which the educational future of a child can be determined by an arbitrary and unscientific test at the incredible age of 11 at all levels ... if neither humanity nor the long-term needs of the nation could afford segregation, educational apartheid at 11 +, equally we could not afford an unfair process of segregation at 18 +. We called for a rapid expansion in higher education, the widening of the gates of opportunity, to every kind of higher education. There were 22 universities in Britain when we were last in Scarborough. Today there are 44. All the former Colleges of Advanced Technology have achieved, or are achieving, university status in a very real sense. Here is one place where an end has been put to the educational snobbery which stood in the way.

When we were last in Scarborough, there were 203,000 students in our universities and other institutions of higher education. Today there are 325,000, an increase of 60 per cent. 105,000 of these are in science and technology, an increase of 32,000 over four years ago. We are now spending £470 millions on higher education, 88 per cent more than four years ago. Capital spending on universities is now double what it was four years ago. The number of teachers in training has risen from 54,000 to 95,000 this year. We are spending £124 millions, nearly 75 per cent more than four years ago, on scientific research at our universities and research councils. We are linking their work more and more with industry and with the regions where they are situated.

2 *Scientific and technological research:*

This year Government spending on all civil scientific research and development will be about £266 millions compared with £158 millions four years ago. And this includes as we then demanded, a massive redeployment from defence research to civil research.

And we are getting priorities into our scientific research – priorities between civil and defence research, priorities within civil research, because we cannot afford at once all the research – and all the equipment – all our scientists would want: Aldermaston scientists working on servo-mechanism for limbs for thalidomide babies.

3 *Technology in industry:* I referred to computers, Giro, the new national data-processing service. The new machine-tool industry.

4 *The humanising of the technological revolution:* I said what had been done to expand training and retraining, and to meet the implications of the new industrial revolution for regions over-dependent on the older industries.

I then announced one of the big talking-points of the conference – the development, on the basis of a partnership between Government and public and private enterprise, of a great new science-based industry, the aluminium smelter projects to be built in three development areas of Scotland, Wales and Northern England.

After a long passage about the conditions of economic success, I turned to the Opposition. I expressed my sympathy for them: for their feeling of deprivation based on a sense that men ordained by Providence to rule our affairs should have had power so rudely wrested from them. Their negative Opposition, including their hostility to every economy we had made in prestige defence expenditure, their demands for increases in every item of public expenditure, and at the same time for cuts in taxation:

On taxation they proclaim the fiscal dreams of a Gladstone, and on expenditure they speak the language of the pork barrel. When the news is good for Britain they pass by in silent embarrassment, too small to proclaim the achievements of a Britain in which they are remote from power. And when the going is hard, they are quick for party advantage to provide aid and comfort to those at home and abroad, the sell-Britain-short brigade who scrutinise every cloud over Britain in the hope of a speculative silver lining for themselves.

I referred to their manoeuvrings:

On the eve of the 1966 Trades Union Congress, they took time off from their reiterated desire to constrict our free Trade Union movement within the legalistic shackles of a corporative state, to tell Congress to reject the Government's appeal for an effective prices and incomes policy, an end for which Tory Chancellor after Tory Chancellor – and even chairman Hogg – had striven, though not one of them was ever prepared to will the means.
The Trades Union Congress treated this appeal with the contempt it deserved.

Now they were instructing industry to fight the Government's Industrial Expansion Bill – in a clear *diktat* to the CBI:

It is my duty to tell them that they misjudge the situation – that the Grand Council of the CBI may share their ignorance of what our proposals mean; they do not share their malice.

The speech secured a standing ovation – it was interesting to see that it was Frank Cousins who was the first to rise to his feet.

The big event of the week was the debate on the Common Market on Thursday, 5th October. A National Executive statement to conference endorsing the Government's application for entry was carried by 4,147,000 to 2,032,000. This two-to-one majority was a great success for George Brown who, more nervous than I had seen him, had in difficult conditions made an excellent speech. But, against his advice, conference rejected the Government's position on Vietnam.

Thursday morning apart, George did not have a good conference. There was a much-publicised incident involving rudeness to press photographers, which led to scathing comments by the press, including a *Daily Mirror* special feature, 'George must go'. Equally, it provided new inspiration for the cartoonists, who had not ceased celebrating the publication of a photograph of George 'frugging' at a party in New York on his visit a few days earlier to the UN.

But there was another incident, potentially more serious, which occurred at the beginning of the week. On the Monday, 2nd October, advance press reports appeared of a document circulated to EEC ministers by the European Commission. It included, according to the reports, some strictures on sterling, and the need for changes in sterling's role if Britain were to join the Community. When the full report became available it was clear that there was no cause for anxiety. But George Brown, reading the first reports on that first Monday, was plunged into gloom. Officials were summoned to fly to Yorkshire, and, lest any wrong conclusions were drawn, he called a few journalists together, whom he addressed in immoderate and over-anxious terms, not troubling to inform me, or the Chancellor, what he was doing. Press comments were acid on his 'momentary loss of nerve' and pointed out that the officials who flew to Scarborough were able to reassure him about the content and meaning of the report.

We returned to London on 6th October to face an economic situation that was by no means out of hand, and a dock strike that was.

Chapter 23

The economic position in October 1967 – the dock strikes – bad trade figures – the rail strike – French manoeuvrings – Lord Attlee's death – by-election losses – the drain on sterling reserves continues – the rise in bank rate – the decision to devalue – run on sterling – devaluation announced – economic measures following devaluation – reflections on the crisis

ON 18th November 1967 the pound sterling was devalued. Devaluation was not forced upon us by any failure to carry through the policies which in three years had transferred an unprecedented overseas deficit to a surplus. What forced us off parity was, basically, the economic consequences of the Middle East crisis, and in particular the closure of the Suez Canal; the proximate causes were the dock strikes in London and Liverpool, and, following their ending, financial manoeuvring within the Six.

As with the seamen's strike of 1966 we had paid a heavy price, against the background of a sterling position whose vulnerability owed nothing to our balance of payments position – until lack of confidence itself undermined that position.

We had begun October with an economy whose strength was not in question. The only arguments were about how soon we should be sufficiently confident to make a decisive move towards reflation. Most economic comment in those days related not to our internal or external position but to the moves designed to further, or to frustrate, entry into the European Economic Community, or about CBI opposition to the Industrial Expansion Bill. There were headlines about the speeches by Sir George Harriman, president of the Society of Motor Manufacturers and Traders, and myself at the eve of the Motor Show dinner, Sir George demanding an easement in hire purchase restrictions on cars. Little did their writers know that Sir George Harriman and Sir Donald Stokes had been my guests at Chequers the previous Sunday, when together we had gone a long way towards setting the seal on the merger between Leyland Motors and BMH, in effect the Austin–Morris complex.

There was no suggestion in the financial columns of the daily press that a new and graver crisis was at hand. They were concerned with the financial aspects of prospective British entry into the Common Market, stimulated, it is true, by a steady drip of French hints about the changes that would be needed in the position of what was called 'the strength of sterling' if Britain were to join. But these added little to the General's press conference five months earlier.

The Liverpool dock strike, part of the aftermath of the Devlin de-casualisation reforms, was entering its fourth week. Parts of the London dock system were out. There was trouble, too, between the drivers and the guards on British Rail, the so-called 'who-sits-where?' dispute about the seating of guards on the new diesels. The two unions involved, the NUR and ASLEF, took it in turns to threaten to bring the railways to a standstill.

By mid-October, unease, though on a minor scale, was spreading to the foreign exchange markets. It had been touched off by bad trade figures, £52 millions deficit, very much affected by the dock strikes. Our hopes of a surplus for the year had gone, with the £200 millions a year 'penalty' from the closure of the Suez Canal and the heavy cost of shipping and high-cost oil from western sources. Even so there was little disposition to panic. There was no public sign of a withdrawal of confidence, but there was a steady – not unmanageable and certainly not critical – outflow of sterling with something of an emphasis on Fridays, quietly contained by Bank of England sales of dollars and convertible currencies. The proba-bility was that the London working balances of international companies were being transferred abroad as a precautionary move, with the added incentive of a rise in interest rates in European capitals and the Euro-dollar market, which an increase in our own bank rate by a half per cent on 19th October did little to stem. There were also clear signs of 'leads and lags' developing; I was told of a public company which had decided to place orders at once for all its imported raw materials for twelve months ahead. Most of the anxiety surrounded the labour troubles. Yet, even at the end of the first week in November, market reports usually described the exchange markets as quiet: depressed sometimes, but not critical. In Liverpool and the areas of the London docks affected, £100 millions of exports were held up.

It seemed urgent to try to settle the Liverpool strike. It was not going to be easy. The Transport and General Workers' Union had virtually lost control of its members and there had certainly not been the local grip on the situation, and two-way consultation between unions and dockers, such as had led to a peaceful and constructive agreement in Hull and certain other ports. This was not so much my view as that of Frank Cousins and of his deputy, Jack Jones, who was increasingly taking charge of union operations and whom I saw on the night of 18th October. Following an urgent telephone call from Jack Jones, Frank Cousins, who was on a union tour in North America, cancelled his arrangements and flew back to London. He met the Minister of Labour, Ray Gunter, and then the two of them came to No. 10. Late in the evening, just before I was due to leave for an industrial tour in Scotland, Ray Gunter returned to No. 10 with Jack Jones.

The Minister had been considering some form of mediation to go with an assertion of national union authority over the situation. The fact that the local strike leadership was in the hands of an unholy – and rare – alliance of Communists, near-Communists and Trotskyites gave some backing to a strong condemnation of industrial militancy in a speech by Ray Gunter the next day. But Jack Jones – in particular – felt that there were real grievances, unexplained facts and a breakdown of intra-union communication, and that these grievances provided fertile ground for the irresponsible militant leadership. I asked for action, and quickly. Jack Jones decided to go to Liverpool to take charge. Meanwhile, Ray Gunter would propose that Mr Jack Scamp be appointed to act as an impartial chairman – above all, to help ascertain the facts, almost all of which were in dispute.

I left on the overnight train for Scotland, for a long-planned industrial tour. I spent 19th October on an exhausting but satisfying day of consultation, meetings and visits to factories and industrial research establishments – and a fascinating tour of a co-operative engineering apprenticeship training unit, run, with the help of the training board levy, for all the smaller Lanarkshire engineering employers, none of whom had the facilities for training in their own factories.

The news which reached me there from Liverpool was bad. The port employers had been reported as rejecting any mediation by Mr Scamp; and the chairman of the national port employers flew to Liverpool to try to overcome the deadlock. The news of the railways, too, was little better. In various parts of the country services were affected by local stoppages as railwaymen refused to accept a reallocation of duties necessitated by the ending of the century-old fireman system.

Stokers in another direction, where over-heating was least needed, were not lacking. Mr John Davies, Director-General of the CBI, dramatically announced that Britain was 'bleeding to death' and called on the Government and TUC to intervene. Lord Cromer, still speaking with the authority of a former Governor of the Bank of England, attacked Government policy on a wide-ranging front.

The railway situation was as serious as that in the docks. I decided to change my arrangements, and return from Glasgow to London by air that night, 19th October, and fly north again the following day for engagements I had in Hull and Liverpool, instead of travelling direct from Glasgow to Hull. That gave me all Friday morning, 20th October, in London for discussions on the industrial crisis.

On that Friday the board of British Rail threatened to withhold guaranteed-week payments for men laid off by the strike. The Government decided in principle to ask for the proclamation of a State of Emergency the following week if the situation worsened, but at the weekend the NUR executive voted by seventeen to seven to resume normal working. Now it was to be the turn of ASLEF, the engine-drivers' union to cause trouble.

After lunch, I flew by executive jet to the RAF station at Leconfield, opened a school in Hull, then flew across to Liverpool, where I attended and spoke at a commercial dinner. I left this function soon after I had spoken, and returned to the Adelphi Hotel, where there was news from Jack Scamp, who had been chairing talks at the town hall from early morning. Jack Jones had asserted control and even the variegated unofficial strike leaders were prepared to join the talks under his leadership. But each hour identified new or resurrected old problems and grievances, over and above those arising from the Devlin reforms providing for decasualisation in the docks. Worst was the fact that agreements made a year or two years earlier on relatively minor issues – the supply of protective clothing, wet work arrangements, sanitary facilities and many more – had apparently not been carried out, creating a general mood of frustration and bitterness among men who might not otherwise have followed so slavishly the hot-headed militant leaders.

The meetings under Jack Scamp's chairmanship went on through the night. I was kept informed. At 3.00 a.m. I had a short sleep, on the bed but fully dressed. At 4.30 a.m. I was awakened with the news that the talks had broken down in dangerous circumstances. The employers – after fourteen hours of discussions – had lost their patience, withdrawn to another room and were drafting a press release couched in provocative terms. I sent a message asking both sides to come to see me at the Adelphi Hotel, after Jack Scamp had been to report. I addressed both sides. I was not concerned, I told them, with the merits of what they were discussing, certainly not with the terms for a settlement. But with so much at stake it would be intolerable if either side broke off, still more so if it were done in terms which would make any early resumption of talks impossible. We argued for an hour and a half. The employers' secretary said that they had no power to settle without a full meeting of their executive, not easy to call at a weekend. I said that he must put them on notice to be available from 9.30 a.m. onwards. By 6.00 a.m. both sides agreed to resume discussions. When I asked if, after the long hours they had been involved in the talks, they would not prefer a break for sleep, both sides said they would prefer to continue.

Soon after 9.00 a.m. agreement was reached and the employers' side called in their colleagues; while they were gathering, Jack Jones secured the agreement of the unofficial strike committee to the proposed terms of settlement. All that remained was for it to be accepted by a mass meeting called for that morning in the Liverpool boxing stadium. A settlement seemed near. But the meeting was a failure. The delay in reporting the terms caused by the consultations with the strike committee led to rumours of a sell-out. Although Jack Jones set out the terms with great clarity and force and indicated the assent of the strike committee, the meeting ended in a shambles. The chairman failed to put the 'return to work' recommendation, no member of the strike committee rose to move it, and the chairman then suggested they sleep on it – a sleep which was to last until the following Wednesday. It was a great – and costly – disappointment. Although Jack Jones was hopeful that the strike would soon end – it did so on the following Friday, 27th October – none could forecast the outcome now that even the ultra-left-wing strike committee had been repudiated by the rank and file.

Despite the rail settlement, continued paralysis in the docks was bad for sterling. Imports were getting through, but exports were piling up. The president of the Chamber of Shipping had spoken truly when he said that imports are always much more successful than exports in finding a way round a stoppage in the docks. The strike was bound to mean bad trade figures for October, due to be published in November; disruption of the trade statistics would continue for months and the inevitable swing-back of exports would be too late for inclusion in the year's trade and payments figures. Together with the effects of the Middle East crisis, it would mean a further deferment of our hopes – which a few months earlier had looked so bright – of the long-awaited surplus.

Financiers on the continent were more and more seizing on the strike situation, despite the repeated reminders of British City editors that our strike statistics were far better than those of most EEC countries.

At this point, with the usual superb French sense of timing, M. Couve de Murville chose to make a blistering attack on sterling in the EEC context. His words were highly publicised throughout Europe. Part of his case was that sterling must become a national, not an international, currency before Britain was ready for entry. But he went further in drawing a comparison between the position we were facing and that of France in 1958; France, he said, had been in similar straits and took the proper measures to overcome them – devaluation. The speech was calculated and clearly mischievous: its fall-out inevitably went further than the EEC context in which it was ostensibly made, The following day he 'half-apologised', at a press conference, said that he was not at all happy at having to speak in public about these things, and went on to upbraid journalists for having taken his remarks in so sensational a manner. But there was no statesman more adept than Couve in calculating the effect of his statements, even the precise percentage of an apology required in any given situation. He was roundly condemned in almost every London City editor's column.

At the annual bankers' dinner at the Mansion House, on 26th October, both the Chancellor and the Governor of the Bank of England spoke with confidence about the over-all position. The Governor, while warning about public expenditure, expressed his 'strong support' for the Government's determination to continue with our policies to achieve the payments surplus needed. He concluded by reminding his audience that had it not been for the closure of the Suez Canal and the slow-down in world production and trade, Britain would have been in surplus. The combined effect of his and the Chancellor's speeches was headlined as 'Devaluation not on agenda'.

This was correct. Though a contingency plan for devaluation of sterling had long been in the Treasury files – *indeed, it had been there when we took office* – a change in parity was not in contemplation. The Governor met with the Chancellor and me at No. 10. I asked him specifically whether a recommendation to devalue was in his mind. He said flatly that it was not. Should we enter the Common Market, then he thought it might be appropriate as one of the associated decisions; in any case, the role of sterling would first have to be thrashed out with the Six before there was any agreement about entry.

As we entered November, sterling was still under pressure but, unlike July 1966, there was hardly a serious commentator pressing for devaluation.

Sterling and industrial troubles had not monopolised Government and No. 10 activities in October. The early days of the month were marked with sadness through the death of Clem Attlee: I dropped all work to prepare my tributes for the House of Commons and television.

'Clement Attlee,' I said in my broadcast, 'was one of the greatest men of our generation – a man of deep compassion and a crisp and efficient administrator and a world statesman of idealism and practical vision. . . .'

After referring to his social work in the East End of London as a young man, and his service in local government, I set out the vital contributions to the winning of the war and the planning of the peace which he made as Winston Churchill's deputy-Prime Minister; his great 1945 election victory, and the creation of the welfare state. But, I went on,

> . . . of all the acts of those years, none was greater in conception or in its consequences than his historic decision to give freedom and self-Government to India and Pakistan, to Burma and Ceylon. This was a controversial and bitterly-fought decision. But he saw clearly that it was charting the path for a new future, a new future which would transform the Empire into a Commonwealth and create a new and free association of nations once bound only by the links of imperial power, and which, too, created new hope for hundreds of millions, giving them at last the chance of taking their destinies into their own hands and raising their lives above the primeval poverty which had been the lot of a greater part of the human family.
>
> It was an act of statesmanship, yes. It was a turning point in the history of world democracy. But it was more than that. It was one of the most decisive blows ever struck for the dignity of man.

International affairs continued to press: Vietnam and Aden in particular. Sir Humphrey Trevelyan, the Governor of Aden, flew back to London to urge on the Foreign Secretary and myself a speeding up of the date of our withdrawal. It was successfully accomplished on 30th November, in good order and with no loss of life: a superb operation in which Sir Humphrey Trevelyan and the C-in-C, Sir Michael le Fanu, deserved high tribute, as did the Foreign Secretary, who handled it coolly and with great skill and imagination throughout. The new People's Republic of South Yemen came into being on that date.

There were visits and speeches in different parts of the country; in addition to the Scottish tour, I opened the Ford company's new research laboratory on 12th October. On the 13th I toured the northern region, beginning with meetings with the Regional Economic Board, followed by the Economic Planning Council, meetings with local trade union officers, then the regional council of the CBI, finally crossing over to Cumberland for meetings with trade-unionists, industrialists and the Cumberland Development Council. There were the usual visits to my constituency. Of all my visits, the least pleasant was to Cambridge, on 28th October, where I was due to address a meeting of the Eastern Regional Council of the Labour party. My car was directed by the police into a narrow alley-way and there stopped by a yelling mob of demonstrators. Probably only a minority were from Cambridge. It had become a familiar routine that when I was known to be visiting any town, particularly the seat of a university, an influx of demonstrators was organised; we frequently saw their cars on the road. This demonstration, ostensibly on Vietnam, was particularly unpleasant; the car was seriously damaged by staves beating down on the bonnet, and the radio and radio-telephone aerials were broken off. My wife was quite badly manhandled, eggs were thrown and a policeman was seriously injured. As a member of my team summarised it as we drove out from Cambridge on to the Royston road, 'They won't be satisfied: a man must die for peace.' The regional Labour party meeting was, by contrast, enthusiastic; the main announcement in my speech was that we intended to introduce controls over rent increases by local councils.

That was not the only diversion that weekend. While I was in my constituency on the previous day I was telephoned by my office about a storm breaking out over some loose words uttered by Lord Chalfont in Lausanne at what he, at any rate, thought was a non-attributable press discussion. They were sensationalised as implying a direct threat that if General de Gaulle blocked our entry into Europe we should retaliate by rethinking our entire European policy, including the maintenance of British troops on the Continent. I intervened at once and on returning to London sent for Alun Chalfont. He began by proffering his resignation and explained that, as he had understood it, his words – which in any case were totally misunderstood – were off the record. I refused his resignation and gave him my full backing against hostile questions in the House.

Friday, 27th October, saw the end of the long session of Parliament which had opened in April 1966.

The prorogation speech, read in the Lords, listed all the measures which had received the Royal Assent: The Industrial Reorganisation Act; the Selective Employment Tax; the regional employment premium; Acts 'to reinforce the voluntary observance of the prices and incomes policy'; decimal currency; the measure to create the Shipbuilding Industry Board and to provide financial assistance to reorganisation; public ownership of the steel industry; the Docks and Harbours Act; the Companies Act; the measure setting up in the Post Office data-processing services for use by industry; the creation of the Meat and Livestock Commission; legislation on road safety, goods vehicles regulations – and the breathalyser; measures to tighten control on drugs; the creation of the Ministry of Social Security; the replacement of National Assistance by supplementary benefits and the increase in pensions and benefits; the housing legislation – subsidies for local authorities for high-rise building and areas with high land costs, and the general subsidy to reduce the effective interest rate for house-building to four per cent, whatever the market rate; the option mortgage scheme to allow owner-occupiers to choose the option of a mortgage rate below the building society rate on surrendering income-tax relief; leasehold enfranchisement; the Land Commission; assistance to local authorities to reduce rate increases for householders, and to provide help for the least well-off ratepayers. The speech went on to list the legislation on Scottish teachers' pay, Scottish water supply and the establishment of a Countryside Commission in Scotland; the Welsh Language Act; the Act against pirate radios and the Act which set up the Ombudsman; statutory reforms in the penal system and criminal court procedure, and, as a further part of the Lord Chancellor's programme of law reform, fifteen Acts giving effect to the reports of the Law Commissions in consolidation and modernisation of the statute law.

Four days later, on 31st October, the Queen's Speech opened the 1967–8 session. In its legislative content it foreshadowed the Industrial Expansion Bill; a National Loans Fund to modernise national borrowing procedures; a measure to give effect to the recommendations of the Aberfan Tribunal; a major Transport Bill, covering better integration of rail and road transport, higher safety standards in the road transport industry, strengthened powers, area by area, in road passenger transport, and the reorganisation of the inland waterways, with particular emphasis on recreation and amenity. Bills were promised to centralise vehicle licensing; to convert the Post Office from a department of State to a public corporation; to modernise town- and country-planning procedures and to establish a Countryside Commission to provide better access to the countryside and widen opportunities for the enjoyment of leisure; to increase compensation to tenant farmers when their land was taken for development, and to safeguard farm animals, especially in factory farming. There was to be a Bill to regulate dumping; a complicated measure on safety and quality of medicines, and a Bill to improve public health and welfare services. Also foreshadowed was legislation to increase family allowances; to widen the scope of the Race Relations Act (by extending it to deal with discrimination in employment and in housing); to reform the law on gaming; and to reduce the powers and reform the constitution of the House of Lords.

Two days later came three more gloomy by-election results. Contrary to forecasts, we held the seat at Manchester, Gorton, as much as anything through the quality of our well-liked local candidate, Ken Marks; Leicester, South West, Bert Bowden's former seat, was lost, his majority of 5,554 swinging to a Conservative lead of 3,939. Even worse, we lost the traditionally safe seat of Hamilton in Scotland to the Scottish Nationalist. True, the Conservatives could gain little comfort here, since their vote fell from over 11,000 to fewer than 5,000 and they lost their deposit. But our vote fell far more, and a 16,576 majority in 1966 gave way to a Scottish Nationalist majority of 1,799. It was very similar to the swing in the Rhondda on 9th March, and with the same ominous portents. Was it just a Poujadist protest, a short-lived reaction, or would it persist, with disastrous results, in a general election? This was what everyone was asking.

The Queen's Speech debate was much more concerned with current affairs than with the proposed legislation. Apart from a surprisingly long exposition on the proposed House of Lords reforms, a good deal of Mr Heath's speech was about the evanescent Chalfont affair, leading up to some lengthy observations in favour of Britain's application to enter the Market.

In succeeding days the attack narrowed. One of the two days traditionally taken up by Opposition amendments was devoted to the transport proposals; the second, and main, one to the economic situation, opened by Mr Macleod. He made a great deal of the unemployment situation – though the figures were lower than during his tenure of the ministry – and with the growth rate. His speech was later taken as spreading gloom in financial circles, but it is fair to say that he joined the Chancellor in rejecting what he called 'blood transfusions' such as devaluation or a floating rate.

We were in fact just eleven days from devaluation and events which could not have been foreseen a week earlier, except in nightmares, took charge with a rush.

On Saturday, 4th November, the Chancellor came to see me about sterling. The situation had suddenly worsened and following widespread rumours on the Continent that we should devalue in mid-November the drain on the reserves had intensified. A telegram had come from one of our representatives in Europe saying that the ministerial finance committee of the Six was due to meet in ten days' time. Its agenda provided for a discussion on what the Six would do if Britain devalued. Some EEC members, it was said, felt that they would have to follow us if we acted. They believed that Sweden, badly hit by the recent Finnish devaluation, would do the same. Loose talk about the forthcoming EEC meeting had started the rumours.

For the first time Jim Callaghan doubted whether we should be able to hold the position and for the first time I had the same doubts. I was anxious that there should be no repetition of the 1966 situation, with lobbying and intrigue on the policy and a feeling among ministers that major decisions were being taken by too small a group of their colleagues. Over the weekend I decided to put the position on the record. I made clear that if the situation worsened, if the Chancellor were to feel that the alternatives to devaluation were unacceptable, I should accept his advice. There would be no question of what had been called a 'political veto'. I warned him, however, that, apart from certain inevitable measures to restrain home consumption, I should be opposed to a major lurch into deflation. On the operational side, either devaluation or a decision to float the pound sterling would have disastrous consequences if our action was followed, voluntarily or involuntarily, by too many others. On the technique of devaluation, I favoured floating, rather than a cut to a lower fixed parity.

On the Monday morning, 6th November, when I handed this minute to him, I found that he had thought the situation through and had decided to take the EEC bull by the horns. He had invited Mr Van Lennep, who was secretary of the financial group of the Six, to come over for a frank discussion, with no holds barred. The Chancellor was already in touch with Secretary Fowler, and had already decided to send the second secretary to the Treasury (Overseas), Sir Denis Rickett, to Washington. While Jim Callaghan was ready to face devaluation, if there were no alternative, he felt that the Six, and the Americans, having peered over the brink might feel that the crisis of competitive currency devaluations which could follow must be averted at all costs. As the foreign exchange markets opened for a new week, they showed themselves to be in a highly neurotic condition; any rumour, any press article, however well-intentioned, could cause millions of pounds to swing for or against any particular currency, not sterling alone. Currency movements were no longer confined to movements of working balances or 'leads and lags'; the professional speculators were in, taking a view, selling spot and forward millions; soon they were selling hundreds of millions they did not own and could not command, hoping to meet their obligations at lower parities. And their operations were by no means confined to sterling. Yet press comment was notably relaxed, and still continued to concentrate mainly on questions about Britain's entry into Europe.

By the Tuesday, 7th November, the dollar was under heavy attack, and sweeping transfers were being made into German marks, and, to a lesser extent, into Swiss francs. Friday's run on sterling had given way on the Monday and Tuesday to a trickle. I forecast that the next rumour would be of a German revaluation, upwards. This proved to be true, and almost all currencies were beleaguered, as holders of first one, then another, switched into Deutschemarks. Chaos and anarchy took control of the markets.

We were waiting for the Van Lennep meeting and also for a clear view of the Washington position: the Governor of the Bank of England and the Federal Reserve chairman, William McChesney Martin, were already in contact. At the weekend the monthly meeting of European central bank governors was due to take place at Basle.

The Chancellor with my agreement proposed to authorise the Governor to tell his colleagues that we were at 'five minutes to midnight'. Sterling's position was extremely precarious; we wanted to know where they stood. Were they ready to see sterling go? Would they want to follow us down? Or did they want us to hold our hand, with a promise on their part to swing in behind sterling to avoid a disruption of world finance? If that was what they wanted, any defences expected must be sufficiently substantial and enduring to keep sterling safe from speculative attack for some years ahead. We had heard that Chancellor Kiesinger was anxious to avoid a major crisis, with its inevitable consequences for Germany, and was talking of using Germany's heavy and unwanted currency accumulation to hold guaranteed sterling, or to buy Treasury bills, to almost any limit.

On the Wednesday morning, 8th November, I held a meeting of the Steering Committee on Economic Policy (SEP). The agenda, fixed the previous week, provided for a discussion on a paper the President of the Board of Trade had been asked to prepare on import quotas, which some ministers tended to favour. I let it be known that the discussion would not be inhibited and that any minister would be free to discuss alternative action. The Board of Trade came down, for good reason, against quotas and Tony Crosland skilfully widened the discussion as I had wanted. I then asked Jim Callaghan to tell our colleagues the position. He spelt out the position in terms of 'free sterling' – our reserves plus drawings then available to us *minus* commitments immediately or at call. He rehearsed the arguments for and against devaluation but stressed that within days we might face a situation where we might have no option. He emphasised my point that if any but a few countries followed us, the operation itself would be frustrated and the effects on the world economic situation might be very grave. I then invited colleagues to discuss the issue freely, and made it clear that there would be no question of a 'political' veto. My mind was open, but, I told them, a decision might be forced upon us without its becoming a matter of considered policy. If other countries followed suit then what we must regard as a political set-back would be followed by an economic and political disaster.

I concluded what was, in all the circumstances, a good discussion by saying that the Chancellor and I would keep the situation under daily review, and, as necessary, would call our colleagues together. At least we were together – as we had been in resisting devaluation in 1966. There would be no talk by others about a determined Chancellor and a resistant Prime Minister. Some colleagues were disturbed by his warning of accompanying domestic measures; as in 1966 they had been persuaded that in some way devaluation was an easy and painless option, a view against which I had consistently warned ministers and the public.

In the evening Jim Callaghan came to see me again. Though sterling had recorded a better day and the Deutschemark rumours were dying down, the Bank's advice about our ability to hold the rate, if we were so minded, was depressing. In his view, while events might dictate another course of action, we should be ready to act on Saturday week, 18th November. We should, he said, consider the accompanying plans in the Treasury 'War Book'. These included increases in taxation; a further cut of £150 millions in Government expenditure; an increase in bank rate by at least two points; tightening of prices and incomes policy, including new statutory provisions; cuts in the investment programmes of public industries; and further reductions, on both public expenditure and foreign exchange grounds, in defence spending.

Ludicrously, he said, the Treasury package also included, as a means to improving foreign confidence, a proposal to remove the limit on overseas tourist expenditure. As I pointed out, that meant that everyone must tighten his belt – unless he could get away to Majorca for a week. The best estimate the Treasury and the Bank could make of countries likely to follow included the Scandinavians, following Finland. The Six were very uncertain; but the US would not devalue. A great deal would depend on Australia. If she devalued, so, almost certainly, would Malaysia, Singapore, Hong Kong and Japan. If the Six and Australia were to follow our change of parity, any gains to us would be extremely problematical.

The Chancellor reported on the Van Lennep discussions. Apparently, the ministerial meeting had been called as a result of a remark by the French delegate to his Italian colleague at a meeting of permanent secretaries of the EEC finance ministries. The Italian was very perturbed, hence the decision to hold a meeting. Mr Van Lennep, who, as we knew, had long taken the view that Britain should devalue, had promised to do all in his power to ensure that the Six did not follow. He felt that there was no case for the Six, as an entity, to do so and if individual countries did so it would totally disrupt the economy of EEC and might break up the Market.

The Chancellor told me that the Treasury considered that the gains to our trade from devaluation would not be immediate. Because of the worsening of the terms of trade, and the slow effect on exports with a long period of production, our balance of payments deficit would be likely to increase in the first six months of 1968 and would not begin to improve until the latter part of the year. I thought this too pessimistic, and gave my reasons, though in the event the Treasury were proved right; indeed, if anything, too sanguine.

We then discussed how much we should tell Washington. It would be right to make the implications clear to the President, especially the implications for our defence policy, including the stationing of British forces in particularly critical areas. It would only be right to warn him, too, of what might be involved for world trade and finance. The US payments position was already serious, largely as a result of the Vietnam War, and the US might be forced into severe deflation – this in an election year.

We considered whether I should fly over to Washington and, if so, for what ostensible reason, for such a visit would carry with it the danger of renewed speculation. In the end, after preliminary soundings, we dropped the idea.

Before our meeting broke up, the Chancellor felt it right to indicate that, as soon as devaluation took place, he would resign. I told him that I should refuse to accept it; it was the policy of the Government, not of one minister, to fight to maintain the parity of the pound.

The following morning, 9th November, bank rate went up another half point to $6\frac{1}{2}$ per cent. The Chancellor and I met to put George Brown in the picture. He accepted that we considered that devaluation was now virtually inevitable, but felt that we should put the issue fairly and squarely before the President of the United States. But, he said, we should emphasise that we were not seeking short-term aid to avert what we were facing. If the US themselves felt that action must be taken in the interests of the dollar, they must be prepared to shoulder our joint burden. In so far as this might mean underwriting the sterling balances, with perhaps our dollar investments as collateral – to be successively realised as required to meet payments against the balances – we could accept this, perhaps combined with a month's moratorium which would give us time to work out a long-term settlement, not excluding an ordered devaluation. George Brown felt, however, that the President had too little authority in Congress to get such an agreement through.

We decided to tell Sir Patrick Dean, HM Ambassador in Washington, of all that was happening, and arranged that he should be briefed by Sir Denis Rickett, who was that day in Bonn and would fly on to Washington. Recognising that westward the land was anything but bright, we discussed our own problems. George Brown, despite the line he had taken in July 1966, was now, as Foreign Secretary, less enamoured of devaluation. I felt that there was something of the Ernest Bevin touch in this. Twenty years earlier, he had felt his position as Foreign Secretary weakened by the convertibility crisis. George Brown's committed 'growthmanship' further rendered him hostile to any deflationary package.

On the Friday, 10th November, I was on a Yorkshire tour, and returned in the evening. Advice from Washington, which reached us on the Saturday, was contradictory. On the political side any hope of US help or a moratorium was discounted. The President would have to go to Congress, where everything held against us – from Cuban trade to Hong Kong-registered ships calling in at Vietnam – would be raised. On the economic side, the US Treasury was horrified at the thought of devaluation. The Under-Secretary to the Treasury, Mr Dening, and then Joe Fowler himself proposed a canvassing of European help – the Germans had been encouraging – plus additional facilities from the International Monetary Fund. This would be put to the President on the Monday, and Secretary Fowler thought that on present form the President would stand his corner. But a lot would depend on the attitudes of the European bankers at Basle. Fowler's messages were flashed to the Governor via the British Embassy at Berne.

On the Sunday, 12th November, George Brown, Jim Callaghan and I met at No. 10. By this time it was clear that an international package designed to avert devaluation was emerging. We were prepared to go along with it, provided that it was sufficiently solid and lasting and that there were no unacceptable conditions attached. It would have to be firm enough to see us through for a period sufficient for us to take a cool decision in the New Year about sterling, on the basis that we should devalue only if it was clear that we were basically over-valued.

While we were talking, the Governor telephoned from Basle and told the Chancellor that the bankers, with one or two exceptions, were hostile to a British devaluation; all wanted to take sterling out of the immediate political and economic cockpit. Washington reported that Dean Rusk had told our Ambassador that he had been fully briefed by the Treasury Secretary, and that he would join Joe Fowler in pressing the President to help.

I was able to summarise the position in a late-night meeting of the three of us on the Sunday: if we could get a long-term package without onerous conditions, guaranteeing us against political and speculative manoeuvrings for a period ahead, we would be ready to consider it, provided that we were free to devalue, from strength, at any time; for example, when the trade returns became normal after the strikes. If we were to devalue against world opinion, causing other countries to follow us, our competitive position would be unimproved. And the fact that we had devalued, after our repeated assurances, might lead sterling-balance holders to rush for cover as fast as they could against the possibility of a second devaluation. Conversions of £100 millions, even £500 millions, could take place, far beyond the capacity of our reserves and our now almost negative free sterling position to meet. For the act of devaluation would not, of itself, alter sterling's international role nor relieve us of the incubus of the sterling balances; nor would that happen unless some altruistic nation, or group of nations, decided to assume them.

On Monday evening, 13th November, the Governor called to report on his meeting with the central bankers at Basle. Opinion there by this time had shifted somewhat from the previous messages; it was about equally divided on whether we should devalue. The Governor was moving rapidly towards devaluation; with our partners so sharply divided, we might no longer be free to take our own decisions. At the same time nearly everyone at Basle – the Americans, particularly, were very strong – took the line that if we decided to hold the parity there should be a massive international operation to back sterling. But, they insisted, it should not be on the basis of a whip-round; it should be a further IMF stand-by of not less than three billion dollars. But Pierre-Paul Schweitzer, Secretary-General of the IMF, who had been consulted, gave a ruling that since this would represent 250 per cent of our quota the rules of the Fund would require not only the agreement of the main banking countries, as members of the General Agreement to Borrow (GAB), but the imposition of rigid restrictions. M. Schweitzer instanced strict credit control, a tightening of prices and incomes policy – presumably statutory – a limitation on growth, and an agreement that, while we might during the currency of the loan decide to devalue, we must pledge ourselves never to float.

On the basis of the agreement which the Chancellor, the Foreign Secretary and I had already reached on the Sunday night, such conditions had to be rejected as unacceptable and intolerable. In the early evening, M. Schweitzer, under American as well as British pressure, sought to qualify the conditions. But whatever *ex gratia* qualifications there might be, GAB agreement from the Group of Ten principal banking countries would still be required. In our view, this must lead to the most searching intrusions not only into our privacy, but even into our economic independence, not least from the French. And all this would be against the background of unacceptably high unemployment, and the play that would be made in Parliament about sacrificing the unemployed to the bankers. Concern about unemployment had been heightened by sensational and innaccurate disclosures the previous Friday – attributed to the Coal Board – that the coal industry was to be run down from 390,000 to 65,000 men by 1980. I had been forced to run the gauntlet of anxiety while touring the Yorkshire coalfield the day they were published.

Meanwhile, we were told that our friends in the US Treasury were reporting to the President at about that time; that they were now thoroughly frightened about the effects of devaluation on the dollar and hence would press the IMF to be more reasonable. The US Under-Secretary to the Treasury would be going to Paris the following day for the OECD Finance Committee meeting in the hope of pressing some of the Basle countries to reconsider their attitude about individual contributions.

Straight after our No. 10 meeting with the Governor I had to go to Guildhall for the Lord Mayor's banquet. Rarely could a prime minister have had a more difficult task in making the principal speech. Not the least of my difficulties was what words to use about sterling which would be true and, at the same time, not a signal to the speculators. These were temporarily in baulk because of rumours from Basle about an international package to back sterling, on which, of course, I could not comment. But the main interest in my speech that evening centred on my remarks about new proposals for a European Technological Community.

On my return to Downing Street at 11.00 p.m., I was shown new tele-grams from Washington, both from the Ambassador and our representative at the IMF. The message was that there was no more that the Americans could do.

At 11.15 p.m. the Chancellor and I, the Cabinet Secretary, Sir Burke Trend, and the Permanent Secretary to the Treasury, Sir William Arm-strong, met in the Cabinet room. We rejected any idea of relying on an international package with, almost certainly, intolerable accompanying domestic measures; the decision, subject to ratification by our Cabinet colleagues, was to devalue. We went straight into a discussion of the steps which, from that hour onward, had to be taken.

The first question for decision was the accompanying financial package. We rejected such Treasury perennials as museum and library charges and – a miserable and unacceptable economy – cuts in hospital-building, and I also refused to accept a rise in the standard rate of income tax. We decided to set up at once a group of ministers who were departmentally concerned to supervise the week's operations. This came to be known in the Treasury's devaluation 'War Book' as the 'Tuesday Club', for it met at No. 10 on the Tuesday, 14th November, at 4.30 p.m. with me in the chair. The other members were the Chancellor, the Foreign Secretary, the Com-monwealth Secretary (to supervise Commonwealth notification), the Defence Secretary, the President of the Board of Trade, and the First Secretary. We set out the facts and found general support for the decision. One or two ministers were prepared to accept some form of international help to tide us over and avoid devaluation provided it would still leave us free to devalue in the spring. There was some criticism of the domestic package.

I had to leave the meeting at 5.30 p.m. to meet the Scottish group of MPs at the House of Commons, and, with such calm as I could muster, dealt with their very real anxieties about unemployment and colliery closures. I refrained from indicating what my immediate anxieties were. This was a meeting I could have done without, but to cancel any scheduled engagement that week could have led to costly rumours.

The ministerial group met again on the Wednesday, 15th November, at 9.00 a.m. and again at 6.30 p.m. Overnight telegrams from Washington suggested that the Americans were 'stiffening', that is, against sterling devaluation. Their Treasury was, in fact, by this time, totally scared. Their Treasury under-secretary was in Paris trying to reconstitute the support package proposed by Mr Fowler. Nevertheless, the group decided to go ahead with devaluation subject to a final confirmation in the evening when later news would have come from Paris. Time was getting late if all the necessary buttons were to be pressed at the right moment. The new rate was agreed and the whole operation ready to be reported to Cabinet the next morning.

When news came at 6.00 p.m. there was no change in the situation, except for a perceptible further stiffening on the part of the Americans. But there was no sign that this was backed by anything in the nature of a cheque-book. We confirmed the decisions: devaluation on the Saturday, 18th November, with a fixed, not floating, rate, this fixed rate to be $2.40 to the pound.

We also reached broad agreement on the accompanying domestic package. George Brown, who arrived very late – he told us he had been thinking – was depressed but didactic. He wanted us to legislate on industrial relations, anticipating the report of the Donovan Commission. There was no opposition in principle, except from Ray Gunter when it was put to him that same evening, and he was concerned simply with the practicability and timing.

The Chancellor told me later that evening that he had just held a meeting with a Bank of England delegate fresh from the Paris meeting. There had been no real change, though much talk of an IMF drawing, easier and speedier to mount than a stand-by. But, if there were to be such a drawing, a Fund mission would have to go through all the books and be free to recommend changes in our policies. Even if it could be arranged at this late minute, it would simply be another form of international loan, with unacceptable conditions. Against this we had firmly set our face. Jim Callaghan, on hearing this latest Paris report, then put the whole issue to his advisers, including the Governor. They were unanimous in sticking to what we had decided.

I was wakened early next morning, 16th November, with a telephone call from Dick Crossman, in a great state and demanding to know what was going on. He was told that all would be revealed when Cabinet met at 10.30 a.m., but this did not satisfy him. I said I could say no more on the telephone. I then opened my morning papers and realised why he had been so upset. They carried splash stories, clearly put out from Paris, about a massive international loan.

The Cabinet met at 10.30 a.m. I said that the agenda as circulated was in abeyance: we would need the morning on the economic situation. To those who had somewhat curtly asked for information the previous Tuesday, I said I had told them that we should be dealing with the economic situation that morning. I then told them of our decision, and called on the Chancellor.

The Chancellor put the whole case gravely, and with, as he said, 'anguish' – but with courage and clarity. I asked for Cabinet confirmation on the question whether we should devalue. Agreement was unanimous, apart from one colleague who asked to reserve his position, mainly because of the accompanying measures. 'When to devalue?' was the next question, and Saturday, 18th November was confirmed. There was some argument about a fixed or floating pound; a number accepting with regret, as I had earlier, our inability to float. There was little disposition to argue for a deeper cut in the rate.

All the accompanying measures were agreed to after considerable discussion, with the exception of the postponement of the raising of the school-leaving age which we left for fuller and calmer evaluation.

During this part of the Cabinet's discussions, a message came in from the whips to say that one of our back-benchers, Robert Sheldon, was tabling a private notice question to the Government about continental reports of a loan. The Chancellor said he must take it himself; he dare not leave it to a junior minister.

The House that afternoon was anxious and noisy, most of the uproar coming from our back-benchers, who were violently opposed to any idea of a loan, with the inevitable strings. I felt that the Chancellor, who played the bowling with a very dead bat, did well. The private notice question asked whether the Government would make 'a statement on the $1,000 million loan being negotiated with foreign banks'. The Chancellor answered, 'The reply is no, Sir. It would clearly be wrong for the Government either to confirm or to deny a press rumour of this kind.'

Further questions, mainly from our side, designed to warn the Chancellor against accepting a loan with strings, because it would almost certainly involve heavier unemployment, were batted aside – 'So far as Her Majesty's Government are concerned, we shall take what decisions are appropriate in the light of our understanding of the needs of the British economy and no one else's.' Mr Macleod, helpfully commenting that while uncertainty was the worst of all worlds, and that the House would expect a statement when these matters were finalised one way or the other, concluded his question by asking, 'Is he aware that if negotiations are in progress I would not wish to comment?'.

The Chancellor thanked him. It was, I think, his answer to a late question by one of our back-benchers, pressing devaluation as preferable to the deflation and other undesirable concomitants of a loan, which led to the disturbance in the markets. His answer was, in fact, on lines I had suggested at Cabinet, when the possibility of such a supplementary was in our minds. 'I have nothing,' the Chancellor said, 'to add to, or subtract from, anything I have said on previous occasions on the subject of devaluation and, in any case, it does not arise from my original answer.'

Within minutes of that answer, the world's foreign exchange markets went mad. But what else could the Chancellor have said? The run on sterling which then developed after a reasonably quiet day, and which intensified to record proportions on the following day, cost us hundreds of millions. The speculators, nearly all of whom sold sterling they had not got and had no hope of repayment unless sterling was devalued, made a killing.

I had sent personal messages to President Johnson and to the Commonwealth leaders principally concerned; others, including the formal notification to the International Monetary Fund, were drafted and ready for despatch in accordance with a strict time-table.

On the Friday, 17th November, I had to leave on the 1.00 p.m. train for Liverpool to address a docks productivity conference called by the two sides of the industry; again, to have cancelled would have fed the speculators. I was in Liverpool for only ninety minutes before I returned to London, arriving at Downing Street at 8.30 p.m. Before leaving, on arrival in Liverpool, and again before leaving Liverpool, I was fed with up-to-the-minute reports on the appalling run on sterling.

In the evening I approved the text of all the personal messages I had to send to heads of government. A reply came from Washington. The President had spoken in the warmest terms to our Ambassador, and said that 'he was putting his stack behind Prime Minister Wilson'. It was essential that the more powerful countries rallied in support of our reaction to help stabilise the post-devaluation currency markets.

In accordance with a decision of ministers on the Friday morning, George Brown, Dick Crossman, Peter Shore and I met to go through the Treasury draft of the announcement, including the accompanying measures, for final approval by the Chancellor and myself in the morning. Jim Callaghan himself was in Cardiff and, for the same reason which had sent me to Liverpool, could not change his arrangements. Unfortunately, he was due to return by car and it was a night of ice and fog. He arrived home, to face a day of great strain, at 8.30 a.m. on the Saturday morning.

After working on the Treasury draft throughout that morning, 18th

November, he and I looked at the outline I had prepared in the train of the ministerial television broadcast I was due to make on the Sunday evening.

With Treasury officials, and keeping in close touch with the Bank of England, decisions had to be taken about timing. The original decision had been that the announcement should be made at 4.30 p.m. on the Saturday, partly because it was understood that the Kuwait and Bahrein banks would be open until Saturday evening. But later information showed that these would be closed by 3.00 p.m., British time. Since the IMF had to circulate our document to their national governors on Saturday morning, there was the danger of a leak at any time after 9.00 a.m. Washington time (2.00 p.m. GMT). However, the Permanent Secretary to the Treasury came round to say that IMF had asked that we should not make the announcement until their meeting had approved the new rate, as required by IMF rules, and that this would not be earlier than 7.00 p.m. London time.

Throughout Saturday, the telegrams were pouring in from every Government, all of them extremely helpful. They were in almost identical terms:

1 They expressed deep sympathy and understanding for us in the decision we had to take;
2 They paid tribute to our courage for fighting so long to hold the rate;
3 They recognised (precisely because we had held out so long) that we were right to say *now* that enough was enough;
4 They accepted that the extent of the devaluation was right;
5 With one or two exceptions, mainly the ones we wanted, they were not proposing to follow us down;
6 They would give us all the backing in their power to stabilise the post-devaluation situation in world currency markets.

Given that this drastic and distasteful step had to be taken, it was going as well as the best that we could hope for and far, far better than we might have feared. Jim Callaghan and I spent the later part of the Saturday morning revising still further the Treasury announcement. When we broke off at 2.00 p.m. most of the replies were in, reiterating the six-point replies of the earlier telegrams. Some of those we had worried about most, and the most doubtful had been France and Japan, had decided not to devalue.

Throughout the day there were vast crowds outside No. 10. I went to the door just for a moment, to see off Dr Ernest Davies, MP for Stretford, and some lady constituents he had brought to see No. 10. The crowds outside gave me a warm and what seemed like an understanding cheer; I was not sure what they understood.

The Treasury statement, which the Chancellor and I had finally cleared in the afternoon, was issued at 9.30 p.m. that evening.

It began by announcing the fact of devaluation, from $2.80 to $2.40, a reduction of 14.3 per cent. It went on to say: 'This change brings with it fresh opportunities – but at a heavy cost. The main opportunity is that our exporters should be able to sell more goods overseas such as motor vehicles and tractors, ships, aircraft, chemicals, textiles and much else.' But it explained that if we were to derive the full benefit we had to reduce demand by consumers at home in order to shift the use of our resources to exports and import-saving. We had to aim at an improvement in our balance of payments of at least £500 millions a year.

The banks were asked to limit their advances except to priority borrowers, especially exporters. Bank rate was being raised immediately to eight per cent. Hire-purchase regulations on cars would be tightened again, with a minimum deposit of $33\frac{1}{3}$ per cent and a maximum repayment period of 27 months.

Public expenditure was to be cut. Expenditure on defence was to be reduced by over £100 millions in the following year. Except in development areas, the SET repayment premia to manufacturers would be withdrawn, saving £100 millions. Other public expenditure, including the capital expenditure of nationalised industries, would be reduced by £100 millions. The export rebate, introduced in 1964, would be abolished, saving just under £100 millions a year, 'since it will no longer be necessary'.

The statement categorically said that the major disadvantage of the change would be a rise in certain prices, though not all at once. New consultations would be held with the TUC and the CBI to ensure that the operation of the agreed prices and incomes policy 'measures up to the requirements of the new situation'. There would be a close watch on dividends: corporation tax was to be raised from 40 per cent to $42\frac{1}{2}$ per cent.

An application was being made to the IMF for new stand-by arrangements of $1.4 billions, and this, together with other assistance being negotiated with overseas central banks, would provide resources of $3 billions, designed to stabilise the new currency situation.

By a Royal Proclamation to be submitted to the Queen in Council the banks were to be closed to the public on Monday, 20th November. The Stock Exchanges would be closed on the same day.

At 9.30 p.m. on the Saturday evening I waited to see the news-flash on television and the announcement on the Downing Street tape-machine. Waiting to see me were George Woodcock for the TUC, John Davies for the CBI and Derek Pritchard, Chairman of the British National Export Council, all of whom I had summoned earlier in the evening. Together with the Chancellor and the Economic Secretary, I saw them, one after another, in the Cabinet Room.

George Woodcock took it very well – and was obviously going to be helpful.

John Davies's reaction surprised me. I dictated my impressions after the meeting in a 'note for the record'.

> Davies took the decision well, but for some reason turned very sour politically. He said CBI leadership had prevented the members running a political campaign and now it was impossible. They were carrying excessive burdens, especially on taxation, and the new package was not making a significant attack on public expenditure. Indeed, corporation tax was going up. I said they should get out into Europe and elsewhere and realise their market opportunities. They had a wonderful opportunity to increase their profits which were supposed to be the motive force of private enterprise. Davies almost implied that they would not do so but spend their time on a political campaign to get rid of the Government.

Throughout my political life, particularly in parliamentary questions and debates, I have always sought to answer in the same spirit in which I have been addressed. This clearly political outburst should be answered politically. In the words of my note at the time: 'His head then got washed.' Perhaps I should have answered differently, and with more fellow-feeling as between politicians, had I then been able to foresee the nature of the political career he was to embark upon as a Conservative Member of Parliament.

Sir Derek Pritchard undertook to make a great rallying-call to exporters to go out and seek the new orders that were open to them.

Looking back in 1971 on those eventful November weeks, what strikes me now as then was the suddenness with which we had been overwhelmed by the operations of a speculative market. The Middle East crisis had frustrated our confident hopes of achieving a soundly based surplus: the dock strikes and railway troubles had undermined trust in sterling. Yet there had been little evidence of a serious break in confidence until manoeuvrings within the Common Market set off damaging rumours in Europe.

The financial pages of the press had not been expressed in crisis terms until the very last week. *The Economist*, usually quick to catch the changing mood of markets, had not devoted any leading article to describe anything in the nature of a gathering crisis – as opposed to unease – until its issue of 11th November. Even this was in the business section at the back and was in part expressed in terms of prospects for the next six months. *The Times*, similarly, while gloomy, hoisted no alarm signals apart from a reference to the effect on the pound of Deutschemark speculation on 8th November. Even on Thursday, 16th November, business columns of *The Times* had been more concerned with my Guildhall speech on European technology than with any impending crisis. It was only as a result of the explosion in the markets the day after the Chancellor's questioning in the House that the storm signals were first hoisted.

It was a crisis different in kind, shorter in duration and – until the last hours – less intense than those which sterling had weathered in the three preceding years. But this time it was lethal.

Chapter 24

*Ministerial broadcast on devaluation – Conservative misrepresentation
– General de Gaulle opposes British entry to the Common Market –
problems in the Parliamentary Labour Party – South African arms sales
– speech on economic policy – a national rail strike averted – Mr Holt's
funeral – President Johnson and Vietnam – cuts in Government spending – party discipline*

THERE was every reason to feel that the operational stage of
devaluation had gone successfully. The political consequences were
still to follow. I was under no illusions about them.

My first task was the ministerial broadcast on both television channels
on the Sunday night, 19th November. The draft I had prepared on the
train back from Liverpool was sombre in tone; devaluation was a
set-back, though this should not be allowed to detract from what we
had achieved in ridding Britain of the £800 millions deficit which we
had inherited. If it was a defeat, it was also a challenge: our task was to
redeploy our resources from home consumption to export. Given restraint and a seizing of our opportunities, we could, with more freedom
than at any time for years, combine a faster rate of industrial expansion
and full employment with a robust balance of payments.

At Friday night's meeting of ministers and my private office staff on
the eve of devaluation I was pressed, above all by Dick Crossman, to
alter the tone of the broadcast, and to drop the references to set-back
and defeat, and almost to exult in our decision. I believe I was wrong to
accept this advice and a comparison today of my original draft with
the text of my Sunday broadcast suggests that I should have stuck to
my first thoughts.

But this had nothing to do with the one sentence in that broadcast
which was most seized on and used against me. In my original draft,
under the heading 'What it means', I drew a distinction between what
had happened to the pound internally, and externally. Recalling the
devaluation of 1949, I was aware that there would be timid and frightened
people thronging the post office and bank counters, pathetically believing
that for every pound of their savings they had invested there, they could
now draw only seventeen shillings. I was anxious to allay these fears.
The act of devaluation meant at the same time that every pound an
individual held or earned abroad automatically, by the very act of
devaluation, would produce not twenty but seventeen shillings on conversion into a foreign currency. That had nothing to do with what
devaluation would, over a period of time, mean for prices. For, clearly,

if we bought a ton of foreign wheat at sixty-five dollars per ton we should have to pay more for it in sterling terms and this would, over a period of time, enter into the price of bread. I recalled that Sir Stafford Cripps, eighteen years earlier, in his post-devaluation broadcast, had forecast a rise of 1½d in the cost of a loaf. Obviously, this would happen again. My draft, written on the train, drew a distinction between the value – in bank, purse and pocket – of the immediate cash to be drawn, and the effect on prices. It said, 'First, say what it means. Not £ at home – a reference to the cashable value of bank holdings – but imports cost more. This means easier exports – but prices. 10s a week (increase in prices per family).'

On returning to London I found a Treasury draft of my broadcast awaiting me. It was far too technical and jargonesque, though this was partly explained by the fact that the original decision had been that the actual announcement of devaluation was to be made in a television broadcast by me on the Saturday, before it was decided that an official announcement would be made by the Chancellor and myself, and that my broadcast would therefore follow on the Sunday evening. But, by pure coincidence, it made the same point about the fact that devaluation *had* not of itself reduced the cash value of savings and other bank deposits. The Treasury draft, quite coincidentally also, had a section headed 'What it means'. It went on, 'Devaluation does *not* mean that the value of the pound in the hands of the British consumer, the British housewife at her shopping, is cut correspondingly. It does not mean that the money in our pockets is worth 14 per cent less to us now than it was this [i.e. Saturday] morning.'

This was the only sentence of the Treasury draft I incorporated in the final version, replacing 'money in our pocket', by the more alliterative 'pound in the pocket'. Though I was cautioned by a civil service adviser, I was reinforced by the words of one of my own staff whose maiden aunt had telephoned to express concern that her Post Office Savings Bank holdings had been slashed by three shillings in the pound. As in my original draft, I kept in the fact in the same paragraph that '... the goods we buy from abroad *will be dearer* ...'. And again, '... I've said that *imports will cost more*, and *this means higher prices over a period for some of our imports, including some of our basic foods*. And it's vital that *price rises* are limited to those cases where increased import costs make this unavoidable.'

Though I referred to the cost value of savings, I made clear that prices would rise. Nothing could have been clearer, as my italics show. Equally, nothing said by any political leader has been more dishonestly or unscrupulously misrepresented and twisted for political purposes, by a hundred Tory speeches and a thousand press features.

The process began, the following evening, in a shrill broadcast by Mr

Heath. Totally out of context he quoted the reference to the 'pound in your pocket', and interpreted it as a misleading pledge that prices would not rise as a result of devaluation.

He disdained to make any reference at all to my statements that prices would rise, or to the clear reason why I had made the point at all.

The Conservative press took up the point, with a degree of misrepresentation unworthy of them. And so it has continued to the present day. When, at question time in Parliament the quotation was explained, the references to rising prices cited, and the Opposition silenced, unaccountably no report appeared in the newspapers which were running the 'pound in your pocket' campaign.

Some newspapers went further. The *Daily Express* began a series of weekly price-schedules each Saturday with an attribution to me twistedly headlined thus, 'The pound in your pocket *will not be* devalued'. They received little comfort in their statistics for some months, the only significant increases being a seasonal rise in the price of tomatoes and dearer beef, due to the most serious foot-and-mouth epidemic in our history.

Neither was Mr Heath above twisting the words. Careful always to omit my references to the inevitability of increased prices, he attributed to me words I had not used, 'the pound in your pocket *will not* be devalued', clearly implying that I had suggested that prices would not rise.

Throughout the rest of the 1966–70 Parliament this was regularly used by the Tory press. When the 1970 election drew near the Conservatives spent thousands of pounds in propagating the phrase, totally out of context, as did leading Conservative newspapers. On the day I write this, long after that election, the *Daily Mail*, who at least had the grace, during the election, to quote my answer to this smear in a television broadcast, repeated it in a leading article. And so, no doubt, regardless of truth, it will continue.

Perhaps the appropriate comment on this sustained political dishonesty occurred in a parliamentary exchange at question-time in 1968. Conservative back-benchers and Mr Heath were hammered into the ground by the quotation of the actual words. Mr Heath rose to deliver his *coup de grâce*. Sweetly, he asked me whether, on consideration, if I had had the chance to reconsider what I had said, whether I would still have said it. Equally politely I replied:

> As to the accuracy of what I said, the answer is, Yes. But recalling the warning of Rudyard Kipling, 'if you can bear to hear the truth you've spoken,
> Twisted by knaves to make a trap for fools. . . .'
> I might have had second thoughts.'

Even Kipling did not stop them.

For the rest, the broadcast set out the facts, the opportunities, the challenge, the cost. But I believe I made an error, in that desperately unreal weekend, in toning down, as compared with my original draft, the extent of the defeat we had suffered, whatever the causes.

Politics were by this time totally dominated by devaluation. When the House met on the Monday, the Chancellor made a statement and bravely withstood Opposition attacks for half an hour.

We had arranged a two-day debate, which was inevitably grim. Mr Macleod was restrained, Mr Heath was not. My own speech was punctuated by interruptions and a determined effort to ensure that I was not heard. But our own people, despite anxieties about the domestic restraints, demonstrated great loyalty. It was partly because some of our backbenchers, particularly on the left, supported our rejection of an 'easy' way out through the acceptance of a loan which would have carried with it intolerable strings; perhaps they were over-optimistic, in that all they had argued failed to allow for the measures we would have to take, then and later, to secure a transfer of £500 millions, in real resource terms, from home consumption to the strengthening of the balance of payments.

Another factor in the new-found unity of our party was the virulence of the Conservative attack. A student of long standing of Conservative attitudes, I had, unusually, some difficulty in forming an assessment. The backbench reaction was easy to assess: they were having a field day. The front bench was more difficult. Their leaders, while seeking relief in raucous tactics, seemed somewhat ill-at-ease. It seemed to be in tune with words of Mr Heath which had been reported to me in the early weeks of the year, when he was said to have asserted that the next election was safely in Conservative hands, 'unless Wilson devalues'. True, so it was said, he had asserted that I would not be prepared to face the short-term political costs, but if I were so prepared – well, there was time for me to await the long-term economic security which would follow, together with its related political gains.

The debate, on a motion to approve the Chancellor's post-devaluation statement, ended in a division won by the Government by 335 to 258.

The day after the debate ended, I appeared on 'This Week' in what the press subsequently described as my 'roughest-ever' grilling on television. It was to be expected, but for once I did not relish the thought. I was desperately tired, perhaps more tired than I had ever been. Before going to the studio I had just twenty minutes free: I went to bed, fell asleep, and woke twenty minutes later a little refreshed. From somewhere – it may have been the stimulation of the questioning – I drew in enough energy to put on a vigorous and lively tone, to my surprise and that of the advisers with me. Surprisingly it got a good press: one phrase clearly anticipated Roy Jenkins' 'two years of hard slog'. There could be no question of any easement in living standards for the next two years, until there had been a secure and lasting transfer of resources from home consumption to exports; the rewards would begin to accrue in 1969, but not before then. Perhaps one reason for the success of the programme was that I allowed myself to be drawn on what the crisis had meant – two weeks of hell for the Chancellor and me, and some hard-hitting attacks on those who had been selling Britain short.

The immediate inquest over, the Government had to get down to the implications of the previous week's decision and succeeding weeks saw the Chancellor's programme carried through by administrative action, statutory orders and legislation. These included measures I had promised in the debate to shield the least well-off families from the higher prices I had said must follow devaluation.

Internationally, all was going well. The IMF stand-by, supplemented by central bank loans, went through easily. Sterling opened strong after devaluation, pressing on the new ceiling. Though the speculators had every reason to congratulate themselves, the purchases of sterling to settle their position meant that a great part of their pre-devaluation sales were offset by post-devaluation purchases at the new rate and foreign exchange flowed into London on a great scale. An attempt to stimulate speculation on an increase in the gold price was scotched by an agreement of the principal monetary powers in the 'Gold Club' to take action to hold the price.

We had been exceptionally fortunate in the decision of individual countries about their own parities. Very few had followed us in devaluing; those who had almost totally coincided with the list I would myself have drawn up. Our trading requirements would have demanded that very few would devalue. But among those few we hoped might devalue in order to limit the inevitable increase in prices were our principal food suppliers and, in the event, Ireland and New Zealand devalued with us; Denmark devalued by eight per cent.

There remained a problem for me. Despite the warm endorsement given to the Chancellor, both in an enthusiastic party meeting and in the House, he renewed his request to be allowed to resign. This I could not accept, as I had told him on one of those feverish nights before devaluation. He had been an international symbol of our determination to fight for sterling, but so had I. There could be no question of a symbolic sacrifice.

Jim Callaghan evaded a challenge from Iain Macleod in Parliament on whether he should resign, saying that he had to see the immediate post-devaluation measures through. He continued to press his resignation. In three days of discussions, from 27th to 29th November, I persuaded him to consider an alternative: that he should become Home Secretary, a post in which he had always shown interest. In the event, he accepted and Roy Jenkins became Chancellor.

It had, in fact, been unfair to Jim Callaghan that he had been kept on at the Treasury tread-mill so long and in such difficult conditions. Earlier in the year he had said he would like to move, and indeed his desire became known in the press. The problem simply was that had sterling's toughest defender moved, it would have been taken all over the world as a sign that we were considering a change in parity. That would undoubtedly have precipitated rumours and speculations on a scale capable of forcing devaluation.

Now that devaluation had taken place there was no such bar on his going to another department. Within a week he told me that he was really enjoying life at the Home Office as he had never enjoyed his period at the Treasury: his record for reform, his assertion of what he preferred to call 'freedom under the law' – in distinction to the Tory cry of 'law and order' – and, above all, his firm and fair handling of the Northern Ireland crisis in 1969–70 were of the utmost benefit to the Government and to the country.

With Roy Jenkins I soon established the closest of relations, as became evident when we saw through together the most difficult public expenditure exercise any Government has attempted since the war.

The day before the exchange of ministerial posts was announced, Tuesday, 28th November, General de Gaulle, in his half-yearly press conference, gave the most resounding *'Non'* to any question of British entry into EEC. He set out his reasons in familiar form and called for a return to the gold standard, but he went on to embellish these familiar themes with a series of allegedly factual comments on Britain and the British.

I decided to reply with a detailed sixteen-point commentary on his misconceptions. To take three points at random:

5. Credit practices – where the President had referred to our discriminatory financing arrangements –

    'If the French President considers perhaps that our arrangements for financing industry on the free market of the City of London are not in accordance with the doctrines of the Treaty of Rome, I feel it right to point out that it is the French credit system, not ours, which controls the allocation of specially favourable credit, industry by industry, in accordance with the *Commissariat du Plan.'*

6. Conditions of work. If the General was referring to strikes in Britain, then, in 1966, Britain lost, through industrial disputes for every 1000 persons employed, 180 man-days against 240 in France.

    Figures to be published tomorrow show that, for the five years 1962–6, our figure was 230 against a French figure of 322. For both of us, the figures are too high. We must both do better. . . .

13. We were told that any attempt to impose British entry would lead to the break-up of a Community whose rules would not bear such a 'monumental exception'. But it was not Britain whose policy in foreign affairs, defence, and international monetary policy was the 'monumental exception' to the European consensus on these questions.

I enjoyed dictating the sixteen points, though I did not affect to believe that they would have any effect on the General. Nor – though they were generally welcomed by the British press – could I have hoped that they would upstage the news of the Jenkins–Callaghan reshuffle; Jim Callaghan had asked for more time to think the matter over and this meant that the announcement of the ministerial changes coincided with the reply to the General.

Roy Jenkins was immediately subject to a baptism of fire in the House. There was acute concern about the conditions the IMF would insist on as part of the stand-by arrangements. With my agreement, the new Chancellor decided to meet the parliamentary pressures head on. We had nothing to hide. He decided that the letter his predecessor had sent to the IMF, on 23rd November, and any subsequent commitments to the IMF, should be made public. Jim Callaghan's letter had been considered line by line by the Cabinet and, in a new exercise in open Government – by no means the last in his period as Chancellor – Roy Jenkins offered to publish it. It was printed in Hansard on 30th November.

When it was finally published, the House quickly lost interest. An emergency debate (under the rules of Standing Order No. 9) on 5th December attracted only seventeen members in the anti-Government lobby.

In early December, there were suggestions that I should be keeping a wary eye on the Parliamentary Party. The first reaction to devaluation was an enthusiastic rallying of the ranks, further reinforced by the hysterical instant opposition of the Conservative leadership. But as the impact of the related domestic measures came to be realised, together with the knowledge that much more would be needed, a certain disenchantment was inevitable. The big doubt was, once we had been forced to give way on a cardinal element of policy – which had been maintained, many of our people felt, at a high cost in domestic terms – whether the new post-devaluation policies would succeed. As one newspaper put it, there was no disposition for a change in high places, but the image was tarnished, and the Government was on trial.

There were rumours of a plot to change the tenancy of No. 10. There never was anything in them, apart from the idle tea-room gossip of a few who could always be counted on to suborn support on behalf of this or that possible candidature, all without any support from their favoured putative leader.

The organised left did get the idea that a *putsch* was contemplated and I was informed by one with impeccable authority to speak for them that if any sought to plant any knives in my back, I should rapidly find the left rallying to my support, weapons turned outwards. They had criticised me enough, Heaven knows, and I had imposed heavy strains on their loyalty, but it appeared that if any action were threatened from elsewhere in the party, I could rely on their determination that no one was going to kill Charles to make anyone else King. It was, perhaps, a pity that this intimation did not become public knowledge: the denial to the cartoonists of the opportunity of presenting the left in their capacity as the Praetorian Guard was a cruel deprivation of their professional human rights.

But, within days, there were new strains within the Parliamentary Party, and, indeed, within the Cabinet, strains more serious than any other in our six years of Government; they came from the always emotive issue of arms to South Africa.

The crisis arose, as so many crises arise, accidentally. After leaving the Treasury, Jim Callaghan, who was exhausted by the devaluation period, decided, with my full encouragement, to take a week's holiday. On his return he attended a dinner of the 'under-forties' club of Labour MPs. In reply to one MP he called in question the ban on arms supplies to South Africa. One who was present later told me that it was anything but considered and was designed, provocatively, to start a discussion. With that interpretation I have always agreed.

Jim Callaghan could not have known how sensitive the issue was. For, at a meeting of the Defence and Overseas Policy committee the previous Friday, 8th December, of which he could not have had knowledge, the issue had been raised. It was the first time that any suggestion that our ban on South African arms shipments should be rescinded had been put to any Cabinet committee. But certain of my colleagues in a mood to question all decisions taken in easier days which might have a bearing on exports, considered that the shopping-list for arms just presented to us by the South African Government should not be turned down out of hand. As far as I was concerned, there was no question about it. But as the argument continued, Dick Crossman, who had certainly no idea in his own mind of supplying arms, suggested that this matter should be left until we had concluded the searching review of Government expenditure and all other economic questions which the new Chancellor had insisted should be undertaken.

The committee was divided. I accepted Dick's proposal, making clear that at the end of the review they would still find me irrevocably opposed to any supply of arms. But, I said, if all matters with an economic bearing were to be called in question, regardless of wider overseas policy issues, regardless of moral issues, then I must insist that the Foreign Office must submit to our scrutiny the, by that time, indefensible and anomalous restrictions on trade with Eastern Europe, under the COCOM regulations. The Foreign Office might still find it desirable to humour American prejudice, but if exports were to be the only criterion, the issue must equally be made subject to rigorous examination and justification on merit.

Jim Callaghan's *jeu d'esprit* inevitably led to a leak to the press. Two days later there were headlines that the Government was considering ending the embargo on arms to South Africa.

Loose talk by the still-small arms lobby in the Cabinet fed the press stories. By the following week the Parliamentary Party was thoroughly alerted.

I was engaged in a series of visits to the regional groups of Labour members. The discussions were usually related to regional economic problems, but at each meeting I stated my willingness to answer questions on any national or international issues. At the northern members' group on 13th December, Tom Urwin, MP, asked me about press rumours on the South African arms issue. I answered that there had been no change in Government policy. Nor had there been.

Two of the younger members of the Parliamentary Party, Kevin McNamara, who had been at the 'under-forties' dinner, and John Ellis became alarmed at the press speculation on the issue. They decided to table a declaratory motion demanding the retention of the embargo. This was published on 12th December and attracted 140 signatures. Since the attitude of the Government Chief Whip, John Silkin, was called in question by ministers at the time, and since the legend surrounding it was still being cited by Conservative ministers in South African debates in the House three years later, it is necessary to state the facts.

The conventions of the Parliamentary Labour Party require that any member proposing to table a parliamentary motion and to seek signatures in support must first show the draft to the Chief Whip. The Chief has three choices: he can approve, if it is clearly in line with party policy or on a 'neutral' issue not inconsistent with it; or he can mark it 'not approved', so that any signatory knows that he is out on his own; or he can ask the sponsor to defer tabling the motion for twenty-four hours, for further consideration or for the purpose of taking advice. In no case does he seek to prevent the tabling of the motion; indeed, to do so might raise questions of parliamentary privilege.

In this case, the sponsors of the motion could not find the Chief, who was temporarily out of the House. His deputy, Brian O'Malley, was approached and he asked for time to put the motion to his Chief. When this was done John Silkin correctly ruled that the motion was in accordance with Government policy and raised no objection. Even if he had known that the matter was in any sense under consideration – which he did not – he could hardly have objected, since that would have alerted members to a possible change of policy.

The Conservative leadership – committed to resuming arms supplies to the South Africans – and our own left and liberal wings were equally in full cry. A private notice question was refused by the Speaker's office only when I gave an undertaking that a question to me on the order paper from

Sir Dingle Foot would be answered orally by me, after questions, if it had not been reached during the question period. Now determined to settle it once for all, I put the matter on the agenda of the Cabinet called for the morning of 14th December.

George Brown was in Brussels at a Western European Union meeting, but he was hoping to be back in time for the Cabinet discussion. Unfortunately, fog closed Brussels Airport and he was unable to take off. When I heard this, I postponed the item until George could be with us, and kept the Cabinet in session pending his arrival; when we further heard that he could not be back until the early evening, I adjourned the Cabinet till then, then deferred it for another hour and, when he was reported to be still fog-bound, to the late evening. In the event, he did not arrive even then. But Dingle Foot's question had to be answered in the afternoon.

I was in great difficulty about it. The question asked, in effect, what shopping-list we had received from the South African Government and what reply we had sent. I confirmed that a list had been received, but said that no reply had been sent. I repeated that the policy remained as announced on 17th November 1964, but 'in view of the widespread interest in this matter I will undertake that the House will be given a fuller statement next week'.

I could hardly hope that matters would be left there. I was at once pressed by Dingle Foot for an '... unequivocable assurance that in no circumstances will the export of arms not already contracted for be permitted to the Republic of South Africa'.

In view of the way in which the matter had been left by the Defence Committee, I could not give the assurance; equally, I could not indicate that any contrary decision had been taken. I was determined to see that it wasn't. In these circumstances I felt it right to indicate that the Cabinet was already looking at the matter but that I had no decision to announce. I replied:

> ... I would have hoped to have been able to make a full statement this afternoon, but my rt. hon. Friend, the Foreign Secretary, who is very much concerned with these matters and should have been back this morning, was prevented by weather conditions from getting back. I think it right that these matters should be the subject of consideration when he is here, and then I will make a fuller statement in answer to my rt. hon. and learned Friend.

It was, of course, perfectly proper and natural for the Cabinet to defer such a decision in the absence of the Foreign Secretary, and I did not intend my words to carry any other meaning. But there had been so much talking to the press that some journalists – and certainly George Brown himself, when he heard about it – concluded that I was making it clear that he was in favour of arms sales.

The Cabinet met on the Friday morning with George Brown there, and

confirmed the OPD decision that all matters considered relevant to exports
and economic policy should be considered in the review which the Defence
Committee had decided to make over the next month. It was agreed that
the House should be so informed when I announced the expenditure
review the following week, making clear that this did not in any sense
mean that a decision was already taken in principle.

That afternoon, the most blatant and inaccurate briefing of the press I
have ever known was organised, damaging alike to the coherence of the
Cabinet and to our standing in the party. The line was that the South
African arms policy was to be reversed, and that I had been defeated on
the issue in Cabinet. I was in no doubt who was responsible; there were
fingerprints all over the place. In any case, George was good enough
to write to me defending his action. More concerned with getting the
right policy on arms than with imposing much-needed discipline, and
conscious that a resignation or a sacking would be a little too much for
our party, which was still bruised by devaluation, I decided to take
no immediate action. Indeed, by taking no action, for the moment, I could
get the result I wanted.

For my part, I gave the strictest instructions that there must be no
retaliatory briefing from my own press officers and, for good measure,
passed on the instructions to all my colleagues who, from anger or a
desire to help, might want to use their own press contacts to set the
record straight. The Saturday press headlined with sickening uniformity
the messages that had been put out. The Sunday papers were as bad.
Friends telephoned me, pleading with me to answer or at least to allow
them to do so. I refused. I had long learnt that persistent briefing, particularly if of a personal nature, whatever its short-term success, almost
invariably produces a counter-reaction, particularly on the minds of colleagues.

I waited, therefore, to strike back at the moment when the attack had
over-reached itself and when the maximum number of ministers was
sickened by its manner and by the inaccuracy of its content.

A Cabinet was called for Monday morning, 18th December, at 10.00
a.m., but colleagues were not informed until late on the Sunday evening, to prevent any meetings of possibly like-minded persons on this
question.

In writing this book I have not felt it appropriate in general to draw
back the veil which rightly covers the detailed transactions of a Cabinet.
But I believe it to be right that, in this case, I should disclose the main
lines of the discussion, which was short: partly because I was unanimously
authorised by the Cabinet to reveal our views to the House, but also
because a legend grew up, arising from the weekend briefing, which in
some minds persists to this day. Recent statements of the present Government have brought the South African arms issue back into the political

arena and ministers have purported to justify their actions and arguments by inaccurate references to the events of December 1967, despite the denial issued with Cabinet authority at the time. Some recent press comment, too, has been based on the legend, not the fact.

I began by speaking in the strongest terms about the leaks to the press, their purpose and effects, and made clear that I had strictly forbidden any counter-attack. What had happened had put the Cabinet, and not least myself, in the most difficult position. Recalling the correct facts – both about the OPD and Cabinet discussions and my own attitude to the arms question – I said that no member of the Cabinet could accept that the briefing had been accurate or fair, to say nothing of its other qualities. This was generally agreed, and no voice was raised in response to my request for any holding a contrary view to speak up.

I then said I had considered whether, in the circumstances, I should not have insisted that the Cabinet decided the issue once and for all, to prevent its poisoning Cabinet and party relations for another month, but this I would not press. What I did insist upon, when announcing in Parliament that afternoon the expenditure and wider economic review, was the inclusion of a statement repudiating the press stories. Further, I must be in a position to say that the repudiation was endorsed by, and made with the authority of, the Cabinet. Certain colleagues who were strongly opposed to the supply of arms – and who could see how Cabinet feeling had swung over the weekend – incredulously asked me whether I was really not pressing for the decision to be taken then and there. I said that I was not.

Then, to my surprise, one of those who – with some regret, I think – had declared himself in favour of arms sales, intervened. He said that the events of the weekend had placed the Prime Minister in an impossible situation: he could not possibly face the House with a delaying statement. The matter should be decided at once and for his part he felt that we had no alternative but to maintain the embargo. He was supported by one colleague after another. In the event the Cabinet decided overwhelmingly against resuming arms supply, and agreed unanimously to the draft of the statement I had insisted should be made repudiating the stories which had been given to the press. At 3.30 p.m., after questions, I made the comprehensive statement we had agreed. Starting from the Government's declared policy of achieving a massive swing of resources from home consumption to export, to import replacement and to investment over the next two years, and recalling the domestic measures announced at the time of devaluation, I spelt out the nature of the further review we had set in hand. Home demand, including Government expenditure, was not to be allowed to endanger the required shift of resources. More must be done to switch the emphasis from a consumer-led to an export-led expansion: 'It will mean reductions in the growth of personal expenditure and in the growth of public expenditure. . . .'

The success of the Government's prices and incomes policy was crucial, I said. The severity of fiscal restraint by the Chancellor would depend on the degree of co-operation we secured on prices and incomes.

On public expenditure, I reminded the House of the difficulty of making immediate cuts in programmes whose scale depended on decisions which had to be taken a long period before the peak of the spending. But decisions taken as a result of the review could, in certain spending areas, have a growing effect in the second year and a decisive effect in the third and subsequent years 'provided that the decisions are taken now'.

I then set out the ground rules for the review.

First, we are not approaching this expenditure review, whether in respect of home or overseas expenditure, on the basis of candle ends, or simply on the basis of minor administrative economies, though we shall not, of course, neglect any opportunities here. Neither are we looking for prospects of under-spending or the shifting of expenditure from one financial year to another. We are bringing under stringent review all major areas of policy, both at home and overseas, where substantial expenditure is involved.

Secondly, no area of expenditure can be regarded... as sacrosanct for the purposes of the searching examination we are making: no spending commitment whether inherited three years ago, or incurred since.

Thirdly it will cover local government expenditure as well as central Government expenditure.

Fourthly... the review will cover defence and overseas expenditure as well as home civil expenditure... at a time when we have been, and are, reassessing Britain's role in the world. This must involve overseas policy.

This brought me to South Africa:

In this connection, the Government have completed their examination of the question of the supply of defence equipment to South Africa and have decided that their policy on this matter, namely to conform to the Security Council Resolution of 18th June, 1963, remains unchanged.

I should add that I have the authority of the whole Cabinet categorically to repudiate as inaccurate reported statements about the position taken by the Cabinet as a whole, by a Cabinet committee which met a week earlier, and also about the position taken by the Prime Minister and other individual ministers.

Mr Heath rose, and with the elegance he had recently imported into his speeches inside and outside the House, produced such oratorical pearls as 'slob of wet blancmange... flatulent and platitudinous'. But what really excited him was the arms decision; did the decision to maintain our policy mean that the South African Government's request for arms for self-defence had been turned down by Her Majesty's Government? (Hon. Members, according to Hansard, 'Yes.') Would the matter be open for reconsideration in the review? I answered that the request had been turned down and that had been decided, in view of the great public interest in the question, ahead of the general package. He was not satisfied. I quote Hansard:

> *Mr Heath:* Does the Prime Minister's last statement mean that this request for arms cannot again be considered under the overseas policy reviews? May we be clear about that?
> *The Prime Minister:* Yes, Sir. That is exactly what it means.

That was the end of the December 1967 South Africa story. It was the first and the last time in our near six years of office that I had to fight rough with any of my colleagues – and I had done it by forbidding a counter-attack against tendentious press briefing.

Two personal interventions I made during that month concerned the Munich air-crash, and the denouement of the 'who-sits-where' rail dispute.

Despite all the inevitable preoccupation with devaluation and its aftermath, including South Africa, I had continued my series of visits to industrial areas and projects. But one visit, on 2nd December, was different. I had been invited by Manchester United Football Club to attend their celebrations for Matt Busby's knighthood. In the afternoon we went to Old Trafford to see United play West Bromwich and in the evening there was a reception. I was called upon to speak and, recalling Sir Matt's great contributions to the game, inevitably found myself referring to the tragic air crash at Munich in 1958. A thought occurred to me, and for a moment, as so often occurs, warning lights flashed: I decided to ignore them and expressed a view I had always held, namely, that Captain Thain, the captain of the BEA aircraft, had been subjected to a raw deal. This was inevitably headlined, and I expected on my return to London to be greeted by a sorrowing Board of Trade minister. On the contrary, Bill Mallalieu welcomed what I had said. He had been working on the possibility of a fresh inquiry, and had met a great deal of bureaucratic objection, including an unwillingness to offend the Germans who had carried out the original investigation. But the results of new research had been published and appeared to give support to the defence advanced by the captain. After my remarks it was impossible for anyone to frustrate the setting up of a new inquiry. It was duly held and, in clearing Captain Thain, removed a long-standing injustice, but many, many years late.

The other event, with wider consequences, was my third personal intervention in a dangerous strike situation.

Just before 11.30 on the night of 5th December I was telephoned by George Woodcock, asking me to receive members of the TUC General Council, together with the executive council of the Associated Society of Locomotive Engineers and Firemen.

The danger of a national rail strike precipitated by the NUR had ended on 21st October when their executive voted to accept British Rail's terms on the allocation of the firemen's duties. But in that agreement there had been no attempt to involve ASLEF, whose members were also concerned. There was the problem of where the guards should sit in the new diesel trains. As British Rail, under the agreement, began to remove brake vans from freight trains the drivers got tough and took their opposition to the point where a damaging go-slow was spreading and it seemed that it would be impossible to avert an almost total national strike. (About one-fifth of the drivers were NUR men, and had they remained at work, skeleton services would have been possible, as in the ASLEF strike in 1955.)

There was something almost ludicrous in the 'who sits where?' dispute, but the danger of a major stoppage was there. The TUC tried to conciliate and by late evening on 5th December George Woodcock felt that the ASLEF executive might be persuaded to call the strike off if he could invoke my authority to tell them that the matter was settled and that there could be no question of asking British Rail to change its policy. He wanted them to know that if there were a prolonged strike it could end only in defeat.

I telephoned Ray Gunter, who had retired to bed; we agreed to accept George Woodcock's advice and he dressed and came round to No. 10. We sent for Mr Len Neal, British Rail's industrial relations chief, lest his advice, or confirmation of what I proposed to say, were needed.

The meeting lasted from 11.30 until 2.00 a.m. I stood firm by the attitude the Government, British Rail and the TUC had taken up and made clear that there was no 'give'. But ASLEF were somewhat mollified by the TUC's expression that the railway authorities had accorded them 'shabby and scurvy treatment', through not bringing them into discussions about the brake vans.

'This has been,' said Mr Woodcock to the press, 'a classic example of how not to conduct industrial relations.'

I proposed – on lines not dissimilar to the formula which had averted the threatened NUR strike in February 1966 – that the omission to consult should be made good by fresh talks between the NUR, ASLEF and British Rail, under the chairmanship of the Minister of Labour. Parity of esteem in the right to consultations having been established, I asked ASLEF to go off and meet in private (in a room in the Cabinet Office adjoining No. 10) and to accept BR's terms, which included the removal of the brake vans and the right of NUR's guards to sit in the rear cab of the locomotive.

After a long discussion, they returned with a decision to accept. There had been no beer, no sandwiches, no sell-out, no concessions. But damaging industrial action had been averted, thanks mainly to the TUC.

Parliament adjourned on 21st December and I was preparing for the usual mad rush to clear my desk, before going for Christmas to Chequers and then to Scilly. But by the time Mr Speaker put the question, I was on the way to Australia.

The previous Sunday, 17th December, I had been wakened with the news that Harold Holt, the Australian Prime Minister, had not returned from a swim in very rough water. He was given up as lost and the Australian Government arranged a memorial service in Melbourne Cathedral. HRH the Prince of Wales offered to go to represent the Queen, Mr Heath agreed to go, and the three of us flew there, via Bahrein and Gan, in a VC 10 of Air Support Command in just over twenty-four hours. We arrived at 10.00 p.m. British time on the Thursday (8.00 a.m. Melbourne time on the Friday), and the RAF's timing, as ever, was so superb that, as had been arranged, ITN's ten o'clock news began with the doors opening and the Prince emerging. It was the beginning of a tiring day, with first the memorial service and then an unending series of meetings with other international mourners.

President Johnson had flown to Australia, a much-appreciated gesture to a Vietnam ally. Less appreciated was the almost total take-over of Melbourne by the US security services. There were, I was told, seven Boeing 707s or C 130s flown in with battle-wagons and security equipment. The convoy which accompanied the President everywhere had forty vehicles, to the annoyance first, and then the ribald amusement, of the Melbourne crowd. In the cathedral there were allegedly a hundred US security men. The British contingent, which included the heir to the throne (of Australia and Britain), the Leader of the Opposition and the Prime Minister, had three. One of these had a sense of humour. He was spotted in the front pew by an American security man, who asked him if he was of that same profession. On being told that he was, he asked how many of his ilk were in the cathedral to guard the British contingent. The American, on being told there were just three, was incredulous. The Prince's detective added that that was, of course, exclusive of the forty others who were at State House, operating the radar. He was pressed, but refused to give details; no doubt the American secret service subsequently spent months evaluating the use of radar in VIP protection.

After the memorial service I had a series of seven or eight meetings with heads of government from different parts of the world, mainly Commonwealth colleagues, but also, in Government House, in a room set aside for us immediately after the service, with President Johnson.

He was principally concerned with the problems of getting North Vietnam to the conference table. He had gone a very long way – much farther than, in the end, he had been prepared to go when Mr Kosygin and I had been negotiating in February. In addition to a long private message to Hanoi, of which he gave me details, he had outlined in his San Antonio speech in September a single formula in which he was prepared to stop the bombing in return for 'prompt and meaningful talks'. He was anxious that in my visit to Moscow early in the New Year I should sound out the Russians on their view of the San Antonio formula.

On the Saturday morning, I had breakfast with the Australian Leader of the Labour Opposition, Mr Gough Whitlam, and then – on the initiative of our High Commissioner, Sir Charles Johnston – met members of the Australian Cabinet. They had been selected to ensure that all possible candidates for premiership were there, in addition to the acting Prime Minister (and almost permanent deputy Prime Minister) 'Black Jack' McEwen, leader of the County party. The High Commissioner directed me to pay careful attention to Senator John Gorton, who, he thought, would be the successful candidate. He was right.

We flew to Perth, where we had to refuel before crossing the Indian Ocean. Time had been provided for the Prince to make an official tour of Perth: this gave me time to meet my thirty relatives there – my mother's sister and her family and other cousins. I had tea in Perth, on Saturday, 23rd December, and Christmas Eve breakfast at Chequers.

After Christmas at Chequers and New Year in the Scillies I returned to London for the most difficult post-devaluation decision, the expenditure review and the decisions on the wider range of economic policy.

Before Christmas, the Chancellor and I had sketched out the outline of the review. It was clear that major reductions would be required in defence and overseas expenditure and in the planned growth of social expenditure. Some very difficult decisions would have to be taken. There was no guarantee that we could get a package of the required scale, with the necessary political balance, even through Cabinet, let alone through the Parliamentary Party.

Cabinet met on 4th January 1968 to consider the Chancellor's proposals. The cuts proposed were sweeping. Those which held out the prospect of greatest difficulty involved the cancellation of the orders for the American F 111A; a speedier withdrawal from south-east Asia and an immediate withdrawal from the Persian Gulf; the restoration of prescription charges; and the postponement of the raising of the school-leaving age. It was a major exercise in restraining the growth of public expenditure. The task of getting it through Cabinet without sensational resignations was the most formidable task I had attempted in over three years of government. My greatest asset was the firmness and determination of the Chancellor in the presentation of his balanced package.

We both knew that there would be the strongest resistance to the defence components of the proposals. The political implications of the restoration of prescription charges and the deferment of the raising of the school-leaving age, plus the cuts in publicly-financed housing and in roads were obvious. While the opposition of defence and overseas ministers to the proposals about south-east Asia and the Persian Gulf were predictable, the commitment of individual ministers on particular items among the domestic proposals provided one of our greatest difficulties.

An expenditure review can take one of two broad courses. There can be a 'ganging-up' of ministers of widely varying spending departments against the Chancellor, even against the very need for cuts. There is always the danger of an implicit deal: 'You support me against the Chancellor on cuts in my programme, and I will support you in defending yours.' The other possibility is that one or two ministers, having accepted cuts in their own expenditure, join the Chancellor in demanding that other ministers are similarly co-operative.

In all our expenditure reviews, before and after the January 1968 operation, Denis Healey was the anchor man. His own grip on defence spending was such that when he responded to the Chancellor's requests he operated as an enthusiast in demanding similar sacrifices by other ministers whose control over their departments, he could argue, was less effective. Since, year by year, defence expenditure was on a downward trend, while domestic spending was moving sharply upwards, he was in a strong position to demand a similar degree of restraint from his domestic colleagues.

This time he was in a more difficult position: he had already accepted a reduction of around £100 millions in his budget in the November package. Moreover, he was heavily committed to the F 111A, since the American contract had been undertaken as a means of saving large sums on costly British alternatives. He had also been involved in intricate overseas negotiations on such issues as south-east Asia and the Persian Gulf, where already he had made major concessions on forward spending plans in previous spending reviews. And he could call on Foreign and Commonwealth Office support. Nor was that unalloyed in fighting for overseas interests against domestic restraint; George Brown was passionate in his defence of previous decisions about the school-leaving age.

There was a further, more general difficulty. The shock to morale, and to Cabinet cohesion, of devaluation, and the aftermath of the South African arms affair led to some weakening of Cabinet solidarity in the matter of unauthorised disclosures. After each meeting, press stories appeared, even with some degree of accuracy on how the Cabinet had divided. As so often when leaks were involved, my suspicion was not so much that individual ministers had proved incontinent in their press contacts, as that there had been too much free discussion with junior ministers, or even PPS's, thus widening the area of knowledge beyond those who, in the familiar security phrase, 'needed to know'. Such a review is even more difficult when Parliament is sitting. Conversations in the Commons tea-room or smoke-room are uninhibited, and members of the press are within yards. At least we did not have this problem, but our discussions were anything but secure. It is a problem all Governments have to face and I did not observe any change in what we had to deal with compared with the Governments that preceded and succeeded us.

Cabinets do not proceed by the counting of heads. I had been trained by Attlee. He was usually able to sum up, as I was, by saying that the Cabinet view was thus and thus, and it was rarely challenged. Both he and I frequently ended a discussion by saying that there was no clear decision, but that one judged that if this or that particular point were dropped the Cabinet might well be disposed to agree on the following proposition, namely XYZ.... He in the forties and I in the sixties were rarely disappointed. A Prime Minister's power, when it comes to summing up a Cabinet discussion, is enormous, provided that the chair remains sufficiently detached and uncommitted and provided above all that he is free of the charge that one of the contending ministers is a court favourite. Attlee's practice, and mine, was never to count heads except on minor questions which were so unimportant that a full discussion would clearly be a waste of Cabinet time.

But in this review so much was at stake, and views were so evenly divided, that any attempt to express a consensus or, indeed, a majority view, would have been challenged. It was the only time in six years that colleagues seemed to be keeping their own tally of the 'voices'. And such were the strains that I was reading day by day in the press that the 'vote' was eleven to ten, or twelve to nine on this or that particular proposal. As I said, every Government goes through such a period; we did not have to face it again.

After the first two meetings, the general attitude was becoming clear, though we had agreed that individual decisions must be reconfirmed at a final round-up. Moreover, the overseas decisions required consultations. Senior ministers were despatched to the Gulf, to south-east Asia and to the United States, and instructed to report before final decisions were taken.

By the end of the first week, two long Cabinet meetings had identified the main points of contention. On the Monday, 8th January and part of Tuesday, 9th January, I carried out a long-scheduled industrial tour in Lancashire, meeting with the Economic Planning Board and Regional Economic Planning Council, with the Industrial Development Association, and visiting factories. On the Monday evening I met representatives of industry, unions and local authority leaders of a very anxious north-east Lancashire. I made a speech supporting the 'I back Britain' campaign, which had begun with a usefully publicised action by some girls who undertook to work unpaid overtime 'for Britain'. This was taken up by the press, a campaign organisation was formed, with posters, button badges, press advertising. Suddenly nearly everyone seemed to be carrying Union Jack shopping bags.

It was a helpful and robust response to the gloom and near-defeatism which might have been expected to follow devaluation. I related the campaign to the needs of the export drive and called on management to set up joint exports committees to help speed overseas shipments, and to gear themselves for getting new orders. Following the speech, we had a long cross-table discussion on the industrial problems of north-east Lancashire. At 9.20 p.m. a message came that it was snowing hard and the road to Liverpool might become impassable. A number of cars in our convoy did go off the road on the way back. Economic ministers accompanying me were puzzled when I said that I was glad the snow had held off until the evening. The point was that it was the second Monday of the month, the day of the unemployment count. January and February are normally the peak months for unemployment; no one wanted bad weather, with its effects on building and other outdoor work to exaggerate an already worrying basic unemployment total.

The next morning I was out at 8.00 a.m. visiting the Liverpool factory of Leyland Motors, where I discussed with a worried Donald Stokes disturbing developments in the projected merger of Leylands with BMH.

The Cabinet was called for 4.00 p.m. that day, 9th January. While I had been away the Chancellor had carried out a series of bilateral meetings with individual spending ministers. Because of snow and ice my train to London was ninety minutes late and the first part of the meeting, in which an uneasy agreement was reached on cut-backs in the still sharply rising roads programme, proceeded without me. A further meeting on the Thursday, 11th January and two on the Friday, the 12th, took us a long way along the road, and we agreed to meet on Monday, 15th January to take final decisions about the main contested items.

I was worried about the number of possible resignations when the package was completed and, still more, about the personalities who might be involved. There had been perfectly legitimate warnings by this or that minister that he must 'reserve his position'. By the Monday I would know. The House had been recalled for the Tuesday, 16th January, a week earlier than usual, and on that day we were to announce the results of the review.

At the Cabinet on Monday, a serious but not heated meeting, the whole package went through, though on some issues, especially in defence and Far-Eastern policy, ministers were almost equally divided. The school-leaving age and, to a lesser extent, prescription charges were also difficult. The package as a whole had an impressive integrity and balance; but I was under no illusions about the certain reaction of the Parliamentary Party and our movement in the country.

The only casualty was Lord Longford, who resigned over the question of the school-leaving age. I invited Eddie Shackleton to succeed him as Lord Privy Seal and Leader in the Lords. After lunch I put Douglas Houghton, as chairman of the PLP, into the picture, and made the announcement of our decision to the House after questions. As in 1966, I felt it right that in a major statement covering all the departments of state, covering, too, important issues of policy going far beyond finance, the Prime Minister should himself present it to the House of Commons and not shelter behind his Chancellor. This practice has been altered since the change of Government in 1970, starting with the mini-Budget of 27th October 1970.

The statement provided for reductions in the existing programmes amounting to £300 millions on the 1968–9 Estimates, and £416 millions in 1969–70. To these were added the revenue from an increase in the National Health stamp, yielding an additional £25 millions in each year, making the totals £325 millions in the first year and £441 millions in 1969–70.

I began with defence. I announced that the withdrawal of forces from stations in the Far East, due to take place, according to the earlier White Paper, by the mid-seventies, was to be completed by the end of 1971; our forces in the Persian Gulf would also be withdrawn by that date. This meant that, apart from our dependencies – and Hong Kong was the most significant here – and 'certain other necessary exceptions', we should not after 1971 be maintaining military bases outside Europe and the Mediterranean. Our forces in Malaysia and Singapore would be included in the withdrawal. Both had been told that we should retain a general capability based on Europe – including Britain – 'which can be deployed overseas as, in our judgment, circumstances demand, including support for United Nations operations'. The number of aircraft based in Cyprus was to be reduced.

The effect of these decisions in terms of manpower would be that the reductions proposed in the earlier White Paper of seventy-five thousand uniformed men and women and eighty thousand civilians would be larger and achieved at an earlier date. The aircraft carrier force was to be phased out as soon as the withdrawal from Malaysia, Singapore and the Persian Gulf had been completed.

The order for fifty F 111A aircraft was to be cancelled, saving some £400 millions over the whole programme, after cancellation charges. The reductions in overseas commitments would make it possible to cut down our requirements for transport aircraft.

The financial results, besides the £110 millions saving in the 1969–70 Estimates announced in November, would mean a saving by 1972–3 of something between £210 millions and £260 millions, at constant prices.

On the civil expenditure side, I began with social security. Total expenditure in the year (1967–8), at £2,909 millions, was forty-eight per cent above 1963–4. It was to rise to £3,106 millions in 1968–9 and £3,126 millions (at constant prices) in 1969–70. There were no cuts. Indeed, our pledge to shelter the least well-off families against the effect of post-devaluation prices increases was to be honoured by a second increase in family allowances, and a further increase in the next reconsideration of supplementary benefits. We were increasing help under the rate rebate scheme for less well-off householders and tenants. I announced that to match the higher family allowances the Chancellor would recover the value of the increase from the better-off by corresponding reductions in child allowances under income tax – the so-called 'claw-back' principle which had been advocated by many concerned with child poverty. The Chancellor would also study the possibility at a later stage of extending 'claw-back' to the whole of the family allowance, not just the 7s increase.

On education, I announced the 'difficult, not to say repugnant' decision to defer from 1971 until 1973 the raising of the school-leaving age to sixteen. But while this would save £33 millions in 1968–9, and £48 millions in the following year, mainly in the related school-building programme, we would make additional resources available, to the extent of £8 millions in each year, for general school-building, partly to help with the progress of comprehensive reorganisation and partly to provide more funds for improving conditions in 'educational priority areas'. Free milk in secondary schools – this was another very emotive issue – was to stop, though in many schools the milk was not being taken up. Capitation grants to direct-grant schools were to be reduced, certain capital projects in higher education were to be held back, and the next increase in students' awards was to be restrained. In education as a whole, there would be a saving, compared with the previous planned increase, of £39 millions in the first year and £58 millions in the second.

In health and welfare, where expenditure was running at £1,619 millions – an increase of forty-five per cent over the figure of four years earlier – our problem was to continue our overriding priority for the record hospital-building programme. This would continue without cuts. But – in full knowledge of the reaction we should be provoking from Labour members and the movement in the country – we announced the reintroduction of the prescriptions charge, at 2s 6d per item, with exemption for those over sixty-five or under fifteen, expectant and nursing mothers, the chronic sick, those on Supplementary Benefit, others with a standard of living at or below Supplementary Benefit levels and war pensioners in respect of disabilities. These exemptions would reduce the £50 millions gross saving to £25 millions; the employees' contribution for the National Health Service was to be increased by 6d in addition to a further increase of 6d on both employers' and employees' contributions to prevent the National Insurance Fund from going into deficit. Dental treatment charges were raised from £1 to 30s. Children and young people under twenty-one, expectant and nursing mothers, and those on Supplementary Benefits remained exempt. A reduction of £5 millions a year in the rapidly rising and record local authority expenditure for the next three years was announced.

Civil defence was to be put on a care and maintenance basis, with a saving of £14 millions in 1968–9 and £20 millions in 1969–70 and succeeding years.

Public sector housing was to be reduced by cutting planned approvals of new houses by 16,500 in each of the two years, saving £27 millions in 1968–9 and £55 millions in 1969–70. I made it quite clear to Parliament that this meant going back on our election pledge on house-building, due to the overriding need in the new situation to swing £500 millions of real resources from home demand to exports.

The road programme, again at a record level of £560 millions – fifty-two per cent up on 1963–4 – would still continue to increase in cash and in real terms, but at a slower rate, saving £53 millions in 1968–9, and £69 millions in 1969–70. These savings would be divided between motorway and other major road projects and local authorities' expenditure on maintenance and improvement of local roads. Plans to assist local passenger transport, provided for in the Transport Bill, would be cut back, saving £10 millions in the first year, and £20 millions in 1969–70.

In expenditure on industry, special provision for the development areas would be maintained; indeed, it continued to grow at a prodigious rate in the next three years. But there were savings in nuclear research and development and in the defence research programme, including aviation. On investment grants – where the Board of Trade had been paying five quarters' worth of payments in a single year to reduce the delay between spending on investment and the receipt of the grant – there would be a cost saving by providing that in the year ahead only four quarters' payments would be made.

The rate of increase in central Government help to local authorities, which had risen by nearly a half over the previous four years, was now to be restricted to three per cent a year, in real terms, over the next three years.

Together with the financial reductions, there was to be a ceiling fixed on the manpower of Government departments. The number at 1st April 1969 was not to exceed the 1968 figure – at an estimated saving of £15 millions.

My statement led to two violent reactions, one entirely predictable, the other less so. That in the House of Commons – with Mr Heath attacking the withdrawal from our stations east of Suez and the run-down of civil defence; the reaction of the left on prescription charges; and the opposition of a wider section of the party to the decisions about the school-leaving age and school milk – was no more violent, and no less, than we had expected.

But what was extraordinary was the reaction of the City of London. When I had foreshadowed the statement in December, I had made it clear that we should be dealing with public expenditure only, the necessary restrictions in private expenditure being the responsibility of the Chancellor of the Exchequer in the Budget and in other ways. All press comment during the succession of Cabinet meetings was related purely to expenditure cuts, and in presenting the programme to the House I made the point five separate times that I was dealing with public expenditure only, and that further action would be taken by the Chancellor to restrain private expenditure. Yet within minutes the City was in a state of confusion and, apparently, anger. This could have been caused by the way in which the news came over the tape, as I saw on the Downing Street machine. There was a series of 'flash' announcements of the measures, with no indication that they were only part of a wider package.

This decision to confine the announcement to public expenditure was deliberate. The Chancellor wanted to make sure that his Budget, which would inevitably mean increases in taxation, would be adequate to the situation. It was too soon after devaluation, with too many of the economic statistics available still relating to the pre-devaluation period, for the Treasury to give him any authoritative estimate of the scale of disinflation he should aim at in the Budget and in other ways. To have introduced an instant January Budget, followed by further measures in April, would have been the worst of all worlds. But however strong the argument, relations between City and Government fell to an all-time and bitter low, with consequential damage to sterling.

The debate on my statement took place over the next two days, 17th and 18th January. It ended, on the Thursday evening, with a vote on the Conservative no-confidence amendment accusing the Government of mismanagement and attacking the defence cuts. Their attack was defeated by 334 votes to 229. When the main motion approving my statement was put, Conservatives abstained and the Liberals alone went into the lobby against us. We won by 304 to nine, but the chief interest lay in the 26 Labour back-benchers who abstained. Two right-wingers carried out the threat of the previous March and abstained to show the impotence of the Whips in dealing with a revolt on the left. Desmond Donnelly went further and resigned the Whip.

The reaction to these abstentions was swift. There were immediate demands from a wide section of the party for disciplinary action to be taken by the Whips against the abstainers. The vote had been on a major issue of policy, the subject of an uncompromising vote of no confidence from the official Opposition.

When I went to my constituency to open a factory, on the Friday morning, 19th January, I had reason to think that the Chief Whip, John Silkin, whose patience was over-strained by what he felt to be an abuse of his liberal attitudes, would move selectively to withdraw the Whip, for a specified period, or *sine die*, from a number of back-benchers, probably those with the worst record of abstentions, particularly those who had voted against the Government on major debates. The correct procedure was for him to report his recommendations to the elected, backbench liaison committee of the party, though his problem was complicated by the fact that one of its leading members, and a vice-chairman of the Parliamentary Party, was an abstainer and had indeed proclaimed on television his disagreement with the Government.

In the event, John Silkin decided on a course of action which was not only unwise but unconstitutional. He had discussed it, so he told me, when I phoned him later, with the Leader of the House, who gave his approval; Dick Crossman subsequently denied this. Without waiting to consult me or the liaison committee, the Chief wrote to all the defaulters telling them that they had 'endangered the existence' of the Government and would be suspended from all party activities, including attendance at party meetings or specialist groups. There was no provision under the rules of the party for any such action; indeed, there were doubts whether the authorities of the House might not rule against an attempt to deny an MP access to a committee-room.

On the Sunday morning, 21st January, when his letter became news, my telephone hardly stopped ringing. I got in touch with Douglas Houghton, the PLP chairman, who was particularly outraged. He had not been consulted, and told me that he must resist the proposal in the liaison committee and in the party meeting. As I had to leave for Moscow on the Monday morning, I decided to take firm action. I did not intend to leave the party in a shambles while I was away. Accordingly I called a meeting at No. 10 of George Brown, Dick Crossman, Douglas Houghton and the Chief Whip, for the Sunday evening.

I began it by indicating that the proposal could not possibly be allowed to go through. The liaison committee was already discussing a code of conduct for Labour members, including disciplinary procedures for defaulters; a text had been agreed for circulation to the party for consideration and early debate. Moreover, the liaison committee had already authorised the Chief Whip, if an emergency arose, to act 'within the spirit' of the code.

At my suggestion we agreed to announce, first that I would address the party meeting the following Thursday; secondly, that the proposed code of conduct would be circulated to the party and that, meanwhile, the Chief was authorised to act within its terms; thirdly, that he would formulate new proposals to put to the liaison committee to deal with the situation which had arisen; and, fourthly, that his new proposals would replace the letter which had been sent to the recalcitrants.

This was reported in Monday morning's press, and immediately stabilised the situation. When, on my return from Moscow, I addressed the PLP the crisis was as though it had never been and the press took almost no interest in the firm words I addressed to the meeting.

Chapter 25

THE Moscow visit was tough going. Outside, the weather was colder than in any of my previous sixteen visits to the Soviet Union. At one point it was 57 degrees (F) of frost, the lowest since 1941, and at the welcome at Vnukovo Airport Mr Kosygin showed genuine concern when he saw that I had left my old fur hat in the aircraft – he immediately seized one from a security guard while mine was sent for.

Mr Kosygin and I had a long private talk in the early evening, followed by dinner together. We were concerned almost exclusively with Vietnam. The next morning, after laying a wreath, in bitter cold, at the tomb of the Unknown Soldier in the Kremlin wall, I called on Mr Brezhnev. Our talk went on far beyond its scheduled time, with Mr Brezhnev doing most of the talking, partly on Vietnam, and still more on Germany. This made us late for the Kremlin lunch where Mr Kosygin, Mr Brezhnev and I, sitting together, argued vehemently for over an hour about Gerald Brooke. As on previous occasions, they kept coming back to the Krogers. I thought I had made some impression and their undertaking to reconsider the matter in the light of what I had said raised my hopes a little. But I was wrong.

My speech after lunch was mainly about Vietnam. Mr Kosygin had delivered a carefully prepared, hard-line speech on Vietnam, later given to the press. I replied off-the-cuff, and shorthand notes of what I said were also given out later. He had said that history would judge us by what we did at this hour.

I took this up: '... because your Government and ours are agreed to bring this violence to an end, to avert dangers of escalation and to end this poisoning of world relations'. I continued:

...I believe that the differences in this tremendously difficult problem have been narrowed and that we can both help to build what is now the much shorter bridge necessary to bring peace.
...Our task is to help narrow the differences and to avoid encouraging the hawks, whether they be in Hanoi or Washington.

As to the hawks, I said that I agreed with a fellow Commonwealth Prime Minister, Mr Gorton, who had said that he was neither a hawk nor a dove but an owl.

We kept the substance of our talks very secret, and this continued up to and after my later visit to Washington. But Mr Kosygin was hopeful that the New Year's Day statement by Nguyen Duy Trinh, the North Vietnam Foreign Minister, might, given an adequate response by Washington, lead to a step forward. He said that just as in London the previous year his starting-point had been the article by the Australian journalist, Mr Burchett, now it was the 'Trinh declaration' which set the stage. This 'declaration' was to the effect that if the US stopped the bombing there would be a speedy response by the DRV in terms of a recourse to the conference-table.

Both of us knew, too, that the White House had initiated new 'palm-tree' talks through a so far unnamed intermediary. It was not until later in the day that I learnt what the Soviet Government thought of him.

We had further talks in the afternoon, and in the evening I was entertained at the Kremlin Theatre at a performance by the Bolshoi Opera Company of *Carmen*. The national anthems were played and we were given a warm reception by the audience.

As on the previous occasion two years earlier, Mr Kosygin took the opportunity of our interval retirement to the private dining-room to begin a very confidential talk about Vietnam. We had not got very far when the signal went for Act II to begin. At various points there were loud 'shushes' from the audience, who looked up, saw who they were shushing and decided to concentrate on the opera.

After giving me his own figure of the destruction of American bombers – attributing more of these to conventional anti-aircraft guns and less to Migs and missiles than I would have expected – he plunged into the political situation. He could not, he said, understand us. What had I possibly meant by saying to him that contacts were going on? There was too much self-delusion in this matter. I referred to what in the previous year we had agreed to refer to as 'talks under a palm-tree'. He said: 'If the Americans have told you that there are significant talks going on now, under a palm-tree or anywhere else, they are lying.'

I asked whether, in saying this, he was in touch with Hanoi and relying on their judgment. He replied that everything Hanoi had told him suggested that there was nothing to justify what I had told him about contacts.

He asked me what President Johnson's aims were. Did he really want a settlement or was it not true that he was simply playing election politics? I said that I felt I knew the President as well as I knew most people and I was absolutely convinced he was sincere in wanting a settlement. It was true that many people in America were taking a hard line, including very many of his electorate, and I felt, therefore, that it required great courage to be going for a settlement which could be misused by anyone to the right of him, as most of them were. Mr Kosygin said – I calculated that it was for the ninth time that week – that he could not understand this, since everyone he met in America wanted peace and denounced Johnson. I had politely not reacted the first eight times; now I told him that people who said that were the sort of people he would be likely to meet. Again, I repeated that among the urban proletariat and the farmers – the repositories in Soviet terms of the higher political wisdom – a very high proportion, certainly a majority in many states, took a line far to the right of the President. Mr Kosygin misread American political opinions if he thought it was easy for the President to take great risks in going for peace at this time, but that, I was convinced, was what he was doing.

After we had stopped to applaud the 'Toreador Song' he shifted his ground and said he thought that the President would win the election if he got peace in Vietnam. Did he want it? I said I thought he would take the same line this year as in any other year, given the circumstances facing him.

He then came back to the contacts. Nothing significant was going on, he insisted. People might think there was. Washington might think so, but from what he knew – and he emphasised 'knew' – this was not so. I said – 'Well, you have your contacts in Hanoi.' 'Ah,' he said, 'these are direct, not based on palm-trees or unsatisfactory intermediaries.'

It became clear that he was not merely cynical but downright furious about the choice of the intermediary. He said that 'all this suggests to us and to *our*' – he seemed to emphasise the word 'our', which may or may not have had significance – 'friends in Hanoi that the Americans are not sincere in a bid for peace'.

I said that his words were disturbing. I was sure that the US were misleading neither themselves nor us. But I pressed him again and asked him to repeat them, to make sure that there had been no misunderstanding through possible errors in translation. He repeated that 'if the Americans were sincere in their contacts – and I do not deny there are probings – they would not proceed in this way'. He had no confidence in them.

He then made his significant statement. 'What we would like to know is whether the Americans really mean business in following up the Trinh declaration. If they do, they could either approach us direct and give us a formulation to pass on to Hanoi, or they could give it to you to give to us to pass to Hanoi. When are you going to Washington?'

This was February 1967 revisited. He was very pressing. I said that I was going in two weeks' time and then I returned to the 'probings'. Again, he was at pains to let me know that the Kremlin were in close touch with Hanoi, in better touch than the Americans. I put it to him: was he saying that what might be happening was true; that the Americans were closely in touch with someone who claimed to be in touch with significant people in Hanoi, but that his own direct contacts in Hanoi discounted the American link as being in any sense meaningful?

That was exactly what he was trying to convey. He made it perfectly plain, and emphasised and re-emphasised it. His contacts with Hanoi were clear and definite; if there had been significant contacts he would have known. There were not.

My interpretation of all this, when I had time to reflect on it, was: that the Americans had contacts through an intermediary whom the Russians regarded as a man of straw or, worse, a choice provocative to them; that the Soviet Government had its own reason through its Hanoi contacts to believe that Hanoi did not take this contact seriously and that the choice of such a person caused Hanoi to doubt American sincerity; that the Soviet Government wanted the Americans to be clear about all this, and to realise that they should get on to a new channel, either direct through Moscow, or via London to Moscow. In either event, once Moscow was clear about the message it would be passed on to Hanoi and to people who counted there; Moscow regarded the 'Trinh declaration', as they called it, as of the first importance. If the US would just stop the bombing there would be a direct response in terms of a move to the negotiating table. This was what the Soviet Government wanted me to convey on my Washington visit – or before.

I concentrated, as far as my thoughts allowed me, on the last two acts of *Carmen*. But it will be a very long time before I can enjoy it again with totally unalloyed pleasure.

When I returned to the Embassy, I dictated a note of our conversation while it was fresh in my mind and asked that it should be sent to the Foreign Office for evaluation. At their discretion it should be passed to the White House. This they did and without editing. When I heard this I wondered how the President would react to my final paragraph, designed only for the British Foreign Office.

> The following questions arise: who is taking whom for a ride? Has Hanoi sold Moscow a bum steer? Is Kosygin trying to sell me one? Or is he for some reason trying to persuade me that the Americans have sold me one? If so why, and who will come unstuck on the evidence available?
> I have stated the facts as well as I remember them in a very colourful Second Act. I think I have put the right questions to the answers. Now I would like to hear from the professionals the answers to the questions.

A lot depended on the identity of the American contact. Incredibly, we did not know; the first thing I was going to raise in Washington was their failure to keep us informed.

A senior Foreign Office personality with me in Moscow hazarded a guess that the American contact was a Rumanian. If he was right, it would explain everything; the choice of a Rumanian behind the back of the Kremlin would be just about the cops-and-robbers level of activity one might expect of certain elements in Washington.

A fortnight later, after remonstrating with the President, I learnt that my FO adviser was right; it was one of Rumania's deputy Foreign Ministers, who, by Soviet standards, was of a somewhat politically off-beat disposition. Rumania was not the most-favoured member of the Soviet bloc. By this time the White House was more disposed to take notice of Moscow's views and the Washington–London–Moscow link.

On the Wednesday morning, 24th January, I called on President Podgorny and then met Mr Kosygin at noon to agree the communiqué. This was expected to be a brief meeting – we were all due at the British Embassy for a lunch I was giving at 1.00 p.m. – but all the argument was about Vietnam and even by 3.00 p.m. we were no nearer an agreement. They wanted a communiqué involving support of Nguyen Duy Trinh's statement and a condemnation of the US position. In the end, we broke up without agreement and left for the Embassy in the hope that we might reach an agreed formula over lunch. The Soviet delegation had a further meeting and arrived very late, but with a form of words we were able to accept.

Mr Mikoyan, my old sparring-partner and friend of the 1947 trade talks, now in honourable retirement, was waiting for us. He rebuked Mr Kosygin and me for our inability to agree by a reasonable hour and said that negotiations were not as well conducted as in the days when he had reached agreement with me on the Anglo-Soviet trade agreement. I pointed out that that agreement had been reached at 6.00 a.m. after a seventeen-hour session and that by contrast Mr Kosygin and I had been an example of speedy negotiation. After a press conference, and the usual good-natured baiting of and by the top Soviet newspaper commentators Mateyev and Mayevski, we left for London in the early evening.

Our talks had produced an interesting situation, though nothing could be said in public. The best comment on our meeting was in the *Guardian* report from Moscow:

> Nothing in the official communiqué (whose drafting yesterday afternoon held up Mr Wilson's departure) or in Mr Wilson's press conference in Moscow gave any sign that anything approaching a breakthrough had been achieved.
> But all the signs are that Mr Wilson has popped some ferret into the Soviet rabbit hole in the hope that something will come out in Hanoi. Not even Mr Wilson can be sure that there is anything in the hole to come out. We can only wait and see....

Things were quieter on my return to London, though substantial sections of the press were again engaged on a 'Wilson-must-go' campaign. It was not a view supported in the PLP or in the public-opinion polls, though it had the enthusiastic backing of Lord Shawcross. In no time at all, the other members of the trinity, Lord Robens and Mr Cecil King, were joining in with demands for a coalition of all the talents – Great Britain Limited – though there were some signs that its leading proponents might

R

not agree on whom the Queen would be advised to send for as Prime Talent.

In one way, the Government's February burdens were lighter than usual. There was no problem of deciding on the expenditure Estimates for they had been settled in the January statement. The same was true of the Defence White Paper, where again the basic decisions had been taken in the expenditure review. The third February annual, the Farm Price Review, also went through with far less difficulty than usual. The preparation of the post-devaluation Budget, however, on which Roy Jenkins was consulting me almost daily, was another proposition.

There were other problems. The country was shocked at this time by the loss with all hands of three fishing trawlers in gales, two of them in the dangerous waters off Iceland. There was an understandable outcry from the unions concerned about safety at sea. In addition to receiving delegations from the fishermen and MPs from the fishing ports, I took a number of ministerial meetings and instructions were given for a 'mother' ship from the Royal Navy to be at hand in dangerous waters. An inquiry was set up under the chairmanship of Admiral Sir Deric Holland-Martin; an inquiry remarkable for the speed with which he won the confidence of the industry, and especially the unions, together with the naturally militant wives in the fishing-ports, and also for the constructive attitude of the trade unions, whose evidence was led by Jack Jones. The Holland-Martin Report, produced with commendable speed and thoroughness, led later to legislation, introduced together with the new legislation to modernise the Merchant Shipping Act, on which Government and the shipping industry had worked incessantly following our pledge after the ending of the seamen's strike.

Another problem was the worst foot-and-mouth outbreak Britain had ever experienced, starting in Cheshire and Shropshire and rapidly spreading down through the Welsh marches to the west country, north into the northern counties, south-east through the midlands. The Northumberland Committee appointed by the Minister of Agriculture later reported that this was due to infected bone, imported from South America, which was sold by a butcher to a farmer for his dogs. There was mass slaughter of cattle on an unprecedented scale and, when the outbreak after several months had been stamped out, a Government compensation scheme to assist farmers who had lost all their herds to re-establish themselves in production.

During this period a number of newspapers were keeping a weekly tally of price increases, in one case, as I have said, with a regular quotation from my 'pound in the pocket' statement, not scrupling to alter the wording in order to suggest that I had undertaken that there would be no price increases following devaluation. Unfortunately for the papers concerned, the figures for a surprisingly long period – surprising to me, among others

– showed very little movement except for a seasonal increase in celery and, later, other seasonal foods; the biggest single increase was for beef prices, as a direct result of the foot-and-mouth outbreak. In fact, by far the largest increase in the cost of living came in April 1968, as a result of necessary taxation changes in the Chancellor's Budget, part of his measures to reduce domestic consumption and divert resources into export.

On 7th February I flew to Andrews Air Force Base, Washington, for my talks with the President. Public comment voiced the lowest expectations of our meeting, partly because of what so much of the press were pleased to deem the devaluation of the Government, partly because any hopes of progress on Vietnam had been damped by the vicious Vietcong offensive during the Tet period (a marked contrast to the situation and hopes of 1967). This had penetrated Saigon and, at one incredible moment, South Vietnamese forces were shelling their own capital. US forces had suffered a humiliating reverse not only in the firing on the American Embassy in Saigon, but in the surrounding of US forces in their strong-point at Khe Sanh, where a total surrender was daily headlined as imminent.

Just as I left, ninety Labour MPs addressed a memorial to me advocating a break in our support of US policy. Mr Heath – without, so the faithful *Times* reported, even consulting his shadow cabinet – gave orders that a motion be tabled calling on me to express full support for the US Vietnam policy. His aim was, of course, to needle our own left. His manoeuvre was described in one London newspaper as 'a shabby piece of party gamesmanship'. In so indulging, he miscalculated the mood. A more general opinion in the press, including papers not normally hostile to the US, urged upon me a certain detachment and wanted a magisterial pronouncement in favour of a change of direction in US policy. If American determination had established that there could be no military settlement imposed by the Vietcong and the DRV, equally the virulence of the Tet offensive showed that any US hope of a military solution was equally ill-founded.

After the usual Embassy briefing, I retired to bed early by Washington time. I awoke early, too, with an idea. There were no plans for any public statements during my visit; I was in what the Americans would have called a 'low-horizon' situation. But at the White House dinner that evening a speech would be required. I felt that the usual routine words expected of a British visitor – with copious references to Magna Carta, our common heritage and our close relationship in two world wars – would appear banal. I decided to be serious, whatever the White House banquet precedents, and to make a definitive statement on Vietnam. By the time my advisers were up and about I had roughed out a manuscript draft of a speech.

In the talks with the President that morning, 8th February, I was concerned to make two points. The first was my strong criticism about the position in which I had been placed in Moscow over the intermediary in the latest 'palm-tree' talks. The second was to urge upon the President the facts of life as I had discovered them in Moscow, reflecting, I was certain, the current position in Hanoi.

Before we left the Embassy, we were faced with a crisis in the protocol field. After the White House dinner, there was to be a musical soirée in the East Room, with stars from the Metropolitan Opera House, New York. A distinguished baritone was due to sing 'The Road to Mandalay' – words by Kipling – including the first formulation of the phrase 'east of Suez'. Since our defence review involving withdrawal from our east of Suez bases was much publicised as a likely bone of contention in the President–Prime Minister talks, Washington protocol chiefs had intervened to propose a variation in the repertoire, and Mrs Johnson had agreed to their recommendations. This was a leading story in the Washington press. I caused a message to be sent to the White House indicating that this was not only a favourite song of mine, but that I could not see any difficulty arising: we had evacuated Mandalay more than twenty years earlier; Burma, in fact, whatever the State Department protocol experts might suggest, had been an independent state, and a member of the United Nations, for the whole of that period. Mrs Johnson duly responded to my plea and, in the event, Mr Robert Merrill rendered 'Mandalay' in a manner which would have pleased even Peter Dawson. I am glad to feel that Mrs Johnson's memoirs confirm my own recollection of this incident, which some contemporary commentators felt might fatally prejudice Anglo-American relations for all the generations to come.

I found the President extremely troubled. Even as we went up from the reception to the Oval Room, he began to talk of Vietnam and North Korea. Two weeks earlier, while I was in Moscow, the USS *Pueblo* had been seized by the Koreans, and I had been asked in an urgent personal message from the President to raise the matter with the Russians and to seek their help. I had done so. The President was very critical of Moscow and doubted whether their writ ran at all in Hanoi. 'Whatever they may want to do they have no power to deliver,' was his judgment. He even seemed undecided whether the Soviet Government were or were not behind or, at any rate, cognisant of, what he regarded as the carefully planned and simultaneous crises in Korea and Vietnam. In Vietnam, the Tet offensive was at its height. Further attacks on South Vietnamese cities were expected. He felt that the motive for the Vietcong offensive was partly to humiliate the US, together with the creation of pressure aimed at a popular uprising. It was also, he thought, designed to draw off to the cities US and South Vietnamese troops and leave the countryside wide open.

He was at pains to defend General Westmoreland, against whom a great attack had been mounted in Congress and the press. At this point he changed the subject to the forthcoming New Hampshire primary; he had received an advance copy of a public-opinion poll, which showed that eighty-four per cent were highly favourable to the General, indeed ninety-six per cent if the undecided were eliminated. Examination of the other poll findings took a good fifteen minutes.

Then we were back to Vietnam. He was still bitter about the Russians. Surely they could influence the North Vietnamese towards a settlement if they wanted to, with all the DRV's dependence on Soviet equipment; if he supplied equipment any time on that scale he would certainly get greater compliance with US policies, he said. I made a mental note that he was not always a hundred per cent successful in South Vietnam. He was finding it difficult to rebut the charge of some of his people that the Russians were causing the maximum trouble in the Middle East and at least conniving at, if not being actually involved in, the recent escalation in Vietnam and Korea. There were those who believed that the Soviets had a powerful interest in keeping the Vietnam struggle going because it led to economic strain in the US, because it created divisions within the US and in the alliance, tied up a large army, and enabled Moscow to exert some influence in Hanoi instead of being left to fight it out with the Chinese in that part of Asia. I told him how fundamentally I disagreed with this analysis and gave him my reasons. They seemed to impress him, and I felt he was looking for arguments rather than stating a case.

I then told him something of our discussion with the Russians about his San Antonio speech, and the relevance thereto of the Trinh declaration. He in turn gave me the facts about San Antonio in even fuller detail than in the account he had given me in Melbourne.

On 25th August a full message had been sent to Hanoi, which he knew had got through. He took it out from his pocket and read it to me. It had gone a great deal further than the San Antonio speech, and spelt out more of what was described there as 'prompt and productive talks' than in the briefing I had had from William Bundy before my Moscow visit.

It had specifically said that the US would be prepared to discuss Phan Vam Dong's four points, in addition to any proposals the Americans themselves would wish to put forward. While it mentioned that military advantage should not be taken by the DRV of the proposed lull in the bombing – it was much less rigorous than the terms on which Washington had wrecked the talks the previous February – it was much more concerned to insist that no action should be taken to make the talks 'impossible'. For example, he said, metaphorically, 'bombing the hut where they were taking place', or intensifying the attacks on that or other areas. It was very fully spelt out, in the document he read to me, that he was concerned not so much in making it a condition that military advantage was not taken of US de-escalation, as in ensuring that there should be no charge of broken faith if the US were to respond to DRV escalation by breaking off the talks or even by resuming bombing.

He then told me that because of the Tet offensive the ban on the bombing of the centre of Hanoi and Haiphong had been ended. I expressed our deep concern. This led to the first exposition I had heard from him of the 'domino theory'. A thoroughly depressing morning.

Nor was he much more cheerful about the economic situation. He had announced tough economic measures, mainly concerned with limiting American capital outflow, which had hit us hard, but which we had accepted. He was counting on Congress accepting his proposals for his tax increases to counter inflation. He was cutting expenditure. If I had ever thought that the President could not turn to economic issues with the same facility with which he approached political and international questions, I would have been thoroughly disabused by his mastery of the budgetary problem. I got the impression that he had lived night and day with his new Director of the Bureau of the Budget. Every figure, every component of the expenditure figures he had at his finger-tips and I felt that he had a firm grip on the problem.

He then expressed concern about our own problem following devaluation. He had been given a brief, which he sent for. Two and a half pages of quarto, single spacing – which I regarded with great gravity. It was drafted in terms which would appeal to him – the pure Roosevelt approach to the dangers of another 1931. The first of the three factors mentioned was the fall in primary prices due to the US recession, with all this would mean for the developing countries – including, in political terms, the increased opening for the Chinese; second, the breakdown of the monetary system; and, third, protectionism. I told him how seriously we viewed the growth of protectionism in the US, and how much we counted on him to resist it. We had had many exchanges about it. On liquidity, we felt that there were dangers from gold speculation and we must keep close together; I reminded him that we had, year by year, sought US support for strong international measures, of which special drawing rights (SDRs) were only a small part of what was needed. For the rest, I did not agree with the analysis. But, I said, I felt that I could trace a feminine hand in its drafting, English at that. He roared with laughter. No one knowing Washington would underrate the importance nor fail to recognise the handiwork of Barbara Ward – Lady Jackson – a brilliant product of *The Economist*. Even if one felt this document was perhaps overdrawn, anyone visiting the White House from London could not fail to be reassured about the high regard in which she was held there. The worry was that there was no Barbara Ward warning him about conventional thinking in international politics and defence. It was time to break off the talks, as we were due to entertain the leading members of his Administration for lunch at the Embassy. In a flash we were invited upstairs, and not for the first time we saw what the White House Commissariat could do in producing twenty-five excellent instant steaks, while a similar number of meals at the Embassy were left to plague the Ambassadress.

In the evening there was the formal dinner at the White House. My travelling advisers and the Embassy staff went through the early-morning draft of my speech with a toothcomb. There was doubt about whether it would be acceptable at a festive occasion; still more doubt about my calculated attack on the hawks. I stuck to my draft, but with the festivity of the dinner, the 'singing strings' and the rest, I grew more doubtful about whether I was right to make such a speech.

President Johnson's speech was elegant, polished and as warm as ever. I rose to deliver mine, all festivity, after-dinner humour and Anglo-American banalities banished. To me, it was a serious occasion. For our hosts, there was the grim reality of the Tet offensive; for us, the danger, reinforced by the anxious words of the troubled President, that the US would lurch into policies from which there might be no easy return.

I plunged straight into the issue of Vietnam, and referred to the indescribable agony and horror of recent events there:

> ... But the sense of outrage this brings can beget dangerous counsels, impatient and exasperated demands to hit back, to escalate in ways which would widen, not end that war. The responsibility of power, Mr President, as you know, means not only loneliness in a democracy, it means facing demands for punitive action wherever national interests are outraged. The hardest part of statesmanship is to show restraint in the face of that exasperation, all those understandable demands for actions, which, however immediately satisfying, could have incalculable effects – effects indeed for the whole world. That is why your Administration's attitude following the *Pueblo* incident is one which will earn tributes from reasoning men everywhere, and indeed from history.
>
> Mr President, the problem of Vietnam, as you have always recognised, can never be settled on a durable and just basis by an imposed military solution.
>
> The events of these past days have underlined yet again that there can be no purely military solution to this problem, that there can be no solution before men meet round the conference table, determined to get peace.
>
> I am frequently urged, as the means to peace, to dissociate the British Government from American action, and in particular to call for the unconditional ending of all bombing.
>
> Mr President, I have said a hundred times in my own country, in Western Europe, in the Kremlin; if I felt that by so doing I could ensure that this war ended one day earlier, or would ensure that peace when achieved was one degree more durable, one degree more just, I would do what I am urged. I have not and I am going to say why.
>
> Over the past three years I have been in a position to know a good deal about the history of negotiations and consultations, contacts and discussions, aimed at getting away from the battleground and round the conference table.
>
> I recall our talks here in Washington at the time of the Baltimore

speech, now nearly three years ago. The Commonwealth Prime Ministers' conference over two and a half years ago when twenty Commonwealth heads of government from Asia and Africa, from the Mediterranean and Caribbean, Australia and Europe, and America, of widely differing views and loyalties over Vietnam called for a cessation of the bombing and in return a cessation of infiltration by the North Vietnamese army into South Vietnam. A hundred proposals to our fellow co-chairman to activate the Geneva conference, or any other forum to get the parties round the table. Washington, London, New York, Moscow – and innumerable less formal consultations through any and everyone who could help find the road to peace. These have failed – failed so far – to find a solution. But it does not mean we were wrong, all of us, to try, to go on trying.

I believe – and this is true even against the deafening background of all that is now happening on the battlefield – that the road to peace was fairly charted, not for the first time, but with greater and more meaningful clarity, at San Antonio last September.

A fortnight ago I was in the Kremlin and in many hours of discussion with the Soviet leaders I sought to spell out what San Antonio and subsequent elucidations of San Antonio meant. I believe the Soviet leaders now know, if they did not understand before, that what that formula means is that the US will stop the bombing, given an assurance that prompt and productive discussions will start, and that this action will not be exploited to create a new situation of military advantage, which would delay a political settlement.

It was our purpose in Moscow to show that once the surrounding misunderstandings have been removed this approach could be reconciled with the conditions laid down by Mr Trinh on 29th December; and this really answers his latest speech this week. There have been some – and not only in Moscow – who have believed that San Antonio meant the US were insisting in advance, as a precondition, on a given outcome to the talks as a condition of stopping the bombing. We believe that this reconciliation is possible once it is clear that all that is needed to start negotiations is assurance that the talks will begin promptly and that they will be meaningful and directed in good faith to a peaceful settlement.

The speech was very well received, particularly by President Johnson and Vice-President Hubert Humphrey. It had been made in the presence of some of the more articulate Senate hawks, and the warning against escalating the war was headlined on both sides of the Atlantic. 'Cage those hawks, L.B.J.! says Wilson' was one main headline in London.

After the concert, including 'Mandalay', we left for the Embassy. The President was particularly friendly – clearly the result of the speech – as we took our leave.

The following morning I tried to telephone him to say that I had secured the agreement of my colleagues to the immediate despatch of a medical relief team to Vietnam, for service in children's hospitals, together with other medical assistance. He was tied up in a meeting. When the message reached him he suggested that, if free, I should go round to see him for a further talk before I left for Canada.

He then said how successful the visit had been, particularly my speech.

Clearly he was more relaxed, and readier to talk in closer and more encouraging terms.

He told me that he had been 'locked in' with the Chiefs of Staff most of the morning, and he gave me a run-down on the latest intelligence reports. He said that it looked as though a further round of attacks would be started in the next twenty-four hours – he thought possibly that night – but he felt that the position would be held. Of all the cities and built-up areas attacked by the Vietcong the previous week all but one or two were now in Allied hands. The Vietcong appeal for a general uprising had failed. He thought that the second round of attacks would confirm the Vietcong's failure to get a hold on the hearts and minds of the general population. Not a single unit or detachment of the South Vietnamese army had defected, even under the strong pressure of the previous week. Though the President and his army commanders had fairly obviously been caught by surprise by the previous week's attacks, I found him optimistic about the future course of the war. To him the defeat of the Tet offensive seemed almost a turning-point in the war. In a sense, so it proved.

He turned to the diplomatic offensive, in which he wanted me to take a hand. It would be useful, he said, following our talks, if I would consider now going straight back to the Russians. But I should begin by telling them first that after three talks in Washington I was absolutely clear that the Americans were dug in and determined, and were going to see this thing through. The Russians must realise that for a start.

Second, he felt that I should pass on to them the American view about the *Pueblo*. It was still possible that the next two meetings might help to resolve the situation but so far there was no sign of it. If the North Koreans maintained their attitude – more particularly, if they took further action, either against the *Pueblo* captives or against South Korea – a situation could be created which would bring all of us in: 'You, the Russians, the rest of us'. The Russians, who had expressed their interest in seeing this issue peacefully settled, should use their influence with North Korea to prevent it from getting out of hand. I later asked HM Ambassador to get from Dean Rusk the text of the State Department note from which the President was speaking, for me to communicate with the Russians.

Third, he turned to the future of the Vietnam problem. He asked that I should inform Moscow of our discussions. I should emphasise – he said this for the second time – that the US were determined to see this thing through to the end. Having done this, I should make clear exactly what the San Antonio formula meant in relation to their comments on the Trinh declaration, in the terms he had employed the previous day, particularly the formulation sent to Hanoi the previous August. I repeated what I had said the previous evening, how impressed I was by the full formulation, so little of which, even at that time, had been made public.

But, if I were to approach the Russians, I should like, for greater accuracy, the full text. He agreed.

After a brief discussion on the economic situation and on the note he had handed to me, we ended, as so often, on a personal and political note. He talked again of New Hampshire and the situation in the Democratic party. He said that it was in no sense certain that he would stand for a further term. He had not made up his mind and it was quite on the cards that he would retire. The one thing he wanted to do was to use all his power and influence to achieve peace in Vietnam on a basis he could defend and be proud of. I said that his spelling out of the San Antonio formula combined with the Trinh statement suggested that the two sides were not so far apart, and that a little more trust was needed. This I would press on Moscow. But was there not another way, I asked? I hesitated to press it; it was all too easy for us, not involved in the fighting, to make suggestions. But – if that trust could not be invoked – was there not a case, as I had urged before, for a US decision to stop the bombing and put the sincerity of North Vietnam to the test? I recognised the difficulties: particularly the political situation and the strength of public feeling in his country. I did not ask him to comment, but this was a view of very many of our people. He did comment. He gave me a very old-fashioned look, and said this was – as he had told me on my previous visit – something which he had repeatedly considered. There could easily come a time – and it could be soon – when he would give me and a lot of other people a big surprise. As he had said this once before I did not give it the value which, seven weeks later, it was proved to merit.

I flew from Washington to Ottawa, where again my talks with Lester Pearson on Anglo-Canadian relations were relaxed and easy. We had to raise the perennial question about the Canadian customs' handling and valuation of British exports. That great maestro managed, probably not by design, to produce the perfect diplomatic squelch.

'Ah, yes,' he said – I reproduce the words as well as I can remember them, but broadly this represents what he said – 'I think I had a brief on this. In fact I was reading it while I was dressing.' He told his secretary to go up to his bedroom and find it.

'Yes,' he said, 'this is it. "Canadian customs valuation. Defensive brief. The Prime Minister is advised not to raise this matter unless raised by the British Prime Minister. If it is raised, the Prime Minister is advised to say no more than...".'

This parody of a Whitehall brief, showing how far British civilisation had spread in what was once an Empire, meant that there was little to be said. The important fact was that in the forthcoming Budget our point was met.

In a private talk with him, later that evening, I raised the question of the next Commonwealth conference. I preferred that following the

Lagos precedent it should take place elsewhere than in Britain. But the country selected would decide the chairmanship. I was anxious that Lester Pearson, with his high standing in the Commonwealth, should chair it and I asked him if he would agree to its being held in Ottawa. This he was willing, indeed flattered, to do, but he said that, nearing seventy, he would shortly be standing down. He could not forecast who would be chosen as his successor, though certain words he used implied that Mr Trudeau was rapidly rising in public esteem, not least through his handling of difficult constitutional questions affecting the relation between the federal government and individual provinces. We left the matter there, since we could not decide the venue without knowing who would be chairman.

I returned to London on 11th February, and reported to the House on my talks in Washington and Ottawa. The report was well received. Mr Sandys tried to raise the question of the US reaction to the withdrawal from east of Suez. With truth, I was able to reply:

> I will leave it to the American administration, and not the right hon. Gentleman, to interpret the views of the American administration about that. In regard to the east of Suez situation, with which the rt. hon. Gentleman is so concerned, he will be happy to know that the only reference made to it while I was in Washington was in the second verse of the Metropolitan Opera House tenor, who sang 'The Road to Mandalay' from which we withdrew twenty years ago.

To questions from our own back-benchers, I stood by the San Antonio formula taken in conjunction with the statement by Mr Trinh on 24th December; the President had repeated to me that he would stop the bombing provided that he was given, in an appropriate form, an assurance that there would be prompt peace-talks thereafter.

The big issue in the latter half of February was the problem of the Kenyan Asians. When Kenya gained independence in December 1963, the very large number of Kenyan residents of Asian – mainly Indian – origin who held British passports were given the choice of becoming Kenyans or continuing to be reckoned as British citizens, though few had any direct relation, either through residence or parentage, with the 'mother' country. Scores of thousands took the 'British' option. Kenya had moved towards their progressive expulsion and there was nowhere for them to go but Britain. In the three months ending January 1968, seven thousand had arrived – more than in the whole of 1966.

Few problems could have presented more difficult issues for the Cabinet or a greater issue of conscience for liberal-minded people throughout the country. On the one hand, there was the human issue presented by homeless persons expelled from their country – for most of them their *native* country – to say nothing of their right to entry conferred by the passports they held. On the other, there was the disruptive effect on national immigration policy from the entry of tens of thousands, possibly hundreds of thousands of Kenyan and other east-African Asians who might be similarly expelled – including the special problem of the strain on the services of the areas where they would have to be assimilated. Counsels were evenly divided. The Cabinet decided to defer the issue for a week, while Malcolm Macdonald, our former roving High Commissioner in Africa, was asked to try to seek a solution by further discussions with President Kenyatta. While this was happening I enjoined the strictest control on any public pronouncement, though it was already an issue, since Mr Enoch Powell had raised it in a manner which was bound to provoke public comment.

Unfortunately, Dick Crossman, talking to journalists that afternoon, was asked about the Kenyan Asians. As a compulsive educator, he could not bear to think that the avid students from the press should remain in ignorance and he treated them to a tutorial setting out the issues. On the one hand, he said – and proceeded to set out the arguments for unlimited entry; and on the other, there were the problems this would set for the established Commonwealth immigration. Never could thirsty students have shown more gratitude to their tutor: with a unanimity he had never achieved at New College the whole press the next morning headlined a 'split in Cabinet over Kenya immigrants', and set out the arguments, with partly fictional attribution to individual protagonists, that were so dividing us.

This did not help in the domestic situation. It manifestly did not help in Kenya. Malcolm Macdonald drew a blank. A week later, after the issue had gone to Cabinet again, Jim Callaghan had to get up in the House and announce that a Bill would be presented the following day bringing Kenyan Asians under immigration control, and limiting the number of special vouchers to be issued to them to 1,500 a year.

The Bill created agony for our back-benchers, as earlier it had for the Cabinet. Nor was this soul-searching confined to the Government side. When the Opposition, who, when in Government, had been responsible for giving to the Asians the right of entry to Britain, cravenly decided to abstain – though Iain Macleod and twelve other Tories joined the Liberals and a number of our own people in the lobby against us – many liberal-minded Conservatives decided to break with Mr Heath. Incredibly, the Conservative leader inscribed a thousand-word message to Mr Humphrey Berkeley on the subject. It was his last genuflection to Tory liberalism. From then on the Monday Club took over the guardianship of the Tory conscience. The issue smouldered throughout the Parliament, and in the later months of 1970, with the ruling of the European Commission on Human Rights, it became a problem again for the Conservatives, with whom it had started.

Financial questions were again calling for urgent attention. In January we had taken hundreds of millions into the reserves and this continued in early February. We had to face a critical situation in mid-February, when forward sales at the time of devaluation were due to mature. In fact, despite some gloomy pronouncements, we took these maturities in our stride without a tremor in the markets. But on Friday, 1st March, and on the following Friday, there were heavy sales of sterling, associated with speculation about an expected increase in the price of gold.

There was much talk about expected revaluations, to the point where there was the greatest doubt whether the price of gold and existing currency parities could be held much longer.

The central bankers were due to meet in Basle on Sunday, 10th March. The Americans were usually represented by Ed Coombs of the New York Federal Reserve; on this occasion William McChesney Martin, Chairman of the Federal Reserve Board, turned up. Nothing could have been more calculated to heighten speculation. The Basle club put out a statement saying that they were standing by the gold price and this was reinforced by on-the-record comments from the Governor of the Bank of England and Bill Martin, which were designed to reassure all concerned. They did not, and by Tuesday the market had taken leave of its senses. Wednesday and Thursday were worse and on the latter afternoon the Paris gold market remained open because, it was officially said, of 'panic buying'.

I raised the matter a number of times with the Chancellor. On the Wednesday evening, 13th March, I said – and this was minuted – that we must stick to our parity with the dollar, whatever might happen to the dollar. Unfortunately, we were out in front and speculation against the dollar inevitably hit us first.

From now on, in this memoir, I rely, almost word for word, on a note I began to dictate that evening while waiting for a reply from the White House – a note I felt would be valuable for monetary history, but which later I continued to supplement in what proved to be a much more significant weekend than anyone could have foreseen.

On Thursday, 14th March, after Cabinet, I asked the Chancellor to stay behind and expressed my concern about the gold situation. I suggested we ought to be taking a view about demonetisation of gold, which would effectively deal with any French activities and which many experts thought to be behind the anarchy ruling in continental markets. I knew he was preoccupied with the Budget and I suggested that we set up a working party to consider all the implications.

When my office subsequently telephoned the Treasury to ensure that all this was on the record it became clear that officials there were thinking of a leisurely working party to get to work after the Budget. I commented that we should not have that amount of time. So it proved. The Chancellor sent me a message to say that he would like to come to my room at the House of Commons at 6.00 p.m. to discuss the situation.

When he came, he said that the worsening gold situation, culminating in panic conditions in Paris at lunch-time, had got the Americans to move. At that moment Bill Martin was with the President. All the Treasury knew (from a telephone call from Martin to the Governor) was that the Americans were thinking in terms of a two-tier arrangement under which the central bankers of the gold pool countries, and any others who would agree to abide by the set of rules to be drawn up, would bind themselves to sell gold only to one another in settlement of monetary deficits. Banks would have to agree that any gold so received, or indeed gold drawn from the reserves, would not be 'leaked' on to the free market at a higher price, or at all. The Bank of England and the Treasury, on a first look at this proposal, were worried, particularly because it might not do the trick and, if it were to fail or to hang fire, then in any interim period of unsettlement sterling would bear the brunt of speculation. The Chancellor said he hoped to hear from the Governor soon after 7.00 p.m. when Martin had ended his White House meeting.

At 6.20 p.m. I asked my principal private secretary, Michael Halls, to come over to the House. I told him to man up an emergency office for the rest of the evening and asked him to ensure that the appropriate Treasury officials were all alerted.

I was due at 6.30 p.m. to meet the Archbishop of Canterbury's Immigration Committee, which was in a militant mood over the Kenyan Asians; this meeting could clearly not be cancelled. Nevertheless, I dictated a message to the President, firing a shot across his bows to ensure that the US did not make any unilateral decision which, however satisfactory to the Americans, would leave those of us in the front line unprotected.

The meeting with the Archbishop's committee began half an hour late, at 7.00 p.m., and went on for just over an hour. The Home Secretary, who had been present, stayed behind to express his anxieties about gold – as he had done after Cabinet that morning. His fear was that 'the gold price was going, and quickly'.

The Archbishop retired, much reassured about our policy for the Asians. I hoped that he had not realised that at that moment of time I was, however regrettably, more concerned with those who were laying up for themselves treasures on earth, where moth and rust were not the only corruption, and were doing so in the hope of a terrestrial gain on the basis of a gold pool price considerably above $35 per fine ounce.

We had still received no news from Washington, though Rostow had informed my office that a full-dress White House meeting was in progress and that we should hear the outcome shortly.

I was concerned that the Foreign Secretary should be put in the picture, for, knowing the President, he might at any time send for our Ambassador. HM Minister (Financial) in Washington had been fully informed on the Treasury network, but George Brown would be entitled to feel aggrieved if he found that these high-level discussions were proceeding without his knowledge. A high-powered Foreign Office search-party was sent to find him, and failed. I waited an hour; still he could not be found. He was supposed to be in the House. One of my secretaries met his personal secretary in the House but got no more information. In the end I returned to No. 10, asking for the search to continue. It was unsuccessful.

The Chancellor came to see me again; he had no more news from Washington, except that the meeting had adjourned for lunch. Nothing was expected before 11.00 p.m. our time. I told him that we were trying to find George Brown. Roy Jenkins said he was due to meet George at ten o'clock to outline his Budget thinking to him, but Foreign Office messages suggested he was unlikely to turn up.

At 10.40 p.m. Secretary Fowler came through on the phone to the Chancellor, who told me he had had a 'bad call' – the line was far from clear – but that Fowler sounded 'battered'. All he could understand was that the Americans wanted us to close down the London gold pool, and that William Martin was talking to the Governor at the same time. Sir Leslie O'Brien would immediately come round to the Treasury to report. At 11.00 p.m. Sir Leslie arrived at No. 11 and Roy brought him in.

It was true, he said, that the Americans wanted us to close the gold pool, and they were calling a meeting in Washington on the Saturday of central bankers and finance ministry representatives of all the gold pool countries. At that meeting, we understood, the Americans were going to advance their 'two-tier proposal'. We were ready to close the gold pool, but this meant that the London foreign exchange must also be closed. This would mean a bank holiday, which in turn, we were advised, would mean an Order in Council, and a Privy Council that night.

I sent Michael Halls over to the House to tell the Lord President of the Council, Dick Crossman, who was fully involved in an all-night session on a guillotine motion on Barbara Castle's Transport Bill. Clearly there could not be a Council without his knowledge, but in all the circumstances I offered to stand in for the customary pre-Council Audience with the Queen.

By this time, with no precedents to guide us, we had sorted out the arrangements for the bank holiday. Bank branches would remain open to cash cheques – for example, those required for paying wages – but there were to be no inter-account settlements. This would be sufficient to prevent foreign exchange transactions. But we were concerned about what might happen to sterling on markets remaining open in other capitals. We decided to let the rate go on all the European markets but felt it essential to see that it was maintained in New York. The Chancellor and I agreed to close the gold pool and the gold market but only on condition that the Americans supported sterling on the New York market, which was remaining open. The deputy-Governor suggested that the New York Federal Bank could be asked to buy and hold guaranteed sterling.

a December 1966 an agreement was signed by Mr Wilson and the Irish Prime Minister, Mr Sean
emass, establishing a free trade area between the United Kingdom and the Irish Republic

Ir Wilson and Mr Brown with President de Gaulle and the French Prime Minister, M. Pompidou
their visit to Paris in January 1967

A
B

NOT

This is what we have to
change

Second, we shall import ...

Third — got to get more
— ~~this~~ unless we ca...
the chance to - includ...
how the — more ov...

Penultimate :-
Break out. Releas...
~~...~~ on own e...
work.

A preliminary draft in his own hand (enlarged) of Mr Wilson's devaluation speech

TUC centenary celebrations at Belle Vue Manchester in June 1968

The General-Secretary of the TUC, Mr Vic Feather with Mr Wilson and Mrs Castle during talks No. 10 on the Government's industrial relations proposals

I pointed out sharply that sterling must be guaranteed in terms of dollars, not gold. This was agreed. The Governor said that, while the Federal Reserve chairman had hinted at support, he could not say that any firm assurance had been given. I said that we could not agree to take action on all the other steps we had been asked to take, including the closure of the gold pool itself, until the assurance was given. The Governor put a call through to Washington. It was not until 12.05 a.m., or soon thereafter, that we were in the clear, and I asked the Clerk to the Privy Council to go ahead with the Council for 12.15 a.m., or as soon afterwards as possible. At this point, having heard that George Brown had surfaced, I sent a senior secretary over to the House to tell him what was happening. A few minutes earlier Peter Shore, who had heard rumours that something was afoot, had telephoned to ask what was going on. I could not tell him anything but, realising we should have to assemble with all speed a quorum for the Council, sent a message asking him to come over. It was an afterthought with cataclysmic results.

After the Council, the Chancellor prepared a public statement and brought it to me at about 1.00 a.m. Shortly afterwards George Brown came through on the telephone in a great state. He had apparently assembled a meeting of ministers in his room and, with a choice of language I should not normally associate with him, demanded my presence there at once. I said that if a meeting were desired, he and they should come over to No. 10 for a properly convened one. This they did, in a very anxious mood. I asked the Chancellor to give a résumé of the facts from 6.00 p.m. that night, to explain what had been done and the acute danger – at least until we knew that markets were to close – of holding a ministerial meeting. This they fully accepted and agreed with the steps we had taken; agreeing, too, that we had had no alternative. Not so George Brown. He was not concerned with the facts and instead of listening to the Chancellor kept up a running commentary, mainly directed to the accusation that Peter Shore had been involved from the outset. He was told that Peter knew nothing of it until sent for; he had learnt the facts only in the Chancellor's car on the way to the Palace. The decibels grew with the strength of the accusations, with all the ministers who had come over with him telling George to control himself.

(I should not have thought it necessary to recount these matters had George not published in the autumn of 1970 a highly tendentious account of the night's events: omitting many relevant facts, some of which he had not known, others of which he must have forgotten. I am drawing, as I said, entirely on the note I dictated at the time.)

The break came when I told him of the efforts we had made to find him, through his office and in other ways, and our failure to do so. He accused both my secretaries and myself of lying and, breathing threats of resignation, came round the table to me, shouting that we had made a great blunder – 'not the first you have made,' he added. He then wandered off through the door. The effect on his colleagues was tremendous. Ray Gunter, in particular, used the words 'disgusting' and 'contempt' to describe his feelings at what had happened. All felt that I could not refuse to accept his resignation this time. I decided to wait until the morning.

While we were talking, Dick Crossman telephoned to say that the news of the gold crisis had appeared on the tapes, that the House was in uproar and that no progress would be made with parliamentary business until the Chancellor intervened to make a statement. Any idea of waiting, as we had intended, until 11.00 a.m. the following morning, after the Cabinet I had called, was out of the question and we trooped over to the House. Roy Jenkins acquitted himself superbly before an anxious but quiet House.

George Brown had ostentatiously seated himself at the end of the second bench, behind his colleagues. After the statement, I was told later, he had gone into the tea-room and loudly proclaimed his resignation and his dissociation from his colleagues. Press reports proliferated in the evening and, later, the Saturday morning papers, quoting him as saying that he was going to save the soul of the party, that the left now had a leader, that he would sign their motions on Vietnam, etc., and much more in similar vein. He was finally, in terse language, told to quieten down by Michael Foot, on behalf of the left, and by Manny Shinwell more generally. Eric Heffer called him to order in further choice Merseyside language. Many Conservative MPs were within earshot and Dick Marsh, who had seen most of the occurrences, told me and other ministers on the Friday that he had 'run into a grinning Heath, who said, "Has he gone yet: if not, why not?" ' Even George Brown's two closest supporters, of many years' standing, told him and other ministers that this time he had gone too far.

In the morning I heard that George had telephoned the Cabinet Secretary, Sir Burke Trend, saying that he had not changed his mind (presumably about resigning) and would not be attending the Cabinet.

When the Cabinet met at 10.30 a.m. the Chancellor explained the night's activities, following which, with no prompting from me, the Cabinet unanimously endorsed the actions we had taken and, further, agreed that consultation would have been impossible. We turned then to the more important task of approving the Chancellor's proposals for the line to be taken at Washington.

Few decisions can have been taken in a more unknown and unpredictable situation. Hardly any of us felt – and we knew this view was widely shared by Treasuries and central banks – that a mere assertion to operate the gold pool rules would hold the situation, which was utterly chaotic as more and more speculators put their weight behind an increase in the world gold price. There were four possible courses: to do nothing, which would have led to disaster; a higher gold price, to which we were opposed and which the Americans would fight to the last ditch; a two-tier gold price system with a fully policed official system, holding the price at the established level, together with a fine market price settled by supply and demand; and demonetisation of the metal. While the last of these was the course to be preferred, it was doubtful whether other countries were ready for it and we reconciled ourselves to a decision in favour of two-tier prices, but fearing that it could not survive the strains for long, perhaps not even for more than a day or so.

Nothing was heard from George Brown all morning, though he sent his unhappy private secretary to see my secretary at lunch-time. He may have been waiting for me to say all was forgiven and that he should not resign. I could not have held the Cabinet together had I done so. I instructed my secretary to inform George's emissary that I had no comment to make. He had missed the Cabinet: an explanation was due.

In the afternoon, I received a message from his PPS, via a member of my political staff, saying that there was just a chance that George Brown might change his mind about resigning if I were to take an initiative. I instructed that he be told to tell the PPS that he did not really know what was in my mind: all I knew was what George Brown had said and his absence from a most important Cabinet. A further visit by his secretary, who said that the Foreign Secretary was drafting a letter, produced no comment.

Meanwhile there was a press story, which might or might not have been inspired, that 'George was not going to resign, but would wait to be sacked'.

At 6.00 p.m. a letter arrived from George, not specifically resigning, but saying, 'I think it better that we should part company'. Recalling the press story, I took it coolly. I had an evening engagement, after which I considered the letter with advisers. My reply was drafted on the basis that his letter was to be regarded as resignation. But to give him time to come through, if he was going to say that his letter did not involve resignation, I deferred taking action on it. There was no response.

I had seen Michael Stewart earlier and asked him to stand by over the Foreign Office appointment. There had been a long-arranged meeting with the Commonwealth Secretary, George Thomson, on another matter and I told him that if George were to resign I should announce that Michael Stewart was to take the Foreign Office, with a mandate to amalgamate the two offices, Foreign and Commonwealth, into a single department. George Thomson would continue as Commonwealth Secretary until the merger took effect.

George Brown did not respond to my letter. The necessary submissions had gone to the Queen at Windsor, with a request that they be not put before her until the situation was clarified. The announcement was made just before 10.30 p.m. The early editions of the morning newspapers were demanding a change at the Foreign Office, the later editions confirmed that there was one.

George Brown's explanation of his resignation related his decision to complaints of presidential, indeed dictatorial, government. When Michael Stewart arrived at the Foreign Office and met George there he rebuked him, in his crispest pedagogical manner, for these references. They were, indeed, a little hard to understand since George, only a few days earlier, had in a private talk criticised my style of government. He had been pressing me to take more decisions myself and not to refer so many issues for collective decision by the Cabinet or Cabinet committees. Every Prime Minister sitting in that chair, he said, would run No. 10 in a different way; were he there he would take more of the decisions. 'Alone,' I asked, 'or in consultation with the deputy Leader?' George found that an embarrassing question. But throughout my premiership he had found my desire to refer major issues for collective discussion irksome.

Despite my feeling for many months past that repeated late-night crises could not continue and that one of them would go beyond what was tolerable, it was sad for all of us to see George Brown go. He was a man of first-class ability, a forceful and indeed imaginative administrator, respected by his parliamentary colleagues, and commanding more affection in the wider Labour movement than any of us. His strengths far exceeded his weaknesses, but it was his weaknesses which ended his ministerial career.

Meanwhile, Mr Heath was busily engaged publicly blaming the world's gold crisis on Britain's devaluation.

The Chancellor and I, for our part, were in constant consultation about the Washington conference, with telegrams arriving almost hourly from our delegation, which consisted of Sir William Armstrong, joint permanent secretary to the Treasury, the Governor of the Bank, and Harold Lever, the Financial Secretary. By Saturday evening, 16th March, we received news that the US were going hard for the two-tier price. I was awakened in the early hours with a telegram which said no more than that the Treasury economic adviser, Mr Michael Posner, was flying back to report. At noon the Chancellor and I met and Mr Posner came to report to us. It was clear that the two-tier system held the field and that there was discussion about possible help for sterling if the markets relapsed into anarchy and gambled on an increased gold price. In such a situation sterling would be in the front line.

We decided that we should not support two-tier aspirations unless there was adequate cover for vulnerable currencies. The Friday bank holiday had been extended to Saturday to stop any nonsense in Middle Eastern banks, and we considered whether to extend the closure into the following week. I was strongly opposed to this, since it might lead to costly speculation about possible further devaluation or a floating of the pound in the following Tuesday's Budget statement.

To forestall criticism from certain of our colleagues, I had formed a small committee of the six ministers directly affected – the President of the Board of Trade, the Foreign Secretary, the First Secretary and the Economic Secretary, as well as the Chancellor and myself. Meeting at 3.30 on the Sunday afternoon, 17th March, the committee endorsed the line we had taken. By early evening the news from Washington was more encouraging and a further meeting of the committee decided to leave things in the hands of the Chancellor and myself. We agreed that there should be no extended bank holiday but that the gold market should remain closed for the time being. Later news from Washington confirmed our decision.

In the small hours of Monday morning, 18th March, the Chancellor and I pronounced benediction on the weekend's events over a drink. Suddenly he made a most moving reference to the fact that this had been his first crisis, and how much he had felt reinforced by my calm throughout.

But, studying Treasury advice, he was gloomy about Monday's markets. Losses of up to $250 millions were expected. Without the slightest evidence to back my view, and purely to reassure him, I told him jokingly that I knew exactly what the day's out-turn would be. We should lose, I said, $3 millions in the morning supporting the rate, and the figure for the day would be $31 millions. Sterling would be higher. I might have plucked any other figures out of the air, but he was reassured.

In the event, over the day, the sterling rate rose by nearly a cent, but exactly $3 millions were expended in holding the rate in the first hour. With a strong sterling demand flowing, the Bank decided to let the rate rise and by lunch-time the loss was still only $3 millions. During the afternoon $9 millions was taken in by the Bank but an unpredicted payment of $40 millions by New Zealand on an IMF debt, which had nothing to do with current events, left a net figure of minus $31 millions – as I had predicted for all the wrong reasons. The odds against getting both figures right must have been hundreds of thousands to one.

On the Tuesday, 19th March, the Chancellor presented his first Budget. It could not be other than tough; in fact it was the most punishing Budget in Britain's peacetime history. It was widely acclaimed as a speech of surpassing quality and elegance and, despite its contents, Roy Jenkins received a great ovation and well-merited compliments from both sides of the House.

In summarising the 'Budget judgment' he made clear that he had accepted the highest figure in the range of advice given him by the Treasury on the amount it was necessary to take out of the economy to reinforce the January measures and to move resources out of home consumption into exports. He decided not to use the always easier option of further hire-purchase restrictions. When we had discussed, day by day, his Budget plans he made it clear that he wanted to keep hire-purchase restrictions in reserve, in case further action was needed to deal with possible trouble in the summer.

In all, he budgeted for increases in taxation amounting to £923 millions in a full year and £775 millions in 1968–9; that is £766 millions and £671 millions respectively, if no account were taken of the previously announced increase in corporation tax and the 'claw-back', recovering tax from recipients of the 7s increase in family allowances.

Betting tax was doubled to five per cent and big increases were made in gaming duties, increasing the yield from the two by £30 millions a year. The duties on wines and spirits were raised, yielding £15 millions; but beer was left alone, as the Chancellor wanted to be as selective and 'unregressive' as possible. Tobacco duty was increased by the equivalent of 2d on a packet of twenty cigarettes – £30 millions more. Hydrocarbon oils, including petrol, were stepped up by 4d a gallon, though the heavy oils duty was left unchanged. The estimated yield here was £76 millions a year, less £3 millions refund to bus operators to help them avoid increases in fares. The lower and medium rates of purchase tax were raised from 11 per cent and 16½ per cent to 12½ per cent and 20 per cent. The higher rate, then 27½ per cent, was split into two categories. Motor-cars, motor cycles, refrigerators and other consumer durables were raised proportionately to 33⅓ per cent while a wide range of 'luxury' and less essential goods – furs, jewellery, gold and silver watches, perfumery and various toiletries – were raised from 27½ per cent to 50 per cent. Tape recorders were brought into the 33⅓ per cent rate and cine projectors, until then surprisingly tax-free, joined cameras at the new rate of 50 per cent.

The increased yield from purchase tax was estimated at £163 millions in a full year, making the total increase in customs and excise duties £314 millions in a full year.

Car licence taxes were raised from £17 10s to £25, in addition to the increase in petrol duty.

The selective employment tax was raised from 25s to 37s 6d a week for men, with other rates in proportion, apart from some degree of shelter for part-time employees and all workers over sixty-five. Because of the effect of the tax on tourism, especially in Wales and Scotland, the Chancellor said that measures would be announced the following day for refunding SET to hotels in certain rural parts of development areas.

The total increased burden from indirect taxes had now reached £592 millions in a full year. The Chancellor, with full agreement, had decided not to raise the standard rate of income tax. Indeed, we both hoped that in the next Budget some selective easement of the burden, particularly for families, might be possible.

On estate duty, he announced that the period before a death on which gifts were dutiable would be extended from five to seven years, with a tapering to lower rates from the fifth to the seventh year. Loopholes were closed on avoidance through insurance policies and discretionary trusts. Further anti-avoidance measures were introduced in the fields of corporation tax and life assurance. Lawyers and others were – as we had frequently urged in Finance Bill debates before 1964 – at long last deprived of their long immunity from tax on their 'post-cessation receipts' of uncollected fees.

Some £15 millions extra, without any change in tax rates, was to be raised by providing that the tax allowance for newly-weds should not extend over the whole year in which they were married, but relate to the actual date of the wedding.

Another blow for progressive taxation came through ending the exclusion from tax enjoyed by children with their own investment income or investment income held or applied on their behalf. From the Budget onwards, such investment income was to be 'aggregated' with the income of the family, as was that of wives. The Chancellor estimated that the yield would be £25 millions, showing, he said, how greatly families with established wealth available to them had benefited over those with the same gross income coming entirely from the efforts of the parents – '...I do not think,' he said, 'any theory of incentives justifies that.'

On the other hand, the age allowance for persons of sixty-five and over was raised, for the second year running, to take account of the increase due during the year in retirement pensions.

His final announcement was in the spirit of Sir Stafford Cripps's 'once-for-all' special assessment, nearly twenty years earlier. Having rejected any increase in the capital gains tax, or a further increase in the corporation tax, he said that he was faced with the question of an impost on the private wealth of individuals, a better method of approach. Instead of a straight wealth tax he proposed that a special charge be assessed on unearned income. Starting at investment incomes of £3,000, and with all the personal and other allowances, it would rise to 9s in the pound for one year only on unearned income above £8,000. At the top ranges it would be more than pound for pound, and would therefore involve a small levy on capital. It was due to yield £100 millions in the year, but for one year only.

The Chancellor was given a great ovation by our side at the end of his two-and-a-half-hour speech.

Chapter 26

AFTER our decision not to sell arms to South Africa it became clear that the Conservatives were not going to allow the question to lie undisturbed. Sir Alec Douglas-Home announced a visit to South Africa where he pledged a future Conservative Government to resume the supply of arms. On his way back to Britain he flew to Salisbury where he had serious talks with Mr Smith in which he reiterated that there could be no agreement which failed to satisfy all the requirements that successive Governments had laid down – the five principles.

His talks had gone into some detail, particularly on the first two principles dealing with unimpeded progress to majority rule. On his return he came to see me, on 29th February, and proudly produced a paper, agreed with Mr Smith, on this question. Mr Smith's mathematics had clearly been superior to those of Sir Alec Douglas-Home. Dividing the total number of legislators by four, I was able to show him that those capable of blocking retrogressive legislation would be fewer than twenty-five per cent of the total. He was a little taken aback but, taking his piece of paper, I quickly demonstrated how by a marginal change involving increasing both sides by a fixed number it would be easy to reach a blocking figure slightly above twenty-five per cent. He was reassured, and felt that Mr Smith would have no difficulty in agreeing to this formula. I was doubtful; for Mr Smith's nimble mind arithmetic was a servant of policy. When Sir Alec had left, George Thomson irreverently commented that my task would have been easier if I had had matches handy.

But within days Rhodesia moved to the centre of the stage again in the most macabre way. After UDI the regime had been careful not to execute the men languishing in Salisbury gaol under sentence of death. Some of these had been sentenced before UDI, some after, and all for offences which were capital when the legal 1961 constitution was in force. In the case of a number of men sentenced after UDI, appeals were before the Privy Council, though the regime did all in its power to

517

frustrate a Privy Council hearing. Early in March it became clear that the executions were shortly to take place of some who had lain under sentence of death for up to two-and-a-half years. The Commonwealth Secretary advised the Queen to exercise the prerogative of mercy. This was provocatively ignored by the regime, which on 6th March proceeded to execute the first three on the list. A last-minute appeal to the Rhodesian Court of Appeal produced from Sir Hugh Beadle and his colleagues a decision that the matter lay within Rhodesian jurisdiction, finally committing himself to the regime as the *de facto* Government. Sir Hugh was met on his impudent return to Government House by the Governor who told him to take himself out, bag and baggage. George Thomson, in a statement in Parliament, announced that the 'dormant commission' appointing Sir Hugh to the governorship in circumstances where Sir Humphrey Gibbs had resigned or was unable to act was revoked.

There was a great outcry in the House about the executions, but even this was as nothing to the storm in the United Nations, with inevitable demands for tighter sanctions and, as ever, the use of force by the British Government to quell the Rhodesian revolt. It is difficult to describe the strength of feeling which overtook the Commons – apart from Rhodesia Front apologists – though the attitude of the Opposition front bench made Pontius Pilate, by comparison, appear one of the decisive figures of history. The Cabinet decided to table an all-party motion of condemnation and abhorrence, but the Conservative leader, when approached, refused to allow his party to be associated with it. We tabled it as a Government motion with Liberal support. More worthy of the traditions of his party were the words of a young Conservative member, Peter Tapsell, who moved the House by a quotation he attributed to Winston Churchill: 'Grass grows quickly over the battlefield: over the scaffold never.'

A little over a week later, grass had grown over any Opposition resentment there had been at the executions. Mr Heath was pressing on me the proposals brought back from Salisbury by Sir Alec Douglas-Home, though these were manifestly outside the five principles as I had demonstrated to Sir Alec himself. But in the United Nations anger took charge, leading inevitably to unreasoning counsels, which Hugh Caradon – and a few were more unhappy than he – had the greatest difficulty in restraining. By the summer the Privy Council had ruled against the regime in test cases before it and rejected the Rhodesian High Court's finding that the regime was a *de facto* Government.

On Saturday, 30th March, I was told on the telephone that a very long telegram was coming in from Washington and would be teleprinted to me at Chequers. It was the text of the broadcast President Johnson would be making the following day.

It began by recalling the San Antonio undertaking to stop the bombing of North Vietnam when it became clear that cessation would lead to prompt and productive discussions. He was now proposing to take a unilateral step along that road by ordering the US Fleet and Air Force to make no further attacks in North Vietnam, except, he laid down:

> in the area north of the demilitarised zone where the continuing enemy build-up directly threatens allied forward positions and where movements of troops and supplies are clearly related to that threat.
> The area in which we are stopping our attacks includes almost ninety per cent of North Vietnam's population and most of its territory. Thus there will be no attacks around the principal populated areas, and in the food-producing areas of North Vietnam.

But he went on to say that he was prepared to order a total cessation of the bombing, given a North Vietnamese response to his offer. He went on:

> Tonight, I call upon the United Kingdom and the Soviet Union—as co-chairmen of Geneva Conference, and as permanent members of the United Nations Security Council—to do all they can to move from the unilateral act of de-escalation I have just announced towards genuine peace in south-east Asia.

He designated Averell Harriman to be ready to go to Geneva, or to any place that could be agreed on, for negotiations with DRV representatives.

This clearly was the 'surprise' move of which he had hinted in the late-morning talk at the White House in February.

After speaking to the Foreign Secretary I immediately replied to the President warmly welcoming his initiative and stating that we would approach the Soviet Union at once.

But when the statement was made on the Sunday evening, 31st March, there was a further shock addition: 'I shall not seek,' he said, 'and I will not accept, the nomination of my party for another term as President.'

This had not been included in the operational text sent to me. Total secrecy had been the aim. The resignation announcement, indeed, was on a separate piece of paper. Even the Vice-President, Hubert Humphrey, I learnt later, was not told until quite late on the Sunday morning, only half an hour before he was due to leave to fly to a conference in Mexico. I recalled then that the President had told me in February that he had not in any way decided to run for a further term and that he was under strong family pressure not to run.

The question was naturally raised how far the President's decision was due to disturbance about the likely trend of the primaries. My own view was that the President, who had more than once hinted to me that he was unwilling to become a 'lame duck' President, was genuine; that he felt this sacrificial step to be necessary to carry conviction. Above all, I think, he felt that his determination to get a settlement would be hard to make effective if every action was regarded as a move in the electoral game. My only doubt was how far Hanoi, and perhaps others, would be able to play a waiting game with him and use their time advantage or, failing to wring concessions, wait in the hope of greater concessions from another President.

At home, at the end of March, three further by-elections were held with, again, devastating results. The deaths of two Labour members, for Acton and Meriden, and the appointment of George Wigg as Chairman of the Racecourse Betting Levy Board, led to elections in which, respectively, Labour majorities of 4,941, 4,581 and 10,022 had been transformed into Conservative gains, with majorities of 3,720, 15,263 and 11,656. The by-election swing to the Conservatives had now broken through the twenty per cent barrier. Gloom settled on the party. The press were re-awakened to reiterate their doubts about my survival. Mr Cecil King lent his declining authority to turning doubts into demands for a new premier. As it turned out, his writ did not run in the Parliamentary Party nor, so far as one could see, outside that part of the country which lay beyond the borders of London E.C.1 and Long Acre.

Before Easter I carried through a major change in ministerial responsibilities designed to reflect changing priorities in administration. Barbara Castle's mammoth Transport Bill, after the guillotine motion carried on the night of the gold crisis, was moving peacefully on to the statute book and I wanted her to be more directly associated with the Government's central economic strategy. We were moving, too, towards the introduction of our long-awaited earnings-related superannuation scheme. Dick Crossman, though carrying the exacting duties of Leader of the House, had played a leading part in it and Michael Stewart, since his reappointment to the Foreign Office, was no longer available as co-ordinator in home affairs.

I was concerned, too, with the machinery of government, being keen to create larger ministries under ministers of proved ability; a risk, always, but one easier to carry out the longer a Government has been in office and ministerial abilities tested. Following the announcement of the merger of the Foreign and Commonwealth Offices, I was determined to bring Health and Social Security together.

Dick Crossman was to give up the Leadership of the House, but was to continue as Lord President, with direct responsibility for co-ordinating the social service departments, including education and housing, and a special responsibility for supervising the preparation of the new superannuation scheme. He was still a non-departmental minister and I was not anxious for any senior colleague to be cut off from a departmental power-base for too long, but his remit included responsibility for merging the two social service departments by the autumn, the date set for the Foreign and Commonwealth Office merger.

I wanted Barbara Castle to take over the Ministry of Labour, to which I intended that all the prices and incomes responsibilities of DEA should be transferred, thus concluding the process begun in 1966. She was not all that keen – for two reasons. The first, as every Prime Minister learns, is that a minister who has transformed a department and lifted it out of the ruck is loath to leave it and, even under pressure, wants to lay down conditions about who his (or her) successor should be. This is understandable. But, second, in Barbara's case there was a psychological problem. The Ministry of Labour image, she felt, was wrong. Recalling Labour's first ever woman minister, forty years earlier, she did not want to be a 'Maggie Bondfield, Mark II'. This I understood, and I wanted her, both in incomes questions and more widely, to take over a responsibility for increased productivity, other than in those purely technological matters which fell within the field of the Ministry of Technology. Apart from taking over incomes policy from DEA, all aspects of manpower productivity would be hers. We discussed a title. She laid claim to Labour and Productivity. I suggested that with a lady minister this might lead to bar-room ribaldry. She took the point and we settled on Employment and Productivity, of which she would become Secretary of State, with the additional status of First Secretary.

I knew that Ray Gunter would be likely to take this change hard. He had enjoyed the Ministry of Labour and, with Sir Dennis Barnes as permanent secretary, had forged an effective machine, particularly on industrial relations. He had set up the Donovan Commission, then finalising its report, and he was looking forward to the post-Donovan phase of refashioning Britain's system of industrial relations in the light of that report. But I wanted him for Power, where, with the strains on the mining industry and the need to get the post-nationalisation steel industry firmly established, a high-level and experienced minister with strong union connections was required. When I told him of the change he was clearly upset but loyally accepted the move. My one reservation was about fuel policy. Important negotiations were afoot on the allocation of North Sea gas and – what I always felt were going to be fruitful – oil franchises, too. I was anxious for a fresh mind to look at these problems, given what I believed was the excessively oil-orientated prejudice of the Department. It had been thus, to my knowledge, for over a quarter of a century. The doubt lay in whether Ray Gunter would be ready to give his mind to the extremely intricate figurings involved in this process and in wider aspects of fuel policy and would be happy in his work. My anxieties were, before long, confirmed.

The Power post was vacant because I wanted Dick Marsh, whose work on steel nationalisation was virtually complete, for Transport. Barbara Castle had to have a keen successor and, in view of the public interest in everything to do with motoring and road safety, one with a good sense of public relations. I was surprised to see how sorry he was at being asked to move; most would have regarded it as a promotion. When he asked about the constitutional position of a minister's being asked to change, I had to tell him – I think this was the only time I had had to do this – that if the captain asked a fielder to move from square leg to cover point, then that was exactly where he had to move. For an ambitious young minister he had been long enough at Power, his first appointment, and had carried through Parliament a major and controversial Bill with distinction; it was in his interest to move. As usually happens, he was wondering a week later why he had been hesitant.

Dick Crossman's successor as Leader of the House was Fred Peart, one of the most popular ministers in the Commons, with an earthy Durham common sense. He was succeeded at Agriculture by Cledwyn Hughes, who had not put a foot wrong at any stage of his ministerial career, and who, from his earlier profession as a solicitor in Anglesey, knew a good deal of the problems of the farmer and the rural community. George Thomas succeeded him as Secretary of State for Wales, a popular choice in the Principality.

Patrick Gordon Walker stood down. I was sorry to have to ask him to do this. He had had a rough ride at Education, almost entirely for reasons outside his control – such as an important court case in which the Department was involved within days of his taking over, and also the school-leaving age decision. He took it with great dignity; the real block to a distinguished ministerial career had occurred at Leyton. In his place I appointed Ted Short, whose administrative and parliamentary successes at the Post Office had become a by-word. He had been a head-master and knew equally the local education authority side as a former leader of the Newcastle City Council. His successor at the Post Office – though, as it turned out, he was not destined to stay there long – was Roy Mason, who had shown his ability to master technological and industrial problems as Minister of Defence (Equipment).

John Morris, Parliamentary Secretary at the Ministry of Transport, who had distinguished himself as chairman of an inquiry into the finances of British Rail, succeeded Roy Mason at Defence.

George Darling, who, as Minister of State at the Board of Trade, had master-minded major legislation on consumer protection, had asked me to be allowed to stand down on health grounds, and he was succeeded by Edmund Dell from DEA.

The Chancellor of the Exchequer, with the load he was carrying, had asked for additional help at the Treasury and Dick Taverne, who had been his Under-Secretary at the Home Office, became Minister of State, Treasury. He was replaced by Elystan Morgan, MP for Cardigan. Tom Urwin replaced Edward Dell at DEA with Minister of State rank; Harold Walker, a whip with long industrial experience, went to DEP; and Bob Brown, a Geordie trade unionist, replaced John Morris at Transport.

The reshuffle meant more than a change of departmental responsibilities. The economic team had been redeployed and there would be a new minister charged with prices and incomes policy and industrial relations.

But more than that. The inner workings of Government would be different. I had often been attracted, as is every Prime Minister, by the idea of a smaller Cabinet, not just marginally smaller by one or two, but something not much larger than half the average size of a post-war Cabinet. On this occasion I made a real effort to see whether I could appoint a Cabinet of no more than eleven or so – with other depart-mental heads outside the Cabinet – along the lines of the two, very differ-ing, War Cabinets in two world wars. But when I drew up such a list, the impossibility became clear. A Cabinet as small as eleven is possible only if it consists almost exclusively of two or three key departmental heads, such as the Foreign Secretary and Chancellor, together with non-departmental ministers and 'overlords' (in the first Churchill Cabinet even the Chancellor was not a member). But all experience was against the appointment of 'overlords', with the divided responsibility between an ivory tower chief on the one hand and, on the other, ministers with statutory duties responsible to Parliament. There is another problem. Prime Ministers who have tried to keep numbers down by leaving out of the Cabinet the minister ultimately responsible for, say, education, agriculture or transport, have alienated very important interests, indeed essential components of our society – as witness Sir Winston Churchill's exclusion of Education from the Cabinet in 1951. Equally, I felt that the Board of Trade, with its responsibility for exports, could not be omitted. Trying to work to a list of eleven and twelve, which I prepared as an experiment, proved conclusively that my hopes must remain unrealised.

Instead I set up the equivalent of an Inner Cabinet, or Parliamentary Committee as it was officially called. It was not intended in any way to replace the Cabinet. It did not take decisions, but it was to give a more coherent political direction to the work of the Government and to ensure that decisions taken with insufficient thought of parliamentary reactions were more carefully worked out in their political context, not least so far as timing was concerned.

On Saturday, 20th April, a speech was made which would justify the claim that, once made, British politics would never be quite the same again. Mr Enoch Powell, speaking in Birmingham on immigration, declared: 'Like the Romans, I seem to see the river Tiber foaming with much blood. . . .'

And with his unrivalled mastery of emotive hyperbole, Mr Powell outlined, with abundant transatlantic analogies, his immigration nightmare: '. . . those whom the gods wish to destroy, they first make mad. We must be mad, literally mad . . .'

Mr Powell's speech created a new and dangerous dimension in British politics. The first impact was on the Conservative party. Late on the Sunday evening Mr Heath dismissed him from the shadow cabinet, and in a statement said that he considered the Birmingham speech 'to have been racialist in tone and liable to exacerbate racial tensions'. It was said that Mr Heath took this action after resignation threats from two leading members of his team. However that may be, there was no doubt that Mr Heath, after some apparent dithering, had asserted his authority. What I noticed with sadness in the months and years ahead was that however deep the personal bitterness between him and Mr Powell, Mr Heath seemed on the run in terms of policy and successively adopted tougher attitudes, on some issues following Mr Powell's line with a delay of three to four months. And this at a time when the tightening up of evasion, by our 1968 Act, was taking effect, and a decline had begun in the arrival of dependants of those immigrants who had come earlier, mostly before 1964. Close relatives of immigrants had, and have, an absolute right of entry and Mr Heath did not challenge this. But, following the arrival of the main body of dependants of the earlier flood of immigrants and the very small numbers of new vouchers issued – together with the attack on evasions – the numbers began to fall markedly. In 1963 the employment voucher holders numbered 30,000. In 1964, 14,500; in 1965, 13,000; in 1966, 5,500; in 1967 they had been 5,000. The figures for the years that followed were 4,700 in 1968, 4,000 in 1969, and 4,000 again in 1970. Though the number of dependants exercising their rights doubled from 26,200 in 1963 to 52,800 in 1967, they had fallen to 22,900 by 1970.

But Mr Powell's words, and Mr Heath's equivocation towards his attitudes – while attacking his language – became an important political factor. It was not so much that Alf Garnett for the first time became a political figure in his own right; he was always that, and he represented a widespread area of prejudice or at least of gut reaction, spreading across all political parties. What Mr Powell had done for the first time was to make him politically articulate and to confer upon him a degree of political respectability by expressing his unspoken thoughts in the sophisticated language of a dedicated political philosopher, skilled in the use of words and, no less, of statistics. A distasteful sight in the days following the Powell speech was the march of a group of London dockers to the House of Commons to demonstrate on behalf of Powell and Powellism. It included, it is true, some well-known members of the National Front, but it would be very far from the truth to pretend that they were all of that persuasion. Many were representative of an attitude which was rooted deep in the docks and other areas of industry.

I decided at once that I must reply to Mr Powell in a major speech. My only engagement the following weekend was a non-party civic dinner in my constituency. It would have been wrong to use such a platform, as my reply would have to be strongly political. I therefore gave notice that I would be saying the following weekend what needed to be said.

My speech, on 5th May, fifteen days after Mr Powell's outburst, was made – as his had been – in Birmingham. It was right that I should meet this problem head-on in one of the areas where the controversy was most heated. It was Birmingham's annual May Day celebration and I devoted the whole of my fifty-five-minute speech to immigration and to Mr Powell. It was a big political risk, made easier by the wholehearted support and enthusiasm of our own party members who filled the City Hall to overflowing. Whether it was politically wise or expedient, others can argue; but it was right. Taking as my May Day theme the brotherhood of man, I decided to challenge racialism directly:

> The battle against racialism here in Britain knows no boundaries, no limits. Its boundaries are not the civic limits of Birmingham or Bradford or Wolverhampton, they extend to Africa, south as well as north of the Zambesi, to Asia, to all the continents of the world. That is why I reject the attitude of those who with their lips – if not their votes – preach

S

against racialism at home and endorse racialism in Rhodesia.

That is why, speaking at this meeting which commemorates those who fought for the right of enfranchisement of all our people, I reject the reasoning of those who in these past days have marched from Smithfield and the docks to the House of Commons to proclaim the doctrines of a new racialism.

I reminded the meeting that in the first fortnight of the administration, in 1964, I had denounced the doctrines propounded in the Smethwick election and taken firm action against racialism in Rhodesia. And now, after three-and-a-half years, the new Race Relations Bill at home and the tabling of a further Rhodesian resolution at the United Nations, had, I said:

> made clear the unequivocal attitude of your Government in the world confrontation between racialism and decency.
>
> That attitude is one from which we will under no circumstances depart. The principles on which that attitude is based are too fundamental for compromise. But if we are to maintain the principle of racial equality we must create practical conditions in which these principles are acceptable to all our people, including those who day by day live their lives alongside immigrant communities.

I then devoted some serious passages to explaining the facts of immigration, and immigration control, the steps we were taking to prevent evasion, and the statistics.

I announced new measures we had been working on to deal with the problems of areas where immigration had been at a high rate. I paid tribute to the work of the ministers who had been charged with this problem – first Maurice Foley then David Ennals – and the thousands of voluntary workers, church members and local administrators who day by day were working to solve community problems. Central government assistance to the fifty-seven local authority areas, identified by the Home Office as having real and substantial immigrant problems, had risen from £480 millions in 1963–4 to £910 millions in 1968–9 – for housing, education, health (excluding the cost of hospitals and the family doctor service) and other community services. I then announced the 'Urban Programme', which had been worked out inter-departmentally under the direction of the Home Secretary, to provide further help in housing, education and health in a number of big towns and cities where these problems were greatest, whether immigration was a factor there or not.

I then swung into my main theme, the treatment and rights of immigrants already settled as British citizens, their right to equality regardless of colour, race or national origin. I cited our action on the Race Relations Bill, against which the Conservatives had voted, with the honourable exception of about twenty of their MPs, led by Sir Edward (later Lord) Boyle, who abstained. Those who had voted against the Bill, I attacked as men who '... play on the fears and anxieties which exist in this country on the subject of immigration and use the Race Relations Bill for the purpose'.

I laid our uncompromising anti-racialism right along the line, and went on:

This century, with the loss of millions of lives, has underlined the fact that democracy survives as long as it is fought for. It is challenged today across the Atlantic. It is for us, living in the home of parliamentary democracy, to decide how we respond to the challenge here in Britain ... This movement of ours has fought steadfastly, regardless of cost, against the prejudice of race and colour.

I referred, as I had seventeen months earlier in the House when dealing with racialism in the Rhodesian context, to the 'Memorial of the Working Men of Lancashire' to Abraham Lincoln:

I cannot help but compare their attitude with the attitude of that vocal minority of workers who marched in London last week.

Today I have dealt at length, to the exclusion of other issues, with an issue which is fundamental to our survival as the kind of nation we are and must remain, because I am not prepared to stand aside and see this country engulfed by the racial conflict which calculated orators or ignorant prejudice can create. Nor in the great world confrontation on race and colour, where this country must declare where it stands, am I prepared to be a neutral, whether that confrontation is in Birmingham or Bulawayo.

In these issues there can be no neutrals, no escape. For in the world of today, while political isolationalism invites danger and economic isolationism invites bankruptcy, moral isolationalism invites contempt.

There are those amongst us who are old enough to remember – and those who are young enough to have read about – the prophetic cartoon that Will Dyson drew for the *Daily Herald* in 1919 when the politicians at Versailles were endangering the peace for which millions had died in the Great War. It was the picture of a baby labelled '1940 Class' and the caption was 'I seem to hear a child weeping'. On our response to this challenge of race and colour on a national scale, in each of our cities and towns, in Birmingham and Smethwick, in Wolverhampton, in Bradford, in Huddersfield, and in the metropolitan boroughs, will depend the future of every child, white or black or brown, for whom we today are the trustees.

... from this historic platform have been heard the words of my Prime Ministerial predecessors speaking in the accents of Victorian complacency, of military and economic imperialism, of nationalism – a generation ago the accents of appeasement.

From this platform I joined with you in denouncing Suez.

Today we face together a different challenge and I have confidence we can meet it together by reasserting our faith in a society of tolerance, of kindliness, and of fair play, qualities for which the British people are admired throughout the world. They must not be able to say what Will Dyson said of the men of Versailles, that we did not heed the weeping of that child. And be it in terms of the survival of this nation, or be it in terms of a world divided by race and colour, I ask not whether that child is black or brown or white ...

The speech was very fully reported. The *Guardian* said that I had preached a 'sermon on the brotherhood of man, which at another time and another place would have seemed routine from the leader of a Labour movement which, Mr Wilson reminded us yet again, "is a crusade or it is nothing" '.

It is significant that the principal Conservative newspapers derided my suggestion that the race and immigration issues should be taken out of politics. Their message was that, regardless of national considerations, there were votes in this issue for the Conservatives: it was an act of impertinence for the Prime Minister to take a national line.

Mr Peter Jenkins of the *Guardian,* one of the few Westminster commentators who troubled to go to Birmingham, had a different interpretation:

> The Prime Minister did the morale of the Government, the Labour party, and himself a power of good by his speech at Birmingham on Sunday. It was the most impressive performance Mr Wilson has given for a very long while. It ranked with the best of those 1964 campaign speeches which caused the most hostile commentators to recognize in him – wrongly as it has mostly turned out – a driving radical force: they wrote about the fire in his belly and compared him with even Lloyd George.
>
> Mr Wilson's task in those days was to take the ordinary material aspirations and basic moral decencies of the Labour movement and supercharge them with combative spirit. And it was by summoning up the practical, down-to-earth characteristically north-country moral force of the historic Labour movement – not by reciting the moral imperatives of metropolitan liberalism – that the Prime Minister spoke to such effect in Birmingham.
>
> On the eve of the municipal elections it would have been all too easy to deliver a bromide exhortation to racial tolerance. But Mr Wilson courageously, and quite deliberately, did not make this sort of speech: instead, at a time when his supporters are feeling pretty sorry for themselves, he gave them something to feel proud about; at a time when their tails are between their legs, he gave them something worth fighting for; at a time when there is a despondent feeling that all politicians are the same, he reminded them that some are a lot more decent than others.

Whatever inspiration this speech might have given our people in the borough elections, the ballot boxes revealed municipal results almost as bad as the previous year's. Ignoring no less serious losses in urban and rural district councils, Labour lost in the boroughs 540 seats net; if urban and rural districts and Scottish burghs are included the net loss was 919. On 9th May, in the London boroughs, where all the seats had to be filled, we lost fifteen of the eighteen boroughs, leaving us in control of only Barking, Tower Hamlets and Southwark.

Yet again we faced a serious problem of morale. There was a further challenge; before the votes were counted, Mr Cecil King, correctly anticipating the results, claimed the boroughs and the parliamentary by-elections, as grist to his demand that 'enough is enough'. Britain needed a new Prime Minister, and Labour a new leader. By a strange coincidence this secured a leading place in the journals he then controlled, though I was left in no doubt about the disgust felt by a considerable number of his employees. But it was a lead-story, too, in the rest of the press and on the television screens.

I was not concerned about Mr King's disenchantment: I alone was in a position to assess the measure, to a person of his calibre, of certain of his personal disappointments. But his doom-laden forecasts about the economy could be damaging. He was a director of the Bank of England and to the ignorant it might be assumed that part-time members of the Court of the Bank 'knew something' of the financial position Britain was facing. This would have been difficult at any time, but this was a bad week for such behaviour. Whether he had realised it or not, we were but a few days from the date when six-month forward sales of sterling made in the week before devaluation were coming up for settlement. The Bank of England had expressed to the Treasury their concern about monetary movements on that day; Mr King's *démarche* could not have been worse timed. But before the Chancellor could act to remove him from the Court he had the grace to resign.

A fortnight later his colleagues on the board of the International Publishing Corporation suddenly realised the meaning of his slogan, 'enough is enough', and found it had an unintended significance for them. He was sacked while shaving.

The borough results and Mr King's *démarche* made the headlines. I was in Bristol on the Friday, 10th May, opening a new zinc smelter at Avonmouth and discussing regional problems with the Planning Board and the Regional Economic Council. I was pursued everywhere for comments on Mr King's statement, which did not seem to me to be important and I told the press and television reporters:

> It is not for me to comment on what Mr King has said. It's a free country, it's a free Press – long may it remain so, and I hope that our newspaper proprietors will always be as free to find space in their papers as other citizens.

In the event, though no longer a newspaper proprietor, he had no difficulty in finding press space for his views and throughout 1968 and the following year, even when our payments were in strong and growing surplus, he steadfastedly maintained his watch for the financial doom which never came.

His attack of 9th May, however, coming as it did from a Bank of England director, did have some effect on the markets. The effect of it, combined with the borough results – hailed as a sign of political disintegration – produced a heavy run on sterling on the Friday. Informing

Parliament of his acceptance of Mr King's resignation from the Bank, on 13th May the Chancellor repudiated the scare-mongering. It was left to an irreverent left-wing member to ask:

> Is my rt. hon. Friend aware that when Mr King called for the resignation of the Prime Minister the value of the pound went down? Therefore would my rt. hon. Friend agree that the value of sterling would go up if he, together with every other Member on this side of the House, stated unequivocally that the Prime Minister will continue for a long time to come?

Immediately after these events the Government put a further strain on a hard-hit Parliamentary Party by publishing the new Prices and Incomes Bill. After devaluation we had said this would be necessary. The Bill provided that existing powers would be continued; it extended to twelve months the time for which a standstill order could be effective, following a reference to the Prices and Incomes Board; new powers were taken to require reductions in existing prices where the Board so recommended; the housing ministers were given new authority to restrain, and where necessary, phase rent increases proposed by local councils and other public authorities, and the Treasury was given power to require notification of dividend increases and prevent excessive distributions. The Part IV powers of the 1966 Bill, under which the six-month incomes freeze of that year had been ordered, had, of course, lapsed in August 1967.

On 13th May I had a meeting with the trade union group of Labour MPs, which went well. Two days later I addressed a crowded and anxious party meeting. I took for my canvas the wider political scene, as well as the Prices and Incomes Bill. Referring to the previous week's local elections as 'the worst defeat we have suffered', and referring to press demands for my resignation, I said, 'There is no question of my nerve giving under the alleged strain of these past days ...'

The Government and the PLP, I went on, faced a situation requiring 'cool heads and strong nerves'. It was a test of the loyalty and determination of the movement outside, 'but it is no good looking to them if we have not got the guts to give a lead'.

That lead was to make a success of the Government's economic policies, '... to win through to surplus and independence, to steady growth based on full employment, to the high wage economy we have set as our objectives'.

And these objectives could not be realised without great risk, until a strong balance of payments was assured. We had a two-year economic strategy on which our political strategy for the rest of the Parliament, and the years beyond that, increasingly depended. '... If we fail, all our speeches, including the speeches of those who demand the right to dissociate at the expense of their fellow members, will be of no avail when the time comes at the end of this Parliament.'

I conceded to the Government's critics that the stringency on family incomes was a major factor in local authority and by-election defeats. But those who sought an easy way out by deserting the Government on prices and incomes policy would not save the day. In addition to the dangers it entailed for the balance of payments, the breakdown of this essential element in our policy would mean further harsh budgets and expenditure cuts.

I left them in no doubt that this was an issue of confidence. No member had the right to abstain and leave it to others to ensure a majority. Every member who abstained, I reminded them, '... is taking an action which but for his neighbour could only produce a Tory majority'.

I then referred to the reasons for our confidence that the two-year strategy would succeed. One was the build-up of export orders, widely reported in the business press, with their expressed expectation of a really significant increase in export shipments in 1969. Another was the growing success of our industrial policies, modernising and improving the efficiency of industries old and new, to which, increasingly, newspapers hostile to us were grudgingly paying tribute.

I ended by warning of the alternatives – either a Conservative Government, or the 'silken trap' our enemies were busy devising for us. This phrase, which caused a little personalised speculation at the time, was a reference to leading articles in certain newspapers calling for a change in the leadership not just in personal terms, but in conditions in which the party would forswear its socialist beliefs and policies and at the same time sever its links with the trade union movement.

The meeting ended with a vote of 205 to 42 in favour of the Government's policies. But more than that, it was widely regarded as decisive in its effect on the morale of the party. Mr Houghton, the PLP chairman, in his report to the press, said I was 'vigorous, confident, and in fighting form' and our members 'very heartened', by the spirit I showed.

The press, after their soundings of PLP members, described it as my 'most forceful for many a day... all his old authority and fighting spirit' (*The Times*); 'a fighting speech which even his critics described as impressive' (*Daily Express*); a 'handsome victory' (*Sun*); while the *Guardian*'s main heading was 'Party rallies to Premier as rebels go to earth'. A number of newspapers headlined my words, 'The great fightback starts today'. And so it proved. Whatever difficulties we were later to face, Labour's fight-back began in May 1968. It was possible in that month, but not again, for a diarist in *The Times* to calculate that the next general election would leave Labour with a rump of 78 seats, after nearly 300 losses, and to speculate on my successor when the 21,000 majority in my own constituency was turned into a defeat. But the public opinion polls remained for a few weeks more at their worst ever and took a little time to recover from the storms of early May.

In the debate the following week, the Prices and Incomes Bill secured its second reading by 290 votes to 255: there were 35 abstentions, and one recognised eccentric, Peter Jackson, voted with the Conservatives.

In the next few weeks I was able to continue my tours of different parts of the country. One memorable visit, on 24th–25th May, was to the General Assembly of the Church of Scotland on the invitation of the Lord High Commissioner, Lord Reith, whom in 1967 and 1968 I had recommended to the Queen for appointment. The Assembly invited me to address them from the floor, the first time a Prime Minister had done so since Mr Attlee in 1946. I devoted the greater part of my speech to the relations between religion and politics, to racial questions at home and abroad – including Rhodesia and South Africa – and to the growth of colour prejudice in some of our great towns and cities. The speech was generously applauded, but listening to the debates, and meeting ministers and others later, it was the tragedy developing week by week in Nigeria and the strong pro-Biafran feeling among members of the Assembly, which dominated the thinking of many of those present.

In the last days of May, France was plunged into chaos, which manifested itself first in her universities, then spread through wide sections of industry. *'Les délices de l'anarchie'*, of which President de Gaulle had spoken as the most likely state of post-de Gaulle France, appeared to have taken charge, and there was a moment when there appeared a strong possibility, perhaps more, of a military coup. Inevitably the French franc plunged to danger levels and there was a massive panic movement of foreign exchange out of the country. It was several weeks before order was re-established. That it was established was in part due to the General's cool acceptance of the risk of calling a general election, which went well for him; but it was due much more, many felt, to the firm and impressive handling of the situation by Prime Minister Pompidou, shortly afterwards dropped by the President. Following the re-establishment of order the franc returned to an uneasy equilibrium – until fresh trouble hit the monetary world in the autumn.

The House adjourned for the Whitsun recess on 31st May. After an arduous winter and spring, with hardly a day off, I had decided that I would plan my Whitsun recess engagements better than in the previous three years and get a few days' rest at Chequers. In the first week of the normal two-week recess the TUC were celebrating their centenary and this meant three engagements, one with a major speech at Belle Vue, Manchester, on Whit Saturday. I had been invited also to go down to Plymouth for the annual conference of the National Association of Head Teachers and was under the strongest pressure from my sister, a prominent local member, to accept it.

But I consoled myself with the thought of a clear break in the second week of the recess. Sadly, the Chief Whip came to me a fortnight before the adjournment and said that if we were to get the legislative programme through Parliament and adjourn by a reasonable date in the summer, the Whitsun adjournment must be cut to a single week. Robbed again.

Nevertheless, these were enjoyable speaking engagements. The TUC historical pageant at Belle Vue was a delight, culminating in a cavalcade of floats and functional vehicles of all kinds. The end of the day saw me hoisted, with George Woodcock, to the top of a fire appliance, some seventy feet up, to wave to the tens of thousands who had come for the celebrations – all to the horror of my Special Branch officers who saw me at that moment as a perfect target for any ill-disposed individual. However, we were clearly among friends.

The speeches were mostly commemorative, but I took the opportunity to draw the moral that, with the accession of the trade union movement over a century to the position of an estate of the realm, with inherent power and with the established right of consultation, it had the duty to show a responsibility commensurate with its power:

> The TUC has arrived. It is an estate of the realm, as real, as potent, as essentially part of the fabric of our national life, as any of the historic Estates.
>
> It is not easy for many within a movement that grew out of revolt to accept all the implications of a role that now is creative, consultative and, in the central economic struggle in which this nation is involved, decisive. Influence and power carry with them the duties of responsibility. Never has this been more clearly illustrated than in the historic decision of the Trades Union Congress, fifteen months ago, to accept the need for an incomes policy which would relate the planned growth of wages to the achieved growth in productivity; which, indeed, went further, in that individual unions, many of them of great power, agreed to surrender to the central organization some part of the historic sovereignty for which they had battled for over a century.

I then drew the moral in terms of the parliamentary struggle over incomes legislation: while in the longer-term the voluntary system alone provided the solution to our national problems, in the short-term we needed both the voluntary system and the backing of statutory safeguards.

This part of my speech, it seemed to me, was less enthusiastically received than the carefully worked out parts designed to commemorate one of the most significant developments in Britain's social and economic history.

My Plymouth speech, on the Bank Holiday, 3rd June, gave me the first opportunity for many months to review the progress of education and the record school-building programme:

> In 1963, 482 new schools were provided, giving a total of over 229,000

new places; in 1967 the figures were 729 new schools providing over 332,000 new school places. Over these years, the number of primary schools has practically doubled and the number of new primary places has more than doubled.

I reported on the provision for help to education under the urban programme and gave the figures for higher education, outstripping all previous estimates.

What attracted most press attention was my account of the progress made towards the establishment of the 'Open University' – the University of the Air I had called for in September 1963:

> This new University institution, which will have its own Chancellor and Vice-Chancellor, governing body and full-time staff, will provide full degree courses with the help of radio and television combined with correspondence and residential courses. We expect the first courses to be provided in 1970 and the rolls for students should be opened next year. The aim of the Open University is to widen the opportunities for higher education by giving a second chance to those who can profit from it, but who have been, for one reason or another, unable to go to a University or a College on leaving school. . . .

On the Wednesday morning, 5th June, I was wakened with the news of the shooting of Senator Robert Kennedy at the end of his successful California primary. Later in the day the news came of his death. He had visited me a few months earlier at No. 10 and we had had a happy and relaxed two hours together.

Now he was victim to the same insensate violence which had murdered his brother, and one could hear the disbelieving scream when the shots were fired – 'Not again!' In a television tribute to Bobby Kennedy, I said,

> It is not only a tragedy for one family or one nation. It is a tragedy in which we are all involved. For the bullets which struck down Robert Kennedy were a symptom of the attacks which, in country after country, and in varying forms, are being aimed at democracy itself.
>
> This is what Robert Kennedy himself condemned a few weeks ago at the funeral for Martin Luther King when, quoting Abraham Lincoln, he said, 'there can be no successful appeal from the ballot to the bullet'. . . .
>
> He himself can do no more to sustain democracy, or to help those for whom he had fought. Rather it is for us to ensure by our response to his death that the seeking after violent solutions, the stirring of hatred against a man because of his race, because of his religion, because of his political convictions, whatever they may be, that these evil things should be outlawed from our great democracies – that because a man has died in the assertion of democracy we should not ourselves, the living, become cynical about democracy and liberty. Because a man has fallen to an assassin's bullet in America we should not fear for the future of democracy in America. Rather should we in Britain, together with the people of America, assert our faith in democracy and liberty on a basis not of conflict and violence but of reasoned solutions.

On Thursday, 13th June, there were by-elections in Sheffield, Brightside, and Oldham West, the first caused by the death of the sitting member, Dick Winterbottom, the second by Leslie Hale's application for the Chiltern Hundreds on grounds of ill-health. The Labour majority of 19,177 in Brightside was reduced to 5,248; that of 7,572 in Oldham was converted into a Conservative majority of 3,311. The swing against the Government in the two constituencies was seventeen per cent, bad enough in all conscience, but an improvement on the catastrophic twenty per cent-plus figures of the spring. A fortnight later we lost Nelson and Colne, Sydney Silverman's seat, the Labour majority of 4,572 giving place to a Tory gain by 3,522. This time the swing was eleven per cent.

Meanwhile the Conservative peers were girding themselves for the challenge of their finest hour, a statutory instrument made under the powers of the post-UDI Southern Rhodesia Act, 1965, imposing a total trade ban on Rhodesia. This was the result of the United Nations' meetings which had followed the executions in Salisbury in March. We had succeeded in holding the understandably violent feelings of African delegates in check and prevented mandatory decisions on the use of force or what would have been a mainly British trade embargo against South Africa. As soon as the order was tabled in the two Houses, there were rumours that the Tories in the House of Lords would use their ancestral majority to throw it out, and without the concurrence of both Houses it could not have effect. How far the move began in their Lordships' House, how far it was a planned operation by the Conservative leadership in the Commons, never became clear, though shadow cabinet briefing claimed credit for Mr Heath's initiative in the matter, and went on to say that it was intended that if a fresh order were laid, it, too, would be voted down and Government policy made unworkable.

The Commons approved the order on 17th June by 319 votes to 246, the Conservatives opposing.

The setting for the Lords' decision could have come from the Savoy Operas. We read of backwoodsmen arriving for the vote who knew neither their own leaders nor the way round the House. Some had never voted before. It was a tense debate, with Lord Shackleton warning the Opposition not only about the constitutional implications of their vote, but about its international repercussions – with Britain unable to carry through its international obligations because of a vote in an unrepresentative chamber.

The order was rejected by a derisory nine votes, 193 to 184. Practically every newspaper recorded it as a moral victory for the Government, and some saw it as a rebuff for Mr Heath's manoeuvring. There was an immediate rush in Conservative circles in the Commons to disclaim responsibility for anything which happened along the corridor. What was gratifying was that 40 cross-benchers and 18 bishops had voted for the order, 26 cross-benchers and no bishops against it. Eight Conservatives, headed by Lord Alport, supported the Government. Interesting, too, was the fact that of the hereditary peers, 142 voted against the order (119 of them Conservatives) and 55 for it; peers of the first creation, including life peers, were 129 to 51 in favour, 47 of the 51 being Conservatives. Among cross-bench first creations, 21 supported the order, with three against.

But a constitutional issue had been raised by this tomfoolery. Since the preceding year, in the hope of securing an all-party agreement on House of Lords reform, talks had been going on between representatives of the three main parties under the chairmanship of the Lord Chancellor. The discussions covered two issues: the powers of the Upper House and its composition. On the question of powers, there was little to argue about. However fierce the constitutional arguments in 1910, to say nothing of the quite deep difference which arose over Lords reform in 1948, there was little disposition to argue in the later sixties that the Lords should have anything more than a very brief delaying power over legislation passed by the elected Chamber. But there was another issue, untouched in the previous reforms – the power of the Lords to reject an Order in Council or a statutory instrument which needed the assent of both Houses to become law. (There was also the related problem of 'negative prayers', that is those orders which automatically became effective on promulgation, but could be nullified by a decision of either House.)

Successive Governments of all parties had come to rely more and more on this kind of delegated legislation, for modern laws are inevitably complex, and detailed provisions, too complicated to be included in the principal act, have to be made by order. Moreover, as facts and requirements change, it is frequently necessary for the law to be altered to keep pace with them. The Southern Rhodesia Act, 1965, was an example. To take another from a very different area of our national life, recent legislation on drug control, introduced by the Labour Government in the spring of 1970, and carried through by our successors, had to take account of the fact that any legislation might become rapidly out of date as new narcotic substances came into the hands of the drug traffickers. Power was given, therefore, to the Home Secretary to make, in effect, new laws by order within the general ambit and purpose of the parent act.

But the power of the Lords to override the wishes of the elected House and negative such delegated legislation was clearly intolerable and there was no difficulty in securing all-party agreement to a reform to circumscribe it.

The discussions on the composition of the Lords were equally constructive. The Conservative leadership in the Upper House was no less keen than our own people in so reforming it as to abolish, for all new accessions, the hereditary qualification for membership. The numbers of life peers (or other peers of the first creation) were to reflect the proportions among the different parties which applied in the Commons, Parliament by Parliament. But there were inevitably many difficult problems to solve, none insoluble or likely to cause disagreement, but some of them inevitably requiring time. There was every reason to hope that an agreed outline could be prepared in time for legislation in the 1968–9 Parliamentary session.

But the action of the Lords on the sanctions order – an order which it was required to give effect to a binding international obligation – raised the whole issue again in an acute form. Many of our back-benchers and some ministers felt that urgent action must be taken to deal with powers, while leaving the issue of composition for later decision. I was pressed to make a statement in the House. Clearly the new situation had to be taken seriously. Deliberate action of the kind taken by the Conservative leadership in the Lords while the discussions were proceeding – whether or not at the instigation of their Commons' leadership, but certainly with their enthusiastic acquiescence – could only be regarded as bad faith.

In my statement I said that this deliberate and calculated decision '... was in direct contravention of the spirit in which these talks were being conducted'.

There was no precedent, I added, for the voting down of a statutory instrument by the non-elected Chamber, in which, in advance of reform, most of its members sat not by the right of creation, but by the right of succession from some near or distant ancestor. I pointed out that not since the Parliament Act of 1911 had the Lords deliberately set themselves out to frustrate in this way the executive actions, and in this case actions to fulfil international commitments, of the elected Government.

Since this decision was clearly taken after the fullest consideration, and after every warning of the consequences, there can be no question of these all-party talks, in the new circumstances, continuing. Although time has not been wasted, and valuable proposals have been put forward both about the powers and the composition of another place, I must tell the House that it is the intention of Her Majesty's Government, at an early date of the Government's choosing, to introduce comprehensive and radical legislation.

While these constitutional arguments were developing, a new and important state paper was published, the Report of the Royal Commission on Trade Unions and Employers' Associations, set up three years earlier, and now simply known by the name of its chairman, Lord Donovan. I had originally had some doubts about Ray Gunter's wisdom, in 1965, in acceding to industrial pressures to include among the membership representatives of the TUC and the employers' organisation; inevitably, attitudes taken on the Commission tended to reflect sectional pressures. But my final judgment, after the publication of the Report and its role in informing the public in the years of acute controversy which followed, is that he was right. The Report gained both in practical knowledge and in authority by the inclusion of men such as Lord Collison, Lord Robens, George Woodcock, Lord Tangley, Sir George Pollock and Mr John Thomson.

Whatever one's attitude to the reform of industrial relations, and whether or not one desires to import legal machinery, one is impressed by Donovan's thorough analysis of industrial relations in Britain over the years. Most striking were the detailed and constructive proposals for reforms patiently achieved within industry, in workshop practice, in the improvement of agreements, negotiating machinery, and disputes procedures, and in the constructive call for better education in the practice of industrial relations at all levels, and on both sides of industry. The tragedy was that we had to wait until 1965 for the appointment of the Commission; for thirteen years nothing had been done. Indeed, Mr Heath, as Minister of Labour, had in 1960 specifically rejected a backbench proposal for an inquiry.

The Report was fundamentally a demand for action by industry itself, for, in the view of the majority, employers and unions were jointly responsible for allowing industrial relations to degenerate into the state of 'indecision and anarchy' which the Commission held to exist.

One of its central findings was that industry-wide negotiations were becoming of less and less importance as factory bargaining became more widespread. But this bargaining usually took place in an informal and fragmented way between managers and shop stewards, resulting in disorderly pay structures, leap-frogging, no procedure for settling disputes and a growing number of unofficial strikes accounting for some ninety per cent of the total days lost by industrial disputes.

For three reasons the majority rejected legal action as a means of dealing with this situation. The first, on which they did not lay great stress, was the traditional view that the law should not concern itself with these questions. The second was that the type of agreement which usually determines pay and working conditions is too vague and informal to form the basis of any action in a court of law. The third was the fact that employers were reluctant to make use even of the legal remedies they already possessed for fear of making relations worse. The Commission felt, and had international experience on their side, that industrialists would be even more reluctant to make use of any new remedies.

The greater part of the Commission's recommendations related to improvements, industry by industry, firm by firm, in procedures and day-to-day relationships. Among the central proposals were, first, the progressive registration by companies, with the Department of Employment and

Productivity, of agreements negotiated at company or plant level, which should increasingly aim to lay down specific rules governing pay negotiations, disputes procedures and the role of shop stewards. Second was a proposal that a Commission on Industrial Relations should be set up to investigate cases referred to it by the DEP in which working arrangements seemed to be unsatisfactory or where industrial relations were fouled by non-recognition of trade unions. On the specific question of unconstitutional strikes, the Commission recorded frankly that they had sought hard to find an interim remedy but had failed. But the use of the law, as a sanction or a deterrent, they specifically ruled out.

As soon as the Report was published, Barbara Castle began formal discussions with both sides of industry to formulate a plan for its implementation.

Less than a fortnight after the Donovan Report came the report of the Fulton Committee, set up to provide for the civil service the first full-dress inquiry since the Harcourt-Trevelyan reforms of the early 1850s. Its terms of reference were wide-ranging, covering the structure, recruitment and management of the home civil service. As with Donovan, the Report was exhaustive, and was backed by volumes of evidence and research, for example the first major examination in our age of the social structure and the recruitment of and entry into the home civil service.

The opening chapter, which gave rise to some controversy, was highly critical of the civil service as the committee had found it, though it conceded that there had been some quiet reforms in the immediately preceding years and that these were gathering momentum. The Report's main finding was that insufficient attention had been paid to management in the service, consequently it called for a new system of training, organisation and career management. Its final chapter included twenty-two conclusions and recommendations.

The main recommendations I accepted in a parliamentary statement on the day of publication. First was the proposal to establish a new, separate civil service department, no longer part of the Treasury. The civil service commission, within the department, would maintain its continued independence and political impartiality in the selection of new entrants. Second, we accepted the proposal for a civil services college – now in being – and third, and most controversial within the service, we accepted the committee's proposals for the abolition of the class system – administrative, executive, clerical – within the civil service, and the creation of a single unified grading structure. This, in force from 1st January 1971, meant, I told the House:

> that for everyone in the civil service, whether from school, whether from a college of technology, or from a university, whether he or she comes in from industry or from a profession – all in future, the school-

leaver, the graduate, the accountant, the engineer, the scientist, the lawyer – for all of them there will be an open road to the top which, up to now, has been, in the main, through the administrative class.

The committee laid great stress on two developments I had repeatedly pressed. The first was a freer two-way movement between the civil service and other areas of our national life, such as private and public industry, local government and the professions. The second was the development of regionalism and, in particular, the intention I confirmed in the House that new recruits to the civil service should be given ample opportunities, at an early stage in their careers, to work in the regions and, where possible, in services which would bring them into contact with the public.

The chairman of the committee had been delegated to ask my opinions on the ministerial responsibility for the new Civil Service Department. He and his colleagues accepted my view, and reported that:

> the new department should be under the control of the Prime Minister. We hope that he will retain direct responsibility for senior appointments, machinery of Government and questions of security. Outside this area, we suggest that the Prime Minister should delegate day-to-day responsibility to a non-departmental minister of appropriate seniority who is also a member of the Cabinet....

The Prime Minister was to hold the title of Minister of the Civil Service as well as the traditional title of First Lord of the Treasury. As I had intended from the first, I nominated Lord Shackleton, the Paymaster General and later in the year once again Lord Privy Seal, as the non-departmental minister to take charge of the day-to-day ministerial work of the department. He was an ideal choice, with long business experience of personnel questions and a dedicated supporter of the Fulton reforms. His work as Leader of the House of Lords left him adequate time for his civil service work. He and Sir William Armstrong, the new head of the civil service, immediately plunged into the negotiations with the staff associations. They, and we, were lucky in the constructive attitude shown by the civil service union leaders, headed by the chairman of the staff side of the Whitley Council, Mr Leslie Williams, and the successive reforms went through smoothly and rapidly. I maintained a very close interest in the progress of the reforms in the civil service. In this I was extremely fortunate in the services, going far beyond his already heavy Downing Street duties, of my principal private secretary, Michael Halls. His civil service training, after his army service, had been mainly in the Board of Trade, where he had served in my private office in the late 1940s. He was the epitome of the new management type envisaged by the Fulton committee but, more than this, his main preoccupation in the latter years of a distinguished career was civil service reform and the speediest possible implementation of Fulton. His annotated comments on the progress reports by the Department were of the greatest value to me and none of the reports was sufficiently comprehensive or urgent to meet the requirements of his exacting and impatient mind. The last of his reports on this subject was in my box on the day, in April 1970, of his tragic death, to which his unremitting devotion to work, at all hours of the day and night, had so critically contributed. He died a few weeks before he was due to be posted to a still more challenging post which would have combined his great administrative qualities with his capacity for executive economic management.

On the late evening of Friday, 28th June, I was at Chequers when my private office telephoned me to say that Ray Gunter, clearly in a determined mood, was calling at No. 10 with a letter. All the signs were that it would involve his resignation, though he had given no hint to me that he was even considering such a step. When it was delivered to my office, and the text teleprinted through to me, I telephoned him to ask him what it was about and invited him to visit me the next morning. He was not prepared to discuss it, but wanted his resignation announced that night and his letter published. This, I explained, was not possible; resignations have no effect, still less can they be announced, until they have been submitted to the Queen. He agreed to await protocol, but made it clear that his decision was final. But he could give no coherent explanation.

I knew that he had never fully accepted his move from Labour to Power. It was only later that I came to the view that he had been told, with malice aforethought, that I had intervened to prevent his appointment to the post of General Secretary of the Labour party. This was not, and could not, be true, but in his mood he might have believed a rumour to this effect. Another theory was that he was upset by press stories and photographs of his successor at his beloved Ministry mately drinking tea with the sewing ladies who had brought sections of the car industry to a standstill with their equal-pay strike; it did not help that tea and sympathy brought a settlement. But one story – subsequently peddled in *The Economist* and elsewhere – that he was a hawk on income policies, would not bear examination. At a ministerial meeting under my chairmanship earlier in the week he had made a moving appeal against too rigid an application of incomes policy in a particular industrial situation.

On the Saturday we spoke again. He was determined to go. I had to begin to make alternative dispositions and a number of colleagues were called to Chequers for the Sunday. Roy Mason, the ex-miner Postmaster-General, was my choice to succeed him, with a seat in the Cabinet. To follow Roy Mason at the Post Office I decided on John Stonehouse who had done well in a succession of ministerial posts and who had shown in the minor and top positions in Aviation a full understanding of the technological issues which a modern PMG required. Bill Mallalieu, who had been concerned with civil aviation matters at the Board of Trade, was moved to Technology to take charge of aviation industry matters and in his place Bill Rodgers, Under-Secretary in the Foreign Office, became Minister of State.

But inevitably Ray Gunter's resignation, expressed in terms of an unwillingness to continue to serve in a Government headed by myself, provided a wonderful opportunity for the predominantly Conservative press.

But there were other issues to attend to. One, on the Monday, 1st July, when Ray Gunter's departure was the main concern of public comment, took place at Lancaster House. It was the signature, simultaneous with other ceremonies in Washington and Moscow, of the non-proliferation treaty which our disarmament ministers – first Lord Chalfont and subsequently Fred Mulley – had laboured so effectively to achieve.

I was involved in troubles over Greece. The take-over there by the colonels was a matter with which we were deeply and intimately concerned. I had used strong words about it in the House and elsewhere, which had caused the colonels to threaten trade reprisals. On the Tuesday, 2nd July, I had to answer questions from members even more affronted than hitherto by repressive actions against freedom in Greece. Off the cuff I accused the regime there of 'bestialities'. It was not the word for which I was groping; it should in fact have been 'barbarities'. Not that that was a word acceptable in Athens; if my limited knowledge of Greek counted for anything, it meant 'alien' or, in Attic terms, un-Greek. But apparently an accusation of bestiality was even more offensive to the Greeks than it would be in English. Further trade threats were issued in Athens and the matter was raised again in the House by an Opposition which never – if trade matters were involved – failed to dissociate itself from any expression by the Government in favour of freedom. It was handled in the most elegant manner by Tony Crosland, whom I had authorised to withdraw my more offensive phrase and substitute the less. Parliamentary peace was re-established and in Athens honour was satisfied. 'Barbarities' was gratefully accepted.

This coincided with a climax in a new 'Wilson must go' campaign run by certain sections of the press. The *Guardian*, however, ran a story headlined 'Wilson must go lobby makes little headway'.

The lobby, such as it was, consisted almost exclusively of a few ex-ministers I had dropped and an equally small number of others who were aggrieved by the fact that I had failed to bring them into Government in 1964 or subsequently. *The Times*, which had not ceased to run leading articles calling for a change at No. 10, published the result of a straw poll their local reporters had taken among leading Labour personalities in different parts of the country. Innocent of Westminster gossip, these grass-roots representatives were almost solidly against pressures for my departure. At the same time Thomson newspapers, through their political correspondents representing newspapers all over the country, approached their MP contacts and reported that only ten per cent of the MPs to whom they had spoken wanted the leadership question re-opened.

The economy was in the news again. The *Director*, the journal of the Institute of Directors, emphatically not a fully-paid up affiliate of the Labour party, asserted that the economy was on the mend. In the indus-trial relations field, a rail go-slow was suddenly imposed and was as quickly ended.

On 6th July I addressed the all-Wales Labour party rally at Newtown, Montgomery. I took the opportunity to carry into the country the fight-back theme of my rallying call to the Parliamentary Party the previous month. In political terms it was perhaps the most important I had made since we entered Government. Starting from a reference to two years of electoral disappointments, the main theme of my speech was 'change' – change in industry, in our institutions, in the social services, in education, with the challenge all this meant and the strains it entailed. But I took the opportunity, too, to hit back, almost for the first time, at our opponents:

It is precisely because we are a Labour Government that we have had to face the bitter hostility of those who resent their own loss of power and our being where we are. No other Government can solve the prob-lems of Britain. Or Wales. They never have.
Being a Labour Government means putting Britain and the British people first and doing it regardless of short-term popularity . . .
Being a Labour Government means that you are fighting a hostile and embittered Establishment, a deprived Establishment, soured by depriva-tion of office and power, which they had been brought up to believe were theirs by divine ordinance. An Establishment which does not scruple to misrepresent or to distort, an Establishment which is prepared to appeal to those who use money to make money, to do their dirty work for them . . .
Economic change, industrial change, change in our barnacled national institutions, social change. But all change hurts. And they exploit the hurts. At every turn they have not scrupled to appeal to their friends in sections of the press, in the aristocratic Establishment, in commerce and finance. They even sought them in the unions . . .
One week they seek to cash in on the prejudices of a small minority of racially-minded dockers. . . . A week or two later they are busy sum-moning up a small majority of racially-minded peers . . .
One week at a fund-raising lunch for industrialists they appeal to their most reactionary prejudices by promising an era of terrorism against the trade unions. . . . The next week they are busy seeking allies in trade union ranks on incomes policy. . . .
One week they are promising the CBI that only wages will be controlled and prices and profits will be let free, and the next week they try to lure

Labour back-benchers into the Tory lobby by voting to let wages rip by rejecting prices and incomes policy . . .

But now their sourness and deprivation are giving way to a new sense of anxiety. For a year the Tory leadership, and their allies in the Tory press, have screamed their heads off in a campaign of distortion and misrepresentation which might make one wonder what Lloyd George was complaining about. Now they are moving into an orchestrated, if inharmonious, double fortissimo. And the source of this musical inspiration is not the confidence they pretend, but the anxiety they feel because they know time is not on their side. They have read the comments of expert and keen-eyed overseas observers. They have read the view objectively expressed that Britain is on the way to an economic miracle.

This contains for them a tantalising alternative of hope and despair. They feel they have only a few months to exploit the hardships of change to a point where they can get us out so that they can enjoy the economic dividends of what we, what the British people, have achieved, are achieving. You will forgive me . . . if the words of Nye Bevan are quoted, and I think I may claim I have the right to do it. In those early fifties, he said the Tories were reaping the fruits of the trees we had planted. They are not going to be allowed to do that a second time.

They are not this time going to cash in on the backache involved in planting those trees and then claim credit for the fruits.

This time we are going to see that that harvest accrues to the British people whose work and sacrifices are earning it. This is why our enemies are stepping up the pace. And let us be ready to face it. They have been throwing everything at us for months now. I have not answered back. Not yet. The time will come. I decline to answer personal attacks whether from them, or from the small minority within this movement who in many cases, I am sure, unwittingly allow themselves to be used . . .

Be warned. In these months before the underlying improvement in the economy takes effect, an improvement which even the business columns of the Tory press are having to concede, the Tories will stop at nothing in order to create an opportunity of getting back to power. Some of their parliamentary experts in sick humour are calling for a general election and claiming in aid recent by-election results. I find this mildly ironic from a group of men who for the first time for a hundred years clung to office until the very last minute allowed by the constitution. And let it be clear, a great deal of the problems we have had to cope with were aggravated beyond measure by that postponement. . . .

They are prepared to attack the whole basis of the country's economy, the country's recovery. And this regardless of the justified charge which has been made, that they risk creating conditions harmful to Britain, laden with sacrifices for the British people. They care not, as long as the conditions thus created can do their dirty work for them.

There are many here, millions more throughout the country, who week by week are working to put Britain right in this devaluation situation. And there is a lot of sweat in a thousand pounds of exports. The Tories are ready, for party advantage, so to misrepresent and decry Britain's achievement, and your achievement, that gullible speculators overseas will be tempted to nullify your efforts by taking out not thousands but millions from the British economy.

This is my warning. We have got to put up a firm and united resistance to what they are doing.

They do not care what kind of a Britain results from their wrecking tactics so long as they rule it. It is power they are after. Power, place, patronage and the social cachet that means so much to them. We sought and won power, we hold power and we shall, when the time comes, seek and win again in order to create a Britain which ensures to all the people of Britain, the workers by hand and brain, whoever and wherever they may be, the full fruits of their labours. We know and they know what is at stake. I have spoken – and these are the words not of any Labour Party speaker but of authoritative foreign opinion – of the great transformation which is coming over British industry. You have not only fought, you have worked for this. See that they don't take it away from you.

Newtown was warmly greeted by the press: 'Wilson blows his top at last.'

But, inevitably, hostile writers seized on the reference to an 'economic miracle' which the text clearly showed (a) was a quotation from a foreign commentator, (b) was related to the early seventies – hence the reference to gathering fruit from the trees we had planted; and (c) referred to the growing success of our policies to strengthen and modernise industry. But a new legend was born, the phrase reappeared again and again out of the context in which it was spoken, and when we ran into acute difficulties through international speculation over the Deutschemark later in the year, it was thrown back in my teeth as a new example of misleading the public. One thing at least – opposition press and politicians had proved the truth of my accusation of deliberate distortion, and had used the very speech in which the accusation was made for the purpose of proving it.

I was pleased to see the main article in the *Daily Telegraph* city page on 2nd February 1971 carry the headline 'Miracle of payments surplus is at hand'. My own timetable for its arrival, in my Newtown speech, had been 'the early seventies'.

The article I quoted, by Marc Ullman of *L'Express*, heralded the economic miracle. But the American press were joining in the new and unaccustomed harmony. The *Washington Post* declared that 'The nation is finally on the right economic track. The trouble is that this has been said so often in the last years when it was not true . . . the same rules apply to the crying of non-wolf or wolf . . .' *Newsweek* commented, 'While there may be no "economic miracle", for the first time in twenty years there is solid reason to hope that Britain may receive its place in the economic sun.'

The same week *The Economist* quoted a German business man as saying of our machine-tool industry, one of the problem industries of four years earlier, 'the British have caught up with us'.

To a growing awareness of Britain's achievement by the international economic fraternity, two new events were added.

After devaluation talks began with a number of overseas central banks aimed at shielding sterling from fluctuations in the sterling balances of sterling area countries, some of whom could, in a moment, convert their sterling holdings into gold, dollars and other convertible currencies. The Financial Secretary, Harold Lever, visited a number of European countries for talks with governments and bankers, and the central bankers conferred among themselves, bilaterally, and at Basle.

The Basle agreement, announced by the Chancellor to the House on 8th July, provided, subject to negotiations between Britain and individual sterling area countries about their holdings, that an international facility would be made available to offset fluctuations in the net total of sterling area balances. It related purely to sterling's international role; it was not available to finance any deficit in Britain's own payments through adverse trade, capital or speculative movements.

The second favourable factor was the improvement in the trade figures, June proving the best since January. Only a single month, it was true, but it held out hopes of a better trend and suggested that the Treasury was accurate in its pre-devaluation estimates that it would take six months to secure the first favourable results of devaluation.

Suddenly the economic mood changed. Sterling rose rapidly to safe levels and a healthy inflow of foreign exchange began to strengthen the reserves.

Mr Heath, however, ignored the signs. His long-heralded speech at Wembley was a major diatribe which could only be taken as an attack on sterling at a critical time. He announced a major two-day debate on the economic situation. He was promptly rebuked by Lord Boothby, who accused him of 'selling sterling down the river'. Whatever Mr Heath's intentions, his speech failed to move the City of London, which was more quickly responding to the better economic news. Mr Maudling referred to 'a glimmer of sunshine'. Suddenly the Opposition decided to abandon their plans for an economic debate. Mr Macleod, defending the decision to his bewildered supporters, said that it 'might misfire'.

In the last week of July an event occurred which rapidly became an unchallenged legend and which, like so many of the destructive legends surrounding me, was devoid of truth.

It concerned the appointment of a new General Secretary of the Labour party in succession to Len Williams, who had been recommended to the Queen as Governor-General of Mauritius. At risk of destroying another myth, which continues to receive the accolade of repetition, the Mauritius appointment was not mine; it was that of the Mauritian Prime Minister. It is true that the independence terms provided that the Mauritius recommendation for the first Governor-General should be discussed with the British Prime Minister. Len Williams was the Mauritian choice. Before I could endorse the recommendation I asked to be assured that it had the support of both parties on the island. This was confirmed in unequivocal terms and I therefore agreed.

Len Williams's post had to be filled in good time for the 1968 party conference. A number of National Executive members asked my view: I expressed none. On being elected leader of the party in 1963 I had, in a statement at my first NEC meeting, made clear that I would not be involved in any matter affecting party organisation, selection or endorsement of parliamentary candidates, disciplinary questions, or appointments.

At the end of April George Brown had asked to see me, the first time since his resignation. He came to my private rooms at No. 10 late on a Sunday evening. His purpose was to discuss the General Secretaryship. I said that I was not going to be involved, but, as the discussion continued, I found myself being drawn in – as it proved, a great mistake. George said he would back anyone I named. I said my first choice would have been Bill Simpson, of the Foundry Workers' Union, who, as chairman of an NEC committee on party organisation, had produced a remarkable report. But, I understood, he was not willing to be a candidate. As the discussion went on, I suggested Harry Nicholas, a former Treasurer, and once again an executive member. George was interested in this suggestion but felt that Harry might be too old, because of the retirement rule which operated at sixty-five. This surprised me – I thought Harry Nicholas was in his middle fifties. I then suggested a TU heavyweight, Fred Hayday, whom George strongly supported. He agreed to go off and sound him out. Fred was unwilling and when I approached him at the TUC centenary celebrations at Manchester on 1st June he made it clear that he would not be a candidate.

Also in April Tony Greenwood came to see me. There had been press rumours that he might be willing to stand. Though I said I would not stand in his way if he wanted to run, I strongly advised him not to do so and I stressed that I wanted him to continue as a minister. At a meeting of the NEC, at which I was not present, a committee was appointed, of which I was a member, to arrange for the post to be advertised, to prepare a short-list and to make any appropriate recommendations.

At the end of June we suggested, on the basis of replies to the advertisement – which were not short-listed – that we should proceed to select a Secretary by invitation from possible candidates and make a recommendation to the Executive. Soundings in the NEC had led a number of my colleagues – but not myself – to propose Tony Greenwood. It was suggested, however, that at a time when relations were difficult with the trade union movement we should approach a senior union leader. After discussion, I proposed Alf Allen of the Shopworkers' Union, USDAW, and Tony Greenwood was proposed as second choice.

The name of Ray Gunter also was proposed. My comment was that I did not want to lose either of the two ministers, though if either felt he could best serve the party in the capacity of General Secretary, I would not stand in his way. As between the two ministers, I refused to express a preference, but the two trade union members of the committee, one of whom was Harry Nicholas, ruled Ray Gunter out. But if he resigned from the Ministry of Power because he had been told that I blocked his selection, he was at the receiving end of a lie.

All of us used our persuasive powers on Alf Allen, but to no effect. The committee met again and despite its previous decision that Tony Greenwood should be our recommendation if we could not persuade Alf Allen, Harry Nicholas – whom I had suggested three months earlier and who had previously been thought to be unwilling to stand – was also proposed and the two names went forward to the NEC. The whole story leaked to the effect that I had demanded Tony Greenwood and been rebuffed. A great press legend that Tony was my candidate was run for weeks on this subject, and Tony's defeat was taken by the Conservative press as conclusive proof that I had lost any grip I ever had on the party. That this story was totally untrue was proved by the agreement by the members of the NEC of a full statement setting out the whole history and the facts as I have outlined them above. But when the NEC, by fourteen votes to twelve, selected Harry Nicholas, the whole story started up again in the press – 'rebuff', 'humiliation', and dark stories of late-night meetings of 'conspirators', of a whip-round to bring sick NEC members in to vote against 'my candidate' and other similar nonsense. But, not for the first time, so much costly newsprint had been expended on the legend that there has been little left to print the truth. The stories, fabricated though they were, had a bad effect on relations within the NEC at what was to prove a critical time.

These diversions apart, July was quiet, the first quiet July we had known in four years. There was another bad by-election, this time at Caerphilly, where Labour's majority of 21,148 was cut to 1,874, due to a successful Welsh Nationalist foray. Labour's vote went down by 10,000, the Nationalists' vote was up by a similar amount, the Conservative's down by 1,500, earning them the indignity of a lost deposit. There was little comfort for the Conservatives there. Within days the ever-volatile Conservative press was warning its own leaders of the snap general election they now thought I might call in the autumn!

As the House adjourned for the summer recess, once again, as in 1967, Aberfan came back into the news. The National Coal Board, following the Tribunal report, had moved speedily to remove the overhanging upper reaches of the disaster tip, and were proceeding to integrate it, by skilful landscaping, into the background. Good engineering but bad psychology. A village which had known that day of terror could not live with that sinister commanding height looming over the village.

Day after day, sorrowing parents would still look up at it; children refused to go to bed in rooms from which it could be seen; if they were cajoled into going to their rooms, they could not sleep.

The Saturday before the House adjourned, 20th July, the Secretary of State had been greeted at his Cardiff office by an angry delegation. The following morning, he telephoned me. We met the next day and I agreed with him: the tip had to go. I called the responsible ministers, including the Treasury, together at a meeting on 26th July. The Coal Board had offered a contribution of £250,000, against an estimated total cost of between £750,000 and £1,000,000. I asked the Secretary of State whether Aberfan would make a contribution from a fund which, subscribed to from all over the world, was almost an embarrassment to its trustees. He said there would be difficulty, but he agreed to ask for it.

I prescribed the contributions which should be made. The costings and contributions should begin from the lower estimate of £750,000. To this the Coal Board should contribute the £250,000 they had offered. The remaining £500,000 should be shared equally between the Government and local donations, including a grant from the Aberfan fund, if the villagers were willing. If expenditure rose above £750,000 the Government would meet the first £50,000 of the additional cost, any further increase being shared equally between the Government and the Coal Board up to a limit of £1,000,000. The Coal Board raised difficulties, and I asked the Minister to remind them of a few facts. There was tough talking between the Ministry and the Board but agreement was reached and George Thomas went down that evening, 26th July, to a meeting of the villagers. They too were willing to provide the share of the cost for which I had asked. To quote *The Times*, usually unemotional:

> He told the Aberfan deputation that although the Government were satisfied that there was no threat to safety, it had accepted representations about the fears expressed last week. 'The best friend I have had in all this has been the Prime Minister', he told the villagers. They received this with loud applause, and invited Mr Thomas to a celebration dinner. One or two were in tears.

Shortly afterwards I accepted an invitation from an Aberfan looking to the future to open the new school they were building for the new generation of their children.

On 20th July the House adjourned and on 7th August Mary and I went to Dawlish for the wedding of our elder son, Robin, and then on to the Isles of Scilly for what I hoped – vainly as it proved – would be an uninterrupted holiday.

Chapter 27

Czechoslovakia – Parliament recalled – the Nigerian civil war – the problem of arms supplies – the Biafran propaganda campaign – relief, food and medical supplies – the search for a negotiated settlement – Lord Hunt's mission to Nigeria – the improved economic situation – the Labour party conference at Blackpool – visit of Sir Max Aitken and Lord Goodman to Rhodesia – the Fearless talks – George Thomson's visit to Salisbury – Mr Smith's rejection of the Government's proposals

MY summer holiday, 1968, was anything but peaceful. In the early days of the holiday I received a succession of teleprinter reports of the progress of individual negotiations with each Commonwealth member of the sterling area to whom Treasury and Bank of England teams had been dispatched. The Basle agreement – providing standby credits to cover fluctuations in the over-all total of sterling balances held by sterling area countries – was dependent on the negotiation, with each country concerned, of an agreement that they would continue to hold a guaranteed proportion of their overseas assets in sterling. This was not easy to accept in the case of some of the newer countries, who had suffered a loss in the real value of their reserves through devaluation; Australia, too, presented special problems. But to each our negotiators had to make clear that we could not make special concessions or derogations to any one country which were not available to all. It was an intricate and well-orchestrated operation and by the end of the month we were home. But there were anxious moments and frequent consultations between the Chancellor, other Treasury ministers and myself.

Before the negotiations were complete, a new international crisis broke. Late at night on Tuesday, 20th August, when I was already in bed, my scrambler telephone rang. It was my private office at No. 10. They reported that the Soviet Ambassador, M. Smirnovsky, had telephoned asking to see me at once. Should that be impossible – as indeed it was – he would call on the minister I nominated to receive him. The Foreign Secretary was on holiday in the west country, and Lord Chalfont was in charge of the Foreign Office. Accordingly Ambassador Smirnovsky went to see him. I had given instructions that Lord Chalfont was to telephone me and report. But just before 1.00 a.m. my office telephoned again to say that the nature of the communication Lord Chalfont had received was such that it should not be passed to me, even over the scrambler telephone. I could only speak on the totally secure instrument which was installed in my office in the Customs and Excise building.

I rapidly dressed – my detectives were standing by – and went down to take the message. It was the Soviet intimation of their intervention in Czechoslovakia.

I decided to return at once and instructed my office to contact, through the Defence Minister, RNAS Culdrose to send a helicopter for me at first light, and to have a fast plane waiting to fly me to London. Unfortunately, I was told, repairs were being made to the runway, and I should have to fly to the RAF station at St Mawgan. Worse, the weather forecast presaged thick fog. There was an RNVR craft on a training exercise at the Quay at Scilly. I sent my Special Branch inspector to alert them to take me over by sea if air travel was ruled out, for I knew they were due to leave early for the mainland. Unfortunately they had engine trouble and could not guarantee to be away before 10.00 a.m. In the event, the fog lifted just as we were due to depart. I left Scilly at 7.00 a.m. and was in Downing Street at 9.10. Michael Stewart arrived five minutes later. We reviewed the situation and worked out instructions to Lord Caradon at the United Nations. He had been informed of the position on my instructions within minutes of my talk with Alun Chalfont. We agreed a message of instruction to our ambassador at NATO headquarters, and to all Commonwealth and foreign posts.

We agreed, too, on the terms of a statement, the first, I think, issued by any country, condemning Soviet intervention as 'a flagrant violation of the United Nations Charter and of all accepted standards of international behaviour'.

By mid-morning the Foreign and Commonwealth Offices had convened a meeting of all Commonwealth High Commissioners.

I decided that Parliament should be recalled. There was little that Government or Parliament could do in the face of this assertion of what later came to be known as the 'Brezhnev doctrine' – that the Soviet Government reserved its freedom to intervene in the internal affairs of any Eastern bloc country – but the action taken by the Soviet Government was so serious that only in Parliament could national anxiety and concern be adequately expressed.

The Leader of the House and the Chief Whip were alerted and Mr Speaker's office informed. Mr Heath was abroad, so I invited Mr Maudling, as his deputy, to call. I was expecting him to press for the recall of Parliament, the normal response of any Opposition, but in this case abundantly justified. On the contrary, he seemed a little taken aback by our decision but undertook to get in touch with the Opposition Chief Whip, who was not immediately available. (He was in fact in Scotland with Sir Alec Douglas-Home, whom we also wanted urgently to contact, as shadow Foreign Secretary, so that Michael Stewart could put him as fully in the picture as the information available to us would permit.)

By this time my Foreign Office secretary, Michael Palliser, who had been holidaying in the Ardennes with his father-in-law, Paul-Henri Spaak, had returned to No. 10, having heard the news on the radio. Only a little later Michael Halls flew in from southern France. We were fully manned.

I decided to move out to Chequers. There was no one to cook for me at No. 10 – and for Michael Palliser – and, in terms of communications, Chequers is simply an extension of the No. 10 switchboard, with full and secure teleprinter facilities.

Reports were coming in every minute – from the White House, from Europe, from the Commonwealth. What was really encouraging was that non-aligned countries in the Commonwealth, especially Africa, and throughout the Afro-Asian world were expressing their sense of shock, and criticism of Soviet action.

The Security Council accepted the inscription of the Czechoslovakian issue on its agenda by 13 votes to 2, both of the minority voters being states involved in the intervention in Czechoslovakia. The resolution of condemnation carried enough votes – 10 in favour, 2 against, with 3 abstentions – to carry the Council, but it was, of course, vetoed by the Soviet delegate. But 13 members were unanimous in calling for the withdrawal of Soviet and other troops from Czechoslovakia. Canada, Britain, France, Denmark, the United States, Paraguay, Brazil and Senegal tabled a further resolution calling for a representative of the Secretary General to go immediately to Prague to satisfy himself about the whereabouts and safety of the Czechoslovak leaders.

Among Commonwealth countries who went on record against the Soviet bloc action were Australia, Canada, Cyprus, Ghana, India, Jamaica, Kenya, Malaysia, New Zealand, Singapore, Tanzania, Uganda and Zambia. Outside the Commonwealth, too, many non-aligned countries suddenly became aligned – in condemnation of Soviet action.

For the next few days we kept in the closest touch with the situation. Meanwhile, in that hot sun, I was marching up and down the terrace of Chequers dictating my speech for the opening of the debate the following Monday, 26th August, a speech which, while it could not disguise the impotence of the whole world outside the Eastern bloc, would express the feelings of members of all parties, from our own left to the rightest of the Conservatives and, still more, the reaction of public opinion throughout the country, of which my very large post-bag provided abundant evidence.

There were quiet cheers from all parts of the chamber when I claimed that we had been right to recall Parliament. The House was quiet, shocked, determined – and impotent.

I recounted the actions of HM Government, including Hugh Caradon's speeches and votes at UN which in readiness for the debate we had published as a White Paper, world reactions, and especially those of the Commonwealth. Justifying the recall of Parliament, I went on,

> There were, perhaps, some who felt that the House would be powerless to do anything beyond recording its profound sense of shock and dismay at this act of blatant aggression, a feeling reflecting a similar doubt as to whether governments here or in any other part of the world could register more than an impotent protest.
>
> But protest need not be impotent. Moreover, even if we here today could do no more than register the strength and unanimity of the feeling throughout the country, that in itself is important and, still more, that is our duty.

I drew the twin lesson which I felt the situation dictated. One was the need for vigilance and greater cohesion of the Western alliance. The other was the need for the greater unity of Europe, so that the view of Europe as a whole could be more strongly concentrated on any threat to freedom with Europe. But there was a further lesson: a vigorous and resilient defence system within the Western alliance was essential, certainly, but not in itself enough. It had to be responsive to political development throughout Europe:

> All of this means change and the willingness to accept change. The Concert of Europe broke down more than a century ago because its inflexible structure made it incapable of adjusting to change, still less of accepting change as an ally. Indeed, it sought to stem the tide of European liberalism in its constituent parts. I believe that we have learned this lesson. It is the Soviet Union which has some hard thinking,. some fast thinking, to do to shake itself free of the posture in which it appears to have frozen itself.
>
> The lesson for us is that not only must our posture in the North Atlantic Treaty be flexible in its defensive postures; it must be flexible equally in its readiness to respond to the opportunities for *détente....*

That needed to be said. In an atmosphere where the only positive response appeared to be a demand for banning visits by ballet companies, sports teams, and trade delegations – which I flatly rejected in my speech – it was not easy to get across the message that *détente* was not less important than determination in defence. Within six months that again reflected a growing public mood.

Parliament had been recalled for two days. It was clear that the House would not wish to debate Czechoslovakia for more than one day. I had proposed to my colleagues that in view of the growing concern about the situation in Nigeria, we should debate it on the Tuesday. It was understood that there would be no vote. I was momentarily on the following day to regret my forthcoming attitude but it was right that we should debate Nigeria.

The Nigeria tragedy had been foreshadowed in Abubakar's last words to me at Lagos Airport in January 1966, when he had wished for me everything except the premiership of a Federal State. Four days later he was dead, the victim of a tribal uprising. The Ibos who had seized power were themselves dispossessed by another military coup, and had retired to Iboland to brood. Their charismatic leader, Colonel Ojukwu, a former close army colleague of the new national leader, General Gowon, was shortly pressing Ibo claims to the point of secession. Throughout the spring of 1967 there was a daily threat of civil war. Through the Commonwealth secretariat, through friendly African Commonwealth countries, and directly, we sought to solve the problem by mediation. First, the High Commissioner in Lagos, together with his deputy in the Ibo capital, Enugu, tried to bring the two sides together. When this failed, Malcolm Macdonald treated with both sides and later co-operated in a new mediatory attempt by General Ankrah, head of the Ghanian Government. But that, too, failed, and on 6th July 1967 fighting broke out.

Although Colonel Ojukwu's aim was to assert the independence of the Eastern region, his early military success led him to carry the war across Nigeria towards the Federal capital. By August, he had captured Benin in the mid-West, and Lagos was threatened. A counter-thrust forced him back on Enugu and from that time forward he was defending the Ibo heartland, together with the Rivers State area around Port Harcourt and the South-Eastern State based on Calabar. The confusion between 'regions' and 'states' is explained by the fact that in Federal Nigeria, following independence, there were three regions, Northern, Western and Eastern, but after the attempted secession the Federal Government created twelve states: the East Central, centring on Enugu, represented purely Ibo territory, but so long as Colonel Ojukwu controlled the Eastern region his writ ran also in the Rivers State with its chief town, Port Harcourt, and the South-Eastern State with Calabar as its capital. In these states there were Ibos in considerable numbers, but it was generally accepted, and certainly the Federal Government claimed, that they were in a minority. As atrocity stories proliferated alleging Northern and Western outrages against Ibos, equally the non-Ibos in Rivers and the South-East alleged corresponding Ibo atrocities in the Calabar and Port Harcourt areas. When I visited these territories in March 1969, I was given evidence, unverifiable but potent, about what had been done to the non-Ibo population under the strains of war and, still more, when the Ibos were forced to withdraw.

By the autumn of 1967 the Federal Government, whose expenditure of ammunition was phenomenal, appealed to Britain for arms supplies. This presented us with a problem which was to be with us for over two years. Britain was, and had been in colonial days as well as in the independence era, Nigeria's traditional supplier of arms. We were equally the nation principally responsible for the military training of Nigeria's armed forces. General Gowon was Sandhurst trained, Colonel Ojukwu had done his officer training at Eaton Hall, Chester. Military cynics claimed to discern an incompatibility in terms of their respective military *Alma Maters.* Others, no less cynical, pointed out that Colonel Ojukwu had the edge through the degree he earned at Lincoln College, Oxford.

The demand for arms supplies meant that our Government was bound to lay itself open to attacks from one side or the other and from their respective supporters in Britain. The following note, dictated by me while flying from Lagos to Calabar at a later stage in the war, set out the position as I saw it at the time:

> George Thomson, Commonwealth Secretary, sponsored the request. I had some doubts about getting involved in a civil war, as did certain other colleagues, but the arguments were overwhelming. As the traditional supplier, a refusal would have meant not a lurch into neutrality but a hostile act against a fellow Commonwealth country whom we recognised, and whose integrity we supported. Moreover, the Russians were in the wings ready to supply everything Nigeria needed but at the price of a growing grip on Nigeria's internal life. There was the problem, too, of British interests in Nigeria. . . .

I spelled out, in particular, the dangers to the 17,000 British citizens resident in Nigeria, many of them in remote communities.

Had Britain not been the traditional arms supplier we could have taken a more detached line, without facing the charge that every death in Nigeria must be laid at our door. But that detached line would still have meant support for the Federal cause. Conferences of the Organisation for African Unity (OAU) at Kinshasa in 1967 and Algiers (1968) had overwhelmingly supported the cause of Nigerian unity. Individual African countries had different reasons for their votes, but central to the thinking of the majority was a determination to resist the break-up of independent African nations on tribal lines. There were 2,000 tribes in Africa, and 'Balkanisation', to use a European analogy, would have produced anarchy and chaos throughout the continent far transcending anything experienced in any other part of the world.

The fighting in the southern areas of Nigeria in the autumn of 1967 involved Britain in a heavy penalty and, through its effect on our supplies, played its part in the devaluation of sterling. These were the principal oil-supplying areas; already ten per cent of our supplies was coming from Nigeria which was the only shorthaul supplying area apart from Libya. The Six-Day War in the Middle East had already led to the embargo on shipments to Britain of Middle East oil, including the temporary loss of Libyan oil.

There was good reason to think that underlying the deep tribal animosities which were the basic cause of the fighting, a struggle for Nigeria's rich oil territories played its part. That was, no doubt, one reason for Colonel Ojukwu's insistence on controlling non-Ibo territories in Rivers and the South-East, though it could fairly be argued that his

Ibo state of 'Biafra' could not survive without access to the sea. It needs no Marxist theory of economic interpretation to explain his fanatical devotion to the Biafran cause, but such an explanation might not be out of place in interpreting the involvement of international financial and oil interests, mainly French, in what was to prove a costly investment in the breakaway State.

Whether inspired by European financial interests, or directly controlled by Colonel Ojukwu himself, the public relations campaign carried out on behalf of Biafra was one of the outstanding features of the war. If Biafra's military prowess had been one-tenth as efficient, the war would have ended in weeks. The purveyors of Biafran propaganda flooded the Western press and Western legislatures with literature, and secured a degree of moral control over Western broadcasting systems, with a success unparalleled in the history of communications in modern democratic societies. Their switch of line was remarkable: as soon as Colonel Ojukwu's forces were pressed back out of the western areas, and indeed out of Enugu and other Ibo heartland areas, the cry was 'genocide'. Should Biafra fall there would be mass extermination, so they said. When food shortages developed, as the result of deliberate and militarily defensible decisions by Colonel Ojukwu to close the supply lines – first by land, and then by daylight flights – the cry was 'starvation' – starvation by all who failed to support the Biafran military cause and especially the 'arch-criminal', Britain. No language was spared in distortion, nor subtlety left unexercised in the supply of filmed 'evidence', avidly snapped up and shown by gullible or committed producers, bringing home to every fireside the responsibility of the Federal Government – and, therefore, Britain – for every death from malnutrition. By 1969 the wildly inaccurate bombing of the Federals' Egyptian pilots brought new accusations of aerial atrocities and when Biafra faced defeat, the 'genocide' reels were revived and run again.

These campaigns had their effect in the Western world and I have never doubted the sincerity of those affected by them. It was a terrible problem for a Government in a democratic country. Within the Parliamentary Party we were under persistent and bitter attack from young and idealistic members, and from Privy Counsellors – such as the highly respected former Colonial Secretary, Jim Griffiths, who, with others, embraced the Biafran cause; from the left, too – despite the fact that with Julius Nyerere and Kenneth Kaunda they were being driven into common cause with South Africa, Rhodesia, Portugal, the Katanga lobby and the mercenaries who had fought their way through one disreputable African campaign after another.

For my colleagues and me in Parliament it meant bitter and indescribably unhappy sessions at question-time and in debates. As we travelled through the country, demonstrations were increasingly hard to bear, as

T

more and more Vietnam gave place to Biafra for their inspiration. But added to those who had urged the case on Vietnam were many, many more, most of them politically uncommitted, who regarded Biafra's sufferings as an outrage. Many of them were young, idealistic students, devout churchgoers, United Nations Association liberals, socialists, pacifists, idealists of every kind. They demonstrated in the streets, often silently – with dignity and sorrow – many for the first and only time in their lives. In the churches, the Roman Catholics with their strong missionary connection with largely-Christian Biafra denounced us from pulpit after pulpit. The Church of Scotland, with its proud African connection, passed a unanimous resolution of condemnation at the Assembly I attended. Many in the Church of England were deeply involved too. One Sunday I wrote letters to twenty-six bishops who had written to me pleading for a change in policy. The nonconformists all, bar a few, condemned us, and placed the guilt for the prolongation of the war, and for every single death through military action or starvation, at our door. One remains silent, or quietly urges the case, without heat, in parliamentary debate; but in the life of a Prime Minister, these are the things that hurt.

By the spring of 1968 the emphasis was on relief, food and medical supplies. Humanitarian organisations in Britain and throughout the civilised world, regardless of the view they took about the rights and wrongs of the war, were ready to pour food and relief supplies into Nigeria, and neighbouring areas, for onward transmission into Biafra. The easiest route would have been along the twenty-mile stretch of road from Enugu to Biafran-held territory; the second easiest by the river systems from Port Harcourt and other coastal areas. I did not blame Colonel Ojukwu for refusing to accept food by these routes. He was fighting a war, and he feared that if he removed his barriers on road- or river-access Federal troops could break through in the wake of the food-bearing transport. Later, when the relief organisations sought to fly the food in, he rejected day flights, because under the cover of night relief flights he could fly in the French arms he so sorely needed to carry on the war. This was militarily defensible: what was not was the use made of the starvation issues by his public relations advisers in Europe and elsewhere. I put this point later, in one of the most difficult parliamentary speeches I have ever had to make, in December 1969. What I did resent was the suggestion that it was our obstinacy, and not Colonel Ojukwu's deliberate military policy, which caused the starvation.

Long before the major parliamentary debates in June and August 1968, Nigeria had replaced Vietnam as our major overseas preoccupation. It took up far more of my time, and that of ministerial colleagues, and far more moral wear and tear than any other issue. Commentators concerned from day to day with nice calculations of parliamentary voting lobbies, or their assessment of the quantitative and qualitative extent of some real or putative split in governing party or Government itself, rarely recognise the impact of these moral pressures, internal as well as external. The head of government has to face these problems not singly or single-mindedly, but simultaneously, against the background of a hundred other issues, economic, financial, diplomatic and political. The headlines, however sensationalised or selective, fail to measure even the tip of the iceberg in the sea of democratic government, where the heaviest and most lethal pressures are below the surface, sometimes concentrated within the heart of the individual.

Throughout 1968 we struggled, with others, to get the parties back to the conference table. Conferences were held in Kampala and Addis Ababa. At the very moment when we were resisting the pro-Biafra pressures in Parliament, George Thomson, Michael Stewart and I were urging on Chief Enahoro in London the need for meaningful talks about a cease fire.

We were concerned equally with the relief problem. In July 1968 I asked Lord Hunt to visit Nigeria as my personal emissary to assess the relief problem; he was accompanied by Sir Colin Thornley, of the Save the Children Fund, Mr A. B. Hodgson of the British Red Cross, and Dr W. J. N. Evans, medical adviser to the mission.

John Hunt was an ideal choice: his organisational ability, demonstrated in the conquest of Everest, and his compassion and dedication to basic human problems – in normal peacetime conditions, as well as in times of crisis – eminently fitted him for a mission of this kind. In March 1969 he was my chief adviser on relief questions on my own visit to Nigeria, and I sent him there again as soon as the fighting ended. Even so, his unimpeachable reputation, his dedication and his ruthless efficiency failed to protect him from those who had an interest in rejecting his honest testimony.

On 12th June 1968 the House had its first major debate on Nigeria, raised, on an adjournment motion, by one of our most passionately sincere pro-Biafran back-benchers, Michael Barnes. George Thomson was abroad and I asked Michael Stewart to reply to the debate, which centred on our responsibility, as arms suppliers, for all Biafra's sufferings. He dealt with the arms issues succinctly and convincingly. We had maintained our traditional supplies, we were not supplying aircraft or aerial bombs. What he could not say was how far Nigeria would have been put in pawn to the Russians had we refused. Whatever military supplies we felt it right to withhold, they did in fact provide; they were tightening their grip on Nigeria's life. The hawks in the Nigerian Military Government gave short shrift to our – as they saw it – pedantic arguments, especially those which linked our arms supplies with pressure to negotiate for a cease fire. They were concerned with the 'quick kill'. It would not have taken more than one false step, perhaps one incautious word in Parliament, to have produced a purge in the Nigerian administration which would have put the pro-Russian hawks in control.

In June I sent Lord Shepherd, Minister of State in the Commonwealth Office, to Lagos for direct talks with General Gowon. His report convinced me, despite my worries, that we had no alternative to the course we were pursuing.

By August 1968 the pressures which had built up led me to propose the debate in our brief recall session. I had been studying the telegrams which reached me day by day on holiday. I had never accepted the view of those who thought that the fighting could end rapidly. But, in fact – and all I learnt subsequently confirmed this – the war was very near its end in the summer and early autumn of 1968. That it lasted a further fifteen or sixteen months was due to one fact – French intervention.

Colonel Ojukwu's worldwide search for arms was failing in its purpose. He did not lack for finance – the French oil interests and his reactionary supporters in Africa ensured that. But he was finding it hard to obtain supplies; and finding it still harder, once he had lost the ports, to fly them in. At this point General de Gaulle took a hand and supplies were made available to the fullest extent that they could be got through to the Colonel's beleaguered troops. The world knew what was going on, yet it could never be proved. Press inquiries to the Quai d'Orsay were tautly answered: 'We know nothing, this is a matter for the Elysée.' At the Elysée, where the energetic M. Foccart was master-minding the operation, all inquiries were blandly referred to the Foreign Ministry. Not that France was supplying arms to Biafra. All the arms went into the arsenals of the Governments of the Ivory Coast and Gabon. As shipments by those Governments to Colonel Ojukwu diminished their national stocks of armaments to danger levels, they were rapidly replenished.

That was why Colonel Ojukwu refused to allow food and other relief by daylight flights, for each sortie would have been monitored, and the arms-carrying planes interdicted. By playing on the idealism of the Church and other relief organisations he secured international agreement that all relief flights should be by night, and under their cover the arms planes flew in. It was war; and he believed in his war. Where his supporters were not justified was in their claim that we and others were responsible for the starvation which could have been quickly ended if daylight flights had been allowed, even more quickly had the surface route been opened.

The debate on the second day of the 27th August recall mainly centred on Britain's arms supplies to Nigeria. The background to it was an OAU initiative, headed by the Emperor of Ethiopia, aimed at a political settlement followed by a cease fire. Nothing came of this; Colonel Ojukwu refused to sit round the table on the basis of a United Nigeria; the Federals refused to contemplate an independent secessionist State. For six weeks the Emperor struggled to find a solution to the problem of moving supplies to the starving in Biafra and he succeeded in getting provisional agreement on a formula; but it failed, mainly because of Colonel Ojukwu's refusal to allow daylight flights. From the Federal side General Gowon announced a great new offensive and said the war would end in four weeks, an injudicious forecast which further angered our critics in Parliament.

It had been understood that the Nigerian debate we had offered, on the adjournment, would end without a division. But the pro-Biafrans decided to organise a vote and since many Government supporters had gone home expecting that there would be no vote it became clear that we could be defeated. In these circumstances the under-secretary, Bill Whitlock, was instructed by the whips to 'talk out' the debate, i.e. not to sit down just in time for a division to be called (there were not enough dissidents to carry a closure motion). His action further intensified the anger of those of our people and of the Conservatives who supported the Biafran line.

In the evening, as I was dealing with papers before going off to resume my holiday, there were sounds of a great commotion in Downing Street. A large group of Biafran students, after a protest meeting in North London, had surprised the police by converging on Downing Street, where they lit an enormous bonfire which was kept going by petrol. It could easily have caused damage, but they then suddenly rushed the door of No. 10, surprising the custodians and almost succeeding in entering in strength. In the mood they were in, who knows what damage they would have done, but enough custodians just managed to get their shoulders to the door to hold it and lock it. From that day on the front door defences were strengthened.

I returned to the Isles for two or three days more before finally coming back to London on 4th September just as, once again, the conference season was beginning.

The TUC's 1968 Congress went right down the line against Government policies, with the engineers, no longer encased in 'Carron's Law', joining the other left-wing unions. A motion opposing the Government's wages policy was carried by 7,700,000 to a million; even an official motion supporting the TUC's own voluntary incomes policy was carried by only 34,000 votes out of a total of eight million.

Changes were taking place in industry. General Electric (GEC), which had already taken over Associated Electrical Industries (AEI), now merged with English Electric to form a company capable of fighting the European giants on equal terms. But there were grave problems of local redundancies, and my colleagues and I had to receive a series of deputations and attempt to agree with industry a code of conduct for redundancy procedures in these and other cases. The Minister of

Technology announced a major reconstruction of the nuclear plant industry, with the principal private enterprise contracting groups entering into partnership with the publicly-owned Atomic Energy Authority, both for research and construction.

The wind of modernisation was invoked in the Foreign and Commonwealth Offices: not only were they due to be merged the following month, but a high-powered inquiry, headed by Sir Val Duncan, chairman of Rio Tinto Zinc, was appointed to recommend changes in the system of British representation abroad. Meanwhile, at my suggestion, Sir Robert Bellinger, who had been a successful and popular Lord Mayor of London, was appointed to head a panel to survey the home departments of the civil service one by one, and to recommend savings in manpower.

The economy was breathing more easily. Good trade figures for August, followed by the announcement of the completion of the Basle agreement negotiations, and the Basle standby of $2 billions, greatly strengthened sterling. Bank rate was reduced to seven per cent. Unemployment showed signs of falling, especially in the main development areas. It was too early to be confident of an export-led boom, but certainly we were beginning to see the results of devaluation. The rapidly growing exports were leading a growth in industrial expansion which though slow was becoming clear.

Our party conference was at Blackpool at the end of September. For the first time for nearly twenty years I missed the pre-conference preliminaries, including the National Executive meetings. I was entertaining, on an official visit, an old friend, Tage Erlander, Prime Minister of Sweden for twenty-two years, who earlier that month had just won a remarkable general election victory, continuing what was already thirty-six years of almost unbroken Social Democratic government. He accepted my invitation to visit Blackpool, and agreed to speak at the pre-conference rally. To what we were trusting would be a 'fight-back' conference he brought fresh hope after his own unexpected election victory. He recalled how two years earlier in Sweden's mid-term local government and senate elections his party had been thrashed but, by making full use of the time left and going over to the offensive, they had won and indeed increased their majority. With a scarcely-veiled hint at the British political scene, he ended: 'Two years is a short time, but it is enough.'

Conference began on the Monday morning. I had experienced some difficulty persuading the NEC to allow the Foreign Secretary and the Chancellor, who were not members of the Executive, to speak from the platform rather than be limited to five minutes from the delegates' rostrum, but eventually it was agreed.

I had been successful, with the help of the General Secretary, in persuading the independent Conference Arrangements Committee to alter the usual order of conference. In the past the big clash of the week – be it economic policy or, in earlier years, issues such as the Common Market or German re-armament – would be held on the Wednesday or even Thursday, and inevitably press interest would be concerned with speculating on the forthcoming debate, and forecasts of the vote results, so that the constructive earlier debates on housing, education or the social services frequently attracted little interest. There was the same danger with the party leader's traditional speech presenting the parliamentary report.

If that took place before the clash of the week it was quickly forgotten; all that was taken back at the end of the week were the memories of division. In 1967 my own speech had been deferred until the Wednesday to get the prices and incomes clash out of the way, but Wednesday is late for a key-note speech.

On this occasion, the Conference Arrangements Committee staged the economic policy clash for the latter part of Monday morning and Monday afternoon. Roy Jenkins and Barbara Castle spoke in support of Government policy, but with the shift of power in the unions, they could not hope to repeat Jim Callaghan's triumph of the previous year. A motion moved by Frank Cousins calling for the repeal of all the incomes legislation was carried by 5,098,000 to 1,124,000.

I opened the next day with my speech: 'This is the conference,' I began, 'they will look back on and say, "That was when Labour came back fighting." ' Following the line of the fight-back speech at Newtown three months earlier, I went on:

It has been a year in which an opportunist Opposition, backed by the special interests which support them, have thrown everything at us. Politically, personally, the lot. And in all these months I have not replied. Not yet. I shall choose my time ...
And the reason they know that time is not on their side is because they have an uneasy and growing fear that Labour has got the measure of the problems not that your Government only is facing but that Britain is facing. The problems not of four years past, but of forty. The problems of moving forward from Imperialism to a modern industrial society. They can see that a pattern is emerging.
It is precisely because they sense this that only a few weeks ago they made that carefully planned, much heralded act of desperation, their campaign directed to suggest that a final and overwhelming economic crisis was only days away. They must have known that there were many in the City, and still more abroad, who, hearing these warnings and believing them, might well have been led to endanger Britain's recovery with an artificially-induced flight of capital. Not for the first time. Next week here they will parade their patriotism. But it always comes off second-best wherever they see a prospect of party gain.

My theme was what I described as the 'emerging pattern'. After four years of Government, with all we had been called upon to do, our declared pattern was taking shape – in balance of payments, industrial modernisation, the regions, defence, housing and planning and education; figure after figure presented our achievements. Sixteen schools built a week compared with the ten of which they boasted. An increase in hospital nursing staff of twenty-three per cent. The rise each year – despite the January restrictions – in health and welfare hospitals and social services. Our attack on the problem of family poverty.

I then dealt with the world problem of violence, and with the growth of racially-inspired conflict in Britain, taking up my Birmingham theme:

> When, before 1964, we charted the path that Britain would follow under a Labour Government, we spoke of a new concept of freedom, the broader freedom without which social democracy would be meaningless. Freedom from contempt, the enhancing of the dignity of man . . .
> This is the only answer to the violent society. We in the Labour movement oppose the importation of violence: equally we oppose the importation of authoritarianism to meet that violence. Some public figures provoke the one, and then invoke the other to deal with it.
> This problem of violence has become a world problem. It is associated in many countries with a swing to the right. Only the forces of reaction, it is urged, have the will and the ruthlessness to stamp out the cult of violence which their words and policies have incited.
> We shall meet the appeal to reaction here in Britain as Swedish social democracy has met it, not by complacent assertions that it can't happen here, but by asserting our faith that social grievances require social solutions – by positive social action by the state. By what the Swedes in their election called the Strong Society.
> We regret equally the apostles of authoritarian violence on the one hand and negative violence on the other. Both are essentially and profoundly anti-democratic. Both seek to destroy. The Conservatives at home and abroad seek to destroy the defences we have built for the weak against those who abuse economic and social power. The Nihilists in their despair seek to destroy the very fabric of organised society.
> We assert that the challenge of violence can be met only by a strong community responsibility to protect the individual against the insolence of economic and social power.

At the end there was again a spontaneous and wild standing ovation, echoed by favourable press comment; 'Wilson Resurgent' headlined the *Daily Telegraph*; 'Wilson comes back with a bounce', and 'Wilson's speech rallies party for Labour's decisive year' were others.

The rest of the week went smoothly. George Brown as deputy leader and chairman of the home policy committee of the Executive showed his old flair in a speech introducing the NEC 'mid-term report', with its programme of new policy projects on which it was working for presentation to the 1969 conference. On Thursday afternoon there were sharp but not unexpected votes against the platform on Rhodesia and Nigeria. I had to miss part of the debate as I was recording a panel interview for the 'This Week' television programme. It was my first major programme for nearly a year. During the preceding months I had kept on with my work and my industrial and housing tours in the regions, but in public relations adopted what the Americans call a 'low profile posture'. It was useless, I had felt, to answer the hostile questions I must expect with a mere reiteration of our hopes and expectations of economic recovery. I preferred to wait until there was something to show. By the autumn of 1968 the improvement in our exports, export orders and the balance of payments gave me something to say.

As I left the temporary 'studio', on the stage of a local cinema, I received a telegram from Rhodesia, the culmination of three months of what Sir Alec Douglas-Home was ever enjoining on me, 'secret diplomacy'.

In June I had decided that the various reports reaching us from Rhodesia suggesting that they would be prepared to accept an honourable settlement must be tested by definite talks. Some came through Conservative politicians, whose official leadership still maintained that Sir Alec Douglas-Home's proposals held the key to a solution. I knew Mr Smith well enough to know that no official soundings would provide a clear answer: he always kept his cards close to his chest pending a high-level confrontation. I decided that any probing should be conducted through other channels.

On Sunday, 30th June, I invited Sir Max Aitken, who had consistently supported an Anglo-Rhodesian settlement, together with Lord Goodman, to meet me at No. 10 on my return from Chequers. Sir Max said I looked well. I replied that I was, 'apart from this appalling deafness'. This was news to him, but I explained it by saying that, for instance, I had thought he had said that he would shortly be visiting Rhodesia. No, he said, I must have misheard. Then, realising what I was after, he said that I had heard correctly, and went on, 'Did you hear me say when I was going?' (Full marks to Sir Max.) I said that we would discuss that, but if he was going there were two points I would wish him to discuss with Mr Smith, whom, no doubt, he would be seeing.

Before we parted that night it had been established that he would shortly be visiting South Africa and that Lord Goodman would be with him as his legal adviser. Mr Smith would be apprised of the visit by Sir Max's representative in Salisbury and arrangements proposed for a private meeting perhaps at Mr Smith's farm at Selukwe, within reasonable reach of the South African border. While he was at No. 10 I dictated a ten-point summary of our requirements for a settlement, concentrated mainly on the blocking quarter, safeguards against any constitutional amendments which would infringe the first and second 'principles' and the need for agreement on the timing and method of assessing the Rhodesian people's acceptance of any agreement reached. We should have new proposals to make about the requirements for the return to constitutional rule. Sir Max Aitken's task would be to establish whether Mr Smith's response was sufficient to justify a meeting between Mr Smith and myself. Sir Max asked when this would be. I said that this would have to be considered, but that I thought it would be on 9th October, probably at Gibraltar, though it might be at Ascension. Unfortunately, the latter, which would have advantages, made it difficult to have one of HM ships off-shore because of the appalling surf. Sir Max asked why, if he were successful in August in securing the necessary conditions for a meeting, we should delay discussions until October. I replied that in my view there should be no meeting before the Rhodesian Front conference at the end of September: I had already had experience of what the grass-roots could do to Mr Smith. After the Rhodesian Front conference I should have my own party conference to attend and, as I wanted to leave adequate time for our meeting, a date around 9th October seemed to be the earliest which seemed practicable.

In August Sir Max Aitken and Lord Goodman went unnoticed to South Africa. I had hoped that they would not have to go to Salisbury because of the danger of speculation about the reason for their visit. But Mr Smith promised full secrecy and carried out his promise. Their aircraft was grounded some distance from the terminal, and on leaving it they were surrounded by as many security guards as Mr Nkomo would have attracted, and whisked off by car to a guarded suite at the hotel. They had meetings with Mr Smith, and explained my message in detail. The answers he gave them – which went further than anything we had so far had, and were certainly better than the proposals brought back by Sir Alec Douglas-Home – were telegraphed under a specially secure cypher to me via Downing Street to Scilly. I dictated a full commentary to those of my colleagues immediately affected, ready for a meeting on my return. The Czechoslovak crisis provided the occasion for a somewhat earlier discussion. One or two ministers were dubious, more so than at the time of the *Tiger* discussions. They feared that a further failure to reach agreement might prove to be an unacceptable rebuff. I did not take this view.

As I pointed out, there are different styles of captaincy and premiership. History was full of top-rank centre-forwards relegated to the reserves for failing to try a shot at goal for fear of missing. I would not mind the accusation of failure if my shot went wide; rather that than be condemned for being afraid to try. Moreover, the Governor was becoming impatient. While being unable to guarantee success, he felt that the chances of success were higher than for some time. He pressed strongly for a 'summit'. I feared that to rebuff him might lead to his resignation, which would precipitate a serious political crisis in Britain.

The time had come, in my view, to test the sincerity of Mr Smith's statements to Sir Alec Douglas-Home and other British visitors that he was ready for a settlement within the six principles. His talks with Sir Max Aitken had been concerned with three issues; the blocking quarter, the question of the right of appeal in constitutional cases to the Privy Council, and the logistics of a return to constitutional rule. On the first two of these his replies to Sir Max Aitken were clear and satisfactory. On the third he reserved his position as he was not clear what I should be proposing. There were two further favourable developments after Sir Max had returned to report to me. Mr Smith got rid of some, though by no means all, of the more objectionable members of his team, including Lord Graham. Secondly, on the provocative issue of the death sentences a large number of prisoners under capital sentence was reprieved and Mr Smith gave notice of measures designed to end mandatory death sentences for certain offences.

I felt that there was enough here to justify a meeting. Official probings, by an Under-Secretary of State at the Commonwealth Relations Office, Mr J. A. R. Bottomley, who had discussions with the Governor, and later with Mr Smith, confirmed his assurances to Sir Max Aitken. They confirmed, too, that Mr Smith was not prepared to negotiate further except on a person-to-person basis. There could be no certainty, or even probability, that a meeting would produce a settlement, but there was some urgency about making the effort. His constitutional experts were hard at work producing a new 'constitution' which all advice suggested would be hard-line in form, segregationist, and designed to ensure that majority rule would be postponed well into the next century. There would be many in our Parliament and among the public – going far beyond the usual fringe of Rhodesian Front supporters – who might find it hard to forgive if we rejected any attempt to negotiate or any attempt to head off a series of totally reactionary and oppressive constitutional moves by the regime.

Moreover, we might be within two years of an election. If no honourable settlement could be reached, the Rhodesian question would be buried as a matter of inter-party controversy for the remainder of the Parliament and over the period of an election. So, indeed, it proved.

Mr Smith agreed to our proposal for the date and showed great skill in holding his Rhodesian Front congress tight and avoiding any commitments which would make a settlement impossible.

Of the various possible venues – Ascension, Malta, even Mauritius, and Gibraltar – I proposed Gibraltar. But on this occasion I saw no objection to the talks being held alongside the quay. Mr Smith, who had complained about being allotted the cabins of the chaplain and medical officer on board *Tiger*, was pleased at the decision that he would have his own accommodation in *Kent* (an admiral's cabin, in fact), moored alongside *Fearless*. This gave him ample facilities to brief the British and world press, to which we made no objection.

Tight security was secured almost to the last minute. At the party conference at Blackpool the week before the meeting, though I had a number of meetings of the ministerial group supervising the arrangements, nothing became known publicly and Mr Smith maintained a similar reticence.

The Commonwealth Secretary, the Attorney General and I, with advisers, left by RAF Comet for Gibraltar on 8th October. *Fearless* and *Kent* had come into the harbour and moored together an hour or two before our arrival. There had been a last-minute leak from Salisbury and the news broke that morning. The London *Evening Standard* correspondent and photographer were there to see them dock and flash the story back under the headline, 'It's the *Fearless* Summit'.

As with *Tiger*, nothing had been spared by the officers and crew of the two ships to make the conference a success. In *Fearless*, the conference ship, the area we should be using from the quarter-deck to the ward-room was sealed off with the imposing notice 'Conference Citadel' at the entrance, and strict security was maintained. Hospitality and accommodation for both parties, and the facilities provided for the hundreds of pressmen who had flocked to Gibraltar, were excellent.

Mr Smith and the Governor could not arrive until the afternoon of the 9th. In the morning the Navy entertained the press on board and showed them the facilities which had been provided. At noon we welcomed the Chief Minister of Gibraltar, Sir Joshua Hassan, who was given the opportunity of talking to a very high-level press corps about Gibraltar's problems and her steadfastness in standing up to Spanish provocation.

The talks with Mr Smith throughout were more agreeable and freer from rancour than those held on board *Tiger*. For one thing we had made clear that there was no deadline. We hoped to carry the discussions as far as we could on board, and, if possible, to reach an agreement there subject to approval in London and Salisbury, and adequate time would be left for consideration in Salisbury and London. If any substantial points were still unsettled we would be agreeable to further consultations between the British Government and Salisbury, through British officials, or, if necessary, ministers.

In all we had some thirty hours of talks, most of them in plenary session, some between Mr Smith and myself, with a secretary for each in attendance. There was, in addition, an informal meeting at which without commitment we discussed possible names for the Royal Commission to test acceptance, and potential ministers for inclusion in an interim constitutional Government.

We had made clear to Mr Smith, through our officials in Salisbury, that there could be no agreement which failed to honour the six principles in full and we insisted on a statement from Mr Smith confirming that he fully understood this as a condition precedent to holding the meeting. The confirmation was duly forthcoming, though he indicated in turn that he regarded certain matters as being of fundamental importance to himself and to those he represented.

After meetings which took place on the Thursday evening, all day Friday and Saturday, it became clear that it would not be possible to reach a definitive understanding at Gibraltar. Substantial progress was made, including Mr Smith's acceptance of an effective blocking quarter. But there remained deep differences, mainly deriving from fundamentally opposed philosophies about Rhodesia's future, which expressed themselves in disagreement about safeguards. We were concerned to find that Mr Smith's repeated proposal to extend the B-roll franchise to a million Africans – which we got him to agree should cover both sexes – held no reality. Because of the requirements of the literacy test for electoral registration, even the Rhodesian leaders estimated that not more than 50,000 would be registered, even after ten years. A great deal of time was devoted to this discussion. A copy of the registration test was produced by one of our officials, and after studying it I felt that it was about as easy to complete as a British income-tax return.

While Mr Smith was urbane throughout the discussions, and Mr J. H. Howman – by this time his 'Foreign Minister' – scarcely less so, we were concerned to note the utterly reactionary and contemptuous line taken up by his 'Secretary for Native Affairs', Mr Nicolle, throughout the discussions. And, as we were to learn, his was the voice of white Rhodesia.

We would have been willing to remain for several more days if we could have felt that this might produce a draft agreement between us. Mr Smith, however, was showing signs of a desire to return home and we heard that his staff were making tentative inquiries about a flight on the Sunday. With his agreement I proposed that overnight we should prepare a definitive document covering the constitutional settlement and our proposals for the return to legality and table it for discussion on the Sunday morning, 13th October, after the church service on the after-deck of *Fearless*. This was duly handed to him in a further meeting at 11.00 a.m. and for an hour he put, and we answered, questions about its provisions. He asked for time to study it and we arranged to meet at 4.30 p.m. This gave me my first opportunity to leave the ship, and for two pleasant hours we cruised in the Admiral's launch in the waters around Gibraltar, including the contested zone improperly 'claimed' by the Spaniards. Other members of my team were in a fast landing craft, part of *Fearless*'s infinitely varied panoply of equipment.

The document we had handed to Mr Smith was later presented to Parliament in Command Paper 3793 the following Tuesday, 15th October, the day after the House resumed. I drew attention to three important features of our proposals.

The first, by no means new, was our insistence on the introduction of a 'vigorous and extended programme for African education', particularly technical education, including agriculture. We were prepared to contribute to this programme a total of £50 millions, spread over ten years, on a pound-for-pound basis. Such a programme, I said, was 'imperative' in the interests of the African population and of Rhodesia as a whole. It would also have an important bearing on the number of Africans able to qualify for the A-roll franchise.

Secondly, I reported, we had included the proposal that the Royal Commission appointed to carry through the fifth principle test of acceptability should be instructed also to inquire into the arrangements for registration under the widely-extended franchise. Thirdly, there were the proposals for a broad-based Government, including Africans, to carry Rhodesia through the process of introducing the new constitution, right up to the election of a new Parliament, elected under that constitution.

I told the House that Mr Smith had said that he would take our proposals back to Salisbury, without commitment, for consideration there, and that I had offered a visit by the Commonwealth Secretary if it were felt that this would assist. I concluded:

> Our position at the end of the talks, as throughout these past years, maintains the position repeatedly stated by the Commonwealth Secretary – no sell out, no slamming the door by us.
> We have insisted that our proposals have to be taken as a whole. Any concessions we have been prepared to offer on matters which do not involve the safeguards required for the six principles are available only as part of an agreement which incorporates the clear guarantees on which we have insisted to safeguard those principles. Now decisions have to be taken in Salisbury. We for our part are keeping the door open. But the key to a settlement is and must remain the six principles, which are cardinal to the future of Rhodesia – the future of all races, for whom the British Parliament stands trustee.

Our proposals were well received by the House, and the Opposition were not disposed to criticise them or to attack us for not going further. The press similarly welcomed them, and considered them fair. The *Daily Telegraph* went so far as to say, in a leading article on 22nd October when Parliament debated the *Fearless* proposals:

> It should be made clear in Parliament today that if Mr Smith and his Cabinet reject the main provisions in *Fearless* there is nothing more to come. There is a limit to what Parliament will accept and it has been reached.

On Wednesday, 16th October, I made a statement in Parliament on the changes in Government departments. The merger of the Foreign and Commonwealth Offices into the new Foreign and Commonwealth Office, announced the previous March on Michael Stewart's reappointment, was to take effect the following day. The necessary preparatory work had been well done. It was no merely formal absorption of the two offices under a single Secretary of State; the new office was integrated on geographical and functional lines. For example, the Africa department was to cover the whole continent, apart from northern Arab States dealt with by the Middle Eastern department, and its responsibilities embraced equally Commonwealth and non-Commonwealth African countries.

Secondly, I said that the amalgamation of the Health and Social Security ministries in the new Department of Health and Social Security, also announced in the spring, would become effective on 1st November with Dick Crossman as Secretary of State. As chairman of the Social Services committee of the Cabinet Dick would continue to exercise a broader co-ordination between the various social departments, including education and housing.

Thirdly, a similar procedure and timetable would govern the transfer of civil service administration from the Treasury to the new Civil Service Department. A debate was arranged on the Fulton Report as a whole.

Two days later I announced the consequential ministerial changes. Dick Crossman was to have two Ministers of State, David Ennals (Health) and Stephen Swingler (Social Security). The two ministers of Cabinet rank who had headed the previous departments, Kenneth Robinson and Judith Hart, were transferred to other duties. Kenneth Robinson became Minister for Planning and Land at the Ministry of Housing and Local Government. Judith Hart, as Paymaster General with a seat in the Cabinet, was entrusted with a number of non-departmental tasks. I had lost the non-departmental work of Eddie Shackleton with his absorption in civil service matters, and she took on a number of Cabinet committees. In addition, she was given a special remit in the fields of youth matters, decentralisation and devolution affecting Scotland and Wales, the co-ordination of Government information and its relationship with the public. She was also given the task of answering questions on the Civil Service Department, except those addressed to me as Prime Minister.

There were changes of title, without functions, resulting from Dick Crossman's appointment as Secretary of State. The Lord Presidency reverted to the Leader of the House, Fred Peart; Lord Shackleton became Lord Privy Seal once more; George Thomson, who was to undertake non-departmental work after his current responsibility for the Rhodesian negotiations was discharged, became Minister without Portfolio. John Diamond, who for four years had fulfilled the exacting duties of Chief Secretary, was promoted to the Cabinet. This was no intended as a reward but was designed, with the increased preoccupation with public expenditure, to enable him to deal on equal terms with the major spending ministers. I had been pressed by two successive Chancellors to find him a seat at the Cabinet table.

To replace the new Ministers of State, in their former departments, Merlyn Rees, Under Secretary of State, Defence (RAF), became Under-Secretary at the Home Office, taking over David Ennals's duties, so devotedly performed, in immigration and community relations questions. Lord Winterbottom moved over from the Ministry of Public Building and Works to the RAF Department and was later succeeded by Charles Loughlin, transferred from Health.

Parliament had resumed against a more favourable background for the Government. The economy was strengthening, the September trade figures had again been good, exports had set up a new record two months running, and the trend of new export orders was rising fast. In addition industrial production was picking up and regional employment policies beginning to show better results. The economic improvement was reflected in better public opinion ratings. The Conservative lead fell to much lower figures; one National Opinion Poll result, which I regarded as highly eccentric, brought it down to 3.9 per cent.

The Chancellor was watching the economy very carefully. He felt that a further touch on the tiller would be required and warned his colleagues that he would have to propose a tightening of hire-purchase restrictions, which he had held in reserve at the time of the Budget in case further disinflationary measures were required in the summer or later. There was some resistance from the industrial ministers who were concerned, in particular, that the effect on automobile production would increase unit export costs. While further industrial evidence was being examined there was a deplorable leak to a national newspaper. This was inevitably seized on by the Conservatives as ammunition for the Bassetlaw by-election, where the poll was due the following week. Barbara Castle, speaking at a by-election meeting there, was asked whether a new 'freeze' was coming immediately after the election. Her denial was perfectly accurate, but her integrity was traduced by the Tories before and, more particularly, after the election, when the hire-purchase restrictions were announced. This was avidly taken up by the press and had its effect not only in Bassetlaw, where our 1966 majority of 10,428 was reduced to 740, but on the Government's standing in the country. The opinion poll gap began to widen again. It is interesting, looking back on December 1968 from two years later, that there was no similar press criticism of the Conservative mini-budget of October 1970, which five days later followed the neatly-timed by-election in St Marylebone. Nor had there been, as I pointed out when the row broke, when Mr Heath was Chief Whip in February 1956, when the then Chancellor, Mr Macmillan, three days after three fiercely-contested by-elections, announced a formidable economic package comparable with those of July 1961 and July 1966.

The turbulent 1967–8 session ended on 22nd October with the Prorogation Speech. As in previous years, this speech provided a comprehensive summary of the legislation carried on to the statute book as the record of the session's work, when all the storms and debates had died away. The 1967–8 Acts included the 1967 Prices and Incomes Act; the Transport Act; the Industrial Expansion Act, strengthening the Government's powers to contribute to industrial projects likely to help the economy; a new Act to regulate the distribution of North Sea gas; major consumer protection legislation tightening the controls on misleading trade descriptions and restrictive trade practices; legislation to clarify the law in relation to hovercraft and tightening controls on aircraft noises and supersonic flight; an anti-dumping Act; the Agriculture Act, helping tenant farmers when their land was taken for development, and safeguarding the welfare of animals; new legislation on health and welfare and a major measure controlling the safety, quality and description of medicines; the Act to provide more effective planning control of town and country development and to increase public participation in local planning decisions; legislation establishing the Countryside Commission, to strengthen conservation powers, and to give greater access for leisure and recreation; the Commonwealth Immigration Act; further legislation outlawing racial discrimination; the Gaming Act, among other provisions eliminating the danger of a Mafia-type invasion which earlier Conservative legislation had facilitated; and further legislation marking the progressive implementation of the prolific work of the Law Commission. Other measures referred to in the Speech included improvements on supplementary benefits, rate rebates and family allowances.

Five days later the Queen's Speech opened the new session, the third of the Parliament, and the fifth of our Administration. It foreshadowed legislation to convert the Post Office from a department of state into a public corporation; to transfer London Transport to the GLC; to centralise, under a new computer system located in the Welsh development area, the issue of driving and vehicle licences; a Bill to assist the tourist industry; the Decimal Currency Bill; new legislation to help the fishing industry and to strengthen the policing and conservation of fisheries; action was promised on the Donovan Report; reform of the Merchant Shipping Acts; legislation 'on the composition and powers of the House of Lords'; a Bill to reduce the voting age to eighteen and to fix eighteen as the age when a man or woman reaches majority; and legislation to protect children and young persons.

There were also Bills to increase public service pensions; on town and country planning; education in Scotland; and to provide an appeals tribunal for would-be immigrants refused entry by the authorities;

legislation to provide further finance for the urban programme, including special new assistance for nursery schools and classes; a Bill, following Aberfan, to enforce safety measures on tips of coal and quarry refuse; most important was the legislation providing for greatly increased financial assistance for the modernisation and repair of older houses 'and their environment'. Finally, there were Bills to increase the Government contribution to the National Theatre; on the administration of justice, and on law reform – in particular, to extend in England and Wales the rights of succession to property by persons who are illegitimate; and to amend the law of heritable securities in Scotland.

Non-legislatively, the speech announced the establishment of a Royal Commission on the Constitution, an idea which had been formulated by Jim Callaghan. In the debate which followed I announced its duties as:

> To examine the present functions of the central legislature and government in relation to the several countries, nations and regions of the United Kingdom;
> To consider, having regard to developments in local government organisation and in the administration and other relationships between the various parts of the United Kingdom, what changes, in the interests of prosperity and good government, are desirable in those functions or otherwise in present constitutional and economic relationships;
> To consider, also, whether any changes are desirable in the constitutional and economic relationships between the United Kingdom and the Channel Islands and the Isle of Man. . . .

I made clear that, since the Commission would inevitably take time to report, its establishment should not be a bar to decisions Government and Parliament might wish to take. The Commission would be required to take account of decisions to Parliament while the Commission was sitting, and I instanced local government reform – on which the Maud Commission was due to report in a few months' time – and Northern Ireland, where the situation was worsening almost daily.

In the economic debate on an official Opposition amendment to the Address in reply to the Queen's Speech, Roy Jenkins put the minor hire-purchase changes in perspective. Contrasting them with crisis package measures of the past, under both Governments, all of which took place against a worsening balance of payments, these latest measures 'were', he said, 'taken against the background of improving trade figures, stronger sterling, and an improving balance of payments prospect. We took them not in a desperate attempt to turn the position round – there was no need for that – but to underpin and accelerate an improvement which was already taking place.'

The Chancellor gave an encouraging report on the progress of the balance of payments. The third quarter of 1968 had shown a striking improvement, though the figures still had to be worked out. The underlying trend was likely to be favourable in the fourth quarter as well.

The Queen's Speech debate on foreign affairs was by contrast a grave one. The worsening internal situation in Czechoslovakia, the fighting in Nigeria, Rhodesia and Vietnam – where there was speculation about a total and now unconditional bombing pause by the President – formed a tapestry of concern which transcended party divisions.

There was still widespread agreement on both sides of the House that the *Fearless* terms were right and should be accepted, though a considerable number of our MPs could not happily accept any settlement other than one based on 'NIBMR', and a small minority would still have preferred the use of force to impose a solution.

The Smith regime had indicated that a visit by George Thomson might be helpful. We were not hopeful that its motive was other than for purposes of public relations. It had to demonstrate to waverers in Rhodesia and to its friends in Britain that it was in earnest about a settlement. A document had come into our hands, circulated to district officials by Mr Smith's Native Affairs adviser, who had not impressed us on board *Fearless*. In this he stated flatly that there was no prospect of a settlement and was particularly scathing in analysing, from a fundamentally racialist view, all our proposals designed to improve the status of Africans, both electorally and in the progressive removal of discriminatory laws.

George Thomson was in Salisbury from 2nd to 9th November. Though his discussions were not completed, he clearly could not remain in Salisbury during the UDI celebrations on 11th November, and he took the opportunity to visit Zambia, Malawi, Uganda, Tanzania and Kenya, and to discuss, with the head of State in each capital, the Rhodesian situation and the forthcoming Commonwealth conference. He was in Salisbury again from 13th to 16th November.

In all he had nine full-scale meetings with Mr Smith and his colleagues. No time-limit was set to the discussion, but by mid-November it became clear that there was no movement at all to an agreement. At this stage Mr Smith and he decided to set out the remaining areas of disagreement so that they could be explained in Parliament. They were formidable. In his statement to the House of Commons on 18th November, George Thomson set out eight major points and even that was not exhaustive.

The first was a *Fearless* sticking-point – the second safeguard against retrogressive constitutional amendments which would impede progress towards majority rule. The *Fearless* terms had made clear our willingness to examine alternative methods to our own proposal, the Judicial Committee of the Privy Council. Some I had spelled out, with the Rhodesian 'constituency' in mind, in the House on 22nd October. George Thomson reported that Mr Smith showed not the slightest interest.

He therefore proposed an alternative, with my authority. Indeed I had worked it out in the aircraft returning from Gibraltar and taken the advice of our constitutional advisers, borrowing, *mutatis mutandis,* from certain provisions of the Australian constitution.

Mr Smith had objected to any external safeguards deriving from outside Rhodesia, despite the encouraging comments he had made to Sir Max Aitken about the Privy Council. George Thomson put forward a proposal which, as he said, would begin in Rhodesia and would also leave the last word with the Rhodesian people. If a constitutional amendment were introduced which was felt to be retrogressive in effect, it could be referred to the Privy Council for advice in one of two circumstances; either on an initiative by a specified number of Rhodesian members of Parliament, or on a decision of Rhodesia's own Constitutional Council. If the Judicial committee had doubts about the amendment they could decide that the matter should be put to the decision of the Rhodesian people as a whole, by means of a referendum of the entire electorate, A- and B-roll electors voting separately, with the requirement that a simple majority on each roll would be sufficient to validate the amendment.

'But Mr Smith told me,' George Thomson reported to the House, 'that he totally rejected the principle on which the alternative proposal was based. I asked Mr Smith whether he had any proposals of his own for a second guarantee. But he had none to offer.'

Mr Smith had reason to know that we were prepared to go further in considering an alternative second safeguard entirely internal to Rhodesia: namely a provision for the A-roll and B-roll referendum on the initiative either of a given number of Rhodesian MPs or of the Constitutional Commission, without necessarily involving the Privy Council.

The second point of disagreement lay in Mr Smith's refusal to agree to the Privy Council's continuing, as under the 1961 constitution, to hear appeals in other than constitutional cases. He had not taken up this attitude in any of our earlier discussions.

Thirdly, the regime wished to extend the period of three months, under the 1961 constitution, for which the legislature could approve the proclamation of a State of Emergency. This would mean extending, perhaps for an intolerable length of time, the period for which Rhodesian citizens could be held in detention without charge or trial, without any opportunity of parliamentary scrutiny.

Fourthly, the regime, while accepting a blocking quarter of elected Africans, wanted for reasons unacceptable to us to alter the number of elected Africans in the Senate or, alternatively, to have more A-roll seats in the lower House and more European seats in the Senate.

Fifthly, they tried to revert to old arguments by reducing the value of the votes to B-roll electors on the A-roll from twenty-five per cent to ten per cent, which would have the effect of postponing the date when majority rule would be achieved.

Sixthly, a technical but important point, they wanted to eliminate the 'delimitation' formula drafted in *Tiger* by Sir Hugh Beadle and not queried either there or on board *Fearless*.

Seventhly, they wanted to extend the criteria by which the Judicial Tribunal had to be guided when deciding which persons in detention should be released to take part in public discussion during the Royal Commission's test of acceptability under the fifth principle. Where the *Fearless* proposals would have excluded those likely to commit or to incite others to commit acts of violence or intimidation, they wanted to include those whose release might lead to a violent response. When this was reported to me, I remembered the dogs they had set on Nkomo's followers.

Lastly, Mr Smith resolutely refused to consider the reinstatement of public servants who had left Rhodesia after UDI in order to remain loyal to the Crown. If we were willing to wipe the slate clean so, we felt, should he. But he was obdurate.

In reporting these disagreements to the House, George Thomson concluded:

I do not want to be unfair to Mr Smith on these points. He did say that he believed that if it were possible to reach agreement on the question of the second safeguard our differences on the other points which I have mentioned could be quickly resolved. That may or may not be so. In so far as Mr Smith meant that he would expect us to give way on them, I made it absolutely clear to him that there could be no question of our doing so. I cannot speak for his own readiness to change his position on them. I can only tell the House as I have sought to do, the position he took on them when talking to me....

My report, I recognise, is a gloomy one. I myself found the last fortnight disappointing and saddening. So fair an opportunity has been turned down that, I am afraid, I could not feel otherwise. But to repeat what I have said before: we for our part are not slamming the door and perhaps one day the response from the other side of that door will be more constructive than it has so far been.

That was, in effect, the last definitive discussion with the regime which could have led to a settlement. In the spring of 1969 there were desultory exchanges, the full text of which were published in a White Paper in June 1969 (Cmnd. 4065). But by that time the regime had introduced its new 'constitution' – racialist, republican, specifically designed to prevent majority rule 'in our lifetime', or ever. It supplemented this with successive acts of discrimination, amounting to active apartheid, so as to rule out – in the absence of a complete change of heart – any move towards the six principles. From the beginning of 1969 every move was away from them.

George Thomson's statement to Parliament marks the end of a chapter.

Chapter 28

A message from President-elect Nixon – further pressure on sterling – the Deutschemark crisis – stern economic measures announced – Mad Friday in the City – financial irresponsibility – Lord Shepherd's visit to Lagos – Chequers conference on the economy – Trade Union reform – the Commonwealth conference of January 1969 – informal talks on Nigeria

AT the end of October 1968, I received a message from Washington informing me that President Johnson had decided to announce an unconditional cessation of all bombing in Vietnam, in the hope of inducing a move on the part of the DRV negotiating team in Paris. When his announcement made this news public, commentators on both sides of the Atlantic were unsure how far it was designed to swing Democratic voters into supporting Hubert Humphrey in the presidential election, or how far it was a last throw, before a new President was elected, to get a move from Hanoi which they would not be able to reverse. But Hanoi made no move. Vice-President Humphrey was defeated, by a small margin, despite a sharp narrowing of the poll gap in the week before the votes were cast.

Richard Nixon, the President-elect, and I exchanged messages, following precedent. Shortly after Mr Nixon's victory, Senator Jack Javits, Republican Senator for New York, an old friend of mine, came to London and asked to see me. But he told me that on this occasion he had come as an emissary from Richard Nixon to discuss the basis of our future working together. Everything he said, he made clear, was under instructions. An early meeting was suggested.

Late on the eve of Thanksgiving Day I received a message from Senator Javits to telephone him the following day. I got through to him during his Thanksgiving lunch. He said – I base myself here on the Downing Street record – that he had just had a further talk with the President-elect who had asked him to let me know that he much looked forward to seeing me as soon as possible after his inauguration. Mr Nixon would wish this first meeting to take place at a time and in circumstances which would underline its importance and make it clear that the purpose was to have a really meaningful exchange of views. *He also hoped that our meeting could be seen to be taking place as soon as possible and ahead of similar talks with other heads of government. Mr Nixon was thinking in terms of a meeting in the latter part of February or in March, and he suggested*

579

*that the details of this could best be worked out in due course through
the normal channels.*

I have italicised the passage in the above paragraph from the official
record because of the subsequent falsification of the situation in the
British press.

The Senator went on to suggest that I should follow up our conversation
with a letter to Mr Nixon as a response to the oral message conveyed by
him.

I duly wrote to Mr Nixon and received a letter from him confirming
the arrangements which had been suggested. After his inauguration, talks
through the diplomatic channels led to provisional arrangements for me to
visit Washington in the last week of February.

In the event, the President decided that instead he would visit Europe
in the very first weeks of his Administration, to demonstrate the importance he attached to the European link – in contrast to his predecessor
who had given the impression that all his interests were in the Pacific –
and to convince Europe that under his presidency the United States would
give a high priority to the Western Alliance. He therefore flew straight
to Brussels, the seat of NATO. His first national visit – and this was
deliberate – was to Britain.

It would not be necessary to tabulate these developments or to attach
any importance to them but for the campaign in the British press in
which one journal after another, in news story, leading article, diary
innuendo and cartoon, set out to assert, as though it were an admitted fact,
that Richard Nixon did not want to meet me and that I must take my
place low down in the queue. The facts were the reverse, as I made clear
in the House. But with an election coming, inconvenient facts could not be
allowed to stop the emergence of a more satisfying fiction, perhaps most
colourfully expressed in a cartoon, soon after the President's inauguration,
showing him at the end of the hot-line telephone, saying, 'Er ... don't
phone us – we'll phone you'. They did not know their Nixon, a man who
had been through the political treadmill and had a long memory. For – as
Jack Javits told me and the President later confirmed – he recalled that
when he was, in American terms, a 'busted flush', having lost the
California governorship election after his presidential defeat by Jack
Kennedy, I had met him at his London hotel. I had then just become
Leader of the Opposition; the American Embassy had telephoned me and
asked me to receive Mr Nixon. Instead, I had called on him and later,
long before his political re-emergence, I had welcomed him at Downing
Street. Of such are political relationships born.

Meanwhile we faced a grim English November. Once again I had the
Guildhall speech to deliver. The speech on 11th November was divided
almost equally between economic and overseas affairs. In addition to
giving an encouraging report on industry I went in some depth into the

'er . . . don't phone us – we'll phone you'

City's record in invisible earnings, with some extremely technical passages about their success in cornering a high proportion of the business in the rapidly expanding Euro-dollar market, estimated by that time to have a total turnover of $20,000 millions.

On overseas affairs I dealt principally with the lessons of Czechoslovakia and my hopes which this time were to be realised for the forthcoming Commonwealth Prime Ministers' conference:

> From the oldest of the former overseas dominions now well past its centenary, to the newest sovereign member of the Commonwealth, still celebrating only a few weeks of independence, there is a fierce desire to assert that independence. A perhaps unnecessary desire – as I have found – to impress on the Mother Country that they are now no longer colonies. What I have had occasion to emphasise, and I fear this may be necessary again, is that Britain has also achieved her independence....

Soon afterwards, sterling came under pressure again. This had nothing to do with our own position, for our balance of payments position was growing stronger week by week. But the Deutschemark was unnaturally strong and rumours of its upward revaluation caused violent currency movements, first out of French francs, then out of dollars and sterling, into Frankfurt. The German coalition was paralysed; while the Social Democrats would have been willing to revalue, as would Bundesbank leaders (who made no secret of it), the CDU majority in the coalition, and, in particular, the Finance Minister, Franz-Josef Strauss, would have none of it. It was an unstable situation, utterly disruptive of values in world exchange markets. We were pressing for a firm and incontestable decision one way or the other, preferably for one which would put the issue beyond doubt by raising the parity of the mark.

Suddenly, on Tuesday 19th November, when both the Chancellor and I were dressing in readiness for the annual dinner of the British National Export Council – which I never failed to attend during my premiership – the Treasury received a summons to attend, at top ministerial level, a conference in Bonn the following day. This was combined with an intimation that while the parity of the mark would remain unchanged, the world's monetary leaders should discuss what other possibilities existed. The Chancellor and I were agreed that inspired lunacy could go no further; if action were ruled out talk could only do harm, since foreign exchange markets would be driven crazy with rumours; rumours bad for the dollar and worse for sterling.

Small matter that our balance of payments was moving into surplus; there was money, possibly big money, to be made out of getting into Deutschemarks, even if only in the short-term. We had abundant experience of what these short-term movements could do to sterling.

The Chancellor and I agreed that, however much we might regret the calling of the Bonn conference, he should go. Meanwhile, he should miss the dinner to deal with the situation and I should attend. We would meet afterwards.

When I returned I called on him at No. 11. He had all his advisers there, and the Governor of the Bank as well. The atmosphere was one of gloom and irritation. The general view was that having created the maximum uncertainty in world markets by its action, the German Government should be pressed to end it by setting a new and definitive rate for the mark. They had informed us that they proposed to meet the situation by a judicious but limited exercise in reducing export subsidies and encouraging imports, amounting to about a four per cent change in export–import relationships. But we were dealing not so much with an imbalance in trading values, though that existed, as with massive movements of speculative capital. Against that background, their tinkering with the terms of trade was, in the Yorkshire phrase, 'neither nowt nor summat'. We brought the Foreign Secretary into our consultations, and decided to ask the German Ambassador, Herr Blankenhorn, to call on us. When he came we expressed ourselves strongly and said that the German Government, having gone so far in conjuring up the uncertainty, should now exorcise it by revaluation. He promised to report our representations to his masters in Bonn.

The next day, 20th November, when the Bonn conference opened, an irritated German Government leaked the story of our summons to Herr Blankenhorn. In no time at all the story had reached the proportions of alleging that I had called the Ambassador from his bed. He and I later agreed that if that story were true we could only conclude that he slept in his dinner jacket, black tie and all. But more harm had been done.

The attacks on sterling had already led earlier in the month to a series of ministerial meetings in Downing Street. When the tightening up of hire-purchase payments had been decided at the end of October, the Chancellor had intimated that he might have to take further action in demand management – though he hoped that this would not be before the New Year. But as the run on sterling assumed serious proportions he felt that we should take immediate action by the use of the 'regulator'. (This had been introduced in Mr Selwyn Lloyd's 1961 Budget; it provided that, at any time, the Chancellor could increase all indirect taxes by up to ten per cent, by order, subject to its confirmation in the following year's Finance Bill). At the same time the Chancellor would have to intensify the monetary squeeze.

Naturally, our Cabinet colleagues wanted to deal with the basic problems of our trade, strong though that was becoming. Import quotas were mentioned but, since our trade balance was moving satisfactorily, these could never have been accepted internationally, since quotas are only permissible, and then with great difficulty, in times of grave trade crisis.

Our problem was monetary movements, speculation and to a lesser extent in terms of British traders, 'leads and lags'. This led us, as part of the projected package, to decide to accept a proposal long urged upon us by our economic advisers – the introduction of import deposits, under which a specific percentage of the value of each import shipment would have to be deposited in cash with Customs and Excise before the documents and goods were cleared. We settled on a rate of fifty per cent. At a time when money was tight, and under the Chancellor's proposals due to become tighter, this would provide a deterrent against speculative imports and, indeed, an argument for holding ordinary imports to minimum levels. We had decided on the tripartite package in principle before the conference of Herr Schiller, the Economics Minister, was called. When the Chancellor left for Bonn I undertook to push it through the Cabinet's Economic committee, and through the Cabinet itself. It would only be reconsidered if the Germans reversed their policy and agreed to revalue. But revaluation was inconceivable to the economic theologians of the Bonn coalition.

I was kept in the closest touch with the progress, if that is the word, of the conference, first by telegrams and then by the early return of Harold Lever, the Financial Secretary, who had been busy in the *couloirs* of the conference and whose sense of humour made an otherwise gloomy report tolerable. Every message confirmed that the conference was a shambles. Two things emerged: first, the Germans were not going to revalue, though they might be prepared marginally to increase their interference with export and import values – this would be as efficacious as Dame Partington's mop in stemming the fury of the Atlantic; second, nothing would be more certain than the fact of French devaluation by 11.11 per cent; its ratification in Paris was regarded as a mere formality. It would take place on the Saturday; the International Monetary Fund was preparing its procedural dispositions. No banker, finance minister or Treasury official who left Bonn on the Friday had any doubt that French devaluation would be in the Sunday morning's headlines. They reckoned without General de Gaulle. On the Saturday night we heard that he had personally rejected the advice of all his quartermasters. The franc was not to be devalued. And, in fact, at its then parity it lived to survive the General's tenure of the Elysée.

At Downing Street we were preparing for a Commons statement by the Chancellor, as soon as he returned on Friday, 22nd November, on our own financial decisions. But there were problems. The ministerial council of the European Free Trade Area was meeting in Vienna. Tony Crosland was our representative and, against the somewhat uncertain timing of our Commons announcement, we controlled the timetable for his announcement, knowing, in the light of the furious EFTA reaction to the import surcharge four years earlier, what he would be facing.

On the Friday morning, as the EFTA council was breaking up, we still had no certainty that the Chancellor would return from Bonn in time to make his announcement before the House adjourned at 4.30 p.m. Fearful of a collapse of Commons business and a premature adjournment, which often happens on a Friday, I instructed the Chief Whip to keep the debate going at all costs and back-benchers were pressed to be ready with last-minute adjournment debates. In the event, the ordinary business ran all day. At noon I authorised Tony Crosland to go ahead, still wondering whether I should have to make the announcement myself in relative ignorance of the details of the Bonn meeting. Harold Lever was instructed to supervise the preparation of a 'shadow' statement for me to make. Meanwhile, punctuated by agonised messages from Vienna, I was carrying the proposals through an unhappy Cabinet.

I was relieved to receive news that the Chancellor had touched down at Heathrow soon after 2.00 p.m. and he had time to discuss the latest situation with me and to show me the draft statement he had prepared before rising to make his statement – nominally on the adjournment of the House – at 3.49 p.m.

Roy Jenkins gave a full account of the development of the Deutschemark crisis and of the Bonn conference. He referred to the speculation against the franc, fed by continued rumours that the French would refuse any credits to deter speculation. But he pointed out that an international support operation of $2,000 million had been assembled in Bonn, in addition to the $1,000 million already available to the Bank of France through other means.

He recounted the progressive improvement in Britain's overseas payments position; on a three-month moving average our trade figures had shown an improvement in every month from May onwards, even including the disappointing October figures. But he mentioned the high level of consumer spending as inhibiting a still faster improvement in our overseas trade performance; he was concerned also about a possible rapid build-up of stocks. He had therefore to announce further domestic measures to reinforce our national effort to get into surplus.

First, he announced the invocation of the Selwyn Lloyd regulator, a surcharge of ten per cent on the duties on beer, on wines, on spirits, on hydrocarbon oils, on petrol substitutes, tobacco, and on every rate of purchase tax. This meant 1d a pint on most beers, 4s on a bottle of whisky, 5d a gallon on petrol, and up to 5d on twenty cigarettes. Purchase tax rates were raised by ten per cent to $13\frac{3}{4}$ per cent, 22 per cent, $36\frac{2}{3}$ per cent and 55 per cent. The total effect was to reinforce the revenue by about £250 millions in a full year. The only remission was the usual refund of the increased petrol and Derv taxes to bus operators.

The Chancellor then announced the measures we had agreed for tightening credit, aimed at reducing private-sector lending by £100 millions by the following March. Legislation would be introduced to impose import deposits, at 50 per cent of their value, on all goods other than basic foods, feeding stuffs, fuel and raw materials and certain categories of goods imported mainly from developing countries. This meant that, roughly, one third of our total imports, some £3,000 millions a year, would be subject to the deposit requirements.

Inevitably, the press reaction was one of righteous outrage and the new decisions, after several months of economic improvement, provided welcome grist to the Opposition's mill. Conservative speeches became increasingly shrill and were more doleful than ever about Britain's economic prospects. The political situation worsened again. Throughout December and into January the Opposition's lead on the public opinion polls widened to over twenty points.

The pound was hit and, as a number of City editors reported, there seemed to be a determined attempt to talk sterling down. During successive periods when sterling had come under attack authoritative comment in the City columns had drawn attention to the fact that, though London financiers had but the most limited opportunity to operate against the pound, one of the City's principal exports to the Continent was a series of hysterical forecasts about the immediate prospects for the economy and for sterling. As the city editor of the *Guardian* put it, 'the gnomes are in London'. This was the message I was regularly receiving from friends in the international banking community. One very senior Swiss banker who had lunched with me on 5th August and who was introduced as the 'top gnome', expressed utter incredulity at the neurotic messages passing from individuals in the City of London to their contacts abroad: he could only speculate on their motives at a time when serious overseas bankers could read the form and were taking an increasingly confident view about Britain's balance of payments.

Whether the motives were basically political, or simply deriving from psychiatric factors, may never be proved. But in early December we saw neurosis reach its apogee in the sudden circulation of rumours which any professional could have deflated by a short telephone call. Professional newsmen, picking up the rumours, did just that; but the professionals in the City preferred the rumours to the facts.

On Thursday, 5th December, after answering my questions in Parliament, I went by train to Cornwall where my eighty-six-year-old father had been taken ill and sent to hospital for observation. It was a natural and filial act on my part which could have no possible bearing on the parity of any international currency. I stayed overnight and at 10.00 a.m. left St Austell, where I was photographed by the press, for Paddington.

By 3.00 p.m. – when I was still on the train – the most incredible rumours were in circulation in the City. The following list appeared in the subsequent *Sunday Times* 'Insight' inquiry into the phenomenon, in their exact words:

1. Jenkins and Wilson have quarrelled bitterly;
2. Healey and Jenkins have quarrelled with Wilson;

3. Barbara Castle and Jenkins have quarrelled;
4. Jenkins has resigned;
5. Wilson has resigned;
6. Wilson has dissolved Parliament and offered the Queen his resignation;
7. Wilson has resigned and (*original touch*) gone to France;
8. Jenkins has resigned with him;
9. Another devaluation is imminent (*this very restrained: the others took devaluation in their stride*);
10. The Queen has abdicated (*surely the apotheosis of rumour*).

Some of these rumours were actually cited by incredulous journalists who telephoned Downing Street and Buckingham Palace. But the formal denial made no difference to the financial lemmings.

This lunacy, in fact, lost Britain $100 millions of our hard-won reserves on that Friday, though it came back in the early days of the following week when ice-packs and strait-jackets took over. Some of our backbenchers, angry at the damage such unfounded and hysterical gossip could have inflicted on the economy and on our society, demanded that a tribunal of inquiry be appointed. This was tempting and would have exposed, once and for all, what we were up against with the wildcat element in the City. But I decided that this was too much of a steam-hammer for those particular nuts. The *Sunday Times*'s 'Insight' team's own inquiry, which was published on Sunday, 15th December, read like the report of an alienist.

It found that '... the affair began with another rumour entirely.' This – three days earlier – was based on a planted report by a chauvinistic French journalist, briefed by the French Finance Minister, saying that Britain's credit was exhausted and that we were applying for a new international loan. By the Friday morning, when I was in the train, the rumours – variously from the Lebanon, Jersey and Blackpool – proceeded to circulate in the City. A partner in the Government broker's office was telephoned while on the floor of the Stock Exchange and told that the gilt-edged market had been closed; his reply: 'Don't be a bloody fool, I'm standing in it.' But he was swimming against the tide. There were wild rumours of a Cabinet minister and a Labour peer telephoning their respective brokers; and a director of the National Westminster Bank was alleged to have spoken indiscreetly at a livery company dinner (that of the playing-card manufacturers). All these stories, too, were untrue. Others were seriously reported as having relied for their rumours on an obscure cartoon in the *Daily Telegraph,* portraying me as a sacked football club manager.

The *Sunday Times,* analysing this welter of rumour, attached importance to those which derived from the fact that when answering questions on the Thursday, my voice had sounded hoarse, the inalienable right of every Englishman in a raw December. '... perhaps, it was suggested, this came from shouting at Jenkins? (No, he simply had a sore throat).'

The *Sunday Times* concluded its inquiry in these words: '... but who needed a specific source?'

Quoting a stockbroker who had helped the team in its inquiries, it went on:

> Rumours are very useful. You needn't believe them. I never believed this one. But it gives you such a good excuse to ring someone up, and say 'have you heard today's story?' And then you see if you can sell him something on the side.

All this took place after nearly a century of compulsory elementary education. When I read all these rumours, I was glad that I had not appointed a judicial tribunal. Under the 1921, Tribunals of Inquiry (Evidence) Act, judicial tribunals, unlike courts of law under recent legislation, cannot reach a verdict of 'diminished responsibility'.

Great harm had nevertheless been done. So-called professionals, responsible for an important area of Britain's economy, had shown themselves fit only to be sent, with their gambling instincts, for training in a betting-shop, where professionalism is better defined, financial disciplines tighter, and where prejudice against any particular horse cannot affect its chance of winning.

Much was being written and said, not least in the City, about the damage done to Britain's recovery by wildcat strikers. My colleagues and I have never hesitated, in Government and – since June 1970 – in Opposition, to condemn wildcat activity in industry as undisciplined and damaging to Britain. Unfortunately Mr Heath could never be brought to condemn this far more serious undisciplined anti-British element in the wider Conservative movement.

The week after 'mad Friday' there was sustained comment on the perilous state of the economy. After the skirmishes, the Imperial Guard of the Establishment, noble Lords, *soi-disant* serious newspapers, Opposition spokesmen swept up the slopes; the publicity given to a speech by Mr Maudling at Greenock must have surprised him, though I noted that in a subsequent radio programme Mr Maudling said, as I had, that we had all under-rated the power of the speculators.

On Thursday, 12th December, the November trade figures were published, showing a very strong and favourable trend. This completed the rout of the speculators.

I pressed the counter-attack home in a five-minute speech at a rally of party workers at Dunstable, on Friday, 13th December – a speech which was reproduced in full on both television channels. I said:

> In Guildhall last month I paid tribute to what the City as a whole is doing to strengthen Britain's balance of payments and the words I used were sharply underlined by yesterday's balance of payments figures,

showing a sharp and sustained increase in earnings on invisible account. In the same speech I criticised a small minority in the City more concerned with making money than with earning money. It was such a minority who by their action last Friday surprised the nation by their naïvety and disregard for the national interest.

Grown men, professionals in a highly technical sense, masters of slide-rule and computer in checking the odds of gain or loss on a foreign exchange transaction, allowed themselves a degree of credulity in simple matters of political fact which would have been scorned by a second-former. Millions upon millions – millions of national assets – changed hands, drained for a short time out of the country, on an assumption – based on nothing more substantial than a gin and tonic or two – that I was at Buckingham Palace ...

This and other no less fantastic rumours were believed and phoned to serious-minded financial experts in Frankfurt and Zürich, and hard-earned national assets were squandered by those who saw a hope of unearned gain or hedge of possible loss ...

... Those who were swift last weekend to make party capital out of this speculative situation knew that they could be undermining the resolve of the vast majority of British people who have kept their nerve, who have got on with the job and who intend to keep on doing so....

... It was not so much the irresponsibility of last Friday afternoon. It was the avid way in which this irresponsibility was seized on.

Did Opposition leaders and their supporters regret what was happening? Or did they welcome it? They did not condemn this damaging strike of speculative capital, as it was their national duty to do. By failure to condemn, they were ready to allow others to draw the conclusions that what had happened suited their purpose.

The last sustained attack on sterling while we were in office had failed. As Britain moved, in the New Year, into strong and growing surplus the area for speculation narrowed. Hard-headed foreign exchange dealers abroad were left to form their own assessment of sterling's strength, unassisted by the kind of London advice we had witnessed. But without the evidence of the improving trade figures, it could have been a near-run thing.

The Nigerian situation continued to worsen. Hopes of a speedy end to the fighting had been ended by the deepening French involvement. Some relief flights were getting through to Biafra at night, but these were far too few to deal with the serious malnutrition in the by then narrow enclave still held and vigorously defended by Colonel Ojukwu.

Only the use of surface routes, or at least the programme of daylight flights which the Federal Government had agreed to allow through, could have had any significant effect.

On 12th December, before the House adjourned for Christmas, a debate on foreign affairs inevitably reflected the preoccupation of members with Nigeria. Many of the speeches dealt with the relief question and the

U

Foreign and Commonwealth Secretary confirmed the willingness of the Federal Government to agree to daylight flights. Lord Shepherd, Minister of State at the Foreign and Commonwealth Office, was in Lagos at that time dealing not only with relief but also renewing our pressure for a cease fire. The difficulty was that Colonel Ojukwu was willing to agree only to a temporary cease fire, which would enable him to regroup his hard-pressed defenders and give more time for much-needed ammunition and other military supplies to be flown in. The Federals, on the other hand, and for military reasons equally compelling to them, were willing to agree to a cease fire only if there were moves towards a permanent settlement.

Lord Shepherd had been authorised to raise with General Gowon a proposal that I should visit Nigeria either just before or just after Christmas. The General was reluctant: some of his people, particularly those ready to switch at any moment to an all-out Russian commitment, resented our humanitarian pressures on the relief question, on our advocacy of a cease fire and other measures to improve the situation. To them, Britain's duty was to give the Federals all-out military support to end the war and the suffering quickly. One of our difficulties with domestic and parliamentary opinion arose from this dilemma: our maintenance of arms supplies gave us some leverage and enabled us to press humane measures on the Federal Government. On the other hand, that leverage was limited because of the threat of a switch to total dependence on the Russians. It was a fact we could not adduce when our critics denounced our 'impotence', despite our 'guilt' in supplying arms.

General Gowon asked me to reconsider my visit, and said that he would be meeting me at the Commonwealth Prime Ministers' conference the following month. In the event he was not able to attend because of a sudden intensification of the fighting in mid-January. But I told him – and at the Commonwealth conference I repeated this to Chief Awolowo, the chief Nigerian delegate – that if the situation were no more satisfactory by the spring I intended to come.

On Sunday, 15th December, I held an all-day conference at Chequers of NEDC, to consider the first draft of the new economic document to replace George Brown's 1965 National Plan. This was followed the next day by a further Chequers conference, this time with the Economic committee of the TUC, to express the Government's reactions to the first draft of its annual economic report. But there was one social event. A few weeks before, as in 1964, I had entertained our Olympic team at Lancaster House and, again following the precedent of four years earlier, I invited our successful paraplegic Olympic team for a celebration party. I asked a number of Olympic athletes to help entertain them, and also a number of my friends in show-business, who received the equivalent of a three-line Whip and generously responded. It was a warm and successful – but like its predecessor, a deeply moving – occasion.

I spent a white Christmas at Chequers and visited Stoke Mandeville paraplegic hospital on Boxing Day. After four days in Scilly I returned on New Year's Day to face the challenge and hopes of 1969. There were two immediate preoccupations: at home, the negotiations with industry about Barbara Castle's post-Donovan proposals on industrial relations and, in the international sphere, the Commonwealth Prime Ministers' conference.

Following the publication of the Donovan Report, the First Secretary, Barbara Castle, had been in almost daily contact with the CBI and the TUC. There were trade union leaders, and a small number of Labour MPs, who were opposed even to the Donovan proposals and to what they saw as an interference with free collective bargaining. But Barbara Castle, with my full backing, was trying to lead the way beyond Donovan. While taking the report as her basis, she felt, as I did, that the confessed failure of the Commission to find any short-term remedy for unofficial strikes could not be accepted; there should at least be an attempt made to secure an immediate step forward while the long-term recommendations about improved negotiating and disputes procedures and registration of agreements and the proposed Commission for Industrial Relations were patiently being pursued. This led to the idea of a 'conciliation pause', applied to local and factory situations. In addition she was examining better procedures than those suggested in Donovan for dealing with inter-union disputes, and the possibility, in official disputes, of an indicative strike ballot to be held if so required in a given situation by the minister. This latter we quickly dropped, when we became satisfied that it was most unlikely to reduce strikes. Indeed, once a ballot had resulted in a majority for strike action, it might well prove impossible for the union leadership to get their members back to work on any agreement which fell short of their full demands. Contrary to surviving legend, by far the greater part of Barbara Castle's proposals were based on improvements within industry, without any use of legal procedures. When on 17th January her proposals were published in *In Place of Strife*, (Cmnd. 3888), only three of the twenty-seven recommendations involved any use of so called 'penal' powers.

In early December, the First Secretary, who had been working with a small group of ministers on her scheme, discussed the proposed time-table with the Chancellor and me. As I understood it, her ministerial group would finalise her draft just after Christmas and would then report to Cabinet on 3rd January. A time-table was worked out for consultations with the TUC and the CBI ready for publication of a definitive White Paper in mid-January. It was clear that once consultation began there would be immediate leaks, possibly selective and tendentious.

I was disturbed to learn, therefore, two days before Christmas, that the meeting with the TUC had been arranged for 30th December, before consideration by the Cabinet. Leaks would be certain to prejudice that consideration. My fears were justified. Looking back on it, my mistake lay in not insisting that the TUC meeting be held back until after the Cabinet meeting. The reason was, as I recall it, the extremely tight time-table on which we were working to bring out both Barbara Castle's White Paper, and Dick Crossman's draft of his revolutionary incomes-related superannuation scheme in good time for parliamentary discussion, when the House resumed on 20th January 1969. But it was an error.

Nearly six months later, after the settlement with the Trades Union Congress, and with the Cabinet and PLP fully united after a period of great strain, Dick Crossman wrote a letter to me, saying that one of the great difficulties for some members of the Cabinet throughout had re-sulted from the scheme becoming public knowledge before the Cabinet could express a view on it. He was right. Moreover, when the Cabinet did react I felt it right to agree that it should have more time to consider the proposals. With the Commonwealth Prime Ministers' conference just then assembling, these meetings had to be held at an early hour in the morning, before my Marlborough House commitments, or in the evening; it was not the best prescription for ensuring a happy and co-operative Cabinet.

It was indeed the Prime Ministers' meeting which provided the other great challenge in the New Year. Despite my efforts to get agree-ment to have it held in another Commonwealth capital, it met, after all, in London, from Tuesday 7th January to Wednesday 15th January 1969.

It was the first conference since the unhappy Rhodesia-dominated gathering of September 1966. Twenty-eight self-governing Common-wealth countries were represented. Tanzania had resumed diplomatic relations with us, and Barbados, Botswana, Lesotho, Mauritius and Swazi-land had attained independent status. Twenty-four countries were repre-sented at head-of-government level, the only absentees being Presidents Ayub Khan and Kenyatta – who were both too ill to attend – General Gowon, fully involved with a new offensive in the Nigerian war, and General Ankrah, the chairman of the Ghanaian National Liberation Council. It was the most representative and top-level Commonwealth gathering in history; despite gloomy forecasts that it would mark the virtual end of the Commonwealth, it proved by far the most successful ever held.

In the advance discussions there was complete agreement on the agenda. Provided there was adequate time for an exhaustive discussion on Rhodesia, no impediment was placed on full debate on all the other issues normally examined in draft at Commonwealth meetings. After a morning session on Tuesday, 7th January, for my speech of welcome, and the conventional courtesies in the afternoon, we went on to a deep examination of world affairs, which lasted for three formal sessions, until our adjournment at 6.00 p.m. on the Wednesday afternoon, by which time twenty heads of government, from every continent of the world, had spoken.

Summarising this part of the discussions, and taking into account, too, the part of the last day's communiqué session which related to the world affairs debate, I gave my impressions to Parliament in a statement after the end of the conference in these terms:

> The debate on the world political situation, in which nearly every delegation took part, was of a kind no other forum would be likely to provide for a serious and authoritative treatment of international problems. While some might have expected the size of the conference to weaken the force and pointedness of the debate, the fact that contributions were made with such authority from every continent of the world, the fact that of the twenty-eight delegations so many were represented at head of government level, the fact that it was so representative a gathering of so many races, in a multi-racial setting, with wide diversity of political approach on many basic world problems – all these facts strengthened rather than weakened the quality of the discussion and the importance of the occasion.
>
> One difference I noticed from previous conferences was the greater emphasis on regional problems – Australasia, south-east and other parts of Asia, Africa, Europe, the Americas, with particular reference to the Caribbean. For each Prime Minister it was as though he was given an angle on world affairs represented not by a world map centring on his own country, as we all instinctively tend to see it, but with each problem sharply highlighted from different geographical angles.

This had been neatly illustrated by a remark of Indira Gandhi, Prime Minister of India, who, in the course of a lengthy discussion on the Middle East, said, 'You have all used the phrase "Middle East"; to us it is known as "West Asia".'

On the Thursday morning we went straight into the most controversial issue of the conference, Rhodesia, which took the whole of the next two days. The debate was frank and hard-hitting, yet however deep the disagreement between us there was a spirit of understanding which had been totally absent from our counsels in 1966.

As I had decided to wind up the debate, I asked George Thomson to open the discussion and set out the British position. He repeated our basic approach over the years we had been in power, our sense of trusteeship for the voteless Africans and our insistence on the Six Principles as the basis of any settlement. After reviewing the progress of sanctions, he took the conference through the history of our successive attempts to reach an honourable settlement, first on *Tiger*, and then *Fearless* and his own subsequent discussions in Salisbury.

The *Fearless* proposals remained on the table, but the British Government's policy on NIBMR remained unchanged. There had as yet been no change in the circumstances of the kind we had sometimes spoken of as justifying a review of the statement of British intentions recorded in the communiqué after the last Prime Ministers' meeting. We had said many times, and George Thomson confirmed it, that if ever there were a change in circumstances justifying a departure from the NIBMR declaration of 1966 so that a fresh look should be taken, we would put the matter before our Commonwealth partners.

I then called on Julius Nyerere to speak. He was at his brilliant best. He made a long statement of the African case, all the more effective in that it was utterly restrained and reliant on withering understatement. His arguments were familiar but, distancing himself from some of his African colleagues, he did not base himself on any assertion that the problem could be solved only by military force. It was on the insistence on NIBMR, on which he had stood out alone in 1965, and on the illegitimacy of the *Fearless* proposals that he rested his case. While our case was that the people of Rhodesia 'as a whole' must have the last word and that they, and not the Commonwealth conference, were the best judge of their interests, Julius Nyerere argued that if a fair test of acceptability showed the Rhodesian people opposed to the *Fearless* proposals, they would be condemned to suffer for a further period under the brutalities of the Smith regime, which we appeared powerless to upset. But if, on the other hand, the test of acceptability showed an acceptance of the *Fearless* proposals, then the Smith regime would remain, with full recognition by Britain. In either case, the Africans would be living in an oppressive system; the only difference would be that in the one case that system would be approved and, in the other, disapproved by Britain.

He concluded by saying that the Commonwealth stood for something basic to the future of mankind; but only while it stood firmly against racialism and minority racial domination. The fact that the Commonwealth was not strong enough to achieve the results it needed quickly must not cause it to surrender its principles. We had to keep on: to maintain and strengthen sanctions, withdraw the *Fearless* proposals at once, before they had besmirched the Commonwealth's reputation for non-racialism and honesty, and unanimously to reaffirm the pledge to NIBMR as the only basis on which a settlement could be made.

The first two speeches had made the points which constituted the warp and woof of a brilliant and never tedious debate. Suffice to say, in the words of an accurate press report, that twenty-three countries, give or take a number of qualifications, were against Britain, and five for us. The Australian Prime Minister, in a highly sensitive and carefully-phrased speech which earned the plaudits even of the minority who disagreed with it, supported us, as did Mr Holyoake of New Zealand. The Tunku, for Malaysia, and President Banda of Malawi, supported us. Pierre Trudeau, attending, as was Mr Gorton, his first Commonwealth conference, basically supported us, but with an elegance of language and a willingness to understand the African point of view which won for him a freshman's laurels. He had gone on record, in a British television interview recorded before he left Ottawa, as expressing great cynicism about the value, even the future, of the Commonwealth. Before the conference ended, he was a committed Commonwealth statesman. British press comments which wrote him off as a playboy, still worse the *Daily Telegraph* which dismissed him as a 'trendy prig', had not begun to appraise his contribution – the beginning, but not the end of his contribution to Commonwealth affairs.

Late in the debate Kenneth Kaunda entered the lists. As ever his speech was deeply sincere and utterly moving. To some extent, he cut himself off from some of his African colleagues and others who supported the African point of view by a passionate plea for the use of force by Britain, on lines made familiar in 1965 and the two 1966 conferences. On the *Fearless* talks, he felt that their acceptance would deprive the Rhodesian Africans of their civil rights for a hundred years and even went so far as to compare them unfavourably with the 1961 constitution in terms of the openings for eventual majority rule.

I began my lengthy reply early enough on the Friday afternoon, 10th January, to allow some of those who had already spoken to have the chance to question me or briefly to reply to my speech. It was in no mere spirit of courtesy that I said that the debate on Rhodesia had been in the very highest standard of Commonwealth meetings. Thanking those who had paid tribute to George Thomson's lucid exposition of the British case, I said that all who had heard President Nyerere's opening of the general debate would agree that his speech, together with the document he had circulated, combined moderation and comradeship in expression with extreme urgency and force, both in its analysis of the Rhodesian situation and in the clear and unequivocal restatement of the Commonwealth ideal. It was a speech marked, as were all those which followed, by a deep sincerity. Strong charges had been made, but I undertook to observe Dr Kaunda's injunction to take the criticism in good spirit.

I began from Britain's standpoint that the Commonwealth's attitude to these questions was not non-racial. It was anti-racial. I then went on, at considerable length, to rebut the arguments of those calling for the use of force. I expressed my understanding of the doubts of those who drew a contrast between Britain's record in repressing colonial revolts in the past and our failure to take action in Rhodesia; and, repeating arguments I had used in previous conferences, I underlined the historical and geographical factors which rendered those analogies irrelevant. I spent some time defending the *Fearless* proposals and reviewed progress on sanctions.

I then turned to the main anxiety which had been expressed. It had always been understood that if there were a substantial change of circumstances it would be right for me to consult with the Commonwealth about the NIBMR declaration of 1966. So far there had been no such change. An agreement with the regime about the *Fearless* terms would not of itself constitute a justification for reconsidering NIBMR. But if the Royal Commission reported that the people of Rhodesia 'as a whole' were willing to accept the agreement as a basis for independence, that would amount to a substantial change of circumstances.

I would then have to put to each of my Commonwealth colleagues the following question; my words were, and I italicise them here:

'If the people of Rhodesia – having had the constitutional proposals put to them, having regard to the consequences of accepting them, and having regard also to the consequences of present conditions continuing, and from their point of view deteriorating – decided for acceptance, should any of my colleagues outside Rhodesia say that the Rhodesians were wrong; that they knew better than the Rhodesians what was good for them?'

I felt, I said, that some of the views I had heard that morning went very close to saying that the future of the Rhodesians must be decided by the Commonwealth conference and not by the Rhodesians themselves. I wondered, I told my colleagues, whether it was not a question of keeping their own consciences clear while the Rhodesians were left to pay the price.

Taking up a charge made by Kenneth Kaunda of 'inconsistency', I pointed out, with great respect to some of my Commonwealth colleagues, a certain 'inconsistency' between all they had been saying during the previous two days and the fact that in the previous month a number of their Governments had voted in the United Nations General Assembly for a resolution purporting to instruct Britain to hand over, manifestly against their will, 23,000 citizens of Gibraltar – fellow Commonwealth citizens – to Spain, a country which would not be regarded by many Prime Ministers as noticeably liberal or democratic in terms of the criteria for democracy which they were laying down for Rhodesia. And this UN vote was after a referendum, supervised by independent Commonwealth observers, had shown that in a secret ballot all but forty-four of the Gibraltarians had come out clearly in favour of maintaining their connection with Britain and rejecting a transfer to Spain.

The British Government was not prepared to impose a political solution in Rhodesia against the will of four million Africans, I said; but the votes of some of my Commonwealth colleagues in the United Nations had shown *them* willing to impose an alien political future on fellow Commonwealth citizens even against their freely-determined wishes.

This really turned the argument, though Julius Nyerere came back smartly with a suggestion that on the Gibraltar analogy I should insist on a referendum in Rhodesia, supervised by independent Commonwealth observers. For the last hour of the day there was a series of exchanges, mainly in the form of questions to, and answers by, me, though Pierre Trudeau joined in with some direct questions to African delegates. In particular, he asked Julius Nyerere whether, if he was satisfied by the test of acceptability, he would be prepared to compromise on the principle of NIBMR? The answer was moderate, mainly criticising the Royal Commission as a means of applying the test. If the people of Canada freely decided to accede to the United States that would be a matter for them, decided by their own democratic processes. He would not propose sending a commission from Tanzania to test Canadian opinions on the question. He did not see why the test in Rhodesia should not be more directly tested; he continued to have serious doubts about the validity of any test of opinion made by a Royal Commission. Pierre Trudeau commented that it seemed clear to him that the question under discussion was not, then, the principle of NIBMR but the method of consultation to be used to gather the opinions of the people of Rhodesia.

The heat was out of the debate. There was no real disposition, however strongly individual Presidents and Prime Ministers felt, to answer my challenge that they were seeking to decide what the Rhodesian people wanted rather than leave it to the Rhodesians themselves to decide their future. But in the last few minutes of the session, concern was expressed about our apparent willingness to leave the *Fearless* proposals 'on the table' indefinitely. Milton Obote and Pierre Trudeau feared that this might encourage intransigence and that if sanctions bit harder the regime might rush to accept *Fearless* for fear of getting something worse. John Gorton interpreted what I had said as meaning that the proposals would remain on the table as long as Britain thought wise. I confirmed this. I did not wish to imply that the proposals would never be withdrawn; 'never' was a word politicians should use with great care. But if Mr Smith continued to reject the offer and moved towards a more extreme policy then the *Fearless* proposals would lapse. If someone more reasonable came along even after the proposals had lapsed, *Fearless*, or some appropriate variant of them, could be revived and again placed on offer. But if the proposals were withdrawn too soon it would set back the emergence of critics of the regime, some of whom were beginning to form multiracial opposition parties.

We adjourned for the weekend, with the week's agenda completed and in very good heart. As the Friday evening party gathered at Chequers, followed by the others on Saturday and Sunday, 11th and 12th January, I noticed that even those who had spoken with the greatest feeling on Rhodesia, were more relaxed and friendlier towards us than they had been for years. From comments dropped by one Commonwealth leader after another, it became clear this conference was developing its own legend of success and mutual confidence. Unprecedentedly, there was no 'lobbying' to be done of individual delegations, but the three Chequers parties provided opportunities for a great number of bilateral exchanges and for old hands to get to know those making their maiden appearance. Pierre Trudeau had stayed with me at Chequers for the weekend before the conference, this second weekend John Gorton and his wife stayed, in both cases creating excellent personal relationships which would have been impossible through merely formal contacts.

The conference resumed on Monday, 13th January. The day was spent on the world economic situation; the debates on this were more constructive than in previous years. Instead of the traditional opening statement by the Chancellor of the Exchequer, I had suggested that the Prime Minister of New Zealand should lead the discussion, and that Lee Kuan Yew should open the next day on Commonwealth co-operation. Both debates produced excellent discussions enabling, as had the world affairs debate, Prime Ministers from different parts of the world to learn a great deal more about problems of the world economy of which they had little direct knowledge, including, in the economic debate, something of the importance and problems of particular commodities on which a country or a wider region was entirely dependent.

Harry Lee of Singapore, who had already distinguished himself in the world affairs discussion with a brilliant unscripted assessment of world politics worthy of comparison with his *tour de force* at Lagos in January 1966, made no less a contribution to the development debate, in which his reference to the problems of developing countries was, by common consent, one of the most remarkable essays in interpretation of the post-imperial world any of us had heard. He has been repeatedly pressed to publish it, and I hope he will do so. With his agreement, I felt it right to include in this memoir of the 1969 conference a brief summary of part of it, describing with brutal realism the economic problems of newly-emancipated countries.

While in no way dissociating himself from the views expressed by others about the 'niggardly' provision made by advanced countries for the needs of developing countries, he wanted, he said, to suggest seven reasons for the failure to realise the visions which the first-generation, anti-colonial nationalist leaders in south-east Asia and elsewhere had held out to rally their people in their quest for freedom.

First, the population explosion had placed a sharply increased burden on the resources of these countries as modern medicine and improved environmental health techniques reduced both infant and adult mortality rates.

Second, 'inter-ethnic peace', previously ensured by the colonial over-lord, had proved difficult to maintain after independence when power often passed into the hands of the ethnic majority. The European powers had created imperial boundaries of convenience. Over the decades, they had brought together an odd mixture of diverse ethnic and cultural groups to complement and supplement the skills required for more effective extraction and exploitation of resources.

Third, power had been handed over to those élite groups who had commanded popular support, but when these new governments attempted to demonstrate continuing legitimacy by retaining support after independence they had brought divisive forces to the surface. For political supremacy, competing leaderships had been unable to resist the temptation to appeal to ethnic, linguistic and religious loyalties. In consequence, the entire country suffered. It had become almost impossible to preserve a complementary balance of the diverse factors and groups previously brought together into one functioning whole by an overlord. Ethnic minorities, who were often the shopkeepers, acted for practical purposes as the village bankers; they knew who was credit-worthy, how each villager could pay in kind for the things he needed on credit, and therefore what to import and store, and what to collect in return and export. When these shopkeepers were forced out of business by rioting or legislation, or both, the villagers lost their bankers. This local knowledge and expertise could be replaced neither by other villagers nor the administrators who had sought by legislative innovation to create native entrepreneurs, nor by members of the USA Peace Corps or the British VSO.

Fourth, the inadequate number of trained men in political leadership, government administration, the professions, commerce and industry had retarded economic development. When political leaders more gifted in arousing their people emotionally than in mundane matters of administration and economics interfered for political ends with what was still working, administrative conditions had deteriorated and the economy had run down further.

Fifth, a number of these States were handicapped by being what had been termed 'soft societies'. With the withdrawal of the unrepresentative (and probably for that reason, decisive) rulers and the introduction of elected governments, a softening took place in the firm framework of administration. Corruption had set in and became a way of life for all those invested with authority, from the highest to the lowest levels of bureaucratic power. Succession by military *coup d'état* had tended to make things worse. There was inability to stem corruption, to resist deficit budgeting and central bank credit creation, leading to an inevitable debasement of their currencies and lack of confidence in the regime, resulting in a drastic slowing down of investment and economic growth.

Sixth, the educated had not been put to best use. Wage differentials between the highly-educated and the untrained were narrowed as politicians sought the popular votes of the masses and sacrificed the interests of the few who happened to be those with professional and technological competence. Worse, educational opportunities for the children of these people became markedly inferior to those available in the developed countries where they could sell their training and skills; this was often the point at which the pulls of social conscience, loyalty and patriotism snapped, and a further brain drain resulted.

Lastly, attitudes towards free enterprise had made a difference in development performance. Almost contiguously with the ethnic and cultural divisions between east Asia and south-east Asia had been the division between the areas where free enterprise had been allowed to flourish and those areas where government planning and controls had stifled enterprise. This had happened either because the State philosophy favoured State planning, or because the entrepreneurs were ethnically a minority and so had their activities circumscribed and restricted for political reasons. On the other hand, it was free enterprise which accounted for the progress of Thailand, Malaysia and Singapore. Thailand was also fortunate in never having been incorporated into a European empire. The Thais were aware that, besides the removal of colonial exploitation, other positive factors were needed, such as managerial and technological skills, enterprise and capital, before national wealth could be increased.

The remaining days, until the communiqué session, were spent in discussion on functional problems of inter-Commonwealth consultation and the working of Commonwealth institutions. The details were set out in the communiqué published as a British White Paper, (Cmnd. 3919).

The communiqué went through more quietly and speedily than in any previous conference I had attended. Apart from a difficulty following our passage on Czechoslovakia – when the Pakistani delegate sought, without support, to equate Israeli 'aggression' in the Middle East with the Soviet action in Czechoslovakia – there was general agreement on the draft prepared by senior officials of the twenty-eight participating countries. What I found particularly impressive was the way in which a number of African countries, previously regarded as at best non-aligned, not merely accepted but insisted on strengthening some of the passages critical of the Soviet Union's action in Czechoslovakia.

But we had run into a difficulty about Nigeria. The Nigerian delegation, led by Chief Awolowo, had had informal meetings with a number of delegations, including – early in the conference – Zambia and Tanzania, who had both recognised the Biafran secessionists. Chequers had provided further opportunities for informal exchanges. But on the day before the communiqué session I received representations from one or two delegations, including one – not recognising Biafra, but regarded by the Federal Government as 'wobbly' – suggesting that the conference would be rendered meaningless if it failed to discuss the most tragic event in the Commonwealth, the Nigerian war. How could they, I was asked, return home and have to tell their Parliaments that it had not been raised? But apart from the fact that the Nigerian delegation would certainly have walked out if any attempt had been made to raise the question, the conventions of Prime Ministers' meetings specifically ruled out any discussion of the internal affairs of an individual Commonwealth country and the fighting in Nigera was a civil war within one country, even though two Commonwealth countries had recognised Biafra. I invited the Nigerian delegation to meet me. They were under instructions, and difficult.

But they said that if any Commonwealth country wanted to assist in getting peace in Nigeria they should put pressure upon the so-called Biafran delegation which was in London and urge it to have discussions with the official Nigerian delegation. This group, headed by Mr Mojekwu, the 'Home Secretary' of Colonel Ojukwu's team, had come to London at the beginning of the conference, gone away, and then returned to London. Chief Awolowo told me that his delegation was authorised by Lagos to have discussions with them without preconditions, though, of course, Nigeria could not accept any final settlement other than one based on the continuing integrity of Nigeria as a single, albeit federal, State. In the view of Chief Awolowo and his colleague, Dr Arikpo, the Nigerian Foreign Minister, it would be particularly useful if the countries which had recognised Biafra and the one or two others who had some measure of acceptance there were to press for the London talks Nigeria had proposed. But there could be no discussions of Nigeria's internal affairs round the conference table.

While we were talking I had an idea which they went away to consider. The following day was the last day of the conference. I suggested that, before settling the communiqué, we should adjourn and go to Lancaster House for drinks and a final social get-together. Informally, and outside the transactions of conference – that was the reason for Lancaster House – I would ask the leader of the Nigerian delegation to say a few words to a group of 'friends', who happened to have gathered, about his Government's assessment of the internal situation in Nigeria and perhaps answer a few questions.

Chief Awolowo agreed. Accordingly, everyone was advised of the nature of the occasion, and there were no absentees from the roster of 'my friends', all of whom happened to be Commonwealth Prime Ministers or acting heads of their delegations. After one or two toasts I called on Chief Awolowo to say a few words. This he did with great restraint, and in carefully chosen phrases set out his Government's clear position. Most of my friends were impressed and there were several questions. At the end, it was the leaders who had insisted on a discussion in conference and a reference in the communiqué who proposed that no more be said. But there was independent agreement that those in a position to do so should put pressure on the Biafrans in London to meet with the Chief and Dr Arikpo.

It was agreed that news of our unofficial meeting and even more unofficial conclusions be given to the press, and the evening papers and those of the next morning made a great deal of the new initiative for peace. But the Biafrans refused to meet the Federal Government delegation.

After the conference was over, Chief Awolowo came to see me before he returned to Nigeria. He was still brimful of confidence that the Federal offensive would provide the long-deferred break-through and the end of the war. I was more doubtful; it was clear that the Federal Government were not yet fully seized of Colonel Ojukwu's ability to hold out following French intervention with arms supplies. His stay in London had brought home to the Chief what the British Government was up against with public opinion and he readily agreed when I said that, while I would hold my hand for the present, if there was no dramatic change in the situation by the end of March I would consider it essential to meet General Gowon personally – in London, Lagos, or some intermediate place – so that we could jointly assess the situation.

On another live issue, the human tragedy of the East African Asians, every initiative we had taken led to disappointment. Various attempts had been made for extra-mural meetings, outside the conference proper, between Britain and the African countries concerned, together with India. Various procedural difficulties led to postponements and cancellations but ultimately Jim Callaghan was able to meet the delegation leaders involved. No progress at all was made and we could get no more than a grudging agreement that the matter would have to be pursued by bilateral diplomatic contacts in the months following.

Press and television comment on the conference, apart from one or two sour notes from papers who found it difficult to accept that any conference presided over by a Labour Prime Minister could be a success, was friendly. Some comment recalled the widespread expectation that the conference would mark the end of the Commonwealth and recorded that it had ended with Commonwealth links greatly strengthened. The *Daily Mirror*, not noted for its support of Commonwealth ideals, reported:

Mr Wilson has undoubtedly scored a big personal triumph in his handling of the conference. He went into the talks knowing that Britain risked
a major drubbing on the issues of Rhodesia and immigration.
Although he was prepared to listen to constructive criticism, he was
determined not to allow any attempt to put Britain in the dock over
these two problems.

His tactics paid off. . . .

An American comment was perceptive and fair. The *Christian Science
Monitor* commented:

The Commonwealth Prime Ministers' Conference did more than defuse
a political time bomb.
It confounded critics by proving the Commonwealth's determination to
survive. It pleased the Commonwealth's friends by demonstrating that
this loose-knit grouping of nations is more united than it was after the
last abrasive conference of 1966. . . .
In what sense then can this conference be called modestly successful?
One way to measure this is to see it relative to the expectations of the
delegates.
Hopes were not high. The 1966 conference, soured by the bitter and
angry denunciations of British policy over Rhodesia, was to blame. . . .
Yet when the delegates left London the Commonwealth was intact, a
showdown on Rhodesia avoided, and, even more important, there was a
fresh desire to see that the Commonwealth flourishes. In a sense the ability
to even survive is progress, though admittedly of a negative kind.
Ironically, those African states who previously had been most critical
of the Commonwealth are increasingly seeing the worth of this organisation and investing more enthusiasm in it.
Some of the traditional antagonisms between Britain and its former
colonies are ebbing. As one informed Commonwealth observer put it . . .
'It (the conference) was no night of the long knives' – a rather lurid
metaphor implying that the practice of African states ganging up on
Britain was noticeably absent this year . . .
Thus while deep divisions exist within the Commonwealth, the conference
at least proved its will to survive and prosper . . .

When I reported to the House on 21st January, I spoke in similar
terms about the success of the conference, and the now-proven value of
the Commonwealth. Mr Heath expressed his agreement.

Chapter 29

The earnings-related superannuation scheme – House of Lords reform – 'L'Affaire Soames' – talks with Dr Kiesinger and Willy Brandt – European technological co-operation – visit to West Berlin – President Nixon's visit to England

D URING January the economic signs were improving and with them came an improvement in the Government's political standing: the Conservative lead of over twenty per cent in December's opinion polls was halved by January. Political comment centred mainly on Barbara Castle's industrial reform measures. Her White Paper was not published until 17th January. But already the TUC reaction, and some comments from Labour MPs, had been whipped up by the press: it was hardly surprising that the public regarded them as consisting entirely of the so-called 'penal clauses'. Special meetings of the trade union group of MPs and of the Parliamentary Labour Party were hastily arranged and before long the National Executive committee was wheeling its heavy artillery into position.

At Walsall on 25th January Mr Heath made a passionate speech – on immigration – in all but his choice of language recalling the thoughts of Enoch Powell – and called for 'immediate legislation'. Jim Callaghan immediately denounced Mr Heath's effort as 'shifty and slick'. Unaccountably, though the Conservatives had a dozen supply days in the months following, when they could have chosen immigration for an all-day parliamentary debate, they never did. As in so many speeches designed to inflame public opinion, our opponents fought shy of submitting their views to the critical analysis of parliamentary debate.

On 28th January, Dick Crossman published his White Paper on the earnings-related superannuation scheme. This set out in definitive form the work he had begun in 1957, when chairman of a National Executive sub-committee. The scheme had been designed to end the social anomaly of what, twelve years earlier, he had called 'two nations in old age'. It had featured in our 1964 and 1966 manifestoes, but had taken what seemed like an infinity of time and patient ingenuity to get into workable form.

The White Paper, (Cmnd. 3883) began from eight principles:

1. That rights to benefit must be earned by the payment of contributions; if pensions were to be financed wholly by taxation their level would inevitably be constrained at too low a level.

2. That benefits and contributions must be related to the contributors' earnings. This would mean differentiation on retirement between individuals, depending on past earnings, but it would end one of the worst features of the flat-rate system, the sudden shock caused by an adjustment of living standards from relatively high wages or salaries earned at work to the bare flat-rate income. But room was still to be left for employers' pension schemes and other ways of providing for old age.

3. That benefits must normally be sufficient to live on, without requiring excessively high contributions during the years of a man's working life. The White Paper provided for this by an ingenious formula which was to give greater weight to the contributions paid on the first third of earnings covered by the scheme.

4. That benefits must take into account changes both in price levels and in general living standards. Earnings-related benefits must not be eroded by increases in the cost of living; but, more, they should, by what was known as the principle of 'dynamism', contain provision to increase statutory benefits to keep pace with increases in the general level of industrial and other earnings.

5. That women were to contribute on the same basis as men and earn similar benefits.

6. That the scheme would not be actuarially funded but be administered on the 'pay as you go' principle. There would be two funds, a National Superannuation Fund covering pensions, widowhood benefits and death grants; and a Social Insurance Fund for all other benefits. The underlying principle was to be that the income from current contributions would be used to meet current expenditure on benefits.

7. That the state scheme would work in partnership with employers' pension schemes. The White Paper accepted that these schemes would have an important part to play and must be assisted to develop, though there would have to be readjustments when they were integrated with, or under the opting-out procedures accepted as a partial replacement for, the state scheme.

8. That people changing jobs must be legally entitled to have their pension rights preserved, if they so wished, or to have their contributions returned to them.

An elaborate schedule of contributions and benefits was drawn up. Those in receipt (at January 1969 standards) of £33 a week, would be paying nearly double their former contributions; those on the (then) national average wage of £22 per week would pay rather less than they had been. The benefit calculations suggested that the lowest-paid workers might get up to sixty per cent of their average earnings in work, higher-paid workers rather less than half; in percentage terms there was, then, a redistributive element in post-retirement pensions, narrowing, though not eliminating, the gap in cash terms. It was announced that existing pensioners receiving only the existing flat-rate benefits, would have their pension scales statutorily reviewed every two years, to take account of price increases and rises in living standards. While twenty years of new contributions would be required before the first pension at the full new rates would be payable, arrangements were proposed for 'blanketing in' those coming on to pension during that period, with pension credits higher than those paid for through previous contributions.

It became increasingly clear that the pension funds were going to declare war on the state scheme, and that they would be backed by the Conservative party. The difference between us was this: while we welcomed the part that employers' pension funds could play in supplementing the state earnings-related pension, and were ready to abate contributions to the state scheme by those paying into a private scheme, we could not accept that society's long-term arrangements for superannuation should be built round the private schemes. For, if that were attempted, as the Opposition wanted, a majority of our people would still be denied equity, on an earnings-related basis, in retirement. From that time forward, Dick Crossman's consultations with the pensions funds and insurance profession mainly related to the discussion of the means and extent of abatement, by the funds and insurance companies, from the national scheme.

Apart from deep and continuing concern about Nigeria, my question periods in Parliament were quiet and free from sensation. My colleagues had done better than in previous years in having their major legislation ready and by the end of January the legislative programme was well-advanced. In terms of the legislative programme, allowing for Supply days and the Budget, the average parliamentary session is halfway through its term by late February or the beginning of March: major Bills not already in committee by that time have an uninsurable expectation of life.

On 3rd February it fell to me to introduce a major Bill, though even its relatively early place in the session failed to guarantee its survival.

The occasion was the second reading of the measure embodying our proposals for Lords reform. The objectives had been foreshadowed, in summary, in my speech in the debate on the Queen's Speech:

Firstly, the hereditary basis for membership should be eliminated; secondly, no one party should possess a permanent majority; thirdly, in normal circumstances the Government of the day should be able to secure a reasonable working majority; fourthly, the powers in the House of Lords to delay legislation should be restricted; and, fifthly, its absolute power to withhold consent to subordinate legislation against the will of the Commons should be abolished.

The more detailed proposals were outlined in a White Paper. They followed very closely the lines provisionally agreed in the all-party talks, until they were suspended following the Lords' vote on the Rhodesian sanctions order. We had considered whether to proceed with the introduction of a short, sharp Bill dealing with powers only, leaving changes in the composition for the indefinite future. But the Lord Chancellor and the Leader of the Lords, who were deeply steeped in the negotiations, both felt strongly that it would not be meaningful to change the powers while leaving the composition to continue to be based on the indefensible hereditary principle. Indeed, what convinced most of their Cabinet colleagues was that if there were not to be major changes in the make-up of the House, Gerald Gardiner and Eddie Shackleton would have wished to recommend a fundamentally different approach to the restriction of its powers. This would mean a fresh start, and would involve postponing legislation to the 1969–70 session.

The Bill, which received its second reading on 3rd February, provided for a two-tier structure. Voting peers would be confined to peers of the first creation and, in their party proportions, would broadly correspond, Parliament by Parliament, to the ratios in the elected Chamber. The right to be a voting-peer would depend on a reasonable attendance record and would be subject to a retirement age. Non-voting peers would consist mainly of those who, at the time of the passage of the Act, held their seats through hereditary succession. No hereditary peer succeeding after that time would be entitled to sit in the House.

On powers, the Lords would have the right to delay a Bill passed by the Commons for six months, but then, on the Commons' support for the Bill being confirmed by a simple resolution, it would become law. On statutory orders, any requiring an affirmative resolution would carry, even if rejected by the Lords, if first approved by the Commons and then confirmed by them after the Lords had rejected it. In the case of an order subject only to negative procedure as described in Chapter 26 above, the decision of the House of Commons would be final.

In moving the second reading I made no effort to suggest that there was any enthusiasm about the Bill, one way or the other. It was in marked contrast to the forecasts of revolution and the end of all Britain's liberties, which the previous reform measures of 1830–32 and 1910–11 had provoked. Indeed, the lack of interest had been shown when a special meeting of our Parliamentary Party called to discuss the proposals had broken up a few minutes later when no one even offered to comment on them.

But during the second reading a most improbable coalition developed against the Bill. While those who were opposed to the Bill were drawn from all sections of parliamentary opinion, the leadership came principally from the Labour left, led by Michael Foot, and the Tory right, led by

Enoch Powell. The former group were principally opposed to any improvements in the Lords' composition which might lead the Upper Chamber to be regarded as a more rational and defensible place and thus lead to an increase in its influence and authority. The latter fought against any curbing of the Lords' powers and abilities to discharge their traditional functions. In his speech, Mr Powell vigorously defended the House's hereditary basis against a chamber consisting of 'nominees'.

The second reading was carried by 285 votes to 135, both front benches voting for the Bill. But as the Bill wearily pursued its committee stage on the floor of the House, the ingenious hostile coalition found little difficulty in moving and debating amendments on a scale which brought progress almost to a standstill. Perhaps progress would have been more rapid in the earlier stages if the Bill had been drafted in a form which placed the clauses dealing with powers ahead of those dealing with the Lord's composition. The combination of this together with anxiety about the Government's industrial relations measures was putting strain on the Parliamentary Party.

The Bill took nine days of parliamentary time – eighty-eight hours of debate on the committee stage – until it was given a merciful release, amid general approval, by an announcement I made on 17th April. In the discussion which followed, I pointed out that though the official Opposition was committed to support the Bill, and had voted for it on second reading, Mr Heath himself voted in only one of fifty-nine subsequent divisions, and then against a Government motion to make progress and get on with the Bill. Other Conservative front-benchers recorded between them sixty-two votes against the Government, all of them on procedural motions designed to move things forward. The truth was, of course, that the Opposition was enjoying seeing the Government's legislative programme getting into difficulties.

On the 11th February I was due to go to Bonn for the annual exchange with the German Chancellor. I could not see much coming out of it: Common Market negotiations were at a low ebb and the French, indeed, were busy trying to make Western Europe Union unworkable. Too much effort was going into the delicate footwork, through Brussels and WEU, which constituted what I called the European quadrille, when the dance-hall proprietor had already made it clear that there was going to be no dance. I was getting concerned, too, about the attitude which the Foreign Office, at least at official level, seemed to be taking against the French, and the joy that some purely procedural victories seemed to give them. The German Chancellor, however warm his protestations, had proved, and was to prove again, that his undoubtedly sincere desire for British entry was not going to be allowed to foul up his relations with General de Gaulle.

On the afternoon of my departure for Bonn, Michael Stewart came to see me. The previous week we had a report from Christopher Soames, the British Ambassador in Paris who had been granted his long-awaited audience with President de Gaulle. It had been affable and forthcoming, though nothing General de Gaulle had said indicated any greater willingness to see Britain in the Community than he had shown in his long talks with me in Versailles. But the Foreign Office saw great significance in some phrases the General had used about possible changes in EEC which would turn it into a looser organisation. He had played no part in the creation of the Common Market, he said, neither did he have any particular faith in it. What was more, he was certain that if we and other applicants joined it, it could no longer be the same. This would not necessarily be a bad thing. It might have been created differently. He by no means excluded that for the future. But we seemed to have set our hearts on joining it for better or for worse. He personally foresaw it changing, and would like to see it change, into a loose form of free trade area with arrangements by each country to exchange agricultural produce. He would be quite prepared to discuss with us what should take the place of the Common Market as an enlarged European Economic Association. He went on to suggest bilateral talks with Britain initially in conditions of great secrecy, on a wide range of economic, monetary, political and defence matters to see whether we could resolve our differences. He said he would like to see a gesture by the British Government proposing that such talks should take place, which he would then welcome.

I did not take this part of his statement – nor, I think, did our Ambassador in Paris – as more than a re-assertion of the words he had used to me in the Elysée in January 1967 when he had suggested two 'alternatives': 'Something entirely new' or an 'agreement – an association'. His proposals for bilateral talks I would have regarded as a friendly gesture, subject to our ensuring that they were not used to divide us in either defence or economic affairs from our partners in EFTA and our prospective partners in EEC. More likely to cause trouble with his EEC partners was his clear hint that the looser association he proposed would be largely directed by France, Britain, Germany and Italy.

But the Foreign Office took the interview much more seriously. In the first place they feared – and they were right to emphasise this – that an acceptance by us of the bilateral proposals might be used by the General as an argument, with his colleagues in the Six, that we were not really serious about entry into EEC; indeed that we were having negotiations with him on an entirely separate basis. To do this would not have been out of character, and certainly, if we were to enter into bilateral talks, we should have had to make clear to the Five the exact basis on which we regarded the talks.

It seemed to me that the Foreign Office were going beyond natural and justified caution. The way they wanted me to handle it in Bonn seemed designed to discredit the French with their EEC partners, and at the same time present ourselves as a rather priggish little Lord Fauntleroy who had resisted the General's anti-EEC blandishments. I expressed my dislike of the manoeuvre but, as I had to leave within minutes, told Michael Stewart that I would discuss the matter with the senior Foreign Office team who were accompanying me to Bonn. My own view was that it should be considered much more carefully before we rushed into any such policy: I was anxious to have a fuller assessment from Christopher Soames. But it was strongly pressed upon me that if I went to Bonn and did not mention it General de Gaulle might make capital out of that, and succeed in convincing Dr Kiesinger that we were flirting with anti-EEC moves in Paris while supporting EEC legitimacy in Bonn.

In our discussions at the Embassy in Bonn late that evening, I continued to express my distaste for the proposal. By the late morning more telegrams were flooding in from London, strongly urging me at least to mention the de Gaulle–Soames talks so that Dr Kiesinger could not, if and when he received information later, accuse me of withholding relevant information from him. This I agreed to do in a few simple sentences with no overtones of the kind that had been proposed.

I had a series of engagements in Bonn that day including a dinner with leading industrialists and bankers from all over Germany. Instead of making a speech I invited questions, a much more rewarding procedure, and they were good questions. I was able to strike a genuinely confident note, including telling them of the trade figures published that morning, with what, for a normal month, was our lowest visible trade deficit for several years – £11 millions. They knew that, together with the surplus on invisible account, this meant, for that month anyway, we had a current account surplus of £30 millions, which if this were maintained would show a comfortable balance of payments position over the year as a whole.

I reached Chancellor Kiesinger's office at four o'clock and asked the Foreign Office team for the brief and anodyne note I had been expecting on the de Gaulle affair. Reading it I found that it was the full works. I made it clear that I was furious; but it was difficult to keep this up in front of the Germans. I therefore made a short statement to Dr Kiesinger of the facts, in as reasoned and unsensational a manner as possible. But when I returned to London I found that the Foreign Office had sent a circular telegram to all relevant posts on the lines they had originally wanted, the recipients to await further instructions. My talks themselves with Dr Kiesinger were friendly and, within their inevitably limited setting, useful. A long-standing Foreign Office aspiration was realised by the signing, on a German initiative, of a joint Anglo-German declaration on European policy, which included a pledge by both Governments to further the aim of British entry into EEC. But any ability Dr

Kiesinger might have had to influence General de Gaulle in this direction, during General de Gaulle's last remaining weeks in office, was destroyed by the Soames affair which Dr Kiesinger took very seriously. When I saw Willy Brandt, Vice-Chancellor and Foreign Minister, at his home – he was ill – he saw nothing new in it. It was, to him, familiar Gaullist language.

We were able to have useful discussions on economic and monetary policy, but clearly with a German Cabinet divided on revaluation – the senior partner in the coalition, the CDU, being opposed to it – there was not likely to be any decision before the Federal elections in September. The same, we feared, would prove true of German signature of the non-proliferation treaty. There was no question of Russian acceptance so long as Germany stood out. The Germans, for their part, were opposed to signature because of a threat made by the Soviet Government to invoke, in appropriate circumstances, the 'enemy states' clauses of the United Nations Charter; clauses which could be used to justify action against Germany. I pointed out that the tripartite declaration made to the Security Council by the United States, Britain and the Soviet Union provided a full guarantee, as did the NATO treaty itself, and said that the Soviet outburst about enemy states had presumably been made in the context of Czecho-slovakia and was meant as a brusque warning to Germany to keep out of Soviet adventures in Eastern Europe, particularly if trouble arose in East Germany. I asked Dr Kiesinger whether his Government's recent exchanges with the Soviet Ambassador had provided any reassurance about the 'enemy states' threat.

I was told – and found, the next day, that Willy Brandt attached great importance to this – that the Soviet Ambassador had made clear in relation to the guarantees against nuclear attack that the Federal German Government would be treated in exactly the same way as every other Government.

Willy Brandt and his party, the SPD, in fact, were pressing for immediate signature and it was clear that Dr Kiesinger's anxieties were largely smoothed away. Herr Franz-Josef Strauss was the stumbling-block and the Chancellor found it difficult to move without his support. But, I was told, he had not pressed his opposition to the point of threatening resignation. Herr Brandt was hopeful of signature by April: if that did not happen it might well have to wait until after the elections. In the event it was the SPD-dominated coalition, which took over in October, that signed the treaty.

More than on any previous European visit we spent a greater part of our time discussing problems of technological co-operation, the most constructive part of the visit. These included ELDO and ESRO, the European air-bus and the competing British BAC–311, and the multi-role combat aircraft (MRCA). The most important discussions centred on the Anglo-German-Dutch collaboration on the centrifuge.

This advanced project had first been brought to my attention by

Frank Cousins shortly before he resigned from the Ministry of Technology. Until that time, the enrichment of uranium 235 had been increasingly concentrated in different countries in varying forms, the conventionally-powered diffusion process as at Capenhurst or the hydro-electric-powered diffusion plant at Pierrelatte. Despite the fact that the French had the great advantage of cheap power their costs were hardly competitive.

For years research had been going on in different countries on the centrifuge process, which is best described as something like a dairy separator, the speed of its spinning producing the desired effect. The breakthrough sought in so many national research establishments depended not only on revolutionary nuclear technology, but on the solution of some formidable problems in mechanical engineering.

In the spring of 1966 Frank Cousins reported to me that the Atomic Energy Authority scientists felt that a breakthrough had been achieved. But no national research establishment knew what progress the others were making. We did not know whether any country and, if so, which country, had reached, as we had, the stage where there was virtual certainty that the method would work. If we were to announce our break-through, even if we gave no details, that would provide an incentive to other countries, some of whom might be considering cancelling the project, to continue. But there were wider and much more difficult considerations. The individual centrifuge was itself quite small, not very much larger than a fire-extinguisher. A production unit to reach a given output was simply built up by aggregating individual centrifuges until the required scale of production was reached, just as one can aggregate individual small dry batteries to equal the capacity of one large one. This meant that if only a small quantity were required, for example by a small nation with nuclear ambitions, a very small unit would be possible. A unit, for any purpose, could be as small as a garage or a cellar.

The implications for nuclear proliferation were clear. Under the older processes a Capenhurst or a Pierrelatte had to be on such a scale that its existence could not be concealed: satellite photography would, in any case, quickly identify its location and, indeed, probable output. With the centrifuge an enrichment unit large enough to service a nuclear weapons programme would be relatively easy to conceal.

A Government committee under my chairmanship was set up on a top-secret basis to handle all questions, including those with disarmament and nuclear weapon implications, relating to what, for secrecy's sake, was for a long time known as the ACARUS project. As the scientists continued to exploit their success, we were taking the necessary decisions against the day when we could discuss its international exploitation. There were difficulties arising from Anglo-American exchanges under the nuclear know-how sharing agreement of 1955, smoothly but, owing to the sensitivity of the problem, not speedily sorted out. Our probings and exchanges with other nations – which had to be confined to technical information, but just frank enough to enable us to assess how far other countries had gone – led us into tripartite discussions with the Dutch and Germans, and finally into the preparation and signature of a plan for a joint research, production and marketing complex. The Cabinet committees concerned, and the Cabinet itself, were fully occupied with these exchanges, and with the text of the agreement and its signature in the very week when we were so preoccupied with the Bonn monetary talks, and the preparation of Roy Jenkins's November mini-Budget.

On 24th November, Tony Benn announced in the House that the three countries were to meet to set up a joint consortium to produce centrifuge enrichment units for their own use and for sale to other countries.

From Bonn I flew to West Berlin on 14th February. It was not the happiest time to go; indeed some Germans I met in Bonn advised against it. The Soviet and East German authorities had been angered by a decision of the Federal Parliament to hold in Berlin its special assembly for the election of the Federal President. Few actions could have been more provocative. I made clear our criticism of it and I found little enthusiasm for it among Federal ministers. The Soviet and East German authorities had reacted sharply by interfering with the movement of vehicles along the Berlin autobahn and threatening the movement of air-craft. The Western authorities were in a state of quasi-alert. But my own aircraft had no difficulty in landing safely. After a welcome at the airport by the Governing Mayor, Herr Schutz, with warm speeches from a cold rostrum, I visited an engineering factory, made an unscheduled stop and speech at the all-German Trades Union conference, and attended a lunch with set speeches, followed by a broadcast on the Berlin radio network.

Before my return to London, I spent the afternoon with the British troops, with formal reviews and informal beers in the several messes, and inspected the RAF base and facilities at Gatow.

In the ten days between my German visit and the visit of President Nixon to London on 24th February, the usual seasonal operations – the Estimates, defence, the Agricultural Price Review – took charge of Cabinet business.

Because we had taken a firm grip on expenditure for 1969–70 as well as 1968–69 in the post-devaluation expenditure review – indeed some of our 1968 decisions were now beginning to work through – the Cabinet's consideration of the Estimates was less harrowing than in the previous year. Our main preoccupations were to restrain the total to an increase in real terms of two per cent, and to take offsetting action for dealing with those limited areas where expenditure was running ahead of the January 1968 White Paper. No further drastic cuts were required and we were, in the main, able to work within the January 1968 decisions. In the field of health and social security, expenditure was outrunning our previously agreed programme, partly because of demographic factors which we were unable to programme or even to forecast with total accuracy. Neither Dick Crossman nor I would have tolerated any cut-back in hospital building and the accounts were in the event balanced by a further increase in social security stamps, which, though in economic terms a tax – and a regressive tax at that – traditionally counted, in the lore of public expenditure convention, as an offset to expenditure. We were thus able to hold the increase to our target figure of two per cent, and, because of our experience of the continual encroachment of Supplementary Estimates on our all-too-small contingency allowance, we provided a further one per cent contingency allowance.

Defence again played its full part. In his White Paper (Cmnd. 3927 published on 20th February), Denis Healey was not only successful, as in previous years, in recording an absolute reduction in real terms – that is in total expenditure measured in constant prices – of £111 millions compared with that of the previous year; but, for the first time since the immediate post-war years, to achieve a real reduction – albeit a small one – in the actual cost provision. Even at current prices expenditure was marginally down on the previous year. Our total saving by this time, compared with the defence expenditure we had inherited from our predecessors, was running at £700 millions in that year and had reached a cumulative saving of over £2,000 millions since 1965.

The Defence White Paper did not announce any new policies. The course had been set a year earlier following the decisions of January 1968. What it did provide was an account of the progress made in the Nuclear Planning Group of NATO – in whose establishment Denis Healey had played so notable a part – constructive collective planning in nuclear questions in marked contrast to the controversial multilateral force which had dominated NATO discussions when we first took office. Equally, it provided the most sophisticated account so far published of the thinking behind NATO's developing attitudes on the doctrine of the controlled nuclear response to any outbreak of fighting in Europe. This was again based mainly on Denis Healey's leadership in NATO and providing, as it did, a means of studied restraint in escalation, was a warning to all concerned to think again before a possible outbreak of fighting in Europe led to thermonuclear exchanges and all-out nuclear war.

Our Estimates were published in the Vote on Account, but as this figure was year by year misunderstood by overseas financial opinion, usually fed by comment from equally ill-informed domestic authorities, the Chancellor announced that from that year onwards, the Vote on Account would be dispensed with and replaced by a much fuller Expenditure White Paper, giving for the two years immediately ahead full details for each item and sub-item – and with projected expenditure in broader classifications for still further ahead. I supported the Chancellor in his demand that from this time on we should publish each year these details. This would not only facilitate parliamentary and public discussion; I was anxious that by the end of 1969 we should publish our firm decisions for 1971–72, as well as for 1970–71, so that there could be no suggestion of a last-minute pre-election spending spree, such as had characterised British political history under our predecessors in 1959 and in 1964. Moreover, facing an Opposition which was attacking the total level of public expenditure while demanding increases in most of the separate items, we would be able to challenge them to say which items they would cut to achieve their promised total and which items they would expand to win their hoped-for votes.

The Agricultural Price Review was particularly difficult. 1968 had been one of those really bad years for farmers, due to the adverse weather conditions which come every few years and to rising costs generally. Farmers' earnings had sunk to a low level; in addition to this there was the continuing impact of the worst foot-and-mouth outbreak in our history. They were facing acute stringency, with a problem of meeting their immediate bills, and it was having a serious effect on farm investment. Productivity was rising, but nothing like enough to deal with the effects of the cataclysmic weather we had suffered. After tough battles in the Price Review sub-committee and at successive meetings of Cabinet, we agreed, for this exceptional occasion, that over eighty per cent of the losses established in the previous year should be recouped in the guaranteed prices for the coming year. This meant a net addition through the Price Review of £34 millions, against an estimated increase of farmers' needs, following the effect of the weather, of £40 millions. Described though it was by the Opposition as a 'hopelessly inadequate award', it was, apart from 1967 and the pre-election bribe of 1964, the highest figure for twenty years. It added to the burden on the Estimates, and it was a first charge on the newly-announced contingency reserve for 1969–70. Because of the parliamentary and agricultural timetables, Estimates have to be published shortly after the middle of February. This is before the Price Review is settled, and as the Estimates have to be agreed some little time before publication the effects of the Price Review have to be added later.

The economic situation was improving. The trade figures were getting better all the time and there was every sign of a strong balance of payments position. Unemployment, on a seasonally corrected basis, had fallen, indeed, since the previous August by nearly 100,000 – although I was bombarding, and had been for a year past, the Central Statistical Office with my doubts about the accuracy of the seasonal correction – and industrial production was showing a real increase.

The CBI's four-monthly industrial survey was the most optimistic for many years past, particularly so far as exports and investment were concerned. But the Treasury and Bank of England were worried about the sharply-rising trend of world interest rates. The Euro-dollar three-month rate stood at 8.1 per cent; it was to rise in the summer to 14 per cent. The New York Treasury Bill rate was 6.1 per cent. Our own bank rate, traditionally a point or two above the New York rate – it had been 5 per cent in the summer of 1964 against a New York rate of 3.5 per cent – was thus relatively 'low' at 7 per cent; at the same time the joint stock banks were straining the Governor's patience with their lending levels, and an increase in bank rate was very much in mind.

On 19th February the Government and the party suffered a deep loss through the sudden death of Stephen Swingler, acknowledged to be one of the most successful of our ministers. When I had appointed him Parliamentary Secretary to the Ministry of Transport in October 1964 there had been some doubts about his ability to settle down to an administrative routine. But in very little time he showed his mettle in both departmental work and in Parliament; for several years he had been in charge of more adjournment debates than any other minister. Barbara Castle's arrival in the Ministry forged a successful partnership, centred on the preparation of the Transport Bill, and in its parliamentary passage he distinguished himself by his untiring work and his mastery of the subject. Despite the controversial nature of the Bill he won great respect from the various transport interests, and I had long considered his promotion. A Cabinet post was already in consideration – I had earlier thought of him as a possible successor to Barbara Castle in Transport – when I recommended him for appointment to Dick Crossman's new department as Minister of State, on the social security side. He quickly mastered the intricacy of the new legislation, but did not live to see it introduced.

I moved David Ennals across to Social Security and in his place appointed Lady Serota, widely respected as a social worker and expert in the local government and health field; in the remaining fifteen months of the Government's life she proved herself, too, one of the most sucessful of my appointments.

Just before President Nixon was due to arrive, '*L'affaire Soames*' broke. From the time of my German visit the French, possibly infuriated by the joint declaration on Europe, but more probably learning of what the Germans and other partners were hearing from our people about Christopher Soames's meeting with the General, erupted in a major way at Western European Union. They accused several countries – and especially the Secretary-General, whose head they demanded – of playing Britain's game by inscribing matters affecting European unity on the agenda. They boycotted the meetings and announced that they would play no further part in the work of the organisation.

Towards the end of the week accounts of the Soames affair began to appear in the French newspapers, with violent attacks on us for passing on an account, which they alleged was an inaccurate one, of the de Gaulle–Soames meeting. The Foreign Office gave the press, on a non-attributable basis, the summary which had been circulated to overseas posts on the day before my talk with Dr Kiesinger.

French fury knew no limit. Anglo-French relations fell back to the low level at which they had been after General de Gaulle's veto in 1963. Recriminations flew across the Channel. On the day that President Nixon arrived, 24th February, the French Embassy handed in a note to the Foreign Office protesting specifically at our action in informing other Governments about the interview. Michael Stewart that day made a statement in Parliament and defended our actions, both in Bonn and elsewhere, saying, 'I think it would have been entirely improper to have allowed those conversations with Dr Kiesinger to conclude without Dr Kiesinger being made aware of what had happened.'

The Conservatives, conscious that they were on to a good thing, pushed it for all they were worth. Only an hour before President Nixon's arrival at London Airport, they succeeded in getting an emergency adjournment debate for the following day. All this – and I cannot blame the Opposition for seizing such an opportunity – presented the President on his fact-finding tour with a Europe in a state of disarray.

Those responsible in the Foreign Office no doubt felt that it was all a famous victory. But, as to what good came out of it, Old Kaspar's judgment was as apposite as any. Christopher Soames was rightly and bitterly upset. He came over to dine with me at Chequers but any thoughts he may have had of resigning were dropped. It was clear to both of us, however, that as long as General de Gaulle remained at the Elysée our relations would be extremely difficult to restore. In the event the General remained in power for only a further two months. In April he submitted new constitutional proposals to a national referendum and surprisingly made his continuance in office conditional on securing a majority for them. Many of those who had consistently opposed him would inevitably vote against him in the referendum and certain of his regional proposals had aroused great opposition. What was probably decisive, however, was the fact that the General was no longer considered essential to the stability of French institutions. M. Pompidou's record during the stormy days of the previous spring was remembered and he had become by this time a popular choice for the succession.

The General was defeated. He resigned his office immediately, as he had said he would, on 28th April. In the ensuing Presidential elections in June M. Pompidou had little difficulty, securing a very strong majority on the second ballot.

President Nixon arrived in London from Brussels on the late afternoon of Monday, 24th February. As he came off 'Air Force One' he was met by the Lord Chamberlain on behalf of the Queen. We then went to the rostrum, where, after the National Anthem and his inspection of the Guard of Honour, I briefly welcomed him. His speech in reply was warm; in his reference to Anglo-American relations – no simple reiteration of a well-worn theme – he caused some surprise by using the phrase 'special relationship'. He again used the phrase during my visit to the White House in January 1970.

I had invited the President to dinner at Chequers and arrangements were made for a short helicopter flight from Heathrow – rehearsed with great noise, the previous day. But in the event there was too much fog around, and we went by car. The forty-five minutes' journey was a useful opportunity to re-establish personal contact. I felt it right to tell him of my first official talk with his predecessor in December 1964, and my proposal that nothing would be said outside our talks that had not been said inside and, except in agreed statements, little of that would be communicated outside. He warmly accepted that, and went on to say something of his hopes for Anglo-American relations. It rapidly became clear, and I am convinced that this was sincere and personal to him, that he had the highest regard for the British tradition in world affairs, especially the judgment and experience of so many of our public servants, with their world view of international problems.

In assessing, as he was beginning to do, the nature of the problems with which he had to deal before he went on to take decisions, he hoped that we would continue to give him our assessment and our views. We then discussed informally Soviet-American relations and the Middle East.

On arrival at Chequers we faced, in the Great Hall, the most daunting assembly of television lights, cables and British and American press photographers that the ancient home of 'rest and recreation' (to quote its donor, Lord Lee of Fareham) had ever seen. Then the President and I retired to the Long Gallery, first for photographs then for serious talking, while Secretary of State William Rogers, Michael Stewart, and advisers on both sides met in my study.

The President and I discussed Vietnam – and he gave me an exposition of his first assessment of the position. We went on to discuss the Middle East, NATO, Europe, my recent German visit; then Rhodesia and Nigeria. After an hour we went downstairs, joined the others for drinks, and then ten in all went in to dinner. The talks during and after dinner, some three hours in all, lasted until well after 11.00 p.m. when he left for London. These discussions, and those which followed in Downing Street the next day, were exploratory, relaxed and extremely friendly. In his first few weeks as President he was collecting all the facts, all the views of those whom he was meeting in London and elsewhere, to help form his first policy assessments.

There was no question of seeking agreement, or of pressure on our part – or his – to secure acceptance of a particular policy. Nevertheless, we were able to form some idea of his initial priorities, the questions to which he was seeking an answer and at least some of his attitudes on them. Above all he was there to listen, and while Chequers was an occasion to establish friendly relations at all levels, Downing Street the next day was much more a series of deep and searching analyses of the main problems. Denis Healey set out our assessment of NATO and wider defence issues; and Michael Stewart those of the Middle East, Europe and East–West relations. Nato was, for the President a 'blue chip' investment: that was what the European part of his journey was about. In the discussions round the Chequers dining-table he began with a reference to a note I had sent to him about the significance of the Commonwealth conference. This took the form, first, of a brief report for him quickly to assimilate, together with a much longer analysis for his special assistant on national security, Dr Henry Kissinger, who could, of course, make any part of it available to the President. It was interesting to see how much importance he attached to the Commonwealth. Over the years, as he said, he had visited the large majority of Commonwealth countries and had been impressed by the common link of the old British heritage – he instanced the Speaker's wig in Ghana – even though these newly-independent countries were pursuing their own interests, individually and with other like-minded countries, within and beyond the Commonwealth connection. Clearly, to him, this provided for us in Britain a window, if not upon the world, at least upon a significant and representative part of it and upon problems which would inevitably become of increasing importance on the world stage.

We discussed, again in an informal way, though this was taken much deeper by Denis Healey the following day, the forthcoming meetings with the Soviet Union about strategic missiles, where, at that point, he was clearly still cautiously feeling his way; what he called the 'measured tread'.

Tuesday's discussion at Downing Street, lasting all morning, was almost exclusively concerned with the political and defence aspects of NATO and wider defence problems. We had also a short and technical discussion about the world monetary and economic situation.

After his lunch at Buckingham Palace, he spent most of his afternoon on engagements which he had asked us or the Embassy to make for him, including a reception he had arranged for some of his old British friends, as well as meetings with Mr Harold Macmillan, Sir Alec Douglas-Home and Mr Heath. He spent half an hour at the House of Commons – it was my question day – and he enjoyed the scarcely-veiled references to our talks and to his presence there, with my elaborate promises to take note of points addressed to him, and my undertaking to bring these points to his attention.

Our, and still more the United States', security authorities had been worried about Mr Nixon's vulnerability if seated in the Diplomatic or Distinguished Strangers' Gallery, but I solved their problem by suggesting he should sit 'under the gallery', on the Opposition side and virtually on the floor of the House itself, visible only to members and to certain of those sitting in the Hansard and press galleries.

In the evening we had another dinner, again a working one. He made it notable by an elegant and generous speech welcoming to Washington John Freeman, our Ambassador-designate, who was present. In one sentence the President eliminated a lot of silly comment about John Freeman's alleged unacceptability on the grounds of words written by him, as Editor of the *New Statesman*, about Richard Nixon some years before. During the meal the President and I talked privately about his assessments of East–West relations, and afterwards we had a cross-table discussion mainly about the Middle East.

For our adjournment, I had arranged, instead of a social reception, for all Cabinet members to join us for coffee. He met each and exchanged a word. He was particularly interested in meeting our ex-miner Minister of Power, Roy Mason, to talk about pneumoconiosis, which the President knew as 'black lung'. This later led HM Chief Inspector of Mines and his health experts to visit the United States to compare notes on these matters. After a few minutes I felt that instead of brief exchanges, the President and his colleagues might like, for as long as he could stay, to meet my colleagues together round the Cabinet table for an informal discussion. He welcomed this and we went downstairs to the Cabinet room.

I began by ruling out of discussion hard issues of foreign and economic affairs, which had already been traversed at length, and suggested that we should discuss broader issues: issues of the future, problems of the environment, of young people, of students, of race and colour, of freedom under the law. Barring myself and other senior ministers who had already met the President from the discussion, I asked our younger colleagues to lead it. Tony Benn, Tony Crosland, Peter Shore, Judith Hart, Dick Marsh, and an older colleague, Gerald Gardiner; each spoke briefly, and to the point: in no time at all the President was joining in an animated discussion, probably without precedent in Anglo-American relations.

The next morning, when I accompanied the President to the airport, he constantly referred to that last hour. He still recalled it a year later as the highlight, unexpected and unplanned though it was, of his tour.

W

Chapter 30

The Fords' strike – Anguilla – discussions with General Gowon – meetings with relief agencies – visits to Enugu and Calabar – further talks in Lagos – talks with Haile Selassie

THE days that followed President Nixon's visit were as intense as ever. DEA, on 26th February, published as a Green Paper the new version of the former National Plan, on indicative lines. This had been intensively discussed by NEDC, first at Chequers and then in a series of meetings at some of which we had had the chairmen of the little Neddies (the committees for individual industries) reporting about the prospects for the industries they covered. It was a realistic document, learning from the experience of its ill-fated predecessor of 1965, and it was well received by industry.

On a different note of realism, came the Fords' strike. Barbara Castle worked all hours of the night to settle it; there was an abortive attempt by the management to involve the law, which further embittered relations. Night after night, until 2.00 a.m. and later, Barbara chaired the attempts to settle.

The crunch came at the weekend. I was at Chequers, but Barbara kept me informed with phone calls right into the small hours. Fords' management were firm and prepared to stand out for a tough settlement. But not so their masters at Detroit, who seemed to want to get Dagenham back in production at all costs. Hugh Scanlon of the engineers and Jack Jones of the transport workers were involved and were decisive in getting settlement which, though involving a big increase in pay, nevertheless met every penny of the increase through productivity. It was in fact a model agreement, on the principle of a high-wave, high-productivity economy.

Bank rate duly went up on 22nd February, from seven to eight per cent and the decision was at once exploited by the Conservatives. Mr Heath attacked it because it might lead to industrial bankruptcies – he had not then been converted, publicly at any rate, to what was to become his new industrial philosophy about the therapeutic effect of company failures.

But what was most worrying me was the continuing, distressing situation in Nigeria. The optimism of January had petered out. There was military failure – on both sides – and a continued stalemate. There was stalemate also in all the world's efforts to get relief supplies moving. Colonel Ojukwu would still not allow the use either of road transport or of daylight flights. The Federals knew that if they could deny Uli Airport to the enemy the war would end, because Colonel Ojukwu's supplies were being flown in, night by night, to that forest airstrip. But the Federal military forces never looked like taking it. New tactics were employed. Using Soviet-supplied aircraft – we had throughout refused to supply aircraft – Egyptian and other pilots carried out bombing flights designed to interdict the supply programme and to destroy the arms supply aircraft on the ground. The air-strikes were anything but efficient: from information we received it seemed that their forays were limited to one or two per pilot, after which he returned home to Egypt, and that in many cases the bombs were unloaded at the earliest possible moment before anti-aircraft fire or Colonel Ojukwu's other defences could intercept them. Inevitably, there were civilian casualties, adding nothing to the conduct of the war except human suffering but providing propaganda material for Colonel Ojukwu's public relations experts in Geneva. The PR offensive had for some time been uneasily poised between the expectation of genocide and the fact of starvation. Now a new story filled the communications media: aerial 'atrocities'. There was even evidence of false reconstructions of atrocity bombing. I tried to get General Gowon to agree that the international observers, which under our pressure the previous year he had invited into Nigeria, should be given access to the site of alleged atrocities. General Gowon was reluctant because, since they could not be on the spot when the bombs fell, many might arrive only to inspect a staged atrocity; Colonel Ojukwu because the public relations aspect of alleged atrocities could be best exploited if there were no independent verification.

Parliamentary pressures on Nigeria inevitably intensified. A most anxious debate took place on 13th March. Because we were supplying arms, for reasons we had repeatedly stated, we were held responsible not only for the starvation but for the aerial 'atrocities'.

I had been making representations to General Gowon about the issues involved, and had raised with him, at the beginning of the month, the question of our postponed meeting. To this he agreed in principle but, with the problems of his further spring offensive, he could not leave Lagos. I therefore agreed to go there. Sir Denis Greenhill, Permanent Under-Secretary of State to the Foreign and Commonwealth Office, went to discuss with General Gowon the arrangements for my visit and the agenda for our talks. Knowledge that I was going to Nigeria leaked out from a Nigerian source to the press and it was published on the day of the debate. All the Opposition and press could say at such a time, in the words of Sir Alec Douglas-Home during the debate, was that this was 'the kind of gimmick we come to expect from the Government on these occasions'.

Though a loyal supporter of the Federal cause, Sir Alec Douglas-Home had persuaded himself of the case for a total embargo on arms supplies to both sides, enforced through the United Nations. This was an unexceptionable proposal in theory: I had proposed it the previous year. Unfortunately it was unworkable because:

The United Nations refused to take cognisance of a purely internal civil war, as it was (rightly) regarded.

The Russians would have rejected it: their increasing permeation of Nigeria depended on their uninhibited supply of arms of all kinds. Had we agreed to suspend our much more limited supplies, which specifically excluded the means of aerial warfare, we would merely have strengthened their influence. Even if the United Nations, against Soviet opposition, had carried a resolution in favour of an arms embargo it would have been unenforceable because the French suppliers of arms to Biafra denied their complicity and would have continued to supply through their agents. As I repeatedly argued, and we were working for this with African support, the only way of enforcing this would be at the receiving end, in Biafra and in the Federal ports and airstrips. But this could only function, with the international supervision required, on the basis of a cease fire. For this we were also working, but the Federals would not agree unless they were satisfied that the arms-run into Biafra was halted: neither side would agree to a cease fire, leading to peace-talks, except on assurances by the other of terms which would be unacceptable. Nigeria would agree only if the talks were directed to a Federal and undivided country: Biafra only if the principle of secession were conceded.

It was an engaging but unrealistic proposal.

The wind-up of a serious debate was mainly characterised by Opposition ribaldry about the announcement of my visit. Nothing can excel the House of Commons debating a great international tragedy as a Council of State, but this was not one of those occasions.

Before the time for my departure to Lagos, trouble erupted from a different part of the Commonweath, this time from a tiny sun-drenched island for which we still had a degree of imperial responsibility. Following the breakdown, in the time of our predecessors, of the imaginative concept of a Caribbean Federation, certain countries had proceeded to independence as sovereign states while others had remained as colonies. For most of these we had introduced in December 1965 the concept of 'associated states', non-sovereign, but with a great degree of local autonomy. For them Britain retained the ultimate responsibility for defence and diplomatic relations.

The associated state of St Kitts, Nevis and Anguilla had been created, but Anguilla, with her leader, Mr Webster, had never been prepared to accept rule from overseas. There had been talk of secession. Parliamentary delegations, in addition to the efforts of Colonial and later Commonwealth Office officials, had sought to resolve the difficulties but without success.

In March 1969, Bill Whitlock, the Under-Secretary responsible for these matters, had visited Anguilla but he had been unceremoniously bundled from it under threat of force. We were advised by our man on the spot that Anguilla was under control of a group of men in close touch with property developers, indeed Mafia-type gangsters, though what we learnt later threw great doubt on this. But the ejection of the Under-Secretary and the islanders' refusal to accept our resident administrators, or St Kitts-Nevis' administration made it necessary for us to act. We decided to take over the island with the use of a minimal force of troops, accompanied by a force of Metropolitan Police, to restore order on a civilian basis. I have, on subsequent occasions, been very doubtful whether the decision we took – to which course I was a fully consenting party – was right. But all that has happened since has, on the whole, convinced me that it was.

The operation leaked – there was no doubt that some elements in the police detachment talked freely; even before the transport aircraft left, the operation was public knowledge. It provided, of course, a field-day for the cartoonists. The musical-comedy atmosphere, the mock-gunboat diplomacy, the colourful personalities of some of the leading police, made it the joke of the year. The cartoonists inevitably had the time of their lives, and who could blame them? The Conservative Opposition made the most of it in the House – though since they took office they have taken the same line as we took, and at the time of writing, January 1971, British troops and police are still there. The troops, in the shape of the Royal Engineers, in fact carried out a number of long-overdue construction jobs to the benefit of the islanders. The problem in diplomatic terms was that Mr Webster, supported by his islanders, would not have rule from St Kitts-Nevis. The equally articulate St Kitts Premier, Mr Bradshaw, would not countenance secession.

With the agreement of other Caribbean Governments, we set up a commission to make recommendations about the constitutional future of the island. When we went out of office in June 1970, the report was still awaited.

I was due to leave for Lagos in the early morning of Thursday, 27th March. The previous day a new crisis had arisen about Barbara Castle's industrial relations proposals. From the day when *In Place of Strife* was published on 17th January, there had been sharp reactions from the Labour movement, the TUC, the Parliamentary Party – and particularly its Trade Union group – and the NEC. A series of PLP meetings had been arranged and Barbara Castle had addressed the TU group. On 3rd March the House debated her White Paper. The Conservatives studiously abstained and the final vote was 224 for the White Paper, 62, including 53 Labour members, against.

At the February meeting of the National Executive the matter had been raised and notice given of a formal motion for the next meeting on 26th March, which, because of the Nigerian crisis, I was not able to attend. I received a full report that afternoon. The details, relating to somewhat complicated resolutions, amendments and counter-amendments, are too involved and tedious to relate at this point of time. The short point was that a resolution was moved expressing the opposition of the National Executive to '*any* legislation designed to give effect to *all* the proposals in the White Paper'. Jim Callaghan moved the deletion of the word 'any', but was reported by the press as voting against an amendment, moved by Tony Greenwood, to delete all the passages in the resolution which appeared to oppose Government policy and, on that amendment being lost, against other amendments to the main resolution. After some consideration, I decided to deal with the matter on my return from Nigeria.

My party reached Lagos at 4.00 p.m. on Thursday, 27th March. I was greeted by General Gowon, whom I had not previously met. We tried to discuss the immediate war situation in the long drive from Ijeka Airport to State House, the former Governor-General's residence where I was staying. But the crowds lining the routes, who must have totalled several tens of thousands, were cheering the whole way, many of them bearing slogans calling for support for a united Nigeria. I could not help recalling that the last time I had driven on that route it was with Abubakar four days before his murder.

We had a short talk at State House, then I got to work with my advisers. HMS *Fearless* had been called from Gibraltar to Lagos and I had a working dinner on board. I had been advised, in case of disturbances, that I should have a safe naval vessel within call. In any case, my hopes of a meeting with Colonel Ojukwu, on which we had encouraging responses, required a possible safe meeting-place in case he could not accept a meeting on land. There was another reason for the presence of *Fearless*: there had been an impressive Soviet naval visit a few days before. *Fearless* trumped that ace, even though she had barely two feet of clear water to get to her berth. In addition to our own aircraft, we had for local use a smaller plane which had flown in laden with relief supplies for the Ibos, and which, in the event, reached Ibos in Federal territory.

The following morning we met for formal discussions at the Federal Military Government headquarters at Dodan Barracks. I was taken aback when General Gowon, a devout Christian, the son of an Anglican missionary, announced that all negotiations in that conference room opened with a dedicatory invocation and he would be obliged if I would lead the meeting in prayer. This was a new experience in an international conference: while I was contemplating the form of an extempore offering a

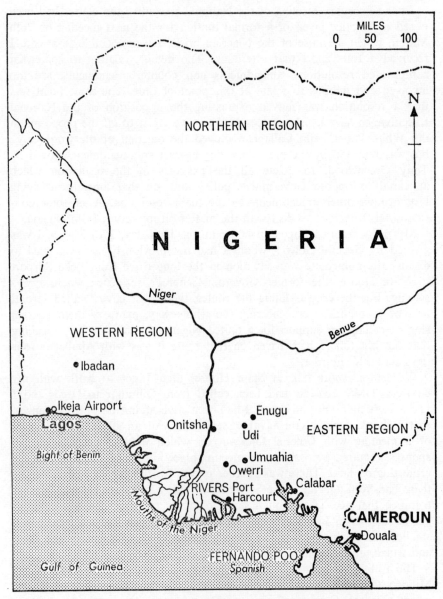

Map of Nigeria showing principal places mentioned in the text.

sergeant provided me with a text – it was in fact the dedicatory prayer used by the local bishop when the barracks were consecrated and which hung on the wall to be used by visiting negotiators.

We proceeded to business. The General welcomed me and expressed thanks for the line we had taken throughout the Nigerian war and particularly our insistence on 'one Nigeria'. The Federal Government, he said, bore no hatred or malice towards the Ibos. He wanted me to see for myself what they were doing for the Ibos in territory regained by the Federal forces.

We discussed arrangements for a visit. I had asked Lord Hunt to join the mission to inquire on my behalf into the relief situation, and I ensured that he would have free access to all the Federal and other authorities, centrally and locally, that he wanted to meet. There was no difficulty: indeed, characteristically, he had met the Federal authorities at 7.00 a.m. that morning before I was awake. Also in my party were two top defence advisers, General Fyffe, Director of Military Intelligence at the War Office, and Air Commodore Evans of the Air Ministry (Plans Department): I asked that they should have full facilities for meeting the top Federal military people. This, too, was agreed.

I reminded General Gowon that Sir Denis Greenhill, in his visit three weeks earlier, had indicated four points that I should want to discuss with him. These I summarised as follows:

1. I wanted to be satisfied about the willingness of the Federal Government to negotiate on anything not involving the dismemberment of Nigeria. I was reassured, I said, by a clear statement to this effect which the General had made in a public statement at our joint press conference at the airport.
2. Equally, I must be satisfied about the willingness of the Federal Government to give guarantees for the safety and well-being of the Ibos after the war and even to accept supervision, of necessity by outsiders, of the effective carrying out of those guarantees. This would be regarded, I said, as an extension of the principle of the offer General Gowon had made to have observers in the country.
3. I wanted assurances about the FMG's readiness to facilitate the flow of relief into the rebel areas as well as into the distressed areas in Federal-occupied territories by the existing night airlifts, pending agreement on surface routes or daylight flights.
4. I asked for an assurance about the Federal Government's determination to refrain from actions which did not help them militarily but which must damage them politically. I had in mind the haphazard bombing by pilots, principally Egyptians. Whether or not they were actually hitting hospitals and schools, and they could hardly be doing this deliberately because they were so incompetent, certainly Biafran propaganda was telling the world that they were.

I then raised two general points. First, I raised the question of the United Nations. For reasons I had given in Parliament I did not feel that consideration in the UN of the Nigerian war was feasible or in accordance with its Charter, and I had stated why a United Nations arms embargo, even if carried, would be unenforceable. But U Thant, in his personal capacity, had suggested certain ideas to the Emperor of Ethiopia, Haile Selassie, about the possible course of mediation by the Organisation of African Unity.

I next referred to recent feelers from Colonel Ojukwu which had reached me through a variety of channels and which appeared to be genuine. Though, in public, he maintained his violent attacks on me, there were clear signs that he wanted to meet me with a view to talks between the two sides. Whether this meant a genuine desire for a solution or was merely a public relations exercise for the benefit of his friends and world opinion, I could not estimate. I should like General Gowon's view – in private rather than in public session if he preferred it.

General Gowon said that this would require careful collective considera-tion by his team. (I could guess the difficulty he might have with his hawks.) But he would comment on some of the other questions. He gave me his appraisal of the military situation with, indeed, a history of the fighting from the outset. He was at pains to say, and to produce evidence in support, that Colonel Ojukwu's original aim had not been merely the Greater Biafra, based on the old Eastern region, but the subjugation of whole country. But, in addition to stopping the drive to the north and west, the rebels had been driven out of the south, the south-east, the mid-west and even the Ibo heartland itself, round Enugu. He was optimistic about the current offensive, and was confident that Umuahia, Colonel Ojukwu's 'capital' and headquarters, would fall that weekend. It did, in fact, fall on 21st April. He made strong criticisms of certain French financial in-terests and claimed that Colonel Ojukwu had traded 'his birthright', in terms of all mineral rights – gold, uranium, bauxite and copper – with a Paris finance house for £10 millions in all, with a cash payment of £6 millions.

General Gowon discussed a matter which had concerned us; the excessive expenditure of small arms ammunition by Federal forces. Within a short period the Federal army got through more than was used by British forces during the whole of the Second World War. As we knew – and as I said to the General – his far from fully-trained troops tended to fire off if they saw a lizard, or even heard a leaf rustle. He commented that he wished automatic weapons had never been invented.

On the anxieties I had expressed, he said that there was no bombing of civilian targets as such; indeed he accused Colonel Ojukwu of faking incidents, by using explosives to create craters near to civilian dwellings or hospitals. The orders to his troops were clear and strictly enforced – the Federal Government had made an example of those who disobeyed orders and a small number had been despatched by the firing squad in the past year.

I said I was more concerned with the foreign pilots, particularly the Egyptians. They were doing the Federal cause little military good but immense political harm. There seemed to be little post-bombing reconnaissance and de-briefing after raids; was it not likely that untrained pilots, many of whom came to Nigeria for a stay of only two or three days, were dumping their bombs and returning to safety as quickly as they could, whatever orders – e.g. to bomb the all-important but defended Uli Airport – they had been given? It was then that I asked whether the international observers, whom he had wisely invited at our suggestion the previous year to examine allegations of 'genocide' in areas overrun by Federal troops, could not go into Biafra. He said this would require agreement by both sides but, in any case, unless they were on the ground right where the bombs were dropped, any 'evidence' they subsequently found could be manufactured. He instanced a colour photograph of such an 'atrocity' in a London newspaper supplement which, on investigation, proved to relate to an accidental chemical explosion. He referred to propaganda on the bombing of 'schools'. These had been closed two years earlier and were at the time of the bombing used for troop-training and other military purposes.

General Gowon discounted my criticisms of the Egyptian pilots, most of whom, he said, were training Nigerian airmen. Nevertheless, one of the concrete results of my visit was an end of these bombing raids, not an easy thing for General Gowon to agree to at the height of a war for survival.

After a short coffee-break, I raised the question of a cease fire and explained the position I had taken up, under attack, in the House of Commons. From the Federal point of view, a cease fire without effective control over arms supply would merely enable the Biafrans to regroup and build up their supplies. I explained the attitude we had taken on Sir Alec Douglas-Home's proposals for an international arms embargo, which he hoped would be followed by negotiations. Since any cease fire would have to be controlled by prior agreement on these questions – which would mean negotiations – should not priority be given to negotiations, including negotiations for a settlement, without waiting either for an arms embargo or a cease fire? He confirmed my understanding that the Federal position on negotiations was that they would sit down with the Biafrans without prior conditions on the Federal side – though there should be none laid down by Colonel Ojukwu either – but they would not ultimately agree to any settlement except on terms of a united Nigeria.

Referring again to the feelers from Colonel Ojukwu about a meeting I raised the question of the venue. There was an invitation to visit 'Biafra', which I was not accepting. But the Colonel had suggested other possible venues, mainly in French-speaking African countries which recognised Biafra. Such a meeting would not involve recognition of Biafra, any more than the *Tiger* and *Fearless* talks had implied recognition of the Rhodesian Front regime. It would enable me to question him about his attitudes to ending the war, and on relief supplies, on which world opinion had the right to be satisfied. General Gowon was reserved, in the absence of consultation with his colleagues, but agreed to discuss it at our next meeting. Unfortunately, this meant losing two days on a very tight timetable.

The afternoon of the 28th and most of 29th March, I spent in travelling to distant parts of the country and in meetings with the relief agencies, the churches, and others concerned with the havoc created by the war. One meeting was with a team of foreign military observers, most of whom agreed with General Gowon about the difficulties of verifying charges about atrocities, even if they were allowed into Biafra. They were a very impressive group, and unequivocal about their findings of earlier genocide or reprisals charges, particularly in areas recaptured by the Federal troops. As I told the House on my return:

> The observers, when I met them, stated that they felt their work to be a success and worth while. The drew attention to their regular and unanimous reports confirming that they had found no evidence whatsoever to support allegations of genocide, or, after a few early and localised cases of indiscipline, of reprisals against the inhabitants of the areas where the Federal advance had taken place.

I had the chance of one or two private talks with General Gowon who accompanied me in the car to a number of engagements. On one of these I pressed upon him the need for an amnesty to include Colonel Ojukwu when the fighting ended. He was at great pains, and I believe he was absolutely sincere, to impress upon me his determination to insist on total reconciliation when the fighting was over. He was as devoted a student of Lincoln as I am and quoted many analogies with the American Civil War and referred specifically to the language and thought of Lincoln's Second Inaugural. He instanced a number of decisions to this end, supplementing his very forthcoming public speech at Zaria a few days earlier. As one example, he had directed that there were to be no campaign medals or ribbons issued to the Federal troops. He envisaged Ibos and Federals sitting down in army messes in the future and such decorations would be a provocation. He mentioned the number of Ibo officials he had placed in top positions in the administration of Ibo areas recaptured by Federal troops.

There would certainly be an amnesty, he went on, but the case of Colonel Ojukwu would be difficult. I warned him of the damaging effects for reconciliation at home, and for opinion abroad, of a state trial. I reminded him of Lincoln's wisdom over Jefferson Davis – no sour apple tree for the Colonel – and this, I was convinced, settled the matter for him. In the event of a military victory, he should let the Colonel slip through his hands to safety abroad.

He raised with us, more than once, the question of our arms supplies. I ruled out any change in our policy of limiting the types we supplied and specifically refused a request for bombs for the Federal Air Force, even though the General argued that bombs of the right type could knock out Uli Airport, through which all the French and other arms were reaching Biafra, and thus end the war.

After the meetings on the morning of 28th March, I flew to Enugu, the former Eastern region capital, by that time under Federal control. I was met by the administrator for the West Central province, an Ibo. We drove through areas uncomfortably close to the battle lines, and visited, at Udi, the Red Cross rehabilitation centre. This was where casualties from the previously Biafran-occupied areas were cared for. The first task was to deal with malnutrition, which in some cases was desperate. The young British doctors and nurses taught me the elementary rules of dealing with advanced malnutrition, a sobering practical lesson for the author of *War on Want*, sixteen years earlier. What impressed me was the selfless devotion of these young people – doctors, nurses, voluntary service workers – working long hours in almost insufferable heat, to save life. These young folk were there not just for hours, as we were, but for months and more. The London journalists with me, in common with my party and myself, were almost overcome with the heat. These volunteers had to stand it the whole time, living in primitive conditions and doing their job with the minimum equipment and supplies. Few experiences have ever impressed me more. Frequently, back in Britain, when I heard facile criticisms of British youth, I referred, often by name, to these young heroes and heroines of Udi and to their opposite numbers in Port Harcourt and Calabar whom I met on the following day. Back in London, I made a point of trying to trace them on their return and subsequently some of them were among other state guests at our Downing Street receptions – notably that for the first men on the moon, and at other receptions for visiting world statesmen. We were glad to greet them again in tolerable conditions and tolerable temperature.

From Udi I went to the new hospital in Enugu where, again, I met dedicated young doctors, nurses and others only with a deep sense of humility. In normal times, their task would have been difficult enough. but they had to cope also with the flood of refugees, the sick and the undernourished casualties of the Nigerian war. This hospital had been financed by Britain's Overseas Development Ministry. When, in subsequent times, I read smug leading articles criticising the 'waste' of Government monies on overseas aid, my first reaction was to recall that hospital, and all it had done and was doing for humanity. I should like to have financed the critics on a one-way ticket to this hospital, where, in the intense heat and primitive conditions, they would be able to see constituents of mine and others hard and devotedly at work. They could have observed and, to the extent of their abilities, helped in the work, which they would have agreed was utterly essential. Having observed and assisted, perhaps as hospital porters, they could come back and write more leading articles.

That evening, 28th March, we returned to Lagos for a dinner with the Federal Government. The following morning we were away from State House at 7.30 a.m. for a flight to Port Harcourt, capital of the Rivers State, and to Calabar. Wherever we went we were greeted with crowds of demonstrators for 'United Nigeria' and with compelling evidence about the desire of the local citizens to be free of Ibo rule. I listened to all the atrocity stories about their sufferings when Colonel Ojukwu's troops were in control, down to the last detail of the sinking of fishing boats and the destruction of nets. Applying a discount of ninety per cent for exaggeration and propaganda, it was still a formidable indictment.

Calabar was more than an official visit, it was a pilgrimage. While thousands waited in the stadium, I insisted on visiting the cemetery to lay a wreath on the grave of Mary Slessor, heroine of countless missionary teachings which I, in common with so many Sunday school children of my generation, had absorbed. I then went to the stadium, where I briefly savoured the ceremonies prepared for me and then, leaving the participants to enjoy their day out, returned to Lagos for a Federal Government reception for the diplomatic corps and business community. Then at 9.00 p.m. back to *Fearless* for a delegation meeting. This was mainly concerned with our communications with Colonel Ojukwu. Clear channels had been agreed: any message I was to send to him, when the lines had been cleared with the Federal Government, was to be routed from the Foreign and Commonwealth Office to their contact in London then via a channel through Lisbon and French African contacts, to Umuahia. I sent clear messages to Whitehall, to be passed on to the Biafran contacts in London, to ensure that the channel was manned throughout Sunday, so that any communication I sent would be flashed through to the Colonel.

The following morning, 30th March, I resumed my formal meeting with General Gowon and his followers. He was ready to answer all the points I had made when we had last met.

On his willingness to negotiate unconditionally, he accepted what I had asked for. On guarantees for the safety and security of all Ibos – including what I had asked for in our private talks, the appointment of OAU observers – he again agreed, without reservation. I asked him once more to make this public.

On relief questions, he confirmed his Government's continuing agreement to the land corridors and daylight flights. Though many of the conditions attached to his relief policy must inevitably help the secessionists to continue fighting, he was not pursuing the policy that 'all was fair in war': this was a different war, he said, where brother was fighting to try to bring brother back into the fold.

On the fourth point, civilian targets, he repeated the orders that he had been given about prohibiting indiscriminate bombing. He still opposed any proposal to send the observers into the areas controlled by Colonel Ojukwu. In the event, as I have said, we found we had made our point and the indiscriminate bombing was speedily ended, and with its ending these particular atrocity stories ended.

He then came to the suggestion that I should meet Colonel Ojukwu. While his colleagues clearly were reluctant that such a meeting should be held, he concluded that he could not make any objection, provided that the meeting was not in 'Biafra', or any country recognising Biafra.

We discussed the basis for a meeting. As I suggested, I would concentrate on relief supplies; I did not intend to mediate, but I would pass on any thoughts Colonel Ojukwu might express to the OAU mediators, and in particular Emperor Haile Selassie. I told General Gowon that I had especially asked that the lines of communication to the Colonel through London and Lisbon should be kept open day and night throughout the weekend. I would send him a message as soon as the meeting ended. General Gowon raised no objection to the long list of possible venues I intended to propose: in West Africa Monrovia, Yaounde, Accra, Lome, Dakar, Ascension, or HMS *Fearless* stationed off Cotonou; in East Africa Nairobi, Entebbe or Addis Ababa.

Telegrams were sent to London at lunchtime Sunday, 30th March, to be passed instantly to the Biafran unofficial representative there, who was to send them via his Lisbon channel to Umuahia. I proposed that we should meet on the following day in any west African capital and would send an Andover, Hercules, or helicopter to pick up Colonel Ojukwu. Alternatively he could meet me in East Africa on the Tuesday or Wednesday. As a reserve proposal, if the only difficulty he raised was that of timing, I was ready to fly back to west Africa after my meeting with Emperor Haile Selassie in Addis Ababa. All necessary plans for this were worked out at a meeting in *Fearless* that evening.

General Gowon and his team joined us for lunch at the British High Commission residence. Full confidence had been established and all his reserve had gone. He invited me to a religious service which he held every Sunday evening at 5.30 at Dodan Barracks. Apparently church parade was compulsory for every member of his Cabinet. As I was due to meet the relief agencies, followed by representatives of all the Nigerian churches, at the time I was not able to accept. He told me some news he had just received, and which was clearly welcome to him. At the passing-out parade for his officer cadets, the sword of honour had been won by a young Ibo. Other news, less welcome to my FCO colleague Maurice Foley, MP for West Bromwich, reached us too: West Bromwich Albion had been defeated in the FA cup semi-final. This led us on to football, and I found that General Gowon was a passionate Manchester United supporter. I gave him the latest news on that front and promised to send him some badges and other trophies I had collected at the Matt Busby celebrations.

In the afternoon, in insufferable heat and humidity, I held a press conference and a series of five television interviews. Because of the heat and humidity I had to change my suit three times and my shirt five. As agreed with General Gowon, I announced the terms of the invitation I had sent to Colonel Ojukwu, together with the list of possible meeting places.

I then went on to the meetings with the US Ambassador who passed on a personal report to me from the negro professor Clyde Ferguson, President Nixon's special emissary on relief questions. Later I met with the Swedish Ambassador, the relief agencies, and the whole spectrum of churches from the Roman Catholic to the Salvation Army. I found that in Lagos, as I had noted in Calabar, the Roman Catholic bishops took a very different line from the pro-Biafran stance of the Church in Britain. The same was true also of the Presbyterians there.

The following morning, 31st March, ready, in the absence of a reply from Colonel Ojukwu, to fly to my meeting with the Emperor of Ethiopia, I found that the London Biafrans had failed to keep their communication lines open, and that the message was due to reach the Colonel only that morning. At 10.00 a.m. we left for Addis Ababa. We were met on arrival with the Emperor's characteristic courtesy, and all the dignities normally reserved for a head of state.

The Emperor, at the airport and at successive private meetings and at the state dinner at the Imperial Palace, never failed to make clear that the warmth of our welcome was due to his undying gratitude to Britain for the liberation of his country from the Italians in the Second World War.

Addis Ababa was fascinating. Of all the places I was only to visit briefly for official meetings it is one I would most want to revisit with more leisure. We were quartered in one of the imperial palaces, formerly occupied by the Duke of Harar. That evening we dined at the Embassy. While we were there we heard that 'Radio Biafra' was said to have made a short statement rejecting my proposal for a meeting. This was to be followed by a full statement by Colonel Ojukwu the next morning. We sent off a further cable through the established channels to .Colonel Ojukwu, pressing for the meeting to take place and proposing to revise the arrangements to meet his convenience. But his statement did not in fact reach me 'the following morning'. I had gone to bed at midnight and was repeatedly wakened by the howling of the wild dogs which at night come from the surrounding hills seeking food. At 3.00 a.m. Michael Palliser, of my private office, came in, switched on the lights and grimly said there would be no more sleep. Colonel Ojukwu's European representative had issued his statement. Neatly timed for the morning European press, it

The British Prime Minister and his Soviet hosts stand for the National Anthems before a performance of *Carmen* in Moscow, January 1968. During this visit extensive discussions took place on the possibilities of reaching a settlement in Vietnam

Mr Wilson with President Johnson on his visit to the United States in February 1968

The 1969 Commonwealth conference. *Back row, left to right:* Mr Keith Holyoake, Prime Minister of New Zealand; Mr Lee Kuan Yew, Prime Minister of Singapore; Mr Arshad Husain, Foreign Minister of Pakistan; Mr Errol Barrow, Prime Minister of Barbados; Mr John W. K. Harlley, deputy chairman, National Liberation Council, Ghana; Mr Dudley Senanayake, Prime Minister of Ceylon; Sir Dauda Jawara, Prime Minister of Gambia; Mr John Gorton, Prime Minister of Australia; Mr Siaka Stevens, Prime Minister of Sierra Leone; Mr Hugh L. Shearer, Prime Minister of Jamaica; Mr Pierre Trudeau, Prime Minister of Canada; Mr Forbes Burnham, Prime Minister of Guyana; President Kaunda of Zambia; Chief Obafemi Awolowo, vice-chairman, Federal Executive Council, Nigeria; Prince Makhosini Dlamini, Prime Minister of Swaziland; President Nyerere of Tanzania. *Front row, left to right:* Chief Leabua Jonathan, Prime Minister of Lesotho; President Obote of Uganda; Dr Eric Williams, Prime Minister of Trinidad and Tobago; Mrs Indira Gandhi, Prime Minister of India; Mr Arnold Smith, the Commonwealth Secretary-General; Mr Harold Wilson; President Hastings Banda of Malawi; President Archbishop Makarios of Cyprus; Dr Borg Olivier, Prime Minister of Malta; Mr James J. Gichuru, Minister of Finance of Kenya; Sir Seewoosagur Ramgoolam, Prime Minister of Mauritius

Mr Wilson with Major-General Gowon on his visit to Nigeria in March 1969 walks past anti-British banners and slogans

In August 1969 Mr Wilson flew to meet President Nixon at the American Airforce base at Mildenhall in Suffolk

The Israeli Prime Minister, Mrs Golda Meir, shares a joke with Harold Wilson and Willy Brandt at the eleventh socialist international conference at Eastbourne in June 1969

was a catalogue of misrepresentations. He claimed that he had assumed the meeting would take place in Biafra. In this connection he made mischief about an answer given by Michael Stewart in the House of Commons a week earlier, when he said that he had 'not entirely ruled out' a visit by me to Biafran territory, though making it clear it was highly unlikely. The Biafran statement went on to throw total doubt on the sincerity of the British Government's motives in proposing the meeting.

My staff was sent for, from the palace and the Embassy, and after consultations I sat up in bed dictating telegrams to London and the text of a statement for issue to the press early that morning. The text said:

The 'Radio Biafra's' statement of 31st March fails to deal with the central fact of the Prime Minister's invitation to a meeting communicated to Mr Kogbara, Colonel Ojukwu's nominated representative in London, on Sunday afternoon: and with the further message sent through the same representative to Colonel Ojukwu early on Monday morning, repeating the invitation and stating the Prime Minister's willingness to return from Addis Ababa via West Africa in order to meet Colonel Ojukwu on Wednesday 2nd April in any one of a number of suggested meeting places. This invitation was further confirmed in a message sent to Colonel Ojukwu on Monday evening after the first reports of a statement on 'Radio Biafra'.

The fact that no attempt has been made to answer these invitations throws doubt on the sincerity of Colonel Ojukwu's earlier message expressing his desire to meet the Prime Minister.

Over a period of several days before the Prime Minister left London messages had reached him through a number of channels indicating that Colonel Ojukwu wished to meet him on his visit to Africa.

It was made clear that the Prime Minister did not intend to visit the territory controlled by Colonel Ojukwu. Indeed, other places were accordingly suggested on Colonel Ojukwu's behalf.

In the informal exchanges between Mr Kogbara and Mr Foley the question was raised of a possible visit to Umuahia by British representatives to discuss arrangements for the proposed meeting. In the event, it became clear that such a visit was not practicable nor was it necessary, since after consultation with the Federal Government the Prime Minister was able to make a definite proposal for a meeting between Colonel Ojukwu and himself at any one of ten convenient places in Africa. All this information was given to Mr Kogbara on Sunday afternoon, at the same time as the Prime Minister announced his invitation to Colonel Ojukwu.

The Umuahia statement claims that Colonel Ojukwu did not receive the invitation until 10.00 a.m. on Monday, 31st March. This long delay in transmission is not the responsibility of the British Government. From Saturday onwards Mr Kogbara had been warned to keep his regular lines of transmission open in case of an urgent message.

As regards the reference in the statement to the answer of the Foreign and Commonwealth Secretary to a supplementary question on Monday, 24th March, further examination of the implications ruled out a visit by the Prime Minister to Umuahia. This was made clear to Mr Kogbara before the Prime Minister left London and already other alternative meeting places outside Nigeria were being considered by both sides before the Prime Minister left London. The Prime Minister's thrice-repeated offer to meet Colonel Ojukwu in one of a number of convenient places in West Africa on Wednesday morning remains open. . . .

At 6.00 a.m. I tried to get some more sleep, but a few minutes later was wakened by two telephone calls, the first in Amharic, the second in indifferent English, asking me if I was the clinic, which I was not. I rang for a household officer lest the call was an urgent one. Soon after that the Imperial Guard outside my window was relieved, with loud orders and stamping of feet, followed by the cheerful efforts of an early-morning bugler. At that point I decided to get up.

The whole morning of 1st April was spent in talks with the Emperor in his palace. Passing the cougars guarding the entrance, and met by the Emperor inside, I was conducted through the palace to his conference room. I gave him a full account of the position as we had found it in Lagos and of my invitation to Colonel Ojukwu. He agreed with our assessment, and went on to describe his own efforts, both on peace talks and the organisation of relief supplies. We discussed the possibilities – not very great in view of Colonel Ojukwu's hardening attitude – of a move forward at the OAU conference in Monrovia later in the month.

In the afternoon I met, for ninety minutes, members of the secretariat of OAU headed by Mr Dialo Telli, the Secretary-General. Most of our discussion was about Nigeria and the OAU representatives expressed themselves in enthusiastic terms, as in succeeding weeks they did publicly, about the line we had taken and the efforts we had made for peace. We then briefly discussed Rhodesia, on which over the years the OAU, and particularly Mr Telli, had attacked us in extravagant terms. I set out the whole story, but was clearly unable to turn them from their publicly-expressed demand for the use of force by Britain. But at least they understood our position better, even if they could not agree with it, and henceforth our relations were considerably better with the OAU and with black Africa generally.

In the evening the Emperor gave an impressive dinner for us in the Imperial Palace. During our private talks at the table he began to break down the air of mystery and majesty that has always surrounded him, and I saw him as a very human, very friendly person.

I was in bed before midnight – we had to be up at 4.30 a.m. (2.30 London time) to catch the aircraft as soon as it was light at 6.00 a.m. I must have had, perhaps, seven hours' sleep in the previous two nights, and as I had to stay up for a state dinner for the President of Niger when I finally reached Downing Street, followed by a short ministerial meeting until 1.00 a.m., this meant a twenty-two-and-a-half-hour day.

Most of the time on the aircraft home I spent preparing a statement on my visit, to be made in the House that afternoon, so there was no time

" You've got to admit he's got guts ! "

for sleep. We refuelled at the British RAF base in Libya, El Adem, where I had a meeting with my advisers to go through the draft I had prepared. Awaiting me was a telegram with the First Secretary's 'final' judgment on the Chancellor's suggestion that a brief interim Industrial Relations Bill should be introduced and that the intention to do so should be announced by him in the Budget speech, when he announced that we should not be renewing the 1967–8 Prices and Incomes legislation when it lapsed at the end of the year. Though Barbara Castle had seen advantage in doing this, if it was physically possible, she had received advice that such a Bill could not be got ready. The telegram I received at El Adem confirmed this.

We reached London Airport at 2.00 p.m. and I went straight to the House to make my statement. This was surprisingly well received – particularly the strong line I had taken about bombing – not least by leading pro-Biafrans who congratulated me on the success of the visit. Despite lack of sleep, I have seldom had so little difficulty in dealing with a long period of supplementaries. From the time of my visit, I was much more confident in dealing with Nigerian questions, mainly because my own private hesitations had been removed by what I had seen and learnt during my visit.

After the statement I had a meeting with Roy Jenkins and Barbara Castle about the Budget announcement and the interim Industrial Relations Bill. To my surprise, Barbara Castle, after further consultations, was now confident that the Bill could be got ready: we agreed to put Roy's proposal to the Cabinet the following day, when it was approved.

At Cabinet the following morning, 3rd April, I opened up on the question raised by press reports of the NEC meeting of 26th March, and of the line taken there by Jim Callaghan. I had no difficulty in accepting his account of what had happened but I felt it right to address a constitutional homily to the Cabinet about the position of a minister when attending a meeting in any other capacity, such as a member of party committees. I stressed that his duty as a minister, including the full acceptance of total collective responsibility for all Government decisions, must transcend all other considerations and loyalties. Should membership of an outside body involve a conflict of loyalties, then that membership must be resigned. I was loth to propose that ministers should not seek election to the NEC, as many of our critics proposed; that would be bad for the party. But in every action, speech and vote, a minister must act as a minister. Any minister not able to accept that doctrine must resign. My statement was accepted by the Cabinet unanimously, and in view of some of the more sensational press references to 'challenges' and forecasts of ministerial resignations, I was authorised to make it public.

After seeing a number of ministers and catching up with some of the work which had accumulated in my absence, I caught the night train to Penzance and went on to Scilly for a short Easter break.

Chapter 31

Industrial relations – discussions with the TUC – speech to the Parliamentary Labour Party – John Silkin succeeded by Bob Mellish – dissensions in the PLP – the borough elections – meeting of the Socialist International at Eastbourne – further discussions with the TUC – agreement reached on dealing with strikes – visit to Aberfan – reflections on strikes and the TUC

ON my return to London on 10th April I was due to meet the TUC. Originally I had intended to call it for the morning of Budget day. But now it had been decided that the Chancellor would be making the statement in the Budget speech about the phasing out of legislation on prices and incomes, and its replacement by a voluntary incomes policy, at the same time announcing the decision to introduce an interim Industrial Relations Bill. I felt therefore that, since at my meeting with the TUC on Budget day we should be concerned with this announcement, there should be an earlier meeting for them to make their formal representations on the White Paper. When we met on the Friday morning, 11th April, the Finance and General Purposes committee of the TUC put with great force their views on what they called 'penal' clauses and asked for an assurance that there would be no legislation during the 1968–69 session. I said that I could not give such an assurance: this heightened their suspicion about our intentions but I undertook to let them know as soon as a decision was taken.

Following a hint Victor Feather had given me in a private talk the previous evening, I repeated Barbara Castle's invitation to the TUC themselves to act to deal with the two main problems with which we were concerned; namely, inter-union disputes in their various forms, and unconstitutional stoppages, such as the recent Girling strike where a handful of men had brought production to a halt over a wide section of the car industry dependent on Girlings for essential components, and thrown thousands of fellow trade unionists out of work. (Vic Feather had mentioned to me action some years earlier when the TUC had forced, under warning of disaffiliation, the National Union of Public Employees to bring some of their Cornish members – ambulance drivers – to heel by threatening their expulsion.)

Would the constituent union, I asked, grant sufficient sovereignty and power to the General Council to enable the TUC to take over this responsibility? Sir Tom O'Brien and others said that over their period as trade unionists the transfer of power to the centre had been no more than marginal and they saw little hope of such development. But others, led by Vic Feather, said that they were prepared to examine what I had said. I did not encourage them to think that this would be enough to enable us to postpone legislative action, but the faster they moved the more all could feel that any legislative powers taken would remain unused and that once the effectiveness of TUC machinery was established the legislation could be repealed.

The Cabinet met on the following Monday, 14th April, for the usual pre-Budget statement by the Chancellor. The proposal finally to let the prices and incomes legislation die out at the end of the year and to introduce interim industrial relations legislation in the current session went through quietly. The next day, before the Budget speech, the TUC and CBI were formally told of our intentions.

Parliamentary and public reaction to this part of the Chancellor's speech was very muted; there was much more criticism expressed about the further increase in SET. At the PLP post-Budget meeting the next day, again little was said, though this, I felt, might have been due to a prior undertaking to discuss industrial relations at the weekly Thursday evening meeting of the party the following day, 17th April.

At this meeting I thought it right to open the discussion since there had been criticism in the past that I had wound up with an important speech, with no further debate possible. This speech has been so often quoted out of context – and this has persisted into the post-June 1970 Parliament – that I must quote both the main pronouncements. After mentioning legislative priorities – I had that afternoon told the House that we were dropping the Parliament Bill, and that we were giving priority to getting the Merchant Shipping Bill ready for introduction in the current session – I said that our industrial relations proposals had already been discussed at three full party meetings and at successive meetings of the trade union group. I said I would deal with the anxieties which remained, and went on:

> We have told the TUC on many occasions – again, yesterday – that if they would come forward with their own measures, equally effective, equally urgent in time, to our proposals to deal with unofficial strikes, we would be prepared to consider their alternative suggestions. So far they have not indicated that this would be possible but they have again been invited to come forward with alternatives if they wish to do so. . . .

I referred to the urgency of the problem caused by stoppages in which a small number of workers, in breach of the constitutional procedures of the unions involved, were threatening the employment of many thousands of workers not a party to their dispute. When I had met the TUC the previous Friday, five such stoppages had been highlighted in the morning's newspapers. I stressed that the only unofficial strikes which would be dealt with under the proposed Bill were those where constitutional procedures agreed to by the unions were being defied, or where agreed procedures did not exist. It was not a question of interfering with trade union rights, which would be strengthened. What was at issue was the right of trade unionists to work, threatened, as many were, almost daily, by unconstitutional stoppages. Compulsory strike ballots would not be in the Bill, for we were concerned with unconstitutional and unofficial strikes; Barbara Castle had taken seriously some weighty arguments from the TUC about compulsory ballots in other countries. I went on,

> The Bill we are discussing tonight is an essential Bill. Essential to our economic recovery. Essential to the balance of payments. Essential to full employment. It is an essential component of ensuring the economic success of the Government. It is on that economic success that the recovery of the nation, led by the Labour Government, depends. That is why I have to tell you that the passage of this Bill is essential to its continuance in office. There can be no going back on that . . .

It was these last two sentences which created yet another legend, unscrupulously fostered by Opposition leaders and Opposition press, and based on yet one more quotation out of context. Wherever it has been quoted, it has never been qualified – as I did at the time it was made – with the prior reference to the invitations to the unions to propose their own means of dealing with the problem, which could have avoided the need to introduce legislation. The apotheosis of the legend, though not its end, came in the middle of the 1970 General Election when, after the Conservatives had exploited it in meeting after meeting, in costly advertising, on television and through their press, a television interviewer, Robert Kee, produced a post card and read the last but one sentence of the quotation above – as he moved in, so he thought, for the kill. When I asked him to read the rest of the quotation from the speech, which would put his question in context, he lamely said it was not on his card – so I repaired his omission.

At the end of the PLP discussions, in which the speeches were mainly from opponents of the Bill, I wound up with a lively speech, specifically referring to the fears expressed. Again I put the point: let the TUC produce proposals which hold out the prospect of being as effective as the Bill, and we would consider them as an alternative to the Bill. In default of such proposals we would have to continue with the legislation. A number of members, including Manny Shinwell, who had previously strongly opposed the Bill, confessed themselves converted by my winding-up speech.

On the following Wednesday, 23rd April, we had yet another party meeting. The Lord Chancellor had been asked to explain the position about the recovery of costs imposed on unofficial strikers who, after being given every chance, first by a conciliation pause laid down by the Minister, and then in hearings before a tribunal, still persisted in unofficial action. He explained the nature of the civil process – for there was no proposal to involve the criminal law in these matters – in a cogent speech. But it had no hope of persuading those who were opposed to any form of statutory intervention, however damaging the dispute.

But the day was Barbara Castle's; in her most impassioned manner she replied to the debate, almost every sentence being cheered. She again took up the TUC point, but referred in scathing terms to the TUC's failure to take action in the previous five years. If, she said, she were to announce that the Bill were to be dropped, there would be no joy in the TUC, for it was the threat of the Bill that was enabling the progressive elements in the TUC to force their colleagues to face up to the problem. If the Bill were dropped, the TUC would go back to sleep for five years more.

In all my years of party meetings I have never seen an ovation such as she received; the applause went on and on and she had to rise to her feet to acknowledge it. If anyone on the platform had risen – and some were tempted to do so – she would have had a standing ovation, something I have never seen in a party meeting. Douglas Houghton, who, as subsequent events showed, was no enthusiast for the proposed Bill, faithfully and accurately recounted her triumph to the press, and was reported to have been greatly moved by it.

But there were other difficulties within the party, different in origin from, but not entirely unconnected with, the battle over the Bill. Discipline was getting more lax in the PLP and while the greater part of the Budget went through unscathed, the proposals to increase SET aroused strong opposition. The Co-operative party was deeply wounded at this, the third increase in four Budgets, and demanded to see me. The party's deputation had rejected an invitation to meet the Chancellor. I refused to see it until it reversed its decision about seeing the Chancellor; when it met my point, I met the deputation. The more restrained were worried about pressure in the Co-operative movement to break up the Co-operative party, all of whose candidates fought their elections on the 'Labour and Co-operative' ticket. I pointed out that if the Co-operative party was to break its link with Labour, none of its members would be able to fight again as Labour candidates, and few, if any, would be elected without Labour support. I reminded them that there had always been a powerful element in the political movement – in the NEC indeed – ready to end the party's constitutional relationship with the Co-op party; this had come to a head a few years earlier, with Hugh Gaitskell leading the move for a change. It was clear from their reaction that this was the last thing they wanted, but their case on SET was strong, for co-operative societies acting as a public service, supplying household needs over a wide range – not just the more profitable items – were particularly vulnerable. I answered as sympathetically as I could, while holding out no hope for any major change in the Budget proposals; they were sufficiently reassured to change their earlier decision to vote against the SET clause in committee to one to abstain. They were helped by a Budget concession remitting SET on co-operative and other establishments concerned with milk distribution.

But when the Budget resolution was reached on 21st April, we had a bad vote. The co-operators were joined by one or two left-wing members and, worse, by some of the right-wing disciplinarians always anxious to reveal the weakness, as they saw it, of John Silkin's liberal regime. Our majority dropped to 28 – 283 for the resolution and 255 against.

John Silkin wanted instructions. Even he felt that his policy of gentle restraint was being abused. I raised the matter at the 'Inner Cabinet'. With the Industrial Relations Bill ahead, I was already considering a change in the post of Chief Whip. In the post-devaluation troubles and manoeuvres, he had come under heavy fire from a number whose real target was the incumbent of No. 10, not of No. 12, Downing Street. Throughout this period I had fought back and defended him successfully; he was my choice, in whom I had every confidence. But he had served for three years. I felt that he was destined to go higher, and quite soon, but he had not had any ministerial experience outside the Whips' Office. I was seriously considering the appointment as Chief Whip of Bob Mellish, Minister of Works, who had been pressed on me by Manny Shinwell (who two years earlier, it will be recalled, had resigned the PLP chairmanship in protest against the 'permissive society' in the PLP). It would mean a nominal step-down in status and salary for Bob, but I found that Manny had sounded him out and found him willing.

On the last Friday in April I mentioned my ideas to certain of my senior colleagues and found them strongly in favour. Over the weekend I decided on the move, and on the Tuesday consulted Douglas Houghton, who was also strongly for the change. I asked him whether he had an alternative candidate to suggest, but he replied there was no better candidate than Bob Mellish. On the Tuesday afternoon I saw Bob, who accepted the post. I saw John Silkin, who was not surprised, though clearly upset. I was sorry that this should be so; he and I had been through a great deal together. That evening I had to attend a Guildhall reception for President Saragat of Italy, who was on a State visit. On my return I received a message that John Silkin, in a mood of acute depression, wanted to see me with his deputy, Brian O'Malley – who felt even more strongly – to press me to change my decision: both indicated their intention, otherwise, to resign. I refused, and enjoined them to sleep on it. This they did and very soon, as so often happens, John Silkin was fully absorbed in one of the most agreeable of all ministerial tasks, the Ministry of Works. A few months later, Brian O'Malley was engaged with no less success and enjoyment in the Department of Health and Social Security.

One or two of my colleagues, particularly when they met left-wing friends, were devastated by the change. Among them was Barbara Castle who wrote demanding to see me late at night. When I received the message it was too late to wake her, so I asked her to come in the morning. Soon she was working wholeheartedly with Bob Mellish. Dick Crossman was all for the appointment: Bob had been his Parliamentary Secretary at Housing and Local Government, and Dick had a high regard for his ability.

Bob Mellish's first task was to deal with the problem of four SET abstainers with a long record of indiscipline and whom John Silkin had chosen for selective suspension from the PLP. He rightly decided to wipe the slate clean as an act of inaugural clemency. At the PLP meeting which had been called to ratify the suspension 'sentences', he announced his decision and went on to talk of his new duties. Unfortunately – despite my strong advice to the contrary – he was carried away three times into asserting that failure to carry the Industrial Relations Bill would mean a dissolution. Only the Prime Minister can talk in this language and in my speech to the party meeting on 17th April, I had qualified any such suggestion. That night, to quote from a diary which I dictated throughout this period, 'all hell was let loose. The left was inflamed by Bob Mellish. Meanwhile the professional WMG [Wilson Must Go] group was also at work.'

It was difficult to estimate how far the left would make common cause. The next day, 1st May, I was in bed for most of the day with a mild gastric complaint, following a dubious fish course at one of the Italian State visit functions. For the first time in four years I looked like having to miss questions through illness. But finding that Michael Stewart was tied up with negotiations with the Foreign Minister of Japan, I went to the House and there I faced attack by Scottish Unionist MPs who, in advance of the following week's Scottish burgh elections, had tabled a series of questions to me, on some of which I was on a sticky wicket. During the five minutes before I was called, I watched them, with increasing anger, mauling Ernie Fernyhough, the mildest and most popular of junior ministers, on Scottish questions closely related to those directed to me. Although feeling about thirty degrees below par, I was roused by their treatment of Ernie, and found enough strength to hit back as hard as I have ever done. Every answer was loudly cheered by our supporters. Whether this was because they knew that I was off-colour, or because they were angry about the treatment Ernie Fernyhough had received, or by a feeling about some of the manoeuvring in the PLP, I do not know. Still less did I know how far manoeuvres had gone. There was, it is true, some activity. Supporters of different possible candidates for the succession, each conscious that there could be no agreement on a winning name, tried to combine forces with the aim of getting rid of me, leaving the choice of my successor to a later fight. One or two proposed – and made this public – the collection of a hundred names to submit to the PLP chairman with a view to a party meeting on the leadership question. One young MP went on television to advocate union to get rid of me and to agree on a successor later. Within six months I invited him to join the Government, telling him that while we had not always seen eye to eye, at least he had shown he had the guts to say, publicly, not behind cupped hands, what he had to say. He was happy to join.

After questions I returned to bed, and at six o'clock a panicky Whip, also disgruntled by Bob Mellish's appointment, came in with dire warnings of a revolt on the left. The Praetorian Guard were deserting: name after fantastic name was cited. Members whose loyalty had never been called in question were said to be in revolt. That evening I made one or two dispositions for handling the matter, but by next morning it transpired that all members named in the whip's report were found to have their knives out; certainly not against me but in my defence. The next day a middle-of-the-road MP telephoned nineteen associates, of whom eighteen joined him in a public statement demanding that the nonsense must stop. The Merseyside group of MPs went unanimously on record in Liverpool with the same message.

I reflected that the trouble-makers had lacked Mr Cecil King's sense of timing. A year earlier he had planned his putsch to coincide with the local elections. This year the move had come a week too early. The 1969 borough elections were still to come. Meanwhile I was dictating my speech for the London May Day rally in the Festival Hall. It was a robust speech, proclaiming our still unpublicised achievements. But I knew that only one sentence would hit the headlines. Referring to the press reports about the Parliamentary Party, I said, 'I know what's going on. I'm going on.' Other ministers, led by Dick Crossman on the Friday, had made public speeches dismissing the speculation about the leadership.

The following day, 5th May, Vic Feather came to lunch at No. 10. Barbara Castle was also there. He was able to report on the TUC's activities, following our appeal to them to show what they could do. He had met me at No. 10 late one evening in the previous week, and had indicated the way in which his and his colleagues' minds were working. One idea, of which he did not have high hopes, was the establishment of joint machinery with the CBI to provide adequate enforcement of agreements within industry. He had, in fact, to leave our lunch early for his meeting with the CBI, which proved abortive. Before going he agreed with our suggestion that I should invite the General Council of the TUC to No. 10 the following week.

That afternoon there was yet another parliamentary disaster. Dick Crossman calmly rose in his place and, on the first day of that week's local elections, announced a £3½ millions increase in National Health Service charges for dentures and spectacle lenses. He did not reassure those concerned about the effect on the local elections by a later admission that he had forgotten that they were taking place. Our machinery for screening parliamentary statements, for content and timing, had some-how allowed this one through. Following inter-departmental agreement, Dick Crossman had given instructions, around Estimates time, for the statement to be drafted: he did not even see the draft until a time had been booked for it and announced. But MPs were horrified. Both the fact of the timing and the announcement they saw as further evidence of ministerial disintegration, or lack of concern for the troops in the field, or both. 'Accident-prone' was the phrase widely used whenever the Government was mentioned. The decision on increased charges had in fact been taken in the PESC (Public Expenditure Survey Committee) discussions at the beginning of the year, when we had settled the over-all expenditure allocations for the 1969–70 Vote on Account, and also for 1970–1, and published them in the annual White Paper.

At that time we had become aware of a serious threat of crisis in the provision of funds for education, with the very real danger of teachers being unemployed and intolerable increases in further education fees. The Secretary of State for Education, Ted Short, had been to see me at mid-night. I had been proposing for some time the introduction of 'block budgeting', under which a group of related departments would be looked at together and priorities assessed, not just within one department but across the group. I put Dick Crossman, in his capacity as chairman of the inter-departmental Committee on the Social Services, in charge to carry out this operation. Loath as he was, as Secretary of State for DHSS, to add to health charges, he was nobly prepared to make a de-partmental sacrifice, with the certainty of a major parliamentary and PLP row, to help education; he agreed, therefore, to postpone by a month the biennial pensions increase on which he had been working, in order to make a once-for-all saving on the Estimates and, at the same time, in-crease the denture and lens charges. Unlike the situation in 1968, we decided not to announce all the decisions, but to phase them over an appropriate period. It was an inauspicious start for the new experi-ment in block budgeting, which had worked well in defence and was, indeed, an essential element in our successive reforms in expenditure control.

After this we tightened up the procedures about parliamentary announce-ments; one obvious change was, so far as possible, to give forty-eight hours' notice of making them so that all the ministers concerned could be alerted to the possible implications.

On the Wednesday morning, 7th May, I was chairing NEDC, when a message was brought in from my PPS saying that Douglas Houghton had opened the third meeting of the PLP on industrial relations with a state-ment from the chair. In this he was said to have told the Government that they could not introduce the Bill, as the Parliamentary Party would not support it.

This was inevitably headlined and a new legend was begun – which again was far from the end of its currency two years later – that we ultimately dropped the Bill because Douglas Houghton told us we could not have it. He came to see me in the afternoon, extremely concerned by the sensational reaction to his words. He had publicly made clear his favourable reaction to Barbara Castle's speech just a fortnight before. He undertook to put the matter right at a further statement at the party meeting due to be held on the Thursday evening.

On Friday 9th May, at No. 10, we held the joint meeting of the Cabinet and NEC, which I had proposed in a message to the NEC meeting on 26th March. I had further proposed that Douglas Houghton should be invited to provide independent representation of the PLP.

The borough and most of the district council results were in. On the face of it, we had done badly again, losing some 917 seats. But it was clearly an improvement on the previous year; the Labour seats won, that is gains plus seats retained, were some twenty per cent above the previous year. Just before lunch, Jim Callaghan intervened with a speech which was taken by a number of ministers as dissociating from Cabinet policies, particularly on the Industrial Relations Bill. Even before our meeting was over this leaked into the evening papers. The leak did not come from Jim Callaghan – I was satisfied about that. It was the main news on television and in the press the next morning. There was much speculation about his future. Some of his colleagues were incensed. On the Monday I told him that while I hoped that there would be no question of resignation, he should quit the Management committee (Inner Cabinet), which had to work on a basis of close trust in the very difficult situation we were facing. He accepted this and devoted himself to his departmental duties.

That night Barbara Castle and I had another No. 10 dinner with Vic Feather. The TUC was making progress and he was submitting a draft to its Finance and General Purposes committee on new and far-reaching powers for the TUC, particularly, though not entirely, in relation to inter-union disputes. A special Congress had been called for 5th June at Croydon. Knowing this we had decided to defer the introduction of the Bill from 22nd May, the eve of the Whitsun recess, to early June, after we had been able to assess the results of it. We discussed arrangements for the meeting with the General Council which we had arranged for the following Monday, 12th May.

On the Sunday, 11th May, I attended the jubilee celebrations of the Union of Post Office Workers in Bournemouth. I had prepared a firm and full speech, again reiterating the need for legislation unless the TUC would take action to put its own house in order, including the issue of union control over disputes. I was given a tremendous reception, outside and inside the hall, and most of all at the end of my speech, delivered to an audience which had sat there in intense heat for three hours.

I returned late that night to Downing Street, where I spent two hours with Ygal Allon, deputy Prime Minister of Israel, who had come over especially to see me in order to discuss the issue of the supply of Chieftain tanks. This had taken up a great deal of my time and that of the Cabinet Defence committee.

The Monday afternoon meeting with the TUC was – I recorded in my diary at the time – markedly friendly and comradely and I could sense a strong desire on their part to avert a split in the movement, 'but not to the extent of showing any give on the so-called "penal clauses".' They had that morning adopted a secretariat draft document, of whose fate Vic Feather had been doubtful. Barbara Castle's judgment on this, as she reported to a meeting of the Inner Cabinet the next day, was that under the threat of our legislation the TUC had moved farther and faster in the previous two weeks than in all the past forty years.

On inter-union disputes the TUC went a very long way. The document went far beyond the narrow issue of inter-union strikes, damaging and frustrating though they were; it covered such issues as recognition, where an employer had to decide which of two or more unions he should recognise for negotiating purposes, and the transfer of workers from one union to another, following a decision on recognition. The major step forward, in the surrender of the sovereignty of individual unions, was the new power to be given to the TUC to intervene in any dispute arising from demarcation or other inter-union questions. The General Council was to be given power to issue an award binding on all the unions concerned. Refusal by an individual union to accept such a decision would mean that the General Council could either suspend the union from membership of the TUC or report it to Congress with a view to disaffiliation. This had been accepted by all the unions; Frank Cousins and Jack Jones both stressed to us how far the TUC had gone.

On the question of unofficial disputes and our proposals for a conciliation pause, the unions were clearly unwilling to go so far. The TUC was to be given powers to act on its own initiative in any unconstitutional strike which might have damaging effects on the economy as a whole, or in causing serious unemployment of other workers, not themselves party to the dispute. But, as I repeatedly stressed at this meeting, and at all the other prolonged discussions up to and including that of the 18th June 1969, there was still no follow-through, no specific programme of action. The General Council had proposed to the CBI that a joint 'fire-fighting' party be sent to deal with the stoppage, but the CBI had turned it down. Would the TUC, I asked, itself send in a team to secure a return to work? Or could it call in the union concerned and ask it to take action? If the union refused to act with determination, would this too be a matter for reporting to Congress? Again, suppose the union did take action but its instructions were ignored by the strikers, would the union be required to discipline them; to suspend or expel them – with all that this might mean in a closed-shop establishment – again under threat of disaffiliation if it were half-hearted? It was clear that the TUC was not prepared to press such action with the same vigour it was ready to employ against a union which failed to act on a demarcation award. It was emphatic that, if an unofficial dispute had been caused by an arbitrary dismissal or by a unilateral change in working practices involving redundancies, there should be a return to the *status quo*, including a return to work, pending negotiations. But there was no indication that employers would agree; the proposal had been specifically rejected in negotiations for a new procedure agreement in the engineering industry. I pointed out that it could be required of the employer under our proposed legislation. To balance this, there would have to be a reversion to the *status quo* in the sense of a return to normal working. While the TUC accepted the principle of this and the engineering unions were prepared to accept it in the new engineering agreement, it was reluctant to give specific commitments to use its rule-book powers to enforce a return to work in every individual case.

On the Wednesday, 14th May, we had the last of the six PLP meetings on the industrial relations issue. In contrast to earlier meetings, a majority of those who spoke demanded action by the Government, in default of a satisfactory response by the TUC. Manny Shinwell, with the support of Douglas Houghton, called on all MPs to 'belt-up' – his words – while negotiations were continuing.

That evening, Vic Feather came to see me. He was as always in a friendly and co-operative mood. He had with him an addendum to the section in the draft document on unconstitutional strikes; it was a big move forward, but not enough. There was still no follow-through in the sense of union guarantees to use every penalty in the rule book to enforce compliance with a TUC call for a return to work. But it was well drafted, and would convince many trade union group MPs that the TUC meant business. Indeed, the wording in the draft which said that 'the TUC will *expect* affiliated unions...' had been amended by the General Council, by the substitution of 'require' for 'expect'. I said we greatly welcomed this move and would consider it, but that in my view it was still not enough. He mentioned, not in any threatening way, a danger he had deduced from some of the General Council discussions: that if we went ahead with the 'penal clauses' the TUC would drop all their own proposals. I pointed out that this would totally destroy their credibility and would lay them open to the charge that their newly-expressed concern about the damage strikes were causing was no more than a response to the threat of legislation; indeed, if the legislation were dropped, the TUC, I said, would 'go back to sleep'.

Barbara Castle and I were due to meet the General Council the following Wednesday, 21st May. After that it would be only a fortnight till the emergency Congress at Croydon. Vic Feather suggested that in that interval I should have a private meeting with himself, the TUC chairman (John Newton), Jack Jones and Hugh Scanlon. I readily agreed, but said that Barbara Castle must be there; or, since she was due to go abroad at Whitsun, Roy Jenkins should attend in her place. I was a little concerned at a number of press reports, totally untrue, suggesting that I was ready to do a deal behind Barbara Castle's back, or even that I was being held in check only by threats of her resignation. All these stories were false. At every stage in the discussions I was at least as demanding as she was.

It was too late to telephone her that night, but, as she was leaving next day for her constituency, I arranged to speak to her early in the morning, and to have a copy of the new TUC text awaiting her at Euston. She was concerned about the hint that the TUC would not go forward with their own proposals if we legislated. Though we had not yet seen the morning papers, this danger was clearly mirrored in them. By this time both she and I felt that we had secured more from the TUC on inter-union disputes than could be gained from any possible legislation. But this was not the case on unconstitutional stoppages.

By the Monday there was fresh trouble over Dick Crossman. He had been subjected to a full hour of questions in the House, and was much pressed about teeth and spectacles, and what the PLP Health group members referred to as the 'alienation' of funds from health to education. In the course of the questioning, and greatly exasperated, he said that no minister could 'alienate' without getting into trouble with his permanent secretary. This caused a fresh explosion, much headlined in the press next morning. Dick Crossman was very low and telephoned me. I said that, as I interpreted him, he was technically right, or what was the machinery of the Comptroller and Auditor-General, the Public Accounts committee, for? The responsibility was laid on Accounting Officers (permanent secretaries) to ensure that not a penny voted by Parliament for any particular spending programme was spent on any other purposes. As I had a question which was close to this subject, I said that I would put it right, though I told him that it was a long way down the Order Paper and might not be reached. He besought me – if it were not reached – to ask leave to answer it after questions. I said I would do better to leave it; I was bound to have a chance of dealing with it on a major television programme on the Tuesday evening. So, in the event, it proved, and Dick Crossman telephoned me long before I was awake the next morning to offer his thanks.

Douglas Houghton then came to see me. He was concerned about a row in which he had been involved with Dick Crossman, following press stories that Dick had implied in the House that his authorised briefing of the press about a PLP discussion of health charges was inaccurate. There was never anything in this, and peace soon reigned. But Douglas was anxious to plan the PLP handling of the Bill, should it be introduced.

I had a brief sleep before my television broadcast which was a BBC innovation involving forty minutes' interviewing in depth, by a single interviewer able to pursue his questions on any subject to the very end. This went well – quite apart from relieving Dick Crossman's anxieties – and I was able to spell out the position we had reached about the Bill and our determination to proceed unless the TUC came up with something likely to be as effective.

That morning the Inner Cabinet met to decide our next step. I felt it right to tell its members of Vic Feather's proposal for a meeting with Jack Jones and Hugh Scanlon, which I had arranged for Sunday, 1st June, at Chequers. The Inner Cabinet agreed to meet again on the Sunday night, 8th June, after the Croydon conference and immediately before the resumption of Parliament. This would be followed by the meeting which Barbara Castle and I were to hold with the General Council on Monday, 9th June, after which the Inner Cabinet would meet again, followed by the full Cabinet. If we had not received evidence of an adequate move forward by the TUC, the Bill would be introduced into Parliament on the Tuesday and published the following day.

The following day, 21st May, Barbara Castle and I met the TUC General Council again. She told me she would like to be at the Chequers meeting and it was agreed to bring her back from her holiday in Italy. A number of the TUC members were extremely complimentary about the broadcast. Again, for two hours, we went over the ground; I was simply asking them to tighten up the provisions on unconstitutional strikes to correspond with the powers they were taking on inter-union disputes. But no agreement was reached. We confirmed our arrangement to meet after Croydon to make a joint appraisal of the situation in the light of the conference. But they were left in no doubt that we should move immediately to the introduction of legislation if the TUC failed to come up with something firm and binding.

The Cabinet met the following morning and reviewed progress. Most of my colleagues went off for Whitsun. I had an enjoyable industrial occasion to attend in Manchester, when some fifty Queen's Award winners, large firms and small, shop stewards and workers at the bench, as well as executives, were entertained by the *Daily Mirror*. It gave a good opportunity, even at a bank holiday weekend, to review our, by this time, remarkable export progress.

The Chequers dinner with TUC representatives took place on 1st

x

June. It was friendly throughout, but tough. Hugh Scanlon and Jack Jones warned us against an excessive preoccupation with unofficial strikes. As power shifted more and more from the centre, they said, to the shop-floor, there would be more ferment at factory level. This would be exacerbated by the fact of the legislation and lead to greater and, they argued, irresistible pressure to turn local unofficial action into officially recognised disputes.

Indeed, Hugh Scanlon said, in the negotiations within the engineering industry for new procedures, negotiating and disputes machinery, to replace the fifty-year-old York Agreement, the employers were insisting that local disputes should be settled locally, instead of taking contested cases to York. This, in his view, would result in many more local disputes being declared official. I stressed and stressed again the challenge to them, and to us, of the Girling-type strike, where Hugh Scanlon himself had been rebuffed by a handful of strikers, even though thousands of his union's members were thrown out of work by the actions of a few. One reply to this worried me: Hugh Scanlon's comment that any fines imposed would be met by sympathetic demonstrations, even by strikes and a whip-round in the area to pay the fines. I knew the militants of Merseyside well enough to know that this would be extremely likely there, and no legislation – ours or the proposed Conservative legislation – could deal with it.

Hugh Scanlon emphasised the problems in his own union, where the Executive had carried by four votes to three a scatty motion requiring the union's vote at Croydon to be thrown against the TUC's proposals, despite his own endorsement of them at the General Council. His trouble was that his National Committee, the engineers' equivalent of an annual conference, had gone on record against any union involvement, whether in the operation of legislation or the acceptance of a TUC discipline. While he might with difficulty secure a reversal of the Executive vote on the Croydon proposals, any pressure to go further would mean a recall conference, where he could not hope to secure acceptance of the proposed TUC powers.

After several hours of discussion we adjourned, and I repeated that at the post-Croydon meetings we would expect a further move by the TUC itself, involving a readiness by its constituent unions to discipline those responsible for unconstitutional action.

Croydon carried the TUC proposal almost unanimously, with overwhelming votes affirming that the trade union movement was unalterably opposed to the proposal that the Government should take powers to impose statutory financial penalties on workpeople or on trade unions in connection either with industrial disputes or with the compulsory registration by trade unions of their rules.

The following Friday, 6th June, I spent the day touring the Tyne shipyards: prosperous, booming, reflecting the success of our interventionist policies. In the evening, Vic Feather came to see me. We discussed the handling of the meeting with the General Council on the following Monday. He was still prepared to help, while making clear that they could not go along with legislation, even on what had come to be known as the 'cold storage proposal'. This was a suggestion which we had examined under which powers would be taken in the Bill but not put into immediate effect. As with Part IV of the Prices and Incomes Act, it could be activated only by specific parliamentary approval: this would give time for the TUC to make its own proposals effective. Only if it failed to do so would the Government ask Parliament to bring the Act's provisions into force.

When we met at Downing Street on the Monday, 9th June, a number of the moderate members of the General Council showed their deep concern about the danger of a split within the Labour movement. But Barbara Castle and I had agreed with Vic Feather to keep the meeting short; to hear their views, following their Croydon Congress, to say we would report them to our colleagues, and to meet again. This went according to plan. But again we warned that unless the TUC was prepared to strengthen its powers for dealing with unconstitutional strikes, legislation would have to be introduced.

The Management committee of the Cabinet met the same day to receive our report, followed by the full Cabinet. This went well, and we were authorised to continue our talks with the TUC. Press stories that Roy Jenkins – who had insisted on the announcement of early legislation in his Budget speech – was weakening were resolutely denied and to my certain knowledge Roy went to great lengths to ensure that the press were so informed.

On the evening of Tuesday, 10th June, we met Vic Feather again. We pressed him further on the Croydon paragraph which related to unconstitutional strikes and asked yet again that it be redrafted on the same basis as that dealing with inter-union disputes. He suggested – and this was new – that we should turn our attention to the idea of a declaratory paragraph being added to the Rules; for the decisive move on inter-union disputes had meant a change of Rule 12. Barbara Castle, sharp as a needle, said that all we needed was a corresponding amendment to Rule 11, dealing with the issues still under dispute and we could all forget about the controversial clauses in the proposed legislation.

I raised with Vic Feather the difficulty of negotiating with a body of forty-one members and asked if they could appoint a negotiating committee? He agreed, and I accordingly proposed this at the meeting with the General Council the following day, 11th June.

It was accepted and Vic Feather, Sir Frederick Hayday, Alfred Allen, Sydney Greene, Hugh Scanlon and Jack Jones were appointed. They had prepared a form of words, which we found woolly and inadequate, designed to give a more detailed interpretation of Rule 11. Any amendment to Rule 11 they rejected as beyond their powers. 'Clarification' was all, and this they offered in the form of a circular to affiliated organisations.

I told them that, without prejudice to our demand for a rule change, their document was too weak. It talked of 'advice' from the General Council to the individual unions: 'advice' described the relationship between a servant and a master, not that between a master and a servant. On inter-union disputes, the word had been 'requirement'; on other aspects of Rule 11 it was 'obligations'.

We adjourned till the following day, when I said that we were prepared to drop those parts of the legislation which they found controversial if they would agree to a 'rule-change'. We did not, of course, propose to drop all the legislation, since there were many proposals, deriving directly from Donovan, or emerging from our post-Donovan discussions with both sides of industry, which must improve industrial relations and negotiating and disputes procedures. But the so-called 'penal clauses' we were prepared – I underlined for the hundredth time – to drop, given an adequate move by them. If they refused we should have to take our own decision, either by implementing the existing proposals, or others equally effective. What I had in mind as an alternative was a proposal we were considering for legislation to prescribe 'Model Rules', including rules to deal with disruptive action, as a condition for registration.

The following Monday, 16th June, I was in Eastbourne all day for a meeting of the Socialist International, marked by successful private meetings with Golda Meir, Prime Minister of Israel, and Willy Brandt. In the evening I returned to London, ready for the Cabinet meeting the following day, where – we had agreed – our final decision was to be taken.

Throughout this book with one justifiable exception – that relating to South Africa – I have maintained the secrecy and collective responsibility of Cabinet. In the case of the Cabinet of 17th June 1969, I feel it wrong to reveal the attitudes of individual ministers, despite the fact that press stories later in the week purported to inform readers – wrongly as it turned out – about the over-all Cabinet position.

But, since a great deal has been written, claiming to describe the view taken by the Cabinet as a whole, I must make this one further exception to dispel the error which has been propagated.

The Cabinet met in the morning at No. 10, and in the afternoon, because of expected divisions in Parliament, we adjourned to my room at the House. This room is too small, overcrowded and uncomfortable, and, I had long learnt, not the best place for conducting business.

It is a fact that at the morning Cabinet many ministers urged that we

should drop all ideas of legislation and be content to accept the tremendous moves forward which the imminence of legislation had forced the
TUC to take. A number of them suggested that we should settle for a
'letter of intent'. I was having none of this. Hawk-eyed opponents of the
Bill were probably right in their calculations that, by lunch-time, a
majority of the Cabinet had expressed either their opposition to the
Bill, or at least strong reservations about it. But after Cabinet, one or
two colleagues spoke to me, some telephoned, one or two sent me brief
notes and others did so in the afternoon. If, they said, I was insisting on
legislation, they were with me all the way.

To some extent, therefore, the afternoon meeting was not so critical
as most commentators have subsequently suggested. They could not know
the line-up, as I did. But I had one disadvantage, a fixed date at 7.00 p.m.
with a very anxious trade union group. Prime Ministers with a critical
meeting should avoid being bound in this way. At 6.00 p.m. I suggested
that the Cabinet might need more time – but Barbara Castle and I had
to meet the General Council the next morning. Should I perhaps postpone the meeting? But provincial members of the General Council were
already on the way to London. Should I then cancel the meeting with
the trade union group? No, it was urged; that might be taken as implying
divided counsels in Cabinet. At five minutes to seven an attempt was
made to take a decision then and there – in favour of shelving the legislation. This was rejected. I summed up. I would address the group, but
not show our hand. This would be difficult but in the circumstances it
was right. For my part, and I knew I spoke for Barbara Castle and others,
the General Council would be told again that, in default of a binding
change in their rules, the legislation would be introduced. If that appeal
failed, the Cabinet would meet the following day at noon and we should
take a firm decision.

My meeting with the trade union group was unsatisfactory from their
point of view. I had intended to speak for a few minutes but went on
for forty. I briefly answered questions, but said that negotiations were
proceeding and I felt that I should say as little as possible. It was an
anxious group I left behind.

That night I met Vic Feather and told him how the situation stood.
And, lest he or others should receive messages that I could not carry the
Cabinet, I told him that I held the proxies. Was a rule-change out of
the question? To my surprise, he said it was not. But, he said, our drafting the previous Thursday gave the impression that the TUC would have
to intervene, with the threat of disciplining recalcitrant unions, in every
stoppage. We discussed possible redrafts.

The next morning we met the General Council. I began by rehearsing
the events which had led up to the meeting. Three courses were open:
legislation on the lines we had proposed; an alternative form of legislation,

omitting the penal clauses but involving the statutory imposition of effective clauses in their rule-books to deal with indiscipline, with the sanction that unions failing to do so would lose the protection accorded to them by the 1906 Act; or a decision by them to alter their procedures on the lines we had suggested. The second course we had considered, and rejected. This brought great relief, as overnight they had feared that this would be our decision. The legislation, I said, must therefore now go ahead, unless they were prepared to move.

It was Rule 11 that we were concerned with. I recognised their anxieties about our earlier formulation, and said that we had a new draft in preparation. After a brief exchange they suggested an adjournment, while we finalised the draft.

Barbara Castle's officials were giving thought to what our course should be if the TUC refused to contemplate a rule-change. One of them brightly suggested that we might agree to an offer by the TUC to print in its Rules our draft as a note of interpretation. Barbara and others were attracted by this. I killed it by saying the headline would be 'Wilson trades legislation for a footnote'.

The General Council then proposed that we should meet the negotiating committee which they had set up the previous week. They were still opposed to a rule-change as such, Alf Allen finally describing it as 'not a runner'. Fred Hayday and other stalwarts supported him, but were at pains to impress on us how specific and binding was the undertaking they were prepared to make. They were, Fred Hayday said, prepared to use our words subject to scrutinising them in detail, and then to enter into 'a solemn and binding undertaking to carry them out'. Vic Feather said that, in practical terms, this would carry greater force than a change in the rules.

Hugh Scanlon then made an impressive point which had obviously already worried his colleagues, and which now, as she said to me, moved Barbara Castle very considerably. He had, he said, been forced to recall his National Committee in order to reverse the adverse vote of the Executive on the granting of powers to the TUC. Even so, he had only carried the day by four votes out of some sixty-odd members. By a decision of that body he had to recall them if there were to be any variations in TUC Rules, going beyond those (to Rule 12) agreed at Croydon. If such a meeting were called, it was virtually certain that he would not only fail to carry the proposed further amendments to the Rules, but would go down to defeat on the rule-changes already agreed. The whole Croydon document and the procedures agreed to both on inter-union disputes and on official stoppages would be destroyed. The other TUC leaders, particularly the right-wingers, were extremely alarmed at this, for without the engineers, and thus the all-important engineering industry, the new procedures would be worthless.

Jack Jones then made an important contribution. He said that we probably did not understand what, under TUC procedures, would be involved in a 'binding agreement'. It would be reported to Congress, and on endorsement, would become 'a rule of Congress'. We might understand better if we were reminded that the Bridlington Regulations of 1939 had, in this way, become 'a rule of Congress', and certainly the Bridlington Regulations, governing inter-union relations, were the most binding Congress had ever imposed. This point was strongly emphasised by the others.

It was getting near to lunch-time, and the rest of the Council, upstairs, were no doubt by this time restive and hungry. I proposed an adjournment for food. Barbara Castle, her officials and I went up to my study to assess the situation. Barbara was clearly attracted by the thought of a Bridlington-type binding agreement, and now summarily rejected the 'footnote' proposal. She came out strongly for the new proposal. This too has to be said, because yet another legend has persisted from that day, repeated and obviously believed by the Conservative press, and assiduously spread in successive speeches by Mr Heath; that I weakened, and forced her to accept. Mr Heath's calculated appeal to masculine chivalry has gained wide support, but unfortunately it was based on a total distortion.

During the lunch-break, we decided to draft for the General Council the terms of a clear statement to be accepted by them as a binding undertaking. At Barbara Castle's suggestion we called the Attorney-General over from his lunch and sat down with him to finalise our own rough draft. The Cabinet having been successively stood down from noon to 12.30, and from 12.30 to 2.30 was now called for 4.00 p.m.

A little after 2.15, the time we had agreed for resuming the talks, Vic Feather asked to meet Barbara Castle and me. We met in the small reception room at No. 10. He emphasised three things:

(1) that he could not get agreement to a rule-change as such;
(2) that what Fred Hayday and others had proposed was more binding and effective from our point of view; and
(3) that he could now confirm that such an undertaking would be unanimous. The importance of this he wanted us to realise: Fred Hayday, as he said, had underlined that never in their history had the TUC made such a proposal, unanimously agreed by the General Council's more than forty members, and totally binding.

I told him that we would be ready to meet his main team in a few minutes, but scrupulously avoided giving him any idea that we were even considering their proposal. When the meeting resumed, ten minutes later, they were obviously totally depressed as a result of what their General Secretary had told them.

I opened the discussion and stressed strongly what we required. But, mentioning that we had been impressed, as they had, by the Scanlon warning, I said that we were prepared to consider a binding undertaking and to recommend it to the Cabinet, provided it was clear, specific, and met all the points on which we had insisted. It was agreed that their committee of seven should meet with us again.

We presented them with our draft and left them to consider it. This took some forty minutes. Before we rejoined them, Barbara Castle and I had agreed that neither of us would accept any amendments, but that we should again withdraw to consider them, with the expert advice both of the Attorney and her DEP officials. The TUC amendments were, in fact, quite small, mainly drafting improvements. They accepted our proposal that 'rule of Congress' be amended to equate the status of their undertaking with the force of the Bridlington Regulations.

Meanwhile Cabinet had assembled. I had them directed to the Cabinet Room, so that there could be no prior knowledge of how things were going as the result of a chance meeting with a roving member of the General Council, which was similarly corralled in the State dining-room.

I told Vic Feather that, before we met, I wanted to be assured of the unanimity he had promised. When we met again, just after 5.00 p.m., he reported that the General Council was unanimous, that the draft had been accepted without amendment and that in the report to Congress the names of all the members of the Council would be appended to it.

There was a changed atmosphere and I stressed again that there must now be an all-out effort, by close relations between Government and both sides of industry, to ensure that the full force deriving from the agreement was directed to dealing with the strike problem. Barbara Castle and I then went to report to Cabinet.

It was by this time 5.15. Our colleagues had waited all day to be summoned to No. 10 and had been waiting in the Cabinet room for over an hour. A colleague later said that I went in looking like thunder, and that Barbara Castle was drawn and white. If that were so, she is a marvellous actress for she was pleased with the commitment the TUC had entered into.

I began by recalling the ending of the Tuesday Cabinet when I had said that Barbara and I would handle the discussions with the TUC in the manner we considered right, and that the Cabinet would then be free to accept or reject the outcome, with all that might mean. Accordingly we had used to the full our intention to introduce legislation if no agreement could be reached. Equally we had made clear that a letter of intent, such as some of our colleagues had proposed, would be quite unacceptable. I said that I took it we had full Cabinet support in taking this line? There was no demur.

I then reported that having negotiated all day within those terms of reference, it was now for the Cabinet to accept or reject our conclusion. What they had, in fact, to accept or reject was the ratification of the agreement we had reached a few minutes earlier upstairs. I made clear that it was a decision. They could accept it or repudiate it.

One enthusiast shouted 'agreed'. I said he had better hear it first. I then read it out, together with the text of the TUC undertaking. There was great excitement, even cheers, as I went on reading and at the end an ovation unparalleled at Cabinet meetings so far as my experience goes. But before our colleagues were allowed to speak, Barbara Castle insisted on intervening. She dressed down the whole Cabinet for placing me in this position: they had left me without a card in my hand, and I had taken the ace, she said.

Michael Stewart, followed by Jim Callaghan, then simply expressed the congratulations of the Cabinet, and their satisfaction at the outcome. Others wanted to join in, but Barbara Castle and I had work to do. There was a joint press conference, followed by a television programme with Barbara and Vic Feather; I had to ask the press to release Barbara as a prior hairdressing appointment was a categorical imperative for her.

Later in the evening I addressed the PLP meeting who were, predictably, ecstatic. When Douglas Houghton said I would answer questions, there was a general shout of 'No'. I knew that the press the next morning would be less ecstatic. We were, after all, in a pre-election atmosphere.

'Surrender, 69' was the headline of the *Daily Express*, 'Surrender' (undated) that of the *Daily Mail*; the *Sun* and *Daily Mirror* were more judicious, and the *Guardian*, which had been pressing me to settle for far less than I was able to announce, seemed to have somewhat lost its bearings. The *Daily Telegraph* was fairer than *The Times*.

In the afternoon I announced the agreement in the House, in answer to three questions already on the Order Paper, amid cheers from our side and cat-calls and twittering from the Opposition.

By the Friday, 20th June, press comment had accelerated in hostility, but by this time I was on my way to South Wales. I had been invited to open the new Aberfan school, to replace the one destroyed in the tragedy of October 1966. I have never had to make a more difficult speech. So many of the children in the school were, by this time, just the same age as their elder brothers and sisters who had died on that ghastly October day in 1966. How far one should refer to the disaster and underline Aberfan's inability to escape from its horror, how far to look to a future of hope – and the parents who were present and the surviving teachers were living equally in the horror of the past and in hope of the future – was the most poignant of decisions. Briefly recalling that October night in Aberfan, I decided to speak of the future.

The warmth of reception Mary and I were given in the streets was in sharp contrast to all that was being said and written in London. One eminent political editor of Merthyr antecedents, John Beavan of the *Daily Mirror*, had gone with me. He was amazed at our reception, though I thought that this was mainly due to appreciation of the fact that I had been in Aberfan on the night of the disaster. But as we drove east, with cheering crowds at every crossing, and as we fought our way into Cartef Aneurin Bevan at Tredegar – the old people's home I was due to open – and on to a great open-air reception, John Beavan found it hard to reconcile the political realities of the grass-roots Labour movement with the currently fashionable comments of those who rarely moved outside the Westminster hot-house. Outside London it had been like this since 1964.

The issues posed in Barbara Castle's White Paper *In Place of Strife* had therefore been settled by a decision to introduce legislation to enact the positive provisions of the Donovan Report, and by our decision of 18th June to follow Donovan in not proceeding with punitive legislation. For good or ill, we had accepted the views of the TUC but only because, under the catalytic action of our legislative proposals, they had 'moved forward forty years in a month'. They had accepted responsibility for dealing not only with the inter-union disputes with which they were best fitted to deal, but also with unconstitutional strikes in a situation where the shop-floor was becoming increasingly militant and determined. It was beyond the hope of any of us that the new TUC procedures would be capable of averting every threatened strike, or speedily to settle every case where embittered men had recourse to strike action. But neither could our proposed legislation have been so capable, still less the legalistic proposals which the Conservative party were peddling.

The advance we had won was the unanimous decision of the TUC to use its powers both in inter-union and in unofficial disputes. Although there would be cases that neither it nor any other agency could hope to settle, there would also be a large number of cases where none but the TUC would have the authority or power to settle.

Strikes did not diminish in number, scale or duration, following the agreement of June 1969, any more than in an increasingly militant situation abroad, where legal restraints operate. But, in that period, the TUC's new powers, aided by some valuable procedure agreements, such as those in shipbuilding, reduced the number of inter-union disputes to a fraction of those experienced in preceding years. Unconstitutional strikes, almost all of them strikes which no legislation could have prevented or which the fussy legalism of the Conservative proposals would have aggravated, were settled speedily and without fuss by the new TUC fire-fighting machinery. All the spectacular strikes in which they failed were disputes where our legislation, directed mainly against unofficial strikes, would have been ineffective or where, equally, the Conservative panacea would have been more likely to exacerbate than to settle the dispute.

The year from the agreement of 18th June 1969, to the General Election of June 1970, was too short to show what the TUC could have achieved. But in case after case where it did intervene, in conditions where no Government, no legislation, could have had any assurance of success, they were successful. The reason why the TUC was involved was because the Downing Street undertaking, itself the direct result of *In Place of Strife*, had created a new and hopeful dimension in industrial relations. As industrial relations, in political speeches and press comments, became more and more an issue in the forthcoming election – with Mr Heath's highly-publicised union-bashing on the eve of each by-election or GLC and other local elections – one question began to assume more importance. Were the Conservatives, for electoral purposes, prepared to put at risk what had been a great achievement between Government and TUC, to sacrifice this new dimension, and make industrial relations the casualty of a drive for political power? All the signs, as the election drew near, were that they were prepared to act in this way. The final answer was not to emerge until after the election, when the TUC's repeated willingness to help avert a strike, or to settle a strike once it had begun, was rudely rebuffed.

Britain's statistics showing the number of strikes, the number of workers affected and the number of man-days lost, are respected internationally for their comprehensiveness and accuracy. But no statistics can show how many strikes could have been avoided since June 1970, or how many of those still to afflict us could similarly be averted, if that new dimension of industrial self-discipline, with all its limitations, all its imperfections, had not been wantonly sacrificed to deliberate and divisive conflict. The dock strike of July 1970, with its attendant State of Emergency, could certainly have been avoided, with no higher wage settlement than that which was ultimately reached and so, also, probably, could the public service workers' (dustmen's) strike, had the new Conservative Government sought to act in the spirit of the Downing Street settlement of June 1969.

This was not all that has been cast away. The TUC's powers and Victor Feather's new interventionist approach made it possible in disputes which were being dealt with by other agencies (such as the use of DEP conciliation or direct negotiating between the parties) for the TUC to take an initiative in bringing the unions together in pursuit of a common, and usually moderate, line.

One example was the newspaper strike in the middle of the 1970 General Election. After Downing Street intervention to end a procedural deadlock resulting from the unwillingness of all the unions to sit round the table with the employers, I telephoned Victor Feather to come to No. 10 once the parties were talking again. His task was to persuade the four unions – five if one counts the two divisions of SOGAT – to agree on a common policy and a common settlement, which unaided by TUC intervention might have taken a very long time. Similarly, during the power dispute of December 1970; in the decision of the electricity unions to resume normal working, following the decision to set up a Court of Inquiry, TUC intervention was decisive in getting the more militant unions to follow the lead of the electricians' union.

This type of action, no less than the effective power of the TUC to settle inter-union disputes, could have been, over a period, one of the most rewarding results of the events of 18th June 1969. It is an essential constituent in any long-term contribution to the solution of Britain's industrial relations problems. Unfortunately, the new and 'abrasive' attitudes which followed the events of the other 18th June – 1970 – must have the costly effect of diminishing the TUC's power to act. Carborundum is not the most appropriate material for lubricating the intricate and delicate mechanism of Britain's system of industrial relations.

Chapter 32

The Budget – the Hunt Report – Spanish action over Gibraltar – emergency debate on Northern Ireland – Major Chichester-Clark succeeds Captain O'Neill – Upper Clyde shipbuilders – the Maud Report – parliamentary boundaries – Liberal victory at Ladywood – the investiture of the Prince of Wales

THE House had met after Easter with the main attention of MPs still concentrated upon the Government's industrial reform proposals. Our people had been inevitably depressed by three further by-elections, on 27th March, the results of which had reached me while I was in Lagos. Two were safe Conservative seats; in Brighton Pavilion their 1966 majority rose from 6,354 to 12,982, and in Weston-super-Mare it increased from 12,393 to 20,472, with Labour falling into third place behind the Liberals. In Walthamstow East, a marginal seat gained by us in 1966, a Labour majority of 1,807 gave place to a Conservative majority of 5,479. Over the three, the anti-Labour swing was around fifteen-and-a-half per cent, better than a year earlier but indicating that we still had a long way to go. In all three, the worsening was caused by a severe drop in Labour votes, the Conservatives only slightly increasing their poll in Brighton and Weston-super-Mare and slightly reducing it in Walthamstow.

The post-Easter session of the Commons was dominated by Roy Jenkins's Budget and the subsequent debate on it. Throughout the previous months, from Christmas onwards, the Chancellor had kept me in touch about the information he was receiving on the prospective Budget out-turn, and the advice he was getting on the forward strategy, together with the way his mind was working – a process enlivened by a parliamentary pantomime mounted by Sir Gerald Nabarro, whose fantasies about the Chancellor's intentions on the road tax were rudely dissipated by the report of the Select Committee appointed to inquire into his allegations.

The Chancellor and I would dearly have liked to have done something in the Budget to relieve taxation, preferably income tax. The overseas trade and payments position was moving firmly into surplus, but we were right not to place it at risk by any premature easement: the Chancellor's two years' hard slog still had a year to go. He decided to reinforce his earlier measures by increasing tax revenue by £270 millions in 1969–70, £340 millions in the first full year.

He presented his Budget on 15th April.

Beginning his proposals with measures which were designed to reform the tax system rather than to provide additional revenue, he announced major changes in the law relating to estate duty, particularly in the field of settled property and discretionary trusts. He eased the rate of duty on smaller estates by raising the exemption limit from £5,000 to £10,000. For larger estates he introduced a series of rising scales on each 'slice' of the estate, in place of the much criticised 'slab system' – under which a single rate applied to the whole estate – with no loss or gain in revenue, but with a clear gain in equity. This was followed by minor changes in the betting and gaming duties.

There was no change in indirect taxation – spirits, tobacco, and beer – which had in any case been raised by the use of the regulator the previous November. But, saying it was 'very much against my own personal inclination', the Chancellor raised the duty on wine, the consumption of which had been rising rapidly. Though the purchase tax rates were left unchanged, one or two minor items were brought into its ambit to remove anomalies. The duties on hydrocarbons was increased, involving 2d a gallon more on the price of petrol.

On direct taxation, he increased corporation tax from $42\frac{1}{2}$ per cent to 45 per cent, yielding £75 millions in 1969–70, and £120 millions in a full year, and bringing our rate into line with those of the US, Canada, Australia, New Zealand, France, Germany, Belgium and the Netherlands. On the other hand, at a cost of £20 millions to the revenue in a full year, he made a number of substantial easements in the position of 'close companies', on which there had been strong representations ever since the introduction of corporation tax four years earlier.

But there was still a long way to go to reach his target. The Chancellor therefore proposed a still further increase in SET, raising the rate for an adult male employee from 37s 6d a week to 48s, representing an increased yield to the Board of Customs and Excise of £123 millions in 1969–70, and £130 millions in a full year, after taking credit for £6 millions net loss as a result of decisions to exclude certain activities from the coverage of the tax.

The Chancellor, indicating his clear desire, had it been possible, to make a substantial reduction in the burden of income tax, and, equally clearly indicating his hope to do so the following year, announced some changes at the margin designed to take 1,100,000 taxpayers out of the tax field, and to give relief to a further 600,000. In addition, he announced some individual reliefs in personal allowances for widows, widowers and others with an unaided responsibility for bringing up young children; an increase in the age exemption limits for taxpayers over sixty-five; and relief for elderly persons living on the income from their savings. Concluding, he announced new incentives in National Savings and the introduction of the new 'contractual savings' (SAYE) scheme, under which tax remission was granted against planned investments in National Savings out of earnings.

The total effect of the tax proposals, combined with the firm grip we were by this time exercising on the increase in Government expenditure, was to change radically the position of the Government as a borrower. A borrowing requirement of £1,956 millions in the financial year 1967–68 was reduced to one of £450 millions in 1968–69; in 1969–70 he aimed at a surplus large enough to increase the debt repayment – and in the event that is what he succeeded in doing. The revolution in the Government's position on internal borrowing was as great as that achieved in the move from record deficit to record surplus in our balance of payments position; indeed it was an important element in our improvement on trade and payments account. But as in the case of the other measures we had had to introduce to make Britain viable overseas, this insistence on austere and responsible financing was carried through only at high political cost.

The Budget had a good reception apart from a major explosion, both from the Conservatives and from our own Co-operative party members, over SET and the reaction to the 2d on petrol from the road-users.

Mr Heath described it as 'a dead-end budget by a fag-end Government'. He went further:

> There is not one single incentive to anyone in this country to make a greater effort to get exports. Is it not strange that there is not one suggestion in this Budget to deal with substitution of imports? ... Judged, then, by the two points which the Chancellor of the Exchequer first made – the whole question of increasing exports which requires incentives and substitution of imports which requires a new policy – this Budget must be condemned as a failure ...

He was reminded of these gloomy words when at the end of the financial year, 1st April 1969 to 31st March 1970, with which the Budget was dealing, Britain's balance of payments recorded the highest surplus in our trading history.

On 24th April the Government made its announcement about help for the 'intermediate areas', on which a committee headed by Sir Joseph Hunt had just submitted a report. These parts of the country, often referred to as 'grey' areas, were not development areas and, therefore, unable to benefit from the Local Employment Act, or from the successive improvements in assistance to development areas introduced since 1964. At the same time a number of them – there was inevitably argument about which should be included – were for one reason or another causing us anxiety, either because the existing level of unemployment was higher than was tolerable, or because of fears about the future, in some areas through prospective colliery closures.

The Government had received the Hunt Report some weeks earlier and I had chaired two meetings on it, before leaving the question for more detailed inter-departmental examination under Peter Shore's direction. I kept a very close interest in this and, a quite unusual procedure, nominated Michael Halls, my principal private secretary, to keep an eye on it for me. He had been for many years in charge of Board of Trade work on development area policy and, indeed, in 1960, after concern about regional unemployment had shaken the then Conservative Government, had been appointed by them as Special Expeditor on regional development, a job held concurrently with that of Board of Trade Regional Controller for the Midlands.

The Hunt committee had made some new and imaginative recommendations. It proposed that the whole of Yorkshire and Humberside and the north-west should qualify for a new form of assistance, a twenty-five per cent building grant for new projects, without any attempt to link them with new jobs: the motive was at least as much to get rid of some of the industrial dereliction, which was a disincentive to attracting new enterprise. These areas, it said, should also qualify for the training grants and direct training assistance already enjoyed by development areas. Second, in 'selected growth zones' within these regions, there should be Government industrial estates and factory building with supporting investment, including link roads. Third, for these two regions and also for the Nottinghamshire, Derbyshire and North Staffordshire sub-divisions of the east and west Midlands regions, there should be an eighty-five per cent grant for derelict land clearance, as in the development areas – and they recommended that land clearance should be speeded up. Fourth, control over the issue of industrial development certificates (idcs) should be relaxed throughout the country by raising the exemption limit from 5,000 to 10,000 square feet. Fifth, the Merseyside development area should be de-scheduled and put on the same basis for incentive as was proposed for the rest of the north-west region.

Our examination of the Report and its thoroughly factual presentation led us to disagree both with the delineation of the areas recommended for action and with the particular choice of assistance proposed.

We rejected the recommendation affecting Merseyside. I resisted this proposal not so much because I was a Merseyside MP but because I opposed, and always had opposed, de-scheduling. When the Conservative Government announced the de-scheduling of Dundee, in the early fifties, I denounced their decision and within a few months I was proved right. Merseyside, though the most prosperous of the development areas by 1969, was very vulnerable to sudden industrial shocks; with a high birth-rate and continued immigration from Ireland, a continual influx of new 'job opportunities' was needed to enable the area even to stand still. The closure or run-down, following industrial mergers, of a number of major factories in the following few months, together with the only narrowly-averted closure of the Cammell Laird shipbuilding yard and the crisis in the Mersey docks, showed how right we were to resist de-scheduling. This placed a limit on the savings on which Hunt had counted for applying financial help elsewhere. Working on a figure of an additional £20 millions a year for helping intermediate areas, in part to be produced by savings in the still rapidly expanding development areas, we agreed on a programme which was announced to Parliament by Peter Shore on 24th April.

Peter Shore announced our decision on new intermediate areas – the Yorkshire coalfield, the Erewash valley area of Derbyshire, parts of Humberside, the main industrial areas of north-east Lancashire east of the proposed new town, a considerable part of south-east Wales, Leith and Plymouth. For these areas, most of the assistance available under the Local Employment Acts was made available – namely, grants at twenty-five per cent of factory building costs, Government-built factories, whether advance factories or custom-built establishments to meet the specific needs of individual manufacturers, and the full range of development area training grants and other training assistance together with assistance for the transfer of key workers. 'Infrastructure' grants, for example for roads in certain areas, help with housing, and, within the enlarged national programme, for derelict land clearance, were announced. Certain of the new intermediate areas in the east Midlands, north Staffordshire and Yorkshire were to qualify for a seventy-five per cent derelict land clearance grant.

The new intermediate area would receive priority in idcs together with development areas; in the rest of the north-west and in the Yorkshire and Humberside areas, control would be liberally administered wherever new factory development was required because of the local employment situation. We rejected the proposal to raise the idcs exemption limit in the more prosperous areas to 10,000 square feet, but the policy would be more liberally administered in new towns and overspill areas. Peter Shore announced that these decisions would be discussed in detail with the Regional Economic Planning Councils – including the exact boundaries of the new intermediate areas – and a further announcement made when the consultations were complete. His further statement was made on 25th June.

Throughout this period, international events, and increasingly Northern Ireland, pressed upon us.

The committee of ministers of the Council of Europe met in London on 6th May, as part of the celebrations of the twentieth anniversary of the Council's foundation. The principal item on the agenda was the question of Greece's membership of the Council. The Greek record on human rights since the take-over by the Colonels in April 1967 was appalling, and the Human Rights Commission was preparing a report on the evidence supplied from inside Greece. In January, the Consultative Assembly of parliamentarians at Strasbourg had passed a resolution calling for the expulsion of Greece from the Council, in default of a speedy restoration of human rights. The ministerial committee decided formally to bring the Assembly resolution to the attention of the Greek Government, to await the report of the Human Rights Commission and, if that were unfavourable and Greece refused to put her house in order, to take a decision at the next meeting. When the committee next met, in December, there had been no improvement, and Greece narrowly avoided expulsion, for which Britain and other countries were pressing, by withdrawing from the Council.

There was continuing trouble over Gibraltar. Spain, rejecting our proposal to refer the dispute to the International Court, continued her policy of intensified harassment. On 30th May, a new constitution for the Rock was promulgated, providing for a greater degree of devolution in domestic matters to Gibraltar's ministers. No change whatsoever was involved in her international status. That did not prevent the Spanish Government from issuing a communiqué describing the constitutional changes as being 'in... open disregard of United Nations resolutions and contrary to the Treaty of Utrecht...'. Nor did it prevent them from completely closing the land frontier between Spain and Gibraltar. Nearly 5,000 Spanish workers, thirty per cent of Gibraltar's labour force, were cut off from their jobs on the Rock.

We had no intention of yielding to this kind of blackmail. The Governor of Gibraltar and the military authorities there, as well as the Gibraltarian ministers, responded quickly to the crisis. As a result, life went on in a fairly normal way and North African workers gained where Spanish workers lost. The worst effect of the cumulative restrictions was to cut off tourists visiting Gibraltar while on holiday in Spain. But, in compensation, Gibraltar was becoming a busy port of call for ships on their long journey round the Cape. In particular, Soviet fishing and other vessels made it a regular haven and local shopkeepers began to build up a thriving trade: their shop-fronts had notices and advertisements in Russian.

The Northern Ireland situation was progressively deteriorating. Following my meeting with Captain O'Neill on 5th August 1966, when he had asked for a short period for Ulster to assimilate his earlier reforms, we had held regular meetings. At the first of these, on 12th January 1967, he was accompanied by two of his hard-liners, Mr Brian Faulkner and Mr William Craig. Roy Jenkins, then Home Secretary, and I took the opportunity to bring home to them our determination to see the reforms pressed home. Captain O'Neill was true to the undertakings he had given us. From the beginning of 1967 he pressed on with domestic reforms, particularly in the field of local government electoral law, and housing. He was under constant pressure from the extremist section of his Stormont party and this came to a head, in a dangerous sense, for the first time, in April 1967, when he dismissed the right-wing Agriculture Minister, Mr Harry West, not on political grounds but on a matter which, Captain O'Neill said in Parliament, raised the question of a conflict of interest. Denounced by the octogenarian former Premier, Lord Brookeborough, and attacked on all sides by right-wing Orangemen, Captain O'Neill's political future was called in question. There were rumours of a takeover by Mr Faulkner which Mr Faulkner promptly denied, though he made no secret of his disagreement with the sacking of Mr West. When the matter came before the Unionist back-benchers' committee, a resolution was carried by a very narrow majority supporting the dismissal of Mr West but acquitting him of any dishonesty.

Throughout that spring and summer there was an uneasy quiet in the streets of Derry and Belfast, and with it an uneasy reprieve for Captain O'Neill. But in October 1968, violence flared up, the beginning of a period of mounting unrest.

On 5th October, a Civil Rights march through the main Unionist areas of Londonderry was banned by Mr Craig, Minister of Home Affairs, following an announcement that an extreme Unionist organisation, the Apprentice Boys' Clubs of Derry, intended to march along part of the same route at the same time. The Apprentice Boys accepted the ban: the Civil Rights marchers ignored it. There was a major clash with the police and batons and water-cannon were used. Gerry Fitt, a Westminster MP, was taken to hospital with a head wound, and many more suffered injury. Three of our back-benchers were there and sent a written report to Jim Callaghan, as well as seeing him.

Once again Northern Ireland became a central issue in the House. On 22nd October I was asked by Paul Rose, a Labour member, whether I would transfer control of the Royal Ulster Constabulary from the Northern Ireland Home Secretary. When he referred to Captain O'Neill as a prisoner of the 'extremists', I took the opportunity of paying one in a long series of tributes to what Captain O'Neill had 'carried through in the way of liberalisation in the face of very great difficulties'. I was then challenged by an Ulster Unionist, Captain Orr, Grand Master of the Ulster Orange Order, who complained that the implication of Paul Rose's question was to 'constitute a slur on what is probably the best and finest police force in the world' (*sic*). I defended the sincerity of Labour back-benchers on these matters and said it was as great as that of Captain Orr. Commenting, '.... I say to the hon. and gallant Member that he is entitled to his view on the matter he has just expressed,' I went on: 'Up to now we have perhaps had to rely on the statements of himself and others on these matters. Since then we have had British television.'

672 The Labour Government 1964-1970

In the Queen's Speech debate Northern Ireland, for the first time in many years, became a focal subject for discussion. On 4th November Captain O'Neill came to see me and the Home Secretary. He had again sent a message saying that he was proposing to bring Mr Faulkner and Mr Craig with him. During the discussions, I made clear our determination about the urgent reforms which were required in the local government franchise, in housing allocations, and in the appointment of a Parliamentary Commissioner with powers comparable to those of our own Ombudsman, to review allegations of maladministration in the Stormont Government. Jim Callaghan and I expressed our concern about some aspects of the Londonderry outbreaks and the operation of their Special Powers Act for which we, as the sovereign power, had to accept international responsibility. I stressed the strength of feeling of many of our members who, while left, right and centre on other issues, were united in their determination to establish human rights in Northern Ireland. Only speedy reform could avert irresistible pressures for legislation at Westminster – under the rights explicitly reserved by Section 75 of the Government of Ireland Act 1920 – intervening in Irish affairs; none of us wanted that. Not only that, but, at a time when we had been forced into unpopular measures to restrain the growth of public expenditure, there was strong feeling among Labour MPs about the large and growing provision of UK finance for Northern Ireland. While this was contributed under the Consolidated Fund and not voted annually on the Estimates, its provision, in the last analysis, depended on the goodwill of the Westminster parliamentary majority.

Finally, as a personal warning and expecting the message to be carried back, I made clear that if Captain O'Neill were overthrown for no other reason than opposition to his reform measures, and if he were replaced by a more extremist leadership, a new situation could arise in which Westminster's inhibitions about taking some of the measures pressed upon us would disappear.

Our joint statement after the talks referred to our discussion on local government, housing, the proposed Ombudsman, the Special Powers Act and the situation in Derry, on which Captain O'Neill had undertaken to report to his colleagues. It also confirmed the pledge I had repeatedly given in the House that the Government would stand by Clem Attlee's declaration on the Ireland Bill, 1949, that partition could not end without the consent of the Northern Irish Parliament.

When I reported to Parliament the next day, 5th November, I repeated, in answer to a question:

We have represented that it is urgent that the local authority franchise should be got on with now, because the principles underlying one man, one vote, the company vote and the rest are just as applicable whatever the form of local government boundaries or local government units there.

For good measure I repeated my private warning of the previous day: in answer to a question by Mr Heath asking for my agreement to the proposition that support should be given to those in Northern Ireland who favoured a moderate policy, I replied:

> I very much agree, and I think that the whole House will, with what he said. Many of us on many occasions have paid tribute to the reforming liberalism, as far as it goes, of Captain O'Neill; it ought to be encouraged to continue. On the other hand, we cannot get into a position where his vulnerability to pressure from the extremists, referred to by the rt. hon. Gentlemen, could be used as an occasion for blackmail and could be used as an occasion where we failed to press for reforms which are necessary.
> If Captain O'Neill were thrown over, or what he is trying to do were thrown over, by extremists, we should ourselves meet to consider a fundamental reappraisal of our relations with Northern Ireland. Meanwhile, therefore, he should be encouraged in pushing on with reform as fast as he can. . . .

Further violent clashes in Derry continued in late October and through most of November. On 22nd November the Northern Ireland Government, after a meeting of the Unionist Parliamentary Party, made an important and courageous announcement of its reform proposals.

Housing allocations were to be based on publicly-announced or 'points' systems; councils would be asked to submit their proposed schemes to the ministry by a given date, and, where necessary, the ministry would advise on the preparation of them. Legislation would be introduced to appoint an Ombudsman in areas covered by 'central government activity'. A 'comprehensive reform and modernisation' of local government structure which would deal, *inter alia*, with the franchise, would be carried through by the end of 1971. Meanwhile the 'company vote' would be abolished at an early date. Recognising our international responsibility, the Stormont Government agreed that as soon as they considered that it could be done 'without undue hazard', those of the special powers that were in conflict with international obligations would be withdrawn from current use, with the right to reintroduce them if it became necessary. The Stormont Government undertook that 'prompt and effective' action would be taken to implement a plan which would 'transform the economic and social conditions of life' in Derry, and Captain O'Neill's Government was prepared to assist by appointing a 'strong, well-qualified and objective Development Commission' with full powers to carry out all the necessary work of planning, co-ordination and physical development.

Captain O'Neill at a press conference the same day went further, saying that consideration would be given to the appointment of an Ombudsman to deal with local grievances. Three days later, on 25th November, the

Government met with members of the Londonderry Corporation and local county and rural district councils, after which it announced that the proposed Development Commission would take over the powers of the Corporation and the district councils, and would have wide powers to implement the Londonderry area plan.

The Northern Ireland Prime Minister continued under heavy pressure. On 11th December – not before time – he dropped Mr Craig from the Cabinet, on the ground that, as he put it, he had known Mr Craig to have been for some time attracted to ideas 'of a UDI nature'.

After the appointment of a Commission to investigate the continuing civil disturbances, Mr Faulkner resigned in opposition to its establishment. His resignation was followed by that of Mr William Morgan, Minister of Health and Social Services. All this produced a fresh revolt in the Unionist party. Captain O'Neill responded with a dash for freedom. On 3rd February he proclaimed a General Election. This was, from his point of view, a disaster. In a number of safe constituencies – including Captain O'Neill's where the Reverend Ian Paisley stood, fresh from gaol – the Unionist vote was split. The Ulster Unionists were returned with an over-all majority of twenty. A number of pro-O'Neill candidates stood as Independent Unionist and gained three seats, but Captain O'Neill was elected on a minority vote; his majority over the Reverend Ian Paisley was only 1,414, on a total poll of 16,400 votes – a shattering blow to his authority. He told a press conference that whether he remained as Prime Minister or not would depend on the party, but he would not stay unless he could carry through his moderate policies. Courageously, he laid his programme before Parliament in the Queen's Speech and, Bill by Bill, his policies made progress. Despite this, he was continually under attack. Riots continued. In April, bombs disrupted water-supply lines and electricity installations. These incidents and other attacks on public utilities – and the belief that the sabotage was from the IRA – led to Captain O'Neill's resignation. (After he had resigned, the outrages were traced to extreme Orangemen.) British troops, as Jim Callaghan announced to Parliament on 21st April, were posted to guard electricity, water and other public service installations in remote areas.

There was an emergency debate at Westminster on 22nd April, made noteworthy by the maiden speech of Miss Bernadette Devlin, who, only an hour earlier, had taken her seat as 'Independent Unity' member following her successful Mid-Ulster campaign. It was a remarkable début, fluent, ordered, confident and not in the slightest degree self-conscious. But, as I commented to Jim Callaghan, sitting on the front bench beside me, it was utterly negative. In Miss Devlin's demonology, the Ulster Unionists were Tories, the Tories were Tories, the Labour front bench were Tories, and so was the Eire Premier, Jack Lynch and his colleagues – Tories all. She examined every possible solution and rejected them all. In particular, she rejected, to the dismay of some of her friends on the Labour benches, the 'Westminster solution' – legislation by us under Section 75 of the 1920 Act. Equally she rejected any idea of British troops taking over responsibility for law and order. Without recounting it, she clearly had in mind the old story of the two Liverpool Irishmen, who, being interrupted in their private fight by a police officer determined to separate the combatants, joined together in an attack on him. The events of the following August proved her wrong.

On 23rd April, the Stormont Unionist Parliamentary Party resolved, by twenty-eight votes to twenty-two, to accept universal adult franchise for the next local government elections. Captain O'Neill had made it an issue of confidence. But at the same time Major Chichester-Clark, a key figure in his Cabinet, resigned from the Agricultural Department on the universal franchise issue. He was not against the principle, but against the timing. The Standing Committee of the Unionist Council was called for early May. But on 28th April the Home Secretary heard, and immediately alerted me, that Captain O'Neill was resigning. His departure was marked by an eloquent and moving broadcast.

The contest to succeed him lay between two ministers who had resigned. In the event, Major Chichester-Clark was preferred to Mr Faulkner by seventeen votes to sixteen. Mr Faulkner joined the new Government and became a tower of strength to the new Prime Minister in carrying through the reform measures. Despite Major Chichester-Clark's resignation on the timing of the egalitarian local government franchise, he quickly became the Prime Minister who saw it through. His amnesty for political offenders was designed to cool the continuing disturbances. But a stormy summer lay ahead.

Meanwhile we faced industrial dangers nearer home. For several months we had been very concerned about Upper Clyde Shipbuilders, formed, as one of the estuarial mergers, from Yarrows, Fairfield and John Brown. Yarrows, with its naval record and future orders was viable; Fairfield's had been saved as a result of George Brown's dramatic intervention and the introduction of unconventional modern management methods involving closer partnership with the workers. But it was facing new difficulties through having accepted low-price orders at a time of rising costs; John Brown's were in difficulty – as had been impressed on me on my visit to Clydebank – once *Queen Elizabeth II* had been delivered. Work was in progress on a new type of standard freighter but it had not reached the point where it could help the exiguous cash flow of the Clydebank component of the group, and thus the economic position of the group as a whole. Ideally, there should have been a single group for the Clyde as a whole, but the more profitable Lower Clyde yards, who had formed their own group, were not willing to join with UCS, with their higher wages, lower productivity and more militant labour record.

The Shipbuilding Industry Board, which we had established under the Shipbuilding Industry Act, 1967, was willing to give help up to a point, but it was required to maintain strict criteria of viability. Tony Benn had held, over three or four months, innumerable meetings on the Clyde; no less than thirteen with local MPs, fifteen with the UCS management, seven with the Scottish TUC and a series with trade union representatives, including a number where he addressed the shop stewards, or other meetings of the workers, in the yards. As a result of his insistence on changes in UCS management and tighter financial control, the agreement by the workers to co-operate fully in reorganisation, and measures for higher productivity – including substantial redundancy – the Shipbuilding Industry Board felt able, at the beginning of June, to add a further £5 millions to its existing loans, with the possibility of a further £4.3 millions for capital investment when it was satisfied that the necessary steps had been taken to secure viability. This was announced to the House on 9th June.

Had this action not been taken, there is little doubt that UCS would have gone under, with mass redundancies in the Clyde yards.

But the yard was soon again in fresh difficulties and Tony Benn, Jack Diamond and, at a later stage, Harold Lever were in constant consultation, and occupied in meetings with the UCS board. From one moment to another it was impossible to get reliable figures of the group's financial position and there was a series of crises over the next six months, when frantic telephone calls made clear that there was no money for the wages due to be paid the following Friday.

By December 1969 the yards faced imminent closure. The ministers concerned brought the matter yet again to the Economic Policy committee and to the Cabinet. On 11th December, Tony Benn was authorised to announce direct Government assistance by way of loans not exceeding £7 millions and, if necessary, completion guarantees in the case of new orders of particular and immediate value to the company's cash-flow position since they were for early completion and payment. In many ways the company was improving its position and reasonably-priced orders were flowing in for the 'Clyde' ships. But time was required – and that meant money. The Government's action – vehemently attacked in the House by the Opposition industry spokesman, at that time Sir Keith Joseph – gave UCS a necessary breathing space, while the improved productivity measures and tighter financial control were given time to become effective.

On 7th June, the Government suffered another sad loss with the death of a senior minister, Gerry Reynolds, Minister of Defence for Administration and Denis Healey's principal deputy. He had been in Defence from

October 1964, beginning as Under-Secretary for the Army. He was an outstandingly successful minister, and would undoubtedly have reached Cabinet rank: he was only forty-one when he died. He was replaced by Roy Hattersley, who had been very much under-graded in his rank of Parliamentary Under-Secretary in Employment and Productivity.

On 11th June one more of the major reports directed at the reform of an important British institution, that of the Royal Commission on Local Government, headed by Lord Redcliffe-Maud, was published. It was a remarkable achievement in three years to have carried out the first thorough analysis of local government – unchanged in its main structure since the Acts of 1888 and 1894 – and to have proposed a radical reconstruction, while at the same time setting out the detailed boundaries for every local government unit in the country.

The Report's dominating theme was the redrawing of local government boundaries not merely to reduce the number of authorities, but to end the artificial division between town and country, in an age when road-building, planning and housing overspill made such a division meaningless. Taking England outside London, in place of 45 administrative counties, 79 county boroughs, 227 non-county boroughs, 449 urban and 410 rural district councils – just over 1,200 in all – the Report proposed that there should be 61 new local government areas. In 58 of these a single authority would be responsible for all services, in place of the two-tier system which covered the greater part of the area of the country. In the three major conurbations, the 'metropolitan' areas centring on Birmingham, Liverpool and Manchester, responsibility would be divided. In each case there would be a metropolitan authority, whose key functions would be planning, transport and major development, together with police and other services requiring authorities of this size. The second tier would consist of 'metropolitan district councils', responsible for education, housing and the local authority personal social services.

Thus 81 'main authorities' would assume the functions of 124 county and county borough councils and over 1,000 county district councils. These authorities, together with those in Greater London, would appoint representatives to form some six or eight 'provincial councils' whose primary task would be to draw up a provincial strategy and planning framework which would be binding on the main authorities.

It was also proposed to establish, below the main authorities, local councils, rather like local consumer councils, mainly to represent local opinion and pressures and to undertake a limited range of purely local functions delegated to them by the main authority concerned.

Three of the commissioners expressed reservation about the pattern of authorities in certain areas, two preferring rather more, and one rather fewer, main authorities. One commissioner, while agreeing with the proposal to end the distinction between town and country authorities, had fundamentally different proposals to make about how this should be done.

In a parliamentary statement on the day of publication, 11th June, I stated the Government's acceptance in principle of the main recommendations of the Report, and announced that we would enter into immediate consultations with local authority associations and others concerned about the proposals. George Thomson, Minister without Portfolio, was entrusted with the task of co-ordinating the work of the different Government departments concerned, with the idea of introducing a Bill as early as possible, probably in the 1970–71 session, after a general election. We had in mind, after consulting local authority associations, to publish a White Paper near the end of the year setting out the Government's conclusions about the structure of local government. This was to be followed by a further White Paper, after more consultations, covering the detailed boundaries.

The Maud Report had an important bearing on an issue of considerable inter-party controversy, the revision of parliamentary boundaries. The House of Commons (Redistribution of Seats) Act, 1949 prescribed boundary changes, and provided thereafter that independent commissioners would have the duty of recommending changes in parliamentary boundaries to keep pace with changes in the distribution of the population. The first redistribution under this procedure took place in 1954, just before the 1955 General Election, and was widely felt to have been too early after the previous changes and, if followed by a further early report, to be likely to involve a too frequent break-up of communities and of constituency parties. Accordingly the Conservative Government introduced a measure, the 1958 Act, lengthening the interval between reviews to not less than seven nor more than fifteen years. The Parliamentary Boundary Commission for England presented its report on 21st April, that for Scotland on 24th April, that for Wales on 19th May and that for Northern Ireland on 10th June: they were published together on 19th June. Under the Act, orders giving effect to them were due to be laid for approval by both Houses. In my view, we made a mistake – once the Royal Commissions on Local Government were set up, with their responsibility for proposing local government boundaries – in not introducing legislation to suspend the work of the Parliamentary Boundary Commissioners, for the parent Act required them to base themselves on local government boundaries and it was clear that very sweeping local authority boundary changes would inevitably be recommended by the local government commissions. Indeed, the Maud recommendations to end the distinction between town and country destroyed the very basis of a great many parliamentary boundaries, including the distinction embodied in the Representation of the People Act between 'borough' and 'county' constituencies.

Therefore, when the Maud recommendations became known, we decided that the recently-proposed parliamentary boundaries should not be implemented and we announced the introduction of legislation to remove the statutory requirement to seek parliamentary approval for them. The Parliamentary Commissioners could then proceed to recommend new boundaries more fully reflecting the new local government areas, once Parliament had declared its view on the White Paper on local authority boundaries. In this way, the House of Commons could more accurately represent the new local communities that would be created.

The Conservatives had been suspicious for some time that we would move to suspend action upon the constituency boundary revision. They believed, and their press with them, that the Commission's recommendations would work strongly to their advantage, to the extent of some twenty seats. I had the strongest reason to doubt this. The view of the Labour party's then national organiser, Miss Sara Barker, an authority on whom I would have always been ready to rely, was that at most six or eight seats, on balance, would be at risk.

When the Home Secretary announced our intention to introduce legislation an immediate storm broke out. Cries of 'gerrymandering', 'fixing', 'destroying the constitution', and 'changing the rules in the middle of the game', filled the air. Where politicians and journalists began, the cartoonists added a new dimension. Tsar Nicholas II, Oliver Cromwell, and all the dictators in history were models of democratic rectitude compared with Her Majesty's Government in the summer of 1969. The Bill went through the Commons with much acrimony but in the autumn was thrown out by the Lords. That unreformed and unelected House, refreshed in its democratic zeal by the reinforcement of long-absent hereditary backwoodsmen, was once again acting in its traditional role of custodian of the people's will, which under our unwritten constitution it is always required to do when a government, other than a Conservative one, is in power, particularly if any action taken is deemed to be injurious to the Conservative interest. It would not have been so, if it had been a Conservative Government, at a time of radical change in local government, which was acting to ensure that parliamentary boundaries reflected, as far as possible, local authority boundaries.

Jim Callaghan was immediately confronted with actions in the High Court, designed to require him to carry out the terms of the Act: that the necessary draft orders to give effect to the Boundary Commissioners' reports be laid before parliament for approval. In the event, he did so by introducing the orders which were then voted down. Thus the status quo was maintained, ending a somewhat disagreeable chapter of controversy.

June was a favourable month for the economy. The trade figures were improving. The balance of payments figures for the first quarter of the year were published, showing a current deficit, unadjusted, of £16 millions, and seasonally adjusted, a surplus of £18 millions. The overall balance, current and capital, was in deficit to the extent of £78 millions in deficit unadjusted, and £52 millions seasonally adjusted.

At the end of June, Roy Jenkins publicly announced that he expected a balance of payments surplus, over the year as a whole, of £300 millions. In the event it was £387 millions, or £457 millions if allowance were made, as was proper, for Euro-dollar borrowing in the computation of the capital account.

But on 27th June we had another bad by-election result. At Ladywood, Birmingham, following the death of Victor Yates, there was a Liberal gain from Labour. In that very small down-town constituency, the Labour vote fell from 8,895 to 2,391, the Liberal vote rose from 3,580 to 5,104 and the Conservative fell from 2,621 to 1,580. The Liberal victory was partly due to the popularity and local government record of their candidate, who represented a local ward on the council. Calculations of the swing from Labour to Conservative on such occasions are meaningless, though that does not stop their being made. Had the Conservative polled no votes at all, the swing would have been calculated, on the conventional basis, as one of five per cent from Labour to Conservative! The seat was duly won back for Labour at the succeeding general election.

On 1st July, the investiture of the Prince of Wales took place in Caernarvon Castle. The ministers principally concerned, Welsh members of both Houses, the diplomatic corps, and representatives of Welsh national life in all its aspects, were in attendance. Although the Chancellor of the Exchequer had kept the Earl Marshal, the Duke of Norfolk (and the Secretary of State), to a tight financial budget, the occasion was superbly organised, and it is difficult to see what more could have been done if the Earl Marshal's much more ambitious demands had been met.

Chapter 33

Discussions in Stockholm with European socialist leaders – the release of Gerald Brooke – the Ombudsman system extended – speech at Guildhall on Europe – discussion with President Nixon at Mildenhall – French devaluation – violence in Northern Ireland – the 'Downing Street Declaration' – the Conservatives and Ulster

NO sooner had we returned to London than a new crisis over Nigerian relief broke out. Malnutrition was more widespread but the ban on surface routes and daylight relief flights was tightly maintained by Colonel Ojukwu. Because of arms smuggling on night flights, the Federal Government placed a ban on them, and a relief aircraft was shot down. New proposals had been worked out internationally, under which aircraft could be loaded in areas outside Nigeria and flown into Uli. The Federal Government was anxious to ensure that arms were not introduced into the relief cargoes, and the proposal was made that each aircraft should touch down in Federal territory for inspection of its cargo. The Nigerian Government, for its part, was willing to agree that neutral observers could be in attendance at Federal airports to ensure that the relief cargoes were not tampered with – Colonel Ojukwu had hinted at the use of poison! Unfortunately – almost certainly because of a clash of temperament between the Red Cross representative in Lagos and members of the Federal Military Government and the need for the International Red Cross representative to reserve his position pending instructions from Geneva – General Gowon ordered the Red Cross to cease its activities in Nigeria. Maurice Foley was despatched to Geneva to sort things out with the International Red Cross. Michael Stewart called a meeting in London, at which he was able to mediate successfully between the Federal Foreign Minister, Dr Arikpo, and the vice-President of the International Red Cross, Professor Freymond. On 7th July Michael Stewart announced in Parliament the terms of a settlement and the Red Cross was re-established in Nigeria.

By this time I was on an official visit to Sweden, my first as Prime Minister. When Tage Erlander, the Swedish Premier and an old friend, was in London in September 1968, I promised to accept his invitation to revisit Sweden – I had been his guest a number of times when in opposition – before his retirement in the autumn. On Friday, 4th July, my party flew to Aengelholm, where we were received informally by the King at his summer residence at Sofiero, and then went on to Stockholm. Anxiety about the Nigerian situation had mounted in Sweden, and there was widespread criticism of the British attitude.

Most of my meetings with the Swedish Government in Stockholm, and later at the Prime Minister's country house at Harpsund, were concerned with Nigeria. I felt that we were able to satisfy the Swedish Government about the situation and Britain's part in it, but only with great difficulty. On the Monday 7th July, we had a very useful informal meeting with socialist leaders from different European countries. In addition to Tage Erlander, Olaf Palme, and other Swedish ministers, the Norwegian leader Trygve Bratteli, Willy Brandt, Mauno Henrik Koivisto, the Finnish Premier, and Jens-Otto Krag, until recently Prime Minister of Denmark, took part. After a brief review of international socialist problems, particularly the tragic split in the Italian Socialist party, we had long discussions about the Soviet proposal for a conference on European security, and the Common Market situation, following the change in the French presidency. Willy Brandt had just paid an official visit to Paris, and brought back reasonably encouraging news about the French attitude towards enlargement of the Community.

I was back in London in time for my questions on Tuesday, 8th July. Two days later there was another debate on Nigeria, centring on the new relief proposals. These were subsequently rejected by Colonel Ojukwu, as was the American proposal, worked out by Professor Fergusson, for the use of military landing craft up the Cross River from Calabar. Despite continuing anxieties, and the outright opposition of the committed pro-Biafrans, Michael Stewart got through the day with relatively little difficulty: I decided that there was no need for me to speak. In the vote that evening, only forty-four MPs of all parties went through the division lobbies against us, nineteen being Labour MPs. On the other hand, some Conservatives voted with us.

The rest of July was a time of intense activity though, with the exception of several meetings I chaired on the deteriorating position in Northern Ireland, it was concerned more with relatively minor and uncontroversial issues and out-of-town visits. But on 10th July, Fred Mulley, as minister responsible for disarmament, announced in the House the tabling, by the British delegation to the eighteen-nation Disarmament Committee in Geneva, of a draft directive on which he had been working for many months. This directive was designed not only to strengthen the 1925 Geneva Protocol on chemical warfare, but also to take a new international initiative to ban the use, production and possession of agents of biological warfare, as the first step towards the complete elimination of both biological and chemical methods of warfare. It was a bold, indeed historic, step forward; the pity of it was that it received so little publicity.

On the Friday, 11th July, I paid a fascinating visit to northern Scotland. Flying first to Wick I visited the experimental reactor development at Dounreay, where the new breeder reactor – whose siting at Dounreay we had announced in 1966, against the strong pressure of the AEA who wanted it at Winfrith Heath in Dorset – was approaching completion. I had lunch with the directors, scientists and senior administrators from AEA headquarters then I flew on to Kinross, for a visit to the Forestry Commission at Culbin Forest; and from there I went on to Inverness, where, after a meeting with the Provost, I spent two hours with the chairman and other members of the Highlands and Islands Development Board. It was in Inverness five years earlier, in May 1964, before we came into office, that I had pledged an incoming Labour Government to establish such a Board. Although originally opposed by the Opposition front bench spokesman, Mr Michael Noble, as 'Marxism', the Conservatives finally dropped their opposition to the Bill when Willie Ross offered to accept an amendment exempting that spokesman's constituency, Argyll, from the benefits of the scheme. It was one of our proudest achievements.

The Board's activities covered some nine million acres, nearly a sixth of the area of Great Britain and 47 per cent of the area of Scotland – though only 5.3 per cent of its population. By the end of 1969 it had approved nearly a thousand projects for financial assistance by grant or loan in agriculture, fisheries, manufacturing and tourism and a wide range of miscellaneous projects, ranging from one-man enterprises to factories employing up to a hundred people. To give examples, financial assistance was provided for the purchase of forty-six new and second-hand fishing boats; £369,000 was invested in fish processing plants; financial assistance was given for working capital and re-tooling for boat-building; £130,000 was provided for research and experiments in sea and fresh-water fish farming; and nearly £2 millions had been advanced, half by grants, to assist tourism; new industry was encouraged by advanced factory building, and assistance in the provision of sites and industrial estates; existing industry was assisted to expand, from cheese, glass, fishing flies, to Harris Tweed; a remote mine facing closure through exhaustion of coal was saved by the Board's sinking test bores, finding new reserves and financing the driving of a new drift mine. New industrial ventures attracted to the area ranged from an American synthetic-fibre firm and a small electronics firm in the Outer Hebrides, to the development, with Dutch co-operation, of bulb-growing in North Uist. In addition the Board acted, in co-operation with the Highlands and Islands Consultative Council and local authorities, as an economic planning authority, assisting infrastructure, planning road and harbour developments, and promoting surveys on mineral resources, transport and marketing. It worked, and works, closely with the Forestry Commission, whose planting programme – as I announced on my visit to the Highlands – was increased yet again and was planned to reach fifty thousand acres in Scotland by 1976.

From what I saw on my visit, and the appreciation of the Board's work I heard on all sides, I could feel that the pledge which I had given at Inverness in May 1964, had been honoured, that the Highlands and Islands Board we intended to create would provide for the vast and remote areas it would serve something in the nature of a miniature Tennessee Valley Authority.

From Inverness I flew to Bradford, for the following day's degree ceremony at the University, where my Chancellor's speech set on the record the progress we had made in expanding facilities for higher education.

At this time, negotiations were proceeding about the release of Gerald Brooke. The Soviet Government was insisting that Brooke could not be released unless there were a prior agreement by us to release the Krogers. We had been, and continued to be, extremely reluctant to agree, not least because there was no comparison between the two cases and because such an agreement might mean that any further arrest of a Soviet agent might lead to the subsequent imprisonment of an innocent British tourist or businessman. But our hand was forced, just as Brooke's term was nearing its end, by further charges being laid against him for alleged offences against the Soviet judicial code while he was in prison. Whatever Soviet diplomats might say, the KGB clearly held the reins. We had to face the possibility of a further sentence of five, or even ten years' imprisonment in intolerable conditions, and with Brooke in an increasingly serious state of health. It was a difficult decision but the Krogers had, in fact, served eight and a half years of their sentence and, on 24th July, Michael Stewart announced that they would be released in October. On receiving this assurance, Moscow had released Brooke, and he reached London that day. When the Krogers' release became effective the Soviet Government had agreed to release other British prisoners, sentenced for smuggling drugs, and also agreed to a number of long-refused marriages between British and Soviet citizens going ahead; Moscow promised, further, to improve arrangements for consular visits to prisoners.

In the same week I announced an extension of the Ombudsman system for local government and for the National Health Service, which, as I had previously informed the House, we were considering. We now accepted that such a system should be established, by statute, for investigating complaints of maladministration in local government. It would be separate from the central government system, but its scope in local government would be similar to that of the Parliamentary Commission in national government. Those responsible for investigating complaints would be independent, and their reports would be considered and, where appropriate, acted on by the local authority concerned.

Similarly, we accepted the need for a similar system in the National Health Service, over and above the proposal for the new hospital advisory service which Dick Crossman had announced. Talks would be started, I announced, with the professional bodies and other parties concerned both in local government and in the National Health Service.

My statement was followed the same day by an announcement by Tony Crosland of another policy decision which we had been carefully examining, this time for the textile industry. Overseas competition, much of it by any standard manifestly unfair, had for many years inflicted the most serious damage on the morale of the cotton and associated industries, with all that meant for their confidence in the future. Voluntary quotas, backed since 1964 with statutory powers, had some effect, but the Board of Trade now proposed to act on the report of the Textile Council (formerly the Cotton Board) and to replace quotas by a tariff of fifteen per cent on imports from the Commonwealth preference area. There was a great outcry from exporting countries, but the new arrangements were widely accepted as fair.

On the financial side Tony Crosland announced a higher depreciation allowance for plant worked on a multi-shift basis in the industry, and new discussions through the consultants appointed by the Board of Trade, working together with the Industrial Reorganisation Corporation (IRC) on merger policy and the structure of the industry.

A few weeks before, a ceremony had taken place of some sentimental, even nostalgic, appeal to me. This was the celebration of the twenty-first anniversary of the second reading of the Bill creating the National Development Research Council; now in this week came a second with a similar appeal; the inauguration of a brain-child of mine, worked out by me privately in the early sixties, announced by me as Leader of the Opposition, and now coming to fruition through the efforts of my ministerial colleagues – the Open University.

The first ceremony was on 11th June, twenty-one years to the day after my speech moving the second reading of the Development of Inventions Bill, 1948. We celebrated also, on the day of his retirement, the achievements of Lord Black (previously Sir William Black, chairman of Leyland), who had directed the work of NRDC for twelve years. When he had taken over, its principal work was still on British computers and hovercraft; soon afterwards came the development of the revolutionary antibiotic, cephalosporin. In the sixties NRDC interests spread much more widely. At this twenty-first anniversary celebration I was able to point to the fact that five hundred inventions that it had developed and sponsored had been licensed for manufacture, while the number of developments in progress was over three hundred, including new techniques for producing micro-electronic components, the development of an automatic foundry, of an automatic multiple bio-medical analysis machine which could revolutionise a wide area of hospital work, an automatic pipe-laying machine, and a process for synthesising

Y

pyrethrum. Its resources had grown with its work; the £5 millions in my original Act had been increased in 1958 to £10 millions, and increased again, in a Bill introduced by Frank Cousins in 1965, to £50 millions. In 1968–69 it had broken even, for the first time, and was able to pay its first dividend to the taxpayer. This was largely as a result of its cephalosporin sales, particularly in the United States.

On 23rd July, the Open University, first announced in a speech in Glasgow in September 1963 as the 'University of the Air', was favourably established at an impressive Charter ceremony at the headquarters of the Royal Society.

The Chancellor of the University, Lord Crowther, in his inaugural speech, defined the new venture:

> We are the *Open* University...We are open, first, as to *people*. Not for us the carefully regulated escalation from one educational level to the next by which the traditional universities establish their criteria for admission...Only in recent years have we come to realise how many such people there are, and how large are the gaps in educational provision through which they can fall. The existing system, for all its great expansion, misses and leaves aside a great unused reservoir of human talent and potential. Men and women drop out through failures in the system, through disadvantages of their environment, through mistakes of their own judgment, through sheer bad luck. These are our primary material. To them we offer a further opportunity...
> We are open as to *places*. This university has no cloisters – a word meaning closed. We have no courts...our only local habitation will be in... Milton Keynes...The rest of the University will be disembodied and airborne. From the start, it will flow all over the United Kingdom. But it is already clear that the University will rapidly become one of the most potent and persuasive, and profitable, of our invisible exports...
> We are open as to *methods*...Every new form of human communication will be examined to see how it can be used to raise and broaden the level of human understanding...
> We are open, finally, to *ideas*. It has been said that there are two aspects of education, both necessary. One regards the individual human mind as a vessel, of varying capacity, into which is to be poured as much as it will hold of the knowledge and experience by which human society lives and moves. This is the Martha of education – and we shall have plenty of these tasks to perform. But the Mary regards the human mind more as a fire that has to be set alight and blown with the divine afflatus. That also we take as our ambition...

My last speaking engagement before the summer holiday was at Guildhall, for a dinner arranged jointly by 'Britain in Europe' and the 'British Council of the European Movement', which were in the process of merging. The three party leaders were due to speak, and the occasion was directed to fund-raising, with a target of £750,000. A few days before it took place I decided to withdraw, as I had heard that the fund-raising firm, Arrow Enterprises, which was in charge of the fund-raising activity, had been promised ten per cent of the proceeds. Recalling all the thousands of voluntary workers who organised functions, for charities and other worthwhile activities, I revolted against this form of professionalism. I particularly disliked the principle that if either of the other two party leaders or I succeeded, through our eloquence, in persuading some rich fellow-diner to contribute £10,000 to the cause, the fund-raising organisation concerned would benefit to the extent of £1,000. My refusal, backed by Jeremy Thorpe, led to a change in the arrangements under which the fund-raiser was promised a flat fee, which I accepted as reasonable.

In my speech I stressed the technological aspects of closer association with Europe, but came down firmly against any commitment to a political union or any other form of federalism. Having emphasised the political arguments for closer association in Europe, which I felt transcended the more arguable economic case, I went on to say:

> I know only too well how quickly any reference to political unity in Europe can become a subject for confusion and even distortion, not least, perhaps, because there are those who find confusion not only diverting but even rewarding.
>
> To succeed in our application to join the Community will of itself have one major political consequence. As Europe's economic strength grows, its political strength will grow and this will underline the need for Europe to speak with a more united voice in the councils of the world.
>
> It is widely acknowledged that if Britain's application succeeds that will not, of itself, involve the acceptance of political obligations going beyond those laid down in the Treaty of Rome, an essential part as they are in the working of the Community....

I then quoted some words of Willy Brandt, made in our joint press conference at Harpsund earlier in the month:

> Some of us expressed, and I think none of us opposed, the view here that experience has shown that economic integration does not lead automatically to political union. This differs very much from the view which was predominant when the Treaty of Rome was put on paper. The view which is shared by many today, and I belong to those who share it, is that, of course, economic integration has certain political results but for what has been called political integration leading towards more than inter-governmental co-operation in the field of developing common views on world politics, this demands special activity, something in addition to what is done in the economic field, and it demands also eventually an apparatus of its own.

Having quoted these words of Willy Brandt, I went on:

> Whether that is so, no one can foretell tonight the direction, still less the pace, or the institutional arrangements, of future moves towards the unity of Europe, particularly when the argument takes on a federalist tinge. I know I would go a great deal less far tonight than many here when I repeat, as I have repeated, Hugh Gaitskell's statement in the debates of seven years ago that whatever the future may hold, the creation of supra-national, federal, political – or defence – institutions is not a reality in, as he put it, ten or twenty years.

The immediate task of this generation is to work, as we are pledged to work, for that degree of political unity which is within our immediate grasp. That is *our* task in the months and years that lie ahead of us.
But we are not here to legislate for the views, still less prejudice the views of those young people whose personal identification with the ideals and aspirations of a wider Europe is one of the hopes of all of us here tonight. They will choose their own course. They will fashion the institutions they think right for the Europe of which they will be a part. Our duty is to create something on which they can build.

I was interested to see the press reaction to Mr Heath's speech, which was in general an unexceptionable reiteration of his well-known European philosophy. In the course of his words, he had referred to the 'real worries' existing in the minds of many citizens about Britain's future in Europe needing to be recognised and met more effectively. He then set out some of the worries in detail, suggesting that the calculations from which these fears stemmed were to a certain extent 'hypothetical'. He was almost certainly referring to articles in the *Guardian* claiming that departmental calculations in Whitehall estimated that the cost to our balance of payments of our adherence to the Common Agricultural Policy of EEC would be of the order of £500 millions. He went on to say that '... every citizen is entitled to have the fullest information on these and other implications of membership'.

Outlining 'a second set of worries' about the dissolution or, at least, weakening of Britain's national identity, and the imposition of institutions on us which had been worked out to serve the interests of others and to build on principles which had no roots in British history or society, he said: 'It would be a great mistake for us to scoff at or belittle these worries, for they stem from a sense of patriotism which provides the foundation for most of what is sound and energetic in Britain today...'

These words were selected for presentation in the anti-Market *Daily Express* the next morning, under the headline, 'Give us the facts on the Six, says Heath'. He was interpreted as moving into a position of detachment on the Market.

Listening to Mr Heath, I did not interpret what he said as a derogation from the total pro-Market philosophy to which he was, and remains rightly regarded as, fully committed. But the press presentation disturbed me, and when in September he received still more striking headlines for an extremely disingenuous series of comments, I became concerned that he was engaged on an uncharacteristic anti-Market manoeuvre. I therefore dealt with his efforts in my speech at our party conference in September. In view of his heavily-publicised demand for 'the facts on the Six', I was subsequently disappointed, seven months later, when on the publication of the White Paper I had commissioned, which set out the best official, objective presentation of the possible costs of joining, he was extremely critical about the fact that I had responded to his demand. It was clear that the White Paper produced a set of figures different from those he had hoped for.

The following Sunday, 3rd August, President Nixon, at the end of a world tour which had begun with his welcome of the triumphant astronauts on board USS *Hornet*, and had then covered a number of Asian countries and Rumania, touched down at the USAF base at Mildenhall, Suffolk, where we had arranged to meet. I flew by Queen's Flight helicopter from Chequers and met him off his aircraft. After a brief official welcome we walked to a room in the commandant's residence. We met alone, while our senior advisers conferred in an adjoining room.

I asked the President about his tour, which had been a great success. He started from the Pacific splashdown of the astronauts, and covered in some detail his visit to Indonesia, Thailand, India and Pakistan. He then went into his up-to-date impression of the position in Vietnam. He repeated what he had said publicly, that he felt that he had gone the last mile for peace, including the offer of free elections following the cessation of bombing. He was prepared to await the response from Hanoi before deciding on his future course of action. We discussed Vietnam and the situation in Laos in some depth. Following his announced decision to withdraw twenty-five thousand troops he indicated his thinking about future withdrawal policy.

He then spoke of his visit to Rumania, where he had been mobbed enthusiastically; clearly this part of his tour had made the deepest impression on him. He explained how the Rumanian visit had come about – a fascinating account later confirmed by the Rumanian Prime Minister, Mr Maurer, when he came to London. The Rumanians had been very frank, as later they were with me, about the situation in Vietnam, with the 'window' they had on Hanoi and on Peking. We covered Western–Soviet relations in the light of the speech Mr Brezhnev had just made and Mr Gromyko's gloss on it, and we went quite deeply into the negotiations on the strategic arms limitation talks (SALT), where, mainly through patient tutorials by Denis Healey, I had more or less mastered the intricacies of the problems involved of MRVs, MIRVs and the rest. Though we were not directly involved, our nuclear expertise and international experience had been of some value to the American negotiations, not least in helping to resolve the anxieties of non-nuclear European allies who feared, as we did not, the consequences of a deal between the United States and the Soviet Union. This recalled my heated exchange with Mr Kosygin during his visit to London in February 1967, which I recounted to the President. We discussed how much more could be done in NATO consultations on SALT, with particular reference to French participation.

We then discussed the Middle East, about which talks between the permanent representatives to the United Nations of the four relevant permanent members of the Security Council (the United States, the Soviet Union, Britain and France) had begun earlier in the summer, as a result of the Security Council remit to make a reality of the United Nations Resolution 242 of 1967, which Britain had initiated. By this time the four-power talks were in recess, while the United States and the Soviet Union were locked in bilateral talks – which, after too long, got nowhere. We agreed to follow this up when the Foreign Secretary visited Washington in September: our Government was anxious to get back to four-power talks and away from the sterilities of the Moscow and Washington bilateral talks.

We then turned to Europe, where I said that I should like, on a more leisured occasion, to develop our thinking. He had pressed me repeatedly during the spring and summer to visit Washington. Indeed, tentative dates had been fixed for May/June. But I had deferred the visit, partly because of my anxieties about the worsening Northern Ireland situation and its possibly deep constitutional implications. I said, however, I looked forward to a visit later in the autumn, or about the turn of the year. We discussed the possibility of a visit to Moscow, which I felt should follow my Washington visit (it should have done so in 1968!) but I found him very interested in my going there earlier, as he wanted to know my assessment on the Soviet approach to a number of questions. In the event, I visited Washington in the following January, and the visit arranged for Moscow was postponed by our General Election until July, and consequently never took place.

After a little time spent assessing Russo-Chinese relations President Nixon and I discussed the struggle, in which the Russians and Chinese were so fully engaged, for the soul of Africa and I raised with great urgency the situation there, particularly in Nigeria. I dealt briefly with the military situation and the manoeuvrings by Biafra on the relief issue. There was no time to deploy all the arguments, but he asked me to send him a detailed assessment. Then and later he made it clear that this was an area of great importance to the United States where our past experience and current high-level contacts put us 'in the lead'. I was to hear that phrase again.

Even after the formal leave-takings and the national anthems, he reverted to this question again, and pressed me to let him have, as quickly as possible, the note I had promised.

After he had left I held a brief press conference. I then dictated a detailed minute of our talks, for the record, and for detailed study by my advisers. It had been valuable, and our advisers, when they had had time to study my minute, were amazed how much we had got through. This was not the view of the Conservative press: we were too near an election for that. The *Daily Mail* in particular devoted its leader column, headed 'Wilson laugh-in', the following morning to the meeting:

...the Prime Minister scurried to Mildenhall to make obeisance on
'Anglo-American' soil.
One cannot imagine, say, former General de Gaulle frisking along in
such circumstances. Nor some of the great denizens of Downing Street.
It was not very dignified nor, we suspect, of lasting value ...
The strains of *Colonel Bogey* seemed a fitting comment on an ill-advised
meeting.

Had I decided not to meet him – and it had been at his suggestion – one
could have imagined how the *Daily Mail* would have thundered its criticism
of my discourtesy. Strangely, it took a very different line about President
Nixon's short visit to Chequers the following October, even though in the
President's subsequent report to the nation on his European tour he
omitted to refer to the fact that he had been to Britain at all: but then
by this time Britain had a Conservative Prime Minister, and the *Daily
Mail*'s well-known objectivity was under strain.

A few days later I left for my summer holiday. Within hours of my
arrival in the Isles of Scilly, on Friday 8th August, telegrams began to
arrive first with the rumour, then the fact, of French devaluation. The
Chancellor was in the south of France and could not be contacted for
some little time. The telegrams continued to pour in. By the end of that
first evening the No. 10 duty clerk who was in charge of my office at
Customs House told me that, on the basis of serial numbers, I had already
received more telegrams on my first day than in any previous three-week
holiday period.

The French devaluation had been well planned and carried through in
total secrecy. There had been no prior speculation or drain on the reserves
and there were not wanting those who compared the French success in
this respect with our lack of it rather less than two years earlier. The
franc was, of course, not an international currency; and, in any event, it
is always easy for those to affect surprise who decide not to comply
with the international rules governing these matters. The International
Monetary Fund had not been given the necessary notice.

There was no rational justification for any concern about sterling in
view of our strong balance of payments position. But we were not dealing
with rational people. Subjective rather than objective factors tend to
govern speculative dealings in foreign exchange markets, not least in
August, when dealings are thin but feverish. The danger was that some
would argue again that where one European currency had gone over the
brink, another might follow. There was a further real danger that, with a
still un-revalued Deutschemark and the outcome of the German election in
the following month very unpredictable, the flood of currency into Frankfurt might resume its earlier proportions. Revaluation had become a central
feature of the German elections, and of the highly personalised Schiller–
Strauss electoral confrontation. Clearly every precaution, national and

international, had to be taken. In the event, for once after a monetary cataclysm the markets were respectably quiet when they opened the following Monday.

But four days later, on 12th August, the Northern Ireland situation flared up to a new level of danger. The Orange celebrations of the Battle of the Boyne on 12th July had passed off reasonably quietly. But for 12th August processions were scheduled to celebrate, nearly three centuries after the event, the unforgotten exploits of the apprentice-boys of Derry – processions in which grown men would feel it an obligation to march, wearing their obligatory sashes and decorations and carrying their inflammatory slogans, through a city that was as dry as tinder and explosive as a gunpowder charge. Consideration had been given to prohibiting the march, and I had originally favoured this course. But unwiser counsels had prevailed; it was argued that a prohibition, and certainly one pressed on Stormont by the Westminster Government, might have provoked such an Orange backlash that Major Chichester-Clark's insecure administration could have been swept from office with total chaos the only possible successor.

Already the police were regarded, not entirely without justification, by the Roman Catholic minority as biased against them. Catholic families in the areas closest to the Orange districts, and particularly those living in mainly Protestant areas, were receiving ugly demands to get out – or else. Night after night, violence continued into the early hours, and even a police force whose impartiality was not in question would have had difficulty in apportioning blame for any particular outbreak. In Londonderry the police were rapidly losing any semblance of control. The Army units in Northern Ireland, already reinforced through the summer, were on alert, but not actively deployed. But they were ready, should the Apprentice Boys' march lead to fresh outbreaks of violence.

On 13th August, the day after the march, the police used CS gas for the first time against Roman Catholic rioters. It was the first time in Northern Ireland, as in any part of the United Kingdom. Some 109 people were injured in the riots, including many officers of the Royal Ulster Constabulary. Petrol bombs were thrown by the Bogsiders and shots were fired by the RUC in Belfast. Jim Callaghan was standing by in Whitehall; I had emergency flying arrangements ready for a return to London. He and I were in close touch on the secret telephone. Despite the Conservative affiliations of the ruling party in Northern Ireland, every London news reporter and leader-writer, whatever the political complexion of the paper for which he was writing, was appalled by the situation he had to describe. It was the culmination of three centuries of atavistic intolerance. It was also the culmination of nearly fifty years of the unimaginative inertia and repression of successive, unchallenged and, because of Ulster's history unchallengeable, Ulster Unionist Governments.

For years the British people, stoically inured to overseas violence – in the United States in the late sixties and more recently in the French troubles of 1968 – had been reassured by the thought that 'it can't happen here'. But the scenes of bloody violence reported in the press, and still more dramatically shown on the television screens, brought home to the British people that law and order had totally broken down. As I later said on television, this was not just 'on our doorstep... it is in our house'. After all, the 'United Kingdom' means the United Kingdom of Great Britain and Northern Ireland.

Jim Callaghan and I spoke later on the night of 13th August and we agreed to meet on the following day. It was important, if it could be avoided, that I should not return to London at this point. He flew down to Culdrose, near Penzance, and I flew by helicopter to meet him.

At my suggestion we were joined, in addition to the advisers he had brought with him, by the commandant of RNAS Culdrose, who had recently been stationed at *Sea Eagle*, by Londonderry, where many of our troops were quartered: his local knowledge helped in the interpretation of the maps and other information before us.

One thing was clear. At any moment there could be a request from Stormont for us to send in the troops to maintain law and order. Jim Callaghan and I considered whether we should propose their intervention and agreed that it would be unwise. But we decided that once the request came, we should meet it. Our Cabinet colleagues had given us the necessary authority before dispersing for the recess. Our worries were needless. Five minutes after Jim Callaghan was airborne to return to London, and before I left Culdrose, the request came, and the order was immediately given. We were in no doubt that this was right, but against the background of Northern Irish history the *Guardian* heading for its leading article the next day was justified: 'A gamble for peace in Derry'. No one could forecast what the outcome might be: in Roman Catholic circles British troops, recalling Black and Tan memories, could be evocative. I remembered that in that remarkable maiden speech of Bernadette Devlin's earlier in the year, she had said that one answer to Northern Ireland's problems must be ruled out; a decision to introduce British troops, which would unite both sides against them. Representing, as I do, the British constituency with pretty well the highest proportion of Irish votes, albeit mostly of the second or third generation, I was disposed to feel that she might have been right. But our decision was hailed enthusiastically in Ulster and above all by the Roman Catholics, who contrasted the strictly impartial conduct of the British forces with what they regarded as the committed partiality of the Ulster police.

General Freeland, who had only recently taken over the command of the augmented British forces there, began as he meant to go on: with firm and authoritative orders enjoining on his troops the strictest impartiality between citizen and citizen in the restoration of law and order. No British Government could have been more fortunate in its Commander-in-Chief.

The British troops were accepted but the violence continued. The divided responsibility between the Army and the RUC, with their hated components, the B-Specials – the armed reserve special constabulary – was inimical to the creation of a peace force which could be accepted and respected by all the combatants.

Jim Callaghan and I remained in constant touch. He had given up any hope of a holiday: mine was continuing in theory. We spoke on Sunday, 17th August, and agreed that I should return to London and invite Major Chichester-Clark to meet me at Downing Street. Before our meeting the Cabinet would be called, for it was clear that we could not go on as we were going. British troops and the British Government were bearing the responsibility for an indefensible situation, exacerbated by the position of the B-Specials, for whose disarmament most British newspapers were pressing. There was pressure, again, for us to suspend the constitution and to exercise direct rule over the Province – a formidable undertaking. By this time, indeed at 5.50 p.m. on that Sunday, British troops in Belfast had virtually taken what the *Sunday Times* later called 'control over the city's war-torn heart'. We were exercising responsibility without power. It was a situation which could not be allowed to continue.

On the Monday, 18th August, in fog so thick that the helicopter sent for me could not find the Scillies – though the relief helicopter, whose task was to pick us out of the sea if we crash-landed, managed to find us – I returned to the mainland, and flew to London. I was at Downing Street by seven-thirty that evening and had all the time I wanted to study the latest situation reports. Most of the following morning was taken up with meetings with Jim Callaghan and his advisers. These included the senior British police officers he had sent to Ulster as advisers and who spoke with utter frankness about the police situation there and, in particular, about the position of the B-Specials. What was impressive was the comment of one of them on the junior ranks in the police, 'men on the verge of policemanship, and genuinely wanting to be policemen', and their comments on the need to enable the police force to become, as in Britain, part of the community, accepted by the community. But what stood in the way was not so much the men higher up as – history.

In the afternoon, such members of the Cabinet as were immediately available in the country met and Jim Callaghan reported on the situation. We were given a free hand on the lines he recommended, and the Cabinet dispersed to allow us to meet Major Chichester-Clark at 5.00 p.m. He was very worried, but more impressive than I had seen him.

The Premier had that morning presided at a security meeting with his Minister of Home Affairs, together with General Freeland and his staff.

Major Chichester-Clark reported the conclusion of the meeting to us: the Army should take over total responsibility for security operations in the Province – including control over the Royal Ulster Constabulary and the USC – holding daily meetings with the Minister of Home Affairs on security questions. The RUC should come under the supreme command of the Commander-in-Chief.

To this, we were ready to agree. But there were necessary conditions to be accepted if the Army, under the political direction of the Secretary of State for Defence, and, ultimately, of the British Cabinet, responsible to Parliament, were to take control. Not only the Army – and here there was no difficulty – but the police authorities subordinate to the Commander-in-Chief, must be, and be seen to be, politically neutral. This must mean – at once – a change in the top direction of the RUC and at the earliest possible moment the standing-down and certainly the disarming of the B-Specials. In addition there was the necessity for a political directive and declaration to govern relationships between the national and the Stormont Governments. During the morning I had personally prepared the text of a declaration for agreement between us. Without this I felt that our political decision to take over the responsibility for security operations would not be acceptable to Parliament; and rightly so, for we could not take over the enforcement of law in a system of society which we could not justify to Parliament. Not only our own people in Parliament, but the whole of the articulate Establishment, including the press, were demanding a fresh start.

When I read out the draft of the declaration, Major Chichester-Clark made no demur. Much of it was by this time acceptable to him. He was prepared to assent to the passage asserting the right of all citizens of Ulster to the same rights, free of discrimination, which were enjoyed by all other citizens of the United Kingdom. He was prepared to agree to an impartial investigation of the police system in Northern Ireland, on which we insisted, and which had been enjoined on me by the Home Secretary's seconded police advisers, one the Chief Constable of Hampshire, the other one of HM Inspectors of Constabulary. But he saw difficulties about the change in the top direction of the RUC, at least until he could inform the then Inspector-General the following morning. After a very tense situation, which at one point involved my insisting that I could proceed no further with the proposal for Army control, we reached provisional agreement.

Half an hour later agreement was reached on the military takeover, on all the outstanding issues, and on what was issued in Cmnd. 4154, as the 'Downing Street Declaration'. This document began by setting out the constitutional position:

> Nothing which has happened in recent weeks in Northern Ireland derogates from the clear pledges made by successive United Kingdom Governments that Northern Ireland should not cease to be a part of the United

Kingdom without the consent of the people of Northern Ireland or from the provision in Section I of the Ireland Act, 1949, that in no event will Northern Ireland or any part thereof cease to be part of the United Kingdom without the consent of the Parliament of Northern Ireland. The border is not an issue. . . .

We also confirmed that responsibility for Northern Irish affairs was a matter of domestic jurisdiction. Our response to the Stormont Government's request for military assistance was 'in that spirit'. But we set out the basis on which British troops were involved, including the assertion of the British Government's views on matters affecting the status of citizens of that part of the United Kingdom and their equal rights and protection under the law.

We went on to welcome the decisions on local government franchise, the revision of local government areas, the allocation of houses, the creation of an Ombudsman to deal with government matters and machinery to consider citizens' grievances against other public authorities, which, after an earlier meeting, I had reported to Parliament in May. And then as Point Six:

The two Governments at their meeting at 10 Downing Street today have reaffirmed that in all legislation and executive decisions of Government every citizen of Northern Ireland is entitled to the same equality of treatment and freedom from discrimination as obtains in the rest of the United Kingdom, irrespective of political views or religion. In their further meetings the two Governments will be guided by these mutually accepted principles . . .

I had drafted the entire seven-point declaration and, subject to one or two minor amendments, it was accepted by Major Chichester-Clark. Its promulgation at Downing Street, at the height of the crisis, will I think be seen as historic, since it held the key to the future. Had a previous United Kingdom Government thought of drafting it, and insisted on its acceptance; more, had its non-discriminatory terms been accepted a generation, or even ten years, earlier, the tragedy of August 1969 could have been averted, and Northern Ireland set peacefully on a new course. In this, as in so many other issues, the Labour Government had to act at the eleventh hour, after years of neglect.

The decisions taken at Downing Street that day had their effect. The assertion of responsibility for law and order by the British troops was accepted, as was the inquiry into the RUC which, at my suggestion, Lord Hunt was appointed to lead. In his military career he had not infrequently had to undertake police responsibilities in colonial situations, which the Northern Ireland position was rapidly in danger of becoming. What I had not realised was that Lord Hunt, as he proclaimed on going to Northern Ireland, was a lineal descendant of one of the apprentice-boys of Derry; unlike so many of those who claimed a bogus collective descent from that group, the Hunt family had over the centuries grown up. Lord Hunt's report, produced at exemplary speed and with characteristic thoroughness, became a further stabilising factor. On the retirement of the Inspector-General, Jim Callaghan nominated Sir Arthur Young, another stabilising factor, to replace him. It was a move calculated to realise the hopes of many police officers on both sides of St George's Channel, that the young, keen professional officers of the RUC could 'become policemen' and help to form part of a police force which could genuinely become part of the community, and not a race apart.

Lord Hunt reported on 3rd October. Among his recommendations was the disbandment of the B-Specials and the creation of a new volunteer force, later to be called the Ulster Defence Regiment, under Regular Army control. This was the subject of legislation carried through Parliament in the 1969–70 session, and the new volunteer force, with a very special appeal for Roman Catholic volunteers, became operational on 1st April 1970. Further legislation to give effect to the Hunt Report was carried through, enabling police authorities in Britain to second their members for service in Northern Ireland and provide mutual support.

The decisions of the meeting on 19th August helped to reduce the violence and stabilise the situation, though it remained tense and strained. Jim Callaghan visited Ulster at the end of the month; a courageous decision which paid off largely because of his insistence on seeing everything and meeting everybody, and through his good-natured, tolerant attitudes throughout his visit. He met everyone from the Reverend Ian Paisley to the Roman Catholic Archbishop – and a number of Catholics a long way beyond him. He visited all the trouble-spots, including the still-barricaded Bogside, where the writ of the RUC even in its anti-crime, as opposed to its law and order, functions, still did not run.

When Jim Callaghan and I had discussed these questions earlier in the month I had suggested that his position should be, and above all should be seen to be, 'firm, cool and fair'. He needed no such admonition. It characterised his attitude throughout, but, above all, on that visit to Northern Ireland. The communiqué issued at the end of the tour was published as a White Paper (Cmnd. 4158), spelling out the principles of the Downing Street Declaration, in more detail but in down-to-earth terms, testified to the facts.

There is no doubt that in the strengthening of the Labour Government's political position and standing during the second half of 1969, Jim Callaghan's handling of the Ulster situation played an important part. This was a problem forcibly brought home to every British household by press and television; and the Labour Government was seen to be acting with manifest firmness and authority in a demonstrably difficult situation.

Throughout this period the Conservative Opposition, in W. S. Gilbert's words, 'did nothing in particular and did it very well'. This applied to the visit to Northern Ireland by Quintin Hogg, shadow Home Secretary, and to his public comments throughout the crisis.

Such reticence was seemly. Their party had ruled Ulster, unchallenged, for the whole of the Province's near half-century's existence as a separate political unit: for nearly three-quarters of that period, a Unionist Government in Stormont had run in double-harness with a Unionist Government, or a Unionist-dominated coalition, at Westminster. Whatever short-run acts of violence and provocation, from any side, may have contributed to the events of August 1969 and subsequently, the inertia and complacency of that infertile Unionist partnership must bear a heavy responsibility.

Chapter 34

Trades Union Congress at Portsmouth – overseas aid – the Labour party conference at Brighton – Labour's achievement – ministerial changes – departmental reorganisation – the No. 10 party for the astronauts

I RETURNED from the west country on Saturday, 30th August, and spent the weekend at Chequers dictating the speech I was to deliver to the Trades Union Congress at Portsmouth two days later. It was not an easy speech to prepare, and it proved still harder to deliver. It was designed to emphasise the things which united us, as well as to urge upon the delegates the necessary conditions for economic advance and higher living standards. I began by setting out the long list of measures, legislative and administrative, which we had carried through in accordance with the speech I had made to Congress on 1st September, the eve of the 1964 General Election. This was my opportunity to justify the claim that the incomes policy, which I had said would be necessary, had been placed against the background of a fairer and more responsible society. There was, for example, the Redundancy Payments Act, leading to payments already amounting to £171 millions to over 785,000 workers; the special help for coal miners made redundant by pit closures; the unprecedented help we had given to bring new work to hard-hit regions; and measures to speed the pace of industrial training – we had established training boards in industries covering over nine million employees, and £120 millions a year had been channelled into industrial training. Equally there was the expansion of the Government Training Centre programme; there were now forty-two centres with 9,000 places, against twenty-five with 3,900 places in 1964, and a further thirteen centres in preparation; there were 40,000 new jobs assisted for training with the doubled grant for development areas.

I went on to outline the measures we had taken to help labour in particular industries – decasualisation in the docks, the reform of the Merchant Shipping legislation in the Bill then before the House – but, I said, more needed to be done. I described our forthcoming legislation providing for joint consultation on safety in industry, for the establishment of an Employment Medical Advisory Service and for other forward steps in occupational medicine for which Congress had been pressing.

But the fair society which I had pledged the Labour Government to create went much wider than this: I set out all we had done in the social services, including earnings – related benefits, the improvement in

699

provision for widows, the abolition of the old system of National Assistance, and the successive increases in industrial injuries benefit, as well as our greatly increased provision for schools and education generally, for hospitals and the National Health Service and for housing.

Outlining the economic task we had faced over these years, including transforming the £800 millions deficit in our overseas payments to the current strong surplus, I repeated what this had meant in terms of restraint on consumer spending, including increased taxation and the prices and incomes policy. I went on:

> Having got so far I must make it clear that, whatever the pressures, we are not going to put these achievements at risk.
> This is not politics. This is Britain's livelihood. We are not going to imperil the hard-worn ground we have won in the battle for economic solvency and economic recovery. We are talking about jobs. We are talking about increasing production which, if it is properly directed, will mean increasing living standards.

I explained that this would mean continued emphasis on productivity, and the maintenance of restraint on prices and incomes. I said:

> There is no escape from this truth. Whatever the system of Government in any country – capitalist, communist, social democratic – if the amount of money paid out on the processes of production exceeds the value of what is produced, then the only result is inflation, hardship for pensioners and the lower paid, cost escalation pricing us out of export markets, and an anarchy from which only the well-heeled can benefit.

The elimination of injustice in our wages system meant also a fair deal for women at work and I foreshadowed the legislation which we were due to introduce in the following parliamentary session. But I added this warning:

> We are ready, to discuss with you a phased implementation of equal pay. We are ready to discuss with you the form of the necessary legislation. But it will be clear to every delegate present that progress on this must be based on restraint in incomes policy generally. You cannot spend the increment to the national dividend, which is provided by the national product, twice over. We believe, all of us believe, in planning. Let us plan this too.

My concluding passages were an unapologetic account of the Government's reasons for introducing *In Place of Strife* and its consequences – the actions which the trade union movement had pledged itself to take in the previous June. I set out what this responsibility meant:

> We recognise, all of us, that you cannot be sure of success with every individual case. Nor would any legislation. That includes the arid proposals of those who seek to take industrial relations out of the field of human relations and make them a happy hunting ground for the legal fraternity.
> Our own British institutions, equally with international experience, show that there is no future in that direction.

Having said that, there are vitally important cases, which the Downing Street undertaking was intended to cover, which must be dealt with speedily and effectively. The Trades Union Congress have accepted this responsibility. There can be no backsliding now by the trade union movement as a whole. The General Council's power to act depends ultimately on the willingness of every individual union to take action against recalcitrant members.

This was strong meat. I did not expect it to be greeted with enthusiasm, nor was it. Press comment the next morning was almost unanimous in its scornful comment on the chilly reception I received. What had they expected? I had no intention of mincing words or concealing the facts in order to get a good reception.

On 11th September the Treasury published the balance of payments figures for the second quarter. They showed not only that for the first half of the year we had been in over-all surplus, but that for the second quarter, that is the quarter immediately following the 'dead-end budget', we had achieved a surplus overall of £190 millions.

When the news was broken to Mr Heath, who was on a Scottish tour, he said, 'Perhaps we had better see the year as a whole before we conclude all is well. The second quarter is always a good quarter. The quarter we are in at the moment is always a difficult quarter of the year.'

The second quarter is, as he suggested, usually favourable for seasonal reasons. But no one had told him that, seasonally corrected, that particular quarter of 1969 showed an overall surplus of £100 millions, in marked contrast to the 'usually favourable' second quarter of 1964, when Mr Heath was in charge of our exports and we were in stark deficit. He was to be reminded of this.

On the Sunday, 14th September, I drove from Chequers to Polesden Lacey, the beautiful National Trust property near Dorking where the Fabian Society had arranged an open-air concert and demonstration in aid of Oxfam. I was one of the speakers and took the opportunity to set out the record of the Government in overseas aid over some very difficult years. We had provided in 1969–70 a flow of official overseas aid (that is aid from the British budget), of £228 millions, and we hoped in 1970–1 to disburse some six per cent more than in the previous year.

There had been rumours that under Treasury pressure the figure for succeeding years was to be cut. I was able to use this occasion to deny the rumours outright. We had not cut our provision for aid out of the budget even in the most difficult years, including the year following devaluation. We were working hard to try to get a substantial increase in the Overseas Development estimate for the following year and well into the seventies as Britain's contribution to the international target set in the Lester Pearson report to the United Nations.

Three days later, 17th September, I went to Scarborough to address the annual conference of the Association of Municipal Corporations. I made it a major speech on relations between central and local government, covering finance, greater freedom for local authorities, the local government Ombudsman, relations between local councils and the communities they serve – with particular reference to admission of the press to their transactions – and, above all, local government reform.

Reminding the conference that local expenditure on current account in 1967–8 amounted, for Great Britain as a whole, to £3,000 millions, of which £1,800 millions came from the Exchequer, I went on to point out that, whereas over the ten years ending in March 1968 central government expenditure had risen by a hundred per cent at current prices, capital and revenue expenditure by local authorities had risen by a hundred and sixty per cent – from £1,900 millions to some £4,900 millions.

Even with the restraints applied in the expenditure review of January 1968, we were providing that for the three years up to 1971, when the increase in central government expenditure was to be held back to three per cent per annum (this was in real terms, at constant prices), that of local government was set to expand at four per cent each year, in real terms. A strict control had to be maintained on Exchequer grants to local authorities, but central controls must themselves be subject to constant questioning and scrutiny. I went on:

> It is my hope that the reorganisation of local government will provide an opportunity and the incentive – and that this opportunity will be taken – for a fresh attack on this problem of central financial control, so that we can reduce the number of points on which decisions are taken by ministers, even by Parliament. I assure you that on this, as on the basic conclusions of Maud, which the Government have already accepted, we mean business, as I know you do.
>
> We want to see more freedom for local authorities on how resources available to local government, for both capital and revenue, are to be used, and on the relative priorities to be given to various functions and activities consistently with overall national policies.

Although, as a result of five years' adverse municipal election results, the great majority of elected representatives present were Conservatives, the speech was remarkably well received. But, of course, the AMC represented the boroughs – county and non-county – and though the former were the more enthusiastic in welcoming the Maud Report, the Association as a whole went along with it. My reception would have been much more restrained had I been addressing the Urban District Councils' or the Rural District Councils' Associations.

The 1969 conference of the Labour party was held at Brighton from 29th September to 3rd October. It was markedly more relaxed and friendlier than in previous years. As I commented in my opening words, 'I read that this is the last Labour conference before your Government seeks a fresh mandate. I wouldn't know – yet.'

But this was not the only reason. Delegates were more confident, partly because of our economic success but also because of the growing political support that our fight-back was producing in the constituencies. Even the Conservative press was reluctantly recording our surer touch. This was seen in economic affairs, but it was, also, a tribute to Jim Callaghan's handling of the Northern Ireland problem.

Inevitably, in what could be a pre-election setting, I spent part of my speech covering our record over our whole five years in office, with the emphasis on the change we had brought over the face of Britain. 'Look around' was my theme: look around at the new hospitals and schools, at our record house-building programme – two million families in new homes built under the Labour Government; at the fresh look on some of our older towns and cities, and our older industrial communities. 'Look around' and sense the hope in the changing north, hope in a reborn Scotland, hope and change in Wales. If we had wanted to tell the Macmillan 1959 story of improved family living standards in terms of the ownership of cars and washing machines, telephones and television sets, refrigerators and transistors, the figures were there to confirm it. But I preferred to instance what we had done to modernise industry. The success abroad of our science-based industries, working, so many of them, in a partnership between public and private enterprise. The old industries we had reclaimed from decline by the injection of public capital through the IRC and the Industrial Expansion Act, both bitterly fought by the Tories, and under threat of a Conservative pledge to scrap them. I asked,

> Can you recognise this Britain of achievement in the welter of propaganda the Tories are pouring out to denigrate the work of their fellow citizens? This sort of Tory propaganda tries to make Britain out to be as dingy as those who peddle the propaganda.
> With the generosity which inspires all my comments on the Opposition party, I said not long ago that I acquitted them, at any rate, of any charge of patriotism so far as the economic welfare of our nation is concerned. When the economic indices in any month give comfort to Britain's critics and enemies abroad, you can see all their top people looking like Victorian undertakers welcoming a wet winter and the promise of a full churchyard.

My reference to the happier state of the economy was not based on a single month. Steadily, indeed rapidly, our monthly trade figures were showing an improving trend. Month after month we were recording an actual surplus on our visible trade, something very rare in Britain's trade figures since the war or before it, and to this our steadily increasing surplus on invisible account had to be added. Taking not one month but the whole year up to that time, I was able to record an increase in the volume of our exports (at constant prices) of nine per cent over the same period of 1968, and thirty per cent over the same period of 1964.

It was a pleasure to quote *The Economist*, which confessing that a few weeks earlier it had been expressing deep fears about Britain's economic situation, printed an editorial just before conference, which read: 'In these past few summer months of 1969, Britain has been running one of the strongest balance of payments among the major powers of the world; indeed, on the face of the latest figures, the second strongest behind only Germany.'

I used the balance of payments position to draw attention to the sour comments of Mr Heath:

> We all recall how Her Majesty's Opposition were dining out on the prospects of our failing to get the balance of payments into surplus; the champagne corks popping. Now, as Britain moves from long years of deficit into surplus, their champagne is turning into gripe-water.

I went on to demonstrate that what he had called the 'favourable' second quarter, had, in 1969 shown '£190 millions *surplus*, that is, *plus*: in 1964, when Mr Heath was in charge of the nation's trade, it was £184 millions *deficit*, that was, *minus*. A turn-round, taking quarter with like-quarter, of £374 millions, not for a year, but a single quarter.'

I criticised the Conservatives for having sold Britain short, offering them, if they sought a new flag as their co-belligerent Ian Smith had done in Rhodesia, a new motto, *Bonum patriae Conservatoribus pessimum*, roughly translated, 'What is good for the country is bad for the Tories'.

I was concerned also with what appeared to be a Conservative manoeuvre on the Common Market. No one has ever excelled Mr Heath as an enthusiast for Europe. But Mr Powell was on the move, and there were murmurings in the Conservative party and at the Beaverbrook end of the Conservative press spectrum.

Mr Heath had appeared at Sheffield the previous week. Apparently there had been no prepared speech. But a question was put to him, no doubt immaculately conceived, which must have come as a surprise to Mr Heath: equally immaculately, a *Daily Express* journalist was there to report his answer, which, surprisingly and exclusively, was the main lead in the following morning's paper and which featured Mr Heath in the improbable role of a Common Market sceptic. All the phrases attributed to Mr Heath suggested an ignorance of the Common Market, of which Mr Heath must be acquitted. I mention only one – that before entry Britain must be satisfied that all of the Six wanted us. 'A brilliant perception,' I said, 'we could not get in otherwise' – none had more reason than Mr Heath to recall that one nation could veto us.

Mr Heath's other comments were equally disingenuous, but they served the purpose. One expressed an anti-federal sentiment. I was flattered, though not long before I had been shouted down in the House by the Conservatives when I had rejected the federal thesis. Another, remarkably, attacked us for our 1967 decision to apply for entry – 'a great deal of damage had been done to Britain's case'. But as I recalled, with my concern to demonstrate historical facts, Mr Heath had on 9th May 1967 specifically welcomed our application in his speech in the House: more, in November 1966, at Harrogate, he had called on the Government for a firm declaration of intent to join the European Economic Community. 'Let it be declared,' he said, 'that Britain wishes to become a full whole-hearted member.... Time is not on our side.... Now is the moment of decision.'

I recalled these words, and went further. If Mr Heath was concerned to out-manoeuvre us by seeking anti-Market votes which, if secured, he would treat with contempt once in office – on the very decision he had demanded from us – I was concerned to show this hypocrisy for what it was: 'Now, nearly three years and one Powell speech later, it apparently was the wrong decision.'

I stated the position of Government and party in simple terms. Terms accepted by conference and the Parliamentary Party as fully representing our stance:

If they, the Six, are ready for negotiations to begin, we are ready. If, in these negotiations, we achieve terms satisfactory for Britain, on the lines we have outlined, then negotiations will succeed.

But, unlike the situation in 1961, we no longer face the challenge of Europe cap in hand. Europe needs us just as much, and many would say more, than we need Europe.

It is the common interest of all of us to achieve economic unity. But, if this cannot be achieved, we can stand on our own feet. At a heavy price for Britain, no doubt, but at a heavier price for Europe, and at a devastating price for Europe's influence in the world.

This remained the basis for the Labour Government's policy and it was one that no one could attack without demanding that Britain should withdraw her application. In the conference debate on the Common Market later in the week the only amendment which proposed that Britain should withdraw her application and proceed no further with negotiations for entry was not even pressed to a division.

Mr Heath had made another point. He had asked that the British people should be given 'every scrap of information available' about these issues. I pointed out that it was he who, when Common Market negotiator, had withheld information about his speech opening the negotiations which set out Britain's terms. It was only published when a leak occurred in Germany. Mr Heath then published a White Paper. We, on the other hand, had published our Foreign Secretary's statement of terms, as a White Paper, at the hour at which it was made. I went further. As I told conference, weeks before I had given instructions that new calculations should be undertaken of the estimates and assessments we – unlike our predecessors – had made, and that these should be published. They would show what entry would mean for the balance of payments and the living conditions – including the cost of living – of the British people.

A White Paper embodying these calculations, drawn up by officials, economists and statisticians, and free from all ministerial interference, was duly published four months later in February 1970. Also duly, it was denounced – as was the very fact of its publication – by Mr Heath, who was again by this time firmly back aboard the Common Market wagon and who felt that so independent an assessment would prejudice public opinion against entry.

In the latter part of my conference speech I turned to the future. Proud as we were of our achievements, forced through against almost continuous economic difficulties, we were not prepared to rest on them:

> ...as socialists we must continuously change our priorities. Change the priorities, because as we change society, as we advance, the problems of society are changing. And as we advance, the standards we set ourselves also advance.
>
> Labour Government always has work to do. That is why a Labour Government can never run out of steam. The politics of the sixties have inevitably been heavily centred on the problems of economic management. The decade that lies ahead will not be free of economic difficulty. But it is already clear that other problems are moving to the centre of the political stage.
>
> First, our environment. There is a two-fold task: to remove the scars of nineteenth-century capitalism – the derelict mills, the spoil heaps, the back-to-back houses that still disfigure so large a part of our land. At the same time we have to make sure that the second industrial revolution through which we are now passing does not bequeath a similar legacy to future generations. We must deal with the problems of pollution – of the air, of the sea, of our rivers and beaches. We must also deal with the uniquely twentieth-century problems of noise and congestion which will increasingly disturb, unless checked, our urban life.
>
> First among the priorities of the seventies is to get rid of the scandal of bad housing and no-housing. That is why all of us here are on the same side as Shelter, indeed we were there first. I am not going to get into an arid and cold argument about how you define homelessness. The problem is those without homes; the problem is those living in slums; and it is the same problem of human misery.
>
> Shelter themselves acknowledged how much has been done by this Labour Government. In a few weeks' time, in little over five years, your Labour Government will have built two million homes. This is a record contrition in rehousing the homeless and the ill-housed. Homes for two million families, in just over five years.
>
> In the last four years, 340,000 slums have been cleared in Great Britain. We are proud of this record but everyone here is determined to do a great deal more. More, to stop four-and-a-half million older houses from becoming the slums of the seventies. This is the task which our Housing Act of this year – a greatly underestimated piece of legislation – was specifically designed to tackle. An advance in housing standards the Tories were too mean to aspire to.
>
> So, on this vital problem of giving all our people decent homes, we wel-

come the job that so many organisations are doing. We welcome, too, the urgent and passionate pressure which organisations like Shelter can bring to this. When it comes down to it, aren't your ideals the same as theirs? And when it comes down to it, can their ideals ever be achieved by the party of the Rent Act, the landlords, the party which let Rachmanism flourish?

I said earlier, look around you at the new schools going up. But we have to look around, too, at the slum schools in our big towns and cities. And in the countryside where the children have an equal right to modern surroundings. Because, even with a record school building programme, we have had to concentrate our resources first in the new housing estates and the new overspill areas where there were no schools at all. And the downtown slum schools have remained. Slum schools can no more be tolerated by any socialist than slum houses. We have already in the past two years made a start on nursery schools. To get the priorities right for nursery schools, primary education, slum schools, time – and a Labour Government – are needed.

Look, too, at the new hospitals that have been built. But look around, too, at the urgent need to replace those Victorian buildings. Bastilles in which too many of our sick, including the mentally sick, have to be treated.

This is a problem that will be with us in the next Parliament and beyond. How we deal with this is the test of a decent society. Time and a Labour Government are needed.

We are building in Britain not an authoritarian society, nor a negatively permissive society, but a strong, tolerant and compassionate society.

That is why we are concerned not only with the physical environment in which our people live and work but the moral and political environment that determines still more the health and happiness of us all . . .

The doctrine of changing priorities, the doctrine that new occasions meant new duties, above all, the doctrine of environmental priority, had for the first time been put in a major way on the political agenda. This was to be reflected a few days later in the appointment of a Secretary of State with specific responsibilities for the environment.

The rest of the week was constructive and without difficulty. The National Executive document, *Agenda for a Generation*, which was to be the basis of our forward policy for the General Election, was carried following a debate introduced by George Brown. No major resolution was carried against the platform. The critics of yesteryear, including left-wing trade union leaders, declared their full support for the Government. In winding up the conference in a five-minute speech I quoted three key-note sentences from the week's debates:

From Roy Jenkins:

We have made good and solid progress. Our aim now must be twofold: to learn from the troubles we have been through, and to make sure that we do not allow hard-won achievements to slip through our fingers. . . .

From Hugh Scanlon:

We know our friends, for we cherish a party committed so clearly to ideals of social justice, equality of opportunity and compassion for the less fortunate members of our community. . . .

From Bill Simpson, a trade union member of the NEC:

I know that we are apt to take for granted some of the achievements of the Government. It has been said that the achievements of this Government have been written boldly in water, its mistakes have been carved in marble. And I want to say to you this, that if political chisellers from other parties want to sculpt our image, to play down their achievements in social policy, why should we whet their tools for them?

On my return to London I went ahead with a major ministerial re-shuffle. I had begun to plan it early in July but, as I intended it to involve drastic changes in the machinery of government, I deferred it until every last detail could be worked out by the Civil Service Department.

But it was not only a question of machinery of government.

I had been considering inviting George Brown to rejoin the Government, either in a non-departmental role, or as possible head of one of the new-merged departments I was contemplating as part of the changes in the machinery of government.

I felt that it would be a pity for his undoubted talents to run to seed; moreover, it would be of assistance in unifying the party in readiness for a general election – he was still popular with wide sections of our rank and file members.

In July I had had a word with him about it, following previous intimations to him that I had hopes this step might be possible. He was insistent, however, that he could return only as deputy Prime Minister since he was still the party's deputy leader. I made it clear that this was impossible; a great deal had happened since he had left the Government in March 1968; new men had come to occupy positions of great prominence. At that I took it that he was no longer interested in joining the Government on the only terms I could offer him.

My first main aim was to concentrate greater areas of departmental responsibility within the field of operations of individual ministers and thus have to rely less on inter-departmental committees for resolving differences which inevitably arose between the departments then existing. My other aim was to highlight, within the administrative machine, new priorities such as I had identified in my conference speech and to lay down a clearer line of authority for dealing with them, both in industrial policy and in environmental questions.

The process of merging departments had been carried some way with the amalgamation of the Foreign Office with the Commonwealth Office (already incorporating the Colonial Office) and of the Ministry of Social Security with Health a year earlier. Throughout July different permutations had been examined. One idea, recommended by the Select Committee on Nationalised Industries, was the merger of all the departments dealing with nationalised industries. This attracted me for it had many advantages. But a serious objection, it seemed to me, lay in the position of transport. Rail transport and certain ancillary enterprises would have had to go into the new ministry and this would either mean separating road from rail and thus frustrating the purposes of the Transport Act for closer co-ordination between them – or separating road haulage operation from road-building, which must necessarily be linked with town and country and regional planning. For some time Whitehall thinking had been in the direction of bringing the housing and local government and transport departments closer together and both were, in fact, due to be housed together in a new government building then under construction.

By the end of July I had decided to bring the Ministries of Transport and of Housing and Local Government under the direction of a single Secretary of State, with a view to amalgamating them at the earliest opportunity in a single administrative department. But on the industrial side, right up to the end of September, we had not moved beyond the transfer of steel from Power to Technology – thus bringing steel production under the same department as the steel-using industries – and the transfer of most of the remaining Board of Trade industries, such as textiles, clothing, pottery and glass and other predominantly consumer-goods industries, also to the Ministry of Technology. The Board of Trade would be left with certain 'transcendental' responsibilities providing services to industry and commerce, including company law, insurance, patents and copyright, and consumer protection, together with responsibility for such non-industrial 'industries' as distribution, newspapers, printing and publishing, and films; for the rest, it would concentrate on exports, shipping and civil aviation. The Board of Trade's responsibilities for regional industrial policy would also go to Technology, thus bringing together the sponsorship of major industries and decisions affecting their location, whether in the development areas or elsewhere.

I was still not satisfied that we had gone far enough. It was a discussion I had with my political office the weekend after conference which provided the key. They proposed that I should put the whole of the Ministry of Power into Technology. My first reaction was that this was too sweeping. But on further thought I saw that this was right. My top civil service advisers reacted very similarly, at first they thought it unworkable, but it was interesting to see how they too soon became attracted by it. It was, at any rate, 'a challenge' and they said they would make it work.

It had several advantages. Atomic energy and electric power generation, together with the other fuel and power industries, were brought under a single political direction; so was responsibility for electricity generation and for the heavy electrical plant industries. Steel was brought together with the steel-using industries, particularly the motor and shipbuilding industries; textiles with textile machinery. Mineral development in both the public and private sectors (except for such building materials as stone, sand and gravel) were brought together, and linked with the industries dependent on the extractive industries. The transfer to Technology of the remaining major industries brought them into the department responsible for NRDC and for industrial productivity generally. Responsibility for IRC was transferred to the newly-constituted Ministry of Technology and, very reluctantly, I decided to bring the DEA experiment to an end, five years after it was set up.

I do not regret the original decision to establish the Department of Economic Affairs. Having thought further on these matters, I still feel that something on DEA lines, however constituted, may have a permanent and central role to play in Britain's future machinery of government. But DEA had not been able, as I had hoped, to present an adequate offset to the Treasury, with the latter's inevitable concentration on monetary and financial questions, overseas and domestic, including demand management. This was no fault of DEA or DEA ministers, nor, indeed, of the Treasury.

The fact was that in the peculiar circumstances of those years, with an inherited balance of payments deficit and hostile speculative activity, both more formidable than we could have forecast, the successful assertion of positive growth policies, often involving valuable long-term industrial investment but at a damaging short-term cost in demand terms, was not possible. But DEA had achieved a great deal which would have been left undone if we had relied on the traditional departmental structure. First, its achievement had been the development of a policy for industry, particularly the modernisation and restructuring of which IRC, DEA's historic invention, was but one example. Second, was its achievement of a policy for regional planning going far beyond the traditional Board of Trade responsibilities for industrial location; it embraced the work of its regional economic planning councils, charged with the task of drawing up plans for each region going far beyond industrial diversification. This task was transferred to the new Secretary of State for Local Government and Regional Planning.

I intended, and ensured, that the areas of work developed by DEA should continue and develop under the new machinery. Indeed, this work would, from that time forward, have the weight of two of the most powerful departments in Whitehall behind it. IRC and industrial planning was now in the hands of the expanded Ministry of Technology and regional development was in the new Environment Department's area. DEA's responsibility for NEDC passed to the Cabinet Office, reporting to me, while the co-ordination of Government documents for presentation to 'Neddy' would be handled by the Treasury. Responsibility for the work of the industrial 'little Neddies' was to be the concern of the relevant sponsoring departments.

On the housing and transport side there would be no immediate merger of the departments. Each, under a minister of Cabinet rank but outside the Cabinet, would maintain its statutory identity, duties and functions, but the two were to work under the general direction of the new Secretary of State for Local Government and Regional Planning, who would normally represent their interests in Cabinet. The Secretary of State was given a special personal responsibility for environmental questions, for regional planning and for the consultations on local government reform, with a small staff working directly to him; he would also have, of course, a call on all the resources of the two departments. I asked Tony Crosland to move from the Board of Trade to become Secretary of State. He had identified himself in numerous speeches and writings with environmental questions and the quality of life and he was widely regarded as the right choice.

The maintenance of the separate identity of the two ministries did not mean that he was to be an 'overlord', a system which I believe, in general, to be unworkable under our administrative parliamentary system. I asked him to work as rapidly as possible for a complete integration of the two departments, recognising that for a time he would have to give his full attention to environmental and local government questions.

By Easter 1970 we had decided to go ahead with integration, but there were some delays concerned with a major allocation of senior permanent and deputy secretaries, and by my decision to bring the Ministry of Public Building and Works into the merged department so that the departments principally responsible for housing would also be together. By May 1970 the plan was ready; indeed, I intended to announce it early in June – an intention which was prevented by the newspaper strike. After the strike ended we were too near polling day and I had to concentrate on other things.

In October 1970, Mr Heath's White Paper on the machinery of government adopted our plan for the environmental, housing and transport departments exactly as we had finalised it for announcement in June.

I believed we had found the right structure. But no structure can work without the right men. This is one reason why I do not think that any system of machinery of government can be laid down for all circumstances. Not only must it reflect the priorities and methods of operation of the Prime Minister, but, more than that, an 'ideal' system on paper cannot work unless the men in charge are of the calibre and enthusiasm to make it work. At Technology I made no change at the top. Tony Benn was to continue in charge but, with the merger with Power, he had two ministers of Cabinet rank to assist him. Power had been a full Cabinet post and I wanted to retain Roy Mason in the Cabinet; indeed, to give him extended responsibilities. He therefore became President of the Board of Trade, the department where he had done so well as Minister of State.

I told him, and announced, that the Board of Trade would now be free to concentrate much more on exports. Its regional offices, losing some industrial work to Technology, should now concentrate on expanding the work of the regional export offices, especially among small manufacturers.

As Tony Benn's principal deputy, with the title of Paymaster General and a seat in the Cabinet, I chose Harold Lever, the Financial Secretary to the Treasury. His great knowledge of industry and finance, his inexhaustible imagination and ingenuity and his high standing in the City and industrial circles eminently fitted him for the post, as the next nine months were to show.

I decided to give Reg Prentice, whom I regarded as another early prospect for a Cabinet appointment, the chance of experience on the industrial side after his successful tenure of Works, and later, Overseas Development. He appeared happy to accept it, subject only to an assurance that this did not portend a Treasury cut in the forward aid and development programmes he would be leaving behind. This reassurance I was able to give him, for I had intervened with the Chancellor to secure his agreement to a sharp increase in the ODM allocation through the seventies, and this we were able to announce a few weeks later. But Reg Prentice clearly thought again after he had left me, and promptly resigned. I asked him to come to see me. I tried to persuade him to change his mind, but without success. Overseas development had become for him not only a ministerial job but his dedicated mission. I could not help saying how much I admired his self-denying stand for something in which he believed, even if I regretted his decision to resign. In his place I recommended the appointment of Lord Delacourt-Smith, formerly Charles Smith, the General Secretary of the Post Office Engineering Union and, before that, Labour MP for Colchester. He took charge – under Tony Benn – of all the aviation work and associated areas of the ministry's duties at a highly critical time for the British aviation industry, which, after June 1970, must be sadly missing him. Tom Urwin, Minister of State with responsibility for regional questions and 'Minister for the North' in DEA, joined Tony Crosland to help on the regional side. I appointed Eric Varley, one of the younger trade union MPs and until then one of my two PPSs, to be Minister of State (regional) to look after the industrial (ex-Board of Trade) functions of Technology. Peter Shore, now that DEA was no more, became Minister without Portfolio and took over many of the duties previously undertaken by George Thomson and some of those exercised by Judith Hart as Paymaster General. She became Minister for Overseas Development, outside the Cabinet.

The two ministers of Cabinet rank nominated to work under Tony Crosland were Tony Greenwood, as Minister of Housing and Local Government, and, at Transport, Fred Mulley replaced Dick Marsh who with great regret I had to ask to stand down: I did not intend that his departure from the Government should be permanent.

With a general expectation that European negotiations might become a reality very soon, I decided that our Common Market negotiator should be in the Cabinet. George Thomson was transferred from his non-departmental post as Minister without Portfolio, to the Duchy of Lancaster, as overall deputy to Michael Stewart and with responsibility for the Brussels negotiations. Alun Chalfont again took over the responsibilities of Disarmament Minister.

In addition to Dick Marsh, two other senior ministers left the Administration. The changes in Housing and Local Government meant that there was no real function for Kenneth Robinson, who had worked with quiet success in both Health and in the land and planning functions of Housing and Local Government. Fred Lee stood down from the Duchy, for with the end of DEA and the change in responsibility for industrial questions, his task had ended.

The Cabinet, as a result, was reduced from twenty-three to twenty-one.

A further list of changes at Minister of State and Under-Secretary level followed a week later. I intended the Administration at the end of this process to be the team which would continue for the rest of the Parliament. In addition to the consequential ministerial movements following on the machinery of government changes and the switching of senior ministers, I wanted to bring in a number of younger MPs who would be the raw material of future Cabinets, including a number of the 1966 intake.

This meant taking leave of a considerable number of junior ministers who had worked well, but who on age grounds would clearly not rise to higher ministerial posts. I wanted to give a chance to the potential 'flyers' of the seventies and to reinforce them with more of our livelier back-benchers after election, if that went in our favour. I wanted also to reduce the size of the Administration.

As successor to Harold Lever as Financial Secretary I chose Dick Taverne, then Minister of State at the Treasury. In his place, Bill Rodgers, Minister of State at the Board of Trade, joined the Treasury team. Goronwy Roberts was moved from the Foreign Office to replace him. The vacant position at DEP caused by the promotion of Roy Hattersley was filled by Edmund Dell, who I had very nearly moved up to Cabinet rank on more than one occasion; because of the increase in the work of DEP – including the prospect of five Bills in the forthcoming session's legislative pro-gramme – he went there as Minister of State. With the resignation of Lord Stonham from the Home Office, after five years of tireless work in the department, and a tremendous legislative record in the Lords, I moved Shirley Williams from the Department of Education and Science to the Home Office. In her place, with the special responsibility for higher education and the Department's functions on 'pure' science, I moved Gerry Fowler from Technology.

Denis Howell, who as Under-Secretary in DES had for five years exercised the duties of 'Minister of Sport' with great force and equal acceptability, went to Housing and Local Government as a Minister of State, still responsible for sport.

After many discussions, I had reached the conclusion that sport was better located in MHLG than in DES. In addition to his responsibilities for general sporting policy and facilities – including his great work on the Edinburgh and Cardiff stadia – for professional sport and contact with the main sporting bodies, amateur and professional, his main duties were concerned mainly with the provision of facilities for young people who had left school. Most of these facilities had, directly or indirectly, to be provided by local authorities. In Scotland, Lord Hughes was promoted from Under-Secretary of State to Minister of State.

Ten ministers resigned, almost all of them over or nearing sixty. They had done a good job, most of them having been in office since October 1964. Two of them were Ministers of State, Lord Stonham and Bill Mallalieu. The others were Parliamentary Under-Secretaries: Jim Boyden (Defence), Ifor Davies (Wales), Ernie Fernyhough (Employment), James MacColl (Housing), Bert Oram (Overseas Development), Joe Slater (ex Post-Office, by this time Posts and Telecommunications), Julian Snow (Health and Social Security), who had been ill, and Bill Whitlock (Foreign and Commonwealth). There were also some lateral transfers: Brian O'Malley, deputy Chief Whip, became Under-Secretary for Social Security; Reg Freeson moved from Power to Housing; Neil Carmichael from Transport to Technology; Norman Pentland from Social Security to Posts. The new appointments were Evan Luard (Foreign and Commonwealth), Dr John Dunwoody (Health), Ivor Richard (Defence, Army); Albert Murray (Transport), Dr Ernest Davies (Technology), Joan Lestor (Education and Science), Ted Rowlands (Wales) and Ben Whitaker (Overseas Development).

The appointment of John Dunwoody created the first husband and wife ministerial team. Joan Lestor's appointment meant that all the ministerial appointments at Education were filled by former teachers: former headmaster Ted Short as Secretary of State, Oxford don and Lancaster lecturer Gerry Fowler as Minister of State for Higher Education, Alice Bacon and Jennie Lee, former secondary school teachers, and Joan Lestor, a nursery school teacher who continued to run her own class until shortly before becoming a minister.

The average age of the resigning junior ministers was sixty, and that of the incoming team thirty-eight.

Two days after the second part of the reshuffle was announced, the American astronauts visited London. In their honour there was a party at

No. 10. Almost from the outset of the Government five years earlier, I had been trying to get away from the stuffy Establishment parties which our predecessors apparently thought gave most pleasure to visiting statesmen and other dignitaries. The usual form had been that a formal dinner would be held from 8.15 or so until 10.00 p.m. after which visitors and other dinner guests would move into the reception rooms, where they would be joined by some two hundred to two hundred and fifty 'reception guests' who stayed until midnight (in our time some of them often until 2.00 or 2.30 a.m.). This continued, but the main difference from pre-1964 days was increasingly the choice of the guests, both for the dinner and the reception. Besides Government and Opposition representatives, and ex-ambassadors, ambassadors, leading businessmen and others with contacts with the country we sought to honour, we increased the number of guests of national and international distinction, whether in science, industry, music, painting and sculpture, the theatre or other areas of achievement, not excluding sport and entertainment. The idea for this change and most of the imagination in drawing up our lists of guests came from my political office. In later years we tried to identify plays and films which we knew the principal guest had enjoyed, or which had secured a favourable reception in his country, and we then invited the stars. For the last two or three parties the Forsyte Saga cast were, for this reason, regular visitors. For example, in the case of the astronauts we found that in their long period of waiting in Houston, they had seen the series right through. Our visitors found these evenings far more acceptable than a stuffed-shirt gathering; many of them knew the reputation of our principal theatrical, television and sports stars almost as well as we did.

The reception for the astronauts, who were touring the world after their successful landing on the moon, was on 14th October. Among the dinner guests we invited British service and aero-space chiefs, leading scientists, and also Britons themselves famous for some great achievement – for example, Lord Hunt, the conqueror of Everest, a number of Nobel prize-winners, the British inventor of Apollo's fuel-cell, the chairman of NRDC which had sponsored it, and others whose research or technology had in some way contributed to Apollo.

The post-dinner guests were even more representative of modern Britain than at any previous reception. But we decided to go further. This was an occasion for an accent on youth. The youth organisations were asked to find truly representative members – from the Scouts and Guides, Red Cross and VSO and the Save The Children Fund – and we invited some of the young nurses and doctors we had met in Uli in Nigeria's East Central province. Religious youth organisations were there, and the organisations representing the handicapped young people, the spastics, the deaf, the blind and others. I told my office 'to find Kevin', a blind Yorkshire boy whom I had met in a children's hospital in Liverpool and who had been entertained at Downing Street when he won a Hansard Society essay prize competition. Kevin came and richly enjoyed himself.

We decided also to invite younger boys and girls, still at school. The problem was one of selection. To avoid too much travelling on the part of quite young children, we decided – with some regret – to confine the selection to London schools. The Inner London Education Authority were asked to suggest four representative schools and to ensure that the choice of those to be invited should be made either by the teachers together, or by a vote of the children, or in some other democratic way, hoping that it would fall on at least some with a special interest in astronavigation.

The reception was a great success and the children received special treatment. After the dinner and the speeches, limited as always on these occasions to five minutes, I took charge of Neil Armstrong, while two other senior ministers took responsibility for the other two members of the Apollo team, Colonel Edwin Aldrin and Lieutenant Colonel Michael Collins, and we piloted them through the kitchens, past the assembling reception guests, and straight to the far room, the white 'boudoir', where all our younger guests were temporarily corralled.

We heard later that the astronauts enjoyed this part of their visit more than anything else to which they were subjected anywhere in their world tour; and their young guests equally were dazzled and delighted – after the astronauts they were left free to meet their sports heroes and heroines, including England's soccer and cricket captains and Olympic athletes, and their favourites from television and other entertainments. Some of the most distinguished among our older visitors were themselves infected by the uncontained excitement of the younger guests.

Chapter 35

The Hunt Report on Northern Ireland's police force – Jim Callaghan's speech on Northern Ireland – five by-elections – Roy Jenkins demolishes Barber – the Royal finances – speech on Vietnam and Nigeria – pollution and the environment – the decision on capital punishment – prices and incomes

PARLIAMENT had reassembled on 13th October to complete the work of the old session. I announced on that day the changes in the machinery of government and then the House went on to debate Northern Ireland. It took place against a background of continuing anxiety. There had been fresh outbreaks of violence in Belfast the previous weekend, involving the murder of an officer of the Royal Ulster Constabulary and serious injuries to members of the British forces. But with the anxiety – perhaps because of it – there was general support of Government policy, which Jim Callaghan, who opened the debate, admirably summarised as:

> One, to keep the peace between the communities; two, to ensure that there is in Northern Ireland, as in the rest of the United Kingdom, a common standard of citizenship; three, that the forces which sustained the state and which for a number of reasons had been unable at that time to maintain law and order should have their role examined in order that the reasons for the breakdown could be made clear and remedies proposed; and, four, that the Government of Northern Ireland should be given every help by Her Majesty's Government to make the necessary changes themselves and to carry on the task themselves.

The report of Lord Hunt's committee on the future of Northern Ireland's police forces, signed on 3rd October, reflected the view that had been put to me in August by the senior police officers who had been seconded for liaison duties in Northern Ireland – that the role of the RUC should be that of a civilian unarmed police force and that its para-military role should be discontinued and dealt with separately.

The Hunt Report, which had been accepted without question by the Northern Ireland Government and by us, included a proposal that between the Minister of Home Affairs and the police force should be interposed, as in the rest of the United Kingdom, a police authority representative of local communities. This authority, the committee urged, should be capable of representing the Roman Catholic as well as the Protestant community. Equally, the committee stressed the importance that in recruitment the RUC should show far more energy than in the past in drawing its members impartially from all classes and from all parts of the Northern Irish community. It was encouraging that this was welcomed by the Roman Catholic authorities, who expressed their willingness to press suitable members of their Church to join the new, unarmed RUC. It was recommended further that the responsibilities of Her Majesty's Inspectorate of Constabulary, whose writ ran in forty-seven police forces in England and Wales, should be extended to cover Northern Ireland. Another valuable recommendation was that police officers from Great Britain could be seconded for service in Northern Ireland, when so requested by the police authority there, reproducing the mobility which had been found useful east of St George's Channel.

A fundamental consequence of the Hunt Report, and of its insistence that the RUC should be stripped of its para-military functions, was the disappearance of the controversial, and, indeed, hated B-Specials.

Summarising the Report and its implications, Jim Callaghan indicated the full support of the UK Government while making clear that its implementation must depend on the acceptance, in a tense political situation, of its recommendations by the Stormont Government. This was forthcoming, and in the succeeding parliamentary session, the Westminster Parliament was asked to carry legislation, first, for the creation of a military reserve force in Northern Ireland, to undertake the border patrol and other quasi-military functions hitherto exercised by the RUC and, second, for the establishment of arrangements to enable police officers in England, Wales and Scotland to be made available for service in Northern Ireland. Apart from a parliamentary storm – arising from our back-benchers – about the Government's proposal that the new reserve force should be known as the 'Ulster' rather than the Northern Ireland Defence Regiment, the two proposals went through without difficulty.

For the rest of his speech, the Home Secretary dealt in great depth with the measures then going through the Stormont Parliament to implement the requirements of the Downing Street declaration about equality of rights in Northern Ireland with those enjoyed in the rest of the United Kingdom. He ended his speech with a forthright attack on the manifestation of Paisleyism, with some illuminating Paisleyite quotations linking the Home Secretary and his ministerial colleagues, Mr Hogg, Mr Heath, and the rest of the House, as creatures of Rome. His most telling words referred to the language of Paisleyism:

> It is the language of war, cast in a biblical mould. 'Fight the good fight' sung in Belfast after a night of rioting is very different when it is sung in an English country chapel in a village. This is what the Reverend Paisley either fails to appreciate or deliberately plays on.

Jim Callaghan's opening speech, in effect, concluded the debate. Apart from a few grunts from Ulster Unionist members – directed mainly against their hereditary foes in Northern Ireland and to a scarcely lesser extent against Labour back-benchers who had asserted the primacy of human rights in the Ulster situation – the rest of the debate was characterised in the main by official Opposition spokesmen meekly supporting the words and actions of the Government, and by our own back-benchers expressing their criticisms of Stormont and the Unionists in speeches designed to strengthen the arm of the Home Secretary.

The remaining days of the session were devoted in large part to further controversy on parliamentary boundaries, already recounted in the previous chapter, to consideration of Lords' amendments to Bills, to the Report and Third Reading stages of, mainly, uncontroversial Bills (such as the Lord Chancellor's Administration of Justice Bill); to debates on the Brambell Report on factory farming, and the report of the Select Committee on Procedure; to the orders giving effect to the changes in the machinery of government which I had announced on 13th October, and to those continuing the powers laid down in the Southern Rhodesia Act, 1965.

These went through easily, with only twenty-six MPs going into the No lobby. And this time there was no subsequent trouble in the Lords.

On 22nd October, the last day of the session, the Queen's Prorogation Speech recounted the legislative achievements of the parliamentary year.

It recorded the appointment of the Commission on Industrial Relations and the Royal Commission on the Constitution, as well as the grant of the Royal Charter to the Open University; measures to help the Lancashire textile industry; an Act to assist the development of tourism; the Decimal Currency Act; the legislation to integrate public transport in London under the Greater London Council; an Act to set up a central system for driving and vehicle licences; new legislation to implement the Aberfan report recommendations to ensure the safety of tips of mine or quarry refuse; the Act to convert the Post Office from a department of state to a public corporation; action to implement the proposals of the Northumberland Inquiry, following the foot-and-mouth outbreak, and the introduction of new codes of practice for animal welfare, particularly in factory farming; a further Act to help the film industry; improvements in National Insurance pensions and benefits, and in supplementary benefits and war pensions, and in public service pensions, together with legislation to make insurance contributions more closely income-related.

There was also the Children and Young Persons Act; legislation to enable Britain to accede to the United Nations Convention on genocide; an Act to allow appeals by would-be immigrants against refusal of entry; the Act to raise the limit on the Government contribution to the National Theatre; the Housing Act, which greatly increased Government aid for the repair and improvement of older houses and their environment; an Act to provide powers and funds for the urban programme for areas of special social need; Acts to modernise the town and country planning system and to bring up to date the law on housing and education in Scotland; legislation to reduce the legal age of majority to eighteen and to provide for voting at eighteen; and a further list of measures of law reform, including those providing for the succession rights of illegitimate children, for changes in the jurisdiction of the county courts and in the system for trying cases of personal injury and real property.

This was again a formidable list of legislation carried through. Much of the press and parliamentary comment on the Queen's Speech which had opened the session a year earlier had related to its 'dullness', or, at best, 'worthiness'; what could be seen when the session ended was how much had been done in the shape of humane legislation affecting the lives of tens of millions of people, including the very old and the very young.

The 1969–70 session was opened on 28th October. It was widely – and rightly – predicted that it would be the last session of the Parliament elected in 1966, and that it might very well not run its full course. But unlike the situation at the end of the 1959–64 Parliament and, it must be admitted, in 1950–51, we were not scraping the barrel. The Legislation committee of the Cabinet, working many months ahead to prepare the programme for the coming session, had throughout the spring and summer been forced to adjudicate between the competing claims of a number of ministers with draft legislation they hoped to see included; inevitably Cabinet consideration of the forward programme gave us the painful duty of deciding on priorities and postponing deeply-cherished measures.

As I had warned the Cabinet when we took office, a reforming Government faces two major restraints: shortage of finance and shortage of parliamentary time. This was as true after six years of the highest legislative productivity in our history, as when we began; when the draft of the Queen's Speech was complete, we had to defer many measures, some of them involving major legislation already in an advanced state of drafting, or with the policy largely decided and ready for the draftsman. The measures postponed, we calculated, were sufficient to occupy some two to two and a half years of future parliamentary legislative time. Certainly our Government, after nearly six years in office, was not running out of steam. Legislatively, as in other ways, we were getting into our stride, as the economic constraints lessened.

The promised legislation included the measure to give effect to the Government's announced policy for intermediate areas; to secure the safety, health and welfare of those employed on off-shore drilling stations; Bills to give effect to the Government's revised policy for industrial relations, to the policies on industrial safety and health, and the Bill to provide for equal pay for men and women. There were to be Bills to rationalise the work of the Monopolies Commission and the Prices and Incomes Board and to combine them in a single body; to deal with the scandal of 'labour-only sub-contracting' in the building industry, under which unscrupulous employers evaded PAYE, social service contributions and, indeed, legal requirements affecting safety; to amend the Merchant Shipping Act – a Bill had been introduced in the previous session, but it was too late to become law; and another to provide for the safety of fishermen, following the succession of disasters in Arctic fishing grounds, and the report of the Holland-Martin inquiry set up by the Government.

The speech also foreshadowed a major Civil Aviation Bill, following the report of the Edwards committee; legislation to reorganise the gas and electricity industries, and to give the Gas Council powers to search for, refine and market petroleum; a minor Bill to assist the film industry, and a major Bill to reorganise Britain's ports on the basis of public ownership and control; legislation to set up the Atomic Energy Authority's nuclear fuel business as a separate Government-controlled company; a Bill to continue the powers given under the Coal Industry Act, 1967, for helping the coal industry, and particularly the older miners; agricultural legislation on egg marketing, grants for fixed capital investment, the reorganisation of smallholdings, and modernisation of the law relating to sales of fertilisers and feeding stuffs; a Bill to require laggard local authorities to come into line with Government policy requiring the preparation of plans to reorganise secondary education on comprehensive lines; a Bill to tighten up the control on dangerous drugs, with much sharper penalties on drug-pushing; a Bill – the biggest of the session – on national superannuation and social insurance, including the protection of occupational pension rights on change of employment; and legislation to follow the Seebohm committee's report on local authority and allied personal social services.

There were proposals – though not yet legislation – to be put forward on local government reform and a revised Green Paper on the future administration of the National Health Service; the powers deriving from prices and incomes policy to control increases in the rents of council houses were to be made permanent by fresh legislation; Scottish law was to be further modernised, including the law on highway construction, and on the feudal system of land tenure and conveyancing; law reform south of the border was to reform provisions for recovering civil debts, substituting the attachment of wages for imprisonment for debt, to humanise the law about the repossession of mortgaged property and to enlarge the powers of the courts on financial provision for wives whose marriages have broken down.

In the debate which followed, Mr Heath, instead of concentrating on the legislative programmes, produced a lively speech attacking the Government's record, especially in the field of economic policy. It was probably the most effective speech he had made as Leader of the Opposition, even if largely unrelated to the world in which we live. But it served its turn and it pleased his troops. My own speech I had prepared on conventional lines, to inform the House about the details of the legislative programme we were supposed to be debating; all that will be remembered of it will be the reference to the pressures then being exercised on one of the more civilised of the Conservative members, Mr Nigel Fisher, MP for Surbiton, and my branding of his right-wing accusers as 'the skinheads of Surbiton'.

Mr Heath may have had a more immediate electoral target in mind than the general election battle. Two days after the Queen's Speech there were five simultaneous by-elections, all in Labour seats – Paddington North, Islington North, Glasgow, Gorbals, Newcastle-under-Lyme and Swindon, the first four caused by deaths, the last by the application by the sitting member for the Chiltern Hundreds.

There was great interest in the 'little election' to see whether Labour would show the improvement currently recorded in the public opinion polls. I was apprehensive because in the London and Glasgow seats Labour support had been eroded by housing movements; there had been complaints about the selection procedure for the Labour candidate in Islington; there was an apparently powerful Scottish Nationalist inter-vention in the Gorbals; and in Swindon there had been considerable political disenchantment with the previous member, Francis Noel-Baker.

Mr Heath took no chances. The night before the poll he descended on Croydon and delivered one of the predictable union-bashing speeches which he usually saved for such occasions. (The weekend before the GLC elections the following April saw the next). There was nothing new in his speech, but it was dutifully splashed the next morning – polling day – by all the loyal Conservative newspapers.

Nor was that all. On the day of the Queen's Speech, the BBC broke with all convention by inviting the Leader of the Opposition to have, at a peak viewing-hour, a quarter of an hour for a party political attack on the Government's legislative programme. No arrangements were made for any Government reply on comparable terms and no thought given, apparently, to the by-elections two days later. Since this was a new de-parture, it was surprising that no inter-party discussions were instituted as with all other programmes – for example on the rules governing post-Budget broadcasts.

To be fair to the BBC, when this broadcast was drawn to their attention the Governors castigated those responsible – it was, of course, too late to offer us redress – and laid down a law as binding as those of the Medes and the Persians, forbidding any invitation to party leaders to broadcast during the currency of a debate. The inviolability of this new rule was demonstrated a few weeks later when it was invoked against me. I had frequently been invited to broadcast on the Nigerian issue, but as I wished to reserve a major contribution for the forthcoming parliamentary debate, I did not accept. I made my speech in Parliament on 8th December, and was then free to take part in the special BBC programme on Nigeria that evening. No, said the BBC – on the grounds that it was a continuing debate. (It was not, in fact; there were two separate debates, but that did not seem to matter). Instead a panel of three sat in judgment on my speech. Two of them were so pro-Biafran that the chairman of the discussion, commenting that the participants were two to one against us, invited Labour's Patrick Gordon Walker, as a compensation, to have the last word.

The by-election situation having been thus teed up by the energy of Mr Heath and the ingenuity of his friends, we duly awaited the declaration of the polls. In Paddington we held the seat, with the Labour majority reduced from 6,464 to 517; housing movements probably accounted for at least half the drop. Islington, too, we held, a great relief in all the circumstances, the majority falling from 7,831 to 1,534 in a very low poll.

In the Gorbals, the Labour majority fell from 9,940 to 4,163 (5,102 over the Conservative), for the Scottish Nationalist took 3,671 votes, and pushed the Conservatives into third place. We also held Newcastle-under-Lyme, again with a big drop from 12,051 to 1,042 in our majority. Only in Swindon, the last to be declared, did the Conservatives register one of the sweeping gains they were expecting, and this for reasons I had foreseen; the Labour majority of 10,443 gave way to a Conservative majority of 478, which we easily erased the following June. The Conservatives were elated on the night's results, but it was not what they expected. In three of the seats they more or less held their 1966 vote while ours slumped; in Swindon they increased it. The swing for the four English constituencies taken together was eleven per cent, an improvement over earlier contests, but clearly we had a long way to go.

The debates on the Queen's Speech continued until the following Tuesday. On the Monday, when the House debated a Conservative economic amendment, members saw as neat a job of parliamentary annihilation as had been witnessed for years when Roy Jenkins took apart Mr Anthony Barber, who had distinguished himself a week earlier in a calculated public speech well-timed for the by-elections. Seizing on a sensational article by Mr Chapman Pincher, the defence correspondent of the *Daily Express* about the fact that it had been discovered that earlier export figures had been under-recorded, Mr Barber gave his support to the allegations in these words:

> The allegation which he [the journalist] makes is as stark as it is simple. It is that for the past two months the official figures have been deliberately designed to deceive – that the British people have been sold a pup.
> What he is saying is that Ministers have *deliberately cheated the nation.*
> And on the face of it that would seem to be just what they have done.

And in a speech in the House, on the eve of the by-election, he had compounded his offence by referring to press and television comment on recent trade figures, saying,

> ... it follows that unless the press and television commentators are regarded by the Government as quite stupid, they were *grossly and inexcusably misled* by Ministers ...

All the italics in these quotations are mine, underlining the normal style of Mr Barber's form of political expression. He had, in fact, far exceeded this choice of words in his weekly references to me, but here at last he was seeking to give chapter and verse to justify his abuse.

What had happened was this. In the spring, the Board of Trade statisticians had discovered that for years the figures of British exports had been understated, by many cargoes being cleared by Customs without the full recording of the exports. At the end of 1963 the then Conservative President of the Board of Trade, Mr Heath – no doubt laudably seeking to reduce the burden on exporters involved in customs documentation – had relaxed the rules about the recording of exports. During trade negotiations with Poland in 1969 the British negotiators had referred to the allegedly unfavourable trade balance between our two countries, quoting figures which the Poles, from their statistics, could not understand. The statisticians of the two sides got together, and the Poles were able to produce verified evidence of British exports to Poland which had not been entered into our monthly or annual Trade and Navigation Accounts. The Board of Trade and the Central Statistical Office set in hand a thorough investigation. It became clear that for four or five years our national export figures had been increasingly under-recorded, to the extent of some £10 millions to £12 millions a month. This had happened during the sensitive years when the monthly figures could provoke damaging raids on sterling. Procedures were tightened up, leading not only to more accurate figures, but to the belated lodgment of certain export documents for previous months.

When the error was discovered, the trade figures published each month were accompanied by a note which estimated the error, under-recording in the early months, over-recording when late entries swelled the figures in a given month.

The point of Mr Barber's attack was to discount the figures for August and September, by which time late recordings were becoming significant. Mr Barber, on the strength of the article he had read, alleged that the trade surplus for August and September should have been £44 millions not £66 millions; a formidable surplus in either event.

The missing £22 millions, which led to his charge of 'cheating' and 'misleading', were the belated returns.

Roy Jenkins tore him apart, calmly and clinically. After disposing of certain allegations about the handling of the statistics of imports and exports of defence equipment, which had misled the journalist and which Mr Barber had characteristically accepted without checking, he went on to the main charge.

Roy Jenkins pointed out that to that extent the figures for May, June and July must have been correspondingly under-estimated, and some of the deficient figures had been published at times of danger for sterling. Mr Barber had not referred to this. But the Chancellor was concerned to learn from where Mr Barber had got his figure of £22 millions – why not £20 or £25 millions? – to justify the charge of cheating. Five times, Roy Jenkins gave the floor to Mr Barber who lamely tried to explain first that it was his estimate, then that it was an estimate based on a conversation with a former Treasury official, and so forth. But why, the Chancellor pressed, £22 millions? Mr Barber offered to accept a lower figure if Roy Jenkins would accept it. But no, the Chancellor confirmed, it was £22 millions, and Mr Barber's informants had got it from the note attached to the trade returns. There was no cheating, no deceit, the great Barber mystery related to the figures we had published with the trade returns.

It was a clean, antiseptic operation, from which Mr Barber had barely recovered a year later, when he himself became Chancellor.

The damage that this kind of reckless charge can do was disregarded by Mr Barber, who was, of course, Conservative party chairman. It justified the bitter comment that the Conservatives were ready to sell Britain short.

As a postscript to this incident it is interesting to note that on 16th November 1970, the Conservative Secretary for Trade and Industry, Mr John Davies, told the House of Commons that in the autumn of 1970 the statisticians had discovered that the 1970 export figures were still subject to substantial under-recording to the extent of £150 millions a year, some £12 millions each month. This meant that all our estimates of the trade balance for 1969 and 1970 were very much too low and our success much greater than we had claimed. It meant, too, though this fact received surprisingly little publicity, that Mr Heath's use, in the election, of the May trade figures, which, published three days before polling day, showed a visible trade deficit of £31 millions, (£13 millions after allowing for the erratic import of two Jumbo jets for BOAC), was based on the wrong facts. Allowing for this and on the facts stated by Mr Davies five months later our visible trade, in that politically important month, must have been approximately in balance; taking into account the strong favourable trend in net invisible earnings, the month's current balance must have shown a surplus of at least £50 millions. Those trade figures, and Mr Heath's unscrupulous use of them, were regarded by many independent commentators, as a turning-point in the election campaign.

Having disposed of Mr Barber, Roy Jenkins was able to present a favourable account of the economy. Industrial production was eight and a half per cent up since devaluation; this was the first period of sustained growth accompanied by an improvement in the balance of payments. In the whole of the Conservative period of office 1951–64, an improvement in overseas payments had occurred only at times of deflation.

We had been helped, for once, by external factors, too.

The IMF Special Drawing Rights scheme, in which Jim Callaghan had played so notable a part, followed by Roy Jenkins who pushed it through international bureaucratic obstruction and French reservations, had come into effect on 28th July, following its adoption by three-fifths of the 100 member countries. This meant that, from January 1970, Britain could draw up to £170 millions a year of additional international currency without incurring new debt obligations. In 1970 we proceeded to draw our allowance and used it for the extinction of overseas debt. Internationally, the Special Drawing Rights scheme was a step in the right direction, a beginning in relating world liquidity to the growth of world trade. It did not go, as yet, anything like so far as we wished nor did it incorporate – as I had urged in a speech in Washington on 1st April 1964 and further developed in another speech to the American Chamber of Commerce in London on 15th May of that year – our proposals for the creation of drawing rights specifically related to the needs of developing countries, enabling them to import investment goods without straining the foreign exchange position either of themselves or of supplying countries.

The second external easement came from Germany. The Bundestag election, resulting in the new coalition between the Social Democrats and the Free Democrats, meant an end to the argument between Dr Schiller and Mr Strauss about revaluation. As soon as the SPD-led coalition was formed the Deutschemark was freed to find its own level, and appreciated by six and a half per cent. When the coalition was confirmed in office by the Bundestag, it was definitively set at a new rate, eight and a half per cent above its previous level. The massive movement of funds into Frankfurt came to an end for the time being, indeed for a while it was reversed.

Though there were occasional flurries in the months ahead, the revaluation of the Deutschemark ushered in a period of international currency stability the like of which we had not known for very many years.

The Queen's Speech debate was hardly over before a crisis over the Royal finances hit the headlines and had to be dealt with in the House. In two broadcasts in the United States in the first week in November, the Duke of Edinburgh had been asked a number of questions about the monarchy. One answer he gave – factually correct – was that the Royal Family would 'go into the red next year', and another, clearly jocular, suggested that 'we may have to move into smaller premises'. Statements made in the United States by public figures, and especially Royal personages, inevitably feed back into this country with a degree of amplification far exceeding the importance of the statement, and for some reason they attract far more attention than they would if uttered in this country. So it proved on this occasion. When the interviews were broadcast at the weekend – a few days after being recorded – the reception was sensational. Mr Anthony Barber, on the Sunday night, 9th November, felt moved to make a statement, while conceding that it was for the Government to initiate action.

By the Monday, according to the press treatment, there had rarely been such a crisis. An attempt was made to raise the issue by way of a Standing Order No. 9 emergency debate in the House, but that failed. Manny Shinwell was reported as saying, 'If we want a monarchy we have to pay them properly. We can't have them going around in rags.'

The shadow cabinet, at their meeting, considered the subject with the deepest gravity and Mr Heath let it be known that, to quote one report, 'circumstances now obliged that a Select Committee should be set up to review what has been called the present position of the Civil List'.

I decided to make a statement in the House the following day, and to set all the facts, which were many and involved, in their proper perspective. While I was dressing for the annual Guildhall dinner, I gave instructions for an announcement to be made that I would make a statement after questions on the Tuesday. The following morning the 'crisis' was running as strongly as ever. My object was to defuse it.

The House was crowded and excited when I made the statement I had dictated with immense care, the preceding night, on returning from Guildhall. I began with the facts. On the Queen's accession, Parliament had fixed the annual amount of the Consolidated Fund grant to the Civil List as £475,000.

In fixing this sum it had been recognised that the real value of any provision would be eroded in real terms over the years. The Select Committee, under the then Chancellor Mr (later Lord) Butler, had included a substantial margin, so that in the early years a reserve could be built up and invested to provide a fund for meeting future deficits. Section 95 of the Civil List Act, 1952, had settled this supplement at £95,000 a year, £25,000 of which was to be available for provision by the Sovereign for members of the Royal Family for whom Parliament had not specifically provided. An amendment by Hugh Gaitskell that the Civil List should be reviewed every ten years had been voted down.

From 1952 to 1961 the Civil List provision showed a surplus, though, with wages and other costs rising in the late fifties and early sixties, the saving from 1959 to 1961 had become very small. After 1962, deficits were incurred. By 1968–69 it had become clear not only that the annual grant was falling far short of outgoings, but that the reserve which had been built up in the early years was being reduced year by year and would be exhausted – meaning that the Civil List over the reign as a whole would be in deficit – by the end of 1970.

For this reason there had been over a period of months detailed discussions between the Queen's advisers and Treasury officials, as a result of which the Government authorised a communication to the effect that a new select committee would be appointed at the beginning of the succeeding Parliament. Earlier action was not required.

I added two facts. The first was that in recent years there had been a progressive transfer of expenditure, previously borne by the Royal Household, to funds provided by departmental votes. Examples were the remuneration of staff engaged on maintenance of the Royal palaces and, more recently, the cost to the Civil List of expenditure on Royal tours overseas and of rail travel on Royal functions in this country. In addition, departmental votes were by this time carrying, to the extent of some £40,000 a year, certain expenses in relation to State entertainment – for example during State visits – which in previous years would have been borne on the Civil List.

The second fact I thought the House would like to know was that, in the previous six years, there had been two efficiency investigations of the Royal Household, one by the Organisation and Methods Division of the Treasury the other by an industrialist commissioned by the Queen's advisers, which had led to a number of cost-saving improvements. I concluded:

> I hope that the House will accept that in this important – and I do not need to stress, delicate – matter, the Government have proceeded in full discussion with the Queen's advisers, on a basis capable of dealing with the problem which is developing, and of dealing with it in time, having regard both to increasing costs and to a proper regard for restraint in public expenditure.

Mr Heath welcomed the statement but, in view of the urgency, tried to press me to set up a select committee at once: after all, my pledge that it would be set up at the beginning of the next Parliament could relate to a point in time which, depending on election timing, might be as late as the spring of 1971, and the reserve would have run out, he was at pains to emphasise, by the end of 1970. But in view of my statement, he was shouting into the wind.

From then on I had no difficulty with the questions which followed.

The Royal advisers had been filled with anxiety. After the parliamentary exchanges I let them know that, while the morning papers would necessarily print a full report on all that had been said, in my view the question, so sensational up to that time, would be as dead as cold mutton by lunch-time the following day. So it proved. The afternoon papers had by that time moved on to other issues.

So indeed had Parliament. The Nigerian situation dominated questions to the Foreign and Commonwealth Secretary and myself, as malnutrition, real and tragic, was exploited for political purposes by supporters of Colonel Ojukwu who could have taken steps to end it by allowing transport of relief supplies, either by surface routes or by daylight flights.

Parliamentary concern was not confined to Nigeria. Towards the end of the month, horrifying but apparently authenticated stories crossed the Atlantic about alleged massacres of South Vietnamese civilians by United States forces. Concern was by no means limited to the substantial body of Labour members who had consistently opposed American involvement in Vietnam. Many commentators, of varying points of view, were critical and it is fair to say that the Cabinet was as concerned at the allegations as any Members of Parliament. I decided that both this issue and the anxieties about relief supplies for Biafra should be brought before the House at the earliest opportunity, and in agreement with the Opposition, who contributed a supply day to supplement the day of Government time we were prepared to make available, it was announced that the House would debate these two issues on 8th and 9th December. MPs would be asked to concentrate on Vietnam on the Monday and on Nigeria on the Tuesday, but in opening the debate, the Lord President told the House I would deal with both issues.

I referred first, and briefly, to the Greek situation. The Council of Europe, later in the week, was due to receive the report on the Greek Government's compliance with the human rights requirements called for at the May meeting of its committee of ministers. I informed the House that, in default of a sudden change of heart by the Greek Government, expressed in a short and specific timetable relating to the restoration both of democracy and human rights, Her Majesty's Government's representative had been instructed to vote for the suspension of Greece from membership of the Council. In the event, at the eleventh hour, Greece withdrew from membership.

The theme of the rest of my speech was that foreign policy in certain circumstances was a choice of evils, and that this was true both in Vietnam and Nigeria.

> We must consider whether one solution will lead more speedily than another to a peaceful settlement and whether it will save lives, either from direct military action or from starvation. If it will, then we must consider whether that will enhance or endanger freedom or create a situation in which new and more horrible atrocities will be likely to result. Peace, freedom and self-determination are all ends in themselves. But, in the tragic context of each of these two countries, they are ends that conflict with one another; where judgment is necessary, but where there can be no certainty of finality of judgment.

Hon. Members will have seen from a report in *The Times* last Saturday that this dilemma – this choice between ends and evils – has arisen for the World Council of Churches, and there may be further controversy over this today when 'Joint Church Aid' meets. The fact that they could even consider suggesting cutting off the food programme to Biafra as a means of shortening the war, with all the dangers that that could mean in terms of relief and starvation, highlights the agony of choosing between ends. . . .

On the alleged atrocities at My Lai I said that what the House had to ask, once the facts were established by the ruthless investigation the President had promised, was whether it was an incident – an aberration, an obscene incident – or whether it was endemic in this kind of war. If the latter, it would be our duty to dissociate from the United States and their conduct of the war. We had, I said, dissociated from aspects of American policy, for example when Michael Stewart had quoted the Declaration of Independence – 'a decent respect for the opinions of mankind' – on the use of gas, and again over the bombing of Hanoi and Haiphong. If it were argued that all war involves such incidents, or still more if it were argued that such an occurrence was unavoidable in this war, then we must accept an editorial view I quoted from the *Guardian* that, '. . . the Americans would deserve to be told that they had lost the war if they believed that they could not win it without the physical elimination of anyone who helps the enemy'.

We must, therefore, I said, await the findings of the judicial examination before we could reach such a decision.

Turning to Biafra, I began again with the choice of evils:

Once again, the parties to the fighting, and their peoples, and we here in Britain, face a situation where every decision of policy is a choice of evils: where what is right – indeed, what to some hon. Members seems to be an over-riding bounden duty – means a denial of what to other hon. Members will seem a categorical imperative which cannot be laid aside. That is the essence of the problem.

I then asked the House to look at this question from the standpoint both of Colonel Ojukwu and of General Gowon.

For Colonel Ojukwu, the security of the Ibo people, their right to live their lives in their own way, is a fundamental principle overriding all others. I do not share – and many hon. Members do not share – his disbelief that these can be secured as part of a negotiated settlement, and as part of a united Nigeria, but what we may feel is not the point.
The failure of every effort to secure peace, or to get to the negotiating table, still rests on the fact that Colonel Ojukwu and those around him have not yet been persuaded that the future of the Ibo people can be safeguarded without further tragic conflict.
It is because this is for him an overriding imperative that he rejects daylight flights or other means of speeding relief supplies from within Nigeria from Governments, including this Government, or the International Red

Cross and from the Churches. For the greater part of the outside world, the obvious solution of this problem is the mercy corridor, such as the road from Enugu into the Biafran enclave, but for Colonel Ojukwu it carries the risk of a military thrust into the heart of his defences. . . .

We can propose, and Her Majesty's Government did so eighteen months ago, possible forms of international assurances as guarantees against this. We were right then and we are right now to play our part in this; but precisely because Colonel Ojukwu insists on this conception of military security every effort, every mediator who has sought to open up the mercy corridor has been met with refusal. That is why the IRC and many Governments have spent many months of effort and a formidable expenditure of money and resources derived from Government treasuries and private charity in trying to mount an airlift.

I understand the arguments of Colonel Ojukwu and his fear that Uli airstrip would lie open to a sudden military air strike. I recognise as a fact in the situation, even if I cannot support his demand, that on military grounds Uli should be kept open by day to mount the air strikes made possible by his acquisition of rocket-firing aircraft and other aircraft from Europe . . . But it does not lie with those who take a different view from ours, and, as I have said, different from over 30 independent Governments in Africa, with those who support Colonel Ojukwu on this – and I understand his position – to put the blame for hunger and malnutrition on the Federal Government or on Her Majesty's Government. . . .

They may say – and I understand this if they say it – that the principle of full self-determination for the Ibos, whether outside or inside the Federation, is over-riding. They may say – and I understand it if they say it – that Colonel Ojukwu is right to prevent daylight flights. They are entitled to say this. But, if that is what they say, they are not entitled at the same time to lay the blame for starvation at the door of the Federal Government or Her Majesty's Government. The logic of their argument – and I concede that it is a respectable argument in logic – is to say that this is Colonel Ojukwu's decision, as it is, and they should proceed to justify that decision on other grounds. . . .

Then turning to the position of General Gowon, I said:

It has not been easy for the Federal Government to agree to this airlift. It is not in the nature of those fighting a war and who have a vital and over-riding principle as they see it, to be over-concerned about the welfare of the enemy's civil population. The whole history of blockade and economic warfare in wars between advanced nations bears testimony to this, including recent wars in Europe, but this is a civil war and throughout history, as we know, civil wars have been even more bloody and unrelenting than wars between nations . . .

I believe that history will pay this tribute, that, faced with a brutal and brutalising civil war, General Gowon felt that his duty lay not in denying but in facilitating the supply of food and medical supplies to those he was fighting – and, in the event, to agree to its being done in this way, that it even permitted the continued supply of arms to the beleaguered and hard-pressed secessionist enclave. Not all my hon. Friends nor all hon. Members opposite will agree, but this is a fact. Those were arms urgently needed by Colonel Ojukwu and if they had been denied or not supplied the war could have ended more quickly.

History may well say that if the Federal Government had hardened their heart against our pressure and the pressure of other Governments and of civilised organisations the whole world over, this war might have ended a good deal earlier, perhaps with far less suffering, fewer casualties, and fewer deaths from starvation. I do not know, but the fact that this can be argued shows the nature of the dilemma that Nigeria, and we, and this House have to face, and are facing, the dilemma now made newly articulate by the World Council of Churches. . . .

I have set out these extracts so fully because this speech represented for me the results of a great deal of heart-searching over more than two years, and was my attempt to rationalise the moral choice which the Government, Parliament and the British people were facing. It was widely accepted even by some who wholeheartedly supported the Biafran cause. Seeing it from Colonel Ojukwu's standpoint seemed fair to them, and some, at least, were ready to agree that for him the rejection of relief missions was enjoined on him by his over-riding principle of Ibo self-determination. This was a long way from the constant assertion of British complicity in murder which we read daily in one or two newspapers, and saw each night in the steady drip, drip of pro-Biafran propaganda on the television screens.

Nigeria was debated for the whole of the next day. Twenty-five of our back-benchers, almost all of them committed pro-Biafrans, voted against the Government in a total of eighty-six in the anti-Government lobby. But many made clear that their vote was more through opposition to our arms supplies than from any desire, now, to blame the British Government for malnutrition in Nigeria.

On 4th December, we faced – at Wellingborough and Louth – the 35th and 36th of the thirty-eight by-elections which took place in the 1966–70 Parliament. As expected, we lost Wellingborough, where a Labour majority of 2,233 gave way to a Conservative gain by 6,049, a swing of under ten per cent. In Louth, on a bitterly cold day, our vote was undoubtedly hit by the weather and fell by nearly two thirds, giving a swing of just under fifteen per cent to the Conservatives.

The last week of the parliamentary sittings before the Christmas recess was a period of intense activity, with ministerial statements and two major debates. On 11th December, the day of Tony Benn's Upper Clyde Shipbuilders' statement, I announced the Government's interim decision on environmental pollution. When I appointed Tony Crosland in October I had asked him for an urgent report on steps which should be taken immediately. He had the advantage of a considerable amount of preparatory work which had been done by Sir Solly Zuckerman, the Government's Chief Scientific Adviser.

I announced the appointment, under him, of a permanent central unit, composed mainly of scientists on his own staff, to assist in co-ordinating inter-departmental work, and to monitor any signs of new dangers to the environment. In addition – and this was why I, rather than Tony Crosland, was making the statement in the House – I announced the Queen's approval to the establishment of a Royal Commission on Environmental Pollution, to be headed by Sir Eric Ashby. Its duty would be, I told the House, 'to advise on matters both national and international, concerning the pollution of the environment: on the adequacy of research in this field; and the future possibilities of danger in the environment'.

Its terms of reference, I explained, envisaged something different from the usual type of Royal Commission required to study the subject referred to it, take evidence, deliberate, make its report, and disband. This was to be a standing Royal Commission, free to report at any time, either on the whole field of pollution, or any specific aspect of it, but also to continue as a permanent watchdog on environmental dangers. In proposing it I had in mind the precedent of the Royal Commission on the Fine Arts, set up in 1924, and that of the Prices and Incomes Board set up in 1965 as a Royal Commission until its establishment had become statutory in 1966.

My short statement, welcomed by the House, paved the way for a major speech on the environment by Tony Crosland the following week, one of the most important and factual statements on the subject ever made. As far as he and I could judge, not a word of it appeared the next day in a single national morning paper.

Pollution in Britain was not our only concern. At this time news reached us, through scientific sources, of a major Soviet proposal to change not only their own environment, but that of a large part of the world. Consideration was being given by them to a proposal to redirect the course of two of the major rivers, the Ob and the Yenesei, so that their outfall would no longer be into the Arctic Ocean. The warmer water entering these rivers from the south and elsewhere had been, almost since the world began, a factor in preventing the Arctic from being even colder than it is. To redirect them might well permanently change the climate of considerable parts of Europe – and indeed a wider area of the world – with major effects on agriculture and fisheries, to say nothing of the like-lihood that Britain would have longer winters, and winters many degrees colder than anything we or our forefathers had known. We sought to get information from the Russians on this proposal, but they were noticeably guarded about it. But we found that our concern was shared by the top scientists of other Governments. We had made no progress in establishing Soviet intentions when the Government left office. It was one of the questions I intended to raise with Mr Kosygin on the visit he had invited me to make in the summer of 1970 after the General Election. This subject will remain on the agenda not only to top-level relations between scientists of different nations, but of still higher-powered international discussion.

Two major and controversial debates had been set for the last three days before the Christmas adjournment. We were due, not later than 31st July 1970, to take a decision on the provision in the 1965 Act abolishing capital punishment, under which capital punishment would be resumed after five years in default of a specific decision of both Houses to end it permanently. The Cabinet had given some thought to this during the late summer and autumn and decided, in November, that it would be desirable to get the question resolved, one way or the other, by Christmas. The amendment which had been carried in the Lords in July 1965 did not permit of any extension of the so-called trial period after 31st July, a course some members would have wished to follow since it would have given them more time to judge the evidence. One fact urged upon us was that it was desirable to settle the issue well before the election, as it would be unhealthy for it to be made an election issue by individual candidates of any party. This election argument was not the decisive factor so far as the Cabinet was concerned, though in the first day's debate on 15th December Shirley Williams disposed of it. But all interested in the question knew that the issue must be settled, and the fact that the Home Secretary was considering it became known early in August. Public discussion was increasingly concentrated on it, and some of it was in danger of becoming unhealthy and morbid. One sickening radio broadcast, enacting the simulated sounds of an execution, was particularly revolting, even though it was done for the best of reasons and even though many abolitionists regarded it as telling and effective.

The arguments against 'rushing it' before Christmas, which were urged by the retentionists, and indeed by some Conservative abolitionists, were based on the fact that we had no official annual figures later than 1968 to show how the number of murders had changed after abolition. Against this it was argued that the figures could not be conclusive; protagonists could interpret them to suit their purpose. The number of murders had increased and so had crimes of violence, but this was true of other countries, where capital punishment had either continued or been discontinued over a longer period. 'Capital murders', those which in the Conservative Government's Homicide Act of 1957 invoked the death penalty, had fallen since abolition.

When the Opposition was told of our intention to bring the matter before the House before Christmas, it reacted sharply and tabled a censure motion, deploring our action in bringing the subject forward for decision before the 1969 figures were available. There were some signs that the Opposition was seeking subtly to enlist for electoral purposes the many supporters of capital punishment. Whatever its intentions may have been at that time, the way Mr Heath subsequently conducted himself disposed of the charge. When I saw the Conservatives' censure motion, I urged, contrary to the views of some of my colleagues, that we should give them every opportunity to debate it, to get any bad blood out of their system or to achieve party unity, whatever it was they wanted, with a full day's debate and a party vote on procedure and timing. This would leave them and the House the freest of free votes on the important issue before us. Even when the idea of separating the debates was agreed, some of my colleagues wanted to confine the censure debate to a half-day. My insistence on a full day was proved right. The censure debate, on 15th December, became monotonously repetitive and Jim Callaghan surprised his critics in his winding-up speech by promising the next day to put before the House the first crude, unqualified 1969 figures.

The next day, free of all rancour, the House debated freely and voted freely. All three party leaders were in the abolitionist lobby, with almost all the front-benchers of the two sides. The vote to end the death penalty was carried by 343 to 185.

But the greatest interest was in the debate in the Lords the following day, 17th December, where a majority for abolition could not be safely predicted, despite the unanimity of the bishops – and almost all, if not all, of the judges – in its favour. The proceedings in the Lords were attended with great drama. There was a packed attendance of peers, public, and many MPs from the Commons. The debate was conducted at a very high level on both sides, but undoubtedly the greatest speech of the day, both for its content and manner and for the effect it had on doubters, was the concluding contribution of Gerald Gardiner, the Lord Chancellor. Some of the most discriminating parliamentarians and commentators of my acquaintance described it to me as the greatest parliamentary speech they had ever heard – and undoubtedly one unprecedented in its power and effect in influencing the results of the debate. When he sat down, the Lords passed the resolution abolishing capital punishment by 220 votes to 174.

By this time the Commons had turned its attention once again to prices and incomes. In all the inter-party and public discussions on legislation, culminating in the Chancellor's announcement in his 1969 Budget speech, we had made clear that the post-devaluation powers in the 1968 Act would lapse at the end of the year and that we should then rely on the more moderate powers in Part II of the 1966 Act. In the Queen's Speech on 28th October, the Government had announced its intention to merge the Prices and Incomes Board with the Monopolies Commission, and in the debate I had said, therefore, that the reactivation of the Part II powers, by a parliamentary resolution, would be a 'bridging operation' until the new Commission for Manpower and Industry was created.

There had been the clearest indication that whenever the motion to reactivate Part II came before the House, there would be a mass revolt in our ranks. There were even forecasts of the Government's defeat, since the Conservatives would undoubtedly vote against us. Their policy for prices and incomes in those pre-election days was inscrutable and indeed so remained for a long period after they formed a government.

What Part II in fact did was confined simply to two main powers. The first was to enable the Government to require early warning of proposals to increase pay or prices, so that the Government could discuss them with those concerned – eighteen per cent of intended price increases had been withdrawn or modified as a result of such discussions – or refer them to the Prices and Incomes Board. Secondly, under the Act the Government could require a standstill, whether of a pay increase or a price increase, for up to thirty days while the Department was evaluating the proposal and having discussions with the interests concerned; and, if a reference was made to the NBPI, defer action for a further three months, pending the publication of the Board's report. There was no further delaying power beyond three months and, even then, it operated only if a NBPI reference were made; if there were no such reference, the delaying power was limited to thirty days.

To the surprise of most of the House, Mr Heath insisted on making a major speech. It was shrill and mainly a repetition of his speeches to the Tory faithful in the country, combining a failure to refer at any point to Part II with an ideological commitment against any form of incomes policy and a crude appeal to Labour back-benchers. There was also a long piece of routine abuse directed at me, whom I had slowly gathered he did not like. After calling for an early election, he dismissed the possibility of my agreeing, for, he said, reaching the oratorical heights, I was 'Bad, bad, bad, but not mad, mad, mad!'

Later I had reason to doubt whether his motive in intervening in the debate was simply to display his oratorical prowess, or whether there was another reason. Reports were appearing in the press – and these were confirmed after the election in a statement by the head of the Conservative Central Office organisation machine – that their private polls were showing that if we had gone to the country in the latter months of 1969 we should have won.

The motion was carried by 289 votes to 261.

I left for Christmas at Chequers, to which, on Boxing Day, instead of visiting Stoke Mandeville Hospital as I had done in previous years, I invited all the paraplegic patients who could come. The party was one of the happiest occasions of my premiership. I was grateful to my show-business friends who came along to help the party get going and no less, to Esme James, the new custodian of Chequers – a member of the No. 10 staff from Winston Churchill's days – and the WRENS and WRAFS who did so much for our guests. Then I went to the Isles of Scilly for the New Year.

This was a short and uneventful rest, marked by one example of parliamentary courtesy and camaraderie which politicians of some countries abroad might have found it difficult to comprehend.

One of my most persistent questioners and critics throughout our years of office was Neil Marten, MP for Banbury. He combined an uncanny and inexplicable ability to get his twice-weekly questions to me high on the order paper – usually at No. 1 – with an unusual topicality and originality in his supplementary questions which kept me fully extended. Just before Christmas he asked me if I would make a ministerial broadcast on New Year's Eve. My opening answer informed him that I had other engagements that evening. Undeterred, he asked whether, if I could escape from them and go on television, I would take the occasion of announcing all the disastrous Government policies of the past year which I proposed to abandon in 1970.

Having no such intention, I made it clear that any change in my arrangements for that evening would be extremely difficult, as I should be preparing for the celebration, on New Year's Day, of our thirtieth wedding anniversary. On 30th December I received from him a specially-constructed card of best wishes on our anniversary, which included a photograph of the hotel, the Old Swan at Minster Lovell, where we had spent our honeymoon – I learnt later that it was in his constituency, and that he had called on the hotel to obtain the photograph. Of such is our parliamentary system, provided it is realised that, courtesies apart, every exchange in Parliament represents a real clash of deeply-held political opinions, unaffected by, and equally unaffecting personal relationships. That is our strength.

Chapter 36

A farmers' demonstration – the end of the civil war in Nigeria – the talk with President Nixon – British relief to Nigeria – visit to Canada and the United States

THE parliamentary recess, from 19th December to 19th January, and a short recess in meetings of the Cabinet and its committees, gave me the chance to make an extended tour in areas of the north, and also to see something of the work of Government research establishments dealing with various aspects of environmental pollution.

The first day – Wednesday 7th January – was devoted to a tour of West Riding areas, where I was concerned principally with pioneering developments in education and new ventures in the arts. At 9.00 a.m. I visited Yorkshire's first purpose-built comprehensive school at Linthwaite in the Colne Valley – a mile from where I was born. Built fifteen years earlier the school had quickly developed its own traditions. I was greatly impressed by what I had found in this and other comprehensive schools; how the very size of the school and staff gives pupils a far greater freedom of choice, in permuting subjects for 'O' and 'A' levels – one of the under-publicised achievements of comprehensive secondary education.

From there I drove across the icy moors to Sheffield where I visited a unique nursery school built within, and as part of, the city's famous Parkhill flats, and then on to a new infants' and junior school, again purpose-built, and with revolutionary teaching methods. Next, I saw the Government industrial rehabilitation unit at Sheffield, where workers who, perhaps after an accident, or illness, or some psychological shock, need to adjust minds or bodies before they can take up or resume factory employment, receive the sympathetic rehabilitation they need to enable them to resume work in industry. I spent half an hour discussing this new industrial service with the social workers and other staff of the unit. In the evening I went to the Playhouse, where a young and enthusiastic company, aided by the new Arts Council policy, was performing its Christmas play.

My journey next morning to Blackburn – via Manchester – gave me the chance to see the enormous progress with the new trunk road schemes designed to link the 'grey areas' of north-east Lancashire with the main industrial areas of the country. The day was hectic, but exciting: the morning at the College of Technology and Design, a civic lunch, a visit to one of Blackburn's two pioneering health centres, which provide almost all modern facilities for out-patients, including schoolchildren, and for the doctors, in industrial or group practice, dental surgeons, radiologists and

739

others, who held their surgeries there; the YMCA and the adjoining young workers' and students' hostel.

As is usual on tours of this kind there were frequent radio and television interviews and press conferences. It was at one of these, with Barbara Castle (Blackburn is her constituency), that in answer to a series of questions on prices and incomes policy, I first used the phrase, quite off the cuff and with no prior thought, 'One man's wage increase is another man's price increase', correct in the context in which I had set it here. From Blackburn I went on to Bolton, where I visited another young theatre group, then, after a dinner with civic leaders, to the Bolton Lads' Club, and finally to Manchester for the sleeper to London.

On the Friday, 9th January, after only an hour at No. 10 I drove to the Water Pollution Research Laboratory at Stevenage, one of whose main tasks is fundamental and practical research into effluent problems. With Tony Crosland and Ernest Davies, Parliamentary Secretary at Technology, I was given a quick course on the theory and practice of pollution, covering industrial effluent and town drainage, and the means – and cost – of combating it. From there I went a short distance to Warren Springs, another Government research establishment, which specialises in the main in oil and other pollution of the seas – they had done the *Torrey Canyon* experiments – and atmospheric pollution, though they had done some interesting new work on recovering valuable materials from town garbage. I saw a demonstration on a simulated beach of the new detergent developed in BP laboratories which quickly removed all traces of a deposit of crude oil.

After lunch I went to the Monks Wood Experimental Station, near Huntingdon, which is one of the Nature Conservancy stations specialising in research into the destruction of wild life. The examination of sea-birds and of near-extinct strains of moorland birds, the effects of coastal and river pollution and of the indiscriminate use of chemical additives and insecticides, were its stock-in-trade. It was encouraging to see the dedicated enthusiasm which animated the staffs here, as in the establishments I had visited in the morning. I was given some fascinating brief explanations by individual researchers about the work they were doing. The work of an entomologist I found interesting, if difficult at first to comprehend, but by the end – aided by diagrams, slides and statistics – I understood how the use of insecticides to combat the depredations of the cabbage moth larvae actually increased the menace by weakening the appetite and the ability to reproduce of other small beings who normally fed on the larvae.

The Huntingdon visit was enlivened by a demonstration from the local farmers, not the first or last that winter. On a number of engagements outside London I had received warnings that militant farmers would disrupt the traffic with their farm vehicles. There was also an intimation from their more moderate leaders that they would like to meet me for a reasoned presentation of their grievances and anxieties. Most farmers had suffered two miserable seasons, and this fact, combined with that of rising costs – including the cost of agricultural credit when they could get it – was pressed on me at meeting after meeting. They faced a financial crisis such as the postwar farming generation had not known. This was the season of the Annual Farm Price Review and it was understandable that they should urge their case on every minister who ventured into their territory. In this case, the message I sent to them via the local police miscarried: they were angered when I sped past their vehicles at the entrance to the long drive up to Monks Wood. They charged me with breach of faith, not knowing that I had offered to meet their leaders in a room set aside for the purpose at the research station.

Because of this misunderstanding they were in a furious mood when we did meet. But we soon settled down to serious discussion. The farmers put their case strongly, and handed me detailed material to study: some I had already seen and examined when I had met NFU national leaders. Whilst we talked their members had broken through the police barrier at the end of the drive and were surrounding the station with angry shouts. I offered, as I usually like to do with demonstrators, to address them at the end of our informal meeting. When I came out of the building, I found the police drawn up in line of battle in front of the entrance, recalling scenes in the second act of *The Pirates of Penzance*. I pushed through them and began to address the farmers. But at that moment they were more concerned to boo and shout slogans, than to listen. It suddenly struck me that this excessive police protection must look ludicrous. I asked the police to withdraw, and in no time got a fair hearing. I spoke seriously, with just the odd couple of jokes – against myself – which they welcomed. At the end there was some encouraging clapping and cheering, friendly although obviously not enthusiastic.

The next morning, 10th January, I left London early for a major political speech at Swansea. In January 1964 I had spoken there on economic plans and policies, with warnings of what we might have to face on taking office.

In January 1967 I had given there an interim progress report, starting from the fact that what we did have to face, in balance of payments terms, had been more than twice as bad as our worst fears. Now, three years later again, I was talking from strength – economic strength. I began my speech by quoting what was being said about us. An article in *The Times Business News* section had made this judgment. 'I believe Britain is leaving the 'sixties in much better underlying shape than she entered them'. The *Daily Express* – under the heading 'The £ Salutes the '70's', declared, 'with export prospects promising, dealers expect the £ to maintain its newfound strength, which means it enters the seventies looking more like the strong man, not the sick man of Europe'. The *Sunday*

Telegraph in a leading article asked 'Who would believe Mr Heath if he argued that all the signs of incipient solvency were fundamentally misleading? The Tories so obviously have a vested interest in pessimism. The *Daily Mail*, in a feature article, quoted Lord Stokes:

> The trouble with we British is that we don't appreciate what we have. This is a great country and it is going to be even greater.
> People go around beating their heads, but the fact is that we've got our national shopping list back, and the balance of payments situation looks as if it will continue for some time. We jolly nearly are in a good position. We can look back with pride to the time when we were an imperial power. And we can take pride in the fact that, unlike any nation previously, we disengaged ourselves without disintegrating.

The *New York Times* – whose report was described as being that of a paper which was not especially pro-British – described Britain's achievement as 'a major 1969 development that deserves great world recognition. Britain has made a spectacular turn around and has moved into one of its strongest world trading positions in many years. . . .'

The remainder of my speech dealt with our social achievements, giving newer and more up-to-date figures of the national provision we were making for all the social services. Pointing out that this had been achieved when our main national effort had been directed to strengthening the economy, I outlined our forward plans for using that strength, once it had been made secure, for a major advance in the conditions of life:

> If we had failed to deal with the economic problem we took over in the sixties then the seventies would have been dominated by the problem of living with richer and more successful neighbours.
> If we fail to deal with the social evils of the seventies we shall have the problem of living with ourselves. . . .

I had devoted a good part of my speech to the transformation which was being wrought in Wales. Between 1951 and 1964 only eight advance factories had been authorised by our predecessors, five of them in their last two years; against that, since 1964, our figure had been fifty-two, of which thirty-six had been let. In new industrial development our predecessors, in their last three years in office, had recorded 2.3 million sq. ft per year, our figure for the three years 1966–68 was 7.9 million sq. ft a year, and in 1969, 8.4 million sq. ft.

Over five years Wales, with five per cent of Britain's population, had gained new industrial development which represented eight per cent of the floor-area of Britain's total new factory space and twelve per cent of the 'job opportunities'. In terms of financial assistance for industrial development, our predecessors in their last full year of office had provided just £1 million for Wales; in our previous year, we had provided £60 millions, and the programme had not reached its peak. In derelict land clearance, under our 1966 Act, fifty-nine schemes covering 1,410 acres had been approved, with a grant of £2.3 millions. We expected to reach a programme of 1,000 acres a year by the end of 1970. Our predecessors' record? With a total grant of £8,700, '... eight lonely acres of derelict land cleared from 1960 to 1964'.

In conclusion I offered a few thoughts on the policies of the Conservative Opposition and made a direct challenge arising out of the public expenditure White Paper (Cmnd. 4234), which the Chancellor had produced the previous month after a long series of meetings of the Cabinet Economic committee. This document set out detailed, costed public expenditure programmes for 1970–1 and 1971–2 and projections based on current trends going as far ahead as 1974, virtually the period of the next Parliament. The expenditure programme representing firm Government decisions, for two years ahead, covered not only major groups of expenditure such as housing, health, education, law and order, but the sub-items, in total detail. An example of the detail in which these programmes had been prepared is shown in the extract covering 'Law and Order':

LAW AND ORDER   £ million

TABLE 2.13   at 1969 Survey prices

	1968–69 provisional outturn	1969–70 estimate	1970–71 estimate	1971–72 estimate
Capital expenditure:				
Home Department's services				
(i) Police	21·0	25·7	28·1	32·8
(ii) Prisons..	9·0	10·5	12·5	17·2
(iii) Probation and after care ..	0·5	0·3	0·3	0·4
(iv) Child care	4·6	4·2	5·5	6·0
(v) Fire Services	9·5	10·6	11·2	11·8
(vi) Other services..	0·3	3·9	5·1	3·5
Total	44·9	55·2	62·7	71·7
Law Courts, etc.	6·3	4·9	6·9	8·4
Total (capital expenditure) ..	51·2	60·1	69·6	80·1
Current expenditure:				
Home Department's services:				
(i) Police	258·4	274·2	289·3	304·6
(ii) Prisons	37·9	40·3	43·8	45·4
(iii) Probation and after care ..	9·8	11·4	12·1	12·9
(iv) Child care	54·9	60·0	63·4	66·9
(v) Fire services	57·2	57·3	58·4	60·5
(vi) Other services	3·3	5·9	8·1	9·7
(vii) Departmental administration	10·3	11·3	12·4	12·8
Total	431·8	460·4	487·5	512·8
Law Courts, etc.	35·0	34·8	36·1	38·3
Legal aid	12·6	12·7	13·3	14·0
Parliament and the Privy Council	6·5	6·8	6·9	7·0
Parliamentary election expenses ..	0·1	0·3	2·1	0·3
Selective employment tax paid by local authorities..	21·0	19·5	19·8	20·2
Total (current expenditure) ..	507·0	534·5	565·7	592·6
Grand total	558·2	594·6	635·3	672·7

The forward projection up to 1974 covered the main programmes, not the detailed sub-programmes. For example, in the case of Law and Order it was what is called above the 'grand total' which was projected forward. The programmed total of £672.7 millions for 1971–2 was due to rise to £700 millions in 1972–3, and £730 millions in 1973–4, all at 1969–70 prices.

The Conservatives, in addition to unrealisable pledges about prices, were committed to sweeping cuts in taxation based on reduced national expenditure and at the same time were making vote-orientated promises to increase most individual spending programmes. Parliament, on its return after the recess, was due to debate, for two days, our expenditure White Paper. And so, at Swansea, after setting out some of the Conservatives' most spectacular spending promises, I challenged them:

> ...Add to that every vote-catching promise, a hint of a promise from Polaris to prisons, and you do in fact have a cast-iron formula for crippling increases in taxes. And if they dispute the implications of what I am saying, it can only be because they have plans for really monumental cuts in Government spending.
>
> What would these cuts be? I issue this challenge to them. When Parliament resumes later this month we shall spend two days debating the Government's White Paper on public expenditure over the next four years ...
>
> In the debate let them say which items they would increase, which they would cut, and the resultant saving – if any. They have all the information they need now – no excuses there.

I returned to London. Throughout the first week we had been receiving news of a dramatic break-through in Nigeria. On the way from Paddington to Chequers, I heard a news flash on the car radio. News from Paris announced the end of the fighting and Colonel Ojukwu's flight to a then unknown destination. As soon as I reached Chequers, I telephoned Michael Stewart at Dorneywood, and asked him to assemble a full team of his officials concerned with Nigeria, including those involved in the relief programme. I asked that Lord Hunt should be alerted and Denis Healey readily agreed that naval and air force movements experts from his department should stand by. My No. 10 team was alerted to report at Chequers early on Sunday morning. Working parties on all the main questions were to meet in London on Sunday morning, and the chief officials were to meet Michael Stewart and me at lunch on the Sunday. There had been some disposition on the Saturday evening on the part of some of his officials to feel that we should defer action until the Monday since they had received no official news yet from Lagos. I adhered to the instructions I had given, which Michael Stewart endorsed. It was as well. At midnight on the Saturday, President Nixon came through on the telephone. We were both concerned that the French – who appeared somewhat rueful at the fall of their protégé – wanted to invoke the

United Nations in taking charge of the situation in Nigeria. I was totally opposed to this. The situation was a civil war which had collapsed. If United Nations intervention had been ruled out during the fighting, it was impossible now. The Federal Government was in complete control, and, knowing it, and the feeling of over-confidence which understandably might overtake it and darken wiser counsels, I felt our most difficult task would be to get them to accept international help. It was no time to think about saving anyone's face; our task was to save lives. President Nixon, who had shown great interest in our own reports on Nigeria, said that while he was prepared to give all the help in his power, he felt we should take the lead. On the subject of relief I told him that my impression was that there were abundant food supplies within close reach of the affected areas; the problem would be getting them in and distributing them. He said he had helicopters 'available in the area' and these would be put in a state of readiness. I promised that when I had been able to make a fuller assessment, in the light of the work I had commissioned, both on relief and cease-fire negotiations, I would get in touch with him again about the steps I felt we should next take.

The working parties made their assessment by lunchtime on Sunday. Maurice Foley was in Yaoundé for the tenth anniversary of the independence of Cameroon. U Thant was also there and through Maurice Foley we were able to let him know our view on the proposed UN reference. I sent Maurice an urgent message telling him to go straight to Lagos, where we hoped he might be able to see General Gowon.

In the early afternoon I sent President Nixon a teleprinter message setting out our appreciation and first decisions, and we arranged to speak again at midnight, by which time he would have had sufficient time to study it and get advice. Meanwhile I gave instructions for an aircraft of Air Support Command to be loaded with a ten-ton emergency kit, mainly of medical supplies, ready to take off when the necessary arrangements were made for its acceptance by Lagos.

I telephoned President Nixon at midnight. He thought we were handling the matter in the right way on the basis of the information available to us. I said that while the military situation was still confused, it was fairly clear that the main issues now were relief and the avoidance of atrocities, which, if they occurred, would be most likely to be caused by trigger-happy young soldiers, or looters in defiance of orders. I had received a message from General Gowon, who had assured me that he would insist on strict compliance with orders he had given, personally and publicly, on the treatment of the population in the areas now falling into Federal hands. We had proposed that the numbers of international observers be increased to monitor allegations of atrocities, and Maurice Foley had told me that U Thant was moving on the same lines. The

Organisation of African Unity, too, had offered to co-operate. On relief, it seemed that the priority should be to get supplies moving by road rather than by air. As a result of earlier contingency planning, including the adoption of the recommendations of President Nixon's emissary, Clyde Fergusson and Lord Hunt, there were thirteen thousand tons of food available in the immediate area – which the Nigerian Red Cross had moved up behind the advancing Federal troops – and over twenty thousand tons in other countries, mainly held by international relief organisations, with an adequate airlift available on the spot. But, I said, we should – all of us – have to work through the Federal Government. We had offered to fly units of the Royal Engineers – two hundred in all – to mend bridges and repair airstrips if necessary. Clyde Fergusson was coming straight to London to confer with Lord Hunt and the Minister of Overseas Development and a message was on its way to General Gowon asking him to agree to a visit by Lord Hunt. We were already shipping a number of lorries, though the first advice we had from the American consultants who had prepared a contingency report said that there were probably enough already there. British businessmen in Nigeria had, two years earlier, on their own initiative built up a register of lorries and other transport equipment in private hands, ready for transfer to relief operations.

I told the President of our offer to send medical supplies and medical teams. It was clear that everything had to go with Nigerian goodwill, and we had already decided that we should work on the principle of asking the Nigerians to tell us what they wanted, and then trying to meet it. The same applied to transport equipment; but owing to the suddenness of the Biafran collapse, and ignorance of road conditions and transport facilities there, it would be a few days before we could get any clear statement of requirements.

In conclusion, I suggested to President Nixon that an international relief fund should be immediately started with Government subscriptions – to be followed, we must hope, by private charitable donations. I indicated that the United States might like to head the list. The President agreed and asked how much I thought he should pledge. I answered: 'Ten million dollars, let's say?.' He said he would get on to 'his people' right away and ten million dollars it was.

A very anxious few days followed. General Gowon's colleagues took a very stiff line against international 'interference'. They had won the war; they were determined without the help of outsiders to bring peace and unity to their country. Organised fighting had stopped and General Gowon had fulfilled every undertaking he had made in previous months not only by the orders he gave to his troops, but also by the public reconciliation with Biafran officers who came to settle the immediate post-cease-fire questions. I had no doubts about their intentions, only about the degree of control over trigger-happy young soldiers in the field and looters, and about the efficiency of the Nigerian relief organisation. The Federal Government resisted any suggestion that the job was in any way too big for them. It rejected relief flights by military transport aircraft which it would have regarded as an assertion of a colonial status for their country.

Maurice Foley had been immediately received by General Gowon and he had secured agreement to the setting-up of liaison machinery on relief, including the despatch of Lord Hunt to Lagos for discussions with the Government there, and to report to London on the relief situation. On the Tuesday afternoon, 13th January, I chaired a meeting at No. 10, with Judith Hart and Foreign and Commonwealth Office ministers, together with representatives of the British relief organisations and British members of international organisations concerned with the Nigerian relief problem. They included Red Cross, Oxfam, Save the Children Fund, Help the Aged and Christian Aid.

Judith Hart and I gave them our assessment. We had to make it clear that we still had no firm information on what was needed, either in supplies or personnel, or of the terms on which the necessary arrangements would be made. Most of the organisations had made their own dispositions; for example, recruiting medical teams and getting them inoculated in readiness, and they were naturally impatient at not being able to begin work. Following the meeting, the Chancellor agreed to a British Government contribution of five million pounds to the international subscription list which I later announced; I wanted our voluntary organisations to know that when the call came nothing they or we had to do would be limited by lack of money.

Later in the day I met Lord Hunt and then Clyde Fergusson and Lord Hunt together. By the weekend, arrangements were working more smoothly. When I reported to the House on 19th January, thirteen tons of medical supplies requested by the Federal authorities had been flown out. Lord Hunt was helping to set up machinery, under the co-ordination of the Secretary to the Nigerian Cabinet, to list requirements in all fields and to transmit them to us, to other Governments and to international organisations. Civil air charter capacity was engaged in a continuing operation to airlift Land Rovers and lorries. Fifteen doctors and twenty nurses had been asked for: and more than half of them were already there.

I had received an interim report from Lord Hunt; one of the most serious problems was the lack of hospital facilities for the war-wounded and for starving children. We were working with the Americans to get emergency field hospitals flown out. There were bad individual incidents of looting and arrogance by some of the incoming troops, and there were one or two incidents of violence by Federal troops, who were severely punished on General Gowon's orders. A step towards healing the nation's wounds had been taken by the public reconciliation of General Gowon with Colonel Effiong, 'Biafran' Chief of Staff, and Sir Louis Mbanefo, 'Biafran' Chief Justice. There were particularly heartening reports of Federal doctors and nurses working in full harmony with their Ibo counterparts. But some Federal authorities were pursuing a vendetta against the local representatives of international relief agencies,

LORD HUNT TO REPORT, SIR.

particularly certain churches whose leaders at some time or another had criticised Federal policy. Cardinal Heenan had come to see me late on the previous Tuesday, with two Roman Catholic missionaries who had just reached London from Biafra, to ask for Nigerian co-operation in mobilising the work of priests and nursing sisters.

But during this time, press and television reports were sensationalising individual incidents and producing heart-rending pictures of starving children. When Lord Hunt returned on Wednesday, 21st January, his public statements to the press, television and radio were viciously attacked as complacent and misleading. The following day, I made a statement to the House on the report which he and Sir Colin Thornley of the Save the Children Fund had made orally to me, supplemented by a written report. What they told me – and their report was backed by Mr Hodson, Deputy Director-General of the Red Cross, who had gone out with Lord Hunt and Sir Colin, and had stayed on in Nigeria to complete his work on the Red Cross side – enabled me to give MPs detailed evidence to support the interim statement of three days earlier. Before the statement, I had spent the whole of lunch-time going through every word of it with Lord Hunt and Sir Colin Thornley, to ensure that it correctly represented their report. I have seldom seen two men so angry with the attacks made upon them by journalists and broadcasters, most of whom had not seen the facts for themselves; those who had reported from Nigeria had seen only individual incidents, and not the whole field. It was hard that, partly for political purposes, partly because of the still-strong Biafran influence in press and television, the critics felt moved to impugn the veracity, honesty and competence of two utterly dedicated and honest public servants.

The press reports had aroused the pro-Biafran members of Parliament, some of whom were only too ready to accept them at their face value rather than to believe Lord Hunt's testimony. In reply not to them but to a question by Mr Heath, who was concerned about the reports by British journalists working in Nigeria, I said:

> I believe that the reports which we have read have been honest, but I believe that, inevitably, both newspaper accounts and newspaper photographers tend to be episodic and deal with individual cases. They naturally do not present a general view of the whole panorama in the sense that we have been able to have from Lord Hunt and his mission, all of whom are highly experienced and expert in the relief field ... I do not think that there is conflict between these reports. I have tried to give the general panoramic view. I know that the press feels strongly about the matter, but the press inevitably – and I understand it – has dealt with individual cases of rape and atrocities. It was right that these things should be reported, but that does not mean that they are necessarily taking place on a total scale. All the evidence is to the contrary.

Mr Heath had referred to the conflict between press reporters and statements made on the relief question by members of the military observers' team when interviewed. I told him that the observers' instructions had nothing to do with relief; their presence was designed to be a guarantee against 'genocide'. Accusations that this would follow a Federal victory had been cynically promoted by Biafran propagandists in the previous two years. The observers reported – and this was not contested by any newspaper – that there was no evidence whatsoever of genocide

AA

or massacres. Unfortunately – and this was the point of Mr Heath's question – they had been interviewed on what they had seen on malnutrition and the organisation of relief, which were outside their terms of reference. Their replies on television gave me, and no doubt many others, an impression of complacency and Blimpishness, which, on the duties with which they were charged, I knew not to be the case. But by roaming wide of their subject they gave an unfortunate impression.

In the main the House was disposed to accept my statement on a still-confused situation. But there was an undercurrent of anxiety and one or two of the pro-Biafrans were again in full cry, with utterly fanciful figures of starvation. One of them succeeded in getting a Standing Order No. 9 adjournment debate for the following Monday. George Thomson replied to it and it was noteworthy that the adjournment motion was not in fact carried to a division by the member who had pressed it, Mr Hugh Fraser.

By this time I was in North America. I had left London Airport for Ottawa at 2.30 p.m. on the previous afternoon, and reached Uplands Air Force base at four o'clock local time. Mitchell Sharp, Canadian Minister of External Affairs, met me and in the car we discussed Nigeria, on which we were in total agreement. He and his Prime Minister had faced, as I had, a formidable last-ditch resistance by pro-Biafran MPs aiming at a retrospective validation of their views, by unjustified attacks upon Federal troops and Federal relief authorities in the new post-war situation. After an audience of the Governor-General, Mr Michener, I had a private talk with Pierre Trudeau at his official residence before we went into an informal working dinner. Again Nigeria was to the fore, together with wider questions about the future of the Commonwealth.

At dinner the conversation was general, but it was interesting and instructive to note the strength of Pierre Trudeau's feelings about ecological questions, especially in the waterways north of Canada following the east–west passage by the United States *Manhattan*. After dinner, we continued the discussions until 10.30 p.m. (by this time it was 4.30 a.m. in Britain). We discussed the timing and venue of the next Commonwealth Prime Ministers' conference. I said that it had been my view – as it had before the 1969 meeting – that we should meet outside London, and suggested Singapore, Port of Spain and Ottawa in that order. This was the first time Singapore had been put forward. Choice of site meant choice of chairman and both of us agreed that either Lee Kuan Yew or Eric Williams would make excellent chairmen. Mr Trudeau would have liked Ottawa, but thought it would be more popular with our colleagues in the summer rather than winter.

The other main subject discussed that Sunday night was the question of British entry into EEC, on which negotiations were imminent. It quickly became, under the sharp cross-questioning of M. Pepin, Minister of Trade, Industry and Commerce, a discussion on the consequential effects on Anglo-Canadian trade if the negotiations then in prospect led to terms which would make British entry a possibility.

We met again early the following morning – at the Prime Minister's office in the Parliament building – where we had a session on East–West relations and the Soviet proposals for a conference on European security questions. We passed on to questions of United Nations peace-keeping forces, where I expressed the hope that the Canadians' unhappy experience in the Middle East in 1967 would not prevent their participation in future peace-keeping operations. Then I raised the question of the Middle East, on which the four-power talks had been resumed. I said that it would be our purpose in those discussions to reach a situation where Ambassador Jarring could resume his mission of mediation.

We then went through to the Cabinet Room, where Mr Trudeau's colleagues were awaiting him, for a more formal session. As on the previous evening, the principal discussion was again about the negotiations for Britain's entry into EEC, opened, at the Prime Minister's request, by M. Pepin. This led us on to a discussion on East–West trade, where we had recently joined, successfully, in pressing for agreement to ease some of the COCOM restrictions on the two-way flow of trade.

After the talks I left for the airport, and reached New York shortly after 2.00 p.m. I went straight to the City Hall, for a meeting with Mayor Lindsay and his municipal chiefs. I had known him when he was a young Congressman and had been greatly impressed with him from that time. Outside the City Hall I was greeted by a demonstration demanding 'Home Rule for Wales'. This meeting was followed by a lively press conference, before I went to the United Nations building for talks with U Thant and his deputy, Mr Narasimhan.

These discussions, which lasted for over an hour and a half, again began with Nigeria. We then passed on to the Middle East, where we went into the main issues before the four-power talks, hopes for a reintroduction of Ambassador Jarring into the scene and the possibility of arms control, which, I said, must in our view await a political settlement. We had a brief discussion on Bahrain, where a long-standing sovereignty dispute between Iran and Bahrain was awaiting the appointment by the Secretary-General of a representative to assess and report on local feeling about the State's future. A few weeks later the Secretary-General's intervention proved successful in the removal of one difficult question from the international agenda.

The greater part of the meeting was on the future of the UN specialised agencies concerned with economic developments following the presentation of an important report by Sir Robert Jackson. We were able to get a number of questions answered by Mr Narasimhan to enable us to take the decisions required before ministers could give instructions to our delegation in the United Nations' discussions about the report.

In the evening, I went on to the headquarters of the United States Foundation for Automation and Employment, with whose British affiliate and international federation I had long had good relations. I had received a number of invitations to make a 'prestige' speech on Britain's economic achievements and policy and had welcomed this one. It was a high-level audience, representing, as did the Foundation itself, the principal leaders of US industry and the trade union movement. American industry had been, and still was, suffering from the effects of a titanic struggle between General Electric and the unions, which had already been on strike for some eleven weeks. That one strike, in one corporation, had already lost more man-days than the whole of British industry had lost during 1969. Reflecting – as I had time for a moment to do – that on my return to Britain, in a pre-election period, I would be plunged into an argument about Conservative proposals to import the legalistic American labour legislation into Britain's system of industrial relations, I found it ironic that the chairman of the US GEC and the leaders of the unions concerned were all present to hear my lecture. I was subsequently told that during the evening the two sides got together on an informal basis: true or not, it did not lead to a settlement, and the dispute continued. It is interesting to note that my chairman was Mr Theodore Kheel, one of America's top labour lawyers and regular Federal arbitrators and chairman of the New York State Public Employees' Commission. I learnt a great deal from Mr Kheel that evening; he was to become a much-cited authority in British politics at the end of the year, after a blistering article by him in *The Times* commenting on the incorporation of large gobbets of US labour law into the Conservative Government's industrial relations legislation. He had set out with devastating candour the failure of such legislation in the land of its birth.

My speech, introduced by Mayor Lindsay, was a confident account of Britain's economic recovery, and of the policies, industrial reorganisation, export priority, demand management, incomes and taxation, which had helped to make it possible. Talking, as I was, mainly to industrialists, I struck a new note about the improvement of management in Britain, contrasting two quotations. The first was from *The Times* in April 1964, which, in an article headed, 'Amateurism in British industry', summarised the sickness in these words:

> Money or a title alone still continues frequently to be the sole criterion for election of men (often holding a score or more similar appointments on other boards) who have but the vaguest idea of how the products of their firms are conceived, developed, made and sold. This is not denying the value of experienced men being brought in. But while

the choice of the dilettante director remains a feature of company control, can this be claimed as anything but amateurism?

On the executive side the trained director is the exception and not the rule. It is an acknowledged fact that the calibre of the lower echelons of managers still leaves a lot to be desired.

Six years later, in 1970, I was able to quote from the *Director*, journal of the British Institute of Directors and normally highly critical of the Labour Government. After, as I said, 'their ritual denunciation of the Government', they went on to say,

For on the brighter side, whole sectors of British industry have grown more efficient. British exporters have achieved staggering success and, despite all the strains imposed by Government and change, Britain goes into the 1970s still the most tolerant and democratic society in the world, with high hopes of industrial resurgence and new bonds with a united Europe. And from the boardroom view, perhaps the most significant achievement of the 1960s was the improvement in the expertise and knowledge, and the sustained enthusiasm, of the young British executive. Ask any international consultant where the best management lies, and he will put Britain high on the list.

I flew to Washington late on the evening of 26th January.

On the following morning just before 10.30 I left Blair House for the White House and after the usual ceremonies on the White House lawn, I began my talks with President Nixon in the Oval Room. He was accompanied by Dr Henry Kissinger, and Sir Burke Trend was with me.

We began with Nigeria, reviewing the situation and comparing notes. Since we were in complete agreement, there was no decision to be taken.

The President had let me know, first at Mildenhall and then in later exchanges through officials, that he would want to discuss all the aspects, economic and political, of Britain's approach to Europe. These we discussed in some depth. The President's view was not very dissimilar from that of his two immediate predecessors. British entry into the EEC would undoubtedly have some effect on the American economy, but nevertheless the US Government supported British entry because of the wider political considerations involved. We then had a brief but useful discussion on a number of issues in East–West relations. President Nixon, I had found at Mildenhall – and indeed in talks with him before he became President – to be one of those international statesmen with whom it is possible to discuss a subject in great depth but with no waste of words. The background is expressed by both almost in shorthand, so that the discussion can proceed directly to the issue which has to be resolved. I expressed to him our view on the Soviet proposal for a conference on security: we – the West – should cease to be negative and should press

THE FICKLE FINGER OF FATE

urgently for a conference, on the condition that it was well prepared and that no restriction was placed by any participant on the proposed agenda.

While we were meeting, our Secretaries of State, and their advisers, were talking in the Cabinet Room. The President and I joined them at 12.40 p.m. and we summarised the main points of our own discussion.

After a lunch given by Mr Rogers at the State Department, I returned to Blair House, where I was host at a discussion on economic affairs. Mr David Kennedy, Secretary to the Treasury; Mr Rogers; Mr Robert Mayo, the director of the Bureau of the Budget; Dr Paul McCracken, chairman of the President's Council of Economic Advisers; and Dr Arthur Burns, the recently appointed chairman of the Federal Reserve Board, all took part. The greater part of the meeting consisted of questions put by me to the Americans on their assessment of the prospects for the American economy. Their interpretation of the various economic indices, and their forecasts about future movements in interest rates, domestic and international, together with the prospects in the Euro-dollar market, and for monetary policy convinced them that the United States was not facing a recession; indeed they did not use the word. I had never put so many questions in ninety minutes since I had stopped holding seminars at Oxford thirty years earlier. Towards the end, one of the senior American representatives interrupted: 'What we should be doing, Prime Minister, is asking you about the recovery in Britain's economy and how your Government did it.'

In the evening there was the traditional White House banquet, very similar to those I had attended in President Johnson's period, though it was white tie and tails now, not dinner jackets. As there was no momentous issue dominating the talks, in the sense that the danger of escalation in Vietnam had dominated those of two years earlier, I had not on this occasion prepared myself with the text of a serious statement, but reverted to the more usual practice of a friendly, off-the-cuff speech of thanks.

The next day, 28th January, I read a report in the *Daily Express*, datelined Washington, which listed the dishes on the dinner menu, and contrasted my assumed food intake with starvation in Nigeria. The distinguished political correspondent whose name appeared in the paper as the author of the story, had also enjoyed a comparatively exotic meal, as the guest of a British Embassy official, and I was angry at this selective comparison. If this was certainly not the nadir of hostile press comment over our five and a half years, it was at any rate a strong bid for the prize. I was glad to find later that, as I would have expected, the signatory of the article had not written this paragraph and that he was as annoyed as I was. It was added – no doubt for 'readers' interest' – in London. They did not pursue such gastronomic comparisons the following weekend, when the no less appetising menu served at a Conservative shadow cabinet conference at the Selsdon Hotel was published.

At ten o'clock that morning Michael Stewart, HM Ambassador John Freeman, and I took part in a unique occasion. President Nixon had made a great point of inviting us to attend, for its whole session, the meeting of his National Security Council. This was without precedent. No British, or indeed European, Prime Minister, had been so invited before, though Mr Holt, because of his contribution to Vietnam, had attended a meeting under President Johnson.

The State Department later authorised press briefing to the effect that the subjects covered by the NSC included Europe and NATO – important because the US was currently settling its European and NATO policy, the Mediterranean, and the Middle East. It would not be appropriate, after so short an interval, to comment on the points made in the discussion. But it was a full and serious one and not an event staged for our benefit.

At noon, the President and I met in the Oval Room for an hour, mainly to draw together the main themes of our own talks and the more detailed discussions between the two Secretaries of State. Apart from a short private discussion on certain aspects of nuclear questions, the wider meetings we held in the Cabinet Room were concentrated on Nigeria, on Rhodesia and on the new protectionist measures threatened against British and other countries' textile industries.

On Rhodesia, I said that we were facing imminent decisions by the regime about their new republican constitution and the further development of apartheid-type measures. It would be necessary for the leading powers to co-ordinate their policies in order to avoid a situation in which the regime and its voluble friends abroad derived encouragement from separatist action by any individual country. When the discussion on this subject ended I was fully satisfied about the strength of American support. Shortly afterwards the United States withdrew their mission from Salisbury – contrary to most forecasts.

In conclusion, we again reverted to the Middle East. In view of the widespread suspicion in a number of capitals and at the United Nations that Britain was moving into a middle position, mediating between Israel and the United States at one end of the spectrum and the Arab powers and the Soviet Union at the other, I said that we would feel it right to help the United States at the appropriate moment by suggesting amendments to their published peace formula, but that we should not regard it as our business to outflank them by conceding points to the Arabs. Were we to do so, the Arabs and their Soviet friends would simply pocket any concessions which they were offered, and accordingly raise their starting bid in the negotiations when the final crunch came.

After lunch at the British Embassy, attended by most of President Nixon's Cabinet colleagues, I had to attend the usual press conference at the Rotunda in the Embassy precinct. It was due to begin at 2.45 p.m. and to be televised live in the United States and, five minutes later, transmitted by satellite live to British television. I went for a quick wash and tidy-up. Leaving the marble-floored bathroom I slipped on the notoriously lethal floor – one of my Cabinet colleagues had similarly suffered a few months earlier. I succeeded in banging my ribs on the door lintel, cutting my lip, and spraining the fingers of both hands. After two minutes to recover my composure, including my own prescription of a large glass of the Ambassador's brandy, I walked as comfortably as I could to the Rotunda. No reference was made to my fall, but observers watching British television later recalled that I had kept my pipe raised in front of my mouth throughout the conference. I did it to keep blood off the television screens. Nevertheless, the conference went well, with a great deal of humour. I was pleased, on reaching London the next day, to read in the *Daily Telegraph* that I was relaxed and fully in command. Later in the day I had to go to have my ribs and hands X-rayed, and this inevitably became known. In the same paper the next day, reference was made to my fall which, it said, sympathetically, explained my 'lacklustre performance'.

Flying through the night, I reached London on the Thursday morning, 29th January, and in the afternoon took my questions in the House.

Chapter 37

Speeches at Nottingham, Camden and Birmingham – the teachers' pay claim – local government reforms – the Common Market and the economy – the Green Paper on the future of the Health Services – visit of the Yugoslav Prime Minister – visit of the German Chancellor – the Farm Price Review – Rhodesia's final break with the Crown – Mr Heath's emissary to Rhodesia – law and order – Roy Jenkins's third Budget – Labour's success in the borough elections – the decision to hold a June election

ON Friday, 30th January, the Conservative shadow cabinet gathered at Selsdon Park, Croydon, for a weekend conference. Its final conclusions were chronicled with a devotion and awe similar to that which, in an earlier age, was accorded to the revelations which followed the descent from Mount Sinai. Every detail, apparently, of future Conservative policy had been worked out, including the first post-election Queen's Speech and a legislative programme going far beyond that, as well as the details of the first Budget and the draft of important Bills. In retrospect, this proved hard to reconcile with the long period of governmental inertia which followed the election; justified for many months by the explanation that every issue was by that time the subject of a detailed and lengthy policy review.

Commentators have advanced three competing theories about the Conservatives' motive in holding the conference. The first, which rather imputes a degree of cynicism, would suggest that the whole operation was no more than a sophisticated and expensive public relations exercise. The second, following the comments which greeted it in the press on Monday, 2nd February, seemed to attribute to it the freshness, decisiveness and breakthrough qualities of the Tamworth Manifesto of 1834. The third speculated that while nothing new had been said, it had been said more abrasively, and that it was then seized on by me, as I wished its regressive implications to be known and understood more widely. This missionary endeavour ultimately failed because the Selsdon themes were successfully muted by the Conservatives throughout the subsequent election campaign – only to be reinstated from, roughly speaking, the end of the first full week in October 1970.

But one thing was clear at the time of the Selsdon conference. 'Tories will campaign for law and order' was the headline in a number of authoritative newspapers; others preferred to stress the undertaking to reduce direct taxation, with the new slant that this would necessitate increases in indirect taxation. Certainly the law and order theme was

757

increasingly pressed, and both press and television were correspondingly impressed. The BBC, on the ground not that Mr Heath should be given the opportunity to present the Opposition's case, which would have been reasonable, but that law and order was now a major political issue for public debate, gave him the top spot in 'Panorama' the day after the conference ended. The Corporation then lost its enthusiasm for the subject and refused the Home Secretary the right of reply on a comparable programme; finally, after complaints of partiality, Jim Callaghan was invited to appear on a late-evening programme, to comment, as Home Secretary, on the arrest of a number of Welsh Nationalists. If he had taken up the invitation it might have landed him and the BBC in contempt proceedings. It would in any case have denied him the opportunity of replying adequately to Mr Heath.

It was disenchanting to the more impressionable of us to read in *The Times* a year later – well after the election – an article by one of the most authoritative interpreters of the Selsdon pronouncements, under the heading 'Cooling off on law and order':

One of the oddities of the politics of 1970 was the cooling down of the issue of law and order from the day that the Conservatives came back to power. Indeed, since Mr Maudling went to the Home Office, the issue has slipped back as a Conservative priority, and it can now be taken for granted that there will be no strong legislation this session and no more than a fairly routine Criminal Justice Bill next session. Once in office the Conservatives have learnt that it is one thing to hew an opportunist plank for an election platform and another thing to draft wise law. All the evidence is that the Selsdon Park Hotel conference gave scant consideration to the issue before they stuck it into a programme that was otherwise unusually well researched. It was raised only in the closing 20 minutes of one of the sessions by Quintin Hogg (now Lord Hailsham), who was then the shadow Home Secretary. The circumstances were such that some Conservative leaders were surprised when law and order was given great prominence as one of the most significant decisions taken at Selsdon Park. But equally there is no doubt that Mr Heath at the time readily awarded the issue priority, although Lord Hailsham's ideas went well beyond the studies made by the several groups of Conservative lawyers who had been at work for years.

The Friday after Selsdon, 6th February, I addressed a party reception at Nottingham. I began with the Conservatives' philosophic stance:

This is not just a lurch to the right, it is an atavistic desire to reverse the course of 25 years of social revolution. What they are planning is a wanton, calculated and deliberate return to greater inequality.
The new Tory slogan is: back to the free for all.
A free for all in place of the welfare state. A free for all market in labour, in housing, in the social services.
They seek to replace the compassionate society with the ruthless, pushing society.

The message to the British people would be simple. And brutal. It would say: 'You're out on your own.'

To depart from the fair society which we have established would be to threaten our system of law and order, which, whatever the strains to which it is subjected in these turbulent days, remains an example of stability to the world.

The unfair society leads to the unstable society. Where law and order has broken down in other advanced countries, this is because the authorities have refused to accept that social grievances must have social solutions. The Tories seek to disturb our society by the creation of social grievances we all thought we had got rid of a generation ago.

It will be our purpose to expose, over the months which lie ahead, exactly what Tory policies mean.

I went on to summarise what their proposals would mean for food prices, housing and the social services. Late on the Saturday Mr Heath issued a strongly-worded repudiation of all that I had said as a description of Conservative policy.

The following week I saw Mr Hogg, now Lord Hailsham of St Marylebone, in a televised presentation of a constituency meeting attacking a reference I had made to the danger of a more unjust Selsdon-type society creating the conditions of bitterness and frustration in which lawlessness would breed. Never one to scorn understatement, he declared: 'The Prime Minister has presided complacently over the century's biggest crime-wave.... To Mr Wilson's foolish and abusive speech I reply with a few names...' He then proceeded to list some well-known criminals of the past decade. Some, as I later pointed out, had operated under successive Governments and had been caught by us. His fancy reached a peak when he attributed to me, personally, the responsibility for the Great Train Robbery, which occurred in 1963, fourteen months before we formed a Government.

On 21st February I addressed the annual conference of the London Labour party in Camden Town Hall. My speech marked the emergence of Selsdon Man as a political figure in his own right. I gave what has since proved to be a prophetic account of the Conservative leadership's repudiation of every traditional Tory attitude since the war, together with the four-point summary of the Selsdon programme:

They now reject the society that has been created since the war, a civilised society in which the community, working through Government and Parliament, provides for the needs of the community, on the basis that everyone counts.

They reject even the Butlerian acceptance of the partnership philosophy in British community life. They even reject the benevolent, paternalistic, father-figure image of Harold Macmillan.

Selsdon Man is designing a system of society for the ruthless and the pushing, the uncaring. His message to the rest is, 'You're out on your own.'

Their policy centres on a simple plan to make life dearer for the many, by paying more for their food, for other essentials, for welfare services, and for the home in which they live – a four-point plan:

One, to force up food prices by the deliberate imposition of levies on imported food, and the abolition of the subsidies on what the housewife buys in the shops.
Two, to force up prices of other essentials by doctrinaire increases in indirect taxation.
Three, to cut down the welfare services to means-tested levels.
Four, to force up rents in a free-for-all in housing.

While this and other speeches provided me with a series of speaking themes for part of each weekend, the continuing tasks of Government occupied the working week.

Many areas were hit by an official, but selective, strike of teachers, who decided not to invoke the profession's arbitration procedures but to continue negotiations. These resulted in an agreement, accepted by the Secretary of State and announced by him in the House on 5th March, providing for a flat-rate increase of £120 to all teachers, and the beginning of talks on a review of the salaries structure, with a partial implementation, to operate from 1st January 1971, of any agreement reached. Industrial action was called off.

Though the teachers were bound by a two-year agreement, they had a very strong case, especially the youngest teachers fresh from college. When representatives of local groups of teachers from my constituency came to see me as their MP, I was touched to hear how older teachers, including head teachers, none of them very well paid, were willing to forgo any increase for themselves if something could be done for their younger colleagues.

On 4th February Tony Crosland published his White Paper (Cmnd. 4276) on local government reform, the first of three to be laid within a week: on Tuesday, 10th February, I tabled the White Paper on Common Market costings, and the following day Dick Crossman laid the consultative Green Paper on changes in the National Health Service.

Tony Crosland's White Paper set out the Government's conclusions on the Redcliffe-Maud recommendations. We accepted the broad proposals on structure, including the amalgamation of town and country districts under all-purpose unitary authorities, with the establishment of metropolitan authorities for the great conurbations. We departed from Maud, first, in our decision that education should be the responsibility of the top tier – that is, the metropolitan authority – and second, in our view that to the Report's proposal that metropolitan authorities should be set up only for Merseyside, south-east Lancashire and north-east Cheshire, and the west Midlands, should be added west Yorkshire and south Hampshire (including the Isle of Wight). Taking careful note of the Commission's view that unitary and metropolitan authorities should contribute members to the proposed regional councils, we said that a final decision should be deferred when we had the report of the Commission on the Constitution. Accepting the proposal for local councils, the paper recorded our decision that their work should not be confined to acting as pressure groups on particular local questions, but should be given a direct voice in the administration of some of the major services operated by the main authorities by having the right to appoint members to district committees which we said the main authorities should establish.

The White Paper listed the Government's proposals for the relaxation both of financial and non-financial controls on local authorities and also controls on the way in which authorities were to manage their internal affairs.

We were in favour of liberating some of the disqualifications in force on prospective councillors and this, together with the Maud proposal for a general election of councillors every three years – instead of the annual retirement of a third of the council – and an improvement in the expenses allowed to councillors through loss of earnings while occupied on council business, were remitted for further consultations. We announced our acceptance of the Commission's recommendation that aldermen should be abolished in the areas covered by their report, and our proposals for the appointment of some ten 'Local Commissioners for Administration', on the model of the Ombudsman, reporting to, but independent of, the individual authorities against whom complaints had been laid. On local government finance, we said that when the Government had completed its consideration of this subject we would report our provisional conclusions in a Green Paper.

The Government intended that a Bill to create the new structure should be introduced in the 1971–2 session, and the new authorities elected in 1973.

On 10th February we laid before Parliament the White Paper (Cmnd. 4289) on the economic assessment of the cost of British entry into the European Communities. It covered a wide range of possible assumptions, updating the more general estimates we had made in the four White Papers published in 1967. The calculation had proved a difficult task as so many alternative assumptions had to be made on questions such as the future price-level – and hence the import levies due – for individual agricultural commodities, and the total and method of budgetary contributions to the Common Agricultural Policy. On some of these the Community itself had not taken decisions, though the pace of decision-taking was quickening. The French had insisted that 'completion' and 'strengthening' of the Community must precede its 'enlargement' and, following the summit meeting of EEC heads of government in December, rapid progress was being made, leading to no less rapid recalculations of our own estimates. But even in cases where decisions on policy were taken there was not always a decision about timing; this again brought further confusion in the preparation of cost estimates. These uncertainties led to a tabular but somewhat negative conclusion, which, based on a spectrum of possible assumptions, indicated a possible range of net burdens to our balance of payments by the later seventies, varying from £100 millions to £1,100 millions. Moreover, we had to point out that some of the items on the positive side, such as the response of British industry to the opportunities of a tariff-free community – offset as it must be by increased exports into Britain – could not be quantified. For this reason pro-Market press and television commentators, as well as MPs, were disposed to condemn the document as biased against entry. It had in fact been prepared on the most independent and objective basis possible by senior officials, with outside economic and statistical assistance, and entirely free – on my instructions – from ministerial interference. Anti-Marketeers for their part concentrated their comments on the upper ranges and, indeed, the median, of the balance of payments cost estimates and on the calculation that retail food prices must be expected to rise by an amount within the eighteen per cent and the twenty-six per cent brackets, and the cost-of-living index as a whole by four to five per cent.

Referring to the most recent decision of the Community, to begin negotiations for the entry of applicant countries in the summer, my statement to the House on the day of publication included these words:

> The negotiations will take place against the background of Britain's economic progress and particularly of the improvement in our balance of payments and in the strength of sterling.
>
> Not only this House but the world outside recognises the sharp contrast of our position today with our position both in 1967 and in the previous negotiations from 1961 to 1963.
>
> These facts create a situation in which Government and Parliament can take their decisions in full confidence that on fair terms we can stand and profit by the far more competitive situation that entry into the Market implies. But, equally, they create a situation which leaves no one in doubt that should the negotiations not lead to acceptable terms for entry, Britain is and will be strong enough to stand on her own feet outside. This was the target – a position of strength – I set for our economic policies when the House debated these matters in 1967.

I concluded:

> The question of entry, what I have called the final decision, does not arise on this White Paper, nor indeed in the debate which will follow. It is in the light of the negotiations which are due to begin in the near future that this decision must be taken. The Government and the House, of course, will recognise that political as well as economic factors are involved. If, when the decision is to be taken, the disadvantages for Britain appear excessive in relation to the benefits which would flow from British

entry, the Government clearly would not propose to Parliament that we should enter the Communities. If, on the other hand, the costs, after negotiations, appear acceptable in relation to the benefits, the Government will recommend entry.

The Government will enter into negotiations resolutely, with good faith, mindful both of British interests and of the advantages of success in the negotiations to all the members of an enlarged community. We have made clear that if the negotiations produce acceptable conditions for British entry we believe that this will be advantageous for Britain, for Europe, and for Europe's voice in the world. Equally, we have made clear that if the conditions which emerge from the negotiations are in the Government's view not acceptable, we can rely on our own strength outside the Communities. But I repeat what I have said on a number of occasions in the House and outside that this outcome – a failure of the negotiations – would involve a cost for Britain, a cost for Europe and a diminution of Europe's influence in world affairs.

My entire statement, as well as the White Paper itself, had been assented to, after careful study of the texts on two successive days, by the whole Cabinet.

When the terms of the White Paper had been examined, Mr Heath and his colleagues did not conceal their anger at what they wrongly conceived to be an anti-Market manoeuvre on my part. It had, in fact, been Mr Heath's stratagems the previous summer and autumn which had strengthened my view that, as he had insisted, all the facts should be assessed and made public. No analytical examination could have been more objective, or more free from political intervention. But in the post-Selsdon mood, Mr Heath had changed his position once again. My strictures on his determination to raise food prices by import levies, drew forth the counter-argument that we should have to do it, in any case, as a condition for Market entry. This *non sequitur* led me, in my Camden Town Hall speech, to comment on the eccentric negotiating posture he seemed to be adopting, in words which, if their comments were any guide, outraged Mr Heath and his colleagues:

Our position, as I have just made clear, is that if, after determined negotiations, we cannot receive acceptable terms, we should have to forgo the benefits. But we should not be called upon to pay the entrance fee. That is our position.

What is incredible, what is incomprehensible and reckless by ordinary standards of prudence and commonsense, is the attitude of the Tory Opposition.

The Conservative position, calculated, considered, carefully thought-out, is to pay the entrance fee in any case.

For it is their purpose to force up the cost of living, deliberately to force up prices, and especially food prices, in Britain. Nothing to do with negotiations for entry into Europe. Irrespective of negotiations. They would put up prices, they would eliminate food subsidies. For the sheer hell of it.

In a world of rising prices, the Labour Government has fought to protect the British consumer.

We have used controls to hold back price increases which in a free market the manufacturer would have imposed. We have limited prices far below what they wanted imposed.

The Tories have made it clear that they would dismantle all the safeguards we have built up against irresponsible price increases. They believe in a free-for-all. But their policy goes beyond this. It means a deliberate and further increase in prices as part of a basic and doctrinaire policy.

This being their policy, the British people would be well advised to bear in mind the warning we shall see posted up at Wembley in a few weeks' time – when the ticket touts come out of hibernation – with its message 'don't put your money down unless you're sure you're getting a ticket which will get you in'.

You've got to say this about the Tory negotiating postures. It's a funny way to run a negotiation to start paying the price before you begin. It's a fairly sure way of getting less satisfactory terms. It's not of itself a recipe for failing to get in, it's a recipe for paying more as the price for getting in. Every case I've heard of, whether in trade negotiations, or industrial negotiations, or foreign policy negotiation, where this has been the nego- tiating posture, has led to one judgment when the deal is complete – 'they saw him coming'.

The Conservative leadership rushed into print with hysterical attacks on me, based on inaccurate information on what I had said: even the *Daily Telegraph* and *The Times* admitted that, when the full text of the speech was available – which it had been at the time – the Conservatives' charges against me 'did not stick'.

On 24th and 25th February the House debated the Common Market on a motion 'to take note' of the White Paper, the appropriate form since the House was not being asked to take any decision in advance of the negotiations. But the debate was an occasion for members on both sides of the House, and on both sides of the question, to express their pro-Market or anti-Market views. There was no vote.

On 11th February, Dick Crossman tabled the Green Paper on the future of the Health Services. A previous Green Paper, laid by Kenneth Robinson, had run into stormy waters in the consultations which followed. One of the advantages of the Green Paper concept we had introduced was that ideas honestly advanced by the Government, but which consultation shows to be unacceptable, can be withdrawn without any loss of face.

In his Green Paper, Dick Crossman sought to achieve three basic purposes: to unite the National Health Service and to integrate its separate local services – the hospital service and the GP service – on a local basis; to provide effective means for co-ordinating the NHS and the local government public health and social services; and to involve local communities in the running of the NHS district services. In consequence, this would decentralise responsibility to local services to the fullest extent compatible with central government responsibility for ensuring maximum value for the resources made available to it from resources contributed by the taxpayer and through the payment of National Health contributions.

The Green Paper set out all the arguments for and against the operation of the Health Service by local government and came down firmly against it, confirming the decision of the Attlee Cabinet more than twenty-three years earlier after a classical confrontation between Herbert Morrison and Aneurin Bevan.

But closer co-ordination at local level was to be provided by matching, in number and in boundaries, NHS district areas to those which would operate in local government following the enactment of the post-Maud reforms. The new NHS authorities, instead of being nominated one hundred per cent by the minister, were to be appointed by a different formula, one third by the local authorities, one third by the profession, and one third by the minister. This had not been easy to get through. The Treasury had clung to the view that a hundred per cent ministerial appointments were needed to get full financial control. My own experience, from 1959 to 1963, as chairman of the Public Accounts Committee, had convinced me of the opposite view.

In the post-Selsdon period I had to keep a wary eye on the behaviour of an Opposition which for two years – some would say more – had not taken a decision unrelated to electoral considerations. But at the same time, the work of government continued at an intensive pace. It was not merely a question of pressing on with the legislative programme – Dick Crossman's Superannuation Bill had received its Second Reading on 19th January, and was going through a marathon committee stage, while Barbara was engaged on five major Bills simultaneously – nor was it the White Paper exercise of foreshadowing the legislation of the succeeding sessions: the day-to-day preoccupation of Government, national and international, seldom slackens.

In the last week of February, the Yugoslav Prime Minister, M. Ribicic, paid an official visit, and in the first week of March the German Chancellor, Willy Brandt, came for a successful series of consultations, equalled only by his success in a number of outside engagements, the highlight of which was his address to a crowded meeting of members of both Houses of Parliament in the Royal Gallery of the House of Lords. Our talks, which showed a total identity of views, were concentrated mainly on discussions of his *Ostpolitik* – which we warmly encouraged – on the Common Market, on the proposed conference on European security, and on our analysis of the world situation. Those invited to the reception for Willy Brandt included past and present members of British forces who had joined in the defence of Berlin, a gesture the Chancellor much appreciated, and – in addition to a glittering assembly of luminaries in the field of science, the arts, industry, entertainments and sport – workers from many of our industries; as well as nurses, ambulance drivers and others from the social services. The press publicised what they called the new swinging style of the Downing Street receptions – they had been going on for three years – and we received for the first time spacious publicity, leading to sour comments from supporters of the *ancien régime* who sought to argue that modern visitors preferred to meet the stuffed shirts of a bygone social order.

Whenever possible I continued with my regional tours. On 20th February I went to Workington to inaugurate the new Leyland bus factory, which my colleagues and I had worked so hard, at so many meetings – with the chairman of British Leyland, Lord Stokes and the chairman of the Cumberland Development Council, Sir Frank Schon – to get established in Cumberland. The full powers of our regional assistance schemes had been invoked and, after strong pressure by me, the decisive last condition was met by the announcement of the road improvements necessary to link West Cumberland with the national motorway and trunk network. The factory, when completed, was to be owned and managed by the Leyland National Company, a partnership between public and private enterprise, owned fifty-fifty by British Leyland and the National Bus Company which was set up under the Transport Act to run bus services in all parts of the country. Its product would be a standardised bus, produced more cheaply than custom-built models tailored to suit the specifications of individual operators, and designed in particular for the export markets. It was a day, therefore, to celebrate: more work and fresh hope for a hard-hit development area, a new export venture, and a fresh and pragmatic experiment in partnership between the public and private sectors.

The following Friday, 27th February, I went to see Bessie Braddock who had been away from the House for several months seriously ill. She was in a hospital which concentrated both on geriatric work and on pioneering work of the most patient and dedicated kind I had ever seen for mentally-handicapped infants. A week later I was in Birmingham to open a new block of homes converted from an old house through the operations of a housing trust, supported by Shelter and financial assistance from the local authority under our new 1969 Act, and then visited the 'Midlands Art Centre for Young People', assisted in this case by the Arts Council. On Friday, 13th March, I was in Merthyr Tydfil, where I received the freedom of the borough. Afterwards I toured many industrial areas and opened newly-occupied Government advance and other factories, some of them on reclaimed derelict land, following our 1966 Act. One Friday after another enabled me to see the new developments of the new Britain we were creating. A welcome change from the earlier years was that my tours were not punctuated by emergency calls informing me of fresh depredations in our sterling reserves, resulting from some new foray by the speculative community. Our balance of payments surplus saw to that, and I was meeting many of the people who had made it possible.

The usual seasonal preoccupations were before Cabinet and Cabinet committees. In one of the most difficult years for agriculture since the war, we had settled the Farm Price Review – in which again I had to take a hand, following meetings with the president of the National Farmers' Union – with the record provision of £54 millions on increases on beef, pig-meat, wheat, barley, milk, sheep and potatoes. To this, we added, exceptionally, special aid to the hard-pressed farmers by raising the rates of fertiliser and lime subsidies by £10 millions over the succeeding year; £5 millions a year on premiums to cattle-breeders to eradicate brucellosis; and increased capital grants, designed to provide a further £20 millions for direct investment over the following two years. Announcing the settlement to the House, Cledwyn Hughes commented that, even excluding the increases in capital grants, the award was higher than in any year since the price review system was introduced by the late Tom Williams in 1948.

The Defence White Paper was published on 19th February and debated by the House on 4th and 5th March. Neither the White Paper nor the debate provided any sensations. Policy had been settled and was working its way through quietly and efficiently, making effective the financial savings on which we had decided. The main interest in the White Paper related to the progress of reorganisation, and the integration more and more of individual service responsibilities into new functional units. Denis Healey had told me that in the next ministerial reorganisation – planned to take place after the election, if we were successful – he would be ready to recommend that parliamentary Under-Secretaries should be no longer appointed for individual services but, reduced by one, be given functional duties comparable to the Ministers of Defence for Administration and for Equipment.

There was great interest in the Government's decision to introduce an unprecedentedly generous pay structure for the armed services, announced in Parliament by Denis Healey on 25th February. It was based on the concept of the 'military salary', which included compensation for payments previously made in kind and now withdrawn. The military salary would not discriminate between single and married men, and would be based on job-evaluation. The new pay scales meant, on the average, an increase of fifteen per cent over the previous value of the servicemen's total real emoluments, that is, over and above the pay and allowances received in cash together with the value of food and accommodation received in kind. The cost in a full year was £41 millions (net) for ending differentiation between single and married men, £75 millions for job-evaluation and the so-called 'X' factor – a Service payment to take special account of the conditions of employment – £5½ millions for improved allowances, a total of £121½ millions. The job-evaluation and X-factor payments were due to be paid from 1st April 1970, together with a first instalment on the ending of differentiation between the single and married man, the full amount to be effective on 1st April 1971.

Meanwhile, on 2nd March Rhodesia had moved to a final break with the Crown. After several false rumours, the regime introduced its new republican 'constitution' and raised its new green and white standard. A number of consequential actions followed, including the inevitable withdrawal of Royal patronage from the Rhodesian services and other institutions. Nothing had changed in legal terms. This latest act of the regime in British, Rhodesian and international law had no more validity than the regime which ordered it. Interest was mainly focused upon international reactions and, in particular, of those countries who, while not recognising the regime – no country did so – had maintained some form of consular or similar representation after our own residual mission had been closed. There was some pressure in the US Congress that America should maintain relations. When the republican constitution was proclaimed, there was a confused moment when a White House spokesman seemed to suggest that the US consulate in Salisbury would remain open; immediately the Secretary of State, whose recent African tour had awakened him and the Administration to the issues at stake in Africa, intervened and the US announced the closure of their consulate. Nine of the eleven other countries which had maintained consular representation until that time took similar action. When the post-republican dust had settled only two nations retained any official representatives in Salisbury – Portugal and South Africa.

Despite the severance of relations with the Crown, Rhodesia was still relevant to Conservative electoral strategy. Just before Christmas it had come to my attention – not through any Government source – that Mr Heath was sending an emissary to Rhodesia on his own responsibility, and without informing the Government. Soon afterwards this information was confirmed by reports in the *Daily Telegraph* by an experienced journalist, who based his story on conversations he had had with the regime. Mr Heath was challenged in the correspondence columns in the *Guardian* to confirm or deny that these contacts had been going on. An article in the *New Statesman* suggested that the Conservatives had compounded Mr Heath's offence by approaching a high official of the American Embassy in London, asking that it should be represented to the White House that it was the Conservative view that the United States should not close its Salisbury consulate. So far as I am aware there was no denial either by the Embassy or by the Conservative party that such representations had been made. Nor did Mr Heath, or any spokesman on his behalf, seek to deny the allegations about the personal emissary to the regime. Certainly Mr Heath specifically refused to answer challenges on either question when they were put to him in Parliament.

The matter of Mr Heath's Rhodesian contacts was raised by our members in the House. Week after week, when I was answering questions on Government policy on Rhodesia, I was asked also about Mr Heath, for whose actions, of course, I had no ministerial responsibility. I suggested that it was for Mr Heath himself to get up and confirm or deny the reports and I gave him every opportunity to do so. He did not respond. By the end of March the questioning was getting rough. Labour members were angry at verified reports that the regime were, under their extended segregationist laws, threatening the Christian churches in their arrangements for education and worship. Sir Roy Welensky had broadcast on the BBC, throwing cold water on the prospects of any new negotiations now that Rhodesia had adopted what he described as 'a racialist constitution'. Against this background our back-benchers were again pursuing Mr Heath who decided, instead of replying, to attack us. Our angry exchange went back over the years, to his 'great divide' of October 1966 over Rhodesia, and to the official Conservative vote on the *Tiger* proposals. When challenged by Mr Jeremy Thorpe, the Liberal leader, he again refused to say what unofficial dealings he had been having with the regime. But, on 26th March, we had the satisfaction of hearing him say that it would be his policy to maintain sanctions ahead of further negotiations; this we had long pressed him to make clear. There was more rejoicing on our side of the House at this announcement than on the Conservative benches.

There the matter rested for another week, until my Presidential address to the annual conference of the United Nations Association in York on 18th April. I said, as part of my reference to our policy in Rhodesia:

And if there are still people in this country – and there are – with powerful political views and powerful economic sponsors behind them, who are still ready to contemplate a sell-out to racialism, they can no doubt take advantage of cheap, empty ex-Consulate premises for maintaining whatever continuing presence they think appropriate.

The following day Mr Heath issued the most petulant statement ever drawn up by any responsible party leader, which was made the main headline in most newspapers on the Monday. His statement read:

If Mr Wilson considers that any offence has been committed by Her Majesty's Opposition, or that there has been any breach of the Official Secrets Act, let him prosecute me and my colleagues. If not, let him shut up.

This ignored the fact that it is possible, in our democracy, to challenge opponents on their actions without imputing criminal practices. The country has a right to know what Opposition leaders, no less than Government, may be doing about controversial political issues. In words Mr

Heath later announced would be his 'style of government', all public figures have a duty to deal 'honestly and openly with the House of Commons, with the press and with the public'. Nor was he on sound constitutional grounds when inviting me to prosecute him. This is a matter for the police, the Director of Public Prosecutions and the Attorney-General: it was a strict rule, under my Administration, that in the discharge of these quasi-judicial functions by these respective authorities, no minister, including myself, could bring any influence to bear on whether a prosecution was instituted or not.

There was a rash of questions on 24th March on Northern Ireland, mainly about the death after a series of heart attacks, following alleged rough treatment at the hands of the Royal Ulster Constabulary, of Mr Samuel Devenney. The previous night, at about ten o'clock, while working on papers, I was told by Michael Halls that Miss Bernadette Devlin, MP for mid-Ulster, was asking to see me urgently about the Devenney case and that if I did not see her she was prepared to spend the night – a cold one – on the steps of No. 10. I sent him to invite her to make an appointment to see the Home Secretary whenever he was free, and to telephone my office for an appointment after questions the next day, as every MP, regardless of party, was able to do; he was further to explain that, if I were to accept the proposition that any MP arriving at the door were to have the right to an immediate meeting – except in case of an emergency – I should have an unending flow of legislators, to an extent which would make administration impossible. After all, there could well be MPs who, unlike Miss Devlin, might wish to indulge in such activities merely for the sake of publicity. Miss Devlin rejected these arguments and settled down for the night. On checking with the Home Office, I found that she had already seen the Home Secretary, who had told her that the Devenney case was being examined by Sir Arthur Young, the RUC chief, in whom he and I had the fullest confidence. But Miss Devlin wanted Scotland Yard called in that night – Sir Arthur Young, following his examination, did in fact decide to call them in, as was his prerogative. We did all we could to persuade her to leave; the best I could do was to ask a messenger to keep her supplied with coffee. The following morning, not wanting ministers to have to step around her when they came to No. 10 for a Cabinet committee meeting, I sent Michael Halls to renew the invitation to her to come at four o'clock. Inevitably the press and television cameras were there. He was successful in his mission, but not before a characteristic display of his unfailing courtesy, when, on his arrival at the door, she began to struggle to her feet, he entreated her, 'Please don't get up'. In the afternoon, she visited me in my room at the House of Commons but stayed only five minutes, satisfied with my reiteration of what the Home Secretary had told her before her chilly and unnecessary vigil.

Questions in the House that day had widened from the Devenney case to issues of reform and developed into a clash between Labour back-benchers and the Ulster Unionist MPs. Two passages in my unprepared answers to supplementaries summarised the position we had reached, and what we had been up against on the Northern Ireland question throughout our Administration. Replying to a question by an Ulster Unionist MP, Captain Orr, about reform measures, a question which unfortunately incorporated provocative and divisive charges against 'malicious people,' I replied:

> The hon. and gallant Gentleman is correct that much of the reform programme for which we have been pressing for four or five years is on the statute book. Other parts of it are through the Northern Ireland Commons and await further parliamentary procedures. Other reform programmes are at present before the Commons in Northern Ireland. I am glad that this has happened. It has been our duty to preserve law and order. But the hon. and gallant Gentleman must search back to see how far the responsibility for these matters is due to the fact that these things have had to be pressed by a Labour Government on Northern Ireland in the last five years. Our problem is to make good in a matter of months what the hon. and gallant Gentleman and his party failed to do in 50 years.

And in reply to a more helpful question by Mr Jeremy Thorpe, I said:

> If occasionally I am a little rough on hon. Gentleman opposite in this matter, I recognise the pressures they are under, both the Westminster Members and the Stormont Members, because of an utterly evil campaign on the part of people who are, if it is possible to conceive it, to the right even of those hon. Gentlemen, and who are trying to put them out of their seats.

For, together with a resurgence of IRA activity, extremist right-wing pressure was the reality in Northern Ireland in the spring of 1970, a development about which Captain O'Neill (by this time Lord O'Neill of the Maine) had warned me after his resignation the previous year. The problem remained with us up to the end of our Government, and was a matter of acute concern during the period of the election.

On successive Thursdays in March, we had the last two by-elections of the Parliament. At Bridgwater on 12th March, the Conservatives increased their majority from 2,986 to 10,915 and their vote by nearly 5,000 – partly at the expense of the Liberals – while our vote fell by just over 3,000. But the swing to them was only a little over eight and a half per cent, in marked contrast to the experience of the past three years. A week later, on 20th March, while I was lunching at the Lancashire Police Headquarters at Hutton, near Preston, the result of the South Ayrshire by-election was brought to me. The intervention of a Scottish Nationalist candidate, the former agent of the greatly-loved Labour MP Emrys Hughes, whose death had caused the election, would, it had been widely expected, upset the result. In the event, our majority over the Conservatives fell only from 12,053 to 10,886: our vote was down by less than 3,000, while the Tory vote was down by 1,664. Commentators set the swing at only 2.9 per cent, almost our best result in the whole Parliament. But this calculation rested on the assumption that the Scottish Nationalist's 7,735 votes were taken equally from the two parties. It was clearly the case that the majority of them were taken from us. It was almost certainly a fact that, if these votes could have been apportioned accurately between the two parties, the swing would have been shown to have been from the Conservatives to Labour, for the first time since Hull North, more than four years earlier.

My visit to the Lancashire police enabled me to see something of the remarkable advance in police communications and crime detection methods by that pioneering police authority. It also enabled me to make a speech there on the law and order issue, at that time a favourite political football of the Conservative Opposition. I was unable to reply in political terms, for this was a non-political occasion; indeed, the Conservative-dominated police authority refused permission for the press and television cameras to be present though I was able to meet the press outside and put the speech on the record.

In my speech, I was able to reply to the Conservative propaganda on law and order, though I did not identify them, by giving the facts:

> The first question is the size of the police force. I read, and have seen on television, some pretty peculiar falsifications of this issue. When the Government which I head came to power there were 80,700 police officers in this country. At the end of 1969, the figure was 91,762. Yes, below the total establishment, but establishments are reviewed and increased and so they should be. The police establishment should at any moment of time always be beyond our grasp, or what is an establishment for? The number of police deployed today is in fact 2,300 greater than the total authorised establishment of five years ago. At the end of 1964 the number of civilians employed in the police service was 18,200. They now total 33,000. And every one of them either makes the policeman more effective or, more directly, releases a policeman to do a police job....
>
> In the last full year before the present Administration took office, the total annual expenditure on equipping the police was running at about £5½ millions. Today we are spending £12 million. The number of police cars on the roads has been doubled. £¼ million then being spent on radio communications for the police has been increased nearly five times to well over £2 millions. Twice as many police cars are now equipped with radio. Against 500 personal radio sets for two-way communication 5½ years ago there are now 23,000 pocket radio sets of an improved design, an increase of 4,500 per cent....
>
> It is right that, when the police are being sold short, for reasons which no doubt seem good to some people, these facts should be stated.
>
> It is easy to make play with crime statistics. It is a sombre fact, transcending the froth of ill-informed public comment, that recorded crime in the

country has been increasing consistently, with some year-to-year fluctuations, certainly since the war, probably for a long time before. When the crime statistics are quoted, let us recognise that because of police vigilance and effectiveness more of the crimes actually committed are being identified and this affects the recorded statistics.

In real terms the rise has been very marked since 1954. There is no advantage, whether to those who are seeking to combat crime or to the general public, in seeking to make political points about this – even about the fact that the annual average rate of crime increase of 5.3 per cent over the past 5 years compares with an overall of 9.6 per cent in the previous years.

Dealing with the speedier detection and punishment of crime, I referred to improvements in the organisation and procedure of the courts, including the introduction of majority verdicts – our answer to gang intimidation of jury-men – our decision to accept the Beeching reforms to ensure speedier trials, and the Lord Chancellor's pressure on magistrates to impose 'realistic' sentences for crimes of violence. But this was not all. I went on:

Whenever we have a situation in which evil can operate and fructify, it is the duty of modern Government to change the climate of society.

I take only two examples. Historians of modern crime would, I think, have devoted a central chapter to the easing of our Gaming Laws in 1960, ten years ago. There was undoubtedly a case for modernisation of the old gaming laws. But the result of the 1960 Act was a new form of brain drain. A brain drain in reverse. While the British scientists and technologists were leaving our shores for other climes, we were laying ourselves open not only to a relatively harmless inward immigration of croupiers and other skilled gaming technicians, but a possible invasion of this country by Mafia types. In the war against organised crime the actions of our Home Secretary in tightening up our laws and our Administration to make it clear that London and our other big cities were not to be a happy hunting ground for the criminal elements of America, and elsewhere, may well prove to have been decisive.

And the other issue is drugs. Taking drugs, and above all, peddling drugs. Parliament is being asked to approve adequate deterrent penalties against those who too easily embark on drug-taking. These are penalties designed to protect weak young men and women against everything that an embarkation on this course can lead to. But in terms of organised crime, the heaviest penalties should be visited against that sinister fraternity who seek to profit by human weakness.

The new legislation now before Parliament rightly lays the heaviest penalty on those who seek to make profit from the peddling of drugs, and I believe that public opinion is solidly behind us.

I turned finally to set the Conservative exploitation against traditional British standards of freedom under the law:

Our joint determination in Britain is so to combine liberty and vigilance as to prevent both violent disturbances on the one hand and an unreasoning backlash on the other....

We are a country with a record and a reputation for order and stability.
We are determined that crime and violence shall not be allowed to under-
mine that order, that stability.

This cannot be achieved on the political hustings. It can and will be
achieved by the British police, given adequate support by a Government
determined to provide the necessary money, resources and legal backing.

Easter 1970 was early – a fact affecting considerations of election timing,
as I had warned colleagues more than four years earlier. I took the overnight train to Penzance, and arrived in the Isles of Scilly on Good Friday
morning; I was back at Downing Street at breakfast-time on the following
Thursday, 2nd April, where, after a morning's meeting with the Chancellor
on the budget, I received the sad news that Michael Halls had suffered a
serious coronary thrombosis, from which he died early the following
morning. In that small village which is No. 10, the news of his coronary,
still more the news of his death, created an atmosphere of utter gloom,
and sympathy for his widow, Marjorie Halls. It seemed a totally inadequate gesture to prepare a tribute for *The Times*, and for the press
generally: but neither that, nor the address Marjorie asked me to contribute at the memorial service in St Margaret's, could begin to assess his
dedicated contribution to the public service; and to me personally.

A depleted and numbed No. 10 staff carried on the work until, several
days later, Sandy Isserlis, an under-secretary in Housing and Local
Government, and formerly principal private secretary successively to
Charles Hill and Quintin Hogg, was appointed to succeed Michael Halls.

Northern Ireland erupted with fresh violence – riots, shooting and bomb
outrages – over the weekend. An Ulster Unionist MP secured a Standing
Order No. 9 adjournment debate for 7th April, the day after the House
returned. Jim Callaghan, who wound up, was able to give a reassuring
report on police reorganisation. The House had passed the two Bills
demanded by the events of the previous autumn, the measure permitting
the secondment of English police officers for police work in Northern
Ireland, and another setting up the Ulster Defence Regiment, for which
recruitment had begun.

In the same week, Olof Palme, the Swedish Prime Minister, a friend for
many years, paid an official visit. Again we had useful discussions, with
no items of controversy – the Nigerian war was over – and a Downing
Street dinner and reception.

The triennial county elections, and those for the Greater London Council
were also taking place in that week.

I was watching the results of the elections carefully. I had already passed
up two spring options for a general election – 19th March, the day of the
South Ayrshire by-election, and 1st May. I was wary of another March
election: British winters had a habit of remaining cold through most of
March, and it seemed too much to hope that we could repeat the mild

weather of March 1966. My caution, in the event, was justified: apart from a cold December, the winter barely began until February and remained cold through most of March and early April.

The county elections were singularly unhelpful in providing guidance to me. Most of them were poor for Labour; hardly any county councils were regained after the débâcle of 1967. Lancashire, which had swung like a pendulum in every election from 1952 onwards, with Labour and the Conservatives alternately gaining control, remained stubbornly Conservative with a strong majority. Only in the Greater London Council elections was there a marked swing, mainly in the downtown urban seats and council housing estates. We did not recapture the GLC, but the 1967 Conservative domination of the council, reduced by one Labour by-election gain in Greenwich, was cut from 81–19 to 65–35 with a number of constituencies returning Conservative candidates by relatively small majorities. More important, our gains in inner London gave us control of the Inner London Education Authority, the old London County Council area. As I continued to watch the situation over the next month I became convinced that if the GLC elections had taken place a month later, at the time of the boroughs, we would have won control, an achievement to be related only to a very good year: the GLC was not created by its Conservative progenitors to be winnable by us in anything but an exceptional year. But for the rest of the week the country elections remained obstinately unhelpful. The signs were that it was the inner urban areas and council estates which were leading the swing to Labour; and there were some signs of this in overspill housing areas and non-county boroughs outside London, as well as in the GLC.

On 14th April, Roy Jenkins introduced his third Budget. He had considered presenting it on the day the House resumed. But, although for the first time for several years it was expected to be a net tax-reducer, he was anxious, as I was, to avoid the charge that the tax reductions were directed to the county and GLC elections. In the event, its moderation was widely regarded as strengthening support for us because of its contrast to the old-style Conservative pre-election Budgets of 1955, 1959 and 1963. (The 1963 Budget had been related to an expected election in the autumn, postponed for other reasons; by 1964 economic difficulties, though skilfully concealed, were mounting, and the Budget was marginally balanced on the side of tax increases.)

During the months before the Budget, the Chancellor in his regular discussions with me had been settling on a net reduction of taxes of some £200–£250 millions. There was no political content in this; his independent Treasury advisers recommended a figure of this order and outside commentators, such as the National Institute for Social and Economic Research, recommended a bigger tax-reduction. The current level of economic activity would have justified a somewhat higher figure, but there were apparently soundly-based expectations of an upward movement in economic activity in the autumn. On fiscal strategy, Roy Jenkins was rightly determined to avoid any increases in taxation of any kind, and to concentrate such remissions as he might recommend on direct taxation. He could have gone for a simple cut in the standard rate: but in his view, with which I concurred, this would have been inequitable in giving too much of the advantage to the better-off. With the expert aid of the Board of Inland Revenue, he examined some ten or eleven alternative dispositions, each known by an alphabetical name, and, as the choice narrowed and refinements were introduced, by numbered sub-categories. Well before Easter, the decision had been taken.

The Chancellor's speech was, in the first instance, a report on his stewardship over two and a half years, and indeed on the Government's responsibility for five and a half years. It was a report, in particular, on the national dividend accruing from the 'two years' hard slog'.

The public sector accounts, he was able to report, had been transformed. A Government borrowing requirement of £1,956 millions in 1967–8 had been reduced to one of £450 millions in 1968–9, and replaced by a surplus of about £600 millions in the year just ended. It was a turn-round in the public sector accounts of about £2,550 millions over two years. Over the same period, the gross national product had risen by about six and a quarter per cent, manufacturing production rising by eleven per cent. That this increase was, as we had planned, export-led was shown by the fact that exports of goods and services rose, in volume terms, by twenty-four per cent – nearly two and a half times the increase in imports and nearly four times the rise in national production. As a result, but it was a causal factor, too, in the increased national production, investment in manufacturing industry had risen by thirteen per cent.

The balance of payments was showing unprecedented strength. The Chancellor had set a target of a £300 millions surplus for the financial year ending March 1970. The figures for the three quarters to December had already reached £451 millions, and the figures of visible trade for the January–March quarter showed a surplus of £36 millions, to which had to be added the assured surplus on invisible account and the net effect of capital transactions. We were in fact, moving into a period of visible surplus over the year as a whole. In January 1971, when the figures were available this was proved to be the case for the calendar year 1970. The Chancellor reminded the House that this was a phenomenon rare in our history: only two years since 1822 had shown a visible trade surplus.

Even taking into account the tough years immediately after 1964, the total deficit for the five years 1965–9, visible, invisible and capital, amounted to £817 millions: the figure for the previous five years was £1,161 millions. On current account alone, the total deficit was £306 millions for our five years, against £436 millions for the last five years of our predecessors. But whether on visible trade, or on the overall balance, there was another significant difference. In the last five years of the Conservative administration, the deficit, serious enough in total, was worsening, reaching an all-time record deficit in the final year. In our five years, with a small total deficit, the movement was improving, reaching, in the final year, an all-time record surplus.

The surplus of the preceding months, and the resulting strength of sterling, had enabled us to pay off large quantities of short-term debt. At the end of 1968, our total short-term and medium-term debt (roughly speaking, central and bank lending and our IMF loans) had amounted to £3,363 millions, against reserves of £1,009 millions. Our net adverse position was thus £2,354 millions. By Budget day, it had been reduced by three-quarters to £525 millions, an improvement of £1,829 millions over fifteen months. In dollar terms, the short- and medium-term debt had been reduced from over $8,000 millions to less than $4,000 millions and reserves had increased.

The changes in taxation did not take long to announce. Allied to the legislation foreshadowed in the Queen's Speech on labour-only sub-contracting in the construction industries, the Chancellor announced fixed charges designed to make unregistered sub-contractors pay tax at the standard rate, since tax evasion, as well as evasion of social security stamp payments, was rife in this 'contracted-out' section of the building industry. Changes were made in the tax treatment of superannuation to take account of the provision in the National Superannuation and Social Insurance Bill. There were minor proposals in the field of estate duty; when decimalisation came, vehicle licences would be rounded down to the nearest new penny; more important, stamp duties on cheques would be abolished on D-day. There would be changes in the betting duties to meet the grievances about the 1969 duties levied on rateable value: in their place the Chancellor settled for the same revenue based on a tax on turnover. At the same time the tax on gaming in clubs was brought into line with the changes in the Gaming Act, 1968. He announced his longer-term proposals for SET based on the Reddaway Report, and made a number of small changes in the tax, including exemption for the production and staging of plays. On industrial building, which the Government decided must be stimulated, he announced, at a cost of £30 millions to the revenue, an increase, for two years from 5th April 1970, in the initial allowance for new buildings from the existing fifteen per cent to thirty per cent outside the development and intermediate areas, and forty per cent in those areas. Age-exemption for income tax was increased yet again, over and above the provision already made to take account of increases in the retirement pension – £50 a year to £475 for single persons, and £60 to £740 for married persons. The personal allowance for women with the sole charge of children was extended from widows to all those bearing similar responsibilities: 100,000 were expected to benefit, at a cost to the revenue of £3 millions. The dependant relative allowance was raised.

Surtax on smaller incomes was cut, mainly to reduce administrative costs. Some 185,000 taxpayers, nearly a third of those liable, were exempted at a cost of £5 millions, and with a saving of three hundred and sixty staff in the surtax offices.

The major change was in income tax. Here, the Chancellor announced an increase of £70 in the single person's allowance to £325, and of £90 in the married allowance to £465. The 'reduced rate band' was to be eliminated – a worthwhile price to pay for raising the tax threshold. Allowing for the earned income allowance, the threshold for single persons and earning wives would thus be raised from £328 to £418 a year, and the relief at this point would be £21 a year. It would be roughly eliminated at £550 a year of earned income. Under his proposals, nearly two million people who would have been paying tax in 1970–71 would be exempt; 100,000 of these were unmarried taxpayers, 800,000 were working wives and over 400,000 were married men. A further eleven million taxpayers would get a continuing benefit of £7 17s 6d a year, and four million others a greater relief. The reliefs would take effect from 5th July – after a June election, though he did not refer to that contingency.

The previous evening, 13th April, I had virtually decided that the election should be held on 18th June. 11th June was still a possibility and, before finally deciding, I needed to refresh my memory about the incidence of wakes weeks and other local holiday periods. Most comment on, and all criticism of, decisions about election timing had ignored the fact that before an election can be held the electoral law requires nineteen days between the dissolution of Parliament and polling-day: convention requires a longer period of notice. An election on 11th June would mean an announcement by 11th May; in practical terms this would have meant before the results of the borough and district council elections. The counties, after all, had not been clear in their electoral message, and while I felt sure what the appropriate date should be, the nature of the decision, to which I have referred in an earlier chapter, must reflect a consensus among one's colleagues.

The public opinion polls, for what they were worth, were moving steadily in our favour, though all showed a small Conservative lead. It was not until 22nd April that the first of the four regular national polls showed a Labour lead. I had just emerged from a railway sleeping compartment at Glasgow when the *Scottish Daily Express* was thrust into my hand, with the headline '*Good* Morning, Mr Wilson' and the news that the Harris poll showed a Labour lead, accompanied by a request for a comment. None was forthcoming.

I was on my way to Oban, to address the Scottish TUC. In addition to making a brief progress report on the economy and on the action we were taking to bring new work to Scotland, I concentrated on industrial relations. I described the action we had taken at Downing Street with the TUC in June 1969, and our determination that the new duties accepted by it should be carried out, and the agreement honoured, and then I went on to attack the Conservative proposals in the field of industrial relations, basing myself on detailed studies of the working of the American Taft-Hartley and Landum-Griffin legislation, on which the Conservative document was largely based. Dealing in particular with enforceability of agreements at law, I summarised American experience in these terms:

> As American experience shows, enforceability at law makes it much harder to get an agreement. The strike lasts longer. In more and more cases cautious union leaders insist on referring an agreement they are prepared to sign to a vote of their members before ratification. In more and more cases these agreements, when referred, are turned down by the members.
>
> More and more agreements are leaving vital issues for settlement later. This leads to secondary strikes.
>
> Nationally enforceable agreements cannot be forced on unwilling local branches and ... groups of workers, except in closed shop conditions. But the Tories have dodged any suggestion of a closed shop. American experience shows that at the end of a strike, most employers are so relieved at getting an agreement and resuming production, that the last thing they would want to do is to provoke fresh trouble by a law suit.

I quoted a recent report by Mr Patrick Lowry, until then a senior official of the Engineering Employers' Federation, who, after a visit to the United States had reported, '. . . to the best of my knowledge none of the employers I met had ever allowed the law to take its full course to the extent that damages were collected from the union.' Employers, he said, who had 'been through it all,' told him that 'lawsuits and the need to live thereafter with the union concerned were quite incompatible...'.

My next major speech was at Bristol on 3rd May for the May Day weekend celebrations. I sensed a new atmosphere from the moment I entered the hall and reports in the next four days said it was building up all over the country; in part stimulated, no doubt, by the transformation in the political situation and by growing speculation about an early general election. Once more my speech was, in the main, an account of our achievements, economic and social, with yet another year's new figures of further increases in our record spending in every branch of the social services.

More and more I was expressing the into-the-seventies theme, first developed in the closing weeks of the old year, and a central element in my Swansea speech; the assertion of our new priorities to help the under-privileged and handicapped, and our developing plans for the environment. Inevitably, I devoted on this occasion more than a few words to the promises of our opponents. They concentrated mainly on an analysis of the Conservative pledges to reduce public expenditure and taxation, while promising vote-catching increases in many major spending programmes. After setting out some of these in detail, I made an offer to them, in these words, '... May Day is one of our great festivals of fraternity and brotherhood. So I promise to mark it with an offer of unparalleled generosity to the leader of the Conservative party.' I went on:

> I will make this unprecedented proposal to him. I am prepared to make available not only the resources of the Administration, but the services of a senior and uniquely qualified minister to help him on what is clearly his major difficulty. To cost his programme. Provided, of course, he tells us what his programme is. What he will no doubt wish to make available for this purpose are his proposals for public expenditure. For increases in public expenditure, for cuts in public expenditure. His proposals for taxation, including the 'sweeping reductions in income tax and surtax' promised by the shadow chancellor in his party political broadcast ...
>
> As soon as the Conservative leader has clarified his policies and programme, I will instruct the Chief Secretary to the Treasury, the greatest authority on public expenditure and taxation any party could produce, to cost his programme. I am further prepared to instruct Mr Diamond to call on all the expert assistance he may need in the Treasury, the Revenue departments, and all the spending departments, to ensure that the costing is as accurate as any costing could ever be. His instructions will be to examine its implications for public expenditure, for taxation, both direct and indirect, and for the cost of living.
>
> He will no doubt begin with the Conservative promises on Government expenditure, which – I am sure this was unintended – are surrounded by a certain degree of dubiety, even approaching mysticism.

The meeting ended in great excitement and enthusiasm. My political press officer said that they sounded as though they would be satisfied by nothing less than an immediate announcement of a general election before I left the platform.

Mr Heath did not appear to share the May Day spirit. He issued a statement to the press that evening and was reported as 'laughing off Mr Wilson's offer of the loan of financial experts. "He must be joking", the Opposition leader said.'

The following week the district councils and the boroughs polled. Before the borough elections, I consulted my senior colleagues on the Cabinet's parliamentary committee about the election timing. Almost all were in favour of June; after the borough elections the following week, the waverers were to express the same view.

I consulted Roy Jenkins on the economic prospects. Regardless of any personal views he might then have held, he gave me his professional view as Chancellor on the election timing. There was nothing known or foreseen by him to influence the decision in favour either of June or of October. But, other things being equal, an early election would remove the uncertainty that was building up – there was widespread public comment in expectation of an early election and, indeed, criticism of my 'dithering'. If I decided to go for June, it would enable decisions to be taken with the minimum of delay.

The voting in the boroughs showed a marked swing to Labour. We gained 447 seats, compared with a loss of 592 in 1967, when the councillors were elected who were defending their seats in 1970. Taking what is to me a more reliable index, the number in 1970 of Labour councillors elected – that is those retaining their seats or gaining seats not previously held by us – the figure was 1,191, compared with 551 in 1969, and 465 in our nadir in 1968; slightly less than the 1,289 in 1966 when post-election euphoria and improved registers resulting from the general election were on our side. The new gains made little difference to the control of individual cities and towns, because of the results of the two previous years, and of the Conservative predominance in controlling 1970s aldermanic elections. But the effect on my colleagues, on the Parliamentary Party, and on the press was electric. There were battle stories of wards won which we had not won for years, of a new enthusiasm and of a tide which must not be missed. My colleagues were now unanimous in favour of an early election, even if those with major legislation in the pipeline had some very natural regrets that their cherished measures would not become law before the election. There was great, indeed unanimous, press comment; I read with wry amusement that I alone was resisting the obvious decision. By this time had I, in fact, decided against a June election I would have been adjudged certifiable. Few of the commentators pronouncing in this sense knew that I had taken my decision on 13th April – some of them, so confident at that time, were to assert in July that my decision to go in June was evidence of a perverse sense of judgment.

On 12th May, my Inner Cabinet colleagues unanimously endorsed my proposal to recommend a dissolution. The Chief Whip reported that a straw poll of MPs showed an almost solid recommendation in favour, the main group of doubtfuls – and this was understandable – being among those who had announced their decision not to stand again.

That evening, at my weekly Audience I informally told the Queen of my likely recommendation. I made the formal submission to her on 18th May. The announcement that the Queen had agreed to a dissolution of Parliament was made in a short statement from No. 10 that evening.

BB

Chapter 38

THE days following the announcement of the General Election were inevitably and completely dominated by it. On Wednesday, 20th May the monthly retail price index was published, showing an increase of 2.1 points during April, due partly to increased potato prices, following the previous year's poor crop – more an act of God than a machination of Her Majesty's Government – and to increased rates and council house rents, mainly imposed by Conservative councils, as Barbara Castle hastened to point out in a press statement. April is, in any case, almost invariably one of the worst months of the year because of seasonal factors. These facts did not prevent the news being sensationalised in the Conservative press and in condemnatory statements issued by Mr Heath.

When a two-point rise in the index was announced for January 1971, one newspaper which had treated the April 1970 rise as a sensation, dismissed it in two paragraphs. Another, equally sensational eight months earlier, kept the news down to two sentences.

For a few days it even appeared that the election was to be fought on the question of a tour of Britain by the racially-selected South African cricketers. Following the disturbances which had attended the visit of the Springbok rugby team the previous winter, there was great anxiety about the reception which the South African cricket team might expect. In a television programme, 'This Week', on 16th April I had answered a question about the tour in these words:

> I think the decision to invite them – to have them coming – was a very ill-judged decision. It's not the first time I've said that if the South Africans behave, as they do, with apartheid – in the matter of sport – then they really have put themselves outside the pale of civilised cricket and civilised everything else, so far as sport is concerned. I think it was a mistake. They are coming. Therefore, I say they should be allowed to play their matches. I do not believe they should be disrupted by digging up pitches or violence. I believe that everyone should be free to demonstrate against apartheid. I hope people will feel free to do that. But not by violent methods – and not by nasty, sneaky little things like, sort of, mirrors to deflect the sunshine into batsmen's eyes and so on. That's a bit of a cheap way out. Let's all express our detestation of apartheid in any peaceful way – let the matches continue. I think the MCC have made a big mistake.

Within hours these words were falsified by some press commentators – and shortly afterwards by Conservative leaders – as being an 'incitement' to violence and breaches of the law. Within days an allegation based on the opposite of what I had said had become mythology: I was inciting violent demonstration. When this charge was thrown up at me in the House, I was able to reject it summarily by quoting the relevant exact words I had used. But the legend continued. Mr Heath himself gave currency to it – outside the House – but was forced to equivocate on a later edition of 'This Week' on 30th April, when confronted with my exact words. The MCC were loath to cancel the tour, even though they were being driven to uncongenial expedients such as buying barbed-wire to surround playing pitches. The Conservatives could hardly conceal their pleasure at the thought that the election campaign would take place against a background of anti-apartheid demonstrations, and that the portrayals of any resulting violence on the television screens of the nation would create a 'law and order' backlash, to say nothing of the guilt by association which they hoped would adhere to the Labour party and its leader. The Conservative press, equally elated, pointed out that the first Test at Lords was due to begin on polling day, a fact I had already noted with some unease before fixing the date. Whatever claims might be made about Waterloo, and the playing-fields of Eton, our opponents hoped that the General Election of 1970 would be fought and won on and around the cricket-pitch at Lords.

On a BBC sports programme on television on 30th April, I appealed to the cricket authorities to think again. It had become clear, through the withdrawal of one Commonwealth country after another, that the Commonwealth games due to be held in the magnificent new sports stadium built, with a large Sports Council grant, in Edinburgh, might be attended by athletes from only a handful of countries. I made a strong appeal that the South African tour be abandoned in the interests of other sports. My warning went wider:

> I hope it won't spread to the point where – but it could you know, if these attitudes persist about South African questions and apartheid – where a British Prime Minister is presiding over a Commonwealth Prime Ministers' conference again cut down to just a rump of the Commonwealth ...

My appeal fell on deaf ears. Keeping the Springbok tour alive seemed to become a point of prestige for the whole Establishment. The Home Secretary made it clear that it would be a matter for the police to handle all disturbances; but he had to report that it was going to be a heavy burden on them.

With the announcement of the election on 18th May, the controversy surrounding the tour acquired a new dimension. On 19th May the Cricket Council at Lords decided by a big majority that the tour would go on. At the same time it warned South Africa that no further tours would be accepted until a South African team came seeking entry which had been selected on a multi-racial basis. This appeared to many critics to be an illogical combination of decisions.

The next day Jim Callaghan came to see me to suggest the time had come for him to take a hand. Many commentators had said that if the Government was opposed to the tour it should use its powers to ban it. That would have been extremely difficult. It would have meant stretching immigration control far beyond any precedent to ban as 'undesirable aliens' men who, in a personal sense, were of unexceptionable character; excluding them simply because the methods of team selection – not they themselves – were racialist. Though the legal powers, were fairly wide, we were advised that such an interpretation of immigration control would certainly require a statement to Parliament, and probably parliamentary approval. With my agreement, Jim Callaghan decided to send for the MCC chiefs and make a direct request to them. This he did on the morning of Thursday, 21st May, and followed his oral request by a formal letter, requesting them on behalf of the Government to cancel the tour 'on grounds of broad public policy'. The Cricket Council met the next day, 22nd May, and took the decision to cancel; 'with deep regret, the Council were of the opinion that they had no alternative but to accede to his request'.

Mr Quintin Hogg, quickly followed by other Conservative leaders, rushed to denounce the Home Secretary. He was clearly expressing a sense of deprivation – not of the opportunity of seeing some lively cricket, but of the prospect of Britain's television screens portraying anti-apartheid demonstrations.

On 29th May Parliament was dissolved. Both Houses met in the morning for Prorogation, and the Queen's Speech recording the work of this truncated session was read. Among the measures which had become law were: equal pay; the Merchant Shipping Act and legislation for safety in fishing; the Films Act; the Agricultural Act on egg marketing and capital investment grants; measures to provide permanent powers to limit increases in council house rents; the Act to reorganise local authority personal services following the Seebohm Report; the Act to reform the Scottish feudal system and a Scottish highways measure. In law reform and judicial procedure Acts had been passed to reconstitute the High Court, with a Family Division, to assist the recovery of civil debts without recourse to imprisonment and to make fair financial provision for wives in matrimonial disputes.

But the Speech included a long list of our Bills which had failed to become law because of dissolution. Some were major measures, such as the Superannuation and Social Insurance Bill, the legislation to merge the Monopolies Commission with the Prices and Incomes Board, the Industrial Relations Bill; and the Bill to reorganise the ports under public ownership. Other important measures caught by the election were: the Dangerous Drugs Bill; the Education Bill, requiring a few laggard or obstructive local authorities to go ahead with comprehensive secondary education and the abolition of 11-plus selection; measures to reorganise the gas and electricity industries; the Bill on industrial health and safety; and the Coal Industry Bill, continuing the powers of the 1967 Act. But I was glad that through providing Government assistance and priority in parliament time, Alf Morris's excellent private members' venture, the Chronically Sick and Disabled Persons' Bill, had received the Royal Assent that morning.

Parliament was nominally prorogued for three days, but in the afternoon the dissolution was proclaimed and the election struggle began in earnest. In the evening, I opened the Labour party campaign at a great rally at Ninian Park, Cardiff:

> Tonight I want to set out the basic issues on which the nation will have to pronounce when it makes its choice between the two alternatives.
> First and foremost the issue of responsibility. How Labour had discharged its duties as a responsible Government. How far, on everything the Tories have told us, they must be convicted of seeking office on a programme of total irresponsibility.
> This is a responsible Government. A Government which has always taken whatever measures were necessary to put the country's economic strength beyond risk.
> A Government which was prepared to face unpopularity – prepared to face the taunts and jibes – and the constant electoral manoeuvring – of an irresponsible Opposition.
> Against this we have to set the record in opposition of the Conservative party. They have barely concealed their partisan delight when it was difficult going for Britain. Their disappointment when it became clear to the world that Britain was paying its way as Britain had not been able to do for years past . . .

We campaigned on our programme of economic and social policy for the seventies, and on the contradictions and unrealisable promises in the Conservative programme; but above all we fought on our record of achievements.

I said in an election broadcast on 16th June:

> In the first years we had to put all our efforts into getting the country strong because without a strong economic base, you can't do what you set out to do. And we are proud of what has been achieved. But economic strength is not an end in itself; it is only a necessary means to an end. The socialism I believe in means above all using all our resources for making Britain a better place to live in and for a Labour government this means sharing prosperity in a way which is fair and just. It means ensuring that our old people are cared for as they should be, that poverty – whatever its cause – is rooted out. It means providing decent homes for families. Housing is an issue in this election; it is an issue because the Government insists that it is an issue. And it will never cease to be

an issue while there is one family poorly housed, while there is one slum street in our big cities. And it means caring for the sick, and that includes the mentally handicapped.

It means helping and protecting ordinary people against the harsh impact of economic change. It means, above all, accepting that individual misfortune is not just a private concern but a community concern, that we are all members one of another.

Even when Britain was up against it, so much was achieved; we strengthened the social services, health and education, as never before; and we can now make faster progress because we are strong. Even this is not enough. It means a deliberate effort by our generation to prepare the way, to give more freedom, more choice for the young people of today and of tomorrow. We have to prepare for the changing Britain and the changing world in which our children are growing up. We must be ready to invest in their future. Better education and equality of opportunity. End the eleven-plus. By a system of comprehensive education which extends to every child the educational opportunities which in the past were available only to a few. But this means spending more on education. It is a question of priorities. This is the first government which is spending more on our children's education than on armaments and defence.

As with the 1966 General Election, I do not propose to recount the cut and thrust, the ebb and flow, of the 1970 contest.

As in 1966 the work of government continued. One development which we noted with interest from the diplomatic telegrams was an improvement in relations between China and Britain. It was, at this point, only at the level of gestures; but in Peking gestures are not accidental – they included a long and friendly talk which Mao Tse Tung chose to have with our *chargé d'affaires* at a diplomatic reception.

The other major event which required my prolonged attention at a difficult time was the national newspaper strike. One of the main groups of printing unions, SOGAT, put in a large wage-claim to replace the existing agreement on its expiry. The Newspaper Publishers' Association refused to negotiate with SOGAT alone, understandably because a new wage-claim was expected within weeks from the big union, the National Graphical Association; for years, wage-settlements and industrial relations in the industry had been bedevilled by the leap-frogging of wage claims. SOGAT refused to sit down with the NGA and the NGA was not willing to join in any round-table discussions. There was total procedural deadlock, and in this situation Richard Briginshaw, General Secretary of SOGAT, gave notice that the printing presses would stop on the following evening, Tuesday 9th June, and then left for his annual conference in Bournemouth. The news reached me just before midnight at Leicester after an arduous election tour. I telephoned London to get a full report from the Employment Department, and then I asked Vic Feather to contact the SOGAT leaders and urge them to stand by and be ready to return to London. Then I left by road, reaching Downing Street at 2.00 a.m.

The following morning I consulted the DEP again and sent a message to Dick Briginshaw asking him to return to London. At 1.00 p.m. he and his executive reached No. 10. I saw him alone, to outline what I had in mind, and then I saw him together with his executive. Meanwhile the newspaper proprietors were asked to be available at two o'clock. My plan to break the procedural deadlock was that all the unions – SOGAT, NGA and representatives of the engineers and the electricians (EPTU) – should each be accommodated in different rooms in Downing Street and the Cabinet office. There would then be separate informal bilateral discussions between the NPA and individual unions, but, to meet the NPA requirement about refusing to settle bilaterally there would be no attempt to reach a definitive agreement until sufficient progress was made to justify a round-table meeting of all the unions with the NPA.

SOGAT accepted my proposal. So did the NPA, stipulating only that bilateral talks with SOGAT should not begin until NGA had accepted the procedure. John Bonfield, General Secretary of the NGA, had been asked to stay at the end of a telephone. Unfortunately, his office was at Bedford and he did not arrive until four o'clock, while the other prospective negotiators had to wait in frustration. On his arrival I put the procedural proposition to him, which he accepted with some reservation of his position about the ultimate wage settlement.

By 6.00 p.m. bilateral talks had produced a situation where there was hope of multilateral negotiations in the evening. One of the big difficulties was the different objectives of the two principal unions, since the higher-paid NGA had less to gain than SOGAT from the increase in basic rates for which SOGAT had asked. Moreover, the NGA representatives had no mandate to negotiate: their claim had not even been formulated. I was a little worried, too, about the AEF and EPTU representatives, who had been corralled hour after hour in a room in the Cabinet office. Inter-union relations could clearly be the key to any settlement. Accordingly, I telephoned Vic Feather and informed him of the procedural position. He was astounded, and said I had brought off a miracle. He agreed to come over and use his good offices to try to persuade the unions to take a common line.

I called all the parties to the Cabinet Room to review progress and appealed to SOGAT to withdraw, or at least postpone, the strike notices. But it was too late, the presses were already stopping and no papers were printed that night.

Both sides agreed with a lecture I gave them on the deplorable state of negotiating procedures and job evaluation in the industry. Progress was made by the acceptance of a suggestion – previously put forward by the NPA – that there should be a long-term review of the pay structure and negotiating procedure, the immediate talks being related to an agreement up to September 1971. I cancelled two big election meetings for that night, the last thing I wanted to do nine days away from polling day. Bilateral negotiations continued with SOGAT until John Bonfield, bored with waiting – and he was not alone in this – insisted on another round-table discussion. If this were not agreed to, he was going home. He then surprised the meeting by proposing a formula for agreement, making it clear that so far as NGA was concerned he was putting it forward on his own responsibility, and his executive's approval would be necessary.

A small working-party was set up and it soon became clear that there was some ambiguity in his proposal. Vic Feather worked like a trojan. By the end of the evening sufficient progress had been made to agree to adjourn to a further meeting – which both sides accepted should be at Congress House – under Vic Feather's chairmanship. For, apart from my desire to get back to the hustings, the occasion for my intervention, the procedural deadlock, was no longer an issue. I had made it clear from the outset that I would play no part in any discussion of the content of the pay claim or any counter-offer. Unfortunately, because members of the NGA executive had to be summoned from all over the country, the adjourned meeting could not take place until Thursday. On the Friday agreement was reached, and newspapers resumed printing at the weekend – in time for the Mondays to print the depressing news of the last-minute defeat of England in the World Cup in Mexico.

I had lost valuable election time. But I felt that it was right to give my full attention to settling the strike. It was not an empty phrase – which was heard so many times that week, frequently from me – that in a general election democracy required the full printing of all the issues before the country, however they might be handled editorially.

My intervention had helped the newspapers to resume full election coverage and enabled some of them in the last few days of the campaign to excel anything they had said about me over the past six years. Two of those who surpassed themselves in this respect might never have resumed printing if the strike had been protracted. But not all were in that situation. One Conservative Sunday newspaper graciously printed a very friendly main leading article paying tribute to me for getting the presses working again: unfortunately it did not appear the Sunday after the settlement; it appeared a week later, three days after the election.

When the Sunday papers appeared on 14th June, there was almost total unanimity about the likely result of the election. The *Sunday Times*'s weekly summary of the five national opinion polls at the latest point before they went to press, recorded variations in the Labour lead from 2.5 per cent (Gallup) to 12.4 per cent (NOP) with a weighted average of 6.4 per cent. One leading national betting chain had virtually ceased taking bets on Labour, having imposed odds, which, allowing for tax, represented 34 to 1 on.

I was one of the few who had doubts, though I would have found it difficult to rationalise them.

They were confirmed from the first results which showed a marked swing to the Conservatives: the Black Country results showed an even larger swing, no doubt representing the publicity given to Mr Enoch Powell's views. When results from other parts of the country confirmed the earlier swing, it became clear that the Conservatives would have a working majority – an outcome which was, I subsequently learnt, as surprising to senior Conservative leaders as to the commentators who had based their forecast on the public opinion polls.

After the declaration of my own majority, marginally up on a larger register to 21,074, but with a 2.4 per cent adverse swing, and after television broadcasts, I set off as planned by road for London. I reached Downing Street at seven o'clock and soon afterwards was facing the cameras which had been installed in the Pillared Room.

I was asked, almost before I had had time to draw breath, much less to sleep, what I thought explained the result. My first reaction, which has hardly been changed since, was expressed in two sentences:

The improvement in our economic position, as in other ways, had not erased all the scars from the tough things we had to do to get that strong position . . .

Asked about our opponents' campaign, I replied,

. . . of course they did exploit the cost of living question. They gave the impression that they would stop the rise in the cost of living. Well now they will have a chance to show whether they can or not.

And in a further reply, I concluded:

No incoming Prime Minister, if Mr Heath takes over, in living memory has taken over a stronger economic situation. I wanted to use that as we have never been able to, in the past five or six years, to use the economic situation for building on what we have done, for example in the social services, health and education and social security and housing – to accelerate what we have been doing, to intensify and develop it. Now we hand over the means to do that, to somebody else.

Index

Aberdeen, 151

Aberfan disaster, 293–8, 424–5, 446, 548–9, 574, 661–2, 719

Abertillery, 101

ACARUS project, 613

Accra, 168, 197, 635

Acton by-election (1968), 520

Addis Ababa, 197, 559, 635–7

Aden: 'ever-readies' required for service in, 96; Sir Arthur Charles assassinated in, 133; state of emergency declared in (25 Sept. 1965), 138; Britain's withdrawal from, 213, 231, 235, 376, 381, 391–2, 396, 399, 405, 444–5; mentioned, 41, 60 117, 173, 189, 415

Adenauer, Dr Konrad, 368, 397, 402

Administration of Justice Bill (1970), 719

Admiralty, 382, 384

Aengelholm, 681

Agenda for a Generation, 707

agriculture: and annual price review (1965), 60; and Britain's proposed entry to EEC, 82, 327–33, 337–44, 369, 386, 389, 410, 688, 761–4; and Australian imports, 118; and Canadian imports, 118; and National Plan, 137; and establishment of Meat and Livestock Commission, 176, 224; and annual price review (1966), 221–2; and factory farming, 447, 719; and annual price review (1968), 495; and annual price review (1969), 614, 616; in Scotland, 683; and Brambell Report, 719; and fixed capital investment grant, 721, 767, 785; and annual price review (1970), 741, 767; mentioned, 10, 225, 524, 733

Agriculture Acts (1947), 60

Agriculture Act (1957), 60

Agriculture Act (1968), 573

Agriculture Act (1970), 785

aid: to underdeveloped countries, 118, 701, 712; to Nigeria, 558–61, 589–90, 623, 627, 629, 632–5, 681–2, 690, 729–32, 744–50

aircraft industry: responsibility for transfered to Ministry of Technology, 9, 62, 245, 326; and Concorde project, 20, 61–2, 411; and TSR 2 project, 40, 42, 60, 61, 78; and P 1154 project, 40, 42, 60, 61; Plowden Report on, 42–3, 61, 190; and proposed European airbus (ESRO), 61, 612; mobility of labour in, 63; Commonwealth consultation on, 118; and Britain's proposed entry to EEC, 337–8, 408, 410; and Anglo-Soviet co-operation in, 350, 352; and D-Notice system, 374; and cancellation of 'swing-wing' aircraft, 411; and reductions in overseas military commitments, 483; and defence research programme, 485; mentioned, 4, 39, 55, 212, 712

Aitken, Frank, 75

Aitken, Sir Max, 565–7, 576

Akrotiri, 153, 197, 307

Albu, Austen, 326

Aldrin, Colonel Edwin, 716

Algeria, 399, 403–4

Algiers, 112, 114, 116, 556

Allen, Alfred, 547, 548, 655, 658

Allon, Ygal, 650

Alport, Lord, 424, 536

Amalgamated Engineering Union (AEU), 193, 194, 226, 227

Amalgamated Union of Engineering and Foundry Workers (AEF), 788

American Challenge, The, Jean-Jacques Servan-Schreiber, 334

Amery, Julian, 61, 62

Amory, Lord, 165

Amsterdam, 423

Anderson, Major-General John, 24

Andronikov, Prince, 92, 334–5, 411

Anglesey, 293, 522

Angola, 197, 307, 407

Anguilla, 625–6

Ankrah, General Joseph Arthur, 555, 592

anti-ballistic missiles (ABMs), 353–4,